The World Book Encyclopedia

U·V Volume 20

World Book, Inc.

a Scott Fetzer company

Chicago London Sydney Toronto

The World Book Encyclopedia

Copyright © 1986, U.S.A.
by
World Book, Inc.

Uu

U is the 21st letter of our alphabet. It came from a letter which the Semitic peoples of Syria and Palestine called *waw*. *Waw* was also the source of *F*, *V*, *W*, and *Y*. The word *waw* meant hook, and was represented by a symbol of a tenthook. The symbol was probably borrowed from an Egyptian hieroglyphic, or picture symbol. The Greeks borrowed the letter from the Phoenicians and gave it a *Y*-shape. The Romans, when they adopted the letter, dropped its bottom stroke and wrote it as *V*. They used it for the vowel sound, *U*, and the consonant sound, *V*. About A.D. 900, people began to write *U* in the middle of a word and *V* at the beginning. During the Renaissance, it became customary among the people to use *u* as a vowel and *v* as a consonant. See ALPHABET.

Uses. *U* or *u* is about the 12th most frequently used letter in books, newspapers, and other printed material in English. As an abbreviation on report cards, *u* means *unsatisfactory*. In geographic names, it may mean *united*, *union*, or *upper*. It frequently stands for *university*. In chemistry, *U* is the symbol for the element *uranium*.

Pronunciation. *U* is a vowel, and has many sounds in English. The sound we associate with its name, *you*, is really a diphthong. It is made by linking two separate sounds pronounced continuously. A person forms this sound by rounding the lips, with the tip of the tongue below the lower teeth, and raising the back of the tongue. Other sounds of *u* are those in *sun*, *duty*, *presume*, *bull*, and *fur*. A silent *u* may occur after *g*, as in *guard* and *guess*. See PRONUNCIATION.   MARIANNE COOLEY

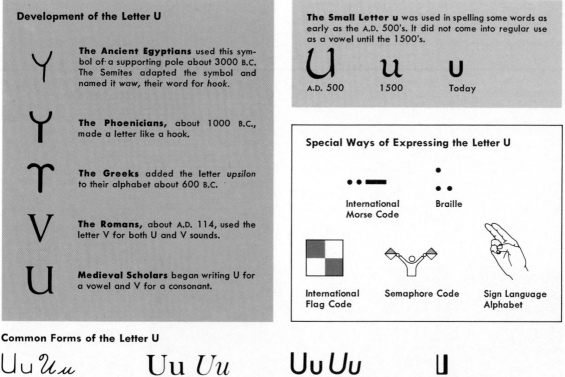

Development of the Letter U

The Ancient Egyptians used this symbol of a supporting pole about 3000 B.C. The Semites adapted the symbol and named it *waw*, their word for *hook*.

The Phoenicians, about 1000 B.C., made a letter like a hook.

The Greeks added the letter *upsilon* to their alphabet about 600 B.C.

The Romans, about A.D. 114, used the letter V for both U and V sounds.

Medieval Scholars began writing U for a vowel and V for a consonant.

The Small Letter u was used in spelling some words as early as the A.D. 500's. It did not come into regular use as a vowel until the 1500's.

A.D. 500   1500   Today

Special Ways of Expressing the Letter U

International Morse Code

Braille

International Flag Code

Semaphore Code

Sign Language Alphabet

Common Forms of the Letter U

Handwritten Letters vary from person to person. *Manuscript* (printed) letters, *left*, have simple curves and straight lines. Cursive letters, *right*, have flowing lines.

Roman Letters have small finishing strokes called *serifs* that extend from the main strokes. The type face shown above is Baskerville. The italic form appears at the right.

Sans-Serif Letters are also called *gothic letters*. They have no serifs. The type face shown above is called Futura. The italic form of Futura appears at the right.

Computer Letters have special shapes. Computers can "read" these letters either optically or by means of the magnetic ink with which the letters may be printed.

1

U-BOAT

U-BOAT. See SUBMARINE (World Wars I and II); WORLD WAR II (U-Boats).

U THANT. See THANT, U.

U-2, reconnaissance plane. See COLD WAR (The U-2 Incident; picture: A U.S. Spy Plane).

U-235 is a radioactive isotope of uranium that is used in nuclear reactors and certain nuclear weapons. The value 235 is the isotope's *mass number*, which indicates the total number of neutrons and protons in the nucleus of the atom. U-235 occurs naturally in such minerals as carnotite and pitchblende. It is always combined with two other uranium isotopes, U-234 and U-238.

The nucleus of U-235 *decays* (breaks apart) by giving off high-energy radiation in the form of *alpha particles*. U-235 emits these particles for a long period of time. It has a *half-life* of about 700 million years (see RADIOACTIVITY [Half-Life]).

U-235 is used as a nuclear fuel because it readily undergoes *fission* when struck by a neutron. Fission is a nuclear reaction in which a nucleus splits into two smaller nuclei of nearly equal size and energy is released. Before U-235 can be used in reactors and atomic bombs, it must be separated from the more abundant U-238, which does not fission easily. This separation produces *enriched uranium*, which contains a higher percentage of U-235 than natural uranium does. U-235 makes up less than 1 per cent of natural uranium but about 3 per cent of the enriched uranium used in most reactors. See URANIUM (Separating Uranium Isotopes).

The fissioning of U-235 produces hundreds of other radioactive isotopes. Many of these isotopes, such as cesium 137 and strontium 90, are extremely hazardous. Large amounts of these fission products are generated during nuclear power production. Their safe disposal has become a serious problem, which experts are working to solve (see NUCLEAR ENERGY [Wastes and Waste Disposal]).

U-235 was discovered in 1935 by Arthur J. Dempster, a Canadian-born physicist. In 1942, a group of physicists at the University of Chicago used U-235 to produce the first self-sustaining *nuclear chain reaction* (series of fissions). The first atomic bomb used in warfare contained U-235. This bomb was dropped by the United States armed forces on Hiroshima, Japan, in 1945, and helped bring an end to World War II.   J. RAYFORD NIX

U-238. See NUCLEAR ENERGY (Nuclear Fission; Present-Day Research); URANIUM (Uranium Isotopes).

U-239. See URANIUM (Radioactivity and Fissionability).

U.A.R. See UNITED ARAB REPUBLIC.

UBANGI, *yoo BANG gee,* is a nickname given to women members of the Sara, a black African tribe living near the Ubangi River in the Central African Republic. Many of the women wear flat wooden disks in their pierced lips.

UBANGI RIVER, *yoo BANG gee,* is the chief northern tributary of the Congo River in Africa. With its main headstream, the Bomu, the Ubangi—also spelled Oubangui—is about 1,400 miles (2,250 kilometers) long. It is formed by the union of the Bomu and Uele rivers, and empties into the Congo near Lake Tumba in Zaire. For about 700 miles (1,100 kilometers), the Ubangi forms the boundary line separating Zaire from Congo on the west, and Central African Republic on the northwest. It is navigable the year around below Bangui, Central African Republic.   WILLIAM A. HANCE

UCAYALI RIVER. See AMAZON RIVER (The Course of the Amazon).

UCCELLO, *oot CHEHL loh,* **PAOLO,** *PAH oh loh* (1397-1475), was one of the first Renaissance painters in Italy. Perspective takes on special emphasis in his work. Its purpose is to bring order into the host of things that people see. Uccello kept it from looking fixed and dead by his bright, almost flat color, and vivid movement. His best-known works include *The Flood* and three scenes of battles. A detail of *The Battle of San Romano* appears in color in the PAINTING article.

Uccello lived in Florence, and was an apprentice to the sculptor Lorenzo Ghiberti. Uccello's real name was Paolo di Dono.   CREIGHTON GILBERT

See also PAINTING (Florentine Masters).

UFFIZI PALACE, *oo FEET see,* a famous building in Florence, Italy, contains one of the world's finest art collections. The collection includes drawings, paintings, prints, and sculptures by many European masters. The palace itself is an outstanding example of the Italian mannerist style of architecture. It was designed by the Italian architect Giorgio Vasari in 1559. Originally intended to house government offices, it was converted into an art gallery about 1575. The palace became a public museum in the 1800's.   WILLIAM J. HENNESSEY

UFO. See UNIDENTIFIED FLYING OBJECT.

Alinari

Uffizi Palace in Florence, Italy, contains classical sculptures and masterpieces of Italian painting from all periods. The palace itself dates from the late 1500's.

Uganda

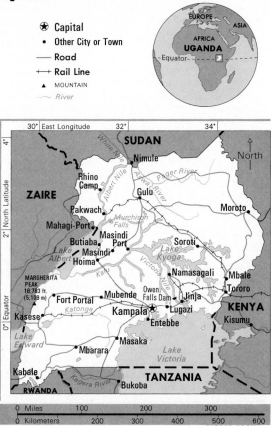

★ Capital
• Other City or Town
— Road
+—+ Rail Line
▲ MOUNTAIN
～ River

WORLD BOOK map

Facts in Brief

Capital: Kampala.

Official Language: English.

Area: 91,134 sq. mi. (236,036 km²).

Population: *Estimated 1986 Population*—15,144,000; distribution, 85 per cent rural, 15 per cent urban; density, 167 persons per sq. mi. (64 per km²). *1980 Census*—12,630,076. *Estimated 1991 Population*—17,387,000.

Chief Products: *Agriculture*—bananas, cassava, coffee, cotton, sweet potatoes, tea, tobacco. *Mining*—copper.

National Anthem: "Uganda."

Flag: A white-crested crane is centered on horizontal stripes of black (for Africa), yellow (sunshine), and red (brotherhood). See FLAG (picture: Flags of Africa).

Money: *Basic Unit*—shilling. See MONEY (table).

UGANDA, *yoo GAN duh* or *oo GAHN dah*, is a thickly populated country in east-central Africa. It is slightly smaller than the state of Oregon. It has a pleasant climate and fertile soil.

The Africans in Uganda belong to several ethnic groups that differ more from one another than do the peoples of Europe. English is Uganda's official language, but the people speak many African languages.

The country's magnificent scenery includes snow-capped mountains, thick tropical forests, and semi-desert areas. Lakes cover more than a sixth of Uganda. Part of Lake Victoria, the world's second largest freshwater lake, lies in the country. Many wild animals roam the vast national parks.

For almost 70 years, Great Britain governed the territory as the *Uganda Protectorate*. Uganda won independence in 1962. Kampala is its capital and largest city.

Government of Uganda is controlled by military leaders. The Military Council, which has from 10 to 15 members, heads the government. The leader of the council serves as head of state. The Military Council appoints a Cabinet, which helps carry out the operations of the government.

People. Most Ugandans are black Africans. Nearly all of the more than 20 ethnic groups have their own language. Uganda has no language that is understood by everyone. The Ganda, also called the Baganda, are the

largest and wealthiest group. They live in central and southern Uganda. Their political and social organization is one of the most highly developed in central Africa. Until 1967, the Ganda had their own *Kabaka* (king) and *Lukiko* (parliament).

Many Ganda are prosperous farmers. Coffee, cotton, and tea are the chief cash crops. Food crops include bananas and vegetables. Women do much of the work on the farms. The Ganda live in houses that have mud walls and corrugated iron roofs.

Like the Ganda, three other ethnic groups in southern Uganda had their own Kabakas until 1967. Most of the people are farmers. But the Karamojong in the northeast and several other ethnic groups in the drier parts of the north lead wandering lives as herders. Karamojong men mat their hair with colored clay in elaborate patterns. A favorite meal consists of milk mixed with ox blood.

Most Ugandans practice traditional African religions. About a fourth of the people are Christians, and many are Muslims. About half of the people cannot read or

Authenticated News Int.

A Cotton Field in Uganda produces one of the nation's most valuable crops. Cotton and coffee are the leading exports.

3

write. Three-fourths of the children receive elementary education. Makerere University is in Kampala.

Land. Most of Uganda is a plateau about 4,000 feet (1,200 meters) above sea level. Thick forests grow in the south. Most of the north is *savanna* (grassland with low trees), but some northeastern areas are semidesert.

Highlands rise near the east and west borders. In the east, Mount Elgon towers 14,178 feet (4,321 meters). Margherita Peak rises 16,763 feet (5,109 meters) in the Ruwenzori Range in the southwest. The Great Rift Valley borders the western highlands and contains Lakes Albert, Edward, and George. The headwaters of the White Nile drain Uganda (see NILE RIVER).

The equator runs through southern Uganda. But because of the high altitude, temperatures are mild. In most areas, the temperature seldom goes above 85° F. (29° C) at midday, or below 60° F. (16° C) at night. Most of Uganda receives over 40 inches (100 centimeters) of rain a year.

Economy. Uganda is an agricultural country. Coffee, cotton, and tobacco are the chief exports. The country has rich deposits of many minerals, but only copper is mined on a large scale. The Owen Falls Dam at Jinja, Uganda's main industrial town, has one of Africa's largest hydroelectric power stations.

Copper ore goes from the mines at Kilembe, near Kasese, to a smelter at Jinja, and then to Kampala and the Kenya seaport of Mombasa. Cargo and passenger ships operate on Lakes Albert, Kyoga, and Victoria, and on the Albert Nile. Uganda has about 3,800 miles (6,120 kilometers) of roads.

History. By the 700's and 800's, the people in parts of what is now Uganda had developed agriculture and the use of iron. By 1200, they had a simple form of government headed by chiefs. Several local kingdoms developed after 1300. The most important early kingdoms were Kitara and Bunyoro.

Arab traders came to the area about 1850. By that time, the Ganda had formed the richest and most powerful kingdom, called Buganda. This kingdom had

Kampala, the Capital of Uganda, is a mixture of the old and new. Many of the women wear colorful ankle-length dresses.

Marc and Evelyne Bernheim, Rapho Guillumette

a large army and a highly developed system of government. Explorers and missionaries from Great Britain arrived in Uganda during the 1860's and 1870's. Great Britain made Buganda a British protectorate in 1894. Buganda and three other kingdoms united and became a British protectorate later in the 1890's. Uganda attained its present boundaries in 1926. The British gradually developed the country's economy. After World War II, Africans played an increasingly important part in governing Uganda. Many Ganda wanted their kingdom to become independent. This caused trouble in the 1950's between the Kabaka of Buganda and the British.

On Oct. 9, 1962, Uganda became independent. Apollo Milton Obote, a member of a northern ethnic group, became prime minister. Buganda got special powers and was more independent of the central government than the other kingdoms.

In October 1963, a Kabaka was elected president. But serious differences arose between the Kabaka and Obote over a land dispute between the Ganda and the Bunyoro. In 1966, Obote charged that the Kabaka was plotting to overthrow the government. He dismissed the Kabaka and announced a new constitution. The constitution made Obote president. The Kabaka fled when government troops attacked his palace. Another constitution was adopted in 1967. It made Uganda a republic and abolished the country's traditional kingdoms, including Buganda.

The Uganda Army overthrew Obote in 1971, and set up a military government. Major General Idi Amin Dada, commander of the country's armed forces, headed the new government as president.

In 1972, President Amin ordered about 47,000 Asians who had been living in Uganda to leave the country. These Asians had not become Ugandan citizens, but they owned many of the businesses in the country. By expelling the Asians, Amin hoped to gain more control of the economy for Ugandans. Amin ruled Uganda as a dictator. Reportedly—at Amin's order—thousands of Ugandans who disagreed with his policies were killed.

In 1978, a border dispute led to fighting between Uganda and Tanzania, which lies to the south. In 1979, Tanzanian troops, aided by Ugandans who opposed Amin, defeated Uganda's army and overthrew Amin's government. The Ugandans who opposed Amin took control of the country's government. In May 1980, military leaders overthrew the government. They formed a new government headed by a commission made up of military leaders and civilians. In December 1980, elections for a new civilian government were held. Obote, who had been living in exile, returned to Uganda. He became a presidential candidate. Obote's political party won the most seats in the National Assembly, and he became president again.

In 1985, military leaders overthrew Obote and took control of the government. General Tito Okello became head of the new military government.   HAROLD INGRAMS

Related Articles in WORLD BOOK include:

Amin Dada, Idi	Lake Albert	Nile River
Ganda	Lake Edward	Obote, Apollo M.
Kampala	Lake Victoria	

UHF WAVE. See ULTRAHIGH FREQUENCY WAVE.

UITLANDERS. See BOER WAR.

Ukraine

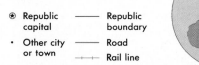

The Ukraine is one of the 15 republics of the U.S.S.R. It is a major farming, industrial, and mining area.

⊛ Republic capital

• Other city or town

——— Republic boundary

——— Road

+—+—+ Rail line

WORLD BOOK map

UKRAINE, *yoo KRAYN* or *yoo KRYN*, is a rich farming, industrial, and mining region in southeastern Europe. It makes up the Ukrainian Soviet Socialist Republic (Ukrainian S.S.R.), one of the 15 republics of the Soviet Union. The Ukraine covers about 233,090 square miles (603,700 square kilometers) and has about 50,667,000 people. About two-thirds of the people live in urban areas. Kiev is the capital and largest city.

People. About three-fourths of the people of the Ukraine are Ukrainians, a Slavic nationality group that has its own customs and language. Russians, a separate group that speaks the Russian language, make up about a fifth of the population. About 1 per cent of the people are Jews, whom the Soviet government also considers a separate nationality group. The Jewish population was sharply reduced during World War II (1939-1945), when the Nazis killed thousands of Ukrainian Jews. Most of the Russians and Jews live in cities.

Many urban Ukrainians speak Russian most of the time. In rural areas, nearly all the people speak Ukrainian. Each region of the Ukraine has its own *dialect* (local form of a language). But the schools teach a standardized form. The universities of Kiev, Lvov, and Odessa rank among the oldest and most famous in the Soviet Union. The Ukraine also has five other universities.

Rural Ukrainians are known for their strong ties to their families and farms. Villagers build their homes and barns of whitewashed stone or adobe, with thatched roofs. Peasant costumes worn on holidays feature white blouses or shirts, decorated with colorful embroidery.

Ukrainians enjoy music, and many of them perform in choruses and dance groups. Ukrainian music often features a stringed instrument called a *bandura*.

Land and Climate. The Ukraine consists largely of a flat plain that stretches from the Pripyat Marshes in the north to the Black Sea in the south. The Carpathian Mountains border the Ukraine on the west. Major rivers include the Dnepr, the Dnestr, and the Donets.

Most parts of the Ukraine have cold winters and hot summers. Temperatures average 23° F. (−5° C) in January and 70° F. (21° C) in July. *Precipitation* (rain, snow, and other measurable forms of moisture) ranges from about 30 inches (76 centimeters) a year in the north to about 9 inches (23 centimeters) in the south.

Economy. Ukrainian farms produce more than half the Soviet Union's sugar beets, nearly a fourth of its meat and dairy products, and a fifth of its grain. Wheat ranks as the main crop in the south. Ukrainian farmers also raise barley, corn, rye, tobacco, and other crops.

The Ukraine has rich deposits of coal, iron ore, manganese, mercury, natural gas, and salt. Heavy industries have developed around these mineral deposits, especially near the cities of Donetsk, Dnepropetrovsk, and Kharkov. About two-fifths of the steel and nearly a third of the coal produced in the Soviet Union comes from the Ukraine. Major manufactured goods include agricultural machinery, cement, chemicals, fertilizer, food products, locomotives, ships, and trucks.

History. During the A.D. 800's, a Slavic civilization called Rus grew up at Kiev and at other points along the river transportation routes from the Baltic Sea to the Black Sea. In time, Kiev became the first of the independent Russian city-states.

During the 1200's, Mongol tribes later known as Tartars swept across the Ukrainian plains from the east and conquered the region. Beginning in the early 1300's, Lithuania and Poland gradually took control of the Ukraine. Under Polish-Lithuanian rule, Ukrainian peasants were bound to the land as serfs. During the

V. Runov, Sovfoto

Ukrainian Women embroider colorful designs on blouses, scarves, pillowcases, tablecloths, and other items. Such embroidery is a distinctive feature of traditional Ukrainian clothing.

5

Kiev is the capital and largest city of the Ukraine. Tree-lined downtown boulevards, such as Kreshchatik Street, *above*, help make Kiev one of the Soviet Union's most picturesque cities.

M. Barabanov, Sovfoto

1400's, many discontented peasants joined bands of independent soldiers called *Cossacks* (see COSSACKS). The Cossacks occupied the territory that lay between the Poles and the Tartars. The region became known as the *Ukraine*, which is a Slavic word meaning *borderland*.

Most of the Ukraine remained under Polish rule until the 1600's. The Cossacks opposed Polish efforts to make them leave the Eastern Orthodox Church and join the Roman Catholic Church. In 1654, this dispute led the Cossack leader Bohdan Khmelnytsky to form an alliance with the Eastern Orthodox *czar* (king) of Russia.

By the mid-1700's, Russia had gained control over almost all the Ukraine. Under Russian rule, the Ukrainians could practice their religion freely, but they remained serfs. Many of them objected to this harsh way of life and to Russia's efforts to replace the Ukrainian language with Russian. Beginning in the mid-1800's, the poet Taras Shevchenko led a revival of Ukrainian culture. The historian Michael Hrushevsky wrote many books on Ukrainian history that stressed the Ukraine's complete separateness from Russia.

In 1917, the Bolshevik Revolution led to the establishment of a Communist government in Russia. After the revolution, many Ukrainians tried to form an independent Ukrainian state. But in time, the Communists brought most of the Ukraine under Communist rule as the Ukrainian Soviet Socialist Republic. In 1922, the Ukraine became one of the four original republics of the Union of Soviet Socialist Republics.

In the Ukraine, as in other parts of the Soviet Union, the Communist government severely limited cultural and political activity. In 1929, the government began to take control of small peasant farms. Hundreds of thousands of Ukrainians were sent to Siberia and Soviet Central Asia for resisting the take-overs of the Communist government. During the 1930's, crop failures and government seizures of grain resulted in millions of deaths from starvation.

After World War II ended in 1945, the Soviet Union took over parts of the Ukraine that had belonged to Czechoslovakia and Poland. The Crimean Peninsula became part of the Ukrainian S.S.R. in 1954.

Since 1950, the economy of the Ukraine has grown rapidly, and standards of living have risen. But many Ukrainians continue to oppose Russian domination and limits on cultural freedom.　　　JOHN A. ARMSTRONG

Related Articles in WORLD BOOK include:

Black Sea	Lvov
Crimea	Odessa
Dnepr River	Ruthenia
Dnepropetrovsk	Sevastopol
Donetsk	Shevchenko, Taras
Kiev	Yalta

UKRAINIAN SOVIET SOCIALIST REPUBLIC. See UKRAINE.

UKULELE, *YOO kuh LAY lee,* is a four-stringed musical instrument related to the guitar. A player strums the ukelele with the fingers of one hand. With the fingers of the other hand, the player picks out chords on the finger board along the neck of the instrument. Most written ukelele music consists of chord symbols that indicate finger positions instead of notes. Thus, the player need not know how to read music. The ukulele was developed from a small guitar brought to Hawaii by the Portuguese in the late 1800's. The ukulele is used mainly to accompany folk and popular singing.　　　ABRAM LOFT

Jim Collins

The Ukulele looks somewhat like a small guitar. It is played by strumming the four strings with the fingers.

ULAN BATOR, *OO lahn BAH tawr* (pop. 402,900), is the capital of Mongolia. For location, see MONGOLIA (map). Its industries produce woolen cloth, felt, saddles, shoes, and meat products. Ulan Bator is a rail center and has a university. Founded in 1649, it has also been called *Urga.*

ULBRICHT, *OOL brihkt,* **WALTER,** *VAHL tuhr* (1893-1973), was the Communist leader of East Germany from 1950 to 1971. He ruled as general secretary of the Communist-dominated Socialist Unity Party. In 1961, Ulbricht ordered the building of the Berlin Wall, which separated the eastern and western sectors of the city.

Ulbricht was born in Leipzig, Germany. He helped found the German Communist Party in 1919, and studied Communist theory in Russia in the mid-1920's.

He was exiled from Germany from 1933 to 1945. He served with Communist forces in Spain during the Spanish Civil War. He returned to Germany in 1945, and helped form the Socialist Unity Party. Ulbricht was deputy premier of East Germany from 1949 to 1960.　　　　　　　　　　　　　　GEORGE G. WINDELL

ULCER, *UHL suhr,* is an open sore in the skin or mucous membrane. During the development of an ulcer, part of the surface tissue breaks down and dies, leaving a raw, inflamed area that heals slowly.

Probably the best-known kinds of ulcers are *peptic ulcers,* which occur in the digestive system. There are two main types of peptic ulcers. *Duodenal ulcers* form in the duodenum, the upper part of the small intestine. *Gastric ulcers* develop in the stomach. During digestion and at certain other times, the stomach produces hydrochloric acid and an enzyme called *pepsin.* These powerful digestive juices can eat through the lining of the stomach and duodenum. Normally, mucous secretions protect the stomach and duodenum from the effects of digestive juices. Duodenal ulcers result from an overproduction of hydrochloric acid and pepsin. Gastric ulcers probably result from a weakening of the stomach's defense against the two digestive juices. The development of peptic ulcers is influenced by such factors as stress and the use of tobacco, both of which stimulate acid production. Overuse of aspirin also promotes ulcer formation by irritating the stomach lining. Some people inherit a tendency toward peptic ulcers.

Most peptic ulcers cause pain in the upper part of the stomach. The pain usually occurs when the stomach is empty, either between meals or during the night. Antacid medications relieve the pain temporarily by neutralizing the stomach acid. Eating may also ease the pain. Patients with peptic ulcers may develop such complications as blockage of the stomach or duodenum, internal bleeding, and perforation of the stomach wall. Most of these conditions require surgery.

Physicians treat peptic ulcers with drugs that neutralize stomach acid or prevent its secretion. If a peptic ulcer continues to recur, surgery may be required.

Other kinds of ulcers include *chronic leg ulcers,* which may result from poor blood circulation caused by diabetes, hardening of the arteries, or varicose veins. *Decubitus ulcers,* commonly called *bedsores,* afflict many patients who are confined to bed or a wheelchair. Ulcers also occur in the mouth, in the wall of the bladder, and on the eyes.　　　　　　　　　　　　　JAMES L. FRANKLIN

See also CANKER; STOMACH (Stomach Diseases); TYPHOID FEVER.

Additional Resources

BERLAND, THEODORE, and SPELLBERG, MITCHELL. *Living with Your Ulcer.* St. Martin's, 1971.
EISENBERG, M. MICHAEL. *Ulcers.* Random House, 1978.
NUGENT, NANCY. *How to Get Along with Your Stomach: A Complete Guide to the Prevention and Treatment of Stomach Distress.* Little, Brown, 1978.

ULITHI, *oo LEE thee,* atoll is one of the western Caroline Islands. It consists of a large atoll, with 183 square miles (474 square kilometers) of lagoon and some detached reefs and islets. The land area totals less than 2 square miles (5 square kilometers). About 710 Micronesians live on the islets. They raise food for their own use and make copra for trade. Like the other Caroline Islands, Ulithi is part of the Trust Territory of the Pacific Islands. The U.S. administers Ulithi. See PACIFIC ISLANDS, TRUST TERRITORY OF THE; PACIFIC ISLANDS (color map).　　　　　　　　　　EDWIN H. BRYAN, JR.

ULNA. See ARM.

ULSTER, *UL ster,* was one of the five provinces of early Ireland. It included what is now Northern Ireland, as well as the counties of Cavan, Donegal, and Monaghan. Northern Ireland is often called Ulster. For location, see IRELAND (color map). See also NORTHERN IRELAND.

ULTIMA THULE, *UL tih muh THYOO lee,* was the name given in ancient literature to the most northern of known lands. A Greek sailor named Pytheas spoke of it in the 300's B.C. He said that the days and nights in Ultima Thule lasted for six months, and that the sea there was so thick the rowers could not get through it. Some think that Pytheas was referring to Norway or Iceland. Others believe Ultima Thule was one of the Shetland Islands. Today Ultima Thule is used to mean any distant place or faraway goal.　　　THOMAS W. AFRICA

See also EXPLORATION (The Ancient Greeks).

ULTIMATUM, *UL tuh MAY tum,* is a final proposition or demand made by one of two negotiating parties. The term is usually used in international affairs. It is a forceful and definite statement of one country's position. It often includes a demand for certain action on the part of the other country within a time limit. The rejection of an ultimatum may mean that one nation breaks off peaceful negotiations with the other.　　PAYSON S. WILD

ULTRAHIGH FREQUENCY WAVE (UHF) is a type of short radio wave. Its frequency ranges from 300 to 3,000 *megahertz.* One megahertz equals 1 million *hertz* (cycles per second). The wavelength of UHF waves measures only from 0.1 to 1 meter.

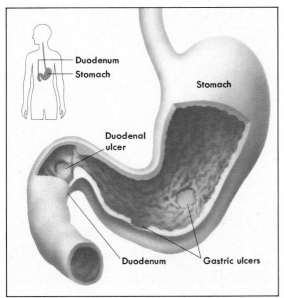

WORLD BOOK illustrations by Leonard E. Morgan

Peptic Ulcers are open sores in the digestive system. There are two main types of peptic ulcers. *Duodenal ulcers* form in the duodenum, the upper part of the small intestine. *Gastric ulcers* develop in the stomach. Both types result from the erosive action of two digestive juices, hydrochloric acid and pepsin.

ULTRAMARINE

UHF waves are widely used in television broadcasting. In the United States and Canada, they carry television signals on channels 14 through 83. UHF waves also are used in aircraft and ship navigation and for police and emergency communication. In some cases, UHF waves provide a communication link between vehicles traveling in space and monitoring stations located on the earth.

UHF waves travel primarily in a straight line, and they cannot pass through the earth. For this reason, the transmission of UHF waves between two points on the earth is limited by the curvature of the earth to 50 miles (80 kilometers) or less. Certain radio waves that have frequencies lower than those of UHF waves can be reflected off the upper layers of the atmosphere to reach beyond the earth's curvature. As a result, they can be transmitted much farther than UHF waves in some cases.   HUGH D. YOUNG

See also SHORT WAVE; TELEVISION (Broadcasting).

ULTRAMARINE is a blue pigment or coloring matter now prepared by artificial means. It usually has a reddish tinge. Ultramarine is made by *calcining* (heating) various combinations of China clay, sodium carbonate, carbon, and sodium sulfate until they form a dry powder. Ultramarine was once ground from the rare mineral lapis lazuli. This old method produced a brilliant, durable blue color, which was much prized by artists, but was very expensive.   EDWARD W. STEWART

See also LAPIS LAZULI.

ULTRAMICROSCOPE is an instrument that allows a person to see objects much smaller than those that can be seen under an ordinary microscope. It is a compound microscope with several lenses. But it differs from other compound microscopes, because it uses a strong horizontal beam of light to illuminate the particles to be seen. This light beam can be brought into intense focus. Usually a powerful arc lamp supplies the light for ultramicroscopic viewing. The rays of light are focused by means of a system of condensing lenses. The last lens brings the rays together into very small, intensely brilliant focus.

Scientists often use this microscope to study *colloidal particles*, or bacteria floating in liquid or in the air. They set the microscope so that it receives only the light scattered by the particles themselves. No part of the direct light that illuminates the objects can enter the instrument. Therefore, the particles shine out as bright "stars" against a dark background. However, like the stars in the sky, these particles appear as points of light without structural detail. Objects as small as $\frac{6}{1,000,000}$ of a millimeter can be seen with an ultramicroscope.   JOSEPH VALASEK

See also ELECTRON MICROSCOPE; ION MICROSCOPE.

ULTRASOUND is sound with *frequencies* above the range of human hearing. Frequency refers to the number of sound waves a vibrating object produces per second. It is measured in terms of *hertz*. One hertz equals one *cycle* (vibration) per second. Most people can hear sounds with frequencies between 20 and 20,000 hertz. However, ultrasound has frequencies above 20,000 hertz. Scientists have developed many uses for ultrasound, especially in medicine and industry.

In addition to its high frequency, ultrasound has other qualities that distinguish it from the sound that is audible to human beings. For example, ultrasonic waves are shorter than the waves of audible sound. When the short waves of ultrasound encounter small obstacles, they are easily reflected, forming echoes. The longer

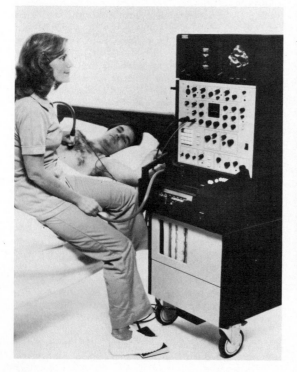

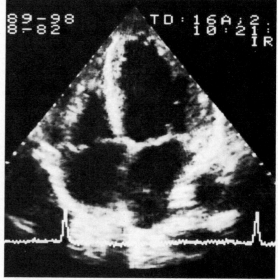

Irex Corporation

Ultrasound is widely used in the diagnosis of heart disease and other disorders. In the photo at the left, an ultrasonic transducer gives off ultrasonic waves and changes the returning echoes into electric pulses. A computer transforms such data as the direction of the echoes and the intensity of the pulses into an image of the four chambers of the heart, as shown above.

waves of audible sound, however, flow around small obstacles, with very little reflection.

Bats, porpoises, and certain other animals that can hear frequencies above 20,000 hertz make important use of ultrasound. For example, some bats give off short, ultrasonic cries that bounce off nearby objects, making echoes. They use these echoes to find insects or other food and to avoid obstacles.

Producing Ultrasound. Scientists have invented whistles and other devices that produce ultrasound. One commonly used device, called an *ultrasonic transducer,* converts electric energy into ultrasonic waves. Some ultrasonic transducers include a special disk made of quartz or of a ceramic material. When charged with electricity, the disk vibrates so rapidly that ultrasonic waves are created.

Many transducers can also convert ultrasonic waves into electric energy. These transducers give off ultrasonic waves at the same time that they change the returning echoes back to electricity. Strong echoes create stronger electric pulses than weak ones do. A computer registers such data as the intensity of the electric pulses and the direction of the returning echoes. The computer can then provide information on the substances that reflected the ultrasonic waves. Some computers transform the data they receive into images on a screen.

Uses. Ultrasound has a wide variety of uses. They can be divided into two basic groups—(1) passive uses and (2) active uses.

Passive Uses of Ultrasound include those in which it is used only to obtain information. For example, doctors use ultrasound to check the development of unborn babies. Special ultrasonic equipment can produce an image of an unborn baby on a screen. Ultrasound can also aid in the diagnosis of tumors, gallstones, heart disease, and other disorders. Most doctors believe that ultrasonic examinations have no dangerous side effects.

Manufacturers use ultrasound to measure the wall thickness of metal or plastic pipes and to test the concentration of particles in inks and paints. Sonar devices locate enemy ships, schools of fish, and underwater obstacles through the use of ultrasound (see SONAR).

Active Uses of Ultrasound include those in which it is used to produce certain effects in materials. For example, brain tumors and kidney stones can be destroyed by ultrasound. Ultrasonic waves can also be used to clean watches and other delicate instruments and to mix chemicals. At certain frequencies, ultrasound can produce enough energy to weld certain metals. LASZLO ADLER

See also REMOTE CONTROL (diagram); MACHINE TOOL (Other Advanced Machining Operations); TRANSDUCER.

ULTRAVIOLET RAYS are an invisible form of light. They lie just beyond the violet end of the visible spectrum (see LIGHT [The Visible Spectrum]). Ultraviolet rays are sometimes known as *black light* because most of them cannot be seen directly by the human eye. These rays can cause sunburn, but they destroy harmful organisms and also have other useful effects.

The sun is the major source of ultraviolet rays. Lightning, or any electrical spark in the air, also produces the rays. Ultraviolet rays can be made artificially by passing an electric current through a gas or a vapor, such as mercury vapor.

Scientists use an instrument called a *spectrometer* to

measure *wavelengths* of ultraviolet rays and other forms of light. A wavelength, the distance between the crest of a wave and the crest of the next wave, is measured in *nanometers.* One nanometer (nm) equals 0.000001 millimeter (0.000000039 inch). Wavelengths of visible light range from about 400 to 800 nm. Ultraviolet rays have wavelengths of about 10 to 400 nm.

The wavelength of an ultraviolet ray determines what materials the ray can pass through. Only long ultraviolet rays can penetrate window glass. Shorter rays can pass through pyrex and quartz. This ability of ultraviolet rays to pass through certain substances enables the rays to be used for specific purposes.

Uses of Ultraviolet Rays. Ultraviolet rays shorter than 320 nm are effective in killing bacteria and viruses. Hospitals use germicidal lamps that produce ultraviolet rays of these short wavelengths to sterilize surgical instruments, water, and the air in operating rooms. Many food and drug companies use germicidal lamps to disinfect various types of products and their containers.

Direct exposure of the skin to ultraviolet rays from the sun or from other sources produces vitamin D in the body. Physicians use ultraviolet rays to treat rickets, a bone disease caused by the lack of vitamin D. Some skin diseases, such as acne and psoriasis, can be treated by ultraviolet rays. Exposure of cereal grains and dairy products to ultraviolet rays kills bacteria and produces vitamin D.

The electronics industry uses ultraviolet rays in manufacturing microcircuits for computers. Researchers are seeking ways of using extremely short ultraviolet rays to produce even smaller electronic devices.

Harmful Effects. Ultraviolet rays irritate the eyes, and so dark glasses should be worn in the presence of these rays. Overexposure of the skin to ultraviolet rays may cause a painful burn. Unlike visible light, ultraviolet rays can penetrate clouds, making sunburn possible even on cloudy days. Some scientists believe ultraviolet rays cause skin cancer.

The sun's shortest ultraviolet rays—those having wavelengths shorter than 290 nm—are particularly harmful to living things. However, most of these rays are absorbed by a form of oxygen called *ozone,* which forms a protective "layer" in the atmosphere. Without this ozone layer, ultraviolet rays would probably destroy most plants and animals. See OZONE.

Scientific Research. Ultraviolet rays originate within the atoms of all elements. Scientists learn about the makeup and energy levels of these particles by studying the rays.

Scientists also study the effect of ultraviolet radiation on the atoms of gases in the atmosphere. High-energy rays cause electrons to separate from atoms, making the atoms electrically charged. These charged atoms, known as *ions,* collect in the upper atmosphere and form a layer called the *ionosphere.* Scientists believe ultraviolet rays broke down water vapor molecules in the atmosphere billions of years ago, resulting in the formation of oxygen in that region. Some scientists believe a similar process may be occurring now on Mars and other planets. JAMES A. R. SAMSON

See also ELECTROMAGNETIC WAVES (diagram: The

ULYSSES

Electromagnetic Spectrum); FOOD PRESERVATION (Ultraviolet Rays).

ULYSSES, *yoo LIHS eez,* was a king of Ithaca and a brave and cunning hero in Greek mythology. His name is *Odysseus* in Greek and *Ulysses* in Latin. Ulysses was noted for his cleverness. In early Greek writings, he also was generous and noble. Some later Greek writers portrayed him as a sly, deceitful trickster.

Most stories about Ulysses tell about his life during and after the Trojan War, a conflict between Greece and the city of Troy. Ulysses is a major character in the *Iliad* and the hero of the *Odyssey,* two epics attributed to the Greek poet Homer. The *Iliad* deals with events in the last year of the Trojan War. The *Odyssey* describes Ulysses' adventures as he returns home after the war.

The Trojan War. Ulysses was the son of Laertes, the king of Ithaca, and Anticleia. But just before her marriage to Laertes, Anticleia had been seduced by Sisyphus, the king of Corinth. Some Greeks believed that Sisyphus was Ulysses' father.

Ulysses married Penelope, the daugther of Icarius, the king of Sparta. Soon after the birth of their son, Telemachus, a group of Greek leaders tried to recruit Ulysses to fight Troy. But Ulysses did not want to go to war. To avoid joining the army, Ulysses pretended to be insane. He yoked an ox and a donkey to a plow and then sowed his fields with salt. Palamedes, a member of the group, suspected that Ulysses was faking insanity. Palamedes took Telemachus and put him in the path of Ulysses' plow. Ulysses turned the plow aside to protect the baby and thus proved that he was sane.

Ulysses reluctantly agreed to sail with the Greek army for Troy, but he never forgave Palamedes. After the Greeks arrived at Troy, Ulysses tricked them into believing that Palamedes was a traitor. The Greek soldiers then killed Palamedes.

During the Trojan War, Ulysses was a valiant fighter and a wise counselor to the Greek leaders. Ulysses showed his bravery by going on dangerous missions to spy on the Trojan forces. The Greeks honored him by giving him the armor of Achilles, the greatest Greek warrior, after Achilles' death.

Return to Ithaca. The Greeks finally defeated the Trojans after 10 years of fighting, and Ulysses set out by ship for Ithaca. During his return voyage, he visited the land of one-eyed giants called Cyclopes. Ulysses was captured by Polyphemus, a Cyclops, but escaped after driving a burning stake through the giant's eye. Polyphemus prayed for revenge to his father, Poseidon, the god of the sea. Poseidon became Ulysses' enemy and tried to prevent his return to Ithaca. Ulysses, largely with the help of the goddess Athena, finally reached home after 10 years of wandering and many thrilling adventures. For the story of his travels, see ODYSSEY.

During Ulysses' long absence, several noblemen had moved into his palace. The men claimed that Ulysses must have died, and they demanded that Penelope marry one of them. Penelope finally agreed to marry the man who could string Ulysses' huge bow and shoot an arrow through 12 hollow axheads.

Ulysses arrived at the palace the day before the archery contest, disguised as a begger. Penelope, unaware of his identity, allowed him to enter the contest. He was the only one who could perform the feat. After revealing his identity, he killed the noblemen with the help of Athena, Telemachus, and loyal servants. He then was reunited with his wife.   ROBERT J. LENARDON

See also TROJAN WAR; PENELOPE.

Additional Resources

EVSLIN, BERNARD. *Greeks Bearing Gifts: The Epics of Achilles and Ulysses.* Four Winds, 1976. A modern, popular treatment of Ulysses and the Trojan War. Includes background material and explains related myths.
FINLEY, M. I. *The World of Odysseus.* Rev. ed. Penguin, 1979.
STANFORD, WILLIAM B. *The Quest for Ulysses.* Praeger, 1974. Traces theme of Ulysses in literature and art from classical period to modern times.

UMAR IBN AL-KHATTAB. See MUHAMMAD (His Religious Life); MUSLIMS (The First Caliphs).

UMBER is a brown mineral pigment used to make certain oil and water-color paints. It is ground, washed, and dried to make *raw umber.* When raw umber is heated, it becomes *burnt umber,* which has a deep reddish color. The name comes from Umbria, Italy, where the mineral was first found.   EDWARD W. STEWART

UMBILICAL CORD, *uhm BIHL uh kuhl,* is a ropelike structure that connects the *fetus* (unborn child) to the *placenta* (see EMBRYO [Human Development]). The cord contains two arteries and one vein. The arteries carry blood containing waste products from the fetus to the placenta. The vein carries blood containing oxygen and food substances obtained from the mother's blood back to the fetus. When the baby is born, the doctor carefully cuts the umbilical cord about 2 inches (5 centimeters) from the baby's abdomen. The remaining stump falls off naturally within 7 to 10 days, leaving a scar that remains throughout life. This scar is called the *umbilicus,* or *navel.* See also CHILDBIRTH.   CARL C. FRANCIS

UMBRA. See PENUMBRA; SHADOW; SUNSPOT.

Painting on a cup (about 490 B.C.) by Douris;
Kunsthistorisches Museum, Vienna

Ulysses was a leader of the Greek army during the Trojan War. The Greeks awarded him the armor of Achilles, the mightiest Greek warrior, after Achilles died in battle. This ancient Greek painting shows Ulysses, *right,* giving the armor to Achilles' son.

UMBRELLA is a device that protects people from rain and sun. It consists of a circular piece of fabric stretched on a frame attached to a central handle. The frame can be folded when it is not needed.

Umbrellas were originally used as sunshades. In many cultures, they were a symbol of rank. In ancient Egypt and Babylonia, for example, only royalty and nobility were permitted to have umbrellas.

Umbrellas were first widely used against rain during the 1700's, when heavy umbrellas made of wood and oilcloth became common in Europe. During the 1800's, light, decorative sunshades called *parasols* became fashionable among women throughout Europe and the United States. Many of these umbrellas had whalebone or metal frames and fine silk coverings edged with lace and fringe. They remained popular until about the 1920's.

Today, umbrellas are used primarily as protection against rain or snow. Most umbrellas are made with metal or plastic frames and covered with plain or patterned fabric or clear plastic. They come in a wide variety of colors. Many umbrellas fold up to fit in purses and briefcases.   LOIS M. GUREL

The Oriental Institute, University of Chicago

Umbrellas Were Used As Sunshades in ancient times. The carving, *above,* shows King Xerxes I of Persia using an umbrella.

UMBRELLA BIRD lives in the tropical forests of South America. It is called the umbrella bird because of the tuft of plumes which rises from its crown and forms an umbrellalike crest over its head. A flap of skin covered with feathers hangs down from its neck. The flap looks like an umbrella handle. The bird is about the size of a crow. It has black feathers, edged with steel-blue.

Little is known about the habits of the umbrella bird. It lives in the tops of the highest trees, often on islands in the Amazon and other rivers.

Scientific Classification. The umbrella bird belongs to the cotinga family, *Cotingidae.* It is genus *Cephalopterus,* species *C. ornatus.*

RODOLPHE MEYER DE SCHAUENSEE

New York Zoological Society
Umbrella Bird

UMBRELLA TREE. See MAGNOLIA.

UMIAK. See ESKIMO (Transportation).

UMPIRE. See BASEBALL (Umpires); BASKETBALL (The Officials); FOOTBALL (The Officials).

UN. See UNITED NATIONS.

UN-AMERICAN ACTIVITIES COMMITTEE was the

name of an investigating committee of the United States House of Representatives. It investigated the threat of *subversion* (overthrowing the government) by groups in the United States and recommended legislation to the House.

The House Committee on Un-American Activities (HUAC) grew from a special investigating committee established in 1938. It became a *standing* (permanent) committee in 1945. In 1969, the House changed the committee's name to the Committee on Internal Security. The House abolished the committee in 1975.

The committee's main interest was to search for Communist influence inside and outside the government. After World War II ended in 1945, many people viewed such investigations as a contribution to the struggle against world Communism. President Harry S. Truman established a loyalty-security program in 1947 after it was discovered that some Communists had held jobs within the government before and during the war. The committee also investigated the activities of other radical or extremist groups.

The committee received attention in 1947 for its hearings on the influence of Communism in the motion-picture industry. But it gained its greatest fame in 1948 during its investigation of Communists in the Department of State. Its hearings led to the perjury trial and conviction of Alger Hiss, a former high official of the department (see HISS, ALGER). Representative Richard M. Nixon of California, a committee member, played a key role in the investigation (see NIXON, RICHARD M. [U.S. Representative]).

After the Hiss case, the Un-American Activities Committee looked into suspected Communist influence in almost all areas of life. Committees in the U.S. Senate and in state legislatures also investigated Communist influence. As a result, public employees and a number of employees in private industries had to take loyalty oaths. Persons accused of Communist associations were *blacklisted* (denied employment) by some firms.

The committee's critics charged that it often abused its investigative power and violated the constitutional rights of witnesses. They maintained that persons labeled as subversives should have the right to cross-examine their accusers. Others believed that the discovery of conspirators should be the responsibility of the police, the FBI, and the courts. Decisions by the Supreme Court of the United States in the 1950's and 1960's curbed the committee's activities. For example, the court ruled that witnesses may refuse to answer any questions that are not related to the matter under investigation.   HARVEY GLICKMAN

Additional Resources

GOODMAN, WALTER. *The Committee: The Extraordinary Career of the House Committee on Un-American Activities.* Farrar, 1968.
KANFER, STEFAN. *A Journal of the Plague Years.* Atheneum, 1973. Chronicles the period of show-business blacklisting, 1947-1958.

UNAMUNO, *oo nuh MOO noh,* **MIGUEL DE,** *mee GEHL deh* (1864-1936), was a Spanish philosophical essayist, poet, novelist, and dramatist. The leading humanist of modern Spain, he argued that individual man—not civilization, society, or culture—was "the subject and supreme object of all thought."

American Antiquarian Society

1834 Uncle Sam was pictured as a young man without a beard or gray hair in early cartoons.

© Punch

1869 Uncle Sam is not always popular. A British cartoonist pictured him as a tightwad after the Civil War.

Library of Congress

1917 Uncle Sam urged men to enlist in the U.S. Army. James Montgomery Flagg painted this poster of World War I.

Jensen, *Chicago Daily News*

1961 An elated Uncle Sam received the news that the first American astronaut had successfully flown into outer space and returned safely.

United Press, Int.

1941 Uncle Sam asked men and women to work in World War II defense plants. McClelland Barclay designed this well-known poster.

Unamuno's best-known work, *The Tragic Sense of Life* (1912), examines the conflict between faith and reason from the Renaissance to the 1900's. In this book, the author evaluates the significance of will, the desire for immortality, and the search for love in human history. Unamuno's study of Spanish culture in *Concerning Traditionalism* (1895) helped stimulate the Spanish intellectual revival known as the Generation of 1898. His finest poem is the long meditation called *The Christ of Velázquez* (1920). His best novel, *Mist* (1914), examines the mysteries of human existence.

Miguel de Unamuno y Jugo was born in Bilbao. He was appointed professor of Greek at the University of Salamanca in 1891 and rector of the university in 1900. In addition to his many books, Unamuno wrote more than 3,000 short essays and articles. A bold political critic, he incurred the hostility of four successive Spanish governments. PETER G. EARLE

UNAU. See SLOTH.

UNCAS, *UHNG kuhs* (1588?-1683?), was a chief of the Mohegan Indians in Connecticut during colonial times. He became noted for his assistance to the English settlers, and his name has been perpetuated in the character Uncas in James Fenimore Cooper's book, *The Last of the Mohicans* (see MOHEGAN INDIANS).

Uncas joined the English in a war against the Pequot Indians in 1637. He defeated the Narraganset tribe in 1643, and five years later fought the Mohawk, Narraganset, and other tribes. Uncas helped the English settlers, but opposed Christianity in his tribe. The English settlements along the Connecticut River probably owed their survival to his help against the Pequot Indians.

A monument to Uncas was erected by the citizens of Norwich, Conn., in 1847. Another monument to his name was erected on the site of the home of James Fenimore Cooper, at Cooperstown, N.Y. WILLIAM H. GILBERT

UNCLE REMUS. See HARRIS, JOEL CHANDLER.

UNCLE SAM is a figure that symbolizes the United States. The term originated as an unfriendly nickname for the U.S. government during the War of 1812.

The term "Uncle Sam" was apparently derived from the large initials "U.S." that Samuel Wilson, an Army meat inspector and provisioner, stamped on barrels of salted meat. People in upper New York and Vermont who opposed the war used the nickname. It first appeared in a Troy, N.Y., newspaper in 1813 and spread rapidly. In 1816, the nickname appeared in a book title, *The Adventures of Uncle Sam*.

The costume of Uncle Sam, decorated with stars and stripes, originated in the cartoons of the 1830's. Seba Smith, a humorous political essayist, was cartooned as Uncle Sam, with such a costume. A clown of the 1800's, Dan Rice, made the costume popular. In 1961, Congress passed a resolution recognizing Uncle Sam as a national symbol. MERRILL JENSEN

See also BROTHER JONATHAN.

UNCLE TOM'S CABIN is a famous antislavery novel by the American author Harriet Beecher Stowe. It first appeared as a serial in the abolitionist magazine *National Era* in 1851 and 1852. The novel was published as a book later in 1852 and quickly became a best seller in the United States and Great Britain.

Stowe wrote *Uncle Tom's Cabin* to criticize slavery, which she considered a national sin. She hoped that her novel would help bring slavery to an early and peaceful end. However, the book increased the hostility of many Northerners toward the South. Southerners, on the other hand, considered Stowe's description of slavery inaccurate. They called the book an insult and an injustice to their region. Historians believe that the bitter feelings aroused by Stowe's book helped cause the Civil War (1861-1965).

The chief character in *Uncle Tom's Cabin* is Uncle Tom, a dignified old black slave. The story describes Tom's experiences with three slaveholders. Two of them

Engraving (1852) by Hammat Billings, The Newberry Library, Chicago

Uncle Tom's Cabin describes the effects of slavery on both slaves and masters. In this scene, Eliza, a young slave, secretly visits Uncle Tom and his wife, Aunt Chloe. Eliza tells them that Tom and her baby have been sold to a slave dealer, and reveals her plan to flee with her child.

—George Shelby and Augustine St. Clare—treat Tom kindly. But the third, Simon Legree, abuses Tom and has him brutally beaten for refusing to tell where two escaped slaves are hiding. Tom dies from the beating. A subplot of the novel tells about the family of slaves—George and Eliza and their baby—who flee to freedom in Canada. In one famous episode, Eliza, clutching her baby, escapes across the frozen Ohio River from pursuing slave catchers. Two other characters in the book are Topsy, a mischievous black girl, and Little Eva, St. Clare's young daughter. The death of Little Eva is another famous episode.

The novel presents a realistic account of American life 10 years before the Civil War. Stowe created a vivid picture of Southern life, with Tom being sold from one slaveowner to another. *Uncle Tom's Cabin* also describes the upper Midwest as seen by George and Eliza as they flee northward into Canada.

After the Civil War, *Uncle Tom's Cabin* became known chiefly through abridgments of the novel and by plays based on the book. However, these versions distorted the original story and characters. By the late 1800's, most people believed that *Uncle Tom's Cabin* dealt primarily with the death of Tom and Little Eva, Topsy's antics, and Eliza's escape. The term "Uncle Tom" came to stand for a black man who, for selfish reasons or through fear, adopts a humble manner to gain favor with whites. But the novel portrayed Tom as a brave man who dies rather than betray two fellow slaves. Few people realized that Simon Legree, the cruel villain, was a Northerner, and that Augustine St. Clare, a Southerner, recognized the evils of slavery.

The famous American critic Edmund Wilson wrote that reading *Uncle Tom's Cabin* for the first time may be a "startling experience." He stated that "it is a much more remarkable book than one had ever been allowed to suspect." JOHN CLENDENNING

See also STOWE, HARRIET BEECHER; AMERICAN LITERATURE (Abolition and *Uncle Tom*).

UNCONSCIOUS, in psychology, is the part of the mind that rarely has awareness, or consciousness. It may contain information that has never been conscious, or that was once conscious but is now unconscious. See also PSYCHOANALYSIS; SUBCONSCIOUS; MYTHOLOGY (Mythology and the Individual).

UNCONSCIOUSNESS. See FIRST AID (Fainting).

UNCTION. See ANOINTING OF THE SICK.

UNDERDEVELOPED COUNTRY. See DEVELOPING COUNTRY.

UNDERGROUND, in political terms, is a secretly conducted movement to overthrow the government or the military occupation forces of a country. Underground tactics have been used since early history, but reached a high point of activity during World War II (1939-1945). Since then, Communist organizations have worked underground in attempts to overthrow many governments.

Adolf Hitler used an underground group called the *fifth column*, especially in the early stages of World War II (see FIFTH COLUMN). German agents worked inside various countries before and during the German invasions of those countries. The agents used espionage, propaganda, and sabotage to aid the German cause and destroy the invaded country's morale.

But once the Germans had conquered a country, the underground of that country's patriots hampered German operations. Underground workers sprang up in France, Belgium, The Netherlands, Denmark, Norway, Yugoslavia, and other conquered countries. They plagued the Germans by blowing up railroad trains and bridges, sabotaging factories, distributing illegal newspapers, rescuing marooned Allied servicemen, and gathering valuable military information.

See also GUERRILLA WARFARE; MAQUIS; PARTISANS; WORLD WAR II (Underground Resistance).

UNDERGROUND RAILROAD was an informal system that helped slaves escape to the Northern States and Canada during the mid-1800's. The system was actually neither underground nor a railroad. It was called the underground railroad because of the swift, secret way in which the runaway slaves escaped. They traveled by whatever means they could, moving about almost entirely at night and hiding during the day. The fugitives and the people who aided them used many railroad terms as code words. For example, hiding places were called *stations*, and people who helped transport the runaways were known as *conductors*.

The underground railroad had no formal organization. Free blacks and some whites in both the South and the North provided the runaways with food, clothing, directions, and places to hide. Southern slaves also helped fugitives escape. In the North, many Quakers and other white abolitionists furnished hiding places and helped slaves move from one refuge to the next.

UNDERGROUND RAILROAD

The term *underground railroad* was first used about 1830. From then until 1860, the system helped thousands of slaves escape. Some settled in the Northern States, but there they could be captured and returned to slavery. Therefore, many fled to Canada, especially after Congress passed a strict fugitive slave law as part of the Compromise of 1850. The major haven for runaways in Canada was southern Ontario, which lies between Michigan and New York.

The most heavily traveled routes of the underground railroad ran through Ohio, Indiana, and western Pennsylvania. Large numbers of fugitives followed these routes and reached Canada by way of Detroit or Niagara Falls, N.Y. Others sailed across Lake Erie to Ontario from such ports as Erie, Pa., and Sandusky, Ohio. In the East, the chief center of the underground railroad was southeastern Pennsylvania. Many runaway slaves followed routes from that area through New England to Quebec.

A few people became famous for their work with the underground railroad. Levi Coffin, a Quaker who was called the "president of the underground railroad," helped more than 3,000 slaves escape. His home in Newport (now Fountain City), Ind., was on three major escape routes. The most famous black leader of the underground railroad was Harriet Tubman, a runaway slave herself. She returned to the South 19 times and helped about 300 blacks escape to freedom.

The underground railroad showed the determination of blacks and many whites to end slavery in the United States. Its operations angered many Southerners and contributed to the hostility between North and South that led to the Civil War.   DAVID HERBERT DONALD

See also ABOLITIONIST; COMPROMISE OF 1850; FUGITIVE SLAVE LAWS; TUBMAN, HARRIET.

Additional Resources

GARA, LARRY. *The Liberty Line: The Legend of the Underground Railroad*. Univ. Press of Kentucky, 1967. Reprint of 1961 ed.
SIEBERT, WILBUR H. *The Underground Railroad from Slavery to Freedom*. Arno, 1968. Reprint of 1898 ed.
STEIN, R. CONRAD. *The Story of the Underground Railroad*. Childrens Press, 1981. For younger readers.

WORLD BOOK map

The Underground Railroad was a network of escape routes used by slaves during the mid-1800's. The routes led from the slave states—shown in gray—to the free states and Canada.

UNDERTAKER. See FUNERAL DIRECTOR.

UNDERWEIGHT. See WEIGHT CONTROL.

UNDERWORLD. See CRIME.

UNDERWRITING is a term first used in England in the 1600's. *Underwriters* (insurers) wrote their names at the bottom of proposed insurance contracts covering a ship and its cargo. They indicated in this way their willingness to assume part of the risk.

Today, every insurance company has an underwriting department which is important to the success of the firm. Underwriting experts must establish the premium rates for various kinds of policies and the amount and degree of risk to be assumed for each policy.

Underwriters also examine all applications for insurance in order to guard against bad risks and to prevent the company from assuming too many of the same kinds of risks. For example, a fire insurance underwriter may find that several suspicious fires have occurred in the building to be insured, and decide the risk is bad.

In finance, underwriting is an agreement to purchase a corporation stock or bond issue.   ROBERT D. PATTON

See also INSURANCE (Careers); LLOYD'S.

UNDOCUMENTED WORKER. See ILLEGAL ALIEN.

UNDSET, *OON seht*, **SIGRID,** *SIHG rihd* (1882-1949), a Norwegian author, won the 1928 Nobel prize for literature. *Kristin Lavransdatter* (1920-1922), her major work, is an epic trilogy of life in Norway during the Middle Ages. It consists of the novels *The Bridal Wreath, The Mistress of Husaby,* and *The Cross.* The novels tell the story of Kristin—her childhood, stormy marriage, and dedication to Christian service after the death of her husband. The displacement of heathen customs by Christian ideals in medieval Norway is dealt with in a second but less impressive epic, *The Master of Hestviken* (1925-1927). The series consists of *The Axe, The Snake Pit, In the Wilderness,* and *The Son Avenger.*

Miss Undset was born in Kalundborg, Denmark. She was the daughter of Ingvald Undset, a distinguished Norwegian archaeologist. Her father awakened in her a strong interest in the Middle Ages. After he died, Miss Undset gave up plans for a career as a painter and went to work in an Oslo business office. While working there from 1899 to 1909, she gathered impressions which she used in her early realistic stories of contemporary lower-middle class life.

Jenny (1911), her first novel to attract widespread attention, deals with the sexual problems of a female artist. Miss Undset wrote other novels about life in her time. They include *The Wild Orchid* (1929) and *The Burning Bush* (1930), stories of a man's conversion to Roman Catholicism. They reflect Miss Undset's own conversion to Catholicism in 1924. Miss Undset took refuge in the United States from 1940 to 1945, while the Nazis occupied Norway. She lectured and wrote while in the United States.   RICHARD B. VOWLES

UNDULANT FEVER, *UHN juh luhnt* or *UHN dyuh luhnt,* is an infectious disease so named because the fever of the patient *undulates* (varies from time to time). British soldiers seem to have acquired it first on the island of Malta. Therefore, they called it *Malta fever.*

A person may get undulant fever by drinking milk from animals which have the disease, or by handling raw meat from infected animals. Many persons in farm communities still drink unpasteurized milk. Undulant fever is a serious danger in such places.

The first symptoms appear from 10 to 15 days after a person becomes infected. The person feels weak, tired, and chilly, suffers a loss of appetite, and has general aches and fevers. The disease often develops so slowly that patients do not realize they are sick. The fever mounts slowly. Only about two out of every 100 cases result in death. But the disease often damages important organs. A combination of streptomycin and sulfa drugs has proved an effective treatment. PAUL R. CANNON

See also BANG'S DISEASE.

UNEARNED INCREMENT. See SINGLE TAX.

UNEMPLOYMENT is the state of a person who wants to work but does not have a job. The term does not refer to people who are not seeking work because of age, illness, or a mental or physical handicap. Nor does it refer to people who are attending school or keeping house. Such persons are classified as out of the labor force rather than unemployed.

Unemployment involves serious problems for both the individual and society as a whole. For the individual, it means loss of income and, in many cases, of self-respect. For society, it results in lost production and, in some cases, criminal or other antisocial behavior.

Until the 1900's, most people considered laziness the main cause of unemployment. But today, they realize that men and women may be out of work through no fault of their own.

Unemployment in the United States

Measuring Unemployment. The Bureau of the Census in the Department of Commerce collects and tabulates unemployment statistics in the United States. The Bureau of Labor Statistics in the Department of Labor analyzes and publishes the statistics. Every month, agents of the bureau visit a certain number of households in all parts of the country. They ask whether the members of each household who are 16 or older have jobs or are looking for work. The answers provide the basis for a monthly estimate of the nation's total labor force. The bureau also reports the *unemployment rate*, the percentage of the total labor force that is unemployed. If 85 million persons were employed and 5 million were unemployed, the bureau would report a total labor force of 90 million and an unemployment rate of 5.6 per cent. Businessmen, economists, and government officials study the reports for indications of the nation's economic health.

The annual U.S. unemployment rate represents the average of the monthly figures for a certain year. It shows the average number of persons unemployed during the year, but not the total number who had some unemployment. In 1984, the average number was about 8½ million. But almost twice that number were jobless at least one week during the year.

The unemployment rate varies greatly among various groups. It tends to be several times as high for teenaged workers as for older persons. Unskilled people experience about three times as much unemployment as do white-collar workers. The unemployment rate among blacks is about twice that among whites.

Economists disagree on the meaning of the unemployment rate. Some believe the rate exaggerates the problem because it includes persons who want only part-time jobs. Others argue that it underestimates the problem because it does not include discouraged work-

ers who have stopped looking for jobs or workers who have taken jobs below the level of their skill.

Types of Unemployment. Some economists classify unemployment into three categories, according to the basic causes. These categories are (1) normal, (2) structural, and (3) deficient demand.

Normal Unemployment exists even when jobs are plentiful. Such unemployment includes workers who have quit their jobs or have been fired, and need some time to find other jobs. It also includes individuals, such as young people and former homemakers, who want employment but have not yet found their first job.

Another kind of normal unemployment, called *seasonal* unemployment, occurs in industries that lay off workers during certain seasons each year. These industries include agriculture, construction, and shipping.

Structural Unemployment exists when individuals seeking work have the wrong skills for the available jobs. For example, many coal miners may be looking for work at the same time that the nation has a shortage of salespeople and stenographers. Structural unemployment also includes individuals in the wrong location to fill available jobs.

Structural unemployment includes *technological* unemployment, which results from the development of new products, machinery, or manufacturing methods. Such developments produce rapid changes in the demand for various skills. The total number of employment opportunities does not decline, but the number of jobs in certain occupations may grow less rapidly than in others or may even decline. In 1947, for example, clerical and professional workers made up only 19 per cent of all employed persons. By the early 1980's, they accounted for about 35 per cent of the total. At the same time, the proportion of unskilled workers declined from about 12 per cent to about 6 per cent of the total. See AUTOMATION (Automation and Jobs).

Deficient Demand Unemployment results from a general lack of need for workers when the nation's total spending is too little. As goods and services remain unsold, industries reduce production and lay off employees. Deficient demand unemployment is called *cyclical* unemployment if it occurs during periods of decreased business activity. But it also can occur during periods of increasing activity if the number of workers grows faster than the number of jobs.

The severest deficient demand unemployment in U.S. history occurred during the Great Depression of the 1930's. The unemployment rate reached about 25 per cent in 1933 and remained above 14 per cent through 1940. After the United States entered World War II in 1941, the government began to spend huge amounts for military purposes. By 1944, the unemployment rate had dropped to 1.2 per cent.

In the late 1950's and early 1960's, the unemployment rate rose to more than 6 per cent. Some economists thought the unemployment was structural and resulted from changes in the types of jobs available. Others thought it was deficient demand unemployment that resulted from too little spending. Then, in 1964, a tax cut allowed people to spend more money, and the government spent more on the Vietnam War. By 1966, unemployment had fallen to a 12-year low. Because the

Employment and Unemployment in the United States*

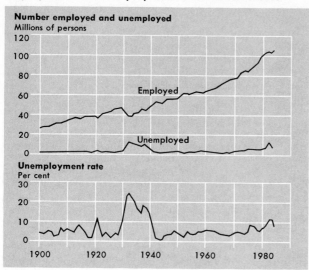

Number employed and unemployed
Millions of persons

Unemployment rate
Per cent

Year	Employed	Unemployed	Unemployment Rate (%)
1900	26,956,000	1,420,000	5.0
1905	30,918,000	1,381,000	4.3
1910	34,559,000	2,150,000	5.9
1915	36,223,000	3,377,000	8.5
1920	39,208,000	2,132,000	5.2
1925	43,716,000	1,453,000	3.2
1930	45,480,000	4,340,000	8.7
1935	42,260,000	10,610,000	20.1
1940	47,520,000	8,120,000	14.6
1945	52,820,000	1,040,000	1.9
1950	58,918,000	3,288,000	5.3
1955	62,170,000	2,852,000	4.4
1960	65,778,000	3,852,000	5.5
1965	71,088,000	3,366,000	4.5
1970	78,678,000	4,093,000	4.9
1975	85,846,000	7,929,000	8.5
1980	99,303,000	7,637,000	7.1
1981	100,397,000	8,273,000	7.6
1982	99,526,000	10,678,000	9.7
1983	100,834,000	10,717,000	9.6
1984	105,005,000	8,539,000	7.5

Sources: Lebergott, Stanley. *Manpower in Economic Growth: The American Record Since 1800.* McGraw-Hill, 1964; U.S. Bureau of Labor Statistics.

*Based on a sample of households throughout the country: for 1900-1946, persons 14 years old and over; after 1946, persons 16 years old and over.

increase in spending reduced unemployment, economists saw that the problem had been deficient demand unemployment. In 1969, the government reduced spending to curb inflation, and unemployment rose again. A recession during the early 1980's led to another rise in unemployment. In December 1982, the jobless rate reached 10.8 per cent, the highest level since 1941.

Fighting Unemployment. The United States government has fought each type of unemployment differently. To combat normal unemployment, the government has established public employment agencies that inform unemployed workers of suitable job openings. To attack structural unemployment, the Manpower Development and Training Act of 1962 set up programs to train workers in skills required for available jobs. The Economic Opportunity Act of 1964 also provided help for workers requiring retraining or other special assistance.

The fight against deficient demand unemployment presents especially serious problems. If unemployment rises, the government may increase its spending in order to create jobs. But such spending can cause rising prices and other problems of inflation. The government may then have to choose between the evils of unemployment and those of inflation.

Some economists believe that unemployment rates as low as 3 to 4 per cent should no longer be expected. They note that beginning in the 1960's higher proportions of women and young people entered the labor force than ever before. These two groups have higher rates of unemployment than the rest of the population.

Some persons believe the government must become the *employer of last resort* if industry cannot use the nation's total labor force. Under such a program, the government would create a job for any person who could not find one. The Emergency Employment Act of 1971 moved toward this goal. It provided federal funds for state and local governments to hire the unemployed.

Unemployment in Canada

Canada has the same types of unemployment that occur in the United States. However, seasonal unemployment is a much more serious problem in Canada because of the longer and colder winter.

In 1961, Canada's annual unemployment rate rose above 7 per cent. After the government took strong action to fight unemployment, the rate fell below 4 per cent in 1965, 1966, and 1967. But Canada's total labor force grew faster than the number of jobs because more and more women sought employment. In 1971, the annual unemployment rate reached a 10-year high of 6.2 per cent. In 1978, unemployment reached 8.4 per cent. A business slump in Canada during the early 1980's contributed to another rise in the jobless rate. By late 1982, unemployment reached 12.8 per cent, the highest level since the nation began recording the jobless rate in 1946.   HERBERT S. PARNES

Related Articles in WORLD BOOK include:

Comprehensive Employment and Training Act	Great Depression
Depression	Poverty
Employment Agency	Recession
Employment Service, U.S.	Unemployment Insurance

Additional Resources

GARRATY, JOHN A. *Unemployment in History: Economic Thought and Public Policy.* Harper, 1978.

JAHODA, MARIE. *Employment and Unemployment: A Social-Psychological Analysis.* Cambridge, 1982.

MAURER, HARRY. *Not Working.* Holt, 1980. Personal interviews with the unemployed.

UNEMPLOYMENT INSURANCE is a means of protecting workers who are out of work and looking for employment. These unemployed workers receive cash payments, usually each week for a limited period. Most of the industrial countries of the world have unemployment insurance systems. About 40 such programs are in effect, mostly in Europe, North America, and Australia.

Trade unions adopted the first plans to help ablebodied wage earners who were temporarily out of work through no fault of their own. In Great Britain, the Journeymen Steam Engine Makers' Society began paying out-of-work benefits as early as 1824. In the late 1800's and early 1900's, Switzerland, Belgium, Den-

mark, France, Norway, and other European countries began public voluntary unemployment insurance plans. In 1911, Great Britain set up the first compulsory unemployment insurance system. After World War I, it began paying various types of allowances, commonly called the *dole*, to unemployed workers who had used up their unemployment benefits. In 1932, Wisconsin adopted the first unemployment insurance law in the United States. A federal-state unemployment insurance plan was established as part of the Social Security Act of 1935.

United States Plan. The Federal Unemployment Tax Act, as amended, levies a 3.4 per cent payroll tax on employers who (1) employ workers in each of 20 weeks in a year or (2) have a quarterly payroll of at least $1,500. No tax is payable on wages over $6,000 a year. The law provides that the federal government gets only 0.7 per cent of the payroll tax in states with unemployment insurance acts meeting federal standards. This amount is returned to the states for administrative expenses and, in some cases, for benefits.

The states determine the tax rate each employer must pay for unemployment insurance. The rate usually depends on the employer's unemployment experience. These rates vary generally from as low as zero to more than 7 per cent. The national average is about 2.5 per cent. In Alabama, Alaska, and New Jersey, employees also contribute a small amount. Each state places the money it collects in the Unemployment Trust Fund of the United States, and withdraws it as needed. The secretary of the treasury administers the fund.

Unemployment insurance protection covers most workers in industry and commerce, and includes civilian federal employees. Some state systems cover more workers than the federal law requires, such as state and local government employees. Some states tax yearly wages of more than $6,000. Railroad workers have their own separate system. In 1955, several large corporations adopted plans to pay their workers unemployment benefits in addition to the amounts paid by the government.

State Regulations. Each state has different benefit provisions. The unemployed worker must apply at the employment service office both for benefit payments and for getting suitable work. The worker must also report regularly to receive benefits and to show a willingness to take a possible job. To qualify for benefits, a worker must have had a certain amount of covered work in a preceding period, usually a year. In most states, the minimum amount of wages required in this period ranges from $300 to $1,440. Most states have a one-week waiting period before benefits are payable. The usual maximum period for payments is 26 weeks.

The amount of the benefit is usually determined from the average wage in the 3 months of the base period that had the highest wages. This average is often adjusted upward to allow for possible unemployment even in that period. The benefit is then computed at half the adjusted average wage, but with certain minimums and maximums. The minimum payment is usually about $15 to $30 a week. The maximum is usually from $90 to $140 a week, but several states pay as high as $180.

About 15 states pay extra benefits for dependents. The benefit is usually a flat amount for each dependent, such as $5 to $10 a week, subject to a maximum total. In these states, the total benefits that workers with de-

pendents can get may be as high as $150 to $210 a week.

In 1980, unemployment insurance benefits paid under state laws totaled about $14 billion. About 10 million workers received weekly benefits. The average benefit totaled about $96 a week. At the same time, the number of workers covered by unemployment insurance averaged about 86 million.

Canadian Plan. The Canadian unemployment insurance plan went into effect in 1941, and applies uniformly in all provinces. About 95 per cent of all Canadian workers are covered. They pay 1.8 per cent of their earnings up to a maximum payment of $5.67 a week. Employers pay 1.4 times the amount paid by each employee. The national government pays for the additional cost of unemployment insurance during periods of high unemployment. After a 2-week waiting period, unemployed workers may collect benefits for as long as 50 weeks. Benefits equal 60 per cent of a worker's earnings up to $189 per week.

Similar benefits apply for sickness and maternity cases, but only up to 15 weeks. Employers with suitable private plans may contract out of the government plan and pay a lower tax rate that applies only to unemployment benefits. ROBERT J. MYERS

See also SOCIAL SECURITY; UNEMPLOYMENT; WELFARE.

UNESCO is a specialized agency of the United Nations. Its full name is UNITED NATIONS EDUCATIONAL, SCIENTIFIC AND CULTURAL ORGANIZATION. UNESCO works for understanding and cooperation among people everywhere. It tries to promote a respect for justice, the rule of law, human rights, and basic freedoms for all people. It was established in 1946 and has headquarters in Paris. About 160 countries are members of UNESCO. The agency carries out programs only at the request of its members. These nations provide most of its funds.

UNESCO stresses education, the spread of culture, and an increase in scientific knowledge. It stimulates scientific research in such areas as energy use and environmental protection. The organization tries to increase the free flow of ideas among the peoples of the world. It encourages artists, scientists, students, and teachers to travel, study, and work in other countries. The agency stresses the use of the social sciences to help solve such problems as inequality and violence. It also works with other UN agencies in providing assistance to developing countries. The *UNESCO Courier*, a monthly magazine printed in 15 languages, reports on the organization's work.

How UNESCO Works

Education. UNESCO considers learning essential for development. It helps countries in their efforts to improve education at all levels. The agency sponsors programs to train teachers, build courses of study, and carry out research in education. UNESCO has started programs in several countries to develop methods of teaching people how to read and write. It also sponsors permanent and mobile libraries.

Science. The agency promotes international scientific cooperation. It encourages research in the basic sciences. It develops studies and research on the environ-

ment and natural resources, and it urges the use of science and technology to help countries develop. For example, the agency helped establish the European Organization for Nuclear Research, which carries on research on the peaceful uses of nuclear energy. UNESCO also distributes scientific information, sponsors training courses, and organizes science conferences and seminars. It operates scientific centers in many developing areas of Africa, Asia, and Latin America.

The organization stimulates the growth of knowledge in the social sciences by sponsoring research and teaching programs. It also promotes the practical application of the social sciences to solving problems. It has supported studies in such areas as race relations, the status of women in society, and the effects of technological growth.

Culture. UNESCO encourages international cooperation to protect and promote culture. In the 1960's, it led efforts to move Nile Valley archaeological treasures that might have been lost under the lake formed by the Aswan High Dam in Egypt. The agency advises governments on how to restore and preserve national monuments. It sponsors exhibits and other efforts to acquaint the public with works of art, literature, and music. It promotes international copyright agreements.

The organization stresses the right to inform and to be informed. It has programs in all major areas of mass communication—including books, films, newspapers, radio, and television. It provides technical aid to developing nations for communications systems.

How UNESCO Is Organized

The General Conference of UNESCO consists of delegates appointed by the member nations. It meets every two years. The conference determines UNESCO policies and programs. It approves the budget and passes on financial and staff regulations. The conference selects the Executive Board and appoints the director-general of UNESCO. It admits new members to UNESCO and adopts conventions and recommendations for approval by the member nations. General Conference delegates have met in several major cities of the world, but most of the conferences have been in Paris.

The Executive Board has 45 members. They serve six-year terms. They are selected from among the delegates to the General Conference. The board meets in regular session at least twice a year. It supervises work on UNESCO programs and prepares the agenda for the General Conference. It recommends new members and nominates the director-general.

The Secretariat carries out UNESCO's programs. About 3,000 persons from most member nations work in the Secretariat. They include administrators, general service personnel, and various kinds of specialists. Some of them work at UNESCO headquarters, and others work in regional offices or in projects in the field.

The director-general, the chief administrative officer of UNESCO, appoints and directs the staff of the Secretariat. This official also makes regular reports on UNESCO activities to member nations and the Executive Board, and submits work plans and budget estimates to the board. The director-general is appointed to a six-year term and has offices in Paris.

The National Commissions of the member nations advise their governments. They also assist the delegations to the General Conference. Most member nations have national commissions to UNESCO. Most commission members come from national organizations interested in education, science, and culture.

History

After World War I (1914-1918), most of the Allies joined in an association called the League of Nations (see LEAGUE OF NATIONS). The League recognized the importance of promoting intellectual cooperation among the nations of the world. During World War II (1939-1945), ministers of education of the Allied nations held conferences regularly. They were especially concerned with reviving educational systems that had been weakened or destroyed by the war.

The United Nations Charter was signed in San Francisco in June 1945. In November of that year, the United Nations Conference for the Establishment of an Educational and Cultural Organization met in London. Representatives of 44 countries attended. They drew up the Constitution of UNESCO, and UNESCO officially came into existence on Nov. 4, 1946. By that date, 20 member countries had ratified the Constitution.

The UNESCO General Conference session of 1954 became an important milestone. The conference set up five important problems on which UNESCO should concentrate. These problems were: (1) illiteracy; (2) primary education; (3) racial, social, and international tensions; (4) mutual appreciation of Eastern and Western cultures; and (5) research on living conditions.

During the 1960's, UNESCO promoted international cooperation in solving world problems. It gave much attention to the problems of the developing nations and stressed conservation of the world's resources.

In 1976, UNESCO adopted a plan in which it recognized that many world problems are interrelated and require coordinated action. The conference emphasized the need to achieve peace, to guarantee human rights and equal opportunity, and to narrow the gap between developed and developing countries.

In 1983, the United States announced it would withdraw from UNESCO unless certain reforms were made. The United States objected to what it viewed as the organization's anti-Western bias, efforts to restrict press freedom, and wasteful management methods. The withdrawal of the United States became official in December 1984.   GABRIEL GUERRA-MONDRAGÓN

See also UNITED NATIONS; LIBRARY (International Library Programs).

Additional Resources

HAJNAL, PETER I. *Guide to UNESCO*. Oceana, 1983.
HOGGART, RICHARD. *An Idea and Its Servants: UNESCO from Within*. Oxford, 1978.
LAVES, WALTER H. C., and THOMSON, C. A. *UNESCO: Purpose, Progress, Prospects*. Indiana Univ. Press, 1957.
SHUSTER, GEORGE N. *UNESCO: Assessment and Promise*. Harper, 1963.

UNEVEN PARALLEL BARS. See GYMNASTICS (The Uneven Parallel Bars).

UNGAVA, *uhn GAY vuh* or *uhn GAH vuh*. All the peninsula of Labrador, except for a narrow strip along the eastern coast, was once included in the district of Ungava, which covered about 351,800 square miles (911,160

square kilometers). In 1912, Ungava became part of the province of Quebec.

UNGRADED SCHOOL. See EDUCATION (Elementary Education).

UNGULATE, *UHNG gyuh liht* or *UHNG gyuh layt,* is any mammal whose toes end in hoofs. The name comes from the Latin word *ungula,* meaning *hoof.* Scientists divide ungulates into two groups. *Odd-toed ungulates* include horses, which have one toe on each foot, and rhinoceroses, with three. *Even-toed ungulates* include deer, with two toes per foot, and pigs, with four. Ungulates are the only horned mammals, but not all ungulates have horns. All ungulates are *herbivores* (animals that eat chiefly plants). Elephants, the largest land animals, are ungulates. WILLIAM V. MAYER

Related Articles in WORLD BOOK include:

Alpaca	Dromedary	Karakul
Antelope	Elephant	Llama
Babirussa	Giraffe	Musk Ox
Bighorn	Goat	Okapi
Boar, Wild	Guanaco	Peccary
Buffalo	Herbivore	Rhinoceros
Camel	Hippopotamus	Ruminant
Carabao	Hog	Sheep
Caribou	Hoof	Vicuña
Cashmere Goat	Horn	Wart Hog
Cattle	Horse	Yak
Deer	Ibex	

UNICAMERAL LEGISLATURE. See LEGISLATURE; NEBRASKA (Legislature).

UNICEF, *YOO nuh sehf,* is the commonly used name for the United Nations Children's Fund. The name comes from the original title of this UN body—United Nations International Children's Emergency Fund. UNICEF aids children in more than 100 countries by helping to solve problems of health, hunger, and education. UNICEF provides supplies for disease-control programs, daycare centers, health centers, school food plans, and other projects. It also provides grants to help train people for such jobs as nursing and teaching. In 1965, UNICEF received the Nobel Peace Prize for its work in aid to children.

When UNICEF was created in 1946, it gave food, clothing, blankets, and medicine to children who

Mallica Vajrathon, UNICEF

UNICEF Programs aid children in more than 100 countries. These youngsters are receiving UNICEF food at a school in India.

needed help after World War II. Following this work, it continued to give aid to children of developing nations.

The people and governments of many countries donate the money used by UNICEF. Some people help by buying UNICEF greeting cards. On Halloween, many children "trick or treat" for UNICEF.   C. LLOYD BAILEY

UNICORN is an imaginary animal that plays a prominent part in medieval European legend and art. The unicorn has the head and body of a horse, the legs of a deer, and the tail of a lion. It is named for a single horn that projects from the middle of its forehead. Unicorns are usually portrayed as white and are generally believed to symbolize purity, chastity, and meekness.

People once believed that the unicorn's horn contained an antidote for poison, and during the Middle Ages, powders supposedly made from such horns sold for extremely

The Unicorn is often used in the design on a coat of arms.

high prices. Most scholars believe the image of the unicorn was derived from hearsay European accounts of the rhinoceros.   C. SCOTT LITTLETON

See also ANIMAL (picture); TAPESTRY (picture).

UNIDENTIFIED FLYING OBJECT (UFO) is a strange light or object that appears in the sky or near the ground and has no known cause. Some people believe UFO's may be spaceships from other planets. Others think UFO's have natural causes, even though scientists cannot explain all UFO reports. Observers have described various kinds of UFO's. Many of these objects resemble a glowing tube or saucer and fly at high speeds, either silently or with a whining sound. UFO's have been reported to have frightened animals, caused static on radios, and landed and left marks on the ground.

For hundreds of years, people have reported seeing mysterious objects in the sky. During World War II (1939-1945), the number of such reports increased greatly. Many military and civilian pilots reported seeing strange moving lights that they called *foo-fighters.* Other reports, some of so-called *flying saucers,* occurred during the mid-1900's in the United States and in other countries. Many came from reliable observers, some of whom photographed what they saw.

Scientists have provided logical explanations for many UFO reports. For example, in many cases, a reported UFO later was identified as a meteor, a planet, a rocket, a star, an artificial satellite, or a weather balloon. Aircraft or their exhaust trails, seen under unusual lighting conditions, have also been reported as UFO's. In addition, atmospheric conditions may produce optical illusions that are described as UFO's.

From 1966 to 1968, the U.S. Air Force sponsored a study of UFO's by scientists at the University of Colorado. The scientists could not explain all the UFO reports, but they found no evidence that UFO's came from other planets. The Air Force also investigated

more than 12,000 UFO reports that occurred from 1947 to 1969. It ended the investigation after concluding that UFO's were no threat to national security. In 1973, a group of scientists established the Center for UFO Studies, which gathers and examines information about UFO reports. The center's headquarters are at 2623 Ridge Avenue, Evanston, Ill. 60201.   J. ALLEN HYNEK

Additional Resources

COHEN, DANIEL. *The World of UFOs.* Harper, 1978. For younger readers.

FITZGERALD, RANDALL. *The Complete Book of Extraterrestrial Encounters: The Ideas of Carl Sagan, Erich Von Däniken, Billy Graham, Carl Jung, John C. Lilly, John G. Fuller, and Many Others.* Macmillan, 1979.

HENDRY, ALLAN. *The UFO Handbook: A Guide to Investigating, Evaluating and Reporting UFO Sightings.* Doubleday, 1979.

HYNEK, J. ALLEN. *The UFO Experience: A Scientific Inquiry.* Contemporary Books, 1972.

JACOBS, DAVID M. *The UFO Controversy in America.* Indiana Univ. Press, 1975.

STORY, RONALD D., ed. *The Encyclopedia of UFOs.* Doubleday, 1980.

UNIFICATION CHURCH. See CULT.

UNIFORM is a style of clothing that identifies persons as members of a group or as workers in a particular field. The most renowned uniforms are the military uniforms.

United States Air Force. In winter, officers and men wear light blue trousers, light blue coats with silver buttons, and visor caps. They wear blue shirts, black ties, and black shoes. In summer, they wear cotton khaki shirts and trousers. Women wear two-piece wool uniforms in winter and cotton dresses in the summer.

United States Army. In winter, men wear light tan shirts with dark green coats and trousers and black ties and shoes. The single-breasted coats have four large gold buttons. Officers' uniforms have black braid on the trousers and coat cuffs. In summer, men wear cotton khaki shirts and trousers. There is narrow braid on the cuffs of officers' coats. Officers wear green visor caps with gold trim. Enlisted men wear visor or overseas caps. Women wear green cotton two-piece summer uniforms and visor or overseas caps.

United States Marine Corps uniforms are of forest-green wool in winter and khaki in summer. For dress occasions, the marines wear dark blue jackets with gold buttons, light blue trousers with scarlet stripes, and white caps and belts. Women in the Marine Corps wear wool suits in winter and cotton suits in summer.

United States Navy. For dress occasions, Navy officers and senior enlisted men have a navy blue double-breasted suit that can be worn the year around. They also wear a white shirt, a white visor cap, a black tie, and black shoes. Officers wear gold buttons, a gold sleeve braid, and a gold hat insignia. Senior enlisted men wear silver buttons and a silver hat insignia. Junior enlisted men wear a blue jumper and round white hat with a black neckerchief and black shoes.

Women wear navy blue suits with a skirt or slacks. This uniform can be worn in any season. Women may wear black berets, overseas caps, or soft-brim hats with high crowns.   THOMAS E. GRIESS

For pictures of uniforms, see AIR FORCE, UNITED STATES; ARMY, UNITED STATES; MARINE CORPS, UNITED STATES; NAVY, UNITED STATES; CLOTHING.

UNIFORM CODE OF MILITARY JUSTICE is a set of laws that governs the conduct of all members of the United States armed forces. It also establishes a system of military courts and judges to try members of the armed forces accused of violating these regulations.

The code provides for three types of military courts and specifies the crimes that each may try. A *general court-martial* may try any military crime, including those punishable by death. A *special court-martial* tries less serious crimes. A *summary court-martial* tries minor offenses.

The code states that a qualified lawyer must be offered to a defendant in any general or special court-martial. The defendant may refuse to have a lawyer, except in cases involving a bad conduct discharge. A defendant may request a trial by a military judge alone, rather than by a court-martial. The code also states that a defendant may be released from confinement while awaiting an appeal of the case. Congress established the code in 1950 and revised it in the Military Justice Act of 1968.   FREDERICK C. LOUGH

See also COURT-MARTIAL.

UNION. See LABOR MOVEMENT; FLAG (table: Flag Terms); SET THEORY.

UNION, ACT OF, in Canadian history, united the colonies of Upper Canada and Lower Canada. The Parliament of Great Britain passed the act in 1840, and it took effect in 1841. The British government had set up the two colonies in 1791 to please a group of British colonists called United Empire Loyalists (see UNITED EMPIRE LOYALISTS). The creation of two colonies was also intended to please the French-speaking majority in Lower Canada.

The Act of Union of 1840 provided for one governor of the united colony, and a legislative council of at least 20 members appointed by the governor. The people in each of the two former individual colonies elected 42 members to a legislative assembly, which met at least once a year. Its members held office for four years, unless the governor dissolved the assembly. The act made English the only official language in council and assembly meetings. But in 1848, French was made the second official language. See CANADA, HISTORY OF (Lord Durham's Report).   JEAN BRUCHÉSI

UNION CITY, N.J. (pop. 55,593), is a manufacturing and residential center just north of Jersey City. The Lincoln Tunnel under the Hudson River links Union City with New York City. For location, see NEW JERSEY (political map). Union City manufactures clothing and automotive, chemical, electrical, heating, paper, tobacco, and wood products. It was formed in 1925, when Union and West Hoboken merged. Union City has a commission form of government.   RICHARD P. MCCORMICK

UNION JACK is the name sometimes used for the national flag of Great Britain, officially called the British Union Flag. The United States Jack has been called a union jack. See also FLAG (picture: Historical Flags of the World).

UNION LABEL is the trademark of organized labor. The label is placed on a finished product to show that members of the union manufactured it. Union labels are registered as trademarks. The purpose of the label is to encourage the use of union-made products. The union label was first used in California during the 1870's. During this time, many Chinese who were

willing to work for low wages entered the United States. The unions protested, and used labels to mark their work. ROBERT D. PATTON

UNION OF SOUTH AFRICA. See SOUTH AFRICA (The Union of South Africa).

UNION OF SOVIET SOCIALIST REPUBLICS. See RUSSIA.

UNION PACIFIC RAILROAD. See CREDIT MOBILIER OF AMERICA; WESTERN FRONTIER LIFE (East Meets West).

UNION PARTY. See REPUBLICAN PARTY (The Civil War).

UNION SHOP is a form of security given to a union in a collective-bargaining agreement. An employer formally recognizes a union as the sole bargaining agent for a specific group of employees. All these employees must belong to the union, or must join it within a specified period, usually 30 or 60 days following the signing of the contract or of their employment, whichever is later. Usually they must remain members of the union as long as the contract or its union shop provision lasts, or they will lose their jobs. GERALD G. SOMERS

See also CLOSED SHOP; OPEN SHOP; LABOR MOVEMENT (What Labor Unions Do).

UNION STATES. See CIVIL WAR (How the States Lined Up).

UNION THEOLOGICAL SEMINARY is a coeducational graduate school of religion in New York City. It has cooperative programs with Columbia University, General Theological Seminary, and the Jewish Theological Seminary of America. Degrees are given in theology and religious education. The seminary, founded in 1836, admits Protestant, Roman Catholic, and Jewish students who wish to prepare for religious work. For enrollment, see UNIVERSITIES AND COLLEGES (table).

Critically reviewed by UNION THEOLOGICAL SEMINARY

UNIONS, LABOR. See LABOR MOVEMENT.

UNIREME. See GALLEY.

UNIT, in measurement, is a quantity adopted as the standard by which any other quantity of the same kind is measured. The standard units of measure used in science, commerce, and industry have been tabulated in groups called *tables of denominate numbers*. There are units of money, of time, of surface, of volume, of weight, and of many other things. PHILIP FRANKLIN

See also DENOMINATE NUMBER; MEASUREMENT; METRIC SYSTEM; WEIGHTS AND MEASURES.

UNIT RULE, in the United States, was a voting rule permitted by the Democratic Party at its presidential nominating conventions from 1860 until 1968. The rule permitted the entire vote of a state delegation to be cast for one candidate, even though a minority of the delegation members favored another candidate. The national convention did not require the unit rule, but it enforced state instructions to delegates to vote as a unit. The practice was abolished at the 1968 Democratic National Convention. The Republican Party has never used the unit rule. CHARLES O. JONES

UNITARIAN UNIVERSALIST ASSOCIATION is a religious denomination formed in 1961 to consolidate the American Unitarian Association and the Universalist Church of America. The association's members are local, self-governing congregations and fellowships. It is organized under a Board of Trustees chosen by a General Assembly.

This denomination developed from protests against the doctrine of the Trinity as held by orthodox Christians, and it supports complete freedom of belief by its members. Hosea Ballou started the Universalist movement in the United States. William Ellery Channing was the founder of Unitarianism. The denomination is historically centered in New England, especially Boston, and has recently spread to urban areas across the United States and Canada. The association is also affiliated with similar groups in Europe and Asia. The association has about 185,000 members. Headquarters are at 25 Beacon Street, Boston, Mass. 02108. For more information on the movement, see UNITARIANS.

Critically reviewed by the UNITARIAN UNIVERSALIST ASSOCIATION

UNITARIANS believe in the unity of God, rather than in the doctrine of the Trinity as found in the historic creeds of the Christian church. The term *Unitarians* also extends to religious groups dating from the 1500's to the present who not only rejected the doctrine of the Trinity, but also rejected creeds as the basis for authority in religion.

History. Early supporters of Unitarianism on the continent of Europe were Francis David (1510-1579) in Transylvania, then part of Hungary; and Faustus Socinus (1539-1604), leader of the Minor Reformed Church in Poland. In England, Unitarian views were advanced by John Biddle (1615-1662). But the main development of English Unitarianism came during the 1700's, when many churches that had previously been Presbyterian became Unitarian. The British and Foreign Unitarian Association was formed in 1825.

In America, Unitarianism developed during the 1700's within the Congregational churches in New England. The movement reacted against Calvinistic doctrines that emphasized human sinfulness, as well as the Trinity. Unitarians argued that such doctrines were inconsistent with the Bible and contrary to reason.

The dispute in the United States between the liberals (Unitarians) and the orthodox Congregationalists became so bitter after 1805 that many churches divided. The Unitarians were forced to organize as a separate religious body. The most prominent supporter of the Unitarians during this period was a Boston clergyman named William Ellery Channing. His sermon "Unitarian Christianity" (1819) was widely accepted as a good statement of their position. The American Unitarian Association was organized in 1825.

Channing believed in Christianity as a divinely inspired religion proved by the miracles of Jesus. Younger Unitarian ministers soon began to argue that religious truth should be based on universal religious experiences, rather than on the record of historical events of long ago. These ministers believed that religious truth and inspiration could be found in traditions other than Christianity.

Such ideas were expressed by Ralph Waldo Emerson in his "Divinity School Address" (1838), and by Theodore Parker in his sermon "The Transient and Permanent in Christianity" (1841). These addresses expressed a new point of view in philosophy and religion. This view was called *transcendentalism* because it stated that people may have an experience of reality that *transcends* (goes beyond) the experience of the senses.

UNITAS, JOHN

Transcendentalism had a lasting effect on Unitarianism, especially in making it more receptive to religious ideas drawn from non-Christian sources. Since that time, two views have emerged in the denomination. One emphasizes liberal religion strongly attached to the Christian tradition. The other refuses to accept any such limits, and often argues that the modern mind, under the impact of science, has moved beyond Christianity altogether. See TRANSCENDENTALISM.

Organization. In 1865, the Unitarian churches in the United States founded a national conference. In 1925, this organization was absorbed into the American Unitarian Association. In 1961, the American Unitarian Association merged with the Universalist Church of America to form a new religious body, the Unitarian Universalist Association. This merger brought together two groups with parallel histories and a similar outlook. The denomination is organized on the basis of congregational church government. That is, the local church exerts basic authority. The local church strongly emphasizes individual freedom of belief and democratic participation in church affairs. Regional and national organizations provide leadership and services for the local churches, but they do not control the churches.

Unitarianism's original area of strength was New England. Today, Unitarian Universalist churches are found in many other parts of the United States and Canada. Most of these churches are in urban areas, and many are in university communities. HENRY WARNER BOWDEN

See also UNITARIAN UNIVERSALIST ASSOCIATION; CHANNING, WILLIAM ELLERY; EMERSON, RALPH WALDO.

UNITAS, JOHN (1933-   ), became one of the greatest quarterbacks in the history of the National Football League (NFL). Unitas ranks second only to Fran Tarkenton among NFL players in total yards passing and pass completions.

Unitas played for the Baltimore Colts from 1956 through the 1972-1973 season. He led the Colts to three world championships —in 1958 and 1959, and again in the 1970-1971 season. Unitas became noted for his daring selection of plays and his passing accuracy. He threw at least one scoring pass in 47 straight league games. In 1959, he threw 32 touchdown passes in 12 games.

Baltimore Colts
John Unitas

Unitas was born in Pittsburgh, and he graduated from the University of Louisville. He joined the Pittsburgh Steelers in 1955, but was released before the season began. He then played with a semiprofessional team before joining the Baltimore Colts. Unitas played for the San Diego Chargers in 1973 and retired as a player in 1974. HERMAN WEISKOPF

UNITED. Many organizations whose names begin with the word *United* are listed in THE WORLD BOOK ENCYCLOPEDIA under the key word in the name. For example, United Steelworkers of America is listed under STEELWORKERS OF AMERICA, UNITED.

United Arab Emirates

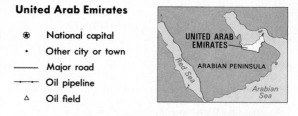

⊛ National capital
· Other city or town
—— Major road
—⊷— Oil pipeline
△ Oil field

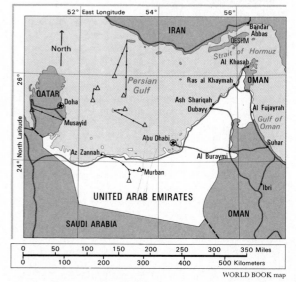

WORLD BOOK map

UNITED ARAB EMIRATES is a federation of seven independent Arab states in southwestern Asia. These states lie along the eastern coast of the Arabian Peninsula, at the south end of the Persian Gulf. They are Abu Dhabi, Al Fujayrah, Ash Shariqah, Dubayy, Ras al Khaymah, Ujman, and Umm al Qaywayn. Each state has a city or town of that same name.

Most people of the United Arab Emirates (UAE) are Arab Muslims. About four-fifths of them live in urban areas. The city of Abu Dhabi is the federation's capital and largest city. Dubayy, the second largest city, is an important port and commercial center.

Beginning in the early 1800's, Great Britain gradually took control of the states' defense and foreign affairs. The states became known as the Trucial States. They remained under British protection until 1971, when they gained full independence. That year, six of the states joined together and formed the United Arab Emirates. Ras al Khaymah joined the union in 1972.

Before the mid-1900's, the region that is now the United Arab Emirates was one of the most underdeveloped in the world. Most of the people earned a living at farming, fishing, or trading, or as nomadic herders. The discovery of oil during the late 1950's brought sudden wealth to the region and led to the development of mod-

Robert Geran Landen, the contributor of this article, is Professor of History and Dean of the College of Liberal Arts at the University of Tennessee at Knoxville, and the author of The Emergence of the Modern Middle East.

ern cities and towns. Many people left their traditional ways of life and took jobs in the oil industry and other fields. By the 1970's, the UAE had one of the world's highest *per capita* (per person) incomes.

Government. A ruler called an *emir* governs each of the seven states, called *emirates*, that make up the UAE. Each emir controls the state's internal affairs.

The federal government controls the UAE's foreign affairs. The seven emirs form the Supreme Council of the United Arab Emirates. The council appoints a president, who serves as chief of state, and a prime minister, who heads the government. The prime minister has a cabinet, the members of which supervise various federal *ministries* (departments). Each emir appoints representatives to the federal legislature, called the Consultative Assembly.

People. Most of the people of the UAE are Arabs. They belong to groups that have lived in the region for hundreds of years. Each group has its own traditions. Rivalries among the various groups have made it difficult to establish a unified nation.

Since the 1960's, thousands of people from neighboring Arab countries and from India, Iran, and Pakistan have come to the UAE to work in the oil industry. The rapid increase in population has caused housing shortages and other problems. But money from the oil industry has enabled the UAE to build apartment buildings,

Facts in Brief

Capital: Abu Dhabi.

Official Language: Arabic.

Form of Government: Federation.

Area: 32,278 sq. mi. (83,600 km²). *Greatest Distances*—north-south, 250 mi. (402 km); east-west, 350 mi. (563 km). *Coastline*—483 mi. (777 km).

Elevation: *Highest*—Jabal Yibir, 5,010 ft. (1,527 m) above sea level. *Lowest*—Salamiyah, a salt flat slightly below sea level.

Population: *Estimated 1986 Population*—1,407,000; distribution, 81 per cent urban, 19 per cent rural; density, 44 persons per sq. mi. (17 per km²). *1980 Census*—1,040,-275. *Estimated 1991 Population*—1,875,000.

Chief Products: *Agriculture*—dates. *Fishing*—fish, shrimp. *Mining*—petroleum.

Flag: The flag has a vertical red stripe and horizontal stripes of green, white, and black. It was adopted in 1971. See FLAG (color picture: Flags of Asia and the Pacific).

Money: *Basic Unit*—dirham. One hundred fils equal one dirham. See MONEY (table: Exchange Rates).

schools, hospitals, and roads to meet the needs of the growing population.

The cities and towns of the UAE have modern houses and apartment buildings. But in rural areas and on the outskirts of the cities, many people live in small

Bruno Barbey, Magnum

Pedestrians and Automobiles Jam a Crowded Street in Dubayy, the second largest city of the United Arab Emirates. Dubayy, an important Middle Eastern port, serves as a commercial center. The city has expanded rapidly since the 1960's, when oil production began in the country.

thatched huts, much as their ancestors did hundreds of years ago. Some of the people wear Western clothing, but most prefer traditional Arab garments.

Arabic is the official language of the UAE. About half of all the people 15 years of age or older can read and write. In the late 1950's, the states had only 8 schools. Today, they have about 450 elementary and high schools.

Land and Climate. The United Arab Emirates covers 32,278 square miles (83,600 square kilometers), including a number of offshore islands in the Persian Gulf. Swamps and salt marshes line much of the northern coast. A desert occupies most of the inland area. Water wells and oases dot the desert. The largest oasis, Al Buraymi, lies in both the UAE and in Oman, the country's neighbor to the east. Hills and mountains cover much of the eastern part of the UAE.

The United Arab Emirates has a hot climate with little rainfall. The humidity is often high along the coast, but the inland desert regions are dry. The mountainous areas are generally cooler and receive more rainfall than the rest of the country. Summer temperatures in the UAE average more than 90° F. (32° C) and often reach 120° F. (49° C). In winter, temperatures seldom drop below 60° F. (16° C). The country receives an average of less than 5 inches (13 centimeters) of rain a year.

Economy of the United Arab Emirates depends largely on the production and export of petroleum. Most of this oil production takes place in the states of Abu Dhabi and Dubayy, which have the country's largest known oil deposits. The rulers of the United Arab Emirates earn large profits from the sale of oil to foreign countries. Much of the country's petroleum is exported in crude form. But the UAE also has refineries that process some of the crude oil. The UAE is a member of the Organization of Petroleum Exporting Countries (OPEC).

Only about 5 per cent of the land of the UAE is suitable for raising crops. Farmers in the desert oases

Bruce McAllister, Black Star

Small Thatched Huts house hundreds of families on the outskirts of cities in the United Arab Emirates. Many of these people are former desert nomads who now work in the cities.

and the hilly regions of the eastern UAE grow bananas, citrus fruits, dates, and other crops. Some farmers also raise cattle. Desert nomads tend herds of camels, goats, and sheep. People who live in the coastal areas catch fish, shrimp, and other seafoods.

Abu Dhabi and Dubayy are the chief ports of the UAE. In addition to oil, the country exports small amounts of dates and fish. Leading imports include building supplies, clothing, food products, household goods, and machinery.

Roads link the major cities and towns of the United Arab Emirates. The country has three international airports. Several of the states operate radio stations, and Abu Dhabi and Dubayy have television stations.

History. People have lived in the region that is now the UAE for thousands of years. The chiefs of Arab groups gradually gained control of the region. Most of the people became Muslims during the A.D. 600's.

The states on the Persian Gulf coast lay along a major trade route between Europe and East Asia. Beginning in the 1500's, various European nations established trading posts in the region. They competed with Arabs, Persians, and Turks for control of the gulf trade. In time, Britain became the strongest European power in the gulf. British ships passed through the gulf on their way to and from British settlements in India.

Battles between British ships and those of the local Arabs occurred frequently during the late 1700's and early 1800's. In 1820, after a British attack on Ras al Khaymah, the Arab rulers of the gulf states signed a treaty with Britain to prevent warfare at sea. The British and the Arab chiefs signed various other agreements during the 1800's and early 1900's, and the region became known as the Trucial States. In time, Britain took control of the states' defense and foreign affairs. But the rulers of Arab groups continued to handle internal matters. Traditional rivalries—and some disputes over boundaries, fishing rights, and other matters —led to wars among the Arab groups during the 1800's and the early 1900's.

The Trucial States remained underdeveloped until the mid-1900's, when foreign oil companies began to drill for oil in the region. In 1958, oil was discovered in the state of Abu Dhabi. Abu Dhabi began to export crude oil in 1962. Four years later, large oil deposits were found in Dubayy. Money from oil production enabled Abu Dhabi and Dubayy to begin to develop into modern states. Other states later began to produce some oil. But they continued to rely chiefly on agriculture and fishing as the basis of their economies.

In 1971, the Trucial States gained full independence from Britain. In spite of traditional rivalries, all the states except Ras al Khaymah joined together and formed the United Arab Emirates on Dec. 2, 1971. That same year, the UAE became a member of the Arab League and the United Nations. Ras al Khaymah joined the UAE in February, 1972.

Under the Provisional Constitution adopted by the UAE in 1971, each emir continued to handle the internal affairs of his state. But the rulers agreed to share their resources and work for the economic development of all the states. ROBERT GERAN LANDEN

See also ABU DHABI.

UNITED ARAB REPUBLIC (U.A.R.) was a union of two independent Middle Eastern countries, Egypt and

Syria. President Gamal Abdel Nasser of Egypt and Shukri al-Kuwatly of Syria proclaimed the union on Feb. 1, 1958. Syrian rebels ended it on Sept. 29, 1961, setting up an independent government for Syria. Egypt continued to use the name United Arab Republic until 1971, when the country changed its official name to the Arab Republic of Egypt.

In April 1963, Egypt, Syria, and Iraq agreed to form a new U.A.R. But because of political differences among the countries, the agreement was not carried out.

Government. The U.A.R. of 1958 had a centralized government, with Cairo as the capital. Egypt and Syria became provinces, with provincial capitals at Cairo for Egypt and Damascus for Syria.

Soon after the merger, the people adopted a provisional constitution and chose Nasser as president. He appointed all members of the National Assembly, selecting half from Egypt and half from Syria. The assembly supposedly exercised legislative power, but Nasser made many decisions without consulting it.

History. Before World War I, most of the Middle East was part of the Ottoman Empire. However, Great Britain had gained control of Egypt in the 1880's, and kept it until Egypt became independent in 1922. After World War I, the Middle East was carved into a number of political divisions. Syria, along with Lebanon, became a League of Nations mandate of France, which controlled them until after World War II.

Following World War II, many Arabs wanted to be united under a single government. Nasser came into power in Egypt during the 1950's, and became the leader of the Arab unity movement. Many Arab leaders suspected the West and turned to Russia for assistance. Nasser accepted Russian aid, although he suppressed Communism within Egypt. The Communists also gained great power in Syria. The desire for Arab unity, the fear of Communist influence in Syria, and Nasser's ambition all contributed to the formation of the United Arab Republic.

Nasser regarded the union of Egypt and Syria as the first step toward uniting all Arab states. On March 8, 1958, Yemen—now Yemen (Sana)—agreed to form a federation with the U.A.R. The union was called the

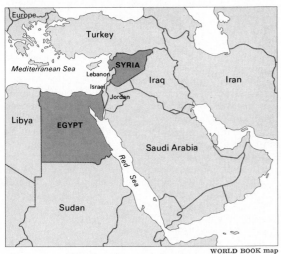

WORLD BOOK map
Location of the United Arab Republic

Europe
Turkey
Mediterranean Sea Lebanon SYRIA
Israel Iraq Iran
Jordan
Libya EGYPT
Saudi Arabia
Red Sea
Sudan

United Arab States, and had Hodeida (now Al Hudaydah), Yemen, as its permanent seat. The United Arab States was not a true federation. Yemen maintained its own membership in the United Nations and separate relations with other countries. Nasser dissolved the United Arab States in December 1961. He declared that the federation was no longer of any value.

Nasser made clear that the U.A.R. would be neutral in world affairs. In 1959, he accused Russia of trying to interfere with the internal affairs of the republic. At the same time, he improved relations with the West.

The government introduced many reforms in both provinces. But many Syrians began to feel that Nasser was raising the level of living in Egypt only by lowering it in Syria. Finally, late in 1961, Syrian officers in the U.A.R. army carried out an almost bloodless revolt and proclaimed an independent Syria. The Baath Party, the ruling party in Syria and Iraq, blocked a new federation attempt in 1963. The party opposed Nasser's attempt to control the new U.A.R.   CHARLES P. SCHLEICHER

See also EGYPT; IRAQ; NASSER, GAMAL ABDEL; SYRIA; YEMEN (SANA).

UNITED ARAB STATES. See UNITED ARAB REPUBLIC.

UNITED AUTOMOBILE WORKERS (UAW) is one of the largest labor unions in the United States. The UAW has local unions throughout both the United States and Canada. Its official name is INTERNATIONAL UNION, UNITED AUTOMOBILE, AEROSPACE AND AGRICULTURAL IMPLEMENT WORKERS OF AMERICA.

To qualify as a member, a worker must be employed in the manufacture or assembly of automobiles, automobile parts or accessories, aircraft, aerospace products, agricultural implements, electrical, or other allied metalworking trades. Office workers and such salaried employees as drafters and engineers in the same field also may become members of the UAW.

The union was organized in Detroit in 1935. It took the place of the National Council of Automobile Workers, which had been affiliated with the American Federation of Labor (AFL). In 1938, the federation expelled the union, along with the other AFL international unions that had made up the Committee for Industrial Organization. The UAW later helped develop the Congress of Industrial Organizations (CIO), which merged with the AFL in 1955. The UAW withdrew from the AFL-CIO in 1968 but rejoined it in 1981. Headquarters are at 8000 E. Jefferson Ave., Detroit, Mich. 48214. For membership, see LABOR MOVEMENT (table).   Critically reviewed by the UNITED AUTOMOBILE WORKERS

See also FRASER, DOUGLAS ANDREW; REUTHER, WALTER P.; WOODCOCK, LEONARD.

UNITED CHURCH OF CANADA is the largest Protestant church in Canada. It was established in 1925 by the union of the Methodist Church in Canada with most Canadian Congregationalist and Presbyterian congregations. A fourth denomination, the Canada Conference of the Evangelical United Brethren Church, joined the union in 1968. The United Church had about 4 million members in the early 1980's.

Doctrine and Organization. In 1924, the Canadian Parliament passed the United Church of Canada Act. This act, which became effective on June 10, 1925, formally established the United Church.

UNITED CHURCH OF CANADA

A constitution called the *Basis of Union* sets forth the administration, legal procedures, and organization of the United Church. The Basis of Union also includes 20 *Articles of Faith* that state the church's doctrine. This doctrine is based on the Bible. The United Church is organized regionally in areas called, from smallest to largest, congregations, presbyteries, and conferences. A General Council, which meets every two years, has considerable authority over the entire church.

The United Church has a presbyterian form of government—that is, the clergy and laity share equal responsibility for church administration. The presbyteries, conferences, and General Council are all governed by bodies made up equally of clergy and laity. All clergy of the United Church are called ministers and have equal rank. Both men and women may be ordained as ministers.

Since the 1960's, the Anglican Church and the Christian Church (Disciples of Christ) in Canada have been negotiating with the United Church concerning union. In 1975, the Anglican Church rejected a "plan of union" prepared by representatives of the three denominations, thereby ending formal negotiations. However, the Anglicans expressed interest in continuing discussions and joint projects, and negotiations between the United Church and the Christian Church (Disciples of Christ) continued.

Activities and Services. The United Church operates several colleges and theological schools that are part of Canadian universities. The church produces much of its own educational material and publishes a monthly periodical called the *United Church Observer*.

The United Church has four training centers that prepare the laity for leadership positions in the church. The United Church and the Anglican Church jointly operate a training center for unordained professional church workers.

In addition to its educational activities, the United Church manages several hospitals and homes for senior citizens in Canada. It also sponsors local rehabilitation centers. A Mission and Service Fund, administered by the national church office, finances mission activities. All congregations contribute to this fund.

On matters of social justice, the United Church tries to guide the thinking of its members and to influence legislation. The church makes public statements on social issues, consults with Canadian government leaders, and presents its views to the provincial legislatures. The church has headquarters at The United Church House, 85 St. Clair Ave. E., Toronto, ON M4T 1M8, Canada. Critically reviewed by the United Church of Canada

UNITED CHURCH OF CHRIST is a Protestant religious denomination. It was formed in 1957 by the merger of the Congregational Christian Churches and the Evangelical and Reformed Church.

The United Church of Christ has a *general synod* (central committee) that directs business affairs, nominates church officials, and performs other duties related to church operations. However, individual congregations have the right to govern themselves.

In 1931, the Congregational churches merged with a union of three small groups that all used the name Christian to form the Congregational Christian Churches. The Evangelical and Reformed Church was formed in 1934 by the union of two American churches of German background.

The church has about 1,700,000 members. Headquarters are located at 105 Madison Avenue, New York, NY 10016. Sandra Sizer Frankiel

See also Congregationalists; National Association of Congregational Christian Churches.

UNITED COLONIES OF NEW ENGLAND. See New England Confederation.

UNITED EMPIRE LOYALISTS were American colonists who moved to British colonies in Canada during and after the Revolutionary War in America (1775-1783). They remained loyal to the British and left the American Colonies to escape persecution by people who supported the Revolutionary War. Many Loyalists also were drawn to Canada by offers of free land. About 40,000 Loyalists moved to Canada. They settled mainly in the western parts of the colonies of Nova Scotia and Quebec.

The Loyalists greatly influenced Canada's cultural and political development. Many of the Loyalists brought their English heritage into areas that had been dominated by people with French traditions. In addition, the French-speaking population quickly lost its status as the overwhelming majority group. Soon, the Loyalists began to demand more authority over their local affairs. These demands led to the creation of the colony of New Brunswick in 1784 and the colony of Upper Canada in 1791. William Morgan Fowler, Jr.

See also Canada, History of (The United Empire Loyalists; picture); New Brunswick (English Settlement); Ontario (Early Settlement).

UNITED FARM WORKERS OF AMERICA is a well-known union of farm laborers. The union, commonly

Duo-Craft Studios, Toronto

The United Church of Canada has headquarters in the United Church House, which is located in Toronto, Ont.

called the UFW, is active in many parts of the United States, especially in California and Florida and in the Northeast. It seeks job security and higher wages for migrant workers and other farm laborers and works to improve their living and working conditions.

Cesar E. Chavez, a leading spokesman for Mexican-American farm workers, founded the National Farm Workers Association in 1962. The association and another union merged in 1966 to form the United Farm Workers Organizing Committee. This union became the UFW in 1973. In its efforts to organize farm workers and obtain union contracts for them, the UFW often urged consumers to boycott farm products produced by nonunion workers. These boycotts brought national attention to the farm labor movement and were supported by many church and student groups, by members of various minority groups, and by other unions.

The UFW is associated with the American Federation of Labor and Congress of Industrial Organizations (AFL-CIO). The union's headquarters are in Keene, Calif., near Bakersfield.

Critically reviewed by the UNITED FARM WORKERS OF AMERICA
See also CHAVEZ, CESAR E.

UNITED FOOD AND COMMERCIAL WORKERS INTERNATIONAL UNION is one of the largest unions in the United States. It is affiliated with the American Federation of Labor and Congress of Industrial Organizations (AFL-CIO). Most of the union's members are butchers, canners, meat packers, supermarket employees, or other workers in the food industry. The union, usually called the UFCW, also represents clerks of department stores, drugstores, and shoe stores; employees of hospitals and nursing homes; workers in the fur and leather industries; and other employees.

The UFCW was formed in 1979 by the merger of the Amalgamated Meat Cutters and Butcher Workmen of North America with the Retail Clerks International Union. UFCW headquarters are at 1775 K Street NW, Washington, D.C. 20006. For membership, see LABOR MOVEMENT (table). Critically reviewed by the UNITED FOOD AND COMMERCIAL WORKERS INTERNATIONAL UNION

UNITED FUNDS. See UNITED WAY OF AMERICA.

UNITED JEWISH APPEAL is an organization in the United States that raises funds for Jewish relief agencies. These agencies aid needy Jews in other countries, and help arrange the transportation and settlement of Jewish immigrants to Israel and other nations. The organization also helps communities organize and conduct their local fund-raising campaigns. The United Jewish Appeal was founded in 1939. Its headquarters are at 1290 Avenue of the Americas, New York, N.Y. 10019. Critically reviewed by the UNITED JEWISH APPEAL

UNITED KINGDOM, officially called United Kingdom of Great Britain and Northern Ireland, is a union of four countries: England, Scotland, Wales, and Northern Ireland. The term *Great Britain* is commonly used in place of *United Kingdom* and is the title of the WORLD BOOK article on that country.

King James I used the term United Kingdom as early as 1604 to show that the kingdoms of England and Scotland were joined under his rule. But it was not until 1707 that the Act of Union formed the Kingdom of Great Britain. An act of 1800 formed the United Kingdom of Great Britain and Ireland, with a unified parliament. The term *United Kingdom* became inappropriate

when the larger part of Ireland won independence in 1921 and became the Irish Free State (now the Republic of Ireland). Six counties in northeastern Ireland remained with Great Britain. They form Northern Ireland.

The Royal Titles Act of 1927 dropped the words United Kingdom, but the phrase was used again during World War II. In 1945, Britain signed the United Nations charter as the United Kingdom of Great Britain and Northern Ireland. The full title was confirmed in the proclamation following the Royal Titles Act of 1953. JOHN W. WEBB

See also ENGLAND; GREAT BRITAIN; NORTHERN IRELAND; SCOTLAND; WALES.

UNITED METHODIST CHURCH is the largest Methodist denomination in the United States. It was formed in 1968 through a union of the Methodist Church and the Evangelical United Brethren Church. The United Methodist Church has about 9,950,000 members and more than 42,000 congregations in the United States. It supports 14 seminaries and over 140 colleges, and has more than 1,500 missionaries in about 50 countries. The church has about 50 bishops supervising administration in the United States. The United Methodist Church takes active stands on social issues. It opposes the use of alcoholic beverages, favors increased reliance on the United Nations to work for world peace, and urges an end to racial discrimination. EARL KENNETH WOOD

See also METHODISTS.

UNITED METHODIST YOUTH FELLOWSHIP is the youth organization of the United Methodist Church. Most United Methodist churches in the United States have at least one youth group. Each group's activities may include study, fellowship groups, choirs, service projects, tours, summer camps, and conferences. The programs are for junior high-school and high-school youth. The fellowship has about 1 million members in 39,000 churches. The youth fellowships of the Methodist Church and the Evangelical United Brethren Church formed the United Methodist Youth Fellowship when the two churches merged in 1968. The organization's address is Box 840, Nashville, Tenn. 37202.

Critically reviewed by the UNITED METHODIST YOUTH FELLOWSHIP

UNITED MINE WORKERS OF AMERICA (UMW) is an industrial trade union that represents the workers in most of the coal mines and coal-processing industries of the United States. It also has local unions in Canada.

The union was organized in Columbus, Ohio, in 1890. It belonged to the American Federation of Labor until 1936. The UMW helped form the Congress of Industrial Organizations in 1935, but withdrew in 1942. It has remained independent, except for a reaffiliation with the AFL that began in 1946 and ended in 1947.

The UMW won fame under John Mitchell in the early 1900's. John L. Lewis served as union president from 1919 until his retirement in 1960. Under Lewis, the union experienced its greatest growth and obtained many benefits for its members. The UMW has headquarters at 900 15th Street NW, Washington, D.C. 20005. Critically reviewed by the UNITED MINE WORKERS OF AMERICA

See also LEWIS, JOHN L.; COAL (Labor Unions); LABOR MOVEMENT (table: Important U.S. Labor Unions); ROOSEVELT, THEODORE (Friend of Labor); WEST VIRGINIA (Labor Troubles).

United Nations Headquarters consists of several buildings along the East River in New York City. The tall Secretariat Building, *center,* has become a well-known symbol of the UN. Other UN buildings include the General Assembly Building, *left,* and the Dag Hammarskjöld Library, *right.*

UNITED NATIONS

UNITED NATIONS (UN) is an organization of 159 nations that works for world peace and security and the betterment of humanity. Countries of every part of the world belong to the UN. They range in size from Russia to St. Christopher and Nevis. Each member nation sends representatives to UN headquarters in New York City, where they discuss and try to solve problems.

The United Nations has two main goals: peace and human dignity. If fighting between two or more countries breaks out anywhere, the UN may be asked to try to stop it. After the fighting stops, the UN may help work out ways to keep it from starting again. But the UN tries above all to deal with problems and disputes before they lead to fighting. It seeks the causes of war and tries to find ways to eliminate them.

The United Nations has met with both success and failure in its work. It has been able to keep some disputes from developing into major wars. It has also

Lincoln P. Bloomfield, the contributor of this article, is Professor of Political Science at the Massachusetts Institute of Technology and the author of The United Nations and U.S. Foreign Policy *and other books on international affairs. The photographs in the article are used through the courtesy of the United Nations unless otherwise credited.*

helped people in many parts of the world gain their freedom and better their way of life. But disagreements among UN members prevent the organization from doing a completely effective job of peacekeeping. Serious financial troubles also weaken the UN.

The United Nations was established on Oct. 24, 1945, shortly after World War II. As the war drew to an end, the nations that opposed Germany, Italy, and Japan decided that such a war must never happen again. Representatives of these nations met in San Francisco in April, 1945, and worked out a plan for an organization to help keep peace in the world. This plan was described in a document called the *Charter of the United Nations.* In June, 1945, 50 nations signed the UN Charter. They were the first UN members. Since then, more than 100 other nations have joined. Many of these were colonies when the UN was founded.

In some ways, the UN resembles the League of Nations, which was organized after World War I (see LEAGUE OF NATIONS). Many of the nations that founded the UN had also founded the League. Like the League, the UN was established to help keep peace between nations. The main organs of the UN are much like those of the League. But the UN differs from the League in two main ways. First, all the great military powers ex-

cept Communist China were UN members from the beginning, and Communist China gained membership in 1971. On the other hand, several powerful countries, including the United States, either did not join the League or withdrew from it. Second, the UN's concern with economic and social problems gives it broader responsibilities than the League had.

The six major organs of the UN carry on the work of the organization. These organs are (1) the General Assembly, (2) the Security Council, (3) the Secretariat, (4) the Economic and Social Council, (5) the International Court of Justice, and (6) the Trusteeship Council. A number of specialized agencies related to the UN deal with such problems as communications, food and agriculture, health, and labor.

United Nations headquarters consists of several buildings along the East River in New York City. The three main buildings are the General Assembly Building, the Secretariat Building, and the Conference Building. A smaller building next to the Secretariat Building houses the library of the United Nations. Members of the United Nations have donated many furnishings and works of art for the UN buildings. The flags of all the members fly in front of UN headquarters.

The United Nations Flag has a map of the world surrounded by a wreath of olive branches. The branches symbolize peace.

Members of the United Nations

The charter members of the UN do not have dates after their names. Other nations are listed with their years of admission.

Afghanistan (1946)
Albania (1955)
Algeria (1962)
Angola (1976)
Antigua and Barbuda (1981)
Argentina
Australia
Austria (1955)
Bahamas (1973)
Bahrain (1971)
Bangladesh (1974)
Barbados (1966)
Belgium
Belize (1981)
Benin (1960)
Bhutan (1971)
Bolivia
Botswana (1966)
Brazil
Brunei (1984)
Bulgaria (1955)
Burkina Faso (1960)
Burma (1948)
Burundi (1962)
Byelorussian S.S.R.
Cameroon (1960)
Canada
Cape Verde (1975)
Central African
    Republic (1960)
Chad (1960)
Chile
China*
Colombia
Comoros (1975)
Congo (1960)
Costa Rica
Cuba
Cyprus (1960)
Czechoslovakia
Denmark

Djibouti (1977)
Dominica (1978)
Dominican Republic
Ecuador
Egypt
El Salvador
Equatorial Guinea (1968)
Ethiopia
Fiji (1970)
Finland (1955)
France
Gabon (1960)
Gambia (1965)
Germany (East) (1973)
Germany (West) (1973)
Ghana (1957)
Great Britain
Greece
Grenada (1974)
Guatemala
Guinea (1958)
Guinea-Bissau (1974)
Guyana (1966)
Haiti
Honduras
Hungary (1955)
Iceland (1946)
India
Indonesia (1950)
Iran
Iraq
Ireland (1955)
Israel (1949)
Italy (1955)
Ivory Coast (1960)
Jamaica (1962)
Japan (1956)
Jordan (1955)
Kampuchea (1955)
Kenya (1963)
Kuwait (1963)

Laos (1955)
Lebanon
Lesotho (1966)
Liberia
Libya (1955)
Luxembourg
Madagascar (1960)
Malawi (1964)
Malaysia (1957)
Maldives (1965)
Mali (1960)
Malta (1964)
Mauritania (1961)
Mauritius (1968)
Mexico
Mongolia (1961)
Morocco (1956)
Mozambique (1975)
Nepal (1955)
Netherlands
New Zealand
Nicaragua
Niger (1960)
Nigeria (1960)
Norway
Oman (1971)
Pakistan (1947)
Panama
Papua New
    Guinea (1975)
Paraguay
Peru
Philippines
Poland
Portugal (1955)
Qatar (1971)
Romania (1955)
Russia (U.S.S.R.)
Rwanda (1962)
St. Christopher and
    Nevis (1983)

St. Lucia (1979)
St. Vincent and
    the Grenadines (1980)
São Tomé and
    Príncipe (1975)
Saudi Arabia
Senegal (1960)
Seychelles (1976)
Sierra Leone (1961)
Singapore (1965)
Solomon Islands (1978)
Somalia (1960)
South Africa
Spain (1955)
Sri Lanka (1955)
Sudan (1956)
Suriname (1975)
Swaziland (1968)
Sweden (1946)
Syria
Tanzania (1961)
Thailand (1946)
Togo (1960)
Trinidad and Tobago (1962)
Tunisia (1956)
Turkey
Uganda (1962)
Ukrainian S.S.R.
United Arab Emirates (1971)
United States
Uruguay
Vanuatu (1981)
Venezuela
Vietnam (1977)
Western Samoa (1976)
Yemen (Aden) (1967)
Yemen (Sana) (1947)
Yugoslavia
Zaire (1960)
Zambia (1964)
Zimbabwe (1980)

*Nationalist China held a seat in the UN until October 1971, when the General Assembly voted to expel Nationalist China and admit Communist China.

The Charter of the United Nations is the constitution of the UN. It includes the plan used for organizing the UN, and the rules by which the UN is governed. UN members agree to carry out the requirements of the charter. The charter has 19 chapters divided into 111 articles that explain the *purposes* (goals), *principles* (basic beliefs), and operating methods of the UN.

Purposes and Principles. The charter lists four purposes and seven principles of the United Nations. The first purpose is to preserve world peace and security. The second purpose is to encourage nations to be just in their actions toward each other. The third is to help nations cooperate in trying to solve their problems. The fourth purpose is to serve as an agency through which nations can work toward these goals.

The first principle of the United Nations is that all members have equal rights. Second, all members are expected to carry out their duties under the charter. Third, they agree to the principle of settling their disputes peacefully. Fourth, they agree not to use force or the threat of force against other nations, except in self-defense. Fifth, members agree to help the UN in every action it takes to carry out the purposes of the charter. Sixth, the UN agrees to act on the principle that non-member states have the same duties as member states to preserve world peace and security. And seventh, the UN accepts the principle of not interfering in the actions of a member nation within its own borders. But these actions must not hurt other nations.

Membership Requirements. The first members of the United Nations were the nations that signed the charter in 1945. Since then, many other nations have requested to join the organization. The charter states that membership in the UN is open to all "peace-loving states" that are "able and willing" to carry out the duties required by the charter. Both the Security Council and the General Assembly must approve applications for membership. A member nation that violates the charter may be suspended or even expelled from the United Nations.

The Six Major UN Organs. The charter sets up the six main organs of the UN and explains the duties, powers, and operating methods of each. The *General Assembly* is the only major organ in which all UN members are represented. The charter permits the Assembly to discuss any question of importance to the UN and to recommend action to be taken by the members or by other UN organs. The *Security Council* has the major responsibility in the UN for keeping the peace. The charter gives the Council special powers to carry out this responsibility. The *Secretariat* has the job of helping all the other organs do their work as efficiently as possible. The charter gives the *Economic and Social Council* several duties, such as advancing human rights and helping people to better their way of life. The *International Court of Justice* handles international legal disputes. The charter established the *Trusteeship Council* to watch over a number of territories that were not self-governing at the time the UN was founded.

The United Nations has established many other agencies, committees, and commissions since the charter was written. But the six main organs are the only UN bodies that operate under rules included in the charter.

Amending the Charter. The UN Charter sets forth the rules for changing the charter. Amendments may be proposed in either of two ways. The General Assembly may propose an amendment if two-thirds of all its members agree to do so. Or two-thirds of the General Assembly members and any nine members of the Security Council may call a *General Conference* to discuss making changes in the charter. As in the General Assembly, a two-thirds vote of a General Conference is required to propose an amendment. A proposed amendment does not go into effect until it has been approved by two-thirds of all UN members, including the five permanent members of the Security Council. In 1965, the charter was amended to increase the size of the Security Council from 11 to 15 members. The amendment was proposed without calling a General Conference.

The charter called for the 10th yearly session of the General Assembly to make plans for a General Conference if one had not already taken place. In 1955, the Assembly took up the question and appointed a planning committee. The committee has met from time to time and has reported to the General Assembly. But the Assembly has taken no further action.

The Preamble to the United Nations Charter

A preamble of about 200 words precedes the chapters of the charter and expresses the guiding spirit of the organization. Jan Christiaan Smuts of South Africa is credited with drafting the preamble (see SMUTS, JAN C.). The complete preamble states:

"We the peoples of the United Nations determined

to save succeeding generations from the scourge of war, which twice in our lifetime has brought untold sorrow to mankind, and

to reaffirm faith in fundamental human rights, in the dignity and worth of the human person, in the equal rights of men and women and of nations large and small, and

to establish conditions under which justice and respect for the obligations arising from treaties and other sources of international law can be maintained, and

to promote social progress and better standards of life in larger freedom,

and for these ends

to practice tolerance and live together in peace with one another as good neighbors, and

to unite our strength to maintain international peace and security, and

to ensure, by the acceptance of principles and the institution of methods, that armed force shall not be used, save in the common interest, and

to employ international machinery for the promotion of the economic and social advancement of all peoples,

have resolved to combine our efforts to accomplish these aims.

Accordingly, our respective Governments, through representatives assembled in the city of San Francisco, who have exhibited their full powers found to be in good and due form, have agreed to the present Charter of the United Nations and do hereby establish an international organization to be known as the United Nations."

The United Nations System

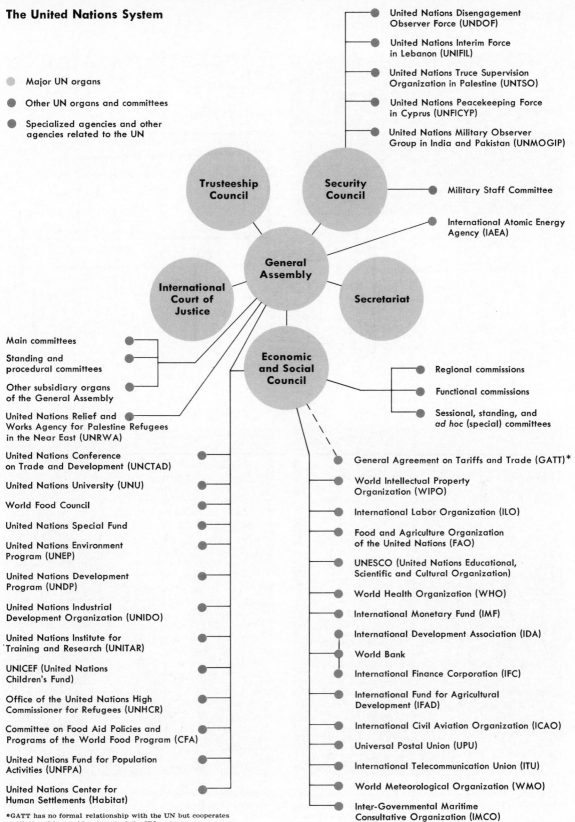

Major UN organs

Other UN organs and committees

Specialized agencies and other agencies related to the UN

Trusteeship Council

Security Council

General Assembly

International Court of Justice

Secretariat

Economic and Social Council

United Nations Disengagement Observer Force (UNDOF)

United Nations Interim Force in Lebanon (UNIFIL)

United Nations Truce Supervision Organization in Palestine (UNTSO)

United Nations Peacekeeping Force in Cyprus (UNFICYP)

United Nations Military Observer Group in India and Pakistan (UNMOGIP)

Military Staff Committee

International Atomic Energy Agency (IAEA)

Main committees

Standing and procedural committees

Other subsidiary organs of the General Assembly

United Nations Relief and Works Agency for Palestine Refugees in the Near East (UNRWA)

United Nations Conference on Trade and Development (UNCTAD)

United Nations University (UNU)

World Food Council

United Nations Special Fund

United Nations Environment Program (UNEP)

United Nations Development Program (UNDP)

United Nations Industrial Development Organization (UNIDO)

United Nations Institute for Training and Research (UNITAR)

UNICEF (United Nations Children's Fund)

Office of the United Nations High Commissioner for Refugees (UNHCR)

Committee on Food Aid Policies and Programs of the World Food Program (CFA)

United Nations Fund for Population Activities (UNFPA)

United Nations Center for Human Settlements (Habitat)

Regional commissions

Functional commissions

Sessional, standing, and ad hoc (special) committees

General Agreement on Tariffs and Trade (GATT)*

World Intellectual Property Organization (WIPO)

International Labor Organization (ILO)

Food and Agriculture Organization of the United Nations (FAO)

UNESCO (United Nations Educational, Scientific and Cultural Organization)

World Health Organization (WHO)

International Monetary Fund (IMF)

International Development Association (IDA)

World Bank

International Finance Corporation (IFC)

International Fund for Agricultural Development (IFAD)

International Civil Aviation Organization (ICAO)

Universal Postal Union (UPU)

International Telecommunication Union (ITU)

World Meteorological Organization (WMO)

Inter-Governmental Maritime Consultative Organization (IMCO)

*GATT has no formal relationship with the UN but cooperates with it and is considered part of the UN system.
WORLD BOOK chart.

27

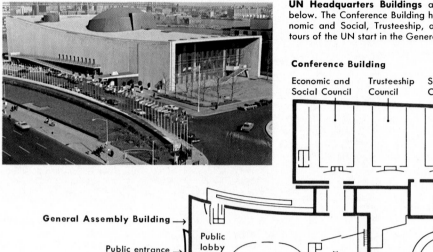

UN Headquarters Buildings are identified in the diagram below. The Conference Building has meeting rooms for the Economic and Social, Trusteeship, and Security councils. Guided tours of the UN start in the General Assembly Building, *left.*

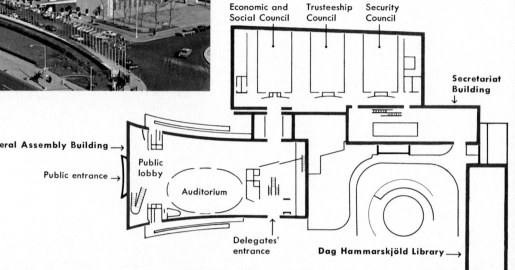

Conference Building

Economic and Social Council

Trusteeship Council

Security Council

Secretariat Building ↓

General Assembly Building →

Public entrance →

Public lobby

Auditorium

Delegates' entrance

Dag Hammarskjöld Library →

The Lobby of the General Assembly Building has displays donated by several UN members. The huge pendulum, *center,* was donated by the Netherlands. The ramp leads to the auditorium, where the General Assembly meets.

WORLD BOOK photo by Dan Budnik

A Statue Representing Peace, called "Let Us Beat Swords into Plowshares," expresses the UN's main goal. The statue, by the Russian sculptor Yevgeny Vuchetich, was a gift to the UN from Russia. It stands on the grounds of the UN headquarters.

The General Assembly is the only major organ of the United Nations in which all members are represented. Each member may send five delegates, five alternate delegates, and as many advisers as it wishes to the General Assembly. However, each member nation has only one vote.

The General Assembly elects a new president and a number of vice-presidents at the beginning of each annual session. The president's main duty is to lead the Assembly's discussions and direct its work.

Powers. The General Assembly is responsible in some way for every other organ of the United Nations. It elects or takes part in electing the members of the other major organs, and it directs the operations of some UN bodies. The General Assembly also controls the UN's budget. It decides how much money each member should contribute and how much of the UN's funds each UN body should receive.

The General Assembly may discuss any question that concerns the work of the UN. It reaches decisions through a vote of its members. As a result of such a vote, the Assembly may suggest actions to be taken by other UN bodies or by member nations. According to the charter, the only decisions of the General Assembly that UN members must obey are votes on the UN budget. All other decisions made by the General Assembly are simply recommendations.

The General Assembly's responsibility for keeping the peace is second only to the similar responsibility of the Security Council. The kind of peacekeeping action that the Assembly can take has been strengthened since the charter was written. In the early years of the UN, sharp disagreements in the Security Council prevented the Council from acting in many cases. In 1950, the General Assembly approved a *resolution* (formal statement) called "Uniting for Peace." This resolution gave the Assembly the power to step in whenever peace is threatened and the Security Council has failed to act. In such an emergency, the Assembly can recommend actions for the UN, including the use of armed force if necessary.

Meetings and Voting. The General Assembly holds one *regular session* each year, beginning on the third Tuesday in September and lasting about three months.

A *special session* may be called if either the Security Council or a majority of member states requests it. Several special sessions have been called to discuss such matters as peacekeeping and finances. The "Uniting for Peace" resolution in 1950 set up a system for calling an *emergency special session* of the Assembly. Such a meeting can be called on 24 hours' notice if peace is threatened and the Security Council has not acted. Any nine members of the Security Council or a majority of UN members may call an emergency special session. Such sessions have been held to deal with serious situations in the Middle East, Hungary, and other parts of the world.

Most questions that are voted on in the General Assembly are decided by a simple majority vote. Some subjects that the charter calls "important questions" need a two-thirds majority vote. These topics include peace and security and the election of new UN members. A simple majority vote of the Assembly may also make any other question an "important" one.

Committees. The UN Charter permits the General Assembly to create as many committees as it needs to help carry on its work. The Assembly has set up seven main committees—the First, Second, Third, Fourth, Fifth, and Sixth committees, and the Special Political Committee. Every member of the General Assembly —thus, every UN member—may have a representative on all these committees.

The First Committee discusses political and security questions and arms control. The Special Political Committee helps the First Committee with its tremendous volume of work. The Second Committee deals with economic and financial questions, the Third with social and cultural matters, and the Fourth with problems of countries that are not self-governing. The Fifth Committee handles administrative and budget matters, and the Sixth handles questions of law. Each committee studies the problems that have been assigned to it and makes recommendations to the General Assembly.

The Assembly has also set up other committees. They help organize and conduct each Assembly session, advise the Second and Fifth committees on financial and budget matters, or deal with problems involving nuclear energy, colonialism, and peacekeeping.

The General Assembly meets to discuss such matters as the UN budget and peace-keeping efforts. The secretary-general, the Assembly president, and an undersecretary sit on stage. Interpreters, reporters, and camera crews work in booths along the wall.

The UN Charter makes the Security Council responsible for keeping the peace. The Council has 15 members, of which 5 are permanent. The permanent members are France, Great Britain, China, Russia, and the United States. The other 10 members of the Council are elected to two-year terms by the General Assembly. Each of the 15 members of the Security Council has one delegate on the Council.

Powers. The Security Council has the power to decide what action the UN should take to settle international disputes. The charter states that the Council's decisions are made in the name of all UN members, who must accept them and carry them out. The Council encourages the peaceful settlement of disputes by calling on the opposing sides to work out a solution. Or the Council may ask the two or more sides to accept a settlement worked out by other nations, individuals, or groups.

The Council itself may investigate a dispute and suggest ways of settling it. For example, the Council may call on UN members to stop trading with a country that is endangering peace and security. It may also ask the members to cut off communications with such a state, or to end contacts with its government. If such actions are not effective, the Security Council may ask UN members to furnish military forces to settle the dispute. The *Working for Peace* section of this article describes some of the actions taken by the Security Council. The final section discusses the UN's peacekeeping difficulties.

The Security Council also has several other important powers. It must approve all applications for membership in the UN. It selects a candidate for secretary-general. And it can recommend plans for arms control.

Meetings and Committees. The Security Council must be able to meet at any time. Meetings may be called to consider any situation serious enough to lead to war. Such a situation can be brought to the attention of the Security Council by any UN member—and in certain cases by nonmembers—by the secretary-general or by any major UN organ. The delegates must be able to attend a meeting as soon as it is called.

The Council makes its own rules for conducting its meetings. In the early years of the UN, it became a custom for the representative of a different nation to serve as president each month. The representatives take turns, in the order that their country's name appears in the English alphabet. UN members that are not members of the Council—and even nations that are not UN members—may be invited to take part in debates that affect them. But these nations have no vote.

The Council may set up as many committees as it needs. The charter calls only for a Military Staff Committee, made up of military representatives of the five permanent members. Other committees have been appointed from time to time, especially to help the Council organize its work and to consider applications for UN membership.

Voting in the Security Council differs from that in any other UN organ. The Council can take action on some questions if any nine members vote in favor of the action. But on many other questions, the Council can act only if nine members—including all five permanent members—agree to do so. A "no" vote by any permanent member defeats such a question, no matter how many other members vote in favor of it. This special voting right of the permanent members is called a *veto*.

Almost any decision of the Council can be vetoed, but the Council has never established what kinds of decisions cannot be vetoed. Through the years, a few customs concerning the veto have developed. For example, a permanent member usually does not veto a decision about what subjects the Council should discuss, or about when the Council should adjourn. But a permanent member sometimes vetoes a decision about the order in which subjects are to be discussed. If a permanent member decides not to vote, or is absent at the time of voting, its action is not considered a veto.

The use of the veto in the Security Council has prevented the United Nations from dealing with a number of major problems. Russia has used the veto over 100 times, much more than the other four permanent members together. The United States used the veto for the first time in March, 1970. It vetoed a Security Council resolution requiring UN members to cut off communications with Rhodesia (now Zimbabwe).

Meetings of the Security Council are held in a special chamber in the Conference Building. Delegates and their assistants sit at the semicircular table. Interpreters and other UN employees sit at the long table in the center.

The Secretariat manages the day-to-day business of the United Nations. Its main job is to provide services for all the other UN organs. The Secretariat is made up of the secretary-general and other administrators assisted by clerks, secretaries, and specialists.

The Secretary-General has broader powers than any other United Nations official. The secretary-general is the chief administrator of the UN and reports to the General Assembly each year on the organization's problems and accomplishments. The secretary-general advises governments and uses the influence of the office to help solve many problems. Most importantly, the charter gives the secretary-general the power to advise the Security Council of any situation that might threaten world peace.

The secretary-general is nominated by the Security Council and appointed by the General Assembly to a five-year term. All five permanent members of the Security Council must agree on a candidate before that person can be nominated. After the Council selects a candidate, it makes a recommendation to the General Assembly. A majority vote of the Assembly appoints a secretary-general.

Trygve Lie of Norway was the first secretary-general. He took office in 1946 and was later reelected. Lie resigned late in 1952 and left office in 1953. He spoke out on important questions and criticized the policies of some UN members.

Dag Hammarskjöld of Sweden followed Lie as secretary-general. Hammarskjöld advanced the right of secretaries-general to act on their own judgment for the UN in a situation threatening peace. Hammarskjöld was elected to a second five-year term in 1958 but was killed in an airplane crash in 1961.

U Thant of Burma was elected to complete Hammarskjöld's term. In 1962, he was appointed to a full five-year term dating from 1961. He was reelected in 1966. In 1972, U Thant was succeeded by Kurt Waldheim of Austria. Waldheim was reelected in 1976. In 1982, Waldheim was succeeded by Javier Pérez de Cuéllar of Peru.

In 1960, the Russians demanded that the UN appoint three persons to serve together as secretary-gen-

© Jim Pozarik, Gamma/Liaison

Javier Pérez de Cuéllar of Peru became secretary-general in 1982. He succeeded Kurt Waldheim of Austria.

eral. They wanted one representative for the Communist members, another for the Western nations, and a third for the uncommitted nations that supported neither side. The Russians called their proposed triple leadership a *troika* (see TROIKA). Their effort failed, but after U Thant took office, he appointed a number of undersecretaries. Communist, Western, and uncommitted nations were all represented.

Other Employees. The Secretariat has about 9,000 employees, of whom about half work at UN headquarters. The rest work at the UN's European headquarters in Geneva, Switzerland, or in special UN missions and agencies throughout the world.

The secretary-general is responsible for appointing and organizing the staff of the Secretariat. The charter instructs the secretary-general to choose staff members from as many different member nations as possible. Employees include accountants, economists, lawyers, mathematicians, translators, typists, and writers. Every UN member country may fill at least six Secretariat jobs if it can provide qualified individuals. A UN employee works for the secretary-general and is not allowed to take orders from any member nation.

The First Four Secretaries-General of the UN were, *from left to right above,* Trygve Lie of Norway, who served from 1946 to 1953; Dag Hammarskjöld of Sweden, 1953 to 1961; U Thant of Burma, 1961 to 1972; and Kurt Waldheim of Austria, 1972 to 1982.

The Economic and Social Council. The United Nations is the first international organization with a major organ devoted to improving the way people live. The Economic and Social Council works to encourage higher standards of living, better health, cultural and educational cooperation among nations, and observance of human rights. It makes recommendations in these areas to the General Assembly, individual nations, and the UN's specialized agencies. For example, the Council recommends to the General Assembly the economic and social projects it considers worthy of UN support. The Assembly then may grant funds for these projects.

The Economic and Social Council is responsible for working with the specialized agencies. In addition to making recommendations to them, the Council communicates recommendations from the agencies to the General Assembly. The Council also cooperates with more than 100 other organizations throughout the world, including the Red Cross and labor unions.

The Council has 54 member nations. Each year, the General Assembly elects 18 members to serve for three years. The Council meets twice a year, but it may also hold special sessions. Each member has one vote, and decisions are made by a simple majority. The Council may allow any UN member or specialized agency to take part in discussions of concern to them. But only Council members may vote.

The Council has a number of commissions that assist in its work. Four commissions deal with the economic problems of certain regions—Africa, Asia and the Far East, Europe, and Latin America. Six others deal with questions of human rights, narcotics, population, social development, statistics, and women's rights. A number of other bodies also assist the Council. They include the governing boards of the United Nations Children's Fund (UNICEF) and the United Nations Development Program.

The International Court of Justice deals with the legal problems of the United Nations. The court has 15 judges, each appointed to a nine-year term. The Security Council and the General Assembly, voting independently, select the judges. No two judges may come from the same country, and the world's major civilizations and legal traditions must be represented. The court traditionally includes one judge from each of the permanent members of the Security Council. It elects a president and vice-president to three-year terms. Headquarters are at The Hague in The Netherlands.

Any UN member may bring a case before the court. The court has helped settle disputes between various countries, including Great Britain and Norway, Belgium and The Netherlands, and Honduras and Nicaragua. These disputes have concerned such matters as fishing rights and the ownership of border territory. The General Assembly and the Security Council have also permitted some nonmember states, such as Switzerland and Liechtenstein, to have cases heard by the court. An individual cannot bring a case to the court unless his government sponsors it.

No nation can be forced to bring its disputes before the International Court of Justice. Many governments have declared that they will seek court rulings in certain types of disputes. Some nations, including the United States, have said that they will decide for themselves what cases to bring before the court. Any nation that seeks a ruling from the court must agree to accept its decision. The court makes its decisions by majority vote.

The International Court gives advisory opinions to the General Assembly upon request. The Assembly also has permitted the Security Council, the Economic and Social Council, the Trusteeship Council, and the specialized agencies to request such opinions.

The Trusteeship Council was designed to help a number of territories that were not self-governing at the end of World War II. Some of these territories were colonies of Italy and Japan. Others were German colonies that had become *mandates* of the League of Nations after World War I (see MANDATED TERRITORY). The UN Charter made the Trusteeship Council responsible for all these territories and for any others that nations might choose to entrust to it. Such areas are called *trust territories*. The Council works to help the trust territories become self-governing or independent.

There were originally 11 trust territories. The UN accepted one or more member nations as *trustees* for each territory. The trustee countries govern the trust territories under the direction of the UN. The Trusteeship Council is made up of representatives of the trustee nations and of all permanent members of the Security Council that do not govern trust territories. The Trusteeship Council meets at least once every year.

Ten trust territories have either become independent or have voted to become a part of other nations. Only one has not decided its own political future—the Trust Territory of the Pacific Islands, governed by the United States.

Present and Former UN Trust Territories

This table lists the 11 original trust areas, their trustees, and the dates that some have achieved independence.

Name	Trustee	Status
Cameroons	Great Britain	Independent as parts of Cameroon and Nigeria, 1961
Cameroons	France	Independent as Cameroon, 1960
Nauru	Australia	Independent, 1968
New Guinea	Australia	Independent as part of Papua New Guinea, 1975
Pacific Islands (Carolines, Marianas except Guam, Marshalls)	United States	Strategic Area Trusteeship (under the Security Council)
Ruanda-Urundi	Belgium	Independent as Rwanda and Burundi, 1962
Somaliland	Italy	Independent as Somalia, 1960
Tanganyika	Great Britain	Independent, 1961
Togoland	France	Independent as Togo, 1960
Togoland	Great Britain	Independent as part of Ghana, 1957
Western Samoa	New Zealand	Independent, 1962

UNITED NATIONS / Specialized Agencies

The specialized agencies are self-governing international organizations related to the United Nations. They deal with such worldwide problems as agriculture, communications, living and working conditions, and health. Some of the agencies are older than the UN itself. Each agency has its own organization, membership, and rules, and each has signed an agreement with the UN. The agency agrees to consider recommendations made by the UN and to report back on steps it takes to carry them out. The Economic and Social Council has the responsibility of helping the UN and the specialized agencies work together effectively.

Each specialized agency was set up to deal with a problem involving the cooperation of many nations. Some of the agencies were established to deal with problems of transportation or communication between countries. Other agencies were set up to help countries that had suffered greatly as a result of war or that had recently become independent. These agencies may provide loans, educational assistance, or other types of aid.

See the *Related Articles* at the end of this article for a list of the specialized agencies that have separate articles in WORLD BOOK.

A Farming Expert of the Food and Agriculture Organization of the United Nations (FAO) teaches two African students how to operate a tractor. Various specialized agencies assist the UN in many countries.

Specialized Agencies of the United Nations

Food and Agriculture Organization of the United Nations (FAO)
Helps nations improve the production of farms, forests, and fishing waters.

Inter-Governmental Maritime Consultative Organization (IMCO)
Encourages cooperation in shipping practices and regulations.

International Civil Aviation Organization (ICAO)
Works for greater safety in air service and for standard international flying regulations.

International Development Association (IDA)
Works with the World Bank. It lends money on easier terms than does the World Bank or the International Finance Corporation.

International Finance Corporation (IFC)
Works with the World Bank. It encourages smaller, private developments. The World Bank mostly lends money for large governmental projects.

International Fund for Agricultural Development (IFAD)
Helps finance projects to increase food production in developing countries.

International Labor Organization (ILO)
Helps improve working and living conditions throughout the world.

International Monetary Fund (IMF)
Helps adjust differences between the money systems used by various countries, making it easier for nations to trade with one another.

International Telecommunication Union (ITU)
Helps nations cooperate to solve problems dealing with radio, telephone, telegraph, and satellite communications.

UNESCO (United Nations Educational, Scientific and Cultural Organization)
Encourages educational, scientific, and cultural progress to increase understanding among nations.

Universal Postal Union (UPU)
Works for international cooperation in the delivery of mail. See POSTAL UNION, UNIVERSAL.

World Bank
Officially called the International Bank for Reconstruction and Development (IBRD). It lends money to help countries with such projects as dams, irrigation works, power plants, and railroads.

World Health Organization (WHO)
The world's principal agency for dealing with health problems.

World Intellectual Property Organization (WIPO)
Works for international cooperation to protect artistic and literary works, inventions, and trademarks against copying.

World Meteorological Organization (WMO)
Encourages nations to cooperate in weather forecasting.

Scientific Conferences, such as this meeting of atomic scientists at UN headquarters, help keep UN members well informed.

Delegations. Each nation has its own rules for appointing delegates to the UN. In the United States, the President nominates the delegates. The nominees are subject to approval by the Senate. In Canada, the prime minister and the Cabinet choose the delegates. The delegation of each country has a *head delegate* who is that nation's official representative at the UN.

Most UN members keep a permanent *mission* of one or more representatives at UN headquarters. They have found that a permanent mission is helpful for taking part in long-term projects and for keeping up with current developments.

Breaking the Language Barrier. Dozens of languages are spoken by United Nations delegates. But when conducting official business, the UN uses only six languages—Arabic, Chinese, English, French, Russian, and Spanish. Delegates may address the General Assembly in any language if they provide a translation into one of the official languages. Skilled interpreters instantly translate the words into each of the other official languages. The delegates wear earphones to listen to the translation they choose.

Groups with Common Interests. As UN membership has grown, most nations with similar interests have banded together. The African nations have their own group, as do the Arab countries and the Asian lands. The Latin-American nations, except for Cuba, form a group, and the Communist nations, including Cuba,

make up another. All these groups meet regularly for various reasons—for example, to decide on a plan of action or to agree on candidates in a UN election. Canada and the other members of the Commonwealth of Nations meet together regularly for discussion but seldom vote as a group. A few nations, including Israel, South Africa, the United States, and Yugoslavia, do not meet or vote regularly with any group.

Publications and Information Services. The UN provides information about its work to member nations and to the public. Each major organ of the UN, as well as many UN agencies, issues documents that give a complete account of its work. These documents give UN members information that helps them carry out their duties. The UN also issues many publications of interest to the public. The *UN Monthly Chronicle*, for example, describes work done by the UN each month. Booklets deal with such subjects as statistics, human rights, or economic development. Many UN publications are issued in several or all of its six official languages.

The UN has an Office of Public Information, which is part of the Secretariat. One of its responsibilities is to direct UN information offices in about 50 cities throughout the world. Each office provides information about the UN to people in nearby regions.

Heads of United States and Canadian Delegations to the UN

Heads of United States Delegations

Name	Served
Warren R. Austin	1947-1953
Henry Cabot Lodge	1953-1960
James J. Wadsworth*	1960-1961
Adlai E. Stevenson	1961-1965
Arthur J. Goldberg	1965-1968
George Ball**	1968
James R. Wiggins	1968-1969
Charles W. Yost	1969-1971
George H. W. Bush	1971-1973
John A. Scali	1973-1975
Daniel Patrick Moynihan	1975-1976
William W. Scranton	1976-1977
Andrew J. Young, Jr.	1977-1979
Donald F. McHenry	1979-1981
Jeane J. Kirkpatrick	1981-1985
Vernon A. Walters	1985-

*Acting head.
**Resigned the day after his nomination was confirmed by the Senate.

Heads of Canadian Delegations

Name	Served
Andrew G. L. McNaughton	1948-1950
R. G. Riddell	1950-1951
E. Herbert Norman*	1951
D. M. Johnson	1951-1955
R. A. Mackay	1955-1958
C. S. A. Ritchie	1958-1962
Paul Tremblay	1962-1966
George Ignatieff	1966-1968
Yvon Beaulne	1969-1972
Saul Rae	1972-1976
William H. Barton	1976-1980
Michel Dupuy	1980-1981
Gerard Pelletier	1981-1984
Stephen Lewis	1984-

*Served as acting head from March to September. Not considered an official head of delegation by the UN.

UNITED NATIONS / *Working for Progress*

An increasingly important goal of the United Nations is to help make the world a better, safer place in which to live. One way the UN works toward this goal is by providing various types of aid for countries and different groups of people. The UN also works for progress in many other fields, including human rights, peaceful uses of nuclear energy, and pollution control.

Economic and Technical Aid consists of grants, loans, training programs, and other means of helping nations develop their resources, production, and trade. After World War II, the International Bank and the International Monetary Fund gave financial assistance to war-torn countries. But the amount of aid they could give was small compared with the amount needed. Most western European countries depended on the United States to help them recover from the war.

As more and more poor countries joined the UN, the organization began to help them. The resources of these countries are either undeveloped or have been developing slowly. Many such nations have become independent since World War II.

The UN dedicated the period from 1961 through 1970 as the first United Nations Development Decade. The UN's goal during this period was to help the developing countries increase their national income by 5 per cent each year. The developed nations were asked to donate 1 per cent of their yearly national income to the program.

The first Development Decade did not meet all its goals, but some progress was made. The International Bank increased the number and size of its loans for the construction of roads, factories, and similar projects. In 1964, the UN held a Conference on Trade and Development (UNCTAD). The main aim of this conference was to encourage international trade, especially between the rich, developed countries and the poor, developing ones. The conference set up a Trade and Development Board, and itself became a permanent organ of the General Assembly. UNCTAD decides on courses of UN action concerning trade and development. The Trade and Development Board carries out UNCTAD's decisions. It meets at least twice a year to consider such matters as improving international shipping or helping the developing countries find markets for their products.

In 1965, the UN combined its technical aid programs to form the United Nations Development Program (UNDP). The UNDP helps nations make studies of their unused natural resources so they can find ways to use them. For example, it suggests ways for nations to make their farms, mines, and water resources more productive. The program also helps people learn the skills needed to develop their country's resources. The UN has helped about half a million men and women learn to manage, as well as work in, industries that will benefit their countries. In 1966, the General Assembly set

Arab Refugees are one of the many groups of people in various parts of the world that receive UN aid. UN agencies also provide loans and other types of aid for developing countries.

up the United Nations Industrial Development Organization (UNIDO) to encourage industrialization in developing countries.

Since the early 1970's, the United Nations has increased its efforts to expand international trade and to provide economic and technical assistance. It also has worked to help the developing countries regulate the growth of their populations, and to promote world disarmament.

Aid to Refugees. The United Nations aids refugees by protecting their legal rights, providing them with food and shelter, and finding them new homes. The UN has declared that the legal rights of refugees include the right to a job, to an education, and to freedom of religion. During World War II, 44 governments cooperated in setting up the United Nations Relief and Rehabilitation Administration (UNRRA) to conduct war relief. After the United Nations was created, UNRRA was replaced by the International Refugee Organization (IRO), a specialized agency. By 1951,

the worst of the war-caused problems were over and the IRO was discontinued.

In 1951, the General Assembly set up the Office of the United Nations High Commissioner for Refugees. This agency has assisted refugees from many countries. The main duty of the High Commissioner is to protect the rights of refugees in foreign countries. The Office of the High Commissioner has a small fund raised by voluntary contributions. But in general, it must work through governments and private agencies.

The UN has a special agency to assist Arab refugees in Palestine—the United Nations Relief and Works Agency for Palestine Refugees in the Middle East (UNRWA). The General Assembly set up the agency to help Arabs made homeless by the 1948 war between Israel and the Arab states. There have been continual wars in this region, and several million Arabs have become refugees. But UNRWA cannot find homes for these refugees so long as Israel and the Arab states continue to fight each other. The most it can do is try to provide them with food, shelter, medical care, and other services. UNRWA's funds are limited, and in the mid-1980's it was able to spend only a small amount of money for each refugee.

Aid to Children. The General Assembly created the United Nations Children's Fund (UNICEF) in 1946. UNICEF'S job was to provide food, clothing, and medical supplies for child victims of World War II. The emergency caused by the war ended by the early 1950's, but UNICEF had become so popular that the General Assembly made it a permanent organization in 1953. Today, UNICEF provides aid for child development and care, job training, and family planning.

UNICEF's funds come from voluntary contributions. About three-fourths of its funds are donated by governments, and the rest is raised privately. The United States Committee for UNICEF raises several million dollars yearly from Halloween trick-or-treat collections and from the sale of UNICEF greeting cards. See UNICEF.

Human Rights. In 1946, the United Nations set up the Commission on Human Rights as part of the Economic and Social Council. The commission wrote the Universal Declaration of Human Rights, which all members of the General Assembly approved in 1948. This declaration expressed the hope that people would learn to respect the rights and dignity of others. Parts of the declaration have been included in the constitutions of El Salvador, Haiti, Indonesia, Jordan, Libya, Puerto Rico, and Syria.

Racial problems have received more attention than any others brought before the UN. These problems—and those of colonialism and economic development—are the main concern of the Asian and African delegates, who make up a majority in the UN. In 1965, the General Assembly approved a treaty called the International Convention on the Elimination of All Forms of Racial Discrimination. The treaty went into effect in 1969, after the governments of 27 nations had approved it. Similar UN treaties deal with slavery, the rights of refugees, and the crime of *genocide* (elimination of an entire national, racial, or religious group).

Small Private Industries in developing countries, such as this textile company in the Philippines, receive financial assistance from UN agencies. The UN also aids large government projects.

Peaceful Uses of Nuclear Energy. In 1953, President Dwight D. Eisenhower of the United States suggested to the General Assembly that governments contribute nuclear materials to an international agency. This agency would use such materials to help develop peaceful uses of nuclear energy.

In 1957, the UN set up the agency that Eisenhower had suggested. The International Atomic Energy Agency (IAEA) is separate from the UN but works closely with it. Its main responsibility is to encourage peaceful uses of nuclear energy. The agency also tries to make certain that no nuclear materials held or supplied by its member nations are used for making weapons. It has developed controls over its members' nuclear materials and conducts inspections of nuclear facilities in many countries each year. All the nuclear projects of IAEA members in Latin America, Asia, and the Pacific area operate under IAEA safeguards. A treaty prohibiting the spread of nuclear weapons went into effect in March, 1970. The IAEA is responsible for inspections that make certain the treaty is not broken.

The IAEA cooperates with many other agencies to encourage the sharing of nuclear information. It also encourages research and experiments dealing with atomic fuels, atomic medicine, *desalination* (removing the salt) of seawater, and other uses of nuclear energy. Money for IAEA projects comes from dues paid by member nations and from voluntary contributions.

Controlling the Environment. The United Nations, like many other organizations, has called attention to air and water pollution and other dangers that threaten the environment. The Economic and Social Council, together with several specialized agencies, studied these problems and made recommendations to the General Assembly. In December, 1968, the Assembly passed a resolution pledging the UN to work for solutions to problems concerning the environment. The UN Conference on Human Environment met in 1972 to discuss ways in which UN members could cooperate to protect the environment. As a result of the conference, the General Assembly established the United Nations Environment Program in 1972. The program encourages international cooperation to fight pollution and preserve the earth's natural resources.

Fighting Hunger has always been a major goal of the UN. The Food and Agriculture Organization of the United Nations (FAO), a specialized agency, was established in 1945. It works to improve the production and distribution of food and other agricultural products. The World Food Program began in 1962 as a joint project of the UN and FAO. It provides emergency food aid and other assistance to developing countries.

In the 1970's, food production in many countries fell behind population growth. As a result, large numbers of people suffered from severe malnutrition. In 1974, the UN World Food Conference met in Rome to discuss the food shortage. This conference established a new UN agency, the World Food Council. The council coordinates the delivery of about 10 million tons of food sent to developing nations every year. It also accumulates world food reserves for use in time of famine. The council works through other agencies that deal with the supply of food, including the FAO, the United Nations Development Program (UNDP), and UNICEF. The Rome conference also created an international warning system to detect future food shortages.

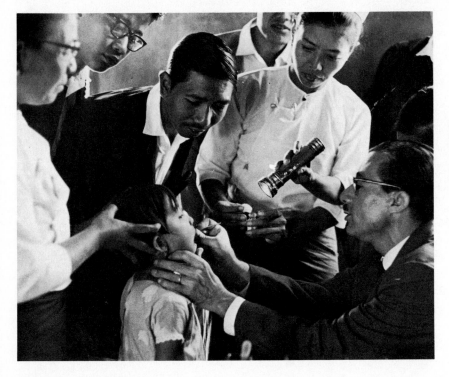

Graduate Medical Students in Burma receive specialized training under the United Nations Development Program (UNDP). This program helps nations develop their human and natural resources.

Early in World War II, the representatives of nine European governments fled to London. Nazi Germany had conquered much of Europe and had driven these leaders from their homelands. Representatives of Great Britain and the Commonwealth nations met in London with leaders of Belgium, Czechoslovakia, France, Greece, Luxembourg, The Netherlands, Norway, Poland, and Yugoslavia. On June 12, 1941, all these nations signed a declaration pledging to work for a free world, where people could live in peace and security. This pledge, usually called the *Inter-Allied Declaration*, was the first step toward building the UN.

The Atlantic Charter followed the Inter-Allied Declaration by two months. It was signed by President Franklin D. Roosevelt of the United States and Prime Minister Winston Churchill of Great Britain. The charter expressed their hope for a world where all people could live free from fear and need. It also expressed their intention to seek eventual disarmament and economic cooperation. See ATLANTIC CHARTER.

On Jan. 1, 1942, representatives of 26 nations signed the *Declaration by United Nations*. This was the first official use of the words *United Nations*. The declaration approved the aims of the Atlantic Charter and was later signed by 21 other nations.

On Oct. 30, 1943, representatives of China, Great Britain, Russia, and the United States signed the *Moscow Declaration on General Security*. This declaration approved the idea of an international organization for preserving world peace. A month later, Roose-velt, Churchill, and Premier Joseph Stalin of Russia met at Teheran, Iran. The three men declared that they recognized the responsiblity of all the United Nations to achieve lasting peace. See TEHERAN CONFERENCE.

The Dumbarton Oaks Conference. From August to October, 1944, representatives of China, Great Britain, Russia, and the United States held a series of meetings at the Dumbarton Oaks estate in Washington. The goal of these meetings was to plan a peacekeeping organization. The four nations succeeded in drawing up a basic plan, though they could not agree on some important questions. The plan's main feature was a Security Council on which China, France, Great Britain, Russia, and the United States would be permanently

Important Dates in UN History

1945 (April 25) The San Francisco Conference opened.

1945 (June 26) The UN Charter was signed by delegates at the San Francisco Conference.

1945 (Oct. 24) The UN was born as the required number of nations approved the charter.

1946 (Jan. 10) The 51-member General Assembly met in London.

1946 (Feb. 14) The UN voted to have its headquarters in the United States.

1948 (Dec. 10) The UN approved the Universal Declaration of Human Rights.

1949 (Dec. 27) The Netherlands granted independence to Indonesia as the result of UN efforts.

1949 (Feb.-July) Israel and the Arab states signed cease-fire agreements worked out by UN officials.

1950 (June 27) The Security Council approved sending UN troops to protect Korea's independence.

1953 (July 27) North Korea and the UN signed a truce.

1954 The Office of the United Nations High Commissioner for Refugees was awarded the Nobel Peace Prize.

1956 (Nov. 6) The UN arranged an Israel-Egypt cease-fire agreement in the Suez Canal dispute.

1960 (July 14) The Security Council approved sending UN forces to Congo (Léopoldville) to keep order.

1962 The UN issued $200-million worth of bonds to help pay its debts.

1964 (March 4) The Security Council approved a peace-keeping force for Cyprus.

1965 UNICEF was awarded the Nobel Peace Prize.

1966 (Dec. 16) The Security Council voted economic sanctions against Rhodesia (now Zimbabwe).

1967 (June) The Security Council arranged cease-fire agreements, ending the six-day Arab-Israeli war.

1968 (June) The General Assembly endorsed a treaty designed to stop the spread of nuclear weapons.

1970 The UN observed its 25th anniversary.

1971 The General Assembly voted to expel Nationalist China and admit Communist China to the UN.

1973 War broke out in the Middle East and the UN helped arrange a partial cease-fire.

1975 The General Assembly declared 1975 as International Women's Year to promote equality between women and men.

1978 (March 19) The Security Council approved a force to try to restore peace in southern Lebanon.

1981 The Office of the United Nations High Commissioner for Refugees was awarded the Nobel Peace Prize.

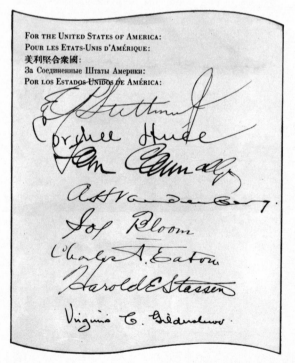

FOR THE UNITED STATES OF AMERICA:
POUR LES ETATS-UNIS D'AMÉRIQUE:
美利堅合衆國:
За Соединенные Штаты Америки:
POR LOS ESTADOS UNIDOS DE AMÉRICA:

The UN Charter was signed by 50 nations at the San Francisco Conference. These are the signatures of the U.S. delegates.

The Signing of the Charter took place on June 26, 1945. President Harry S. Truman, *far left,* stood by as Secretary of State Edward R. Stettinius, Jr., signed for the United States.

represented. The permanent members of the organization would have the power to veto decisions that had been approved by the rest of the Council. See DUM-BARTON OAKS.

In February 1945, Roosevelt, Churchill, and Stalin met at Yalta in the Crimea. At this meeting, they agreed that some minor actions of the Security Council could not be vetoed by the permanent members. The three leaders announced that a conference of United Nations would open in San Francisco on April 25, 1945. This conference would use the plan worked out at Dumbarton Oaks to help prepare a charter for the United Nations.

The San Francisco Conference. Delegates from 50 nations met in San Francisco for the United Nations Conference on International Organization. The conference opened on April 25, 1945, 13 days after the death of President Roosevelt and 12 days before the surrender of Germany. Victory over Japan was still four months away.

At the conference, some major disagreements arose between the Big Three (Great Britain, Russia, and the United States) and the smaller, less powerful nations. The Big Three believed they could guarantee future peace only if they continued to cooperate as they had during the war. They insisted that the UN Charter should give them the power to veto actions of the Security Council. The smaller nations opposed the veto power but could not defeat it. They did succeed in adding to the importance of other UN organs, such as the General Assembly and the Economic and Social Council. In these bodies, responsibilities could be shared more equally than in the Security Council. Such efforts by smaller nations helped create an organization that had far-reaching powers and responsibilities.

On June 26, 1945, all 50 nations present at the conference voted to accept the charter. Poland had been unable to attend but later signed the charter as an original member. The charter then had to be approved by the governments of the five permanent members of the Security Council and of a majority of the other nations that signed it. The charter went into effect on Oct. 24, 1945, a date that is celebrated every year as United Nations Day.

Building UN Headquarters. The first session of the General Assembly opened in London early in 1946. The delegates took up the question of where the permanent headquarters of the United Nations should be located. They considered invitations from various countries and finally agreed that the headquarters should be in the United States. On Dec. 14, 1946, the Assembly accepted a gift of $8½ million from John D. Rockefeller, Jr., of the United States to buy 18 acres (7 hectares) of land along the East River in New York City. The city itself donated additional land in the area. In 1947, the General Assembly approved plans for the headquarters buildings. The next year, the U.S. Congress approved an interest-free loan of $65 million for their construction. The buildings were completed in the fall of 1952.

UNITED NATIONS/*Working for Peace*

The Indonesian Dispute. In July 1947, fighting broke out in Indonesia between the Republic of Indonesia and The Netherlands. Indonesia had been a Dutch colony before Japan occupied it during World War II. The Dutch wanted to regain control after the war, but the Indonesians demanded independence.

The Security Council took up the question and on Aug. 1, 1947, called for a cease-fire. On Jan 17, 1948, a committee appointed by the Council persuaded Indonesia and The Netherlands to sign a cease-fire agreement. But in December 1948, The Netherlands announced that it no longer accepted the agreement. Fighting broke out again.

On Jan. 28, 1949, the Security Council approved a plan for an independent Indonesia and set up the UN Commission for Indonesia. The commission arranged another cease-fire agreement in August 1949, and brought the two sides together for a conference at The Hague in The Netherlands. After this conference, the Dutch granted independence to Indonesia on Dec. 27, 1949. The new nation included all the Netherlands Indies except West New Guinea (now Irian Jaya).

The Netherlands wanted to continue ruling West New Guinea until its people could decide their future. But Indonesia claimed it had inherited West New

Guinea as part of the Netherlands Indies. In December 1961, fighting broke out between Dutch and Indonesian forces. Acting Secretary-General U Thant, worried over the possibility of war, brought the two sides together for talks. In August 1962, The Netherlands and Indonesia agreed to let the UN govern the area until May 1963, when Indonesia would take control. They also agreed that in 1969, Indonesia would let the people of West New Guinea vote on their future. As a result of the 1969 vote, West New Guinea remained part of Indonesia.

The India-Pakistan Conflict. In January 1948, the Security Council sent a commission to try to settle a war between India and Pakistan. The two nations had gone to war in 1947 over the region of Kashmir, which both claimed. After a year of effort by the UN commission, India and Pakistan agreed to let the people of Kashmir vote on the question. The two sides approved a cease-fire line in July 1949. But the UN could not persuade either side to remove enough troops from the area to assure peaceful voting.

Fighting broke out again between India and Pakistan in August 1965. One of the causes of this war was again the question of Kashmir. In September, the Security Council demanded that both nations stop fighting and withdraw their forces to the 1949 cease-fire line. The secretary-general met with both sides, and a cease-fire was finally arranged on Sept. 20, 1965. Two UN observer groups enforced the cease-fire. In 1966, Russia persuaded India and Pakistan to sign an agreement pledging to give up the use of force in the dispute. The dispute itself was not settled, and the UN observer groups continued to administer the cease-fire.

The Arab-Israeli Wars. In 1947, the General Assembly approved a plan to divide Palestine into a Jewish state and an Arab state, with Jerusalem to be administered by the UN. The Arabs opposed the plan and fighting broke out between Arabs and Jews. Nevertheless, the state of Israel was born on May 14, 1948. The next day, armies from Egypt, Iraq, Lebanon, Syria, and Transjordan (now Jordan) invaded Israel.

The General Assembly and the Security Council both tried to stop the fighting. On May 20, 1948, the Assembly sent Count Folke Bernadotte of Sweden to try to make peace. He was shot and killed in Jerusalem a few months later. Ralph J. Bunche of the UN Secretariat replaced him. By July 1949, Bunche had arranged cease-fires between Israel and each of its Arab neighbors. Bunche won the 1950 Nobel peace prize for his achievement.

The cease-fire agreements did not establish boundaries between Israel and the Arab states. They stated only that the two sides would not go beyond the points they occupied when the fighting stopped. When the cease-fire went into effect, Israel occupied more territory than had been approved by the United Nations in 1947. Jerusalem was divided. About 700,000 Arabs fled Israel and went to neighboring Arab countries, where they became refugees. During the next several years, an equal number of Jews left Arab countries to go to Israel. The cease-fire agreements called for UN groups representing both Arabs and Israelis to report

any new fighting. The UN set up a truce organization to investigate such reports.

The truce organization worked effectively for several years, but no progress was made toward lasting peace. The Arabs blockaded Israeli ships in the Suez Canal and the Gulf of Aqaba. In 1955, Arabs from Egypt began terrorist raids against Israel. Israel returned the attacks. In July 1956, Egypt seized the Suez Canal from its British and French owners.

Great Britain and France tried unsuccessfully to reach an agreement with Egypt. They then asked the Security Council to act. The Council proved unable to reverse the Egyptian action, and Israeli troops invaded Egypt. Great Britain and France then vetoed action by the Security Council and sent forces to defend the Suez Canal. The General Assembly called for a cease-fire, which was finally achieved on Nov. 6, 1956. The Assembly agreed that UN troops should guard the borders between Israel and Egypt. A United Nations Emergency Force (UNEF) was organized, and 10 UN members furnished troops. In March 1957, Israel withdrew its forces behind the 1949 cease-fire lines.

The 1956 cease-fire did not lead to peace. The Arab nations continued to call for destruction of the Jewish state. Russia supplied arms to the Arab countries, and Western nations supplied them to Israel. UNEF troops guarded the border between Egypt and Israel, but the Arabs raided Israel from Jordan and Syria. Israeli forces raided those countries in return.

In May 1967, Egypt demanded that the UN withdraw its forces from Egyptian territory. The secretary-general yielded to the demand, and Egypt once again blockaded Israeli ships in the Gulf of Aqaba. On May 30, Jordan signed a military agreement with Egypt. On June 5, Israel responded to an expected Arab invasion by attacking Egypt, Jordan, and Syria. The two sides did not agree to a cease-fire until June 10. By that time, Israel had seized Jordan's West Bank, including all of Jerusalem; Egypt's Sinai Peninsula and Gaza Strip; and Syria's Golan Heights. Israel also gained control of the entry to the Gulf of Aqaba.

In November 1967, the United Nations Security Council called on Israel to give up all Arab territory occupied in June and accept a promise of secure borders in return. Secretary-General Thant appointed Gunnar V. Jarring of Sweden to conduct peace talks with the Arabs and Israelis. But Jarring could accomplish little. Both the Arabs and the Israelis continued to raid and to build up arms supplies.

In October 1973, Egyptian forces made a surprise attack on Israel on the Jewish holiday of Yom Kippur. Israel again fought Egypt and Syria. Major battles occurred in the Sinai Peninsula and in the Golan Heights. Cease-fires ended most of the fighting by November.

In January 1974, Egypt and Israel agreed to a separation of their forces in the Sinai Peninsula. Syria and Israel reached a similar agreement on the Golan Heights in May. The UN established two new international peacekeeping forces to supervise both fronts. These forces were the United Nations Disengagement Observer Force (UNDOF) in the Golan Heights and the United Nations Emergency Force II (UNEF II) in the

Sinai Peninsula. Despite the presence of UN troops, Israel claimed legal and political authority in the Golan Heights in 1981. Syria refused to recognize Israel's claim.

In 1974, the UN invited Palestinian leader Yasir Arafat to open a two-week debate on the status of the Palestinian people. Arafat was chairman of the Palestine Liberation Organization (PLO), a group approved by the Arab countries to represent the Palestinian Arabs. After the debate, the General Assembly adopted a resolution recognizing the Palestinians' right to nationhood. A second resolution gave the PLO *observer status*—that is, the right to attend Assembly sessions but not to take part. The next year, the Assembly passed a resolution declaring that Zionism is "a form of racism." Zionism is the Jewish nationalistic movement that helped establish the state of Israel. This move angered many Western nations in the UN and worsened relationships in all UN agencies where the same resolution was passed.

During the late 1960's and the 1970's, the PLO established a number of bases in the southern part of Lebanon. A civil war that broke out in Lebanon in the mid-1970's enabled the PLO to carry out raids against neighboring Israel. On March 11, 1978, PLO terrorists bombed a bus on the outskirts of Tel Aviv-Yafo, Israel's largest city, and many Israeli civilians were killed. Three days later, Israeli troops crossed the Lebanese border and established a "protective zone" consisting of much of the southern third of Lebanon.

Both Lebanon and the United States asked the Security Council to act. The Council called on Israel to withdraw from Lebanese territory and be replaced by a new international peacekeeping force. This force was the United Nations Interim Force in Lebanon (UNIFIL). The last Israeli troops withdrew from Lebanon by June 1978. However, PLO raids on Israeli settlements continued. In 1982, Israeli troops staged a full-scale invasion of Lebanon and drove the PLO forces from their strongholds in the south and from Beirut. In 1985, the Israeli troops withdrew from all of Lebanon except a buffer zone along the Israeli border.

In 1978, Israel agreed to return the Sinai area to Egypt. Egypt and Israel also agreed on autonomy for the Gaza Strip and the Israeli-occupied West Bank of Jordan. Most Arab nations opposed the resulting peace treaty, which was signed in 1979. That same year, the secretary-general withdrew UNEF II from the Sinai and substituted personnel from the UN Truce Supervision Organization (UNTSO). In 1982, Egypt regained full control of the Sinai Peninsula.

The Korean War. At the end of World War II, Russian troops occupied Korea north of the 38th parallel and United States troops occupied it to the south. In 1947, the UN appointed a commission to find ways to unite the country and form a national government. The northern part of Korea refused to take part in this plan. But elections were held in the south and the Republic of Korea was set up. In 1948, the General Assembly declared that the government of the Republic of Korea (South Korea) was the only legal government.

On June 25, 1950, Communist armies from North Korea invaded the Republic of Korea. Two days later, the Security Council voted to ask members of the UN to send troops to assist South Korea. Russia could not veto the Council's action because it had temporarily withdrawn its delegate to protest Nationalist China's membership on the Council.

On July 7, 1950, the Council formed a UN military command under the leadership of the United States. Of the 60 UN members, 16 sent troops to Korea and 41 sent supplies. But the United States contributed more than 95 per cent of the troops and supplies.

In October 1950, Chinese Communist forces entered the war. The Security Council met to discuss the situation, but the Russian delegate had returned and vetoed any attempt of the Council to act. The General Assembly then accused the Chinese Communists of attacking the Republic of Korea. The Chinese ignored the Assembly's demands that they withdraw their forces. The fighting finally ended on July 27, 1953, when North Korea and the United Nations signed a cease-fire agreement. See KOREAN WAR.

Conflict on Cyprus. In 1954, Greece informed the UN that it supported the demand of Cyprus to decide its own political future. The island was then under British rule. About 80 per cent of its people are Greek, and most of the rest are Turkish. The two groups oppose each other strongly. Some of the Greeks on the island demanded that Cyprus become a part of Greece. The General Assembly discussed the situation in 1954 and in following years, but the UN took no action.

By February 1957, disturbances between the Greeks and Turks on Cyprus had become so serious that the General Assembly urged Britain, Greece, and Turkey to find a solution. The three nations worked out an acceptable plan. On Aug. 16, 1960, Cyprus became an independent republic. Britain, Greece, and Turkey guaranteed the independence of Cyprus.

In December 1963, President Makarios of Cyprus withdrew some rights of the Turkish population. Turkey's fleet appeared off the island, and Cyprus appealed to Russia for help. Cyprus also joined Great Britain in seeking assistance from the Security Council. In March 1964, the Council approved the creation of a UN military force to keep peace between the Greeks and Turks on Cyprus. This force, which was supported by voluntary contributions from UN members, helped prevent conflict on the island during the 1960's and early 1970's.

In July 1974, conflict between the Greeks and Turks broke out again. Cypriot troops led by Greek army officers forced Makarios to flee the country. Turkey claimed that Greece had violated the independence of Cyprus, and Turkish troops invaded the island. Fighting continued until Turkey had seized over a third of the island. In 1983, the Turkish Cypriots proclaimed their third of Cyprus a separate republic, called the Turkish Republic of Northern Cyprus. The Security Council condemned the Turkish proclamation. See CYPRUS (History).

The Congo Emergency. On June 30, 1960, Congo (Léopoldville)—now Zaire—became an independent republic after 55 years of Belgian rule. As the Belgian

administrators and army withdrew, riots broke out. A total breakdown threatened the country. Belgian troops returned to keep order. See ZAIRE (Civil Disorder).

The Congolese government asked the United Nations for military assistance. The Security Council approved both the creation of a special UN force and civilian aid to restore order in the country. During the months that followed, Russia vetoed further action by the Security Council, and the General Assembly took over the Congo operation.

The UN force helped the Congolese government regain control of the country, and order was restored. The UN withdrew its force from the Congo on June 30, 1964.

The UN force in the Congo totaled 20,000 troops at its peak. The cost of supporting this force was nearly $400 million, and another $50 million was spent on economic aid for the Congolese. France, Russia, and several other UN members refused to pay their share of these expenses. They argued that only the Security Council could make assessments for peacekeeping. The Congo assessments had been made by the General Assembly. In a short time, the UN ran deeply into debt, and its ability to meet future emergencies was reduced.

The Cuban Missile Crisis. On Oct. 22, 1962, President John F. Kennedy of the United States told the world that Russia was building secret missile bases in Cuba. Russian ships were bringing the missiles and the equipment for these bases. The missile bases could launch nuclear attacks on the United States and other nations from Cuba, which lies only 90 miles (145 kilometers) from Florida. Kennedy demanded that Russia remove all the missile bases and missiles from Cuba, and he announced a naval *quarantine* (blockade) of Cuba. He asked both the Organization of American States (OAS) and the UN Security Council to act.

Acting Secretary-General U Thant immediately began to seek ways to avoid a head-on clash between the two powers. On October 24, Thant announced that he had suggested actions for Russia and the United States to settle the dispute. Several days later, Russia ordered its ships not to proceed to Cuba. The United States in turn promised to do everything possible to avoid war. On October 28, Russian Premier Nikita S. Khrushchev agreed to Kennedy's demands. Russia and the United States then agreed that the UN should supervise the removal of the missiles and missile bases. But Thant could not persuade Cuba to accept UN inspectors. See CUBA (The Cuban Missile Crisis).

The Problem of Southern Africa has been especially difficult for the UN. In South Africa—the largest country of southern Africa—a minority of whites rules a large majority of blacks. In 1920, the white South African government began to rule Namibia (South West Africa), a large, adjacent territory inhabited chiefly by blacks. In Rhodesia (now Zimbabwe), another southern African country, whites ruled the black majority long after white rule had ended in most of Africa.

Some UN members urged that the UN take military action against the white governments. Some suggested that South Africa be expelled from the UN. But most members preferred different action.

The UN has taken action against South Africa, which enforces *apartheid*, the separation of the races. Almost all UN members oppose apartheid, and the General Assembly has frequently spoken out against it. In 1962, the Assembly set up a special committee to deal with the situation in South Africa. The next year, the Security Council declared that apartheid threatened world peace and security. It urged UN members not to supply South Africa's rulers with weapons or other materials that could be used against the black population. In 1974, the General Assembly excluded South Africa's delegation from that year's session because of the nation's apartheid policy. This action deprived South Africa of the right to speak or vote at the session. In 1976, the General Assembly passed a new series of resolutions against South Africa's racial policy. The resolutions urged UN members to stop trading with South Africa, to halt arms shipments there, and to refuse sports competition with South African athletes. In 1977, the Security Council ordered all UN members to stop selling weapons to South Africa. The council's order was the first such action ever taken against a UN member.

In 1966, the General Assembly voted to set up a UN council to govern Namibia, until Namibia was ready for independence. The League of Nations had given control of Namibia to South Africa, which refused to make it a UN trust territory. South Africa refused to let the UN council enter Namibia and introduced apartheid there. Since the late 1970's, South Africa has sometimes appeared to come close to agreement with Western members of the UN Security Council on conditions for Namibia's independence. The talks on Namibia continued into the 1980's.

The UN also took action against Rhodesia. In 1966, it ordered UN members to stop trading with Rhodesia and to halt weapons shipments to the Rhodesian government. These economic *sanctions* (penalties) were the first ever approved by the UN. Black Rhodesians fought a long guerrilla war to end white control of the country. In 1980, general elections were held under British supervision. Rhodesia then became the independent nation of Zimbabwe with a government in which blacks held a majority of the offices.

The Iranian Crisis. In February 1979, a movement led by Ayatollah Ruhollah Khomeini, a Muslim religious leader, overthrew the government of the *shah* (king) of Iran. The deposed shah, Mohammad Reza Pahlavi, had left Iran in January. In October he entered the United States for medical treatment. In November, Iranian revolutionaries took over the U.S. Embassy in Teheran, the capital of Iran. They seized members of the embassy staff and other U.S. citizens there and held them as hostages. The revolutionaries demanded that the United States return the shah to Iran for trial in exchange for the prisoners. However, the U.S. government refused.

In December, the Security Council held an emergency meeting seeking an end to the crisis. The Council adopted a unanimous resolution "urgently" calling for Iran to free the hostages. But the revolutionaries continued to hold the Americans, even after the shah had

left the United States. In July 1980, he died in Egypt.

Separate visits to Teheran in early 1980 by Secretary-General Kurt Waldheim and by a five-member UN commission failed to end the crisis. In May, the International Court of Justice, the UN's judicial branch, issued a ruling calling for the immediate release of all American hostages in Iran. But the Iranian revolutionaries held the Americans until January 1981.

Arms Control. The UN Charter mentions only briefly the need for arms control. But the charter was written before the nuclear age began. By 1949, both Russia and the United States had atomic bombs. They agreed that controls were needed for such weapons, but they could not agree on what kind of controls. The UN studied the problem, and the General Assembly issued many appeals for nations to reduce their arms production.

In 1961, Russia and the United States agreed on a plan to establish a disarmament committee. The UN approved the plan, and an 18-nation committee was set up. More nations were added in 1969. In 1979, the number was increased to 40, and the Committee on Disarmament became an official UN organ.

The Cuban missile crisis of 1962 convinced both Russia and the United States to work harder for control of nuclear weapons. In 1963, the two nations, along with Great Britain, signed a treaty outlawing nuclear tests in the atmosphere, in outer space, and underwater —but not underground. These countries also agreed not to put weapons of mass destruction in orbit.

In 1968, the United Nations approved a *nonproliferation treaty*. This treaty prohibits the nuclear powers that signed and ratified it—Great Britain, Russia, and the United States—from giving nuclear weapons to nations that do not already have them. China and France have nuclear weapons but refuse to sign the treaty. The treaty went into effect in 1970.

In 1971, the UN General Assembly approved a treaty banning the production and stockpiling of biological weapons. The treaty took effect in 1975.

Peaceful Uses of Outer Space. In 1958, the UN secretary-general called on all nations to agree not to claim territory in outer space. The General Assembly declared in 1963 that outer space should be used to benefit all people and that no nation could claim any of it. In 1967, Great Britain, Russia, and the United States signed a treaty reflecting the aims of the Assembly.

Peaceful Uses of the Seabed. The question of uses of the seabed came before the General Assembly for the first time in 1967. The Assembly noted that new inventions allowed nations to use the seabed as a source of valuable minerals and in other new ways. The Assembly appointed a permanent 42-nation committee to study the problem. The committee agreed that a large area of the seabed should be beyond the control of individual nations and should be used only for the benefit of all people. In 1971, the UN worked out a treaty barring the testing or use of nuclear weapons from the seabed beyond a 12-nautical-mile coastal zone. The treaty went into effect in 1972. In 1982, a UN conference approved a draft of a Law of the Sea Treaty. The treaty, which covered many uses of the ocean, would not take effect until 60 nations ratified it.

Peacekeeping Difficulties. The UN has only limited ability to maintain peace. Its members have never been able to agree on a permanent police force to deal with international disputes. However, the United Nations has military forces stationed in several Middle Eastern countries and in Cyprus to keep warring groups apart. The organization only sends such peacekeeping forces if both sides in a conflict want them and agree to have them come.

Powerful members, such as Russia and the United States, prefer to use their own forces to deal with certain types of conflicts. Some members of the organization, especially those from Asia and Africa, think the peacekeeping efforts of the United Nations should be concerned mainly with fighting racial discrimination in southern Africa.

Finances. Every UN member is expected to pay a share of the organization's day-by-day expenses. The amount each member pays depends on its ability to pay. According to UN rules in the early 1970's, no member could pay more than 30 per cent or less than 0.04 per cent of the UN's ordinary expenses. But in 1972, the maximum contribution was reduced to 25 per cent at the request of the United States, the only member paying that much. In 1977, the minimum contribution for any member of the organization was lowered to 0.01 per cent.

The UN has been seriously weakened by a debt that once reached $134 million. But its financial problem involves more than money. The members do not agree on what UN organ should conduct and finance peacekeeping operations. The International Court of Justice ruled in 1962 that all UN members should share the cost of peacekeeping operations in the Middle East and the Congo. The General Assembly approved the funds for these operations. But Russia and other Communist countries, along with France, have refused to pay their peacekeeping assessments. They claim that only the Security Council can make assessments for peacekeeping.

In 1964, Russia fell two years behind in some of its UN payments. The charter states that such a member "shall have no vote." The United States tried to enforce this rule but could not win the support of a majority of other members. A special committee set up in 1965 and a special session of the General Assembly in 1967 made no progress toward solving the UN's financial problems. The organization has avoided bankruptcy by tight control of expenses, by a $200-million bond issue in 1962, and by a voluntary "rescue fund" established in 1964.

Membership Questions. Most nations are UN members. The question of membership for Communist China came up at every General Assembly session from 1950 to 1971. In 1971, the Assembly voted to expel Nationalist China and admit Communist China to the United Nations.

Nations join the UN for various reasons. Membership gives some nations a place in the international community that they might not otherwise have. Some of these nations are so small that they cannot afford their own embassies. Through one mission at the UN, they

UNITED NATIONS

Y. Nagata, United Nations

United Nations Peacekeeping Troops were sent to the Golan Heights after fighting between Israel and Syria ended there in 1974. The area lies on the border between the two nations.

can keep in contact with most of the world's governments. Membership in the UN enables these small nations to bring their problems to public attention and to take part in UN programs of economic and technical assistance.

The presence of many small nations in the UN has also created some problems. The vote of the smallest state counts the same as the vote of the largest. Some nations have suggested that very small countries be given less than a full vote after joining the UN.

Only one nation—Indonesia—has ever withdrawn from the UN. Indonesia rejoined less than two years later. Most countries appear unwilling to try to get along without the UN. They also realize the value of international effort in dealing with certain kinds of economic and social problems. Above all, members understand that UN peacekeeping and peacemaking can help prevent a third world war.   LINCOLN P. BLOOMFIELD

UNITED NATIONS/Study Aids

Questions

How many UN member nations are represented in the General Assembly?

What are the two main goals of the UN?

What are the duties of the secretary-general of the UN?

How does voting in the Security Council differ from voting in other UN organs?

What are the two main differences between the UN and the League of Nations?

What are the official languages of the UN?

Which United Nations organ works with the specialized agencies?

What nations are permanent members of the Security Council?

Why was the Dumbarton Oaks Conference held?

Has any nation ever withdrawn from the UN?

Reading and Study Guide

See *United Nations* in the RESEARCH GUIDE/INDEX, Volume 22, for a *Reading and Study Guide*.

Additional Resources

Level I

EPSTEIN, EDNA. *The United Nations.* 6th ed. Watts, 1973.

LARSEN, PETER. *The United Nations at Work Throughout the World.* Morrow, 1971.

Worldmark Encyclopedia of the Nations, Vol. 1: The United Nations. 6th ed. Wiley, 1984.

Level II

BAEHR, PETER R., and GORDENKER, LEON. *The United Nations: Reality and Ideal.* Praeger, 1984.

LUARD, EVAN. *The United Nations: How It Works and What It Does.* St. Martin's, 1979. *A History of the United Nations, Vol. 1: The Years of Western Domination, 1945-1955.* 1982.

REID, ESCOTT. *On Duty: A Canadian at the Making of the United Nations, 1945-1946.* Kent State Univ. Press, 1983.

UNITED NATIONS DEPARTMENT OF PUBLIC INFORMATION. *Everyone's United Nations.* 9th ed. United Nations, 1979.

The U.S., the UN, and the Management of Global Change. Ed. by Toby Trister Gati. Columbia Univ. Press, 1983.

UNITED NATIONS CHILDREN'S FUND. See UNICEF.

UNITED NATIONS DAY is October 24. It commemorates the date in 1945 that the required number of nations signed the United Nations Charter, officially establishing the UN. In the United States, the President issues a proclamation urging citizens, communities, government officials, and organizations to plan United Nations Day programs. In Canada, the prime minister issues a statement, and many communities plan observances.

UNITED NATIONS DEVELOPMENT PROGRAM. See UNITED NATIONS (Working for Progress).

UNITED NATIONS EDUCATIONAL, SCIENTIFIC, AND CULTURAL ORGANIZATION. See UNESCO.

UNITED NATIONS UNIVERSITY is a worldwide research and advanced training institution established by the United Nations (UN). Unlike a traditional university, it has no campus, students, or faculty, and it does not grant degrees. Rather, the university is a central planning agency for networks of cooperating institutions and scholars. It promotes joint study and the exchange of knowledge to solve global problems. The university organizes and coordinates research, training, and information services throughout the world. It has three major areas of interest—world hunger, human and social development, and use and management of natural resources.

The UN General Assembly chartered the United Nations University in 1973, and it began operations in 1975. The university chooses its own programs and the institutions and individuals through which it works. It receives most of its funds from a permanent endowment established by voluntary contributions from members of

UNITED SOCIETY OF BELIEVERS

the United Nations. The university has headquarters in Tokyo.   P. A. MCGINLEY

UNITED NEGRO COLLEGE FUND is a nonprofit fund-raising organization. Its membership consists of 41 predominantly black colleges and universities in the United States. The fund was set up in 1944 to raise money to help operate the schools, all of which are private. It also provides other services to the schools, including educational and administrative counseling.

The organization receives contributions from corporations, foundations, and individuals. By the late 1970's, it had raised more than $200 million. Headquarters are at 500 E. 62nd Street, New York, N.Y. 10021.

Critically reviewed by the UNITED NEGRO COLLEGE FUND

UNITED PARCEL SERVICE (UPS) is the largest package delivery company in the United States. It operates in all the states; in Ontario, Canada; and in West Germany. UPS offers both ground and air transportation of packages. The company operates the largest private delivery fleet in the United States.

In 1907, two teen-agers named James Casey and Claude Ryan borrowed $100 and started a messenger service for businesses in Seattle. The company later began delivering packages. In 1919, the firm was named United Parcel Service. By the early 1950's, it was providing delivery service for retail stores in more than a dozen metropolitan areas. Since 1952, UPS has been a *common carrier*, offering pickup and delivery service for both businesses and individuals.

Critically reviewed by UNITED PARCEL SERVICE

UNITED PRESBYTERIAN CHURCH IN THE U.S.A. See PRESBYTERIAN CHURCH (U.S.A.).

UNITED PRESS INTERNATIONAL (UPI) is one of the largest independent news agencies in the world. It distributes news, photographs, television news film, radio news, and cable television news programming to about 6,000 clients. Its clients include newspapers, radio and television stations, news magazines, and cable television outlets in more than 100 countries. UPI has about 200 bureaus, including about 110 in the United States. It employs over 1,700 persons.

Subsidiaries include United Press International of Canada, Ltd., United Press International (U.K.), Ltd., in Great Britain, and Unicom News. UPI also operates a television film service, UPITN, Inc. United Press International was formed in 1958, when United Press and International News Service merged.   WILLIAM C. PAYETTE

UNITED SERVICE ORGANIZATIONS (USO) is a civilian nonprofit organization that provides assistance to men and women in the U.S. armed forces and to their families. USO provides informal education, information about foreign cultures, recreational activities, shows, travel assistance, and other programs and services. More than 40,000 volunteers throughout the world assist a small professional staff to make possible the many USO programs. USO is a congressionally chartered organization that receives its funding from individual donations and corporate gifts, and from United Way of America.

The USO was founded in 1941. Its world headquarters are at 601 Indiana Avenue NW, Washington, DC 20004.   Critically reviewed by UNITED SERVICE ORGANIZATIONS

UNITED SOCIETY OF BELIEVERS. See SHAKERS.

The United States is a land of great beauty and natural wealth. Its many famous and interesting sights include the Statue of Liberty in New York Harbor, *above left;* quaint cable cars on hilly San Francisco streets, *top right;* and areas of rich farmland in the fertile Midwest, *bottom right.*

UNITED STATES

UNITED STATES OF AMERICA is the fourth largest country in the world in both area and population. Only Russia, Canada, and China have larger areas. China, India, and Russia are the only countries with more people. The United States covers the entire midsection of North America, stretching from the Atlantic Ocean in the east to the Pacific Ocean in the west. It also includes Alaska, in the northwest corner of North America; and Hawaii, far out in the Pacific. The United States is often called the *U.S., U.S.A.,* or *America.*

The land of the United States is as varied as it is vast. It ranges from the warm beaches of Florida and Hawaii to the frozen northlands of Alaska, and from the level Midwestern prairies to the snow-capped Rocky Mountains. This huge and beautiful country is unbelievably rich in natural resources. It has great stretches of some of the most fertile soil on earth, a plentiful water supply and excellent water routes, and large stretches of forests.

The contributors of this article are John Edwin Coffman, Associate Professor of Geography at the University of Houston; and Teresa A. Sullivan, Associate Professor of Sociology at the University of Texas at Austin.

Huge deposits of valuable minerals, including coal, iron ore, natural gas, and petroleum, lie under the ground.

Economically, the United States is one of the world's most highly developed and productive nations. No other country equals the United States in the value of its agricultural, manufactured, and mined products. The people of the United States enjoy one of the world's highest standards of living.

Until the 1500's, what is now the United States was largely a wilderness. Small groups of Indians lived scattered over the land between the Atlantic and Pacific. Eskimos inhabited what is now Alaska, and Polynesians lived in Hawaii. People in Europe saw in this vast "new world" a chance to build new and better lives. Small groups of Spaniards settled in what is now the Southeastern and Western United States in the 1500's. People from England and some other European countries began settling along and near the East Coast during the 1600's. In 1776, colonists in the East founded an independent nation based on freedom and equal opportunity for all. Through the years, large numbers of people from Europe continued to settle in the United States. In addition, people from almost every other part of the world settled in the country. Except for black Africans brought in as slaves, these *immigrants* came seeking the rights and opportunities that had become

Breathtaking Scenery makes Yellowstone National Park one of America's favorite vacationlands. The park, located chiefly in Wyoming, is home to buffaloes and other wild animals.

John Running, Black Star

Facts in Brief

Capital: Washington, D.C.

Form of Government: Republic. For details, see UNITED STATES, GOVERNMENT OF THE.

Area: 3,618,770 sq. mi. (9,372,614 km²), including 79,481 sq. mi. (205,856 km²) of inland water but excluding 60,788 sq. mi. (157,440 km²) of Great Lakes and Lake Saint Clair and 13,942 sq. mi. (36,110 km²) of coastal water. *Greatest Distances Excluding Alaska and Hawaii*—east-west, 2,807 mi. (4,517 km); north-south, 1,598 mi. (2,572 km). *Greatest Distances in Alaska*—north-south, about 1,200 mi. (1,930 km); east-west, about 2,200 mi. (3,540 km). *Greatest Distance in Hawaii*—northwest-southeast, about 1,610 mi. (2,591 km). *Extreme Points Including Alaska and Hawaii*—northernmost, Point Barrow, Alaska; southernmost, Ka Lae, Hawaii; easternmost, West Quoddy Head, Me.; westernmost, Cape Wrangell, Attu Island, Alaska. *Coastline*—4,993 mi. (8,035 km), excluding Alaska and Hawaii; 12,383 mi. (19,929 km), including Alaska and Hawaii.

Elevation: *Highest*—Mount McKinley in Alaska, 20,320 ft. (6,194 m) above sea level. *Lowest*—In Death Valley in California, 282 ft. (86 m) below sea level.

Physical Features: *Longest River*—Mississippi, 2,348 mi. (3,779 km). *Largest Lake Within the United States*—Michigan, 22,300 sq. mi. (57,757 km²). *Largest Island*—island of Hawaii, 4,038 sq. mi. (10,458 km²).

Population: *Estimated 1986 Population*—240,854,000; density, 67 persons per sq. mi. (26 per km²); distribution, 74 per cent urban, 26 per cent rural. *1980 Census*—226,545,805. *Estimated 1991 Population*—253,140,000.

Chief Products: *Agriculture*—beef cattle, milk, corn, soybeans, hogs, wheat, cotton. *Fishing Industry*—shrimp, salmon, crabs. *Manufacturing*—nonelectric machinery; transportation equipment; chemicals; food products; electric machinery and equipment; fabricated metal products; primary metals; printed materials; paper products; rubber and plastics products; clothing. *Mining*—petroleum, natural gas, coal.

Flag: Adopted June 14, 1777.

Motto: *In God We Trust*, adopted July 30, 1956.

National Anthem: "The Star-Spangled Banner," adopted March 3, 1931.

Bird: Bald Eagle, adopted June 20, 1782.

Money: *Basic Unit*—dollar.

---

part of the American way of life. As a result of this immigration from so many lands, the United States today has one of the world's most varied populations. It has been called "a nation of immigrants."

The vast space and resources of the land, the ideals of freedom and equal opportunity, and hard work by the people all helped build the United States into the economic giant it is today. The Americans—as the people are commonly called—also made major contributions to world progress in such fields as technology, science, and medicine. Americans developed the mass production system of manufacturing, the electric light bulb, the telephone, the reaper and steel plow, and polio vaccine. They also developed new art forms, including jazz, musical comedy, and the skyscraper.

At times, the U.S. economy has run into difficulty. Even so, it remains one of the most productive systems ever developed. In some cases, groups of Americans have suffered socially and economically from discrimination. But the country's laws have helped many people overcome discrimination and achieve better lives.

This article discusses the regions, people, way of life, land, climate, and economy of the United States. For detailed information on the country's government and history, see UNITED STATES, GOVERNMENT OF THE, and UNITED STATES, HISTORY OF THE.

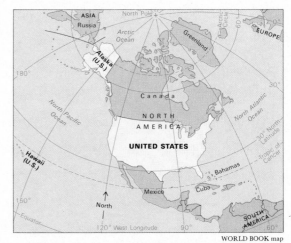

WORLD BOOK map

The United States stretches across North America between the Pacific and Atlantic oceans. It also includes Alaska, in the northwest corner of the continent; and Hawaii, far out in the Pacific.

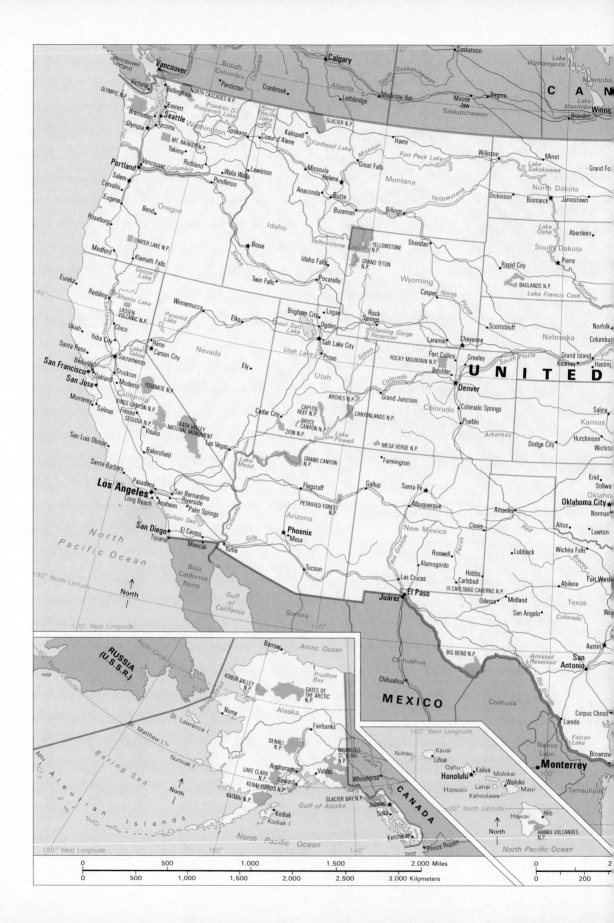

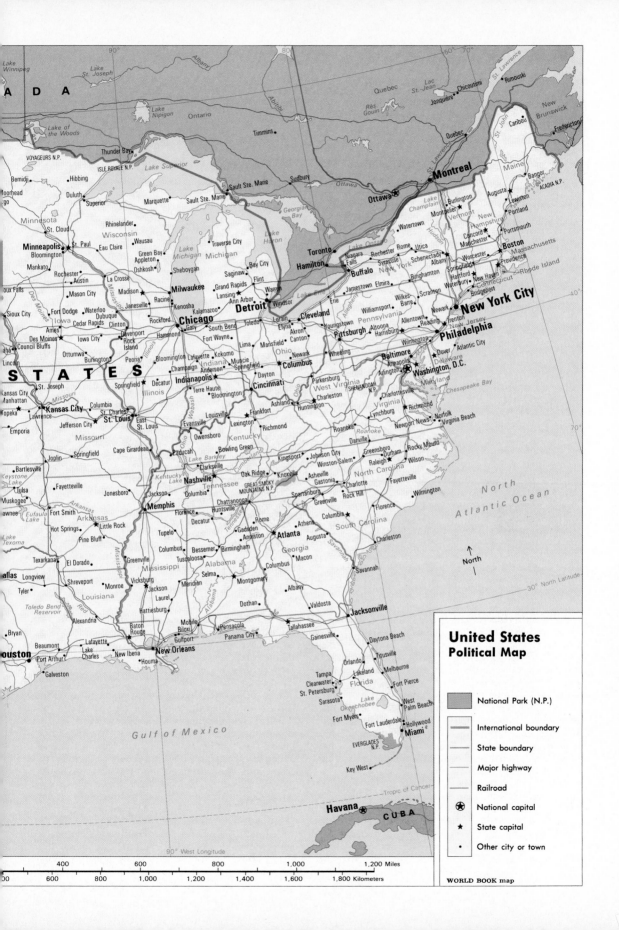

United States
Political Map

Michael Philip Manheim

Giant Cactuses in Arizona are symbols of the "wide open spaces" of the Southwest. A warm, dry climate has made the Southwest one of the nation's fastest-growing areas.

Tom Pantages

A Snow-Covered Village nestles among low hills in Vermont. Such tiny, picturesque settlements are common in much of the far Northeastern part of the United States.

Shrout & Shrout

A Southern Mansion in Alabama dates from 1853. Originally a private home, it is now a government-owned museum and a reminder of the life style and architecture of the pre-Civil War South.

Political Divisions. The United States consists of 50 states and the District of Columbia. The District of Columbia is a piece of land set aside by the federal government for the nation's capital, Washington, D.C. For a list of the states, see the table in this article titled *Facts in Brief About the States*.

In area, population, and economic output, some of the states are comparable to many nations. The United States has a federal system of government, which gives the states many powers that national governments have in most other countries. For example, the states have broad control over public education and the establishment of civil and criminal laws.

Regions. The states of the United States, excluding Alaska and Hawaii, are often divided into seven major regions. Each region is made up of states that have similarities in geography, climate, economy, traditions, and history. The regions are: (1) New England, (2) the Middle Atlantic States, (3) the Southern States, (4) the Midwestern States, (5) the Rocky Mountain States, (6)

the Southwestern States, and (7) the Pacific Coast States. For a list of the states in each region, see the table titled *Regions of the United States* in this article. The map that accompanies the table shows the location of each of these regions.

New England is a small region in the northeast corner of the country that is known for picturesque rural villages, numerous fishing harbors, and colorful autumn scenery. New England was the nation's first industrial center, and manufacturing is still its leading source of income. Industrial cities dot southern New England. Much of the region's land is too hilly or rocky to grow crops. But New England produces large amounts of dairy and poultry products and is famous for its maple syrup. Many tourists visit the region to see its many historic sites—especially those from colonial times—and to enjoy its natural beauty.

Many New Englanders, especially in the rural north, are descendants of English Puritans who settled the region during the 1600's. The more densely populated

southern section of New England has people of many backgrounds, including blacks, Irish, Italians, and French Canadians. The southern section includes Boston, New England's largest city by far.

The Middle Atlantic States Region stretches inland from the Atlantic Ocean southwest of New England. Deepwater harbors help make the region a major center of international trade. The busiest harbor is at New York City, the largest city in the United States. Factories in and near such Middle Atlantic cities—in order of size—as New York City, Philadelphia, Pittsburgh, Buffalo, and Newark produce a wide variety of goods. Coal mining and related industries are important economic activities in the western part of the Middle Atlantic States Region. Farms dot hillsides and fertile plains in various parts of the region. Forested mountains, sandy seashores, scenic lakes and rivers, historic sites, and big-city attractions draw many visitors to the region.

The Middle Atlantic States Region ranks as the nation's most densely populated area. Its urban population includes people of varied European backgrounds, and large groups of people of black African, Latin-American, and Asian ancestry. Many of the region's rural dwellers are of British descent.

The Southern States Region is an area of rolling hills, mountains, and plains bordered by broad beaches along the Atlantic Ocean and the Gulf of Mexico. Until the mid-1900's, the region's economy was based heavily on agriculture. Such warm-weather crops as sugar cane, tobacco, and—especially—cotton contributed greatly to the economy. Agriculture has retained importance in the South. But an industrial boom that began in the mid-1900's has greatly increased manufacturing and has improved the balance of the region's economy. Tourists flock to coastal resorts in the South—especially in winter, when temperatures are usually relatively mild. Baltimore is the largest city of the Southern States Region. Memphis, Washington, D.C., New Orleans, Jacksonville, and Nashville rank next in size. Washington, D.C., is not part of any state, but it is located within the region.

Large numbers of Southerners are descended from early English, Irish, and Scottish immigrants. From the 1600's to the 1800's, many black Africans were brought to the region to work on plantations as slaves. Today, blacks form a large minority group in the Southern States Region. Many Southerners have a strong sense of regional loyalty and take pride in the South's history and traditions.

The Midwestern States Region is a vast area of generally flat land that covers much of the center of the United States. The Midwest is famous for its large stretches of fertile soil. Farms in the region produce enormous quantities of corn, wheat, and other crops; and also dairy products and livestock. In addition, the Midwest has a number of large industrial cities. The cities include, in order of size, Chicago, Detroit, Indianapolis, Milwaukee, and Cleveland.

The Mississippi River system, the Great Lakes, and many railroads give the region an excellent transportation network. Lakes and rivers—some set among rolling

Regions of the United States

The map below shows the location of the seven regions of the United States that are discussed in this section of the article. The table below the map lists the states within each region.

WORLD BOOK map

New England
Connecticut, Maine, Massachusetts, New Hampshire, Rhode Island, Vermont

Middle Atlantic States
New Jersey, New York, Pennsylvania

Southern States
Alabama, Arkansas, Delaware, Florida, Georgia, Kentucky, Louisiana, Maryland, Mississippi, North Carolina, South Carolina, Tennessee, Virginia, West Virginia

Midwestern States
Illinois, Indiana, Iowa, Kansas, Michigan, Minnesota, Missouri, Nebraska, North Dakota, Ohio, South Dakota, Wisconsin

Rocky Mountain States
Colorado, Idaho, Montana, Nevada, Utah, Wyoming

Southwestern States
*Arizona, *New Mexico, Oklahoma, Texas

Pacific Coast States
California, Oregon, Washington

*Arizona and New Mexico are often grouped with the Rocky Mountain States.

Main Outlying Areas of the United States

Name	Acquired	Status
American Samoa	*	Unorganized unincorporated territory
Baker Island and Jarvis Island	1856	Unincorporated territory
Guam	1898	Organized unincorporated territory
Howland Island	1856	Unincorporated possession
Johnston Island and Sand Island	1858	Unincorporated territory
Kingman Reef	1922	Unincorporated territory
Midway Island	1867	Unincorporated territory
Palmyra Island	1898	Unincorporated possession
Puerto Rico	1898	Commonwealth
Trust Territory of the Pacific Islands	1947	UN trust territory (U.S. administration)
Virgin Islands of the United States	1917	Organized unincorporated territory
Wake Island	1898	Unincorporated possession

*Acquired in stages between 1900 and 1925.

hills and rugged bluffs—provide numerous recreation areas there.

The Midwestern States Region has a varied population. Its rural areas include large groups of descendants of settlers from Germany, Great Britain, Norway, Sweden, and eastern and southern Europe. The region's city population includes many descendants of people who came from northern, southern, and eastern Europe. Blacks make up a large minority group in the big cities of the Midwest.

The Rocky Mountain States Region lies west of the Midwest. It is named for the rugged, majestic Rocky Mountains, which cut through it. In addition to the mountains, the region has areas of deserts, plains, and plateaus. Although much of it is a thinly populated wilderness, some of its cities and towns are among the nation's fastest-growing areas. Denver ranks as the region's largest city by far.

Rich deposits of gold, silver, and other metals first attracted settlers to the region. Mining remains an important economic activity, but manufacturing is now

the chief source of income. Cattle and other livestock graze on dry, grassy ranges, and farmers grow a variety of crops in the Rocky Mountain States Region. Many tourists visit the region to enjoy its scenic beauty and numerous ski resorts.

The population of the Rocky Mountain States Region includes persons of European descent, as well as blacks, Mexican Americans, and American Indians. Mormons, whose ancestors founded a religious community in Utah in the 1800's, form an important cultural group in the region.

The Southwestern States Region spreads out over a vast area that is sometimes called the "wide open spaces." There, cattle graze on huge ranches, and vast fields of cotton and other crops soak up rays of blazing sunshine. However, petroleum has brought the region most of its wealth. The region has large deposits of petroleum and natural gas, as well as various other minerals. In the 1900's, refineries and petrochemical factories led the way to industrialization in the Southwest.

The industrialization has helped bring about much

Facts in Brief About the States

State	Capital	Popular Name	Area (sq. mi.)	Area (km²)	Rank in Area	Population*	Rank in Pop.*	Population Density* (sq. mi.)	Population Density* (km²)
Alabama	Montgomery	Yellowhammer State	51,705	133,915	29	3,893,978	22	75	29
Alaska	Juneau	Last Frontier	591,004	1,530,700	1	401,851	50	0.7	0.3
Arizona	Phoenix	Grand Canyon State	114,000	295,260	6	2,718,425	29	24	9
Arkansas	Little Rock	Land of Opportunity	53,187	137,754	27	2,286,419	33	43	17
California	Sacramento	Golden State	158,706	411,049	3	23,668,562	1	149	58
Colorado	Denver	Centennial State	104,091	269,595	8	2,889,964	28	28	11
Connecticut	Hartford	Constitution State	5,018	12,977	48	3,107,576	25	619	239
Delaware	Dover	First State	2,044	5,295	49	594,338	47	291	112
Florida	Tallahassee	Sunshine State	58,644	151,939	22	9,746,421	7	166	64
Georgia	Atlanta	Empire State of the South	58,910	152,576	21	5,463,087	13	93	36
Hawaii	Honolulu	Aloha State	6,471	16,759	47	964,691	39	149	58
Idaho	Boise	Gem State	83,564	216,432	13	944,038	41	11	4
Illinois	Springfield	Land of Lincoln	56,345	145,934	24	11,427,414	5	203	78
Indiana	Indianapolis	Hoosier State	36,185	93,720	38	5,490,260	12	152	59
Iowa	Des Moines	Hawkeye State	56,275	145,753	25	2,913,808	27	52	20
Kansas	Topeka	Sunflower State	82,277	213,098	14	2,364,236	32	29	11
Kentucky	Frankfort	Bluegrass State	40,409	104,660	37	3,660,257	23	91	35
Louisiana	Baton Rouge	Pelican State	47,752	123,677	31	4,206,098	19	88	34
Maine	Augusta	Pine Tree State	33,265	86,156	39	1,125,030	38	34	13
Maryland	Annapolis	Old Line State	10,460	27,092	42	4,216,941	18	403	156

*1980 Census

urban growth in the Southwestern States Region. The region includes many of the nation's fastest-growing cities. Its largest cities are, in order of size, Houston, Dallas, San Antonio, Phoenix, El Paso, and Oklahoma City. The region also has many retirement communities. Tourist attractions in the Southwest include huge, unspoiled areas of incredible natural beauty, such as the Grand Canyon and the Painted Desert.

Many cultures come together in the Southwest. The population includes people of various European backgrounds, and black, Mexican-American, and American Indian minority groups.

The Pacific Coast States Region, which borders the Pacific Ocean, is known for its dense forests, rugged mountains, and dramatic ocean shore. The scenic beauty and relatively mild climate of the region encourage an outdoor life style enjoyed by both residents and tourists.

Fertile valleys in the Pacific Coast States Region produce a large part of the nation's fruits, nuts, vegetables, and wine grapes. The region also has abundant timber, minerals, and fish. Much manufacturing takes place in its large cities, which include—in order of size—Los Angeles, San Diego, San Francisco, San Jose, and Seattle.

The discovery of gold and the opening of the Oregon Territory in the mid-1800's brought a stream of settlers to the Pacific Coast. New residents have continued to pour in ever since. Today, the population includes people of European ancestry, and black and Mexican-American minority groups. The region also has more people of Asian ancestry than any other part of the United States, and a large number of American Indians.

Outlying Areas. The United States has possession of various island territories in the Caribbean Sea and the Pacific Ocean. Some of them, such as Guam and the Virgin Islands, have a large degree of self-government. Puerto Rico, one of the areas, is a commonwealth associated with the United States that has been given wide powers of self-rule by the U.S. Congress. It sends to Congress a representative who votes only in committees. See the table titled *Main Outlying Areas of the United States* in this article.

State Abbreviation†	State Bird	State Flower	State Tree	State Song	Admitted to the Union	Order of Admission	Members of Congress Senate	House
Ala.	Yellow-hammer	Camellia	Southern pine (Longleaf pine)	"Alabama"	1819	22	2	7
**	Willow ptarmigan	Forget-me-not	Sitka spruce	"Alaska's Flag"	1959	49	2	1
Ariz.	Cactus wren	Saguaro (Giant cactus)	Paloverde	"Arizona"	1912	48	2	5
Ark.	Mockingbird	Apple blossom	Pine	"Arkansas"	1836	25	2	4
Calif.	California valley quail	Golden poppy	California redwood	"I Love You, California"	1850	31	2	45
Colo.	Lark bunting	Rocky Mountain columbine	Blue spruce	"Where the Columbines Grow"	1876	38	2	6
Conn.	Robin	Mountain laurel	White oak	"Yankee Doodle"	1788	5	2	6
Del.	Blue hen chicken	Peach blossom	American holly	"Our Delaware"	1787	1	2	1
Fla.	Mockingbird	Orange blossom	Cabbage (Sabal) palm	"Old Folks at Home" ("Swanee River")	1845	27	2	19
Ga.	Brown thrasher	Cherokee rose	Live oak	"Georgia on My Mind"	1788	4	2	10
**	Nene (Hawaiian goose)	Hibiscus	Kukui	"Hawaii Ponoi" (Hawaii's Own)	1959	50	2	2
Ida.	Mountain bluebird	Syringa (Mock orange)	Western white pine	"Here We Have Idaho"	1890	43	2	2
Ill.	Cardinal	Native violet	White oak	"Illinois"	1818	21	2	22
Ind.	Cardinal	Peony	Tulip tree, or yellow poplar	"On the Banks of the Wabash, Far Away"	1816	19	2	10
Ia.	Eastern goldfinch	Wild rose	Oak	"The Song of Iowa"	1846	29	2	6
Kans. or Kan.	Western meadow lark	Sunflower	Cottonwood	"Home on the Range"	1861	34	2	5
Ky. or Ken.	Kentucky cardinal	Goldenrod	Kentucky coffeetree	"My Old Kentucky Home"	1792	15	2	7
La.	Brown pelican	Magnolia	Bald cypress	"Give Me Louisiana"; "You Are My Sunshine"	1812	18	2	8
Me.	Chickadee	White pine cone and tassel	White pine	"State of Maine Song"	1820	23	2	2
Md.	Baltimore oriole	Black-eyed Susan	White oak (Wye oak)	"Maryland, My Maryland"	1788	7	2	8

†For the two-letter state abbreviations used by the U.S. Postal Service, see the table with the POST OFFICE article.
**The state has no traditional abbreviation.

Facts in Brief About the States

State	Capital	Popular Name	Area (sq. mi.)	Area (km²)	Rank in Area	Population*	Rank in Pop.*	Population Density* (sq. mi.)	Population Density* (km²)
Massachusetts	Boston	Bay State	8,284	21,456	45	5,737,081	11	693	268
Michigan	Lansing	Wolverine State	58,527	151,586	23	9,262,070	8	158	61
Minnesota	St. Paul	Gopher State	84,402	218,601	12	4,075,970	21	48	19
Mississippi	Jackson	Magnolia State	47,689	123,515	32	2,520,631	31	53	20
Missouri	Jefferson City	Show Me State	67,697	180,516	19	4,916,759	15	71	27
Montana	Helena	Treasure State	147,046	380,848	4	786,690	44	5	2
Nebraska	Lincoln	Cornhusker State	77,355	200,350	15	1,569,825	35	20	8
Nevada	Carson City	Silver State	110,561	286,532	7	799,184	43	7	3
New Hampshire	Concord	Granite State	9,297	24,032	44	920,610	42	99	38
New Jersey	Trenton	Garden State	7,787	20,169	46	7,365,011	9	946	365
New Mexico	Santa Fe	Land of Enchantment	121,593	314,925	5	1,303,445	37	11	4
New York	Albany	Empire State	49,108	127,189	30	17,558,072	2	358	138
North Carolina	Raleigh	Tar Heel State	52,669	136,413	28	5,881,813	10	112	43
North Dakota	Bismarck	Flickertail State	70,702	183,119	17	652,717	46	9	3
Ohio	Columbus	Buckeye State	41,330	107,044	35	10,797,624	6	261	101
Oklahoma	Oklahoma City	Sooner State	69,956	181,186	18	3,025,495	26	43	17
Oregon	Salem	Beaver State	97,073	251,419	10	2,633,149	30	27	10
Pennsylvania	Harrisburg	Keystone State	45,308	117,348	33	11,864,751	4	262	101
Rhode Island	Providence	Ocean State	1,212	3,140	50	947,154	40	781	302
South Carolina	Columbia	Palmetto State	31,113	80,582	40	3,122,814	24	100	39
South Dakota	Pierre	Sunshine State	77,116	199,730	16	690,768	45	9	3
Tennessee	Nashville	Volunteer State	42,114	109,152	34	4,591,120	17	109	42
Texas	Austin	Lone Star State	266,807	691,030	2	14,227,574	3	53	20
Utah	Salt Lake City	Beehive State	84,899	219,889	11	1,461,037	36	17	7
Vermont	Montpelier	Green Mountain State	9,614	24,900	43	511,456	48	53	20
Virginia	Richmond	Old Dominion	40,767	105,586	36	5,346,797	14	131	51
Washington	Olympia	Evergreen State	68,139	176,479	20	4,132,204	20	61	24
West Virginia	Charleston	Mountain State	24,231	62,759	41	1,950,258	34	80	31
Wisconsin	Madison	Badger State	56,153	145,436	26	4,705,642	16	84	32
Wyoming	Cheyenne	Equality State	97,809	253,326	9	469,557	49	5	2

*1980 Census

State Abbreviation†	State Bird	State Flower	State Tree	State Song	Admitted to the Union	Order of Admission	Members of Congress Senate	House
Mass.	Chickadee	Arbutus	American elm	"All Hail to Massachusetts"	1788	6	2	11
Mich.	Robin	Apple blossom	White pine	"Michigan, My Michigan"**	1837	26	2	18
Minn.	Common loon	Pink and white lady's-slipper	Norway, or red, pine	"Hail! Minnesota"	1858	32	2	8
Miss.	Mockingbird	Magnolia	Magnolia	"Go Mis- sis- sip- pi"	1817	20	2	5
Mo.	Bluebird	Hawthorn	Flowering dogwood	"Missouri Waltz"	1821	24	2	9
Mont.	Western meadow lark	Bitterroot	Ponderosa pine	"Montana"	1889	41	2	2
Nebr. or Neb.	Western meadow lark	Goldenrod	Cottonwood	"Beautiful Nebraska"	1867	37	2	3
Nev.	Mountain bluebird**	Sagebrush**	Single-leaf piñon	"Home Means Nevada"	1864	36	2	2
N.H.	Purple finch	Purple lilac	White birch	"Old New Hampshire"	1788	9	2	2
N.J.	Eastern goldfinch	Purple violet	Red oak	None	1787	3	2	14
N.Mex. or N.M.	Roadrunner	Yucca flower	Piñon, or nut pine	"O, Fair New Mexico"	1912	47	2	3
N.Y.	Bluebird	Rose	Sugar maple	"I Love New York"	1788	11	2	34
N.C.	Cardinal	Flowering dogwood	Pine	"The Old North State"	1789	12	2	11
N.Dak. or N.D.	Western meadow lark	Wild prairie rose	American elm	"North Dakota Hymn"	1889	39	2	1
O.	Cardinal	Scarlet carnation	Buckeye	"Beautiful Ohio"	1803	17	2	21
Okla.	Scissor-tailed flycatcher	Mistletoe	Redbud	"Oklahoma!"	1907	46	2	6
Ore. or Oreg.	Western meadow lark	Oregon grape	Douglas fir	"Oregon, My Oregon"	1859	33	2	5
Pa. or Penn.	Ruffed grouse	Mountain laurel	Hemlock	None	1787	2	2	23
R.I.	Rhode Island Red	Violet	Red maple	"Rhode Island"	1790	13	2	2
S.C.	Carolina wren	Carolina jessamine	Palmetto	"Carolina"	1788	8	2	6
S.Dak. or S.D.	Ring-necked pheasant	American pasqueflower	Black Hills spruce	"Hail, South Dakota"	1889	40	2	1
Tenn.	Mockingbird	Iris	Tulip poplar	"My Homeland, Tennessee"; "My Tennessee"; "Rocky Top"; "The Tennessee Waltz"; "When It's Iris Time in Tennessee"	1796	16	2	9
Tex.	Mockingbird	Bluebonnet	Pecan	"Texas, Our Texas"	1845	28	2	27
Ut.	Sea Gull	Sego lily	Blue spruce	"Utah, We Love Thee"	1896	45	2	3
Vt.	Hermit thrush	Red clover	Sugar maple	"Hail, Vermont!"	1791	14	2	1
Va.	Cardinal	Dogwood	Dogwood	"Carry Me Back to Old Virginia"	1788	10	2	10
Wash.	Willow goldfinch	Coast rhododendron	Western hemlock	"Washington, My Home"	1889	42	2	8
W. Va.	Cardinal	Rhododendron	Sugar maple	"The West Virginia Hills"; "This is My West Virginia"; "West Virginia, My Home Sweet Home"	1863	35	2	4
Wis.	Robin	Wood violet	Sugar maple	"On, Wisconsin!"	1848	30	2	9
Wyo.	Meadow lark	Indian paintbrush	Cottonwood	"Wyoming"	1890	44	2	1

†For the two-letter state abbreviations used by the U.S. Postal Service, see the table with the POST OFFICE article.
**Unofficial

Population. The U.S. Census Bureau reported that in 1980 the country had a population of 226,545,805. In 1985, the United States had an estimated population of about 240,854,000.

Whites make up about 83 per cent of the country's population. Blacks form the largest minority group. They account for about 12 per cent of the population. American Indians make up about one-half of 1 per cent of the population. Most of the rest of the people are of Asian descent.

The white population includes many Spanish-speaking people, such as Mexican Americans, Puerto Ricans, and immigrants from Cuba. The Census Bureau classifies the Spanish-speaking people as a minority group. The group makes up about 6 per cent of the population, and is the second largest minority in the United States.

About 51.5 per cent of all Americans are females. People under the age of 20 make up about a fifth of the population. People from 20 to 34 years old and those 35 to 59 years old each make up about a fourth. Those people who are 60 or older account for about a sixth. Improvements in medical care and other developments have increased the life expectancy of Americans. In 1900, the life expectancy—or average number of years a person is expected to live—was 47.3. Today, it is 73.6.

Approximately 94 per cent of the total population was born in the United States. The largest foreign-born groups are, in order of size, Mexicans, Germans, Canadians, Italians, British, and Cubans. The United States has an overall average population density of about 67 persons per square mile (26 persons per square kilometer). But the density varies widely from place to place. See the map in this section of the article for the density throughout the country.

Ancestry. The United States has one of the world's most varied populations in terms of ancestry. The population includes descendants of people from almost every part of the world.

The first people to live in what is now the United States were Indians, Eskimos, and Hawaiians. The Indians and Eskimos are descended from peoples who migrated to North America from Asia thousands of years ago. The ancestors of the Hawaiians were Polynesians who sailed to what is now Hawaii from other Pacific islands about 2,000 years ago.

Most white Americans trace their ancestry to Europe. Some Spaniards settled in what is now the United States during the 1500's. European settlement increased sharply during the 1600's. At first, most of the settlers came from England. But America soon attracted large numbers of immigrants from other nations of northern and

Population Density and Centers of Population

This map shows the population density throughout the United States. Population density is the average number of persons who live on each square mile or square kilometer in an area. The map also shows how the country's center of population moved westward between 1790 and 1980.

WORLD BOOK map

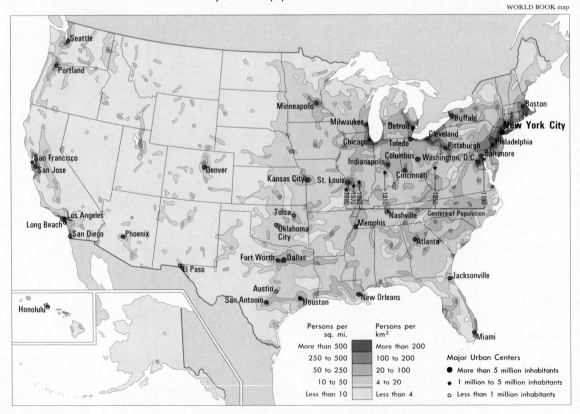

Persons per sq. mi.	Persons per km²
More than 500	More than 200
250 to 500	100 to 200
50 to 250	20 to 100
10 to 50	4 to 20
Less than 10	Less than 4

Major Urban Centers
● More than 5 million inhabitants
• 1 million to 5 million inhabitants
o Less than 1 million inhabitants

The Population of the United States

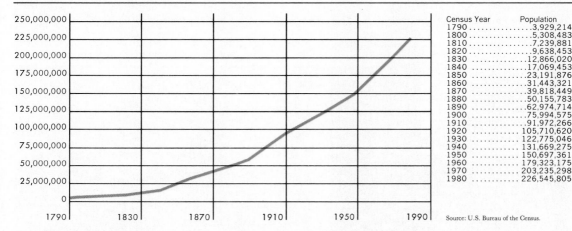

Census Year	Population
1790	3,929,214
1800	5,308,483
1810	7,239,881
1820	9,638,453
1830	12,866,020
1840	17,069,453
1850	23,191,876
1860	31,443,321
1870	39,818,449
1880	50,155,783
1890	62,974,714
1900	75,994,575
1910	91,972,266
1920	105,710,620
1930	122,775,046
1940	131,669,275
1950	150,697,361
1960	179,323,175
1970	203,235,298
1980	226,545,805

Source: U.S. Bureau of the Census.

The population of the United States has risen steadily since the country's first census was taken in 1790. The above graph illustrates the country's population growth since the first census. The table at the right lists the population figure for each census year.

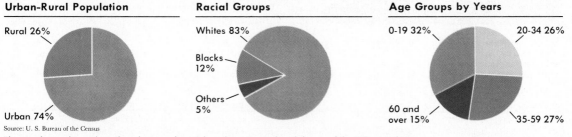

Source: U. S. Bureau of the Census

The pie charts above show the urban-rural, racial, and age-group breakdowns of the U.S. population in 1980. Nearly 75 per cent of the people live in urban areas. Whites account for about 83 per cent of the population, and blacks for about 12 per cent. Persons under 20 make up the largest age group. This group accounts for about 32 per cent of the country's population.

western Europe. The nations included France, Germany, Ireland, The Netherlands, and Scotland; and the Scandinavian lands of Denmark, Norway, and Sweden. Until the late 1800's, northern and western Europe continued to provide most of the immigrants. Then, large waves of people began flocking to America from southern and eastern European nations, including Austria-Hungary, Greece, Italy, Poland, and Russia.

The white population of the United States also includes Spanish-speaking people. A small percentage of them trace their ancestry directly back to Spain. But most of them are people who immigrated—or whose ancestors immigrated—to the U.S. from Latin America. Some have mainly Spanish ancestry. Others have mixed Spanish and Latin-American Indian ancestry.

Most black Americans are descendants of Africans who were brought to the United States as slaves during the 1600's, 1700's, and 1800's and forced to work on plantations. See SLAVERY (Slavery in the United States).

Since the 1800's, the United States has attracted immigrants from Asia. Most Americans of Asian descent trace their ancestry to China, Indochina, Japan, or the Philippines. For more details on the flow of people into the United States through the years, see IMMIGRATION.

The United States has often been called a *melting pot*. This term refers to the idea that the country is a place where people from many lands have come together and formed a unified culture. Americans do have many things in common. For example, the vast majority of them speak English, and people throughout the country dress similarly and eat many of the same kinds of foods. Public education, mass communication, and other influences have helped shape a common identity for Americans. But in other ways, U.S. society is an example of *cultural pluralism*. That is, large numbers of its people have retained features of the cultures of their ancestors. Many Americans take special pride in their origins. They preserve traditions—and in some cases the languages—of their ancestors. In many cities, people of different national, ethnic, or racial origins live in separate neighborhoods, and shops and restaurants reflect their cultural backgrounds. Ethnic festivals, parades, and other events in various parts of the United States emphasize the nation's cultural pluralism.

Tony Kelly   John Running

Urban and Rural Life in the United States contrast sharply. Motor vehicles move slowly along a street lined by big buildings in downtown San Antonio, *above left.* At a county fair, *right,* farm people show their sheep in a livestock competition.

For census purposes, the United States is divided into *urban areas* and *rural areas*. An urban area, as defined by the U.S. Census Bureau, is a community with 2,500 or more people. A rural area is a community with fewer than 2,500 people.

In 1790, the year of the first census, about 95 per cent of the nation's people lived in rural areas, and only about 5 per cent were urban dwellers. Through the years, these percentages changed steadily and dramatically. Today, about 74 per cent of all the people live in urban areas, and only about 26 per cent live in rural areas.

Several factors contributed to the dramatic population shift from the countryside to urban areas. Through the years, Americans greatly improved agricultural methods and equipment. From the 1800's onward, farm work has become more and more efficient, farm production has soared, and fewer and fewer people have been needed to work on the nation's farms. At the same time, an industrial boom has created large numbers of new jobs in the nation's urban areas. As a result of these economic changes, a steady flow of people from rural to urban areas has taken place. Also, large numbers of immigrants—many of whom had been farmers in their homelands—found jobs in cities and settled there when they reached the United States. In addition, the fast-paced life of cities seemed glamorous to many rural people, especially the young. Large numbers of rural people left home to seek excitement in cities.

Urban Life. Urban areas, which range from giant cities surrounded by suburbs to small towns, dot the U.S. landscape. Although the urban areas cover less than 2 per cent of the land, they are the home of about three-fourths of the people. New York City, with about 7 million people, is the largest U.S. city by far. Los Angeles and Chicago both have about 3 million people. Three other U.S. cities—Houston, Philadelphia, and Detroit—each have more than 1 million people.

Networks of suburbs surround many U.S. cities. The central cities and their suburbs form units called metropolitan areas. There are about 330 metropolitan areas in the United States. The three largest are, in order of size, the New York City, Los Angeles-Long Beach, and Chicago areas. The New York City metropolitan area has about $8\frac{1}{4}$ million people, the Los Angeles-Long Beach area has about $7\frac{1}{2}$ million people, and the Chicago area has about 6 million people.

For many years, the vast majority of the country's urban population lived in the central cities. But during the mid-1900's, suburban population soared throughout the United States, while central city growth slowed down or decreased. In 1980, more Americans lived in suburbs than in central cities.

The Northeast and Midwest have long had most of the nation's largest urban areas. But during the 1900's, other parts of the country have experienced dramatic urban growth. Since the early 1900's, many California urban communities—especially Los Angeles—have grown tremendously. Since the mid-1900's, the populations of many more urban areas in the West, and in the South and Southwest, have soared. Such metropolitan areas as Atlanta, Dallas, Denver, Houston, and Phoenix grew rapidly. Large numbers of people were attracted to the West, South, and Southwest by jobs created by new

industries. Also, many of the fastest-growing communities have warm, sunny climates, which helped attract many of the newcomers. Parts of the South, Southwest, and West are sometimes called the *Sunbelt* because they have such climates.

Urban economies provide jobs for a great variety of workers, including office and factory workers, bankers, doctors, fire fighters, medical personnel, police officers, teachers, trash collectors, and construction and transportation workers. Urban life also has many other positive features. Because of their large populations, urban areas generally offer a wide variety of specialized services and shops. Urban dwellers can take advantage of an assortment of restaurants, recreation facilities, and places of entertainment. Because of such facilities as art galleries, museums, libraries, theaters, and concert halls, many cities are important cultural centers. These and other features make urban areas exciting and interesting places to live for many people.

The people of most U.S. urban areas represent a variety of ethnic and racial backgrounds. Most cities include neighborhoods in which almost all the people belong to the same ethnic or racial group. The people of large urban areas are also divided economically. Urban society includes extremely wealthy and extremely poor people, and a huge middle class. The wealthy live in luxurious apartments or condominiums, or in large, comfortable single-family houses. Middle-class housing also includes apartments, condominiums, and single-family houses. In general, the housing of the middle class is comfortable, though not as luxurious as that of the wealthy. In contrast, large numbers of urban poor people live in substandard housing. They rent small, crowded apartments or run-down single-family houses.

In addition to substandard housing, urban areas have a number of other negative features. Such features include high crime rates, racial and ethnic friction, noisy surroundings, pollution, and traffic jams. See CITY (City Problems).

Rural Life. More than 98 per cent of all the land of the United States is classified as rural. But much of the rural land is uninhabited or only lightly inhabited. About 25 per cent of all Americans live in rural areas.

Farms provide the economic basis of the nation's rural areas. But only about 9 per cent of the country's rural people work as farmers. Many other rural people own or work in businesses related to agriculture, such as grain and feed stores and warehouses. Mining and related activities and light industries also employ many rural people. Still other rural Americans work as teachers, police officers, salesclerks, or in other occupations. Many farmers hold other jobs for part of the year to add to their incomes.

American farmers of today lead vastly different lives from those of their grandparents. Machines have eliminated much backbreaking farm work. Farmers use machines to help them plow, plant seeds, harvest crops, and deliver their products to market. Many farms have conveyor systems so that the farmer no longer has to shovel feed to farm animals. Milking machines make morning and evening chores easier. In the home, farm families may have all the comforts and conveniences of people who live in cities. During the 1900's, the automobile, telephone, radio, and television have brought American farm families into close contact with the rest of the world.

The steady decline in the percentage of the country's rural population showed signs of slowing down

Sprawling Suburbs surround many American cities. Rows of comfortable houses line the streets of most of them. Highways connect the suburbs with their central cities, where large numbers of suburban dwellers work.

somewhat during the 1970's. Although many people continued to move away from rural areas, others chose to move into rural towns and farm communities. Many of the newcomers wanted to escape the overcrowding, pollution, crime, and other problems that are part of life in urban areas and to take advantage of benefits of country living. Rural areas have lower crime rates and less pollution than urban areas. They are also far less noisy and crowded.

Because of their small populations, rural communities collect less tax revenues than urban communities do, and they generally cannot provide the variety of services that urban areas can. For example, rural communities have cultural and recreational facilities that are more limited than those available in urban areas. For many rural Americans, social life centers around family gatherings, church and school activities, special interest clubs, and such events as state and county fairs.

Rural areas generally have less diversified economies than urban areas. Because there are fewer and a smaller variety of jobs to choose from, rural communities may experience more widespread economic hardships than urban communities. A single economic downturn—a drop in farm prices, for example, or the closing of a mine —can cause economic hardship for an entire rural community.

The nation's rural areas, like its urban areas, have wealthy, middle class, and poor people. For the most part, however, the gaps between economic classes are not as large in rural areas as in urban areas. Most rural Americans live in single-family houses. The majority of

the houses are comfortable and in good condition. But some people, including many who live in parts of Appalachia—in the eastern United States—and other pockets of rural poverty, have run-down houses and enjoy few luxuries.

See FARM AND FARMING; RANCHING.

Education has been an important factor in the economic development of the United States and in the achievement of a high standard of living for most Americans. It has also contributed to the enjoyment of life for many people. Americans are among the best-educated people in the world. Schools, libraries, museums, and other educational institutions in the country provide learning opportunities for people of all ages.

Schools. During the early history of the United States, most schools were privately owned. Church groups owned and operated many of them. In the early 1800's, the idea of free public schools began to gain widespread support in the country. State and local governments took the responsibility for establishing public school systems. By 1918, every state had laws requiring children to attend school until they reached a certain age or completed a certain grade. Today, about 80 per cent of the nation's elementary and high schools, and about 45 per cent of its institutions of higher learning, are public schools. The rest are private schools run by religious organizations or private groups.

The United States has about 78,000 elementary schools and about 30,000 high schools. In addition, there are approximately 3,200 colleges, universities, and community—or junior—colleges in the country.

John Launois, Black Star

WORLD BOOK photo by Joseph A. Erhardt

Central Cities of most U.S. urban areas have neighborhoods where most people belong to the same racial or ethnic group. In New York City's Harlem area, *above left,* most people are blacks. A Chicago neighborhood, *right,* has many Spanish-speaking people and some signs in Spanish.

Chicago Academy of Fine Woodworking (WORLD BOOK photo)   Ken Firestone

The Educational System of the United States includes many learning opportunities outside formal classrooms. An adult education class, *above left,* offers woodworking lessons. At a museum,
right, people study exhibits dealing with space travel.

Many American children begin their schooling before
enrolling in first grade. About 35 per cent of all the children aged 3 and 4 attend nursery schools, and about 85
per cent of all 5-year-olds attend kindergarten. More
than 99 per cent of all U.S. children complete elementary school, and about 70 per cent of them graduate
from high school. Approximately 65 per cent of the high
school graduates go on to colleges or universities. About
20 per cent of the country's people complete at least four
years of higher education.

Adult education is an important part of the school
system in the United States. Millions of adults take
courses at universities, colleges, vocational schools, recreation centers, or other institutions. Many adults continue their schooling to improve their job skills or to get
training for a new job. Others attend classes simply to
develop new hobbies or to find out more about topics
that interest them. A growing number of part-time and
full-time college and university students are men and
women who have held jobs or raised families and are
returning to school to get a degree.

Public schools in the United States are supported
mainly by taxation. Private schools get their operating
funds chiefly from tuition and contributions of private
citizens. The nation's schools, like its private businesses,
have always had to deal with financial problems. Since
the 1960's, rapidly rising material and salary costs have
increased the financial problems of the schools. Some
schools, both public and private, have cut back on programs and reduced their faculties to try to keep expenses
in line with revenues. Many colleges and universities
have sharply increased their tuition and fee charges.

Schools in the United States face a number of other
problems. Many schools, particularly in large cities,
have run-down buildings, a shortage of teachers, inadequate supplies, and overcrowded conditions. A far higher percentage of young people in these areas fail to
complete secondary school than in other areas. Some
people claim that schools in their areas fail to provide
students with the basic skills necessary to obtain and
hold jobs. Schools with large numbers of students from
foreign countries face the problem of educating some
children who cannot speak English. Demands for bilingual education increased in the 1970's, especially in
school districts with large numbers of Spanish-speaking
students. Bilingual education involves instruction in
both English and the native language of the students.
Also in the 1970's, a decline in the nation's birth rate
caused a reduction in the number of children of school
age. Some schools closed or reduced their staffs because
of the declining enrollment. Many teachers lost their
jobs. See EDUCATION.

Libraries provide the American people with access to
books, periodicals, pamphlets, and other printed matter.
In addition, many libraries offer audio-visual materials,
research services, lectures, and educational exhibits.

There are about 8,500 public libraries in the United
States. They range from one-room libraries in small
towns to huge city libraries and their branches. There
are more than 4,000 university and college libraries in
the United States, as well as thousands of libraries in
elementary schools and high schools.

The nation's library system also includes large numbers of private research libraries and special libraries that

57

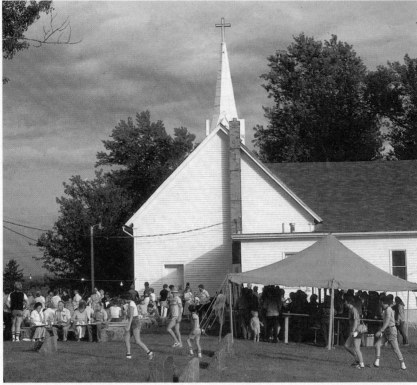

Archie Lieberman

Religion plays an important role in the lives of millions of Americans. The country's churches provide people with moral guidance and places for worship. Many churches are also centers for social gatherings, such as the church picnic shown at the left.

have collections limited to certain fields of knowledge. In addition, many government agencies and businesses operate their own libraries. Three of the government's many libraries are considered national libraries because of their large and varied collections and because of the many services they provide. They are the Library of Congress, the National Agricultural Library of the Department of Agriculture, and the National Library of Medicine of the Department of Health and Human Services. See LIBRARY.

Museums. There are about 5,500 museums in the United States. They include museums of art, history, natural history, and science. In addition, a number of historic houses and villages are classed as museums. The collections of many of the nation's museums are devoted to a single topic of interest, such as the history of baseball or railroads. Some museums have huge collections of items from many parts of the world. Others feature exhibits of local interest. In addition to exhibits, many U.S. museums offer classes, lectures, films, field trips, and other educational services. The most famous museums in the United States include the Metropolitan Museum of Art in New York City, the Museum of Science and Industry in Chicago, and the Smithsonian Institution in Washington, D.C. See MUSEUM.

Religion. About 60 per cent of all the American people are members of an organized religious group. Among them, about 55 per cent are Protestants, 38 per cent Roman Catholics, 4 per cent Jews, and 3 per cent are members of Eastern Orthodox Churches. Relatively

small numbers of Americans belong to other faiths, such as Islam and Buddhism. Roman Catholics make up the largest single religious denomination in the United States. About 50 million Americans are Roman Catholics. The country's largest Protestant groups are, in order of size, Baptists, Methodists, Presbyterians, Lutherans, and Episcopalians.

Religion has played an important role in the history of the United States. Many people came to the American Colonies to escape religious persecution in other lands. The early colonists included Puritans in New England, Roman Catholics in Maryland, and Quakers in Pennsylvania. The early Americans made religious freedom one of the country's basic laws. The First Amendment to the Constitution of the United States, which was adopted in 1791, guarantees every American freedom of religion. It also provides that no religious group be given official recognition as a state church. These provisions were intended to prevent persecution of religious minorities and the favoring of one church over another. The country's religious freedom was one of the reasons immigrants continued to flock to the United States through the years.

Although all religious groups in the United States enjoy freedom, Christian traditions have had a stronger influence on American life than those of any other faith. For example, most offices, factories, and other places of employment are closed on Sunday, the Sabbath of most Christians. The influence of Christianity results from the fact that a majority of the people are Christians.

WORLD BOOK photo

Bill Grimes, Black Star

Recreational Activities provide the people of the United States with leisure-time enjoyment. Baseball fans thrill to the excitement of the duel between a major-league pitcher and batter, *above left*. A large group of runners compete—and get exercise—in a marathon race, *right*.

Throughout the country's history, religion has influenced everyday life in a number of ways. For example, in colonial America many religious rules were enforced by local governments (see COLONIAL LIFE IN AMERICA [The Church]). Some of the laws that prohibited activities on Sunday were enforced by local communities as late as the 1900's.

Today, religion has relatively less influence in the everyday lives of most Americans. But churches and other religious organizations continue to play important roles in American life. Their chief functions are to provide moral guidance and places for worship. However, religious groups also operate many elementary and secondary schools, colleges, universities, hospitals, and nursing homes. They provide aid for refugees, the poor, the elderly, orphans, and other persons in need. Social gatherings are held at many churches. Some religious groups take active roles in discussing such issues as birth control and rights for minorities and women.

Recreation. Most Americans have a great deal of leisure time, and they spend it in a variety of ways. They pursue hobbies; take part in sports activities; attend sporting and cultural events; watch movies and television; listen to records, tapes, and radios; and read books and magazines. They enjoy trips to museums, beaches, parks, playgrounds, and zoos. They take weekend and vacation trips, eat at restaurants, go on picnics, and entertain friends at home. These and other activities contribute to the richness and diversity of American life.

Sports rank as a leading American pastime. Millions of Americans enjoy watching such sports events as automobile races, horse races, and baseball, basketball, and football games—either in person or on television. Many Americans, especially children and other young people, play baseball, basketball, football, and soccer. People of most ages participate in such sports as bicycle riding, boating, bowling, fishing, golf, hiking, hunting, running, skiing, softball, swimming, and tennis.

Motion pictures, plays, concerts, operas, and dance performances attract large audiences in the United States. Americans find entertainment at home, as well. About 98 per cent of all American homes have a television set. On the average, a set is in use in each home for about six hours a day.

Hobbies occupy much of the leisure time of many Americans. Large numbers of people enjoy raising flower or vegetable gardens or indoor plants. Other popular hobbies include stamp collecting, coin collecting, and photography. Since the mid-1900's, interest in such crafts hobbies as needlepoint, quilting, weaving, pottery making, and woodworking has increased sharply.

Most Americans spend part of their leisure time traveling. Many take annual vacations, as well as occasional one-day excursions or weekend trips. Some people have vacation homes near lakes or seashores, in the mountains, or in other recreation areas. Others own motor homes or trailers, which provide comfortable living and sleeping quarters during trips. Some people enjoy camping in tents. Others prefer to stay in hotels or motels while on trips.

European colonists arrived in America during the early 1600's, bringing European art traditions with them. But within a few years, colonists were building houses that probably rank as the first major American works of art. During the 1700's, American craftworkers began to produce outstanding examples of furniture, sculpture, and silverwork. By the mid-1700's, colonial painters were creating excellent portraits.

The first important American literature appeared in the early 1800's with the works of such authors as Washington Irving and James Fenimore Cooper. During the late 1800's, American architects began designing skyscrapers that revolutionized urban architecture throughout the world. Two uniquely American art forms, jazz and musical comedy, developed during the late 1800's and early 1900's. In the early 1900's, the United States gained international leadership in the new art forms of motion pictures and modern dancing.

Today, American architects, authors, composers, painters, and sculptors have achieved worldwide recognition and influence. Many of them have shown a keen interest in developing new styles, new ways of expressing themselves, and even new forms of art.

Oil painting on canvas (1904); Woolaroc Museum, Bartlesville, Okla.

Museum of the American Indian,
New York City, Heye Foundation

Oil painting on canvas (1773);
the Historical Society of Pennsylvania

Early Painting and Sculpture emphasized American themes. Most colonial painters concentrated on portraits. John Singleton Copley painted a famous portrait of soldier and politician Thomas Mifflin and his wife, *above*. The portrait shows Copley's ability to capture the human character of colonial leaders. In the 1800's and early 1900's, many painters turned to the West for subjects. Charles Marion Russell's *The Bolter*, pictured at the upper right, is typical of this artist's scenes of cowboy life. For generations, the Hopi Indians of Arizona have carved wooden figures called Kachina dolls, *right*. The Hopi used the statues in religious ceremonies.

Oil paint, enamel, and aluminum paint on paper (1949); private collection

Modern Painting and Sculpture have produced both abstract and realistic styles. Jackson Pollock gained fame for such paintings as *Number 13, 1949,* shown above. These paintings consist of rhythmic patterns dribbled onto the painting surface. George Segal placed plaster figures among actual objects, as in *The Butcher Shop,* shown at the right.

Architecture in the United States developed the skyscraper as one of the most characteristic types of modern building. The Sears Tower, *lower left,* dominates the Chicago skyline. Frank Lloyd Wright ranks as America's most important architect. Wright's Falling Water house, *lower right,* shows his ability to blend a structure with its natural setting.

Everett C. Johnson, Lensman

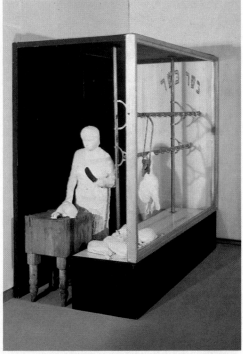

Plaster sculpture with wood, metal, vinyl, and plexiglass (1965); Art Gallery of Ontario

Western Pennsylvania Conservancy

King Oliver's Creole Jazz Band; Ramsey Archive

Sean Shaver

Grandpa Jones performing at the Grand Ole Opry;
George L. Walker III, Gamma/Liaison

Popular Music has taken many forms in the United States. Jazz relies on spontaneous playing by musicians. Trumpeter Louis Armstrong, standing in the center of the group shown at the upper left, was the first great jazz soloist. Country music, *left,* began as the folk music of Southern whites but soon gained widespread acceptance. Singer Elvis Presley, *above,* helped make rock music the country's leading type of popular music in the mid- and late 1900's.

© 1937 Walt Disney Productions

Diane Keaton and Woody Allen in a scene from *Annie Hall;*
© 1977 United Artists Corporation, All Rights Reserved

Motion Pictures have been one of the most popular and influential art forms in the United States since the early 1900's. The animated films of Walt Disney, such as *Snow White and the Seven Dwarfs,* shown at the left, have charmed moviegoers throughout the world. Woody Allen became a leading actor, director, and writer with the success of *Annie Hall,* shown at the right, and other comedies.

Martha Swope

Dancing in the United States often explores American subjects. The famous dancer and dance composer Martha Graham created *Appalachian Spring,* shown above, a ballet that celebrates the courage and dignity of American pioneers during the early 1800's.

© Eileen Darby

Theater has produced many masterpieces of serious drama and musical comedy. Arthur Miller's drama *Death of a Salesman,* shown at the left, deals with a salesman who discovers that his search for success has brought him only disappointment and failure. Frank Loesser wrote the music and words for *Guys and Dolls,* shown at the right, a musical about colorful characters who live in New York City.

63

© Norman Prince

Rolling Hills dotted by farm buildings stretch across the Appalachian Highlands, which extend from Maine to Alabama. The scene shown above is in West Virginia.

David Muench

A Swamp that includes bald cypress trees lies in Florida's Everglades National Park in the southernmost part of the Coastal Lowlands. The Coastal Lowlands extend from New England to Texas.

The United States has an area of 3,618,770 square miles (9,372,614 square kilometers). The country, excluding Alaska and Hawaii, can be divided into seven major land regions. The regions are: (1) the Appalachian Highlands; (2) the Coastal Lowlands; (3) the Interior Plains; (4) the Ozark-Ouachita Highlands; (5) the Rocky Mountains; (6) the Western Plateaus, Basins, and Ranges; and (7) the Pacific Ranges and Lowlands. For a discussion of the land regions of Alaska and the islands of Hawaii, see the articles on those states.

The Appalachian Highlands extend from the northern tip of Maine southwestward to Alabama. The region has three main subdivisions. They are, from east to west: (1) the Blue Ridge Mountains Area, (2) the Ridge and Valley Region, and (3) the Appalachian Plateau.

The Blue Ridge Mountains Area consists of various ranges that are among the oldest mountains in the United States. Many of the peaks are worn and rounded. The Great Smoky Mountains of Tennessee and North Carolina are among the highest and most rugged mountains in the area. The area is named for the Blue Ridge Mountains, which stretch from southeastern Pennsylvania to northeastern Georgia. Northern extensions of the Blue Ridge range include the Adirondack Mountains of New York and the White Mountains and Green Mountains of New England.

In much of the Blue Ridge area, mountains form barriers to land transportation. But several mighty rivers, including the Delaware, Hudson, Potomac, and Susquehanna, cut through the mountains to form *water gaps*. The gaps provide low, level land for highways and railroads. Forests cover the mountains of the Blue Ridge

area, and lumbering is an important industry there.

The Ridge and Valley Region consists of the Great Valley in the east and a series of alternating ridges and valleys in the west. The rolling Great Valley is actually a series of valleys, including the Hudson Valley in New York; the Cumberland, Lebanon, and Lehigh valleys in Pennsylvania; and the Shenandoah Valley in Virginia. The region has some forests, but other wooded areas have been cleared to take advantage of fertile soil and relatively level land for farming. About 50 dams on the

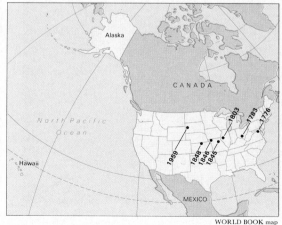

WORLD BOOK map

The Geographic Center of the United States has moved westward as the country has added new territory. Since 1959, when Alaska and Hawaii were added, it has been in South Dakota.

Tennessee River and its branches in the southern Great Valley provide flood control and hydroelectric power.

The Appalachian Plateau extends from New York to Alabama. Glaciers covered the northern plateau during the Ice Age and carved out natural features, including the Finger Lakes in New York. Deep, narrow river valleys cut through the plateau in some areas, creating steep, rugged terrain. Deposits of coal, iron ore, oil, and other minerals lie beneath the surface, and many people in the region work in mining. Parts of the region have good farmland. But thin, rocky soil covers much of the plateau, and the steep hillsides are badly eroded.

The Coastal Lowlands extend from southeastern Maine, across the eastern and southern United States, to eastern Texas. Forests of hickory, oak, pine, and other trees are common throughout the lowlands. The region has three subdivisions: (1) the Piedmont, (2) the Atlantic Coastal Plain, and (3) the Gulf Coastal Plain.

The Piedmont is a slightly elevated rolling plain that separates the Blue Ridge Mountains from the Atlantic Coastal Plain. It stretches from southern New York to Alabama. The eastern boundary of the Piedmont is called the *Fall Line*. Rivers that reach the Fall Line tumble down from the Piedmont to the lower coastal plains in a series of falls and rapids. In the early days of settlement of the eastern United States, boats traveling inland on coastal rivers stopped at the Fall Line and unloaded their cargoes. The rapids prevented the boats from traveling farther. They also provided water power for early industries. As a result, many cities grew up along the Fall Line. Tobacco is a leading agricultural product of the Piedmont, and the region also has many orchards and dairy farms. See PIEDMONT; FALL LINE.

The Atlantic Coastal Plain extends eastward from the Piedmont to the Atlantic Ocean. It ranges from a narrow strip of land in New England to a broad belt that covers much of North and South Carolina, Georgia, and Florida. In colonial times, the broad southern part of the plain encouraged the development of huge plantations for growing cotton. Cotton is still grown there. Other farm products include vegetables, citrus fruits, peanuts, and tobacco. In New England, where the plain narrows to a width of about 10 miles (16 kilometers) in some places, crop farming has always been less important. Many New Englanders turned to manufacturing, fishing, or shipping instead of farming.

Numerous rivers cross the plain and flow into the Atlantic Ocean. They include the Delaware, Hudson, James, Potomac, Roanoke, Savannah, and Susquehanna. Bays cut deeply into the plain in some areas, creating excellent natural harbors. They include Cape Cod Bay, Boston Bay, Chesapeake Bay, Delaware Bay, and Long Island Sound.

Many resort areas flourish around the beautiful sandy beaches and offshore islands that line much of the Atlantic shore from New England to Florida. In some inland regions, swamps form large wilderness areas, where trees and grasses rise up from shallow waters and tangled vines and roots form masses of vegetation.

The Gulf Coastal Plain borders the Gulf of Mexico from Florida to southern Texas. Numerous rivers—including the Alabama, Mississippi, Rio Grande, and Trinity—cross the plain and flow into the Gulf. The Mississippi, which originates in the Interior Plains to the north, is the most important of these rivers. Barges carrying cargoes from many parts of the country travel along the river. Soil deposited along the banks of the Mississippi and other rivers in the Gulf Coastal Plain creates fertile farmland. The plain also has belts of hilly forests and grazing land, and large deposits of petroleum

Michael S. Crummett, Black Star

Fields of Wheat grow near a rural Montana community on the Interior Plains. The plains, America's vast heartland, stretch from the Appalachian Highlands to the Rocky Mountains.

Robyn Horn, Arkansas Department of Parks and Tourism

Rugged Hills border a valley in northwestern Arkansas, which is part of the Ozark-Ouachita Highlands. This region also includes parts of Missouri and Oklahoma.

65

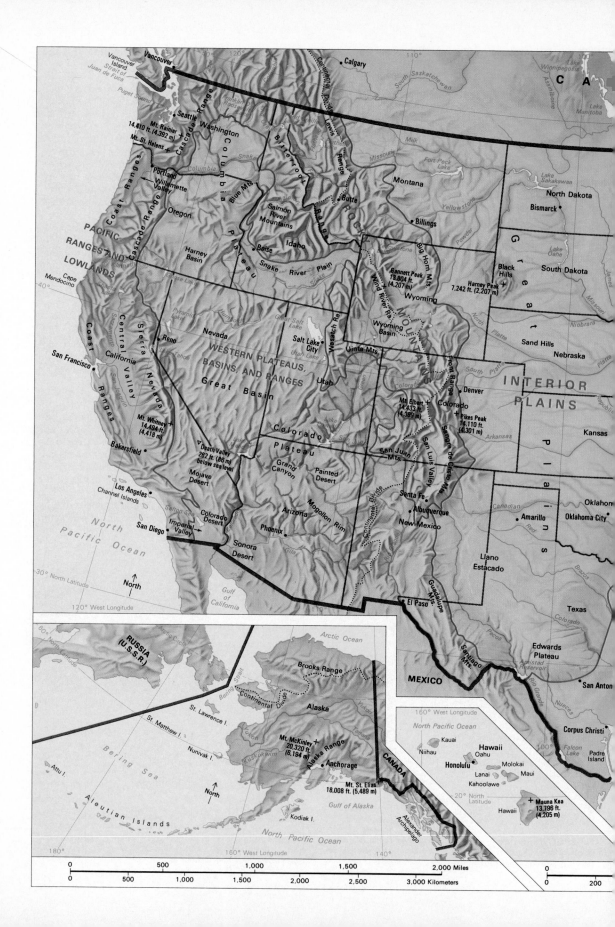

Vancouver
Island
Strait of
Juan de Fuca
Puget Sound
Vancouver
Seattle
Washington
Mt. Rainier
14,410 ft. (4,392 m)
Mt. St. Helens
Portland
Willamette
Valley
Oregon
Cascade Range
Franklin
Mts.
Columbia
Columbia Plateau
Snake
Blue Mts.
Bitterroot Range
Lewis Range
Calgary
Continental Divide
South Saskatchewan
Missouri
Milk
Fort Peck
Lake
Montana
Yellowstone
Butte
Billings
Big Horn Mts.
Gannett Peak
13,804 ft.
(4,207 m)
Wind River Range
Wyoming
PACIFIC
RANGES AND
LOWLANDS
Coast Ranges
Cape
Mendocino
40°
Salmon
River
Mountains
Boise
Idaho
Snake   River   Plain
Harney
Basin
Goose Lake
Sierra Nevada
Reno
Pyramid
Lake
Humboldt
Nevada
Great Salt
Lake
Salt Lake
City
Utah Lake
Wasatch Rd.
Uinta Mts.
Wyoming
Basin
Lake
Winnipegosia
C   A
Lake
Manitoba
Lake
Sakakawea
North Dakota
Bismarck
Lake
Oahe
South Dakota
Black
Hills
Harney Peak
7,242 ft. (2,207 m)
Sand Hills
Nebraska
James
Missouri
Niobrara
North Platte
Platte
G   r   e   a   t
San Francisco
California
Valley
Central Valley
Coast Ranges
San Joaquin
Mt. Whitney
14,494 ft.
(4,418 m)
Bakersfield
Los Angeles
Channel Islands
North
Pacific Ocean
30° North Latitude
120° West Longitude
San Diego
WESTERN PLATEAUS,
BASINS, AND RANGES
Great   Basin
Death Valley
282 ft. (86 m)
below sea level
Mojave
Desert
Colorado
Desert
Imperial
Valley
Salton Sea
Sonora
Desert
Gulf
of
California
North
Colorado   Plateau
Grand
Canyon
Painted
Desert
Arizona
Mogollon Rim
Phoenix
Gila
Utah
Colorado
Colorado
Mt Elbert
14,433 ft.
(4,389 m)
Denver
Pikes Peak
14,110 ft.
(4,301 m)
Front Range
Sangre de Cristo Mts.
San Juan
Mts.
San Luis Valley
Santa Fe
Albuquerque
New Mexico
Continental Divide
Rio Grande
Guadalupe Mts.
El Paso
South Platte
Arkansas
Canadian
Red
Llano
Estacado
MEXICO
Santiago Mts.
Edwards
Plateau
Amistad
Reservoir
Pecos
INTERIOR
PLAINS
P   l   a   i   n   s
Kansas
Republican
Oklahoma
Oklahoma City
Amarillo
Texas
Colorado
Brazos
Edwards
Plateau
San Anton
Rio Grande
Nueces
Corpus Christi
Padre
Island
Falcon
Lake

RUSSIA
(U.S.S.R.)
60° North Latitude
Arctic Ocean
Brooks Range
Continental Divide
Alaska
Bering Strait
St. Lawrence I.
St. Matthew I.
Nunivak I.
Kuskokwim
Yukon
Mt. McKinley
20,320 ft.
(6,194 m)
Alaska Range
Anchorage
Kuskokwim
CANADA
Mt. St. Elias
18,008 ft. (5,489 m)
Attu I.
Aleutian   Islands
Kodiak I.
Gulf of Alaska
North Pacific Ocean
Alexander
Archipelago
Bering
Sea
North
160° West Longitude
160° West Longitude
North Pacific Ocean
Kauai
Niihau
Hawaii
Oahu
Honolulu
Lanai
Molokai
Maui
Kahoolawe
Hawaii
Mauna Kea
13,796 ft.
(4,205 m)
20° North
Latitude
100°
140°

0	500	1,000	1,500	2,000 Miles
0	500	1,000	1,500	2,000	2,500	3,000 Kilometers

0   200

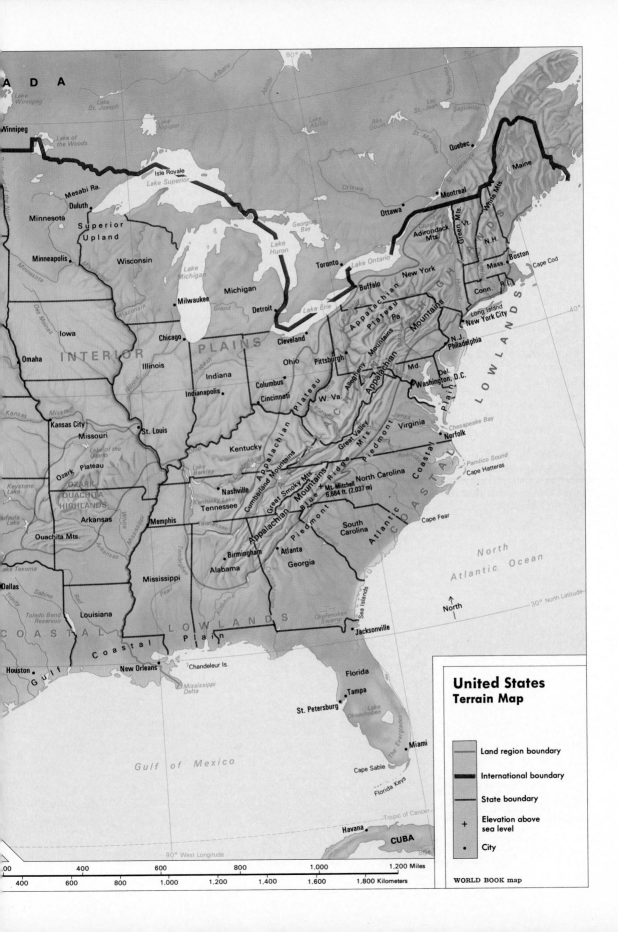

CANADA

Winnipeg
Lake Winnipeg
Lake St. Joseph
Albany
Abitibi
Lac St. Jean
Saguenay

Isle Royale
Lake Superior
Mesabi Ra.
Duluth
Minnesota
Superior Upland
Lake Nipigon
Georgian Bay
Lake Huron
Ottawa
St. Maurice
Quebec
Maine
White Mts.

Minneapolis
Wisconsin
Lake Michigan
Michigan
Grand
Milwaukee
Detroit
Lake Erie
Toronto
Lake Ontario
Buffalo
Ottawa
Montreal
Adirondack Mts.
Green Vt.
N.H.
Mass. Boston
Cape Cod

Iowa
INTERIOR
PLAINS
Chicago
Illinois
Cleveland
Ohio
Pittsburgh
Appalachian Plateau
Pa.
Mountains
Appalachian
New York
New York City
Long Island
Conn. R.I.

Omaha
Des Moines
Kansas
Missouri
Kansas City
Missouri
St. Louis
Indiana
Indianapolis
Columbus
Cincinnati
Ohio
W. Va.
Allegheny Mountains
Plateau
Md.
Washington, D.C.
Del.
N.J.
Philadelphia

Ozark Plateau
Lake of the Ozarks
Keystone Lake
OZARK-OUACHITA HIGHLANDS
Arkansas
Kentucky
Lake Barkley
Tennessee
Nashville
Cumberland Mountains
Appalachian
Great Smoky Mts.
Mt. Mitchell 6,684 ft. (2,037 m)
Blue Ridge
Great Valley Mts.
Piedmont
James
Virginia
Roanoke
North Carolina
Norfolk
Chesapeake Bay
Pamlico Sound
Cape Hatteras

Ouachita Mts.
Eufaula Lake
Memphis
Tennessee
Alabama
Birmingham
Alabama
Atlanta
Georgia
Piedmont
Chattahoochee
South Carolina
Sea Islands
Cape Fear
ATLANTIC COASTAL PLAIN

Dallas
Toledo Bend Reservoir
Sabine
Red
Trinity
Louisiana
Mississippi
Pearl
COASTAL
LOWLANDS
Coastal Plain
North Atlantic Ocean
North
30° North Latitude

Houston
Gulf
New Orleans
Chandeleur Is.
Mississippi Delta
Florida
Tampa
St. Petersburg
Lake Okeechobee
Jacksonville
The Everglades
Miami
Cape Sable
Florida Keys

Gulf of Mexico

Tropic of Cancer
Havana
CUBA

90° West Longitude
80°

United States
Terrain Map

Land region boundary
International boundary
State boundary
+ Elevation above sea level
• City

400   600   800   1,000   1,200 Miles
400 600 800 1,000 1,200 1,400 1,600 1,800 Kilometers

WORLD BOOK map

and natural gas lie beneath it and in the offshore Gulf waters. The Gulf Coastal Plain has many sandy beaches, swamps, bays, and offshore islands.

The Interior Plains occupy a huge expanse of land that stretches from the Appalachian Highlands in the east to the Rocky Mountains in the west. Glaciers covered much of the region during the Ice Age. They stripped the topsoil from parts of Michigan, Minnesota, and Wisconsin and carved out hundreds of lakes. Today, much of this area is heavily forested. Farther south —in parts of Illinois, Indiana, Iowa, and Ohio—the glaciers flattened the land and deposited rich soil ideal for growing crops. The plains slope gradually upward from east to west and get progressively drier.

The western part of the region, called the Great Plains, has vast grasslands where livestock graze and areas of fertile soil that yield corn, wheat, and other crops. Few trees grow on the Great Plains. Rugged hills, including the Black Hills of South Dakota and Wyoming, rise up out of the plains in some places.

Deposits of iron ore and coal provide raw materials for many manufacturing industries in the eastern part of the Interior Plains. Important deposits of petroleum and metal ores lie in the western part.

Glaciers carved out the five Great Lakes in the Interior Plains. The lakes—Erie, Huron, Michigan, Ontario, and Superior—are the largest group of freshwater lakes in the world. The lakes provide a vital transportation route for shipping the agricultural and industrial products of the Interior Plains. The Mississippi River is the region's other great waterway. The Mississippi and its many branches, including the Missouri and Ohio rivers, form a river system that reaches into all parts of the Interior Plains.

The Ozark-Ouachita Highlands rise up between the Interior Plains and Coastal Lowlands. The highlands form a scenic landscape in southern Missouri, northwest Arkansas, and eastern Oklahoma. The region is named for the Ozark Plateau and the Ouachita Mountains. Rivers and streams have cut deep gorges through the rugged highland terrain. The highlands include forested hills, artificial lakes, and many underground caves and gushing springs. Much of the region has poor soil for farming but fertile land lies along the river valleys. Deposits of coal, iron ore, and other minerals are valuable natural resources of the highlands.

The Rocky Mountains form the largest mountain system in North America. They extend from northern Alaska, through Canada and the western United States to northern New Mexico. Many peaks of the Rockies are more than 14,000 feet (4,270 meters) high. The *Continental Divide*, or *Great Divide*, passes through the mountains. The divide is an imaginary line that separates streams that flow into the Pacific Ocean from those that flow into the Atlantic. Many important rivers, including the Colorado, Missouri, and Rio Grande, have their sources in the Rockies.

Forests cover the lower mountain slopes. The *timber line* marks the elevation above which trees cannot grow. Grasses, mosses, and lichens grow above the line, and wild flowers color the slopes. Bighorn sheep, elk, deer, bears, mountain lions, and other animals make their homes in the mountains. Lakes and streams set among the rugged peaks add to the region's spectacular beauty.

Lumbering and mining are important industries in the Rockies. The mountains are a storehouse of such metals as copper, gold, lead, silver, and zinc. The region also has large deposits of oil and natural gas. Mountain

David Muench

The Rocky Mountains, west of the Interior Plains, soar to heights of more than 14,000 feet (4,270 meters) above sea level. The majestic scene above is in Colorado.

David Muench

Desert Areas cover much of the Western Plateaus, Basins, and Ranges land region, west of the Rockies. The land shown above is in the Nevada portion of the Great Basin, a part of the land region.

The Pacific Coast forms the western border of the Pacific Ranges and Lowlands region, which extends from Canada to Mexico. Rugged rock formations line parts of the coast, including the California area shown at the left.

Jerry Howard, Stock, Boston

meadows provide grazing land for beef and dairy cattle, and valleys are used for growing crops.

For many years, the Rockies formed a major barrier to transportation across the United States. In the 1860's, the nation's first transcontinental rail line was built, passing through the Rocky Mountain region at the Wyoming Basin. Today, other railroads and highways cut through tunnels and passes in the mountains, and airplanes fly over the mountains.

The Western Plateaus, Basins, and Ranges lie west of the Rocky Mountains. This region extends from Washington south to the Mexican border. It is the driest part of the United States. Parts of it are wastelands with little plant life. But the region has some forested mountains, and some fertile areas where rivers provide irrigation water necessary for growing crops. In other areas, livestock graze on huge stretches of dry land.

The Columbia Plateau occupies the northernmost part of the region. It has fertile volcanic soil, formed by lava that flowed out of giant cracks in the earth thousands of years ago. The Colorado Plateau lies in the southern part of the region. It has some of the nation's most unusual landforms, including natural bridges and arches of solid rock and huge, flat-topped rock formations. The plateau's spectacular river gorges, including the Grand Canyon of the Colorado River, rank among the world's great natural wonders.

The Basin and Range part of the region is a vast area of mountains and desert lowlands between the Columbia and Colorado plateaus. It includes Death Valley in California. Part of Death Valley lies 282 feet (86 meters) below sea level and is the lowest place in the United States. The Great Basin is an area within the larger Basin and Range area. Great Salt Lake is the largest of

many shallow, salty lakes in the Great Basin. Bathers cannot sink in Great Salt Lake because it is so heavy with salt. Near the lake is the Great Salt Lake Desert, which includes a large, hard, flat bed of salt.

The Pacific Ranges and Lowlands stretch across western Washington and Oregon and most of California. The region's eastern boundary is formed by the Cascade Mountains in the north and by the Sierra Nevada in the south. Volcanic activity formed the Cascades. Two of the Cascades—Lassen Peak in California and Mount Saint Helens in Washington—are active volcanoes. Some of the range's highest peaks have glaciers and permanent snowfields. Evergreen forests cover the lower slopes and provide the raw materials for lumber and paper products industries. The Sierra Nevada are granite mountains, dotted with lakes and waterfalls.

Broad, fertile valleys lie west of the Cascade and Sierra Nevada mountains. They include the Puget Sound Lowland of Washington, the Willamette Valley of Oregon, and the Central Valley of California. Valley farms produce large amounts of fruits and vegetables.

West of the valleys, the Coast Ranges line the Pacific shore. In many places, they rise up abruptly from the ocean, creating craggy walls of rock. In other areas, the mountains lie behind sandy coastal plains. Deep bays that jut into the coast include Puget Sound, Columbia River Bay, San Francisco Bay, and San Diego Bay.

The San Andreas Fault runs through the Coast Ranges in California. It is a break in the earth where movements of the earth's crust cause occasional earthquakes. Giant redwood trees grow on the mountains in northern California. Set among the Coast Ranges are a number of rich agricultural valleys that produce much of the nation's lettuce, dried fruit, and wine grapes.

The climate of the United States varies greatly from place to place. Average annual temperatures range from 9° F. (−13° C) in Barrow, Alaska, to 78.2° F. (25.7° C) in Death Valley, California. The highest temperature ever recorded in the country was 134° F. (57° C). It was registered at Death Valley on July 10, 1913. The lowest recorded temperature was −80° F. (−62° C). It was registered at Prospect Creek, Alaska, near Barrow, on Jan. 23, 1971.

Precipitation varies from a yearly average of less than 2 inches (5 centimeters) at Death Valley to about 460 inches (1,170 centimeters) at Mount Waialeale in Hawaii. In general, however, most parts of the United States have seasonal changes in temperature and moderate precipitation. The Midwest, the Middle Atlantic States, and New England experience warm summers and cold, snowy winters. In the South, summers are long and hot, and winters are mild. Along the Pacific Coast, and in some other areas near large bodies of water, the climate is relatively mild all year. Mountains also affect the climate. In the West, for example, the mountainous areas are cooler and wetter than the neighboring plains and plateaus. Parts of the West and Southwest have a desert climate.

The moderate climate in much of the United States has encouraged widespread population settlement. It has also helped make possible the production of a great variety of agricultural goods.

See NORTH AMERICA (Climate). See also the section on Climate in each state article.

David Muench

Death Valley, California, the country's driest place, receives less than 2 inches (5 centimeters) of precipitation yearly. It recorded the highest U.S. temperature ever, 134° F. (57° C).

David Muench

Waimea Canyon, Hawaii, was formed by water flowing from Mount Waialeale. The mountain, the wettest place in the U.S., receives about 460 inches (1,170 centimeters) of precipitation a year.

Steve McCutcheon

Prospect Creek, Alaska, recorded the lowest U.S. temperature ever, −80° F. (−62° C). The nearby town of Barrow has the country's lowest average annual temperature, 9° F. (−13° C).

Average January Temperatures

The southern and far western parts of the United States have milder winters than the rest of the country. This map shows how average January temperatures generally decrease from south to north.

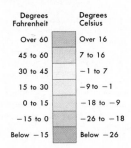

Degrees Fahrenheit	Degrees Celsius
Over 60	Over 16
45 to 60	7 to 16
30 to 45	−1 to 7
15 to 30	−9 to −1
0 to 15	−18 to −9
−15 to 0	−26 to −18
Below −15	Below −26

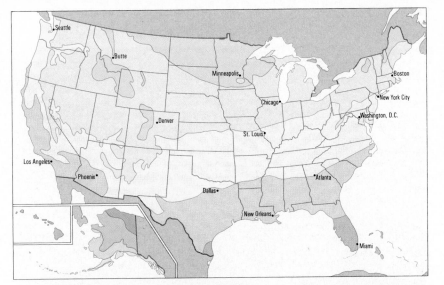

Average July Temperatures

Average July temperatures in most of the country are between 75 and 90° F. (24 and 32° C) or 60 and 75° F. (16 and 24° C). Temperatures are lower in most of Alaska and some mountains, and higher in the southwest desert.

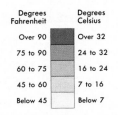

Degrees Fahrenheit	Degrees Celsius
Over 90	Over 32
75 to 90	24 to 32
60 to 75	16 to 24
45 to 60	7 to 16
Below 45	Below 7

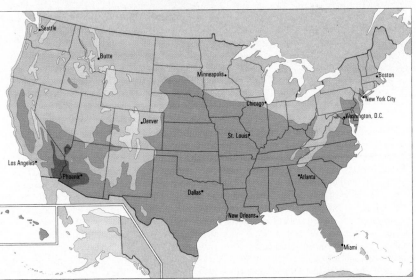

Average Yearly Precipitation

This map shows that the amount of yearly precipitation in the United States generally increases from west to east. But some areas along the west coast and in Alaska and Hawaii receive the most precipitation.

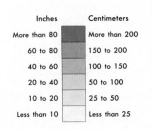

Inches	Centimeters
More than 80	More than 200
60 to 80	150 to 200
40 to 60	100 to 150
20 to 40	50 to 100
10 to 20	25 to 50
Less than 10	Less than 25

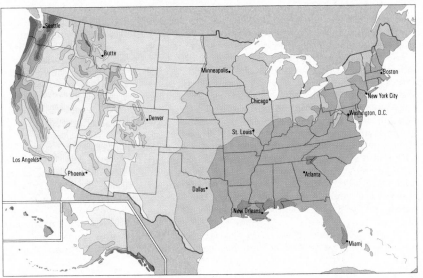

America's Economy produces a greater value of agricultural, manufactured, and mined products than any other country. A huge warehouse, *left,* stores grain before it is shipped to distant markets. Barges, railroad cars, trucks, and other transportation facilities are used to transport products.

Milt & Joan Mann

The United States ranks first among the nations of the world in the total value of its economic production. The nation's *gross national product (GNP)*—the value of all the goods and services produced—amounted to about $3⅔ trillion in 1984. This total was more than twice the GNP of any other country in the world.

The United States economy is based largely on a *free enterprise system.* In such a system, individuals and companies are free to make their own economic decisions. Individuals and companies own the raw materials, equipment, factories, and other items necessary for production, and they decide how best to use them in order to earn a profit.

Even though the U.S. economy is based on free enterprise, the government has placed regulations on economic practices through the years. It has passed antitrust laws, which are designed to keep one company or a few firms from controlling entire industries. Such control, called a monopoly, does away with competition and enables controlling companies to charge high prices and reduce the quality of goods. Government regulations have protected consumers from unsafe merchandise and protected workers from unsafe working conditions and unreasonably low wages. The government has also enacted regulations designed to reduce environmental pollution. Some people argue that the government interferes in the economy too much. Others say it should do more. In spite of involvement by the government, the United States still has one of the least regulated economies in the world. See CAPITALISM; MONOPOLY AND COMPETITION.

In spite of its overall strength, the United States economy has faced problems from time to time. The problems include *recessions* (mild business slumps), *depressions* (severe business slumps), and *inflation* (rising prices). See DEPRESSION; GREAT DEPRESSION; RECESSION; INFLATION.

Natural Resources. A variety of natural resources provide the raw materials that support the economy of the United States. In addition to a moderate climate, the most valuable resources are minerals, soils, water, forests, and fish.

Minerals. The United States has large deposits of coal, iron ore, natural gas, and petroleum, which are vital to the country's industrial strength. Its many other important minerals include copper, gold, lead, nickel, phosphates, potash, silver, sulfur, and zinc. To meet its needs, the country must import additional amounts of iron ore, petroleum, and some other minerals.

Soils. The United States has vast expanses of fertile soil that is well-suited to growing crops. The most fertile soils include the dark soils of the Interior Plains and the *alluvial* (water-deposited) soils along the lower Mississippi River Valley and other smaller river valleys. Rich, wind-blown soil called *loess* covers parts of eastern Washington and the southern Interior Plains.

Water. Lakes, rivers, and underground deposits supply water for households, farms, and industries in the United States. The nation uses about 400 billion gallons (1,500 billion liters) of water daily. Households use only about 10 per cent of this total. The vast majority of the rest is used to irrigate farms and to operate manufacturing industries.

Forests cover nearly a third of the United States, and they yield many valuable products. About a fourth of the nation's lumber comes from the trees of forests in the

John Running, Stock, Boston

Forests are one of the many natural resources that contribute to the U.S. economy. Logs from forests are used for lumber and in making other valuable products.

Pacific Northwest. Forests in the South supply lumber, wood pulp—which is used to make paper—and nearly all the turpentine, pitch, rosin, and wood tar produced in the United States. The Appalachian Mountains and parts of the Great Lakes area have fine hardwood forests. Hickory, maple, oak, and other hardwood trees cut from these forests provide quality woods for the manufacture of furniture.

Fish. Americans who fish for a living catch about $4\frac{1}{2}$ million short tons (4 million metric tons) of sea products annually. The greatest quantities are taken from the Gulf of Mexico, where important catches include menhaden, oysters, and shrimp. The Pacific Ocean supplies anchovies, crabs, salmon, tuna, and other fish. The Atlantic yields cod, flounder, haddock, hake, herring, menhaden, and other fish; and such shellfish as clams, lobsters, oysters, and scallops.

Energy Sources. The farms, factories, households, and motor vehicles of the United States consume vast amounts of energy annually. Various sources are used to generate the energy. Petroleum provides about 45 per cent. It is the source of most of the energy used to power motor vehicles, and it heats millions of houses and factories. Natural gas generates about 25 per cent of the energy used. Many industries use gas for heat and power and millions of households burn it for heat, cooking, and drying laundry. Coal is the source of about 20 per cent of all the energy. Its major uses are in the production of electricity and steel. The electricity lights buildings and powers factory and farm machinery. Water and nuclear power each generate about 5 per cent of America's energy. Water is used chiefly to power hydroelectric plants, which produce electricity for some industries and homes.

Nuclear power, like coal and water, generates electricity for industries and homes.

Since the mid-1900's, the cost of energy—especially the petroleum portion—has risen dramatically. The rising cost became a major contributor to inflation in the United States and other countries. For more details, see ENERGY SUPPLY.

Manufacturing is the single most important economic activity in the United States. It accounts for about 21 per cent of the gross national product and employs about 20 per cent of the workers. The value of American manufactured goods is greater than that of any other country. Factories in the United States turn out a tremendous variety of *producer goods*, such as sheet metal and printing presses; and *consumer goods*, such as cars, clothing, and TV sets. The leading U.S. manufactured products are, in order of value, nonelectric machinery, transportation equipment, chemicals, food products,

U.S. Gross National Product

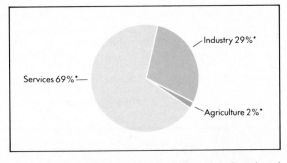

Services 69%*

Industry 29%*

Agriculture 2%*

The gross national product (GNP) is the total value of goods and services produced by a country in a year. The GNP measures a nation's total annual economic performance and can also be used to compare the economic output and growth of countries. The U.S. GNP was $3,661,300,000,000 in 1984.

Production and Workers by Economic Activities

Economic Activities	Per Cent of GDP Produced*	Employed Workers Number of Persons	Employed Workers Per Cent of Total
Manufacturing	21	19,589,000	20
Finance, Insurance, & Real Estate	17	5,665,000	6
Wholesale & Retail Trade	16	21,790,000	22
Community, Social, & Personal Services	15	20,666,000	21
Government	12	15,973,000	16
Transportation, Communication, & Utilities	9	5,169,000	5
Construction	4	4,315,000	5
Mining	4	999,000	1
Agriculture, Forestry, & Fishing	2	3,750,000	4
Total	100	97,916,000	100

*Based on gross domestic product (GDP). GDP is gross national product adjusted for net income sent or received from abroad.
Sources: U.S. Bureau of Economic Analysis; U.S. Bureau of Labor Statistics; U.S. Department of Agriculture.

electric machinery and equipment, fabricated metal products, primary metals, printed materials, paper products, and rubber and plastic products.

The Midwest and Northeast have long been major manufacturing centers. Since the mid-1900's, the nation's fastest-growing manufacturing areas have been in California, the Southwest, and the South. Today, California ranks first among the states in the value of its manufactured goods, followed by New York, Ohio, Illinois, Michigan, and Pennsylvania. Manufacturers in California produce aircraft, aerospace equipment, computers and electronic components, food products, and many other goods. Midwestern factories turn out much of the nation's iron and steel, automobiles, and other heavy industrial products. The Northeast has many clothing factories, food processors, printing plants, and manufacturers of electronic equipment. Petroleum refineries and petrochemical industries account for much of the manufacturing activity in Texas and other states bordering the Gulf of Mexico. Atlanta, Dallas-Fort Worth, and Wichita are important centers for the manufacture of aircraft and related equipment.

Through the years, Americans have developed manufacturing processes that have greatly increased productivity. During the early 1900's, U.S. automobile firms introduced the moving assembly line and identical interchangeable parts for cars. This led to mass production, in which large numbers of goods could be produced in less time and at a lower cost than ever before. Beginning in the mid-1900's, industries in the United States turned increasingly to *automation*—the use of machines that operate with little human assistance. American inventors and engineers developed computers to bring automation to an even higher level. Today, computers operate machines, handle accounting, and perform many other important functions in American industries. See MANUFACTURING.

Agriculture accounts for less than 3 per cent of the U.S. gross national product and employs less than 4 per cent of the nation's workers. Yet, the United States leads the world in agriculture production. The average food production of a U.S. farmer is enough to feed nearly 80 persons. As a result, the country's farms turn out as much food as the nation needs, with enough left over to export food to other countries. About a sixth of the world's food exports come from U.S. farms.

Beef cattle rank as the most valuable product of American farms. Millions of beef cattle are raised on huge ranches in the western United States. The South and Midwest also produce large numbers of beef cattle. Other leading farm products, in order of value, include milk, corn, soybeans, hogs, wheat, and cotton. Farmers

United States Land Use This map shows major land uses in the United States, and also offshore fishing areas. Labels on the map identify chief products of various areas. The label size generally indicates product importance. Other labels on the map locate major manufacturing centers in the country.

WORLD BOOK map

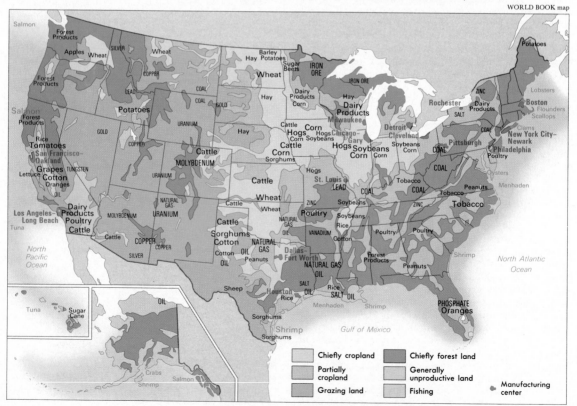

72b

Boeing

Manufacturing ranks as the single most important economic activity in the United States. The steps in the manufacture of an airplane include building a full-sized model, *above*.

Milt & Joan Mann

Agriculture includes the raising of both crops and livestock. A mechanized system for fattening cattle for market, *above*, is one example of the efficient methods used by American farmers.

throughout the country raise dairy cattle for milk and other products. Much of the dairy production is concentrated in a belt that extends from Minnesota through New York. Midwestern states account for much of the nation's corn, soybeans, and hog production. The nation's chief wheat-growing region stretches across the Great Plains. The South, Southwest, and California raise almost all the country's cotton. Farmers in various areas also produce poultry, eggs, fruits, vegetables, nuts, and many other crops.

The United States has played a major role in the modernization of agriculture. During the 1800's, American inventors developed the first successful harvesting machine, threshing machine, and steel plow. American scientists have made important contributions to the development of improved plant varieties and livestock breeds, as well as agricultural chemicals for fertilizer and pest control.

The use of modern farm machinery and agricultural methods has helped make U.S. farms the most efficient in the world. But it has also contributed to rapidly rising production costs. Many farmers who have been unable to meet these rising costs have been forced to quit farming and sell their land. Since 1925, the number of farms in the United States has decreased from about 6,500,000 to about 2,300,000. At the same time, average farm size increased from about 143 acres (58 hectares) to about 440 acres (178 hectares). Some of the largest farms in the United States are owned by business corporations. But more than 95 per cent of all the farms are owned by individuals or by corporations or partnerships made up of members of farm families. See AGRICULTURE; FARM AND FARMING.

Mining. The United States leads the world in the value of its mineral production. Mining accounts for about 4 per cent of the gross national product and employs about 1 per cent of the workers.

The country's chief mineral products are, in order of value, petroleum, natural gas, and coal. The United States ranks first in the world in production of coal and natural gas, and second in petroleum—after Russia. Most coal deposits lie in the Interior Plains and the Appalachian Highlands. Major deposits of petroleum and natural gas occur in Alaska, California, Louisiana, Oklahoma, and Texas. Other important U.S. minerals include building stone, copper, gold, iron ore, lead, phosphate, potassium, salt, sand and gravel, silver, uranium, and zinc.

Although mining accounts for a small share of the total U.S. economic output, it has been a key to the growth of other parts of the economy. Coal and iron ore, for example, are needed to make steel. Steel, in turn, is used to make automobiles, buildings, bridges, and many other goods. Coal is also a fuel for electric power plants. Refineries turn petroleum into gasoline; fuel oil for heating and industrial power; and petrochemicals used in plastics, paint, drugs, fertilizers, and synthetic fabrics. Stone is used in the construction of buildings, and sand and gravel in building highways. Phosphates and potassium are important ingredients in fertilizers. See MINING.

Construction Industry accounts for about 4 per cent of the U.S. gross national product and provides jobs for about 5 per cent of the work force. It employs such workers as architects, engineers, contractors, bricklayers, carpenters, electricians, plumbers, roofers, ironworkers, and plasterers.

Service Industries is a general name for a large, varied category of economic activities. Most of the services provided by the government, including education, are included in this category. Banking, trade, and other financial activities are also service industries. The many other service industries include the operations of transportation, communication, data processing, and insurance companies; and of hotels, restaurants, and barber and beauty shops. Taken together, service industries account for the largest part of the country's GNP—about 69 per cent—and they employ about 70 per cent of the workers. Many service industries are discussed in sections that follow this section.

Finance. Banks finance much of the economic activity in the United States by making loans to both individuals and businesses. American banks loan billions of dollars annually. Most of the loans to individuals are for the purchase of houses, automobiles, or other major items. Bank loans to businesses provide an important source of money for *capital expansion*—the construction of new factories and the purchase of new equipment. As a business expands, it hires more workers. These workers, in turn, produce more goods and services. In this way, the nation's level of employment and its economic output both increase. In addition to borrowing money from banks, most business corporations issue stocks and bonds to raise money for expansion. See BANK; STOCK, CAPITAL; BOND.

Trade. Various kinds of trade play major roles in the American economy. Wholesale trade takes place when a buyer purchases goods directly from a producer. The goods may then be sold to other businesses for resale to consumers. Retail trade involves selling products to the final consumer. Grocery stores, department stores, and automobile dealerships are examples of retail trade establishments. Together, wholesale and retail trade account for about 16 per cent of the U.S. gross national product and employ about 22 per cent of the workers.

Some kinds of trade take place at special *exchanges* (markets). For example, people buy and sell corporate stocks and bonds at stock exchanges. The New York Stock Exchange is the largest in the United States. Commodity exchanges trade agricultural *commodities* (goods), including corn, cotton, soybeans, wheat, and metals. The Chicago Board of Trade is the world's largest commodity exchange.

Foreign trade provides markets for surplus agricultural goods and many raw materials and manufactured goods produced in the United States. The nation imports goods that it lacks entirely or that producers do not supply in sufficient quantities. It also imports goods produced by foreign companies that compete with U.S. firms. The United States leads the world in the value of its foreign trade. Throughout much of the country's history, the value of U.S. exports has exceeded, or been about the same as, the value of its imports. But since the mid-1960's, the value of imports has been much higher than the value of exports most of the time. See BALANCE OF PAYMENTS (United States Balance of Payments); INTERNATIONAL TRADE.

The nation's many important exports include: (1) machinery and transportation equipment, such as computers, electronic power generators, aircraft, automobiles, trucks, and tractors; (2) agricultural products, including corn, cotton, feed grains, livestock, soybeans, and wheat; (3) chemicals, such as dyes, fertilizers, medi-

Collier/Condit, Stock, Boston

Mining provides vital raw materials for American industry. For example, a strip mine, *left,* yields coal. Coal, in turn, is used to fuel electric power plants and to make steel for many manufactured products.

James R. Holland, Stock, Boston

WORLD BOOK photo

The Construction Industry provides jobs for many Americans. Construction workers help put up a high-rise building in the center of a city, *above*.

Service Industries are those economic activities that provide services rather than products. Data processing, *above,* is one of the many service industries. Others include government services and the operation of hotels and restaurants.

cines, and plastic material and resins; and (4) crude materials, including cotton, metal ores, and soybeans.

The leading U.S. imports include (1) machinery and transportation equipment, such as radios, stereo equipment, television sets, and automobiles and their parts; (2) minerals, especially petroleum; and (3) manufactured goods, including iron and steel and other metals, newsprint, and textiles.

Canada is the country's chief trading partner. Other U.S. trading partners in order of importance, include Japan, Mexico, and Great Britain. See INTERNATIONAL TRADE.

Government Spending plays a major role in the economy. Federal, state, and local governments employ about a sixth of the workers in the United States. Many government employees are directly involved in making public policies. Others—including police officers, postal workers, teachers, and trash collectors—provide public services.

Federal, state, and local governments buy a fifth of all the goods and services produced in the United States. Government purchases range from paper clips to office buildings. The federal government ranks as the nation's largest single buyer of goods and services. Its agencies buy billions of dollars worth of equipment from private companies. In addition, federal grants finance much of the nation's research activity. State governments spend most of their income on education, health care and hospitals, highways, and public welfare. Local governments spend more than half their income on education, and smaller amounts for police and fire protection, hospitals, streets, sanitation and sewerage, and parks.

In addition to its roles as an employer and purchaser

of goods and services, government influences the economy by providing income to certain groups of people. For example, the federal government makes social security payments to retired and disabled persons. Federal, state, and local governments provide welfare assistance to the needy. Such government programs are the only source of income for some Americans.

Transportation. A sprawling transportation network spreads out over the United States. Motor vehicles drive on about 4,000,000 miles (6,400,000 kilometers) of streets, roads, and highways in the country. Americans use automobiles for most of their personal travel. Trucks carry nearly a fourth of the freight in the United States. See ROAD; AUTOMOBILE; TRUCK.

The United States has about 322,000 miles (518,000 kilometers) of railroad track. Railroads rank as the leading freight carriers in the United States, handling more than 33 per cent of the freight. But they account for less than 1 per cent of all passenger traffic in the United States. See RAILROAD.

Airlines handle more than 12 per cent of all U.S. passenger traffic, but less than two-tenths of 1 per cent of the freight traffic. More than 30 domestic and international airlines operate in the United States. Chicago-O'Hare International Airport is the country's—and the world's—busiest airport. See AIRPORT; AVIATION.

About 15 per cent of the freight traffic in the United States travels on waterways. The Mississippi River system handles more than half of this freight. Ships and barges traveling on the Mississippi and its branches, including the Arkansas, Missouri, and Ohio rivers, can reach deep into the country's interior. The Great Lakes form the nation's other major inland waterway. The St.

A Network of Highways crisscrosses the United States. Highways form a key part of the nation's excellent transportation system. The construction and repair of highways provides jobs for people throughout the country.

James R. Holland, Stock, Boston

Lawrence Seaway links the lakes with the Atlantic Ocean. See INLAND WATERWAY.

There are many major ports in the United States. New Orleans ranks as the busiest port in the nation. The ports of New York City and Houston rank as the next busiest U.S. ports. See PORT.

Pipelines that carry crude oil, petroleum products, and natural gas account for nearly 25 per cent of the total freight handled in the United States. The nation's vast pipeline network is about 1,250,000 miles (2,012,-000 kilometers) long. See PIPELINE.

Communication. Private corporations operate the publishing and broadcasting industries in the United States. The First Amendment of the Constitution guarantees freedom of the press and speech. These guarantees allow newspapers and broadcasters to operate without government censorship. Laws prohibit the publishing or broadcasting of libelous, obscene, and treasonous materials. But, for the most part, the government interferes little in the operation of the communication industry. The free exchange of ideas and informa-

tion is a vital part of the nation's democratic heritage.

Publishers in the United States issue about 1,800 daily newspapers, which have a total circulation of more than 60 million copies. The nation also has about 7,150 weekly and 540 semiweekly newspapers. The newspapers provide information on local, national, and international events. Many also include such special features as opinion columns, articles on health and fashion, and comic strips and crossword puzzles. In the United States, most newspapers chiefly serve a local region. Many other countries have newspapers with national circulations. See NEWSPAPER.

There are more than 9,800 radio stations and about 1,000 television stations in the United States. Radio and television stations provide the public with entertainment programs, news coverage, and various public interest programs. In the United States, both national networks and local stations broadcast radio and television programs. Almost every American household has at least one television set and one or more radios. See RADIO; TELEVISION.   JOHN EDWIN COFFMAN and TERESA A. SULLIVAN

UNITED STATES/*Study Aids*

Related Articles. See UNITED STATES, GOVERNMENT OF THE; and UNITED STATES, HISTORY OF THE, with their lists of *Related Articles.* See also the separate article on each state with its *Related Articles.* Additional related articles include:

EDUCATION

Education	School	Universities and Colleges

INDUSTRIES AND PRODUCTS

For the rank of the United States among other coun-

tries in production, see the following articles:

Aluminum	Corn	Lead
Automobile	Cotton	Lemon
Barley	Electric Power	Lumber
Cattle	Fishing	Nuclear Energy
Cheese	Industry	Oats
Chemical	Forest Products	Orange
Industry	Gas	Paper
Clothing	Gold	Petroleum
Coal	Horse	Potato
Copper	Iron and Steel	Rubber

Rye
Salmon
Salt
Ship
Silver
Sugar
Sugar Beet
Sugar Cane
Textile

Tobacco
Tuna
Tungsten
Uranium
Vegetable
Wheat
Wine
Zinc

NATIONAL PARKS AND MONUMENTS

See NATIONAL PARK SYSTEM (tables: National Parks; National Monuments).

OUTLYING AREAS

American Samoa
Caroline Islands
Guam
Line Islands
Mariana Islands

Marshall Islands
Midway Island
Puerto Rico
Virgin Islands
Wake Island

PHYSICAL FEATURES

See DAM; LAKE; MOUNTAIN; RIVER, with their lists of *Related Articles*.

SOCIAL AND CULTURAL LIFE

American Literature
Architecture
Book
Christmas
Dancing
Drama
Easter
Holiday
Library

Motion Picture
Museum
Music
Painting
Recreation
Religion
Sculpture
Theater

OTHER RELATED ARTICLES

Air Force, United States
Army, United States
Bicentennial Celebration, American
Census
Citizenship
City
Clothing
Coast Guard, United States
Conservation
Farm and Farming
Flag

Food
Housing
Immigration
Marine Corps, United States
Minority Group
Money
Navy, United States
RAND Corporation
Segregation
Transportation

Outline

I. **The Nation**
   A. Political Divisions
   B. Regions
   C. Outlying Areas
II. **People**
   A. Population
   B. Ancestry
III. **Way of life**
   A. Urban Life
   B. Rural Life
   C. Education
   D. Religion
   E. Recreation
IV. **The Arts**
V. **The Land**
   A. The Appalachian Highlands
   B. The Coastal Lowlands
   C. The Interior Plains
   D. The Ozark-Ouachita Highlands
   E. The Rocky Mountains
   F. The Western Plateaus, Basins, and Ranges
   G. The Pacific Ranges and Lowlands

VI. **Climate**
VII. **Economy**
   A. Natural Resources
   B. Energy Sources
   C. Manufacturing
   D. Agriculture
   E. Mining
   F. Construction Industry
   G. Service Industries
   H. Finance
   I. Trade
   J. Government Spending
   K. Transportation
   L. Communication

Questions

How does the United States rank among the countries of the world in population and area?

Why is the country called a *melting pot?*

What are the country's main land regions?

How does mineral production contribute to other parts of the American economy?

What are some of the leading farm products in the United States?

What are some of the reasons why the United States changed from a rural nation to an urban nation?

Where is the lowest land in the United States?

What are some problems faced by schools in the United States?

What are the major religions in the United States?

What are some positive and negative features of U.S. urban life and rural life?

Additional Resources

Level I

CARPENTER, ALLAN. *Far-Flung America.* Childrens Press, 1979. An introduction to the geography of the U.S.

FROME, MICHAEL. *The National Parks.* Rev. ed. Rand McNally, 1981.

ROSS, FRANK X. *Stories of the States: A Reference Guide to the Fifty States and the U.S. Territories.* Harper, 1969.

SCOTT, JOHN A. *The Story of America: A National Geographic Picture Atlas.* National Geographic Society, 1984.

Level II

ARNOLD, EVE. *In America.* Knopf, 1983. Photographic essay.

COOKE, ALISTAIR. *The Americans: Fifty Talks on Our Life and Times.* Knopf, 1979.

Discovering Historic America. Ed. by S. Alien Chambers. 2 vols. Dutton, 1982. Regional travel guides.

ESTALL, ROBERT C. *A Modern Geography of the United States: Aspects of Life and Economy.* Quadrangle, 1972.

FISHER, RONALD M. *Still Waters, White Waters: Exploring America's Rivers and Lakes.* National Geographic Society, 1977.

FROME, MICHAEL. *Rand McNally National Park Guide.* Rev. ed. Rand McNally, 1982.

LORD, SUZANNE. *American Travelers' Treasury: A Guide to the Nation's Heirlooms.* Morrow, 1977.

PEIRCE, NEAL R., and HAGSTROM, JERRY. *The Book of America: Inside 50 States Today.* Norton, 1983.

RIFKIND, CAROLE. *A Field Guide to American Architecture.* New American Library, 1980.

SOWELL, THOMAS. *Ethnic America: A History.* Basic Books, 1981.

TERKEL, STUDS. *American Dreams: Lost and Found.* Pantheon, 1980. Presents a wide cross-section of American people.

TOCQUEVILLE, ALEXIS DE. *Democracy in America.* First published between 1835 and 1840 and now available in many editions, this has become a classic interpretation of American life.

U.S. BUREAU OF THE CENSUS. *Statistical Abstract of the United States.* U.S. Government Printing Office. Published annually. A useful collection in one volume of information on all aspects of American life.

The Declaration of Independence and the United States Constitution provide the basis of the U.S. government. These documents are displayed in the National Archives Building in Washington, D.C. The Declaration stands in an upright case above the Constitution.

UNITED STATES GOVERNMENT

UNITED STATES, GOVERNMENT OF THE. The government of the United States represents, serves, and protects the American people at home and in foreign countries. From the nation's capital in Washington, D.C., its activities and influence reach every part of the world.

The three branches of the United States government—executive, legislative, and judicial—are usually represented by the President, Congress, and the Supreme Court. Generally speaking, the President enforces the laws that Congress passes, and the Supreme Court interprets these laws if any question arises.

United States military forces stationed in many parts of the world support American policy and help preserve peace. Representatives of the government work in international organizations, provide technical assistance, and negotiate with other governments. Millions of civil service employees and other workers at home and abroad carry out the programs of the government.

The United States government shares governmental powers with the states under the *federal* system established by the United States Constitution. The national governments of most other countries are *unitary* (centralized). They have final authority in all matters, and grant only limited powers to state and local governments.

Government in the United States operates on three levels: national, state, and local. The federal government in Washington cannot abolish the states or re-arrange their boundaries. It can exercise only powers that are delegated or implied by the Constitution. The states exercise powers reserved to them or not denied them by the Constitution. In some areas, the federal and state governments have *concurrent* powers. That is, they both have the right to exercise authority. The American judicial system keeps the federal and state governments within their proper fields of power.

The United States government makes and enforces laws, collects taxes, provides services for the people, protects individuals and their property, and works for national and international security. But it is noted for the way it encourages the people to take part in government, seeks to protect the rights of the people from the government itself, and assures the self-government of the states. Abraham Lincoln described the United States government in his Gettysburg Address as being "of the people, by the people, for the people."

For a description of the United States, its history, and its Constitution, see UNITED STATES; UNITED STATES, HISTORY OF THE; CONSTITUTION OF THE UNITED STATES.

Government in American Life

The United States government, through its activities, services, and authority, directly affects the lives of the American people in many ways. It collects taxes and customs duties to finance government work. It borrows money and issues bonds. It coins money and prints currency. It establishes uniform weights and measures. It issues patents and copyrights. It controls immigration and emigration, and naturalizes noncitizens. It operates the postal system, and builds roads and highways. It manages a social security system. It has powers to regulate agriculture, business, and labor through its authority to regulate interstate commerce. It negotiates with other governments, and participates in international organizations to promote peace, health, and education. It has the power to declare war and to conclude peace pacts. It maintains the armed forces and

can draft citizens for military service. It admits new states into the union. It governs the District of Columbia and the territories, including American Samoa, Guam, and the Virgin Islands. The U.S. government also governs islands in the Pacific Ocean under a United Nations trusteeship.

The United States seeks not only to govern, but also to protect the liberty of the states and the people. The Bill of Rights in the Constitution guarantees that all persons shall have freedom of speech and of religion, freedom of the press, the right of assembly, and freedom from arbitrary interference by the federal government. It guarantees a person freedom from arbitrary arrest and imprisonment. It also guarantees the right to trial by jury and justice in the federal courts. The United States government acts to see that no state deprives any person of life, liberty, or property without due process of law, or denies equal protection of the law. See BILL OF RIGHTS.

The Executive Branch

The executive branch of the United States government consists of (1) the Executive Office of the President, (2) the executive departments, and (3) the independent agencies.

The President of the United States is the nation's chief executive and chief of state. The President lives in the White House in Washington, D.C., and has offices there. As chief executive, the President has the responsibilities of enforcing federal laws and appointing and removing high federal officials. The President commands the armed forces, conducts foreign affairs, and recommends laws to Congress. The President also appoints American representatives to international organizations and to diplomatic missions in other lands. As chief of state, the President performs many ceremonial duties. Elected by the people to hold office for a four-year term, the President cannot be elected to more than two terms.

The Executive Office of the President includes: (1) the White House Office, (2) the Office of Management and Budget, (3) the National Security Council, (4) the

Symbols of the United States include the American flag and the Great Seal. The eagle on the seal holds an olive branch and arrows, symbolizing a desire for peace but the ability to wage war. The reverse side bears the Eye of Providence, representing God, and a pyramid dated 1776.

Stacy Pick, © Lensman

The United States Capitol in Washington, D.C., is where Congress meets to make the nation's laws. The House of Representatives uses the wing at the left, and the Senate the one at the right.

Office of Policy Development, (5) the Council of Economic Advisers, (6) the Office of the United States Trade Representative, (7) the President's Intelligence Oversight Board, (8) the Office of Administration, (9) the Council on Environmental Quality, (10) the Office of the Vice-President, (11) the Office of Science and Technology Policy, and (12) the President's Foreign Intelligence Advisory Board. See PRESIDENT OF THE UNITED STATES.

Executive Departments conduct the administration of the national government. These 13 departments are: (1) State, (2) Treasury, (3) Defense, (4) Justice, (5) Interior, (6) Agriculture, (7) Commerce, (8) Labor, (9) Health and Human Services, (10) Housing and Urban Development, (11) Transportation, (12) Energy, and (13) Education. Department heads are appointed by the President, with the approval of the Senate. They form the *Cabinet* (see CABINET). Twelve are called *secretaries*. The attorney general heads the Department of Justice.

The typical executive department has a deputy or undersecretary and two or more assistant secretaries. The President appoints these officials, and may remove them without giving any reason. High officials usually resign when a new President takes office.

Generally, each executive department is divided into bureaus, bureaus into divisions, divisions into branches, branches into sections, and sections into units. Most officials below the highest level serve under civil service appointments (see CIVIL SERVICE). All executive departments have headquarters in Washington, but about 90 per cent of the employees work in *field services* (activities that are not a part of headquarters).

Independent Agencies developed with the growth of government regulation. They operate in many fields, including aeronautics and space, nuclear energy, banking and finance, civil service, communications, farm credit, home loans, information services, interstate commerce, labor relations, railroad retirement, science, securities and exchange, selective service, small business, tariffs, trade, and veterans affairs. Administrators or directors head most of the agencies. But the regulatory agencies, such as the Interstate Commerce Commission, are headed by several persons of equal rank, although one may serve as chairperson. The President appoints the members of these agencies with Senate approval, and must state reasons for removing them.

The Legislative Branch

The legislative branch of the United States government includes Congress, which consists of the Senate and the House of Representatives. This branch also includes nine administrative agencies: (1) the Architect of the Capitol, (2) the Congressional Budget Office, (3) the Copyright Royalty Tribunal, (4) the Cost Accounting Standards Board, (5) the General Accounting Office, (6) the Government Printing Office, (7) the Library of Congress, (8) the Office of Technology Assessment, and (9) the United States Botanic Garden.

The Senate and the House of Representatives meet in separate chambers in the Capitol in Washington, D.C. Congress makes, repeals, and amends federal laws. It also levies federal taxes and appropriates funds for the government. See CONGRESS OF THE UNITED STATES.

The Senate has 100 members. Each state, regardless of size or population, has two senators, who serve six-year terms. The Vice-President of the United States presides over the Senate. The Senate has certain exclusive powers. It alone can sit as a court of impeachment to try federal officials impeached by the House of Representatives. It alone has the power to approve the President's nominations for major federal offices. Any treaty made by the United States is subject to the Senate's approval. See SENATE.

The House of Representatives consists of 435 members. A state's representation is based on population. It ranges from California's 45 members to one each from Alaska, Delaware, North Dakota, South Dakota, Vermont, and Wyoming. The number of representatives from a state changes as its population changes. Reapportionment takes place every 10 years, after each national census in a year ending with zero. Only the House can bring charges of impeachment against high federal officials. It alone can initiate tax bills. See HOUSE OF REPRESENTATIVES.

The Judicial Branch

The Supreme Court of the United States is the highest court in the land. It has a chief justice and eight associate justices. The President appoints all justices with the approval of the Senate. The justices hold office for life. See SUPREME COURT OF THE UNITED STATES.

Other Federal Courts. About 95 federal *district courts* are located in various cities. Above the district courts are 13 federal *courts of appeals*, often called *circuit courts*. Above the courts of appeals is the Supreme Court. Decisions of a district court may be appealed to an appeals court, and from the appeals court to the Supreme Court. Federal courts decide cases that involve the Constitution and federal laws. Judges of these courts hold office for life. The President appoints them with the approval of the Senate. See COURT.

Principles of American Government

Separation of Powers. The Constitution divides the powers of the United States government among the executive, legislative, and judicial branches. Each branch is generally independent of the other two, and has the authority to check or balance the others. *Checks and balances* give each branch some powers that affect the other two. For example, Congress holds a check over the President with its authority to make government appropriations. It checks the courts with its powers to organize courts and create rules for their procedures. One of the President's checks on Congress is the power to veto bills. The President influences the courts by the kind of judges he or she appoints. The courts can check the President and Congress by declaring executive orders and legislative acts unconstitutional.

A Written Constitution provides the basis of government in the United States. It divides powers and duties between the federal and state governments. It specifies the powers of each branch of the national government. A written constitution is a unique American contribution. British royal governors had ruled the colonies in America under written charters granted by the monarch. However, the idea of a written constitution as the basic law of an independent country was new.

The Constitution not only grants powers, but also

How a Bill Becomes Law in the United States

The drawings on this page and the next three pages show how federal laws are enacted in the United States. Thousands of bills are introduced during each Congress, which lasts two years, and hundreds become law. All bills not enacted by the end of the two-year period are killed.

WORLD BOOK illustrations by David Cunningham

Ideas for New Laws come from many sources. The President, members of Congress, and other government officials may propose laws. Suggestions also come from individual citizens; special-interest groups, such as farmers, industry, and labor; newspaper editorials; and public protests. Congressional committees, in addition to lawyers who represent special-interest groups, actually write most bills and put them into proper legal form. Specialists called *legislative counsels* in both the Senate and House of Representatives also help prepare many bills for congressional action.

Individual citizens

Public protests

Newspaper editorials

Special-interest groups

The President

Members of Congress and
other government officials

Each Bill Must Be Sponsored by a Member of the House or Senate. Up to 25 representatives and any number of senators may co-sponsor a bill. A bill may originate in either house of Congress unless it deals with taxes or spending. The Constitution provides that all such bills must be introduced in the House. The tradition that money bills must begin in the lower house of the legislature came from England. There, the lower house—the House of Commons—is more likely to reflect the people's wishes because the people elect its members. They do not elect the upper house, the House of Lords. The rule has little meaning in the United States because voters elect both houses.

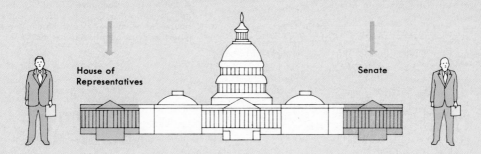

House of
Representatives

Senate

How a Bill Goes Through Congress

The drawings on this page and the next show the normal path of a bill introduced in the House of Representatives. The process is the same for a bill introduced in the Senate, except that the House action comes after the Senate action. A bill may die at almost any stage of the process if no action is taken on it. A majority of the bills introduced in Congress fail and never become law.

Introduction in the House. A sponsor introduces a bill by giving it to the clerk of the House or placing it in a box called the *hopper*. The clerk reads the title of the bill into the *Congressional Record* in a procedure called the *first reading*. The Government Printing Office prints the bill and distributes copies.

Assignment to Committee. The speaker of the House assigns the bill to a committee for study. The House has about 20 *standing* (permanent) committees, each with jurisdiction over bills in a certain area.

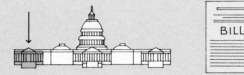

The Bill Goes to the Senate to await its turn. Bills normally reach the Senate floor in the order that they come from committee. But if a bill is urgent, the leaders of the majority party might push it ahead.

Committee Action. The committee or one of its subcommittees studies the bill and may hold hearings. The committee may approve the bill as it stands, revise the bill, or table it.

Assignment to Committee. The Vice-President of the United States, who is the presiding officer of the Senate, assigns the proposed law to a committee for study. The Senate has about 15 standing committees.

The Senate Considers the Bill. Senators can debate a bill indefinitely, unless they vote to limit discussion. When there is no further debate, the Senate votes. Most bills must have a simple majority to pass.

A Conference Committee made up of members of both houses works out any differences between the House and Senate versions of the bill. The revised bill is sent back to both houses for their final approval.

The Committee Studies the Bill and hears testimony from experts and other interested persons. In some cases, a subcommittee conducts the study. The committee may release the bill with a recommendation to pass it, revise the bill and release it, or lay it aside so that the House cannot vote on it. Releasing the bill is called *reporting it out*, and laying the proposed law aside is called *tabling*.

The Bill Goes on a Calendar, a list of bills awaiting action. The Rules Committee may call for quick action on the bill, limit debate, and limit or prohibit amendments. Without the committee's help, a bill might never reach the floor of the House.

Consideration by the House begins with a second reading of the bill, the only complete reading in most cases. A third reading, by title only, comes after any amendments have been added and before the final vote. If the bill passes by a *simple majority* (one more than half the votes), it goes to the Senate.

Introduction in the Senate. To introduce a bill, a senator must be recognized by the presiding officer and announce the introduction of the bill. A bill that has passed either house of Congress is sometimes called an *act*, but the term usually means legislation that has passed both houses of Congress and become law.

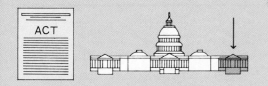

The Bill Is Printed by the Government Printing Office in a process called *enrolling*. The clerk of the house of Congress that originated the bill certifies the final version.

The Speaker of the House Signs the Enrolled Bill, and then the Vice-President signs it. Finally, Congress sends the proposed new legislation to the White House for consideration by the President.

Action by the President

A bill passed by Congress goes to the President, who has 10 days—not including Sundays—to sign or veto it. The President may also let a bill become law by letting 10 days pass without acting.

Approval. After approving a bill, the President signs it, dates it, and often writes the word *approved* on it.

Veto. A vetoed bill must be returned to Congress with an explanation of the President's objections.

No Action. The President might not veto the bill but may fail to sign it to show disapproval of some parts.

Reconsideration by Congress. If two-thirds of those members present approve the vetoed bill, it becomes law despite the President's veto.

Ten Days Pass. If the President holds the bill for 10 days—excluding Sundays—while Congress is in session, it becomes law without the signature of the chief executive. A bill that reaches the President fewer than 10 days—excluding Sundays—before Congress adjourns cannot become law without the President's signature. If the President fails to sign the proposed law, it dies. This procedure is called a *pocket veto*.

The Bill Becomes Law and is given a number that indicates which Congress passed it. For example, a law enacted by the 95th Congress might be designated Public Law 95-250.

limits them. However, it does not answer all questions. For example, who in the government is to say that a state is trying to use a power that belongs to the federal government? Who is to say that the federal government is attempting to exercise a power that belongs to the states? Who is to say that the President, Congress, or the Supreme Court are acting unconstitutionally?

Judicial Review is the method used to answer the basic question: Who is to say what the Constitution means in cases of dispute? Courts have the power to declare legislative acts and executive orders (1) constitutional, or legal; or (2) unconstitutional, or illegal.

Judicial review confines the state and national governments within their constitutional limits. Generally, the state courts interpret the state constitutions, and federal courts interpret the United States Constitution. The Supreme Court can declare unconstitutional executive orders and legislative acts of the federal or the state governments. The Constitution clearly states that it and all federal laws and treaties are the supreme law of the land.

Popular Sovereignty allows the American people to change the Constitution. Congress initiates amendments to the Constitution. A proposed amendment must have the approval of two-thirds of both the Senate and the House of Representatives. It then goes to the states for their approval. Congress may call a national convention to propose amendments, if two-thirds of the state legislatures request it. The amendment becomes a part of the Constitution after legislatures or conventions in three-fourths of the states have ratified it. The American people may adopt an entirely new constitution by calling a new constitutional convention, like the one at Philadelphia in 1787. If such a convention were held, the constitution it adopted would be sent to the states for approval. It would become effective when ratified in the same way as an amendment.

Political Parties and Elections

The American people have a strong voice in their government. They can exercise their democratic rights by voting in national, state, and local elections, and by working in political parties and campaigns.

The Two-Party System. The United States has two major political parties, the Democratic and the Republican. Both parties receive support from individuals and groups in all parts of the country. Members of these two parties hold almost all the offices in the national, state, and local governments.

Minor political parties of the United States rarely elect candidates to government offices. They serve chiefly to call attention to problems that the major parties may have neglected. Often, one or both of the major parties may then attempt to solve such a problem. Then the third party, which brought attention to the problem, may disappear. See POLITICAL PARTY.

National Elections to elect a President and Vice-President are held every four years on the first Tuesday after the first Monday in November. All members of the House of Representatives and about one-third of the members of the Senate are elected at this same time. Between the presidential elections, all of the representatives and another one-third of the senators are elected. This election is held on the same day in November in even-numbered years.

Federal and state laws regulate elections and the qualifications of voters. Most states hold *primary* elections in which party members nominate candidates for state and local offices. Some states use the primary to nominate candidates for Congress. National political conventions nominate candidates for President and Vice-President. See POLITICAL CONVENTION; PRIMARY ELECTION.

Presidential elections are held to select electors to the Electoral College (see ELECTORAL COLLEGE). Each state has as many electors as the total of its senators and representatives in Congress. The District of Columbia has three electors. The electors usually vote for the candidate who receives the most votes in their state. A candidate for President must receive a majority of the electoral votes to be elected.

The Development of American Government

English Background. The United States inherited many government practices from the English rulers of colonial days. In England, the people, particularly in the middle classes, had fought their kings to win the right to representative government. They had also won civil rights and liberties that would protect them and their property from arbitrary acts of government.

The English colonists brought with them the ideas of representative government and civil liberties when they came to America. American frontier life produced much individual independence and self-reliance because of the equal opportunity offered each person. Representative government and many civil liberties became even broader than they had been in Great Britain.

Early American Government. The colonies became states after the Declaration of Independence in 1776. They founded the first independent general government in the United States under the *Articles of Confederation* (see ARTICLES OF CONFEDERATION). Under the Articles, the 13 states guarded their individual powers so strictly that they failed to give Congress the power to tax or to regulate interstate and foreign commerce. Congress could not even create an army without asking the state governments for men and money. Such leaders as George Washington, Benjamin Franklin, James Madison, and Alexander Hamilton feared that the weak national government would collapse. They led a constitutional convention in Philadelphia in 1787 that wrote the United States Constitution. The document was ratified by the first nine states by June, 1788, and went into effect in 1789.

The Constitution gave the national government more powers than it had possessed under the Articles of Confederation. The federal government exercises these powers directly over the people, not through the state governments, as it had done under the Articles.

The Growth of American Government. Congress gave the western territories of the United States local representative government as they grew in population. The Northwest Ordinance, passed under the Articles of Confederation in 1787, became a model for future territorial governments (see NORTHWEST ORDINANCE). After a territory had enough people, Congress admitted it into the Union as a state.

The United States purchased Alaska in 1867, and in

1 CARPENTERS' HALL,
PHILADELPHIA (1774)

2 INDEPENDENCE HALL, PHILADELPHIA
(1775-1776; 1777; 1778-1783)

3 CONGRESS HALL,
BALTIMORE (1776-1777)

Meeting Places of American Congresses

The Earliest American Congresses met in the buildings shown here. The Continental Congress first met in 1774 in Carpenters' Hall, Philadelphia. In 1776, Philadelphia's Independence Hall became the first Capitol of the new nation. In 1800, the Congress of the United States moved into the first Capitol in Washington, D.C.

4 OLD COURT HOUSE,
LANCASTER, PA. (1777)

10 CONGRESS HALL,
PHILADELPHIA
(1790-1800)

5 YORK COUNTY COURT HOUSE,
YORK, PA. (1777-1778)

9 FEDERAL HALL,
NEW YORK CITY (1785-1790)

8 FRENCH ARMS TAVERN,
TRENTON, N.J. (1784)

7 STATE HOUSE,
ANNAPOLIS, MD. (1783-1784)

6 NASSAU HALL,
PRINCETON, N.J. (1783)

1898 it acquired Puerto Rico, Hawaii, and the Philippines. At first, these territories did not receive as democratic and representative a government as the other territories within the borders of the United States. But the Philippines gained full independence in 1946. Puerto Rico became a commonwealth in 1952. Alaska and Hawaii became the 49th and 50th states in 1959.

Problems of Government. Since 1789, all governments—national, state, and local—have taken on more powers and duties. They have been forced to do so by the increase in population, the growth of cities and towns, the development of industries, and the growth of transportation and communications. Problems that were once local, such as conservation and transportation, have become national. The belief has developed that people should use government and other organizations to provide themselves with services, such as social security, made possible by modern wealth and science. As a result, the federal government has grown even faster than the state and local governments.

Many persons object to the expansion of federal authority, particularly over state and local matters. Others insist that public interest demands federal rather than state control in cases that involve more than one state. When conflicts arise, the courts must decide how to balance the rights of the states with the needs of the national government.

WILLIAM G. CARLETON

Related Articles in WORLD BOOK include:

EXECUTIVE DEPARTMENTS

Agriculture, Department of
Commerce, Department of
Defense, Department of
Education, Department of
Energy, Department of

Health and Human Services, Department of
Housing and Urban Development, Department of

Interior, Department of the
Justice, Department of
Labor, Department of
State, Department of

Transportation,
Department of
Treasury, Department
of the

EXECUTIVE OFFICE OF THE PRESIDENT

Economic Advisers,
Council of
Management and
Budget, Office of

National Security Council
President of the United
States

INDEPENDENT AGENCIES

Civil Rights,
Commission on
Consumer Product
Safety Commission
Environmental
Protection Agency
Equal Employment
Opportunity Commission
Export-Import Bank
of the United States
Farm Credit
Administration
Federal Communications
Commission
Federal Deposit Insurance
Corporation
Federal Election Commission
Federal Home Loan
Bank Board
Federal Maritime
Commission
Federal Mediation and
Conciliation Service
Federal Reserve System
Federal Trade Commission
General Services
Administration

Indian Claims Commission
International Trade
Commission, U.S.
Interstate Commerce
Commission
National Aeronautics and
Space Administration
National Foundation
on the Arts and
the Humanities
National Labor Relations
Board
National Mediation
Board
National Science
Foundation
Nuclear Regulatory
Commission
Postal Service, U.S.
Railroad Retirement Board
Securities and Exchange
Commission
Small Business
Administration
Tax Court, United States
Tennessee Valley Authority
Veterans Administration

JUDICIAL BRANCH

Court of Appeals
Court of Claims
Court of International Trade,
United States

Court of Military Appeals
District Court
Supreme Court of
the United States

LEGISLATIVE BRANCH

Congress of the United States
General Accounting Office
Government Printing Office
House of Representatives

Library of Congress
Senate
Vice President of
the United States

SYMBOLS OF GOVERNMENT

Columbia
E Pluribus
Unum
Flag

Great Seal of the
United States
Liberty Bell
Pledge of Allegiance

Star-Spangled
Banner
Statue of Liberty
Uncle Sam

OTHER RELATED ARTICLES

American's Creed
Ballot
Bill of Rights
Census
Checks and Balances
Citizenship
City Government
Civil Service
Constitution of the
United States
County
Court
Democracy
Electoral College
Foreign Service
Government
Hoover Commission
Immigration

Initiative and
Referendum
Law
Local Goverment
Money
National Debt
Naturalization
Political Party
Presidential Succession
Public Lands
Radio Free Europe/
Radio Liberty
Social Security
Spoils System
State Government
States' Rights
Statuary Hall
Tariff

Taxation
Territory
United States, History of the
United States Capitals
Veto

Voice of America
Voting
Washington, D.C.
White House
Yankee

Outline

I. Government in American Life
II. The Executive Branch
  A. The President
  B. Executive Departments
  C. Independent Agencies
III. The Legislative Branch
  A. The Senate   B. The House of Representatives
IV. The Judicial Branch
  A. The Supreme Court   B. Other Federal Courts
V. Principles of American Government
  A. Separation of Powers
  B. A Written Constitution
  C. Judicial Review
  D. Popular Sovereignty
VI. Political Parties and Elections
  A. The Two-Party System   B. National Elections
VII. The Development of American Government
  A. English Background
  B. Early American Government
  C. The Growth of American Government
  D. Problems of Government

Questions

How does the United States government differ from most other national governments?

What are the three branches of the United States government?

What is *popular sovereignty? Judicial review?* Why are they important in the United States government?

How does each branch of the government exercise its powers of checks and balances?

How does the United States Constitution divide powers among the national and state governments?

What is an *independent agency?* What does it do?

How did the ideas of representative government develop in the colonies?

What steps must be taken to amend the United States Constitution?

What are two exclusive powers of the House of Representatives?

What are some typical questions of government left unanswered by the United States Constitution?

Reading and Study Guide

See *United States Government* in the RESEARCH GUIDE/INDEX, Volume 22, for a *Reading and Study Guide.*

Additional Resources

Level I

ACHESON, PATRICIA C. *Our Federal Government, How It Works: An Introduction to the United States Government.* Rev. ed. Dodd, 1984.

COOK, FRED J. *The Rise of American Political Parties.* Watts, 1971.

COY, HAROLD. *Congress.* Rev. ed. Watts, 1981. *The Supreme Court.* Rev. ed. 1981.

ELTING, MARY, and GOSSETT, MARGARET. *We Are the Government.* Rev. ed. Doubleday, 1967.

Level II

LISTON, ROBERT A. *Defense Against Tyranny: The Balance of Power in Government.* Messner, 1975.

MAGRUDER, FRANK A. *Magruder's American Government.* Rev. ed. Allyn & Bacon, 1982.

PAGE, BENJAMIN I. *Who Gets What from Government.* Univ. of California Press, 1983.

United States Government Manual. U.S. Government Printing Office. Published annually.

Kennedy Galleries, Inc.

Walters Art Gallery

West Point Museum

Independence

The Westward Movement

The Civil War

The History of the United States spans more than 200 years. It is an exciting tale of the birth and growth of one of the world's freest, richest, and most powerful nations.

UNITED STATES HISTORY

UNITED STATES, HISTORY OF THE. The history of the United States is the story of a great nation that was carved out of a wilderness by a brave and freedom-loving people. The men and women who built the United States came from almost every part of the world. They represented many different nationalities, races, and religions. Through the years, the people and their descendants learned to live and work together, and to take pride in being Americans. This spirit of cooperation and pride helped make the United States the huge, powerful, and wealthy nation it is today. It also helped the country and its people survive many challenges and hardships—including dangers in the wilderness, wars, social turmoil, and economic depressions.

Background

As late as the 1400's, Indians and Eskimos were the only inhabitants of the Western Hemisphere. During the next 200 years, people from several European countries sailed across the Atlantic Ocean to North and South America. Among them were colonists—chiefly British—who settled along the eastern coast of North America between what are now Maine and Georgia. These hard-working colonists built up a series of thriving permanent settlements in the wilderness. They lived under British rule for many years. But their dedication to liberty led them to declare their independence and form the United States of America in 1776.

Growth and Expansion

The American people dedicated their new nation to the principles of democracy, freedom, equality, and

opportunity for all. From the start, the United States welcomed immigrants to its shores. Attracted by the opportunity for freedom and a chance for a better life, newcomers from many lands poured into the United States by the millions. Immigration and natural growth caused the country's population to mount steadily—from fewer than 3 million in 1776 to more than 235 million today.

As the population grew, the American people spread out across North America. Wherever they went, these pioneers worked hard to turn the wilderness into a place where they could earn a living. They formed thriving farms in places where the soil was good. They searched for minerals and other valuable resources, and established towns where they found resources. Cities grew up along the main transportation routes and business and industry prospered there.

America's rapid growth made it one of the world's largest nations in both size and population. The country's bustling economic activity turned it into a land of enormous wealth.

Today, the United States ranks as the world's leading producer of farm products and manufactured goods, and its people have the highest standard of living in the world. The United States also became a world leader in many other fields, including science, medicine, technology, and military strength.

Challenges and Hardships

The United States grew and prospered in spite of many challenges and hardships. At the start, the very survival of the new nation was in doubt. The colonists

86

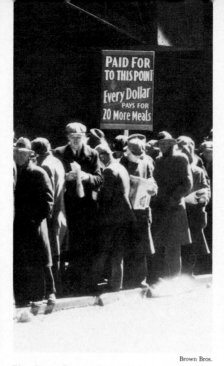

The Metropolitan Museum of Art

Industrialization

Brown Bros.

The Great Depression

NASA

The Space Age

who founded the United States had to defeat the mighty British Empire in the Revolutionary War to make their claim to independence stick. They succeeded despite great odds against them.

Both the colonists and the pioneers who moved westward across the country faced many dangers, including disease, starvation, and attacks by Indians. In the 1860's—less than 100 years after the Revolution—the survival of the United States was threatened again. Eleven Southern states withdrew from the Union and tried to establish an independent nation. The tragic, bloody Civil War between the North and the South followed. The North won the Civil War and the country remained united.

The American ideals of equality and opportunity for all did much to help the United States grow and prosper. Yet the ideals have not always been followed in practice. From colonial times until the end of the Civil War, many black Americans were slaves. In addition, some Americans have suffered from discrimination in jobs and other areas because they were immigrants, or because of their race or religion.

America's economic growth, though amazingly rapid, has not always been smooth. Periodically, severe depressions have brought the economy to a near standstill. At such times, large numbers of Americans lost their jobs and lived in poverty.

During the 1900's, the United States became one of the world's strongest military powers. As such, it took on the role of defending democracy throughout the world. This role led the United States into two World Wars and other conflicts. In the mid-1900's, many Americans began protesting against their country's military role, while others defended it. This issue led to bitter disputes among the people.

Today, like always, the United States faces many problems. They include the existence of poverty amid great wealth, recurring slumps in the economy, disputes over foreign policy, and pollution of the environment. But Americans retain deep pride in their country and the belief and hope that they can overcome their difficulties as their ancestors did.

About This Article

The contributor of this article is Oscar Handlin, Carl M. Loeb University Professor at Harvard University. He is the author of many books on American history, including The Uprooted—*a winner of the Pulitzer Prize—and* The Americans: A New History of the People of the United States.

The article traces the history of the United States from its beginnings to the present day. The outline below shows the major sections of the article. WORLD BOOK *also has many individual articles on important events and people in United States history. Cross-references within this article refer to other* WORLD BOOK *articles for details on key topics. The Study Aids section includes a listing of related articles.*

Article Outline:

87

The French Arrive in Florida (1591), an engraving by Theodore de Bry based on a painting by Jacques le Moyne; Library of Congress

European Explorers from several countries made voyages to America during the 1500's. The scene above shows French explorer Jean Ribaut and his crew approaching the Florida coast in 1562. Friendly Indians gathered along the shore to greet the newcomers.

UNITED STATES HISTORY / *America Before Colonial Times*

For thousands of years, Indians were the only inhabitants of the Western Hemisphere. They had wandered into North America from Asia more than 20,000 years ago. They spread across the hemisphere to the tip of South America. About 10,000 years ago, Eskimos—another Asian people—moved to the Western Hemisphere. But they settled only in the far north, near the Arctic Circle (see ESKIMO).

The Vikings were probably the first white men to reach America. A band of these venturesome seamen is believed to have explored part of the east coast of North America about 1,000 years ago. But European exploration and settlement of America did not begin for another 500 years. Then, in 1492, Christopher Columbus sailed westward from Spain, seeking a short sea route to the Far East, or Orient. He found, instead, a vast New World. Following Columbus' voyage, explorers, soldiers, and settlers from several European countries flocked to America. The process through which white men took control of the Indian homeland was underway.

The First Americans

About 20 million Indians were living in the Americas when Columbus reached the New World. About 15 to 20 million Indians lived between what is now Mexico and the tip of South America. About 1 million Indians lived in what are now the United States and Canada.

The American Indians formed hundreds of tribes, with many different languages and ways of life. Some tribes in the south—including the Aztec, Inca, and Maya—established advanced civilizations. They founded cities that had huge, magnificent buildings. They also accumulated gold, jewels, and other riches. Most American Indians north of Mexico lived in small villages. They hunted game and raised such crops as *maize* (corn), beans, and squash. Some tribes traveled continuously in search of food and never established permanent settlements.

Some Indian tribes of North America helped early European settlers survive in the wilderness of the New World. But as settlers moved westward, they became a threat to the Indian way of life, and Indians and whites became enemies. For a detailed story of the first Americans, see INDIAN, AMERICAN.

European Discovery

The Vikings. About A.D. 1000, Vikings from Greenland explored part of the North American mainland—probably what is now Newfoundland, Canada. Led by Leif Ericson, they were probably the first white men to reach the mainland of the continent. But the Vikings did not establish permanent settlements, and their voyages were soon forgotten.

Columbus. Before Columbus' voyage, Europeans did not know the Western Hemisphere existed. During the 1400's, Europeans became interested in finding a short sea route to the Far East—a region of spices and other valuable goods.

Columbus, an Italian navigator, believed he could find a short route to the East by sailing west. Financed by the Spanish king and queen, he set sail westward from Spain on Aug. 3, 1492. Columbus reached land on October 12, and assumed he had arrived in the Far East. Actually, he landed on San Salvador, one of the islands just east of the North American mainland.

Columbus died in 1506, still believing he had sailed to the Far East. But other Europeans realized he had come upon an unexplored land. They called it the *New World*, and honored Columbus as its discoverer. Europeans also called the Western Hemisphere *America*, after Amerigo Vespucci. An Italian, Vespucci claimed he made voyages to the New World for Spain and Portugal beginning in 1497.

Exploration and Early Settlement

The discovery of the existence of America caused a wave of excitement in Europe. To many Europeans, the New World offered opportunities for wealth, power, and adventure. European rulers and merchants wanted to gain control of the hemisphere's resources in order to add to their wealth. Rulers also sought to gain New World territory, and thus increase their power and importance. Christian clergymen were eager to spread their religion to the Indians. Explorers and others viewed the New World as a place to seek adventure, as well as gain personal fame and fortune. Before long, Europeans from several countries sailed across the Atlantic to explore America and set up trading posts and colonies.

For details on the early exploration, see EXPLORATION AND DISCOVERY.

The Spanish and Portuguese. During the 1500's, the Spanish and Portuguese spread out over the southern part of the Western Hemisphere in search of gold and other riches. The Spaniards quickly conquered the Inca of Peru, the Maya of Central America, and the Aztec of Mexico. The Portuguese took control of what is now Brazil. By 1600, Spain and Portugal controlled most of the hemisphere from Mexico southward.

Also during the 1500's, Spaniards moved into what is now the Southeastern and Western United States. They did not discover riches there, as they did farther south. But they took control of Florida and of the land west of the Mississippi River. In 1565, the Spanish founded St. Augustine, Fla., the oldest city in what is now the United States. They also established missions and other settlements in the West and South. See MISSION LIFE IN AMERICA; SPAIN (The Spanish Empire).

The British and French began exploring eastern North America about 1500. At first, both nations sent only explorers and fur traders to the New World. But after 1600, they began establishing permanent settlements there. The French settlements were chiefly in what is now Canada. The British settlements included the 13 colonies that later became the United States.

For many years, Great Britain and France struggled for control of the land between the Atlantic Ocean and the Mississippi River, and for Canada. Britain finally won out in 1763 when it defeated France in the French and Indian War.

The Land That Became the United States

The explorers who came to the northern part of the hemisphere did not find gold and other riches, as did the Spanish in the south. Nor did these explorers find large Indian civilizations to help supply their needs. Instead, they found a wilderness sparsely inhabited by Indians.

The first settlers encountered many hardships as they attempted to establish colonies along the eastern coast. They had no way of knowing that beyond their settlements lay a vast and unbelievably rich and varied land. But later, the resources of this new land—its fertile soils, abundant water supplies, and plentiful minerals— would help the United States grow into one of the world's largest and most prosperous nations.

Period Facts in Brief

Important Dates

1492 Christopher Columbus sailed from Spain to the Western Hemisphere. Europeans honored him as the discoverer of America.

1497 John Cabot made the first voyage to North America for England.

1500 Portuguese explorer Pedro Álvares Cabral reached what is now Brazil.

1513 Ponce de León of Spain began exploring Florida, seeking the Fountain of Youth.

1521 Spanish conquistador Hernando Cortés defeated the Aztec of Mexico.

1534 Jacques Cartier of France became the first European to reach the Gulf of St. Lawrence in Canada.

1540-1542 Francisco Coronado of Spain explored the American Southwest.

1565 Spaniards founded St. Augustine, Fla., the oldest city in what is now the United States.

1585 Sir Walter Raleigh tried unsuccessfully to establish a permanent British settlement in America.

Kevin L. Martin

An Acoma Indian Village, *above,* is one of the oldest continuously inhabited settlements in the United States. Located on a *mesa* (flat-topped hill) in New Mexico, it probably dates from the 1300's.

Penn's Treaty with the Indians (1771), an oil painting on canvas by Benjamin West; Pennsylvania Academy of the Fine Arts, Philadelphia

Early Colonists worked to maintain good relations with the Indians. William Penn, *arms extended*, made his first treaty with the Indians in 1682. His fair dealings with the Indians helped the colony of Pennsylvania grow and prosper.

UNITED STATES HISTORY: 1607-1753 / *The Colonial Heritage*

The first British attempt to establish a colony in what is now the United States took place in 1585. Sir Walter Raleigh sent settlers to Roanoke Island, off the coast of North Carolina. But this attempt at colonization failed (see LOST COLONY).

In 1607, a small band of about 100 British colonists reached the coast near Chesapeake Bay. They founded Jamestown, the first permanent British settlement in North America (see JAMESTOWN). During the next 150 years, a steady stream of colonists came to America and settled near the coast. Most of them were British, but they also included people from France, Germany, Holland, Ireland, and other countries.

The earliest colonists faced great hardship and danger in the wilderness. They suffered from lack of food and from disease, and were sometimes attacked by Indians. But the colonists soon established productive farms and plantations; built towns, roads, churches, and schools; and began many small industries. They prospered economically and, for the most part, maintained peaceful relations with the Indians.

The American colonists also developed political practices and social beliefs that have had a major influence on the history of the United States. They made strides toward democratic government, and they placed a high value on individual freedom and on hard work as a means of getting ahead.

The Thirteen Colonies

In the early 1600's, the British king began granting charters for the purpose of establishing colonies in America. The charters went to companies of merchants and to individuals called *proprietors*. The merchants and proprietors were responsible for recruiting people to settle in America and, at first, for governing them. By the mid-1700's, most of the settlements had been formed into 13 British colonies. Each colony had a governor and legislature, but each was under the ultimate control of the British government.

The 13 colonies stretched from what is now Maine in the north to Georgia in the south. They included the New England Colonies of Massachusetts, Connecticut, Rhode Island, and New Hampshire in the far north; the Middle Colonies of New York, New Jersey, Pennsylvania, and Delaware; Virginia and Maryland along Chesapeake Bay; and the Southern Colonies of North Carolina, South Carolina, and Georgia in the far south.

Virginia and Maryland were among the earliest British colonies. They were founded for different reasons, but they developed in much the same way.

Virginia began with the Jamestown settlement of 1607. The London Company, an organization of English merchants, sent the settlers to America, hoping that they would find gold and other treasures. But the settlers found no treasures, and faced great hardships. Captain John Smith played a leading role in helping the colony survive in its early days. In about 1612, some Jamestown colonists began growing tobacco, which the London Company sold in Europe. The crop soon became popular, and—as tobacco production mounted—Virginia prospered. New farms and settlements sprang up in the colony.

Maryland was founded by the Calverts, a family of wealthy English Roman Catholics. Catholics were persecuted in England, and the Calverts wanted to provide a place where Catholics could enjoy freedom. In 1632, Cecilius Calvert became proprietor of the Maryland area. Colonists, led by Leonard Calvert, established the first Maryland settlement in 1634. The Maryland settlers also raised tobacco. As tobacco production increased, their colony grew and prospered.

The people of Virginia and Maryland made important strides toward democracy and individual liberty. The Virginians appealed to the London Company for a voice in their local government. The company wanted to attract newcomers to its colony, and so it agreed. In 1619, it established the House of Burgesses, the first representative legislature in America (see HOUSE OF BURGESSES). Maryland attracted both Catholic and Protestant settlers. In 1649, the Calverts granted religious freedom to people of both faiths. This was the first religious toleration act in North America.

New England. Puritans, originally financed by English merchants, founded the New England Colonies. Puritans were English Protestants who faced persecution because of their opposition to the Church of England, Britain's official church. See PURITAN.

In 1620, a group of *Separatists* (Puritans who had separated from the Church of England) and other colonists settled in New England. Called *Pilgrims*, they founded Plymouth Colony—the second permanent British settlement in North America. Between 1628 and 1630, Puritans founded the Massachusetts Bay Colony at what are now Salem and Boston. Plymouth became part of Massachusetts Colony in 1691. See PLYMOUTH COLONY; MASSACHUSETTS BAY COLONY.

Settlers spreading out from Massachusetts founded the three other colonies in New England. Connecticut was first settled in 1633 and became a colony in 1636. Colonists settled in Rhode Island in 1636. Rhode Island became a colony in 1647. New Hampshire, first settled in 1623, became a colony in 1680.

Important Puritan leaders of the New England Colonies included governors William Bradford of Plymouth and John Winthrop of Massachusetts, and Roger Williams, the founder of Rhode Island.

Life in New England centered around towns. Each family farmed its own plot of land, but they all lived close together in a town. The early New England colonists relied on farming to earn a living. But before long, the New Englanders started many small industries, including fishing, lumber, and crafts.

The Puritans also contributed to democracy in

Period Facts in Brief

First Permanent Settlement, Each Colony

Virginia (1607), Massachusetts (1620), New Hampshire (1623), New York (1624), Connecticut (1633), Maryland (1634), Rhode Island (1636), Delaware (1638), Pennsylvania (1643), North Carolina (about 1653), New Jersey (1660), South Carolina (1670), Georgia (1733).

Important Dates

1607 About 100 colonists founded Jamestown, the first permanent British settlement in North America.

1619 Virginia established the House of Burgesses, the first representative legislature in America.

1620 The Pilgrims founded Plymouth Colony, the second permanent British settlement in North America.

1624 The Dutch established the settlement of New Netherland.

1636 Harvard—the first college in the colonies—was founded.

1638 People from Sweden established the settlement of New Sweden.

1647 Massachusetts established the first colonial public school system.

1649 Maryland passed the first religious toleration act in North America.

1664 England took control of New Netherland and New Sweden.

1672 The Boston Post Road was completed, linking Boston and New York City.

1704 *The Boston News-Letter,* the first successful colonial newspaper, began publication.

1752 Benjamin Franklin flew a homemade kite during a storm to prove that lightning is a form of electricity.

Population Growth and Change

Total population, about 100

1607 |

Rural, 100%

Total population, 1,328,000

1753

Rural, 98%   Urban, 2%

WORLD BOOK map

The Thirteen Colonies stretched along the eastern coast of North America. French territory lay to the north and west of the colonies, and Spanish territory lay to the south.

America. The Pilgrims created the *Mayflower Compact*, an agreement among the adult males to provide "just and equal laws" for all (see MAYFLOWER COMPACT). The New England Puritans also held town meetings, where the adult males worked together to frame laws.

The Middle Colonies. Soon after British settlement started, the Dutch founded New Netherland, a trading post and colony that included what are now New York and northern New Jersey. They began a permanent settlement in New York in 1624, and in New Jersey in 1660. In 1638, the Swedes established a trading post and settlement called New Sweden in present-day Delaware and southern New Jersey. The Dutch claimed New Sweden in 1655. But in 1664, the British—far better established in America than the Dutch—took over New Netherland and New Sweden.

King Charles II of England gave the New York and New Jersey territory to his brother, James, Duke of York. Friends of the duke founded huge farming estates in northern New York. New York City developed from the Dutch city of New Amsterdam in southern New York. It became a shipping and trading center. The Duke of York gave New Jersey to two of his friends who allowed much political and religious freedom. As a result, New Jersey attracted many settlers.

Swedes established a small settlement in what is now Pennsylvania in 1643. In 1681, William Penn of England received a charter that made him proprietor of Pennsylvania. Penn was a *Quaker*—a religious group that was persecuted in many countries (see QUAKERS). At Penn's urging, Quakers and other settlers who sought freedom flocked to Pennsylvania. Penn carefully planned settlements in his colony, and Pennsylvania thrived. Philadelphia, one of the settlements, became the largest city in colonial America. Penn also became proprietor of the Delaware area.

The Southern Colonies. In 1663, King Charles II gave the land between Virginia and Florida, called Carolina, to eight proprietors. Virginians had set up a settlement in the northern part of Carolina about 10 years earlier. After 1663, Carolina attracted British settlers, French Protestants called Huguenots, and Americans from other colonies. In 1712, the northern two-thirds of the region was divided into two colonies, North Carolina and South Carolina. North Carolina developed as a colony of small farms and fur trading activity. In South Carolina, wealthy landowners established rice and indigo plantations. The plantations required many laborers, and landowners filled this need by bringing many blacks to the colony as slaves. The coastal settlement of Charleston, S.C., became a rich seaport and lively social center.

The southern one-third of Carolina remained largely unsettled until 1733. Then, James Oglethorpe of England founded Georgia there. Oglethorpe hoped Georgia would become a colony of small farms. The colony's charter prohibited the importation of blacks so that neither slavery nor plantations would develop. But by 1750, Georgia law had been changed to allow settlers to bring in slaves, and plantations soon developed.

Life in Colonial America

Reports of the economic success and religious and political freedom of the early colonists attracted a steady flow of new settlers. Through immigration and natural growth, the colonial population rose to $1\frac{1}{3}$ million by 1753. Most of the settlers came from Britain, but the colonies also drew newcomers from almost every other country of Western Europe. In addition, the slave trade brought in so many Africans that, by the 1750's, blacks made up about 20 per cent of the population. Yet despite the varied backgrounds of the early settlers, Americans of the mid-1700's had—as one writer said— "melted into a new race of men."

The Colonists. Europeans knew that a person who went to America faced great hardship and danger. But

Detail of *Baltimore in 1752* (about 1807), an aquatint by Daniel Bowley based on a drawing by John Moale; Maryland Historical Society, Baltimore

Many of the Early Settlers grouped together in small villages. Baltimore, Md., *above*, began as a cluster of houses and other buildings along the banks of the Patapsco River. Colonists fished in the river, *left foreground*, and grew tobacco in a large field, *far right*.

Library of Congress

A TOBACCO PLANTATION

New York Public Library, Arents Collection

The Industrious Colonists worked hard to establish communities in the wilderness. A Northern colonist, *left,* shaves a board to size for a house he is building. Slaves on a Southern plantation, *right,* pack tobacco for shipment to Europe as plantation owners look on.

the New World also offered people the opportunity for a new start in life. As a result, many people were eager to become colonists.

Some Europeans came to America seeking religious freedom. In addition to the Puritans, Roman Catholics, Quakers, and Huguenots, they included Jews and members of German Protestant sects.

Other Europeans became colonists for economic reasons. Some of them were well enough off, but saw America as a place where they could become rich. Many poor Europeans also became colonists. Most of them came to America as *indentured servants.* An indentured servant agreed to work for another person, called a *master,* in America. In return, the master paid for the servant's transportation and provided him with food, clothing, and shelter. Agreements between servants and masters lasted up to seven years, after which the servant was free to work for himself.

Still other people who came to America had no choice in the matter. They included prisoners from overcrowded English jails, Irishmen captured by the English in battle, and black Africans captured in intertribal warfare and sold to European traders. The prisoners and captives were sold into service in America.

At first, the blacks had the same legal status as white indentured servants. But by about 1660, black equality had faded. Many masters began extending the period of service of their black servants indefinitely. This marked the beginning of slavery in North America. Some people in all the American colonies owned slaves, but slavery became more common in the South than in the North. The South had plantations that required large numbers of laborers, and the plantation owners found it profitable to buy slaves to do the work.

The Economy. The earliest colonists had to struggle to produce enough food to stay alive. But before long, colonial America had a thriving economy. Planters

grew large crops of rice, indigo, and tobacco. Small farmers raised livestock and such crops as corn and wheat. When not busy in their fields, many farmers fished or hunted. Some cut lumber from forests to provide the materials for such products as barrels and ships. The colonists used part of what they produced, but they exported large quantities of goods. They traded chiefly with Britain, whose manufacturing firms depended on raw materials from its colonies. In return, they received manufactured goods. The colonies also traded with the French, Dutch, and Spanish.

Economic and Social Opportunity. Colonial America, like Europe, had both wealthy upper-class people and poor lower-class people. But in Europe, old traditions made economic and social advancement rare. America had no such traditions. Advancement was possible for everyone willing to work hard except slaves. In the New World, land was plentiful and easy to obtain, and there were many opportunities to start new businesses. Indentured servants often obtained land or worked in a trade after their period of service ended. Often, they or their sons became well-to-do merchants or landowners. The colonies had a great need for professional people, such as clergymen, lawyers, physicians, and schoolteachers. Because little training was required for these jobs, they were open to almost everyone.

The Colonists and Government. The colonists rejected the old idea that government was an institution inherited from the past. Instead, they regarded it as something they themselves had created for their own use. The colonists lived under British rule. But to them, laws made in Britain meant little until they were enforced on the spot. They often ignored British laws. This independent attitude would soon lead to a clash between the Americans and the British.

For more information on life in the American Colonies, see COLONIAL LIFE IN AMERICA.

Detail of *Raising the Liberty Pole*, an engraving by John McRae; Kennedy Galleries, Inc., New York City

Joyful Celebrations followed the signing of the Declaration of Independence on July 4, 1776. The scene above shows colonists raising a liberty pole to mark the occasion. At the right, colonial army officers sign up a volunteer for service in the war for independence against Great Britain.

UNITED STATES HISTORY: 1754-1783 / *The Movement for Independence*

Relations between the American Colonies and Great Britain began to break down during the mid-1700's. Little by little, Britain tightened its control over the colonies. Its leaders passed laws that taxed the colonists and restricted their freedom. The colonists had become accustomed to governing themselves, and had developed a sense of unity and independence. As a result, they deeply resented what they considered British interference in their affairs. Friction between the Americans and British mounted, and, on April 19, 1775, the Revolutionary War broke out between the two sides. During the war—on July 4, 1776—the colonists boldly declared their independence from their mighty British rulers. In 1783, they defeated the British and made their claim to independence stick.

Background to the Revolution

The French and Indian War. Great Britain and France had struggled for control of eastern North America throughout the colonial period. As their settlements moved inland, both nations claimed the vast territory between the Appalachian Mountains and the Mississippi River. The struggle led to the outbreak of the French and Indian War in 1754.

The British won the war, and, under the Treaty of Paris of 1763, Britain gained control of: (1) all of what is now Canada, and (2) all French territory east of the Mississippi River except New Orleans. Britain also received Florida from Spain in 1763. As a result, the British controlled all of North America from the Atlantic Ocean to the Mississippi River.

The French and Indian War was a turning point in American history. It triggered a series of British policy changes that eventually led to the colonial independence movement. See FRENCH AND INDIAN WARS (The French and Indian War).

British Policy Changes. The French and Indian War created problems for the British. After the war, Britain had to find ways to strengthen its control over its enlarged American territory. Also, Britain had spent so much money fighting the French and Indian War that its national debt had nearly doubled. George III, who

94

had become king of Great Britain in 1760, instructed the British Parliament to establish policies to solve these problems. Parliament soon began passing laws that restricted the freedom of the American colonists, taxed them, or both.

In 1763, Parliament voted to station a standing army in North America to strengthen British control. Two years later, in the Quartering Act, it ruled that colonists must provide British troops with living quarters and supplies. Britain also sought to keep peace in North America by establishing good relations with the Indians. The Indians had already lost a good deal of territory to the white settlers. A British proclamation of October, 1763, prohibited American colonists from settling west of the Appalachian Mountains until treaties with the Indians might open up areas there.

King George and Parliament believed the time had come for the colonists to start obeying trade regulations and paying their share of the cost of maintaining the British Empire. In 1764, Parliament passed the Sugar Act. This law provided for the efficient collection of taxes on molasses brought into the colonies. It also gave British officials the right to search the premises of persons suspected of violating the law. The Stamp Act of 1765 extended to the colonies the traditional English tax on newspapers, legal documents, and other printed matter (see STAMP ACT).

Colonial Reaction. The colonists bitterly opposed the new British policies. They claimed that Britain had no right to restrict their settlement or deny their freedom in any other way. They also strongly opposed British taxes. The colonists were not represented in Parliament. Therefore, they argued, Britain had no right to tax them. The colonists expressed this belief in the slogan, "Taxation Without Representation is Tyranny."

To protest the new laws, colonists organized a widespread boycott of British goods. Many colonists joined secret clubs called *Sons of Liberty.* These groups threatened to use violence to prevent enforcement of the laws (see SONS OF LIBERTY). In 1765, representatives of nine colonies met in the Stamp Act Congress to consider joint action against Britain.

A Brief Easing of Tensions. The colonial boycott and resistance alarmed Britain's leaders. In 1766,

Parliament repealed the offensive Stamp Act. But at the same time, it declared that Britain still had the right to make laws for the colonies.

The Road to Independence

Renewed Conflict. The relaxation of tensions between the Americans and the British proved to be short-lived. In 1767, Parliament passed the Townshend Acts, which taxed lead, paint, paper, and tea imported into the colonies. These and other laws renewed discontent among the colonists. As tensions between the Americans and British grew, Britain reacted by sending troops into Boston and New York City.

The sight of British troops in the city streets aroused colonial anger. On March 5, 1770, Boston civilians taunted a group of troops. The troops fired on the civilians, killing three persons and wounding eight others, two of whom died later. This incident, called the Boston Massacre, shocked Americans and unnerved the British. See BOSTON MASSACRE.

In 1770, Parliament repealed all provisions of the Townshend Acts with one exception—the tax on tea. Three years later, Parliament reduced the tax on tea sold by the East India Company, a British firm. The British actions offended the colonists in two ways. They reaffirmed Britain's right to tax the colonists and gave

Period Facts in Brief

Important Dates

1756 A stagecoach line linked New York City and Philadelphia.

c. 1757 The first street lights in the colonies were installed in Philadelphia.

1763 Britain defeated France in the French and Indian War and gained control of eastern North America.

1763 Britain stationed a standing army in North America and prohibited colonists from settling west of the Appalachian Mountains.

1765 The British Parliament passed the Stamp Act, taxing newspapers, legal documents, and other printed matter in the colonies.

1770 British troops killed American civilians in the Boston Massacre.

1773 Colonists staged the Boston Tea Party, dumping British tea into Boston Harbor.

1774 The Intolerable Acts closed Boston Harbor and included other steps to punish the colonists.

1774 The First Continental Congress met to consider action against the British.

1775 The Revolutionary War between the colonists and the British began.

1776 The colonists adopted the Declaration of Independence and formed the United States of America.

1781 The Americans defeated the British at Yorktown, Va., in the last major battle of the Revolutionary War.

1783 The Treaty of Paris officially ended the Revolutionary War.

Population Growth and Change

Total population, 1,360,000

1754

Rural, 98%   Urban, 2%

Total population, 3,125,000

1783

Rural, 96%   Urban, 4%

affix the STAMP.

This is the Place to

The Stamp Act, passed by Parliament in 1765, required colonists to buy stamps as a tax on printed matter. A tax stamp appears at the left, *above.* A colonial illustrator drew a skull and crossbones—a symbol of death—*right,* to protest the law.

the East India Company an unfair advantage in the tea trade. Furious Americans vowed not to use tea and colonial merchants refused to sell it. On Dec. 16, 1773, a group of American colonists staged the Boston Tea Party to dramatize their opposition. Dressed as Indians, the colonists boarded East India Company ships and threw tea the ships contained into Boston Harbor. See BOSTON TEA PARTY.

In 1774—in the Quebec Act—Britain extended the boundary of its colony of Quebec to include territory north of the Ohio River. Quebec had a large French population, and the Americans resented the expansion of the colony. See QUEBEC ACT.

The Intolerable Acts. Angered by the Boston Tea Party, Parliament passed laws to punish the colonists early in 1774. Called the Intolerable Acts by the Americans, the laws included provisions that closed the port of Boston, gave increased power to the British royal governor of the colony of Massachusetts, and required the colonists to house and feed British soldiers. See INTOLERABLE ACTS.

The First Continental Congress. The Intolerable Acts stirred colonial anger more than ever before. On Sept. 5, 1774, delegates from 12 colonies met in the First Continental Congress in Philadelphia. The delegates were serious men who disliked lawlessness, and they still hoped for a settlement with the British. They reaffirmed American loyalty to Britain and agreed that Parliament had the power to direct colonial foreign affairs. But at the same time, the delegates called for an end to all trade with Great Britain until Parliament repealed the Intolerable Acts. King George shattered hope for reconciliation by insisting that the colonies either submit to British rule or be crushed. See CONTINENTAL CONGRESS.

The Revolutionary War Begins. On April 19, 1775, British troops tried to seize the military supplies of the Massachusetts militia. This action led to the start of the Revolutionary War. Colonists—first at Lexington, and then at Concord, Mass.—took up arms to turn back the British. At Concord, the determined Americans stopped the British advance. Word of their success spread, and hope for victory over Britain grew. Colonial leaders met in the Second Continental Congress on May 10, 1775. The Congress faced the task of preparing the colonies for war. It organized the Continental Army, which colonists from all walks of life joined. On June 15, the Congress named George Washington of Virginia commander in chief of the army.

King George officially declared the colonies in rebellion on Aug. 23, 1775. He warned the Americans to end their rebellion or face certain defeat by Britain. But the threat had no effect on the colonists' determination to fight on. Some of the people—called *Loyalists*—favored submission to British rule, but a growing number of Americans now supported the fight for independence. Many people who had been unsure were convinced by reading Thomas Paine's pamphlet *Common Sense*. Paine—in this brilliant plea for the cause of freedom—stated the simple alternatives open to the Americans: They must either accept the tyranny of the British Crown or throw off their shackles by proclaiming a republic.

The Declaration of Independence. On July 4, 1776, the Second Continental Congress officially declared independence and formed the United States of America by adopting the Declaration of Independence. Written by Thomas Jefferson of Virginia, the declaration was a sweeping indictment of the king, Parliament, and the British people. It also set forth certain self-evident truths that were basic to the revolutionary cause. It said that all men are created equal, and are endowed by their Creator with rights to life, liberty, and the pursuit of happiness. To protect those rights, men organized governments, and the governments derived their powers from the consent of the governed. But

Detail of *The Battle of Lexington, April 19th, 1775* (1775), an engraving by Amos Doolittle; Connecticut Historical Society, Hartford

The Revolutionary War began on April 19, 1775, on the village green in Lexington, Mass., *left.* British troops, *in red coats,* routed the Americans. But later in the day, colonists at nearby Concord stopped a British advance.

when a government ceased to preserve the rights, it was the duty of the people to change the government, or abolish it and form a new one.

Thus the colonists were fighting for philosophical principles as well as specific objectives. The spirit aroused by the Declaration of Independence was an important factor in the ultimate American victory. See DECLARATION OF INDEPENDENCE.

Victory Over a Great Empire. The Americans were challenging the world's most powerful empire in the Revolutionary War. They lacked a well-trained army, officers who were accustomed to commanding troops, and munitions and money. But they had the advantage of fighting on their home territory. The British, on the other hand, had well-trained and well-equipped troops and officers, but they were fighting in an unfamiliar land thousands of miles from home. The American cause was also helped by aid from France and other European nations that opposed Britain.

The Revolutionary War raged on through the 1770's. Then, on Oct. 19, 1781, the Americans won a decisive victory at the Battle of Yorktown in Virginia. The main part of the British Army surrendered there, and the Americans had—in effect—won the war. Two years of peace negotiations and occasional fighting followed. Finally, on Sept. 3, 1783, the Americans and the British signed the Treaty of Paris of 1783, officially ending the Revolutionary War.

For a detailed account of the war for independence, see REVOLUTIONARY WAR IN AMERICA.

American Attitudes and Independence

Through the years, the American people had developed attitudes that help explain their strong desire to gain freedom from the British. These attitudes included a deep belief in government by the people, a sense of unity, an optimistic view of the future, and strong nationalistic feelings.

Government by the People. When the American colonies were first settled, merchants and large landowners held most of the political power. But little by little, other colonists began to use the political process to express their views on important issues. Such issues included the ownership of land, representation in government, taxation, and the role of the church in society. The colonists learned to back candidates for public office who would represent their views and challenge the power of the ruling class.

The ruling merchants and landowners presented only half-hearted resistance to this widening of political power. They needed the aid of the lower classes to back their opposition to British policy. Furthermore, the very argument for self-government that the colonial leaders used against the British justified those seeking to share political power within the colonies. By 1774, America no longer was a society in which the few ruled with the passive consent of the many. Instead, large numbers of people had an active voice in government.

Unity, Optimism, and Nationalism. Through the years, the colonists had developed feelings of unity. Their opposition to the British led them to rely on one another more and more. Groups called *Committees of Correspondence* were set up throughout the colonies to provide organized opposition to Britain. Supported voluntarily by the people, the committees decided what action should be taken against the British in times of crisis. See COMMITTEES OF CORRESPONDENCE.

The colonial Americans also shared an optimistic view of their future. They were impressed by the rapid growth of their colonies, and they loved to calculate how much more their population and wealth would yet increase.

Unity and progress led to an increasing sense of nationalism among the people. By 1774, the colonists no longer thought of themselves as transplanted Europeans, but rather as Americans.

Congress Voting Independence (begun late 1700's), an oil painting on canvas by Robert Edge Pine and Edward Savage; Historical Society of Pennsylvania, Philadelphia

The Vote for Independence from Great Britain took place on July 2, 1776. On July 4, the Second Continental Congress officially adopted the Declaration of Independence, and the United States of America was born.

Election Day at the State House (1816), India ink and water color on paper by John Lewis Krimmel; Historical Society of Pennsylvania, Philadelphia

Democratic Elections were among the important features written into the new nation's Constitution by the Founding Fathers. Large numbers of voters, *above*, turned out in Philadelphia for an election in 1816. American flags waving in the breeze added to the patriotic spirit of the event.

UNITED STATES HISTORY: 1784-1819 / *Forming a New Nation*

As a result of the Treaty of Paris of 1783, the new nation controlled all of North America from the Atlantic Ocean to the Mississippi River between Canada and Florida. Canada, to the north, remained British territory. Great Britain returned Florida to Spain, and Spain continued to control the area west of the Mississippi River.

The original 13 colonies made up the first 13 states of the United States. Eventually, the American land west of the Appalachian Mountains was divided into territories.

At the end of the Revolutionary War, the new nation was still a loose confederation of states. But in 1787, American leaders got together and wrote the Constitution of the United States. The Constitution became the country's basic law and welded it together into a solid political unit. The men who wrote it included some of the most famous and important figures in American history. Among them were George Washington and James Madison of Virginia, Alexander Hamilton of New York, and Benjamin Franklin of Pennsylvania. The authors of the Constitution, along with other early leaders such as Thomas Jefferson of Virginia, won lasting fame as the Founding Fathers of the United States.

At the start of its history, the United States faced severe financial problems. But before long, the skill of its leaders and the spirit and hard work of its people put the country on a sound economic footing. Early America also faced threats from powerful European nations. But masterful diplomacy by Washington and other leaders guided the country through its early years in peace. The peace ended with the War of 1812, in which the United States and Great Britain fought to a standstill. After the war, America focused its attention on its own development, and entered a period of bustling economic growth.

Establishing a Government

The American people began setting up a new system of government as soon as they declared their independence. Each of the new states had its own constitution before the Revolutionary War ended. The state constitutions gave the people certain liberties, usually including freedom of speech, religion, and the press. In 1781, the states set up a federal government under laws called the Articles of Confederation. But the Articles proved to be inadequate for running the government. The shortcomings of the Articles led to the formation of a new government under the Constitution.

Background to the Constitution. The Articles of Confederation gave the federal government the power to declare war and manage foreign affairs. But the Articles did not allow the government to collect taxes, regulate trade, or otherwise direct the activities of the states.

Daniel Boone Coming Through the Cumberland Gap by George Caleb Bingham; Courtesy of Washington University, St. Louis

THE GROWTH OF A NATION

The development of the United States is an exciting and remarkable adventure story. It is the record of a brave and freedom-loving people who built a wilderness into one of the world's greatest nations. This special Trans-Vision® unit illustrates major stages in the growth of the United States. The base map shows the strip of land that the 13 English colonies occupied along the Atlantic Coast in 1776. The Trans-Vision® traces the westward expansion of the United States in a series of transparent maps. The series opens with a look at the new nation in 1791, when 14 states had ratified the United States Constitution. At that time, the nation's boundaries stretched westward to the Mississippi River. During the first half of the 1800's, courageous explorers and hardy pioneers pushed across the continent. By 1821, the United States had 24 states and included the vast territory of the Louisiana Purchase, which had been bought from France in 1803. By 1854, the general boundaries of the mainland United States had been formed and the nation consisted of 31 states. When New Mexico and Arizona became the 47th and 48th states in 1912, the mainland United States was completed. This unit also examines the various ways in which the United States added the territories that helped form its boundaries. The map on the inside back cover outlines these territories, and the text on the back cover describes the impact of each acquisition.

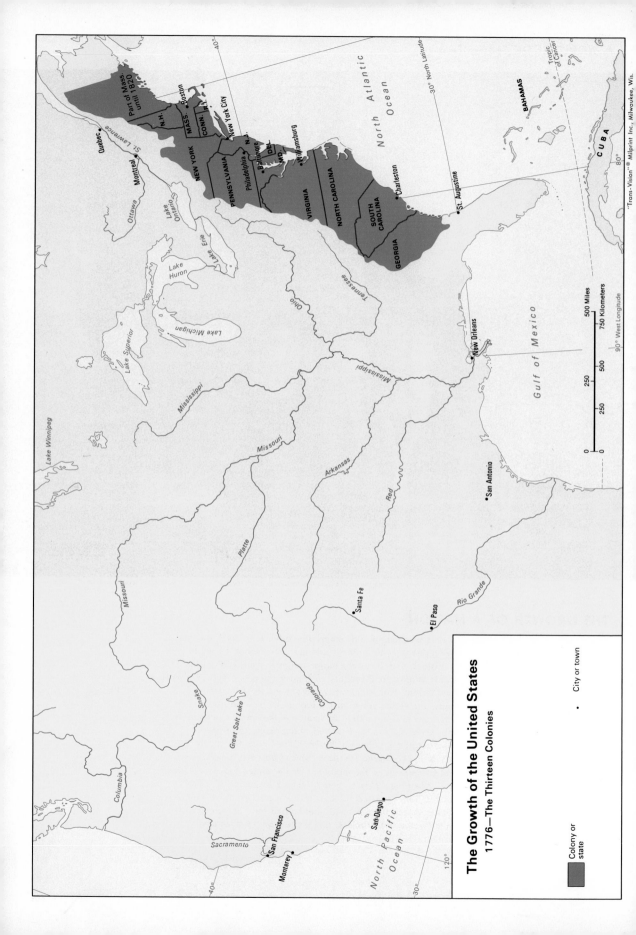

The Growth of the United States
1776—The Thirteen Colonies

Colony or state

• City or town

"Trans-Vision"® Milprint Inc., Milwaukee, Wis.

Part of Mass. until 1820

N.H.
MASS.
CONN.
R.I.
Boston
New York City
NEW YORK
PENNSYLVANIA
N.J.
Philadelphia
Baltimore
DEL.
MD.
Williamsburg
VIRGINIA
NORTH CAROLINA
SOUTH CAROLINA
GEORGIA
Charleston
St. Augustine

Quebec
Montreal
Ottawa
St. Lawrence

Lake Ontario
Lake Erie
Lake Huron
Lake Michigan
Lake Superior
Lake Winnipeg

North Atlantic Ocean

BAHAMAS
CUBA

Tropic of Cancer
30° North Latitude
40°

Tennessee
Ohio
Mississippi
Missouri
Arkansas
Red
San Antonio
New Orleans

Gulf of Mexico

500 Miles
250
0

750 Kilometers
500
250
0

90° West Longitude

Santa Fe
El Paso
Rio Grande

Missouri
Platte
Snake
Colorado
Great Salt Lake
Columbia
Sacramento
San Francisco
Monterey
San Diego

North Pacific Ocean

120°
40°
30°

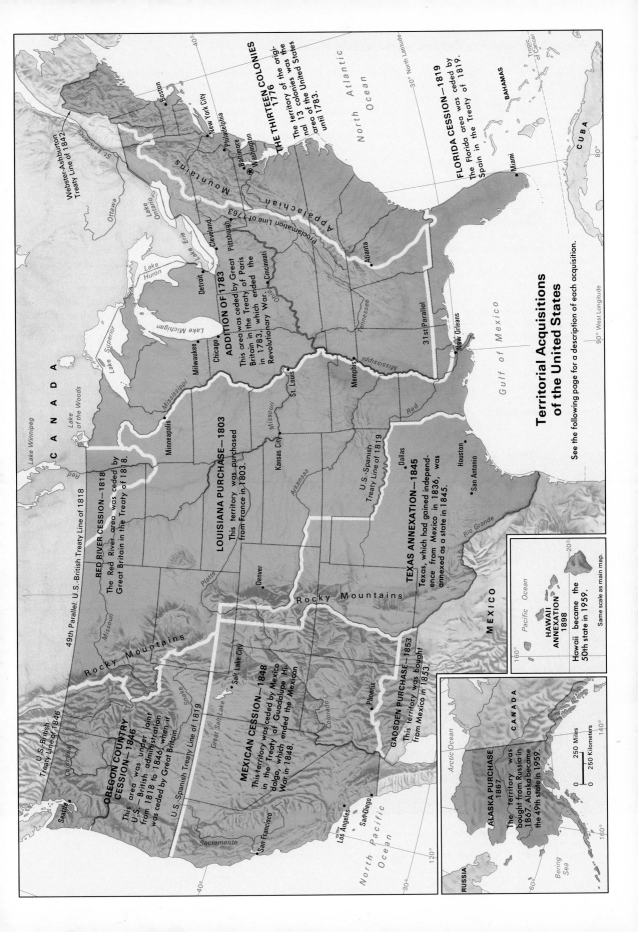

Territorial Acquisitions
of the United States

See the following page for a description of each acquisition.

THE THIRTEEN COLONIES 1776
The territory of the original 13 colonies was the area of the United States until 1783.

FLORIDA CESSION—1819
The Florida area was ceded by the Treaty of 1819 with Spain in the Treaty of 1819.

ADDITION OF 1783
This area was ceded by Great Britain in the Treaty of Paris in 1783, which ended the Revolutionary War.

RED RIVER CESSION—1818
The Red River area was ceded by Great Britain in the Treaty of 1818.

LOUISIANA PURCHASE—1803
This territory was purchased from France in 1803.

TEXAS ANNEXATION—1845
Texas, which had gained independence from Mexico in 1836, was annexed as a state in 1845.

OREGON COUNTRY CESSION—1846
This area was under joint U.S.–British administration from 1818 to 1846, when it was ceded by Great Britain.

MEXICAN CESSION—1848
This territory was ceded by Mexico in the Treaty of Guadalupe Hidalgo, which ended the Mexican War in 1848.

GADSDEN PURCHASE—1853
This territory was bought from Mexico in 1853.

HAWAII ANNEXATION 1898
Hawaii became the 50th state in 1959.

Same scale as main map.

ALASKA PURCHASE 1867
The territory was bought from Russia in 1867. Alaska became the 49th state in 1959.

Webster-Ashburton Treaty Line of 1842

49th Parallel, U.S.-British Treaty Line of 1818

U.S.-British Treaty Line of 1846

U.S.-Spanish Treaty Line of 1819

U.S.-Spanish Treaty Line of 1819

Proclamation Line of 1763

31st Parallel

250 Miles
250 Kilometers

Major Territorial Acquisitions of the United States

The United States added territory in many ways. It bought vast areas, gained others by treaty, and won much land through war. Following are brief descriptions of the nation's major territorial acquisitions from 1776 to 1898.

The 13 Colonies occupied what became the original area of the United States. The 13 original states and parts of Maine, Vermont, and West Virginia were formed from this area.

The Addition of 1783 extended the nation's boundaries north to the Great Lakes, south to the 31st parallel, and west to the Mississippi River. All or most of nine states were formed from this region, which more than doubled the territory of the United States.

The Louisiana Purchase of 1803 added 827,987 square miles (2,144,476 square kilometers) of land to the United States. The federal government paid France about $15 million for the territory. Part or all of 15 states were formed from the area.

The Red River Cession was included in a treaty between the United States and Great Britain in 1818. Parts of Minnesota, North Dakota, and South Dakota were formed from this area. The treaty also made the 49th parallel the northern boundary of the United States between the Lake of the Woods and the high land in the Rocky Mountains called the *Continental Divide*.

The Florida Cession of 1819 gave the United States the areas then called East Florida and West Florida. Parts of Louisiana, Mississippi, and Alabama and all of Florida were formed from this territory.

The Texas Annexation of 1845 added what was then the nation's largest state. Most of the present boundaries of Texas were established in 1850, when the state gave up claims to western lands.

The Oregon Country Cession extended the western border of the United States to the Pacific Ocean in 1846. This cession also established the 49th parallel as the nation's northern boundary in the area west of the Continental Divide. Idaho, Washington, and Oregon were formed from the Oregon region.

The Mexican Cession of 1848 added 525,000 square miles (1,360,000 square kilometers) of land to the United States. The government paid Mexico $15 million for this region, which became California, Nevada, Utah, and part of four other states.

The Gadsden Purchase of 1853 gave the United States 29,640 square miles (76,770 square kilometers) of land in what is now Arizona and New Mexico. The United States paid Mexico $10 million for the land.

The Alaska Purchase of 1867 added 586,000 square miles (1,518,000 square kilometers) of territory to the country. The government paid Russia $7,200,000 for this region.

The Hawaii Annexation of 1898 gave the United States its largest present overseas possession. The Hawaiian Islands cover 6,450 square miles (16,710 square kilometers).

Detail of an oil painting (1912); Montana Historical Society, Helena

The Exploration of the West increased rapidly after the Louisiana Purchase in 1803. The American artist Charles Marion Russell painted this scene of the meeting between the explorers Meriwether Lewis and William Clark, *far right*, and the Flathead Indians in Montana in 1805.

Under the Articles, each state worked independently for its own ends. Yet the new nation faced problems that demanded a strong federal government. The United States had piled up a huge national debt during the Revolutionary War. But since the federal government could not collect taxes, it was unable to pay the debt and put the country on a sound economic footing. The government even lacked the means for raising money to provide for national defense. The federal government had no power to regulate the nation's trade. In addition, some states issued their own paper money, causing sharp changes in the value of currency and economic chaos. See ARTICLES OF CONFEDERATION.

Creating the Constitution. In 1786, Virginia persuaded five states to send delegates to a convention at Annapolis, Md., to discuss interstate commerce. The delegates decided that the Articles of Confederation would have to be revised and wrote a report calling for all states to join in a new convention. In 1787, delegates from every state except Rhode Island met in Philadelphia's Independence Hall to consider revisions to the Articles. Rhode Island did not take part because it resented "outside interference" in its affairs. The delegates decided against simply revising the Articles of Confederation. Instead, they agreed to write an entirely new Constitution. The convention chose George Washington as presiding officer.

The delegates debated long and hard over the contents of the Constitution. Some of them wanted a document that gave much power to the federal government. Others wanted to protect the rights of the states and called for a weak central government. Delegates from large states claimed their states should have greater representation in Congress than the small states. But small-state delegates demanded equal representation.

The delegates finally reached agreement on a new Constitution on Sept. 17, 1787. The document they produced has often been called a work of political genius. The authors skillfully worked out a system of government that satisfied the opposing views of the people of the 1780's. At the same time, they created a system of government flexible enough to continue in its basic form to the present day.

The Constitution provided for a two-house legislature—a House of Representatives and a Senate. Representation in the House was based on population in order to satisfy the large states. All states received equal representation in the Senate, which pleased the small states. The Constitution gave many powers to the federal government, including the rights to collect taxes and regulate trade. But it also reserved powers for the states. The Constitution provided for three branches of government: the executive, headed by a President; the legislature, made up of the two houses of Congress; and the judiciary, or federal court system. In a master stroke of government organization, the creators of the Constitution provided for a system of checks and balances among the three branches. Each branch received powers and duties that ensured that the other branches would not have too much power.

Adopting the Constitution. Before the Constitution became law, it needed *ratification* (approval) by nine states. Some Americans still opposed the Constitution,

Period Facts in Brief

Presidents (with political parties and dates of service)
George Washington, no political party, 1789-1797
John Adams, Federalist, 1797-1801
Thomas Jefferson, Democratic-Republican, 1801-1809
James Madison, Democratic-Republican, 1809-1817
James Monroe, Democratic-Republican, 1817-1825

States in the Union

The 13 states that ratified the Constitution:
Delaware (1787), Pennsylvania (1787), New Jersey (1787), Georgia (1788), Connecticut (1788), Massachusetts (1788), Maryland (1788), South Carolina (1788), New Hampshire (1788), Virginia (1788), New York (1788), North Carolina (1789), Rhode Island (1790).

New states added through 1819:
Vermont (1791), Kentucky (1792), Tennessee (1796), Ohio (1803), Louisiana (1812), Indiana (1816), Mississippi (1817), Illinois (1818), Alabama (1819).

Important Dates

1787 The Founding Fathers wrote the Constitution.
1790's The first U.S. political parties developed.
1790 Samuel Slater built the country's first successful water-powered machines for spinning cotton.
1793 Eli Whitney invented the cotton gin.
1800 Washington, D.C., became the national capital.
1803 The Louisiana Purchase doubled the size of the United States.
1811 Work began on the National Road, which—when completed—linked the East and the Midwest.
1812-1814 The United States and Great Britain fought the War of 1812.
1814 Francis Scott Key wrote "The Star-Spangled Banner."

Population Growth and Change

Total population, 3,240,000

1784

Rural, 96%   Urban, 4%

Total population, 9,358,000

1819

Rural, 93%   Urban, 7%

WORLD BOOK map

The United States After the Revolution extended from the Atlantic Ocean to the Mississippi River. British territory lay to the north, and Spanish territory lay to the west and south.

and fierce debate over ratification broke out. Hamilton, Madison, and John Jay responded to criticism of the document in a series of letters to newspapers. Called *The Federalist*, the letters gained much support for the Constitution (see FEDERALIST, THE). On June 21, 1788, New Hampshire became the ninth state to ratify.

The Bill of Rights. Much opposition to the new Constitution stemmed from the fact that it did not specifically guarantee enough individual rights. In response, 10 amendments known as the Bill of Rights were added to the document. The Bill of Rights became law on Dec. 15, 1791. Among other things, it guaranteed freedom of speech, religion, the press, and the rights to trial by jury and peaceful assembly.

For more details, see CONSTITUTION OF THE UNITED STATES; BILL OF RIGHTS.

Setting Up the Government. The Constitution provided that the President be elected by an Electoral College, a group of men chosen by the states (see ELECTORAL COLLEGE). In 1789, the Electoral College unanimously chose Washington to serve as the first President. It re-elected him unanimously in 1792. The people elected the members of the first House of Representatives, as they do today. But the senators were chosen by the state legislatures, a practice that continued until the early 1900's. The government went into operation in 1789, with its temporary capital in New York City. The capital was moved to Philadelphia in 1790, and to Washington, D.C., in 1800.

Early Problems and Politics

Solving Financial Problems. Financial problems plagued the new government. The national debt piled up during the Revolutionary War threatened the financial structure of the United States. The nation also needed internal improvements such as roads and bridges, but the federal government could not afford to pay for them.

Americans split over how to deal with the financial problems. One group, led by Secretary of the Treasury Alexander Hamilton, wanted the federal government to take vigorous action. Another group, headed by Secretary of State Thomas Jefferson, opposed government participation in economic affairs.

Hamilton proposed that the government increase tariffs and tax certain products made in the United States, such as liquor. The government would use the tax money to pay both its debts and those of the states. It would also have money for ongoing expenses and internal improvements. Hamilton also proposed a government-supported national bank to control government finances.

Jefferson and his followers, who included many Southerners, denounced all of Hamilton's plans. But Jefferson later agreed to support some of Hamilton's financial proposals. In return, Hamilton agreed to support a shift of the national capital to the South. Congress approved Hamilton's financial plan and agreed to locate the capital in the South. Jefferson continued to oppose the national bank proposal. But in 1791, Congress chartered a national bank for 20 years (see BANK OF THE UNITED STATES).

Enforcing Federal Law. The new tax program led to the Whiskey Rebellion. In 1794, farmers in Pennsylvania who made whiskey refused to pay the tax on liquor. President Washington sent in troops who ended the rebellion. Washington's action did much to establish the federal government's authority to enforce its laws within the states. See WHISKEY REBELLION.

Foreign Affairs. The new government also faced problems in foreign affairs. In 1793, France went to war against Britain and Spain. France had helped the Americans in the Revolutionary War, and it now expected U.S. assistance in its war. Americans disagreed over which side to support. Jefferson and his followers wanted the United States to back France, while Hamilton and his group favored the British.

President Washington insisted that the United States

Signing the Constitution (1860's), an oil painting on canvas by Thomas Rossiter; Independence National Historical Park Collection, Philadelphia

The Signing of the Constitution, *above,* ranks among the most historic events in American history. The delegates to the Constitutional Convention signed the document in 1787. Ratified in 1788, the Constitution has served as the basic law of the United States ever since.

remain neutral in the European war. He rejected French demands for support, and also sent diplomats to Britain and Spain to clear up problems with those countries. Chief Justice John Jay, acting for Washington, negotiated the Jay Treaty with Britain in 1794. The treaty's many provisions included a trade agreement with Britain which—in effect—ended American trade with France. It also included a British promise to remove troops still stationed on U.S. territory. In 1795, Thomas Pinckney negotiated the Pinckney Treaty, or Treaty of San Lorenzo, with Spain. This treaty settled a dispute over the Florida border between the United States and Spain and also gave the United States free use of the Mississippi River. See Jay Treaty; Pinckney Treaty.

In 1796, Washington—annoyed by the disputes within his Administration—refused to seek a third term as President. John Adams succeeded him in 1797. At about that time, French warships began attacking American merchant vessels. Adams, like Washington, hoped to use diplomacy to solve foreign problems. He sent diplomats to France to try to end the attacks. But three agents of the French government insulted the diplomats with dishonorable proposals, including a demand for a bribe. The identity of the agents was not revealed. They were simply called X, Y, and Z, and the incident became known as the XYZ Affair.

The XYZ Affair created a furor in the United States. Hamilton and his followers demanded war against France. But Adams was determined to keep the peace. In 1799, he again sent diplomats to France. This time, the United States and France reached a peaceful settlement. See XYZ Affair.

Establishing Political Parties. Washington and many other early American leaders opposed political parties. But in the 1790's, the disputes over government policies led to the establishment of two parties. Hamilton and his followers, chiefly Northerners, formed the Federalist Party. The party favored a strong federal government and generally backed Britain in international disputes. Jefferson and his followers, chiefly Southerners, established the Democratic-Republican Party. The party wanted a weak central government and generally sided with France in foreign disputes. See Federalist Party; Democratic-Republican Party.

The Alien and Sedition Acts. The XYZ Affair had a major impact on American internal policies and politics. After the affair, the Federalists denounced the Democratic-Republicans for their support of France. The Federalists had a majority in Congress. They set out to silence their critics, who included Democratic-Republicans and foreigners living in the United States. In 1798, the Federalist Congress and President Adams —also a Federalist—approved the Alien and Sedition Acts. These laws made it a crime for anyone to criticize the President or Congress, and subjected foreigners to unequal treatment.

A nationwide outcry against these attacks on freedom followed. The protests included the Kentucky and Virginia Resolutions. The resolutions were statements by the Kentucky and Virginia state legislatures that challenged the constitutionality of the Alien and Sedition Acts. The most offensive parts of the Acts soon expired

George Washington, *far right,* became the first American President in 1789. The other men in the picture are the members of his first Cabinet. They are, *left to right,* Henry Knox, Thomas Jefferson, Edmund Randolph, and Alexander Hamilton.

or were repealed. However, the Alien and Sedition Acts gave the Federalists the reputation as a party of oppression. See Alien and Sedition Acts; Kentucky and Virginia Resolutions.

Jeffersonian Democracy

Public reaction to the Alien and Sedition Acts helped Jefferson win election as President in 1800 and again in 1804. Jefferson's political philosophy became known as *Jeffersonian democracy.* Jefferson envisioned the United States as a nation of small farmers. In Jefferson's ideal society, the people would lead simple, but productive, lives and be able to direct their own affairs. Therefore, the need for government would decline. Jefferson took steps to reduce government expenses and the national debt. But in spite of his beliefs and practices, Jefferson found that as President he could not avoid actions that expanded the role of government.

The Louisiana Purchase, the first major action of Jefferson's presidency, almost doubled the size of the United States. In 1801, Jefferson learned that France had taken over from Spain a large area between the Mississippi River and the Rocky Mountains called Louisiana. Spain was a weak nation, and did not pose a threat to the United States. But France—then ruled by Napoleon Bonaparte—was powerful and aggressive. Jefferson viewed French control of Louisiana as a danger to the United States.

In 1803, Jefferson arranged the purchase of the area from France for about $15 million. The Constitution did not authorize the government to buy foreign territory. Jefferson, a defender of strict interpretation of the Constitution, had to admit that he had "stretched the Constitution until it cracked."

The Louisiana Purchase of 1803 added to the United States the territory between the Mississippi River and the Rocky Mountains. The purchase almost doubled the size of the country.

The Louisiana Purchase added 827,987 square miles (2,144,476 square kilometers) of territory to the United States. In 1804, Jefferson sent Meriwether Lewis and William Clark to explore the land. Lewis and Clark traveled all the way to the Pacific Ocean. Their reports provided valuable information about the Indians and the natural wealth of the West. See LOUISIANA PURCHASE; LEWIS AND CLARK EXPEDITION.

The Supreme Court. John Marshall became chief justice of the United States in 1801. Under Marshall, the Supreme Court became a leading force in American society. In 1803, in the case of *Marbury v. Madison*, the court asserted its right to rule on the constitutionality of federal legislation (see MARBURY V. MADISON). From then until Marshall's death in 1835, the court reviewed about 50 cases involving constitutional issues. This role of Marshall's court strengthened the nation by providing a way to ensure that government remained within constitutional bounds. But the Supreme Court also did much to increase the power of the federal government, a development Jefferson had opposed. For example, in *McCulloch v. Maryland* (1819), the court ruled that the federal government has implied powers in addition to those specified in the Constitution. It also said federal authority prevails over state authority when the two conflict (see MCCULLOCH V. MARYLAND).

Jefferson and Foreign Policy. In 1803, Great Britain and France went to war again, and both nations began seizing American merchant ships. The British also *impressed* American seamen, seizing them and forcing them into British service.

Jefferson again found it necessary to use government powers, this time to protect American shipping. At his request, Congress passed trade laws designed to end British and French interference. The Embargo Act of 1807 made it illegal for Americans to export goods to foreign countries. But the embargo threatened to ruin the nation's economy, and was repealed in 1809. The Non-Intercourse Act of 1809 prohibited Americans from trading with Britain and France. But the warring nations still interfered with American trade.

The War of 1812

James Madison succeeded Jefferson as President in 1809. France soon promised to end its interference with American shipping, but Britain did not. Also, people believed the British were encouraging Indians to attack American pioneers moving westward. For these reasons, many Americans demanded war against Britain. They were led by members of Congress from the West and South called *War Hawks*, including Henry Clay of Kentucky and John C. Calhoun of South Carolina. Other Americans, especially New Englanders, opposed the War Hawks' demand. But on June 18, 1812, at Madison's request, Congress declared war on Britain and the War of 1812 had begun.

Neither side gained much advantage early in the war. But on Aug. 24, 1814, British troops captured Washington, D.C., and burned the Capitol and other government buildings. This British action made Americans

Capture of the City of Washington (1815), an anonymous engraving;
Anne S. K. Brown Military Collection, Brown University Library, Providence, R.I.

British Troops captured Washington, D.C., in 1814—during the War of 1812. The British set fire to the United States Capitol, the White House, and other government buildings in the city.

realize their nation's survival was at stake. Large numbers of volunteers rushed into service, and helped stop the British offensive. The Treaty of Ghent of Dec. 24, 1814, officially ended the War of 1812. Neither side won the war and little was gained from the struggle. See WAR OF 1812.

Growing Nationalism

A strong spirit of nationalism swept through the United States following the War of 1812. The war itself gave rise to increased feelings of self-confidence and unity. The peace that followed enabled the nation to concentrate on its own affairs. The bitterness that had marked political disputes eased with the breakup of the Federalist Party. Meanwhile, the nation expanded westward, new states entered the union, and the economy prospered. Historians sometimes call the period from about 1815 to the early 1820's *The Era of Good Feeling* because of its relative peace, unity, and optimism about the future.

Nationalism and the Economy. After the War of 1812, Henry Clay and other nationalists proposed economic measures that came to be called the *American System*. They said the government should raise tariffs to protect American manufacturers and farmers from foreign competition. Industry would then grow and employ more people. More employment would lead to greater consumption of farm products, and so farmers would prosper and buy more manufactured goods. In addition, tariff revenues would enable the government to make needed internal improvements.

The government soon put ideas of the American System into practice. In 1816, Congress enacted a high tariff, and it chartered the second Bank of the United States, to give the government more control over the economy. The government also increased its funding of internal projects, the most important of which was the National Road. Begun in 1811, the road stretched from Cumberland, Md., to Vandalia, Ill., when completed. It became an important route for the shipment of goods and the movement of settlers westward (see NATIONAL ROAD).

A National Culture. Many early Americans had tried to pattern their culture after European civilization. Architects, painters, and writers tended to imitate European models. But in the late 1700's and early 1800's, art and culture more and more reflected American experiences. Architects designed simple, but beautiful, houses that blended into their surroundings. Craftworkers built sturdy furniture that was suited to frontier life, yet so simply elegant as to be considered works of art. The furniture of the Shakers, a religious group, is an example. The nation's literature flourished when it began reflecting American experiences. Political writings such as the works of Thomas Paine and the authors of *The Federalist* had high literary merit. The works of Washington Irving, one of the leading early authors, helped gain respect for American literature.

Decline of the Federalists. In 1814 and 1815, New England Federalists held a secret political meeting in Hartford, Conn. Their opponents charged that they had discussed the *secession* (withdrawal) of the New England States from the Union (see HARTFORD CONVENTION). The Federalists never recovered from the charge, and the party broke up about 1816. James Monroe, the Democratic-Republican presidential candidate in the election of 1820, was unopposed.

New Territory. The United States gained two new pieces of territory between 1815 and 1820. In 1818, a treaty with Britain gave the country the Red River Basin, north of the Louisiana Territory. Spain ceded Florida to the United States in 1819.

"A Fire Bell in the Night." The Era of Good Feeling did not mean an end to all the country's disputes. The issue of slavery was causing deep divisions among the people. Many Northerners were demanding an end to slavery, while Southerners were defending it more and more. Jefferson, then retired, accurately viewed the growing dispute as a warning of approaching disaster, "like a fire bell in the night."

Detail of *Fairview Inn* (1889), a water color on paper by Thomas C. Ruckle; Maryland Historical Society, Baltimore

The National Road was a transportation route in early America. When completed, it stretched from Maryland to Illinois. A steady stream of pioneers moved westward along the road. Inns, like this one near the National Road, provided resting and eating stops for travelers.

Prairie Scene: Mirage (1837), a water color by Alfred Jacob Miller; Walters Art Gallery, Baltimore

Americans Moved Westward by the thousands during the early 1800's. Hardy pioneers, *above*, piled all their belongings into covered wagons and set out to find new homes in the West. The push westward continued until the nation stretched from coast to coast.

UNITED STATES HISTORY: 1820-1849/*Expansion*

During the early 1800's, settlers by the thousands moved westward over the Appalachian Mountains into the new states and territories. Many of these pioneers even settled beyond the country's western boundary. They flocked into Texas, California, and other western lands belonging to Mexico. Americans also settled in the Oregon Country, a large territory between California and Alaska claimed by both Britain and the United States. In the mid-1800's, the United States gained control of the Mexican lands and the southern part of the Oregon Country, and the nation extended from coast to coast.

The pioneers were brave, hardy people who went west in search of a better life. They were attracted by the West's open land, good farmland, and rich mineral and forest resources. Through hard work, they settled the Western wilderness—as earlier Americans had done in the East.

The build-up of the West gave rise to changes in American politics. As areas in the West gained large populations, they were admitted to the Union as states. But wealthy Easterners continued to control governmental and economic policy. Western farmers and frontiersmen, as well as city laborers and craftsmen, soon banded together politically to promote their interests. They found a strong leader in Andrew Jackson, and helped elect him President in 1828. Jackson took steps to reduce the power of wealthy Easterners and aid the "common man." At the same time, other Americans were working for such reforms as women's rights, im-

provements in education, and the abolition of slavery.

The United States and Europe maintained peaceful relations during the Expansion Era. But in 1823, President James Monroe issued the Monroe Doctrine, a statement that warned European countries not to interfere with any of the free nations of the Western Hemisphere (see MONROE DOCTRINE).

America Moves West

By 1820, American pioneers had established many frontier settlements as far west as the Mississippi River. By the 1830's, the Westward Movement had pushed the frontier across the Mississippi, into Iowa, Missouri, Arkansas, and eastern Texas. The land beyond, called the *Great Plains*, was dry and treeless, and seemed to be poor farmland. But explorers, traders, and others who had journeyed farther west told of rich farmland and forests beyond the Rocky Mountains. In the 1840's, large numbers of pioneers made the long journey across the Great Plains to the Far West.

The Pioneers included Easterners from both the North and South. Many other pioneers came from Europe seeking a better life. Some people went west in search of religious freedom. The best known of these were the Mormons, who settled in Utah in 1847.

Most of the pioneers became farmers who owned their own plots. But urban life also moved westward with the frontier. Bustling towns and cities grew up in the West. There, traders in farm goods and other products of the West carried on brisk businesses. The urban

centers also attracted churches, banks, stores, and hotels; and clergymen, craftsmen, doctors, lawyers, lawmen, and schoolteachers.

For more details on the pioneers, see PIONEER LIFE IN AMERICA; WESTWARD MOVEMENT.

Manifest Destiny. By the mid-1840's, thousands of Americans lived in the Oregon Country and on the western land claimed by Mexico. By then, large numbers of Americans had come to believe in the doctrine of *manifest destiny*. That is, they thought the United States should control all of North America. Stirred by this belief, Americans demanded control of Oregon and the Mexican territory.

The conflicting claim with Britain over Oregon was settled with relative ease. Britain decided that the effort needed to hold all of Oregon was not worth while. In 1846, the British turned over to the United States the part of the territory south of the 49th parallel, except Vancouver Island. See OREGON TERRITORY.

The struggle over the Mexican territory was more complicated. It began in Texas in 1835, when the American settlers there staged a successful revolt against Mexican rule. In 1836, the settlers proclaimed Texas an independent republic, but also requested U.S. statehood. Nine years later, the United States annexed Texas and made it a state.

The United States gained more Mexican territory as a result of the Mexican War. In 1846, President James K. Polk sent General Zachary Taylor to occupy land near the Rio Grande that both the United States and Mexico claimed. Fighting broke out between Taylor's troops and Mexican soldiers. On May 13, 1846, at Polk's request, Congress declared war on Mexico. The United States quickly defeated its weak neighbor. The Treaty of Guadalupe Hidalgo, signed on Feb. 2, 1848, officially ended the war. The treaty gave the United States a vast stretch of land from Texas west to the Pacific and north to Oregon.

In 1853, in the Gadsden Purchase, America bought

Period Facts in Brief

Presidents (with political parties and dates of service)
- James Monroe, Democratic-Republican, 1817-1825
- John Quincy Adams, Democratic-Republican, 1825-1829
- Andrew Jackson, Democrat, 1829-1837
- Martin Van Buren, Democrat, 1837-1841
- William H. Harrison, Whig, 1841
- John Tyler, Whig, 1841-1845
- James K. Polk, Democrat, 1845-1849
- Zachary Taylor, Whig, 1849-1850

States in the Union

Number at start of period: 22
Number at end of period: 30
States added during the period:
Maine (1820), Missouri (1821), Arkansas (1836), Michigan (1837), Florida (1845), Texas (1845), Iowa (1846), Wisconsin (1848).

Important Dates

1820 The Missouri Compromise ended a slavery dispute.
1823 The Monroe Doctrine warned Europeans against interference in Western Hemisphere affairs.
1825 The Erie Canal opened, providing a water route from the Atlantic Ocean to the Great Lakes.
1830 The *Tom Thumb*, the nation's first commercial steam locomotive, operated in Baltimore.
1832 South Carolina threatened secession over a tariff.
1834 Cyrus McCormick patented the reaper.
1837 Samuel F. B. Morse demonstrated the first successful telegraph in the United States.
1846 Britain ceded the southern part of the Oregon Country to the United States.
1848 Victory in the Mexican War gave the United States vast new territory in the West.
1848 The discovery of gold in California triggered the Gold Rush.

Population Growth and Change

Total population, 9,638,453
1820
Rural, 93%   Urban, 7%

Total population, 22,488,000
1849
Rural, 85%   Urban, 15%

Settlement of Immigrants in Missouri (about 1850), a lithograph by E. Sachse; Missouri Historical Society, St. Louis

A Pioneer Homestead in Missouri, *above*, consisted of a log cabin and a small piece of farmland. The farmer cleared timber from the surrounding forest to build his house and to burn as fuel.

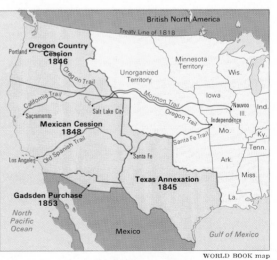

WORLD BOOK map

Expansion in the Mid-1800's extended the nation westward to the Pacific Ocean. The Oregon Country was ceded to the U.S. by Britain. The rest of the new territory came from Mexico.

Detail of *The Trail of Tears* (1942), an oil painting on canvas by Robert Lindneux; Woolaroc Museum, Bartlesville, Okla.

Eastern Indians were forced to move west of the Mississippi River during the Expansion Era as whites took over their land. The difficult journey, above, became known as the *Trail of Tears* among the Cherokee and Choctaw Indians.

from Mexico the strip of land that makes up the southern edge of Arizona and New Mexico. The United States then owned all the territory of its present states except Alaska (purchased from Russia in 1867) and Hawaii (annexed in 1898). See MEXICAN WAR; GADSDEN PURCHASE.

The western territory gained by the United States added to the American spirit of national pride and was a key factor in the nation's economic growth. But it also helped widen the split between the North and South, and helped bring on the Civil War. See *The Irrepressible Conflict* section of this article.

Expansion and the Indians. As the pioneers moved westward, they took over much of the land that Indians had occupied for thousands of years. Fighting often broke out between the pioneers and Indians. The United States government sent soldiers to battle the Indians and the soldiers won most of these so-called Indian Wars. By the 1840's, the soldiers had driven most eastern Indians west of the Mississippi River. See INDIAN WARS (Along the Frontier).

Expansion and the Economy. Expansion into the rich interior of the continent enabled the United States to become the world's leading agricultural nation. Many of the pioneer farmers found they could produce more than they needed for their families. They then concentrated on products with high sales value. Cotton was in great demand by textile mills in Europe and the Eastern United States. Farmers in the South as far west as Texas raised cotton to supply the mills. Many settlers in Kentucky and Tennessee prospered by growing tobacco. Midwesterners produced large crops of corn and wheat, and also raised much livestock. Farmers in the Far West raised wheat, fruit, and other valuable products.

New techniques and machines boosted the output of America's farms. The cotton gin, invented by Eli Whitney in 1793, came into widespread use in the 1800's. It enabled cotton growers to separate cotton fiber from the seeds as fast as 50 people could by hand. The reaper, patented by Cyrus McCormick in 1834, allowed farmers to harvest grain much more quickly than before. See COTTON GIN; REAPER.

The discovery of minerals in the West also aided America's economy. The most famous mineral strike took place in 1848, when gold was discovered at Sutter's Mill in California. See FORTY-NINER; GOLD RUSH.

The period also marked the beginning of large-scale manufacturing in the United States. Previously, most manufacturing was done by craftworkers at home or in small shops. But beginning in the early 1800's, businesses erected factories equipped with modern machinery that enabled them to produce goods more rapidly. Manufacturing remained centered in the East, but some Western towns developed industries.

Developments in transportation also contributed immensely to America's economic growth. New or improved roads—such as the National Road in the East and the Oregon and Santa Fe trails in the West—eased the difficulty of traveling and shipping goods by land (see TRAILS OF EARLY DAYS with its *Related Articles*).

In 1807, Robert Fulton demonstrated the first commercially successful steamboat, the *Clermont*. The steamboat soon became the fastest and most important means

Detail of *A Cotton Plantation on the Mississippi* (1884), a Currier and Ives lithograph based on a painting by W. A. Walker; Museum of the City of New York

Cotton Plantations sprang up throughout the South in the 1800's. Cotton became so important to the Southern economy that people called the crop "King Cotton." Many whites used black slaves to work in their fields. They claimed that slave labor was vital to the South's economy.

The Camden and Amboy Railroad with the Engine "Planet" in 1834 (1904), an oil painting on canvas by Edward Lamson Henry; Graham Gallery, New York City

Railroads and Steamboats became important means of transportation during the Expansion Era. In the scene above, New Jersey travelers transfer from a steamboat, *background,* to a train. A stagecoach and a carriage—two other means of transportation—appear at the right.

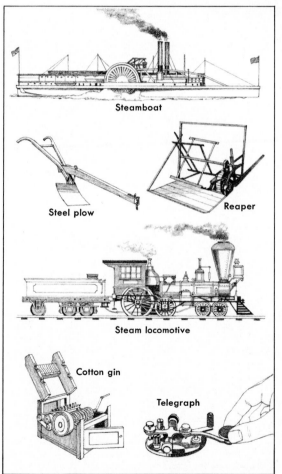

Steamboat

Steel plow

Reaper

Steam locomotive

Cotton gin

Telegraph

WORLD BOOK illustrations by David Cunningham

Technological Advances in transportation, farming, and communication greatly aided America's economic growth during the early 1800's. Some of the developments are shown above.

of shipping goods. Americans of the early 1800's built many canals to connect their natural waterways. The Erie Canal, the most important one, was completed in 1825. It opened a water passage from the Hudson River in New York to the Great Lakes in the Midwest. Boats used the canal to carry manufactured products from the East to the West and farm products and raw materials from the West to the East (see ERIE CANAL).

The steam-powered railroad soon rivaled the steamboat in importance as a means of shipping. In the 1820's, American railroads were still in the experimental stage. But by 1850, about 9,000 miles (14,500 kilometers) of railroad lines were in operation.

In 1837, Samuel F. B. Morse demonstrated the first successful telegraph in the United States. The telegraph soon gave businessmen the fastest means of communication yet known. An expanded postal system also helped speed communications.

Cultural Change. After 1820, the wilderness seemed less and less hostile to the American people. Increasingly, society glorified the frontier and nature. The public eagerly read the novels of James Fenimore Cooper, which described Indians and frontiersmen as pure of heart and noble in deeds. Ralph Waldo Emerson and other American philosophers praised nature as a source of truth and beauty available to all people, rich and poor alike.

Developments in printing spread art and information to more people than ever before. A new printing process called *lithography* enabled artists to produce many copies of their works cheaply. Large numbers of Americans bought and decorated their homes with lithographs. The lithographs of Nathaniel Currier and James Merritt Ives were especially popular. They depicted everyday American scenes, customs, and events—often in a sentimental style. Faster printing presses reduced the cost of printing newspapers. After 1835, many newspaper publishers lowered the cost of their papers to a penny, a price even poor people could afford. But the spoken word remained an important means of mass communication. Large numbers of people attended gatherings

Detail of *Stump Speaking* (1854), an oil painting on canvas
by George Caleb Bingham; Boatmen's National Bank of St. Louis

Political Candidates and other orators traveled far and wide to bring their messages to frontier audiences. Public speeches from platforms like the one at the left became known as *stump speeches*.

where political candidates, pleaders of special causes, and famous clergymen and lawyers made speeches.

City people of the Expansion Era flocked to theaters to enjoy plays, minstrel shows, and other forms of entertainment. Groups of entertainers also toured the country, performing before small-town audiences. P. T. Barnum, the most famous showman of the time, fascinated the public with exhibitions of midgets, "fat ladies," and other unusual attractions.

Politics and the "Common Man"

The Election of 1824 led to renewed political friction in the United States. Four Democratic-Republicans, including John Quincy Adams and Andrew Jackson, sought to succeed Monroe as President. Jackson received the most electoral votes. But he did not win a majority, so it fell upon the House of Representatives to select the new President. The House chose Adams. Embittered, Jackson and his followers formed a separate wing of the Democratic-Republican Party, which soon developed into the Democratic Party.

Jacksonian Democracy. Adams and all the earlier Presidents came from well-to-do Eastern families. Jackson, by contrast, was born in a log cabin into a poor family. He won national fame as an Indian fighter and as a hero of the War of 1812.

Jackson ran for President again in 1828. He appealed for support from Western farmers and frontiersmen, and city laborers and craftsmen. He promised to end what he called a "monopoly" of government by the rich and to protect the interests of the "common man." His policy of equal political power for all became known as *Jacksonian Democracy*. Jackson's background and policies gained him much support in the West and in the nation's growing cities. The voters elected him President by wide margins in 1828 and again in 1832.

Jackson as President. When Jackson became President, many wealthy Easterners held what were, in effect, lifelong appointments to federal government jobs. Jackson dismissed many of these people from office, replacing them with his supporters. Some historians consider this action the start of the spoils system in the federal government. See SPOILS SYSTEM.

Jackson's main crusade against the wealthy involved the second Bank of the United States. The bank's duties included regulating the nation's money supply. Jackson believed the bank operated as a monopoly that favored the wealthy. In 1832, Congress voted to recharter the bank, but Jackson vetoed the bill. He soon withdrew the government's money from the bank, and the bank later collapsed.

The other great issue of Jackson's Administration involved the tariff and nullification. In 1828, Congress passed a bill that placed high tariffs on goods imported into the United States. The South believed the bill favored New England manufacturing interests, and denounced it as a "Tariff of Abominations." Speaking for South Carolina, Calhoun (then the Vice-President) claimed any state could nullify a federal law it deemed unconstitutional. In 1832, Congress lowered tariffs somewhat, but not enough to please South Carolina. South Carolina declared the tariff acts "null and void," and threatened to secede from the Union if the federal government tried to collect tariffs in the state. This action created a constitutional crisis. Jackson believed in states' rights, but maintained the Union must be preserved. In 1833, he persuaded Congress to pass the *Force Bill*, which allowed him to use the armed forces to collect tariffs. But Congress lowered tariffs to a point acceptable to South Carolina, and the nullification crisis ended. See NULLIFICATION.

Politics After Jackson. Jackson's influence on politics continued after he left office. As undisputed leader of the Democrats, Jackson designated Martin Van Buren to be the party's candidate in the 1836 presidential election. Jackson's opponents had formed the

Whig Party four years earlier. In an attempt to attract followers of Jackson, most Whigs supported William Henry Harrison to oppose Van Buren. Harrison, like Jackson, had won fame as a war hero. But the voters, still loyal to Jackson, elected Van Buren.

A depression called the Panic of 1837 crippled the American economy shortly after Van Buren took office, but prosperity later returned. The presidential election of 1840 again matched Van Buren and Harrison. In their campaign, the Whigs made some attempt to criticize Van Buren's economic policies, but for the most part they ignored issues. Instead, they promoted Harrison as a war hero and associated him with hard cider, the log cabin, and other symbols of the frontier. In this way, they appealed to many of Jackson's frontier supporters, and Harrison won the election.

Social Reform

During the Expansion Era, many Americans came to believe that social reforms were needed to improve their society. Churches and social groups set up charities to aid the poor and teach them how to help themselves. Reformers worked to reduce the working day of laborers from the usual 12 or 14 hours to 10 hours. Prohibitionists—convinced that drunkenness was the chief cause of poverty and other problems—persuaded 13 states to outlaw the sale of alcohol between 1846 and 1855. Dorothea Dix and others worked to improve the dismal conditions in the nation's prisons and insane asylums. Other important targets of reformers were women's rights, improvements in education, and the abolition of slavery.

The Drive for Women's Rights. Early American women had few rights. There were almost no colleges for women, and most professional careers were closed to them. A married woman could not own property. Instead, any property she had legally belonged to her husband. In addition, American women were barred from voting in all elections.

A women's rights movement developed after 1820, and brought about some changes. In 1835, Oberlin College became the first men's school to admit women. Other men's colleges soon began admitting women, and new colleges for women were built. In 1848, New York became the first state to allow married women to own real estate. That same year, Lucretia Mott and Elizabeth Cady Stanton organized a Woman's Rights Convention in Seneca Falls, N.Y. The convention issued the first formal appeal for *woman suffrage* (the right to vote). But nationwide suffrage did not come about until 1920.

Education Reform. In the early 1800's, most good schools in the United States were expensive private schools. Poor children went to second-rate "pauper," or "charity," schools, or did not go at all. During the 1830's, Horace Mann of Massachusetts and other reformers began demanding education and better schools for all American children. States soon began establishing public school systems, and more and more children received an education. Colleges started training teachers for a system of public education based on standardized courses of study. As a result, schoolchildren throughout the country were taught much the same lessons. For example, almost all children of the mid-1800's studied the *McGuffey*, or *Eclectic, Readers* to learn to read. These books taught patriotism and morality as well as reading (see McGuffey, William H.).

The Abolition Movement became the most intense and controversial reform activity of the period. Beginning in colonial times, many Americans—called *abolitionists*—had demanded an end to slavery. By the early 1800's, every Northern state had outlawed slavery. But through the years, the plantation system of farming had spread throughout the South, and the economy of the Southern States depended more and more on slaves as a source of cheap labor.

The question of whether to outlaw or allow slavery became an important political and social issue in the early 1800's. Through the years, a balance between the number of *free states* (states where slavery was prohibited) and *slave states* (those where it was allowed) had been sought. This meant that both sides would have an equal number of representatives in the United States Senate. As of 1819, the federal government had achieved a balance between free states and slave states. There were 11 of each.

When the Territory of Missouri applied for admission to the Union in 1818, bitter controversy broke out over whether to admit it as a free or slave state. In either case, the balance between free and slave states would be upset. But in 1820, the nation's leaders worked out the Missouri Compromise, which temporarily maintained the balance. Massachusetts agreed to give up the northern part of its territory. This area became the state of Maine, and entered the Union as a free state in 1820. In 1821, Missouri entered as a slave state, and so there were 12 free and 12 slave states.

The Missouri Compromise had another important provision. It provided that slavery would be "forever prohibited" in all the territory gained from the Louisiana Purchase north of Missouri's southern border, except for Missouri itself. See Missouri Compromise.

The Missouri Compromise satisfied many Americans as an answer to the slavery question. But large numbers of people still called for complete abolition. In 1821, Benjamin Lundy, a Quaker, pleaded for gradual abolition in a journal called *The Genius of Universal Emancipation*. William Lloyd Garrison, a fiery New England journalist, opposed even gradual abolition. Garrison demanded an immediate end to slavery. He founded *The Liberator*, an important abolitionist journal, in 1831. Many blacks who had gained their freedom became important speakers for the abolition movement. They included Frederick Douglass and Sojourner Truth. See Abolitionist.

The growing strength of the abolition movement raised fears among Southerners that the federal government would outlaw slavery. Increasingly, the South hardened its defense of slavery. Southerners had always argued that slavery was necessary to the plantation economy. But after 1830, some Southern leaders began arguing that blacks were inferior to whites, and therefore fit for their role as slaves. Even many Southern whites who owned no slaves took comfort in the belief that they were superior to blacks. As a result, Southern support of slavery increased.

The First Day at Gettysburg (1863), an oil painting on canvas by James Walker; West Point Museum, U.S. Military Academy

The Civil War ranks among the most tragic events of United States history. Fought between 1861 and 1865, it pitted Northerners against Southerners in bloody battle. In the Battle of Gettysburg, *above*, about 40,000 Americans were killed or wounded in just three days.

UNITED STATES HISTORY: 1850-1869 / *The Irrepressible Conflict*

The long dispute between the North and South over the issue of slavery came to a head after the Mexican War ended in 1848. The vast new area the United States had acquired in the West during the 1840's created a problem Americans could not evade. It was obvious that the new land would sooner or later be split up into territories, and then into states. Proslavery Americans—chiefly Southerners—argued against any restraints on slavery in the new territories and states. Antislavery Americans—mainly Northerners—wanted the federal government to outlaw slavery in the newly acquired lands. Still others proposed the doctrine of *popular sovereignty*. That is, they said the people of the territories and states should decide whether or not to allow slavery.

At first, the sides tried to settle their differences through debate and compromise. But the dispute over slavery proved to be an "irrepressible conflict," as Senator William H. Seward of New York termed it. During the 1850's, the North and South drew further and further apart over the issue. In the early 1860's, 11 Southern states seceded from the Union. The North insisted that the South had no right to secede and that the Union must be preserved at all costs. On April 12, 1861, the Civil War broke out between the North and South. In this tragic chapter of United States history, Americans faced Americans in bloody battle. The Civil War took more American lives than any other war. It left large parts of the South in ruins, and created long-lasting feelings of bitterness and division between the people of the North and South.

The North won the Civil War in 1865. The North's victory preserved the Union. And, soon after the war, slavery was outlawed throughout the United States.

Debate and Compromise

California applied for statehood in 1849. The application triggered debate over whether California should be admitted as a free state or a slave state. It also heightened the long-standing argument over how to deal with the slavery question.

Congressional Views. Members of Congress became spokesmen for the various views about slavery. Calhoun, then a senator from South Carolina, expressed the views of Americans who believed in the right to own slaves. Senator Seward was one of many spokesmen for people with strong antislavery beliefs. He said moral law—a higher law than the Constitution—required that the government abolish slavery nationwide. Senator Clay of Kentucky represented Americans who held views between those of Calhoun and Seward. Clay urged both the North and South to compromise because—he said—the alternative was the end of the Union.

The Compromise of 1850. Clay and others succeeded in bringing about agreement on the California slavery question. They won approval of the Compromise of 1850, a series of laws that made concessions to both the North and South. Measures designed to satisfy the North included the admission of California to the Union as a free state and the abolition of the slave trade in Washington, D.C. As part of the Compromise, Congress created the territories of New Mexico and Utah. To try to satisfy Southerners, Congress ruled that when these territories became states, the residents would de-

cide whether or not to allow slavery. Also for the South, Congress agreed to strict measures designed to aid the capture of runaway slaves.

Many Americans thought the Compromise of 1850 provided a final solution to the slavery problem. The Compromise did cool the heated argument over the issue—but only for a while. See COMPROMISE OF 1850.

The Kansas-Nebraska Act. In the early 1850's, Congress began considering the creation of new territories in the area roughly between Missouri and present-day Idaho. Bitter debate flared up over whether the territories should ban or allow slavery. Those who called for a ban cited the Missouri Compromise to back their position. The land under consideration was part of the area in which the Compromise had "forever prohibited" slavery. But on May 25, 1854, Congress passed the Kansas-Nebraska Act, a law that changed this provision. The law created two territories west of Missouri— Kansas and Nebraska. It provided that the people of Kansas and Nebraska would decide whether or not to allow slavery. See KANSAS-NEBRASKA ACT.

Nationwide Turmoil

Few, if any, American laws have had more far-reaching effects than the Kansas-Nebraska Act. Furious antislavery Americans denounced both Northerners and Southerners who had supported the act. Others staunchly defended the act. Everywhere, attitudes toward the slavery question hardened, and capacity for further compromise diminished. Political and social turmoil swept through the country, and the United States was on the road to war.

Political and Institutional Splits. Angered by the Kansas-Nebraska Act, a group of antislavery Americans formed the Republican Party in 1854. Many Democrats and Whigs who opposed slavery left their parties and became Republicans. Other Americans, puzzled by the national turmoil, sought simple answers to the country's problems. They joined the Know-Nothing (or Ameri-

Period Facts in Brief

Presidents (with political parties and dates of service)

Zachary Taylor, Whig, 1849-1850
Millard Fillmore, Whig, 1850-1853
Franklin Pierce, Democrat, 1853-1857
James Buchanan, Democrat, 1857-1861
Abraham Lincoln, Republican, 1861-1865
Andrew Johnson, National Union, 1865-1869
Ulysses S. Grant, Republican, 1869-1877

States in the Union

Number at start of period: 30
Number at end of period: 37
States added during the period:
California (1850), Minnesota (1858), Oregon (1859), Kansas (1861), West Virginia (1863), Nevada (1864), Nebraska (1867).

Important Dates

1850 The Compromise of 1850 temporarily ended a national crisis over the slavery question.
1854 Passage of the Kansas-Nebraska Act led to nationwide turmoil over the slavery issue.
1856 The first American kindergarten opened in Watertown, Wis.
1860 Pony express riders began carrying mail from St. Joseph, Mo., to the Far West.
1861-1865 The North and the South fought each other in the Civil War.
1863 The Emancipation Proclamation declared freedom for all slaves in Confederate-held territory.
1865 The 13th Amendment outlawed slavery throughout the United States.
1867 The United States bought Alaska from Russia.
1868 The House of Representatives impeached President Andrew Johnson, but the Senate did not remove him from office.

Population Growth and Change

Total population, 23,191,876
1850
Rural, 85%   Urban, 15%

Total population, 38,925,000
1869
Rural, 75%   Urban, 25%

The Old Print Shop, Inc., New York City

The Compromise of 1850 temporarily cooled the heated dispute over slavery between the North and South. Henry Clay, *center above*, led the effort in Congress to pass the Compromise.

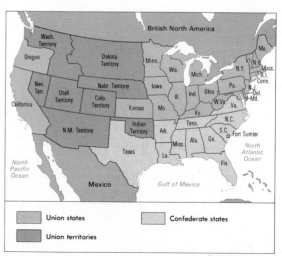

WORLD BOOK map

The Civil War (1861-1865) split the nation into two parts— the Confederacy and the Union. The Confederacy was made up of 11 Southern States that withdrew from the Union in 1860 and 1861.

III

Detail of *The Slave Auction* (1862), an oil painting on canvas by Eyre Crowe; Kennedy Galleries, Inc., New York City

Slaves Were Sold at public auctions in the South. Pictures of blacks being sold like merchandise stirred much resentment against slavery in the North.

can) Party, which blamed the problems on immigrants and Roman Catholics.

The stability of the two main political parties before 1854 had helped keep the nation together. Thus, the political splits deprived the country of an important unifying force. Religious denominations had also been a unifying force. But beginning in the 1840's, large church groups split along sectional lines and another unifying institution was lost. By the mid-1850's, the Supreme Court seemed to be the only institution to command nationwide respect. But in 1857, the court ruled—in the Dred Scott Decision—that Negroes were not citizens and that laws limiting the spread of slavery were unconstitutional. The court then lost much of its influence in the North. See DRED SCOTT DECISION.

Social Disorder. After 1854, Southerners increasingly referred to themselves as a separate national group. In the North, abolitionists stepped up their campaign against slavery. Harriet Beecher Stowe's novel *Uncle Tom's Cabin* (1851-1852) became one of the most widely read books in America. This powerful work about the horrors of slavery helped stir antislavery feelings to a fever pitch. In Kansas, fierce fighting broke out in 1856 between proslavery and antislavery settlers. See UNCLE TOM'S CABIN; KANSAS ("Bleeding Kansas").

On Oct. 16, 1859, abolitionist John Brown and a small band of followers seized the federal arsenal at Harpers Ferry, Va. (now W. Va.). Brown intended the action as the first step in a general slave uprising. But federal troops easily captured him, and—after a trial—he was hanged. Brown's plan had almost no chance of success. The odds against him were so great that many people believe he was insane at the time of the Harpers Ferry incident. Even so, many Northerners thought of him as a martyr, while many Southerners genuinely believed his attack was part of an organized movement to end slavery. These attitudes perhaps best show how divided the United States had become in the 1850's.

The Election of 1860 also reflected the nation's division. The Democratic Party split into Northern and Southern wings, with each wing slating its own candidate for President. The Whig Party, weakened by desertions, disbanded before the election. Conservative Whigs and Know-Nothings formed the Constitutional Union Party, which ran its own candidate for President. Only the Republicans remained united. They nominated Abraham Lincoln, an Illinois lawyer, for President. The Republican unity helped Lincoln win the election on Nov. 6, 1860.

Secession. Lincoln had earned a reputation as an opponent of slavery, and his election was unacceptable to the South. Southerners feared the new President would restrict or end slavery. Alarmed by this prospect, South Carolina seceded from the Union on Dec. 20, 1860, well before Lincoln took office. Alabama, Florida, Georgia, Louisiana, and Mississippi seceded in January, 1861. The six seceded states formed the Confederate States of America in February. Later in 1861, Arkansas, North Carolina, Tennessee, Texas, and Virginia seceded and joined the Confederacy.

Lincoln took office on March 4, 1861. The new President insisted above all else on the preservation of the Union. To him, the seceded states were still part of the United States, and there was yet hope for reconciliation. But a little more than a month later, the North and South were at war.

The Civil War and Reconstruction

The Civil War began on April 12, 1861, when Southern troops fired on Fort Sumter, a military post in Charleston Harbor. Both sides quickly prepared for battle after the Fort Sumter clash. The North had superior financial and industrial strength, and more manpower than the South. But the South fought valiantly to defend its cause. The South gained the upper hand at first, but the North gradually turned the tide. Finally, Confederate resistance wore down, and Union armies swept through the South. On April 9, 1865, General

Library of Congress

The South Lay in Ruins at the end of the Civil War. A scene showing shells of burned-out buildings in Richmond, Va., above, provides an example of the destruction brought on by the war.

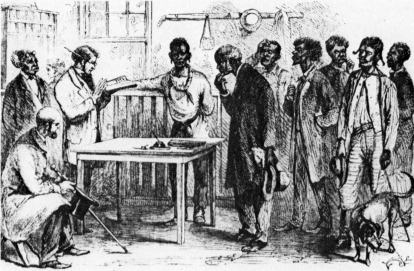

Reconstruction Measures passed by Congress after the Civil War included the establishment of election boards to register black voters. The scene at the left shows blacks lined up to register in Macon, Ga.

Robert E. Lee—commander of the Confederate Army—surrendered to the Union commander General Ulysses S. Grant at Appomattox Court House in Virginia. The last Confederate troops surrendered on May 26.

The four years of bloody fighting between the North and South had staggering effects on the nation. About 360,000 Union troops and perhaps 260,000 Confederate troops—all Americans—died in the conflict. No other war in history has taken so many American lives. Property damage was enormous, especially in the South. Many Southern cities, towns, plantations, factories, and railroads lay in ruin. The war also took an emotional toll on the nation. It caused deep and long-lasting feelings of bitterness and division between the people of the North and the South.

For a detailed account of the war, see CIVIL WAR.

The Emancipation Proclamation. At the start of the Civil War, Lincoln's main goal was the preservation of the Union. But as battlefield casualties mounted, he decided that another goal—the emancipation of the slaves—was necessary to justify the cost of the war. On Jan. 1, 1863, Lincoln issued the Emancipation Proclamation. The proclamation declared freedom for all slaves in the areas under Confederate control at the time. See EMANCIPATION PROCLAMATION.

Reconstruction. Toward the end of the Civil War, the North set out to establish terms under which Confederate States would be readmitted to the Union. The process through which the South returned, as well as the period following the war, is called *Reconstruction*.

Northerners divided into two groups over Reconstruction policy. One group, called the *moderates*, wanted to end the bitterness between the North and South and favored avoiding harsh treatment of the rebels. Members of the other group, the *radicals*, believed the South should be punished for its rebellion. They also wanted a policy that would ensure that blacks received better treatment in the South than they had before the war.

President Lincoln might have worked out a compromise. But assassin John Wilkes Booth shot him on April 14, 1865. Lincoln died the next day, less than a week after Lee's surrender. Vice President Andrew Johnson became President. He tried to carry out Lincoln's policy, but he was unable to overcome radical opposition. The radicals included many of the most powerful Republicans in Congress. They controlled enough votes in Congress to push through their own Reconstruction policy and override Johnson's vetoes. Johnson's opposition to the radicals almost led to his removal from office. In 1868, the House of Representatives impeached him. But the Senate voted against removing him from office by the margin of a single vote. For details, see JOHNSON, ANDREW.

The Reconstruction program drafted by Congress included laws to further the rights of blacks. The 13th Amendment to the Constitution (1865) outlawed slavery throughout the United States. The 14th Amendment (1868) confirmed the citizenship of blacks, and the 15th Amendment (1870) made it illegal to deny the right to vote on the basis of race.

Congress also stationed troops in the South. Republicans, protected by the troops, took control of local Southern governments. White Southerners loyal to their old traditions bitterly resented the new political system. Many of them joined the Ku Klux Klan, a secret society that used violence to keep blacks from voting and trying to achieve equality (see KU KLUX KLAN).

Congress insisted that the Confederate States agree to follow all federal laws before being readmitted to the Union. Between 1866 and 1870, all the Confederate States returned to the Union. By the early 1870's, interest in Reconstruction in the North had faded. However, Reconstruction did not end until 1877, when the last federal troops left the South.

Reconstruction had limited success. It expanded the legal rights of blacks and set up public school systems. But the old social order, based on white supremacy, soon returned to the South. The fundamental problem of the black's place in society remained to haunt future generations. See RECONSTRUCTION.

Forging the Shaft: A Welding Heat (1877), an oil painting on canvas by John Ferguson Weir;
The Metropolitan Museum of Art, New York City, Gift of Lyman G. Bloomingdale, 1901

America Became an Industrial Giant during the late 1800's. The nation's factories, such as the
iron foundry above, began turning out products on a much larger scale than before. Millions of rural
Americans and immigrants flocked to the country's cities to work in the booming industries.

UNITED STATES HISTORY: 1870-1916 / Industrialization and Reform

The industrial growth that began in the United States in the early 1800's continued steadily up to and through the Civil War. Still, by the end of the war, the typical American industry was small. Hand labor remained widespread, limiting the production capacity of industry. Most businesses served a small market and lacked the capital needed for business expansion.

After the Civil War, however, American industry changed dramatically. Machines replaced hand labor as the main means of manufacturing, increasing the production capacity of industry tremendously. A new nationwide network of railroads enabled businessmen to distribute goods far and wide. Inventors developed new products the public wanted, and businessmen made the products in large quantities. Investors and bankers supplied the huge amounts of money that businessmen needed to expand their operations. Many big businesses grew up as a result of these and other developments. They included coal mining, petroleum, and railroad companies; and manufacturers and sellers of such products as steel, industrial machinery, automobiles, and clothing.

The industrial growth had major effects on American life. The new business activity centered in cities. As a result, people moved to cities in record numbers, and the cities grew by leaps and bounds. Many Americans amassed huge fortunes from the business boom, but others lived in extreme poverty. The sharp contrast between the rich and the poor and other features of American life stirred widespread discontent. The discontent triggered new reform movements, which—among other things—led to measures to aid the poor and control the size and power of big business.

The industrial growth centered chiefly in the North. The war-torn South lagged behind the rest of the country economically. In the West, frontier life was coming to a close.

America's role in foreign affairs also changed during the late 1800's and early 1900's. The country built up its military strength and became a world power.

The Rise of Big Business

The value of goods produced by American industry increased almost tenfold between 1870 and 1916. Many interrelated developments contributed to this growth.

Improved Production Methods. The use of machines in manufacturing spread throughout American industry after the Civil War. With machines, workers

could produce goods many times faster than they could by hand. The new large manufacturing firms hired hundreds, or even thousands, of workers. Each worker was assigned a specific job in the production process. This system of organizing laborers, called the *division of labor*, also sped up production. The increased production speed had a tremendous impact on the economy. It enabled businessmen to charge lower prices for products. Lower prices, in turn, meant more people could afford the products, and so sales soared.

Development of New Products. Inventors created, and businessmen produced and sold, a variety of new products. The products included the typewriter (1867), barbed wire (1873), the telephone (1876), the phonograph (1877), the electric light (1879), and the gasoline automobile (1885). Of these, the automobile had the greatest impact on the nation's economy. In the early 1900's, Ransom Eli Olds and Henry Ford began turning out cars by mass production. Automobile prices dropped, and sales soared. The number of automobiles owned by Americans jumped from 8,000 in 1900 to almost 3,500,000 in 1916.

Natural Resources. America's rich and varied natural resources played a key role in the rise of big business. The nation's abundant water supply helped power the industrial machines. Forests provided lumber for construction and wooden products. Miners took large quantities of coal and iron ore from the ground. Andrew Carnegie and other businessmen made steel from these minerals. Steel played a vital role in the industrialization process. It was used to build machines, railroad tracks, bridges, automobiles, and skyscrapers. Other industrially valuable minerals included copper, silver, and petroleum. Petroleum—the source of gasoline—became especially important after the automobile came into widespread use in the early 1900's.

A Growing Population. More than 25 million immigrants entered the United States between 1870 and

Period Facts in Brief

Presents (with political parties and dates of service)

Ulysses S. Grant, Republican, 1869-1877
Rutherford B. Hayes, Republican, 1877-1881
James A. Garfield, Republican, 1881
Chester A. Arthur, Republican, 1881-1885
Grover Cleveland, Democrat, 1885-1889
Benjamin Harrison, Republican, 1889-1893
Grover Cleveland, Democrat, 1893-1897
William McKinley, Republican, 1897-1901
Theodore Roosevelt, Republican, 1901-1909
William H. Taft, Republican, 1909-1913
Woodrow Wilson, Democrat, 1913-1921

States in the Union

Number at start of period: 37
Number at end of period: 48
States added during the period:
Colorado (1876), North Dakota (1889), South Dakota (1889), Montana (1889), Washington (1889), Idaho (1890), Wyoming (1890), Utah (1896), Oklahoma (1907), New Mexico (1912), Arizona (1912).

Important Dates

1876 Alexander Graham Bell invented the telephone.
1877 Thomas Edison invented the phonograph.
1879 Edison invented the electric light.
1884 The world's first skyscraper was begun in Chicago.
1886 The American Federation of Labor was founded.
1898 The United States defeated Spain in the Spanish-American War.
1903 The Wright Brothers made the first successful airplane flight at Kitty Hawk, N.C.
1913 The 16th Amendment gave the federal government the power to levy an income tax.
1914 World War I began in Europe.

Population Growth and Change

Total population, 39,818,449
1870
Rural, 74%   Urban, 26%

Total population, 99,871,604
1916
Rural, 51%   Urban, 49%

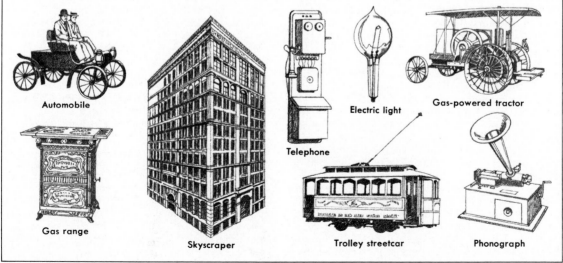

Automobile

Gas range

Skyscraper

Telephone

Electric light

Gas-powered tractor

Trolley streetcar

Phonograph

WORLD BOOK illustrations by David Cunningham

Many New Products came into use during the period of industrialization. Their manufacture and sale contributed greatly to the economic boom. Some of the new products are shown above.

The Granger Collection, New York

Immigrants flocked into the United States by the millions during the late 1800's and early 1900's. A shipload of newcomers from Europe is shown above.

Immigration to the United States Between 1870 and 1916

The largest number of immigrants between 1870 and 1916 came from southern and eastern Europe. Earlier, the number of immigrants from northern and western Europe had far surpassed the total from any other part of the world.

Source: U.S. Bureau of the Census

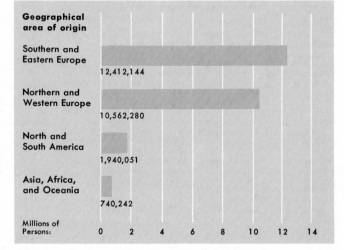

Geographical area of origin	
Southern and Eastern Europe	12,412,144
Northern and Western Europe	10,562,280
North and South America	1,940,051
Asia, Africa, and Oceania	740,242

Millions of Persons: 0 2 4 6 8 10 12 14

1916. Immigration plus natural growth caused the U.S. population to more than double during the same period, rising from about 40 million to about 100 million. Population growth helped the economic boom in two ways. It increased the number of consumers, and thus enlarged the market for products. It also provided the additional workers needed for the jobs created by the new business activity.

Distribution, Sales, and Communication. In the late 1800's, the American railroad system became a nationwide transportation network. The distance of all railroad lines in operation soared from about 9,000 miles (14,500 kilometers) in 1850 to almost 200,000 miles (320,000 kilometers) in 1900. A high point in railroad development came in 1869, when workers laid tracks that joined the Central Pacific and Union Pacific railroads near Ogden, Utah. This event marked the completion of the world's first transcontinental railroad system. The system linked the United States by rail from coast to coast.

The new railroads spurred economic growth. Mining companies used them to ship raw materials to factories over long distances quickly. Manufacturers distributed their finished products by rail to points throughout the country. The railroads became highly profitable businesses for their owners, including Cornelius Vanderbilt and Jay Gould.

Improved sales methods also aided economic growth. Owners of big businesses sent salespeople to all parts of the country to promote their products. Enterprising merchants opened huge department stores in the growing cities. They included Marshall Field of Chicago, R. H. Macy of New York, and John Wanamaker of Philadelphia. The stores offered a wide variety of products at reasonable prices. Other merchants—including Montgomery Ward and Richard Sears—began mail-

order companies, chiefly to serve people who lived far from stores. The companies published catalogs that showed their products. Buyers used the catalogs to order goods by mail.

Advances in communication provided a boost for the economy. Railroads replaced such mail-delivery systems as the stagecoach. In 1876, Alexander Graham Bell invented the telephone. These developments, along with the telegraph, provided the quick communication that is vital to the smooth operation of big business.

Investment and Banking. The business boom triggered a sharp increase in investments in the stocks and bonds of corporations. As businesses prospered, persons eager to share in the profits invested heavily. Their investments provided capital that companies needed to expand their operations.

New banks sprang up throughout the country. Banks helped finance the nation's economic growth by making loans to businesses. Some bankers of the era, especially J. P. Morgan, assumed key positions in the American economy because of their ability to provide huge sums of capital.

Monopolies. The government did little to regulate business during the 1800's. Unrestricted, American business executives struggled to wipe out competition and gain complete control of their industries. They formed monopolies, which—for the most part—are illegal today. Some business owners in the same industry *merged* (united to form a single company) in order to reduce or eliminate competition. Others formed *trusts*. A trust was a monopoly in which a group of managers controlled rival businesses without formal ownership (see MONOPOLY AND COMPETITION; TRUST).

The monopolies had some favorable effects on the economy. They helped make possible the giant, efficient corporations that contributed so much to economic

growth. The monopolies also enabled businessmen to avoid sharp fluctuations in price and output, and thus keep sales steady. On the other hand, monopolies gave some businessmen so much power that they could take unfair advantage of others. A businessman with little or no competition could demand goods from suppliers at low cost, while charging high prices for his products. The businessman could also save money by reducing the quality of his products.

The South and the West

The War-Torn South. After the Civil War, Americans in the South faced the task of rebuilding their war-torn society. The South lagged behind the rest of the nation economically. Some industry developed in the region, but the South remained an agricultural area throughout the period of industrialization.

Many Southern farmers—both black and white—owned the land they worked. But in general, the land of these small, independent farmers was poor. The best land was given over to tenant farming—a system in which laborers farm the land and pay rent in money or crops to the owner. The tenant farming system had neither the virtues of the plantation system of pre-Civil War days nor of the independent owner system. The tenant farmers lacked the incentive to improve land that was not their own, and the owners did not have full control over production. For these and other reasons, agriculture remained more backward in the South than elsewhere.

The End of the Western Frontier. The long process of settling the United States from coast to coast drew to a close after the Civil War. In 1862, Congress passed the Homestead Act, which offered public land to people free or at very low cost. Thousands of Americans and immigrants started farms in the West under the provisions of the act. They settled chiefly on the Great Plains, which—contrary to earlier beliefs—included much excellent farmland. Miners flocked to the West as the demand for minerals soared. Towns sprang up near the mines. Cattle ranching spread throughout the Southwest after the Civil War.

After 1870, settlement became so widespread in the West that it was no longer possible to draw a continuous frontier line. The United States Census of 1890 officially recognized the fact that America's frontier had ended. See WESTWARD MOVEMENT (The Last Frontiers); WESTERN FRONTIER LIFE.

The settlement of the West brought an end to the American Indian way of life. Farmers occupied and fenced in much of the land. White men moving westward slaughtered buffalo herds on which Indians depended for survival. Some Indians retaliated against the whites by attacking wagon trains and homes. But as in earlier days, the federal government sent soldiers to crush the Indian uprisings. In the end, the Indians were no match for the soldiers and their superior weapons. Through the years, the federal government pushed more and more Indians onto reservations. Reservation Indians suffered from poverty and illness, and could not adjust to the new way of life forced upon them. By 1900, the separate Indian way of life had become a thing of the past. For more details, see INDIAN, AMERICAN (The

Western History Collections, University of Oklahoma Library
Farmers Flocked to the Great Plains during the late 1800's. The Kansas farm family above built their house from sod. The Plains had few trees, and so lumber for building was scarce.

Fall of Indian America); INDIAN RESERVATION; INDIAN TERRITORY; INDIAN WARS.

Life During the Industrial Era

The industrial boom had major effects on the lives of the American people. The availability of jobs in industries drew people from farms to cities in record numbers. In 1870, only about 25 per cent of the American people lived in urban areas. By 1916, the figure had reached almost 50 per cent.

The lives of people in the cities contrasted sharply. A small percentage of them had enormous wealth and enjoyed lives of luxury. Below them economically, the larger middle class lived comfortably. But at the bottom of the economic ladder, a huge mass of city people lived in extreme poverty.

The Wealthy. The business boom opened up many opportunities for financial gain. The economic activity it generated enabled many people to establish successful businesses, expand existing ones, and profit from investments. Some businessmen and investors were able to amass huge fortunes. The number of millionaires in the United States grew from perhaps about 20 in 1850 to more than 3,000 in 1900. Among the millionaires was a small group who accumulated fortunes of more than $100 million each. They included Andrew Carnegie, Marshall Field, J. P. Morgan, John D. Rockefeller, and Cornelius Vanderbilt. The wealthy Americans built enormous mansions, wore the finest clothing, ate in the best restaurants, and could afford to buy almost anything they desired.

The Middle Class. Other city people prospered enough to live lives of comfort, if not wealth. They included owners of small businesses, and such workers as factory and office managers. They became part of America's growing middle class.

The Underprivileged. The laborers who toiled in factories, mills, and mines did not share in the benefits of

Jacob A. Riis photo; Museum of the City
of New York, Jacob A. Riis Collection

The Antique Shop, an oil painting on canvas by Louis Charles Moeller;
Collection of Mr. and Mrs. George J. Arden

The Lives of the Poor and the Rich contrasted sharply during the industrial period. Poor city people, *left,* lived in a crowded tenement and could barely afford the necessities of life. But the wealthy, such as the well-dressed antique shoppers at the right, enjoyed lives of luxury.

the economic growth. They usually worked at least 60 hours a week for an average pay of about 20 cents an hour, and had no fringe benefits.

As the nation's population grew, so did the competition for jobs. The supply of workers outstripped the demand. Businessmen felt little pressure to improve the lot of workers. They knew that job competition meant poor people would work under almost any conditions. The oversupply of workers led to high unemployment. In addition, depressions slowed the economy to a near standstill in 1873, 1884, 1893, and 1907. Unemployment soared during the depressions. Workers suffered through the periods of idleness without the unemployment benefits that are available today. Such economic hardship meant that, in many cases, every family member except very young children had to seek a job.

The everyday life of the city poor was dismal and drab. The poor lived crowded together in slums. Much of their housing consisted of cheap apartment buildings called *tenements.* The crowded slum neighborhoods bred crime. Overwork, poor sanitation, and inadequate diet left slum dwellers vulnerable to disease. Many poor children received little or no education, because they had to work to contribute to their families' welfare. In addition, schools in the slums were poorly equipped for educating those who attended them.

In spite of harsh living conditions, hope made the lives of many of the poor tolerable. The poor knew that economic advancement was possible in the United States. Some families, through hard work and saving, were able to start small businesses. And—even if a worker himself could not advance economically—he believed that in America his children would.

The Farmers. American farmers also suffered hardships after the Civil War. Advances in agricultural equipment and techniques had enabled most of the

farmers to increase their production. However, *middlemen* between the farmers and the consumers took a large share of the money earned from farm products. The middlemen included owners of railroads, grain elevators, mills, and gins.

The Gilded Age. American author Mark Twain called the era of industrialization "The Gilded Age." Twain used this term to describe the culture of the newly rich of the period. Lacking tradition, the wealthy developed a showy culture supposedly based on the culture of upper-class Europeans. The enormous mansions of the newly rich Americans imitated European palaces. The wealthy filled the mansions with European art works, antiques, rare books, and gaudy decorations. They spent their leisure time attending operas, relaxing at luxurious resorts, or engaging in other functions they believed were signs of refinement.

Most Americans, however, had a far different idea of culture. They enjoyed fairs that exhibited industrial machines, the latest inventions, and other items related to America's material progress. The fairs included the Philadelphia Centennial Exposition of 1876 and the Chicago World's Columbian Exposition of 1893. The American people were eager spectators at circuses, vaudeville shows, and sporting events. Baseball became so popular after 1900 that it was called the *national pastime.* Also after 1900, a new kind of entertainment, the motion picture, began attracting public interest. Many Americans of the industrial era enjoyed playing popular songs from sheet music on parlor pianos, or, after 1877, from records on crude phonographs. The people liked magazines filled with pictures, and *dime novels*—inexpensive books that emphasized adventure and the value of hard work and courage.

Government and the People. After the Civil War, the Democratic and Republican parties developed strong *political machines.* Members of these organizations kept

in contact with the people, and did them favors in return for votes. But in general, political and government leaders strongly favored business interests. They did little to interfere with business or to close the gap between the rich and poor.

Government of the era was also marked by widespread corruption. Ulysses S. Grant became President in 1869. Members of Grant's Administration used their government positions for their own financial gain (see GRANT, ULYSSES S. [Political Corruption; Government Frauds]). Corruption also flourished in state and local government. The people seemed little concerned, however. For example, in 1872, Grant won a second term and received more votes than he did the first time.

Reform

A strong spirit of reform swept through the United States during the late 1800's and early 1900's. Many Americans called for changes in the country's economic, political, and social systems. They wanted to reduce poverty, improve the living conditions of the poor, and regulate big business. They worked to end corruption in government, make government more responsive to the people, and accomplish other goals.

During the 1870's and 1880's, the reformers made relatively little progress. But after 1890, they gained much public support and influence in government. By 1917, the reformers had brought about many changes. Some reformers called themselves *progressives*. As a result, the period of American history from about 1890 to about 1917 is often called the *Progressive Era*.

Early Reform Efforts included movements to organize laborers and farmers. In 1886, skilled laborers formed the American Federation of Labor (AFL)—now the American Federation of Labor-Congress of Industrial Organizations (AFL-CIO). Led by Samuel Gompers, this union bargained with employers and gained better wages and working conditions for its members. Farmers founded the National Grange in 1867 and Farmers' Alliances during the 1870's and 1880's. These groups helped force railroads to lower their charges for hauling farm products and assisted the farmers in other ways.

Unskilled laborers had less success in organizing than did skilled laborers and farmers. The Knights of Labor, a union open to both the unskilled and skilled workers, gained a large membership during the 1880's. But its membership declined sharply after the Haymarket Riot of 1886. In this incident, someone threw a bomb during a meeting of workers in Haymarket Square in Chicago, and a riot erupted. Eight police officers and two other persons were killed. Many Americans blamed the disaster on the labor movement. The Haymarket Riot aroused antilabor feelings and temporarily weakened the cause of unskilled workers.

The drive for woman suffrage became strong after the Civil War. In 1869, Susan B. Anthony and Elizabeth Cady Stanton founded the National Woman Suffrage Association. The Territory of Wyoming gave women the right to vote the same year. Soon, a few states allowed women to vote, but only in local elections.

Early reformers brought about some changes in government. In 1883, their efforts led to passage of the Pendleton, or Civil Service, Act. This federal law set up the Civil Service Commission, an agency charged with granting federal government jobs on the basis of merit, rather than as political favors. The commission was the first federal government regulatory agency in the nation's history. In 1884, Democrats and liberal Republicans joined together to elect Grover Cleveland President. A reform-minded Democrat, Cleveland did much to enforce the Pendleton Act.

The Progressive Era. The outcry for reform increased sharply after 1890. Members of the clergy, social workers, and others studied life in the slums and reported on the awful living conditions there. Educators criticized the nation's school system. A group of writers—called *muckrakers* by their critics—published exposés about such evils as corruption in government and how some businesses cheated the public. The writers included Upton Sinclair, Lincoln Steffens, and Ida M. Tarbell. Increasingly, unskilled workers resorted to strikes in an attempt to gain concessions from their employers. Often, violence broke out between strikers and strikebreakers hired by the employers. Socialists and others who opposed the U.S. economic system of capitalism supported the strikers and gained a large following.

Corning-Painted Post Historical Soc., Corning, N.Y.   Sy Seidman (WORLD BOOK photo)   Culver

Popular Entertainment of the period included circuses, dime novels, and—after 1900—motion pictures. A circus parade through a small-town street, *left,* was a highly exciting event. A dime novel, *center,* taught the value of courage. Many movies featured slapstick comedy, *right.*

These and other developments caused many middle-class and some upper-class Americans to back reforms. The people wondered about the justice of a society that tolerated such extremes of poverty and wealth. More and more, the power of big business, corruption in government, violent strikes, and the inroads of socialism seemed to threaten American democracy.

As public support for reform grew, so did the political influence of the reformers. In 1891, farmers and some laborers formed the People's, or Populist, Party. The Populists called for government action to help farmers and laborers. They gained a large following, and convinced many Democrats and Republicans to support reforms. See POPULISM.

Reformers won control of many city and some state governments. They also elected many people to Congress who favored their views. In addition, the first three Presidents elected after 1900—Theodore Roosevelt, William Howard Taft, and Woodrow Wilson—supported certain reform laws. These political developments resulted in a flood of reform legislation on the local, state, and federal levels.

Local and State Legislation. Reformers in local and state government passed many laws to help the poor. Such laws provided for tenement house inspection, playgrounds, and other improvements of life in the slums. Some reform governments expanded public education and forced employers to protect workers against fires and dangerous machinery in factories. The many reformers in local and state government included mayors Samuel M. "Golden Rule" Jones of Toledo, Ohio, and Tom L. Johnson of Cleveland; and governors Woodrow Wilson of New Jersey and Robert M. "Battling Bob" La Follette of Wisconsin. Wisconsin went so far as to pass an income tax, a measure bitterly opposed by the wealthy Americans.

Federal Legislation. In 1890, the federal government passed the Sherman Antitrust Act. This act outlawed trusts and other monopolies that hindered free trade. But the government did little to control monopolies until after Theodore Roosevelt became President in 1901. Roosevelt was a liberal Republican who called for a "square deal" for all Americans. He won lasting

fame as a "trust buster." Roosevelt did not oppose monopolies altogether, but he believed they should be regulated whenever they operated against the public interest. In 1903, Roosevelt established the Bureau of Corporations, an agency that collected information on businesses. When the bureau found that a business was violating the Sherman Antitrust Act, the government sued. During Roosevelt's presidency, the government brought suits against more than 40 companies. The most famous suit broke up John D. Rockefeller's Standard Oil Company in 1911.

Roosevelt became the first President to aid laborers in a strike against employers. In 1902, the United Mine Workers struck for better wages and working conditions. Roosevelt asked the miners and the mine owners to settle their differences through arbitration, but the mine owners refused. Angered, the President threatened to have the Army take over the mines. The owners gave in, and reached a compromise with the miners.

In 1906, Upton Sinclair published *The Jungle,* a novel about unsanitary conditions in the meat-packing industry. Roosevelt ordered an investigation of Sinclair's charges, and found they were true. At Roosevelt's urging, Congress passed the Meat Inspection Act and the Federal Food and Drugs Act to regulate food and drug processing.

Republican William Howard Taft succeeded Roosevelt in 1909. Although a conservative, Taft helped further the cause of reform. He brought twice as many suits against businesses as Roosevelt did. He also extended civil service and called for a federal income tax.

In 1912, conservative Republicans backed Taft for their party's presidential nomination, and liberal Republicans supported Roosevelt. Taft won the nomination. The liberals then formed the Progressive, or "Bull Moose," Party and nominated Roosevelt for President. The Republican split enabled reform Democrat Woodrow Wilson to win the presidency. The Democrats also gained control of Congress.

The reform movement flourished under Wilson. Two amendments to the Constitution proposed during Taft's Administration were ratified in 1913. The 16th Amendment gave the federal government the power to levy an

The Progressive Era was marked by widespread demands for reform. Young socialist women, *left,* marched in a parade to demand better treatment of laborers. Such public demonstrations became common tactics among the reformers of the era.

Detail of *Battle of Manila Bay, May 1, 1898*, a lithograph by an unknown Japanese artist; Chicago Historical Society

Victory in the Spanish-American War set the United States on the road toward becoming a world power. The war lasted less than a year. In the Battle of Manila Bay, *above,* American ships commanded by Commodore George Dewey destroyed a Spanish fleet in the Philippines.

income tax. The 17th Amendment provided for the election of U.S. senators by the people, rather than by state legislatures. The Clayton Antitrust Act of 1914 struck a blow against monopolies. It prohibited corporations from grouping together under interlocking boards of directors. It also helped labor by making it impossible to prosecute unions under antitrust laws. In 1914, the government set up the Federal Trade Commission (FTC) to handle complaints about unfair business practices. The many other reform measures passed during Wilson's presidency included the Underwood Tariff Act of 1913, which lowered a high tariff that protected American business from foreign competition.

For more details on this era of reform in the United States, see PROGRESSIVE MOVEMENT.

Foreign Affairs

During the 1870's and 1880's, the United States paid relatively little attention to foreign affairs. In comparison to such European nations as France, Germany, and Great Britain, America was weak militarily and had little influence in international politics. Among Europeans, American diplomats had the reputation of being bumbling amateurs. German leader Otto von Bismarck summed up the European attitude toward America. He said, "A special Providence takes care of fools, drunkards, and the United States." During the 1890's and early 1900's, however, the United States developed into a world power and took a leading role in international affairs.

The Spanish-American War of 1898 marked a turning point in U.S. foreign policy. Spain ruled Cuba, Puerto Rico, the Philippines, and other overseas possessions during the 1890's. In the mid-1890's, Cubans revolted against their Spanish rulers. Many Americans demanded that the United States aid the rebels. On Feb. 15, 1898, the U.S. battleship *Maine* blew up off the coast of Havana, Cuba. No one was certain what caused the explosion, but many Americans blamed the Spaniards. Demands for action against Spain grew, and "Remember the *Maine*" became a nationwide war cry. On April 25, 1898, at the request of President William McKinley, Congress declared war on Spain. The United States quickly defeated Spain, and the Treaty of Paris of Dec. 10, 1898, officially ended the war. Under it, the United States received Guam, Puerto Rico, and the Philippines from Spain. Also in 1898, the United States annexed Hawaii. See SPANISH-AMERICAN WAR; HAWAII (History).

A World Power. Roosevelt succeeded McKinley as President in 1901. He expressed his foreign policy strategy with the slogan, "Speak Softly and Carry a Big Stick." Roosevelt meant that the country must back up its diplomatic efforts with military strength.

The United States built up its armed forces under Roosevelt. In 1902, Germany, Great Britain, and Italy blockaded Venezuela in an attempt to collect debts from that South American nation. Citing the Monroe Doctrine, Roosevelt forced the Europeans to withdraw. In 1903, the President used a threat of force to gain the right to dig the Panama Canal (see PANAMA CANAL [History]). America took over the finances of the Dominican Republic in 1905 to keep that country stable and free from European intervention. In 1916, during Wilson's Administration, American troops occupied the Dominican Republic to keep order there. These and other actions showed that the United States had emerged as a world power.

War Clouds in Europe. In 1914, long-standing problems among European nations led to the outbreak of World War I. In this fierce, destructive struggle, the *Central Powers* (Germany and a few other nations) lined up against the *Allies* (France, Great Britain, Italy, Russia, and many smaller countries). Before long, events would drag the United States into the war and test its new role as a world power.

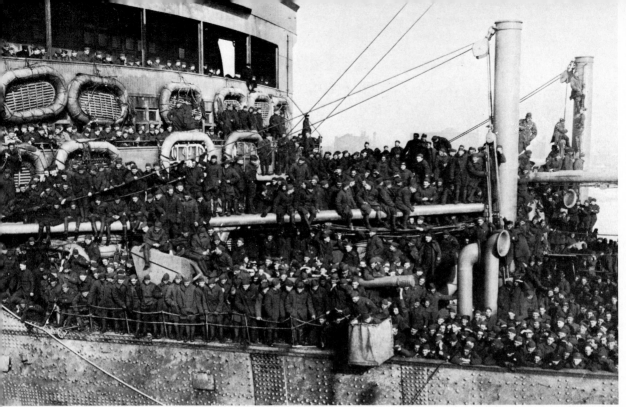

World War I marked the first time the United States had fought a full-scale war on foreign territory. In 1917 and 1918, troopships carried about 2 million American fighting men across the Atlantic to Europe. Called *doughboys,* the Americans helped the Allies defeat Germany.

UNITED STATES HISTORY: 1917-1929 / A New Place in the World

The United States stayed out of World War I until 1917. But then, German acts of aggression convinced President Wilson and most other Americans of the need to join the war against Germany in order to make the world "safe for democracy." For the first time in its history, the United States mobilized for a full-scale war on foreign territory. About 2 million American fighting men soon crossed the Atlantic in troopships. The *doughboys,* as the troops were called, played an important role in the Allied victory in 1918.

The decade following World War I brought sweeping changes to American life. The economy entered a period of spectacular—though uneven—growth. Spurred on by the good times and a desire to be "modern," large numbers of Americans adopted new attitudes and life styles. The booming economy and fast-paced life of the decade gave it the nickname of the *Roaring Twenties.* But the good times ended abruptly. In 1929, a stock-market crash triggered the worst and longest depression in America's history.

World War I and the Peace

The United States in the War. After World War I began in 1914, the United States repeatedly stated its position of neutrality. But increasingly, German acts of aggression brought America closer to joining the Allies. On May 7, 1915, a German submarine sank the British passenger ship *Lusitania.* The attack killed 1,198 people, including 128 American passengers. Wilson and other Americans bitterly protested this killing of defenseless civilians, and Germany agreed to stop such attacks.

Wilson won reelection in November 1916, using the slogan, "He Kept Us Out of War." But three months later, German submarines began sinking American merchant ships. This and other acts of aggression led the U.S. to declare war on Germany on April 6, 1917.

The American people rallied around their government's decision to go to war. Almost 2 million men volunteered for service, and about 3 million were drafted. The doughboys fought valiantly in the trenches, forests, and fields of France and helped the battered Allies turn back a major German offensive. On the home front, the spirit of patriotism grew to a fever pitch. Americans willingly let the government take near full control of the economy for the good of the war effort. The people bought billions of dollars worth of Liberty Bonds to help pay the cost of the war. Movie stars, including Charlie Chaplin and Mary Pickford, toured the country to promote bond sales. Fiery patriotic songs such as George M. Cohan's "Over There" and "You're a Grand Old Flag" gave a lift to the spirits of the doughboys and the public alike.

World War I ended in an Allied victory with the signing of an armistice on Nov. 11, 1918. For a detailed account of the conflict, see WORLD WAR I.

The Peace Conference and Treaty. In 1919, the Allies held the Paris Peace Conference to draw up the terms of the peace with Germany. Wilson viewed the conference as an opportunity to establish lasting peace among nations. He proposed a list of terms called the *Fourteen Points* to be used as a guide for the peace settlement. The terms included arms reductions and settlement of disputed territorial claims (see FOURTEEN POINTS). But the other leading Allies were chiefly interested in gaining territory and war payments from Germany. They adopted the Treaty of Versailles, which ignored almost all of Wilson's proposals. The treaty stripped Germany of its armed forces and much territory, and forced it to pay high war damages.

The Treaty of Versailles did make provision for one of Wilson's proposals—an association of nations (later called the League of Nations) that would work to maintain peace. But Wilson suffered a final blow to his peace plans when the United States Senate failed to ratify the Treaty of Versailles. Thus, the Senate rejected U.S. participation in the League of Nations. See VERSAILLES, TREATY OF; LEAGUE OF NATIONS; WILSON, WOODROW (Wilson's Second Administration).

Life During the Roaring Twenties

In many ways, the 1920's marked the point at which the United States began developing into the modern society it is today. During and after World War I, people continued to move from farms to cities in record numbers. The 1920 United States Census reported that, for the first time, a majority of Americans lived in urban areas. By the end of the Roaring Twenties, such features of modern life as the automobile, telephone, radio, and electric washing machine had become part of millions of American households. In 1927, aviation pioneer Charles A. Lindbergh helped launch the modern air age when he made the first solo flight across the Atlantic Ocean.

The role of American women changed dramatically during the 1920's. The 19th Amendment to the Constitution, which became law on Aug. 26, 1920, gave women the right to vote in all elections. In addition, many new opportunities for education and careers opened up to women during the decade.

Modern Life and Social Change. Developments of the 1920's broadened the experiences of millions of Americans. The mass movement to cities meant more people could enjoy such activities as movies, plays, and sporting events. Radio broadcasting began on a large scale during the 1920's. It brought news of the world and entertainment into millions of urban and rural homes. The automobile gave people a new way to get around—whether for business, or to see far-off places, or just for fun. Motion-picture theaters became part of almost every city and town during the 1920's. They became known as *dream palaces* because of their fancy design and the excitement and romance that movies provided for the public. The new role of women also changed society. Many women who found careers outside the home began thinking of themselves more as the equal of men, and less as housewives and mothers.

Change and Problems. The modern trends of the 1920's brought about problems as well as benefits.

Many Americans had trouble adjusting to the impersonal, fast-paced life of cities. This disorientation led to a rise in juvenile delinquency, crime, and other anti-social behavior. The complex life in cities also tended to weaken the strong family ties that had always been part of American society. See CITY (City Problems [Social Problems]).

The 18th Amendment to the Constitution, called the prohibition amendment, caused unforeseen problems. It outlawed the sale of alcoholic beverages throughout the United States as of Jan. 16, 1920. Large numbers of otherwise law-abiding citizens considered prohibition a violation of their rights. They ignored the law and bought liquor provided by underworld gangs. The supplying of illegal liquor, called *bootlegging*, helped many gangs prosper. In addition, competition for control of the lucrative bootlegging business led to many gang wars. See PROHIBITION.

The Flaming Youth. In an effort to be modern, many young men and women of the Roaring Twenties adopted a life style that earned them the nickname of the *Flaming Youth*. Women began wearing radically new clothing styles. Short skirts, rolled-down stockings, and short "bobbed" hair replaced the full-length dresses and long hair of earlier days. Women who wore such clothes became known as *flappers*. The flappers and their *beaus* (boyfriends) enjoyed such new thrills as speeding around in automobiles. They—along with many of their elders—often visited supposedly secret

Period Facts in Brief

Presidents (with political parties and dates of service)
Woodrow Wilson, Democrat, 1913-1921
Warren G. Harding, Republican, 1921-1923
Calvin Coolidge, Republican, 1923-1929
Herbert C. Hoover, Republican, 1929-1933

States in the Union
Number at start of period: 48
States added during the period: none.

Important Dates
1917-1918 The United States fought in World War I.
1920 The U.S. Senate rejected American participation in the League of Nations.
1920 The U.S. Census showed that, for the first time, the majority of Americans lived in urban areas.
1920 The 18th Amendment, prohibiting the sale of alcoholic beverages nationwide, became effective; the 19th Amendment gave women complete suffrage.
1922 The government raised tariffs to the highest level ever.
1925 The Scopes Trial in Dayton, Tenn., upheld the right of a state to ban the teaching of evolution in public schools.
c. 1925 The Golden Age of radio broadcasting began.
1927 Charles A. Lindbergh made the first solo flight across the Atlantic Ocean.
1927 *The Jazz Singer,* the first successful motion-picture "talkie," appeared.
1929 The stock-market crash brought financial ruin to thousands of investors.

Population Growth and Change

Total population, 101,297,851

1917

Rural, 50%   Urban, 50%

Total population, 121,670,000

1929

Rural, 44%   Urban, 56%

Ford Archives, Henry Ford Museum, Dearborn, Mich.

Automobile Ownership soared in the 1920's. During the decade, the number of automobiles in the United States nearly tripled. Cars soon crowded the streets of every American city and town.

Jazzmen Photo from Ramsey Archive

A Jazz Band and dancers dressed in flapper costumes entertain a nightclub audience, *above.* Jazz became so popular in the 1920's that the decade is sometimes called the *Jazz Age.*

Brown Bros.

Revival Meetings attracted large numbers of people during the 1920's. At these meetings, evangelists such as Billy Sunday, *on platform above,* delivered emotional sermons.

Wide World   Culver

Heroes of the 1920's included Babe Ruth and Charles A. Lindbergh. Ruth became the most famous sports star of the decade. Lindbergh made the first solo flight across the Atlantic Ocean.

nightclubs called *speakeasies.* At the speakeasies, people drank bootleg liquor; listened to jazz, the latest craze in popular music; and danced the Charleston and other modern steps.

An Age of Heroes. Americans of the Roaring Twenties developed strong admiration for individual accomplishment. Lindbergh's transatlantic flight made him a national hero. Sports superstars of the 1920's won the public's admiration for their ability to excel within the rules of the game. The stars included Red Grange of football, Jack Dempsey of boxing, Bobby Jones of golf, Bill Tilden and Helen Wills of tennis, and—most of all—baseball's Babe Ruth. Even attitudes toward big businessmen changed during the 1920's. Despised by many in earlier days, businessmen gained widespread admiration for their accomplishments.

The movies provided the public with daring fictional heroes, including good, strong cowboys who always defeated bad Indians or outlaws. In literature, F. Scott Fitzgerald created fictional characters whose pleasure-seeking lives won public admiration. But other authors saw little glamour in American life. For example, Sinclair Lewis won fame for novels that portrayed the "average American" as narrow-minded and dull. Ernest Hemingway scorned society's values and made heroes of the "lost generation"—people who did not fit into modern life.

Looking Backward. Not all Americans saw the changes brought about during the Roaring Twenties as being desirable. Many people yearned for a return to old American traditions, a trend that was reflected in many areas of life. In politics, it led to the return of a conservative federal government. In his successful presidential campaign of 1920, Warren G. Harding used the slogan "A Return to Normalcy." To many people, returning to "normalcy" meant ending the strong role of the federal government that marked the early 1900's. It also meant *isolation,* a turning away from the affairs of the outside world. Isolation—a reaction to World

War I—became a feature of American foreign policy during the 1920's.

In religion, the trend toward tradition led to an upsurge of *revivalism* (emotional religious preaching). Revival meetings were most common in rural areas, but also spread to cities. Billy Sunday, once a major-league baseball player, drew wildly enthusiastic crowds to his revivals in big cities.

The conservative Americans of the Roaring Twenties also called for a return to law and order. They denounced violations of prohibition and other crimes. However, few people seemed too bothered when, in 1923, investigators revealed widespread corruption in the Harding Administration (see HARDING, WARREN G. [Government Scandals]; TEAPOT DOME).

The Ku Klux Klan had died out in the 1870's, but a new Klan gained a large following during the 1920's. The new Klan had easy answers for Americans troubled by modern problems. It blamed the problems on "outsiders," including blacks, Jews, Roman Catholics, foreigners, and political radicals. Both Northerners and Southerners joined the Ku Klux Klan. At its height, the Klan had more than 2 million members. See KU KLUX KLAN (The Early 1900's).

The Economy—Boom and Bust

During the 1920's, the American economy soared to spectacular heights. Wartime government restrictions on business ended. Conservatives gained control of the federal government and adopted policies that aided big business. New technological developments also contributed to business growth.

But in spite of its growth and apparent strength, the economy was on shaky grounds. Only one segment of the economy—manufacturing—prospered. The distribution of wealth grew lopsided. Business executives grew rich, but farmers and laborers became worse off than before the war. Finally, in 1929, wild speculation led to a stock-market crash that toppled the economy like a house of cards.

Government and Business. The American people grew tired of the federal government's involvement in society that marked the Progressive Era and the war years. They elected to Congress conservatives who promised to reduce the role of government. Also, all three Presidents elected during the 1920's—Harding, Calvin Coolidge, and Herbert Hoover—were Republicans who agreed with the policy.

The federal government, however, did what it could to promote American business. In 1922, the government passed the Fordney-McCumber Act, which raised tariff duties to the highest level ever in order to keep foreign goods from competing with American products. This and other measures did much to help American business flourish.

Technology enabled American manufacturers to develop new products, improve existing ones, and turn out goods much faster and more cheaply than ever before. Sales of such items as electric washing machines, refrigerators, and radios soared. But the manufacturing boom depended most heavily on the growth of the automobile industry. Before and during the 1920's, Henry Ford and others refined car manufacturing to a science.

The cost of automobiles continued to drop and sales soared. In just 10 years between 1920 and 1930, the number of cars registered in the United States almost tripled, growing from about 8 million to 23 million. The thriving automobile industry triggered growth in such related industries as steel, road construction, gasoline sales, and tourism.

Agriculture and Labor did not share in the prosperity. A reduced market for farm goods in war-torn Europe and a slowdown in the U.S. population growth led to a decline in the demand for American farm products. Organized labor suffered major setbacks during the 1920's. A lack of government support reduced the power of unions in their dealing with employers, and workers in many new industries remained unorganized. Widespread poverty among farmers and laborers cut into the demand for manufactured goods, a contributing factor to the upcoming depression.

Investments, Speculation, and the Crash. The economic growth of the 1920's led more Americans than ever to invest in the stocks of corporations. The investments, in turn, provided companies with a flood of new capital for business expansion. As investors poured money into the stock market, the value of stocks soared. The upsweep led to widespread speculation, which pushed the value of stocks far beyond the level justified by earnings and dividends. Much of the speculation involved buying stocks *on margin;* that is, paying a fraction of the cost and borrowing the rest.

Such unsound investment practices led to the stock-market crash of 1929. In late October, a decline in stock prices set in. Panic selling followed, lowering stock prices drastically and dragging investors to financial ruin. When the year ended, the government estimated that the crash had cost investors $40 billion. The crash combined with the other weaknesses in the economy to bring on the Great Depression of the 1930's.

For more details on the decade of the 1920's, see ROARING TWENTIES.

Wide World

The Stock-Market Crash of 1929 brought an abrupt end to the prosperity of the Roaring Twenties. Crowds of panic-stricken investors gathered aimlessly on Wall Street after the crash, *above.*

The Great Depression of the 1930's spread poverty throughout the United States. Hungry, unemployed Americans stood in long "bread lines" to receive food paid for by charitable donations. The hard times dragged on until 1942, after the United States entered World War II.

UNITED STATES HISTORY: 1930-1959 / Depression and a World in Conflict

The United States suffered through the Great Depression that followed the stock-market crash of 1929 for more than 10 years. During the depression, millions of workers lost their jobs and large numbers of farmers were forced to abandon their farms. Poverty swept through the nation on a scale never before experienced.

The Great Depression was not limited to the United States. It struck almost every other country in the world. In some countries, the hard times helped bring to power dictators who promised action to restore the economy. The dictators included Adolf Hitler in Germany and a group of military leaders in Japan. Once in power, both Hitler and the Japanese rulers began conquering neighboring lands. Their actions led to World War II, the most destructive conflict in the history of man. The United States fought in the war from 1941 to 1945, and played a key role in defeating Germany and Japan.

Victory in World War II brought a spirit of great relief and joy to the United States. The postwar economy boomed. More people shared in the prosperity than ever before, creating a huge, well-to-do middle class. Even so, Americans still faced problems. Chief among them were the new threat of nuclear war, the growing strength of Communism, and discontent among Americans who did not share in the prosperity.

The Great Depression

The Road to Ruin. The stock-market crash sent shock waves through the American financial community. Banks greatly curtailed their loans to businesses, and businessmen then cut back on production. Millions of people lost their jobs because of the cutbacks. Spending then dwindled, and businesses suffered even more. Factories and stores shut down, causing even higher unemployment. Consumption of farm products declined, and farmers became worse off than ever. Thousands of banks failed during the depression and foreign trade decreased sharply. By the early 1930's, the nation's economy was paralyzed.

The Depression and the People. At the height of the depression in 1933, about 13 million Americans were out of work, and many others had only part-time jobs. Farm income declined so sharply that more than 750,000 farmers lost their land. The Dust Bowl, the result of a terrible drought on the western Great Plains, also wiped out many farmers (see DUST BOWL). Hundreds of thousands of people lost their life savings as a result of the bank failures.

Throughout the depression, many Americans went hungry. People stood in "bread lines" and went to "soup kitchens" to get food provided by charities. Often, two or more families lived crowded together in a small apartment. Some homeless people built shacks of tin and scraps of wood in vacant areas. They called these clumps of shacks *Hoovervilles*—a scornful reference to Herbert Hoover, President when the depression struck. In 1932, about 15,000 World War I veterans marched on Washington, D.C., to demand an early

payment of a government bonus owed them. Hoover ordered troops to drive them out of the city.

Roosevelt, Recovery, and Reform. Early in the Great Depression, Hoover promised that prosperity was "just around the corner." But the depression deepened as the election of 1932 approached. The Republicans slated Hoover for re-election. The Democrats chose Franklin Delano Roosevelt. In his campaign, Roosevelt promised government action to end the Great Depression and reforms to avoid future depressions. The people responded, and Roosevelt won a landslide victory.

Roosevelt's program for recovery and reform was called the *New Deal*. Its many provisions included public works projects to provide jobs, relief for farmers, aid to manufacturing firms, and the regulation of banks. A solidly Democratic Congress approved almost every measure Roosevelt proposed. Many new government agencies were set up to help fight the depression. The agencies included the Civilian Conservation Corps (CCC) and the Works Progress Administration (WPA), both of which provided jobs; the Farm Credit Administration (FCA), which extended credit to farmers; and the Social Security Board, which developed the social security system.

The New Deal helped relieve the hardship of many Americans. But hard times dragged on until World War II military spending stimulated the economy.

Roosevelt's efforts to end the depression made him one of the most popular U.S. Presidents. The voters elected him to four terms. No other President won election more than twice. Roosevelt's New Deal was a turning point in American history. It marked the start of a strong government role in the nation's economic affairs that has continued and grown to the present day. See GREAT DEPRESSION; NEW DEAL.

The United States in World War II

World War II began on Sept. 1, 1939, when German troops overran Poland. France, Great Britain, and other nations (called the Allies) went to war against Germany.

Period Facts in Brief

Presidents (with political parties and dates of service)
Herbert C. Hoover, Republican, 1929-1933
Franklin D. Roosevelt, Democrat, 1933-1945
Harry S. Truman, Democrat, 1945-1953
Dwight D. Eisenhower, Republican, 1953-1961

States in the Union
Number at start of period: 48
Number at end of period: 50
States added during the period:
Alaska (1959), Hawaii (1959).

Important Dates
1930's The United States suffered through the Great Depression.
1933 President Franklin D. Roosevelt began the New Deal program to try to end the depression.
1941-1945 The United States fought in World War II.
1945 An American airplane dropped the first atomic bomb used in warfare on Hiroshima, Japan.
1945 The United States became a charter member of the United Nations (UN).
1947 President Truman announced the Truman Doctrine, which pledged American aid to nations threatened by Communism.
1950's Television became part of most American homes.
1950 Senator Joseph R. McCarthy gained national fame by charging that Communists had infiltrated the federal government.
1950-1953 The United States fought in the Korean War.
1954 The Supreme Court ruled compulsory segregation in public schools unconstitutional.
1955 Martin Luther King, Jr., began organizing a movement to protest discrimination against blacks.
1957 Russia launched *Sputnik I*—the first space satellite—causing the United States to place more emphasis on space research.

Population Growth and Change
Total population, 122,775,046
1930
Rural, 44%   Urban, 56%

Total population, 175,608,490
1959
Rural, 31%   Urban, 69%

Library of Congress

The Dust Bowl spread across the Great Plains and the Southwest during the Depression, destroying much farmland. It was caused by a drought accompanied by severe dust storms.

Wide World

World War II Defense Workers included many women. The women filled jobs vacated by men who entered the armed forces. They helped supply the men with planes, ships, and weapons.

U.S. Energy Research and Development Administration

American Planes Dropped Atomic Bombs on the Japanese cities of Hiroshima and Nagasaki in 1945. The destruction from these blasts caused Japan to surrender, ending World War II.

At first, America stayed out of the war. But on Dec. 7, 1941, Japanese planes bombed the U.S. military base at Pearl Harbor, Hawaii. The United States declared war on Japan on December 8, and on Germany and Italy—Germany's chief ally—three days later.

The War Effort. The American people backed the war effort with fierce dedication. About 15 million American men served in the armed forces. They ranged from teenagers to men well over 40. More than 200,000 women volunteered for service. At home, automobile plants and other factories were converted into defense plants where airplanes, ships, weapons, and other war supplies were made. The country had a shortage of civilian men, and so thousands of women worked in the defense plants. With a combination of humor and admiration, people called the women defense workers "Rosie the Riveter." Even children took part in the war effort. Boys and girls collected used tin cans, old tires, and other "junk" that could be recycled and used for war supplies.

Allied Victory. On May 7, 1945, after a long, bitter struggle, the Americans and other Allies forced the mighty German war machine to surrender. Vice-President Harry S. Truman had become President upon Roosevelt's death about a month earlier. Truman demanded Japan's surrender, but the Japanese continued to fight on. Truman then made one of the major decisions in history. He ordered the use of the atomic bomb, a weapon many times more destructive than any previous weapon. An American airplane dropped the first atomic bomb used in warfare on Hiroshima, Japan, on Aug. 6, 1945. A second atomic bomb was dropped on Nagasaki on August 9 (see ATOMIC BOMB). Japan formally surrendered on September 2, and the war was over. For more details, see WORLD WAR II.

The Threat of Communism

The United States and Russia both fought on the side of the Allies during World War II. But after the war, the two countries became bitter enemies. Russia,

as a Communist country, opposed democracy. It helped Communists take control of most of the countries of Eastern Europe and also aided Communists who seized control of China.

Russia and China then set out to spread Communism to other lands. The United States, as the world's most powerful democratic country, took on the role of defending non-Communist nations threatened by Communist take-over. The containment of Communism became the major goal of U.S. postwar foreign policy.

The Cold War and Foreign Policy. The postwar struggle between the American-led non-Communist nations and Russia and its Communist allies became known as the *Cold War*. It was so named because it did not lead to fighting, or a "hot" war, on a major scale.

Both the United States and Russia built up arsenals of atomic bombs, more powerful hydrogen bombs, and other nuclear weapons. The nuclear weapons made each nation capable of destroying the other. The threat of nuclear war made both sides cautious. As a result, Cold War strategy emphasized threats of force, propaganda, and aid to weak nations. The United Nations (UN), founded in 1945, provided a forum where the nations could try to settle their Cold War disputes.

Truman and Dwight D. Eisenhower, the first two Presidents of the Cold War era, pledged American military support to any nation threatened by Communism. Also, the United States provided billions of dollars to non-Communist nations. See COLD WAR.

The Korean War resulted from the Cold War friction. On June 25, 1950, troops from Communist North Korea, equipped by Russia, invaded South Korea. The UN called on member nations to help restore peace. Truman sent American troops to aid South Korea, and the UN sent a fighting force made up of troops from many nations. The war lasted for three years, ending in a truce on July 27, 1953. See KOREAN WAR.

Communism and Internal Friction. The spread of Communism caused deep divisions within the United States. Conservatives blamed the Roosevelt and Truman Administrations for allowing the Communist postwar gains. They also claimed that Communists were infiltrating the American government. The charges led to widespread investigations of—and debate over—the extent of Communist influence in American government and society. Conservatives believed the investigations were needed to save the country from Communist control. Liberals charged the conservatives with conducting "witch hunts"; that is, trying to fix guilt on people without evidence. See UN-AMERICAN ACTIVITIES COMMITTEE; HISS, ALGER; McCARTHY, JOSEPH R.

Postwar Society

After World War II, the United States entered the greatest period of economic growth in its history. Periods of *inflation* (rapidly rising prices) and *recession* (mild business slumps) occurred. But overall, businesses and people prospered. Prosperity spread to more Americans than ever before, resulting in major changes in American life. However, not all people shared in the prosperity. Millions of Americans—including a high percentage of the nation's blacks—continued to live in poverty. The existence of poverty amid prosperity

Suburban Housing Developments sprang up around American cities after World War II. The postwar prosperity enabled millions of people to afford new houses in the suburbs.

A Civil Rights Law banning compulsory school segregation led to a dramatic incident in 1957. President Eisenhower sent federal troops to escort black students into an all-white Arkansas school.

brought on a period of active social protest that has continued to the present day.

Prosperity Returns. Military spending during World War II drew the United States out of the Great Depression. Major industries, such as automobile manufacturing and housing construction, had all but stopped during the war. After the war, these industries resumed production on a much larger scale than ever. Relatively new industries such as electronics, plastics, frozen foods, and jet aircraft became booming businesses.

The shortage of goods during the war and other factors combined to create a vast market for American products. A soaring birth rate boosted the number of consumers. Between 1950 and 1960 alone, the population of the United States grew by about 28 million. Labor unions became stronger than ever, and gained high wages and other benefits for their members. Wage laws and other government regulations also helped give workers a greater share of the profits of business. These developments also meant that more Americans had more money to spend on goods.

A New Life Style resulted from the prosperity. After the war, millions of people needed, and were able to afford, new housing. Construction companies quickly built up huge clusters of houses in suburbs around the nation's cities. Vast numbers of Americans moved from cities to suburbs. The suburbs attracted people for many reasons. They offered newer housing, more open space, and—usually—better schools than the central cities. See Suburb; City (Metropolitan Cities).

A rise in automobile ownership accompanied the suburban growth. The majority of suburbanites worked in the central cities and depended on cars to get to and from work. Most suburbs lacked good local transportation systems, and so families relied on cars to go shopping or almost anywhere else. Between 1940 and 1960, the number of automobiles registered in the United States jumped from about 27½ million to 61½ million. By 1960, over three-fourths of all American families

owned a car, and almost a fifth owned more than one.

Increased automobile traffic led to the building of a nationwide network of superhighways. The car and prosperity enabled more people than ever to take vacation trips. New motels, fast-service restaurants, and gas stations sprang up to serve the tourists.

Prosperity and technological advances changed American life in other ways. Television—an experimental device before the war—became a feature of most American homes during the 1950's. This wonder of modern science brought scenes of the world into the American living room at the flick of a switch. Fascinated, large numbers of people made TV watching one of their main leisure-time activities (see Television [History]). New appliances made household work easier for American families. They included automatic washers, driers, dishwashers, and garbage disposers.

Poverty and Discrimination. In spite of the general prosperity, millions of Americans still lived in poverty. The poor included members of all races, but the plight of the nation's poor blacks seemed especially bleak. Ever since emancipation, blacks in both the North and South had faced discrimination in jobs, housing, education, and other areas. A lack of education and jobs made poverty among blacks widespread.

During the early 1900's, blacks, joined by many whites, had begun a movement to extend civil rights to blacks. The movement gained momentum after World War II. Efforts of civil rights leaders resulted in several Supreme Court decisions that attacked discrimination. In the best-known case, *Brown v. Board of Education of Topeka* (1954), the court ruled compulsory segregation in public schools illegal.

In spite of the gains, many civil rights leaders became dissatisfied with the slow progress of their movement. In 1955, Martin Luther King, Jr., a Baptist minister, began organizing demonstrations protesting discrimination. Before long, the public protest would become a major tool of Americans seeking change.

A Photograph of the Earth taken by astronauts orbiting the moon, above, is an example of America's leading role in science and technology. But despite its many accomplishments, the United States today faces a variety of problems and challenges—just as it has throughout its history.

UNITED STATES HISTORY/*America Since 1960*

The period of American history since 1960 has been marked by a continuation of many postwar trends. For much of the period, the country's foreign policy remained focused on the containment of Communism. The economy continued to expand, despite recurring periods of inflation and recession. The movement of people from cities to suburbs continued steadily. The 1970 U.S. Census showed that, for the first time, more Americans lived in suburbs than in cities.

The country continued to be a leader in scientific and technological advancements. It made great strides in medicine that helped reduce human suffering, and its technological skill provided the means for a new and exciting field of exploration—outer space.

At the same time, events and new public attitudes brought dramatic social changes to the United States. The black civil rights movement grew in intensity during the 1960's. Many other groups—including American Indians, Mexican Americans, and women—also began demanding fuller rights. In the mid-1960's, many Americans began challenging their government's foreign-policy decisions. Protesters of all kinds staged demonstrations to try to bring about change. Most demonstrations were conducted peacefully. But in some cases, they led to violence.

Crime and violence soared in the United States after 1960, and pollution threatened the environment. Concern over political corruption grew in the 1970's, and helped bring about the first resignation of an American President, Richard M. Nixon.

As in every other period of history, the list of the nation's problems was long. But at the same time, most Americans maintained a deep pride in their country. In 1976, the American people celebrated the *bicentennial* (200th anniversary) of its founding. They marked the occasion with parades, reenactments of historical events, and other patriotic celebrations.

The 1960's

The Civil Rights Movement. The black civil rights movement became the main domestic issue in the United States during the early 1960's. Increasingly, blacks—joined by whites—staged demonstrations in order to dramatize their demands for rights and equality. One of the highlights of the movement came on Aug. 28, 1963, when more than 200,000 people staged a *freedom march* called the March on Washington in Washington, D.C.

John F. Kennedy, who became President in 1961, urged Congress to pass legislation outlawing discrimination on the basis of race. Kennedy was killed by an assassin on Nov. 22, 1963, and Vice-President Lyndon B. Johnson became President. Johnson, a former U.S. senator skilled in dealing with legislators, persuaded Congress to pass many major civil rights laws.

The Civil Rights Act of 1964 outlawed discrimination in employment, voter registration, and public accommodations. The Civil Rights Act of 1968 was designed to end discrimination in the sale and renting of housing. Congress, at Johnson's urging, also provided financial

aid for the needy as part of a program that Johnson called the War on Poverty. For a detailed account of the civil rights movement, see BLACK AMERICANS.

Urban Unrest. In spite of government aid and a generally booming economy, poverty remained a major problem in America's central cities. Discontent among blacks in poor, decaying neighborhoods grew. In the mid-1960's, blacks staged riots in the ghettos of Chicago, Cleveland, Detroit, Los Angeles, New York City, Newark, and other cities. Many blacks also rioted in 1968, following the assassination of Martin Luther King, Jr.

The number of such crimes as murder, robbery, and rape soared during the 1960's. The crime rate was especially high in the central cities, but also increased rapidly in suburbs and elsewhere. Sociologists attributed the rising crime rate to many factors, including the weakening of the family, poverty, mental illness, drug addiction, and a feeling of hopelessness and alienation.

The Vietnam War brought further turmoil to the United States in the 1960's. The war had begun in 1957 as a battle for control of South Vietnam between the non-Communist government and Communists. In the late 1950's and early 1960's, Presidents Eisenhower and Kennedy sent military aid and advisers to support the South Vietnam government. Soon after Johnson became President, the Communists threatened to topple the government. Johnson responded to the threat by sending hundreds of thousands of American combat troops to help South Vietnam fight the Communists. By the mid-1960's, the United States was deeply involved in the Vietnam War.

Public response to the Vietnam War differed sharply from the near unanimous public support in World Wars I and II. A majority of Americans supported the war effort at first, but others bitterly opposed it. In the late 1960's, opposition to the war grew. The war critics argued that the United States had no right to interfere in Vietnamese affairs. Throughout the nation, college students and others staged antiwar demonstrations.

Johnson, discouraged by the criticism of his Vietnam policy, refused to run for reelection in 1968. The people elected Richard M. Nixon, partly because he pledged to end U.S. involvement in the war. But as the 1960's ended, U.S. troops were still in Vietnam.

Space Exploration by American astronauts provided a high note during the troubled 1960's. On May 5, 1961, astronaut Alan B. Shepard, Jr., soared into space from a launching pad at Cape Canaveral, Fla. Shepard earned the distinction of becoming the first American in space. During the 1960's, the United States and the Soviet Union matched their technological skills in a race to land the first person on the moon. Then, on July 20, 1969, millions of people watched on television as U.S. astronaut Neil A. Armstrong climbed down from his spacecraft and became the first person to set foot on the moon. For the story of America's accomplishments in space, see SPACE TRAVEL.

The 1970's

Political Scandals rocked the United States in the 1970's. Investigators revealed many cases of graft and other corruption in local and state government, but the nation's attention focused chiefly on charges of corruption on the federal level.

In 1973, Spiro T. Agnew, Nixon's Vice President,

Period Facts in Brief

Presidents (with political parties and dates of service)
Dwight D. Eisenhower, Republican, 1953-1961
John F. Kennedy, Democrat, 1961-1963
Lyndon B. Johnson, Democrat, 1963-1969
Richard M. Nixon, Republican, 1969-1974
Gerald R. Ford, Republican, 1974-1977
James E. Carter, Jr., Democrat, 1977-1981
Ronald W. Reagan, Republican, 1981-

States in the Union

Number at start of period: 50
States added during the period: none.

Important Dates

1961 Astronaut Alan B. Shepard, Jr., became the first American in space.
1962 Russia removed missiles from Cuba, ending a threat of war with the United States.
1964 Congress passed a flood of important civil rights laws.
1965 American combat troops entered the Vietnam War.
1969 Astronaut Neil A. Armstrong became the first person to set foot on the moon.
1973 The United States removed its last ground troops from Vietnam. The war ended in 1975.
1974 Richard M. Nixon became the first American President to resign from office.
1976 The United States celebrated its bicentennial.
1981-1982 A recession led to the highest rate of unemployment in the United States since the Great Depression of the 1930's.

Population Growth and Change

1960 — Total population, 179,323,175
Rural, 30%   Urban, 70%

1986 — Total population, 240,854,000
Rural, 26%   Urban, 74%

Wide World

Civil Rights for Blacks became a major national issue during the 1960's. About 200,000 persons, including both blacks and whites, took part in the March on Washington in 1963.

David Burnett

Protest Demonstrations became a common tool among Americans seeking change in the 1960's. The young people above called for an end to U.S. participation in the Vietnam War.

Alex Webb, Magnum

The Watergate Scandal forced President Richard M. Nixon, *left on carpet,* to resign from office in 1974. Vice President Gerald R. Ford, *right,* succeeded Nixon as President.

came under criminal investigation. A federal grand jury began hearing charges that he participated in widespread graft in Maryland. The investigation covered the period Agnew had served as an officeholder in Maryland and as Vice President. Agnew resigned from the vice presidency on Oct. 10, 1973. See AGNEW, SPIRO T.

In 1972, campaign workers for President Nixon's re-election committed a burglary at the Democratic political headquarters in the Watergate building complex in Washington, D.C. Nixon was later charged with covering up the burglary and with other illegal activities. In July 1974, the Judiciary Committee of the House of Representatives voted articles of impeachment against the President. Evidence against Nixon mounted until it became apparent that the full House of Representatives would impeach him and that the Senate would remove him from office. On Aug. 9, 1974, he resigned as President. He was the only U.S. President ever to resign.

Gerald R. Ford, who had been appointed Vice President following Agnew's resignation, succeeded Nixon. He pardoned Nixon for all federal crimes the former President might have committed while in office. See WATERGATE and NIXON, RICHARD M., for more details on the Watergate scandal and resignation.

The Spreading Drive for Equality. The drive for equality that began with blacks spread to other minority groups. American Indians, Mexican Americans, and others organized active movements aimed at gaining equality (see INDIAN, AMERICAN [Indians Today]; MEXICAN AMERICANS). In addition, large numbers of women began calling for an end to discrimination based on sex. Their activities became known as the Women's Liberation Movement. The movement helped bring about greater equality for women in employment and other areas (see WOMAN [Woman's Roles Today]).

Pollution and Conservation. As the country's industry and population grew, so did the pollution of its

environment. Smoke from factories and fumes from automobiles filled the air with dangerous gases. Wastes from factories and other sources polluted many rivers and lakes. Many Americans began demanding government action to control environmental pollution. In response, the government passed many antipollution laws. But the pollution problem remains severe. See ENVIRONMENTAL POLLUTION.

The need to conserve energy has become another pressing problem for the country. America's many industries, households, cars, and other energy users place a drain on the nation's limited energy supply. The energy crisis was highlighted in 1973, when a fuel shortage reduced the supply of oil available for heating homes and the gasoline supply for automobiles and other vehicles. In 1979, another gasoline shortage hit parts of the nation. See ENERGY SUPPLY.

Foreign Affairs. The chief U.S. foreign policies in the 1970's were aimed at ending the Vietnam War and easing world tensions. Nixon removed America's last ground forces from Vietnam in 1973. Two years later, South Vietnam fell to the Communists. For fuller details on the conflict, see VIETNAM WAR.

Nixon also took steps to reduce tensions between the United States and China and the Soviet Union, the two leading Communist powers. In 1972, he visited these countries. Nixon reached agreements with the Chinese and Soviet leaders that seemed to improve U.S. relations with the Communist powers.

Jimmy Carter, elected President in 1976, worked to end a long-standing dispute with Panama over control of the Panama Canal. In 1978, the United States approved a treaty negotiated by the Carter Administration that will give Panama control of the canal on Dec. 31, 1999. Another treaty will give the United States the right to defend the canal's neutrality.

Carter also tried to improve U.S. relations with China

and Russia. In early 1979, the United States and China established normal diplomatic relations. Later that year, Carter and Leonid I. Brezhnev, leader of the Soviet Communist Party, signed a treaty that would limit the use of U.S. and Russian nuclear arms. But relations between the United States and the Soviet Union declined sharply when Soviet troops invaded Afghanistan in late 1979. Partly to protest the invasion, the United States Senate ended consideration of the arms treaty.

Troubles in the Middle East, a region that is important to U.S. security, also challenged the United States. In 1978, Carter arranged meetings that led to a peace agreement between Egypt and Israel. In Iran, a revolution overthrew the government of the shah in February 1979. In November of that year, revolutionaries took over the U.S. Embassy in Teheran, Iran's capital, to protest American aid to the deposed shah. The revolutionaries held a group of U.S. citizens as hostages, and they demanded that the United States return the shah to Iran for trial. The U.S. government refused to meet the demands and denounced the Iranian action as a violation of international law. In April 1980, Carter ordered a military mission into Iran to rescue the hostages. However, the mission failed. The shah died in Egypt in July, but the revolutionaries held the hostages until January 1981. See CARTER, JAMES E., JR. (The Iranian Crisis); IRAN (The Islamic Republic).

Domestic Problems. The worst period of inflation in American history began in the late 1960's. During the early 1970's, a severe recession led to high unemployment. Historically, recessions have brought an end to inflation. During the early 1970's, however, inflation continued to plague the nation's consumers in spite of the severe business slump. The economy recovered during the mid-1970's, when the recession ended and the rate of inflation slowed down. Inflation began to rise sharply again during the late 1970's. The rate of inflation was slowed somewhat by a recession that occurred in early 1980.

Recent Developments

The economy became the main concern of President Ronald Reagan, who succeeded Carter in 1981. Reagan wanted to slash the inflation rate and balance the federal budget. Inflation slowed again, largely due to another recession which began in mid-1981. But sharp declines in construction, manufacturing, and retail trade led to rising unemployment. Many people postponed purchases because of record high interest rates.

To stimulate the economy, Reagan proposed the largest federal income tax reduction in U.S. history. Congress approved the tax-cut program, which scheduled cuts in 1981, 1982, and 1983. But high interest rates continued to limit spending by consumers and investment by business. The recession worsened, and the nation experienced its highest rate of unemployment since 1941. An economic recovery began in 1983, and unemployment fell sharply. Inflation remained low. But the tax cuts and heavy government defense spending helped bring about record deficits in the federal budget.

Automation and increasing foreign competition created major problems for U.S. industrial workers during the early 1980's. Many workers lost their jobs when companies installed robots and other advanced technology. The new machines greatly outproduced the workers they replaced and demanded new skills that those workers lacked. Many more jobs were lost as a result of growing imports in many industries, including automobiles and steel. This competition forced many U.S. companies to go out of business. Others closed their factories in the United States and opened plants in Mexico, South Korea, Taiwan, and other nations where labor costs were far below those in the United States.

In foreign affairs, the United States became increasingly concerned with unrest in Central America. Much fighting has taken place between rebels and government troops in Nicaragua and El Salvador. Cuba and the Soviet Union gave aid to the government of Nicaragua and rebels in El Salvador. The United States supported a rebellion against the Nicaraguan government and provided military aid to El Salvador's government.

The United States launched a huge military buildup during the early 1980's. It also held talks with officials of the Soviet Union to reduce nuclear arms, but the talks failed. The United States then began to carry out a program to supply its allies in Western Europe with hundreds of nuclear missiles. This program further strained U.S.-Soviet relations.   OSCAR HANDLIN

UNITED STATES HISTORY / *Study Aids*

Related Articles. See the articles on each President and the *History* section of the articles on each state. Other related articles in WORLD BOOK include:

HISTORICAL PERIODS AND WARS

Civil War	Exploration
Cold War	French and Indian Wars
Colonial Life in America	Gay Nineties

Lehtikuva, Photoreporters

Freed U.S. Hostages arrive in West Germany in January 1981, before returning to the United States. Iranian revolutionaries held them 14 months to protest U.S. aid to the deposed shah of Iran.

Great Depression
Indian Wars
Industrial Revolution
Korean War
Mexican War
Pioneer Life in America
Progressive Movement
Reconstruction
Revolutionary War in America

Roaring Twenties
Spanish-American War
Vietnam War
War of 1812
Western Frontier Life
Westward Movement
World War I
World War II

IMPORTANT DOCUMENTS

Articles of Confederation
Atlantic Charter
Compromise of 1850
Constitution of the United States
Declaration of Independence
Emancipation Proclamation
Federalist, The
Four Freedoms

Fourteen Points
Gettysburg Address
Homestead Act
Kansas-Nebraska Act
Mayflower Compact
Missouri Compromise
Monroe Doctrine
Northwest Ordinance

OTHER RELATED ARTICLES

American Literature
Bicentennial Celebration, American
Continental Congress
Flag
Gold Rush
Immigration
Indian, American
Lewis and Clark
    Expedition
Louisiana Purchase

Money
Panama Canal
Political Party
Slavery
States' Rights
United States
United States,
    Government of the
United States Capitals
World, History of the

Outline

I. America Before Colonial Times
  A. The First Americans
  B. European Discovery
  C. Exploration and Early Settlement
  D. The Land That Became the United States
II. The Colonial Heritage (1607-1753)
  A. The Thirteen Colonies
  B. Life in Colonial America
III. The Movement for Independence (1754-1783)
  A. Background to the Revolution
  B. The Road to Independence
  C. American Attitudes and Independence
IV. Forming a New Nation (1784-1819)
  A. Establishing a Government
  B. Early Problems and Politics
  C. Jeffersonian Democracy
  D. The War of 1812
  E. Growing Nationalism
V. Expansion (1820-1849)
  A. America Moves West
  B. Politics and the "Common Man"
  C. Social Reform
VI. The Irrepressible Conflict (1850-1869)
  A. Debate and Compromise
  B. Nationwide Turmoil
  C. The Civil War and Reconstruction
VII. Industrialization and Reform (1870-1916)
  A. The Rise of Big Business
  B. The South and the West
  C. Life During the Industrial Era
  D. Reform
  E. Foreign Affairs
VIII. A New Place in the World (1917-1929)
  A. World War I and the Peace
  B. Life During the Roaring Twenties
  C. The Economy—Boom and Bust
IX. Depression and a World in Conflict (1930-1959)
  A. The Great Depression
  B. The United States in World War II
  C. The Threat of Communism
  D. Postwar Society

X. America Since 1960
  A. The 1960's
  B. The 1970's
XI. Recent Developments

Questions

What were the 13 original colonies?
What was the Stamp Act? The Sugar Act?
When was the Declaration of Independence adopted?
Why did the early American leaders decide to write the Constitution?
What was the doctrine of manifest destiny?
How did westward expansion contribute to America's economic growth?
What was the nullification crisis?
What were some effects of the Civil War?
What was the Louisiana Purchase?
What was prohibition?

Additional Resources

Level I

BOORSTIN, DANIEL J. *The Landmark History of the American People from Plymouth to Appomattox.* Random House, 1968. *The Landmark History of the American People from Appomattox to the Moon.* 1970.
Coming to America. Dial, 1980-1981. A 5-volume series on immigration.
COMMAGER, HENRY S. *The First Book of American History.* Watts, 1957.
COY, HAROLD. *The Americans.* Little, Brown, 1958. *Presidents.* Rev. ed. Watts, 1977.
JONES, JAYNE CLARK. *The American Indian in America.* 2 vols. Lerner, 1973.
LANDAU, ELAINE. *Hidden Heroines: Women in American History.* Simon & Schuster, 1975.
MAY, CHARLES PAUL. *The Uprooted.* Westminster, 1976.
THUM, MARCELLA. *Exploring Black America: A History and Guide.* Atheneum, 1975.

Level II

AMERICAN HERITAGE. *Great Historic Places.* Rev. ed. Simon & Schuster, 1980.
BAILEY, THOMAS A. *A Diplomatic History of the American People.* 10th ed. Prentice-Hall, 1980.
BILLINGTON, RAY ALLEN. *Westward Expansion: A History of the American Frontier.* 5th ed. Macmillan, 1982.
BURNS, JAMES MACGREGOR. *The Vineyard of Liberty: The American Experiment.* Knopf, 1982.
COMMAGER, HENRY S., ed. *Documents of American History.* 2 vols. 9th ed. Prentice-Hall, 1974.
DEBO, ANGIE. *A History of the Indians of the United States.* Univ. of Oklahoma Press, 1970.
Encyclopedia of American History. Ed. by Richard B. Morris. 6th ed. Harper, 1982.
FRANKLIN, JOHN H. *From Slavery to Freedom: A History of Negro Americans.* 5th ed. Knopf, 1980.
HANDLIN, OSCAR. *A Pictorial History of Immigration.* Crown, 1972.
HARDING, VINCENT. *There Is a River: The Black Struggle for Freedom in America.* Harcourt, 1981.
HOCHMAN, STANLEY. *Yesterday and Today: A Dictionary of Recent American History.* McGraw, 1979.
HOFSTADTER, RICHARD. *The American Political Tradition and the Men Who Made It.* Rev. ed. Knopf, 1973.
HYMOWITZ, CAROL, and WEISSMAN, MICHAELE. *A History of Women in America.* Bantam, 1978.
LECKIE, ROBERT. *The Wars of America.* Rev. ed. Harper, 1981.
LINGEMAN, RICHARD R. *Small Town America: A Narrative History, 1620—The Present.* Putnam, 1980.
MORISON, SAMUEL ELIOT, and others. *A Concise History of the American Republic.* 2nd ed. Oxford, 1983.
TINDALL, GEORGE BROWN. *America: A Narrative History.* 2 vols. Norton, 1984.
WHITE, THEODORE H. *America in Search of Itself: The Making of the President, 1956-1980.* Harper, 1982.

Insigne of the United States Air Force Academy

UNITED STATES AIR FORCE ACADEMY

UNITED STATES AIR FORCE. See AIR FORCE, UNITED STATES.

UNITED STATES AIR FORCE ACADEMY prepares young men and women for careers as officers in the United States Air Force. It stands on an 18,000-acre (7,280-hectare) site in the foothills of the Rocky Mountains, near Colorado Springs, Colo. The academy is an agency of the Department of the Air Force.

Students at the academy are called *Air Force cadets.* Cadets take four years of academic work leading to a Bachelor of Science degree. They also take professional military training to earn regular commissions in the United States Air Force. When students enter the academy, they agree to serve four years as a cadet and five years as an Air Force officer. The United States government provides food, housing, and medical care for the cadets. Each cadet receives a monthly salary to pay for uniforms, textbooks, and personal expenses.

Entrance Requirements. Candidates for appointment to the academy must be: (1) citizens of the United States, (2) at least 17 and not yet 22 years old on July 1 of the year for which they seek appointment, (3) unmarried, (4) in good physical condition, and (5) of good moral character. A catalog containing full information may be obtained from the Registrar, United States Air Force Academy, Colorado 80840.

Nomination and Selection of Cadets. Each candidate for the academy must be nominated by one of the

Selection of Candidates

Candidates for the United States Air Force Academy are nominated by the sources listed below. The figures represent the total number of candidates each nominating source may select for the Academy.

- **100** by the President of the United States
- **5** by the Vice President of the United States
- **500** by United States Senators
- **2,175** by United States Congressmen
- **600** from qualified alternates selected by Senators and Congressmen
- **65** sons and daughters of deceased or disabled veterans or prisoners of war
- **5** from the District of Columbia
- **6** from Puerto Rico
- **1** from Guam
- **1** from American Samoa
- **1** from the Virgin Islands
- **85** from the regular United States armed forces
- **85** from the reserve United States armed forces
- **20** from honor military schools
- **24** cadets from other countries

An unlimited number of sons and daughters of Medal of Honor winners may also attend.

legally established nominating sources. Candidates must then pass the qualifying medical examination, the physical aptitude examination, and college entrance examinations in order to qualify for appointment.

Cadet Life. Cadets live in cadet dormitories. A cadet's normal weekday begins with *reveille* at 6 A.M. Before classes, they eat breakfast and prepare their rooms for morning inspection. Classes are held from 7:30 A.M. to noon and from 1:30 P.M. to 3:30 P.M. Most classes are conducted in small classrooms and laboratories in Fairchild Hall.

After classes, the cadet takes part in sports, drill, or extracurricular activities. After supper, the cadet must study in the dormitory or in the academy library until 10:15 P.M. Taps sounds at 11:00 P.M.

Cadets may attend Sunday or Sabbath services of their faith in the academy chapel. The chapel's 17 towering aluminum spires make it an academy land-

Air Force Cadets march past the cadet chapel on the campus of the U.S. Air Force Academy near Colorado Springs, Colo. The academy is located in the foothills of the Rocky Mountains.

UNITED STATES AIR FORCE ACADEMY

U.S. Air Force Academy

Air Force Cadets Take Target Practice at the shooting range under the expert guidance of an instructor.

mark. The chapel is divided into sections for Protestant, Roman Catholic, and Jewish religious services. Cadets may also participate in services held in nearby communities.

Cadets live by an *honor code* that stresses complete integrity in word and deed. The code says, "We will not lie, steal, or cheat, nor tolerate among us anyone who does." The cadets themselves enforce the code, and violation of the code is cause for dismissal.

Social functions for the cadets are held on weekends in Arnold Hall. Privileges to leave the campus on weekends increase as the cadet progresses through the academy. Each year, all cadets receive a 12-day Christmas *leave* (vacation), a 1-week spring leave, and a 3-week summer leave.

The Academy Curriculum consists of the academic program, military training, and physical education. The academic program includes courses in the basic and applied sciences, social sciences, and humanities. The cadet must take certain courses that provide a general background in all subject areas. The cadet also majors in one subject or area of concentration. Cadets who have completed previous college work and cadets with special ability may take advanced courses in their major fields. Cadets are also permitted to compete with students from other universities for fellowships and scholarships.

The academy prepares cadets for a role of leadership through military training. This training provides the basic military knowledge required of an Air Force officer. The training includes flying instruction and field trips. Each summer during their sophomore, junior, and senior years, cadets participate in training programs at the academy and other military installations.

Cadets develop a high degree of physical fitness through a varied program of physical education and athletics. Each cadet must participate in either intramural or varsity athletic contests.

History. In the 1920's, Brigadier General Billy Mitchell urged that the government set up an Air Force acad-

emy (see MITCHELL, BILLY). In 1949, the Secretary of Defense appointed a service academy board to study the need for another academy. The board recommended that an academy to train future Air Force officers be established without delay.

On April 1, 1954, Congress authorized the establishment of an Air Force academy. A committee appointed by the Secretary of the Air Force chose the academy's permanent location. The Air Force dedicated the academy in 1955. Lt. Gen. Hubert R. Harmon became its first superintendent. The first class of 306 cadets trained at the temporary academy site at Lowry Air Force Base, near Denver, Colo. The academy moved to its permanent site near Colorado Springs in 1958. In 1976, the academy admitted women students for the first time. <small>Critically reviewed by the AIR FORCE ACADEMY</small>

See also COLORADO (Places to Visit; picture: United States Air Force Academy at Colorado Springs).

UNITED STATES ARMY. See ARMY, UNITED STATES.

UNITED STATES BANK. See BANK OF THE UNITED STATES.

UNITED STATES BORDER PATROL. See BORDER PATROL, UNITED STATES.

UNITED STATES BOTANIC GARDEN in Washington, D.C., exhibits over 10,000 species and varieties of plants, many of them rare. The collection includes products of the United States and other countries. The garden is located on the southwest side of Capitol Hill.

As a public service, the garden identifies plants and recommends methods of growing them. It also presents special displays and furnishes educational facilities to botanists around the world.

A private organization founded the garden in 1820. In 1842, the government assumed control of the garden to display botanical collections assembled by government expeditions. The Congressional Joint Committee on the Library has supervised the United States Botanic Garden since 1856. <small>JOHN C. BOLLENS</small>

UNITED STATES CAPITALS. The federal government had no permanent capital from 1776, when the Declaration of Independence was signed, until 1800, when the government took up its residence in Washington, D.C. The Continental Congress, and, later, the Congress authorized under the Articles of Confederation, had many different meeting places. The earliest American Congresses met in the cities that are listed below, with the dates Congress met in each city.

Philadelphia, September 5, 1774, to December 12, 1776.
Baltimore, December 20, 1776, to March 4, 1777.
Philadelphia, March 5, 1777, to September 18, 1777.
Lancaster, Pa., September 27, 1777.
York, Pa., September 30, 1777, to June 27, 1778.
Philadelphia, July 2, 1778, to June 21, 1783.
Princeton, N.J., June 30, 1783, to November 4, 1783.
Annapolis, Md., November 26, 1783, to June 3, 1784.
Trenton, N.J., November 1, 1784, to December 24, 1784.
New York City, January 11, 1785, to August 12, 1790.
Philadelphia, December 6, 1790, to May 14, 1800.

In 1789, the United States Constitution authorized the new Congress to accept a gift of land from the states for the establishment of a new capital. But jealousy among the states blocked every attempt to choose a location. At last, Alexander Hamilton of New York agreed to the selection of Virginia as a site. In return, Con-

gressional delegates from Virginia agreed to support a bill in Congress which Hamilton wanted passed. Finally, both Virginia and Maryland gave land for the new capital. In 1791, President George Washington chose the site on the Potomac River where the capital was to be built. A commission was appointed to survey the ground and plan the city. The commission named the capital *The City of Washington* in honor of President Washington.

Congress met in Philadelphia from 1790 until 1800, when the government moved to Washington. After 1801, several attempts were made to change the capital's location, but all of them failed.   GEORGE E. MOWRY

See also UNITED STATES, GOVERNMENT OF THE (pictures: Meeting Places of American Congresses); DISTRICT OF COLUMBIA; WASHINGTON, D.C.

UNITED STATES COAST GUARD. See COAST GUARD, UNITED STATES.

UNITED STATES COAST GUARD ACADEMY prepares young men and women to be commissioned officers in the United States Coast Guard. It covers 100 acres (48 hectares) on the banks of the Thames River in New London, Conn. The academy is comparable to those of the other armed forces. But the enrollment of the academy is smaller and entrance is by annual nationwide competitive test rather than by congressional appointment.

Students at the academy are called *cadets.* Graduates receive bachelor of science degrees and commissions as ensigns in the United States Coast Guard.

Entrance Requirements. Cadets are selected through nationwide competition based on college entrance examinations. Applicants must be U.S. citizens at least 17, but not yet 22, years of age. They must also meet other requirements established by the commandant of the United States Coast Guard. In 1976, the academy admitted women students for the first time.

The academy has an enrollment of about 1,100 stu-

UNITED STATES COAST GUARD ACADEMY

A Summer Cruise gives Coast Guard Academy cadets training in knot-tying, *above,* and many other sailing skills.

dents. Cadets are organized as a brigade for military training. Senior cadets serve as brigade officers under the supervision of career Coast Guard officers.

The Course of Instruction offers a four-year program of academic, military, and physical education training. Cadets must take certain courses that provide a background in all subject areas. They also choose one of 13 fields for in-depth study. Such fields include marine engineering and ocean science. Military training includes such academic courses as navigation and seamanship, plus summer training. During summers, cadets participate in Coast Guard operations aboard modern cutters and the academy's training bark *Eagle.* Summer programs include aviation training, small arms training, and search-and-rescue training.

Coast Guard Cadets assemble for review on the campus parade ground, *left.* The Coast Guard Academy prepares young men and women to be commissioned officers in the United States Coast Guard. The seal of the Coast Guard Academy is shown above.

History. The Coast Guard cadet training system began in 1876 with the assignment of the cutter *Dobbin* as a combination training ship, classroom, and berthing quarters. Cadets had their winter quarters at New Bedford, Mass., and later at Arundel Cove, Md. In 1910, the Coast Guard established the academy on shore at New London. The original Georgian-style buildings were built in 1932. Today, more than 30 buildings make up the academy.   Critically reviewed by the COAST GUARD ACADEMY

See also COAST GUARD, U. S. (Training an Officer).

UNITED STATES CONGRESS. See CONGRESS OF THE UNITED STATES.

UNITED STATES CONSTITUTION. See CONSTITUTION OF THE UNITED STATES.

UNITED STATES DEPARTMENT . . . Each executive department of the U.S. government has an article in WORLD BOOK. For a list of the departments, see the article UNITED STATES, GOVERNMENT OF THE (Executive Departments).

UNITED STATES EMPLOYMENT SERVICE. See EMPLOYMENT SERVICE, UNITED STATES.

UNITED STATES FLAG. See FLAG.

UNITED STATES FOREST SERVICE. See FORESTRY (History); FOREST SERVICE.

UNITED STATES GOVERNMENT. See UNITED STATES, GOVERNMENT OF THE.

UNITED STATES HISTORY. See UNITED STATES, HISTORY OF THE.

UNITED STATES INFORMATION AGENCY. See INFORMATION AGENCY, UNITED STATES.

UNITED STATES INTERNATIONAL TRADE COMMISSION. See INTERNATIONAL TRADE COMMISSION, UNITED STATES.

UNITED STATES MARINE CORPS. See MARINE CORPS, UNITED STATES.

UNITED STATES MARINE CORPS WAR MEMORIAL. See WASHINGTON, D.C. (color picture); IWO JIMA.

UNITED STATES MERCHANT MARINE ACADEMY trains young men and women to become officers in the United States Merchant Marine. The academy, often called *Kings Point*, occupies 65 acres (26 hectares) on the north shore of Long Island at Kings Point, N.Y., about 20 miles (32 kilometers) northeast of New York City.

The United States Merchant Marine Cadet Corps was established in 1938. Its academy, founded in 1943, became a permanent, government-sponsored school in 1956, and received equal status with the academies of the armed forces. The United States Department of Transportation operates the academy.

Entrance Requirements. Candidates for the school must be citizens of the United States, not less than 17 and not yet 22 years of age by July 1 of the year in which they seek admission. They must be of good moral character. They must also have 15 high school credits, including 3 units in mathema-

U.S. Merchant Marine Academy

The U.S. Merchant Marine Academy Color Guard carries the American flag and flags of the academy during a drill.

tics, 1 unit in science, and 3 units in English. Competitive examinations are held each year among candidates nominated to the academy by United States senators or representatives. In 1974, the academy accepted its first women students.

Enrollment. Appointments to the academy are governed by a state and territory quota system based on population. The academy has an authorized strength of 1,000 midshipmen. They represent the 50 states, the District of Columbia, Puerto Rico, Guam, American Samoa, and the Virgin Islands. The academy may also admit not more than 12 candidates from Central and South America.

The School Program. The academy offers a four-year course of undergraduate study designed to prepare its graduates for the many problems that may confront merchant marine officers during their careers. Midshipmen study and gain practical experience in an atmosphere of order and discipline. Their practical experience subjects include training aboard a ship. Their academic subjects deal with marine engineering, navigation, electricity, ship construction, naval science and tactics, economics, business, languages, and history.

Midshipmen spend their first year as Fourth Classmen at the academy. Their second year, as Third Classmen, is spent aboard a merchant ship. Their third year, as Second Classmen, and fourth year, as First Classmen, are both spent at the academy. On completion of the four-year program, midshipmen are examined for their original licenses as third deck, third assistant engineer, or dual license officers in the merchant marine. They may then serve on any merchant ship. Graduates also receive bachelor's degrees and commissions as ensigns in the naval reserve.

Critically reviewed by the UNITED STATES MERCHANT MARINE ACADEMY

U.S. Merchant Marine Academy

The Academy Seal

The U.S. Military Academy at West Point, N.Y., prepares young men and women for a career as a military officer. Washington Hall, *left*, is the center of many cadet activities at the academy. The main parade ground, called *The Plain*, lies in front of the hall. The academy's official seal is shown above.

U.S. Army

U.S. Army

A Cadet undergoes a four-year training program that leads to a Bachelor of Science degree and a commission in the Army.

UNITED STATES MILITARY ACADEMY at West Point, N.Y., is the oldest military college in the United States. It prepares young men and women for careers as officers in the United States Army. The academy is supported by the federal government, and is supervised by the Department of the Army.

Students at the academy are called *cadets*. After four years of training, they earn Bachelor of Science degrees and they receive commissions in the United States Army.

The academy is part of a military reservation that occupies 16,000 acres (6,470 hectares) on the west bank of the Hudson River, about 50 miles (80 kilometers) north of New York City. The superintendent, an Army lieutenant general, commands the academy and the military post associated with it.

Entrance Requirements. A candidate for the school must be at least 17 years old, and not yet 22 years of age on July 1 of the year of admission. A candidate must be a U.S. citizen and must be unmarried. The Director of Admissions and Registrar, United States Military Academy, West Point, N.Y. 10996, provides information on admissions.

A candidate must obtain a nomination to the academy before taking the academic, physical aptitude, and medical examinations. About three-fourths of the vacancies for the academy are filled by nominees of U.S. Senators and Representatives. In addition, qualified enlisted members of the regular and reserve components of the Army may be nominated under separate quotas. Other candidates may receive nominations from the President or Vice-President. Quotas also have been

U.S. Army

Students at West Point take courses in engineering, the humanities, mathematics, and the sciences. They study composition in a freshman English course, *above*. Extracurricular activities include working at the cadet radio station, *below*.

U.S. Army

established for sons and daughters of deceased or disabled veterans, and for certain other categories.

Cadets are members of the Regular Army. They are paid about $345 a month. From this amount, they must pay for uniforms, textbooks, and incidental expenses. Housing, meals, and medical care are provided.

SELECTION OF CANDIDATES

Candidates for the United States Military Academy are appointed as follows. The figures represent the total number of candidates each nominating source may select for the academy.

- **100** by the President of the United States
- **5** by the Vice-President of the United States
- **500** by United States Senators
- **2,175** by United States Representatives
- **600** from qualified alternates selected by Senators and Congressmen
- **40** sons and daughters of deceased or disabled veterans or prisoners of war
- **5** from the District of Columbia
- **6** from Puerto Rico
- **1** from Guam
- **1** from American Samoa
- **1** from the Virgin Islands
- **1** from the Philippines
- **85** from the regular United States armed forces
- **85** from the reserve United States armed forces
- **20** from honor military schools
- **20** cadets from other countries

An unlimited number of sons and daughters of Medal of Honor winners may also attend.

The Student Body is called the Corps of Cadets. The corps is broken down into regiments, battalions, and companies. The academy's *honor code* is a cherished possession of cadets and graduates. Administered by the cadets themselves, the code states simply that a cadet will not lie, cheat, or steal, or tolerate those who do. The code requires complete integrity in word and deed. It is strictly enforced, and any intentional violation is a cause for dismissal from the academy.

The cadet academic year extends from August to May. *Graduation Week* climaxes the year's events for the graduating *First* (senior) class. Other classes are called the *Fourth* (freshman) class; *Third* (sophomore) class; and *Second* (junior) class.

A Cadet's Day starts with the first call for reveille at 6:20 A.M. All cadets live in barracks, two or three to a room. They eat their meals in Washington Hall. Classes and study time extend from 7:50 A.M. until 3:15 P.M. From that time until the 6:15 P.M. supper hour, cadets participate in extracurricular activities, parades, or intramural and intercollegiate athletics. The day ends with taps at 11 P.M.

Education and Training. The four-year undergraduate program seeks to prepare students for service as career regular Army officers. It stresses academic, military, and physical fitness skills. The academic curriculum provides a basic education in engineering, mathematics, science, and the social sciences and humanities. Advanced and elective courses enable cadets to concentrate in areas of particular interest.

The cadet receives training in military skills through participation in the Corps of Cadets, through courses taken during the academic year, and through summer training sessions. Summer training is held at West Point, at nearby Camp Buckner, or at selected military posts. It includes instruction in Army weapons and field maneuvers. A cadet also spends time as a platoon leader with an actual Army combat unit. Students develop physical fitness skills through required participation in varsity or intramural sports.

History. The idea of a military academy was first proposed in the late 1700's by such early American leaders as George Washington. In March, 1802, Congress established the U.S. Military Academy on an Army site at West Point, N.Y. The school opened officially in July of the same year. Under Col. Sylvanus Thayer, who served as superintendent from 1817 to 1833, the academy became a pioneer in civil engineering. Thayer also introduced many educational reforms that remain important ingredients of academy life. During the Civil War (1861-1865), the school dropped its strict emphasis on engineering. Today, the academy provides a broad educational background, plus specialized and elective programs. In 1976, the academy admitted women students for the first time.

Among the great American military leaders who received their training at West Point were Robert E. Lee, Ulysses S. Grant, Stonewall Jackson, Philip Sheridan, John J. Pershing, Douglas MacArthur, Dwight D. Eisenhower, and George S. Patton, Jr.

Critically reviewed by UNITED STATES MILITARY ACADEMY

See also NEW YORK (picture); THAYER, SYLVANUS.

UNITED STATES NATIONAL MUSEUM. See NATIONAL MUSEUM OF AMERICAN HISTORY; NATIONAL MUSEUM OF NATURAL HISTORY.

Precision Drill gives midshipmen a chance to display their ability at marching in complicated formations. The United States Naval Academy band takes part in the elaborate performances. The academy coat of arms is shown above.

U.S. Navy

UNITED STATES NAVAL ACADEMY at Annapolis, Md., is a government-operated military college that educates and trains young men and women to become officers in the United States Navy and Marine Corps. The academy and adjacent naval activities occupy about 1,100 acres (449 hectares) along the Severn River. George Bancroft, secretary of the navy under President James K. Polk, founded the academy in 1845.

Students at the Naval Academy are called *midshipmen*. Their training takes four years. Those who complete the work are awarded a bachelor of science degree, and are commissioned as ensigns in the Navy or as second lieutenants in the Marine Corps.

Entrance Requirements. Each year, about 1,300 young men and women are selected for admission to the *plebe* (freshman) class at the Naval Academy. A candidate for the school must be at least 17 years old, and not older than 21, on July 1 of the year of admission. A candidate must be unmarried and must be a U.S. citizen and a high school graduate.

To be considered for an appointment to the academy, a candidate must obtain a nomination from an official source. Such sources include U.S. senators and representatives, the President, and the secretary of the navy. Most candidates apply for nomination during the spring of their junior year in high school because some congressmen select nominees the following summer.

An admissions board at the academy examines each candidate's school records and college entrance examination scores. The board also studies the results of a candidate's medical and physical aptitude tests and other evidence of character, leadership potential, academic aptitude, and physical fitness. Most young persons who are accepted by the academy rank academically in the top 20 per cent of their high school class.

After the midshipmen have been admitted, the U.S. government pays for their tuition, room and board, and medical and dental care. Each midshipman is paid about $330 a month, which is one-half the pay of an ensign. Midshipmen must use this salary to pay for books, uniforms, equipment, and personal services. After these expenses are deducted, they usually have a remaining cash allowance of $40 to $50 each month. They receive an increased allowance for leave periods and other special occasions.

Complete information about entering the academy can be obtained by writing the Director of Candidate Guidance, United States Naval Academy, Annapolis, Md. 21402.

───────── **SELECTION OF CANDIDATES** ─────────

Candidates for the United States Naval Academy are appointed as follows. The figures represent the total number of candidates each nominating source may select for the academy.

- **100** by the President of the United States
- **5** by the Vice-President of the United States
- **500** by United States senators
- **2,175** by United States congressmen
- **600** from qualified alternates selected by senators and congressmen
- **65** sons and daughters of deceased or disabled veterans or prisoners of war
- **5** from the District of Columbia
- **6** from Puerto Rico
- **1** from Guam
- **1** from American Samoa
- **1** from the Virgin Islands
- **1** from the Philippines
- **85** from the regular United States armed forces
- **85** from the reserve United States armed forces
- **20** from honor military schools
- **20** from other countries

An unlimited number of qualified sons and daughters of Medal of Honor winners may also attend.

UNITED STATES NAVAL ACADEMY

U.S. Navy

Midshipmen Learn to Shoot at the firing range, *above.* In addition to military skills, the academy stresses academic training, physical fitness, and the development of leadership ability. Graduates receive commissions in the Navy or the Marine Corps.

The Life of a Midshipman. The program at Annapolis seeks to develop students for positions of military leadership. The academy emphasizes both academic training and the development of leadership, physical, and professional skills. During the academic year, midshipmen devote their major efforts to academic studies. But they also must participate in a varsity sport or in the intramural sports program. The Army-Navy football game between the U.S. Military Academy at West Point, N.Y., and the U.S. Naval Academy ranks as the biggest sports event of the year. For extracurricular activity, students choose from more than 70 clubs and organizations, ranging from dramatics to scuba diving.

During the midshipmen's first summer, they learn the basics of military life, including how to shoot and sail. Physical tests, drills, and athletics are required for physical fitness. During their remaining summers, the midshipmen spend time at sea and at naval installations learning about ships, submarines, and aircraft.

Graduates receive their diplomas and Navy or Marine Corps commissions at the end of June Week. They celebrate by tossing their midshipmen caps high in the air. One of the academy songs, "Anchors Aweigh," was composed for the June Week of 1907.

The Academic Program. The Naval Academy offers a four-year undergraduate program. The curriculum provides a broad education in mathematics, science, engineering, and the social sciences and humanities. It also supplies a background in leadership, navigation, weaponry, and other professional areas. Each midshipman follows a specialized program that provides in-depth study in a field of interest. Such fields include aerospace engineering, oceanography, and international security affairs.

History. Midshipmen were trained at sea before the academy was founded as the Naval School in 1845. George Bancroft established the school in Annapolis on the site of Fort Severn, a former U.S. Army post. In 1850 and 1851, the school was reorganized as the U.S. Naval Academy. During the Civil War (1861-1865), Annapolis was considered too close to the battle lines, so the midshipmen were moved to Newport, R.I. In 1865, midshipmen returned to Annapolis. At about the same time, the academy began adding athletics and more recreation to the program.

The Spanish-American War, in 1898, demonstrated the school's importance to the Navy, and the course of study was greatly expanded. New buildings were constructed between 1899 and 1907, and most of them are still used. Fort Severn and many other landmarks were torn down to make room for the new structures. Another large building program, including several engineering buildings and a library, was completed in 1976. Women midshipmen were first admitted to the academy in 1976.   Critically reviewed by the U.S. NAVAL ACADEMY

See also MARYLAND (picture: Graduation).

UNITED STATES NAVAL OBSERVATORY. See NAVAL OBSERVATORY, UNITED STATES.

UNITED STATES NAVY. See NAVY, UNITED STATES.

UNITED STATES NOTE. See MONEY (The Rebirth of Paper Money).

UNITED STATES POST OFFICE. See POST OFFICE.

UNITED STATES POSTAL SERVICE. See POSTAL SERVICE, UNITED STATES.

UNITED STATES PRESIDENT. See PRESIDENT OF THE UNITED STATES.

UNITED STATES SEAL. See GREAT SEAL OF THE UNITED STATES.

UNITED STATES SHIPPING BOARD. See MERCHANT MARINE (The United States Merchant Marine).

UNITED STATES STEEL CORPORATION is one of the world's largest steel producers. It makes nearly a fourth of the steel manufactured in the United States and about 6 per cent of the Free World's total.

The company also produces iron ore, limestone, and coal, and manufactures oil field drilling and pumping equipment. It produces agricultural and industrial chemicals, and basic materials for the plastics industry. The firm manufactures aluminum and steel siding and other building products for homes and businesses. Other activities of the company include the development, financing, and leasing of real estate; and mortgage operations. In 1982, U.S. Steel merged with Marathon Oil Company, one of the largest oil companies in the United States. For sales, assets, and number of employees of U.S. Steel, see MANUFACTURING (table).

The company was organized in 1901, chiefly by Elbert H. "Judge" Gary, a Chicago lawyer. Gary aimed to produce steel in large quantities more efficiently and economically than had been done in the past. J. P. Morgan, a famous American banker, financed the corporation, which began business with assets of $1,400,000,000. The firm was the first billion-dollar corporation in the nation's history.

The corporation originally included a number of companies that manufactured steel bridges, sheet steel, steel tubing, steel hoops, tin plate, and other metal products. Through the years, U.S. Steel gradually absorbed these companies. The corporation's head-

quarters are located in New York City and Pittsburgh.

Critically reviewed by UNITED STATES STEEL CORPORATION

See also GARY, ELBERT H.

UNITED STATES SUPREME COURT. See SUPREME COURT OF THE UNITED STATES.

UNITED STATES WEATHER BUREAU. See WEATHER SERVICE, NATIONAL.

UNITED STEELWORKERS OF AMERICA. See STEELWORKERS OF AMERICA, UNITED.

UNITED WAY OF AMERICA is the national organization for many local groups that raise money to support health, recreation, and welfare agencies. Local United Way groups, including United Funds and Community Chests, operate in more than 2,300 communities. These groups combine the fund-raising activities of many independent organizations into a single, coordinated campaign.

United Way funds help more than 200 major national organizations, including the American Red Cross, Boy Scouts of America, Girl Scouts of the U.S.A., Travelers Aid, and the Urban League. In all, more than 37,000 agencies and programs benefit from United Way. About 20 million volunteer workers, who are backed by business, labor, and government, conduct United Way campaigns. They raise about $1½ billion a year in contributions from more than 39 million individuals and corporations.

The organization was established in 1918 as Community Chests and Councils of America. It became known as United Way of America in 1970. Headquarters of United Way of America are at 801 N. Fairfax Street, Alexandria, Va. 22314.

Critically reviewed by UNITED WAY OF AMERICA

UNIVALVE is the name given to a class of mollusks whose shells are in one piece. Limpets and snails are univalves. See also MOLLUSK (Kinds); SHELL (Kinds; pictures).

UNIVERSAL COPYRIGHT CONVENTION. See COPYRIGHT (International Copyright).

UNIVERSAL DECLARATION OF HUMAN RIGHTS. See HUMAN RIGHTS, UNIVERSAL DECLARATION OF.

UNIVERSAL JOINT. See AUTOMOBILE (The Drive Train).

UNIVERSAL LANGUAGE. Language is the main means of communication between peoples. But so many different languages have developed that language has often been a barrier rather than an aid to understanding among peoples. For many years, people have dreamed of setting up an international, universal language which all people could speak and understand.

The arguments in favor of a universal language are simple and obvious. If all peoples spoke the same tongue, cultural and economic ties might be much closer, and good will might increase between countries. However, many persons consider the promoters of universal languages to be impractical idealists, and discourage the idea.

René Descartes, a French philosopher, is believed to have originated the idea of a universal language in the 1600's. John Comenius, a Bohemian bishop and educator of the same period, also suggested the idea. More than 200 other languages designed for universal use have been invented since that time.

Volapük was the earliest of these languages to gain much success. The name of the language comes from

two of its words meaning *world* and *speak*. Johann Martin Schleyer, a German priest, invented the suggested language in 1879. Later, Idiom Neutral, a simplified form of Volapük, was suggested. Other proposed languages include Esperanto; a revised form of Esperanto called Ido; Interglossa; Interlingua; Novial; and Spelin. However, only Esperanto is used widely.

English is close to being an international language. During the last several hundred years, it has become a second language in many countries as a result of economic, political, and social developments. To promote such widespread use, scholars invented Basic English (see BASIC ENGLISH). ROBERT J. KISPERT

See also ESPERANTO; INTERLINGUA; VOLAPÜK; LANGUAGE (Universal Languages).

UNIVERSAL POSTAL UNION. See POSTAL UNION, UNIVERSAL.

UNIVERSAL SET. See SET THEORY (Kinds of Sets).

UNIVERSALIST CHURCH OF AMERICA. See UNITARIAN UNIVERSALIST ASSOCIATION.

UNIVERSE consists of all the matter, light, and other forms of radiation and energy that have been discovered. The universe also consists of everything that scientists, as a result of their theories, believe to be present somewhere in space and time.

The universe includes the earth and everything on it. It also includes everything in the solar system. All the stars, of which the sun is one, are part of the universe. More than 100 billion stars are grouped in the shape of a giant circular galaxy called the Milky Way. The Milky Way is about 100,000 *light-years* across. A light-year is the distance that light travels in a year—about 5.88 trillion miles (9.46 trillion kilometers).

Studies of distant space with optical and radio telescopes indicate that there are at least as many galaxies in the universe as there are stars in the Milky Way. Galaxies tend to be grouped together into *clusters*, and clusters are grouped into *superclusters*. Most astronomers believe that superclusters are the largest groups that can be told apart in the universe.

Size of the Universe. Scientists do not know if the universe has a certain size. Most astronomers think that bright, unusual galaxies called *quasars* may be the most distant objects in the universe. Quasars may be as far away as 10 billion light-years from the earth. Light from quasars takes so long to reach the earth that it must have been given off several billion years ago to be seen today.

Scientists cannot tell how far away a quasar is from studying its brightness alone. When an object that gives off light moves away from an observer, that person sees the light as longer wave lengths. This apparent change in the wave lengths of light is called a *red shift* (see RED SHIFT). Scientists can study the red shift of a quasar to find out how far away the quasar is. The amount of red shift depends on the speed at which the object moves away from the observer. All the distant galaxies and quasars have enormous red shifts. Scientists believe this means that the universe is expanding, with every part of the universe moving away from every other part. This is the fundamental feature of the universe that scientists try to explain with various theories about the universe.

UNIVERSE

Exploring the Universe. In ancient times, people thought the universe consisted only of their own locality, distant places of which they had heard, and the sun, moon, planets, and stars. They thought of the heavenly bodies as gods and spirits. During the 1400's and 1500's, voyages of discovery showed that the world was round, not flat as most people had believed. The Polish astronomer and mathematician Nicolaus Copernicus demonstrated that the earth was like the other planets and revolved around the sun.

Later astronomers showed that the sun was a typical star, and that stars visible to the unaided eye were many light-years away. The development of the telescope, the spectroscope, and the photographic plate led to a great expansion of astronomical knowledge. Astronomers then discovered that the sun was in the outer part of the Milky Way. About 1900, they realized that many of the fuzzy patches of light, called *nebulae*, among the stars were other galaxies. Many of these galaxies were at enormous distances from the Milky Way. The discovery of the red shift in distant galaxies led to the theory of the expanding universe. This discovery also formed the basis of *cosmology*, the study of the behavior of the universe.

Cosmological Theories. Most cosmological theories about the universe are based on the idea that any part of the universe is like any other part having the same age. Albert Einstein's general theory of relativity also forms part of the basis for theories about the behavior of the universe. This theory, in turn, is based on two beliefs: (1) that no signal can travel faster than the speed of light, and (2) that the laws of physics are the same everywhere in the universe.

Theories resulting from these ideas involve a universe that expands and contracts. From observing the red shift in distant galaxies, scientists conclude that the universe is expanding. But the overall behavior of the universe depends on the average density of matter in the universe at the present time.

Suppose that all the matter that can be seen in the universe were spread out evenly. There would be only about one atom of hydrogen—the most abundant element in the universe—in 10 cubic yards (7.6 cubic meters) of space. Under these conditions, the universe would be *open*. That is, it would continue to expand indefinitely and would approach zero density at an infinite time in the future. If people were still living then, they would not see any galaxies beyond those in their local supercluster. All other galaxies would have receded to an infinite distance. The stars would have exhausted all the energy that makes them shine, so they would be dark.

On the other hand, large amounts of matter may exist in space in some form that scientists do not know about. If the spread-out density of matter in space were as much as 100 atoms of hydrogen in 10 cubic yards (7.6 cubic meters), the universe would be *closed*. A light beam sent into space in this kind of universe would return to its sender many billions of years later. At some time in the future, perhaps 100 billion years, the expansion would stop. The galaxies in the universe would start coming together again, and matter in the universe would approach infinite density.

Some scientists have suggested theories about the universe that are based on different ideas. For example, the *steady state* theory is based on the belief that any part of the universe is like all other parts at all times. According to this theory, matter is continuously created and formed into new galaxies that replace those which recede to infinite distances. Other scientists believe that Einstein's general theory of relativity is incomplete. They have suggested changes in this theory that predict different things for the expanding universe.

No one knows which, if any, of the theories may prove to be correct. Scientists must wait until the progress of radio and optical astronomy, plus space research, provides certain information. Scientists need to know the average density of the matter in space, the age of the universe, the behavior of red shifts at very large distances, and whether or not Einstein's theory of relativity is correct. A. G. W. CAMERON

Related Articles in WORLD BOOK include:

Astronomy	Quasar
Cosmology	Relativity
Earth	Solar System
Galaxy	World

See also *Universe* in the RESEARCH GUIDE/INDEX, Volume 22, for a *Reading and Study Guide*.

UNIVERSITIES AND COLLEGES are schools that continue a person's education beyond high school. A university or college education helps men and women enjoy richer, more meaningful lives. It prepares many people for professional careers as doctors, engineers, lawyers, or teachers. It also gives a person a better appreciation of such fields as art, literature, history, human relations, and science. In doing so, a university or college education enables individuals to participate with greater understanding in community affairs.

Modern universities developed from the European universities of the Middle Ages. These institutions took their name from the Latin word *universitas*. This word referred to a group of people organized for a common purpose. Properly speaking, a school that is called a *university* should deal with nearly all fields of learning. But universities today may differ in the variety of their educational programs, and in their specialized fields of study. Most universities provide a wide range of graduate programs and have a number of undergraduate schools. They may also have graduate professional schools or colleges. But few universities teach as many branches of learning as the word *university* implies.

The first European colleges were merely groups of students who banded together through common interests. In English universities, colleges were formed to provide living quarters and a dining room for various groups of students. Usually these students took similar studies, and so the word *college* came to refer to a specific field of learning.

Harvard University, the oldest institution of higher learning in the United States, was established chiefly to prepare men for the ministry. Today, we would call such a school a *college of theology*, or a *seminary* (see SEMINARY). Later, schools broadened their courses to teach the liberal arts (see LIBERAL ARTS). These became known as *colleges of liberal arts*. The first universities in the United States divided their courses into various fields of learning, and called the departments that taught each branch *colleges* or *schools*. Thus, the word

college has come to have two meanings in the United States. It may refer to a part of a university that teaches a special branch of knowledge, or it may designate a separate institution which specializes in a single branch of knowledge.

The type of learning available at individual colleges can often be determined from their names. Liberal-arts colleges usually call themselves simply *colleges*. Other schools may be identified by such names as *teachers colleges*, *agricultural colleges*, or *dental colleges*. Modern universities have many kinds of colleges or schools, from liberal arts to law, medicine, theology, dentistry, and fine arts. *Junior colleges*—also called *community colleges*—mainly offer two-year programs. Some of these programs prepare a person for a semiprofessional career or occupation. After completing a junior college program, some students transfer to a "senior" college or university for additional study. See COMMUNITY COLLEGE.

Going to College

Most high school students at some time in their studies face two questions: "Should I attend college?" and "What college will serve my purposes best?" Students should take stock of their personal abilities and desires. They must decide whether or not they will receive specific preparation in college that will help them in their future work. For example, some students may find that special vocational training, rather than a college education, will better prepare them for the careers they want (see VOCATIONAL EDUCATION).

Decisions about attending college should be made only after serious thought about one's life goals. Individuals who enroll in a college without being strongly motivated may find it difficult to be successful students. A person who decides against attending college must realize that such a decision does not necessarily prevent an individual from increasing in earning ability or social status.

Selecting a School. Students who decide to attend college must choose the school that most nearly fits their needs, finances, and personal likes. They can discover many of the facts by talking to friends and teachers. They can learn about particular schools by writing to them for information.

There are a number of basic questions a student should ask about any school being considered.

1. Does the school offer the courses in which I am interested?

2. How well is the school equipped in general buildings, libraries, laboratories, and other property?

3. What teaching methods does the school use? What is the average size of each class?

4. What is the standing of the school? Is it accredited? What is the standing of the particular college or department of the school in which I intend to do most of my work?

5. What are the school's tuition, fees, and living expenses? Are opportunities available for earning all, or part of, my expenses while I attend school?

6. Does the school offer the *extracurricular* (nonacademic) activities in which I am interested?

7. How is the school located with regard to transportation, living quarters, and general conveniences?

Entrance Requirements of the various universities and colleges may differ considerably. In general, they

require satisfactory completion of a high school course. Most require that freshmen have taken certain courses in high schools. Many schools will not admit students whose high school grades are below a certain average. As more students seek to attend universities or colleges, entrance requirements tend to become higher.

Many institutions require students to pass an entrance examination. Schools may also give students intelligence tests and aptitude tests for later counseling. For example, a student's adviser may use the results of the tests to guide the student's work. See COLLEGE ENTRANCE EXAMINATION.

Colleges and universities state their entrance requirements in their catalogs. They nearly always require a *transcript* (copy) of an applicant's high school credits, as well as letters of recommendation. Entrance examinations are generally given several months before the school term begins. Freshmen usually take the intelligence and aptitude tests during an orientation period, frequently called *Freshmen Week* at colleges and universities in the United States.

Persons without a high school diploma should not assume that higher education is closed to them. Many colleges and universities admit men and women who have not completed high school. This procedure allows the schools to serve an increasing number of adults seeking continuing education. It also helps extend educational opportunities to such persons as military veterans and members of minority groups. Before enrolling such applicants, the university or college evaluates their work experience and reviews their scores on special tests. These tests are designed to measure whether a person's knowledge is equivalent to that of an average high school graduate.

Accrediting. A prospective college student should know the standing of the institution he or she intends to enter. Colleges and universities in the United States are accredited by six regional accrediting authorities. They are the Middle States Association of Colleges and Schools, the New England Association of Schools and Colleges, the North Central Association of Schools and Colleges, the Northwest Association of Schools and Colleges, the Southern Association of Colleges and Schools, and the Western Association of Schools and Colleges. These authorities base their judgment on the equipment, financial status, requirements, and teaching standards of the schools.

Professional societies accredit the various professional schools. For example, the American Medical Association accredits medical schools. State boards of education also accredit schools in their states. Students may use credits from approved schools in order to obtain teaching certificates and professional licenses within the state.

The table with this article includes all universities and colleges fully accredited by one of the six regional accrediting associations recognized by the Council on Postsecondary Accreditation. This list was compiled from the *HEP 1985 Higher Education Directory*, which is published by Higher Education Publications, Inc. Enrollment figures are also from this directory.

For a complete list of degree-granting universities and colleges in Canada, and a discussion of higher educa-

tion in Canada, see the WORLD BOOK article on CANADA (Education).

Size. Universities and colleges in the United States range in enrollment from fewer than a hundred students to more than 300,000. Universities with enrollments over 100,000, in order of enrollment of all campuses, are California State University, State University of New York, University of Wisconsin, University of California, University of North Carolina, University of Texas, and City University of New York. Canada's largest university, the University of Toronto, has an enrollment of more than 30,000.

Many universities have more than one campus. For example, the State University of New York has more than 60 campuses. When choosing a school, a prospective student should take into consideration the enrollment of individual campuses as well as the enrollment of the whole university.

College Costs vary widely. Most college catalogs list the average living costs for one year, as well as the tuition, and other fees. During the mid-1980's, the average cost of tuition, fees, room, and board at public universities for all students was about $3,600. The cost for residents averaged less than this amount, and that for nonresidents was higher. The cost at private universities averaged about $9,300 for all students.

Working Your Way. Many college students earn all or part of their expenses. Many have part-time jobs while they attend school, such as working in stores and restaurants. Most schools offer students jobs, such as waiting on tables in dormitories or working in the library. Schools often operate employment bureaus to help find part-time jobs for their students. Some students work during summer vacations, and others drop out of college for a time to work. Many husbands or wives of students work to help their spouses. Sometimes both spouses are students and work part-time.

Financial Help. Students may receive all or part of their college expenses through various aid programs. These programs include scholarships and fellowships; federal, state, and private loan programs; and benefits for veterans and certain other groups such as war orphans. There are so many programs of this kind that almost every college and university has a financial aid office to serve its students. A prospective student who needs financial assistance should consult this office at the schools he or she is considering. In general, there are enough financial aid programs to make it possible for any person to attend some college or university in spite of financial problems. See FELLOWSHIP; SCHOLARSHIP; GI BILL OF RIGHTS.

Kinds of Universities and Colleges

Universities and colleges in the United States may be classified as (1) those operating under private sponsorship, and (2) those operating under public sponsorship. Private institutions may be church-related or nonsectarian. Public institutions may be sponsored by local government, state government, or the federal government. The military academies are examples of federally supported institutions. Most private liberal arts colleges are church-related, while most privately sponsored universities are not now associated with any

church. Most public universities are sponsored by state governments. Most junior or community colleges are sponsored by local governments.

Income. All universities and colleges receive funds from a variety of sources. Private colleges depend primarily on student fees and on endowments and gifts for their operating income. Public institutions also have these sources, but depend mainly on state and local taxes for operating funds. Both public and private institutions may receive federal funds for research activities. The federal government distributes aid among colleges and universities according to various formulas. These formulas are based on the number of students in scholarship and loan programs, and on the enrollment of graduate students and veterans.

Both public and private institutions receive funds for construction from several sources. These sources include federal, state, and local grants or loans; gifts; student fees; and endowments.

Governing Boards. Most universities and colleges are controlled by a *board of trustees* or a *board of regents*. Boards of trustees of private institutions usually elect their own members. The church body may elect the trustees of a church-related institution. The alumni association of a private institution often elects some of the trustees. The trustees of public institutions are usually appointed by the governor of the state. The voters sometimes elect the trustees or regents.

Boards of trustees or regents approve educational policies. They also appoint the chief administrative officer of the institution. In some states, coordinating committees and boards exercise supervision over those institutions financially assisted by the state.

Most church-related colleges except seminaries admit students of any religious denomination. Some of them expect all students to attend chapel exercise and to study some religious courses. But some church-related colleges apply these rules only to students of the same religious faith.

In the United States, the federal government has encouraged the development of universities and colleges since the time of the Northwest Ordinance of 1787. The Morrill Act of 1862 provided land grants to all states to support colleges that, among other subjects, would teach agriculture and the mechanical arts. In some instances, these land grants were given to existing state universities. In other cases, new institutions were established. Many are now major universities.

Seven Canadian provinces sponsor and support universities. Some provinces have also founded technical, agricultural, and junior colleges. The first provincial university was the University of Toronto. It was founded in 1827 as King's College.

School Organization

Campus is the land on which a college or university stands. The main buildings on a campus usually include classroom buildings, an administration building, a library, laboratories, a gymnasium, an athletic field and stadium, and dormitories. Many institutions have a building, often called a *union*, where social gatherings, plays, and dances may be held. Many of today's universities and colleges have more than one campus.

Administration. The organization of state, province, and city-supported institutions is generally about the

(text continued on page 165)

Universities and Colleges

Each of the universities and colleges listed in this table is fully accredited by one of the six regional associations recognized by the Council on Postsecondary Accreditation. All of these schools grant bachelor's or advanced degrees. For a list of Canadian universities and colleges, see CANADA (table: Universities and Colleges).

Name	Location	Founded	Control	Student Body	Enrollment
Abilene Christian University	Abilene, Tex.	1906	Private	Coed.	4,518
Academy of the New Church	Bryn Athyn, Pa.	1876	General Church of the New Jerusalem	Coed.	159
Adams State College	Alamosa, Colo.	1921	State	Coed.	1,875
Adelphi University	Garden City, N.Y.	1896	Private	Coed.	11,208
Adrian College	Adrian, Mich.	1859	Methodist	Coed.	1,222
Agnes Scott College	Decatur, Ga.	1889	Private	Women	533
Air Force Institute of Technology	Wright-Patterson Air Force Base, Ohio	1919	Federal	Coed.	957
Akron, University of	Akron, Ohio	1870	State	Coed.	26,569
Alabama, University of	Tuscaloosa, Ala.	1831	State	Coed.	15,987
	Birmingham, Ala.	1966	State	Coed.	13,894
	Huntsville, Ala.	1950	State	Coed.	5,959
Alabama Agricultural and Mechanical University	Normal, Ala.	1875	State	Coed.	4,126
Alabama State University	Montgomery, Ala.	1874	State	Coed.	4,044
Alaska, University of	Anchorage, Alaska	1976	State	Coed.	3,470
	Fairbanks, Alaska	1917	State	Coed.	4,525
	Juneau, Alaska	1956	State	Coed.	1,835
Alaska Pacific University	Anchorage, Alaska	1957	Methodist	Coed.	782
Albany College of Pharmacy	Albany, N.Y.	1881	Private	Coed.	551
Albany Medical College of Union University	Albany, N.Y.	1839	Private	Coed.	580
Albany State College	Albany, Ga.	1903	State	Coed.	1,896
Albertus Magnus College	New Haven, Conn.	1925	Roman Catholic	Coed.	499
Albion College	Albion, Mich.	1835	Methodist	Coed.	1,742
Albright College	Reading, Pa.	1856	Methodist	Coed.	2,110
Albuquerque, University of	Albuquerque, N.Mex.	1920	Roman Catholic	Coed.	1,808
Alcorn State University	Lorman, Miss.	1871	State	Coed.	2,442
Alderson-Broaddus College	Philippi, W.Va.	1871	Baptist	Coed.	827
Alfred Adler Institute of Chicago	Chicago	1952	Private	Coed.	130
Alfred University	Alfred, N.Y.	1836	Private	Coed.	1,614
New York State College of Ceramics at Alfred University	Alfred, N.Y.	1900	State	Coed.	762
Alice Lloyd College	Pippa Passes, Ky.	1923	Private	Coed.	483
Allegheny College	Meadville, Pa.	1815	Private	Coed.	1,946
Allentown College of St. Francis de Sales	Center Valley, Pa.	1964	Roman Catholic	Coed.	1,101
Alliance College	Cambridge Springs, Pa.	1912	Private	Coed.	289
Alma College	Alma, Mich.	1886	Presbyterian	Coed.	1,059
Alvernia College	Reading, Pa.	1958	Roman Catholic	Coed.	771
Alverno College	Milwaukee	1936	Roman Catholic	Women	1,359
Amber University	Garland, Tex.	1971	Private	Coed.	1,052
American College	Bryn Mawr, Pa.	1927	Private	Coed.	675
American College of Puerto Rico	Bayamón, P.R.	1963	Private	Coed.	3,518
American Conservatory Theatre	San Francisco	1969	Private	Coed.	83
American Graduate School of International Management	Glendale, Ariz.	1946	Private	Coed.	1,037
American International College	Springfield, Mass.	1885	Private	Coed.	2,055
American Technological University	Killeen, Tex.	1973	Private	Coed.	466
American University	Washington, D.C.	1893	Methodist	Coed.	11,219
Amherst College	Amherst, Mass.	1821	Private	Coed.	1,541
Ana G. Méndez Educational Foundation:					
Metropolitan University College	San Juan, P.R.	1980	Private	Coed.	4,358
Turabo University College	Caguas, P.R.	1972	Private	Coed.	6,469
Anderson College	Anderson, Ind.	1917	Church of God	Coed.	2,008
Andover Newton Theological School	Newton Centre, Mass.	1807	Private	Coed.	453
Andrews University	Berrien Springs, Mich.	1874	Adventist	Coed.	2,851
Angelo State University	San Angelo, Tex.	1928	State	Coed.	5,834
Anna Maria College	Paxton, Mass.	1946	Roman Catholic	Coed.	1,655
Antillian College	Mayagüez, P.R.	1957	Private	Coed.	919
Antioch University	Yellow Springs, Ohio	1852	Private	Coed.	3,249
Aquinas College	Grand Rapids, Mich.	1923	Roman Catholic	Coed.	2,743
Aquinas Institute	St. Louis	1951	Roman Catholic	Coed.	78
Arizona, University of	Tucson, Ariz.	1885	State	Coed.	30,669
Arizona State University	Tempe, Ariz.	1885	State	Coed.	39,287
Arkansas, University of	Fayetteville, Ark.	1871	State	Coed.	16,052
	Little Rock, Ark.	1927	State	Coed.	9,565
	Monticello, Ark.	1909	State	Coed.	1,817

Sources: *HEP 1985 Higher Education Directory*. Higher Education Publications.

Name	Location	Founded	Control	Student Body	Enrollment
	Pine Bluff, Ark.	1873	State	Coed.	2,731
Medical Sciences	Little Rock, Ark.	1879	State	Coed.	1,391
Arkansas College	Batesville, Ark.	1872	Presbyterian	Coed.	550
Arkansas State University	State University, Ark.	1909	State	Coed.	7,791
Arkansas Tech University	Russellville, Ark.	1909	State	Coed.	3,267
Armstrong College	Berkeley, Calif.	1918	Private	Coed.	381
Armstrong State College	Savannah, Ga.	1935	State	Coed.	2,992
Art Center College of Design	Pasadena, Calif.	1930	Private	Coed.	1,474
Art Institute of Chicago, School of the	Chicago	1866	Private	Coed.	1,373
Arthur D. Little Management Education Institute	Cambridge, Mass.	1973	Private	Coed.	57
Asbury College	Wilmore, Ky.	1890	Private	Coed.	1,179
Ashland College	Ashland, Ohio	1878	Brethren	Coed.	2,876
Assemblies of God Theological Seminary	Springfield, Mo.	1972	Private	Coed.	207
Associated Mennonite Biblical Seminaries					
Goshen Biblical Seminary	Elkhart, Ind.	1946	Mennonite	Coed.	153
Mennonite Biblical Seminary	Elkhart, Ind.	1945	Mennonite	Coed.	70
Assumption College	Worcester, Mass.	1904	Roman Catholic	Coed.	2,800
Athenaeum of Ohio	Cincinnati, Ohio	1829	Roman Catholic	Coed.	165
Athens State College	Athens, Ala.	1822	State	Coed.	1,002
Atlanta College of Art	Atlanta, Ga.	1928	Private	Coed.	271
Atlanta University	Atlanta, Ga.	1865	Private	Coed.	1,080
Atlantic, College of the	Bar Harbor, Me.	1969	Private	Coed.	163
Atlantic Christian College	Wilson, N.C.	1902	Disciples of Christ	Coed.	1,537
Atlantic Union College	South Lancaster, Mass.	1882	Adventist	Coed.	597
Auburn University	Auburn, Ala.	1856	State	Coed.	18,401
	Montgomery, Ala.	1967	State	Coed.	5,041
Augsburg College	Minneapolis, Minn.	1869	Lutheran	Coed.	1,502
Augusta College	Augusta, Ga.	1925	State	Coed.	4,140
Augustana College	Rock Island, Ill.	1860	Lutheran	Coed.	2,352
Augustana College	Sioux Falls, S.Dak.	1860	Lutheran	Coed.	1,968
Aurora College	Aurora, Ill.	1893	Adventist	Coed.	1,314
Austin College	Sherman, Tex.	1849	Presbyterian	Coed.	1,186
Austin Peay State University	Clarksville, Tenn.	1927	State	Coed.	3,892
Austin Presbyterian Theological Seminary	Austin, Tex.	1902	Presbyterian	Coed.	175
Averett College	Danville, Va.	1859	Private	Coed.	916
Avila College	Kansas City, Mo.	1916	Roman Catholic	Coed.	1,876
Azusa Pacific University	Azusa, Calif.	1899	Private	Coed.	2,467
Babson College	Babson Park, Mass.	1919	Private	Coed.	3,229
Baker University	Baldwin City, Kans.	1858	Methodist	Coed.	839
Baldwin-Wallace College	Berea, Ohio	1845	Methodist	Coed.	3,755
Ball State University	Muncie, Ind.	1918	State	Coed.	18,208
Baltimore, University of	Baltimore, Md.	1925	State	Coed.	5,379
Baltimore Hebrew College	Baltimore, Md.	1919	Private	Coed.	251
Bangor Theological Seminary	Bangor, Me.	1814	United Church of Christ	Coed.	86
Bank Street College of Education	New York City	1916	Private	Coed.	595
Baptist Bible College of Pennsylvania	Clarks Summit, Pa.	1932	Baptist	Coed.	792
Baptist Bible Institute	Graceville, Fla.	1943	Baptist	Coed.	397
Baptist College at Charleston	Charleston, S.C.	1960	Baptist	Coed.	2,170
Barat College	Lake Forest, Ill.	1858	Roman Catholic	Coed.	640
Barber-Scotia College	Concord, N.C.	1867	Presbyterian	Coed.	374
Bard College	Annandale-on-Hudson, N.Y.	1860	Private	Coed.	733
Barrington College	Barrington, R.I.	1900	Private	Coed.	430
Barry University	Miami Shores, Fla.	1940	Roman Catholic	Coed.	3,019
Bartlesville Wesleyan College	Bartlesville, Okla.	1910	Wesleyan	Coed.	799
Bates College	Lewiston, Me.	1855	Private	Coed.	1,452
Bayamón Central University	Bayamón, P.R.	1970	Roman Catholic	Coed.	1,724
Baylor College of Dentistry	Dallas	1905	Private	Coed.	652
Baylor College of Medicine	Houston	1903	Private	Coed.	902
Baylor University	Waco, Tex.	1845	Baptist	Coed.	10,473
Beacon College	Washington, D.C.	1971	Private	Coed.	111
Beaver College	Glenside, Pa.	1853	Presbyterian	Coed.	2,046
Belhaven College	Jackson, Miss.	1883	Presbyterian	Coed.	938
Bellarmine College	Louisville, Ky.	1950	Roman Catholic	Coed.	2,730
Bellevue College	Bellevue, Nebr.	1965	Private	Coed.	2,720
Belmont Abbey College	Belmont, N.C.	1876	Roman Catholic	Coed.	801
Belmont College	Nashville, Tenn.	1951	Baptist	Coed.	1,927
Beloit College	Beloit, Wis.	1846	Private	Coed.	1,081

Universities and Colleges

Name	Location	Founded	Control	Student Body	Enrollment
Benedict College	Columbia, S.C.	1870	Private	Coed.	1,371
Benedictine College	Atchison, Kans.	1858	Roman Catholic	Coed.	957
Bennett College	Greensboro, N.C.	1873	Methodist	Women	542
Bennington College	Bennington, Vt.	1925	Private	Coed.	643
Bentley College	Waltham, Mass.	1917	Private	Coed.	7,645
Berea College	Berea, Ky.	1855	Private	Coed.	1,532
Berklee College of Music	Boston	1945	Private	Coed.	2,463
Berry College	Mount Berry, Ga.	1902	Private	Coed.	1,499
Bethany Bible College	Santa Cruz, Calif.	1919	Assemblies of God	Coed.	511
Bethany College	Lindsborg, Kans.	1881	Lutheran	Coed.	790
Bethany College	Bethany, W.Va.	1840	Private	Coed.	778
Bethany Nazarene College	Bethany, Okla.	1899	Nazarene	Coed.	1,400
Bethany Theological Seminary	Oak Brook, Ill.	1905	Brethren	Coed.	121
Bethel College	Mishawaka, Ind.	1947	Missionary Church	Coed.	410
Bethel College	North Newton, Kans.	1887	Mennonite	Coed.	661
Bethel College	St. Paul, Minn.	1871	Baptist	Coed.	2,067
Bethel College	McKenzie, Tenn.	1842	Presbyterian	Coed.	471
Bethel Theological Seminary	St. Paul, Minn.	1871	Baptist	Coed.	493
Bethune-Cookman College	Daytona Beach, Fla.	1904	Methodist	Coed.	1,636
Biola University	La Mirada, Calif.	1908	Private	Coed.	3,096
Birmingham-Southern College	Birmingham, Ala.	1856	Methodist	Coed.	1,553
Bishop Clarkson College of Nursing	Omaha, Nebr.	1888	Private	Coed.	517
Bishop College	Dallas	1881	Baptist	Coed.	1,186
Black Hills State College	Spearfish, S.Dak.	1883	State	Coed.	1,916
Blackburn College	Carlinville, Ill.	1857	Private	Coed.	429
Bloomfield College	Bloomfield, N.J.	1868	Presbyterian	Coed.	1,830
Bloomsburg University	Bloomsburg, Pa.	1839	State	Coed.	6,240
Blue Mountain College	Blue Mountain, Miss.	1873	Baptist	Women	328
Bluefield College	Bluefield, Va.	1920	Private	Coed.	402
Bluefield State College	Bluefield, W.Va.	1895	State	Coed.	2,804
Bluffton College	Bluffton, Ohio	1899	Mennonite	Coed.	593
Boise State University	Boise, Idaho	1932	State	Coed.	11,092
Boricua College	New York City	1974	Private	Coed.	1,060
Borromeo College of Ohio	Wickliffe, Ohio	1954	Roman Catholic	Men	113
Boston College	Chestnut Hill, Mass.	1863	Roman Catholic	Coed.	14,069
Boston Conservatory	Boston	1867	Private	Coed.	414
Boston University	Boston	1839	Private	Coed.	28,157
Bowdoin College	Brunswick, Me.	1794	Private	Coed.	1,392
Bowie State College	Bowie, Md.	1865	State	Coed.	2,233
Bowling Green State University	Bowling Green, Ohio	1910	State	Coed.	17,173
Bradford College	Bradford, Mass.	1803	Private	Coed.	370
Bradley University	Peoria, Ill.	1897	Private	Coed.	5,637
Brandeis University	Waltham, Mass.	1948	Private	Coed.	3,557
Brenau College	Gainesville, Ga.	1878	Private	Coed.	1,555
Brescia College	Owensboro, Ky.	1950	Roman Catholic	Coed.	912
Briar Cliff College	Sioux City, Iowa	1929	Roman Catholic	Coed.	1,260
Bridgeport, University of	Bridgeport, Conn.	1927	Private	Coed.	6,343
Bridgeport Engineering Institute	Bridgeport, Conn.	1924	Private	Coed.	901
Bridgewater College	Bridgewater, Va.	1880	Brethren	Coed.	894
Bridgewater State College	Bridgewater, Mass.	1840	State	Coed.	7,366
Brigham Young University	Provo, Utah	1875	Church of Jesus Christ of Latter-day Saints	Coed.	29,695
Hawaii Campus	Laie, Oahu, Hawaii	1955	Church of Jesus Christ of Latter-day Saints	Coed.	1,607
Brooks Institute	Santa Barbara, Calif.	1945	Private	Coed.	775
Brown University	Providence, R.I.	1764	Private	Coed.	6,942
Bryan College	Dayton, Tenn.	1930	Private	Coed.	543
Bryant College	Smithfield, R.I.	1863	Private	Coed.	6,582
Bryn Mawr College	Bryn Mawr, Pa.	1880	Private	Women	1,810
Bucknell University	Lewisburg, Pa.	1846	Private	Coed.	3,256
Buena Vista College	Storm Lake, Iowa	1891	Presbyterian	Coed.	1,403
Burlington College	Burlington, Vt.	1972	Private	Coed.	131
Butler University	Indianapolis	1855	Private	Coed.	4,030
Cabrini College	Radnor, Pa.	1957	Roman Catholic	Coed.	784
Caldwell College	Caldwell, N.J.	1939	Roman Catholic	Women	749
California, University of	Berkeley, Calif.	1868	State	Coed.	29,296
	Davis, Calif.	1905	State	Coed.	19,321
	Irvine, Calif.	1965	State	Coed.	11,270
	Los Angeles	1919	State	Coed.	34,568
	Riverside, Calif.	1954	State	Coed.	4,787
	San Diego	1912	State	Coed.	13,102

Universities and Colleges

Name	Location	Founded	Control	Student Body	Enrollment
	San Francisco	1864	State	Coed.	3,819
	Santa Barbara, Calif.	1898	State	Coed.	16,158
	Santa Cruz, Calif.	1962	State	Coed.	6,817
California Baptist College	Riverside, Calif.	1950	Baptist	Coed.	660
California College of Arts and Crafts	Oakland, Calif.	1907	Private	Coed.	1,044
California College of Podiatric Medicine	San Francisco	1914	Private	Coed.	424
California Family Study Center	Burbank, Calif.	1971	Private	Coed.	300
California Institute of Integral Studies	San Francisco	1968	Private	Coed.	193
California Institute of Technology	Pasedena, Calif.	1891	Private	Coed.	1,810
California Institute of the Arts	Valencia, Calif.	1964	Private	Coed.	858
California Lutheran College	Thousand Oaks, Calif.	1959	Lutheran	Coed.	2,467
California Maritime Academy	Vallejo, Calif.	1929	State	Coed.	488
California School of Professional Psychology	Berkeley, Calif.	1969	Private	Coed.	325
	Fresno, Calif.	1969	Private	Coed.	188
	Los Angeles	1969	Private	Coed.	284
	San Diego	1969	Private	Coed.	321
California University of Pennsylvania	California, Pa.	1852	State	Coed.	4,528
California State University					
California State College Stanislaus Campus	Bakersfield, Calif.	1965	State	Coed.	3,641
	Turlock, Calif.	1957	State	Coed.	4,574
California State University	San Bernardino, Calif.	1960	State	Coed.	5,167
	Chico, Calif.	1887	State	Coed.	14,289
	Fresno, Calif.	1911	State	Coed.	16,374
	Fullerton, Calif.	1957	State	Coed.	24,385
	Hayward, Calif.	1957	State	Coed.	12,433
	Long Beach, Calif.	1949	State	Coed.	36,397
	Los Angeles	1947	State	Coed.	22,663
	Northridge, Calif.	1958	State	Coed.	28,134
	Sacramento, Calif.	1947	State	Coed.	21,671
Dominguez Hills Campus	Carson, Calif.	1960	State	Coed.	10,391
California Polytechnic State University	San Luis Obispo, Calif.	1901	State	Coed.	15,826
California State Polytechnic University	Pomona, Calif.	1938	State	Coed.	17,146
Consortium	Long Beach, Calif.	1973	State	Coed.	1,200
Humboldt State University	Arcata, Calif.	1913	State	Coed.	7,322
San Diego State University	San Diego	1897	State	Coed.	33,937
San Francisco State University	San Francisco	1899	State	Coed.	26,245
San Jose State University	San Jose, Calif.	1857	State	Coed.	26,274
Sonoma State University	Rohnert Park, Calif.	1960	State	Coed.	6,664
Calumet College	Whiting, Ind.	1951	Roman Catholic	Coed.	1,269
Calvin College	Grand Rapids, Mich.	1876	Reformed	Coed.	3,807
Cambridge College Institute of Open Education	Cambridge, Mass.	1970	Private	Coed.	363
Cameron University	Lawton, Okla.	1909	State	Coed.	5,497
Campbell University	Buies Creek, N.C.	1887	Baptist	Coed.	3,052
Campbellsville College	Campbellsville, Ky.	1906	Baptist	Coed.	702
Canisius College	Buffalo, N.Y.	1870	Roman Catholic	Coed.	4,354
Capital University	Columbus, Ohio	1850	Lutheran	Coed.	2,560
Capitol Institute of Technology	Laurel, Md.	1932	Private	Coed.	821
Cardinal Glennon College	St. Louis	1898	Roman Catholic	Men	99
Cardinal Newman College	St. Louis	1976	Roman Catholic	Coed.	86
Cardinal Stritch College	Milwaukee	1937	Roman Catholic	Coed.	1,261
Caribbean Center for Advanced Studies	San Juan, P.R.	1966	Private	Coed.	486
Caribbean University College	Bayamón, P.R.	1969	Private	Coed.	2,692
Carleton College	Northfield, Minn.	1866	Private	Coed.	1,884
Carlow College	Pittsburgh	1929	Roman Catholic	Women	963
Carnegie-Mellon University	Pittsburgh	1900	Private	Coed.	5,998
Carroll College	Helena, Mont.	1909	Roman Catholic	Coed.	1,330
Carroll College	Waukesha, Wis.	1846	Presbyterian	Coed.	1,380
Carson-Newman College	Jefferson City, Tenn.	1851	Baptist	Coed.	1,733
Carthage College	Kenosha, Wis.	1847	Lutheran	Coed.	1,376
Case Western Reserve University	Cleveland	1826	Private	Coed.	8,529
Castleton State College	Castleton, Vt.	1787	State	Coed.	2,043
Catawba College	Salisbury, N.C.	1851	United Church of Christ	Coed.	987
Cathedral College of the Immaculate Conception	Douglaston, N.Y.	1914	Roman Catholic	Men	103

Universities and Colleges

Name	Location	Founded	Control	Student Body	Enrollment
Catholic Theological Union	Chicago	1967	Roman Catholic	Coed.	331
Catholic University of America	Washington, D.C.	1887	Roman Catholic	Coed.	7,057
Catholic University of Puerto Rico	Ponce, P.R.	1948	Roman Catholic	Coed.	13,048
Cedar Crest College	Allentown, Pa.	1867	Private	Women	1,030
Cedarville College	Cedarville, Ohio	1887	Baptist	Coed.	1,730
Centenary College	Hackettstown, N.J.	1867	Private	Women	1,257
Centenary College of Louisiana	Shreveport, La.	1825	Methodist	Coed.	1,441
Center for Advanced Studies on Puerto Rico and the Caribbean	San Juan, P.R.	1976	Private	Coed.	230
Center for Creative Studies- College of Arts and Design	Detroit	1926	Private	Coed.	1,113
Center for Early Education, College of the	Los Angeles	1939	Private	Coed.	64
Center for Humanistic Studies	Detroit	1981	Private	Coed.	56
Central Arkansas, University of	Conway, Ark.	1907	State	Coed.	5,875
Central Baptist Theological Seminary	Seminary Heights, Kans.	1901	Baptist	Coed.	148
Central Connecticut State University	New Britain, Conn.	1849	State	Coed.	12,487
Central Florida, University of	Orlando, Fla.	1963	State	Coed.	14,180
Central Methodist College	Fayette, Mo.	1853	Methodist	Coed.	569
Central Michigan University	Mount Pleasant, Mich.	1892	State	Coed.	17,132
Central Missouri State University	Warrensburg, Mo.	1871	State	Coed.	9,526
Central New England College of Technology	Worcester, Mass.	1888	Private	Coed.	306
Central State University	Wilberforce, Ohio	1887	State	Coed.	2,424
Central State University	Edmond, Okla.	1890	State	Coed.	12,304
Central University of Iowa	Pella, Iowa	1853	Reformed	Coed.	1,465
Central Washington University	Ellensburg, Wash.	1890	State	Coed.	6,989
Central Wesleyan College	Central, S.C.	1906	Wesleyan	Coed.	413
Centre College of Kentucky	Danville, Ky.	1819	Private	Coed.	718
Chadron State College	Chadron, Nebr.	1911	State	Coed.	1,913
Chaminade University of Honolulu	Honolulu, Hawaii	1955	Roman Catholic	Coed.	1,925
Chapman College	Orange, Calif.	1861	Private	Coed.	5,585
Charleston, College of	Charleston, S.C.	1770	State	Coed.	5,394
Charleston, University of	Charleston, W.Va.	1888	Private	Coed.	2,215
Charter Oak College	Hartford, Conn.	1973	State	Coed.	1,124
Chatham College	Pittsburgh	1869	Private	Women	658
Chestnut Hill College	Philadelphia	1924	Roman Catholic	Women	1,088
Cheyney University of Pennsylvania	Cheyney, Pa.	1837	State	Coed.	1,867
Chicago, University of	Chicago	1890	Private	Coed.	9,013
Chicago School of Professional Psychology	Chicago	1979	Private	Coed.	72
Chicago State University	Chicago	1867	State	Coed.	7,389
Chicago Theological Seminary	Chicago	1855	United Church of Christ	Coed.	135
Christ College Irvine	Irvine, Calif.	1972	Lutheran	Coed.	265
Christ the King Seminary	East Aurora, N.Y.	1974	Roman Catholic	Coed.	129
Christian Brothers College	Memphis	1871	Roman Catholic	Coed.	1,518
Christian Heritage College	El Cajon, Calif.	1970	Private	Coed.	344
Christian Theological Seminary	Indianapolis	1958	Disciples of Christ	Coed.	301
Church Divinity School of the Pacific	Berkeley, Calif.	1893	Episcopal	Coed.	103
Cincinnati, University of	Cincinnati, Ohio	1819	State	Coed.	32,905
Citadel, The Military College of South Carolina	Charleston, S.C.	1842	State	Coed.	3,252
City University	Bellevue, Wash.	1973	Private	Coed.	2,190
Claflin College	Orangeburg, S.C.	1869	Methodist	Coed.	645
Claremont Graduate School	Claremont, Calif.	1925	Private	Coed.	1,649
Claremont McKenna College	Claremont, Calif.	1946	Private	Coed.	830
Clarion University of Pennsylvania	Clarion, Pa.	1867	State	Coed.	4,951
Venango Campus	Oil City, Pa.	1961	State	Coed.	510
Clark College	Atlanta, Ga.	1869	Methodist	Coed.	1,966
Clark University	Worcester, Mass.	1887	Private	Coed.	3,242
Clarke College	Dubuque, Iowa	1843	Roman Catholic	Coed.	892
Clarkson University	Potsdam, N.Y.	1896	Private	Coed.	4,037
Clemson University	Clemson, S.C.	1889	State	Coed.	12,093
Cleveland Chiropractic College	Kansas City, Mo.	1922	Private	Coed.	398
Cleveland Institute of Art	Cleveland	1882	Private	Coed.	562
Cleveland Institute of Music	Cleveland	1920	Private	Coed	269
Cleveland State University	Cleveland	1964	State	Coed.	18,944
Coe College	Cedar Rapids, Iowa	1851	Private	Coed.	1,471
Cogswell College	San Francisco	1887	Private	Coed.	456
Coker College	Hartsville, S.C.	1908	Private	Coed.	300
Colby College	Waterville, Me.	1813	Private	Coed.	1,685

Universities and Colleges

Name	Location	Founded	Control	Student Body	Enrollment
Colby-Sawyer College	New London, N.H.	1837	Private	Women	561
Colgate University	Hamilton, N.Y.	1819	Private	Coed.	2,652
College Misericordia	Dallas, Pa.	1924	Roman Catholic	Coed.	1,253
Colorado, University of	Boulder, Colo.	1861	State	Coed.	22,177
	Colorado Springs, Colo.	1965	State	Coed.	5,288
	Denver	1912	State	Coed.	10,720
Health Sciences Center	Denver	1924	State	Coed.	1,385
Colorado College	Colorado Springs, Colo.	1874	Private	Coed.	1,961
Colorado School of Mines	Golden, Colo.	1874	State	Coed.	2,948
Colorado State University	Fort Collins, Colo.	1870	State	Coed.	18,909
Colorado Technical College	Colorado Springs, Colo.	1965	Private	Coed.	602
Columbia Bible College	Columbia, S.C.	1923	Private	Coed.	877
Columbia Christian College	Portland, Ore.	1949	Private	Coed.	220
Columbia College	Chicago	1890	Private	Coed.	4,158
Columbia College	Columbia, Mo.	1851	Disciples of Christ	Coed.	2,358
Columbia College	Columbia, S.C.	1854	Methodist	Women	1,198
Columbia Theological Seminary	Decatur, Ga.	1828	Presbyterian	Coed.	444
Columbia Union College	Takoma Park, Md.	1904	Adventist	Coed.	507
Columbia University:					
Main Division	New York City	1754	Private	Coed.	16,091
Barnard College	New York City	1889	Private	Women	2,416
Teachers College	New York City	1887	Private	Coed.	4,155
Columbus College	Columbus, Ga.	1958	State	Coed.	4,245
Combs College of Music	Bryn Mawr, Pa.	1885	Private	Coed.	85
Conception Seminary College	Conception, Mo.	1883	Roman Catholic	Men	91
Concord College	Athens, W.Va.	1872	State	Coed.	2,262
Concordia College	River Forest, Ill.	1864	Lutheran	Coed.	1,312
Concordia College	Ann Arbor, Mich.	1962	Lutheran	Coed.	540
Concordia College	Bronxville, N.Y.	1881	Lutheran	Coed.	455
Concordia College	Portland, Ore.	1905	Lutheran	Coed.	315
Concordia College	Mequon, Wis.	1881	Lutheran	Coed.	647
Concordia College at Moorhead	Moorhead, Minn.	1891	Lutheran	Coed.	2,553
Concordia College-St. Paul	St. Paul, Minn.	1893	Lutheran	Coed.	718
Concordia Lutheran College	Austin, Tex.	1926	Lutheran	Coed.	435
Concordia Seminary	Clayton, Mo.	1839	Lutheran	Coed.	735
Concordia Teachers College	Seward, Nebr.	1894	Lutheran	Coed.	1,062
Concordia Theological Seminary	Fort Wayne, Ind.	1846	Lutheran	Men	553
Connecticut, University of	Storrs, Conn.	1881	State	Coed.	22,800
Connecticut College	New London, Conn.	1911	Private	Coed.	1,933
Conservatory of Music of Puerto Rico	San Juan, P.R.	1959	Territory	Coed.	264
Converse College	Spartanburg, S.C.	1889	Private	Women	952
Cooper Union	New York City	1859	Private	Coed.	978
Coppin State College	Baltimore	1900	State	Coed.	2,310
Cornell College	Mount Vernon, Iowa	1853	Private	Coed.	830
Cornell University	Ithaca, N.Y.	1865	Private; State	Coed.	10,615
Statutory Colleges	Ithaca, N.Y.	1865	State	Coed.	7,552
Cornish Institute	Seattle	1915	Private	Coed.	506
Covenant College	Lookout Mountain, Ga.	1955	Presbyterian	Coed.	520
Covenant Theological Seminary	St. Louis, Mo.	1956	Presbyterian	Coed.	132
Cranbrook Academy of Art	Bloomfield Hills, Mich.	1932	Private	Coed.	140
Creighton University	Omaha, Nebr.	1878	Roman Catholic	Coed.	5,682
Culver-Stockton College	Canton, Mo.	1853	Disciples of Christ	Coed.	619
Cumberland College	Williamsburg, Ky.	1889	Baptist	Coed.	1,747
Curry College	Milton, Mass.	1879	Private	Coed.	1,257
Daemen College	Amherst, N.Y.	1947	Roman Catholic	Coed.	1,683
Dakota State College	Madison, S.Dak.	1881	State	Coed.	1,151
Dakota Wesleyan University	Mitchell, S.Dak.	1885	Methodist	Coed.	514
Dallas, University of	Irving, Tex.	1956	Roman Catholic	Coed.	2,684
Dallas Baptist College	Dallas	1965	Baptist	Coed.	1,337
Dallas Theological Seminary	Dallas	1924	Private	Coed.	1,173
Dana College	Blair, Nebr.	1884	Lutheran	Coed.	552
Daniel Webster College	Nashua, N.H.	1965	Private	Coed.	1,053
Dartmouth College	Hanover, N.H.	1769	Private	Coed.	4,504
David Lipscomb College	Nashville, Tenn.	1891	Private	Coed.	2,262
Davidson College	Davidson, N.C.	1837	Presbyterian	Coed.	1,402
Davis and Elkins College	Elkins, W.Va.	1904	Presbyterian	Coed.	952
Dayton, University of	Dayton, Ohio	1850	Roman Catholic	Coed.	10,958
Defense Intelligence College	Washington, D.C.	1962	Federal	Coed.	456
Defiance College	Defiance, Ohio	1850	Private	Coed.	815
Delaware, University of	Newark, Del.	1833	State	Coed.	18,615
Delaware State College	Dover, Del.	1891	State	Coed.	2,151
Delaware Valley College of Science and Agriculture	Doylestown, Pa.	1896	Private	Coed.	1,620

Universities and Colleges

Name	Location	Founded	Control	Student Body	Enrollment
De Lourdes College	Des Plaines, Ill.	1927	Roman Catholic	Women	279
Delta State University	Cleveland, Miss.	1924	State	Coed.	3,480
Denison University	Granville, Ohio	1831	Private	Coed.	2,162
Denver, University of	Denver	1864	Private	Coed.	8,230
Denver Conservative Baptist Seminary	Denver	1950	Baptist	Coed.	480
DePaul University	Chicago	1898	Roman Catholic	Coed.	12,867
DePauw University	Greencastle, Ind.	1837	Private	Coed.	2,394
De Sales School of Theology	Washington, D.C.	1949	Roman Catholic	Coed.	23
Detroit, University of	Detroit	1877	Roman Catholic	Coed.	5,967
DeVry Institute of Technology	Chicago	1931	Private	Coed.	6,562
DeVry Institute of Technology	Columbus, Ohio	1952	Private	Coed.	4,333
DeVry Institute of Technology	Phoenix, Ariz.	1967	Private	Coed.	4,785
Dickinson College	Carlisle, Pa.	1773	Private	Coed.	1,813
Dickinson State College	Dickinson, N.Dak.	1918	State	Coed.	1,162
Dillard University	New Orleans	1869	Private	Coed.	1,142
District of Columbia, University of the	Washington, D.C.	1976	Federal; Municipal	Coed.	14,105
Divine Word College	Epworth, Iowa	1964	Roman Catholic	Men	99
Doane College	Crete, Nebr.	1872	Private	Coed.	680
Dr. Martin Luther College	New Ulm, Minn.	1884	Lutheran	Coed.	725
Dominican College of Blauvelt	Orangeburg, N.Y.	1952	Private	Coed.	1,712
Dominican College of San Rafael	San Rafael, Calif.	1889	Roman Catholic	Coed.	618
Dominican House of Studies	Washington, D.C.	1902	Roman Catholic	Coed.	27
Dominican School of Philosophy and Theology	Berkeley, Calif.	1932	Roman Catholic	Coed.	93
Don Bosco College	Newton, N.J.	1928	Roman Catholic	Men	72
Dordt College	Sioux Center, Iowa	1955	Private	Coed.	1,077
Dowling College	Oakdale, N.Y.	1959	Private	Coed.	2,153
Drake University	Des Moines, Iowa	1881	Private	Coed.	6,492
Drew University	Madison, N.J.	1866	Methodist	Coed.	2,335
Drexel University	Philadelphia	1891	Private	Coed.	12,339
Dropsie College for Hebrew and Cognate Learning	Philadelphia	1907	Private	Coed.	42
Drury College	Springfield, Mo.	1873	Private	Coed.	2,532
Dubuque, University of	Dubuque, Iowa	1852	Presbyterian	Coed.	1,286
Theological Seminary	Dubuque, Iowa	1852	Presbyterian	Coed.	166
Duke University	Durham, N.C.	1838	Private	Coed.	9,794
Duquesne University	Pittsburgh	1878	Roman Catholic	Coed.	6,298
Dyke College	Cleveland	1848	Private	Coed.	1,441
D'Youville College	Buffalo, N.Y.	1908	Roman Catholic	Coed.	1,309
Earlham College	Richmond, Ind.	1847	Quaker	Coed.	1,146
East Central Oklahoma State University	Ada, Okla.	1909	State	Coed.	3,826
East Stroudsburg University	East Stroudsburg, Pa.	1893	State	Coed.	4,066
East Tennessee State University	Johnson City, Tenn.	1911	State	Coed.	9,628
East Texas Baptist University	Marshall, Tex.	1912	Baptist	Coed.	882
East Texas State University	Commerce, Tex.	1917	State	Coed.	7,768
	Texarkana, Tex.	1971	State	Coed.	1,142
East-West University	Chicago	1980	Private	Coed.	547
Eastern Baptist Theological Seminary	Philadelphia	1925	Baptist	Coed.	334
Eastern College	St. Davids, Pa.	1952	Baptist	Coed.	845
Eastern Connecticut State University	Willimantic, Conn.	1889	State	Coed.	3,416
Eastern Illinois University	Charleston, Ill.	1895	State	Coed.	10,354
Eastern Kentucky University	Richmond, Ky.	1906	State	Coed.	13,041
Eastern Mennonite College	Harrisonburg, Va.	1917	Mennonite	Coed.	1,028
Eastern Michigan University	Ypsilanti, Mich.	1849	State	Coed.	18,078
Eastern Montana College	Billings, Mont.	1927	State	Coed.	4,177
Eastern Nazarene College	Wollaston, Mass.	1900	Nazarene	Coed.	841
Eastern New Mexico University	Portales, N.Mex.	1927	State	Coed.	5,571
Eastern Oregon State College	La Grande, Ore.	1929	State	Coed.	1,881
Eastern Washington University	Cheney, Wash.	1882	State	Coed.	8,156
Eckerd College	St. Petersburg, Fla.	1959	Private	Coed.	1,051
Eden Theological Seminary	Webster Groves, Mo.	1850	United Church of Christ	Coed.	204
Edgewood College	Madison, Wis.	1927	Roman Catholic	Coed.	750
Edinboro State College	Edinboro, Pa.	1857	State	Coed.	5,636
Edward Waters College	Jacksonville, Fla.	1866	African Methodist Episcopal	Coed.	859
Elizabethtown College	Elizabethtown, Pa.	1899	Brethren	Coed.	1,841
Elmhurst College	Elmhurst, Ill.	1871	Private	Coed.	3,521
Elmira College	Elmira, N.Y.	1855	Private	Coed.	2,548
Elon College	Elon College, N.C.	1889	United Church of Christ	Coed.	2,625

Universities and Colleges

Name	Location	Founded	Control	Student Body	Enrollment
Embry-Riddle Aeronautical University	Bunnell, Fla.	1926	Private	Coed.	8,076
Emerson College	Boston	1880	Private	Coed.	2,231
Emmanuel College	Boston	1919	Roman Catholic	Women	1,037
Emory and Henry College	Emory, Va.	1836	Methodist	Coed.	769
Emory University	Atlanta, Ga.	1836	Methodist	Coed.	8,228
Emporia State University	Emporia, Kans.	1863	State	Coed.	5,768
Episcopal Theological Seminary of the Southwest	Austin, Tex.	1952	Protestant Episcopal	Coed.	82
Erskine College	Due West, S.C.	1837	Presbyterian	Coed.	661
Eureka College	Eureka, Ill.	1855	Private	Coed.	537
Evangel College	Springfield, Mo.	1955	Assemblies of God	Coed.	1,809
Evansville, University of	Evansville, Ind.	1854	Private	Coed.	4,761
Evergreen State College	Olympia, Wash.	1967	State	Coed.	2,611
Fairfield University	Fairfield, Conn.	1942	Roman Catholic	Coed.	4,960
Fairleigh Dickinson University	Madison, N.J.	1958	Private	Coed.	4,974
	Rutherford, N.J.	1942	Private	Coed.	4,172
	Teaneck, N.J.	1954	Private	Coed.	7,970
Fairmont State College	Fairmont, W.Va.	1865	State	Coed.	5,190
Felician College	Lodi, N.J.	1942	Roman Catholic	Women	631
Ferris State College	Big Rapids, Mich.	1884	State	Coed.	11,008
Ferrum College	Ferrum, Va.	1913	Methodist	Coed.	1,638
Fielding Institute	Santa Barbara, Calif.	1974	Private	Coed.	415
Findlay College	Findlay, Ohio	1882	Church of God	Coed.	1,190
Fisk University	Nashville, Tenn.	1866	Private	Coed.	753
Fitchburg State College	Fitchburg, Mass.	1894	State	Coed.	6,609
Flagler College	St. Augustine, Fla.	1963	Private	Coed.	981
Florida, University of	Gainesville, Fla.	1853	State	Coed.	34,252
Florida Agricultural and Mechanical University	Tallahassee, Fla.	1887	State	Coed.	4,825
Florida Atlantic University	Boca Raton, Fla.	1961	State	Coed.	9,089
Florida Institute of Technology	Melbourne, Fla.	1958	Private	Coed.	6,963
Florida International University	Miami, Fla.	1965	State	Coed.	13,620
Florida Memorial College	Miami, Fla.	1879	Private	Coed.	931
Florida Southern College	Lakeland, Fla.	1885	Methodist	Coed.	3,318
Florida State University	Tallahassee, Fla.	1851	State	Coed.	22,022
Fontbonne College	St. Louis	1917	Roman Catholic	Coed.	905
Fordham University	New York City	1841	Roman Catholic	Coed.	13,110
Forest Institute of Professional Psychology	Des Plaines, Ill.	1979	Private	Coed.	132
Fort Hays State University	Hays, Kans.	1902	State	Coed.	5,488
Fort Lewis College	Durango, Colo.	1911	State	Coed.	3,528
Fort Valley State College	Fort Valley, Ga.	1895	State	Coed.	1,735
Framingham State College	Framingham, Mass.	1839	State	Coed.	5,869
Francis Marion College	Florence, S.C.	1970	State	Coed.	2,911
Franciscan School of Theology	Berkeley, Calif.	1968	Private	Coed.	153
Franklin and Marshall College	Lancaster, Pa.	1787	Private	Coed.	2,917
Franklin College of Indiana	Franklin, Ind.	1834	Private	Coed.	536
Franklin Pierce College	Rindge, N.H.	1962	Private	Coed.	1,805
Franklin University	Columbus, Ohio	1902	Private	Coed.	4,983
Freed-Hardeman College	Henderson, Tenn.	1869	Church of Christ	Coed.	1,220
Fresno Pacific College	Fresno, Calif.	1944	Mennonite	Coed.	812
Friends University	Wichita, Kans.	1898	Quaker	Coed.	813
Frostburg State College	Frostburg, Md.	1898	State	Coed.	3,654
Fuller Theological Seminary	Pasadena, Calif.	1947	Private	Coed.	2,728
Furman University	Greenville, S.C.	1826	Baptist	Coed.	3,105
Gallaudet College	Washington, D.C.	1864	Private	Coed.	1,292
Gannon University	Erie, Pa.	1933	Roman Catholic	Coed.	4,135
Gardner-Webb College	Boiling Springs, N.C.	1905	Baptist	Coed.	1,740
Garrett-Evangelical Theological Seminary	Evanston, Ill.	1853	Methodist	Coed.	363
General Theological Seminary	New York City	1817	Private	Coed.	179
Geneva College	Beaver Falls, Pa.	1848	Presbyterian	Coed.	1,267
George Fox College	Newberg, Ore.	1891	Quaker	Coed.	744
George Mason University	Fairfax, Va.	1957	State	Coed.	14,930
George Washington University	Washington, D.C.	1821	Private	Coed.	19,150
George Williams College	Downers Grove, Ill.	1890	Private	Coed.	1,243
Georgetown College	Georgetown, Ky.	1829	Baptist	Coed.	1,211
Georgetown University	Washington, D.C.	1789	Roman Catholic	Coed.	12,020
Georgia, Medical College of	Augusta, Ga.	1828	State	Coed.	1,977
Georgia, University of	Athens, Ga.	1785	State	Coed.	25,886
Georgia College	Milledgeville, Ga.	1889	State	Coed.	3,467
Georgia Institute of Technology	Atlanta, Ga.	1885	State	Coed.	11,377
Southern Technical Institute	Marietta, Ga.	1948	State	Coed.	3,242

Universities and Colleges

Name	Location	Founded	Control	Student Body	Enrollment
Georgia Southern College	Statesboro, Ga.	1906	State	Coed.	6,826
Georgia Southwestern College	Americus, Ga.	1906	State	Coed.	2,326
Georgia State University	Atlanta, Ga.	1913	State	Coed.	21,254
Georgian Court College	Lakewood, N.J.	1908	Roman Catholic	Women	1,499
Gettysburg College	Gettysburg, Pa.	1832	Private	Coed.	1,926
Glassboro State College	Glassboro, N.J.	1923	State	Coed.	9,790
Glenville State College	Glenville, W.Va.	1872	State	Coed.	1,785
GMI Engineering and Management Institute	Flint, Mich.	1919	Private	Coed.	2,433
Goddard College	Plainfield, Vt.	1938	Private	Coed.	151
Golden Gate Baptist Theological Seminary	Mill Valley, Calif.	1944	Baptist	Coed.	571
Golden Gate University	San Francisco	1901	Private	Coed.	10,950
Goldey Beacom College	Wilmington, Del.	1886	Private	Coed.	2,069
Gonzaga University	Spokane, Wash.	1887	Roman Catholic	Coed.	3,491
Gordon College	Wenham, Mass.	1889	Private	Coed.	1,059
Goshen College	Goshen, Ind.	1894	Mennonite	Coed.	1,113
Goucher College	Towson, Md.	1885	Private	Women	1,021
Governors State University	University Park, Ill.	1969	State	Coed.	4,886
Grace College	Winona Lake, Ind.	1948	Brethren	Coed.	900
Grace Theological Seminary	Winona Lake, Ind.	1937	Brethren	Coed.	396
Graceland College	Lamoni, Iowa	1895	Reorganized Church of Jesus Christ of Latter Day Saints	Coed.	1,086
Graduate Theological Union	Berkeley, Calif.	1962	Private	Coed.	379
Grambling State University	Grambling, La.	1901	State	Coed.	3,970
Grand Canyon College	Phoenix	1949	Baptist	Coed.	1,257
Grand Rapids Baptist College and Seminary	Grand Rapids, Mich.	1941	Baptist	Coed.	1,077
Grand Valley State Colleges	Allendale, Mich.	1960	State	Coed.	6,366
Grand View College	Des Moines, Iowa	1896	Lutheran	Coed.	1,247
Gratz College	Philadelphia	1895	Private	Coed.	258
Great Falls, College of	Great Falls, Mont.	1932	Roman Catholic	Coed.	1,272
Green Mountain College	Poultney, Vt.	1834	Private	Coed.	328
Greensboro College	Greensboro, N.C.	1838	Methodist	Coed.	585
Greenville College	Greenville, Ill.	1892	Methodist	Coed.	755
Grinnell College	Grinnell, Iowa	1846	Private	Coed.	1,187
Grove City College	Grove City, Pa.	1876	Private	Coed.	2,200
Guam, University of	Agana, Guam	1952	Territory	Coed.	2,574
Guilford College	Greensboro, N.C.	1837	Quaker	Coed.	1,625
Gulf-Coast Bible College	Houston	1953	Church of God	Coed.	366
Gustavus Adolphus College	St. Peter, Minn.	1862	Lutheran	Coed.	2,307
Gwynedd-Mercy College	Gwynedd Valley, Pa.	1948	Roman Catholic	Coed.	2,160
Hahnemann University	Philadelphia	1848	Private	Coed.	1,987
Hamilton College	Clinton, N.Y.	1812	Private	Coed.	1,642
Hamline University	St. Paul, Minn.	1854	Methodist	Coed.	1,882
Hampden-Sydney College	Hampden-Sydney, Va.	1776	Presbyterian	Men	777
Hampshire College	Amherst, Mass.	1965	Private	Coed.	1,212
Hampton University	Hampton, Va.	1868	Private	Coed.	3,824
Hannibal-LaGrange College	Hannibal, Mo.	1858	Baptist	Coed.	507
Hanover College	Hanover, Ind.	1827	Private	Coed.	994
Hardin-Simmons University	Abilene, Tex.	1891	Baptist	Coed.	1,948
Harding University	Searcy, Ark.	1924	Church of Christ	Coed.	2,972
Graduate School of Religion	Memphis	1958	Church of Christ	Coed.	268
Harris-Stowe State College	St. Louis	1857	Municipal	Coed.	1,027
Hartford, University of	West Hartford, Conn.	1877	Private	Coed.	8,564
Hartford Graduate Center	Hartford, Conn.	1955	Private	Coed.	1,930
Hartford Seminary	Hartford, Conn.	1834	Private	Coed.	97
Hartwick College	Oneonta, N.Y.	1928	Lutheran	Coed.	1,422
Harvard University	Cambridge, Mass.	1636	Private	Coed.	13,971
Radcliffe College	Cambridge, Mass.	1879	Private	Women	2,595
Harvey Mudd College	Claremont, Calif.	1955	Private	Coed.	510
Hastings College	Hastings, Nebr.	1882	Presbyterian	Coed.	777
Haverford College	Haverford, Pa.	1833	Private	Coed.	1,025
Hawaii, University of	Hilo, Hawaii	1947	State	Coed.	3,746
Manoa Campus	Honolulu, Hawaii	1907	State	Coed.	20,880
West Oahu College	Aiea, Hawaii	1976	State	Men	408
Hawaii Loa College	Kaneohe, Hawaii	1963	Private	Coed.	385
Hawaii Pacific College	Honolulu, Hawaii	1965	Private	Coed.	2,268
Hawthorne College	Antrim, N.H.	1962	Private	Coed.	711
Health-Sciences-Chicago Medical School, University of	North Chicago, Ill.	1912	Private	Coed.	825
Hebrew College	Brookline, Mass.	1921	Private	Coed.	182

Name	Location	Founded	Control	Student Body	Enrollment
Hebrew Union College—Jewish Institute of Religion	Los Angeles	1954	Jewish Congregations	Coed.	80
	New York City	1922	Jewish Congregations	Coed.	112
	Cincinnati, Ohio	1875	Jewish Congregations	Coed.	145
Heidelberg College	Tiffin, Ohic	1850	Private	Coed.	840
Hellenic College-Holy Cross Greek Orthodox School of Theology	Brookline, Mass.	1937	Greek Orthodox	Coed.	240
Henderson State University	Arkadelphia, Ark.	1890	State	Coed.	2,966
Hendrix College	Conway, Ark.	1884	Methodist	Coed.	961
High Point College	High Point, N.C.	1924	Methodist	Coed.	1,355
Hillsdale College	Hillsdale, Mich.	1844	Private	Coed.	1,044
Hiram College	Hiram, Ohio	1850	Private	Coed.	1,223
Hobart and William Smith Colleges	Geneva, N.Y.	1822	Private	Coordinate	1,855
Hofstra University	Hempstead, N.Y.	1935	Private	Coed.	10,809
Hollins College	Roanoke, Va.	1842	Private	Women	954
Holy Apostles College	Cromwell, Conn.	1956	Roman Catholic	Coed.	152
Holy Cross, College of the	Worcester, Mass.	1843	Roman Catholic	Coed.	2,519
Holy Family College	Fremont, Calif.	1946	Roman Catholic	Coed.	73
Holy Family College	Philadelphia	1954	Roman Catholic	Coed.	1,296
Holy Names College	Oakland, Calif.	1868	Roman Catholic	Coed.	629
Holy Redeemer College	Waterford, Wis.	1968	Roman Catholic	Men	60
Hood College	Frederick, Md.	1893	Private	Women	1,676
Hope College	Holland, Mich.	1866	Private	Coed.	2,530
Houghton College	Houghton, N.Y.	1883	Wesleyan	Coed.	1,227
Houston, University of:					
Clear Lake City Campus	Houston	1971	State	Coed.	6,586
Downtown College	Houston	1974	State	Coed.	6,353
University Park Campus	Houston	1927	State	Coed.	30,544
Victoria Campus	Victoria, Tex.	1973	State	Coed.	836
Houston Baptist University	Houston	1960	Baptist	Coed.	2,688
Howard Payne University	Brownwood, Tex.	1889	Baptist	Coed.	1,123
Howard University	Washington, D.C.	1867	Private	Coed.	11,445
Huntingdon College	Montgomery, Ala.	1854	Methodist	Coed.	721
Huntington College	Huntington, Ind.	1897	United Brethren in Christ	Coed.	429
Huron College	Huron, S.Dak.	1883	Presbyterian	Coed.	372
Husson College	Bangor, Me.	1898	Private	Coed.	1,499
Huston-Tillotson College	Austin, Tex.	1876	Methodist; United Church of Christ	Coed.	577
Idaho, College of	Caldwell, Idaho	1891	Presbyterian	Coed.	696
Idaho, University of	Moscow, Idaho	1889	State	Coed.	9,195
Idaho State University	Pocatello, Idaho	1901	State	Coed.	7,132
Iliff School of Theology	Denver	1892	Methodist	Coed.	276
Illinois, University of	Urbana-Champaign, Ill.	1867	State	Coed.	34,914
	Chicago	1896	State	Coed.	21,003
Illinois Benedictine College	Lisle, Ill.	1887	Roman Catholic	Coed.	2,362
Illinois College	Jacksonville, Ill.	1829	Private	Coed.	766
Illinois College of Optometry	Chicago	1872	Private	Coed.	547
Illinois Institute of Technology	Chicago	1892	Private	Coed.	6,926
Illinois School of Professional Psychology	Chicago	1976	Private	Coed.	296
Illinois State University	Normal, Ill.	1857	State	Coed.	20,565
Illinois Wesleyan University	Bloomington, Ill.	1850	Methodist	Coed.	1,667
Immaculata College	Immaculata, Pa.	1920	Roman Catholic	Women	1,672
Immaculate Conception, Seminary of the	Huntington, N.Y.	1926	Roman Catholic	Coed.	189
Incarnate Word College	San Antonio	1881	Roman Catholic	Coed.	1,357
Indiana Central University	Indianapolis	1902	Methodist	Coed.	3,290
Indiana Institute of Technology	Fort Wayne, Ind.	1930	Private	Coed.	557
Indiana State University	Terre Haute, Ind.	1865	State	Coed.	11,933
Indiana University	Bloomington, Ind.	1820	State	Coed.	32,711
	Kokomo, Ind.	1945	State	Coed.	2,808
	South Bend, Ind.	1940	State	Coed.	5,912
Indiana University Northwest	Gary, Ind.	1921	State	Coed.	4,897
Indiana University-Purdue University	Fort Wayne, Ind.	1964	State	Coed.	10,128
	Indianapolis	1969	State	Coed.	23,258
Indiana University Southeast	New Albany, Ind.	1969	State	Coed.	4,640
Indiana University of Pennsylvania	Indiana, Pa.	1875	State	Coed.	12,503
Institute of Paper Chemistry	Appleton, Wis.	1929	Private	Coed.	104
Insurance, College of	New York City	1947	Private	Coed.	1,622
Inter American University of Puerto Rico:					
Arecibo Branch	Arecibo, P.R.	1957	Private	Coed.	3,604

Universities and Colleges

Name	Location	Founded	Control	Student Body	Enrollment
Metropolitan Campus	San Juan, P.R.	1960	Private	Coed.	16,608
San Germán Campus	San Germán, P.R.	1912	Private	Coed.	7,431
International Institute of the Americas of World University	San Juan, P.R.	1965	Private	Coed.	5,327
International Training, School for	Brattleboro, Vt.	1964	Private	Coed.	735
Iona College	New Rochelle, N.Y.	1940	Roman Catholic	Coed.	6,183
Iowa, University of	Iowa City, Iowa	1847	State	Coed.	28,948
Iowa State University of Science and Technology	Ames, Iowa	1858	State	Coed.	25,333
Iowa Wesleyan College	Mount Pleasant, Iowa	1842	Private	Coed.	715
Ithaca College	Ithaca, N.Y.	1892	Private	Coed.	5,111
Jackson State University	Jackson, Miss.	1877	State	Coed.	6,523
Jacksonville State University	Jacksonville, Ala.	1883	State	Coed.	6,284
Jacksonville University	Jacksonville, Fla.	1934	Private	Coed.	2,419
James Madison University	Harrisonburg, Va.	1908	State	Coed.	9,779
Jamestown College	Jamestown, N. Dak.	1883	Presbyterian	Coed.	616
Jarvis Christian College	Hawkins, Tex.	1912	Disciples of Christ	Coed.	547
Jersey City State College	Jersey City, N.J.	1927	State	Coed.	8,918
Jesuit School of Theology at Berkeley	Berkeley, Calif.	1934	Roman Catholic	Coed.	161
Jewish Theological Seminary of America	New York City	1886	Private	Coed.	133
John Brown University	Siloam Springs, Ark.	1919	Private	Coed.	768
John Carroll University	Cleveland	1886	Roman Catholic	Coed.	3,767
John F. Kennedy University	Orinda, Calif.	1964	Private	Coed.	1,652
Johns Hopkins University	Baltimore	1876	Private	Coed.	9,955
Peabody Institute	Baltimore	1857	Private	Coed.	417
Johnson Bible College	Knoxville, Tenn.	1893	Christian Church/ Churches of Christ	Coed.	367
Johnson Cay Smith University	Charlotte, N.C.	1867	Private	Coed.	1,192
Johnson State College	Johnson, Vt.	1828	State	Coed.	1,214
Judaism, University of	Los Angeles	1947	Private	Coed.	208
Judson College	Marion, Ala.	1838	Baptist	Women	375
Judson College	Elgin, Ill.	1963	Baptist	Coed.	414
Juilliard School	New York City	1905	Private	Coed.	1,242
Juniata College	Huntington, Pa.	1876	Private	Coed.	1,286
Kalamazoo College	Kalamazoo, Mich.	1833	Baptist	Coed.	1,234
Kansas, University of	Lawrence, Kans.	1864	State	Coed.	24,400
Medical Center	Kansas City, Kans.	1905	State	Coed.	1,765
Kansas City Art Institute	Kansas City, Mo.	1885	Private	Coed.	438
Kansas Newman College	Wichita, Kans.	1933	Private	Coed.	759
Kansas State University of Agriculture and Applied Science	Manhattan, Kans.	1863	State	Coed.	19,497
Kansas Wesleyan	Salina, Kans.	1885	Methodist	Coed.	578
Kean College of New Jersey	Union, N.J.	1855	State	Coed.	12,984
Kearny State College	Kearney, Nebr.	1903	State	Coed.	7,276
Keller Graduate School of Management	Chicago	1973	Private	Coed.	1,219
Kendall College	Evanston, Ill.	1934	Private	Coed.	406
Kendall School of Design	Grand Rapids, Mich.	1928	Private	Coed.	578
Kennesaw College	Marietta, Ga.	1963	State	Coed.	4,754
Kenrick Seminary	St. Louis	1893	Roman Catholic	Men	86
Kent State University	Kent, Ohio	1910	State	Coed.	19,927
Kentucky, University of	Lexington, Ky.	1865	State	Coed.	22,267
Kentucky State University	Frankfort, Ky.	1926	State	Coed.	2,199
Kentucky Wesleyan College	Owensboro, Ky.	1860	Methodist	Coed.	901
Kenyon College	Gambier, Ohio	1824	Private	Coed.	1,414
Keuka College	Keuka Park, N.Y.	1890	Private	Coed.	500
King College	Bristol, Tenn.	1867	Presbyterian	Coed.	429
King's College	Briarcliff Manor, N.Y.	1938	Private	Coed.	798
King's College	Wilkes-Barre, Pa.	1946	Roman Catholic	Coed.	2,306
Knox College	Galesburg, Ill.	1837	Private	Coed.	939
Knoxville College	Knoxville, Tenn.	1875	Presbyterian	Coed.	501
Kutztown University	Kutztown, Pa.	1866	State	Coed.	5,861
Laboratory Institute of Merchandising	New York City	1939	Proprietary	Coed.	230
Lafayette College	Easton, Pa.	1826	Private	Coed.	2,398
LaGrange College	La Grange, Ga.	1831	Methodist	Coed.	960
Lake Erie College	Painesville, Ohio	1856	Private	Coordinate	964
Lake Forest College	Lake Forest, Ill.	1857	Private	Coed.	1,138
Lake Forest School of Management	Lake Forest, Ill.	1946	Private	Coed.	382
Lake Superior State College	Sault Ste. Marie, Mich.	1946	State	Coed.	2,494
Lakeland College	Sheboygan, Wis.	1862	United Church of Christ	Coed.	809
Lamar University	Beaumont, Tex.	1923	State	Coed.	14,638

Name	Location	Founded	Control	Student Body	Enrollment
Lambuth College	Jackson, Tenn.	1843	Methodist	Coed.	722
Lancaster Bible College	Lancaster, Pa.	1933	Private	Coed.	349
Lancaster Theological Seminary	Lancaster, Pa.	1825	United Church of Christ	Coed.	242
Lander College	Greenwood, S.C.	1872	State	Coed.	2,004
Lane College	Jackson, Tenn.	1882	Methodist	Coed.	731
Langston University	Langston, Okla.	1897	State	Coed.	1,856
La Roche College	Pittsburgh, Pa.	1963	Roman Catholic	Coed.	1,613
La Salle University	Philadelphia	1863	Roman Catholic	Coed.	7,068
La Verne, University of	La Verne, Calif.	1891	Brethren	Coed.	3,988
San Fernando Valley College of Law	Sepulveda, Calif.	1962	Private	Coed.	249
Lawrence Institute of Technology	Southfield, Mich.	1932	Private	Coed.	5,868
Lawrence University	Appleton, Wis.	1847	Private	Coed.	1,067
Lebanon Valley College	Annville, Pa.	1866	Methodist	Coed.	1,239
Lee College	Cleveland, Tenn.	1918	Church of God	Coed.	1,125
Lehigh University	Bethlehem, Pa.	1865	Private	Coed.	6,287
Le Moyne College	Syracuse, N.Y.	1946	Roman Catholic	Coed.	2,131
LeMoyne-Owen College	Memphis	1862	Baptist; United Church of Christ	Coed.	1,073
Lenoir-Rhyne College	Hickory, N.C.	1891	Lutheran	Coed.	1,382
Lesley College	Cambridge, Mass.	1909	Private	Coed.	2,059
LeTourneau College	Longview, Tex.	1946	Private	Coed.	1,033
Lewis and Clark College	Portland, Ore.	1867	Private	Coed.	3,054
Lewis-Clark State College	Lewiston, Idaho	1893	State	Coed.	2,048
Lewis University	Romeoville, Ill.	1932	Roman Catholic	Coed.	2,744
Liberty Baptist College	Lynchburg, Va.	1971	Baptist	Coed.	3,386
Limestone College	Gaffney, S.C.	1845	Private	Coed.	1,536
Lincoln Memorial University	Harrogate, Tenn.	1897	Private	Coed.	1,356
Lincoln University	Jefferson City, Mo.	1866	State	Coed.	2,847
Lincoln University	Lincoln University, Pa.	1854	State	Coed.	1,230
Lindenwood College	St. Charles, Mo.	1827	Presbyterian	Coed.	1,916
Linfield College	McMinnville, Ore.	1849	Baptist	Coed.	1,496
Livingston University	Livingston, Ala.	1835	State	Coed.	1,458
Livingstone College	Salisbury, N.C.	1879	Methodist	Coed.	618
Lock Haven University	Lock Haven, Pa.	1870	State	Coed.	2,619
Loma Linda University	Loma Linda, Calif.	1905	Adventist	Coed.	5,157
Long Island University:					
Brooklyn Center	New York City	1926	Private	Coed.	6,899
C. W. Post Campus	Greenvale, N.Y.	1954	Private	Coed.	12,356
Southampton Center	Southampton, N.Y.	1963	Private	Coed.	1,221
Longwood College	Farmville, Va.	1839	State	Coed.	2,589
Loras College	Dubuque, Iowa	1839	Roman Catholic	Coed.	1,784
Loretto Heights College	Denver	1918	Roman Catholic	Coed.	811
Los Angeles Baptist College	Newhall, Calif.	1927	Private	Coed.	308
Louisiana College	Pineville, La.	1906	Baptist	Coed.	1,049
Louisiana State University	Shreveport, La.	1965	State	Coed.	4,280
Agricultural and Mechanical College	Baton Rouge, La.	1855	State	Coed.	31,100
Medical Center	New Orleans	1931	State	Coed.	2,553
University of New Orleans	New Orleans	1956	State	Coed.	15,901
Louisiana Tech University	Ruston, La.	1894	State	Coed.	11,055
Louisville, University of	Louisville, Ky.	1798	State	Coed.	19,714
Louisville Presbyterian Theological Seminary	Louisville, Ky.	1853	Presbyterian	Coed.	210
Lourdes College	Sylvania, Ohio	1958	Roman Catholic	Coed.	762
Lowell, University of	Lowell, Mass.	1894	State	Coed.	15,514
Loyola College	Baltimore	1852	Roman Catholic	Coed.	6,182
Loyola Marymount University	Los Angeles	1911	Roman Catholic	Coed.	6,433
Loyola University	New Orleans	1912	Roman Catholic	Coed.	3,933
Loyola University of Chicago	Chicago	1870	Roman Catholic	Coed.	14,457
Lubbock Christian College	Lubbock, Tex.	1957	Private	Coed.	992
Luther College	Decorah, Iowa	1861	Lutheran	Coed.	2,053
Luther Northwestern Theological Seminary	St. Paul, Minn.	1869	Lutheran	Coed.	841
Lutheran Bible Institute of Seattle	Issaquah, Wash.	1944	Private	Coed.	217
Lutheran School of Theology at Chicago	Chicago	1860	Lutheran	Coed.	307
Lutheran Theological Seminary at Gettysburg	Gettysburg, Pa.	1826	Lutheran	Coed.	275
Lutheran Theological Seminary at Philadelphia	Philadelphia	1864	Lutheran	Coed.	234
Lutheran Theological Southern Seminary	Columbia, S.C.	1830	Lutheran Church of America	Coed.	174
Lycoming College	Williamsport, Pa.	1812	Methodist	Coed.	1,192

Name	Location	Founded	Control	Student Body	Enrollment
Lynchburg College	Lynchburg, Va.	1903	Private	Coed.	2,357
Lyndon State College	Lyndonville, Vt.	1911	State	Coed.	1,060
Macalester College	St. Paul, Minn.	1874	Private	Coed.	1,695
MacMurray College	Jacksonville, Ill.	1846	Private	Coed.	632
Madonna College	Livonia, Mich.	1947	Roman Catholic	Coed.	3,409
Maharishi International University	Fairfield, Iowa	1971	Private	Coed.	734
Maine, University of	Augusta	1965	State	Coed.	3,423
	Farmington, Me.	1864	State	Coed.	1,880
	Fort Kent, Me.	1878	State	Coed.	679
	Machias, Me.	1909	State	Coed.	782
	Orono, Me.	1865	State	Coed.	11,651
	Presque Isle, Me.	1903	State	Coed.	1,187
University of Southern Maine	Portland-Gorham, Me.	1878	State	Coed.	8,166
Maine Maritime Academy	Castine, Me.	1941	State	Coed.	649
Mallinckrodt College	Wilmette, Ill.	1918	Roman Catholic	Coed.	285
Malone College	Canton, Ohio	1892	Quaker	Coed.	872
Manchester College	North Manchester, Ind.	1889	Brethren	Coed.	1,011
Manhattan College	New York City	1853	Private	Coed.	4,841
Manhattan School of Music	New York City	1917	Private	Coed.	715
Manhattanville College	Purchase, N.Y.	1841	Roman Catholic	Coed.	1,267
Mannes College of Music	New York City	1916	Private	Coed.	439
Mansfield University	Mansfield, Pa.	1857	State	Coed.	2,713
Marian College	Indianapolis	1851	Roman Catholic	Coed.	857
Marian College of Fond du Lac	Fond du Lac, Wis.	1936	Roman Catholic	Coed.	528
Marietta College	Marietta, Ohio	1834	Private	Coed.	1,438
Marion College	Marion, Ind.	1920	Wesleyan	Coed.	1,077
Marist College	Poughkeepsie, N.Y.	1946	Private	Coed.	3,158
Marlboro College	Marlboro, Vt.	1946	Private	Coed.	197
Marquette University	Milwaukee	1864	Roman Catholic	Coed.	11,664
Mars Hill College	Mars Hill, N.C.	1856	Baptist	Coed.	1,525
Marshall University	Huntington, W. Va.	1837	State	Coed.	11,741
Mary Baldwin College	Staunton, Va.	1842	Presbyterian	Women	867
Mary College	Bismarck, N. Dak.	1955	Roman Catholic	Coed.	1,121
Mary Hardin-Baylor, University of	Belton, Tex.	1845	Baptist	Coed.	1,170
Mary Immaculate Seminary	Northampton, Pa.	1939	Roman Catholic	Men	40
Mary Washington College	Fredericksburg, Va.	1908	State	Coed.	2,936
Marycrest College	Davenport, Iowa	1939	Roman Catholic	Coed.	1,407
Marygrove College	Detroit	1910	Roman Catholic	Coed.	1,189
Maryknoll School of Theology	Maryknoll, N.Y.	1912	Roman Catholic	Coed.	171
Maryland, University of:					
Baltimore County	Catonsville, Md.	1963	State	Coed.	7,384
Baltimore Professional Schools	Baltimore	1807	State	Coed.	4,800
College Park Campus	College Park, Md.	1856	State	Coed.	37,046
Eastern Shore	Princess Anne, Md.	1886	State	Coed.	1,214
University College	College Park, Md.	1947	State	Coed.	11,275
Maryland Institute, College of Art	Baltimore	1826	Private	Coed.	1,454
Marylhurst College for Lifelong Learning	Marylhurst, Ore.	1893	Roman Catholic	Coed.	675
Marymount College	Tarrytown, N.Y.	1919	Roman Catholic	Women	1,271
Marymount College of Kansas	Salina, Kans.	1922	Roman Catholic	Coed.	706
Marymount College of Virginia	Arlington, Va.	1950	Roman Catholic	Coed.	1,669
Marymount Manhattan College	New York City	1936	Roman Catholic	Women	2,197
Maryville College	St. Louis	1872	Roman Catholic	Coed.	1,927
Maryville College	Maryville, Tenn.	1819	Presbyterian	Coed.	582
Marywood College	Scranton, Pa.	1915	Roman Catholic	Women	2,966
Massachusetts, University of	Amherst, Mass.	1863	State	Coed.	26,517
	Boston	1964	State	Coed.	11,448
Massachusetts College of Art	Boston	1873	State	Coed.	2,017
Massachusetts College of Pharmacy and Allied Health Sciences	Boston	1835	Private	Coed.	986
Massachusetts Institute of Technology	Cambridge, Mass.	1861	Private	Coed.	9,575
Massachusetts Maritime Academy	Buzzards Bay, Mass.	1891	State	Coed.	839
Mayo Foundation					
Mayo Graduate School of Medicine	Rochester, Minn.	1915	Private	Coed.	941
Mayo Medical School	Rochester, Minn.	1971	Private	Coed.	161
Mayville State College	Mayville, N. Dak.	1889	State	Coed.	695
McCormick Theological Seminary	Chicago	1829	Presbyterian	Coed.	568
McKendree College	Lebanon, Ill.	1828	Private	Coed.	750
McMurry College	Abilene, Tex.	1923	Methodist	Coed.	1,329
McNeese State University	Lake Charles, La.	1938	State	Coed.	7,270

Name	Location	Founded	Control	Student Body	Enrollment
McPherson College	McPherson, Kans.	1887	Brethren	Coed.	496
Medaille College	Buffalo, N.Y.	1875	Roman Catholic	Coed.	807
Medical College of Ohio at Toledo	Toledo, Ohio	1964	State	Coed.	561
Medical College of Pennsylvania	Philadelphia	1850	Private	Coed.	539
Meharry Medical College	Nashville, Tenn.	1876	Private	Coed.	747
Memphis Academy of the Arts	Memphis	1936	Private	Coed.	208
Memphis State University	Memphis	1912	State	Coed.	20,624
Menlo College	Menlo Park, Calif.	1927	Private	Coed.	644
Mennonite Brethren Biblical Seminary	Fresno, Calif.	1955	Mennonite	Coed.	129
Mercer University	Atlanta, Ga.	1960	Baptist	Coed.	1,808
	Macon, Ga.	1833	Baptist	Coed.	2,950
Southern School of Pharmacy	Atlanta, Ga.	1903	Baptist	Coed.	323
Mercy College	Dobbs Ferry, N.Y.	1950	Private	Coed.	9,399
Mercy College of Detroit	Detroit	1941	Roman Catholic	Coed.	2,106
Mercyhurst College	Erie, Pa.	1926	Roman Catholic	Coed.	1,606
Meredith College	Raleigh, N.C.	1891	Baptist	Women	1,615
Merrimack College	North Andover, Mass.	1947	Roman Catholic	Coed.	3,751
Mesa College	Grand Junction, Colo.	1925	State	Coed.	4,602
Messiah College	Grantham, Pa.	1909	Private	Coed.	1,502
Methodist College	Fayetteville, N.C.	1956	Methodist	Coed.	810
Methodist Theological School in Ohio	Delaware, Ohio	1958	Methodist	Coed.	241
Metropolitan State College	Denver	1963	State	Coed.	14,410
Miami, University of	Coral Gables, Fla.	1925	Private	Coed.	14,656
Miami University	Oxford, Ohio	1809	State	Coed.	14,872
Michigan, University of	Ann Arbor, Mich.	1817	State	Coed.	35,072
	Dearborn, Mich.	1959	State	Coed.	6,390
	Flint, Mich.	1956	State	Coed.	5,025
Michigan State University	East Lansing, Mich.	1855	State	Coed.	42,730
Michigan Technological University	Houghton, Mich.	1885	State	Coed.	7,640
Mid-America Baptist Theological Seminary	Memphis	1972	Baptist	Coed.	316
Mid-America Nazarene College	Olathe, Kans.	1966	Nazarene	Coed.	1,218
Middle Tennessee State University	Murfreesboro, Tenn.	1911	State	Coed.	10,948
Middlebury College	Middlebury, Vt.	1800	Private	Coed.	1,951
Midland Lutheran College	Fremont, Nebr.	1883	Lutheran	Coed.	872
Midwest College of Engineering	Lombard, Ill.	1967	Private	Coed.	255
Midwestern Baptist Theological Seminary	Kansas City, Mo.	1957	Baptist	Coed.	488
Midwestern State University	Wichita Falls, Tex.	1922	State	Coed.	4,818
Miles College	Birmingham, Ala.	1905	Methodist	Coed.	736
Millersville University	Millersville, Pa.	1852	State	Coed.	6,420
Milligan College	Milligan College, Tenn.	1866	Private	Coed.	660
Millikin University	Decatur, Ill.	1901	Presbyterian	Coed.	1,547
Mills College	Oakland, Calif.	1852	Private	Women	911
Millsaps College	Jackson, Miss.	1890	Methodist	Coed.	1,203
Milwaukee School of Engineering	Milwaukee	1903	Private	Coed.	2,536
Minneapolis College of Art and Design	Minneapolis, Minn.	1886	Private	Coed.	509
Minnesota, University of	Duluth, Minn.	1947	State	Coed.	10,872
	Morris, Minn.	1959	State	Coed.	1,735
Twin Cities Campus	Minneapolis-St. Paul, Minn.	1851	State	Coed.	64,515
Minnesota State University System:					
Bemidji State University	Bemidji, Minn.	1913	State	Coed.	4,882
Mankato State University	Mankato, Minn.	1866	State	Coed.	14,083
Metropolitan State University	St. Paul, Minn.	1971	State	Coed.	3,406
Moorhead State University	Moorhead, Minn.	1885	State	Coed.	7,103
St. Cloud State University	St. Cloud, Minn.	1869	State	Coed.	11,555
Southwest State University	Marshall, Minn.	1963	State	Coed.	2,127
Winona State University	Winona, Minn.	1858	State	Coed.	5,304
Minot State College	Minot, N. Dak.	1913	State	Coed.	2,695
Mississippi, University of	University, Miss.	1844	State	Coed.	9,408
Medical Center	Jackson, Miss.	1955	State	Coed.	1,733
Mississippi College	Clinton, Miss.	1826	Baptist	Coed.	2,775
Mississippi State University	Mississippi State, Miss.	1878	State	Coed.	13,376
Mississippi University for Women	Columbus, Miss.	1884	State	Women	1,894
Mississippi Valley State University	Itta Bena, Miss.	1946	State	Coed.	2,238
Missouri, University of	Columbia, Mo.	1839	State	Coed.	24,763
	Kansas City, Mo.	1929	State	Coed.	11,419
	Rolla, Mo.	1870	State	Coed.	7,795
	St. Louis	1963	State	Coed.	12,035

Universities and Colleges

Name	Location	Founded	Control	Student Body	Enrollment
Missouri Baptist College	St. Louis	1963	Private	Coed.	406
Missouri Southern State College	Joplin, Mo.	1965	State	Coed.	4,478
Missouri Valley College	Marshall, Mo.	1888	Presbyterian	Coed.	480
Missouri Western State College	St. Joseph, Mo.	1915	State	Coed.	4,269
Mobile College	Mobile, Ala.	1961	Baptist	Coed.	940
Molloy College	Rockville Centre, N.Y.	1955	Roman Catholic	Coed.	1,638
Monmouth College	Monmouth, Ill.	1853	Presbyterian	Coed.	645
Monmouth College	West Long Branch, N.J.	1933	Private	Coed.	4,067
Montana, University of	Missoula, Mont.	1893	State	Coed.	9,101
Montana College of Mineral Science and Technology	Butte, Mont.	1893	State	Coed.	2,195
Montana State University	Bozeman, Mont.	1893	State	Coed.	11,233
Montclair State College	Montclair, N.J.	1908	State	Coed.	14,754
Monterey Institute of International Studies	Monterey, Calif.	1955	Private	Coed.	411
Montevallo, University of	Montevallo, Ala.	1896	State	Coed.	2,600
Moore College of Art	Philadelphia	1844	Private	Women	524
Moravian College	Bethlehem, Pa.	1807	Moravian	Coed.	1,847
Morehead State University	Morehead, Ky.	1922	State	Coed.	6,337
Morehouse College	Atlanta, Ga.	1867	Private	Men	1,933
Morgan State University	Baltimore	1867	State	Coed.	4,720
Morningside College	Sioux City, Iowa	1893	Methodist	Coed.	1,253
Morris Brown College	Atlanta, Ga.	1881	Methodist	Coed.	1,326
Morris College	Sumter, S.C.	1908	Baptist	Coed.	628
Mount Angel Seminary	St. Benedict, Ore.	1887	Roman Catholic	Men	118
Mount Holyoke College	South Hadley, Mass.	1837	Private	Women	1,968
Mount Marty College	Yankton, S. Dak.	1936	Roman Catholic	Coed.	592
Mount Mary College	Milwaukee	1913	Roman Catholic	Women	1,111
Mount Mercy College	Cedar Rapids, Iowa	1928	Roman Catholic	Coed.	1,167
Mount St. Alphonsus Seminary	Esopus, N.Y.	1907	Roman Catholic	Coed.	50
Mount St. Clare College	Clinton, Iowa	1895	Roman Catholic	Coed.	336
Mount St. Joseph on the Ohio, College of	Mount St. Joseph, Ohio	1920	Roman Catholic	Women	1,699
Mount St. Mary College	Newburgh, N.Y.	1954	Roman Catholic	Coed.	1,038
Mount St. Mary's College	Los Angeles	1925	Roman Catholic	Women	1,099
Mount St. Mary's College	Emmitsburg, Md.	1808	Roman Catholic	Coed.	1,696
Mount St. Vincent, College of	New York City	1847	Roman Catholic	Coed.	1,147
Mount Senario College	Ladysmith, Wis.	1962	Private	Coed.	516
Mount Union College	Alliance, Ohio	1846	Methodist	Coed.	981
Mount Vernon College	Washington, D.C.	1875	Private	Women	521
Mount Vernon Nazarene College	Mount Vernon, Ohio	1966	Nazarene	Coed.	1,027
Muhlenberg College	Allentown, Pa.	1848	Lutheran	Coed.	2,353
Mundelein College	Chicago	1930	Roman Catholic	Women	1,282
Murray State University	Murray, Ky.	1922	State	Coed.	7,542
Muskingum College	New Concord, Ohio	1837	Presbyterian	Coed.	1,040
NAES College	Chicago	1974	Private	Coed.	25
National College of Chiropractic	Lombard, Ill.	1906	Private	Coed.	998
National College of Education	Evanston, Ill.	1886	Private	Coed.	1,721
National University	San Diego	1971	Private	Coed.	6,824
Naval Postgraduate School	Monterey, Calif.	1909	Federal	Coed.	1,519
Nazareth College	Nazareth, Mich.	1924	Roman Catholic	Coed.	571
Nazareth College of Rochester	Rochester, N.Y.	1924	Roman Catholic	Coed.	2,423
Nebraska, University of	Lincoln, Nebr.	1869	State	Coed.	25,075
	Omaha, Nebr.	1908	State	Coed.	14,024
Medical Center	Omaha, Nebr.	1869	State	Coed.	2,564
Nebraska Wesleyan University	Lincoln, Nebr.	1887	Private	Coed.	1,179
Neumann College	Aston, Pa.	1962	Roman Catholic	Coed.	847
Nevada, University of	Las Vegas, Nev.	1955	State	Coed.	11,452
	Reno, Nev.	1886	State	Coed.	9,613
New College of California	San Francisco	1971	Private	Coed.	617
New England, University of	Biddeford, Me.	1943	Roman Catholic	Coed.	725
New England College	Henniker, N.H.	1946	Private	Coed.	1,312
New England Conservatory of Music	Boston	1867	Private	Coed.	717
New Hampshire, University System of					
University of New Hampshire	Durham, N.H.	1866	State	Coed.	12,415
Keene State College	Keene, N.H.	1909	State	Coed.	3,705
Plymouth State College	Plymouth, N.H.	1871	State	Coed.	3,544
School for Life Long Learning	Durham, N.H.	1972	State	Coed.	1,876
New Hampshire College	Manchester, N.H.	1932	Private	Coed.	6,820
New Haven, University of	West Haven, Conn.	1920	Private	Coed.	7,298
New Jersey, University of Medicine and Dentistry of	Newark, N.J.	1956	State	Coed.	1,883
New Jersey Institute of Technology	Newark, N.J.	1881	State; Municipal	Coed.	6,874
New Mexico, University of	Albuquerque, N. Mex.	1889	State	Coed.	24,056

Name	Location	Founded	Control	Student Body	Enrollment
New Mexico Highlands University	Las Vegas, N. Mex.	1893	State	Coed.	2,312
New Mexico Institute of Mining and Technology	Socorro, N. Mex.	1889	State	Coed.	1,371
New Mexico State University	Las Cruces, N. Mex.	1888	State	Coed.	13,395
New Orleans Baptist Theological Seminary	New Orleans	1917	Baptist	Coed.	1,547
New Rochelle, College of	New Rochelle, N.Y.	1904	Roman Catholic	Coed.	5,729
New School for Social Research	New York City	1919	Private	Coed.	4,381
Parsons School of Design	New York City	1896	Private	Coed.	2,710
Otis Art Institute	Los Angeles	1918	Private	Coed.	627
New School of Music	Philadelphia	1943	Private	Coed.	70
New York, City University of:					
Bernard Baruch College	New York City	1919	Municipal; State	Coed.	15,238
Brooklyn College	New York City	1930	Municipal; State	Coed.	15,568
City College	New York City	1847	Municipal; State	Coed.	13,528
College of Staten Island	New York City	1955	Municipal; State	Coed.	11,121
Graduate School and University Center	New York City	1961	Municipal; State	Coed.	3,051
Hunter College	New York City	1870	Municipal; State	Coed.	17,353
John Jay College of Criminal Justice	New York City	1964	Municipal; State	Coed.	5,881
Lehman College	New York City	1931	Municipal; State	Coed.	9,591
New York City Technical College	New York City	1946	Municipal; State	Coed.	12,261
Queens College	New York City	1937	Municipal; State	Coed.	17,335
York College	New York City	1966	Municipal; State	Coed.	4,094
New York, State University of, College at:	Brockport, N.Y.	1835	State	Coed.	7,401
	Buffalo, N.Y.	1867	State	Coed.	11,430
	Cortland, N.Y.	1866	State	Coed.	5,994
	Fredonia, N.Y.	1867	State	Coed.	5,192
	Geneseo, N.Y.	1867	State	Coed.	5,231
	New Paltz, N.Y.	1823	State	Coed.	7,418
	Old Westbury, N.Y.	1967	State	Coed.	3,755
	Oneonta, N.Y.	1887	State	Coed.	6,124
	Oswego, N.Y.	1861	State	Coed.	7,841
	Plattsburgh, N.Y.	1889	State	Coed.	6,019
	Potsdam, N.Y.	1816	State	Coed.	4,920
	Purchase, N.Y.	1967	State	Coed.	3,688
College of Ceramics at Alfred University	Alfred, N.Y.	1900	State	Coed.	762
College of Environmental Science and Forestry	Syracuse, N.Y.	1911	State	Coed.	1,587
College of Optometry	New York City	1971	State	Coed.	254
College of Technology	Utica, N.Y.	1966	State	Coed.	3,054
Cornell University Statutory Colleges	Ithaca, N.Y.	1865	State	Coed.	7,552
Downstate Medical Center	New York City	1860	State	Coed.	1,414
Empire State College	Saratoga Springs, N.Y.	1971	State	Coed.	5,201
Fashion Institute of Technology	New York City	1944	Municipal; State	Coed.	9,704
Maritime College	New York City	1874	State	Coed.	1,126
State University of New York at:	Albany, N.Y.	1844	State	Coed.	15,726
	Binghamton, N.Y.	1946	State	Coed.	11,725
	Buffalo, N.Y.	1846	State	Coed.	23,479
	Stony Brook, N.Y.	1957	State	Coed.	14,741
Health Sciences Center	Buffalo, N.Y.	1846	State	Coed.	3,360
Upstate Medical Center	Syracuse, N.Y.	1834	State	Coed.	927
New York Institute of Technology	Old Westbury, N.Y.	1955	Private	Coed.	8,122
	New York City	1955	Private	Coed.	3,477
New York Regents College Degrees, University of the State of	Albany, N.Y.	1784	American Evangelical Lutheran Church	Coed.	18,695
New York University	New York City	1831	Private	Coed.	32,460
Newberry College	Newberry, S.C.	1856	Lutheran	Coed.	684
Niagara University	Niagara University, N.Y.	1856	Roman Catholic	Coed.	3,825
Nicholls State University	Thibodaux, La.	1948	State	Coed.	7,226
Nichols College	Dudley, Mass.	1815	Private	Coed.	992
Norfolk State University	Norfolk, Va.	1935	State	Coed.	7,346
North Adams State College	North Adams, Mass.	1894	State	Coed.	2,709
North Alabama, University of	Florence, Ala.	1872	State	Coed.	5,269
North American Baptist Seminary	Sioux Falls, S.D.	1858	Baptist	Coed.	147
North Carolina, University of	Asheville, N.C.	1927	State	Coed.	2,520
	Chapel Hill, N.C.	1789	State	Coed.	22,071
	Charlotte, N.C.	1965	State	Coed.	10,336

Universities and Colleges

Name	Location	Founded	Control	Student Body	Enrollment
	Greensboro, N.C.	1891	State	Coed.	10,332
	Wilmington, N.C.	1947	State	Coed.	5,766
Appalachian State University	Boone, N.C.	1899	State	Coed.	10,437
East Carolina University	Greenville, N.C.	1907	State	Coed.	14,510
Elizabeth City State University	Elizabeth City, N.C.	1891	State	Coed.	1,532
Fayetteville State University	Fayetteville, N.C.	1867	State	Coed.	2,410
North Carolina Agricultural and Technical State University	Greensboro, N.C.	1891	State	Coed.	5,228
North Carolina Central University	Durham, N.C.	1910	State	Coed.	4,990
North Carolina School of the Arts	Winston-Salem, N.C.	1963	State	Coed.	535
North Carolina State University	Raleigh, N.C.	1887	State	Coed.	22,669
Pembroke State University	Pembroke, N.C.	1887	State	Coed.	2,191
Western Carolina University	Cullowhee, N.C.	1889	State	Coed.	6,361
Winston-Salem State University	Winston-Salem, N.C.	1892	State	Coed.	2,259
North Carolina Wesleyan College	Rocky Mount, N.C.	1956	Methodist	Coed.	932
North Central College	Naperville, Ill.	1861	Methodist	Coed.	1,388
North Dakota, University of	Grand Forks, N. Dak.	1884	State	Coed.	10,905
North Dakota State University	Fargo, N. Dak.	1890	State	Coed.	9,463
North Florida, University of	Jacksonville, Fla.	1965	State	Coed.	5,444
North Georgia College	Dahlonega, Ga.	1873	State	Coed.	1,984
North Park College and Theological Seminary	Chicago	1891	Evangelical Covenant Church of America	Coed.	1,316
North Texas State University	Denton, Tex.	1890	State	Coed.	18,782
Northeast Louisiana University	Monroe, La.	1931	State	Coed.	11,075
Northeast Missouri State University	Kirksville, Mo.	1867	State	Coed.	7,205
Northeastern Bible College	Essex Fells, N.J.	1950	Private	Coed.	301
Northeastern Illinois University	Chicago	1961	State	Coed.	10,349
Northeastern Oklahoma State University	Tahlequah, Okla.	1851	State	Coed.	6,512
Northeastern University	Boston	1898	Private	Coed.	38,926
Northern Arizona University	Flagstaff, Ariz.	1899	State	Coed.	11,925
Northern Baptist Theological Seminary	Lombard, Ill.	1913	Baptist	Coed.	217
Northern Colorado, University of	Greeley, Colo.	1889	State	Coed.	9,671
Northern Illinois University	De Kalb, Ill.	1895	State	Coed.	25,676
Northern Iowa, University of	Cedar Falls, Iowa	1876	State	Coed.	11,180
Northern Kentucky University	Highland Heights, Ky.	1968	State	Coed.	8,951
Northern Michigan University	Marquette, Mich.	1899	State	Coed.	8,377
Northern Montana College	Havre, Mont.	1929	State	Coed.	1,687
Northern State College	Aberdeen, S. Dak.	1901	State	Coed.	2,716
Northland College	Ashland, Wis.	1892	Private	Coed.	700
Northrop University	Inglewood, Calif.	1942	Private	Coed.	1,445
Northwest Christian College	Eugene, Ore.	1895	Disciples of Christ	Coed.	227
Northwest College of the Assemblies of God	Kirkland, Wash.	1934	Assemblies of God	Coed.	719
Northwest Missouri State University	Maryville, Mo.	1905	State	Coed.	5,102
Northwest Nazarene College	Nampa, Idaho	1913	Nazarene	Coed.	1,221
Northwestern College	Orange City, Iowa	1882	Reformed	Coed.	891
Northwestern College	Roseville, Minn.	1902	Private	Coed.	884
Northwestern College	Watertown, Wis.	1865	Lutheran	Men	269
Northwestern Oklahoma State University	Alva, Okla.	1897	State	Coed.	1,721
Northwestern State University of Louisiana	Natchitoches, La.	1884	State	Coed.	6,443
Northwestern University	Evanston, Ill.	1851	Private	Coed.	15,703
Northwood Institute	Midland, Mich.	1959	Private	Coed.	2,119
Norwich University:					
Military College of Vermont	Northfield, Vt.	1819	Private	Coed.	1,490
Vermont College	Montpelier, Vt.	1834	Private	Coed.	1,023
Notre Dame, College of	Belmont, Calif.	1868	Roman Catholic	Coed.	1,360
Notre Dame, University of	Notre Dame, Ind.	1842	Roman Catholic	Coed.	9,298
Notre Dame College	Manchester, N.H.	1950	Roman Catholic	Women	716
Notre Dame College	Cleveland	1922	Roman Catholic	Women	671
Notre Dame of Maryland, College of	Baltimore	1873	Roman Catholic	Women	1,668
Notre Dame Seminary Graduate School of Theology	New Orleans, La.	1923	Roman Catholic	Coed.	78
Nova University	Fort Lauderdale, Fla.	1964	Private	Coed.	5,567
Nyack College	Nyack, N.Y.	1882	Christian and Missionary Alliance	Coed.	761

Name	Location	Founded	Control	Student Body	Enrollment
Oakland City College	Oakland City, Ind.	1885	Private	Coed.	562
Oakland University	Rochester, Mich.	1957	State	Coed.	11,721
Oakwood College	Huntsville, Ala.	1896	Adventist	Coed.	1,418
Oberlin College	Oberlin, Ohio	1833	Private	Coed.	2,809
Oblate College	Washington, D.C.	1916	Roman Catholic	Coed.	40
Oblate School of Theology	San Antonio	1903	Roman Catholic	Coed.	77
Occidental College	Los Angeles	1887	Private	Coed.	1,593
Oglala Lakota College	Kyle, S. Dak.	1971	Federal	Coed.	665
Oglethorpe University	Atlanta, Ga.	1835	Private	Coed.	1,160
Ohio Dominican College	Columbus, Ohio	1911	Roman Catholic	Coed.	1,019
Ohio Northern University	Ada, Ohio	1871	Methodist	Coed.	2,625
Ohio State University	Columbus, Ohio	1870	State	Coed.	53,438
	Lima, Ohio	1960	State	Coed.	901
	Mansfield, Ohio	1958	State	Coed.	1,095
	Marion, Ohio	1957	State	Coed.	729
	Newark, Ohio	1957	State	Coed.	911
Ohio University	Athens, Ohio	1804	State	Coed.	15,734
Ohio Valley College	Parkersburg, W. Va.	1958	Churches of Christ	Coed.	275
Ohio Wesleyan University	Delaware, Ohio	1842	Methodist	Coed.	2,004
Oklahoma, University of	Norman, Okla.	1890	State	Coed.	21,802
Health Sciences Center	Oklahoma City, Okla.	1900	State	Coed.	2,378
Oklahoma, University of Science and Arts of	Chickasha, Okla.	1908	State	Coed.	1,378
Oklahoma Baptist University	Shawnee, Okla.	1910	Baptist	Coed.	1,416
Oklahoma Christian College	Oklahoma City, Okla.	1950	Private	Coed.	1,614
Oklahoma City University	Oklahoma City, Okla.	1901	Methodist	Coed.	3,158
Oklahoma Panhandle State University	Goodwell, Okla.	1909	State	Coed.	1,323
Oklahoma State University	Stillwater, Okla.	1890	State	Coed.	23,354
Old Dominion University	Norfolk, Va.	1930	State	Coed.	15,781
Olivet College	Olivet, Mich.	1844	Private	Coed.	561
Olivet Nazarene College	Kankakee, Ill.	1907	Nazarene	Coed.	1,907
Oral Roberts University	Tulsa, Okla.	1965	Private	Coed.	4,024
Oregon, University of	Eugene, Ore.	1872	State	Coed.	15,405
Oregon Graduate Center	Beaverton, Ore.	1963	Private	Coed.	76
Oregon Health Sciences University	Portland, Ore.	1974	State	Coed.	1,431
Oregon Institute of Technology	Klamath Falls, Ore.	1946	State	Coed.	2,668
Oregon State University	Corvallis, Ore.	1868	State	Coed.	16,754
Ottawa University	Ottawa, Kans.	1865	Baptist	Coed.	2,074
Otterbein College	Westerville, Ohio	1847	Methodist	Coed.	1,628
Ouachita Baptist University	Arkadelphia, Ark.	1886	Baptist	Coed.	1,691
Our Lady of Holy Cross College	New Orleans, La.	1922	Roman Catholic	Coed.	770
Our Lady of the Elms, College of	Chicopee, Mass.	1928	Roman Catholic	Women	778
Our Lady of the Lake University of San Antonio	San Antonio	1911	Roman Catholic	Coed.	1,577
Ozarks, College of the	Clarksville, Ark.	1834	Presbyterian	Coed.	674
Ozarks, School of the	Point Lookout, Mo.	1906	Private	Coed.	1,293
Pace University	New York City	1906	Private	Coed.	14,285
White Plains Campus	White Plains, N.Y.	1923	Private	Coed.	4,460
Pleasantville/Briarcliff Campus	Pleasantville, N.Y.	1963	Private	Coed.	4,400
Pacific, University of the	Stockton, Calif.	1851	Private	Coed.	5,997
Pacific Christian College	Fullerton, Calif.	1928	Disciples of Christ; Churches of Christ	Coed.	459
Pacific Graduate School of Psychology	Palo Alto, Calif.	1975	Private	Coed.	169
Pacific Lutheran University	Tacoma, Wash.	1890	Lutheran	Coed.	3,583
Pacific Northwest College of Art	Portland, Ore.	1909	Private	Coed.	201
Pacific Oaks College	Pasadena, Calif.	1951	Private	Coed.	242
Pacific School of Religion	Berkeley, Calif.	1866	Private	Coed.	237
Pacific Union College	Angwin, Calif.	1882	Adventist	Coed.	1,592
Pacific University	Forest Grove, Ore.	1849	Private	Coed.	1,071
Paine College	Augusta, Ga.	1882	Multiple Protestant denominations	Coed.	817
Palm Beach Atlantic College	West Palm Beach, Fla.	1968	Baptist	Coed.	656
Pan American University	Edinburg, Tex.	1927	State	Coed.	8,847
Park College	Parkville, Mo.	1875	Private	Coed.	3,179
Patten College	Oakland, Calif.	1945	Private	Coed.	143
Paul Quinn College	Waco, Tex.	1872	African Methodist Episcopal	Coed.	467
Pennsylvania, University of	Philadelphia	1740	Private	Coed.	22,317
Pennsylvania College of Optometry	Philadelphia	1919	Private	Coed.	579
Pennsylvania State University	University Park, Pa.	1855	State	Coed.	36,162
Behrend College	Erie, Pa.	1926	State	Coed.	1,850
Capitol Campus	Middletown, Pa.	1966	State	Coed.	2,711
Hershey Medical Center	Hershey, Pa.	1964	State	Coed.	517

Name	Location	Founded	Control	Student Body	Enrollment
King of Prussia Center for Graduate Studies	Radnor, Pa.	1963	State	Coed.	438
Pepperdine University	Malibu, Calif.	1937	Private	Coed.	6,499
Peru State College	Peru, Nebr.	1867	State	Coed.	926
Pfeiffer College	Misenheimer, N.C.	1885	Methodist	Coed.	812
Philadelphia College of Art	Philadelphia	1876	Private	Coed.	1,617
Philadelphia College of the Bible	Langhorne, Pa.	1913	Private	Coed.	566
Philadelphia College of Pharmacy and Science	Philadelphia	1821	Private	Coed.	1,107
Philadelphia College of Textiles and Science	Philadelphia	1884	Private	Coed.	3,091
Philadelphia College of the Performing Arts	Philadelphia	1870	Private	Coed.	346
Philander Smith College	Little Rock, Ark.	1877	Methodist	Coed.	461
Phillips University	Enid, Okla.	1906	Disciples of Christ	Coed.	1,132
Phoenix, University of	Phoenix	1976	Private	Coed.	1,982
Piedmont College	Demorest, Ga.	1897	Congregational Christian Churches	Coed.	386
Pikeville College	Pikeville, Ky.	1889	Presbyterian	Coed.	560
Pine Manor College	Chestnut Hill, Mass.	1911	Private	Women	591
Pittsburg State University	Pittsburg, Kans.	1903	State	Coed.	5,117
Pittsburgh, University of	Bradford, Pa.	1963	Private; State	Coed.	1,023
	Johnstown, Pa.	1927	Private; State	Coed.	3,227
	Pittsburgh	1787	Private; State	Coed.	29,358
Greensburg Campus	Greensburg, Pa.	1963	State	Coed.	1,274
Pittsburgh Theological Seminary	Pittsburgh	1794	Presbyterian	Coed.	342
Pitzer College	Claremont, Calif.	1963	Private	Coed.	740
Point Loma Nazarene College	San Diego	1902	Nazarene	Coed.	1,870
Point Park College	Pittsburgh	1960	Private	Coed.	2,666
Polytechnic Institute of New York	New York City	1854	Private	Coed.	4,930
Pomona College	Claremont, Calif.	1887	Private	Coed.	1,390
Pontifical College Josephinum	Worthington, Ohio	1892	Roman Catholic	Men	209
Portland, University of	Portland, Ore.	1901	Private	Coed.	2,872
Portland School of Art	Portland, Me.	1882	Private	Coed.	274
Portland State University	Portland, Ore.	1946	State	Coed.	14,449
Post College	Waterbury, Conn.	1890	Private	Coed.	1,484
Pratt Institute	New York City	1887	Private	Coed.	4,072
Presbyterian College	Clinton, S.C.	1880	Presbyterian	Coed.	913
Presbyterian School of Christian Education	Richmond, Va.	1914	Presbyterian	Coed.	97
Prescott College	Prescott, Ariz.	1966	Private	Coed.	133
Princeton Theological Seminary	Princeton, N.J.	1812	Presbyterian	Coed.	881
Princeton University	Princeton, N.J.	1746	Private	Coed.	6,153
Principia College	Elsah, Ill.	1898	Private	Coed.	788
Providence College	Providence, R.I.	1917	Roman Catholic	Coed.	5,915
Puerto Rico, University of	Mayagüez, P.R.	1911	Commonwealth	Coed.	9,241
Bayamón Technological University College	Bayamón, P.R.	1971	Commonwealth	Coed.	4,444
Cayey University College	Cayey, P.R.	1967	Commonwealth	Coed.	3,319
Humacao University College	Humacao, P.R.	1962	Commonwealth	Coed.	3,134
Medical Sciences Campus	San Juan, P.R.	1950	Commonwealth	Coed.	2,911
Rio Piedras Campus	Rio Piedras, P.R.	1903	Commonwealth	Coed.	19,755
Puget Sound, University of	Tacoma, Wash.	1888	Methodist	Coed.	4,199
Purdue University	West Lafayette, Ind.	1869	State	Coed.	32,635
Calumet Campus	Hammond, Ind.	1943	State	Coed.	7,719
North Central Campus	Westville, Ind.	1943	State	Coed.	2,544
Indiana University-Purdue University	Fort Wayne, Ind.	1964	State	Coed.	10,128
	Indianapolis	1969	State	Coed.	23,258
Queens College	Charlotte, N.C.	1857	Presbyterian	Coed.	1,102
Quincy College	Quincy, Ill.	1860	Roman Catholic	Coed.	944
Quinnipiac College	Hamden, Conn.	1929	Private	Coed.	3,631
Radford University	Radford, Va.	1910	State	Coed.	5,903
Ramapo College of New Jersey	Mahwah, N.J.	1969	State	Coed.	4,515
Rand Graduate Institute of Policy Studies	Santa Monica, Calif.	1970	Private	Coed.	53
Randolph-Macon College	Ashland, Va.	1830	Private	Coed.	925
Randolph-Macon Woman's College	Lynchburg, Va.	1891	Private	Women	739
Redlands, University of	Redlands, Calif.	1907	Baptist	Coed.	2,634
Reed College	Portland, Ore.	1909	Private	Coed.	1,094
Reformed Theological Seminary	Jackson, Miss.	1965	Private	Coed.	221
Regis College	Denver	1877	Roman Catholic	Coed.	3,390
Regis College	Weston, Mass.	1927	Roman Catholic	Women	1,146

Universities and Colleges

Name	Location	Founded	Control	Student Body	Enrollment
Rensselaer Polytechnic Institute	Troy, N.Y.	1824	Private	Coed.	6,673
Rhode Island, University of	Kingston, R.I.	1892	State	Coed.	10,834
	Narragansett, R.I.	1937	State	Coed.	190
	Providence, R.I.	1944	State	Coed.	2,941
Rhode Island College	Providence, R.I.	1854	State	Coed.	8,451
Rhode Island School of Design	Providence, R.I.	1877	Private	Coed.	1,688
Rhodes College	Memphis	1848	Presbyterian	Coed.	1,006
Rice University	Houston	1891	Private	Coed.	3,881
Richmond, University of	Richmond, Va.	1830	Baptist	Coordinate	4,411
Rider College	Lawrenceville, N.J.	1865	Private	Coed.	5,462
Ringling School of Art and Design	Sarasota, Fla.	1931	Private	Coed.	459
Rio Grande College	Rio Grande, Ohio	1876	Private	Coed.	1,359
Ripon College	Ripon, Wis.	1851	Private	Coed.	918
Rivier College	Nashua, N.H.	1933	Roman Catholic	Women	2,219
Roanoke College	Salem, Va.	1842	Lutheran	Coed.	1,384
Robert Morris College	Coraopolis, Pa.	1921	Private	Coed.	5,689
Roberts Wesleyan College	Rochester, N.Y.	1866	Methodist	Coed.	612
Rochester, University of	Rochester, N.Y.	1850	Private	Coed.	8,561
Rochester Institute of Technology	Rochester, N.Y.	1829	Private	Coed.	16,146
Rockford College	Rockford, Ill.	1847	Private	Coed.	1,469
Rockhurst College	Kansas City, Mo.	1910	Roman Catholic	Coed.	3,183
Rockmount College	Denver, Colo.	1914	Private	Coed.	295
Rocky Mountain College	Billings, Mont.	1878	Private	Coed.	388
Roger Williams College	Bristol, R.I.	1945	Private	Coed.	2,505
	Providence, R.I.	1945	Private	Coed.	1,455
Rollins College	Winter Park, Fla.	1885	Private	Coed.	3,415
Roosevelt University	Chicago	1945	Private	Coed.	6,685
Rosary College	River Forest, Ill.	1901	Roman Catholic	Coed.	1,607
Rose-Hulman Institute of Technology	Terre Haute, Ind.	1874	Private	Men	1,322
Rosemont College	Rosemont, Pa.	1921	Roman Catholic	Women	607
Rush University	Chicago	1972	Private	Coed.	1,146
Russell Sage College	Troy, N.Y.	1916	Private	Women	3,135
Rust College	Holly Springs, Miss.	1866	Methodist	Coed.	826
Rutgers The State University of New Jersey	Camden, N.J.	1927	State	Coed.	5,013
	New Brunswick, N.J.	1766	State	Coed.	32,826
	Newark, N.J.	1892	State	Coed.	9,548
Sacred Heart, University of the	San Juan, P.R.	1935	Roman Catholic	Coed.	7,275
Sacred Heart College	Belmont, N.C.	1892	Roman Catholic	Coed.	395
Sacred Heart Seminary College	Detroit	1919	Roman Catholic	Men	198
Sacred Heart University	Bridgeport, Conn.	1963	Roman Catholic	Coed.	5,008
Saginaw Valley State College	University Center, Mich.	1963	State	Coed.	4,370
St. Alphonsus College	Suffield, Conn.	1963	Roman Catholic	Men	50
St. Ambrose College	Davenport, Iowa	1882	Roman Catholic	Coed.	2,138
St. Andrew's Presbyterian College	Laurinburg, N.C.	1958	Presbyterian	Coed.	756
St. Anselm College	Manchester, N.H.	1889	Roman Catholic	Coed.	1,795
St. Augustine's College	Raleigh, N.C.	1867	Episcopal	Coed.	1,581
St. Benedict, College of	St. Joseph, Minn.	1913	Roman Catholic	Coordinate	2,262
St. Bonaventure University	St. Bonaventure, N.Y.	1858	Roman Catholic	Coed.	2,751
St. Catherine, College of	St. Paul, Minn.	1905	Roman Catholic	Women	2,285
St. Charles Borromeo Seminary	Philadelphia	1832	Roman Catholic	Men	554
St. Edward's University	Austin, Tex.	1885	Roman Catholic	Coed.	2,572
St. Elizabeth, College of	Convent Station, N.J.	1899	Roman Catholic	Women	880
St. Francis, College of	Joliet, Ill.	1925	Roman Catholic	Coed.	3,613
St. Francis College	Fort Wayne, Ind.	1890	Roman Catholic	Coed.	1,264
St. Francis College	New York City	1859	Roman Catholic	Coed.	2,839
St. Francis College	Loretto, Pa.	1847	Roman Catholic	Coed.	1,565
St. Francis Seminary School of Pastoral Ministry	Milwaukee	1856	Roman Catholic	Coed.	81
St. Hyacinth College-Seminary	Granby, Mass.	1927	Roman Catholic	Men	44
St. John Fisher College	Rochester, N.Y.	1948	Roman Catholic	Coed.	2,318
St. John Vianney College Seminary	Miami, Fla.	1959	Roman Catholic	Men	56
St. John's College	Winfield, Kans.	1893	Lutheran	Coed.	251
St. John's College	Annapolis, Md.	1696	Private	Coed.	395
	Santa Fe, N. Mex.	1964	Private	Coed.	342
St. John's College and Seminary	Camarillo, Calif.	1939	Roman Catholic	Men	203
St. John's Provincial Seminary	Plymouth, Mich.	1949	Roman Catholic	Coed.	189
St. John's Seminary	Brighton, Mass.	1884	Roman Catholic	Men	204
St. John's University	Collegeville, Minn.	1857	Roman Catholic	Coordinate	2,028
St. John's University	New York City	1870	Roman Catholic	Coed.	18,961
St. Joseph College	West Hartford, Conn.	1932	Roman Catholic	Women	1,212
St. Joseph Seminary College	St. Benedict, La.	1891	Roman Catholic	Coed.	119

Universities and Colleges

Name	Location	Founded	Control	Student Body	Enrollment
St. Joseph the Provider, College of	Rutland, Vt.	1954	Roman Catholic	Coed.	338
St. Joseph's College	Mountain View, Calif.	1898	Roman Catholic	Men	101
St. Joseph's College	Rensselaer, Ind.	1889	Roman Catholic	Coed.	963
St. Joseph's College	North Windham, Me.	1912	Roman Catholic	Coed.	3,762
St. Joseph's College	New York City	1916	Private	Coed.	1,007
Suffolk Campus	Patchogue, N.Y.	1916	Private	Coed.	1,318
St. Joseph's Seminary	Yonkers	1896	Roman Catholic	Men	178
St. Joseph's University	Philadelphia	1851	Roman Catholic	Coed.	6,086
St. Lawrence University	Canton, N.Y.	1856	Private	Coed.	2,432
St. Leo College	St. Leo, Fla.	1889	Roman Catholic	Coed.	4,677
St. Louis College of Pharmacy	St. Louis	1864	Private	Coed.	633
St. Louis University	St. Louis	1818	Roman Catholic	Coed.	8,727
Parks College	Cahokia, Ill.	1927	Roman Catholic	Coed.	1,029
St. Martin's College	Olympia, Wash.	1895	Roman Catholic	Coed.	517
St. Mary, College of	Omaha, Nebr.	1923	Roman Catholic	Women	1,141
St. Mary College	Leavenworth, Kans.	1923	Roman Catholic	Women	802
St. Mary of the Plains College	Dodge City, Kans.	1952	Roman Catholic	Coed.	619
St. Mary-of-the-Woods College	Saint Mary-of-the-Woods, Ind.	1840	Roman Catholic	Women	662
St. Mary Seminary	Cleveland	1848	Roman Catholic	Coed.	72
St. Mary's College	Notre Dame, Ind.	1844	Roman Catholic	Women	1,769
St. Mary's College	Orchard Lake, Mich.	1885	Roman Catholic	Coed.	195
St. Mary's College	Winona, Minn.	1912	Roman Catholic	Coed.	1,404
St. Mary's College of California	Moraga, Calif.	1863	Roman Catholic	Coed.	2,956
St. Mary's College of Maryland	St. Marys City, Md.	1839	State	Coed.	1,296
St. Mary's Seminary and University	Baltimore	1791	Roman Catholic	Coed.	314
St. Mary's Seminary College	Perryville, Mo.	1818	Roman Catholic	Men	72
St. Mary's University of San Antonio	San Antonio	1852	Roman Catholic	Coed.	3,311
St. Meinrad College	St. Meinrad, Ind.	1857	Roman Catholic	Men	180
St. Meinrad School of Theology	St. Meinrad, Ind.	1861	Roman Catholic	Men	148
St. Michael's College	Winooski, Vt.	1903	Roman Catholic	Coed.	2,000
St. Norbert College	De Pere, Wis.	1898	Roman Catholic	Coed.	1,672
St. Olaf College	Northfield, Minn.	1874	Lutheran	Coed.	3,061
St. Patrick's Seminary	Menlo Park, Calif.	1894	Roman Catholic	Men	87
St. Paul Bible College	Bible College, Minn.	1916	Christian and Missionary Alliance	Coed.	593
St. Paul School of Theology	Kansas City, Mo.	1958	Methodist	Coed.	218
St. Paul Seminary	St. Paul, Minn.	1894	Roman Catholic	Men	86
St. Paul's College	Lawrenceville, Va.	1888	Episcopal	Coed.	687
St. Peter's College	Jersey City, N.J.	1872	Roman Catholic	Coed.	4,199
St. Rose, College of	Albany, N.Y.	1920	Roman Catholic	Coed.	2,728
St. Scholastica, College of	Duluth, Minn.	1912	Roman Catholic	Coed.	1,165
St. Teresa, College of	Winona, Minn.	1907	Roman Catholic	Women	553
St. Thomas, College of	St. Paul, Minn.	1885	Roman Catholic	Coed.	5,854
St. Thomas, University of	Houston	1947	Roman Catholic	Coed.	2,040
St. Thomas Aquinas College	Sparkill, N.Y.	1952	Private	Coed.	1,973
St. Thomas Seminary	Denver	1907	Roman Catholic	Men	134
St. Thomas University	Miami, Fla.	1962	Roman Catholic	Coed.	3,333
St. Vincent College and Seminary	Latrobe, Pa.	1846	Roman Catholic	Coed.	983
St. Vincent de Paul Regional Seminary	Boynton Beach, Fla.	1960	Roman Catholic	Coed.	103
St. Xavier College	Chicago	1846	Roman Catholic	Coed.	2,346
Salem College	Winston-Salem, N.C.	1772	Moravian	Women	619
Salem College	Salem, W. Va.	1888	Private	Coed.	788
Salem State College	Salem, Mass.	1854	State	Coed.	8,551
Salisbury State College	Salisbury, Md.	1925	State	Coed.	4,341
Salve Regina, The Newport College	Newport, R.I.	1934	Roman Catholic	Coed.	1,961
Sam Houston State University	Huntsville, Tex.	1879	State	Coed.	10,476
Samford University	Birmingham, Ala.	1841	Baptist	Coed.	4,161
San Diego, University of	San Diego	1949	Private	Coed.	5,003
San Francisco, University of	San Francisco	1855	Roman Catholic	Coed.	6,251
San Francisco Art Institute	San Francisco	1871	Private	Coed.	633
San Francisco Conservatory of Music	San Francisco	1917	Private	Coed.	215
San Francisco Theological Seminary	San Anselmo, Calif.	1871	Presbyterian	Coed.	965
Sangamon State University	Springfield, Ill.	1969	State	Coed.	3,327
Santa Clara, University of	Santa Clara, Calif.	1851	Roman Catholic	Coed.	7,231
Santa Fe, College of	Santa Fe, N. Mex.	1947	Roman Catholic	Coed.	978
Sarah Lawrence College	Yonkers, N.Y.	1926	Private	Coed.	1,026
Savannah College of Art and Design	Savannah, Ga.	1978	Private	Coed.	452
Savannah State College	Savannah, Ga.	1890	State	Coed.	2,115
Saybrook Institute	San Francisco, Calif.	1970	Private	Coed.	154
Scarritt College for Christian Workers	Nashville, Tenn.	1892	Methodist	Coed.	87
School of Theology at Claremont	Claremont, Calif.	1885	Methodist	Coed.	247

Name	Location	Founded	Control	Student Body	Enrollment
Schreiner College	Kerrville, Tex.	1923	Presbyterian	Coed.	513
Scranton, University of	Scranton, Pa.	1888	Roman Catholic	Coed.	4,620
Scripps College	Claremont, Calif.	1926	Private	Women	580
Seabury-Western Theological Seminary	Evanston, Ill.	1933	Episcopal	Coed.	97
Seattle Pacific University	Seattle	1891	Methodist	Coed.	2,720
Seattle University	Seattle	1891	Roman Catholic	Coed.	4,508
Seton Hall University	South Orange, N.J.	1856	Roman Catholic	Coed.	10,349
Immaculate Conception Seminary	South Orange, N.J.	1860	Roman Catholic	Coed.	177
Seton Hill College	Greensburg, Pa.	1883	Roman Catholic	Women	968
Shaw University	Raleigh, N.C.	1865	Private	Coed.	1,832
Sheldon Jackson College	Sitka, Alaska	1878	Private	Coed.	222
Shenandoah College and Conservatory of Music	Winchester, Va.	1875	Methodist	Coed.	874
Shepherd College	Shepherdstown, W. Va.	1871	State	Coed.	3,138
Shippensburg State University	Shippensburg, Pa.	1871	State	Coed.	5,882
Shorter College	Rome, Ga.	1873	Baptist	Coed.	775
Siena College	Loudonville, N.Y.	1937	Roman Catholic	Coed.	3,403
Siena Heights College	Adrian, Mich.	1919	Roman Catholic	Coed.	1,404
Sierra Nevada College	Incline Village, Nev.	1969	Private	Coed.	212
Silver Lake College	Manitowoc, Wis.	1935	Roman Catholic	Coed.	411
Simmons College	Boston	1899	Private	Women	2,847
Simon's Rock of Bard College	Great Barrington, Mass.	1964	Private	Coed.	315
Simpson College	San Francisco	1921	Christian and Missionary Alliance	Coed.	306
Simpson College	Indianola, Iowa	1860	Private	Coed.	1,065
Sinte Gleska College	Rosebud, S. Dak.	1970	Private	Coed.	246
Sioux Falls College	Sioux Falls, S. Dak.	1883	Baptist	Coed.	870
Skidmore College	Saratoga Springs, N.Y.	1911	Private	Coed.	2,457
Slippery Rock University	Slippery Rock, Pa.	1889	State	Coed.	5,782
Smith College	Northampton, Mass.	1871	Private	Women	2,987
Sojourner-Douglass College	Baltimore	1980	Private	Coed.	457
South, University of the	Sewanee, Tenn.	1860	Episcopal	Coed.	1,097
South Alabama, University of	Mobile, Ala.	1963	State	Coed.	9,411
South Carolina, Medical University of	Charleston, S.C.	1824	State	Coed.	1,857
South Carolina, University of	Aiken, S.C.	1961	State	Coed.	1,835
	Columbia, S.C.	1801	State	Coed.	24,671
	Spartanburg, S.C.	1967	State	Coed.	2,583
Coastal Carolina College	Conway, S.C.	1959	State	Coed.	2,511
South Carolina State College	Orangeburg, S.C.	1896	State	Coed.	3,901
South Dakota, University of	Vermillion, S. Dak.	1862	State	Coed.	8,263
South Dakota School of Mines and Technology	Rapid City, S. Dak.	1885	State	Coed.	2,808
South Dakota State University	Brookings, S. Dak.	1881	State	Coed.	7,981
South Florida, University of	Tampa, Fla.	1956	State	Coed.	25,743
South Texas, University System of:					
Corpus Christi State University	Corpus Christi, Tex.	1971	State	Coed.	3,251
Laredo State University	Laredo, Tex.	1969	State	Coed.	900
Texas A&I University	Kingsville, Tex.	1925	State	Coed.	5,245
Southeast Missouri State University	Cape Girardeau, Mo.	1873	State	Coed.	9,091
Southeastern Baptist Theological Seminary	Wake Forest, N.C.	1950	Baptist	Coed.	1,106
Southeastern Louisiana University	Hammond, La.	1925	State	Coed.	9,530
Southeastern Massachusetts University	North Darmouth, Mass.	1895	State	Coed.	6,843
Southeastern Oklahoma State University	Durant, Okla.	1909	State	Coed.	4,179
Southeastern University	Washington, D.C.	1879	Private	Coed.	1,597
Southern Arkansas University	Magnolia, Ark.	1909	State	Coed.	2,095
Southern Baptist College	Walnut Ridge, Ark.	1941	Baptist	Coed.	405
Southern Baptist Theological Seminary	Louisville, Ky.	1858	Baptist	Coed.	2,141
Southern California, University of	Los Angeles	1880	Private	Coed.	29,411
Southern California College	Costa Mesa, Calif.	1920	Assemblies of God	Coed.	740
Southern California College of Optometry	Fullerton, Calif.	1904	Private	Coed.	405
Southern College of Optometry	Memphis	1932	Private	Coed.	528
Southern College of Seventh-Day Adventists	Collegedale, Tenn.	1892	Adventist	Coed.	1,801
Southern Colorado, University of	Pueblo, Colo.	1933	State	Coed.	5,432
Southern Connecticut State University	New Haven, Conn.	1893	State	Coed.	10,481
Southern Illinois University	Carbondale, Ill.	1907	State	Coed.	23,733
	Edwardsville, Ill.	1957	State	Coed.	11,098
Southern Indiana, University of	Evansville, Ind.	1965	State	Coed.	3,664

Name	Location	Founded	Control	Student Body	Enrollment
Southern Methodist University	Dallas	1911	Private	Coed.	9,156
Southern Mississippi, University of	Hattiesburg, Miss.	1910	State	Coed.	13,003
Southern Oregon State College	Ashland, Ore.	1926	State	Coed.	4,326
Southern University	New Orleans	1956	State	Coed.	2,622
Agricultural and Mechanical College Main Campus	Baton Rouge, La.	1880	State	Coed.	9,125
Southern Utah State College	Cedar City, Utah	1897	State	Coed.	2,378
Southern Vermont College	Bennington, Vt.	1926	Private	Coed.	460
Southwest, College of the	Hobbs, N. Mex.	1956	Private	Coed.	204
Southwest Baptist University	Bolivar, Mo.	1878	Baptist	Coed.	1,428
Southwest Missouri State University	Springfield, Mo.	1906	State	Coed.	15,015
Southwest Texas State University	San Marcos, Tex.	1899	State	Coed.	16,397
Southwestern Adventist College	Keene, Tex.	1893	Adventist	Coed.	712
Southwestern Baptist Theological Seminary	Fort Worth, Tex.	1908	Baptist	Coed.	3,447
Southwestern College	Winfield, Kans.	1885	Methodist	Coed.	588
Southwestern College of Christian Ministries	Bethany, Okla.	1946	Pentecostal Holiness Church	Coed.	51
Southwestern Louisiana, University of	Lafayette, La.	1898	State	Coed.	15,702
Southwestern Oklahoma State University	Weatherford, Okla.	1901	State	Coed.	4,560
Southwestern University	Georgetown, Tex.	1840	Methodist	Coed.	990
Spalding University	Louisville, Ky.	1814	Roman Catholic	Coed.	971
Spelman College	Atlanta, Ga.	1881	Private	Women	1,458
Spertus College of Judaica	Chicago	1925	Private	Coed.	328
Spring Arbor College	Spring Arbor, Mich.	1873	Methodist	Coed.	975
Spring Garden College	Philadelphia	1851	Private	Coed.	1,398
Spring Hill College	Mobile, Ala.	1830	Roman Catholic	Coed.	1,061
Springfield College	Springfield, Mass.	1885	Private	Coed.	2,349
Stanford University	Stanford, Calif.	1885	Private	Coed.	13,784
Stephen F. Austin State University	Nacogdoches, Tex.	1921	State	Coed.	11,881
Stephens College	Columbia, Mo.	1833	Private	Women	1,295
Sterling College	Sterling, Kans.	1887	Presbyterian	Coed.	394
Stetson University	De Land, Fla.	1883	Baptist	Coed.	2,898
Steubenville, University of	Steubenville, Ohio	1946	Roman Catholic	Coed.	915
Stevens Institute of Technology	Hoboken, N.J.	1870	Private	Coed.	3,086
Stillman College	Tuscaloosa, Ala.	1876	Presbyterian	Coed.	523
Stockton State College	Pomona, N.J.	1969	State	Coed.	5,056
Stonehill College	North Easton, Mass.	1948	Roman Catholic	Coed.	2,745
Strayer College	Washington, D.C.	1904	Private	Coed.	1,773
Suffolk University	Boston	1906	Private	Coed.	6,330
Sul Ross State University	Alpine, Tex.	1917	State	Coed.	2,313
Susquehanna University	Selinsgrove, Pa.	1858	Lutheran	Coed.	1,714
Swarthmore College	Swarthmore, Pa.	1865	Private	Coed.	1,278
Sweet Briar College	Sweet Briar, Va.	1901	Private	Women	738
Syracuse University	Syracuse, N.Y.	1870	Private	Coed.	21,124
Utica College	Utica, N.Y.	1946	Private	Coed.	2,345
Tabor College	Hillsboro, Kans.	1908	Mennonite	Coed.	421
Talladega College	Talladega, Ala.	1867	Private	Coed.	539
Tampa, University of	Tampa, Fla.	1931	Private	Coed.	2,002
Tarkio College	Tarkio, Mo.	1883	Presbyterian	Coed.	586
Taylor University	Upland, Ind.	1846	Private	Coed.	1,460
Temple University	Philadelphia	1888	Private; State	Coed.	29,643
Tennessee, University of	Chattanooga, Tenn.	1886	State	Coed.	7,544
	Knoxville, Tenn.	1794	State	Coed.	27,041
	Martin, Tenn.	1927	State	Coed.	5,525
Center for Health Sciences	Memphis	1911	State	Coed.	2,026
Tennessee State University	Nashville, Tenn.	1912	State	Coed.	8,008
Tennessee Technological University	Cookeville, Tenn.	1915	State	Coed.	7,872
Tennessee Wesleyan College	Athens, Tenn.	1857	Methodist	Coed.	511
Texas, University of	Arlington, Tex.	1895	State	Coed.	22,171
	Austin, Tex.	1881	State	Coed.	48,039
	El Paso, Tex.	1913	State	Coed.	15,129
	San Antonio	1969	State	Coed.	11,145
	Tyler, Tex.	1971	State	Coed.	2,623
Dallas Campus	Richardson, Tex.	1969	State	Coed.	7,376
Health Science Center at:	Dallas	1943	State	Coed.	1,335
	Houston	1972	State	Coed.	2,676
	San Antonio	1959	State	Coed.	2,326
Medical Branch	Galveston, Tex.	1881	State	Coed.	1,655
Permian Basin Campus	Odessa, Tex.	1969	State	Coed.	1,825
Texas A&M University System:					
Prairie View A&M University	Prairie View, Tex.	1876	State	Coed.	4,499

Name	Location	Founded	Control	Student Body	Enrollment
Tarleton State University	Stephenville, Tex.	1899	State	Coed.	4,231
Texas A&M University	College Station, Tex.	1871	State	Coed.	36,127
	Galveston, Tex.	1971	State	Coed.	590
Texas Christian University	Fort Worth, Tex.	1873	Private	Coed.	6,881
Texas College	Tyler, Tex.	1894	Methodist	Coed.	619
Texas Lutheran College	Seguin, Tex.	1891	Lutheran	Coed.	1,249
Texas Southern University	Houston	1947	State	Coed.	8,298
Texas Tech University	Lubbock, Tex.	1923	State	Coed.	22,849
Texas Wesleyan College	Fort Worth, Tex.	1891	Methodist	Coed.	1,603
Texas Woman's University	Denton, Tex.	1901	State	Women	7,827
Thiel College	Greenville, Pa.	1866	Lutheran	Coed.	807
Thomas A. Edison State College	Trenton, N.J.	1972	Municipal; State	Coed.	3,643
Thomas Aquinas College	Santa Paula, Calif.	1969	Private	Coed.	120
Thomas College	Waterville, Me.	1894	Private	Coed.	934
Thomas Jefferson University	Philadelphia	1824	Private	Coed.	1,870
Thomas More College	Fort Mitchell, Ky.	1921	Roman Catholic	Coed.	1,224
Tift College	Forsyth, Ga.	1849	Baptist	Coed.	609
Toccoa Falls College	Toccoa Falls, Ga.	1907	Private	Coed.	649
Toledo, University of	Toledo, Ohio	1872	State	Coed.	21,386
Tougaloo College	Tougaloo, Miss.	1869	Private	Coed.	775
Touro College	New York City	1970	Private	Coordinate	2,233
Towson State University	Baltimore	1866	State	Coed.	14,869
Transylvania University	Lexington, Ky.	1780	Private	Coed.	701
Trenton State College	Trenton, N.J.	1855	State	Coed.	9,940
Trevecca Nazarene College	Nashville, Tenn.	1942	Nazarene	Coed.	972
Trinity Christian College	Palos Heights, Ill.	1959	Private	Coed.	440
Trinity College	Hartford, Conn.	1823	Private	Coed.	1,972
Trinity College	Deerfield, Ill.	1897	Evangelical Free Church of America	Coed.	556
Trinity College	Burlington, Vt.	1925	Roman Catholic	Women	870
Trinity College	Washington, D.C.	1897	Roman Catholic	Coed.	714
Trinity Evangelical Divinity School	Deerfield, Ill.	1897	Evangelical Free Church of America	Coed.	891
Trinity Lutheran Seminary	Columbus, Ohio	1830	Lutheran	Coed.	305
Trinity University	San Antonio	1869	Presbyterian	Coed.	3,103
Tri-State University	Angola, Ind.	1884	Private	Coed.	1,093
Troy State University	Troy, Ala.	1887	State	Coed.	6,921
	Montgomery, Ala.	1965	State	Coed.	2,118
Tufts University	Medford, Mass.	1852	Private	Coed.	7,006
Tulane University of Louisiana	New Orleans	1834	Private	Coed.	10,512
Tulsa, University of	Tulsa, Okla.	1894	Private	Coed.	5,944
Tusculum College	Greeneville, Tenn.	1794	Presbyterian	Coed.	366
Tuskegee Institute	Tuskegee Institute, Ala.	1881	Private	Coed.	3,440
Union College	Barbourville, Ky.	1879	Methodist	Coed.	818
Union College	Lincoln, Nebr.	1891	Adventist	Coed.	1,024
Union College	Schenectady, N.Y.	1795	Private	Coed.	3,421
Union Theological Seminary	New York City	1836	Private	Coed.	312
Union Theological Seminary in Virginia	Richmond, Va.	1812	Presbyterian	Coed.	244
Union University	Jackson, Tenn.	1825	Baptist	Coed.	1,374
U.S. Air Force Academy	Colorado Springs, Colo.	1954	Federal	Coed.	4,477
U.S. Army Command and General Staff College	Fort Leavenworth, Kans.	1881	Federal	Coed.	971
U.S. Coast Guard Academy	New London, Conn.	1876	Federal	Coed.	939
U.S. International University	San Diego	1952	Private	Coed.	2,208
U.S. Merchant Marine Academy	Kings Point, N.Y.	1943	Federal	Coed.	1,140
U.S. Military Academy	West Point, N.Y.	1802	Federal	Coed.	4,472
U.S. Naval Academy	Annapolis, Md.	1845	Federal	Coed.	4,617
U.S. Sports Academy	Mobile, Ala.	1972	Private	Coed.	36
United Theological Seminary	New Brighton, Minn.	1962	Private	Coed.	246
United Theological Seminary	Dayton, Ohio	1871	Methodist	Coed.	278
Unity College	Unity, Me.	1966	Private	Coed.	327
Upper Iowa University	Fayette, Iowa	1857	Private	Coed.	1,606
Upsala College	East Orange, N.J.	1893	Lutheran	Coed.	1,543
Urbana University	Urbana, Ohio	1850	Private	Coed.	547
Ursinus College	Collegeville, Pa.	1869	Private	Coed.	2,085
Ursuline College	Cleveland	1871	Roman Catholic	Women	1,264
Utah, University of	Salt Lake City, Utah	1850	State	Coed.	24,364
Utah State University	Logan, Utah	1888	State	Coed.	11,112
Valdosta State College	Valdosta, Ga.	1906	State	Coed.	5,525
Valley City State College	Valley City, N. Dak.	1889	State	Coed.	1,081
Valparaiso University	Valparaiso, Ind.	1859	Lutheran	Coed.	4,251
Vanderbilt University	Nashville, Tenn.	1873	Private	Coed.	8,715
VanderCook College of Music	Chicago	1909	Private	Coed.	168

Universities and Colleges

Name	Location	Founded	Control	Student Body	Enrollment
Vassar College	Poughkeepsie, N.Y.	1861	Private	Coed.	2,356
Vermont and State Agricultural College, University of	Burlington, Vt.	1791	State	Coed.	11,103
Vermont Law School	South Royalton, Vt.	1972	Private	Coed.	383
Villa Julie College	Stevenson, Md.	1947	Private	Coed.	900
Villa Maria College	Erie, Pa.	1925	Roman Catholic	Women	622
Villanova University	Villanova, Pa.	1842	Roman Catholic	Coed.	11,716
Virgin Islands, College of the	St. Thomas, U.S. Virgin Is.	1962	State	Coed.	2,744
Virginia, University of	Charlottesville, Va.	1819	State	Coed.	17,118
Clinch Valley College	Wise, Va.	1954	State	Coed.	1,202
Virginia Commonwealth University	Richmond, Va.	1837	State	Coed.	20,031
Virginia Intermont College	Bristol, Va.	1884	Baptist	Coed.	610
Virginia Military Institute	Lexington, Va.	1839	State	Men	1,321
Virginia Polytechnic Institute and State University	Blacksburg, Va.	1872	State	Coed.	22,921
Virginia State University	Petersburg, Va.	1882	State	Coed.	4,526
Virginia Union University	Richmond, Va.	1865	Baptist	Coed.	1,297
Virginia Wesleyan College	Norfolk, Va.	1961	Methodist	Coed.	837
Visual Arts, School of	New York City	1947	Private	Coed.	4,823
Viterbo College	La Crosse, Wis.	1890	Roman Catholic	Coed.	1,165
Voorhees College	Denmark, S.C.	1897	Episcopal	Coed.	625
Wabash College	Crawfordsville, Ind.	1832	Private	Men	766
Wadhams Hall Seminary and College	Ogdensburg, N.Y.	1924	Roman Catholic	Men	68
Wagner College	New York City	1883	Lutheran	Coed.	2,305
Wake Forest University	Winston-Salem, N.C.	1834	Baptist	Coed.	4,795
Walla Walla College	College Place, Wash.	1892	Adventist	Coed.	1,717
Walsh College	Canton, Ohio	1958	Roman Catholic	Coed.	1,150
Walsh College of Accountancy and Business Administration	Troy, Mich.	1968	Private	Coed.	1,811
Warner Pacific College	Portland, Ore.	1937	Church of God	Coed.	441
Warner Southern College	Lake Wales, Fla.	1964	Private	Coed.	304
Warren Wilson College	Swannanoa, N.C.	1894	Presbyterian	Coed.	535
Wartburg College	Waverly, Iowa	1852	Lutheran	Coed.	1,131
Wartburg Theological Seminary	Dubuque, Iowa	1854	Lutheran	Coed.	257
Washburn University of Topeka	Topeka, Kans.	1865	Municipal	Coed.	6,515
Washington, University of	Seattle	1861	State	Coed.	34,468
Washington and Jefferson College	Washington, Pa.	1781	Private	Coed.	1,267
Washington and Lee University	Lexington, Va.	1782	Private	Coed.	1,708
Washington College	Chestertown, Md.	1782	Private	Coed.	794
Washington State University	Pullman, Wash.	1890	State	Coed.	16,746
Washington Theological Union	Silver Spring, Md.	1969	Private	Coed.	176
Washington University	St. Louis	1853	Private	Coed.	10,700
Wayland Baptist University	Plainview, Tex.	1908	Baptist	Coed.	1,469
Wayne State College	Wayne, Nebr.	1909	State	Coed.	2,321
Wayne State University	Detroit	1868	State	Coed.	29,775
Waynesburg College	Waynesburg, Pa.	1849	Presbyterian	Coed.	685
Webb Institute of Naval Architecture	Glen Cove, N.Y.	1889	Private	Coed.	79
Webber College	Babson Park, Fla.	1927	Private	Coed.	297
Weber State College	Ogden, Utah	1889	State	Coed.	10,361
Webster University	St. Louis	1915	Private	Coed.	4,954
Wellesley College	Wellesley, Mass.	1870	Private	Women	2,257
Wells College	Aurora, N.Y.	1868	Private	Women	509
Wentworth Institute of Technology	Boston	1904	Private	Coed.	3,737
Wesley College	Dover, Del.	1873	Methodist	Coed.	1,194
Wesley Theological Seminary	Washington, D.C.	1882	Methodist	Coed.	333
Wesleyan College	Macon, Ga.	1836	Methodist	Women	340
Wesleyan University	Middletown, Conn.	1831	Private	Coed.	3,006
West Chester University	West Chester, Pa.	1871	State	Coed.	9,704
West Coast University	Los Angeles	1909	Private	Coed.	886
Orange County Center	Orange, Calif.	1963	Private	Coed.	492
West Florida, University of	Pensacola, Fla.	1963	State	Coed.	5,294
West Georgia College	Carrollton, Ga.	1933	State	Coed.	6,005
West Liberty State College	West Liberty, W. Va.	1837	State	Coed.	2,513
West Los Angeles, University of	Culver City, Calif.	1966	Private	Coed.	705
West Texas State University	Canyon, Tex.	1909	State	Coed.	6,805
West Virginia College of Graduate Studies	Institute, W. Va.	1972	State	Coed.	2,988
West Virginia Institute of Technology	Montgomery, W. Va.	1895	State	Coed.	3,353
West Virginia State College	Institute, W. Va.	1891	State	Coed.	4,352
West Virginia University	Morgantown, W. Va.	1867	State	Coed.	21,337
West Virginia Wesleyan College	Buckhannon, W. Va.	1890	Methodist	Coed.	1,579
Westbrook College	Portland, Me.	1831	Private	Coed.	1,036
Western Baptist College	Salem, Ore.	1935	Private	Coed.	280

Universities and Colleges

Name	Location	Founded	Control	Student Body	Enrollment
Western Connecticut State University	Danbury, Conn.	1903	State	Coed.	5,996
Western Conservative Baptist Seminary	Portland, Ore.	1927	Private	Coed.	520
Western Evangelical Seminary	Portland, Ore.	1945	Private	Coed.	204
Western Illinois University	Macomb, Ill.	1899	State	Coed.	12,404
Western Kentucky University	Bowling Green, Ky.	1906	State	Coed.	12,796
Western Maryland College	Westminster, Md.	1867	Methodist	Coed.	1,814
Western Michigan University	Kalamazoo, Mich.	1903	State	Coed.	20,580
Western Montana College	Dillon, Mont.	1893	State	Coed.	984
Western New England College	Springfield, Mass.	1919	Private	Coed.	5,364
Western New Mexico University	Silver City, N. Mex.	1893	State	Coed.	1,571
Western Oregon State College	Monmouth, Ore.	1856	State	Coed.	2,458
Western State College of Colorado	Gunnison, Colo.	1911	State	Coed.	2,865
Western State University College of Law	Fullerton, Calif.	1966	Private	Coed.	1,316
Western Washington University	Bellingham, Wash.	1893	State	Coed.	9,352
Westfield State College	Westfield, Mass.	1838	State	Coed.	4,503
Westmar College	Le Mars, Iowa	1890	Methodist	Coed.	505
Westminster Choir College	Princeton, N.J.	1926	Private	Coed.	417
Westminster College	Fulton, Mo.	1851	Presbyterian	Coed.	687
Westminster College	New Wilmington, Pa.	1852	Private	Coed.	1,591
Westminster College of Salt Lake City	Salt Lake City, Utah	1875	Private	Coed.	1,233
Westminster Theological Seminary	Philadelphia	1929	Private	Coed.	422
Westmont College	Santa Barbara, Calif.	1940	Private	Coed.	1,010
Wheaton College	Wheaton, Ill.	1860	Private	Coed.	2,490
Wheaton College	Norton, Mass.	1834	Private	Women	1,257
Wheeling College	Wheeling, W. Va.	1954	Roman Catholic	Coed.	990
Wheelock College	Boston	1888	Private	Coed.	1,112
Whitman College	Walla Walla, Wash.	1859	Private	Coed.	1,209
Whittier College	Whittier, Calif.	1887	Private	Coed.	1,541
Whitworth College	Spokane, Wash.	1890	Private	Coed.	1,802
Wichita State University	Wichita, Kans.	1892	State	Coed.	16,632
Widener University	Chester, Pa.	1821	Private	Coed.	5,669
Wilberforce University	Wilberforce, Ohio	1856	Methodist	Coed.	979
Wiley College	Marshall, Tex.	1873	Methodist	Coed.	543
Wilkes College	Wilkes-Barre, Pa.	1933	Private	Coed.	2,967
Willamette University	Salem, Ore.	1842	Private	Coed.	1,860
William and Mary, College of	Williamsburg, Va.	1693	State	Coed.	6,521
Christopher Newport College	Newport News, Va.	1960	State	Coed.	4,214
William Carey College	Hattiesburg, Miss.	1906	Baptist	Coed.	1,477
William Jewell College	Liberty, Mo.	1849	Baptist	Coed.	1,569
William Paterson College	Wayne, N.J.	1855	State	Coed.	12,139
William Penn College	Oskaloosa, Iowa	1873	Quaker	Coed.	470
William Woods College	Fulton, Mo.	1870	Private	Women	793
Williams College	Williamstown, Mass.	1793	Private	Coed.	1,971
Wilmington College	New Castle, Del.	1967	Private	Coed.	877
Wilmington College	Wilmington, Ohio	1870	Quaker	Coed.	1,346
Wilson College	Chambersburg, Pa.	1869	Private	Women	254
Wingate College	Wingate, N.C.	1896	Southern Baptist	Coed.	1,481
Winthrop College	Rock Hill, S.C.	1886	State	Coed.	4,881
Wisconsin, Medical College of	Milwaukee	1913	Private	Coed.	866
Wisconsin, University of	Eau Claire, Wis.	1916	State	Coed.	10,883
	Green Bay, Wis.	1965	State	Coed.	4,681
	La Crosse, Wis.	1909	State	Coed.	8,659
	Madison, Wis.	1849	State	Coed.	42,230
	Milwaukee	1956	State	Coed.	26,119
	Oshkosh, Wis.	1871	State	Coed.	10,683
	Platteville, Wis.	1866	State	Coed.	5,335
	River Falls, Wis.	1874	State	Coed.	5,334
	Stevens Point, Wis.	1894	State	Coed.	9,016
	Superior, Wis.	1893	State	Coed.	2,171
	Whitewater, Wis.	1868	State	Coed.	10,321
Parkside Campus	Kenosha-Racine, Wis.	1965	State	Coed.	5,850
Stout Campus	Menomonie, Wis.	1893	State	Coed.	7,595
Wisconsin Conservatory of Music	Milwaukee	1899	Private	Coed.	120
Wittenberg University	Springfield, Ohio	1845	Lutheran	Coed.	2,245
Wofford College	Spartanburg, S.C.	1854	Methodist	Coed.	1,057
Woodbury University	Los Angeles	1884	Private	Coed.	1,084
Wooster, College of	Wooster, Ohio	1866	Presbyterian	Coed.	1,757
Worcester Polytechnic Institute	Worcester, Mass.	1865	Private	Coed.	3,634
Worcester State College	Worcester, Mass.	1874	State	Coed.	6,170
World College West	San Rafael, Calif.	1971	Private	Coed.	57
Wright Institute	Berkeley, Calif.	1969	Private	Coed.	161

Name	Location	Founded	Control	Student Body	Enrollment
Wright State University	Dayton, Ohio	1964	State	Coed.	13,914
Wyoming, University of	Laramie, Wyo.	1886	State	Coed.	10,209
Xavier University	Cincinnati, Ohio	1831	Roman Catholic	Coed.	6,950
Xavier University of Louisiana	New Orleans	1915	Roman Catholic	Coed.	2,176
Yale University	New Haven, Conn.	1701	Private	Coed.	10,332
Yankton College	Yankton, S.Dak.	1881	Private	Coed.	277
Yeshiva University	New York City	1886	Private	Coordinate	4,384
York College of Pennsylvania	York, Pa.	1787	Private	Coed.	4,364
Youngstown State University	Youngstown, Ohio	1908	State	Coed.	15,590

same as that of other universities and colleges. They usually offer about the same courses of study, although state institutions often emphasize technical and professional education more than private schools.

In most cases, a *president* or *chancellor* is the chief administrator of a university or college. Other officials handle educational programs, registration, management of funds, and collection of tuition. A *dean of students* helps direct discipline and advise students.

Each college or separate school of a university generally has an *academic dean* or *director*. He or she leads the faculty in preparing the course of study for the college or school, and takes part in university planning.

Faculty includes the teachers of a college or university. The faculty of a college is divided into *departments*. Each department deals with one general course of study, such as English, mathematics, or physics. Each department has a *chairman*, who is usually a *professor*. Under the chairman are other professors, *associate professors*, *assistant professors*, and *instructors*. Some departments also have *teaching fellows* or *research fellows*. These are graduate students who teach or do research part time. Some university faculties include scientists or other research workers who do not teach. Their research is supported by the institution or by funds granted the institution by individuals or groups having specific research interests. Universities and colleges do much research under government contract.

The Student Body of a university or college is divided into graduates and undergraduates. *Graduates* have already received their bachelor's degree and are working more or less independently for a master's or doctor's degree. *Undergraduates* are studying for their bachelor's degree. The undergraduates belong to one of four classes, according to their year of study. These are the *freshman*, *sophomore*, *junior*, and *senior* classes. Most schools also admit *special students*. These students take a number of courses, but are not working toward a degree.

Most institutions are *coeducational*, with both men and women students. Others admit students of only one sex. A *coordinate* institution generally has separate men's and women's colleges. They are controlled by the same central authority and are usually located on the same or nearby campuses. See COEDUCATION.

The Calendar is the program of a school year. It is divided according to one of three systems. The most common system divides the calendar into two *semesters* of about 16 weeks each. The first semester begins in August or September. The second semester begins in January or early February. The school year ends in May or June with *commencement*, or graduation exercises (see GRADUATION). Many schools also hold a six- to eight-week summer session. By attending school all year, students may graduate in three years instead of four.

College calendars may also be arranged according to the *quarter* system. The school year is divided into four quarters of 10, 11, or 12 weeks each. The first quarter begins in the fall. The Christmas holidays come between the first and second quarters, and the spring holidays between the second and third quarters. Many students do not attend the fourth, or summer, quarter. The popularity of the quarter system increased during World War II, when many people wanted to finish college as quickly as possible before entering the armed forces. The *trimester* system divides the school year into three trimesters of about 15 weeks each.

Selecting Courses

Curriculum. The courses given by a college or university are called the school's curriculum. The catalog of the institution outlines the complete curriculum. It gives the requirements for taking each course, as well as the credits given for the course. Each course is designated as giving a specified number of *credits*. These usually equal the number of class hours devoted each week to the course. For example, a course that meets three times a week usually gives three credits for graduation. Schools using the semester calendar require about 120 credits for graduation. Between 30 and 40 of the required credits must be in the student's major subject.

Institutions vary considerably in the amount of freedom given students in selecting their courses. Almost all colleges and universities have a certain number of required subjects. Students usually can also choose nonrequired courses called *electives*. Liberal arts colleges usually give a student more opportunity to choose courses than do professional schools. Many institutions have *general education programs* for freshmen and sophomores. These programs give students a range of courses in different fields of knowledge.

When college freshmen register, they usually indicate the major subject they want to study. During the first two years, they take largely the basic required courses, such as English composition. The last two years are devoted mostly to the student's major. Many schools permit a student to have two majors.

Undergraduate Study. The programs of study provided by universities and colleges are divided into undergraduate and graduate levels. Colleges generally do not offer graduate programs, although some may offer the master's degree. An undergraduate program usually requires four years to complete. Some engineering programs and most architectural programs require five years to complete. Undergraduate study may be in the arts and sciences, or in a discipline such as English, economics, or chemistry. Undergraduate programs may also be given in a professional field such as agriculture, teacher education, or business administration.

Social Sororities are a part of college life for some women students. Members usually live together in sorority houses.

University of Pittsburgh

Laboratory Work offers students opportunities to apply principles they have studied in science or engineering classes.

University of Chicago

Graduate Study may also be in the arts and sciences, or in a profession. It ordinarily begins only after a person has completed undergraduate study. Some professional fields will only admit a student who has completed undergraduate study. This is generally true of medicine, law, dentistry, and theology. Graduate study is more intensive and specialized than undergraduate study. It usually involves more reading, and some research experience. The time required to earn a graduate degree varies. It is usually three years in law and theology, and four years in medicine. Some graduate programs may be completed in one or two years.

Degrees. The bachelor of arts or bachelor of science degree is the common degree for completing a four or five year program. One or two years of graduate study are usually required for the master of arts or master of science degree. A doctor's degree signifies more extensive graduate study. Many institutions also award honorary degrees for outstanding achievement in a profession or in public service. See DEGREE, COLLEGE.

College Life

College life gives students a welcome measure of independence. But students should realize that new responsibilities go with this independence. They must balance hard work with recreation, allow enough time and energy for social activities, and learn to use to the best advantage the opportunities their school offers.

Residence. Most colleges have *residence halls* or *dormitories*. Dormitory life offers many opportunities for friendships. Many schools also have student-controlled residences called *cooperatives*. In these, the students can cut expenses by doing their own housework. Students may also live in private homes or apartments.

Many students live with their parents and *commute* (travel daily) between home and campus. Some colleges and universities whose campuses are in large cities provide *commuter centers*, where students who commute may spend free time while on campus.

Fraternities and Sororities have houses at many schools. These organizations choose their own members according to the rules set up by the school. Educators do not agree on the value of the fraternity and sorority

system. Some approve the social advantages gained by membership in these organizations. Others believe that they tend to dominate college life, and to become undemocratic. Some colleges prohibit social fraternities and sororities on their campuses. See FRATERNITY; SORORITY.

Instruction. College freshmen find they have much more time to do as they choose than they had in high school. Classes generally take up only about 15 hours each week, although there may be additional hours of laboratory work. The rest of the time between classes is free for study or recreation.

Most classes are either lecture or discussion groups. In larger institutions, *lectures* may be given to several hundred students at a time, sometimes with the assistance of closed-circuit television. The student should take careful notes on the information given. *Discussion groups*, or *seminars*, are much smaller. Students often work on individual projects outside of class and report on them to the group.

Many universities and colleges offer courses known as *individualized-study* or *self-directed* courses. Such courses have no formal classroom sessions. Students work independently on assignments outlined by course materials. They complete the assignments at their own pace, under the guidance of a faculty member. In this kind of course, the student may use computers, individually assigned laboratory booths, and other special learning aids.

For a general discussion of tests and grading, see GRADING; TESTING.

Libraries. University and college libraries are vast storehouses of knowledge. Some hold several million volumes. The library must be used to the fullest extent if the student is to receive the greatest benefit from a college course. At best, routine classwork can only scratch the surface of any field of knowledge. Students can round out their education only by consistent and intelligent independent reading. See LIBRARY (College and University Libraries).

Research and Laboratory Work. The college teacher tries to do more than merely hand the student facts to memorize. It is far more important to develop the student's ability to find information and to learn to think

intelligently. For this reason, the teacher tries to direct the student in independent study and research by recommending books for outside reading and by suggesting new avenues of study in a certain field. Students in the sciences and engineering have laboratories in which to work. World-famous scientists direct some of these laboratories. In them they have made many important discoveries, often with the help of graduate students. For example, much of the original work on the use of atomic energy was done in the laboratories of the University of Chicago and the University of California.

Extracurricular Activities outside the normal routine of classes and study help develop the student's personality, and provide a proper balance for the daily routine. Athletics are one of many possible activities (see SPORTS). Students may also work on the staffs of school newspapers and magazines. They may take part in such activities as dramatics, music, writing, hobbies, debating, politics, religion, and student government (see STUDENT GOVERNMENT). These activities are valuable, but the wise student remembers that learning is the main purpose of attending college.

History

European Universities. Modern universities had their origin in Europe during the 1100's. But European universities were not the first in the world. The Arabs had universities at earlier dates. The University of Al-Azhar, founded in Cairo in about 970, is one of the oldest universities in the world still operating.

European universities developed from the cathedral and monastery schools. Their development took place so slowly that it is difficult to know the point at which they became universities. Many scholars believe the oldest European university is the University of Bologna, Italy. It came into existence about 1100. The University of Paris developed during the late 1100's. Many other universities appeared in Europe in the 1200's and 1300's.

These first schools were founded largely to serve the professions. They provided the first unified teaching of law, medicine, and theology. Most of them were mod-

eled on one of two plans—the Bologna plan or the Paris plan. At Bologna, the university was a corporation of the students. They hired the teachers and controlled the school's policies. The University of Paris was a corporation of the teachers. They collected fees from the students and directed the policies of the university.

Control of the schools gradually passed to a permanent body of administrators. The courses of study also broadened. During the Renaissance in the 1400's, the universities helped direct the revival of interest in Greek and Roman learning. From this revival developed the modern concept of the liberal-arts curriculum.

First Universities in the Americas. The first university in the Western Hemisphere, the University of Santo Domingo, was founded in the Dominican Republic in 1538. The University of San Marcos at Lima, Peru, was founded in 1551, as was the National Autonomous University of Mexico. Other universities appeared shortly afterward in the other Spanish colonies.

The first university to be planned in what is now the United States was at Henricopolis, Va. It was authorized in 1619, but plans were dropped after the Indian massacres of 1622. Harvard University is the oldest school of higher education still active in the United States. It was founded in 1636. The oldest university in Canada, Laval University, was founded as the Seminary of Quebec in 1663. It became a university in 1852. The first English-speaking university in Canada was established in 1789. It was the University of King's College at Windsor, N.S.

Higher education in the United States began at a time when knowledge was limited. The modern scientific spirit had not yet developed. The early settlers regarded colleges chiefly as a means of training ministers.

Many of the people who came to America came in search of religious freedom. The influence of this fact may be seen in the development of the American system of higher education. Each faith wanted to train its own leaders, and each set up schools to do so. As a result, many small church colleges were founded during

Rick Friedman, Black Star

Laval University

The Oldest Universities in the United States and Canada are Harvard University, *left*, and Laval University, *right*. Harvard, in Cambridge, Mass., was founded in 1636. Laval, in Ste.-Foy, Que., was founded as the Seminary of Quebec in 1663. It became a university in 1852.

UNIVERSITIES AND COLLEGES

The Oldest U.S. Universities and Colleges

Name	Location	Year*
Harvard University	Cambridge, Mass.	1636
William and Mary College	Williamsburg, Va.	1693
Yale University	New Haven, Conn.	1701
Princeton University	Princeton, N.J.	1746
Columbia University	New York City	1754
University of Pennsylvania	Philadelphia	1756
Brown University	Providence, R.I.	1764
Rutgers The State University of New Jersey	New Brunswick, N.J.	1766
Dartmouth College	Hanover, N.H.	1769

*Year institution became a bachelor's degree-granting institution.

the 1700's and 1800's, particularly in the Middle West. These colleges were general rather than specialized. They taught liberal arts rather than technical subjects. Early in U.S. history, some leaders saw the need for education that went beyond religious concerns. The state university was one response to this need.

Another development was the granting of land in new territories for the establishment of schools. In addition, wealthy citizens gave gifts for the founding of nonchurch schools. A number of schools which had been established by churches also came under private control.

Growth of Specialization. During the 1800's and through the mid-1900's, specialization in knowledge increased. Many colleges were created to train students in such fields as agriculture, medicine, engineering, and commerce. Specialization also resulted in an increased emphasis on advanced study. As a result, graduate schools were established at many larger schools. In turn, professional and research interests came to dominate all other educational interests. Education for professions overshadowed the liberal arts.

Specialization has resulted in the multiplying of the fields of knowledge. Educators have been asked to decide whether the college should become a preparatory school for the professions or whether the professional schools should lengthen their courses. Actually, both have happened. Today there is no set idea of what a college should be.

Another cause of specialization has been the increase in the number of students attending college. In the early days, universities served only a relatively limited group. But the people of the United States insisted that higher education should be available to anyone who wanted it. Obviously, the more the college population grew, the more courses had to be offered to satisfy many different individual interests and abilities.

Recent Developments. During World War II, American colleges contributed to the national effort by developing special programs of study and research. After the war, the typical veteran who entered a university was a young man in a hurry. He wanted to obtain a college education or vocational training as quickly as possible, and start the career that had been interrupted by the war. This development brought into sharp focus the whole problem in modern higher education. An additional factor was Russia's rapid postwar advances in science. Educators agree that students need a broad education as a basis for whatever field attracts them.

Some colleges now emphasize the study of classic works of literature. Others have combined campus study with practical training in factories and offices. Some colleges have made special studies of the needs of young people to discover what to emphasize in their programs. State universities generally try to use knowledge in as many ways as possible to serve society.

During the 1960's and early 1970's, programs were developed to help members of minority groups obtain a higher education. The federal government established *Upward Bound*, a project designed to encourage and prepare students from low-income homes to attend college. Some schools modified their admissions standards for members of minority groups to encourage their enrollment. Curriculum designers also fashioned new programs, such as Afro-American, American Indian, and Chicano studies. These programs were intended to broaden the student's understanding of the contributions of various ethnic groups to American society.

Other developments centered on the changing role of women in society. The enrollment of women increased in courses leading to professions that had traditionally been considered the work of men. Some colleges developed programs to encourage women to enter such fields as engineering, law, and medicine. In addition, many colleges that had admitted only men began to enroll women.

Another major development in American universities and colleges has been their increasing contribution to the world outside the campus. University laboratories have become important centers of experiment and discovery. College extension services, home study, correspondence courses, and radio and television programs have spread knowledge far beyond the narrow limits of the campus. JOHN E. CORBALLY, JR.

Related Articles. See the separate articles on outstanding universities and colleges, such as HARVARD UNIVERSITY; WILLIAM AND MARY, COLLEGE OF. See also the Career section in the various articles on different fields of human knowledge, such as MEDICINE (Careers in Medicine); ENGINEERING (Choosing an Engineering Career). Other related articles in WORLD BOOK include:

Academic Freedom
American Association
  of University Women
Careers
Coeducation
College Entrance
  Examination
Community College
Degree, College
Education
Extension Service

Fellowship
Fraternity
Land-Grant College
  or University
Library
Research
Scholarship
Sorority
Teaching
United Negro
  College Fund

Outline

I. Going to College
  A. Selecting a School
  B. Entrance Requirements
  C. Accrediting
  D. Size
  E. College Costs
  F. Working Your Way
  G. Financial Help

II. Kinds of Universities and Colleges
  A. Privately Controlled Schools
  B. Church-Controlled Schools
  C. Publicly Controlled Schools

III. School Organization
  A. Campus
  B. Administration
  C. Faculty
  D. The Student Body
  E. The Calendar

IV. Selecting Courses
  A. Curriculum
  B. Preprofessional Courses
  C. Graduate Study
  D. Degrees

V. College Life
    A. Residence   D. Libraries
    B. Fraternities   E. Research and Laboratory Work
       and Sororities   F. Extracurricular Activities
    C. Instruction
VI. History

Questions

What information should you get when you select a university or college?

How does a university differ from a college?

How is a university faculty usually organized?

In what two ways are school-year programs divided?

In addition to instruction, what opportunities does a university or college offer?

What is the oldest university in the United States? In Canada?

From what sources can a student obtain financial aid?

What kinds of courses did the first universities and colleges in the United States offer? Why?

Why has specialization developed in higher education?

What is the largest university in the United States? In Canada?

Additional Resources

Barron's Profiles of American Colleges. 11th ed. Barron's, 1978.

COLLEGE SCHOLARSHIP SERVICE. *The College Cost Book.* College Entrance Examination Board. Pub. annually.

HARRIS, ROBIN S. *A History of Higher Education in Canada, 1663-1960.* Univ. of Toronto Press, 1971.

HAYDEN, THOMAS C. *Handbook for College Admissions: A High School Student's Guide to Understanding the College Admissions System.* Atheneum, 1981.

JOHNSON, S. W. *The Freshman's Friend.* Barron's, 1976. Dictionary of terms relating to college life.

ROSS, MURRAY G. *The University: The Anatomy of Academe.* McGraw, 1976. History of universities in Canada, England, and U.S. from medieval times to present.

The World of Learning. 2 vols. Europa. Pub. annually.

UNIVERSITY EXTENSION. See CORRESPONDENCE SCHOOL; EXTENSION SERVICE.

UNIVERSITY OF . . . See articles on universities listed under their key word, as in CHICAGO, UNIVERSITY OF.

UNKNOWN SOLDIER. After World War I, officials of the Allied countries found that the bodies of many soldiers killed in battle could not be identified. The governments of Belgium, France, Great Britain, Italy, and the United States decided to honor in some special way the memory of these soldiers. Each government chose a symbolic unknown soldier, buried the remains near the national capital, and built a monument in honor of the soldier. Belgium placed its unknown soldier in a tomb at the base of the Colonnade of the Congress in Brussels. France buried its unknown soldier beneath the Arc de Triomphe in the center of Paris, and keeps a flame always burning over the grave. Great Britain buried its unknown soldier in Westminster Abbey. Italy's unknown soldier lies in front of the monument to Victor Emmanuel in Rome.

The Unknown Soldier of the United States was one of four war dead taken from American cemeteries in France. An American soldier, Sergeant Edward Younger, selected the soldier from these four. The remains were brought to the U.S. Capitol to lie in state. On Armistice Day (Nov. 11), 1921, they were buried in Arlington National Cemetery in Virginia, across the Potomac River from Washington, D.C. The tomb, completed in 1931, has a white marble sarcophagus over the grave bearing the inscription, "Here rests in honored glory an American soldier known but to God."

and for 23 years worked as a businessman by day and as a writer by night. After he became a vice president of the company, he resigned to write full time. He went to Europe and lived and studied there for three years. Then he published many volumes of poetry and lectured extensively. He became best known, however, as an anthologist of poetry. He edited about 18 collections of poetry, including *Modern British Poetry* (1920), *Modern American Poetry* (1919), and *Stars to Steer By* (1941). He also wrote an autobiography, *From Another World* (1939). He served as consultant in poetry in English for the Library of Congress. He was born in New York City.   JAMES WOODRESS

UNTOUCHABLE. See CASTE; INDIA (Religion).

UPANISHADS, *oo PAN uh shadz*, are a group of writings that make up the last section of a collection of Hindu scriptures called the Vedas. The Upanishads form a basic part of Hinduism and have influenced most Indian philosophy.

The Upanishads are sometimes called the *Vedanta*, which means *the summing up of the Veda*. The word *Upanishads* means *to sit close to*. It suggests that this sacred material was originally secret. Most of the Upanishads were composed as dialogues between a teacher and a student. The most important ones appeared between 800 and 600 B.C.

Several important Hindu schools of thought, including the sankhya and yoga schools, were founded on the teachings of the Upanishads. These teachings follow two basic philosophies. One states that there is a single fundamental reality, called *Brahman*, or God, which corresponds to *Atman*, the soul. Thus, there is no real distinction between the soul and God. The other Upanishadic philosophy states that each soul is individually divine.   CHARLES S. J. WHITE

See also HINDUISM; VEDAS.

UPAS, *YOO puhs*, is the name of a large forest tree that grows in southeastern Asia and Indonesia. Supposedly, tribespeople mixed its poisonous milky sap with other plant poisons to poison arrows and darts. Tales about the deadliness of this poison terrified early explorers and travelers in the East Indies. Fabulous but false stories started regarding the poison and the plant producing it. People said that nothing could grow in the shade of the tree. They said the tree brought death to birds that perched on it or flew above it. Some people believed that only persons completely covered with clothes could approach the tree without danger.

Scientific Classification. The upas belongs to the mulberry family, Moraceae. It is *Antiaris toxicaria*.   K. A. ARMSON

UPDIKE, JOHN (1932-   ), is an American author of novels, short stories, essays, and poetry. Updike became noted for his elaborate, lyrical prose style. He served as a staff writer for *The New Yorker* magazine from 1955 to 1957 and built his literary reputation as a frequent contributor to *The New Yorker*.

Much of Updike's fiction explores the superficial but attractive materialism he sees in middle-class American life. Typical Updike characters are self-absorbed, guiltridden, and obsessed with their own unimportance and the prospect of their death. They relieve their anxieties through marital unfaithfulness, but this fails to help them in their search for spiritual salvation. These characters appear in such novels as *A Month of Sundays* (1975) and *Marry Me* (1976).

In the novel *Couples* (1968) and the stories collected in *Museums and Women* (1972), Updike dramatized the disintegrating morals and marriages in several suburban families. The autobiographical stories in *Too Far to Go* (1979) narrate the course of the Maple family from newlywed happiness to divorce.

© Jill Krementz
John Updike

Updike's first popular work, *Rabbit Run* (1960), is a novel about Rabbit Angstrom, a former high school basketball star bewildered by family responsibilities. In *Rabbit Redux* (1971), Rabbit confronts such issues of the late 1960's as drug use, racial violence, and the Vietnam War. *Rabbit Is Rich* (1981) portrays Rabbit in middle age, wealthy but spiritually unfulfilled. *Rabbit Is Rich* won the 1982 Pulitzer Prize for fiction.

Updike was born in Shillington, Pa. Many of the early stories collected in *Pigeon Feathers* (1962) deal with the experiences of young people in a town based on Shillington. Updike's other novels include *The Centaur* (1963), *The Coup* (1978), and *The Witches of Eastwick* (1984). His essays appear in *Hugging the Shore* (1983). Updike's poems have been collected in *Midpoint* (1969) and *Tossing and Turning* (1977).   EUGENE K. GARBER

UPHOLSTERY is the material used to cushion and cover furniture. It makes furniture more comfortable and attractive. Most upholstery is added to the seat, back, arms, and sides of chairs and couches.

Furniture makers upholster a chair or couch after they have built a frame of wood, metal, or plastic. Upholstery consists of four major parts: (1) webbing, (2) springs, (3) padding, and (4) a cover.

First, the upholsterer stretches strips of heavy cloth, called *webbing*, across the bottom of the frame. The strips are crisscrossed for greater support. The webbing is then firmly fastened to the frame.

The *springs* used in upholstering the seat must be strong enough to support the weight of a person. Upholsterers use chiefly two types of springs, *coil springs* and *zigzag springs*. Coil springs are attached to each point of intersection between the webbing strips. The tops of the coils are bound together and fastened to the frame with strong cord. Zigzag springs are stretched across the seat and fastened to the frame. Lighter springs may be used on areas of the furniture that receive less pressure, such as the arms and back.

Next, the upholsterer covers the springs with burlap, or some other sturdy material, as a foundation for the *padding*. The chief materials used for padding are cotton, polyester fibers, and such flexible foams as urethane foam and foam rubber. Padding may also consist of animal hair or plant fibers. The padding may be thin if the furniture will have cushions. Most cushions are filled with foam or polyester fibers, but some have feather fillings. Some chairs or couches, called *tight seats*, have no cushions and require thicker padding. *Overstuffed furniture* has extra layers of padding, plus loose cushions.

Finally, the upholsterer stretches a cover over the padding and fastens it to the frame with tacks or staples. Upholstery covers are manufactured in a wide range of colors, patterns, and materials. Most covers are made of fabric. Upholsterers use natural fabrics like cotton and wool, or such manufactured fabrics as acetate and polyester. Plastic is often used to cover automobile seats and furniture that is heavily used because it is durable and easy to clean. Leather covers last longer than those that are made of many other materials, but they are more expensive. EDWARD L. CLARK

UPLAND PLOVER is a North American bird of the sandpiper family. It is usually found on wet prairies or meadows. It is the only member of the tattler group of sandpipers that does not live by the sea.

The upland plover is sometimes known as the Bartramian sandpiper. It is about 1 foot (30 centimeters) long, and it has an especially long tail for a sandpiper. Its color is blackish-brown and buff above, and buff with dark streaks on the breast and sides. Its belly is white. The upland plover breeds from Alaska to Montana and Maine. In fall, it migrates to southern Brazil and Argentina. There, the bird winters on the pampas.

The upland plover makes its nest in clumps of prairie grass or dry leaves on the prairie. The female lays four cream-colored or pale buff eggs, speckled with dark brown. The color of the birds blends with the grass, making them hard to see. The young birds can fly by midsummer, and start south almost at once. Upland plovers destroy many harmful insects, such as locusts and cutworms. The birds are protected from hunters by law.

Karl H. Maslowski
The Upland Plover destroys many harmful insects.

Scientific Classification. Upland plovers are in the sandpiper family, Scolopacidae, and not in the true plover family. Upland plovers are classified as *Bartramia longicauda*. GEORGE E. HUDSON

UPPER CANADA. See ONTARIO (History).
UPPER VOLTA. See BURKINA FASO.
UPS. See UNITED PARCEL SERVICE.
UPSILON PARTICLE, *YOOP suh lahn,* is the heaviest known subatomic particle. It has a mass about 10 times as large as that of a proton. The upsilon particle is unstable and quickly breaks down into lighter particles. It has no electric charge.

Upsilon particles are a type of *meson,* a particle made up of smaller units called *quarks.* Upsilon particles consist of a quark and its antimatter counterpart, an *antiquark.* When an upsilon particle breaks down, the quark and antiquark destroy each other. This process results in the release of energy and the creation of lighter particles.

A group of American physicists, led by Leon M.

Lederman, discovered the upsilon particle in 1977. They produced the particle by causing high-energy protons to collide with light atomic nuclei. The upsilon particle decays too rapidly to be observed directly. It was detected by observing the lighter particles that resulted from its breakdown. The large mass of the upsilon indicated that its quark was heavier than other quarks. This new quark was named *b-quark.* ROBERT H. MARCH

See also ANTIMATTER; QUARK.

UR, *ehr* or *oor,* a city in the ancient region of Sumer (now southeastern Iraq), was one of the world's first cities. It stood on the Euphrates River near the Persian Gulf and thrived as a commercial center and port from about 3500 to at least 1850 B.C. Nearby communities came under Ur's control during this period, and Ur became a strong city-state. A shift in the course of the Euphrates later isolated Ur from river traffic.

Between about 3000 and 2000 B.C., Ur served as the capital of three major ruling families. The third of these families, founded by King Ur-Nammu about 2100 B.C., controlled a large empire that extended from Assyria in the northwest to Elam in the southeast. This family's reign ended about 2000 B.C., when Elam conquered Ur. The Bible states that the Hebrew leader Abraham came from Ur. JOHN A. BRINKMAN

See also BABYLONIA; CITY (pictures); SCULPTURE (The Beginnings [picture]); SUMER.

URAL MOUNTAINS, *YUR uhl,* extend for 1,500 miles (2,410 kilometers) through western Russia. They run south from the Arctic Circle to near the Aral Sea. Many geographers consider them to be one of the boundaries between Europe and Asia. See RUSSIA (physical map).

The industrial and mineral development of the Ural Mountains played an important part in supplying the armies of Russia during World War II. These mountains are remarkable in the variety and amount of mineral wealth which they contain. Salt, silver, and gold have been mined in the Ural Mountains since the 1500's. By the 1800's, the Ural region was famous for its gems and semiprecious stones, which include emerald, beryl, amethyst, topaz, and sapphire. Other mining activities produce aluminum, chromium, coal, cobalt, copper, diamonds, iron ore, magnesium, nickel, platinum, and potash. Oil is found west of the Urals, and new gas and oil fields have been developed on the northeastern sides of the mountains. The Urals also have one of the world's largest reserves of asbestos.

The mountains are geologically old. They were formed about 225 million years ago, at the end of the Paleozoic Era. Since then, they have been worn down to rounded hills, most of which rise only from 1,000 to 6,000 feet (300 to 1,800 meters). The highest peak of the Ural Mountains is Mount Narodnaya (6,214 feet, or 1,894 meters). THEODORE SHABAD

URAL RIVER, *YUR uhl,* is a shallow stream that rises in the southern Ural Mountains in Russia. For location, see RUSSIA (physical map). The Ural flows south for about 1,570 miles (2,527 kilometers) and enters the Caspian Sea through several mouths. Salmon and sturgeon fisheries are along the Ural. Railroads cross it at Orenburg and Ural'sk. A steel center, Magnitogorsk, lies on the upper Ural. THEODORE SHABAD

URANIA. See MUSES.

Shelly Katz, Black Star

Yellowcake, a Form of Processed Uranium

Westinghouse Electric Corporation

The Anaconda Company

A Uranium Mine

Pellets of Uranium Fuel

Production of Uranium as Nuclear Fuel involves several steps. Trucks carry uranium ore from the mine to processing plants. There, a uranium concentrate called *yellowcake* is produced. After much further processing, the uranium is compressed into fuel pellets.

URANIUM, a silvery-white, radioactive metal, is the main source of nuclear energy. It is more plentiful than such "common" elements as iodine, mercury, and silver. But only tiny amounts of uranium are present in most of the rocks in which it is found. Uranium is highly reactive, and it combines with most other elements to form chemical compounds. These compounds are always extremely poisonous.

Uranium is used chiefly as a fuel for nuclear reactors. The reactors produce nuclear energy with which nuclear power plants generate electricity. About 1 pound (0.45 kilogram) of uranium produces as much energy as 1,140 short tons (1,030 metric tons) of coal. Uranium is also used in making atomic bombs and some other nuclear weapons. Medical researchers use it to produce radiation for certain experiments. In addition, uranium is used in scientific research to produce various radioactive isotopes and such artificial elements as neptunium and plutonium.

Uranium was discovered in 1789 by the German chemist Martin H. Klaproth. He found it in pitchblende, a dark bluish-black mineral. Klaproth named uranium in honor of the planet Uranus, which had been discovered eight years earlier. In 1841, pure uranium was isolated from the other elements in pitchblende by the French chemist Eugène Péligot.

Sources of Uranium

Many rocks contain bits of uranium. But large amounts occur only in such minerals as pitchblende and carnotite. Pitchblende, which contains various uranium oxides, is the richest uranium ore. Carnotite is the most important uranium ore mined in the United States. It consists of uranium, oxygen, potassium, and vanadium.

In the late 1970's, the non-Communist countries had a total of about 2,000,000 short tons (1,800,000 metric tons) of uranium ore that could be mined. These countries also had large amounts of uranium in deposits of shale and phosphate, in granite, and in the oceans. However, such deposits cannot yet be mined at a reasonable cost.

The United States produces more uranium oxide than any other non-Communist country, followed by Canada and South Africa. The non-Communist nations produce a total of about 55,000 short tons (50,000 metric tons) of uranium oxide annually. The annual production totals for Communist countries are not available.

The chief deposits of uranium ore in the United States are in Colorado, New Mexico, Texas, Utah, and Wyoming. About 65 per cent of Canada's uranium comes from the province of Ontario. Much of the uranium that is produced in South Africa is a by-product of gold mining. The gold mines in the Witwatersrand area, near the city of Johannesburg, provide large amounts of uranium.

Uranium Isotopes

In nature, uranium consists of a mixture of three isotopes—U-238, U-235, and U-234. These isotopes of

Uranium is found on most of the continents. This map shows the location of major known uranium deposits. The United States has the largest known deposits, followed by Canada and Australia. Information on uranium deposits in Communist countries is not available.

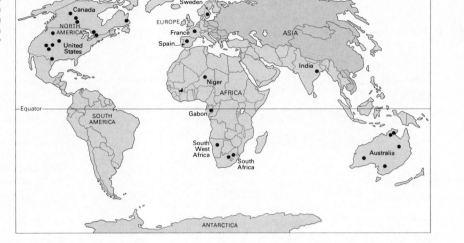

• Major uranium deposit

☐ No information available

WORLD BOOK map

uranium have different weights, but each has 92 protons in its nucleus. Uranium isotopes differ in weight because they have different numbers of neutrons in their nuclei.

Each isotope has its own *mass number*, which is the total number of protons and neutrons in the nucleus. U-235, the most important isotope of uranium, has a mass number of 235. U-235 is used in nuclear reactors and some nuclear weapons. It can be used for such purposes because it is the only natural isotope of uranium that can easily be made to *fission*—that is, split into two nearly equal parts. U-235 makes up only about 0.71 per cent of all natural uranium. U-238, which is the heaviest natural uranium isotope, accounts for approximately 99.28 per cent of the natural uranium. U-234 makes up only about 0.006 per cent of the world's supply.

Scientists have produced 11 artificial isotopes of uranium. U-233, which is made from thorium, is the most important one because it can be used in nuclear reactors (see THORIUM).

Properties of Uranium

Uranium has an atomic weight of 238.029 and is the heaviest natural element. It has the atomic number 92, and its chemical symbol is U. It melts at 1132° C and boils at 3818° C. At 20° C, uranium has a density of 19.07 grams per cubic centimeter (see DENSITY). Uranium belongs to the group of elements called the *actinide series* (see ELEMENT, CHEMICAL [Periodic Table]).

Ability to Form Compounds. Uranium combines directly with most substances to form chemical compounds. For example, it combines with oxygen to produce several oxides, including uranium oxide (UO_2) and uranium trioxide (UO_3). Uranium also decomposes acids, forming certain types of salts, called *uranyl salts*.

Uranium reacts with fluorine to create such fluorides as uranium tetrafluoride (UF_4) and uranium hexa-

Leading Uranium-Producing States and Provinces

State/Province	Production
New Mexico	6,570 short tons (5,960 metric tons)
Ontario	5,360 short tons (4,860 metric tons)
Wyoming	4,450 short tons (4,040 metric tons)
Texas	3,240 short tons (2,940 metric tons)
Saskatchewan	2,920 short tons (2,650 metric tons)
Colorado	1,990 short tons (1,810 metric tons)
Utah	1,450 short tons (1,320 metric tons)

Sources: U.S. Department of Energy; Statistics Canada. Figures are for 1981.

Leading Uranium-Producing Countries

Country	Production
United States	19,560 short tons (17,740 metric tons)
Canada	8,280 short tons (7,510 metric tons)
South Africa	7,970 short tons (7,230 metric tons)
Niger	4,700 short tons (4,300 metric tons)
France	3,300 short tons (3,000 metric tons)
Australia	3,150 short tons (2,860 metric tons)
Gabon	1,500 short tons (1,360 metric tons)

Sources: U.S. Bureau of Mines; U.S. Department of Energy. Figures are for 1981.

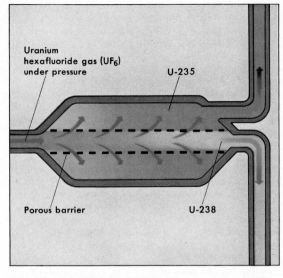

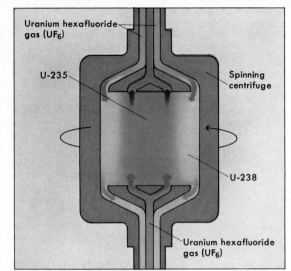

The Gaseous Diffusion Method of isotope separation, shown in the diagram above, uses porous barriers to separate uranium isotopes. Separation occurs because the molecules of uranium hexafluoride gas containing the isotope U-235 pass through the barriers faster than those containing U-238.

The Centrifugal Method of separating isotopes uses an artificial gravitational field, produced in a spinning cylinder, to separate uranium isotopes. The gravitational field forces uranium hexafluoride molecules containing U-235 and those containing U-238 to travel in different directions, away from each other.

fluoride (UF_6). It can also combine with carbon, chlorine, hydrogen, nitrogen, and many other elements.

Radioactivity and Fissionability. All isotopes of uranium are radioactive. Their nuclei *decay* (break apart), releasing energy and particles, chiefly in the form of *alpha rays*, *beta rays*, and *gamma rays* (see ALPHA RAY; BETA RAY; GAMMA RAY). In nature, the loss of such radiation and particles from the uranium nuclei eventually changes uranium into a lead isotope that is not radioactive (see TRANSMUTATION OF ELEMENTS).

Uranium isotopes give off radiation for long periods of time. For example, U-238 loses half its radioactivity every $4\frac{1}{2}$ billion years. This length of time is called a *half-life*. U-235 has a half-life of 700 million years, and U-234 has a half-life of only 250,000 years.

A uranium nucleus fissions into two fragments when a neutron strikes it. U-235 fissions much more readily than U-238. When a U-235 nucleus fissions, it releases a large amount of energy. It also releases two or more neutrons. These neutrons split other nuclei, which then release neutrons that split still more U-235 nuclei. This series of fissions is called a *nuclear chain reaction*.

A U-238 nucleus does not fission easily because it absorbs most of the neutrons that strike it. But a U-238 nucleus that continues to be struck by neutrons of extremely high energy may change into U-239, an artificial isotope of uranium. U-239 decays into neptunium by giving off beta rays. The neptunium then decays by beta radiation into an isotope of plutonium, Pu-239 (see NEPTUNIUM; PLUTONIUM). Pu-239 fissions easily and can be used in nuclear reactors and weapons. It can be produced from U-238 in a special type of nuclear reactor, called a *breeder reactor*.

How Uranium Is Mined and Processed

Locating and Mining Uranium. Since the end of World War II in 1945, geologists have made extensive efforts to locate deposits of uranium ore. Traditionally, uranium prospectors have used Geiger counters or scintillation counters to locate uranium deposits. These instruments detect the radiation given off by uranium. See GEIGER COUNTER.

Today, scientists also use other instruments to locate uranium. One device is a camera carried in a space satellite. The camera is equipped with color film or film that is sensitive to infrared rays. The camera takes photographs of an area of land, and the pictures are transmitted to geologists on the earth. Such photographs may reveal certain land formations that contain uranium ore.

Another device for locating uranium is an instrument called a *gamma ray recorder*. It detects radiation and indicates how far uranium lies below the surface of the earth. The recorder is lowered into a hole drilled into the ground. An electric cable connects the device to instruments in a truck. The recorder sends data via the cable to these instruments, which enable uranium prospectors to compute and log in the information.

Uranium near the earth's surface is mined by a process called *strip mining*. Huge power shovels remove the rocks and soil that cover the deposits, and smaller shovels then dig out the uranium ore.

Miners use explosives and drills to excavate uranium ore that lies deep below the ground. The explosives loosen the ore, and the miners drill into the walls of the mine to remove it. They load the ore into buckets that are hoisted by cables to the surface. The ore is then dumped into trucks.

Refining and Processing Uranium Ore. The uranium ore is taken from the mine to a *uranium-concentrating plant*. There, workers use sulfuric acid to extract an oxide of uranium, U_3O_8. This uranium oxide forms a uranium concentrate called *yellowcake*. The yellowcake is shipped to another plant, where it is combined with fluorine to produce uranium hexafluoride (UF_6).

The uranium hexafluoride then goes to an *enrichment*

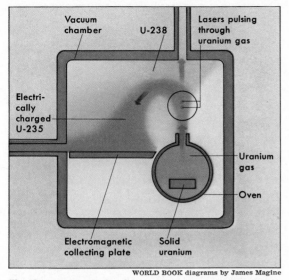

| Vacuum chamber | U-238 | Lasers pulsing through uranium gas |

The Spectroscopic Method separates uranium isotopes by the use of two lasers. The lasers cause only the U-235 atoms to acquire an electric charge. A charged collecting plate produces an electric field, which sweeps the U-235 atoms onto the plate. The electric field does not affect the uncharged U-238 atoms.

WORLD BOOK diagrams by James Magine

plant, where the isotopes U-235 and U-238 are separated from each other. The separation of these isotopes produces *enriched uranium*, which contains a higher percentage of U-235 than does natural uranium. The enriched uranium used in nuclear reactors contains about a 3 per cent concentration of this isotope. Nuclear weapons use enriched uranium that has about a 90 per cent concentration of U-235. U-235 is the only natural isotope of uranium that fissions easily and can sustain a chain reaction.

The enriched uranium goes to a *fuel fabrication plant*, where the uranium hexafluoride is converted to uranium dioxide (UO_2). The uranium dioxide is compressed into solid, cylinder-shaped pellets. The pellets are placed in hollow rods made of zirconium or stainless steel. These rods are shipped to nuclear power plants, where they are used as nuclear reactor fuel.

Separating Uranium Isotopes. Scientists have developed several methods of separating uranium isotopes. In the late 1970's, however, industry used only the *gaseous diffusion method* and the *centrifugal method*. Researchers are experimenting with two *spectroscopic methods*, which seem to be more efficient and economical than the gaseous diffusion and centrifugal processes. The spectroscopic techniques may eventually replace the other methods.

The Gaseous Diffusion Method of isotope separation is used by the uranium enrichment plants in the United States. In this process, molecules of uranium hexafluoride gas are pumped through barrierlike structures that have millions of tiny holes in them. The composition of these barriers is classified as secret by the United States government.

The weight of the gas molecules determines the rate at which they pass through the holes in the barriers. Molecules that contain U-235 atoms pass through the barriers faster than the heavier molecules, which contain U-238. The different weights of the uranium isotopes produce the difference in the weights of the uranium hexafluoride molecules.

The percentage of molecules containing U-235 increases only slightly in the gas that has passed through a barrier. Highly enriched uranium is obtained by passing the gas through the barrier about 2 million times.

The Centrifugal Method is used in several enrichment plants in Europe. The centrifuge in this process consists of vertical cylinders that spin rapidly. Uranium hexafluoride gas enters each rotating cylinder through openings in the top and bottom.

The spinning motion of the cylinders produces an artificial gravitational field inside them. The weight of the uranium hexafluoride molecules determines how they are affected by this gravitational field. The field forces the heavier molecules, which contain U-238 atoms, out of openings at the bottom of the cylinder near its walls. Molecules that contain U-235 are forced out through openings near the middle of the top of the cylinder. The molecules containing U-235 are then pumped to another cylinder. This process is repeated until the desired concentration of U-235 is obtained.

The Spectroscopic Methods separate uranium isotopes by means of lasers. A laser is a device that produces a thin beam of light having only one frequency (see LASER). The light absorbed by an atom depends on the mass of the atom and the frequency of the light. Light of some frequencies is absorbed by U-235, but not by U-238.

In one spectroscopic technique, two lasers are used to separate isotopes in uranium gas. The lasers produce light of different frequencies, but only the U-235 atoms absorb it. One electron in each U-235 atom goes into an *excited* (high-energy) state when it absorbs light from the first laser. The light from the second laser strikes the excited electron and knocks it out of its orbit around the nucleus of the atom. Each of the atoms that loses an electron acquires a positive electric charge. An electric field sweeps the positively charged U-235 atoms onto smooth, negatively charged pieces of metal called *collecting plates*. The electric field does not affect the U-238 atoms because they have no electric charge.

The other spectroscopic method separates uranium isotopes by using molecules of such compounds as uranium hexafluoride and uranium borohydride ($U[BH_4]_4$). Light from a laser excites only the molecules that contain U-235. Continued radiation of light from a second laser changes the chemical properties of the excited molecules. The change in the molecules that contain U-235 causes them to have chemical properties different from those of the molecules containing U-238. Chemical reactions that affect only the molecules containing U-235 are used to separate them from the molecules with U-238.

History of the Uses of Uranium

Uranium and its compounds have been used for various purposes for more than 2,000 years. Colored glass produced about A.D. 79 contains uranium oxide, and this substance has been used through the centuries to color glass. For nearly 100 years after the discovery of uranium in 1789, it continued to be used chiefly as a pigment in glass manufacturing. Uranium was also

used as a pigment in painting china and as a chemical for processing photographs.

In 1896, the French physicist Antoine Henri Becquerel discovered that uranium is radioactive. His achievement marked the first time that any element had been found to be radioactive. Becquerel's discovery led to a surge of scientific interest in uranium.

In 1938, the German chemists Otto Hahn and Fritz Strassman used uranium to produce the first artificial nuclear fission. In 1942, Italian-born physicist Enrico Fermi and his co-workers at the University of Chicago produced the first artificial nuclear chain reaction. They used uranium as the fissionable material. Fermi's work led to the development of the atomic bomb.

Scientific research also led to peacetime uses of uranium. In 1954, the U.S. Navy launched the *Nautilus*, the first submarine powered by nuclear fuel. In 1957, the first nuclear power plant in the United States began to operate in Shippingport, Pa., near Pittsburgh.

Since the early 1970's, nuclear energy has become an important source of energy. Many scientists predict that it will continue to play a major role in the future. However, the supply of easily obtainable uranium is decreasing, and the cost of locating, refining, and enriching uranium remains high. In addition, many people are concerned about the safety of nuclear energy production.   ELLIOT R. BERNSTEIN

Related Articles in WORLD BOOK include:

Atom (diagram:	Atomic Bomb	Nuclear Reactor
How Atoms	Isotope	Radioactivity
Compare)	Nuclear Energy	U-235

Additional Resources

BICKEL, LENNARD. *The Deadly Element: The Story of Uranium.* Stein & Day, 1979.
GRAINGER, LESLIE. *Uranium and Thorium.* Putnam, 1958.
LIBBY, LEONA M. *The Uranium People.* Crane, Russak, 1979. Personal account of the American uranium project during and after World War II.

URANIUM-235. See U-235.

URANUS, *yu RAY nuhs* or *YUR uh nuhs,* was the earliest god of the sky in Greek and Roman mythology. He was the son and husband of Gaea, the earth. Uranus and Gaea were the parents of the Titans, the first race of mythological beings.

Uranus feared his children and confined them deep within their mother, the earth, immediately after their birth. Gaea plotted revenge for their imprisonment. With her help, Cronus, the youngest Titan, attacked Uranus while he slept. Cronus wounded Uranus with a sickle and made him unable to father any more children. Because of his wound, Uranus became separated forever from Gaea. The Greeks and Romans used this myth to explain the separation of the earth from the sky.

After being separated from Gaea, Uranus played little part in mythology. His functions as god of the sky were taken over by his grandson, called Zeus by the Greeks and Jupiter by the Romans.   C. SCOTT LITTLETON

See also MYTHOLOGY (Greek Mythology); TITANS.

URANUS, *yu RAY nuhs* or *YUR uh nuhs,* is the seventh planet from the sun. Only Neptune and Pluto are farther away. Uranus has a diameter of about 31,570 miles (50,800 kilometers), which is more than four times the diameter of the earth.

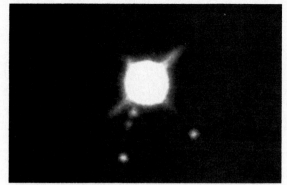

Lowell Observatory

Four of Uranus' Five Satellites formed a triangle directly below the planet when this telescopic picture was taken. The rays of light that seem to come from Uranus' edges were created when light from the planet was scattered by the telescope's lenses.

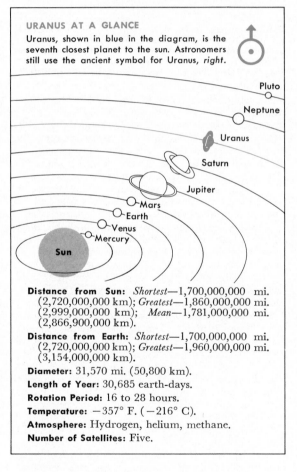

URANUS AT A GLANCE

Uranus, shown in blue in the diagram, is the seventh closest planet to the sun. Astronomers still use the ancient symbol for Uranus, *right.*

Pluto
Neptune
Uranus
Saturn
Jupiter
Mars
Earth
Venus
Mercury
Sun

Distance from Sun: *Shortest*—1,700,000,000 mi. (2,720,000,000 km); *Greatest*—1,860,000,000 mi. (2,999,000,000 km); *Mean*—1,781,000,000 mi. (2,866,900,000 km).

Distance from Earth: *Shortest*—1,700,000,000 mi. (2,720,000,000 km); *Greatest*—1,960,000,000 mi. (3,154,000,000 km).

Diameter: 31,570 mi. (50,800 km).

Length of Year: 30,685 earth-days.

Rotation Period: 16 to 28 hours.

Temperature: −357° F. (−216° C).

Atmosphere: Hydrogen, helium, methane.

Number of Satellites: Five.

Uranus travels around the sun in an oval-shaped orbit. Its mean distance from the sun is about 1,781,000,000 miles (2,866,900,000 kilometers). The planet takes 30,685 earth-days to go around the sun. At its closest approach to the earth, Uranus is about 1,700,000,000 miles (2,720,000,000 kilometers) away.

As it orbits the sun, Uranus rotates on its *axis,* an

Name	Mean Distance from Uranus		Diameter of Satellite		Year of Discovery
	In miles	In kilometers	In miles	In kilometers	
Miranda	80,800	130,000	75	120	1948
Ariel	119,300	192,000	217	350	1851
Umbriel	165,900	267,000	155	250	1851
Titania	272,200	438,000	310	500	1787
Oberon	364,100	586,000	280	450	1787

imaginary line through its center. The axes of most planets are almost *perpendicular* (at an angle of 90°) to the planets' paths around the sun. But the axis of Uranus is tilted 98° from the perpendicular position, so that it is almost level with the planet's path around the sun. Uranus takes 16 to 28 hours to spin on its axis. The large angle of tilt and the rapid spin of the planet make it appear to roll along in its orbit. See PLANET (illustration: The Axes of the Planets).

The British astronomer Sir William Herschel discovered Uranus in 1781. Little is known about the planet's surface. Astronomers believe Uranus is surrounded by clouds. They estimate the temperature of the planet to be −357° F. (−216° C).

Five small *satellites* (moons) move around Uranus. The planet also has at least nine thin rings around it. The rings, which are much fainter than those of Saturn, appear to consist of countless particles and always remain parallel to Uranus' equator. HYRON SPINRAD

See also PLANET; SOLAR SYSTEM; HERSCHEL (Sir William).

URBAN was the name of eight popes of the Roman Catholic Church. Urban II and Urban VIII were the most important. The popes' reigns were:

Urban I, Saint	(222-230)	Urban V	(1362-1370)
Urban II	(1088-1099)	Urban VI	(1378-1389)
Urban III	(1185-1187)	Urban VII	(1590)
Urban IV	(1261-1264)	Urban VIII	(1623-1644)

Urban II (1042?-1099), a Frenchman, vigorously supported the Cluniac reform movement within the Roman Catholic Church. Pope Urban was opposed by Guibert of Ravenna, the antipope who called himself *Clement III*, a candidate of Emperor Henry IV of Germany. Urban was successful against Clement III and the emperor. He presided at the Council of Clermont in 1095. There, he gave one of the most effective talks in history, in which he called Christians to a crusade to take the Holy Land from the Turks. The cry, "God wills it!" at the conclusion of his speech inaugurated the First Crusade (see CRUSADES). The crusaders drove Clement III from Rome. Then, they established Urban on the papal throne before going to Jerusalem.

Under Urban's direction, the Council of Clermont issued a number of strict reform decrees, deposed the emperor's nominee for the see of Cambrai, excommunicated the king of France for adultery, and extended the Truce of God to all Christendom. Urban was born in the province of Champagne, in France.

Urban VIII (1568-1644) was pope during most of the Thirty Years' War (1618-1648). He held foremost the welfare of the Roman Catholic Church. Urban founded an international seminary to train priests for the missions. In 1633, he opened China and Japan as mission territory for all religious orders. Urban was born in Florence, Italy. THOMAS P. NEILL and FULTON J. SHEEN

URBAN COALITION, NATIONAL, is an organization that works to solve urban problems in the United States. It seeks to identify the most urgent problems of urban areas, to make the nation aware of the problems, and to begin action on them.

The coalition includes representatives of business, labor, and minorities; and leaders of civic, community, and religious organizations. These individuals try to find solutions to problems in economic development, education, employment, housing, and health care for urban residents. The coalition is financed by corporations, foundations, government contracts, individuals, labor unions, and religious groups. A committee of about 60 national leaders establishes policies for the national group. The coalition has approximately 40 local groups in about 20 states and Washington, D.C.

The National Urban Coalition was formed in 1970 through the merger of the Urban Coalition and Urban America, Inc. The Urban Coalition was created in 1967 following riots in several of the nation's largest cities. It sought to improve the conditions that had bred the disorders. Urban America, Inc., was established in 1965 to gather and distribute information and to give technical assistance in housing and urban design and planning. The National Urban Coalition has headquarters at 1201 Connecticut Avenue NW, Washington, D.C. 20036. Critically reviewed by the NATIONAL URBAN COALITION

URBAN LEAGUE is an interracial nonprofit community service organization in the United States. Its full name is the National Urban League. The organization works to end racial discrimination and to increase the economic and political power of blacks and other minority groups.

The league has local chapters in more than 100 cities. The chapters conduct community programs that provide health care, housing, job training and placement, voter education, and other services. The league works to influence national policy by testifying before legislative bodies and issuing reports on such matters as equal employment opportunities, income maintenance, and welfare reform. It also conducts research on the problems of minority groups and publishes its findings.

The league was founded in 1910. Its national headquarters are at 500 E. 62nd Street, New York, N.Y. 10021. Critically reviewed by the NATIONAL URBAN LEAGUE

See also JORDAN, VERNON E., JR.

URBAN RENEWAL refers to city programs to eliminate slums and replace them with improved residential, commercial, or industrial areas. Urban renewal programs also try to upgrade areas that show signs of becoming slums and to improve the environment generally. In the United States, cities receive financial and technical aid from the federal government to plan and carry out urban renewal programs.

How Urban Renewal Works. Some declining neighborhoods can be renewed through building-repair programs, cleanup campaigns, or enforcement of housing and health codes. Other areas may have to be destroyed completely and then rebuilt. A city buys such areas, demolishes them, and sells the cleared land for private development projects or public use. For example, the land may become the site of a new shopping and office center, a college, or a private or public hous-

Urban Renewal Projects replace old, run-down buildings with modern, functional structures. Constitution Plaza in Hartford, Conn., is shown before urban renewal, *above,* and after the project was completed, *below.*

Travelers Corporation

ing development. The city may build a new playground, school, hospital, or some other public facility on part of the land. To acquire a large enough site, a city may have to use the power of *eminent domain*—that is, force the sale of private property for public use.

Urban renewal projects are planned and carried out by a local public agency. The agency may be a housing authority, a department of a city government, or a separate agency that handles only urban renewal problems. Federal grants pay for either two-thirds or three-fourths of the net cost of an urban renewal project, depending on the size of the city. To qualify for federal assistance, a city must adopt a community development program that is approved by the U.S. Department of Housing and Urban Development. The city must also hold public hearings before land can be purchased for urban renewal. In this way, arguments for and against a proposed urban renewal program can be brought to public attention.

Before a run-down neighborhood can be cleared, the residents and business establishments must be relocated. The city is required to provide displaced families with decent, safe, and sanitary housing at prices and rents they can afford. Financial aid is given to residents and businesses in the neighborhood for their moving expenses and property losses. Families and elderly persons may receive government payments to help them relocate.

Achievements and Problems. Urban renewal has helped provide better housing for thousands of urban families. Parks, schools, hospitals, libraries, and museums have been built on cleared slum land. Urban renewal has also revived declining downtown areas and brought about new industrial and commercial development. This development has created large numbers of new jobs and has provided more tax money for cities. In many cities, urban renewal areas are the only areas with stable, racially integrated communities.

The most serious challenge faced by urban renewal is the relocation of families displaced by various projects. A large proportion of the displaced people have been blacks and members of other minorities. In spite of laws outlawing discrimination in the sale and rental of housing, these families have had difficulty finding adequate homes. Many have moved into already overcrowded areas, thus helping to create new slums. Some renewal projects have displaced low-income families so that luxury apartments and other facilities for higher-income persons could be built. Some social scientists argue that urban renewal destroys the community spirit of established neighborhoods. Others claim the benefits of urban renewal outweigh its disadvantages.

History. The federal government made its first major attempt at slum clearance in the 1930's. The United States Housing Act of 1937 set up the U.S. Housing Authority to help clear slums and provide public housing for low-income families. In 1949, Congress passed a bill providing for large-scale slum clearance and private rebuilding of these areas. A 1954 law granted aid to cities to rehabilitate older housing. During the 1970's, many cities tried a new type of renewal program called *urban homesteading.* It offered, at low cost, abandoned houses owned by the city to people who would repair and live in them. During the 1980's, several states created areas called *urban enterprise zones* to attract new businesses to slums. Businesses within the zones receive tax cuts and freedom from such regulations as rent controls and zoning laws.   JACK MELTZER

Related Articles in WORLD BOOK include:

City (City Problems)
City Planning
Eminent Domain
Housing

Housing and Urban
    Development,
    Department of
Slum

Additional Resources

CASSIDY, ROBERT. *Livable Cities: A Grassroots Guide to Rebuilding Urban America.* Holt, 1980.
LOTTMAN, HERBERT R. *How Cities Are Saved.* Universe Books, 1976. Provides an international perspective.
MAYER, MARTIN. *The Builders: Houses, People, Neighborhoods, Governments, Money.* Norton, 1978.
ROSENTHAL, DONALD B., ed. *Urban Revitalization.* Sage, 1980.

UREA, *yu REE uh* or *YUR ee uh,* also called *carbamide,* is a nitrogen-rich organic compound produced by the bodies of human beings and many other animals. It is also made artificially for use in such products as cattle feed, fertilizers, pharmaceuticals, and *plastics.*

Urea is a white crystal or powder that dissolves readily in water. The human body produces urea as a means of ridding itself of excess nitrogen. Urea forms chiefly in the liver, and is eliminated mostly in the urine.

Urea was the first organic compound to be produced artificially. In 1828, the German chemist Friedrich Wöhler made urea by heating a water solution of ammonium cyanate, an inorganic compound. Wöhler's work helped to overthrow the belief that organic compounds could be formed only by natural forces operating within living organisms. Urea's chemical formula is $CO(NH_2)_2$.   ROBERT J. OUELLETTE

UREMIA, *yu REE mee uh,* is a condition that occurs when poisonous wastes build up in the blood. Such wastes normally pass out of the body in the urine, which is produced by the kidneys. Uremia results if the kidneys do not rid the body of these wastes. The word *uremia* means *urine in the blood.*

Uremia occurs mostly in adults who have a kidney disease. Uremia develops gradually as more and more poisons accumulate because of the damaged kidneys. Physicians can successfully treat a few of the diseases that cause uremia. But in most cases, the diseased kidneys cannot be repaired, and advanced uremia occurs. The symptoms of advanced uremia include nausea, vomiting, hiccups, loss of appetite, breath that smells of urine, drowsiness, and itchy, yellowish-tan skin. Patients may also have muscular twitching, mental disturbances, and convulsions. In time, they become unconscious, a condition called *uremic coma.* Death follows in most cases.

Physicians use two methods to keep advanced uremia victims alive. A *dialysis machine* cleanses the blood in much the same way as the kidneys do. Surgeons also perform kidney transplants to replace diseased kidneys with healthy ones.   LAURENCE H. BECK

See also KIDNEY; NEPHRITIS; TISSUE TRANSPLANT.

URETHRA. See BLADDER; KIDNEY.

UREY, *YOO ree,* **HAROLD CLAYTON** (1893-1981), was an American chemist who made important contributions in two main fields. During his early career, he conducted research on *isotopes,* which are atoms of the same element that differ in atomic weight. Urey's later work centered on the history and chemical nature of the solar system. During the late 1960's and early 1970's, he played a prominent role in the interpretation of lunar samples gathered by Apollo astronauts.

Urey won the 1934 Nobel Prize for chemistry for the discovery of deuterium, a rare isotope of hydrogen (see DEUTERIUM). During World War II (1939-1945), he directed a laboratory where isotopes of boron, hydrogen, and uranium were produced for use in the development of the atomic bomb.

Urey's study of the earth and solar system began after the war. He calculated the temperature of ancient oceans by determining the amount of certain isotopes in fossil shells. He also studied the chemical composition of the sun, moon, and planets and formulated theories on the origin of the solar system.

Urey was born in Walkerton, Ind. He earned a Ph.D. degree in chemistry from the University of California at Berkeley. He served on the faculty of Columbia University from 1929 to 1945, at the University of Chicago from 1945 to 1958, and at the University of California at San Diego from 1958 until his death.   DANIEL J. KEVLES

URINE, *YUR uhn,* is a liquid waste product of the body. The kidneys take urine out of the blood. A healthy person's urine is amber-colored and slightly acid. Urine is a little heavier than water with an average specific gravity of 1.022. It is made up of water, urea, creatinine, uric acid, and inorganic salts. The inorganic salts include sodium, potassium, ammonia, calcium, and magnesium.

Blood reaches the kidneys through the *renal* arteries. Waste matter and water removed from this blood passes from the kidneys to the bladder through two small tubes, the *ureters.* The urine is expelled from the bladder to the outside through another tube, the *urethra.*

The kidneys do not always give off the same amount of urine. During sleep, the amount is smaller and more concentrated. They form less urine when a person perspires, and more when a person drinks large amounts of liquid. The *antidiuretic hormone,* given off by the pituitary gland, controls the amount of water held by the *nephrons* (tiny kidney tubes). Certain diseases may also change the amount and strength of urine.

The condition of urine is often an index to a person's health. Sugar in the urine is a symptom of diabetes. Albumin and blood in the urine may mean the kidneys have been damaged.   EWALD D. SELKURT

See also BLADDER; DIURETIC; KIDNEY; UREMIA.

URIS, *YOO rihs,* **LEON MARCUS** (1924-   ), an American author, is known for his best-selling novels based on historical events and issues. Uris wrote *Battle Cry* (1953), his first novel, about the U.S. Marines in World War II (1939-1945). *Exodus* (1958) deals with the founding of the state of Israel. *Mila 18* (1961) describes the Jewish revolt in the Warsaw ghetto during World War II. Uris used the Berlin airlift of 1948 and 1949 as the background for *Armageddon* (1964). *Trinity* (1976) concerns the conflicts between Ireland and Great Britain. Uris was born in Baltimore.   SHERMAN PAUL

UROLOGY. See MEDICINE (table: Major Medical Specialty Fields).

URSA MAJOR AND URSA MINOR. See BIG AND LITTLE DIPPERS.

URSULA, *UR suh luh,* **SAINT,** is a saint of the Roman Catholic Church. According to legend, Ursula was a maiden from Britain, who was martyred, together with 11,000 maiden companions. Returning from a pious pilgrimage to Rome, they were attacked by Huns at Cologne, and killed for their faith. Saint Ursula's feast day is October 21. See also URSULINES.   WILLIAM J. COURTENAY

URSULINES, *UR suh lihnz,* are members of a Roman Catholic order of women. The order was named for Saint Ursula, its patron saint. The order, also called the *Nuns of Saint Ursula,* was established at Brescia, Italy, in 1535, by Saint Angela Merici. The primary work of the Ursulines is the teaching of girls and young women. From the first, the community observed strict discipline. It became a cloistered order through the aid of Saint Charles Borromeo. In 1574 the Ursuline nuns entered France, and a convent was built for them near Paris in 1611. The order spread rapidly to most countries of Europe and to America. Convents were established in Quebec in 1639 and in New Orleans in 1727. The number of Ursuline nuns in all countries totals about 4,500. See also URSULA, SAINT.   FULTON J. SHEEN

URUGUAY

Pan American World Airways; Screen Traveler, Gendreau

The Gauchos Are the Cowboys and Sheepherders Who Developed Uruguay's Rich Livestock Industry.

URUGUAY, *YUR uh GWAY* or *YUR uh GWY,* is a country in South America. A land of low hills and green pasturelands, it lies on the southeast coast of South America. It is smaller than Kansas, but it has about 600,000 more people than that state. Nearly half the people raise sheep and cattle. The country has one of the highest living standards in South America.

From 1951 to 1967, Uruguay had one of the most unusual democratic governments in the world. A nine-member national council headed the government, instead of a president or prime minister. But the constitution adopted in 1967 provided for a government headed by a president.

Before 1828, people in the Spanish colony of Buenos Aires, Argentina, called Uruguay the *Banda Oriental* (East Bank), because it lay east across the Río de la Plata (Silver River). Uruguay became independent in 1828. Its name in Spanish, the official language, is LA REPÚBLICA ORIENTAL DEL URUGUAY (THE EASTERN REPUBLIC OF URUGUAY). Montevideo is the capital.

The Land and Its Resources

Uruguay is separated from Argentina on the south and west by the Río de la Plata and the Uruguay River. It has three land regions: (1) the coastal lowlands, (2) the highlands, and (3) the pasturelands.

The Coastal Lowlands form a narrow belt of sand dunes like those of North and South Carolina. This region stretches along Uruguay's Atlantic coast and along the Río de la Plata.

The Highlands. The land rises gradually from the eastern coast to highlands that extend from the Brazilian border almost to the southern coast. Uruguayans call these highlands *Cuchilla Grande* (Big Knife), because knifelike formations of granite jut through the surface

Facts in Brief

Capital: Montevideo.

Official Language: Spanish.

Form of Government: Republic.

Area: 68,037 sq. mi. (176,215 km²). *Greatest Distances*—north-south, about 330 mi. (531 km); east-west, about 280 mi. (451 km). *Coastline*—about 600 mi. (966 km).

Population: *Estimated 1986 Population*—3,008,000; distribution, 85 per cent urban, 15 per cent rural; density, 44 persons per sq. mi. (17 per km²). *1975 Census*—2,788,429. *Estimated 1991 Population*—3,053,000.

Chief Products: *Agriculture*—linseed, meat, wheat, wool. *Manufacturing and Processing*—canned meat, glass, leather, linseed oil, textiles. *Mining*—granite, gravel, limestone, marble, sand.

National Anthem: "Himno Nacional del Uruguay" ("National Hymn of Uruguay").

Flag: A gold sun on a white canton appears on a field of nine white and blue horizontal stripes. The stripes represent Uruguay's original nine political subdivisions. See FLAG (picture: Flags of the Americas).

National Holiday: Independence Day, August 25.

Money: *Basic Unit*—peso. For the value of the peso in dollars, see MONEY (table: Exchange Rates). See also PESO.

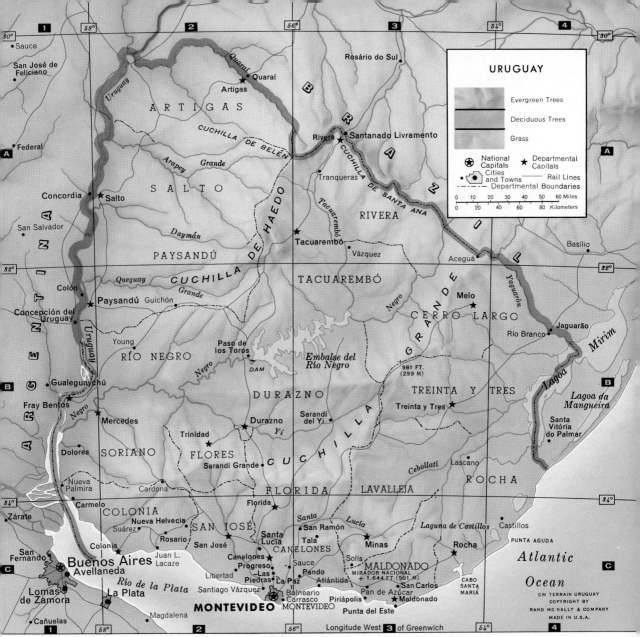

Specially created for **World Book Encyclopedia** by Rand McNally and World Book editors

Departments

ARTIGAS	.57,530..A 2
CANELONES	318,860..C 2
CERRO LARGO	.73,200..B 3
COLONIA	110,860..C 2
DURAZNO	54,990..B 2
FLORES	.24,680..B 2
FLORIDA	.66,090..B 2
LAVALLEJA	.65,240..B 3
MALDONADO	.75,620..C 3
MONTEVIDEO	1,229,750..C 2
PAYSANDÚ	98,730..A 2
RÍO NEGRO	.49,820..B 2
RIVERA	.79,330..A 3
ROCHA	.59,950..B 3
SALTO	100,410..A 2
SAN JOSÉ	.88,280..C 2
SORIANO	.80,110..B 2
TACUAREMBÓ	84,830..B 3
TREINTA Y TRES	.45,680..B 3

Source: 1975 census.

Cities and Towns

Acequá	.......930..A 3
Artigas	.29,260..A 2
Atlántida	...2,270..C 3
Barros Blancos*	.8,430..C 3
Canelones	.15,940..C 2
Cardona	...4,130..B 2
Carmelo	.13,630..B 1
Castillos	...6,450..C 4
Colonia	.16,900..C 2
Delta del Tigre y Villas*	.9,620..C 2
Dolores	.12,770..B 1
Durazno	.25,810..B 2
Florida	.25,030..C 2
Fray Bentos	.19,570..B 1
Guichón	...4,720..B 2
Juan L. Lacaze	.11,130..C 2
La Paz	.14,400..C 2
Lascano	...6,040..B 3
Las Piedras	.54,000..C 2
Libertad	...6,070..C 2
Maldonado	.22,160..C 3
Melo	.38,260..B 3

Mercedes	...34,670..B 2
Minas	...35,430..C 3
Montevideo	1,229,750..C 2
Nueva Helvecia	.8,600..C 2
Nueva Palmira	.6,930..B 1
Pan de Azúcar	.4,860..C 3
Pando	.16,180..C 3
Paso Carrasco*	.8,560..C 2
Paso de los Toros	13,180..B 2
Paysandú	.62,410..B 2
Piriápolis	...5,220..C 3
Progreso	...8,260..C 2
Punta del Este	.6,910..C 3
Río Branco	...5,700..B 4
Rivera	.49,010..A 3
Rocha	.21,550..C 3
Rosario	...8,300..C 2
Salto	.71,880..A 2
San Carlos	.16,880..C 3
San José	.28,430..C 2

San Ramón	...6,570..C 3
Santa Lucía	.14,100..C 2
Santiago Vázquez	.1,320..C 2
Sarandí del Yi	.6,330..B 3
Sarandí Grande	...5,600..B 2
Sauce	...3,940..C 2

Solís	.......1,770..C 3
Suárez	...3,520..C 2
Tacuarembó	34,150..A 3
Tala	...3,620..C 3
Tranqueras	.3,920..A 3
Treinta y Tres	...25,760..B 3
Trinidad	....17,600..B 2
Vázquez	........A 3
Young	...11,080..B 2

Physical Features

Arapey Grande River	........A 2
Cabo Santa María (Cape)	.....C 3
Cebollatí River	...B 3
Cuchilla de Belén (Mountains)	...A 2
Cuchilla de Haedo (Mountains)	...B 2
Cuchilla Grande (Mountains)	..A 3
Daymán River	...A 2
Embalse del Río Negro (Reservoir)	..B 3
Lagoa Mirim (Lake)	....B 4

Laguna de Castillos (Lake)	......C 4
Mirador Nacional (Mountain)	.....C 3
Negro River	......B 2
Punta Aguda (Point)	.......C 4
Queguay Grande River	........A 2
Río de la Plata (Estuary)	...C 2
Santa Lucía River	.C 3
Tacuarembó River	..A 3
Uruguay River	.....B 1
Yaguarón River	...B 3
Yi River	.........B 2

*Not on map; key shows general location.

176a

Cattlemen Sell Their Livestock at an auction yard near Montevideo, *above*. The city, which has a large meat packing industry, ships beef and cowhides to many parts of the world.

Punta del Este, *above,* one of Uruguay's most fashionable resort spots, has fine beaches, hotels, and nightclubs. The seaside city lies about 70 miles (113 kilometers) east of Montevideo.

soil on many of the ridges. The highest point in Uruguay is 1,644-foot (501-meter) Mirador Nacional in the Cuchilla Grande. Highlands also run along parts of the northern border.

The Pasturelands begin at the highlands in eastern Uruguay and spread across the country to the Uruguay River. They cover about four-fifths of the country.

Uruguay Covers an Area Smaller than Kansas.

WORLD BOOK map

Location of Uruguay

Rivers. The major rivers are the Uruguay and the Negro. The Río de la Plata is really the bay formed by the Paraná and Uruguay rivers.

Natural Resources. Uruguay's vast pasturelands are its most valuable resource. Pastures, often with grass 3 feet (91 centimeters) high, support the sheep and cattle industries. Uruguay has no important forests. Its few minerals include limestone, granite, and marble.

Climate. Uruguay's climate is generally mild. July (winter) temperatures average from 50° to 55° F. (10° to 13° C). January (summer) temperatures average from 70° to 75° F. (21° to 24° C). Rainfall averages only about 45 inches (114 centimeters) a year, and it is spread throughout the year. Droughts sometimes occur.

Life of the People

About 15 of every 100 persons in Uruguay live in *rural* (farm) areas. About 85 of every 100 live in *urban* (city) areas. Montevideo has about 50 per cent of the urban population.

Most of the people speak Spanish and have Spanish or Italian ancestry. Early European settlers drove out nearly all the Charrua Indians, the original inhabitants. Indians make up less than one-tenth of the population today. Most of them live in farm areas.

Uruguay has complete religious freedom. About two-thirds of the people are Roman Catholics. The rest belong mostly to the Anglican and Methodist churches.

Way of Life. The father of a typical family in Uruguay works on a ranch, in a meat-packing plant, or in a wool warehouse. The mother cares for the home.

Shelter. Most people in the cities live in small, tile-roofed houses made of stucco, brick, or concrete, although some live in modern apartment buildings. The houses and apartment buildings often resemble those in Florida and southern California. The government of

Ernst A. Jahn, DPI

Montevideo's Harbor, *above,* is an inlet of the Río de la Plata. The port, which serves ships from many parts of the world, helps make Montevideo the transportation center of Uruguay.

177

URUGUAY

Uruguay has built numerous low-rent housing developments.

Most ranch owners live in one-story brick houses, plastered on the outside and roofed with tile. Ranch workers and their families usually live near the ranch owner in one- or two-room thatch-roofed houses made of stone, brick, or *adobe* (sun-dried clay brick).

Food. The people eat much meat, particularly beef. Popular dishes include *pavesa* (a type of beef broth) and *asado con cuero* (beef barbecued in its hide). *Yerba maté*, a South American tea, is a favorite drink.

Clothing. Most Uruguayans wear clothing similar to that worn in the United States and Canada. Men on the ranches sometimes wear the boots, loose trousers, neckerchiefs, and broad-brimmed hats worn by the gauchos more than 100 years ago.

Recreation. Uruguayan soccer teams have won several Olympic championships. Other popular sports include polo, swimming, boating, golf, and tennis.

Uruguayans celebrate their most colorful festival, the *carnaval*, during the three days before Lent. They sing, dance, and parade in masks and colorful costumes.

City Life. Montevideo is the only city in Uruguay with more than 100,000 people. It has a population of

Ernst A. Jahn, DPI

The Palacio Salvo, a landmark of Montevideo, faces the Plaza Independencia, *foreground,* in the heart of the business district. Many people view the city from the top of this 27-story building.

about 1¼ million. The cities of Uruguay are clean and modern, with tall buildings, broad streets, beautiful parks and homes, good sewerage systems, and electricity. For details on the major cities, see MONTEVIDEO; SALTO.

Country Life centers around farms, ranches, and small villages. Cattle herded by roving bands of gauchos once roamed over open plains. As the herds increased, cattle owners built fences to keep them separate. This was the beginning of the modern *estancias* (ranches). Gauchos still herd cattle on the larger ranches, which sometimes cover more than 12,000 acres (4,860 hectares). Small villages usually consist of one or two stores and a cluster of brick or adobe houses.

Work of the People

Nearly two-thirds of Uruguay's people work in service industries, which include government, trade, construction, transportation, and communication. About 20 per cent work in manufacturing, and about 15 per cent work in agriculture. The average income, about $3,200 a year, is exceeded in South America only in Venezuela. The government owns all the railroads, power plants, and telephone and telegraph services in the country. Government plants and businesses compete with private companies in many industries.

Manufacturing. Meat packing and tanning are the main manufacturing industries. Other industries produce beverages, clothing, foods, furniture, glassware, leather goods, linseed oil, and tobacco products.

Agriculture, particularly sheep and cattle raising, is an important industry. Sheep and cattle graze on the vast pasturelands throughout the year, because of the mild, even climate. Farmers cultivate less than one-tenth of the farmland. Most of them live in the south, where their goods can be transported easily to markets in Montevideo. They grow wheat on about half the farmland, and also raise alfalfa, barley, citrus fruits, corn, and oats. Uruguay is a leading flaxseed producer.

The government helps the farmers by paying them subsidies for such items as wheat, dairy products, and cattle. The government often pays part of the cost of shipping cattle to meat-packing plants. Since 1948, the government has bought many large ranches and sold them in smaller parcels to farmers.

Electric Power plants provide as much power as is needed by Uruguay's farms and factories. A hydroelectric plant on the Negro River at Rincón del Bonete produces more than half the nation's power.

Trade. Uruguay imports more goods than it exports. Wool and meat account for more than half the exports. Wool shipments average 40,000 short tons (36,000 metric tons) a year and rank among the world's largest. Hides make up about 14 per cent of the exports. Uruguay imports raw materials and such goods as automobiles, cotton, iron and steel, and machinery. It trades mostly with the United States and Western European countries. It belongs to the Latin American Integration Association, an economic union.

Transportation is centered in Montevideo. Roads, railroads, and airlines connect the main cities. The country has about 1,900 miles (3,060 kilometers) of railroad tracks and more than 25,000 miles (40,200 kilometers) of roads and highways. Uruguay's section of the Pan American Highway runs from Rio Branco to Colonia.

The Legislative Building Is One of Many Government Structures in Montevideo.

Communication. Montevideo has 15 of the nation's 25 newspapers, and several magazine- and book-publishing firms. Television stations in Montevideo, and radio stations throughout the country, entertain and inform the people. Many cities have telegraph, radio-telegraph, and radio-telephone service.

Education

About 90 per cent of Uruguay's people can read and write. The law requires all children to attend elementary school, starting at age 6. The government operates free schools from kindergarten through college.

The University of the Republic in Montevideo was founded in 1849. Students from any country may attend this university without charge. The Technical University consists of 74 different technical schools located throughout the country. Students in these schools learn such subjects as architecture, engineering, and agriculture. There are also several teachers colleges, and schools for the blind and handicapped students.

The Arts

Juan Manuel Blanes, the first important Uruguayan painter, gained fame in the late 1800's for his paintings that illustrated the nation's history. The paintings of Pedro Fígaro also achieved fame. Prominent Uruguayan artists of the 1900's include the painter José Cúneo and the sculptor José L. Zorrilla de San Martín.

Horacio Quiroga was a famous Uruguayan writer and poet of the early 1900's. Alberto Zum Felde, a writer and critic, also became an outstanding literary figure in Uruguay. One of Uruguay's best-known musicians is Héctor Tosar Errecart, a pianist and composer who has won world recognition. Much Uruguayan folk music comes from the legends of the gauchos.

What to See and Do in Uruguay

Beaches and resorts at such places as Montevideo, Balneario Carrasco, and Punta del Este make the country a favorite vacation spot. People flock to Solís, Santiago Vázquez, Vázquez, Atlántida, and many other river and coastal cities to enjoy fishing and boating.

Uruguayans call Montevideo the *City of Roses*, because of the thousands of roses in its gardens and parks. Museums, theaters, and libraries have made the capital a main cultural center of South America.

Government

Under the constitution adopted in 1967, the people elect a president to head the government of Uruguay. The president serves a five-year term and may not be re-elected until five years after leaving office. Under the constitution, the president appoints a Council of Ministers (cabinet), whose members head various government departments. The constitution also provides for a two-house legislature, called the General Assembly, whose members are elected by the people. The Chamber of Deputies has 99 members, and the Senate has 30 members.

Courts. The supreme court controls all the courts. A chief justice and four associate justices are appointed to 10-year terms. They may not be reappointed until after five years following their term. The supreme court appoints judges in the lower courts and all justices of the peace. Uruguay's laws come from the constitution and from laws passed by the federal government and local governments.

Taxation. The government operates many businesses that sell to people at low prices. It must levy many taxes to run these businesses. The people of Uruguay pay a general income tax, and also pay a 20 per cent general sales tax. An additional tax is placed on such things as motion-picture admissions, matches, rentals, and gasoline.

Politics. All citizens 18 or older may vote in Uruguayan elections. The country's two major political parties are the Colorados and the Blancos. In general, the Colorados represent the interests of urban people. They believe the government should support national industries and increase job opportunities. The Blancos represent rural people. They want the government to control land ownership and distribute it evenly.

URUGUAY

Armed Forces. A total of about 30,000 men and women serve in Uruguay's army, navy, and air force. In addition, the country has a large military reserve unit. Service in the armed forces is voluntary.

History

Early Years. In 1516, the Spanish navigator Juan Díaz de Solís became the first white man to land in Uruguay. But when Solís and part of his crew went ashore, fierce Charrua Indians killed them.

In 1680, the Portuguese established the first white settlement in Uruguay. They built a fort at Colonia, across the Río de la Plata from Buenos Aires, Argentina. Spain wanted to check Portuguese expansion in Uruguay, so Spanish colonists founded Montevideo in 1726. By the 1770's, the Spaniards had settled most of Uruguay. They attacked Colonia in 1777, and drove the last of the Portuguese out of the country.

In 1810, José Gervasio Artigas organized an army to fight for independence from Spain. Artigas had served with the Spanish cavalry. He had almost defeated the Spanish by 1817, when Portuguese troops from Brazil attacked both the Spanish and the Uruguayans and captured Montevideo. In 1820, the Portuguese annexed Uruguay to Brazil and drove Artigas into exile. Artigas never returned to Uruguay. But a group of his followers, called "The Immortal Thirty-three," revolted against Brazil in 1825. Their armies held most of Uruguay within a few months. Uruguay then decided to unite with Argentina for protection against Brazil.

Independence. In 1825, Argentina joined Uruguay in the war against Brazil. Great Britain intervened in 1826 because a Brazilian blockade of Montevideo and Buenos Aires interfered with British trade. In 1828, because of the British intervention, Brazil and Argentina recognized Uruguay as an independent republic. Uruguay adopted its first constitution in 1830.

Civil War. In 1830, the revolutionary leader Fructuoso Rivera was elected the first president of Uruguay. After his term ended in 1836, he tried to regain power by leading a revolt against his successor, Manuel Oribe. In this civil war, Oribe's forces called themselves *Blancos* (Whites), and Rivera's men called themselves *Colorados* (Reds). The Colorados won the war in 1852.

Struggles for Power. Uprisings and rebellions continued, as control of the government changed from one party to another. The Colorados won in 1865, and held power until 1958. But revolutions upset the nation until the 1900's. From 1865 to 1870, Uruguay fought a war with Paraguay. See PARAGUAY (History).

Reforms in the Early 1900's. José Batlle y Ordóñez was elected president in 1903. He soon put the government in control of the banks, improved the labor laws, and gave credit and aid to farmers. He also encouraged the construction of new harbors, factories, homes, and public buildings.

Batlle thought the great powers of the presidency had caused the country's many revolutions. He worked for a new constitution, which was adopted in 1917. It established a national council. President Gabriel Terra dissolved the council in 1933.

Recent Events. In 1942, Uruguay severed relations with the Axis powers. Uruguay declared war on Germany and Japan in 1945, but no Uruguayan troops went into battle. The country became a charter member of the United Nations that same year.

In 1951, a new constitution dissolved the presidency and replaced it with a nine-member national council as head of the government. The council was set up to ensure that both the Blanco and Colorado political parties would share in the government. But it was inefficient and too slow in acting on economic problems. Foreign trade declined, and government spending increased to provide welfare benefits demanded by the people. In 1967, Uruguay adopted a new constitution and returned to the presidential system of government.

In 1961, the Organization of American States met at Punta del Este to sign the charter for the Alliance for Progress, a Latin-American aid program. It met again at Punta del Este in 1962 to suspend Cuba from participation in OAS affairs because of that country's Communist revolutionary activities in Latin America. In 1964, Uruguay joined other OAS nations in breaking relations with Cuba because of Cuban interference in Venezuela. In 1967, the presidents of the American nations met at Punta del Este to approve the formation of a Latin-American common market.

General Oscar Daniel Gestido, a member of the Colorado Party, was elected president in 1967. He died in December of that year and was succeeded by the

Leon Kofod

The Spanish Pioneers who settled in Uruguay during the 1700's and 1800's are honored by a life-sized bronze monument called *La Carreta* (The Cart). The monument stands in a park in Montevideo.

vice president, Jorge Pacheco Areco. In 1971, agriculture minister Juan M. Bordaberry of the Colorado Party was elected president.

During the mid-1900's, inflation, unemployment, and other economic problems caused unrest in Uruguay. At the same time, antigovernment terrorist groups became active. One group, the Tupamaros, kidnapped and murdered Uruguayan and foreign officials.

In June 1973, military leaders forced President Bordaberry to dissolve Uruguay's national legislature and local government councils. The government then began to rule by decree. Although Bordaberry remained in office, the military leaders dominated the government. In 1976, the military leaders removed Bordaberry from office and named Aparicio Mendez to replace him. Mendez's term ended in 1981. The military leaders appointed Lieutenant General Gregorio Alvarez Armellino to succeed Mendez as president.

In November 1984, Uruguay held its first elections since 1973. Julio Maria Sanguinetti of the Colorado Party was elected president. The people also elected provincial leaders and members of the General Assembly. In February 1985, the assembly met for the first time since military rule. Sanguinetti and his cabinet were sworn in the following month. Sanguinetti also became commander in chief of the army.　　　JOHN TATE LANNING

Related Articles in WORLD BOOK include:

Outline

Questions

What is Uruguay's most valuable natural resource?
What Uruguayan export ranks among the largest in the world?
Who were Uruguay's first white settlers?
Why is José Artigas important in Uruguay's history?
How does Uruguay rank in size among South American republics?
How did the *Blancos* and *Colorados* get their names?

URUGUAY RIVER, *YUR uh GWAY* or *YUR uh GWY*, is part of the great Paraná and La Plata river system of South America. The Uruguay rises in the state of Santa Catarina in southern Brazil and flows west, and then south for about 1,000 miles (1,600 kilometers). It empties into the bay of the Río de la Plata. The Uruguay forms part of the boundary between Brazil and Argentina, and all the boundary between Uruguay and Argentina. Before it joins the Río de la Plata, the river becomes a lake from 4 to 7 miles (6 to 11 kilometers) wide. For the location of the river, see URUGUAY (map); BRAZIL (map).　　　MARGUERITE UTTLEY

U.S. See UNITED STATES.

U.S.A. See UNITED STATES.

USES. See EMPLOYMENT SERVICE, UNITED STATES.

USO. See UNITED SERVICE ORGANIZATIONS.

U.S.S.R. stands for Union of Soviet Socialist Republics, the official name of Russia. See RUSSIA.

USTINOV, *YOO stih nawf,* **DIMITRIY FEDOROVICH** *duh MYEE tryuh ih FYAW duh RAW vyihch* (1908-1984), was an important leader in the Soviet Union. From 1976 until his death, he served as minister of defense and a marshal of the Soviet Army. As minister of defense, Ustinov directed the Soviet armed forces. Also from 1976 until his death, he was a full member of the Politburo, the main policymaking body of the Soviet Communist Party. Ustinov contributed greatly to the growth of the military power of the Soviet Union.

Baldev, Sygma
Dimitriy Ustinov

Ustinov was born in Samara, now called Kuybyshev. He joined the Communist Party in 1927. Ustinov received a degree in mechanical engineering in 1934 and worked for several years as an engineer in the weapons industry. In 1941, during World War II, he was appointed people's commissar of armaments. As commissar, Ustinov directed weapons production in the Soviet Union. In 1946, his title was changed to minister of armaments. Ustinov served in this post until 1953. He later held a series of other high Soviet and Communist Party positions.　　　MELVIN CROAN

USUMBURA. See BUJUMBURA.

USURY, *YOO zhuhr ee,* is interest at a higher rate than the law allows. The person who charges more than the maximum legal rate is a *usurer*.

In Biblical times, all payments for the use of money were regarded as usury, and were forbidden. Any money lender was then called a usurer. Romans forbade interest charges during the period of the Roman Republic, but permitted them during the time of the Roman Empire. In general, people regarded interest and usury as synonymous until the late Middle Ages, because most of the borrowers were poor persons who needed money in order to obtain the necessities of life.

But the development of modern business, which required the use of large amounts of borrowed funds, made it clear that the borrower used the funds in productive operations, and should expect to pay for their use. In time, interest came to be recognized as legitimate.

A difficulty arose because the risks and costs of making small loans were so great that legitimate dealers would not handle such loans. This gave illegitimate "loan sharks" their opportunity. Eventually, people recognized that the government should permit much higher rates on small loans. The result was a uniform small-loan law, adopted by many states. It permits licensed lenders to charge as high as $3\frac{1}{2}$ per cent interest per month on an unpaid balance. The interest usually varies with the amount of money borrowed. Service charges and discounts may make the real interest rate much higher than the rate advertised. A 1968 law called the Truth in Lending Act, which became effective in 1969, requires lenders to state clearly the actual annual interest on loans.　　　JOHN ALAN APPLEMAN

See also INTEREST; LOAN COMPANY.

The Wasatch Range in Northern Utah

Valley West by Harrison T. Groutage from the WORLD BOOK Collection

UTAH

The Beehive State

UTAH is an important mining state in the Rocky Mountain region. It also serves as a vital link in the transportation and communications systems of the western United States. Salt Lake City, Utah's capital and largest city, is an industrial and banking center. The city is the headquarters of the Church of Jesus Christ of Latter-day Saints. The members of this church are called *Mormons*. Mormons make up about 70 per cent of Utah's population.

Utah has rich mineral deposits. About a seventh of the nation's copper comes from Bingham Canyon near Salt Lake City. Utah ranks second only to Arizona in the production of copper, and third behind South Dakota and Nevada in gold production. It stands among the leading states in its production of uranium ore. It is also a leading producer of molybdenum, potassium salts, silver, and vanadium. It is the only state that produces gilsonite, a solid form of asphalt.

The annual value of Utah's manufacturing is greater than that of its mining and farming combined. But Utah's manufacturing plants depend on the products that are mined and farmed in the state. The smelting and refining of *nonferrous metals* (metals containing no iron), and also the processing of iron and steel are important industries. Also important in the state's economy is the processing of such farm products as fruits, grain, meat, poultry, sugar beets, and vegetables.

Utah has snow-covered mountains and beautifully

colored canyons. The wind and rain have formed rocks into many arches and natural bridges. Great Salt Lake is the largest natural lake west of the Mississippi River. People can easily float in this lake because it is from four to seven times as salty as the ocean. Deserts cover much of Utah, but artificially created reservoirs provide irrigation water for farmland. The largest reservoirs are Lake Powell, created by Arizona's Glen Canyon Dam, and Flaming Gorge, behind Flaming Gorge Dam.

Mormon pioneers led by Brigham Young settled the Utah region in 1847. They called the region *Deseret*. This Mormon word means *honeybee*, and it stands for hard work and industry. Utah's nickname is the *Beehive State*. The Congress of the United States organized the region as a territory in 1850, and named it *Utah* for the Ute Indian tribe that lived there. The early white settlers fought several battles against these Indians. In 1861, the first transcontinental telegraph message was sent across wires that met in Salt Lake City. The first transcontinental railroad system was completed at Promontory in 1869. Utah was admitted to the Union as the 45th state on Jan. 4, 1896.

The contributors of this article are Everett L. Cooley, Professor of History and Collections Specialist at the University of Utah; Robert Layton, Professor of Geography at Brigham Young University; and William B. Smart, Editor and General Manager of The Deseret News.

Utah Travel Council

Statue of Brigham Young in Salt Lake City

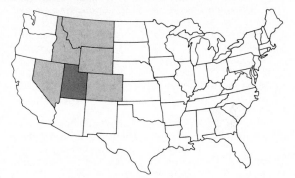

Utah (blue) ranks 11th in size among all the states, and 5th in size among the Rocky Mountain States (gray).

Facts in Brief

Capital: Salt Lake City.

Government: *Congress*—U.S. senators, 2; U.S. representatives, 3. *Electoral Votes*—5. *State Legislature*—senators, 29; representatives, 75. *Counties*—29.

Area: 84,899 sq. mi. (219,889 km²); including 2,826 sq. mi. (7,320 km²) of inland water; 11th in size among the states. *Greatest Distances*—north-south, 345 mi. (555 km); east-west, 275 mi. (443 km).

Elevation: *Highest*—Kings Peak, 13,528 ft. (4,123 m) above sea level. *Lowest*—Beaverdam Creek, in Washington County, 2,000 ft. (610 m) above sea level.

Population: *1980 Census*—1,461,037; 36th among the states; density, 17 persons per sq. mi. (7 persons per km²); distribution, 84 per cent urban, 16 per cent rural. *1970 Census*—1,059,273.

Chief Products: *Agriculture*—beef cattle, milk, hay, turkeys, sheep. *Manufacturing*—primary metals; nonelectrical machinery; transportation equipment; food products; electrical machinery and equipment; stone, clay, and glass products; fabricated metal products; petroleum and coal products. *Mining*—petroleum, coal, copper, uranium, molybdenum, gold.

Statehood: Jan. 4, 1896, the 45th state.

State Abbreviations: Ut. (traditional); UT (postal).

State Motto: *Industry*.

State Song: "Utah, We Love Thee." Words and music by Evan Stephens.

Scenic Monument Valley, a Navajo Indian Tribal Park in Southeastern Utah

Hal Rumel, Publix

Constitution. Utah adopted its constitution in 1895, the year before it became a state. Constitutional *amendments* (changes) may be proposed by the state legislature or by a constitutional convention.

An amendment proposed by the legislature must receive the approval of two-thirds of the members of each house. The amendment must then be approved in a general election by a majority of the persons voting on the issue.

Before a constitutional convention can meet, it must be approved by two-thirds of the members of each house of the legislature. The constitutional convention must then be approved by a majority of the voters in a general election. Amendments proposed by a constitutional convention must receive a majority of the votes cast in a general election.

Executive. The governor of Utah serves a four-year term and may be reelected any number of times. The governor receives a yearly salary of $53,000. For a list of all the governors of Utah, see the *History* section of this article.

Other elected state officials include the attorney general, lieutenant governor, state auditor, and state treasurer. All of these officials serve four-year terms and may be reelected. The lieutenant governor serves as governor if the governorship becomes vacant.

The governor appoints various state officials who are not elected, including the director of finance and the director of social services. The governor appoints members of state division boards who name certain state department heads. Most of the appointments must be approved by the senate.

Legislature of Utah consists of a 29-member senate and a 75-member house of representatives. Members of both legislative houses are elected from districts drawn up according to population. State senators serve four-year terms, and state representatives serve two-year terms.

The legislature meets annually on the second Monday in January. Regular sessions of the legislature last 45 days. The governor may call special sessions of the legislature. Such sessions last up to 30 days.

Courts. Utah's highest court is the state supreme court. This court has five justices, elected to 10-year terms. The justice with the shortest remaining period in office serves as chief justice.

Utah is divided into seven judicial districts. Each district has one or more district court judges, depending on population. District court judges are elected to six-year terms.

Other Utah courts include circuit courts, juvenile courts, and justice of the peace courts. Circuit court judges are elected to six-year terms. The governor, with the advice of a juvenile court commission, appoints juvenile court judges to six-year terms. Justices of the peace are either elected or appointed. They serve four-year terms.

Local Government. Each of Utah's 29 counties is managed by a three-member board of county commissioners. Two of the members of each board are elected to four-year terms. The third member is elected for two years. The board is responsible for county affairs and for supervising county departments and officers. All other county officers are elected to four-year terms. They include an assessor, attorney, auditor, clerk, recorder, sheriff, surveyor, and treasurer.

Municipalities in Utah are divided into four classes, according to population. These classes are: (1) first-class cities, (2) second-class cities, (3) third-class cities, and (4) towns. First-class cities have 100,000 or more people. Second-class cities have between 60,000 and 99,999 people. Third-class cities have between 800 to 59,999 people. Towns have fewer than 800 people.

Any city or town may use a council-manager or a mayor-council form of government if it elects to do so.

Gerald Silver

The Governor's Residence is in Salt Lake City. The mansion, built in 1904, was the home of former Senator Thomas Kearns of Utah. His widow, Mrs. Jennie J. Kearns, donated it to the state in the late 1930's.

The State Seal

Symbols of Utah. On the state seal, the beehive on the shield represents industry. The sego lilies surrounding the beehive symbolize the time when Mormon pioneers ate lily bulbs to avoid starvation. "Industry" is the state motto, and 1847 was the year the Mormons came to Utah. The seal was adopted in 1896 and appears on the state flag. The flag was adopted in 1913.

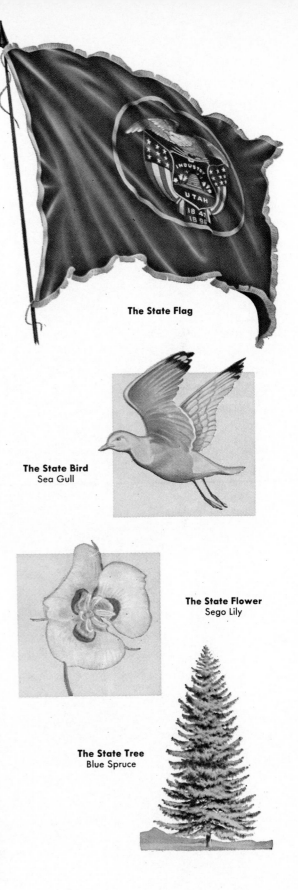

The State Flag

The State Bird
Sea Gull

The State Flower
Sego Lily

The State Tree
Blue Spruce

Otherwise, first- and second-class cities use the commissioner form of government, third-class cities have a mayor-council form, and towns are governed by a town council. The state constitution gives municipalities the right to adopt their own charters. This right is called *home rule*, but few Utah municipalities have used it.

Revenue. Sales taxes account for nearly 25 per cent of the state government's *general revenue* (income). Other important sources of revenue include individual income taxes, corporate income taxes, and licenses. About 30 per cent of the state government's revenue comes from federal grants and other programs of the United States government.

Politics. Political strength in Utah has been fairly evenly divided between the Democratic and Republican parties. About an equal number of Democrats and Republicans have served as governor of the state. Since 1970, each party has controlled the legislature about half the time. For Utah's electoral votes and voting record in presidential elections, see ELECTORAL COLLEGE (table).

The State Capitol is in Salt Lake City, Utah's capital since 1856. Fillmore was the capital from 1851 to 1856.

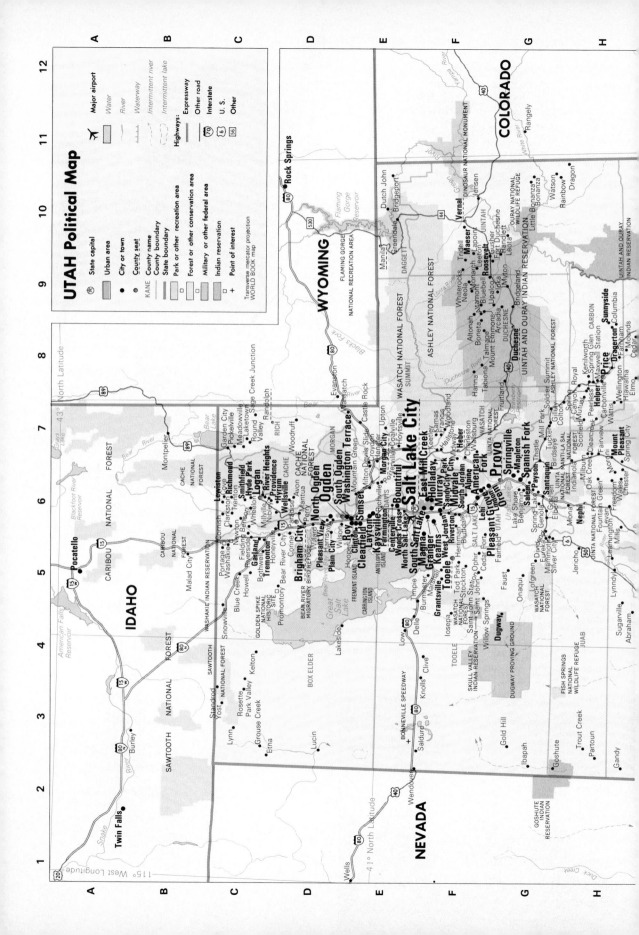

UTAH Political Map

⊗ State capital

◻ Urban area

● City or town

◉ County seat

KANE County name

County boundary

State boundary

◻ Park or other recreation area

◻ Forest or other conservation area

◻ Military or other federal area

◻ Indian reservation

+ Point of interest

Water

~ River

~~ Waterway

Intermittent river

Intermittent lake

Highways:

═══ Expressway

─── Other road

70 Interstate

6 U.S.

56 Other

✈ Major airport

Transverse mercator projection
WORLD BOOK map

IDAHO

NEVADA

WYOMING

COLORADO

Salt Lake City

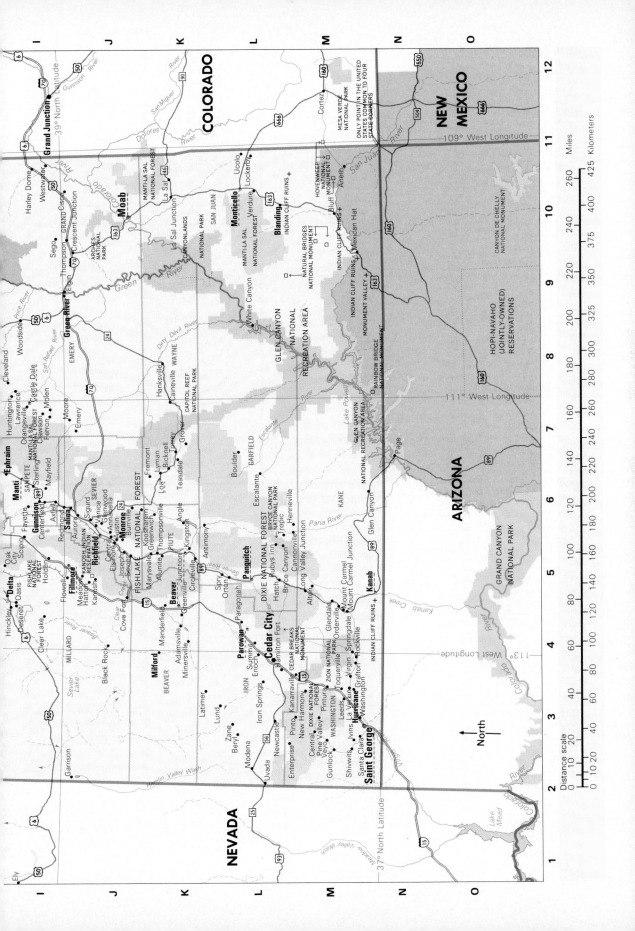

Utah Map Index

Population

1,461,037 ..Census .. 1980
1,059,273 ....".....1970
890,627 ....".....1960
688,862 ....".....1950
550,310 ....".....1940
507,847 ....".....1930
449,396 ....".....1920
373,351 ....".....1910
276,749 ....".....1900
210,779 ....".....1890
143,693 ....".....1880
86,786 ....".....1870
40,273 ....".....1860
11,380 ....".....1850

Metropolitan Areas

Provo-Orem 218,106
Salt Lake
City-Ogden 910,222

Counties

Beaver........ 4,378. .K 3
Box Elder .... 33,222. .D 3
Cache .... 57,176. .D 6
Carbon ...... 22,179. .H 9
Daggett .... 769. .E 9
Davis ....146,540. .E 6
Duchesne .... 12,565. .G 8
Emery .... 11,451. .I 8
Garfield .... 3,673. .L 7
Grand .... 8,241. .I 10
Iron .... 17,349. .L 3
Juab .... 5,530. .H 4
Kane .... 4,024. .M 6
Millard .... 8,970. .I 4
Morgan .... 4,917. .D 7
Piute .... 1,329. .K 5
Rich .... 2,100. .D 7
Salt
Lake ......619,066. .F 6
San Juan ..... 12,253. .K 10
Sanpete ..... 14,620. .I 6
Sevier .... 14,727. .J 6
Summit ...... 10,198. .E 8
Tooele .... 26,033. .F 4
Uintah .... 20,506. .F 10
Utah ....218,106. .G 6
Wasatch ...... 8,523. .F 7
Washington ... 26,065. .M 3
Wayne .... 1,911. .K 8
Weber ......144,616. .D 7

Cities and Towns

Abraham ....H 4
Adamsville ....K 4
Alpine .... 2,649. .F 6
Alta* .... 381. .F 6
Altamont .... 247. .F 9
Alton .... 75. .M 5
Altonah ....F 9
Amalga* .... 323. .C 6
American
Fork .... 12,564. .F 6
Aneth ....M 11
Angle ....K 6
Annabella .... 463. .J 6
Antimony .... 94. .K 6
Aurora .... 874. .J 6
Austin ....J 5
Avon ....D 6
Axtell ....I 6
Ballard* .... 558. .G 9
Bear River City .... 540. .D 6
Beaver......... 1,792.°K 5
Benjamin ....G 6
Bennion* ...... 9,575. .E 6
Benson ....C 6
Beryl ....L 3
Bicknell .... 296. .K 6
Bingham Canyon* ......F 6
Birdseye ....G 6
Black Rock ....J 4
Blanding .... 3,118. .L 10
Blue Creek ....C 5
Bluebell ....F 9
Bluff ....M 10
Bluffdale ...... 1,300. .F 6
Bonanza ....G 10
Boneta ....F 8
Bothwell ....C 5
Boulder .... 113. .L 7
Bountiful ..... 32,877. .E 6
Brian Head* ...... 77. .L 4
Bridgeland ....G 9
Bridgeport ....E 10
Brigham
City .... 15,596.°D 6
Bryce Canyon ....L 5
Burmester ....F 5
Burrville ....J 6
Caineville ....K 7
Cannonville ...... 134. .M 6
Carbonville ....H 8
Castle Dale .... 1,910.°I 7
Castle Rock ....E 7
Cedar ....H 8
Cedar City .... 10,972. .L 4
Cedar Fort ...... 269. .F 6
Cedar Hills* ..... 571. .F 6
Centerfield ...... 653. .I 6
Centerville ..... 8,069. .E 6
Central ....J 6
Central ....M 3
Charleston ...... 320. .F 7
Chester ....H 6
Circleville .... 445. .K 5
Cisco ....I 10
Clarkston .... 562. .C 6
Clawson ....I 7
Clear Lake ....I 4
Clearcreek ....H 7
Clearfield .... 17,982. .E 6
Cleveland .... 522. .I 8
Clinton .... 5,777. .E 6
Clive ....F 4
Coalville ...... 1,031.°E 7
Colton ....G 7
Columbia ....H 8
Corinne .... 512. .D 6
Cornish .... 181. .C 6
Cottonwood* . 11,554. .F 6
Cottonwood
Heights* ... 22,665. .E 6
Cove ....C 6
Cove Fort ....J 5
Crescent Junction ......I 9
Croydon ....E 7
Defas Park* ....G 6
Delle ....E 4
Delta .... 1,930. .I 5
Deseret ....I 5
Devils Slide ....E 6
Deweyville* ...... 311. .C 6
Dividend ....G 6
Dragerton ....H 8
Dragon ....H 11
Draper* .... 5,530. .F 6
Duchesne ...... 1,677.°G 8
Dugway .... 1,646. .G 4
Dutch John ....E 10
East Carbon* .. 1,942. .H 8
East Layton* ... 3,531. .E 6
East Midvale, see
Cottonwood
[-East Midvale]
East Mill
Creek ...... 24,150. .F 6
Elberta ....G 6
Elgin ....I 9
Elk Ridge* .... 381. .G 6
Elmo .... 300. .H 8
Elsinore .... 612. .J 5
Elwood* .... 481. .C 5
Emery .... 372. .J 7
Enoch .... 678. .L 4
Enterprise .... 905. .L 3
Ephraim ...... 2,810. .I 6
Escalante .... 652. .L 6
Etna ....C 2
Eureka .... 670. .G 5
Fairfield ....G 5
Fairview .... 916. .H 7
Farmington ..... 4,691.°E 6
Farnham ....H 8
Faust ....G 5
Fayette .... 165. .I 5
Ferron .... 1,718. .I 7
Fielding .... 325. .C 6
Fillmore .... 2,083.°I 5
Flowell ....I 5
Fort Duchesne ....G 9
Fountain
Green .... 578. .H 6
Francis .... 371. .F 7
Freedom ....H 6
Fremont ....K 6
Fruit Heights* .. 2,728. .E 6
Fruitland ....G 8
Gandy ....H 2
Garden City ...... 259. .C 7
Garland .... 1,405. .C 5
Garrison ....I 2
Genola .... 630. .G 6
Gilluly ....G 7
Glen Canyon ....N 6
Glendale .... 237. .M 5
Glenwood .... 447. .J 6
Gold Hill ....G 3
Goshen .... 582. .G 6
Goshute ....G 2
Grafton ....M 4
Granger ....F 6
Granite Park .... 5,554. .F 6
Grantsville .... 4,419. .F 5
Green River .... 1,048. .I 9
Greendale ....E 10
Greenville ....K 4
Greenwich ....K 6
Grouse Creek ....C 3
Grover ....K 7
Gunlock ....M 3
Gunnison ...... 1,255. .I 6
Gusher ....F 9
Hailstone ....F 7
Hamilton Fort ....L 4
Hanksville ....K 8
Hanna ....F 8
Harley Dome ....I 11
Harrisville ..... 1,371. .D 6
Hatch .... 121. .L 5
Hatton ....J 5
Heber .... 4,362.°F 7
Helper .... 2,724. .H 8
Henefer .... 547. .E 7
Henrieville ...... 167. .M 6
Herriman ....F 6
Hiawatha .... 249. .H 7
Highland* ..... 2,435. .F 6
Hildale* .... 1,009. .N 4
Hinckley .... 464. .I 5
Holden .... 364. .I 5
Holladay ..... 22,189. .F 6
Honeyville .... 915. .D 6
Hooper ....E 5
Howell .... 176. .C 5
Hoytsville ....E 7
Huntington .... 2,316. .I 7
Huntsville* ...... 577. .D 6
Hurricane ..... 2,361. .M 3
Hyde Park ..... 1,495. .C 6
Hyrum .... 3,952. .D 6
Ibapah ....G 2
Indianola ....H 7
Ioka ....G 9
Iosepa ....F 4
Iron Springs ....L 3
Ivins .... 600. .M 3
Jensen ....F 10
Jericho ....H 5
Joseph .... 217. .J 5
Junction .... 151.°K 5
Kamas .... 1,064. .F 7
Kanab .... 2,148.°N 5
Kanarraville ..... 255. .M 4
Kanosh .... 435. .J 5
Kaysville ...... 9,811. .E 6
Kearns .... 21,353. .F 6
Keetley ....F 7
Kelton ....C 4
Kenilworth ....H 8
Kingston .... 146. .K 5
Knolls ....F 4
Koosharem .... 183. .J 6
Lake Shore ....G 6
Lakeside ....D 4
Laketown .... 271. .C 7
Lapoint ....F 9
La Sal ....K 10
La Sal Junction ....K 10
Latimer ....K 3
La Verkin ..... 1,174. .M 3
Lawrence ....I 8
Layton .... 22,862. .E 6
Leamington ...... 113. .H 5
Leeds .... 218. .M 3
Leeton ....F 9
Lehi .... 6,848. .F 6
Leota ....G 10
Levan .... 453. .H 6
Lewiston ...... 1,438. .C 6
Lindon .... 2,796. .F 6
Little Bonanza ....G 10
Loa .... 364.°K 6
Lockerby ....L 11
Lofgreen ....G 5
Logan .... 26,844.°C 6
Long Valley
Junction ....M 5
Low ....E 4
Lucin ....D 3
Lund ....L 3
Lyman ....K 6
Lynn ....C 3
Lynndyl .... 90. .H 5
Maeser .... 2,216. .F 10
Magna .... 13,138. .F 6
Mammoth ....G 5
Manderfield ....K 5
Manila .... 272.°E 10
Manti .... 2,080.°I 6
Mantua .... 484. .D 6
Mapleton ...... 2,726. .G 6
Marshall ....F 5
Marysvale .... 359. .K 5
Maxwell Station ....H 8
Mayfield .... 379. .I 6
Meadow .... 265. .J 5
Meadowville ....C 7
Mendon* .... 663. .C 6
Mexican Hat ....M 9
Midvale ...... 10,146. .F 6
Midway .... 1,194. .F 7
Milburn ....H 7
Milford .... 1,293. .K 4
Mill Fork ....G 7
Mills ....H 6
Millville .... 848. .C 6
Milton ....E 6
Minersville ...... 552. .K 4
Moab .... 5,333.°J 10
Modena ....L 2
Molen ....I 7
Mona .... 536. .H 6
Monarch ....F 9
Monroe .... 1,476. .J 6
Monticello ..... 1,929.°L 10
Moore ....I 7
Morgan City ... 1,896.°E 7
Moroni .... 1,086. .H 6
Mounds ....H 8
Mount Carmel ....M 4
Mount Carmel
Junction ....M 4
Mount Emmons ....F 9
Mount
Olympus* ... 6,068. .F 6
Mount
Pleasant .... 2,049. .H 7
Mountain Green ....E 6
Murray ...... 25,750. .F 6
Mutual ....H 7
Myton .... 500. .G 9
Neola ....F 9
Nephi .... 3,285.°H 6
New Harmony ... 117. .M 3
Newcastle ....L 3
Newton .... 623. .C 6
Nibley .... 1,036. .C 6
North Logan* .. 2,258. .C 6
North
Ogden ...... 9,309. .D 6
North Salt
Lake .... 5,548. .E 6
Oak City .... 389. .I 5
Oak Creek ....H 7
Oakley* .... 470. .E 7
Oasis ....I 5
Ogden .... 64,407.°D 6
Onaqui ....G 5
Ophir .... 42. .F 5
Orangeville .... 1,309. .I 7
Orderville .... 423. .M 5
Orem .... 52,399. .F 6
Orton ....L 5
Panguitch ..... 1,343.°L 5
Paradise .... 542. .D 6
Paragonah ...... 310. .L 4
Park City ...... 2,823. .F 7
Park Valley ....C 3
Parowan ...... 1,836.°L 4
Partoun ....H 2
Payson .... 8,246. .G 6
Peerless ....H 8
Perry .... 1,084. .D 6
Peterson* ....E 6
Pickelville ....C 7
Pine Valley ....M 3
Pinto ....M 3
Pintura ....M 3
Plain City ...... 2,379. .D 6
Pleasant
Grove ..... 10,833. .F 6
Pleasant View .. 3,983. .D 6
Plymouth* ...... 238. .C 5
Portage .... 196. .C 5
Porterville ....E 6
Price .... 9,086.°H 8
Promontory ....D 5
Providence .... 2,675. .C 6
Provo .... 74,108.°G 6
Rainbow ....G 10
Randlett ....G 9
Randolph .... 659.°C 7
Redmond .... 619. .I 6
Richfield ...... 5,482.°J 6
Richmond ..... 1,705. .C 6
Richville ....E 6
River Heights .. 1,211. .C 6
Riverdale* .... 6,031. .D 6
Riverside ....C 5
Riverton ...... 7,293. .F 6
Rockville ....M 4
Roosevelt ..... 3,842. .F 9
Rosette ....C 3
Round Valley ....C 7
Roy .... 19,694. .E 6
Royal ....H 8
Rubys Inn ....L 5
Rush Valley* ..... 356. .F 5
Sage Creek Junction ....C 7
St. George ... 11,350.°N 3
St. John ....F 5
St. John Station ....F 5
Salduro ....E 3
Salem .... 2,233. .G 6
Salina .... 1,992. .I 6
Salt Lake
City ......163,034.°E 6
Sandy City ... 52,210. .F 6
Santa Clara .... 1,091. .M 3
Santaquin ..... 2,175. .G 6
Scipio .... 257. .I 6
Scofield .... 105. .H 7
Sego ....I 10
Sevier ....J 5
Shivwits ....M 3
Sigurd .... 386. .J 6
Silver City ....G 5
Smithfield ..... 4,993. .C 6
Snowville .... 237. .C 5
Soldier Summit ... 12. .G 7
South Cotton-
wood* ..... 11,117. .E 6
South Jordan .. 7,492. .F 6
South Ogden . 11,366. .D 6
South Salt
Lake .... 10,413. .F 6
South Weber* . 1,575. .E 6
Spanish Fork .. 9,825. .G 6
Spring Canyon ....H 8
Spring City ...... 671. .H 7
Spring Glen ....H 8
Spring Lake ....G 6
Springdale ...... 258. .M 4
Springville ... 12,101. .G 6
Spry ....L 5
Standrod ....C 3
Sterling .... 199. .I 6
Stockton .... 437. .F 5
Sugarville ....H 5
Summit ....L 4
Sunnyside .... 611. .H 9
Sunset .... 5,733. .E 6
Syracuse* ..... 3,702. .E 6
Tabiona .... 152. .F 8
Talmage ....F 8
Taylors-
ville* ...... 17,448. .E 6
Teasdale ....K 7
Thistle ....G 7
Thompson ....I 10
Thompsonville ....K 5
Timpie ....E 5
Tod Park ....F 5
Tooele .... 14,335.°F 5
Toquerville ...... 277. .M 3
Torrey .... 140. .K 7
Tremonton .... 3,464. .C 5
Trenton .... 447. .C 6
Tridell ....F 9
Tropic .... 338. .L 6
Trout Creek ....H 3
Tucker ....G 7
Ucolo ....L 11
Uintah* .... 439. .E 6
Union [-East
Midvale]* ... 9,665. .E 6
Upalco ....G 9
Upton ....E 7
Uvada ....L 2
Val Verda* .... 6,422. .E 6
Venice ....J 6
Verdure ....L 10
Vernal .... 6,600.°F 10
Vernon* .... 181. .G 5
Veyo ....M 3
Virgin .... 169. .M 4
Wahsatch ....D 7
Wales .... 153. .H 6
Wallsburg .... 239. .F 7
Washakie ....C 5
Washington .... 3,092. .M 3
Washington
Terrace ..... 8,212. .E 6
Watson ....G 10
Wattis ....H 7
Wellington ..... 1,406. .H 8
Wellsville ..... 1,952. .D 6
Wendover ..... 1,099. .E 2
West
Bountiful* ... 3,556. .E 6
West Jordan . 27,315. .F 6
West Point* ... 2,170. .E 6
West
Valley* ..... 72,433. .E 6
Westwater ....I 11
Wheelon ....C 6
White Canyon ....L 8
White City* .... 7,267. .F 6
Whiterocks ....F 9
Willard .... 1,241. .D 6
Willow Springs ....F 5
Wilson ....D 6
Woodland ....F 7
Woodland Hills* ... 60. .G 6
Woodruff .... 222. .D 7
Woods Cross .. 4,263. .E 6
Woodside ....I 8
Yost .... 67. .C 3
Zane ....L 3

*Does not appear on map; key shows general location.
°County seat.
Source: 1980 census. Places without population figures are unincorporated areas.

The 1980 United States census reported that Utah had 1,461,037 people. This figure was an increase of 38 per cent over the 1970 figure of 1,059,273.

More than four-fifths of Utah's people live in urban areas. That is, they live in or near cities and towns of 2,500 or more people. The rest of the people live in rural areas. About three-fourths of the people live in the state's two metropolitan areas (see METROPOLITAN AREA). For the populations of Utah's two metropolitan areas—Provo-Orem and Salt Lake City-Ogden—see the *Index* to the political map of Utah.

Salt Lake City is the capital and largest city of Utah. There are four other cities in the state with populations of more than 50,000. They are, in order of size, Provo, Ogden, Orem, and Sandy City. See the separate articles on the cities of Utah listed in the *Related Articles* at the end of this article.

About 97 per cent of Utah's people were born in the United States. The largest groups of people born in other countries came from Canada, Germany, Great Britain, and Mexico.

About 70 per cent of Utah's people are Mormons. Most of the other church members are Roman Catholics or Protestants.

Salt Lake Valley Convention & Visitors Bureau

The Great Salt Lake is a popular recreational area. The high salt content of the water provides great buoyancy, enabling swimmers to float with ease. The lake also attracts many boaters.

Population Density

Utah is thinly populated except for a number of cities and towns in the north. More than three-fifths of the state's residents live in the Salt Lake City-Ogden metropolitan area.

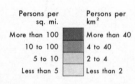

Persons per sq. mi.	Persons per km²
More than 100	More than 40
10 to 100	4 to 40
5 to 10	2 to 4
Less than 5	Less than 2

© John & Barb Enlow

Mormons Gather in Salt Lake City's Temple Square, the symbolic center of Mormonism. Salt Lake City is Utah's capital and largest city. About 70 per cent of the state's people are Mormons.

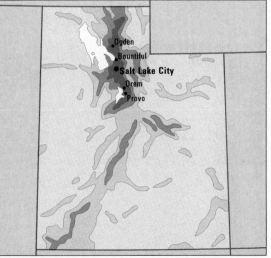
WORLD BOOK map; based on U.S. Bureau of the Census data.

Paul Gillette, Stock, Boston

A Miner Drills for Ore in a Utah uranium mine. Many rich mineral deposits are located throughout the state.

Schools. Utah's first school was a tent in the Salt Lake Valley. It was set up in 1847, the year the Mormons first settled in the region. By the mid-1850's, the Utah region had more than 200 schools. Parents had to pay to send their children to these early schools because of a shortage of tax money. The region's first free public school opened in American Fork in 1866. A law passed in 1890 made all public elementary schools free. In 1895, a constitutional convention provided for the establishment and support of free public high schools in Utah.

Today, Utah has one of the highest percentages of high school graduates in the United States. It also has one of the highest percentages of people who attend college.

The state board of education supervises the public school system in Utah. The board of education has nine members, who are elected to four-year terms. The board appoints a superintendent of public instruction as its executive officer. A 17-member state board of regents supervises the colleges and universities in Utah. Utah requires children to attend school from age 6 through 17. For the number of teachers and students in Utah, see EDUCATION (table).

Libraries. Utah's first library was established with books hauled to the region by oxen in the 1850's. In 1897, a state law provided for free public libraries. The Salt Lake City Public Library opened the next year. The Carnegie Free Library (now Weber County Library) in Ogden was the first building in the state to be used only as a library. It opened in 1903. In 1957, the Utah State Library Commission was established.

UTAH/*A Visitor's Guide*

Millions of tourists visit Utah every year. The state's forests, mountains, lakes, and rivers are excellent for boating, fishing, hunting, sightseeing, skiing, and swimming. One of Utah's most popular places to visit is the center of Mormonism—Temple Square in Salt Lake City. Three important Mormon church buildings stand in the square. These are the majestic Mormon Temple, which took 40 years to build; the Salt Lake Tabernacle, famous for its huge organ and choir; and the Visitor Center. The Temple is not open to the general public.

Bryce Canyon National Park, Land of Brilliant Color

Hal Rumel, Publix

Places to Visit

Following are brief descriptions of some of Utah's many interesting places to visit:

Beehive House, in Salt Lake City, is the restored home of Brigham Young. This stately, two-story adobe house was built in 1855.

Bingham Canyon Copper Pit, near Salt Lake City, is the largest open-pit copper mine in North America. It is nearly ½ mile (0.8 kilometer) deep, and over 2 miles (3 kilometers) across at its widest point.

Bonneville Salt Flats, near Wendover, is famous for automobile racing trials. The area has about 50 square miles (130 square kilometers) of flat salt beds that are as hard as cement.

Great Salt Lake, near Salt Lake City, has water four to seven times saltier than any ocean.

Monument Valley, in southeastern Utah, has red sandstone formations that rise 1,000 feet (300 meters). In the evening, a formation called the *totem pole* casts a shadow 35 miles (56 kilometers) long.

Ruins of Indian Cliff Dwellings line mountain ledges near Blanding, Bluff, Kanab, Moab, Parowan, Price, and Vernal. These cliff dwellings housed Indians who lived in the Utah region hundreds of years ago.

Trolley Square, in Salt Lake City, is a colorful center of restaurants and shops in a remodeled trolley service area. The square is a state historic site.

National Parks, Monuments, and Forests. Utah has five national parks—Arches, Bryce Canyon, Canyonlands, Capitol Reef, and Zion. The state shares Dinosaur and Hovenweep national monuments with Colorado. Other Utah national monuments are Cedar Breaks, Natural Bridges, Rainbow Bridge, and Timpanogos Cave. The Golden Spike National Historic Site is at Promontory. Utah shares the Glen Canyon National Recreation Area with Arizona. There are nine national forests in Utah—Ashley, Cache, Caribou, Dixie, Fishlake, Manti-La Sal, Sawtooth, Uinta, and Wasatch.

State Parks. Utah has 44 state parks. For information on these parks, write to Director, State Park and Recreation Commission, 1596 W. North Temple, Salt Lake City, UT 84116.

Today, Utah has about 50 public libraries. There are large collections of Mormon literature at the libraries of Brigham Young University in Provo and of the University of Utah and the Utah State Historical Society—both in Salt Lake City. One of the world's largest collections of genealogical records and research is maintained by the Genealogical Department Library of the Church of Jesus Christ of Latter-day Saints in Salt Lake City.

Museums. Utah's art museums include the Salt Lake City Art Center; the Utah Museum of Fine Arts, at the University of Utah in Salt Lake City; the B. F. Larsen Gallery of Art, at Brigham Young University in Provo; and the Springville Museum of Art. Historical museums include the Utah Museum of Natural History, at the University of Utah; the Utah State Historical Society's

Museum in Salt Lake City; and the Pioneer Memorial Museum in Salt Lake City.

Universities and Colleges

Utah has six universities and colleges accredited by the Northwest Association of Schools and Colleges. For enrollments and further information, see UNIVERSITIES AND COLLEGES (table).

Name	Location	Founded
Brigham Young University	Provo	1875
Southern Utah State College	Cedar City	1897
Utah, University of	Salt Lake City	1850
Utah State University	Logan	1888
Weber State College	Ogden	1889
Westminster College of Salt Lake City	Salt Lake City	1875

Annual Events

Each July, Utahns observe the 1847 arrival of Mormon pioneers in the Salt Lake Valley. Many Utah cities stage celebrations. The symphony season at the Salt Lake City Symphony Hall extends from November to March. Other annual events in Utah include:

January-April: U.S. Film Festival in Park City (January); Intermountain Utah Boat, Sports, and Travel Show in Salt Lake City (March); St. George Arts Festival (April).

May-August: Friendship Cruise in Green River (May); Uinta Basin Junior Livestock and Horse Show in Vernal (May); Reenactment of the Driving of the Golden Spike at Promontory (May 10); Strawberry Days Festival in Pleasant Grove (June); Utah Arts Festival in Salt Lake City (June); Festival of the American West in Logan (July and August); Mormon Miracle Pageant in Manti (July); Shakespearean Festival in Cedar City (July and August); Park City Arts Festival (August).

September-December: Bonneville National Speed Trials on Bonneville Salt Flats (September); Utah State Fair in Salt Lake City (September); Oktoberfest at Snowbird Resort southwest of Salt Lake City (August to October); Ballet West, *The Nutcracker*, at Utah State University in Logan and Salt Lake City (December); Utah Oratorio Society, *The Messiah*, in the Salt Lake Tabernacle in Salt Lake City (Sunday before Christmas).

Brigham Young University

Brigham Young University Library in Provo

Mormon Temple in Salt Lake City's Temple Square
Lorin D. Wiggins

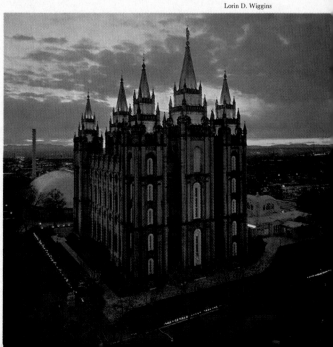

Automobile Racing on the Bonneville Salt Flats
Utah Travel Council

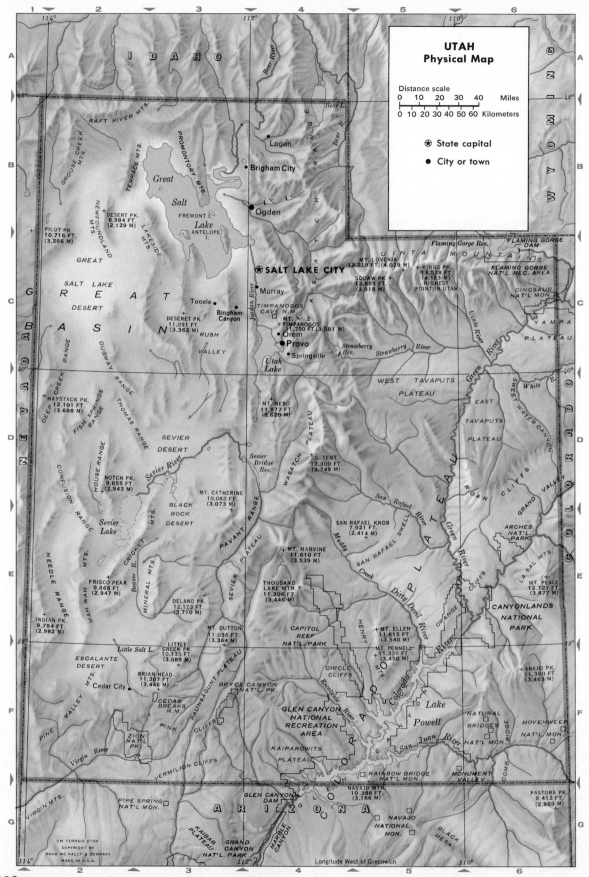

UTAH
Physical Map

Distance scale

0 10 20 30 40 Miles

0 10 20 30 40 50 60 Kilometers

⊛ State capital

● City or town

Specially created for **World Book Encyclopedia** by Rand McNally and World Book editors

Land Regions.

Utah includes parts of three major land regions: (1) the Rocky Mountains, (2) the Basin and Range Region, and (3) the Colorado Plateau.

The Rocky Mountains extend generally north and south across a large part of western North America. In Utah, two ranges of the Rocky Mountains—the Uinta and the Wasatch—form an angle in the northeast corner of the state. The Uinta Range extends westward from Colorado almost to Salt Lake City. It is the only major range of the Rocky Mountains that runs east and west. Several peaks in the Uinta Range are more than 13,000 feet (3,960 meters) high. Kings Peak, the highest point in Utah, rises 13,528 feet (4,123 meters) near the center of the range. Many lakes and flat-bottomed canyons in the Uinta Range were formed by glaciers that once covered the area.

The Wasatch Range extends from Mount Nebo, near Nephi, northward into Idaho. The western side of this rugged range is very steep. It rises 6,000 to 8,000 feet (1,800 to 2,400 meters) above the valleys that border it. The Wasatch Range also has many canyons. The canyons provide water and serve as recreation areas for the people in Utah's largest cities, just west of the mountains. Some of the canyons were formed by glaciers. The Ogden, Provo, and Weber Canyons were cut by rivers.

The Basin and Range Region covers parts of several states, including the western part of Utah. It is one of the driest regions in the United States. Small mountain ranges and broad basins cover the center of the region. Higher ranges and plateaus border it on the east and the west. Great Salt Lake lies in the northeast part of the region. West and southwest of the lake is a barren area called the Great Salt Lake Desert. The desert has about 4,000 acres (1,600 hectares) of flat salt beds that are as hard as concrete.

The extreme southwestern corner of Utah's Basin and Range region is known as *Utah's Dixie*. The early settlers grew cotton and grapes there.

The Colorado Plateau stretches over parts of Utah, Arizona, Colorado, and New Mexico. It covers most of the southern and eastern sections of Utah. This region consists of broad, rough uplands cut by deep canyons and valleys. High plateaus in the western part of the region include the Aquarius, Fish Lake, Markagunt, Paunsagunt, Pavant, Sanpitch, Sevier, and Tushar. These plateaus have elevations of more than 11,000 feet (3,350 meters). The famous Bryce, Cedar Breaks, and Zion canyons are in this area. The Henry Mountains rise west of the Colorado River, and the Abajo and La Sal mountains are east of the river. Utah's southeastern corner meets the corners of Arizona, New Mexico, and Colorado. This is the only point in the United States where four states meet (see ARIZONA [picture: Four Corners]).

Rivers and Lakes.

Utah's rivers are used to provide irrigation for great stretches of farmland that otherwise would be desert. The Colorado River and its main tributary, the Green River, are the largest rivers in the state. These rivers and their many branches drain the eastern half of Utah. The Snake River of Idaho and its branches drain Utah's northwest corner. The Bear, Provo, and Weber rivers begin in the Uinta Range and flow through the Wasatch Mountains into Great Salt Lake. The Sevier is the chief river of south-central Utah. It begins in the Paunsagunt Plateau and flows north, then bends to the southwest. Most of the Basin and Range Region, which extends across several western states, has no outlet to the sea. It is the largest area of interior drainage in the United States.

Thousands of years ago, a huge body of fresh water

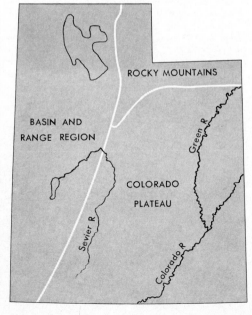

Land Regions of Utah

ROCKY MOUNTAINS

BASIN AND RANGE REGION

COLORADO PLATEAU

Green R.

Sevier R.

Colorado R.

UTAH

covered parts of Utah. Scientists have named this ancient sea Lake Bonneville. The Bonneville Salt Flats, in the middle of the Great Salt Lake Desert, cover part of the bed of Lake Bonneville. Great Salt Lake and Utah Lake are also part of what remains of Lake Bonneville. Great Salt Lake is the largest natural lake west of the Mississippi River. It is four to seven times as salty as the ocean, and becomes even saltier when the water level drops during dry periods. Great Salt Lake is salty because its waters are not drained by outflowing streams. Instead, some of the water evaporates and leaves salt deposits behind. The Jordan River drains Utah Lake and keeps its waters fresh. Utah Lake and Bear Lake, which Utah shares with Idaho, are important reservoirs in which irrigation waters are stored. Many small lakes lie in the Boulder, Uinta, and Wasatch mountains.

Deserts cover about a third of Utah. Few plants can grow in these deserts because of the lack of rainfall. The Great Salt Lake Desert lies west and south of Great Salt Lake. Other deserts include the Sevier Desert in west-central Utah, and the Escalante Desert in the southwestern part of the state.

Plant and Animal Life. Forests cover about 30 per cent of Utah. The forest land is found in the mountains. Common trees include aspens, firs, junipers, pines, and spruces. Many kinds of grasses, shrubs, and wild flowers grow in the mountains. The dry sections of the state have cactus, creosote bush, greasewood, mesquite, and shadscale. The state's wetter sections have grasses and sagebrush.

Common small animals in Utah include badgers, foxes, martens, muskrats, rabbits, ringtails, skunks, and weasels. Among the larger animals are black bears, bobcats, coyotes, lynxes, and mountain lions. The mule deer is the most common game animal. Buffaloes, elks, moose, and pronghorns are also found in the state. Ducks, geese, grouse, pheasants, and quail are common game birds of Utah. The state has such reptiles as lizards, toads, tortoises, and several kinds of snakes. Trout is the state's most common fish. Other fish that are found in Utah include bass, catfish, graylings, perch, and whitefish.

Lorin D. Wiggins

Bear River, fed by melting snow, offers excellent fishing in the Uinta Mountains of Utah's Rocky Mountains region.

W. R. Wilson

Lake Powell, in the Colorado Plateau region, was formed by Glen Canyon Dam on the Colorado River in Arizona.

Great White Throne, *left,* rises nearly ½ mile (0.8 kilometer) from the canyon floor in Zion National Park. Zion Canyon in the Basin and Range Region is a spectacular example of river erosion.

Union Pacific Railroad

UTAH /Climate

Average July temperatures in Utah range from 60° F. (16° C) in the northeast to 84° F. (29° C) in the southwest. January temperatures average 20° F. (−7° C) in the north and 39° F. (4° C) in the southwest. Utah's record high temperature, 116° F. (47° C), occurred at St. George on June 28, 1892. The state's lowest temperature was −50° F. (−46° C), at Woodruff on Feb. 6, 1899, and at Strawberry Tunnel on Jan. 5, 1913.

Yearly *precipitation* (rain, melted snow, and other moisture) varies from less than 5 inches (13 centimeters) in the Great Salt Lake Desert to up to 50 inches (130 centimeters) in the northeast. The southwest gets little snow, but Alta, a ski area near Salt Lake City, has over 400 inches (1,000 centimeters) a year.

FPG

A Hot, Dry Climate causes the Great Salt Lake Desert to crack and makes it one of the most desolate regions in the world.

SEASONAL TEMPERATURES

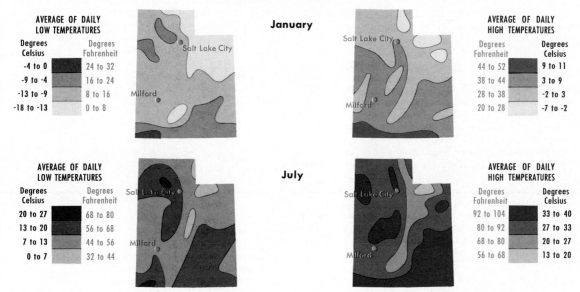

AVERAGE OF DAILY LOW TEMPERATURES

January

Degrees Celsius	Degrees Fahrenheit
-4 to 0	24 to 32
-9 to -4	16 to 24
-13 to -9	8 to 16
-18 to -13	0 to 8

AVERAGE OF DAILY HIGH TEMPERATURES

Degrees Fahrenheit	Degrees Celsius
44 to 52	9 to 11
38 to 44	3 to 9
28 to 38	-2 to 3
20 to 28	-7 to -2

AVERAGE OF DAILY LOW TEMPERATURES

July

Degrees Celsius	Degrees Fahrenheit
20 to 27	68 to 80
13 to 20	56 to 68
7 to 13	44 to 56
0 to 7	32 to 44

AVERAGE OF DAILY HIGH TEMPERATURES

Degrees Fahrenheit	Degrees Celsius
92 to 104	33 to 40
80 to 92	27 to 33
68 to 80	20 to 27
56 to 68	13 to 20

AVERAGE YEARLY PRECIPITATION
(Rain, Melted Snow and Other Moisture)

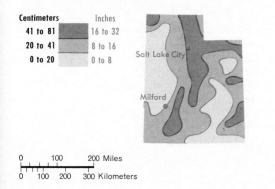

Centimeters	Inches
41 to 81	16 to 32
20 to 41	8 to 16
0 to 20	0 to 8

```
0      100      200 Miles
0  100  200  300 Kilometers
```

WORLD BOOK maps

AVERAGE MONTHLY WEATHER

	SALT LAKE CITY					MILFORD				
	Temperatures				**Days of Rain or Snow**		**Temperatures**			**Days of Rain or Snow**
	F°		C°				F°		C°	
	High	Low	High	Low			High	Low	High	Low	
JAN.	36	17	2	-8	10	JAN.	36	12	2	-11	8
FEB.	43	24	6	-4	8	FEB.	43	19	6	-7	5
MAR.	52	30	11	-1	9	MAR.	53	25	12	-4	6
APR.	63	37	17	3	9	APR.	64	32	18	0	4
MAY	73	45	23	7	8	MAY	74	40	23	4	6
JUNE	82	58	28	14	5	JUNE	84	48	29	9	2
JULY	92	61	33	16	5	JULY	93	56	34	13	5
AUG.	90	59	32	15	6	AUG.	89	54	32	12	4
SEPT.	79	49	26	9	4	SEPT.	81	44	27	7	2
OCT.	67	39	19	4	7	OCT.	67	33	19	1	4
NOV.	50	29	10	-2	7	NOV.	53	22	12	-6	4
DEC.	40	23	4	-5	9	DEC.	41	15	5	-9	4

Service industries, such as wholesale and retail trade, play a leading role in Utah's economy. They account for almost three-fourths of the *gross state product*—the total value of all goods and services produced in a state in a year. Manufacturing, mining, and agriculture are other important economic activities. The federal government is also a major factor in Utah's economy. It owns about two-thirds of the land in the state.

Natural Resources of Utah include rich mineral deposits, and mountain and valley soils.

Minerals. Bingham Canyon, near Salt Lake City, has rich deposits of copper, gold, molybdenum, and silver. Coal, natural gas, and oil are found in the Colorado Plateau. Sand and gravel deposits are found throughout the state. Large deposits of oil and gas are found in the northwest area, in a region called the Overthrust Belt. Utah has some of the nation's richest deposits of oil shale and tar sands, which may someday be used as sources of oil. Other Utah minerals include beryllium, clay, gilsonite, gypsum, potassium salts, salt, stone, uranium, and vanadium.

Soils of Utah are generally poor for farming. Most of the mountain soils are poorly developed. Valley soils are often mixtures of sand, gravel, and clay carried down by mountain streams. Where water is available these valley soils can produce good crops.

Service Industries account for 74 per cent of the gross state product of Utah. Most of the service industries are concentrated in the state's two metropolitan areas.

Wholesale and retail trade ranks as the most valuable service industry. It accounts for 18 per cent of the gross state product and is Utah's largest employer. Salt Lake City is the state's major trade center. Government, the second most valuable service industry, accounts for 17 per cent of the gross state product. State government offices are in Salt Lake City, the capital. The federal government also employs many of the workers in Salt Lake City.

Three service industries each account for 13 per cent of Utah's gross state product. They are (1) community, social, and personal services, (2) finance, insurance, and real estate, and (3) transportation, communication, and utilities. Community, social, and personal services include education and health care; advertising; and the operation of beauty shops and cleaning establishments. Salt Lake City is one of the chief centers of finance and transportation of the Rocky Mountain States.

Manufacturing, including processing, accounts for 17 per cent of the gross state product of Utah. Goods manufactured there have a *value added by manufacture* of about $3½ billion annually. Value added by manufacture represents the increase in value of raw materials after they become finished products. Utah's chief manufactured products, in order of importance, are (1) nonelectrical machinery, (2) transportation equipment, and (3) food products.

Nonelectrical Machinery has a value added of about $640 million yearly. The industry's chief products include office, computing, and accounting machinery and construction, mining, and materials handling equipment. Salt Lake City is the industry's major production center.

Transportation Equipment manufacturing has an annual value added of about $543 million. Brigham City in northern Utah has the largest transportation equipment plant in the state. It produces aircraft engines and parts. The plant also manufactures propulsion systems for missiles and spacecraft.

Food Products have a value added by manufacture of about $400 million yearly. Utah cities with food processing plants include Ogden and Salt Lake City.

Other Leading Industries. The electrical machinery and equipment industry ranks fourth in importance in Utah. Other leading industries, in order of importance, include printing and publishing, petroleum and coal products, fabricated metals, chemical products, and stone, clay, and glass products. Instruments and textiles are also important to Utah's economy.

Mining accounts for 3 per cent of Utah's gross state product. The mining industry earns about $2 billion a year. Petroleum is the state's most valuable mineral. Most of Utah's petroleum comes from Duchesne, San Juan, and Uintah counties. Coal is the second most

Utah's Gross State Product

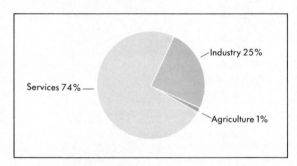

Services 74% —
Industry 25%
Agriculture 1%

The gross state product (GSP) is the total value of goods and services produced in a state in a year. The GSP measures a state's total economic performance and can also be used to compare the economic output and growth of states. Utah's GSP was $17,006,000,000 in 1983.

Production and Workers by Economic Activities

Economic Activities	Per Cent of GSP Produced	Number of Persons	Per Cent of Total
		Employed Workers	
Wholesale & Retail Trade	18	133,200	22
Government	17	128,600	22
Manufacturing	17	85,300	14
Community, Social, & Personal Services	13	112,600	19
Finance, Insurance, & Real Estate	13	28,100	5
Transportation, Communication, & Utilities	13	35,900	6
Construction	5	28,600	5
Mining	3	13,900	2
Agriculture	1	30,000	5
Total	100	596,200	100

Sources: *Employment and Earnings*, May 1984, Bureau of Labor Statistics; 1982 Census of Agriculture, Census Bureau; WORLD BOOK estimates based on data from Department of Agriculture and Bureau of Economic Analysis.

valuable mineral in the state. Utah is among the leading coal producers west of the Mississippi River. Carbon, Emery, and Sevier counties supply nearly all the state's coal. Utah is second only to Arizona in copper production. Most of the state's copper is taken from a huge open-pit mine in Bingham Canyon. Utah is also among the leading producers of gold, silver, uranium, and vanadium.

Uintah County is the nation's only producer of gilsonite, a solid form of asphalt. The water of Great Salt Lake is used to produce natural salts. Utah is a leading producer of molybdenum and potassium salts. Nearly every county in the state produces sand and gravel. Other minerals produced in Utah include beryllium, clays, lime, natural gas, phosphate rock, and stone.

Agriculture in Utah accounts for 1 per cent of the gross state product. It provides a yearly income of about $580 million. Farmland covers about 12 million acres (4.9 million hectares), or about a fourth of the state's land area. About 1 million acres (400,000 hectares) are irrigated by water stored in reservoirs. About 800,000 acres (320,000 hectares) can be farmed without irrigation by using dry farming methods (see DRY FARMING). Utah's 12,000 farms average 1,050 acres (425 hectares) in size. But most of the irrigated farms are under 650 acres (263 hectares). Many of the dry farms and ranches are much larger.

Livestock and Livestock Products have an annual value of about $433 million. Beef cattle, Utah's leading farm product, earn about $175 million yearly. Milk ranks second. Eggs, hogs, sheep, turkeys, and wool are other important livestock products. Utah is a leading wool-producing state, and a sheep-raising center of the western United States.

Crops have an annual value of about $146 million in Utah. Hay, the chief crop, earns about $40 million a year. Wheat is the second leading crop, and cherries rank third. Other important crops include alfalfa seed, apples, barley, greenhouse and nursery products, onions, potatoes, and sugar beets. Most of the wheat and sugar beets come from the northern and central counties. Farmers in the north-central section raise apples, apricots, beans, cherries, corn, peaches, pears, peas, and tomatoes. The largest potato crops are in Beaver, Davis, Iron, Millard, and Washington counties.

Electric Power. Most of Utah's electricity comes from coal-powered steam plants in Emery and Uintah counties. Hydroelectric facilities at Flaming Gorge and Glen Canyon generate the rest of the state's power.

Transportation. The first transcontinental railroad system in the United States was completed in Utah on May 10, 1869. On that date, the Central Pacific and Union Pacific railroads were joined at Promontory.

Today, railroads operate on 1,725 miles (2,776 kilometers) of track in Utah. About 10 rail lines provide freight service, and passenger trains link Utah cities to other cities. The state also has about 49,000 miles (78,900 kilometers) of roads, and 95 airports and airfields. Fourteen major airlines serve the state. The largest commercial airport in Utah is in Salt Lake City.

Communication. Utah's first newspaper, the *Deseret News*, was established in Salt Lake City in 1850. Today, the state has about 45 newspapers and 20 periodicals. The largest newspapers are the *Deseret News* and the *Salt Lake Tribune*, both of Salt Lake City. The state's first radio station, KZN (now KSL), began broadcasting in Salt Lake City in 1922. In 1948, Utah's first television station, KTVT (now KTVX-TV), began operating. Today, Utah has about 70 radio stations, 6 commercial television stations, and 2 educational TV stations.

Farm and Mineral Products

This map shows where the state's leading farm and mineral products are produced. The major urban areas (shown on the map in red) are the state's important manufacturing centers.

Bingham Canyon Copper Mine is the largest open-pit copper mine in North America. Utah is a leading producer of copper.

W. R. Wilson

HISTORIC UTAH

"This Is The Place," Brigham Young, the Mormon leader, is supposed to have said on seeing the Great Salt Lake Valley. His pioneer party came to the site of Salt Lake City on July 24, 1847.

Jim Bridger, who later became a famous army scout, may have been the first white person to see Great Salt Lake. He reached its shores in the winter of 1824-1825.

Promontory

SALT LAKE CITY

The First U.S. Transcontinental Railroad System was completed at Promontory, Utah, on May 10, 1869. The system linked the Central Pacific and Union Pacific railroads.

The Bingham Canyon Mine supplies about a seventh of U.S. copper. The mine boomed after surface mining began in 1906.

The Sugar Beet Industry began in Utah in the 1850's when the Mormons first planted beet seeds. The Lehi plant, opened in 1890, was the third in the country to succeed in beet-sugar manufacture.

The Discovery of Uranium near Moab in 1952 touched off a uranium rush. People came to Utah from all over the country hoping to "strike it rich."

Moab

The Mormons Began Irrigation of the land in Utah in 1847, the year of their arrival. They diverted City Creek, now in Salt Lake City, to flood the hard ground before plowing.

The Bonneville Speedway stretches over hard salt beds of the Great Salt Lake Desert. Here, in 1947, John Cobb, a British driver, was the first to travel more than 400 miles (640 kilometers) per hour on land.

Indian Days. Indians probably lived in the Utah region several thousand years ago. These early Indians made their homes in pueblos and in cliff dwellings. White explorers who came to the region in 1776 found four major tribes—the Gosiute, Paiute, Shoshoni (Snake), and Ute. The Navajo arrived in the 1860's, and now occupy large areas in southwestern Utah.

Early Exploration. In 1540, Spanish explorers arrived at the Grand Canyon in what is now Arizona. They may have traveled into the Utah region, although many historians doubt that they did. More than 235 years passed before white people again came to Utah. In 1776, while American colonists were fighting for their independence from Great Britain, two Spanish Franciscan friars led an expedition into the Utah region. They were Silvestre Velez de Escalante and Francisco Atanasio Domínguez. The friars explored the region and reached Utah Lake. Later, a few other Spaniards visited the region. But Spain was not interested in setting up colonies there. The first Americans to visit the region probably crossed what is now northern Utah in 1811-1812. They were part of a fur trading expedition.

Jim Bridger, a famous scout, was probably the first white person to see Great Salt Lake. He reached its shores during the winter of 1824-1825. Bridger tasted the salty water, and thought he had found an ocean. Hundreds of fur trappers and traders soon came to the Great Salt Lake area. By 1830, travelers were crossing central Utah to get from Santa Fe, in New Mexico, to Los Angeles.

The Mormons were Utah's first permanent settlers. This religious group belonged to the Church of Jesus Christ of Latter-day Saints. Joseph Smith established the church in Fayette, N.Y., in 1830. Brigham Young became leader of the Mormons after Smith's death in 1844. The Mormons were persecuted nearly everywhere they went. They traveled to Ohio, Missouri, and Illinois in search of religious freedom. In 1846, Young led a group of his people west. They reached the Great Salt Lake region in 1847, and Young settled there. He planned communities for all his followers. See MORMONS.

Many groups of Mormons settled in the valleys of north-central Utah. They irrigated the valleys and made farming productive. In 1848, swarms of grasshoppers invaded the valleys and threatened to ruin the settlers' crops. But sea gulls from Great Salt Lake wiped out the grasshoppers. The sea gull later became the state bird, and a monument was built in Salt Lake City to honor the gulls. The kind of grasshopper that attacked the settlers' crops became known as the Mormon cricket.

In 1849, the Mormons established their Perpetual Emigrating Fund. This fund helped bring to Utah many Mormons who could not pay for the trip. The fund operated for about 40 years. It brought about 50,-000 Mormons to Utah, including many from Denmark, England, Norway, Scotland, Sweden, and Wales.

Indian Troubles. Relations between the Mormons and the Indians were peaceful at first. But some of the Indians resented the settlers who had taken their land. Beginning in 1853, a Ute chief named Walker led attacks against several Mormon settlements. These attacks were known as the *Walker War*. In 1854, Brigham Young persuaded Walker to end the attacks. For several years, the settlers and Indians lived peacefully. Another Ute chief, Black Hawk, led an uprising against the Mormon settlers in 1865. The attack started the Black Hawk War. Other tribes joined in the fighting. About 50 Mormons were killed, and the settlers suffered losses of more than $1 million. Black Hawk and his followers agreed to peace terms in 1867, but other Indians made occasional raids until late 1872. Most of the Ute settled on a reservation in the Uinta Basin.

Territorial Days and Statehood. The Utah region belonged to Mexico when the Mormons first arrived in 1847. At the time, the United States and Mexico were fighting the Mexican War (1846-1848). The United States won the war and acquired from Mexico a large area of land, including the Utah region.

In 1849, the Mormons established the *State of Deseret*. They set up a temporary government with Brigham Young as governor. Church leaders filled other government offices. The settlers adopted a constitution and asked to be admitted to the Union. But Congress was engaged in a bitter debate over the question of slavery in the United States. This debate resulted in a series of acts called the *Compromise of 1850*. Part of the compromise established the Utah Territory, with Young as the first territorial governor. The territory extended far to the east and west of present-day Utah. See COMPROMISE OF 1850.

Between 1849 and 1895, Utah asked several times to be admitted to the Union. But Congress refused each time because of the Mormon practice of *polygamy* (one

Important Dates in Utah

1776 Silvestre Velez de Escalante and Francisco Atanasio Domínguez made the first far-reaching exploration of the Utah region.

1824-1825 Jim Bridger probably was the first white person to see Great Salt Lake.

1847 Brigham Young and the first Mormon pioneers arrived in the Great Salt Lake region.

1848 The United States won the Utah area from Mexico.

1849 The Mormons created the State of Deseret, and adopted their first constitution.

1850 Congress established the Utah Territory.

1860-1861 The pony express crossed Utah.

1861 Telegraph lines met at Salt Lake City, providing the first transcontinental telegraph service.

1869 The first transcontinental railroad system was completed at Promontory.

1890 The Mormons in Utah prohibited polygamy.

1896 Utah became the 45th state on January 4.

1913 The U.S. Bureau of Reclamation completed the Strawberry River reservoir, the state's first large reclamation project.

1952 Rich uranium deposits were found near Moab.

1959 Utah became an important missile-producing state.

1964 Flaming Gorge and Glen Canyon dams were completed.

1967 Construction began on the Central Utah Project, a program to provide water for Utah's major growth areas.

1974 Oil companies invested millions of dollars to lease federally owned oil-shale land in Utah.

man having more than one wife). Actually, few Mormon men had more than one wife. But Utah was refused statehood as long as Mormons practiced polygamy.

President James Buchanan wanted to take control of the Utah Territory away from the Mormons. In 1857, he appointed Alfred Cumming of Georgia as territorial governor, in place of Brigham Young. Buchanan sent federal troops to enforce the appointment. This period became known as the *Utah*, or *Mormon, War*. The soldiers marched toward Utah, stopping along the way during the winter of 1857-1858. In September, 1857, a group of Utahns and Indians, nervously awaiting the federal troops, attacked a party of about 140 travelers passing through Utah. Most of the travelers were murdered. Only a few small children were permitted to live. The incident became known as the *Mountain Meadows Massacre*. John D. Lee, who took part in the massacre, was later convicted and executed.

The federal troops, guided by Jim Bridger, arrived in Utah in the spring of 1858. The war ended shortly afterward, though the troops stayed three years. Bad feeling between the Mormons and the soldiers existed throughout this period. Brigham Young was no longer territorial governor, but he remained the real leader of the Mormons. The troops left Utah when the Civil War began in 1861.

During the 1860's, Utah's boundaries were changed several times. Parts of the territory were given to Nevada, Colorado, and Wyoming. Congress established Utah's present boundaries in 1868.

The pony express began carrying mail on April 3, 1860. Pony express riders crossed Utah on their journeys between St. Joseph, Mo., and Sacramento, Calif. On Oct. 26, 1861, the operators of the pony express announced the closing of the express. Two days earlier, telegraph lines from Washington, D.C., and from San Francisco had met in Salt Lake City. This was the nation's first transcontinental telegraph. It provided a link between the eastern and western United States, and so the pony express was no longer needed.

In 1862, Congress passed a law forbidding polygamy. That same year, federal troops were again sent to Utah, under the command of Colonel Patrick E. Conner. Conner was interested in mining, and he encouraged his troops to prospect for minerals. In 1863, gold and silver were discovered in Bingham Canyon. Conner sent out word of the discovery. He hoped that a mining boom would bring a flood of non-Mormons into Utah and reduce Mormon control of the territory. But profits from Utah's minerals were small during the 1860's, mostly because of transportation problems. Few prospectors came to the territory. By the 1870's, however, many mining companies were operating in Utah.

Plans for a transcontinental railroad had first been made during the 1850's. In 1863, the Central Pacific Railroad began building eastward from Sacramento, and the Union Pacific built westward, starting in Omaha, Neb. The two lines met at Promontory, Utah, on May 10, 1869. A railroad-building boom soon began in Utah.

During the 1880's, federal courts began enforcing federal laws against polygamy. Hundreds of Mormons were fined and sent to prison. A law passed in 1887 permitted the U.S. government to seize church property of the Mormons for use by public schools. In 1890, Wilford Woodruff, the church president, advised the Mormons to give up polygamy. In October of that year, the church officially prohibited polygamy.

In 1895, Utah submitted a new constitution to Congress. This constitution outlawed polygamy and prevented control of the state by any church. Utah was admitted to the Union as the 45th state on Jan. 4, 1896. The people elected Heber M. Wells, a Republican, as their first governor.

The Early 1900's brought expansion of the railroad construction that had begun after the Civil War. The railroads opened new markets for Utah's farm and mining products. Utah farmers increased livestock operations, and beef cattle and sheep became important prod-

Deseret Store in Salt Lake City accepted grain as payment for goods in the 1800's.

Culver

First Transcontinental U.S. Rail System was completed in 1869 in Promontory. Central Pacific and Union Pacific officials drove in the last spike.

Union Pacific Railroad

ucts. Surface mining methods were introduced in Bingham Canyon in 1906. The state's copper production increased greatly. A huge federal irrigation project on the Strawberry River, completed in 1913, increased the amount of Utah's irrigated farmland.

Large smelters were built in the Salt Lake Valley during the early 1900's, and Utah's smelting industry grew. After the United States entered World War I in 1917, Utah mines supplied the Allies with large supplies of *nonferrous metals* (metals containing no iron).

Utah was hit hard by the Great Depression of the 1930's. The mining industry suffered. Farm prices dropped. Utah had one of the nation's highest percentages of unemployed workers. The state's economy improved in the late 1930's when the depression eased.

The Mid-1900's. Utah's manufacturing and mining industries prospered during World War II (1939-1945). After the war, the government increased its activities in Utah. Military installations established during the war were expanded. In the middle and late 1950's, missile plants were built in Brigham City, Ogden, and Salt Lake City. By 1959, the state had become a center of missile production.

During the 1950's and 1960's, Utah changed from an agricultural to an industrial state. The manufacture of steel products became an important industry. In 1952, a rich uranium deposit was discovered near Moab. Oil and gas fields were developed in eastern and southeastern Utah. In the early 1960's, the construction of Flaming Gorge Dam, Glen Canyon Dam, and many smaller dams brought further industrial growth.

Tourism became an important industry in the state during the 1950's and 1960's. An increase in the number of urban residents led to demands for more recreational facilities, and development of outdoor recreation areas in the state boomed. Ski resorts in the Wasatch Mountains attracted visitors from throughout the nation.

During the 1960's, the Utah economy suffered a series of setbacks. The need for missile parts produced in the state declined in 1963, and the value of Utah's missile industry fell. A slump in mineral prices caused the value of the state's mineral products to drop.

The cost of operating Utah's schools soared between the late 1940's and early 1960's. In 1963, Utah educators requested an additional $25½ million in state aid to education. The state legislature provided $11 million. Governor George D. Clyde then set up a commission to examine Utah's educational needs. In 1964, the commission urged that aid to education be increased by another $6 million. Clyde refused to approve the increase because he felt it would cripple the state's economy.

The National Education Association (NEA) urged teachers throughout the United States not to accept jobs in Utah until the problem was solved. Never before had U.S. educators organized a protest against an entire state. In 1965, the legislature increased school aid by $25½ million over a two-year period. The NEA then ended its protest.

During the 1960's, environmental concerns received increased attention in Utah. In 1968, nerve gas being tested in western Utah by the U.S. Army accidentally poisoned about 6,000 sheep. Utahns demanded an end to the testing and storing of such chemicals in the state. In addition, the Utah legislature set up a statewide program in 1969 to fight increasing air pollution.

Morton Thiokol, Inc.

A Testing Station for Large Rocket Nozzles operates in Brigham City. The giant motor uses solid fuel.

The Governors of Utah

	Party	Term
Heber M. Wells	Republican	1896-1905
John C. Cutler	Republican	1905-1909
William Spry	Republican	1909-1917
Simon Bamberger	Democratic	1917-1921
Charles R. Mabey	Republican	1921-1925
George H. Dern	Democratic	1925-1933
Henry H. Blood	Democratic	1933-1941
Herbert B. Maw	Democratic	1941-1949
J. Bracken Lee	Republican	1949-1957
George D. Clyde	Republican	1957-1965
Calvin L. Rampton	Democratic	1965-1977
Scott M. Matheson	Democratic	1977-1985
Norman H. Bangerter	Republican	1985-

Utah Today is influenced heavily by the federal government, which owns and administers about two-thirds of Utah's land. Most of the state's water comes from lakes and streams in national forests and is stored behind federally built dams. About 7 per cent of Utah's workers are employed by the federal government.

Education costs remain a problem in Utah. Because of the Mormon emphasis on education, Utahns average more years of school than people in any other state. Utah also spends a greater percentage of its funds on education than almost any other state.

A nationwide oil shortage during the early 1970's led to increased coal production in Utah. Also, several oil companies invested millions of dollars to lease federally owned oil-shale land in Utah. But in the late 1970's, the high cost of producing oil from shale rock and concern over possible pollution problems delayed the development of Utah's oil-shale resources.

Conservation is an important issue in Utah today. Disputes regarding land use exist between conservationists and other Utah residents. Conservationists work to preserve Utah's desert and mountainous areas. Other residents favor using part of this land for power plants, mining, grazing livestock, and other purposes.

Utah has a limited supply of water. Construction of the Central Utah Project, begun in 1967, is scheduled for completion in the 1990's. This project will provide large amounts of water to the part of Utah that has a high rate of population and industrial growth.

EVERETT L. COOLEY, ROBERT LAYTON, and WILLIAM B. SMART

UTAH/*Study Aids*

Related Articles in WORLD BOOK include:

BIOGRAPHIES

Bridger, James	Browning, John M.	Young, Brigham

CITIES

Ogden	Provo	Salt Lake City

HISTORY

Cliff Dwellers	Mormons
Deseret	Ute Indians
Guadalupe Hidalgo, Treaty of	Western Frontier Life
Jefferson Territory	

NATIONAL PARKS AND MONUMENTS

Arches National Park	Hovenweep National
Bryce Canyon	Monument
National Park	Natural Bridges National
Canyonlands National Park	Monument
Capitol Reef National Park	Rainbow Bridge Na-
Cedar Breaks National	tional Monument
Monument	Timpanogos Cave Na-
Dinosaur National	tional Monument
Monument	Zion National Park

PHYSICAL FEATURES

Colorado River	Great Salt Lake	Rocky Mountains
Great Basin	Desert	Wasatch Range
Great Salt Lake	Lake Powell	

Outline

I. Government
  A. Constitution
  B. Executive
  C. Legislature
  D. Courts
  E. Local Government
  F. Revenue
  G. Politics
II. People
III. Education
  A. Schools
  B. Libraries
  C. Museums
IV. A Visitor's Guide
  A. Places to Visit
  B. Annual Events
V. The Land
  A. Land Regions
  B. Rivers and Lakes
  C. Deserts
  D. Plant and Animal Life
VI. Climate
VII. Economy
  A. Natural Resources
  B. Service Industries
  C. Manufacturing
  D. Mining
  E. Agriculture
  F. Electric Power
  G. Transportation
  H. Communication
VIII. History

Questions

What lake once covered most of present-day Utah? What two lakes are remnants of that body of water? How do they differ?

What historic event occurred at Promontory in 1869?

What event ended the pony express?

Why did the Mormons come to Utah? Who was their leader?

What are some of Utah's manufactured products?

Where is the Sea Gull Monument? Why was it built?

What is Utah's most valuable mineral?

What two features of Utah's 1895 constitution helped the territory be admitted to the Union?

What is unusual about the drainage of the Great Basin and Range region of Utah?

Additional Resources

Level I

CARPENTER, ALLAN. *Utah.* Rev. ed. Childrens Press, 1979.

ELLSWORTH, S. GEORGE. *The New Utah's Heritage.* Rev. ed. G. M. Smith, 1985.

FRADIN, DENNIS B. *Utah in Words and Pictures.* Childrens Press, 1980.

LUCE, WILLARD and CELIA. *Utah.* Rev. ed. G. M. Smith, 1980.

Level II

ANDERSON, NELS. *Desert Saints: The Mormon Frontier in Utah.* Univ. of Chicago Press, 1942. A classic study.

ARRINGTON, LEONARD J. *Great Basin Kingdom: An Economic History of the Latter-Day Saints, 1830-1900.* Univ. of Nebraska Press, 1966. Reprint of 1958 edition.

Atlas of Utah. Ed. by Wayne L. Wahlquist, and others. Brigham Young Univ. Press, 1980.

LONG, EVERETTE B. *The Saints of the Union: Utah Territory During the Civil War.* Univ. of Illinois Press, 1981.

The Peoples of Utah. Ed. by Helen Z. Papanikolas. Utah State Historical Society, 1976.

PETERSON, CHARLES S. *Utah: A Bicentennial History.* Norton, 1977.

Utah: A Guide to the State. Rev. ed. Western Epics, 1982. From the American Guide Series.

Utah's History. Ed. by Richard D. Poll, and others. Brigham Young Univ. Press, 1978.

UTAH, UNIVERSITY OF, is a state-supported co-educational university in Salt Lake City, Utah. It has colleges of humanities, science, and social and behavioral science; and professional schools of architecture, business, education, engineering, fine arts, health, law, medicine, mines, nursing, pharmacy, and social work. It also has a graduate school and a division of continuing education. Courses lead to bachelor's, master's, and doctor's degrees. The university was founded in 1850 as the University of Deseret. It received its present name in 1892. For the enrollment of the University of Utah, see UNIVERSITIES AND COLLEGES (table).

Critically reviewed by the UNIVERSITY OF UTAH

UTAMARO, *OO tah MAH raw* (1753-1806), was a leading Japanese printmaker. He turned public taste in the direction of bold drawing, striking poses, and unusual color contrasts. His beautiful women or pairs of lovers are tall and graceful. He often showed them only from the waist up, and drew faces and hands with great elegance under masses of jet-black hair. Toward the end of his life, he turned for novelty to exaggerations and distortions, which some of his followers carried even further. Utamaro was born in Kawagoe, Japan. See also JAPANESE PRINT (picture).   ALEXANDER C. SOPER

UTE INDIANS, *yoot,* are a tribe of the Western United States. They live on three major reservations in Utah and Colorado. The name of the state of Utah comes from the Ute Indians.

The Ute are governed by tribal councils that are elected by popular vote. Members of the tribe work in agriculture, forestry, and tourism. They are also developing the coal, gas, oil, and other mineral deposits that lie under the reservations.

The Ute once lived in the mountains and plains of Colorado and Utah and in northern New Mexico. They built cone-shaped houses of brush, reeds, and grasses. They assigned hunting grounds to families and hunted antelope, buffalo, and deer in annual game drives.

Each fall, the Ute traveled to New Mexico to trade with the Pueblo Indians and the Spaniards. During the 1600's, they obtained horses from the Spaniards, which increased the tribe's mobility. The Ute hunted over a wider area and developed an advanced economy that involved trading meat and hides for material goods.

196

They became powerful warriors and fought the Arapaho, Cheyenne, Comanche, and Kiowa tribes.

The best-known chief of the Ute was Ouray, who became prominent in the 1800's. Ouray spoke Spanish, English, and several Indian languages. He settled disputes between the Ute and the white settlers and arranged the first treaty between the Ute and the United States government. The government assigned reservations to the Ute in the late 1800's.   JAMES M. JEFFERSON

See also INDIAN WARS (The Southern Plains).

UTERUS, *YOO tuhr uhs,* or *WOMB,* is a hollow organ of the female reproductive system in which an unborn baby develops. The organ is near the base of the abdomen. In a woman who is not pregnant, the uterus resembles an upside-down pear in shape and is about the size of a fist. The bottom of the uterus consists of a necklike opening called the *cervix,* which leads into the vagina. At birth, a baby passes down through the cervix and the vagina and then out of the woman's body.

Each month during a woman's childbearing years, blood vessels, glands, and cells build up in the lining of the uterus. This process prepares this organ to receive a fertilized egg. If fertilization does not occur, the built-up lining is discharged during menstruation. If fertilization takes place, the fertilized egg attaches itself to the lining of the uterus. The egg develops into an embryo, and tissues from the uterus and the embryo form a disk-shaped organ called the *placenta.* The placenta provides the unborn baby with food and oxygen and carries away its waste products (see PLACENTA).

The uterus expands to about 24 times its normal size during pregnancy. During childbirth, the muscles of the uterus contract and force the baby out of the mother's body. A second wave of contractions then expels the placenta. The uterus returns to normal size a few weeks after the birth of the baby.   GRETAJO NORTHROP

See also HYSTERECTOMY; MENSTRUATION; REPRODUCTION.

UTICA, *YOO tih kuh,* an ancient North African city, was the oldest Phoenician colony in the western Mediterranean Sea. It stood about midway between present day Tunis and Bizerte, Tunisia. According to legend, Utica was founded in 1101 B.C. But scholars now believe it was founded in the 700's B.C. Utica was an important seaport, but its site is now about 7 miles (11 kilometers) from the sea. Some ruins of the city remain.

At first, Utica and the neighboring colony of Carthage were almost equal in power. With Motya, a colony in western Sicily, they gave Phoenicia control of the Mediterranean passage to the Straits of Gibraltar, threatening Greek sea trade.

Carthage later became an independent power, and began to challenge Rome by the 300's B.C. Utica sided with Rome during the Third Punic War (149-146 B.C.) between Rome and Carthage. Rome won the war and made Utica capital of its new province of Africa. Utica was conquered by Arabs in the A.D. 600's.   LOUIS L. ORLIN

UTICA, *YOO tih kuh,* N.Y. (pop. 75,632), is an important commercial and industrial center in the Mohawk Valley along the New York State Barge Canal System. It lies about 90 miles (140 kilometers) northwest of Albany in a rich agricultural and dairy region.

Utica covers an area of about 17 square miles (44 square kilometers). With Rome, N.Y., it forms a metropolitan area of 320,180 persons.

Industry and Trade. During the late 1800's and early 1900's, Utica ranked first among the cities of New York in the production of cotton cloth. After World War II, when many textile companies began to move to southern states, Utica factories started to produce a variety of tools, machines, and manufactured articles. Important products include heating, ventilating, refrigerating, and air-conditioning equipment; electronic tools and products; pneumatic tools; paper products; air compressors; and men's and boys' clothing. Utica is also a trading center for farmers of the Mohawk Valley.

Utica lies on the only water-level pass through the Appalachian Mountains. An airport, and railroad, bus, and truck lines serve the city. Utica is a major New York State Barge Canal System terminal. Utica College, an affiliate of Syracuse University, is in Utica.

History. A king's grant to William Cosby and his associates in 1734 included the site of Utica. Fort Schuyler was built on the site during the French and Indian War (1754-1763). After the Revolutionary War, many persons from New England and the lower Mohawk Valley settled there. Utica was incorporated as a village in 1798. The name (from that of an ancient North African town) was drawn from suggestions placed in a hat. Utica was chartered as a city in 1832. It has a mayor-council form of government.   WILLIAM E. YOUNG

UTILITARIANISM, *yoo TIHL uh TAIR ee uh NIHZ uhm,* is the doctrine that the goal of life is "the greatest happiness of the greatest number." Whatever brings about this happiness has "utility." Anything that obstructs such happiness is useless. Utilitarians hold that the most definite mark of happiness is pleasure. Jeremy Bentham, "the father of the Utilitarians," first developed this idea in England. The name *Utilitarianism* was not used until John Stuart Mill, a disciple of Bentham, formed the Utilitarian Society in 1823. The society became a great center of liberal thought and helped to bring about many reforms.   H. M. KALLEN

See also BENTHAM, JEREMY; MILL (family).

UTILITY, PUBLIC. See PUBLIC UTILITY.

UTOPIA, *yoo TOH pee uh,* is the name commonly given to an imaginary land where everything is supposed to be perfect. The name *utopia* comes from the Greek words *ou* and *topos,* meaning *no place.* The name refers particularly to a type of society with ideal economic and social conditions. People often apply the adjective *utopian* to plans of reform that they consider to be impractical and visionary.

The word *utopia* was used as the title of a famous book by Saint Thomas More. *Utopia* was first published in Latin in 1516 and was translated into English in 1551. It is partly in the form of a dialogue. The book gives More's views on the ideal government. But, like most writings on utopias, it also criticizes social and economic conditions of More's times.

More's *Utopia* is the report of a Portuguese sailor Raphael Hythlodaye. The sailor has made three voyages to America with the explorer Amerigo Vespucci, and tells of his travels through wild and unexplored places. The greatest wonder is the island of Utopia, where all men are equal, prosperous, educated, and wise.

Several other books have presented an imaginary ideal state of society. One of the first books describing

a utopia was Plato's *Republic*, written about 375 B.C. More recent utopias are described in Samuel Butler's *Erewhon*, which almost spells *nowhere* backwards (1872); Edward Bellamy's *Looking Backward* (1888); and H. G. Wells' *A Modern Utopia* (1905).   GOERGE A. WICKES

See also BELLAMY, EDWARD; COMMUNAL SOCIETY; MORE, SAINT THOMAS; PLATO; WELLS, H. G.

UTRECHT, *YOO trehkt* (pop. 231,769; met. area 494,-898), a Dutch city, lies on the Rhine River, about 22 miles (35 kilometers) southeast of Amsterdam (see NETHERLANDS [map]). Utrecht is called the *City of Spires and Bridges* because of its many churches and bridges. A triple avenue of trees, the *Maliebaan*, is a popular sight in Utrecht. Industries include sawmills, machine shops, breweries, carpet works, and factories that make velvets, cottons, linens, and musical instruments.

Much Dutch history centers about this interesting old city. In 1579, the seven northern Protestant provinces united in Utrecht. The nation of the Netherlands grew out of this union. A treaty that helped end the War of the Spanish Succession was signed at Utrecht in 1713 (see UTRECHT, PEACE OF).   BENJAMIN HUNNINGHER

UTRECHT, *YOO trehkt*, **PEACE OF,** was one of the great international peace settlements of history. It ended the War of the Spanish Succession (1701-1714) and established a balance of power in Europe. The settlement consisted of the Treaty of Utrecht, the Treaty of Rastatt, and the Treaty of Baden.

The death of King Charles II of Spain in 1700 led to the War of the Spanish Succession. Charles left a will that gave the Spanish crown to a French prince, Philip of Anjou. Philip was the grandson of King Louis XIV of France, and so other European countries feared that France might add Spain's empire to its own. In the war, France fought against the Grand Alliance, consisting of Austria, England, Prussia, the Netherlands, and smaller states in the Holy Roman Empire. The conflict spread to North America, where it was known as Queen Anne's War (1702-1713). Finally, in 1712, representatives of all the participants met in Utrecht, the Netherlands, to formally discuss peace terms.

The Treaty of Utrecht, signed in 1713, marked the declining power of France and the growing worldwide strength of Great Britain. The treaty recognized Philip as king of Spain, but France agreed that Spain and France would never be united under one ruler. Britain gained the Spanish colonies of Gibraltar and Minorca and received a contract to supply all the Spanish colonies in America with African slaves. In North America, France gave Britain the Hudson Bay Territory, Newfoundland, and the Nova Scotia region of Acadia.

Holy Roman Emperor Charles VI refused to sign the Treaty of Utrecht. He claimed that he was the heir to the Spanish throne. Fighting between France and Austria, the chief state in the Holy Roman Empire, continued until 1714. That year, the two nations signed the treaties of Rastatt and Baden, which confirmed most of the terms of the Treaty of Utrecht.   CLAUDE C. STURGILL

See also ACADIA; FRENCH AND INDIAN WARS (Queen Anne's War); SUCCESSION WARS.

UTRILLO, *oo TREE loh*, **MAURICE,** *mow REES* (1883-1955), was a French artist known for his paintings of Paris street scenes. His favorite subject was the Mont-

martre district, with its steep streets and picturesque windmills. Most of Utrillo's paintings have a melancholy feeling. The streets are empty, or a few lonely figures wander through them. New-fallen snow and leaden skies often lend a gloomy air. He increased the gloominess by the use of deep perspectives. From 1908 to 1914, Utrillo used white and off-white colors with soft, warm ones. His later paintings have brighter colors.

Utrillo was born in Paris. His mother was Suzanne Valadon, a well-known painter and artists' model. She introduced him to painting, but he was essentially self-taught. Utrillo painted his scenes from memory or used picture postcards as aids.   WILLARD E. MISFELDT

Sacré Coeur de Montmartre (1937), a painting on paper mounted on canvas; Indianapolis Museum of Art, Indianapolis, Ind., Delavan Smith Fund

A Typical Utrillo Painting portrays lonely figures on the narrow, twisting streets of Montmartre, a district of Paris.

UZBEKISTAN, *ooz behk ih STAN*, is a region that makes up the Uzbek Soviet Socialist Republic, one of the 15 republics of the Soviet Union. The Uzbek republic is the third most populated Soviet state. It lies in the foothills of the Tien Shan and Pamir mountains in Turkestan, and extends northwest to the Aral Sea (see RUSSIA [map]). The state covers 172,700 square miles (447,400 square kilometers) and has about 17,498,000 people. Most of the people live in the Fergana Valley, along the upper part of a river called Syr Darya.

Uzbekistan produces large quantities of almonds, apricots, cotton, and raisins and other dried fruit. Stock and sheep raising and horse breeding are important activities. Mineral resources of Uzbekistan include natural gas, petroleum, and sulfur. Tashkent, the largest city in the Asian part of the Soviet Union, is the capital of the Uzbek republic.   ROBERT A. LEWIS

See also SAMARKAND; TASHKENT; TURKESTAN.

Vv

V is the 22nd letter of our alphabet. It came from a letter used by the Semites, who once lived in Syria and Palestine. They called the letter *waw*, their word for *hook*. They wrote the letter with a symbol borrowed from an Egyptian *hieroglyphic*, or picture symbol. The Greeks borrowed the letter from the Phoenicians and gave it a *Υ*-shape. The Romans, when they adopted the letter, dropped the vertical stroke. They used it for the vowel sound, *u*, and the consonant sound, *v*. About A.D. 900, people began to write *v* at the beginning of a word and *u* in the middle.

During the Renaissance, people began using the letter *v* for the consonant and *u* for the vowel. But the change was not final for several hundred years. See ALPHABET.

Uses. *V* or *v* is about the 21st most frequently used letter in books, newspapers, and other material printed in English. *V* is the Roman numeral for five. As an abbreviation, *V* may stand for *veteran* or *volunteer*. It is the abbreviation for *verb* in grammars and dictionaries. In music, it stands for *violin* or *voice*. It may mean *various*, *volt*, *volume*, or *versus*. In chemistry, *V* is the symbol for the element *vanadium*.

Pronunciation. A person pronounces *v* by placing the lower lip on the upper teeth, closing the *velum*, or soft palate, and forcing the breath through the teeth and lips, vibrating the vocal cords. This sound may be spelled *ph*, as in *Stephen*. In German, it may sound like the English *f*. In Spanish it may have a *b* sound. See PRONUNCIATION.   MARIANNE COOLEY

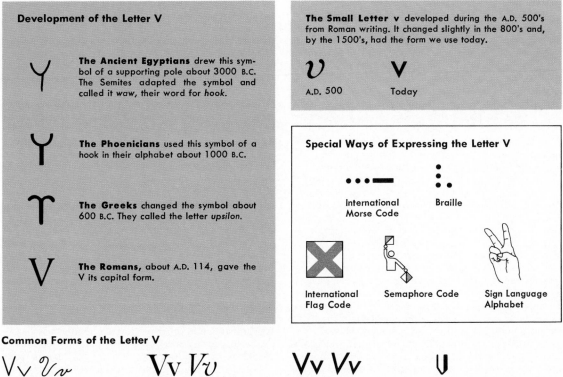

Development of the Letter V

The Ancient Egyptians drew this symbol of a supporting pole about 3000 B.C. The Semites adapted the symbol and called it *waw*, their word for *hook*.

The Phoenicians used this symbol of a hook in their alphabet about 1000 B.C.

The Greeks changed the symbol about 600 B.C. They called the letter *upsilon*.

The Romans, about A.D. 114, gave the V its capital form.

The Small Letter v developed during the A.D. 500's from Roman writing. It changed slightly in the 800's and, by the 1500's, had the form we use today.

A.D. 500   Today

Special Ways of Expressing the Letter V

International Morse Code

Braille

International Flag Code

Semaphore Code

Sign Language Alphabet

Common Forms of the Letter V

Handwritten Letters vary from person to person. *Manuscript* (printed) letters, *left,* have simple curves and straight lines. Cursive letters, *right,* have flowing lines.

Roman Letters have small finishing strokes called *serifs* that extend from the main strokes. The type face shown above is Baskerville. The italic form appears at the right.

Sans-Serif Letters are also called *gothic letters*. They have no serifs. The type face shown above is Futura. The italic form of Futura appears at the right.

Computer Letters have special shapes. Computers can "read" these letters either optically or by means of the magnetic ink with which the letters may be printed.

V-1, V-2. See Guided Missile (The First Guided Missiles); Rocket (Rockets of the Early 1900's).

V-E DAY, which stands for Victory in Europe Day, was officially proclaimed by President Harry S. Truman on Tuesday, May 8, 1945. It marked the surrender of the German armed forces and the end of the fighting against Germany.

The German surrender was signed at the headquarters of General Dwight D. Eisenhower in Reims, France, at 2:41 A.M. on May 7. Colonel General Alfred Jodl, chief of staff of the German armed forces, signed for Germany.   George E. Mowry

See also World War II (Victory in Europe).

V-J DAY, which stands for Victory over Japan Day, marked the end of World War II. At 7 P.M. on August 14, 1945, President Harry S. Truman announced that Japan had agreed to surrender unconditionally. Japan had been trying to end the war, and surrender rumors had raced through the United States for the four days before August 14.

September 2, 1945, has since been declared the official V-J Day. On that day, the Japanese signed the terms of surrender aboard the battleship U.S.S. *Missouri* in Tokyo Bay.   George E. Mowry

See also World War II (Victory in the Pacific).

VACA, ÁLVAR NÚÑEZ CABEZA DE. See Cabeza de Vaca, Álvar Núñez.

VACCINATION. See Immunization.

VACUUM is a space that has no matter in it. However, there is no such thing as a complete vacuum because no one has ever been able to remove all the air molecules in a space. A vacuum may also be described in terms of the pressure of the air or another gas that remains in a partially evacuated container. In this sense, a vacuum is any enclosed space in which pressure is less than *normal atmospheric pressure*. Normal atmospheric pressure is the pressure of the atmosphere at sea level—14.7 pounds per square inch (101.3 kilopascals).

Scientists speak of *high* or *low* vacuums, depending on how much gas has been removed from a container. The fewer the number of gas molecules in a container, the less the pressure is. The highest vacuum measured so far, approximately 0.0000000001 pascal, is only about one-quadrillionth of normal atmospheric pressure. Even at this extremely low pressure, 1 cubic inch (16 cubic centimeters) of gas contains about 540,000 molecules. In contrast, 1 cubic inch of air at normal atmospheric pressure contains about 410 billion billion gas molecules.

Various kinds of pumps are used to produce different degrees of vacuums. For example, a *diffusion pump* is used to attain high vacuums. This device sprays streams of vapor that sweep gas molecules out of the enclosed space. Lower vacuums can be produced by means of mechanical pumps equipped with rotors and valves.

Vacuums have many practical uses. Gases and liquids tend to flow from areas of high pressure to those of lower pressure—that is, into a vacuum. Drinking liquid through a straw involves this principle. Sucking on the straw produces a partial vacuum inside the mouth and in the top part of the straw. The greater pressure of the air outside pushes the liquid up the straw. A vacuum cleaner operates on the same basic principle. The cleaner has a fan that produces a vacuum inside of it. Air out-

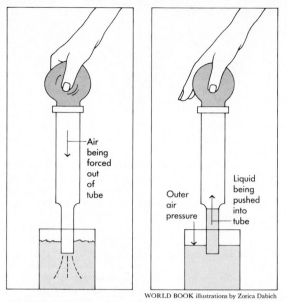

WORLD BOOK illustrations by Zorica Dabich

How a Vacuum Works is shown in these illustrations of a meat baster. When the bulb is squeezed, *left,* air is forced from the tube. When the bulb is released, *right,* the greater air pressure outside pushes liquid into the tube to fill the vacuum.

side the machine rushes in to fill the vacuum, carrying with it particles of dust and dirt.

A vacuum conducts heat poorly, and so it is an effective insulator. A thermos bottle used to keep liquids hot or cold consists of a double-walled container with a vacuum in the space between the walls. A similar type of vacuum bottle called a *Dewar flask* is used in laboratories to store extremely cold liquefied gases.

In a vacuum, water and many other liquids evaporate rapidly at a temperature much lower than their normal boiling point. For this reason, vacuum chambers are used in drying operations where it is essential to remove moisture from a substance quickly without burning it. Such operations include sugar refining and the freeze-drying of food.

Many kinds of electronic devices require a vacuum. The picture tube of a television set and the visual display of a computer system are familiar examples of vacuum tubes. The vacuum in such a tube allows beams of electrons to travel directly to the screen, where they form a picture. If too many air molecules were present in the tube, the electrons would collide with the molecules and scatter, destroying the picture.

Other kinds of devices, such as those employed in industry and scientific research, use vacuum tubes or chambers for a similar reason. For example, cyclotrons, synchrotrons, and other particle accelerators used to increase the energy level of atomic particles require extremely high vacuums.   Hugh D. Young

See also Thermos Bottle; Vacuum Cleaner; Vacuum Tube.

VACUUM BOTTLE. See Thermos Bottle.

VACUUM CLEANER is an electric appliance that cleans primarily by suction. Vacuum cleaners remove dirt and waste material from carpets, rugs, and bare floors. They also may be used to clean clothing, cur-

tains, furniture, machinery, woodwork, and other items.

A vacuum cleaner works by means of a suction fan, which creates a partial vacuum within the machine. Outside air, which always tries to fill a vacuum, flows rapidly into the cleaner, sweeping up loose dirt. A cloth or paper bag, or other container, traps the dirt, and the cleaned air is blown out of the machine. The container must be emptied or changed regularly. In some models, dirt is deposited in a tank of water, which filters out dust better than a bag does.

There are two main kinds of vacuum cleaners, *canisters*, or *tanks*, and *uprights*. A canister vacuum cleaner contains a bag and a powerful suction fan. Dirt is pulled into the bag through a flexible hose to which a variety of nozzles can be attached. An upright vacuum cleaner has a small fan and an *agitator* in its base. The agitator is a rotating cylinder with bristles that loosen dirt. Waste is sucked into a bag attached to the handle of the machine. Some cleaners combine various features of canisters and uprights. Such *combination vacuum cleaners* have both an agitator in their nozzle and a canister unit to provide powerful suction.

Other types of vacuum cleaners include *hand* models, *lightweight* models, and *wetvacs*. A hand vacuum cleaner can be carried easily in one hand. It is convenient for cleaning surfaces that cannot be reached with a conventional machine. A lightweight vacuum cleaner is used for light cleaning and dusting. It looks like an upright but weighs less, produces little suction, and has no agitator. A wetvac is a canister-type machine that cleans up liquids.

The first vacuum cleaning devices were developed

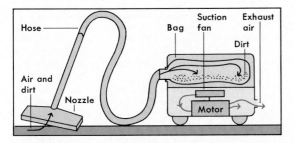

The Two Main Kinds of Vacuum Cleaners are the *canister, or tank,* and the *upright.* In a canister, *above,* a suction fan pulls dirt through a flexible hose and into a bag. In an upright, *below,* a suction fan draws in waste material that has been loosened by an *agitator,* a rotating cylinder with bristles.

WORLD BOOK diagrams by Arthur Grebetz

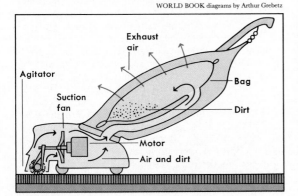

about 1900. Several inventors produced various types of vacuum cleaners in the early 1900's.   JANE GOLTERMANN

VACUUM GAUGE. See GAUGE.

VACUUM PUMP. See PUMP.

VACUUM TUBE is a device once widely used in such electronic equipment as radios, television sets, and computers. Vacuum tubes control the electric currents, called *electronic signals*, that are necessary to the operation of such equipment. The tubes help to create these signals, strengthen them, combine them, or separate them from one another.

The outer part of a vacuum tube consists of a tube-like glass or metal shell. Inside the shell are specially designed wires and small metal plates that control the electronic signals. The vacuum tube gets its name from the fact that almost all the air must be removed from the tube for it to work. A *partial vacuum* is created inside the tube by pumping out as much air as possible.

Vacuum tubes played an important part in the development of the science of electronics. From the 1920's through the 1950's, all electronic equipment used vacuum tubes. Since that time, the vacuum tube has been replaced in most kinds of electronic equipment by a newer device called the *transistor*. Transistors do the same jobs as vacuum tubes but are smaller and more reliable (see TRANSISTOR). Certain electronic equipment still uses various types of vacuum tubes. For example, the screen of a television set is one end of a large vacuum tube. See ELECTRONICS (Devices and Circuits).

How a Vacuum Tube Works. The outer part of most common vacuum tubes is a glass or metal container called an *envelope* or *bulb*. The envelope encloses two or more metal parts called *electrodes*. The electrodes create and control a flow of electrons within the tube. This flow of electrons corresponds to the electronic signal being controlled by the tube. The electrodes are connected to wires that pass through the *base* (bottom) of the envelope. Electronic signals enter and leave the vacuum tube by means of these wires.

Two basic electrodes in a vacuum tube are the *emitter*, or *cathode*, and the *collector*, or *anode*. The emitter gives off electrons. These electrons flow to the collector, which surrounds the emitter. The emitter has a coating that gives off electrons when it gets hot. Close to the emitter is a *filament* (glowing wire) much like the filament of a light bulb. Electricity from outside the tube flows through the filament and heats it. The filament heats the emitter, causing it to give off electrons.

The emitter usually has a negative electric charge and the collector usually has a positive charge. The electrodes get their charges from a battery or other source of direct current. The emitter's negative charge helps to push away the electrons produced by the emitter. This happens because electrons have a negative charge, and two negative charges—or two positive charges—always push away from each other. But a negative and a positive charge always attract each other. Thus, the positive collector attracts the negative electrons. In this way, a current of electrons flows from the emitter to the collector.

Another basic vacuum tube electrode is the *grid*. It consists of a wire mesh located between the emitter and the collector. The grid controls the amount of electrons

flowing through the tube. A strong negative charge on the grid prevents many of the electrons from reaching the collector. If the negative charge becomes weaker, more electrons get past the grid and reach the collector. The strength of the charge on the grid corresponds to the strength of the electronic signal entering the tube.

A vacuum tube may have several other parts between the emitter and collector. It may also have charged metal plates that can "bend" a stream of electrons created in the tube. Magnets outside the tube can also bend the stream of electrons.

Kinds of Vacuum Tubes. There are many hundreds of vacuum tubes having various sizes and functions. But electrical engineers classify all tubes into a few basic types. Receiving tubes, the kind once widely used in radio and television receiving sets, are classified by the number of electrodes they have. Receiving tubes include (1) *diodes* (two-electrode tubes), (2) *triodes* (three-electrode tubes), and (3) multielectrode tubes. Other types of tubes include (1) cathode-ray tubes, (2) microwave tubes, and (3) gas-filled tubes.

Diodes have only an emitter and a collector. These tubes are used chiefly as *rectifiers*. A rectifier changes alternating current into direct current. An alternating current is one that keeps reversing its direction of flow. An electrode connected to a source of alternating current gets a charge that constantly changes from positive to negative and back again. If an alternating current is sent to a diode, the tube will pass the current only when the emitter has a negative charge. This happens only when the current is flowing in one direction. Thus, the current leaving the tube is direct current.

Diodes were used in receiving sets as rectifiers and also as *detectors*. A detector changes the weak alternating current of the radio waves into direct

The Audion was the first vacuum tube that could strengthen an electronic signal. It made possible the development of electronics.

current, from which the receiver produces a sound or picture. See ELECTRONICS (Rectification).

Triodes have a grid, as well as an emitter and a collector. The triode *amplifies* (strengthens) weak signals. A weak signal connected to the grid controls the much larger current flowing from the emitter to the collector. The large current thus becomes a stronger copy of the signal on the grid. A triode can also produce an alternating current without using an outside signal. When the triode operates in this way, it is called an *oscillator*. See ELECTRONICS (Amplification; Oscillation).

Multielectrode tubes have more than one grid between the emitter and collector. Two important multielectrode tubes are the *tetrode* and *pentode*. A tetrode contains two grids—the basic one and a second grid called the *screen*. The screen prevents the tube from producing unwanted oscillations. A pentode has a third grid, called the *suppressor*. The suppressor improves the tube's amplifying power. Other multielectrode tubes have even more grids, but such tubes have limited use.

Cathode-ray tubes (CRT's) are used in electronic equipment to display pictures or other information. The picture tube of a television set is a CRT. In a radar set, a CRT shows tiny spots of light that locate the position of ships or airplanes. A CRT in an electronic instrument called an *oscilloscope* may display wavy-line "pictures" of electronic signals.

All CRT's work in basically the same way. The tube has a round or rectangular screen at one end. The tube tapers from the screen to a narrow neck at the opposite end. In the neck, there is a special type of emitter, called an *electron gun*. The electron gun "shoots" a beam of electrons toward the screen. Wherever the beam strikes the screen, it causes a special coating on the screen to glow. Electrically charged metal plates inside the CRT, or electromagnets outside the CRT, move the beam across the entire screen. The beam thus "paints" a picture on the screen with spots of light. See TELEVISION (The Picture Tube).

Microwave tubes produce or control radio waves of extremely high frequencies. Radar sets, long distance tele-

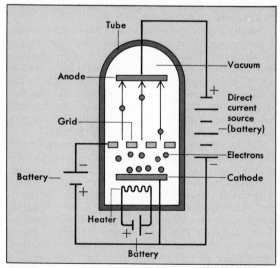

A Triode Vacuum Tube creates and controls a flow of electrons in a vacuum. The heater causes electrons to leave the cathode. A source of direct current connected to the tube pulls these electrons toward the anode. Voltage from a battery connected to the grid controls the number of electrons that reach the anode.

phone and television systems, and microwave ovens use such waves. Three types of microwave tubes are *klystrons*, *magnetrons*, and the *traveling-wave* tube.

Gas-filled tubes contain a small amount of such gases as argon, mercury vapor, and neon. These gases increase the amount of current that can flow through a tube. The atoms of gas become *ionized* by losing some of their electrons and thus becoming positively charged. The ionized atoms can carry much more electrical current than would otherwise flow through the tube. A typical gas-filled tube is the *thyratron*.

Development of the Vacuum Tube. Electrical experimenters began working with devices that resembled vacuum tubes during the mid-1800's. These devices were glass tubes with the air partially removed. The experimenters noticed a glow around the tubes, as well as other unusual effects, when electricity flowed through the tubes. See ELECTRONICS (Early Experiments).

The American inventor Thomas A. Edison invented the first electronic vacuum tube. But he did not realize the importance of his invention. In the early 1880's, Edison sealed an extra electrode into one of his electric lights. When the light was on, Edison found that a current flowed from the filament to the extra electrode. This phenomenon became known as the *Edison effect*. Edison failed to make any use of his discovery, which was actually a diode vacuum tube.

A British scientist, John Ambrose Fleming, experimented with the Edison effect. His experiments led him to develop a diode in 1904 to detect "wireless" radio signals. Fleming's *valve*, as he called his device, was the first practical radio tube.

In 1906, the American inventor Lee De Forest patented a two-electrode tube much like the Fleming valve. De Forest called his tube an *audion*. In 1907, De Forest patented an audion with a zigzag wire between the other two electrodes. This tube was the first triode.

In 1912, Harold D. Arnold, an American physicist, began experimenting with the audion. He changed its internal construction and removed as much air as possible to create a partial vacuum in the tube. In 1914, De Forest's audion worked successfully as an amplifier on a long-distance telephone line. Beginning in 1912, several inventors contributed to the development of the audion as an oscillator. They included De Forest and the American radio pioneer Edwin H. Armstrong. During World War I (1914-1918), Walter Schottky, a German physicist, invented an experimental four-element tube. From this tube, Albert W. Hull, an American engineer, developed a practical tetrode tube in 1924. A Dutch engineer, Benjamin D. H. Tellegen, invented the pentode in 1926.

Two vacuum tubes that represented significant steps in the development of television were invented in 1923. Vladimir K. Zworykin, a Russian-born American scientist, made the *iconoscope*—the first successful television camera tube. That same year, Zworykin built a workable television picture tube, the *kinescope*. His tubes were forms of the cathode-ray tube.

Electrical engineers turned their attention away from vacuum tubes after the transistor and similar devices were developed in the early 1950's. In the future, transistor devices are expected to replace all but a few vacuum tubes. BERNARD S. FINN

See also ELECTRONICS with its list of *Related Articles*.

VADUZ, *VAH doots* (pop. 4,704), is the capital of the principality of Liechtenstein. The city lies in an Alpine valley, in the shadow of high mountains (see LIECHTENSTEIN [map]). The major industry is cotton manufacturing. Vaduz was founded early in the Middle Ages, and many of the original buildings are still standing. The castle of the princes of Liechtenstein stands on a mountain high above the city. GEORGE KISH

VAGINITIS, *VAJ uh NY tihs*, is an inflammation of the vagina. It is characterized by itching and swelling, plus an abnormal vaginal discharge. The inflammation may also affect the *vulva*, the folds of skin outside the vagina. Vaginitis occurs most frequently during the childbearing years of women.

Most cases of vaginitis result from infection by certain bacteria, fungi, and protozoans. The infectious organisms produce great amounts of waste material that irritates the vagina and vulva, causing swelling and itching. One of the most common of the various bacteria that cause vaginitis is *Hemophilus vaginalis*. These bacteria cause the whitish, filmy fluid normally present in the vagina to thicken and turn gray or yellow. A fungus called *Candida*, also known as *Monilia*, turns the vaginal fluid thick and white. A protozoan called *Trichomonas* causes the fluid to turn yellow-green or gray and become thin and foamy.

The infectious bacteria, fungi, and protozoans may be present in the vagina without causing vaginitis. They are normally kept in balance so that none exists in harmful quantities. Vaginitis occurs when the balance is upset, allowing one or more of the organisms to reproduce in great numbers. The balance can be disturbed by many factors, including pregnancy, poor health or diet, lack of sleep, or the use of certain drugs. Cuts, scrapes, or irritation from laundry detergents or perfumed soaps or powders can increase the likelihood of vaginal infection.

A physician treats vaginitis by first examining the vaginal fluid to determine which organism is causing the infection. Certain antibiotics and other medicines are used to cure vaginitis. The infections discussed in this article have no permanent effect on a woman's ability to bear children. TIMOTHY T. MILLER

VAGRANCY, *VAY gruhn see*. A person who wanders from place to place, and who lives in idleness and without any settled home, is called a *vagrant*, or *vagabond*. Most states of the Union have laws against vagrancy, based on the idea that a vagrant has "no visible means of support" and may become a public charge. A person arrested for vagrancy may be sentenced to a term in jail. Law enforcement officers often arrest beggars and criminals as vagrants. FRED E. INBAU

VALDEZ, *val DEEZ*, Alaska (pop. 3,079), is the city in which the southern end of the Trans-Alaska pipeline is located. The pipeline carries oil about 800 miles (1,300 kilometers) to Valdez from Prudhoe Bay on the Arctic Coastal Plain (see ALASKA [political map]). The city has huge tanks that store the oil until tankers transport it to ports on the U.S. mainland. Valdez, which lies on the south-central coast of Alaska, is the northernmost ice-free port in North America.

Valdez grew rapidly during the mid-1970's, when large numbers of people moved there to work on the

pipeline. The population increased from only 1,005 in 1970 to about 8,300 in 1977, when the pipeline was completed. Many people then moved from Valdez, and the population decreased.

Valdez was founded in 1790 by the Spanish explorer Salvador Fidalgo. It was named for Antonio Valdes, a Spanish naval official. Through the years, Valdez has served as a fishing, shipping, and trading center for the surrounding area. In 1964, the city was heavily damaged by an earthquake. Valdez has a council-manager form of government.   CLINTON T. ANDREWS, JR.

VALENCE, *VAY luhns,* also called *valency,* is a number that indicates the ability of a chemical element to combine with other elements. In the past, valence had several slightly different meanings. The term is now gradually being replaced by more precise chemical descriptions.

Valence was first defined as the number of hydrogen atoms that can combine with each atom of an element. For example, each atom of oxygen can combine with two hydrogen atoms to form water (H_2O). Therefore, oxygen has a valence of two. A second definition of valence is based on the charges of ionized atoms. Sodium ions have one positive charge, so the valence of sodium is one. A third definition is based on the number of *bonds* (chemical links) that an atom forms with other atoms. Carbon atoms usually form four bonds, as in the compound *methane* (CH_4). As a result, carbon is said to have a valence of four. Many elements can combine in so many ways that they have several valences. Sulfur has common valences of 2, 4, and 6.   JOHN P. FACKLER, JR.

See also CHEMISTRY (Valence); BOND (chemical); LEWIS, GILBERT N.

VALENCIA, *vuh LEHN shee uh* (pop. 751,734), lies in the fertile northern part of Venezuela, a short distance from the coast. For location, see VENEZUELA (political map). It is the country's largest manufacturing center. Industries include sugar mills, textile mills, and tanneries. Valencia was founded in 1555.

VALENCIA, *vuh LEHN shee uh* (pop. 751,734), is the third largest city in Spain. Only Madrid and Barcelona are larger than Valencia. Valencia lies on the Turia River, 3 miles (5 kilometers) from the Mediterranean coast and its port of Villanueva del Grao (see SPAIN [political map]). Hundreds of years ago, the Romans built walls around their settlement at Valencia. These walls were torn down in 1871. A gate called Torres de Serranos was built in 1238. Two towers were added in the late 1300's, and restored in 1930.

The city is one of the railroad centers of eastern Spain, and carries on a large export trade in oranges and other fruits. Valencia is noted for its silk, colored tiles, tobacco, textiles, and iron and bronze wares. The city's products also include cement, furniture, musical instruments, paper, toys, and perfumes and cosmetics.

Valencia was long occupied by the Moors. It has rows of white houses built in the Moorish style, and many famous public buildings dating from the 1200's, although today much of the city is modern. The University of Valencia is well known.   STANLEY G. PAYNE

VALENS, *VAY luhnz* (A.D. 328-378), was the Roman emperor who allowed large numbers of barbarians to settle on Roman territory. In A.D. 376, the Visigoths,

threatened by other barbarians, sought refuge along the empire's northern boundaries. Valens let them settle there, hoping to integrate them into his army. But Roman officials mistreated the Visigoths, and they revolted. In 378, they killed Valens and destroyed his army at Adrianople (now Edirne, Turkey). The Visigoths soon became the first independent barbarian nation in the Roman Empire (see GOTHS). Valens was born in what is now Hungary. His brother, Emperor Valentinian I, named him co-emperor to administer the eastern provinces in 364. A believer in *Arian heresy,* which denied the divinity of Christ, Valens persecuted many orthodox Christians.   WILLIAM G. SINNIGEN

See also ARIANISM.

VALENTINE, SAINT, is the name associated with two martyrs of the early Christian church. Little is known about them. The Roman history of martyrs lists two Saint Valentines as having been martyred on February 14 by being beheaded. One supposedly died in Rome and the other at Interamna, now Terni, 60 miles (97 kilometers) from Rome. There is no conclusive evidence for doubting the existence of either man.

The Saint Valentine who died in Rome seems to have been a priest who suffered death during the persecution of Claudius the Goth about A.D. 269. A basilica was built in his honor in Rome in A.D. 350, and a catacomb containing his remains was found on this location.

Another history of martyrs mentions a Saint Valentine who was bishop of Interamna and who may have been martyred in Rome. By being remembered both in Rome and in Interamna, he may have come to be considered as two persons, but this is not entirely certain.

The custom of exchanging valentines on February 14 can be traced to the English poet, Geoffrey Chaucer. He mentioned that birds began to pair off on that day (see VALENTINE'S DAY).   JAMES A. CORBETT and FULTON J. SHEEN

VALENTINE'S DAY is a special day observed on February 14. On this day, people send greeting cards called *valentines* to their sweethearts, friends, and members of their families. Many valentines have romantic verses, and others have humorous pictures and sayings. Most say, "Be my valentine."

For weeks before February 14, stores sell valentines and valentine decorations. Schoolchildren decorate their classrooms with paper hearts and lace for the occasion. On Valentine's Day, many people give candy, flowers, and other gifts to their friends.

Valentine's Day Around the World

In the United States and Canada, children exchange valentines with their friends. In some schools, the children hold a classroom party and put all the valentines into a box they have decorated. At the end of the day, the teacher or one child distributes the cards. Many children make their own valentines from paper doilies, red paper, wallpaper samples, and pictures cut from magazines. Sometimes they buy kits that include everything needed to make valentines. Many children send their largest, fanciest cards to their parents and teachers.

Older students hold Valentine's Day dances and parties. They make candy baskets, gifts, and place cards trimmed with hearts and fat, winged children called *cupids.* Many people send flowers, a box of candy, or some other gift to their wives, husbands, or sweethearts.

WORLD BOOK photo

Modern Valentines include both humorous and romantic cards. Special ones are printed for sweethearts and for husbands, wives, and relatives. Most cards say, "Be my valentine."

Hallmark Historical Collection; Hallmark Cards (WORLD BOOK photo)

Three-Dimensional Valentines open to stand by themselves. They fold flat for mailing. Many of them, such as this German card from the late 1800's, are decorated with birds and flowers.

Most valentine candy boxes are heart-shaped and tied with red ribbon.

In Europe, people celebrate Valentine's Day in many ways. British children sing special Valentine's Day songs and receive gifts of candy, fruit, or money. In some areas of England, people bake valentine buns with caraway seeds, plums, or raisins. People in Italy hold a Valentine's Day feast.

In Great Britain and Italy, some unmarried women get up before sunrise on Valentine's Day. They stand by their window, sometimes for hours, watching for a man to pass. They believe that the first man they see, or someone who looks like him, will marry them within a year. William Shakespeare, the great English playwright, mentioned this belief in *Hamlet* (1603). Ophelia, a woman in the play, sings:

> Good morrow! 'Tis St. Valentine's Day
> All in the morning betime,
> And I a maid at your window,
> To be your valentine!

In Denmark, people send pressed white flowers called *snowdrops* to their friends. Danish men also send a type of valentine called a *gaekkebrev* (joking letter). The sender writes a rhyme but does not sign his name. Instead, he signs the valentine with dots, one dot for each letter of his name. If the woman who gets it guesses his name, he rewards her with an Easter egg on Easter. Some people in Great Britain also send valentines signed with dots.

History

Beginnings. Different authorities believe Valentine's Day began in various ways. Some trace it to an ancient Roman festival called *Lupercalia*. Other experts connect the event with one or more saints of the early Christian church. Still others link it with an old English belief that birds choose their mates on February 14. Valentine's Day probably came from a combination of all three of those sources—plus the belief that spring is a time for lovers.

The ancient Romans held the festival of Lupercalia on February 15 to ensure protection from wolves. During this celebration, young men struck people with strips of animal hide. Women took the blows because they thought that the whipping made them more fertile. After the Romans conquered Britain in A.D. 43, the British borrowed many Roman festivals. Many writers link the festival of Lupercalia with Valentine's Day because of the similar date and the connection with fertility.

The early Christian church had at least two saints named Valentine. According to one story, the Roman Emperor Claudius II in the A.D. 200's forbade young men to marry. The emperor thought single men made better soldiers. A priest named Valentine disobeyed the emperor's order and secretly married young couples.

Another story says Valentine was an early Christian who made friends with many children. The Romans imprisoned him because he refused to worship their gods. The children missed Valentine and tossed loving notes between the bars of his cell window. This tale may explain why people exchange messages on Valentine's Day. According to still another story, Valentine restored the sight of his jailer's blind daughter.

Many stories say Valentine was executed on Febru-

205

Valentines Through the Years

The custom of sending romantic messages on Valentine's Day may have begun as early as the 1400's. At first, people made their own valentines. Commercial cards were not printed until the early 1800's. Many early valentines were blank, with space for the sender to write his or her own message.

Smithsonian Magazine
(Charles H. Phillips)

The Oldest American Valentine is a handmade card from the early 1700's. It has a handwritten verse in German.

A Card by Louis Prang, a famous Boston card maker, dates from the late 1800's.

A Movable Card from the early 1900's has a boy whose left arm moves to reveal a valentine.

Romantic Valentines of the 1830's, such as this British card, featured brokenhearted lovers. Many of the verses were about love that was not returned.

Valentines by Kate Greenaway, a British artist, showed garden scenes. This card was printed in the 1880's by Marcus Ward & Company, a London greeting card company.

206

An American Valentine from the Civil War Period, which lasted from 1861 to 1865, has tent flaps that open. The photograph on the left shows the card closed. The one on the right shows the tent flaps open, revealing a Union soldier writing to his sweetheart at home.

A Card by Esther A. Howland, one of the first U.S. valentine manufacturers, dates from about 1850. This card has a lace frame and a stuffed satin center decorated with cutouts.

An American Valentine from the 1890's features lace, pansies, and a cupid, the symbol of love. The tiny printing above the cupid's head says, "To one I love."

ary 14 about A.D. 269. In A.D. 496, Pope Gelasius named February 14 as St. Valentine's Day.

In Norman French, a language spoken in Normandy during the Middle Ages, the word *galantine* sounds like *Valentine* and means *gallant* or *lover*. This resemblance may have caused people to think of St. Valentine as the special saint of lovers.

The earliest records of Valentine's Day in English tell that birds chose their mates on that day. People used a different calendar before 1582, and February 14 came on what is now February 24. Geoffrey Chaucer, an English poet of the 1300's, wrote in *The Parliament of Fowls*, "For this was on St. Valentine's Day, / When every fowl cometh there to choose his mate." Shakespeare also mentioned this belief in *A Midsummer Night's Dream*. A character in the play discovers two lovers in the woods and asks, "St. Valentine is past; / Begin these woodbirds but to couple now?"

Early Valentine Customs. People in England probably celebrated Valentine's Day as early as the 1400's. Some historians trace the custom of sending verses on Valentine's Day to a Frenchman named Charles, Duke of Orléans. Charles was captured by the English during the Battle of Agincourt in 1415. He was taken to England and put in prison. On Valentine's Day, he sent his wife a rhymed love letter from his cell in the Tower of London.

Many Valentine's Day customs involved ways that single women could learn who their future husbands would be. Englishwomen of the 1700's wrote men's names on scraps of paper, rolled each in a little piece of clay, and dropped them all into water. The first paper that rose to the surface supposedly had the name of a woman's true love.

Also in the 1700's, unmarried women pinned five bay leaves to their pillows on the eve of Valentine's Day. They pinned one leaf to the center of the pillow and one to each corner. If the charm worked, they saw their future husbands in their dreams.

In Derbyshire, a county in central England, young women circled the church 3 or 12 times at midnight and repeated such verses as:

> I sow hempseed.
> Hempseed I sow.
> He that loves me best,
> Come after me now.

Their true loves then supposedly appeared.

One of the oldest customs was the practice of writing women's names on slips of paper and drawing them from a jar. The woman whose name was drawn by a man became his *valentine*, and he paid special attention to her. Many men gave gifts to their valentines. In some areas, a young man gave his valentine a pair of gloves. Wealthy men gave fancy-dress balls to honor their valentines.

One description of Valentine's Day during the 1700's tells how groups of friends met to draw names. For several days, each man wore his valentine's name on his sleeve. The saying *wearing his heart on his sleeve* probably came from this practice.

The custom of sending romantic messages gradually replaced that of giving gifts. In the 1700's and 1800's, many stores sold handbooks called *valentine writers*. These books included verses to copy and various suggestions about writing valentines.

Commercial Valentines were first made in the early 1800's. Many of them were blank inside, with space for the sender to write a message. The British artist Kate Greenaway became famous for her valentines in the late 1800's. Many of her cards featured charming pictures of happy children and lovely gardens.

A woman named Esther A. Howland, of Worcester, Mass., became one of the first U.S. manufacturers of valentines. In 1847, after seeing a valentine from Great Britain, she decided to make some of her own. She made samples and took orders from stores. Then she hired a staff of young women and set up an assembly line to produce the cards. One woman glued on paper flowers, another added lace, and another painted leaves. Howland soon expanded her business into a $100,000-a-year enterprise.

Many valentines of the 1800's were hand painted. Some featured a fat cupid or showed arrows piercing a heart. Many cards had satin, ribbon, or lace trim. Others were decorated with dried flowers, feathers, imitation jewels, mother-of-pearl, sea shells, or tassels. Some cards cost as much as $10.

From the mid-1800's to the early 1900's, many people sent comic valentines called *penny dreadfuls*. These cards sold for a penny and featured such insulting verses as:

> 'Tis all in vain your simpering looks,
> You never can incline,
> With all your bustles, stays, and curls,
> To find a valentine.

Many penny dreadfuls and other old valentines have become collectors' items.   CAROL BAIN

See also LUPERCALIA; VALENTINE, SAINT.

Additional Resources

BARTHA, EDNA. *Hearts, Cupids, and Red Roses: The Story of the Valentine Symbols.* Clarion, 1982. Reprint of 1974 ed.

CORWIN, JUDITH. *Valentine Fun.* Simon & Schuster, 1982. Includes a brief history of Valentine's Day and directions for projects.

YAROSLAVA, ed. (pseud. of Yaroslava Surmach Mills). *I Like You, and Other Poems for Valentine's Day.* Scribner, 1976.

VALENTINE'S DAY MASSACRE. See CHICAGO (The Roaring Twenties).

VALENTINIAN was the name of three western Roman emperors. Two of them were important.

Valentinian I (A.D. 321-375) was born in Pannonia (now parts of Austria, Hungary, and Yugoslavia) to a poor family. He became a famous army officer. In A.D. 364, he was chosen emperor after the death of Jovian. Valentinian appointed his brother Valens coruler, and gave him the eastern provinces to rule. Valentinian was a capable emperor who ruled with absolute power. He tried to protect the poor from dishonest government officials and powerful senators. He allowed his people almost complete religious freedom. Throughout his reign, the Alamanni, the German tribes in the north, and the desert tribes in Africa rebelled, and he fought many wars against them. He died during a campaign against the Quadi, a German tribe living in what is now a region in Czechoslovakia called Moravia.

Valentinian III (A.D. 419-455) was the son of the Emperor Constantius and grandson of Theodosius I. He became emperor in 425, at the age of six. His mother, Galla Placidia, governed for him during his boyhood.

He became so dependent on her that after she died he was a weak and purposeless ruler. When barbarians attacked the West Empire on all sides, Valentinian's general, Flavius Aëtius, won great victories over the Huns and Visigoths in Gaul (now France). But the empire was too weak to resist fully, and was gradually broken up. The Vandals conquered Africa, the Scots and Picts won Britain, and the Visigoths and the Suevi took over much of Spain and Gaul. Valentinian levied high taxes to replace the lost revenues from these provinces, and the people grew rebellious. In 454, Valentinian had Aëtius murdered, and a year later he was assassinated by Aëtius' followers.　WILLIAM G. SINNIGEN

VALENTINO, RUDOLPH (1895-1926), was the most popular romantic star of American silent motion pictures. He gained fame for his roles as a handsome, passionate lover.

Wide World
Rudolph Valentino

Valentino's real name was Rodolfo d'Antonguolla. He was born in Castellaneta, Italy, near Taranto. He came to New York City in 1913 and worked briefly as a gardener and laborer. Valentino then toured the country as a dancer in stage musicals. He probably began his film career in *Alimony* (1918). He became a star in *The Four Horsemen of the Apocalypse* (1921). Valentino played a desert warrior in *The Sheik* (1921) and *Son of the Sheik* (1926) and portrayed a bullfighter in *Blood and Sand* (1922). His other films included *Camille* (1921), *Monsieur Beaucaire* (1924), *Cobra* (1925), and *The Eagle* (1925). He died at the age of 31 following surgery for peritonitis.　CHARLES CHAMPLIN

Additional Resources

TAJIRI, VINCENT. *Valentino.* Bantam, 1977.
WALKER, ALEXANDER. *Rudolph Valentino.* Stein & Day, 1976.

VALERA, EAMON DE. See DE VALERA, EAMON.

VALERIAN, *vuh LIHR ee uhn,* family includes more than 300 different kinds of perennial or annual herbs and some shrubs. These grow mostly in the Northern Hemisphere. Several members of this family are grown as garden or border flowers, and two as potherbs for flavoring food.

One group of valerians has strong-smelling underground parts. Its flowers are small and colored white or reddish. A well-known species is the *common valerian,* or *garden heliotrope.* It yields an oil used in medicine.

The two species grown as potherbs are called *corn salad,* or *lamb's-lettuce,* and *Italian corn salad.* Both grow about 1 foot (30 centimeters) high. They are native to southern Europe, but corn salad has been introduced in Central Europe and North America. Italian corn salad has pink flowers. Corn salad has blue flowers. Both are grown in spring and fall. Plants should be about 6 inches (15 centimeters) apart.

Scientific Classification. Valerians belong to the valerian family, Valerianaceae. Common valerian is *Valeriana officinalis;* corn salad is *Valerianella olitoria;* Italian corn salad is *Valerianella eriocarpa.*　THEODOR JUST

VALÉRY, *vah lay REE,* **PAUL** (1871-1945), was a French poet. He wrote two famous long poems, *The Young Fate* (1917) and *The Graveyard by the Sea* (1920), and a collection of shorter poems, *Charmes* (1922). Valéry completed few poems because he believed that poets should work carefully and deliberately rather than be guided by inspiration. He thought that a bad poem resulting from long, careful calculation was better than a masterpiece resulting from chance. Valéry's model of the perfect artist was Leonardo da Vinci. In the essay *Introduction to the Method of Leonardo da Vinci* (1895), he maintained that structure is the basic quality of artistic creation and compared the work of the poet to that of the engineer.

Most of Valéry's nonfiction reflects the attitude of the late 1800's that only through a thorough knowledge of oneself can a person understand the universal psyche. In his book *Regarding the Real World* (1931), Valéry viewed modern man as a Hamlet wavering between self-destruction and self-preservation.　ANNA BALAKIAN

See also FRENCH LITERATURE (The Four Masters).

VALHALLA, *val HAL uh,* was the great hall of the dead heroes in Norse mythology. The word means *Hall of the Slain.* It was the most magnificent palace in Asgard, and Odin feasted there with his heroes.

Valhalla had walls of gold and a roof of battle shields. Huge spears held up its ceiling. They were so highly polished that the gleam from them was the only light needed. The 540 doors were so wide that 800 men could enter side by side. The guests sat at long tables. They were the dead heroes who had been brought to Valhalla by the Valkyries, or battle maidens. The Valkyries waited on the tables and served luxurious food.

The heroes rode out to the battlefield to fight every morning. They often wounded each other terribly, but their hurts were healed before they returned to Valhalla for the noonday feast.　PADRAIC COLUM

See also ODIN; VALKYRIE.

VALKYRIE, *val KIHR ee,* was one of the warlike goddess-maidens of Norse mythology. The Valkyries rode on swift horses and were armed with spears, shields, and helmets. Odin sent them to battlefields to choose dead heroes, take them to Valhalla, and serve them feasts. The name means *those who choose the fallen.* Brunhild, the maiden Sigurd awakened from a magic sleep, was a Valkyrie. Richard Wagner built his opera *Die Walküre* around this theme. See also BRUNHILD; ODIN; OPERA (*Ring of the Nibelung, The*); VALHALLA.　EINAR HAUGEN

VALLANDIGHAM, *vuh LAN dih guhm,* **CLEMENT LAIRD** (1820-1871), an Ohio politician, criticized President Abraham Lincoln's Civil War policies. Vallandigham was one of the best known of the northern Copperheads or Peace Democrats. He favored compromise with the South, and was arrested and charged with treason in 1863. President Lincoln banished him to the Confederacy, but he escaped to Canada.

Vallandigham was born in New Lisbon, Ohio. He served in the Ohio state legislature in 1845 and 1846, and in the U.S. Congress from 1858 to 1863. During his exile in 1863, Ohio Democrats nominated him for governor, but he lost the election. Vallandigham returned to the United States in 1864, but he never regained political prominence.　FRANK L. KLEMENT

VALLE, JOSÉ CECILIO DEL

VALLE, *VAH yay,* **JOSÉ CECILIO DEL** (1780-1834), a Central American patriot and statesman, wrote the Central American Declaration of Independence, proclaiming freedom from Spain on Sept. 15, 1821. He became a leader of Guatemala's independence movement in 1821. Mexico annexed Guatemala in 1822, and imprisoned Valle briefly. He was elected vice-president of the Central American Confederation in 1823, but refused to serve. Valle was born in Honduras.   HARVEY L. JOHNSON

VALLETTA, *vahl LEHT tah* (pop. 14,249), is the capital and chief seaport of Malta. It lies on a narrow peninsula between the harbors on Malta's northeast coast. Valletta is the administrative, cultural, and commercial center of Malta. Valletta is the home of the Royal Malta Library. The Royal University of Malta, the island's only university, is at Msida, just outside Valletta. The Cathedral of Saint John and the Palace of the Grand Masters (now the governor general's residence) are among the city's sights.

Valletta became the capital of Malta in 1571. It had been founded about five years earlier. Valletta was named for Jean Parisot de la Vallette, grand master of the Knights of Malta. The British maintained a naval base at Valletta from the early 1800's until 1979.

See also MALTA (map; picture).

VALLEY is a natural trough in the earth's surface. It is the most important feature of the landscape. Systems of valleys extend through plains, hills, and mountains. Streams and rivers flowing through valleys drain interior land regions to the ocean. Many valleys have fertile soil and make excellent farmland.

All valleys are similar in shape. The bottom of a valley is called its *floor*. The floor usually slopes gradually in one general direction. Mountain valleys usually have narrow floors. But in low-lying plains, a valley floor may be several miles or kilometers wide. The part of the valley floor along river banks is called the *flood plain*. The flood plain is part of the river channel, but it is used only during a flood. Buildings on the flood plain may be damaged when the river floods. A valley's sides are called *valley walls* or *valley slopes*. The ridge formed where the walls of neighboring valleys meet is a *divide*.

Kinds of Valleys. Various kinds of valleys are named according to their appearance. A deep valley with steep walls is called a *canyon*. One of the most famous canyons is Grand Canyon in Arizona. Along coastlines, valleys that are flooded by the ocean are called *drowned valleys*. Chesapeake Bay and Delaware Bay are drowned valleys. Where a valley joins a larger valley from the side, the two floors usually meet at the same level. But sometimes the floor of the side valley is higher than the floor of the main valley where they join. The side valley is then called a *hanging* valley. A river flowing through a hanging valley may form a waterfall where the water enters the main valley.

Not all valleys are on land. Many deep *submarine* canyons are found on the slopes leading up from the ocean floor to the edge of the continental shelf. Hudson Canyon is a submarine canyon. It extends south-eastward down the continental shelf to the Atlantic Ocean floor from a point near New York City.

How Valleys Are Formed. Most valleys on dry land are formed by the running water of streams and rivers,

and by the erosion of slopes leading to them. Erosion moves material down the slopes to the valley floor where the stream carries it to a lake or to the ocean. In addition, the stream may erode its channel deeper.

A valley may also be formed when a long, narrow section of the earth's crust sinks below the surrounding area. A valley formed in this way is called a *rift valley*. One system of rift valleys extends about 4,000 miles (6,400 kilometers) from the Sea of Galilee south through the Red Sea, and into southeastern Africa.

Glaciated valleys are valleys that were enlarged by the action of glaciers. These valleys are often found high in mountains. They are U-shaped rather than V-shaped.   SHELDON JUDSON

Related Articles in WORLD BOOK include:

Canyon	Imperial Valley
Death Valley	Ocean (illustration: The
Delaware Water Gap	Land Beneath the Oceans)
Erosion	Shenandoah Valley
Hanging Valley	Valley of the Kings
Ice Age (Effects of the	Wyoming Valley
Ice Sheets)	

VALLEY FORGE, Pa., is an area along the Schuylkill River, about 25 miles (40 kilometers) west of Philadelphia. General George Washington and his men camped there in the winter of 1777 and 1778, during the Revolutionary War. These months were discouraging for the Americans. Washington's Continental Army had to endure several months of suffering.

Conditions at Valley Forge. Washington led his troops to Valley Forge after his defeats at Brandywine and Germantown, Pa. These defeats left Philadelphia under British control.

Washington's soldiers had little food, and too little clothing to protect themselves from the cold. The Continental Congress could not provide additional supplies to fill the soldiers' needs. The army of about 11,000 lived in crude log huts that they built themselves. On Dec. 23, 1777, Washington wrote: "We have this day no less than 2,873 men in camp unfit for duty because they are barefooted and otherwise naked."

More than 3,000 soldiers died during this period. Many others were either too weak or too sick to fight, because of a smallpox epidemic. But the people around Valley Forge enjoyed all the comforts of a rich countryside, because little fighting took place at this time. The British lived a carefree life in Philadelphia.

The winter at Valley Forge tested the loyalty of the American troops. Only dedicated patriots stayed with the Continental Army. Many people criticized Washington, but he held his position at Valley Forge throughout the winter and spring. In spite of all the difficulties, he improved his troops with the help of Baron von Steuben, a former Prussian soldier. Steuben drilled the soldiers in a system of field formations. By spring, Washington had a disciplined, well-trained army. The news of the alliance between France and the United States reached Valley Forge on May 6, 1778. It cheered Washington, and helped him to move successfully against the British in June.

Valley Forge National Historical Park covers the campsite. For area, see NATIONAL PARK SYSTEM (table: National Historical Parks). The park's buildings and monuments were built in memory of Washington's Continental Army. The old stone house he used as headquarters still stands there. Other buildings in the park in-

Soldiers at Valley Forge, cold, hungry, and sick, endured what has been often called the "Winter of Despair" in 1777 and 1778.

clude the Washington Memorial Chapel, National Memorial Arch, Cloister of Colonies, and Valley Forge Museum of Natural History.   WILLIAM MORGAN FOWLER, JR.

See also REVOLUTIONARY WAR IN AMERICA; WASHINGTON, GEORGE; STEUBEN, BARON VON.

VALLEY OF TEN THOUSAND SMOKES. See KATMAI NATIONAL PARK.

VALLEY OF THE KINGS is a rocky, narrow gorge, which was used as a cemetery by the *pharaohs* (kings) of ancient Egypt between 1550 and 1100 B.C. The Valley, sometimes called the Valley of the Tombs of the Kings, lies on the west bank of the Nile River at Thebes. Sixty-two tombs have been discovered in the Valley of the Kings and in the adjoining Western Valley.

The tombs are in the form of corridors and chambers cut into rock. Carved and painted religious scenes and hieroglyphic texts cover the walls. The art work deals mainly with the activities of a dead king in the hereafter. The tomb of Seti I, discovered in 1817, is the largest and most ornate tomb. Other tombs in the Valley include those of Tutankhamen, Thutmose III, Ramses II, and Ramses III.   LEONARD H. LESKO

VALMY, BATTLE OF. See ARMY (table: Famous Land Battles).

VALOIS, *vah LWAH,* was the family name of a branch of the great Capetian line of French kings (see CAPETIAN DYNASTY). The House of Valois ruled France from 1328 to 1589. Philip VI, the first of the Valois kings, came to the throne after Charles IV died. Charles VIII died in 1498 without any sons, and the throne passed to Louis, Duke of Orléans. He died in 1515 without a male heir and the throne passed to Francis of Angoulême. Francis was crowned Francis I and became the first of the Angoulême branch of the House of Valois. Henry III, who died in 1589, was the last of the Angoulêmes, and Henry IV, who followed him, was the first Bourbon.   FRANKLIN D. SCOTT

See also CHARLES (VIII); FRANCIS (I) of France; HENRY (III) of France; LOUIS (XII); PHILIP (VI).

VALPARAÍSO, *vahl pah rah EE soh* or *VAL puh RY soh* (pop. 266,876), is the principal seaport and third largest city of Chile. Valparaíso lies on a wide inlet of the Pacific Ocean about 70 miles (110 kilometers) northwest of Santiago. For location, see CHILE (political map). *Valparaíso* is Spanish for *Valley of Paradise.*

Valparaíso is a modern and progressive city, and an important manufacturing center. The chief products include cotton goods, machinery, tobacco, refined sugar, and liquor. The city has many fine public buildings and schools. An electric railroad joins Valparaíso with Santiago, and another line joins the city with the mining section of inland Chile. In 1906, a severe earthquake destroyed parts of the city.   KALMAN H. SILVERT

See also SOUTH AMERICA (picture: Steamships).

VALUE, in economics, means the power of a commodity to command other commodities in exchange. Value relates to the terms upon which one commodity exchanges for others. It must not be confused with price. A commodity's *price* means its exchange power in terms of money (see PRICE). Its *value* means its exchange power in terms of other commodities.

Value and Utility. In order to possess value, an article must have *utility.* That is, it must have the power to satisfy a want. For example, farm products always have value because everyone desires them. So farmers can usually find a market for their products. The desire for articles must be backed by purchasing power. No article will have any value if those who want it have no money or commodities to offer in exchange for it.

A thing may have great value and still be used in ways which harm humanity. For example, drugs and alcohol possess great utility. They are of benefit when used properly. But they become harmful when people misuse them or become addicted to them.

Value and Scarcity. In order to possess value, an article must be scarce. That is, it must be so limited in quantity that those who have it are able to get something else in exchange for it. Air, which has great utility, seldom has any value. There is so much of it that ordinarily everyone can have all he wants without having to pay anyone for it. But under certain conditions, air does have value. A good illustration is compressed air, which is bought and sold.   HAROLD G. MOULTON

VALUE, in color. See COLOR (The Munsell Color System; illustration).

VALUE ADDED BY MANUFACTURE is a statistic used to measure and compare manufacturing activity. For example, if a state had a total value added by manufacture of $10 billion in 1965 and $20 billion in 1975, its manufacturing activity has doubled. Value added by manufacture is one of the chief measures of economic activity used by the U.S. government.

Value added by manufacture is the increase in value of raw material after it becomes a finished product. It

VALUE-ADDED TAX

represents the effect of manufacturing in terms of money. To compute this value, economists subtract the cost of materials, supplies, containers, fuel, electricity, and contract work from the value of manufactured products as they leave the factory.   LEONARD S. SILK

VALUE-ADDED TAX is a tax imposed by a government at each stage in the production of a good or service. The tax is paid by every company that handles a product during its transformation from raw materials to finished goods. The amount of the tax is determined by the amount of the value that a company adds to the materials and services it buys from other firms.

Suppose that a company making scratch pads buys paper, cardboard, and glue worth $1,000. Then it spends an additional $100 on rent, telephone calls, and delivery costs. It sells the scratch pads for $1,600. The company would pay a value-added tax on $500. This figure is arrived at by subtracting the cost of materials ($1,000) and operating expenses ($100) from the sale price ($1,600). Thus, $1,600 − 1,000 − 100 = $500.

Most firms that pay a value-added tax try to pass this expense on to the next buyer. As a result, most of the burden of this tax eventually falls on the consumer. The tax is levied at a fixed percentage rate and applies to all goods and services. In 1954, France became the first nation to adopt a value-added tax. Several other European countries have since done so.   JOHN R. COLEMAN

VALVE is a term used for various mechanical devices which open and close to control the flow of fluids in pipes and vessels. The term also is used in physiology for natural growths in the body which serve much the same purpose as mechanical valves. Among these are the valves of the heart, which open and close to control the flow of blood through the chambers of the heart.

There are also several types of mechanical valves, including the *automatic*, the *nonautomatic*, and *slide* valves.

Automatic valves are opened and closed by the pressure and back pressure of the fluid. The valve proper is a little gate which swings open on one side of an opening. When the liquid pressure is behind the valve, the pressure forces the valve open, and pushes through. Then pressure on the other side forces the valve back against the opening, closing the valve. The valves in the heart operate in this way. Nonautomatic valves are operated by an outside force. The valve in a common water faucet is opened and shut by turning a handle.

A slide valve works like the valve on a steam-engine cylinder. The moving part of the valve slides back and forth across the openings made in the cylinder, opening and closing them by changing the direction of motion of the sliding part of the valve.   OTTO A. UYEHARA

See also CARBURETOR; GASOLINE ENGINE; SAFETY VALVE.

VAMPIRE is a corpse that supposedly returns to life at night to suck people's blood. According to many folk stories, a vampire must have a constant supply of fresh blood obtained by biting the neck of sleeping victims. The victims lose strength, die, and become vampires themselves.

Stories of vampirelike creatures have come from many parts of the world. But most vampire tales originated in Eastern European and Balkan countries, such as Albania, Greece, Hungary, and Romania. There are

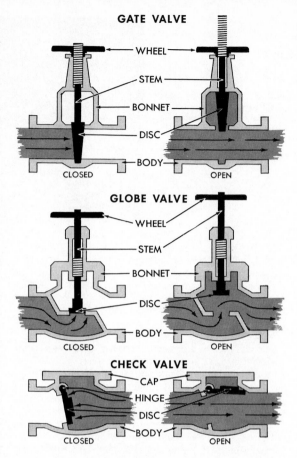

Principal Types of Valves. The nonautomatic gate and globe valves are used to turn on or shut off the flow of liquids. The check (automatic valve) allows a liquid to flow in one direction, but it closes shut to stop flow in the opposite direction.

many superstitions about vampires. People who commit suicide, die violently, or are condemned by their church supposedly become vampires. According to folklore, a vampire can be destroyed by driving a wooden stake through its heart. In Europe, from the late 1600's to the early 1800's, people dug up graves looking for vampires.

The horror novel *Dracula* (1897), by the English author Bram Stoker, ranks as the most famous vampire story. Stoker based the character of Dracula on an actual person, Vlad Tepes, a cruel prince from Walachia (now part of Romania). Vlad was nicknamed Dracula, which in Romanian means *son of the devil* or *son of a dragon*. A number of motion pictures have been made about Dracula.   ALAN DUNDES

See also STOKER, BRAM.

VAMPIRE BAT is the name given several different bats. The name is given particularly to certain bats in Central America and tropical America, which attack men, fowl, and other warm-blooded animals, and drink their blood. The best known is the *common vampire bat*, a small reddish-brown animal about 3 inches (8 centimeters) long. It has very sharp triangular-shaped front teeth, which cut like a razor. Its esophagus is short and narrow, and will permit nothing but fluids to pass.

Vampire bats sometimes attack persons who are sleeping. The bite itself is harmless and soon heals, but many vampire bats carry rabies. Vampire bats have destroyed livestock and other animals in some localities, and have also infected humans.

Weird stories have been told about the viciousness of these mammals. Their peculiar name comes from the superstitious legends about the vampire, an imaginary being that sucked the blood from humans.

William A. Wimsatt &
David G. Allen

Vampire Bat

Scientific Classification. True vampire bats make up the vampire bat family, Desmodontidae. They form three genera, *Desmodus, Diaemus,* and *Diphylla.* The common vampire bat is genus *Desmodus.*   FRANK B. GOLLEY

See also BAT; VAMPIRE; STOKER, BRAM.

VANADIUM, *vuh NAY dee uhm,* a chemical element, is a silvery-white metal that is used to toughen steel and other metals. Mixtures of vanadium and other metals form very strong alloys (see ALLOY). Vanadium resists attack from many chemicals, and its alloys do not rust. Vanadium steels are used to make automobile frames, gears, springs, and axles. Carbon-vanadium steels are used to make locomotive parts.

Vanadium remains strong at high temperatures and conducts heat rapidly. It also allows atomic particles called *neutrons* to pass through it. For these reasons, vanadium is used in some atomic reactors.

Vanadium never occurs as a metal. It is found combined with other elements. Sources of vanadium include the minerals patronite, a combination of vanadium and sulfur; vanadinite, a combination of lead, chlorine, and vanadium; and carnotite, a compound of uranium and vanadium.

Most commercial vanadium is made from patronite. Patronite is heated to remove the sulfur, and sodium carbonate is added to form sodium vanadate (Na_3VO_4). Sulfuric acid is then added, causing the vanadium to combine with oxygen and form vanadium pentoxide (V_2O_5). The pentoxide is heated with carbon or aluminum in order to remove the oxygen and leave fairly pure vanadium.

Small amounts of pure vanadium can be prepared by the iodide-decomposition process. This process is based on the thermal decomposition of vanadium iodide (VI_2) on an electrically heated filament.

Vanadium forms few compounds. Vanadium pentoxide is used in the chemical industry as a *catalyst,* a substance that speeds up certain chemical reactions. Vanadium pentoxide is also used as a *mordant* (colorfixer) in dyeing, and to make the dye aniline black.

Vanadium has the chemical symbol V. Its atomic number is 23 and its atomic weight is 50.9415. Vanadium melts at 1890° C ($+10°$ C) and boils at about 3000° C. It was first discovered in 1801 by Andrés del Río of Mexico, who called it *erythronium.* Later, he thought erythronium was only impure chromium. Nils Sefström, a Swedish chemist, rediscovered the element in 1830, and called it vanadium.   ALAN DAVISON

VAN ALLEN, JAMES ALFRED (1914-   ), a physicist, discovered the Van Allen belts, two zones of electrically charged particles that surround the earth. His team of scientists used data from the United States Explorer and Pioneer satellites to make the discovery in 1958. See VAN ALLEN BELTS.

Van Allen was born in Mount Pleasant, Iowa, and graduated from Iowa Wesleyan College and the University of Iowa. He became head of the University of Iowa department of physics and astronomy in 1951. He was one of the chief planners of the International Geophysical Year of 1957-1958.   R. T. ELLICKSON

VAN ALLEN BELTS are two zones of electrically charged particles that surround the earth high above its surface. The belts were named for James A. Van Allen, an American physicist, who discovered the first of the zones in 1958. He based his discovery on data sent by *Explorer I,* America's first space satellite.

The Van Allen belts surround the earth somewhat like doughnuts. The inner belt extends from about 600 to 3,000 miles (1,000 to 5,000 kilometers) above the earth. The outer belt reaches from about 9,300 to 15,500 miles (15,000 to 25,000 kilometers).

Astronomers originally thought the belts consisted of radiation and called them Van Allen radiation belts. The scientists later determined that the belts contained high concentrations of charged particles, such as protons and electrons. The earth's magnetic field traps such particles and directs them toward the magnetic poles. The trapped particles move in spiral paths along a system of imaginary lines of the magnetic field. These lines, called *flux lines,* curve from the north magnetic pole to the south magnetic pole. As particles approach either pole, the converging lines of the magnetic field reflect them back toward the opposite pole. This "magnetic mirror" effect keeps particles in the Van Allen belts bouncing between the poles. The belts acquire new particles from the *solar wind,* a continuous stream of charged particles from the sun. Violent eruptions on the sun's surface called *solar flares* provide additional particles.

Intense solar activity disrupts the Van Allen belts and leads to *magnetic storms* (see MAGNETIC STORM). Disruptions of the belts also interfere with radio reception, cause surges in power transmission lines, and produce auroras.   JAY M. PASACHOFF

See also EARTH (diagram: The Earth Has a Magnetic "Tail"); VAN ALLEN, JAMES A.; AURORA.

VANBRUGH, *van BROO,* **SIR JOHN** (1664-1726), was an English playwright and architect. He was the last of the Restoration period writers who satirized the manners of his day. In his first and most famous play, *The Relapse* (1696), he attacked the preference for sentimentality in drama. Aside from *The Provoked Wife* (1697), his other plays are adaptations from the French. They are carelessly written, but contain passages of genuine wit.

Vanbrugh was more successful as an architect. He designed Blenheim Palace in Oxfordshire and the Queen's Theater in London, and helped design the Clarendon Building in Oxford. The Queen's Theater was an ornate structure that was used for opera and pantomime in the 1700's. Vanbrugh was born in London.   ALAN S. DOWNER

MARTIN VAN BUREN

W. Van Buren

Oil painting on canvas (1864) by George Peter Alexander Healy;
© White House Historical Association (National Geographic Society)

The United States Flag had 25
stars when Van Buren took office.

J. Q. ADAMS
6th President
1825—1829

JACKSON
7th President
1829—1837

W. H. HARRISON
9th President
1841

TYLER
10th President
1841 — 1845

8TH PRESIDENT OF THE UNITED STATES 1837-1841

VAN BUREN, MARTIN (1782-1862), ran for President three times, but won only the first time. He served during the nation's first great depression, the Panic of 1837. The panic brought financial ruin and misery to millions. Many turned to the government for help, but Van Buren refused all public aid. He believed in Thomas Jefferson's theories that government should play the smallest possible role in American life. "The less government interferes," Van Buren explained, "the better for general prosperity."

Van Buren's erect bearing and high, broad forehead gave him a dignified appearance. He had served as Vice-President under Andrew Jackson, and, as President, Van Buren inherited much of Jackson's popularity. But during the three years of the panic, Van Buren bore the anger of a disappointed people. His enemies accused him of being a sly, scheming politician. They called him "The Little Magician" and "The Fox of Kinderhook." They ridiculed his courteous manners. When Van Buren continued to deal politely with his political rivals, they said this showed his lack of deep convictions.

By defending his Jeffersonian ideals, Van Buren demonstrated that actually he had both deep convictions and courage. Partly because he refused to compromise, Van Buren was defeated for re-election in 1840 by William Henry Harrison, whom he had beaten in 1836. Van Buren ran again for President in 1848, but finished a poor third.

In Van Buren's time, Washington, D.C., was still a city of muddy streets and few trees. One traveler said: "It looks as if it had rained naked buildings upon an open plain." But life in the capital reflected the excitement of a growing country. The first railroad into Washington was completed in time to bring visitors from New York City and Philadelphia to Van Buren's inauguration. Frontiersmen such as Sam Houston mingled with courtly Southerners and proper New Englanders. Washington hostesses sought out the popular author, Washington Irving, for their dinner parties. Out West, the frontier town of Chicago became an incorporated city, and the Republic of Texas began its fight for statehood.

Early Life

Childhood and Education. Martin Van Buren was born in the Dutch community of Kinderhook, N.Y., on Dec. 5, 1782. He was the third of the five children of Abraham and Maria Hoes Van Buren. Martin had an older brother and sister, and two younger brothers. His mother was the widow of Johannes Van Alen, and had three other children by her first marriage. Abraham Van Buren ran a truck farm and a tavern. As a child, Martin enjoyed listening to the tavern patrons as they argued politics in the Dutch language.

—— IMPORTANT DATES IN VAN BUREN'S LIFE ——

1782 (Dec. 5) Born in Kinderhook, N.Y.
1807 (Feb. 21) Married Hannah Hoes.
1812 Elected to the New York Senate.
1819 (Feb. 5) Hannah Hoes Van Buren died.
1821 Elected to the United States Senate.
1828 Elected Governor of New York.
1829 Appointed Secretary of State.
1832 Elected Vice-President of the United States.
1836 Elected President of the United States.
1840 Defeated for re-election by William H. Harrison.
1848 Nominated for President by the Free Soil party.
1862 (July 24) Died in Kinderhook, N.Y.

214

Martin attended the village school. At the age of 14, he began to study law under Francis Sylvester, a local attorney. He showed great talent, and Sylvester soon let him work in court. Martin first took part in a court trial at the age of 15. Another lawyer from Sylvester's office had tried the case. As he was about to sum up his arguments, he turned to Martin and said: "Here, Mat, sum up. You may as well begin early." The boy was rewarded that day with a silver half dollar. He soon became a familiar sight in the village court.

In 1801, Van Buren moved to New York City to continue his studies. He was admitted to the bar in 1803, and opened a law office in Kinderhook with his half brother, James I. Van Alen.

Van Buren's Family. On Feb. 21, 1807, Martin Van Buren married his distant cousin and childhood sweetheart, Hannah Hoes (March 8, 1783-Feb. 5, 1819). Mrs. Van Buren died 18 years before her husband became President. The couple had four sons. Abraham, the eldest, was his father's White House secretary, and later

served on the staff of General Zachary Taylor during the Mexican War. John, the second son, became attorney general of New York.

Political and Public Career

Van Buren's enthusiasm for the ideas of Thomas Jefferson took him into politics as a Democratic-Republican (see DEMOCRATIC-REPUBLICAN PARTY). He was elected to the New York senate in 1812. Shortly after his re-election to the senate in 1816, Van Buren was appointed attorney general of New York.

U.S. Senator. In 1820, a split in the Democratic-Republican party of New York gave Van Buren a chance to show his ability as a political leader. Governor De Witt Clinton tried to get John C. Spencer into the U.S. Senate through a special election. Van Buren split with Clinton, and successfully managed the election of Rufus King, an independent Federalist. A year

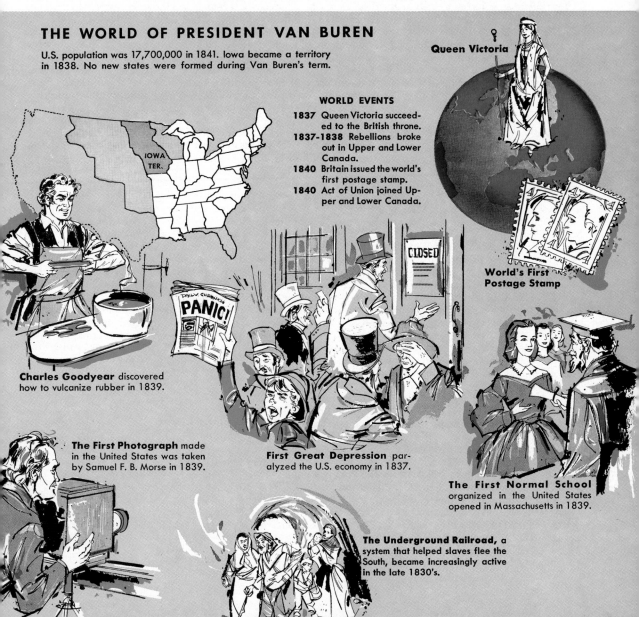

THE WORLD OF PRESIDENT VAN BUREN

U.S. population was 17,700,000 in 1841. Iowa became a territory in 1838. No new states were formed during Van Buren's term.

Queen Victoria

WORLD EVENTS

1837 Queen Victoria succeeded to the British throne.
1837-1838 Rebellions broke out in Upper and Lower Canada.
1840 Britain issued the world's first postage stamp.
1840 Act of Union joined Upper and Lower Canada.

World's First Postage Stamp

Charles Goodyear discovered how to vulcanize rubber in 1839.

The First Photograph made in the United States was taken by Samuel F. B. Morse in 1839.

First Great Depression paralyzed the U.S. economy in 1837.

The First Normal School organized in the United States opened in Massachusetts in 1839.

The Underground Railroad, a system that helped slaves flee the South, became increasingly active in the late 1830's.

From *A History of Old Kinderhook* by Edward A. Collier,
G. P. Putnam's Sons, 1914

Van Buren's Birthplace was in the Dutch community of Kinderhook, N.Y. The only record of what it looked like comes from drawings made during Van Buren's lifetime.

later, when the other Senate seat was vacated, Van Buren's standing had so increased that the legislature elected him.

Van Buren took his seat in the Senate on Dec. 3, 1821. He became a leader in the fight against imprisonment for debt, a great social evil of the time. In 1828, Congress passed a law abolishing such imprisonment. Van Buren also tried to stop the extension of the slave trade. He introduced a bill forbidding the importation of slaves into Florida unless they were owned by settlers. This bill was defeated. Van Buren won re-election to the Senate in 1827. He soon became a supporter of Andrew Jackson for the presidency.

Secretary of State. Late in 1828, Van Buren resigned from the Senate after being elected governor of New York. He served as governor only two months, then resigned to become Secretary of State under President Jackson. Van Buren successfully pressed claims for damages to American shipping by French and Danish warships during the Napoleonic Wars. Under his leadership, the United States re-established trade with the British West Indies. The British had closed West Indian ports to American shipping in 1826 in retaliation for high American tariffs on British goods.

Vice-President. In 1831, Jackson appointed Van Buren U.S. Minister to Great Britain. But the Senate, by one vote, refused to confirm the appointment. By this act, Van Buren's enemies thought they had destroyed his career. Jackson took the Senate's action as a personal insult. In 1832, he supported Van Buren's nomination to the vice-presidency. He also made it clear that Van Buren was his choice to be the next President.

As Vice-President, Van Buren supported Jackson's decision to withdraw federal deposits from the Bank of the United States (see BANK OF THE UNITED STATES). Senate debates over the issue became increasingly bitter. At the height of the dispute, rumors sprang up of a plot to assassinate Van Buren. For a time, Van Buren carried loaded pistols as he presided over the Senate.

Election of 1836. With Jackson's support, Van Buren easily won the Democratic nomination for President in 1836. He defeated William Henry Harrison, the main Whig candidate, by 97 electoral votes. In the vice-presidential race, no candidate won a majority of the electoral votes. The Senate then chose Van Buren's running mate, Representative Richard M. Johnson of Kentucky. No other Vice-President has ever been elected by the Senate.

Van Buren's Election

Place of Nominating Convention . . .	Baltimore
Ballot on Which Nominated	1st
Whig Opponent	William Henry Harrison
Electoral Vote*	170 (Van Buren) to 73 (Harrison)
Popular Vote	765,483 (Van Buren) to 549,508 (Harrison)
Age at Inauguration	54

* For votes by states, see ELECTORAL COLLEGE (table).

Van Buren's Administration (1837-1841)

The Panic of 1837. Van Buren owed the presidency to Andrew Jackson. But many of the problems that faced him as President had developed during Jackson's administration. Congress had failed to limit the sales of public lands to actual settlers, even though Jackson urged such action during his last year in office. Everyone was speculating in public lands, even clerks and shoeshine boys. State banks and branches of the Bank of the United States had joined the speculative splurge. They made vast loans without security in gold or silver. Unable to limit land sales, Jackson had issued his *Specie Circular* of July 11, 1836. It required the government to accept only gold and silver in payment for public lands. Banks could no longer make loans without security, and the speculation ended. A financial crash was inevitable. It came on May 10, 1837, just 67 days after Van Buren took office. Banks in Philadelphia and New York City closed, and soon every bank in the country did likewise. The first great depression in U.S. history had begun.

The Independent Treasury. Van Buren felt no responsibility for the effects of the depression on the people. As President, he was worried only because federal funds on deposit in private banks were in danger. He therefore proposed that an independent treasury be created to hold government funds. A bill putting this plan gradually into effect passed Congress on July 4, 1840. The independent treasury was abolished in 1841, after Van Buren left office. It was reestablished in 1846 under President James K. Polk.

Life in the White House. Van Buren avoided extravagant White House parties because of the depression. He limited his entertaining to simple dinners. Many visitors to the Executive Mansion found the atmosphere formal and austere, even with Van Buren's four sons present. The people of Washington admired the modesty and personal charm of the youths, all in their 20's. But many, especially Dolley Madison, regretted the lack of a woman in the household. She introduced the President's eldest son, Abraham, to Angelica Singleton

Vice-President and Cabinet

Vice-President	*Richard M. Johnson
Secretary of State	John Forsyth
Secretary of the Treasury	Levi Woodbury
Secretary of War	Joel R. Poinsett
Attorney General	Benjamin F. Butler
	Felix Grundy (1838)
	Henry D. Gilpin (1840)
Postmaster General	Amos Kendall
	John M. Niles (1840)
Secretary of the Navy	Mahlon Dickerson
	James Paulding (1838)

*Has a separate biography in WORLD BOOK

of South Carolina. A romance soon developed, and the young people were married in late 1838. Angelica Van Buren assumed the role of White House hostess.

Growing Unpopularity. The depression was only one of many disturbances during Van Buren's administration. Border disputes developed with Canada. In 1839, a boundary dispute between Maine and New Brunswick nearly resulted in open warfare. Van Buren handled the problem with tact, and the dispute was settled peacefully. However, he received little credit for his efforts. See NEW BRUNSWICK (The Aroostook War).

Antislavery leaders blamed Van Buren for the expensive war to drive the Seminole Indians from Florida. They feared the region might become a new slave state. Proslavery leaders attacked the President for not working to annex Texas. They believed he did not want to admit a new slave state into the Union.

Election of 1840. The Democrats nominated Van Buren for re-election in 1840 in spite of his unpopularity. Vice-President Johnson had so many enemies that he failed to gain renomination. The Democrats could not agree on any vice-presidential candidate. As a result, Van Buren became the only presidential candidate in American history to seek election without a running mate. The Whigs again nominated William Henry Harrison for President, and chose former Senator John Tyler of Virginia as his running mate.

Harrison launched a boisterous campaign in which he attacked Van Buren as an aristocrat who had no interest in the unemployment caused by the depression. Using the slogan "Tippecanoe and Tyler too," Harrison campaigned on the basis of his colorful military career. Few persons were surprised when Van Buren lost by an electoral vote of 234 to 60. But many were amazed by the close popular vote. Of 2,400,000 votes cast, Van Buren lost by fewer than 150,000. See HARRISON, WILLIAM HENRY (Elections of 1836 and 1840).

Later Years

Van Buren retired to his country estate, Lindenwald, near his birthplace. He remained active in politics for more than 20 years. In 1848, the antislavery Free Soil party nominated him for President (see FREE SOIL PARTY). He lost the election, but took so many New York votes from Democrat Lewis Cass that the Whig candidate, Zachary Taylor, was elected.

As the slavery disputes grew hotter, Van Buren made his antislavery position clear. But he remained a loyal Democrat, supporting Franklin Pierce in 1852 and James Buchanan in 1856. He opposed Abraham Lincoln at first in 1860, but gave him loyal support after the election. Van Buren died at Lindenwald on July 24, 1862, and was buried beside his wife in Kinderhook. The Lindenwald estate became the Martin Van Buren National Historic Site in 1974.   HUGH RUSSELL FRASER

Related Articles in WORLD BOOK include:

Depression	Johnson, Richard Mentor
Harrison, William Henry	President of the United States
Jackson, Andrew	Vice President of the U. S.

Outline

I. Early Life
　A. Childhood and Education
　B. Van Buren's Family
II. Political and Public Career
　A. U.S. Senator
　B. Secretary of State

　C. Vice-President
　D. Election of 1836
III. Van Buren's Administration (1837-1841)
　A. The Panic of 1837
　B. The Independent Treasury
　C. Life in the White House
　D. Growing Unpopularity
　E. Election of 1840
IV. Later Years

Questions

Whose support assured Van Buren's nomination for President?

What events caused Van Buren to lose popularity?

What social evil did Van Buren oppose as Senator?

Why did Van Buren refuse to give federal aid to the people during the Panic of 1837?

Why was Van Buren called "The Fox of Kinderhook"?

What was Van Buren's plan to protect federal funds from the effects of a depression?

Why did Vice-President Van Buren carry loaded pistols while presiding over the Senate?

Why was Van Buren the only person ever to run for President without a vice-presidential running mate?

Additional Resources

BOARDMAN, FON W., JR. *America and the Jacksonian Era, 1825-1850.* Walck, 1975. Has section on Van Buren. For younger readers.

CURTIS, JAMES C. *The Fox at Bay: Martin Van Buren and the Presidency, 1837-1841.* Univ. Press of Kentucky, 1970.

NIVEN, JOHN. *Martin Van Buren and the Romantic Age of American Politics.* Oxford, 1983.

REMINI, ROBERT V. *Martin Van Buren and the Making of the Democratic Party.* Norton, 1970. Reprint of 1959 edition.

VANCE, CYRUS ROBERTS (1917-   ), served as secretary of state from 1977 to 1980 under President Jimmy Carter. Vance, a lawyer and former official in the Department of Defense, came to the Department of State as an experienced diplomat. In 1967, he settled a dispute between Greece and Turkey over Cyprus. In 1968 and 1969, he served as deputy United States negotiator at the Paris peace talks on the Vietnam War.

As secretary of state, Vance played a major role in establishing full diplomatic relations between the United States and China. He also helped negotiate a peace treaty between Egypt and Israel. He resigned because he could not support a plan by the Carter Administration to rescue American hostages held in Iran (see CARTER, JAMES E., JR.).

Vance was born in Clarksburg, W. Va. He graduated from Yale University and from Yale Law School. He enlisted in the Navy in 1942, during World War II. In 1947, he joined a New York City law firm.

In 1961, President John F. Kennedy named Vance general counsel of the Department of Defense. Vance became secretary of the Army in 1962, and President Lyndon B. Johnson appointed him deputy secretary of defense in 1964.   NANCY H. DICKERSON

VANCE, ZEBULON BAIRD (1830-1894), was a Confederate governor of North Carolina and a Democratic United States Senator. He opposed secession, but served in the Confederate Army. He became governor of North Carolina in 1862, and devoted himself to supplying North Carolina soldiers. He was elected to the United States Senate in 1870, but was refused his seat. He was elected governor again in 1876 and served in the U.S. Senate from 1879 until his death. He was born in Buncombe County, North Carolina. Vance represents North Carolina in Statuary Hall.   W. B. HESSELTINE

VANCOUVER

© Creative Concepts from West Stock

Vancouver Is North America's Leading Pacific Coast Port. It also ranks as the largest city and chief industrial and commercial center of British Columbia. Skyscrapers rise near the white-domed B.C. Place Stadium, *above*. The stadium is part of a complex built for the Expo 86 exposition.

VANCOUVER, *van KOO vuhr,* is the largest city in British Columbia and the busiest port on the Pacific coast of North America. It also ranks as the seventh largest city in Canada. About half of British Columbia's people live in the Vancouver metropolitan area. The city is the province's major center of commerce, culture, industry, and transportation.

Vancouver lies in southwestern British Columbia, about 25 miles (40 kilometers) north of the Canadian-United States border. The city's chief asset is its natural harbor in Burrard Inlet. The harbor is connected with the Pacific Ocean by English Bay, the Strait of Georgia, and Juan de Fuca Strait. Ships can use the port the year around because the harbor's waters never freeze. The port handles nearly all of Canada's trade with Japan and other Asian nations. Vancouver is often called *Canada's Gateway to the Pacific.*

The first permanent settlement on the site of what is now Vancouver grew up near a sawmill built in 1865. Rich timber resources helped the settlement become a bustling lumber town. In 1884, the Canadian Pacific Railway (now CP Rail) chose the site as the western terminal of Canada's first transcontinental railroad. William Van Horne, the railroad's general manager, named the town for Captain George Vancouver, a British explorer who had sailed into Burrard Inlet in 1792.

Greater Vancouver

Vancouver covers about 44 square miles (114 square kilometers) on the southern shore of Burrard Inlet. The city lies in a beautiful setting, near the Coast Mountains and the ocean. The protective mountains, and warm winds blowing in from the Pacific, help provide a surprisingly mild climate for a city so far north.

Vancouver's temperatures average 36° F. (2° C) in January and 63° F. (17° C) in July.

The Vancouver metropolitan area, called *Greater Vancouver,* occupies 1,077 square miles (2,786 square kilometers). Greater Vancouver is Canada's third largest metropolitan area. Only the Montreal and Toronto metropolitan areas have a larger population.

The City lies on two ridges that are separated partly by a shallow inlet called False Creek. Stanley Park, the main recreational area, is on the shorter, northern ridge. Farther south and east on this ridge are downtown Vancouver and rows of high-rise apartment buildings in a section known as the West End. The broader, southern ridge includes the East End, a large section of single-family homes.

The intersection of Granville and Georgia streets is the heart of downtown Vancouver. The 30-story Toronto Dominion Bank Tower rises over the intersection.

Facts in Brief

Population: 414,281. *Metropolitan Area Population—* 1,268,183.

Area: About 44 sq. mi. (114 km²). *Metropolitan Area—* 1,077 sq. mi. (2,786 km²).

Altitude: 38 feet (11.6 m) above sea level.

Climate: *Average Temperature—*January, 36° F. (2° C); July, 63° F. (17° C). *Average Annual Precipitation* (rainfall, melted snow, and other forms of moisture)— 47 inches (119 cm). For the monthly weather in Vancouver, see BRITISH COLUMBIA (Climate).

Government: Mayor-council. *Terms—*2 years for the mayor and the 10 council members.

Founded: 1865. Incorporated as a city in 1886.

It stands in Pacific Centre, a complex that also has a department store and an underground shopping center. The city's tallest building, the 33-story Royal Bank Tower, stands nearby at Georgia and Burrard streets. It rises 466 feet (142 meters) in Royal Centre, a development that includes a hotel and shopping mall.

Vancouver's Coat of Arms, adopted in 1969, includes a lumberman and a fisherman. These figures represent two industries that have contributed much to the city's growth.

Several other downtown streets have special characteristics. Robson Street, also known to Vancouver residents as *Robsonstrasse,* its German name, is a fascinating center of European import stores. Restaurants that specialize in French, German, Greek, Italian, and other types of cooking help give the street an international charm. Most of Vancouver's Chinatown, the second largest Chinese community in North America, is on Pender Street. Only San Francisco's Chinatown has a larger population. More than 30,000 persons of Chinese descent live on or near Pender Street, which is lined by restaurants, gift shops, and nightclubs.

Gastown, the original center of Vancouver, consists of a few redeveloped blocks just north of Chinatown. Gastown's old brick buildings and cobblestone streets recall the city's early days. This area has several antique shops and art galleries.

The Metropolitan Area. The Coast Mountains, including two snow-capped peaks called the Lions, rise majestically north of Vancouver. Point Grey, a peninsula, juts into the Strait of Georgia at the west end of the city. The flat, green, delta lands of the Fraser River basin spread south of Vancouver.

Surrey, Vancouver's largest suburb, is located east of the city. It has a population of about 150,000. Other suburbs include Burnaby, Coquitlam, Delta, North Vancouver, and Richmond.

People

About 70 per cent of Vancouver's people were born in Canada. People of British ancestry make up the largest group. Other large groups include those of Chinese, German, Italian, or Scandinavian descent. The first Chinese residents came during the late 1800's to help build the Canadian Pacific Railway. Many Europeans arrived after World War II ended in 1945.

Vancouver's mild climate has helped make the city a popular retirement center. The climate also attracts large numbers of young people from other parts of Canada. But many of them lack job skills and cannot find work. As a result, they contribute to the city's relatively high rate of unemployment. Poverty is an-

City of Vancouver

BRITISH COLUMBIA

• Vancouver

Vancouver, the largest city in British Columbia, is the busiest port in Canada. The map shows the city and its major points of interest.

— City boundary
═ Main road
— Other road
+—+ Rail line
• Point of interest
▢ Built-up area
▢ Nonbuilt-up area
▢ Park
▢ Indian reserve

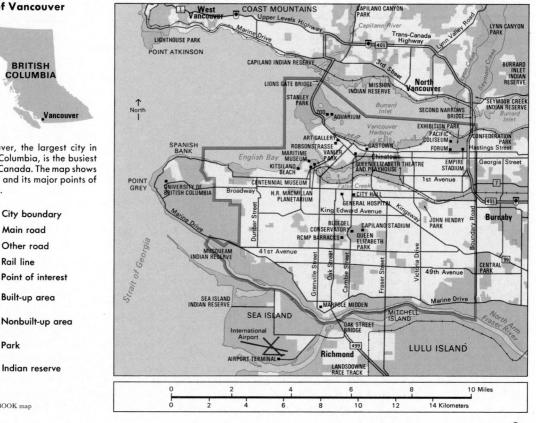

Lumbering is a chief industry of the Vancouver area. Huge forests near the city provide logs for local sawmills, plywood plants, and pulp and paper mills.

other major problem in Vancouver. Most of the poor live in run-down buildings just east of the downtown section and in parts of the East End.

Members of the United Church of Canada form the largest religious group in Vancouver. The city also has many Anglicans, Lutherans, Presbyterians, and Roman Catholics.

Economy

Trade and Finance. Vancouver is Canada's second busiest port behind only Sept-Îles, Que. Vancouver's port handles about 25 million short tons (23 million metric tons) of cargo annually. It serves as the main center for the distribution of goods shipped between Canada and Asia. The port is also the center of an important northern coastal trade. More than 50 steamship lines serve Vancouver.

Vancouver is the largest wholesale and retail trading center of Western Canada. About 100,000 workers in Greater Vancouver are employed by wholesale and retail companies. The sales of these firms exceed $2½ billion annually. Almost every large business in British Columbia has its headquarters in the city. The tourist industry ranks among Vancouver's fastest-growing sources of employment.

Vancouver has more banks, loan companies, and other financial institutions than any other city in Western Canada. Trading on the Vancouver Stock Exchange totals about $500 million yearly.

Transportation. Vancouver serves as the western terminal of Canada's two transcontinental railroads, CP Rail and the Canadian National Railways. The British Columbia Railway, owned by the provincial govern-

ment, has its general offices in the city. The Burlington Northern connects Vancouver with U.S. cities.

About 2½ million passengers use Vancouver International Airport yearly. Among Canadian airports, only those at Montreal and Toronto serve more passengers. Three major Canadian airlines and several U.S. airlines use Vancouver's airport.

Local transportation facilities in the city include a bus system. An elevated rapid transit system was scheduled to begin operating early in 1986. Ferry lines connect Vancouver and nearby Vancouver Island. The Lions Gate Bridge spans Burrard Inlet. It is 1,550 feet (472 meters) long and links Stanley Park and West Vancouver. The Trans-Canada Highway connects Vancouver and other Canadian cities.

Industry. Greater Vancouver ranks as the most important Canadian industrial center west of Ontario. The approximately 2,000 factories in Greater Vancouver produce about $2 billion worth of goods annually. They employ about 72,000 workers.

The area's leading industries are food processing and the manufacture of wood and wood products. Fish processing and meat packing rank as the chief activities of the food products industry. Vast evergreen forests in and near Greater Vancouver provide the raw materials for the area's sawmills, pulp and paper mills, and veneer and plywood plants. Other leading industrial activities include metal fabricating, the making of paper and related products, and the manufacture of petroleum and coal products.

Communication. Vancouver has two major daily newspapers, *The Province* and *The Sun*. Eight radio stations and three television stations serve the city.

Education

Schools. Vancouver has about 100 public elementary schools and about 20 public high schools, with a total of 70,000 students. The public school system also operates the Vancouver School of Art and the Vancouver Vocational Institute. In addition Vancouver has about 40 church-supported schools and private schools.

The University of British Columbia, on Point Grey, is the second largest university in Canada. It has about 18,000 students, and only the University of Toronto has a bigger enrollment. Simon Fraser University is in Burnaby.

Libraries. The Vancouver Public Library system includes a downtown central library and about 15 branches. The University of British Columbia Library owns nearly 1½ million volumes.

Cultural Life and Recreation

The Arts. The Vancouver Opera Association performs in the Queen Elizabeth Theatre. Major stage attractions are presented in the Playhouse Theatre next door. The Vancouver Symphony Orchestra performs nearby in the Orpheum Theatre. The Vancouver Art Gallery features paintings by European and Canadian artists.

Museums. The Centennial Museum and the H. R. MacMillan Planetarium form part of a modern cultural center at the mouth of False Creek. The museum features exhibits on the settlement of Western Canada. The planetarium, topped by a tent-shaped dome, presents

films about the universe. Nearby on the waterfront, the Maritime Museum displays the famous Arctic exploring ship *St. Roch.* This vessel was the first to sail through the Northwest Passage from both the west and the east. It made the voyages between 1940 and 1944.

Parks. Vancouver has about 135 parks that cover a total of about 2,700 acres (1,090 hectares). Stanley Park occupies 1,000 acres (400 hectares) and ranks among the largest city parks in Canada. It includes the Stanley Park Zoo and the Vancouver Public Aquarium. The aquarium is one of the finest marine centers in the world and the largest in Canada. It has more than 8,000 specimens and presents shows with two trained killer whales. Stanley Park is also known for its flower gardens. Queen Elizabeth Park includes an arboretum and the Bloedel Conservatory.

Vancouver's mild climate makes it attractive the year around for many outdoor activities, including fishing, golfing, and tennis. Vancouver also has many fine beaches. The Pacific National Exhibition, Western Canada's largest fair, attracts many tourists to Vancouver in late August and early September every year. It includes agricultural and industrial displays and many kinds of entertainment.

Sports. The British Columbia Lions of the Canadian Football League play in the domed B. C. Place Stadium. The Vancouver Canucks of the National Hockey League play in Pacific Coliseum.

Government

Vancouver has a mayor-council form of government. The voters elect the mayor and the 10 members of the city council to two-year terms. Property taxes provide most of the city government's income. But these and other taxes do not provide enough money to pay for public services and needed improvements. As a result, Vancouver depends on funds from the federal and provincial governments to meet its expenses.

Other problems in Vancouver include air and water pollution, and a shortage of low-rent housing. City leaders are also concerned about the increasing rate of construction on land that may be needed for parks or for other recreational use.

History

Salish Indians lived in what is now the Vancouver area before white men arrived. In 1791, Don Jose Marie Narvaez, a Spanish seaman and explorer, became the first European to see the area. Captain George Vancouver sailed into Burrard Inlet in 1792.

The settlement that became Vancouver was founded in 1865, when lumbermen built Hastings Mill on the site. In 1867, John Deighton, a former English sailor, built a saloon nearby to serve the loggers. He had the nickname "Gassy Jack" because he was so talkative, and the community soon became known as Gastown.

Early Growth. In 1884, the Canadian Pacific Railway chose the site of Vancouver as its western terminal. The young lumber town was incorporated as the city of Vancouver in April, 1886. At that time, about 2,000 people lived there. A fire destroyed most of Vancouver two months later, but the city was quickly rebuilt.

The first Canadian Pacific train reached Vancouver from Eastern Canada in 1887. The city's population rose to 8,000 in 1889. Vancouver began to grow as a seaport in 1891, when ships of the Canadian Steamship Company started to sail between the city and the Orient. By 1901, Vancouver's population had soared to 42,000.

The Great Boom. Between 1900 and 1910, job opportunities made Vancouver the fastest-growing city in Canada. The salmon-canning and wood-processing industries created many of these jobs. Immigrants poured into the city from China, Great Britain, India, Japan, and the United States. In 1904, the Great Northern Railway linked Vancouver with Seattle and other U.S. transportation centers. By 1911, about 86,000 people lived in Vancouver.

The opening of the Panama Canal in 1914 resulted in a tremendous increase of business for Vancouver's port. The canal provided a cheaper way to ship fish, grain, and lumber from Western Canada to Eastern Canada, Europe, and the Eastern United States. By 1921, Vancouver had a population of 163,220. In 1929, the neighboring communities of Point Grey and South Vancouver became part of Vancouver. In 1931, nearly 250,000 people lived in the city.

The Mid-1900's. Vancouver suffered severely during the Great Depression of the 1930's. Thousands of unemployed and homeless people moved to the city from other parts of Canada to seek jobs and relief from the cold winters. Many of these people found no work and took part in several demonstrations against the provincial and federal governments.

World War II (1939-1945) brought prosperity to the city as shipbuilding and other industries expanded. During the war, Vancouver served as headquarters of the coastal defense staffs of the Canadian Army.

The city changed rapidly after the war. Tall apartment buildings appeared in the West End, and modern office towers replaced old structures in downtown Vancouver. In addition, shopping centers were built near many residential areas.

Recent Events. Vancouver's seaport became increasingly important during the late 1960's because of a rapid growth of trade between Canada and Japan. In 1970, a coal-loading terminal equipped to handle the world's largest cargo ships opened just south of Vancouver at Roberts Bank.

Private developers gave the city a new skyline during the 1960's and early 1970's. They erected more tall apartment buildings in the West End and office towers in the downtown area. The downtown developments included Pacific Centre and Royal Centre. In 1974, the city prohibited automobile traffic on a part of Granville Street in downtown Vancouver and turned this section into an attractive mall.

Project 200, another private development, began in 1970 on a 23-acre (9.3-hectare) site on the waterfront. A 32-story office building opened there in 1972. Plans for Project 200 also include the construction of a second office tower. Expo 86, an international exposition of communication and transportation technologies, was scheduled to be held in Vancouver in 1986.   ERIC NICOL

See also BRITISH COLUMBIA (pictures); CANADA (picture); PARK (picture: Urban Parks).

VANCOUVER

VANCOUVER, Wash. (pop. 42,834), is a port on the Columbia River, directly across from Portland, Ore. (see WASHINGTON [political map]). It is one of the state's largest cities and the seat of Clark County. Its mills produce lumber, veneer, plywood, wood pulp, and paper. Power from the nearby Bonneville Dam aids in the production of aluminum. The city also has food-processing plants. Vancouver is an important port. Its major exports include grain and lumber.

The oldest city in the state, Vancouver was founded by the Hudson's Bay Company in 1824. Captain George Vancouver, for whom the city is named, had entered the mouth of the Columbia River on an exploration trip in 1792. The old trading post site now lies in Vancouver Barracks, an army post established in 1849. Vancouver was incorporated as a city in 1857. It has a council-manager government.   HOWARD J. CRITCHFIELD

VANCOUVER, GEORGE (1758-1798), was a British explorer. Vancouver Island and cities in the state of Washington and in British Columbia, Canada, are named after him.

He was born at King's Lynn, Norfolk, England. He entered the navy as an able seaman at the age of 13. His early experiences were on Captain James Cook's two last voyages (see COOK, JAMES). Vancouver served as a midshipman on the last voyage.

An incident concerning Nootka Sound, off the west coast of Vancouver Island, threatened war between Great Britain and Spain. Vancouver was ordered there, and he sailed in April, 1791. He sailed by way of the Cape of Good Hope, Australia, and New Zealand, following Cook's example. He made valuable maps

Brown Bros.
George Vancouver

of the coasts of these areas. He reached the American continent in 1792. Vancouver participated in certain formalities involving Nootka Sound, and then sailed through Juan de Fuca Strait and around Vancouver Island, becoming the first white person to sight the Strait of Georgia. He surveyed the Pacific Coast north of San Francisco for the first time. He returned to England via Cape Horn in 1795.

His book, *A Voyage of Discovery to the North Pacific Ocean and Round the World in the Years 1790-1795,* was published in 1798.   WILLIAM P. BRANDON

VANCOUVER ISLAND is the largest island on the Pacific Coast of North America, and an important part of the Canadian province of British Columbia. Vancouver Island extends for 285 miles (459 kilometers) along the southwestern coast of Canada and is from 40 to 80 miles (64 to 130 kilometers) wide. Victoria, the largest city on the island, is the capital of British Columbia. The other chief cities are Nanaimo and Port Alberni. The total population of the island is 495,125.

Location, Size, and Surface Features. Vancouver Island is separated from the mainland of British Columbia by Queen Charlotte Strait, Johnstone Strait, and

WORLD BOOK map
Location of Vancouver Island

the Strait of Georgia. Juan de Fuca Strait lies south of the island. Vancouver Island covers 12,079 square miles (31,284 square kilometers). It is the southern end of a partly sunken mountain chain, the Island, or Vancouver, Range. The tops of the range rise sharply from the Pacific Ocean to heights of 5,000 to 7,000 feet (1,500 to 2,100 meters). Dangerous reefs and small, rocky islands are common along the western shore. The valleys of the sunken range form many winding, fiordlike bays. Quatsino, Nootka, and Barkley sounds reach into the heart of the island. Pacific Rim National Park is on the western coast. The eastern shore is less rugged and broken, and has a few level stretches.

Vancouver Island has the mildest climate in Canada because of the Japan Current. There is little winter in the southern part around Victoria, but in the northern and western mountains the winters are often severe.

The Island's Resources. The slopes of the mountains on Vancouver Island are covered with fir, cedar, and hemlock forests. Lumbering is the chief industry. The island has several large pulp mills, sawmills, and plywood plants. Farms are cultivated in the valleys. The southeast coast produces many berries and flower bulbs. Excellent game fishing attracts many tourists.

History. In 1774, the Spanish explorer Juan Perez became the first European to sight Vancouver Island. In 1778, the British navigator James Cook became the first European to land on the island. George Vancouver, a member of Cook's expedition, returned to Vancouver Island in 1792 and sailed around it. The island is named for him. See VANCOUVER, GEORGE.

During the 1800's, the United States claimed the island and nearby territory on the mainland. But the United States surrendered these claims to Great Britain in 1846. The first settlement on the island was made in 1843, when the Hudson's Bay Company built Fort Victoria. In 1849, Vancouver Island became a British colony. In 1866, it was united with mainland settlements to form British Columbia.   RODERICK HAIG-BROWN

See also NOOTKA INDIANS; VICTORIA (B.C.).

VANDALIA STATE HOUSE. See ILLINOIS (Places to Visit).

VANDALISM is criminal damage to property. It includes breaking the windows of public or privately owned buildings, painting slogans on the walls of public places, breaking furniture or machinery, and many

other forms of damage. Vandalism may be an act of revenge or a way of expressing a political opinion. Both young people and adults sometimes commit the crime just for "fun." For example, football fans may tear down the goal posts after an important game.

In the United States, the damage caused by vandalism totals millions of dollars yearly. In most cases, the costs are paid by the business, school, or government that has been vandalized, or by individual victims.

Vandalism is punishable by fine or imprisonment. Some local governments have laws that hold parents responsible for vandalism committed by their children. But most acts of vandalism are not punished. Law enforcement is difficult in such cases, and the cost of most individual acts of damage is not large enough to make legal action worthwhile.   JAMES F. SHORT, JR.

VANDALS were a Germanic tribe of barbarians that invaded the Roman Empire during the early A.D. 400's. The Vandals, and other barbarians, helped bring about the empire's decline. The Vandals were probably no more destructive than other barbarians, but the word *vandal* has come to mean someone who destroys or damages valuable things.

The Vandals were originally a group of tribes that lived along the southern coasts of what are now Norway, Sweden, Denmark, and the Danish islands. They migrated to central Europe about 100 B.C., and settled in Silesia and Galicia (now in southern Poland). In the late A.D. 300's, the Vandals moved westward because they were threatened by the Huns from the east. The Vandals crossed the northwest boundaries of the Roman Empire in 406, and raided the province of Gaul (now France). In 409, they moved into Spain.

The Vandals reached the peak of their power under King Genseric, who ruled from 428 to 477. They conquered northern Africa and ruled the Mediterranean Sea. In 455, they looted Rome. Byzantine Emperor Justinian I sent forces against them in 533. In 534, these forces captured the Vandals' territories, destroying the Vandals as a nation.   WILLIAM G. SINNIGEN

VAN DE GRAAFF, *VAN duh GRAF*, **ROBERT JEMISON** (1901-1967), an American physicist, invented the electrostatic generator named after him. The Van de Graaff generator builds up a high-voltage electric charge useful for nuclear research (see VAN DE GRAAFF GENERATOR).

Van de Graaff was born in Tuscaloosa, Ala. He graduated from the University of Alabama in 1922 and did postgraduate work at the Sorbonne in Paris and at Oxford University in England. After doing research in physics at Princeton University, he joined the Massachusetts Institute of Technology staff in 1931. He built the first model of his generator that year and added improvements in later models.   ROGER H. STUEWER

VAN DE GRAAFF GENERATOR, *VAN duh GRAF*, also known as an *electrostatic generator*, is a device for building up a high electrical charge. It is a source of charged particles that may be used for atom smashing. In general, the generator is used to boost protons and other nuclear particles to energy of about 10 million electron volts (10 Mev.). The chief value of the machine is that narrow beams of protons of known energies can be produced. Scientists use these beams to study nuclear forces.

Robert J. Van de Graaff made the first generator of this kind at the Massachusetts Institute of Technology.

Massachusetts Institute of Technology

The First Van de Graaff Generator was built at the Massachusetts Institute of Technology in 1931. Physicists use these particle accelerators for nuclear research.

In the generator, a continuous belt of an insulating material moves past a source of negative electricity. This source sprays electrons on the belt. The belt then goes into a hollow metal dome where a fine metallic brush moves the electrons onto the dome surface. When the charge at the top of the dome is high enough, electrically charged particles are hurled at targets at the bottom of the generator.

Van de Graaff machines work at higher energy when they are enclosed in a pressure vessel. To prevent leakage of the electricity, a gas such as Freon or air under pressure as high as 150 pounds per square inch (10.5 kilograms per square centimeter) is put in the vessel. Electrostatic generators are widely used because they generate a constant supply of voltage.   RALPH E. LAPP

See also PARTICLE ACCELERATOR.

VANDENBERG, ARTHUR HENDRICK (1884-1951), was an American statesman and political leader. He was appointed United States senator from Michigan in 1928. He was elected to the Senate a few months later and was reelected in 1934, 1940, and 1946. He became a Republican leader in the Senate, and was active in molding United States foreign policy.

Vandenberg served as a United States representative at the United Nations conference in San Francisco in 1945. The next year he was a delegate to the Paris Peace conference. In 1947, Vandenberg became president pro tem of the Senate. He gave up his Senate duties in 1950 because of illness. Vandenberg was born in Grand Rapids, Mich.   F. JAY TAYLOR

VANDENBERG AIR FORCE BASE, Calif., is the training center for U.S. Air Force ballistic missile crews. Space satellites are launched from the base and from nearby Point Arguello. The base covers about 98,400 acres (39,820 hectares) and lies about 10 miles (16 kilometers) northwest of Lompoc. It was established as Camp Cooke, an Army post, in 1941. It became an Air Force base in 1956 and was renamed for General Hoyt S. Vandenberg. In 1985, construction was completed on facilities that enable the base to serve as a launching and landing site for space shuttles, which are reusable manned spacecraft.   RICHARD M. SKINNER

VANDERBILT, CORNELIUS

VANDERBILT, CORNELIUS (1794-1877), was the most successful and powerful American businessman of his time. He made his fortune in steamship lines and railroads but also had investments in manufacturing and banking. Vanderbilt was often called "Commodore" because of his steamship interests.

Vanderbilt was born in Port Richmond on Staten Island, N.Y. At the age of 16, he bought a small boat, which he used to carry freight and passengers between Staten Island and New York City. During the War of 1812, Vanderbilt transported supplies to forts along New York Harbor. He formed a steamship company in 1829 and soon dominated shipping along the Atlantic coast and on the Hudson River. After the California gold rush began in 1849, Vanderbilt established a steamship line that carried prospectors from New York City to San Francisco. The route included an overland crossing through Nicaragua. By the mid-1850's, his ships made regular trips to and from Europe, and he had become the leading American steamship owner.

In 1865, Vanderbilt gained control of the Hudson River Railroad. In 1869, he merged this line with the New York Central Railroad to form a network that ran from New York City to Buffalo, N.Y. By 1873, he owned rail lines that extended as far west as Chicago.

Vanderbilt helped build the nation's transportation system. In several cases, however, he used questionable business tactics. These actions helped create unstable conditions in the stock market, which drove many firms into bankruptcy. Vanderbilt did not support charities. But late in life, he gave $1 million to Central University (now Vanderbilt University) in Nashville, Tenn., and donated $50,000 to the Church of the Strangers in New York City. At his death, Vanderbilt left a fortune of more than $105 million, the largest in American history up to that time. ROBERT SOBEL

See also GOULD, JAY.

Additional Resources

HOYT, EDWIN P. *The Vanderbilts and Their Fortunes.* Doubleday, 1962. Primarily devoted to Cornelius.

LANE, WHEATON J. *Commodore Vanderbilt: An Epic of the Steam Age.* Johnson Pub. Co., 1973. Reprint of 1942 ed. A biography.

VANDERBILT UNIVERSITY is a coeducational, privately controlled university in Nashville, Tenn. It has a college of arts and science; schools of divinity, education, engineering, law, management, medicine, and nursing; and a graduate school. Courses lead to bachelor's, master's, and doctor's degrees. Vanderbilt also offers undergraduate study programs at universities in England, France, Israel, Spain, and West Germany.

The school was first chartered in 1872 as Central University. It was renamed Vanderbilt University in 1873 after Cornelius Vanderbilt, an American businessman, gave $1 million to build and support the school. For enrollment, see UNIVERSITIES AND COLLEGES (table).

Critically reviewed by VANDERBILT UNIVERSITY

VAN DER GOES, *van duhr GOOS,* **HUGO** (1440?-1482), was the leading Flemish painter of his generation. He was influenced by Jan van Eyck and Rogier van der Weyden, earlier Flemish artists. But he surpassed them in the earthy solidity of his figures and in his greater understanding of human psychology.

Virgin and Child with Saint Anne and Franciscan Donor (about 1470), an oil painting on wood; Royal Museum of Fine Arts, Brussels, Belgium

A Van der Goes Painting shows the expressive portraits and realistic landscape background that are typical of his style.

A few of Van der Goes' pictures prove him one of the best portrait artists of his time, but his main contribution to Flemish art consists of several large altarpieces. Among them is the *Adoration of the Shepherds,* painted for an Italian merchant who lived in Bruges, Belgium. It is famous for the vivid portrayal of three adoring shepherds and the charming heads of the merchant's children. His last work is the *Death of the Virgin,* an unforgettable study of human pathos.

Little is known about Van der Goes' youth. In 1467, he was accepted as a master in the artists' guild in Ghent. About 1478, he entered a monastery near Brussels as a lay brother. JULIUS S. HELD

VAN DER WAALS, *vahn duhr VAHLS,* **JOHANNES DIDERIK,** *yoh HAH nuhs DEE duh rihk* (1837-1923), a Dutch theoretical physicist, became famous for his work on the behavior of liquids and gases. He won the 1910 Nobel prize in physics for developing the famous equation of state which bears his name. The equation takes into account the forces between the molecules of a gas. Van der Waals was born at Leiden, the Netherlands, on Nov. 23, 1837. He served as professor of physics at Leiden from 1877 until his retirement in 1907. See also MOLECULE (Molecules and Matter). R. T. ELLICKSON

VAN DER WEYDEN, *van duhr VYD uhn,* **ROGIER,** *roh GEER* (1399?-1464), was a Flemish painter, and a founder of the Flemish movement in painting. He is celebrated for the courtly dignity of his figures, his skillful manner of composition, and his subtle observation of human emotion. He was also a keen student of nature, and painted everything down to the smallest detail in his panels. With an unfailing sense for the beauty of line and the gracefulness of motion, he created masterpieces which influenced Flemish, German, and French art for many years.

Some of Van der Weyden's works are lost, but many of his paintings are still preserved. These include *The Madonna with St. Luke, The Last Judgment,* and the *Adoration of the Magi,* a *triptych,* or a picture in three panels. His painting *The Descent from the Cross* appears in color in the PAINTING article.

Van der Weyden was born in Tournai, Belgium. He

moved to Brussels in the 1430's, where he was appointed "painter of the town." In 1450 he made a trip to Italy. He received commissions from Duke Philip the Good of Burgundy and members of his court. Van der Weyden's portraits preserved the haughty manners and proud bearing of these nobles.   JULIUS S. HELD

VAN DEVANTER, VAN *dih* VAN *tuhr*, **WILLIS** (1859-1941), served as an associate justice of the Supreme Court of the United States from 1911 to 1937. His opinions as a Supreme Court justice were consistently conservative. He also served from 1903 to 1910 as a federal circuit judge. Van Devanter was born in Marion, Ind., and graduated from DePauw University and the Cincinnati Law School. He practiced law in Indiana and Wyoming, and served as chief justice of the Supreme Court of Wyoming in 1889 and 1890.   H. G. REUSCHLEIN

VAN DINE, S. S. (1888-1939), is the pen name of Willard Huntington Wright, an American author of detective fiction. Van Dine's novels featured the scholarly and snobbish amateur detective Philo Vance. Van Dine introduced Vance in *The Benson Murder Case* (1926). The detective also appears in 11 other novels, including *The Canary Murder Case* (1927) and *The Bishop Murder Case* (1929). In the Philo Vance stories, the murderers use unusual methods to commit their crimes. Wright was born in Charlottesville, Va. He also wrote art and literary criticism.   FREDERICK J. HOFFMAN

VAN DOREN, CARL (1885-1950), was an American biographer and critic. He won the 1939 Pulitzer Prize for biography for *Benjamin Franklin* (1938). Van Doren also wrote *Swift* (1930), a biography of the English author Jonathan Swift, and *Jane Mecom* (1950), a book about Benjamin Franklin's sister.

Painting on wood panel (1464); the Louvre, Paris

Van der Weyden's *Saint Mary Magdalene* **shows his skill at portraying dignified figures and realistic landscapes.**

Van Doren wrote many critical essays about American authors. Much of his literary criticism was collected in *The Roving Critic* (1923) and *Many Minds* (1924). Van Doren wrote a number of books about the Revolutionary War in America (1775-1783). They include the *Secret History of the American Revolution* (1941) and *Mutiny in January* (1943). He also wrote an autobiography, *Three Worlds* (1936). Carl Clinton Van Doren was born in Hope, Ill., near Urbana. His younger brother, Mark Van Doren, was also a noted author.   SAMUEL CHASE COALE

VAN DOREN, MARK (1894-1972), was an American poet, critic, and educator. He wrote more than 50 works of prose and poetry and won a Pulitzer prize in 1940 for his *Collected Poems* (1939).

Many of Van Doren's poems describe the beauty of nature and New England's changing seasons. Others are based on American legends and reveal his love for the nation's cultural heritage. Some poems that Van Doren wrote during the 1940's reflect his somber thoughts about World War II (1939-1945). These war poems are included in *Collected and New Poems: 1924-1963* (1963). In *Good Morning: Last Poems* (published in 1973 after his death), Van Doren expressed calm acceptance of the prospect of death.

Van Doren's career as a critic began with *Henry David Thoreau* (1916), a study of Thoreau's writings. Van Doren also wrote essays on the works of other writers, including John Dryden, Nathaniel Hawthorne, and William Shakespeare. His major critical writings appear in *Private Reader* (1942) and *The Happy Critic* (1961). In addition, he wrote novels, plays, short stories, and *Autobiography* (1958).

Mark Albert Van Doren was born in Hope, Ill., near Urbana. From 1920 to 1959, he taught English at Columbia University. His older brother, Carl Clinton Van Doren, was also a noted writer.   ELMER W. BORKLUND

VAN DRUTEN, *van* DROOT *uhn,* **JOHN WILLIAM** (1901-1957), was a playwright who became known for his polished comedies. His plays are noted for their sophisticated dialogue and strong portrayals of women. Van Druten's comedies include *Old Acquaintance* (1940), *The Voice of the Turtle* (1943), *I Remember Mama* (1944), and *Bell, Book and Candle* (1950). He adapted his best-known serious play, *I Am a Camera* (1951), from Christopher Isherwood's stories, *Goodbye to Berlin*.

Van Druten was born in London and taught at University College, Wales. He turned to literature as a career after *Young Woodley* (1925), his second play, succeeded in New York City. The play had been banned in England as an attack on its public school system. Van Druten came to America in 1926, and became a United States citizen in 1944.   THOMAS A. ERHARD

VAN DYCK, *van* DYK, **ANTON** (1599-1641), was the most famous portrait painter of the 1600's. His portraits had an especially strong influence on English art. Van Dyck also painted mythological and religious scenes and was a fine engraver and etcher.

Van Dyck was born in Antwerp, Belgium. He showed great talent for painting as a boy and had his own studio and pupils at the age of 16. From 1618 to 1620, Van Dyck worked with the famous painter Peter Paul Rubens. Van Dyck visited England briefly in 1620 and then lived in Italy from about 1621 to 1627. He painted

in several Italian cities, including Genoa, Rome, and Venice. His portraits of Genoese nobles and their children rank among his finest works. Throughout his career, Van Dyck admired the style of the Venetian artist Titian. Van Dyck's Italian paintings show Titian's influence in their warm colors and free brushwork.

Van Dyck returned to Antwerp in 1627 and worked there for about five years. During this period, he painted his largest and finest religious pictures, including *The Resurrection of Christ*.

In 1632, Van Dyck moved to England, where King Charles I made him court painter. The artist became popular with English nobles and completed about 350 portraits of them, including 38 of the king. *Portrait of Charles I Hunting*, perhaps the most famous of these works, appears in the PAINTING article. Van Dyck set new standards for English portrait painting through the dignity, elegance, and grace of his interpretations, and his ability to paint clothing and accessories in vivid

Robert Rich, Earl of Warwick (about 1635), an oil painting on canvas; the Metropolitan Museum of Art, New York City, the Jules S. Bache Collection, 1949 (WORLD BOOK photo by Malcolm Varon)

A Typical Van Dyck Portrait shows a full-length figure posed against a landscape background. The portrait above illustrates Van Dyck's drawing skill and his ability to paint rich fabrics.

detail. He established a tradition closely followed by Thomas Gainsborough and Sir Joshua Reynolds, the leading English portrait painters of the 1700's.

Van Dyck created a series of engravings and etchings portraying artists and writers of his day. The portraits in this series, called the *Iconographie*, rank among the masterpieces of printmaking.   ROBERT F. REIFF

See also CHARLES (I) of England (picture); CLOTHING (pictures: The Ruff, Clothing of the 1600's).

Additional Resources

BROWN, CHRISTOPHER. *Van Dyck*. Cornell Univ. Press, 1983.
MARTIN, JOHN RUPERT, and FEIGENBAUM, GAIL. *Van Dyck as Religious Artist*. Princeton, 1979.

VAN DYKE, HENRY (1852-1933), was an American Presbyterian clergyman, educator, novelist, essayist, poet, and religious writer. His writing is delicate, vivid, and full of idealism, as in his *Companionable Books* (1922). He also wrote *The Poetry of Tennyson* (1889) and many other works. Van Dyke was born in Germantown, Pa.   HARRY H. CLARK

VAN EYCK, *van EYEK,* **JAN,** *yahn* (1380?-1441), was one of the founders of the Flemish realistic style of painting. This style dominated northern European painting for more than 100 years. Van Eyck, working with his brother, Hubert, was also the first great artist to use the technique of oil painting.

Van Eyck's style emphasizes natural lighting effects; vivid colors; and rich, precise details of clothing and jewels. His works also show skillful handling of atmosphere and perspective. Van Eyck's paintings reflect the influence of the Flemish painter Robert Campin. Like Campin, Van Eyck used symbolism. For example, in his earliest surviving work, *Madonna in a Church* (1425), Van Eyck painted the Virgin Mary extremely large in comparison to her surroundings. Her size symbolizes her importance to Christianity.

The Van Eyck brothers probably collaborated on the *Ghent Altarpiece* (1432), a huge work consisting of 26 panels in a frame. The artists filled the work with so many figures and symbolic references that the viewer must study it closely to understand all its meanings.

Van Eyck painted several portrait heads and a famous interior scene, *The Arnolfini Wedding* (1434). This painting shows a couple being married before the artist and his assistant, whose images are reflected in a mirror on the rear wall. *The Arnolfini Wedding* is reproduced in the WORLD BOOK article on PAINTING. Van Eyck was born in the province of Limburg in the Netherlands.   ROBERT F. REIFF

See also PAINTING (The Flemish Style); JEROME, SAINT (picture).

VAN GOGH, *van GOH,* **VINCENT** (1853-1890), is one of the most famous painters in modern art. Yet during his lifetime, he received no recognition and sold only one painting. Van Gogh failed in every career he attempted and felt unloved and friendless throughout his life. He turned to art to express his strong religious feelings and his deep need for love and respect. During the last five years of his life, Van Gogh completed more than 800 oil paintings.

Van Gogh was born in Groot-Zundert, near Breda, the Netherlands. When he was 16, his parents sent him to The Hague to work for an uncle who was an art dealer. But Van Gogh was unsuited for a business career.

Oil painting on wood (1435); Städelsches
Kunstinstitut, Frankfurt, Germany (Kunst-Dias Blauel)

Van Eyck's *Lucca Madonna* shows the artist's skillful handling
of light and his ability to paint fabrics and jewels in precise detail.
Van Eyck's realistic style influenced many painters.

produced in color in the PAINTING article. During a
seizure late in 1888, he threatened to kill the French
painter Paul Gauguin, who was visiting him. Van Gogh
cut off one of his own ears during this seizure. He committed suicide in 1890.

Throughout his life, Van Gogh corresponded with his
brother Theo and other people. Van Gogh's *Complete
Letters*, published in three volumes in 1958, provide an
intimate view of his life and thought. See LETTER
WRITING (picture).   ROBERT F. REIFF

See also IMPRESSIONISM; EXPRESSIONISM.

Additional Resources

HAMMACHER, ABRAHAM M. and RENILDE. *Van Gogh: A Documentary Biography*. Macmillan, 1982.
LEYMARIE, JEAN. *Van Gogh*. Rev. ed. Rizzoli, 1978.
VAN GOGH, VINCENT. *The Complete Letters of Vincent Van Gogh*.
3 vols. 2nd ed. New York Graphic Society, 1978.
WALLACE, ROBERT. *The World of Van Gogh, 1853-1890*. Time Inc.,
1969.

VANGUARD. See SPACE TRAVEL (Artificial Satellites).

VAN HORNE, SIR WILLIAM CORNELIUS (1843-
1915), was a railroad executive of great ability. He became, in turn, general manager, vice president, and president of the Canadian Pacific Railway (now CP Rail).
Van Horne's driving force helped make possible the
prompt construction of that railroad. His executive skill
enabled the company to pull through its difficult early
years. He was born near Joliet, Ill.   WILLIAM R. WILLOUGHBY

VANIER, GEORGES PHILIAS (1888-1967), served as
governor general of Canada from 1959 to 1967. He

In 1878, Van Gogh applied for admission to a theological school but was rejected. He then decided to
become an unordained preacher and received his training from a missionary society in Brussels, Belgium. Late
in 1878, Van Gogh represented the society as a minister
in the Borinage, a poor coal-mining district in Belgium.
He took his work so seriously that he went without food
and other necessities so he could give more to the poor.
The missionary society objected to Van Gogh's un-
orthodox behavior and relieved him in the summer of
1879. Van Gogh began to draw while in the Borinage,
and late in 1880 he decided to become a painter.

Van Gogh's first pictures were still lifes and scenes
of peasants at work. He favored dark brown and olive
colors and heavy brushstrokes. *The Potato Eaters* (1885)
is his finest and most ambitious work of this period.
In 1886, Van Gogh went to Paris to visit his brother
Theo and was immediately attracted to the impres-
sionist art he saw there. Under the influence of impressionism, he lightened his brushstrokes and used
bright, clear colors.

In 1888, Van Gogh moved to Arles in southern
France. There, he painted his most expressive and original pictures. An example of his work of this period is
The Postman Roulin, reproduced in color in the PAINTING
article. In Arles, Van Gogh suffered from occasional
violent seizures, which were diagnosed after his death
as epilepsy. The intense color and slashing brushstrokes of Van Gogh's paintings reflect his disturbed
mind. An example is his picture *The Night Café*, re-

Oil painting on canvas; courtesy of the Fogg Art Museum, Harvard
University, Cambridge, Mass., Bequest—Collection of Maurice Wertheim

Van Gogh Painted This Self-Portrait in 1888.

VANILLA

was the first French Canadian and the first Roman Catholic to hold the office. Vanier won fame as a soldier and diplomat. He lost a leg while fighting in France in World War I. Later he became a major general.

Georges Philias Vanier

Vanier served as Canadian ambassador to France from 1945 to 1953. He was born in Montreal.

VANILLA is the name of a group of climbing orchids. The vanilla extract which is used to flavor chocolate, ice cream, pastry, and candy comes from these plants. The vanilla vine has been cultivated in Mexico for hundreds of years. This type of vanilla has been introduced into other tropical areas. Comoros, Indonesia, Madagascar, and Reunion produce much of the world's supply. Another variety of vanilla grows on the island of Tahiti in the South Pacific Ocean.

The vanilla vine has little rootlets by which the plant attaches itself to trees. The cultivated plant lives about 10 years. It produces its first crop after three years.

The plant produces a fruit in the shape of a cylindrical *pod* (bean) from 5 to 10 inches (13 to 25 centimeters) long. The fruit has an oily black pulp that contains many tiny black seeds. The pods are gathered when they are a yellow-green in color. Then the curing, or drying, process takes place. This process shrinks the bean and turns it a rich, chocolate-brown color. The process also gives the bean the flavor and aroma of vanilla as we know it.

Vanilla extract is prepared by a complicated and expensive process. The beans are chopped into small

A Bean of the Vanilla Plant, *above,* undergoes a drying process that turns it a chocolate-brown color. The top photo shows a worker inspecting a wild vanilla vine in Mexico.

pieces and then percolated with alcohol and water. Food scientists have developed artificial vanilla flavors because of the high cost of vanilla.

Scientific Classification. Vanilla is in the orchid family, *Orchidaceae.* The vine of Mexico and Madagascar is genus *Vanilla,* species *V. fragrans.*   G. W. TAYLOR

VAN LAWICK-GOODALL, JANE. See GOODALL, JANE.

VAN LEEUWENHOEK, ANTON. See LEEUWENHOEK, ANTON VAN.

VAN LEYDEN, *LIE dun,* **LUCAS** (1494?-1533), a Dutch engraver, was also a painter, draftsman, and designer of woodcuts. He produced an astonishingly large number of works. Born in The Netherlands, he was influenced by the German, Albrecht Dürer, and the Italian, Marcantonio Raimondi. Most of Van Leyden's engravings have Biblical subjects, but some show the life of his time. Among his paintings are *The Last Judgment* and *Moses Striking the Rock.*   JULIUS S. HELD

Abraham and Isaac (early 1500's); The Metropolitan Museum of Art, New York City, Harris Brisbane Dick Fund, 1925
A Woodcut by Lucas Van Leyden shows the landscape setting and skillful use of perspective that are typical of his work.

VAN RENSSELAER, *van REHN suh ler,* was the name of a family of Dutch landowners who settled in New York state.

Kiliaen Van Rensselaer (1595-1643) was one of the leading colonizers of the territory that later became New York. In 1629, the Dutch West India Company authorized large grants of land in New Netherland to company members who promised to colonize their lands. As a result, a class of great landowners, called *patroons,* developed. Kiliaen Van Rensselaer was the greatest of them. He established the huge manor of Rensselaerswyck, which included two counties and

part of a third on both banks of the Hudson River south of Albany. Van Rensselaer, a wealthy diamond merchant of Amsterdam, where he was born, was successful because he invested much money and supplied his farmers with cattle, horses, tools, and mills. But he never visited his colony on the Hudson.

Stephen Van Rensselaer (1764-1839), an American army officer and politician, was the eighth and last of the Dutch patroons of Rensselaerswyck. He was lieutenant governor of New York and a U.S. representative. He helped bring about construction of the Erie and Champlain canals. He served as a major general in the War of 1812, and was chancellor of New York University from 1835 to 1839. He was born in New York City. IAN C. C. GRAHAM

VAN'T HOFF, *vahnt HAHF,* **JACOBUS HENRICUS,** *yah KOH buhs hehn REE kuhs* (1852-1911), was a Dutch chemist who received the first Nobel Prize for chemistry in 1901. He discovered the laws of chemical dynamics and osmosis. He was the first to note that the properties of solutions depend upon the number, not the kind, of dissolved particles. He also showed that the simple gas laws apply to dilute solutions. Van't Hoff also did fundamental work in stereochemistry, which is concerned with the arrangement of atoms in the spaces of the molecules. Van't Hoff was born in Rotterdam. While teaching at the Prussian Academy of Sciences in Berlin, he did important research on the formation and decomposition of double salts. K. L. KAUFMAN

VANUATU, *vah NOO ah too,* is an island country in the southwest Pacific Ocean. It consists of 80 islands with a total land area of about 5,700 square miles (14,-763 square kilometers). For location, see PACIFIC ISLANDS (map). The largest islands are, in order of size, Espiritu Santo, Malekula, Efate, Erromango, and Tanna. Vanuatu has a population of about 137,000. Port-Vila (pop. 25,000)—on Efate—is the nation's capital and largest urban community. Vanuatu's national anthem is "Yumi, yumi, yumi" ("We, we, we").

From 1906 to 1980, Great Britain and France jointly governed the islands, which were then called the New

Hebrides. In 1980, the islands became the independent nation of Vanuatu.

Government. Vanuatu is a republic. A Parliament, whose 39 members are elected by the people to four-year terms, makes the country's laws. A prime minister, who heads the majority party in Parliament, runs the government with the aid of a Council of Ministers. Village, regional, and island councils handle local government affairs. The Parliament and the regional council presidents elect a president to a five-year term. The president's role is chiefly ceremonial.

People. More than 90 per cent of Vanuatu's people are Melanesians. Asians, Europeans, and Polynesians make up the rest of the population. About three-fourths of the people live in rural villages. Many village houses are made of wood from nearby forests and of bamboo and palm leaves. Port-Vila and Santo—on Espiritu Santo—are the only urban communities. More than 100 languages are spoken in Vanuatu. Bislama, a language that combines mainly English words and Melanesian grammar, is commonly used throughout the country. Vanuatu has about 300 elementary schools and several high schools. About 85 per cent of the people are Christians and most of the rest practice local religions.

Land and Climate. The islands of Vanuatu form a Y-shaped chain that extends about 500 miles (800 kilometers) from north to south. Most of the islands have narrow coastal plains and mountainous interiors. Several islands feature active volcanoes. The northern islands have a hot, rainy climate, with a year-round temperature of about 80° F. (27° C) and annual rainfall of about 120 inches (305 centimeters). Temperatures in the southern islands range from about 67° to 88° F. (19° to 31° C), and the yearly rainfall totals about 90 inches (230 centimeters).

Economy of Vanuatu is based on agriculture. Rural families produce nearly all the food they need. They grow fruits and vegetables, raise chickens and hogs, and catch fish. Some families produce *copra* (dried coco-

Vanuatu is a country that consists of 80 islands in the southwest Pacific Ocean. People enjoy boating on sparkling blue water near the sandy shore of one of the islands, *left*.

nut meat) for sale. Tourism is important to the economy.

Small ships and airplanes serve as the main means of transportation among the islands. Vanuatu has few good roads and no railroads. The government publishes a newspaper and operates a radio station.

History. Melanesians have lived in what is now Vanuatu for at least 3,000 years. In 1606, Pedro Fernandez de Queirós, a Portuguese explorer in the service of Spain, became the first European to see the islands. The British explorer James Cook mapped the region in 1774 and named the islands the New Hebrides after the Hebrides islands of Scotland.

British and French traders, missionaries, and settlers began coming to the islands during the 1820's. In 1887, Great Britain and France set up a joint naval commission to oversee the area. In 1906, the commission was replaced by a joint British and French government called a condominium (see CONDOMINIUM).

After the United States entered World War II in 1941, the New Hebrides became an important military base for the Allies. American troops built many roads, bridges, and airstrips there. A movement for independence began in the islands during the 1960's. The New Hebrides became the independent nation of Vanuatu on July 30, 1980. ROBERT LANGDON

VAN VLECK, JOHN. See NOBEL PRIZES (table: Nobel Prizes for Physics—1977).

VAN WINKLE, RIP. See RIP VAN WINKLE.

VANZETTI, BARTOLOMEO. See SACCO-VANZETTI CASE.

VAPOR, *VAY pur,* in physics, is the term applied to the gaseous state into which solids and liquids pass when they are heated. In a technical sense, both steam and oxygen are vapors. It is customary, however, to make a distinction between gases and vapors. Gases remain gases when compressed at ordinary temperatures. Vapors resume their liquid or solid state under high pressure at ordinary temperatures. The process of converting a substance from solid or liquid form into a vapor is called *vaporization. Evaporation* and *boiling* of liquids are forms of vaporization. In evaporation, the change to a vaporous condition takes place slowly. In boiling, it occurs very rapidly. The formation of vapor directly from a solid state is called *sublimation.* Vaporization in connection with atmospheric conditions bears an important relation to climate. Water vapor is always present in the air. When condensed under varying conditions, water vapor forms clouds, dew, rain, and snow. See also BOILING POINT; EVAPORATION; GAS. LOUIS MARICK

VAPOR LAMP is a source of electric light that uses a vapor or gas, rather than a wire, to produce light. The first vapor lamp consisted of a tube filled with vapor and a small pool of mercury at one end. When the tube was tipped, the mercury rolled through the gas, causing it to glow. Modern vapor lamps are rather short and stocky. They are used outdoors for street and highway lighting. A short quartz tube inside a larger glass tube causes the gas between them to glow. Different gases give various colors. For example, sodium gives yellow or orange light. Fluorescent lights are a form of vapor lamp. See also ELECTRIC LIGHT. KARL A. STALEY

VAPOR LOCK occurs in a gasoline engine when some of the gasoline boils in the fuel-supply system.

Excessive heating of the engine may cause boiling, or *vaporization,* of the fuel. This reduces the amount of fuel pumped to the engine, because vapor takes up more space than liquid. The engine then runs erratically or stops until the vaporized gasoline cools and turns to liquid. Vapor locks occur most frequently during long, steep climbs on hot days, or when slowing suddenly after a hard drive. See also FUEL INJECTION. WILLARD L. ROGERS

VAPOR TRAIL. See CONTRAIL.

VARA. See WEIGHTS AND MEASURES (Miscellaneous Weights and Measures).

VARENNES, PIERRE GAULTIER DE. See LA VÉRENDRYE, SIEUR DE.

VARÈSE, *vah REHZ,* **EDGARD** (1883-1965), was a leading experimental composer of the early 1900's. He refused to follow any school or system of musical composition and did not even consider himself a composer. Varèse declared that he was merely an "organizer of sounds." His works influenced many American and European composers of the mid-1900's.

Varèse composed almost all his important works from 1921 to 1935. He was one of the first to write for percussion instruments only. His most famous composition, *Ionisation* (1931), requires 13 performers who play 39 percussion instruments, including piano, celesta, and chimes. The work also includes two sirens. Varèse pioneered in the development of electronic music (see ELECTRONIC MUSIC). His *Poème Electronique* (1958) is a major work in this field.

Varèse was born in Paris and settled in the United States in 1915. He became a U.S. citizen in 1926. Varèse founded the New Symphony Orchestra in 1919 and helped establish the International Composers' Guild in 1921. Both organizations were dedicated to promoting modern music. MILOŠ VELIMIROVIĆ

VARIABLE STAR. See STAR (Variable Stars).

VARIATIONS, in music, consist of repeating some elements of a musical idea while altering others. This technique is the principle behind the development of musical ideas, and gives variety while retaining coherence.

Composers of all periods have freely used the variation technique. Early variations used by classic composers usually repeated the melody clearly, changing the accompaniment and sometimes the harmonies. Variations became more complicated in the romantic music of the 1800's. In this and later music, it is often difficult to see any resemblance between variations and the original theme. GRANT FLETCHER

See also CLASSICAL MUSIC (The Variation Form).

VARICELLA. See CHICKEN POX.

VARICOSE VEIN, *VAR ih kohs,* is a swollen vein caused by some body condition that interferes with the flow of blood toward the heart. Veins in the legs often become varicose, especially when a person stands a great deal. Heart and liver diseases, gout, pregnancy, abdominal tumors, and tight garters are among the various other causes of varicose veins.

In advanced cases of varicose veins, bluish knotty lumps form along the vein. The patient feels considerable pain in the leg. The chief danger is that the vein will burst, and cause hemorrhage. The diseased veins can also keep the tissues from getting enough nourishment. Water may collect under the skin and cause dropsy. Then the leg is likely to develop ulcers.

Physicians recommend wearing an elastic stocking or

bandage, which will support the varicose vein with steady pressure. Physicians often inject the veins with drugs that tend to shrink them or they may remove the veins by surgery. A disorder known as *hemorrhoids* is varicose veins of the rectum. HYMAN S. RUBINSTEIN

See also HEMORRHOIDS.

VARIETY MEATS. See MEAT.

VARIOMETER. See GLIDER (Flying a Glider; History).

VARLEY, FRED. See GROUP OF SEVEN.

VARNISH is a transparent liquid used to protect wood, metal, and other materials from air and moisture, and to improve their appearance. A varnish leaves a hard, glossy film when it dries.

Clear varnishes protect the surface of wood while allowing the natural grain of the wood to show through. *Varnish stains* contain dyes that change the color of the wood but still bring out the grain. Varnishes used on metal are sometimes called lacquers. Lacquers help prevent corrosion without dulling the metallic appearance. Varnishes are also used to protect insulating wires, masonry, and paper from moisture.

Varnishes can be baked on by heating the varnished articles in ovens at temperatures of 150° to 400° F. (66° to 200° C). Baking improves the wearing quality of the varnished object.

Types of Varnish. There are two main classes of varnishes, spirit and oleoresinous. *Spirit varnishes* are made of chemicals called *resins*. The resins are dissolved in a quickly-evaporating solvent such as alcohol. These varnishes dry when the solvent evaporates. Shellac is a common spirit varnish. Other spirit varnishes include Japan, dammar, and pyroxylin lacquers.

Oleoresinous varnishes are mixtures of resins and drying oils that are heated and dissolved in turpentine or petroleum products. These varnishes dry in two ways, by evaporation of the solvent, and by the hardening of the resin-oil mixture when it combines with oxygen. Oleoresinous varnishes withstand outdoor conditions well. Spar varnish, used on the wood exterior of boats, is an oleoresinous varnish.

Making Varnish. Both natural resins and synthetic resins are used in making varnish. *Natural resins* are extracted from living plants and from fossil plants. Shellac, dammar, and rosin are common natural resins. *Synthetic resins* include such chemical compounds as phenol-formaldehyde, urea-formaldehyde, alkyd (glyceryl phthalate), and cumar.

In making spirit varnishes, the resin is dissolved by churning it with the solvent. Small amounts of heat are sometimes used to speed the dissolving process. After the resin is dissolved, the varnish is refined by filtering and is then ready for use.

In making oleoresinous varnishes, the oil and resin are cooked in closed kettles that hold 5,000 gallons (19,000 liters) or more. The mixture is kept at a temperature of 450° to 700° F. (230° to 370° C) until it reaches the desired *body* (thickness). Then the mixture is cooled and thinners are added. Some natural resins will not dissolve easily in oils. These resins are *run* (heated at about 600° F., or 320° C, until 15 to 30 per cent evaporates).

Drying oils are added to the varnish to hasten the drying time. Linseed oil was probably the first oil to be used in varnishes. Many other drying oils such as perilla,

tung, dehydrated castor, soybean, and fish oils are used today. Compounds of lead, cobalt, or manganese are often added to quicken drying.

Varnishes are named by giving the number of gallons of oil that have been mixed with 100 pounds of resin. For example, a 30-gallon tung-oil kauri varnish is made with 30 gallons of tung oil and 100 pounds of kauri resin. Varnishes used on surfaces exposed to weather contain more oil than those used indoors. JOHN R. KOCH

See also LACQUER; SHELLAC; RESIN; AIRBRUSH.

VASCO DA GAMA. See DA GAMA, VASCO.

VASE, *vays* or *vayz;* in Great Britain, often *vahs* or *vahz.* A vase is a hollow vessel of pottery, stone, metal, glass, or other material. It is usually rounded and deeper than it is wide. A vase is generally decorative, or ornamental, and designed to please the eye by its graceful shape, color, or patterns applied on its surface. Vases are now used chiefly for ornament or to hold flowers. Sometimes they are used for other household purposes. Vases also hold the ashes of the cremated dead.

Pottery or earthenware vases have been made in almost every age of the world's history. Many relics have been preserved and new ones are constantly being discovered. Pictures on these relics often reveal the artistry of the people and sometimes something of their life. One of the most famous ancient vases is the Portland vase, found near Rome in the 1600's. It was found in a tomb believed to be that of Alexander Severus. The Portland vase is of transparent dark blue, coated with milky-white glass cut in cameo style. It is located in the British Museum. EUGENE F. BUNKER, JR.

See also DELFT (picture); PORCELAIN (picture).

VASECTOMY. See SURGERY (table).

VASELINE. See PETROLATUM.

VASODILATOR NERVES. See BLUSHING.

VÁSQUEZ DE CORONADO, FRANCISCO. See CORONADO, FRANCISCO VÁSQUEZ DE.

VASSAL. See FEUDALISM.

VASSAR, MATTHEW (1792-1868), was an American brewer who founded Vassar College. He was born in East Tuddingham, England, and was brought to the United States in 1796. He established a successful brewery in Poughkeepsie, N.Y., and made a large fortune. He also owned a whaling dock in Poughkeepsie, and was part owner of a whaling fleet. Vassar became interested in higher education for women, and in 1861 gave a large sum of money to found Vassar College. The wide publicity given to the venture created interest in college education for women throughout the world. Gifts by Vassar to the college during his life totaled over $800,000. Vassar became a coeducational college in 1968. ROBERT H. BREMNER

VASSAR COLLEGE is a coeducational liberal arts college at Poughkeepsie, N.Y. It is privately controlled and offers courses in languages and literature, arts, physical sciences, and social sciences. Vassar students live in residence houses on a 1,000-acre (400-hectare) campus. Vassar was founded as a school for women in 1861. It was the first women's college to have the equipment and resources equal to those of men's colleges. It became a coeducational school in 1968. For enrollment, see UNIVERSITIES AND COLLEGES (table). See also VASSAR, MATTHEW. Critically reviewed by VASSAR COLLEGE

VATICAN CITY, *VAT ih kuhn* (pop. 1,000), is the smallest independent state in the world. It serves as the spiritual and governmental center of the Roman Catholic Church, the largest Christian church in the world. Vatican City covers only 108.7 acres (44 hectares). But it exercises spiritual sway over millions of Roman Catholics. Its ruler is the pope. Vatican City lies entirely within the city of Rome, Italy. But it is foreign soil to Italian citizens. Vatican City has been an independent sovereign state since the signing of the Treaty of the Lateran in 1929. For location, see ITALY (political map); ROME (map: Inner Rome).

The official name of Vatican City in Italian is Stato della Città del Vaticano (The State of Vatican City). *The Vatican* is a short name for the state and for the city that makes up the state. People often use the term *Vatican* to refer to the pope and the government of Vatican City, in much the same way as they use the term *Washington* to refer to the President of the United States and the U.S. government.

Description

Vatican City is about as large as an average city park. It lies on Vatican Hill in northwestern Rome, just west of the Tiber River. High stone walls surround most of the city. The irregularly shaped area within these walls contains picturesque buildings in several architectural styles. It also contains many courtyards, landscaped gardens, and quiet streets. The huge St. Peter's Church, with its stately dome, dominates the entire city.

St. Peter's Church is the largest Christian church in the world. Contrary to popular belief, it is a basilica, not a cathedral. St. John Lateran, in Rome, is the cathedral church of the pope (see BASILICA; CATHEDRAL; LATERAN). For a history and description of St. Peter's Church and St. Peter's Square, see SAINT PETER'S CHURCH.

The Boundaries of Vatican City, marked by a white line in this picture, enclose an area of about ⅙ square mile (0.4 square kilometer) in northwestern Rome. The dome of the famous St. Peter's Church dominates the skyline of the Papal State.

Vatican Palace is a group of connected buildings with well over 1,000 rooms. The various chapels, apartments, museums, and other rooms cluster around several open courts. The pope's apartment, the offices of the Secretariate of State, and reception rooms and halls occupy one part of the palace. The remainder is devoted largely to the Vatican Museums, the Vatican Archive, and the Vatican Library.

Vatican Museums have a priceless collection of statuary, including the famous *Apollo Belvedere* and the *Laocoön* (see the pictures in the articles on APOLLO and LAOCOÖN). The museums also have large sections devoted to pagan and Christian inscriptions, to Egyptian and Etruscan antiquities, and to modern religious art. The many rooms and chapels within the museums are decorated by the works of such master artists as Fra Angelico, Pinturiccio, Raphael, Titian, and Leonardo da Vinci. Some of Michelangelo's greatest paintings decorate the ceiling and one large wall of the Sistine Chapel (see MICHELANGELO; SISTINE CHAPEL).

Vatican Archive contains important religious and historical documents. Pope Paul V organized the archive in 1612. It houses such important documents as the original report on the trial of Galileo (1633), the request of the English Parliament for the annulment of the marriage of Henry VIII to Catherine of Aragon (1530), and the concordat of Napoleon (1801). Pope Leo XIII opened the archive to scholars in 1881. Since then, many European nations have created historical institutes to search the archives for information on their particular countries.

Vatican Library has one of the world's largest and most valuable collections of early manuscripts and books. See VATICAN LIBRARY.

Other Buildings belonging to Vatican City but located outside the city walls include the basilicas of St. John Lateran, St. Paul's-outside-the-Walls, and St. Mary Major, all in Rome; and the pope's summer villa and the Vatican observatory at Castel Gandolfo.

Administration

The pope, as absolute ruler of Vatican City, heads all branches of the government. But, since he devotes his time primarily to spiritual and ecclesiastical matters, he delegates most of his temporal authority to other officials.

The internal domestic affairs of Vatican City are directed by a Governor, whose duties resemble those of the mayor of a city. Foreign affairs are handled by the Cardinal Secretary of State, who also coordinates ecclesiastical and political affairs. The Vatican has civil law courts in addition to the Tribunal of the Sacred Roman Rota, which handles religious cases. But most civil criminal cases are prosecuted by the Italian government. The Congregation of the Ceremonial directs papal ceremonies and audiences, and also handles matters of protocol and etiquette. Vatican finances are controlled by a number of administrations, or departments. Each administration handles a different set of funds.

Vatican City issues its own postage stamps, coins,

and automobile license plates. The pope's yellow-and-white banner is the official state flag (see FLAG [picture: Flags of Europe]).

Public Works. The Vatican maintains its own mail system, telephone and telegraph systems, water supply, and lighting and street-cleaning services. It also has its own bank, a large printing plant, and a rarely occupied jail. Although the state has its own railroad station, no one has ever bought a ticket to Vatican City. The 300 yards (270 meters) of track that connect the station in Vatican City with an Italian railroad carries only freight.

Armed Forces. Vatican City does not have an army or navy capable of fighting a war. The Vatican does, however, maintain a military corps known as the Swiss Guard. The function of the Swiss Guard is to maintain a constant watch over the pope and his personal residence (see SWISS GUARDS). In addition, the Central Office of Vigilance guards Vatican City. Also, the St. Peter and Paul Association provides everyday police services for Vatican City.

Diplomatic Corps of Vatican City includes about 60 *legates* (ambassadors), as well as other diplomatic personnel. The highest ranking legates are the *nuncios*. Legates of lesser rank are called *internuncios*. Nuncios

SCALA

The Sistine Chapel is a famous structure in the Vatican Palace. It was named for Pope Sixtus IV, who ordered its construction during the 1470's. The chapel is noted for the paintings by Michelangelo that cover the ceiling and the rear wall behind the altar. Other artists decorated the side walls.

and internuncios head the Vatican's delegations to other countries. They also look after the welfare of the Roman Catholic Church in those countries. Most European and Latin-American countries receive nuncios or internuncios from the Vatican. Papal representatives in countries that have no formal diplomatic relations with the Vatican are called *apostolic delegates*. Such delegates have no diplomatic status and hold authority only in ecclesiastical matters. Apostolic delegates serve in the United States, Great Britain, Mexico, and several other countries.

Communications. The Vatican publishes *L'Osservatore Romano*, one of the most influential daily newspapers in the world. Other Vatican publications include *Osservatore della Domenica*, a weekly publication; and the *Acta Apostolicae Sedis*, which prints official church documents. The Vatican's powerful radio transmitter broadcasts news and papal messages in 30 languages, including Latin.

History

Vatican Hill was once the site of Roman emperor Nero's public gardens and circus. Many early Christians suffered martyrdom there. According to tradition, St. Peter was crucified on the hill and buried nearby. The early popes believed that a shrine built in the A.D. 100's marked the site of Peter's tomb. Because of this belief, they erected Vatican City on that spot.

In the A.D. 300's, the Christian emperor Constantine the Great built a basilica over the tomb in which St. Peter was believed to be buried. The Vatican Palace and other structures were gradually built around the basilica. But the main residence of the popes during the Middle Ages was the Lateran Palace in Rome, not the Vatican. From 1309 to 1377, the popes lived at Avignon, France. On their return to Rome, they found the Lateran Palace burned, so they moved to the Vatican. Beginning in the 1500's, St. Peter's Church was built on the site of the Old Basilica of Constantine.

Through the years, the popes gained control over an area in central Italy called the Papal States. In 1870, after a series of political defeats, Pope Pius IX lost his power over the Papal States. In protest, he and his successors withdrew inside the Vatican and refused to deal with the Italian government. Finally, in 1929, the Treaty of the Lateran was signed. By this treaty, the pope gave up all claim to the Papal States, and Italy agreed to the establishment of the independent State of Vatican City. For the provisions of the Treaty of the Lateran, see PAPAL STATES.

In 1939, Pope Pius XII initiated a series of excavations beneath St. Peter's Church. These excavations unearthed, among other things, a tomb thought to be the original tomb of St. Peter.   JOACHIM SMET

See also POPE; ROMAN CATHOLIC CHURCH.

VATICAN COUNCIL is the name of two *ecumenical* (general) councils of the Roman Catholic Church that were held in Vatican City in Rome. An ecumenical council is a meeting of church leaders called by a pope for a special purpose. There have been 21 ecumenical councils.

The first Christian council, the Council of Nicaea, took place in 325. The 20th and 21st councils are called *Vatican Councils* I and II. Vatican I was held in 1869 and 1870. Vatican II was held from 1962 to 1965. This article describes the Vatican councils. For background information on these councils, see ROMAN CATHOLIC CHURCH. For information on earlier councils, see NICENE COUNCILS; TRENT, COUNCIL OF.

Vatican I

Vatican I was called by Pope Pius IX. It opened Dec. 8, 1869, and is remembered primarily for approving the doctrine of *papal infallibility*. This doctrine states that the pope can commit no error when he speaks as head of the church to proclaim, in matters of faith and morals, what is to be accepted by all Roman Catholics as the teaching laid down by Jesus Christ and His apostles. At the outbreak of the Franco-Prussian War in 1870, the council was suspended. It never reconvened.

Vatican II

Pope John XXIII announced his intention of calling a worldwide church council on Jan. 25, 1959. He said the council would provide an *aggiornamento* (renewal or updating) of Roman Catholic religious life and doctrine.

Pope John opened the first session Oct. 11, 1962, and closed it Dec. 8, 1962. He died on June 3, 1963, and the remaining three sessions were held under his successor Pope Paul VI. The second session ran from Sept. 29 to Dec. 4, 1963; the third session from Sept. 14 to Nov. 21, 1964; and the final session from Sept. 14 to Dec. 8, 1965.

Vatican II was one of the most widely-discussed religious events of the century. Religious officials, journalists, and other observers—both Catholic and non-Catholic—from all over the world reported and interpreted the actions of the council.

The Documents. The council *promulgated* (officially announced) 16 documents. The documents defined the nature of the church, gave the bishops greater influence in church affairs, and gave the laity a more active part in the liturgy. The documents also proclaimed a historic church position on religious liberty, and expressed new and liberalized positions on the church's relations with non-Catholic and non-Christian faiths.

The council approved these documents in the form of four *constitutions*, three *declarations*, and nine *decrees*. Constitutions were the council's most solemn documents.

The Constitution on the Church was the most important of the documents. It set the theological basis for all other council documents, and described the nature of the church. It described the laity and hierarchy as "members of the people of God," and forbade any separation between them. The constitution portrayed the bishops and the pope as a "college," with the pope as head. It implied a greater sharing by the bishops in the exercise of the authority of the church and gave the bishops a larger role in church government.

The Constitution on the Sacred Liturgy permitted the use of the *vernacular* (local language) in place of Latin in parts of the Mass. The Mass liturgy was revised to allow greater participation by the congregation. The vernacular was also approved for other sacraments, such as baptism, eucharist, and marriage.

The Constitution on Divine Revelation emphasized the vital part sacred scriptures (the Bible) play in the

church's life and liturgy. By stressing the importance of the Bible, this constitution narrowed the differences between Roman Catholics and Protestants on the issue of divine revelation.

The Pastoral Constitution on the Church in the Modern World was the first ecumenical document to be addressed to all people, not just Roman Catholics. The first part discussed people's relationship to the world, to the church, and to God. The church rejected atheism, but said that atheists should be respected and loved because they are God's creatures.

The second part took up urgent problems facing humanity. One chapter dealt with family life, and others dealt with social, economic, and political problems of today. The council condemned all forms of war as a means of settling international disputes, but it said countries had the right to self-defense. It called for the community of nations to organize and work to relieve the suffering of poor and starving peoples.

The Declaration on Christian Education endorsed the right of parents to choose freely the type of education they wish for their children.

The Declaration on the Relationship of the Church to Non-Christian Religions emphasized the respect owed to all people as children of a common Creator. The document said the church rejects nothing that is "true and holy" in religions such as Hinduism, Buddhism, Islam, and Judaism. It condemned any form of discrimination, particularly anti-Semitism. It stated the Jews had no collective responsibility for the death of Christ.

The Declaration on Religious Freedom stated that all people have the right to religious freedom. This was a dramatic change in the church's historical position. The declaration, however, repeated the church's claim to be the one true faith.

The Decree on the Instruments of Social Communication declared that means of communication such as the press and motion pictures should be used for moral purposes.

The Decree on Ecumenism pledged the church to work for the unity of all Christianity, and encouraged Roman Catholics to participate in the ecumenical movement. The decree permits Catholics to join non-Catholics in common prayer, with the permission of local bishops.

The Decree on Eastern Catholic Churches reasserted the equality of Eastern Rite Catholic churches with the Western Latin rite. The decree set forth circumstances under which Catholics and Eastern Orthodox Church members could participate together in the sacraments and liturgy.

The Decree on the Bishops' Pastoral Office in the Church discussed in detail the collegiality of bishops described in the *Constitution on the Church*. It directed the bishops to form national and regional conferences to meet local conditions and problems. It also called for a synod of bishops to meet with the pope periodically in Rome to act as an international senate or advisory board.

The Decree on the Appropriate Renewal of the Religious Life gave directions for modernizing the religious life of monks, priests, brothers, and nuns.

The Decree on Priestly Formation urged reforms in both the intellectual and spiritual training of candidates for the priesthood. It granted national church leaders more authority to regulate seminaries.

The Decree on the Ministry and Life of Priests reaffirmed the laws of *celibacy* (unmarried state) for Roman Catholic priests, without modifying the Eastern Rite discipline allowing married or celibate clergy.

The Decree on the Apostolate of the Laity expanded the examination of the role of Catholic laity in church affairs described in the *Constitution on the Church*. The decree urged the laity to use its initiative in both religious and temporal affairs.

The Decree on the Church's Missionary Activity called for greater cooperation and support between well-established churches and missionary churches.

Other Events. On Oct. 4, 1965, Pope Paul made a historic journey to speak before the United Nations in New York City. The pope made the trip in the name of the entire council "for the cause of peace in the world." He pleaded for the support of all nations in promoting peace and outlawing war.

The final days of the council witnessed two other historically significant events. On December 6, Pope Paul met with Protestant observers of the council and more than 1,000 bishops in a joint prayer service.

On December 7, the pope read a declaration removing a sentence of excommunication on the patriarch of Constantinople that dated back to 1054. A similar declaration read in Istanbul by the patriarch of Constantinople removed a sentence of excommunication passed against a group of papal legates in 1054. The declarations were a step toward ending the division between the Roman Catholic and Eastern Orthodox churches. MARK J. HURLEY

Additional Resources

JOHN PAUL II, POPE. *Sources of Renewal: The Implementation of the Second Vatican Council.* Harper, 1980.
LINDBECK, GEORGE A. *The Future of Roman Catholic Theology: Vatican II—Catalyst for Change.* Fortress Press, 1970.

VATICAN LIBRARY, *VAT uh kuhn,* is the library of the Roman Catholic Church in Vatican City. It has one of the world's most important collections of early manuscripts and books. The Vatican Library was founded by Nicholas V, pope from 1447 to 1455, as a library for handwritten manuscripts.

The Vatican Library is still chiefly a manuscript library, though it now also has about 350,000 printed books in its collection. The library's manuscripts number more than 50,000, over 31,000 of which are valuable old Latin works. There are also nearly 4,000 Greek and Oriental manuscripts in the library.

Many of the manuscripts are kept in closed rooms and may be seen only with the permission of the librarian. But the current practice of the Vatican Library is to make such materials available to all competent scholars. FULTON J. SHEEN

See also LIBRARY (picture: Vatican Library).

VAUDEVILLE, *VAW duh vihl* or *VOHD vihl,* is a kind of theatrical entertainment that features a wide variety of acts. It was the most popular form of entertainment in the United States from the 1880's to the early 1930's. Vaudeville developed many stars who later gained great success in other types of entertainment, especially motion pictures and radio. These stars included Jack Benny, George Burns, Eddie Cantor, W. C. Fields, Al Jolson, Ed Wynn, and Sophie Tucker.

Some vaudeville theaters presented 20 or more acts in

a single *bill* (performance). However, the standard pattern was 8 to 10 acts. The range of material and performers in a vaudeville bill was enormous. A vaudeville show presented jugglers, animal acts, skits, recitations, celebrities of the day, singers, and, most popular of all, comics and magicians. The arrangement of these acts might have seemed unplanned. But theater managers carefully organized their bills to present a selection of dissimilar acts intended to create excitement and expectation among viewers.

Because of the efforts of powerful producers and theater owners, vaudeville became a highly organized nationwide big business. A number of individuals controlled large *circuits* (chains) of theaters. The best known of these circuits were operated by E. F. Albee, Martin Beck, Willie Hammerstein, B. F. Keith, Marcus Loew, William Morris, Alexander Pantages, and F. F. Proctor. All vaudeville performers wanted to star in "big-time" theaters that presented only two shows a day. However, most performers appeared in "small-time" theaters that offered 3 to 12 shows a day. Some theaters presented continuous shows that began about 9:30 A.M. and lasted until about 10:30 P.M.

The term *vaudeville* comes from a French word for a light play with music that was popular in France during the 1800's. The American form grew out of attempts by saloon owners to attract more customers by offering free shows with their drinks. These shows were known as *variety*. At first, variety had a bad reputation because it took place in saloons and often included vulgar material. But by the 1890's, it had achieved respectability under the more elegant French name of *vaudeville*. Soon vaudeville had become the major form of live entertainment for family audiences. Showman Tony Pastor is credited with converting vaudeville into entertainment suitable for families by prohibiting drinks and upgrading the quality of the performers. Pastor presented many famous vaudeville stars at Tony Pastor's Opera House in New York City.

Vaudeville's popularity declined with the development of sound motion pictures in the late 1920's. But vaudeville style acts are still presented in some night clubs and on television. DON B. WILMETH

Additional Resources

DiMEGLIO, JOHN E. *Vaudeville U.S.A.* Bowling Green Univ. Press, 1973.
SAMUELS, CHARLES and LOUISE. *Once Upon a Stage: The Merry World of Vaudeville.* Dodd, 1974.
SLIDE, ANTHONY. *The Vaudevillians: A Dictionary of Vaudeville Performers.* Arlington House, 1981.

VAUGHAN, *vawn,* **HENRY** (1622-1695), was one of the leading English poets of the 1600's. He began his career with a volume of nonreligious verse, *Poems* (1646), and then wrote the deeply religious *Silex Scintillans* (two parts, 1651 and 1655). The Latin *Silex Scintillans* means "the flashing flint," and refers to the way God's love and a knowledge of divine mysteries can strike fire into the stoniest hearts of people. Vaughan described these moments of illumination with fine natural imagery. His greatest poem, "The World," is a complex meditation that tells how he "saw Eternity the other night." He is often considered the forerunner of the romantic poet William Wordsworth.

Vaughan was born in Wales. He retired there about 1660 and became a country doctor. RICHARD S. SYLVESTER

See also METAPHYSICAL POETS.

VAUGHAN WILLIAMS, *vawn WIHL yuhmz,* **RALPH** (1872-1958), was one of Great Britain's foremost composers. His music mingles the flavors of English folk songs and Tudor church music, both of which he studied intensively. He produced such distinguished music as the *Sixth Symphony* (1947); an opera, *The Pilgrim's Progress* (1951); *Seventh Symphony,* or *Sinfonia Antartica* (1952); and *Eighth Symphony* (1956). He composed music for the coronation of Queen Elizabeth II in 1953.

Vaughan Williams was born in the parish of Down Ampney, Gloucestershire. In 1904, he became active in the Folk Song Society, and edited *The English Hymnal* in 1905. By 1914, he had written *A Sea Symphony* (1910), *A London Symphony* (1914), and several other choral and orchestral works. His other popular works include *The Lark Ascending* (1921), *Sir John in Love* (1929), and *Flourish for a Coronation* (1937). HALSEY STEVENS

VAULT, in architecture, is a roof or ceiling in the form of an arch. The four main kinds of vaults are the barrel vault, the dome, the groined vault, and the ribbed, or Gothic, vault. The simplest form is the *barrel vault,* which is a continuous arch. Each part is held in place by the part next to it. The *dome* is a vault in the form of a hemisphere built upon a circular base. Some domes are oval or slightly pointed. The *groined vault* is formed by joining together two or more barrel vaults at right angles. The lines at which the vaults join are called *groins.* In a *ribbed vault,* arched ribs are built in the places where groins would otherwise be. The ribs rest on pillars and make massive walls unnecessary. In Gothic architecture, ribs were both structural and decorative.

The word *vault* also applies to rooms designed for the safekeeping of valuables. Such a vault is usually made of steel, with heavy walls and ceiling, and it is entered through a steel door (see BANK [picture]). In cemeteries, enclosures or buildings called vaults are used as temporary or permanent places of burial. TALBOT HAMLIN

See also ARCHITECTURE (table: Architectural Terms).

VD. See VENEREAL DISEASE.

VEAL is the flesh of cattle that are too young and small to be sold as beef. These cattle are divided into *vealers* and *calves.* Vealers are animals under 14 weeks old that are fed with milk. Calves—like older cattle—eat grass or grain, but calf flesh is not as tasty as beef. Most beef sold at stores comes from animals one to two years old.

In the United States, vealers and calves sell by weight and according to grades set up by the federal government. The U.S. grades are *prime, choice, good, standard, utility,* and *cull.* The best grades of veal are plump, and range in color from light pink to grayish pink. The flesh of lower grades is thin and watery.

Calf flesh is darker and has more definite grain than vealer flesh. Calves also have much more fat covering than vealers. The meat of both calves and vealers has little trimming waste when sold in stores.

Veal is similar to beef. Veal contains more water than beef, but it has less fat. Veal is more tender than beef, but the older age of beef cattle makes beef tastier than veal. People in the United States eat much more beef than veal. JOHN C. AYRES

See also BEEF; CATTLE (Beef Cattle); MEAT.

VEBLEN, *VEHB luhn,* **THORSTEIN BUNDE** (1857-1929), an American economist, was one of the most original and creative thinkers in the history of American economic thought. His first book, *The Theory of the Leisure Class* (1899), is a scholarly and satirical protest against the false values and social waste of the upper classes. *The Theory of Business Enterprise* (1904) criticizes the capitalist system, and predicts that it will drift into either fascism or socialism. In *The Engineers and the Price System* (1921), Veblen assigned to scientists and engineers an important position in building a new planned economic society. Veblen was born in Cato, Wis. He was graduated from Carleton College and received his Ph.D. from Yale University. DUDLEY DILLARD

VECELLIO, TIZIANO. See TITIAN.

VECTOR. See MOTION (Newton's Laws of Motion).

VEDAS, *VAY duhz,* are the oldest sacred books of Hinduism. The Vedas include most of the doctrines concerning Hindu divinities. They also present philosophical ideas about the nature of Brahman, the supreme divine being of the Hindu religion. The word *veda* means *knowledge.*

There are four Vedas. They are, in order of age beginning with the oldest, *Rig-Veda, Sama-Veda, Yajur-Veda,* and the *Atharva-Veda.* Each Veda is divided into three parts: (1) the *Samhitas,* consisting of hymns and prayers written in verse; (2) the *Brahmanas,* dealing mainly with ideas about Brahman and with religious ceremonies; and (3) the *Upanishads,* philosophical works.

The Vedas were composed during the 1,000 years before the birth of Christ. For hundreds of years, certain Hindu families memorized parts of the Vedas and passed them down orally. Hindu law permitted only certain persons to hear the Vedas recited, and so the works became surrounded by mystery. Nevertheless, the ideas presented in the Vedas spread throughout Indian culture. The Vedas were probably first put in writing about the time of Christ's birth. CHARLES S. J. WHITE

See also BRAHMAN; HINDUISM; SANSKRIT LANGUAGE AND LITERATURE; UPANISHADS.

VEERY, *VIHR ee,* is a North American bird of the thrush group. It lives in the northeastern parts of the United States and Canada. The veery is also known as Wilson's thrush or as the nightingale. It has brownish upper parts, a whitish, faintly spotted breast, and is about 7 inches (18 centimeters) long. It builds its nest of leaves in the lower branches of bushes or small trees. The female lays from three to five greenish-blue eggs.

Scientific Classification. The veery and other thrushes make up the subfamily Turdinae of the family Muscicapidae. (Some authorities consider the thrushes a separate family, Turdidae.) The veery is *Catharus fuscescens.* LEON A. HAUSMAN

VEGA, *VEE guh,* is the brightest star in Lyra, a constellation in the Northern Hemisphere. It is also called *Alpha Lyrae.* Vega appears bluish-white because it is extremely hot. Its surface temperature is about 18,000° F. (10,000° C). Vega is about 26 light-years from the earth (see LIGHT-YEAR). In about 13,000 years, it will become the earth's North Star.

In 1983, the Infrared Astronomical Satellite (IRAS), an observatory orbiting the earth, detected a giant ring or shell of solid particles surrounding Vega. These particles probably grew from the remains of the cloud of gases and smaller dust particles that formed the star. The discovery by IRAS represented the first direct evidence of such particle growth around any star except the sun. Many astronomers believe the material around Vega might be a solar system that is in the process of formation. SUMNER STARRFIELD

See also ASTRONOMY (map: The Stars and Constellations of the Northern Hemisphere); NORTH STAR.

VEGA, *VAY gah,* **LOPE DE,** *LOH pay day* (1562-1635), was the most important playwright of Spain's Golden Age. He wrote more plays than any other author. Lope was once credited with 1,800 full-length plays and 400 *autos sacramentales* (short religious plays). This total is an exaggeration, but scholars generally agree that he wrote over 400 plays. The two largest categories are "cloak-and-sword" plays of intrigue, and historical plays, such as *The Best Mayor, the King* (1616?) and *The Sheep Well* (1619?).

Lope described his theory of drama in *The New Art of Writing Plays* (1609). He rejected the dramatic unities that restricted action to a single place during a specific length of time. He believed that the best themes were conflicts of passion and the Spanish honor code. His characters usually lack individuality, but his style is poetic and his situations are exciting. Lope's influence on the dramatists of his time was strong, and he is credited with creating a Spanish national drama.

Lope Félix de Vega Carpio was born in Madrid. He led an adventurous and troubled life. Several of his love affairs ended sadly, particularly his relationship with Marta de Nevares, whom he met after becoming a priest in 1614. PETER G. EARLE

See also DRAMA (The Golden Age of Spanish Drama); SPANISH LITERATURE (Drama).

VEGETABLE is any of many nutritious foods that come from the leaves, roots, seeds, stems, and other parts of certain plants. People eat vegetables raw or cooked and use them as part of a main meal, in salads and soups, and as snacks.

Vegetables are an important part of a healthy diet. They are excellent sources of vitamins, especially niacin, riboflavin, thiamin, and vitamins A and C. Vegetables also supply the minerals calcium and iron. Most vegetables do not have many calories.

The growing of vegetables is a branch of *horticulture,* a field of agriculture that also includes the raising of fruits. Horticultural scientists define a vegetable as the edible product of a *herbaceous plant.* A herbaceous plant has stems that are softer and less fibrous than the woody stems of trees and shrubs. Most vegetables are *annuals—* plants that live for only one year or one growing season.

The horticultural definition of vegetables distinguishes them from fruits, which grow annually on trees and other woody plants that live more than two years. In some cases, common usage differs from scientific definitions. For example, most people consider muskmelons and watermelons as fruits. But horticulturists regard them as vegetables because these melons grow on vines that must be replanted annually.

The hobby of growing a home vegetable garden is becoming increasingly popular. Home gardening can help reduce food costs, produce high-quality vegetables, and provide exercise and fun. The most popular vegetables grown in home gardens include beans, cabbage, cucumbers, lettuce, onions, radishes, squash, and to-

Plant Parts Used as Vegetables

Vegetables are nutritious foods that come from various parts of certain plants. Bulbs, flower clusters, fruits, leaves, roots, seeds, stems, and tubers may be eaten as vegetables.

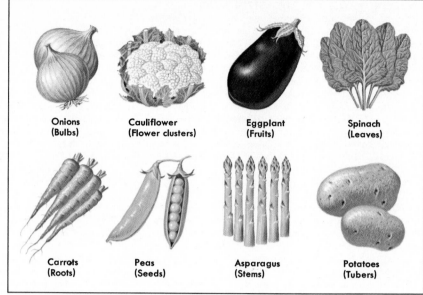

Onions
(Bulbs)

Cauliflower
(Flower clusters)

Eggplant
(Fruits)

Spinach
(Leaves)

Carrots
(Roots)

Peas
(Seeds)

Asparagus
(Stems)

Potatoes
(Tubers)

matoes. This article deals mainly with the commercial production of vegetables. For more information on home vegetable growing, see GARDENING.

Most vegetables grown commercially in the United States and Canada are canned, dehydrated, frozen, or processed in some other way. Vegetables raised for processing include peas, potatoes, snap beans, sweet corn, and tomatoes. Those grown to be eaten fresh include cabbage, carrots, lettuce, onions, and tomatoes.

The leading vegetable-producing states are, in order of rank, California, Illinois, Iowa, Minnesota, and Missouri. In Canada, most vegetables come from British Columbia, Ontario, and Quebec.

Plant Parts Used as Vegetables

Vegetables can be grouped according to the part of the plant from which they come. Plant parts eaten as vegetables include bulbs, flower clusters, fruits, leaves, roots, seeds, stems, and tubers.

Bulbs consist of many fleshy leaves that surround a short stem. The base of these leaves is large and grows underground, and it is the part usually eaten. Garlic, leeks, onions, and shallots are bulbs used as vegetables and seasonings.

Flower Clusters. The most common flower clusters used as vegetables are broccoli and cauliflower. Broccoli plants have *heads* (thick clusters of flower buds) that are green and branched. The heads of cauliflower are tight, round, and white.

Fruits are the seed enclosures, along with the seeds, produced by a flowering plant. Horticulturists consider the edible fruits of herbaceous annuals as vegetables. Fruits of vegetable plants include cucumbers, eggplants, muskmelons, okra, peppers, pumpkins, snap beans, squashes, tomatoes, and watermelons.

Leaves eaten as vegetables include Brussels sprouts, cabbage, chard, Chinese cabbage, cress, endive, kale, lettuce, mustard, and spinach. Some of the vegetables are cooked before being eaten, but most are eaten raw in salads. Celery and rhubarb are *petioles* (leafstalks).

Petioles support the leaf blades and are connected to the stems of a plant.

Roots that are vegetables may be *fibrous roots* or *taproots*. Fibrous roots branch and spread sideways underground. Sweet potatoes are enlarged, fleshy parts of fibrous roots. A taproot is the enlarged part of a root that grows straight down. Beets, carrots, horseradish, parsnips, radishes, rutabagas, and turnips are examples of taproots.

Seeds. People eat the seeds of plants when they eat cowpeas, garden peas, kidney beans, lima beans, navy beans, and sweet corn. Certain seeds, such as kidney beans and navy beans, are harvested after they become hard. Other seeds, such as garden peas and sweet corn, are picked when they are still soft.

Stems support the leaves, flowers, and fruits of a plant. The two chief stems eaten as vegetables are asparagus and kohlrabi. Asparagus stems are tall and slender. Kohlrabi plants have large bulblike stems.

Tubers. Most tubers are a specialized kind of stem that grows underground. The main ones used as vegetables are potatoes and Jerusalem artichokes. Potatoes make up about a fifth of all the vegetables produced in the United States and Canada.

Growing Vegetables

The choice of a location for raising any vegetable commercially depends chiefly on the climate. For example, sweet corn grows best during the wet summers of Minnesota, Oregon, and Wisconsin. Potatoes thrive in the cool growing conditions of Idaho, Maine, and Washington. The irrigated desert areas of California are ideal for raising tomatoes. The cool summers of other sections of California are just right for lettuce. During the winter, the warm climate of Arizona, Florida, and Texas makes those states important producers of fresh vegetables for the northern United States.

There are four basic steps in commercial vegetable production: (1) planting, (2) caring for the crop, (3) harvesting, and (4) packing and shipping. Most vegeta-

ble growers use various kinds of machines for these operations.

Planting. Many vegetables are planted as seeds in the field where they will grow until harvested. This method is called *direct seeding*. Some vegetable farmers plant *pregerminated seeds*. These seeds are first sprouted in partly decayed plant matter called *peat*. The mixture of peat and sprouted seeds is then planted in the field. Some vegetables, such as cabbage and tomatoes, may be grown from transplanted seedlings that were started in a greenhouse or in a field in a warmer climate. A vegetable grower can produce a crop earlier in the season by using transplants than would be possible by direct seeding.

The planting date varies with the type of vegetable. Some vegetables grow best in cool weather and are planted early in spring. They include beets, carrots, lettuce, potatoes, radishes, and spinach. Others, such as cabbage, onions, and peas, can withstand frost and are planted even earlier. Growers in the Southern States can plant cool-weather vegetables during winter.

Some vegetables, among them eggplants, squash, and sweet corn, require warm weather. These crops are planted so that the seedlings emerge after the last frost of the season. Cucumbers, lima beans, muskmelons, and tomatoes are planted only after the final frost. In the North, warm-season vegetables can be planted in late spring, usually after April. In the Southern States, these vegetables can be planted as early as February.

Caring for the Crop begins by preparing the soil before the seeds are planted. The vegetable grower cultivates and fertilizes the fields and also may apply weedkiller. After planting the crop, the grower may cultivate the fields again to kill weeds and improve the circulation of air and water through the soil. More fertilizer may also be applied.

Vegetable farmers inspect their crops periodically for destructive insects and plant diseases. Farmers use a variety of chemicals and methods of control because different insects and diseases attack different plants. Fields of vegetables may have to be irrigated if they do not receive enough rain. In areas with arid and semi-arid climates, irrigation is a necessity.

Harvesting vegetables at the proper time is extremely important. Vegetables sent directly to a local market or to a processing plant can be more mature when harvested than those that must be shipped long distances. Farmers may harvest some vegetables, such as carrots

and potatoes, over a period of several weeks. However, other crops must be picked and transported rapidly to ensure freshness and quality.

Packing and Shipping. Most vegetables are graded according to quality and size. Harvested vegetables may be taken to a building where they are sorted, washed, trimmed, packaged, and labeled. But some machines can pick, sort, and package the crops while moving through the fields.

Most vegetables are washed to remove dirt and prevent wilting. The outer leaves of lettuce and cabbage are removed to improve the appearance of the vegetables. Cucumbers are waxed to prevent water loss. Some vegetables, including lettuce and sweet corn, must be cooled to prevent spoilage after being harvested.

Vegetables are shipped by refrigerated trucks or railroad cars to local or distant markets and processing plants. Some vegetables, such as onions and potatoes, can be stored for long periods of time before being shipped.　　　　　　　　　　　　W. E. SPLITTSTOESSER

Related Articles. See the *Agriculture* section of the various state, province, and country articles for a discussion of vegetables grown there, such as ARKANSAS (Agriculture). Additional related articles in WORLD BOOK include:

VEGETABLES

Artichoke	Collards	Muskmelon	Salsify
Asparagus	Corn	Mustard	Shallot
Bean	Cowpea	Okra	Sorrel
Beet	Cress	Onion	Soybean
Broccoli	Cucumber	Parsley	Spinach
Brussels	Eggplant	Parsnip	Squash
Sprouts	Endive	Pea	Sweet Potato
Cabbage	Garlic	Peanut	Swiss Chard
Carrot	Horseradish	Pepper	Taro
Cauliflower	Kale	Potato	Tomato
Celery	Kohlrabi	Pumpkin	Turnip
Chayote	Leek	Radish	Watermelon
Chinese	Lentil	Rhubarb	Yam
Cabbage	Lettuce	Rutabaga	Zucchini
Chive	Lima Bean		

OTHER RELATED ARTICLES

Agriculture	Horticulture
Canning	Nutrition (Basic
Farm and Farming	Food Groups)
Food	Plant
Food, Frozen	Truck Farming
Food Preservation	Vegetable Oil
Gardening	Vegetarianism

Leading Vegetable-Growing States

California	
	11,302,000 short tons (10,253,000 metric tons)
Illinois	
	10,965,000 short tons (9,947,000 metric tons)
Iowa	
	9,934,000 short tons (9,020,000 metric tons)
Minnesota	
	5,878,000 short tons (5,332,000 metric tons)
Missouri	
	4,775,000 short tons (4,332,000 metric tons)

Source: *Agricultural Statistics, 1982,* USDA. Figures are for 1981.

Leading Vegetable-Growing Countries

China	
	266,342,000 short tons (241,621,000 metric tons)
Russia	
	116,752,000 short tons (105,916,000 metric tons)
United States	
	107,489,000 short tons (97,512,000 metric tons)
India	
	75,663,000 short tons (68,640,000 metric tons)
Brazil	
	54,635,000 short tons (49,564,000 metric tons)

Source: *FAO Production Yearbook, 1981.* Figures are for 1981.

VEGETABLE IVORY

VEGETABLE IVORY. See IVORY PALM.

VEGETABLE OIL is a fatty substance obtained from certain plants. Most vegetable oils are liquids. But several, including cocoa butter, coconut oil, and palm oil, are solids at temperatures below about 75° F. (24° C). People use vegetable oils in various foods and in making paint, soap, and other products.

Most vegetable oils are obtained from fruit or seeds. Oils extracted from fruit include olive and palm oil. Seeds provide cocoa butter and such oils as coconut, corn, cottonseed, linseed, palm kernel, peanut, rapeseed, safflower, soybean, and sunflower oil.

Uses. Vegetable oils are used mainly in producing or cooking many kinds of foods. These oils consist almost entirely of fat, an essential part of a healthful diet. For more information on the food value and chemical composition of vegetable oils, see FAT.

The chief vegetable oils used in the United States are cottonseed, soybean, and sunflower oil. People use these oils, as well as corn, olive, and peanut oil, in frying food and as salad oil. Most salad dressings include soybean oil. Margarine and other solid shortenings are made from corn, cottonseed, palm, safflower, soybean, and sunflower oil. Candy manufacturers use cocoa butter, coconut oil, and palm kernel oil.

Many nonfood products also contain vegetable oil. For example, manufacturers make cosmetics, shampoos, and soaps from coconut, palm, and palm kernel oil. Some medicines contain cocoa butter or castor, olive, or wheat germ oil. Many paints and varnishes include a *drying oil*, such as linseed, soybean, or tung oil. Drying oils combine with oxygen from the air to form a tough coating. See OIL (Fixed Oils).

Production of vegetable oils begins with their extraction from fruit or seeds. Many oils are simply squeezed out. For example, processors use a powerful machine called a *high-pressure press* to squeeze out coconut and palm oil and some cottonseed oil. This procedure removes nearly all the oil from the fruit or seeds. But the high pressure heats the oil, which develops a dark color and a strong flavor as a result. Oils may also be squeezed out under low pressure in a process called *cold pressing.* This process, which does not heat the oil, results in a light-colored, mild-flavored product. But low-pressure extraction does not remove all the oil from the plant. Cold pressing is used chiefly to obtain olive oil.

A process known as *solvent extraction* is sometimes used to remove the oil. In this process, the manufacturer soaks the fruit or seeds in a liquid called a *solvent* that dissolves oil. A mixture of plant material, solvent, and oil results. Machines then remove the plant material and evaporate the solvent to obtain the oil. Most soybean oil is produced by solvent extraction.

Processors squeeze part of the oil from some sources, including corn, cottonseed, and peanuts. They remove the remaining oil from the seeds with solvents.

Oils obtained by high-pressure or solvent extraction are bleached, deodorized, and purified to produce a high-quality product. Cold-pressed oils require no further processing.   THEODORE J. WEISS

Related Articles in WORLD BOOK include:

Castor Oil	Copra	Cottonseed Oil	Linseed Oil
Chocolate	Corn Oil	Hydrogenation	Margarine

Olive Oil	Palm Oil	Rape	Soybean	Tung Oil
Paint	Peanut	Safflower	Sunflower	Varnish

VEGETARIANISM is the practice of not eating meat. Vegetarians regard the flesh of all animals, including that of fish and poultry, as meat. Most vegetarians avoid eating meat because of moral or religious beliefs. They believe it is wrong to kill animals for food. Many vegetarians also think that eating meat is unhealthy.

Some vegetarians exclude milk and eggs, as well as meat, from their diet because these foods come from animals. Vegetarians are divided into three groups, based on their attitude toward milk and eggs. *Lacto-ovo-vegetarians* include milk and eggs, and foods made from milk and eggs, in their diet. *Lacto-vegetarians* do not eat eggs, but they drink milk and eat such milk products as butter and cheese. *Vegans* avoid milk and eggs and all foods made from these animal products.

A vegetarian diet must be well planned to provide the protein and certain other nutrients that the body needs and that meat contains. Most lacto-ovo-vegetarians and lacto-vegetarians can easily plan a healthy diet because milk and eggs are good sources of high-quality protein. Milk also provides large amounts of calcium, which helps strengthen bones. Milk and eggs both contain vitamin B_{12}, which forms a part of red blood cells and helps the nerves function properly.

Vegans must plan their diet especially well because no single fruit, vegetable, or grain contains the nutritionally complete protein found in meat, milk, and eggs. Beans, nuts, peas, and many other vegetarian foods contain large amounts of protein. However, these foods must be eaten in particular combinations to provide the body with nutritionally complete protein. For example, beans and rice eaten together provide complete protein, but neither food does when eaten alone. To obtain calcium, vegans must eat sesame seeds or certain green leafy vegetables, such as broccoli or spinach. Most vegans take vitamin B_{12} tablets to obtain the necessary amount of this nutrient.

Most vegetarian diets contain fewer calories than diets that include meat. As a result, vegetarians in general are thinner than meat-eaters. Most vegetarians also consume less saturated fat and smaller amounts of a fatty substance called *cholesterol* than most meat-eaters do. These lower dietary levels of saturated fat and cholesterol result in lower levels of cholesterol in the blood. Medical research indicates that a high level of cholesterol in the blood is associated with heart disease. Some studies have shown that vegetarians in the United States are healthier and live longer than other Americans.

Vegetarianism is practiced by some religious groups, including Hindus and Seventh-day Adventists. Some Americans practice vegetarianism because they believe the high consumption of meat, especially beef, in the United States reduces the world food supply. They object to the fact that American cattle are fed grain to fatten the animals for market. These people think the grain should be used for human consumption rather than as animal feed because the livestock consume more calories than they produce. Some people also believe that the land on which livestock graze should be used to grow grain. But many agricultural experts disagree. They argue that most grazing land is not suitable for farming.   RICHARD A. AHRENS

VEGETATION. See GRASSLAND; PLANT; DESERT.

VEIN. See LEAF (The Parts of a Leaf).

VEIN is a blood vessel which carries blood toward the heart. The blood circulates in the body through a system of tubes called blood vessels. The three kinds of vessels are arteries, capillaries, and veins. Most veins return blood to the heart after it has given out nourishment to the tissues and taken up waste products and poisons. Blood in veins is called *venous* blood. See the Trans-Vision three-dimensional picture with HUMAN BODY.

The blood returning from the body cells has lost much of its oxygen, and is dull, brownish-red. It circulates through the right side of the heart and then goes to the lungs. Here it gives off its waste carbon dioxide and takes on a new supply of oxygen. Bright red blood from the lungs returns to the heart through the pulmonary veins. Then it begins its trip through the body.

The veins begin at the capillaries. At first they are very tiny, and are called *venules*. Small veins join to form larger ones. Finally all the venous blood of the body pours into two very large veins which open into the heart. One of these, the *superior vena cava*, carries blood from the head and arms. The other, the *inferior vena cava*, carries it from the trunk and legs.

Veins, like arteries, have walls made of three layers. But the vein walls are thinner, less elastic, and less muscular than those of the arteries. The lining membrane of the veins is the *intima*. In many of the larger veins, the intima has folds which serve as valves. These folds lie against the wall when the blood is flowing freely. Several things can cause the blood to slow down or stop—the weight of blood above the vessel, effects of gravity, pressure on a vein, or low fluid pressure. Then the valves open out, and stop the blood from flowing backward. The valves are usually just above the place where two veins join. There are no valves in the veins of the abdomen, brain, and lungs, or in the smaller veins.

Veins that are swollen, stretched, or coiled on themselves are *varicose* veins. *Phlebitis* is inflammation of a vein. In this disease a blood clot forms, and causes pain and stiffness.   JOHN B. MIALE

Related Articles in WORLD BOOK include:

Aneurysm	Bloodletting	Jugular Vein	Varicose
Artery	Heart	Phlebitis	Vein

VELÁZQUEZ, *vuh LAHS kuhs,* **DIEGO,** *DYAY goh* (1599-1660), was an important Spanish baroque painter. Many characteristics of his style can be seen in one of his masterpieces, *Las Meninas* (*Maids of Honor*), which is reproduced in color in the PAINTING article. *Las Meninas* shows Velázquez' use of realism, rich colors, light and shadow, and his ability to place his subjects in space. Despite the apparent effortless quality of his paintings, Velázquez was a painstaking craftsman who constantly reworked his canvases. His pictures have influenced such later artists as Gustave Courbet, Édouard Manet, and Pablo Picasso. See BAROQUE (Baroque Painting).

The Metropolitan Museum of Art

Velázquez painted this well-known portrait of himself.

The Metropolitan Museum of Art

Gaspar Cardinal de Borja Velasco, by Velázquez, shows how well the painter portrayed the personality of his subjects.

Diego Rodriquez de Silva y Velázquez was born in Seville. As a youth, he studied with Francisco Pacheco. Pacheco taught him the style of the Italian artist Michelangelo Caravaggio, characterized by its realism and use of somber light and dark tones. Velázquez began to paint for King Philip IV in 1623, and was a successful court painter for the rest of his life.

In 1629, Velázquez went to Italy, where he studied the art of ancient Rome and perfected his ability to paint nudes. After his return to Spain in 1631, he produced a series of great royal portraits as well as *The Surrender of Breda* (*The Lances*), one of the world's finest historical paintings.

Velázquez again visited Italy from 1649 to 1651. While in Rome he did a penetrating portrait of Pope Innocent X and also painted his only pure landscapes. After his return to Spain, Velázquez painted some of his greatest pictures. These include his most dazzling court portraits—*Venus with a Mirror*, one of the few nudes in Spanish art, and *Las Meninas*.   MARILYN STOKSTAD

VELD. See PRAIRIE.

VELLUM is fine animal skin used for paper. See BOOK (Early Books); PARCHMENT.

VELOCIPEDE, *vuh LAHS uh peed,* is a name for any relatively light vehicle propelled by the rider or riders. The name was applied especially to early forms of bicycles and tricycles. See also BICYCLE.

VELOCITY, *vuh LAHS uh tee,* is the rate at which a body moves in space in a given direction. Velocity is expressed in distance and time, such as miles per hour or meters per second. There is an important difference between speed and velocity. *Speed* indicates the rate of motion in any direction. When a body is said to have a speed of 40 miles per hour, it indicates that that is the

rate in any direction. But *velocity* indicates the rate in one fixed direction. This means that a body may have a velocity of 40 miles per hour north of one particular point. Mathematically, velocity is a *vector* quantity, because it has both speed and direction.

Types of Velocity. Velocity may be *uniform*, which means the spaces traveled during a given unit of time are the same throughout the motion. To find the uniform velocity of a body we need only divide the distance traveled by the time. This could be stated in the formula $V = \frac{d}{t}$ where V is equal to velocity, d is equal to distance, and t is equal to time.

Velocity may be *variable*. This means that the spaces passed in a given unit of time are not equal throughout the motion. For example, a moving object could have a velocity of 30 meters per second at a certain instant and then speed up to 60 meters per second. If the object gained speed uniformly, its average velocity would equal its initial velocity plus its final velocity divided by two. This could be written

Av. $V = \frac{V_1 + V_2}{2}$ where Av. V represents the average velocity, V_1 is equal to the initial velocity and V_2 is equal to the final velocity.

Accelerated Velocity. Variable velocity may be positively or negatively accelerated. A *positively accelerated* velocity means that, during each portion of time, the body passes through a greater space than during the preceding portion of time. A falling body has a positively accelerated velocity. In *negative acceleration*, such as a train stopping, a smaller space is traveled in each successive unit of time.   ROBERT F. PATON

See also MOTION; FALLING BODIES, LAW OF; CALCULUS.

VELVET is a cloth with a soft, deep *nap* (surface) called the *pile*. Velvet is made of silk, rayon, nylon, cotton, or a mixture of two or more of these yarns.

To make the pile, manufacturers weave two pieces of material at the same time, using three *warp* (lengthwise) yarns and two *weft* (crosswise) yarns. In each piece, they weave one set of weft yarns with one set of warp yarns in a plain or twill weave. Then they weave the extra warp yarn into the two pieces of material, first into one and then into the other. Finally, the two pieces of velvet are cut apart. Manufacturers also produce velvet in a single layer fabric. They insert wires as weft yarns and then withdraw the wires. As the wires are withdrawn, a small knife on the end of them cuts the warp yarns to produce a soft pile.

Velvet is usually made with silk yarn in the pile and cotton in the background. Silk velvet has only silk yarn. Velvet cloth comes in 36- to 39-inch (91- to 99-centimeter) widths.

A pile fabric that is woven by using extra weft yarn is called *velveteen*. When the pile is woven in ridges and cut, the cloth is *corduroy*. If thicker than $\frac{1}{8}$ inch (3 millimeters), the cloth is *plush*.   KENNETH R. FOX

See also CORDUROY.

VELVET LEAF. See INDIAN MALLOW.

VENA CAVA. See HEART (How the Heart Works).

VENATION. See BOTANY (table: Terms Used in Botany).

VENDETTA, *ven DET uh,* is a family feud once common in Italy, especially in Corsica and Sicily. One family fought another, often savagely, to avenge a personal injury or murder. The victim's nearest relative had to take revenge on the offender. If the offender could not be punished, vengeance had to be taken on the next of kin. Vendettas were similar to the family feuds that have taken place in the hills of Kentucky and Tennessee. See also FEUD.   WILLIAM H. MAEHL

VENDING MACHINE is a device that dispenses a product or service when money is put into it. Vending machines dispense many types of merchandise, including candy, cigarettes, chewing gum, and soft drinks. In some areas, drive-in vending machine centers are open 24 hours a day. They sell prepared foods, grocery items, and beverages.

Many businesses, schools, and hospitals use special types of vending machines in their lunchrooms. These machines dispense beverages, soup, sandwiches, complete hot meals, and desserts. Vending machines in some airports sell air travel insurance. Coin-operated washing machines and dry-cleaning machines are familiar service vending machines.

How Vending Machines Work. Most vending machines accept coins only. With some types, the user must insert the exact change before the machine will operate. With others, the user can insert a coin larger than the purchase price. The machine will refund the proper amount of change along with the item. Some vending machines, known as *currency-changers*, will even accept paper money and make change. Some vending machines can distinguish between bills of different denominations. They return the proper amount of change for each denomination that they can accept.

The Vending Machine Industry is composed of manufacturing companies, operating companies, and companies that supply the products sold in the machines. The manufacturers produce the machines. The operating companies place them in suitable locations, and keep them stocked and in proper working order. Operating companies usually pay a fee to the owner of the location where a machine is placed for the use of his space. The fee paid to the owner of the location is based on the sales the vending machine makes.

History. A device that dispensed holy water in a Greek temple in Alexandria, Egypt, in the 200's B.C. is the earliest known vending machine. The first vending machines in the United States, chewing gum dispensers, appeared on New York City train platforms in the late 1880's. Cigarette vending machines first appeared during the 1920's. Since that time, vending machines have developed into a major U.S. industry. In the early 1980's, over $14 billion a year worth of goods were sold using vending machines.   THOMAS B. HUNGERFORD

VENEER, *vuh NIHR,* is a thin sheet of wood of uniform thickness cut by peeling, slicing, or sawing logs. It is used primarily for plywood panels made by gluing sheets of veneer together. Single sheets of veneer are used to make such items as fruit baskets, crates, and packing boxes.

Most veneer is cut from the Douglas fir, but many other varieties of wood are also used. There are several ways of cutting veneer, but the most popular is the *rotary-cut* method. In this method, the log is placed in a lathe and then revolved against a knife extending across

the length of the log. The veneer is unwound in a long ribbon, much like unrolling a bolt of wrapping paper or cloth. Veneers vary in thickness from $\frac{1}{110}$ to $\frac{3}{8}$ inch (0.23 to 9.5 millimeters). Most rotary veneers are cut in thicknesses from $\frac{1}{20}$ to $\frac{1}{7}$ inch (1.3 to 3.6 millimeters).

The United States produces about $1\frac{1}{2}$ billion cubic feet (41 million cubic meters) of veneer logs a year. Canada produces about 29,770,000 cubic feet (843,000 cubic meters) of veneer yearly.   HARRY E. TROXELL

See also FURNITURE (Louis XIV Furniture); MAHOGANY; PLYWOOD.

VENERABLE BEDE, THE. See BEDE.

VENEREAL DISEASE, *vuh NIHR ee uhl,* often called *VD* or *sexually transmitted disease* (STD), is any of several serious diseases spread almost entirely by sexual contact with an infected person. These diseases are rarely transmitted by contaminated objects because the germs that cause them die quickly outside the body. The word *venereal* comes from *Venus,* the ancient Roman goddess of love.

This article discusses the venereal diseases gonorrhea, syphilis, genital herpes, and chlamydia. In addition to these diseases, AIDS and more than a dozen other disorders are thought to be passed primarily by sexual contact (see AIDS).

Gonorrhea is caused by a bacterium called *Neisseria gonorrhoeae.* The disease affects chiefly the moist surfaces of the sex organs. However, other parts of the body may become infected if the bacteria come into direct contact with them.

In men, the most common point of infection is just inside the tip of the penis. About 3 to 10 days after infection, most men develop a discharge from the penis and experience a burning sensation when urinating. However, some men become infected without developing any symptoms. In women, the infection usually starts in the *cervix,* the lower part of the womb. Infected women may experience a vaginal discharge, but about half of all infected women develop no symptoms.

Gonorrhea is especially serious for women. It can spread through the female reproductive organs, causing *pelvic inflammatory disease.* This severe condition may result in *sterility,* the inability to bear children. In addition, babies born to infected women may pick up the bacteria during the birth process. These infants may develop gonorrhea in the eyes, which can lead to blindness if not treated promptly. Most states of the United States require that the eyes of newborn babies be treated with drops of silver nitrate or an antibiotic solution. This treatment prevents blindness from gonorrhea.

Most cases of gonorrhea can be cured with penicillin or other antibiotics, especially if the disease is diagnosed early. However, some types of the gonorrhea bacterium can resist antibiotics.

Syphilis is caused by a corkscrew-shaped germ called *Treponema pallidum.* In most cases, the germs enter the body through breaks in the moist surfaces of the sex organs or of other areas.

Syphilis occurs in four main stages: (1) primary, (2) secondary, (3) latent, and (4) late. The symptoms of primary syphilis develop about three weeks after infection. A small sore called a *chancre* appears in the area where the germs entered the body. The person may not notice the chancre, which disappears in about three weeks if not treated. Secondary syphilis occurs six weeks

to six months later. The victim may feel ill and develop a rash and fever. The rash may be unnoticed, and all of the symptoms disappear within several weeks.

There are no symptoms during the latent stage, and a blood test is then the only means of detecting the disease. If the condition is not treated, late syphilis occurs within 10 to 30 years. The germs may attack the brain, heart, skin, spinal cord, or other parts of the body. At this stage, the disease can cause blindness, deafness, heart disease, insanity, or paralysis.

A pregnant woman who has syphilis but is not treated can pass it to her unborn child. The woman may have a miscarriage, or the infant may die at birth. If the baby lives, he or she may be born with the disease.

If syphilis is treated during the first three stages, it can be cured easily with penicillin or other antibiotics. During the late stage, treatment can prevent the disease from becoming worse but probably cannot cure it.

Genital Herpes is caused by a virus called *herpes simplex type 2.* This infection produces blisters, followed by painful sores, on the skin of the genital area. The sores gradually heal by themselves after a few weeks. However, the disease may recur frequently. There is no cure, though a drug called acyclovir can speed the healing of the skin sores and reduce or prevent recurrent attacks. Herpes simplex type 2 also can infect newborns, causing brain damage or death, and many scientists suspect that it may cause cancer of the cervix.

Chlamydia is caused by a bacterium called *Chlamydia trachomatis.* This infection is the most widespread venereal disease in the United States. Researchers estimate that chlamydia strikes 3 million to 10 million Americans each year. The symptoms of chlamydia are almost identical to those of gonorrhea, and physicians cannot distinguish between the two diseases without laboratory tests. If it infects the eyes, the chlamydia bacterium may produce *conjunctivitis,* an inflammation of the eyes. In women, chlamydia can cause especially severe cases of pelvic inflammatory disease. Babies born to infected women can pick up chlamydia during delivery. These babies may develop pneumonia. Chlamydia may be cured with tetracycline antibiotics.   RONALD K. ST. JOHN

See also DISEASE (graph: Main Contagious Diseases in the U.S.; table: Some Communicable Diseases); EHRLICH, PAUL; HERPES; TABES.

Additional Resources

CHASE, ALLAN. *The Truth about STD: The Old Ones—Herpes and Other New Ones—The Primary Causes—The Available Cures.* Quill, 1983. STD stands for "sexually transmitted diseases."
CORSARO, MARIA, and KORZENIOWSKY, CAROLE. *STD: A Commonsense Guide.* St. Martin's, 1980.
HYDE, MARGARET O. *VD-STD: The Silent Epidemic.* 2nd ed. McGraw, 1983. Suitable for younger readers.

VENETIAN BLIND, *vuh NEE shuhn,* is a window blind made of slats. Venetian blinds are given this name because they were widely used in Venice during the 1600's. Similar curtains had been developed earlier by the Japanese, who used bamboo rods. Today, Venetian blinds have slats made of metal, wood, or some other sturdy material. The slats are hung on tapes so that each slat slightly overlaps the next one when they are closed. The slats are operated by cords and pulleys that can be adjusted to keep out sunlight but admit breezes.

WORLD BOOK photo by Milt and Joan Mann

A Residential Area in Caracas, Venezuela's capital and largest city, has many high-rise apartments. In most Venezuelan cities, modern apartment buildings like these are rapidly replacing traditional Spanish-style houses, which have one story and center on a courtyard.

VENEZUELA

VENEZUELA, *VEHN ih ZWAY luh,* is a South American country that ranks as one of the world's leading producers and exporters of petroleum. Before its petroleum industry began to boom during the 1920's, Venezuela was one of the poorer countries in South America. The economy of Venezuela was based on such agricultural products as cacao and coffee. Since the 1920's, however, Venezuela has become one of the wealthiest and most rapidly changing countries on the continent. Income from petroleum exports has enabled Venezuela to carry out huge industrial development and modernization programs.

Venezuela lies on the north coast of South America along the Caribbean Sea. Mountain ranges extend across much of northern Venezuela, which is the most densely populated region of the country. Caracas, the capital and largest city, lies in this region. Vast plains called the *Llanos* spread across central Venezuela. High plateaus and low mountains cover the south.

About three-fourths of Venezuela's people live in cities and towns. Nearly all Venezuelans speak Spanish. Most of the people are descendants of Europeans, American Indians, and Africans who intermarried.

Christopher Columbus landed in what is now Venezuela in 1498 on his third voyage to the New World. It was his first landing on the mainland of the Americas. Later, European explorers in northwestern Venezuela found Indian villages where the houses were built on

---

William J. Smole, the contributor of this article, is Professor of Anthropology at the University of Pittsburgh.

---

poles over the waters of the Gulf of Venezuela and Lake Maracaibo. Some of the explorers were reminded of the Italian city of Venice, where buildings stood along the water. They named the area *Venezuela,* which is Spanish for *Little Venice.* Later, the name Venezuela was applied to a large area of northern South America. Spain ruled Venezuela for about 300 years. In 1811, Venezuela declared its independence.

Government

Venezuela is a republic. All citizens 18 years and older may vote. Since 1811, the country has had 26

Facts in Brief

Capital: Caracas.

Official Language: Spanish.

Official Name: República de Venezuela (Republic of Venezuela).

Form of Government: Federal republic.

Area: 352,145 sq. mi. (912,050 km²). *Greatest Distances*—north-south, 790 mi. (1,271 km); east-west, 925 mi. (1,489 km). *Coastline*—1,750 mi. (2,816 km).

Elevation: *Highest*—Pico Bolívar, 16,411 ft. (5,002 m) above sea level. *Lowest*—sea level along the coast.

Population: *Estimated 1986 Population*—19,014,000; distribution, 76 per cent urban, 24 per cent rural; density, 54 persons per sq. mi. (21 per km²). *1981 Census*—14,516,735. *Estimated 1991 Population*—22,365,000.

Chief Products: *Agriculture*—cotton, sugar cane, corn, coffee, rice. *Manufacturing*—refined petroleum products, petrochemicals, processed foods, textiles. *Mining*—petroleum, iron ore, diamonds, gold.

National Anthem: "Gloria al Bravo Pueblo" ("Glory to the Brave People").

Money: *Basic Unit*—bolívar. For its value in U.S. dollars, see MONEY (table: Exchange Rates). See also BOLÍVAR.

constitutions. Venezuela's present Constitution was adopted in 1961.

National Government. A president, elected by the people, serves as Venezuela's head of state and as head of the executive branch of government. The National Congress, which forms the legislative branch, consists of the 203-member Chamber of Deputies and the 49-member Senate. Voters elect the deputies and senators to five-year terms. The Supreme Court of Justice is the highest court in the country.

Local Government. Venezuela is divided into 20 states, 2 federal territories, and the Federal District. Each state and territory, and the Federal District, has a legislature elected by the people and a governor appointed by the president. The country also has many islands in the Caribbean that are federal dependencies.

Armed Forces. About 54,000 persons serve in Venezuela's army, navy, air force, and national police force. Men may be drafted for two years of military service after reaching 19 years of age.

People

Population. Venezuela has a population of over 19 million. About 75 per cent of the people live in cities and towns. The rest live in rural areas. Caracas, the capital and largest city, has about 1 million people. About $2\frac{3}{4}$ million persons live in the Caracas metropolitan area. Venezuela has five other cities with populations of over 300,000. They are Barquisimeto, Maracaibo, Maracay, Petare, and Valencia.

Ancestry. Numerous Indian tribes lived in what is now Venezuela before the 1500's, when Spain colonized the area. The Spanish conquered many of the Indian tribes. They also imported black slaves from Africa. Many of the Indians, Spaniards, and blacks intermarried. Today, about 65 per cent of Venezuela's people are of mixed ancestry. People of unmixed white, black, or Indian ancestry make up the rest of the population.

Since 1945, many Europeans and Colombians have moved to Venezuela to seek jobs. Most of the Europeans came from Spain, Italy, and Portugal.

Languages. Almost all Venezuelans speak Spanish, the country's official language. Indians in remote areas speak various tribal languages.

Ways of Life. Compared with some other Latin-American countries, Venezuela has a fairly open society. In general, the people are not rigidly segregated on the basis of racial or class differences. Venezuela thus differs from Latin-American countries that have a strict class system based on ancestry.

Since the 1940's, many Venezuelans have moved from rural areas to the cities. As the cities have grown, so has the country's middle class. Members of the middle class include business people; government workers; and doctors, lawyers, teachers, and other professionals. Most middle-class Venezuelans live comfortably, dress well, own a car, and take vacations regularly. Some families live in one-story, Spanish-style houses that center on a courtyard. But in most cities, such houses are being rapidly replaced by high-rise apartments.

Even though Venezuela's middle class has grown, poverty remains a major problem. Many poor Venezuelans live in crowded slums on the outskirts of the cities. Most of these people are unskilled workers from rural areas. Many build and live in small shacks called

The Venezuelan Capitol in Caracas houses the National Congress. This view of the Capitol shows part of its large courtyard. The building was completed in 1872.

Venezuela's State Flag, used by the government, was adopted in 1954. The national flag omits the coat of arms.

Coat of Arms. The running horse symbolizes liberty; the wheat sheaf, unity; and the swords, independence.

Venezuela lies on the north coast of South America along the Caribbean Sea. It borders Colombia, Brazil, and Guyana.

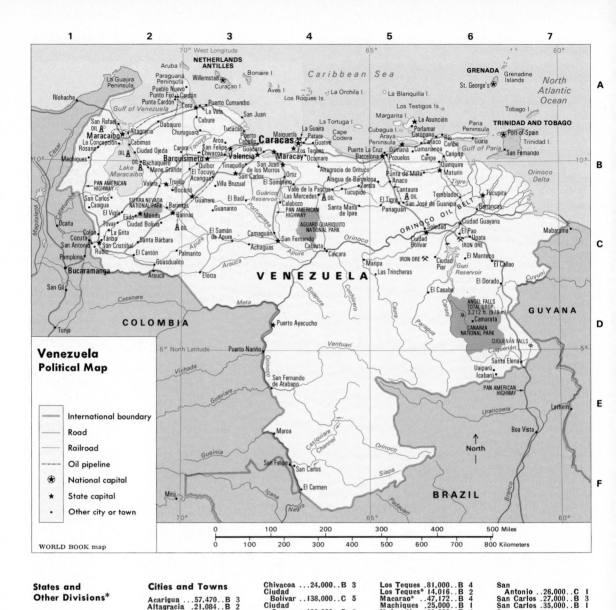

Venezuela
Political Map

International boundary
Road
Railroad
Oil pipeline
National capital
State capital
Other city or town

WORLD BOOK map

States and Other Divisions*

Amazonas (federal territory) ...26,369	E 4
Anzoátegui 616,518	B 5
Apure ...198,280	C 3
Aragua ...676,117	B 4
Barinas ...285,990	C 2
Bolívar ...487,634	D 6
Carabobo ...819,380	B 3
Cojedes ...113,629	B 3
Delta Amacuro (federal territory) ...56,690	B 6
Federal dependencies ...463	A 4
Federal District ...2,322,209	B 4
Falcón ...486,954	A 3
Guárico ...386,061	C 4
Lara ...810,851	B 2
Mérida ...415,421	C 2
Miranda 1,074,236	B 4
Monagas ...357,452	B 6
Nueva Esparta .142,075	A 5
Portuguesa 364,847	B 3
Sucre ...552,301	B 5
Táchira ...612,762	C 1
Trujillo ...449,710	B 2
Yaracuy ...267,835	B 3
Zulia ..1,598,631	B 1

Cities and Towns

Acarigua ...57,470	B 3
Altagracia ...21,084	B 2
Altagracia de Orituco ...24,000	B 4
Anaco ...39,000	B 5
Antímano* 168,772	B 4
Aragua de Barcelona 9,107	B 5
Araure* ...27,011	B 5
Barcelona ...76,410	B 5
Barinas ...80,000	C 2
Barinitas ...9,148	C 2
Barquisimeto ...459,000	B 3
Baruta* ...121,066	B 4
Boconó ...15,915	B 2
Cabimas ...168,000	B 2
Cabudare* ...14,593	B 3
Cagua* ...37,000	B 4
Calabozo ...47,000	B 4
Cantaura ...19,816	B 5
Caraballeda* ...20,765	B 4
Caracas 1,279,600 *2,755,000	B 4
Cariaco ...8,060	B 5
Caripe ...8,584	B 5
Caripito ...24,000	B 6
Carirubana* ...15,701	A 2
Carora ...43,000	B 2
Carúpano ...76,000	B 6
Catia La Mar* ...62,200	B 4
Chacao* ...78,528	B 4
Chivacoa ...24,000	B 3
Ciudad Bolívar ...138,000	C 5
Ciudad Guayana 193,000	C 6
Ciudad Ojeda ...115,000	B 2
Colón ...20,000	C 1
Coro ...87,000	A 3
Cúa* ...12,880	B 4
Cumaná ...158,000	B 5
Cumanacoa .9,524	B 5
Ejido ...13,375	C 2
El Recreo* 113,583	B 4
El Sombrero 8,373	B 4
El Tigre ...49,801	B 5
El Tocuyo ...24,000	B 3
El Valle* ..186,149	B 4
El Vigía ...28,000	C 2
Guacara ...50,000	B 3
Guanare ...43,000	B 3
Guarenas* ..44,000	B 4
Guasdualito .7,793	C 2
Guatire ...25,000	B 4
Güigüe* ...21,000	B 4
Güiria ...17,000	B 6
La Asunción 6,334	A 5
La Concepción ..13,885	B 2
La Guaira ..20,344	B 4
La Vega* .106,630	B 4
La Victoria* ...51,000	B 4
La Victoria* ...17,664	B 2
Los Dos Caminos* 59,211	B 4
Los Teques .81,000	B 4
Los Teques* 14,016	B 2
Macarao* ..47,172	B 4
Machiques .25,000	B 1
Maiquetía ..59,238	B 4
Maracaibo 845,000	B 2
Maracay ..322,000	B 4
Mariara* ..32,000	B 4
Maturín ..165,000	B 6
Mene Grande ..17,621	B 2
Mérida ...91,000	C 2
Morón* ...25,000	B 3
Ocumare ...30,000	B 4
Palo Negro* ..25,000	B 4
Pariaguán ..7,968	B 5
Petare ..225,419	B 4
Porlamar ..40,000	B 5
Pozuelos ..45,391	B 5
Puerto Ayacucho 10,417	D 4
Puerto Cabello ..87,000	B 3
Puerto Cumarebo 10,064	A 3
Puerto La Cruz ..63,276	B 5
Punta Cardón ..18,182	A 2
Punto Fijo ...112,000	A 2
Quíbor ..12,216	B 3
Quiriquire .12,671	B 6
Río Caribe 10,062	B 6
Rosario ..23,000	B 1
Rubio ...24,000	C 1
San Antonio ..26,000	C 1
San Carlos ..27,000	B 3
San Carlos .35,000	B 1
San Cristóbal 257,000	C 1
San Felipe ..52,000	B 3
San Fernando 49,000	C 4
San José de Guanipa ..22,330	B 5
San Juan de los Morros ..48,000	B 4
San Mateo* 22,000	B 4
San Rafael .12,304	A 2
Santa Bárbara ..8,473	C 2
Santa Rita* ..15,668	B 2
Tacarigua* ..14,493	B 3
Tinaquillo .12,015	B 3
Tovar ...12,814	C 2
Trujillo ..40,000	B 2
Tucupido ..11,081	B 4
Tucupita ..26,000	B 6
Turmero* ..57,000	B 4
Upata ...31,000	C 6
Valencia ..471,000	B 3
Valera ...105,000	B 2
Valle de la Pascua ..47,000	B 4
Villa Bruzual ..15,184	B 3
Villa de Cura ..34,000	B 4
Yaritagua* ..26,000	B 3
Zaraza ...15,480	B 5

*Does not appear on the map; key shows general location.
*Population of metropolitan area, including suburbs.

Sources: 1978 official estimates for states, territories, the Federal District, and large cities; 1971 census for federal dependencies and some small cities.

ranchos. Thousands of ranchos cover large expanses of land in and around many cities.

Since the 1960's, the Venezuelan government has carried out massive programs to improve the living conditions of the poor. For example, it has furnished building materials, electricity, water, and sewerage facilities for some rancho dwellers. In addition, large public housing units have been built in many cities. The government also has taken steps to improve rural life so that people will stay on farms rather than move to the already crowded cities. In many rural areas, for example, the government has built paved roads, extended electric service, and set up educational and health facilities.

Food. Traditional Venezuelan foods include black beans, cooked bananas, and rice, which are usually eaten with beef, pork, poultry, or fish. The traditional bread is a round corn-meal cake called *arepa*. However, Venezuelans also buy prepared foods in supermarkets and commonly eat wheat bread.

The national dish of Venezuela is the *hallaca*, which is served mainly at Christmas. Hallacas consist of corn-meal dough filled with a variety of foods and cooked in wrappers made of a type of banana leaf.

Recreation. Baseball and soccer are the most popular spectator sports in Venezuela. Professional teams play before large crowds in city stadiums. Several cities have bullfights, but they do not attract as many people as competitive sports events do.

Venezuelans enjoy music and dancing. Popular dances include the exciting, rhythmic *salsa* and such fast, lively Caribbean dances as the *merengue* and *guaracha.* The national folk dance of Venezuela is the *joropo.* This stamping dance is performed to the music of *cuatros* (four-stringed guitars), the harp, and *maracas* (rattles made of gourds). Rock music is also popular among young Venezuelans.

Religion. Roman Catholicism has long been the traditional religion in Venezuela, and most of the people are baptized Catholics. However, Roman Catholicism is not an official religion, and the Constitution guarantees freedom of worship.

Education in Venezuela has improved greatly since the 1960's. Today, about 86 per cent of the people 15 years of age or older can read and write, compared with about 63 per cent in 1960. Yet one of Venezuela's chief problems is a shortage of skilled workers and scientists. In 1974, the government began a massive scholarship program. In its first stage, the program granted 10,000 scholarships to college-age Venezuelans.

Venezuelan law requires all children from ages 7 through 13 to attend school. Venezuelans can receive a free public education from kindergarten through university graduate school. The country has 10 public and 5 private universities. The largest and most important is the Central University of Venezuela, a public university in Caracas. It has about 50,000 students.

The Arts. During the 1900's, several Venezuelan writers and artists have won international fame. The novelist Teresa de la Parra and the poet Andrés Eloy Blanco were among the most important writers. But probably the best-known writer was Rómulo Gallegos, who also served as president of the country in 1948. Gallegos portrayed the distinctive character of different regions of Venezuela in such novels as *Doña Bárbara*

Crowded Slums cover large areas in and around many Venezuelan cities. In Caracas, almost a third of the people live in small shacks like those above. The shacks are called *ranchos.*

A Sunny Sidewalk Cafe provides a pleasant place to relax in Caracas. The cafe is on a street in the Sabana Grande, the name of one of the city's main shopping and business districts.

WORLD BOOK photos by Milt and Joan Mann

A Rodeo, held near the city of Barinas, attracts many young Venezuelans. Barinas is the capital of the state of Barinas, a cattle-raising area in the western part of the country.

VENEZUELA

(1929), *Canaima* (1935), and *Pobre Negro* (1937). The leading Venezuelan artists of the 1900's include the abstract painters Alejandro Otero and Jesús Soto.

Venezuela also has produced some spectacular modern architecture. Outstanding examples can be found on the campus of the Central University of Venezuela, where boldly designed buildings have been integrated with imaginative murals and sculptures.

Land Regions

Venezuela has four major land regions. They are (1) the Maracaibo Basin, (2) the Andean Highlands, (3) the Llanos, and (4) the Guiana Highlands.

The Maracaibo Basin lies in northwestern Venezuela and consists of Lake Maracaibo and the lowlands around it. Lake Maracaibo is the largest lake in South America. It covers 5,217 square miles (13,512 square kilometers). The continent's largest known petroleum deposits lie in the Maracaibo Basin.

The Andean Highlands begin southwest of the Maracaibo Basin and extend across northern Venezuela. Most of Venezuela's people live in this region. The region has three sections. They are, from west to east:

WORLD BOOK photo by Milt and Joan Mann

The Andean Highlands begin southwest of the Maracaibo Basin and extend across northern Venezuela. Many small farms and towns lie in the mountains. This farmer is tending a crop of carrots.

(1) the Mérida Range, (2) the Central Highlands, and (3) the Northeastern Highlands.

The Mérida Range consists of mountain ranges and high plateaus. Pico Bolívar, the highest point in Venezuela, rises 16,411 feet (5,002 meters) above sea level.

The Central Highlands consist of two parallel mountain ranges along the Caribbean coast. Fertile valleys lie between the mountain ranges. The Central Highlands have more people and more industries than any other area in Venezuela.

The Northeastern Highlands consist of low mountains and hilly land. A famous natural feature of this area is the Cave of the Guácharo, near the town of Caripe. Thousands of large birds called *guácharos* live in the cave. These birds are found only in northern South America and chiefly in this cave.

The Llanos lie between the Andean Highlands and the Guiana Highlands. The Orinoco River, which begins in the Guiana Highlands, flows from west to east along the southern border of the Llanos. The river and its tributaries drain most of Venezuela. The Orinoco extends 1,284 miles (2,066 kilometers) and is the longest river in the country.

Large cattle ranches cover much of the Llanos. The cowhands on these ranches are called *llaneros*. The Llanos also have farmland. But the region has a long dry season, and irrigation is needed to grow such crops as rice and sesame. Important oil fields lie in the eastern part of the Llanos.

The Guiana Highlands rise south of the Llanos and cover nearly half of Venezuela. The region's high plateaus have been deeply eroded by swift-flowing rivers. Angel Falls, the world's highest waterfall, is in the Guiana Highlands. It plunges 3,212 feet (979 meters). Tropical forests cover much of the southern part of the region. See SOUTH AMERICA (picture: Angel Falls).

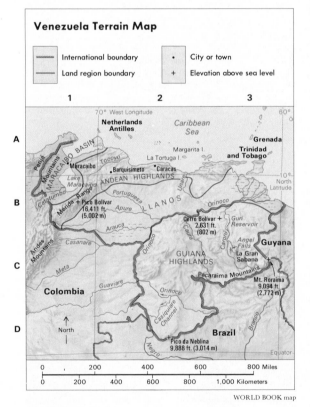

Venezuela Terrain Map

——— International boundary		• City or town
——— Land region boundary		+ Elevation above sea level

WORLD BOOK map

Physical Features

Andean Highlands	B	2
Angel Falls	C	3
Apure River	B	2
Casiquiare Channel	D	2
Guiana Highlands	C	2
Guri Reservoir	B	3
La Gran Sabana (Plateau)	C	3
Lake Maracaibo	B	1
Llanos (Plains)	B	2
Maracaibo Basin	A	1
Margarita Island	A	2
Mérida Range	B	1
Orinoco River	B	3
Pacaraima Mountains	C	3
Pico Bolívar (Peak)	B	1

242

The Llanos consist of gently sloping plains that stretch across central Venezuela. The region has many large ranches on which cowhands called *llaneros* herd cattle on horseback, *left.*

Scattered tribes of Indians live in the Guiana Highlands, but many areas have no inhabitants. The region has valuable deposits of iron ore, gold, and diamonds. Some of the rivers near Ciudad Guayana have been dammed and provide large amounts of electricity.

Climate

Venezuela lies entirely within the tropics. However, the average temperatures vary throughout the country, depending chiefly on altitude. Lowland areas are warm the year around. The highest average annual temperature—83° F. (28° C)—occurs in the central Llanos and the northern part of the Maracaibo Basin. At higher elevations, the weather is much cooler. In the Andean Highlands at Mérida, the annual temperature averages 67° F. (19° C).

The amount of rainfall also varies greatly in different parts of Venezuela. Annual rainfall averages about 120 inches (305 centimeters) in the Perijá Mountains, which are west of Lake Maracaibo, and in the southern Guiana Highlands. In contrast, much of the Caribbean coast is dry, and some areas receive only 16 inches (41 centimeters) of rainfall yearly. Most of the rest of the country has alternate wet and dry seasons. In the eastern Llanos, annual rainfall averages about 40 inches (100 centimeters).

Economy

Venezuela's economy is based largely on the petroleum industry. Since the early 1960's, the country has used much of its oil income to develop new industries and to promote agriculture.

Natural Resources. Petroleum is Venezuela's most important natural resource. The most productive oil fields lie in the Maracaibo Basin and in the eastern Llanos. Large amounts of natural gas occur with the oil deposits. Venezuela also has huge deposits of iron ore, as well as nickel ore, diamonds, and gold. The Guri Dam on the Caroní River in the Guiana Highlands is one of the world's largest dams. Many other rivers in that region could be dammed to provide electricity.

The Petroleum Industry provides 95 per cent of Venezuela's earnings from exports. Venezuela is one of the world's largest exporters of petroleum. The country produces an average of about $1\frac{1}{2}$ million barrels of oil a day,

most of which it exports to the United States. The petroleum industry is highly mechanized.

Commercial production of petroleum began in Venezuela in 1917, but the industry did not begin to boom until the 1920's. Foreign firms, especially U.S. companies, produced and marketed the oil. They shared the profits with the Venezuelan government. In 1960, Venezuela helped found the Organization of Petroleum Exporting Countries (OPEC). OPEC promotes the interests of member countries, whose economies depend heavily on oil exports. The Venezuelan government gradually bought out the foreign oil companies in the country, and it *nationalized* (took control of) the entire petroleum industry by 1976.

Mining. Venezuela produces about 20 million short tons (18 million metric tons) of iron ore a year. United States firms began mining iron ore in Venezuela in the 1940's. In 1975, Venezuela nationalized the industry. Venezuela exports more iron ore to the United States than to any other country. It also exports ore to other Latin American countries and to European countries.

Venezuela also mines diamonds and gold. Less than 2 per cent of the country's workers are employed in mining. This percentage includes the workers employed in the petroleum industry.

Agriculture declined in Venezuela after the oil industry developed. But since the 1960's, the government of Venezuela has worked successfully to increase farm production.

About 20 per cent of Venezuela's workers are farmers. The main crops include cotton, sugar cane, corn, coffee, and rice. Farmers also raise beef and dairy cattle. About three-fourths of the farms cover fewer than 50 acres (20 hectares) each. But large farms and ranches raise most of Venezuela's commercial farm products.

About half of all Venezuelan farms are operated by their owners, and nearly 13 per cent are rented. Many people farm land that they do not own or rent. Most of these people live in isolated areas where they cultivate small plots called *conucos*. They produce only enough food to support themselves. During the 1960's, the government began programs that provided farmland for many landless rural families.

Manufacturing. Venezuela's chief manufactured goods are refined petroleum products and *petrochemicals*

VENEZUELA

The Petroleum Industry provides 95 per cent of Venezuela's export earnings. Most of the oil comes from wells in the Maracaibo Basin. Many of the wells are in Lake Maracaibo itself, *above.*

Iron-Ore Mining is one of Venezuela's major industries. Cerro Bolívar, *above,* and other mountains of high-grade ore lie in the Guiana Highlands of southern Venezuela.

Modern Expressways link the major Venezuelan cities. This expressway interchange in Caracas is popularly called the *araña,* which is a Spanish word meaning *spider.*

(chemicals made from petroleum or natural gas). The country also processes food and manufactures textiles, lumber, and other products. Most of the goods made in Venezuela are sold within the country. Manufacturing employs about 17 per cent of the labor force.

Trade. Venezuela has a favorable trade balance—that is, it earns more money from exports than it spends on imports. Petroleum and petroleum products and iron ore are the leading exports. The main imports include industrial machinery and transportation equipment. Venezuela trades chiefly with the United States, West Germany, and Japan.

Transportation and Communication. Venezuela has about 29,000 miles (46,400 kilometers) of roads, of which nearly half are paved. The country has few railroads. Three national airlines serve the country. The largest airport is at Maiquetía. The leading seaports include La Guaira, Puerto Cabello, and Maracaibo.

Telegraph and postal services are available throughout Venezuela, but telephone service is limited chiefly to the cities and towns. The country has more than 200 radio stations and about 40 television stations. About 25 daily newspapers are published in Venezuela.

History

Many Indian tribes lived in what is now Venezuela before European settlers arrived. The chief tribes belonged to two groups—the Carib and the Arawak. The Carib Indians lived in the eastern part of Venezuela, and the Arawak Indians lived in the west. Both groups lived by farming, hunting, fishing, and gathering wild plants. After the Europeans arrived, large numbers of Indians died of diseases brought by the Europeans. Many others starved or were killed in warfare.

European Exploration and Settlement. Christopher Columbus was the first European explorer to reach Venezuela. In 1498, he landed on the Paria Peninsula. In 1498 and 1499, the Spanish explored most of the Caribbean coast of South America. Spanish settlers soon followed the explorers.

During the early 1500's, the Spaniards came to Venezuela to collect pearls from oyster beds around the islands of Margarita and Cubagua. They called the area from the Araya Peninsula to Cape Codera the Pearl Coast. The Spanish also worked the extensive salt ponds on the Araya Peninsula. These ponds produced salt for several centuries.

From 1528 to 1546, King Charles I of Spain leased Venezuela to a German banking group to pay off his debts to them. The Germans did little to advance the economy of the colony.

By the 1700's, Venezuela was one of Spain's poorest South American colonies. To increase trade and develop the economy, Spain gave the Royal Guipuzcoana Company of Caracas, a private trading company, the right to control all trade in Venezuela. The company began to operate in 1730. It expanded the colony's economy, which was based on cacao, indigo, and hides. But the colonists resented the company's rigid control over trade. The firm eventually lost much of its power and went out of business in 1784.

The Struggle for Independence. During the early 1800's, Spain's South American colonies began to fight for independence. The chief leaders in the independence movement included the Venezuelans Simón Bolívar,

Francisco de Miranda, and Antonio José de Sucre. They and their followers fought for many years to free all of northern South America from Spanish rule.

Venezuela was the first Spanish colony in South America to demand its independence. The colony declared its freedom on July 5, 1811, though Spanish forces still occupied much of the country. Venezuela did not become truly independent until 1821. That year, Bolívar won a great victory against the Spanish at Carabobo (near Valencia), which ended Spanish rule in Venezuela. Meanwhile, in 1819, Bolívar had set up and become president of Gran Colombia, a republic that eventually included what are now Venezuela, Colombia, Ecuador, and Panama.

Venezuela broke away from Gran Colombia in 1829 and drafted a separate constitution in 1830. General José Antonio Páez, a leader in Venezuela's independence movement, became the first president of the new Venezuelan republic in 1831.

Rule by Dictatorships. After achieving independence, Venezuela had many periods of civil unrest. A series of dictatorial *caudillos* (leaders) ruled the country until the mid-1900's. Two of these caudillos, Generals Antonio Guzmán Blanco and Juan Vicente Gómez, greatly influenced Venezuela's development.

Guzmán Blanco ruled Venezuela from 1870 to 1888. Before he came to power, the country had been torn by civil wars and political instability. Guzmán Blanco established order in Venezuela. He built roads and communication systems, and foreign firms began to invest in the country.

Gómez ruled Venezuela from 1908 to 1935. He cruelly put down all opposition to his rule. During his administration, the petroleum industry began to develop. With the oil profits, Gómez paid off Venezuela's huge national debt and created a strong army. But he also used some of the profits for personal benefit.

The Road to Democracy. After 1935, opposition to dictatorship increased greatly among the Venezuelan people. New, reformist political parties were organized. Leaders of a party called the Acción Democrática (AD), supported by the army, seized power in 1945. In 1947, the people elected Rómulo Gallegos of the AD as president. But in 1948, the army overthrew him.

For the next two years, three military leaders jointly ruled Venezuela. In 1950, Marcos Pérez Jiménez became dictator. A revolt against Pérez Jiménez broke out in 1958, and he was forced into exile. Later that year, the voters elected Rómulo Betancourt, a leader of the AD, as president. Since 1958, all Venezuelan presidents have been chosen in democratic elections.

Venezuela Today. In 1974, Carlos Andrés Pérez of the AD became president. Luis Herrera Campins of the Social Christian Party succeeded Pérez in 1979. Jaime Lusinchi of the AD became president in 1984.

Some experts predict that much of Venezuela's petroleum resources will be used up by about the year 2000. But by careful planning and by exploring for new oil, the government hoped to maintain a high level of production for much longer. In addition, the growth of other industries would enable Venezuela's economy to continue to expand even after the country's petroleum resources are exhausted. Venezuela's population is increasing rapidly. Economic expansion is necessary to meet the needs of a growing population.

In the early 1980's, a worldwide decline in the use of petroleum led to reduced oil production in Venezuela. This reduction helped cause a severe recession in Venezuela.
WILLIAM J. SMOLE

Related Articles in WORLD BOOK include:

BIOGRAPHIES

Bolívar, Simón	Miranda, Francisco de
Columbus, Christopher (Third Voyage to America)	Sucre, Antonio José de

CITIES

Barquisimeto	Ciudad Bolívar	Valencia
Caracas	Maracaibo	

PHYSICAL FEATURES

Andes Mountains	Cuquenán Falls
Angel Falls	Lake Maracaibo
Caribbean Sea	Orinoco River

OTHER RELATED ARTICLES

Bolívar	Roosevelt, Theodore
Latin America	(Foreign Policy)
Organization of Petroleum	South America
Exporting Countries	Spanish Main
Petroleum (map)	

Outline

I. **Government**
　　A. National Government　　C. Armed Forces
　　B. Local Government
II. **People**
　　A. Population　　D. Ways of Life　　G. Religion
　　B. Ancestry　　E. Food　　H. Education
　　C. Languages　　F. Recreation　　I. The Arts
III. **Land Regions**
　　A. The Maracaibo Basin　　C. The Llanos
　　B. The Andean Highlands　　D. The Guiana Highlands
IV. **Climate**
V. **Economy**
　　A. Natural Resources　　E. Manufacturing
　　B. The Petroleum Industry　　F. Trade
　　C. Mining　　G. Transportation and
　　D. Agriculture　　　　Communication
VI. **History**

Questions

What is the most densely populated region of Venezuela?

How did Venezuela get its name?

Where in Venezuela are South America's largest known petroleum deposits?

What is the ancestry of most Venezuelans?

What are the *Llanos?*

When did Venezuela become an independent country?

What are Venezuela's main crops?

How has Venezuela used much of its oil income?

What is the religion of most Venezuelans?

Who was the first European explorer to reach what is now Venezuela?

Additional Resources

BETANCOURT, RÓMULO. *Venezuela: Oil and Politics.* Rev. ed. Houghton, 1979. A political history of Venezuela since the late 1800's by one of its presidents.

CARPENTER, ALLAN, and HAAN, E. R. *Venezuela.* Childrens Press, 1970. A history and travel book. For younger readers.

LOMBARDI, JOHN V. *Venezuela: The Search for Order, the Dream of Progress.* Oxford, 1982.

RAY, TALTON F. *The Politics of the Barrios of Venezuela.* Univ. of California Press, 1969.

WILCOCK, JOHN. *Traveling in Venezuela.* Hippocrene, 1979. A general introduction and travel guide.

Bruno Pellegrini, Publifoto

Venice occupies about 120 islands off the northeast coast of Italy. In Saint Mark's Square, the heart of the city, a bell tower called the Campanile, *center,* rises above the domed roof of the Basilica of Saint Mark. The Doges' Palace stands next to the basilica.

VENICE, *VEHN ihs,* Italy (pop. 332,775), is one of the world's most famous and unusual cities. Venice lies on about 120 islands in the Adriatic Sea and has canals instead of streets. Its people use boats instead of automobiles, buses, taxis, and trucks. Venice also includes part of the Italian mainland.

Fine architecture and priceless works of art have long helped make Venice a major tourist center. The city also ranks as one of Italy's largest ports. Venice is the capital of Venetia, one of the 20 political regions of Italy. The city's name in Italian is Venezia.

Venice lies at the north end of the Adriatic Sea, $2\frac{1}{2}$ miles (4 kilometers) off the coast of Italy. For location, see ITALY (political map).

The city's location on the Adriatic made it an important trading center as early as the A.D. 800's. Venice became a strong sea power and gradually built a colonial empire that extended throughout much of the eastern Mediterranean area. At the height of its power, Venice was known as the "Queen of the Adriatic."

Through the years, Venice lost much of its economic and political strength. But the city's art treasures helped it keep its place as a cultural center of the world. Today, floods and polluted air and water threaten to slowly destroy the city. People from many parts of the world have joined various campaigns to save Venice.

The City forms a governmental unit of Italy called a *commune.* The islands of Venice make up the historic center of the city. The modern industrial centers of Marghera and Mestre on the mainland are part of the commune of Venice. See ITALY (Local Government).

A lagoon separates the islands of Venice from the mainland. A roadway over the lagoon carries traffic between the mainland and two of the islands. Automobiles, buses, and trains use terminals on those islands. More than 150 canals take the place of streets on all the islands of Venice, and boats provide transportation. Black, flat-bottomed boats called *gondolas* once served as the chief means of transportation on the islands. Today, motorboats have replaced most of the gondolas (see GONDOLA). More than 400 bridges cross the canals and link the main islands of Venice. Narrow alleyways called *calli* run between the buildings on the islands.

The Grand Canal, the city's main canal, winds through the heart of Venice. Marble and stone palaces built between the 1100's and 1800's stand along both sides of the Grand Canal. The Rialto Bridge crosses the canal in the heart of the city. Venice's chief shopping district lies along the Merceria, a narrow street that runs from the Rialto Bridge to Saint Mark's Square.

Saint Mark's Square is the center of activity in Venice. The Basilica of Saint Mark, on the east side of the square, ranks as one of the world's outstanding examples of Byzantine architecture (see SAINT MARK, BASILICA OF). A bell tower called the Campanile stands nearby. Buildings in the Renaissance style of architec-

ture rise along the other three sides of the square. Cafes in front of these buildings are favorite meeting places for tourists and for residents of the city. The Doges' Palace, just off the square, was built as a residence for early Venetian rulers called *doges* (see DOGE).

Priceless artworks may be seen in buildings throughout Venice. The Academy of Fine Arts has an outstanding collection of famous paintings, including works by such Venetian masters as Titian, Tintoretto, and Paolo Veronese. The largest theater in Venice, the Fenice, presents operas and plays. Hundreds of students attend Venice's schools of architecture, art, and music. The University of Venice has about 6,000 students.

Venice has few parks or gardens. But the Lido, a narrow sandbar that borders the islands on the east, is one of Europe's most popular beach resorts.

Venice's location gives the city unique characteristics, but it has also caused serious problems. For example, during winter storms, floodwaters sweep through the islands, covering public squares and walkways and damaging buildings. The constant exposure to water is also weakening the foundations of Venice's buildings. In addition, air pollution is eroding the buildings, as well as many of the city's outdoor art treasures. The islands of Venice were sinking an average of about $\frac{1}{5}$ inch (5 millimeters) yearly until the mid-1970's.

Scientists believe the sinking resulted partly from the removal of underground water for use by industries. The Italian government restricted the use of water from the city's underground wells. Water pressure then built up under the islands, and the city stopped sinking.

The People of Venice's islands are continually affected by the water that surrounds them. The water influences their food and housing as well as their transportation. For example, seafood is the main course of a typical Venetian lunch or dinner. Houses and other buildings do not stand on solid ground but on wooden *piles* (posts) driven into the mud.

Almost all Venetians are Roman Catholics. Several annual events, in addition to religious holidays, attract large crowds to the city. One of these events, the Feast of the Redeemer, commemorates the end of a plague that struck Venice in 1575. During this all-night festival in July, musicians perform in lighted boats along the canals. A *regatta* (gondola race) is held in September.

Since about 1950, thousands of Venetians have left the islands to live in the mainland communities of Marghera and Mestre. They have moved chiefly because the mainland offers greater job opportunities and a lower cost of living. The modern apartment buildings in Marghera and Mestre also attract many Venetians. Most of the buildings on the islands were erected hun-

City of Venice

Venice, founded in A.D. 452, was built on islands in the Adriatic Sea. The small map at the right shows the city boundary. The map below locates important historic and artistic sites of Venice.

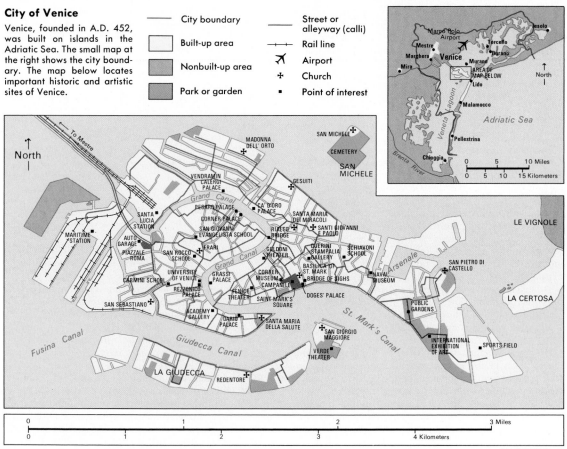

WORLD BOOK map

VENICE

Bullaty/Lomeo, Rapho Guillumette

Canals take the place of streets in Venice, and boats are used for transportation. Most of the buildings that line the canals are hundreds of years old. Bridges link the city's main islands.

dreds of years ago, and there is no room to build new housing.

Economy. Tourism is the chief economic activity of the islands of Venice. About 3 million tourists a year visit the historic center of the city. They make up an important market for goods produced by craftworkers who live on the various islands. The islands of Murano have won fame for fine crystal and glassware. Lace and embroidered work come from Burano.

The industrial and trade activities of Venice center in Marghera and Mestre. Factories in these communities produce aluminum, chemicals, coke, fertilizer, paint, petroleum products, steel, and other goods. Venice's port facilities are centered at Marghera.

Industrial development in the mainland portion of Venice has created thousands of jobs for Venetians. But it has also been a major cause of the serious air and water pollution that threaten the city.

History. The first settlers of Venice fled to the islands during the A.D. 400's to escape barbarians who were invading Italy from northern Europe. The early Venetian economy was based on fishing and trading. The Venetians traveled along the Adriatic coasts in search of new markets. By the 800's, Venice was trading with Constantinople (now Istanbul) and cities on the Italian mainland and northern coast of Africa. Venice developed into an independent city-state, ruled by nobles.

Venetian ships provided the transportation for the Fourth Crusade, which lasted from 1201 to 1204. The Venetians joined the crusaders in battle and conquered the Byzantine Empire, including Constantinople (see CRUSADES [The Fourth Crusade]). The growing strength of Venice led the city into a series of wars with Genoa, a rival sea power. Venice finally defeated Genoa in 1380 and gained control over trade in the eastern Mediterranean Sea. Venice reached the height of its power during the 1400's, when its colonial empire included Crete, Cyprus, the Dalmatian coast (now part of Yugoslavia), and part of northeastern Italy. Venetian ships carried almost all the silks, spices, and other luxury items that reached Europe from Asia. Venice became a leading center of Renaissance art in the late 1400's and 1500's (see RENAISSANCE).

In the late 1400's, Christopher Columbus journeyed to America and Vasco da Gama discovered a sea route to India. The center of trade in Europe then shifted to the Atlantic Ocean, and Venice's power declined. The city gradually lost its eastern colonies to the Turks.

In 1797, French forces led by Napoleon Bonaparte occupied Venice. Napoleon divided what was left of the Venetian empire between France and Austria. The city itself came under Austrian control. In 1866, Venice became part of the independent Kingdom of Italy.

The industrialization of Marghera and Mestre began in the early 1900's. During World War II (1939-1945), German troops took over the city. Allied planes bombed the port at Marghera but spared Venice's islands.

In 1966, a disastrous flood that struck much of Italy caused millions of dollars in damage in Venice. The flood badly damaged or destroyed many of the city's paintings and statues. International organizations and private citizens donated money to help the Italian government pay the repair costs. Following the flood, government committees and private researchers began studies on pollution control. During the mid-1970's, the Italian government took steps to restore many of the city's ancient structures damaged by floodwaters and pollution.   EMILIANA P. NOETHER

Related Articles in WORLD BOOK include:

Bridge of Sighs
Campanile
Doge
Europe (picture:
  Modern Art)

Flag (picture: Historical
  Flags of the World)
Glass (The Middle Ages)
Venetian Blind

VENISON. See DEER.

VENIZELOS, *VEH nee* Z*EH laws*, **ELEUTHERIOS** (1864-1936), was the dominant figure in Greek politics from 1910 to 1935. He helped Greece acquire many Aegean islands, Crete, and other territories. He brought Greece into World War I in 1917 on the side of the Allies. He prepared for the unsuccessful Greek invasion of Turkey from 1920 to 1922. Venizelos served as prime minister six times, and persuaded the Greeks to establish a republic. He was born on Crete. See also GREECE (History).   R. V. BURKS

VENN DIAGRAM. See SET THEORY (Diagraming).

VENOM is a poisonous substance produced by many kinds of animals. These animals, which include certain species of snakes, bees, fish, scorpions, and spiders, use venom to kill and digest prey. The poison is manufactured by a venom gland and is injected into the victim in various ways.

Venom contains many toxic substances that act together to poison a victim. These substances differ among the species of animals that produce venom. Some venoms include poisons that block the transmission of nerve impulses to muscle cells, causing numbness and paralysis. Certain substances in venom slow or stop the heart. Many venoms also break down the walls of blood capillaries, causing swelling and massive bleeding. Some venoms contain poisons that cause the victim's blood to clot. Others contain substances that prevent clotting.

Animals that produce venom use various body parts to inject the poison into their victims. Snakes have fangs through which the poison passes into a victim's body. Many kinds of fish use sharp, bony spines to inject venom. Bees, hornets, and wasps have stingers for poisoning their prey. Most kinds of spiders inject venom by biting a victim. Scorpions use claws on their tail to shoot venom into prey.

Venom has many uses in the treatment of illness. For example, physicians use the venom of the Malayan pit viper to treat certain types of heart attacks. Cobra venom is used to relieve some cases of severe pain, and bee venom helps in the treatment of arthritis. Venoms are also used in biological research. For instance, venoms that block the transmission of nerve impulses serve as a tool in the study of nerve function.   ANTHONY T. TU

Related Articles in WORLD BOOK include:

Bee (Sting)	Snake (Fangs and Venom Glands)
Hornet	Snakebite
Scorpion	Wasp

VENTILATION supplies fresh air to indoor places and removes stale air from these places. For people to feel comfortable, they need fresh air free from dust, soot, and odors. The air must not be too warm or too cool, and it must have the right amount of moisture.

Even if the air in a room is fresh to begin with, important changes take place when people come into the room. The air becomes warmer because the human body gives off heat. The amount of moisture in the air increases because of the water vapor given off as people breathe and perspire. Also, the air becomes stale because of perspiration and the oily matter given off from people's skins, noses, throats, and clothing. Smoking especially makes the air stale.

People remove the gas oxygen from the air they inhale, and give off another gas, called *carbon dioxide*, to the air they exhale. Many people once thought that the carbon dioxide gas breathed out was harmful to anyone who breathed it in again. Although breathing increases the carbon dioxide and decreases the oxygen in a room, these changes are so slight that they have little or no effect on a person's health.

The more people there are in a room, or the harder they work, the faster the air becomes stale. Stale air must be removed and replaced with fresh air. If the air outside is fresh, simply opening a window and perhaps turning on a fan will ventilate the room. However, if the outside air is not fresh or the room is on the inside of a building, special equipment is needed to clean the air, cool or heat it, and remove or add moisture. This equipment is called *air conditioning* (see AIR CONDITIONING).   MERL BAKER

See also HUMIDITY; AIR CLEANER.

VENTRICLE. See HEART.

VENTRILOQUISM is the art of projecting, or "throwing," the voice so that it seems to come from a different source. It takes long and steady practice to develop this ability. The sounds are produced in the usual method adopted in talking, but the lips are held as nearly motionless as possible. The tongue is drawn well back and only the tip is moved. A deep breath is taken in and exhaled very slowly. Sounds are modified, or changed, by the muscles of the throat and the palate. Consonants are often changed to avoid lipmoving syllables. For instance, the letter *p* becomes a *k*. *B* is treated in the same way, and is quickly slurred into a *g* or *k*. Lack of facial expression on the part of the performer helps to fool the audience. The performer also constantly directs the attention of the audience to the place from which the sound is supposed to come. Theatrical ventriloquists often use a puppet with whom they pretend to carry on a conversation (see PUPPET).

Ventriloquism is an ancient art. The Greeks thought it was the work of demons. They believed the voice came from the abdominal region. The word ventriloquism comes from the Latin *venter*, meaning *belly*, and *loqui*, meaning *to speak*.   GLENN HUGHES

VENTRIS, *VEHN trihs*, **MICHAEL GEORGE FRANCIS** (1922-1956), a British architect, solved one of the great mysteries of archaeology. He deciphered *Linear B*, a system of writing used by the ancient Greeks about 3,500 years ago. Inscriptions in Linear B were first found on clay tablets discovered at Knossos, Crete, about 1900. But all efforts to decipher them failed until Ventris, an amateur cryptographer, succeeded in 1953. He proved that Linear B was Greek written in the alphabet used by the Minoans, the people of ancient Crete. As a result, scholars changed their views about the early history of ancient Greece. Ventris was born at Wheathampstead, England. See also GREECE, ANCIENT (Beginnings); AEGEAN CIVILIZATION.

VENUS, *VEE nuhs*, was a major goddess in Roman mythology. She originally was the goddess of love and beauty, but later she also symbolized the creative force that sustains all life. Cupid, the Roman god of love, was her son. Venus closely resembled the Greek goddess Aphrodite.

Venus was also the mother of Aeneas, an ancestor of the legendary founders of Rome. The Romans worshiped her because of her association with the city's early history. They dedicated some of Rome's most important temples to her. They believed the family of the ruler Julius Caesar descended from Venus.

Venus was born full-grown from the foam of the Mediterranean Sea. She married Vulcan, the lame and ugly blacksmith god. Venus had a love affair with Mars, the god of war, and she also fell in love with Adonis, a mortal.

Venus plays an important part in a famous myth called the Judgment of Paris. Venus and the goddesses Juno and Minerva all claimed a golden apple, a prize reserved for the most beautiful goddess. To settle the argument, the god Jupiter ordered Paris, the son of King Priam of Troy, to choose the most beautiful of the three. Paris awarded the apple to Venus. In revenge, Juno and Minerva made certain that Troy was destroyed during the Trojan War.

VENUS

Venus has been a popular subject of painters. Many paintings show her admiring herself in a mirror. Others portray the Judgment of Paris or show Venus with Mars or Adonis.

PAUL PASCAL

See also APHRODITE; ADONIS; PARIS (in mythology); VENUS DE MILO; VULCAN; PAINTING (picture: *Birth of Venus*).

VENUS is known as the earth's "twin" because the two planets are so similar in size. The diameter of Venus is about 7,520 miles (12,100 kilometers), about 400 miles (644 kilometers) smaller than that of the earth. No other planet comes closer to the earth than Venus. At its closest approach, it is about 25,000,000 miles (40,200,000 kilometers) away.

As seen from the earth, Venus is brighter than any other planet or even any star. At certain times of the year, Venus is the first planet or star that can be seen in the western sky in the evening. At other times, it is the last planet or star that can be seen in the eastern sky in the morning. When Venus is near its brightest point, it can be seen in daylight. Ancient astronomers called the object that appeared in the morning Phosphorus, and the object that appeared in the evening Hesperus (see EVENING STAR). Later, they realized these objects were the same planet. They named Venus in honor of the Roman goddess of love and beauty.

Orbit. Venus is closer to the sun than any other planet except Mercury. Its mean distance from the sun is about 67,250,000 miles (108,230,000 kilometers), compared with 93,000,000 miles (150,000,000 kilometers) for the earth and 36,000,000 miles (57,900,000 kilometers) for Mercury.

Venus travels around the sun in a nearly circular orbit. The planet's distance from the sun varies from about 67,700,000 miles (109,000,000 kilometers) at its farthest point to about 66,800,000 miles (107,500,000 kilometers) at its closest point. The orbits of all the other planets are more *elliptical* (oval-shaped).

Lowell Observatory

The Phases of Venus can be seen through a telescope. The planet appears as a large halo when on the same side of the sun as the earth. It looks like a crescent as it moves away from the earth, and like a small disk when near the opposite side of the sun.

Venus takes about 225 earth-days, or about $7\frac{1}{2}$ months, to go around the sun once, compared with 365 days, or one year, for the earth.

Phases. When viewed through a telescope, Venus can be seen going through "changes" in shape and size. These apparent changes are called *phases*, and they resemble those of the moon. They result from different parts of Venus' sunlit areas being visible from the earth at different times.

As Venus and the earth travel around the sun, Venus can be seen near the opposite side of the sun about every 584 days. At this point, almost all its sunlit area is visible. As Venus moves around the sun toward the earth, its sunlit area appears to decrease and its size seems to increase. After about 221 days, only half the planet is visible. After another 71 days, Venus nears the same side of the sun as the earth, and only a thin sunlit area can be seen.

Venus is at its closest point to the earth when it is on the same side of the sun as the earth. Although its sunlit half faces away from the earth at this point, Venus is still visible as a thin halo. As Venus moves away from the earth, its sunlit area increases for about two months, and then decreases as the planet moves toward the opposite side of the sun.

When Venus is moving toward the earth, the planet

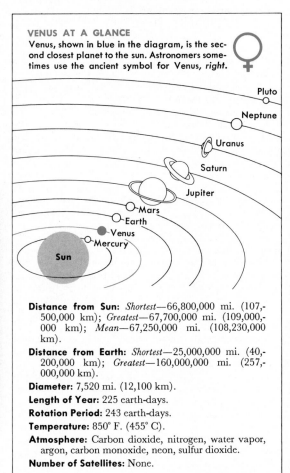

VENUS AT A GLANCE

Venus, shown in blue in the diagram, is the second closest planet to the sun. Astronomers sometimes use the ancient symbol for Venus, *right*.

Pluto
Neptune
Uranus
Saturn
Jupiter
Mars
Earth
Venus
Mercury
Sun

Distance from Sun: *Shortest*—66,800,000 mi. (107,500,000 km); *Greatest*—67,700,000 mi. (109,000,000 km); *Mean*—67,250,000 mi. (108,230,000 km).

Distance from Earth: *Shortest*—25,000,000 mi. (40,200,000 km); *Greatest*—160,000,000 mi. (257,000,000 km).

Diameter: 7,520 mi. (12,100 km).

Length of Year: 225 earth-days.

Rotation Period: 243 earth-days.

Temperature: 850° F. (455° C).

Atmosphere: Carbon dioxide, nitrogen, water vapor, argon, carbon monoxide, neon, sulfur dioxide.

Number of Satellites: None.

can be seen in the evening sky. When moving away from the earth, it is visible in the early morning sky.

Rotation. As Venus travels around the sun, it rotates slowly on its axis, an imaginary line drawn through its center. Venus' axis is not *perpendicular* (at an angle of 90°) to the planet's path around the sun. The axis tilts at an angle of approximately 175° from the perpendicular position. For an illustration of the tilt, see PLANET (The Axes of the Planets). Venus is the only planet that does not rotate in the same direction in which it travels around the sun. It rotates in the *retrograde* (opposite) direction. Venus spins around once every 243 earth-days.

Surface and Atmosphere. Although Venus is called the earth's "twin," its surface conditions appear to be very different from those of the earth. Astronomers have had difficulty learning about the surface of Venus because the planet is always surrounded by thick clouds of sulfuric acid and sulfur. They have used radar, radio astronomy equipment, and space probes to "explore" Venus and to form some idea of the conditions on the planet.

The surface of Venus is extremely hot and dry. Photographs and radar measurements indicate that the planet has surface features as varied as those of the earth. These features include mountains, canyons and valleys, and flat plains. Some parts of Venus' surface are covered with fine dust and others with large sharp-edged rocks. There is no water on the planet's surface because the high surface temperature would make the water boil away.

The atmosphere of Venus is heavier than that of any other planet. It consists primarily of carbon dioxide, with small amounts of nitrogen and water vapor. The planet's atmosphere also contains minute traces of argon, carbon monoxide, neon, and sulfur dioxide. The *atmospheric pressure* (force exerted by the weight of the gases) on Venus is estimated at 1,352 pounds per square inch (95 kilograms per square centimeter), compared with about 14.7 pounds per square inch (1.03 kilograms per square centimeter) on the earth.

The plants and animals that live on the earth could not live on Venus, because of the high temperature and the lack of sufficient oxygen. Astronomers do not know whether any form of life exists on Venus.

Temperature. The temperature of the uppermost layer of Venus' clouds averages about 55° F. (13° C). However, the temperature of the planet's surface is approximately 850° F. (455° C)—higher than that of any other planet.

Most astronomers believe that Venus' high surface temperature can be explained by the "greenhouse" heat theory. A greenhouse lets in radiant energy from the sun, but it prevents much of the heat from escaping. The thick clouds and dense atmosphere of Venus work in much the same way. The sun's radiant energy readily filters into the planet's atmosphere. But the large particles of sulfur in Venus' clouds—and the water vapor and great quantity of carbon dioxide in the atmosphere—seem to trap much of the solar energy at the planet's surface.

Mass and Density. The *mass* of Venus is about four-fifths that of the earth (see MASS). The force of gravity on Venus is slightly less than on the earth. For this reason, an object weighing 100 pounds on the earth would

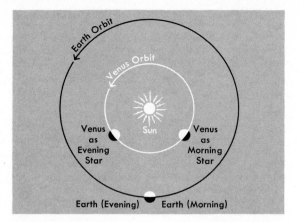

Venus Appears in the Evening Sky when moving toward the earth. It is in the morning sky after it has passed between the sun and the earth and begins moving away from the earth.

weigh about 89 pounds on Venus. Venus is also slightly less *dense* than the earth (see DENSITY). A portion of Venus would weigh a little less than an equal-sized portion of the earth.

Flights to Venus. Venus was the first planet to be observed by a passing spacecraft. The unmanned U.S. spacecraft *Mariner II* passed within 21,600 miles (34,760 kilometers) of Venus on Dec. 14, 1962, after traveling through space for more than 3½ months. It made various measurements of conditions on and near Venus. For example, instruments carried by the spacecraft measured the high surface temperatures of the planet.

Two unmanned Russian spacecraft "explored" Venus in 1966. *Venera 2* passed within 25,000 miles (40,200 kilometers) of the planet on February 27, and *Venera 3* crashed into Venus on March 1.

In October 1967, spacecraft from both the United States and Russia reached Venus. On October 18, the Russian spacecraft *Venera 4* dropped a capsule of instruments into Venus' atmosphere by parachute. On October 19, the U.S. spacecraft *Mariner V* passed within 2,480 miles (3,991 kilometers) of Venus. Both probes reported large amounts of carbon dioxide in the planet's atmosphere. On Dec. 15, 1970, the Russian spacecraft *Venera 7* landed on Venus. The U.S. planetary probe *Mariner X* flew near Venus on Feb. 5, 1974. The probe reported that the planet has no magnetic field.

On October 22, 1975, the unmanned Russian spacecraft *Venera 9* landed on Venus and provided the first close-up photograph on the planet's surface. Three days later, another Russian space vehicle, *Venera 10*, reached Venus. It photographed Venus' surface and measured its atmospheric pressure.

Four unmanned spacecraft reached Venus in December 1978. The U.S. *Pioneer Venus 1* began orbiting the planet on December 4. It transmitted radar photographs of Venus and measured temperatures at the top of the planet's clouds. On December 9, the U.S. *Pioneer Venus 2* entered the planet's atmosphere and measured its density and chemical composition. On December 21, the Russian craft *Venera 12* landed on Venus. A second Russian lander, *Venera 11*, reached the planet's surface

VENUS DE MILO

four days later. Both probes sent back data on Venus' lower atmosphere. Two more Russian spacecraft landed on Venus in 1982—*Venera 13* on March 1 and *Venera 14* on March 5. Both probes transmitted color photographs of the planet and analyzed soil samples.   Hyron Spinrad

See also PLANET; SOLAR SYSTEM; SPACE TRAVEL.

Additional Resources

Dunne, James A., and Burgess, Eric. *The Voyage of Mariner 10: Mission to Venus and Mercury.* NASA, 1978.

Hunten, D. M., and others, eds. *Venus.* Univ. of Arizona Press, 1983.

Motz, Lloyd. *On the Path of Venus.* Pantheon, 1977. For younger readers.

VENUS DE MILO, *VEE nuhs duh MEE loh,* is a magnificent Greek statue. It is made of marble and represents Venus, or Aphrodite. It is one of the great treasures of the Louvre museum, in Paris. It received the name *Venus de Milo,* or *Venus of Melos,* because a peasant found it on the Greek island of Melos in 1820. For hundreds of years, the statue had remained hidden in an underground cave near the ruins of an ancient theater. During these centuries, it had suffered considerable damage. It was in two parts when found. Pieces of the arms were found with it, as well as a pedestal with an inscription. These later disappeared, and no one has ever found them. The Marquis de Rivière, French ambassador to Turkey, bought the statue. After it was repaired, he gave it to Louis XVIII of France, who presented it to the Louvre. No one knows who made the Venus de Milo, or exactly when. It was probably made during the first or second century B.C., under the influence of a master whose work belonged to an earlier, greater period of Greek art. See also PARIS (picture).   Florence Hope

VENUS'S-FLYTRAP, *VEE nuhs sihz,* is a plant found in a small area of the coastal regions of North and South Carolina. It is also called *dionaea* (pronounced *DY uh NEE uh*). This plant traps insects in its leaves and digests them. Because of this habit it is called a *carnivorous* (meat-eating) plant. Venus's-flytrap grows in bogs in which the soils lack nitrogen. The insects take the place of nitrogen in the plant's diet. It grows best in a damp atmosphere but needs sunshine.

Venus's-flytrap grows about 1 foot (30 centimeters) high. It bears a cluster of small, white blossoms

Hugh Spencer, NAS
Venus's-Flytrap

at the top of the flower stalk. The blossoms rise from a tuft of oddly shaped leaves. The leaves have two parts —a lower bladelike portion and an upper part with two lobes hinged to a rib. The surface of each lobe has three sensitive hairs, and the edges are fringed with sharp bristles. When an insect lights on one of these hairs, the two lobes close like a trap and hold the insect inside. The soft parts of the insect are digested by a fluid that is secreted by special glands of the leaf. After the plant has taken in the food, the trap opens, and the leaf is in position to capture another victim. When a leaf has caught several insects, it withers and dies.

Scientific Classification. Venus's-flytrap belongs to the family Droseraceae. It is *Dionaea muscipula.*   Theodor Just

See also PLANT (picture: Plants That Eat Insects).

VENUS'S-GIRDLE. See CTENOPHORE.

VERACRUZ, *VEHR uh KROOZ* (pop. 295,297), is the chief port of Mexico. Its official name is Veracruz Llave (pronounced *YAH vay*). The city overlooks a fine harbor on the Gulf of Mexico, 200 miles (320 kilometers) east of Mexico City (see MEXICO [political map]). The city's products include cement, chocolate, cigars, flour, seafood, shoes, and textiles.

Hernando Cortés founded Veracruz in 1519 (see CORTÉS, HERNANDO). The city was the first Spanish settlement in Mexico. The United States Army captured the city in 1847 during the Mexican War. The French occupied it during their invasion of Mexico in the 1860's. United States Marines occupied Veracruz for a time in 1914, after a dispute with Mexico over the arrest of a group of American sailors.   John A. Crow

VERB is a part of speech that expresses an action or a state of being. A verb may consist of one word, such as *send,* or a group of words, such as *has been sending.* Verbs occupy characteristic positions in a sentence. For example, only a verb makes sense in the blank spaces in the following sentences:

She _____ the letter. (sent, began)
He _____ my father. (is, answered)
We _____ immediately. (went, arrived)
Did they _____? (go, begin)

Some words, such as *theft* and *loneliness,* express an action or a state of being but are not verbs. These words are nouns. They cannot be used in the verb position of a sentence. In addition, they do not possess other features of verbs called *formal characteristics.*

Formal Characteristics of verbs can be illustrated by the different forms of the verb *fall.* These forms are *fall, falls, fell, fallen,* and *falling. Fall* is the base form, or infinitive, with or without the preceding particle *to. Fall* is also the form of the first and second person singular and plural, as in *I fall, you fall, we fall. Falls* is the form of the third person singular, used with a noun or a pronoun subject. *Fell* is the past tense form. *Fallen* is the past participle. It is used after an auxiliary verb, such as *be* and its forms (*am, is, are, was,* and *were*) or *have* and its forms (*has* and *had*). It is also used alone when the verb is used as a modifier, as in Fallen *leaves covered it. Falling* is the present participle, used as a modifier, as in The *falling snow blinded him,* and after forms of *be,* as in He *was* falling.

Auxiliary Verbs, such as *can, may, should, might,* and *must,* do not have the same characteristics as other verbs. They are usually followed by the base form of a verb, as in *John can go but Peter must stay.* The verbs *do, be,* and *have* serve a double function. They may be used as independent verbs (*He has it*) and also as auxiliary verbs (*She has tried*).

Regular and Irregular Verbs are classified according to the way they form the past tense and past participle. A verb's base form, past tense form, and past participle are called its *principal parts.*

Most English verbs are regular. The past tense form and the past participle of a regular verb are created by adding *-ed* to the base form, as in *happen, happened, happened.* The principal parts of all verbs of recent origin are

formed by adding -*ed* to the base form, as in *computerize, computerized, computerized.*

Irregular verbs change in other ways to form the past tense and past participle. One kind of irregular verb changes in the past tense and then keeps that same form in the past participle. Examples include *feed, fed, fed;* and *win, won, won.* Another kind adds an -*n* or -*en* to the base form or to the past tense form to make the past participle. Examples include *know, knew, known;* and *speak, spoke, spoken.* Other verbs have irregular changes in spelling for each principal part, as in *slay, slew, slain.* Still others use the same form for all principal parts. They include *cost, cut, set,* and *shut.* These verbs are called *invariables.*

A large group of irregular verbs shows a change of vowel in both the past tense and past participle: *begin, began, begun; swim, swam, swum.* Through usage, many verbs of this type are gradually changing into regular verbs with -*ed* endings. For example, the verb *strive* has the irregular forms *strive, strove, striven* and also has the regular forms *strive, strived, strived.*

Transitive and Intransitive Verbs. Verbs may be classified as either transitive or intransitive. A transitive verb has an object, as in *He found the money.* The object of *found* is *money.* An intransitive verb has no object, as in *She is speaking.* Many verbs may be transitive in one sentence and intransitive in another. For example, *The chorus sang a popular song* (transitive); *The chorus sang well* (intransitive).

Linking, or Copulative, Verbs occur in two general structures. In one, the verb is followed by an adjective, as in *He is good* or *It smelled good.* Verbs such as *seemed, looked, tasted, smelled, became, sounded, turned,* and various others can be used as linking verbs. In the other linking-verb structure, a noun following the verb refers to the subject, as in *She is my mother; He became mayor;* and *She seemed an interesting person.* In American English, *be, become, remain,* and *seem* are the only verbs commonly used in this construction. British English uses a few others.

Finite and Nonfinite Verbs. A finite verb, together with a subject, can form a grammatically complete sentence: *She drives; She is driving.* A nonfinite verb, or *verbal,* is derived from a verb but acts as another part of speech. There are three forms of verbals: *gerunds, participles,* and *infinitives.* A gerund is used as a noun: *Swimming is fun.* Participles serve as adjectives: *Susan held the winning ticket.* Infinitives can be used as nouns, adjectives, or adverbs. In the sentence *To run a mile is difficult,* the infinitive *to run* serves as a noun. In the sentence *I have reading to do,* the infinitive *to do* is used as an adjective. In the sentence *Alice practiced to become a better singer,* the infinitive *to become* serves as an adverb.

Nonstandard Usage of Verbs involves the use of verb forms that are not suited to the rest of a sentence. Such usage occurs mainly in two ways. One way consists of dropping a standard verb ending: *He fall* instead of *He falls.* The other common nonstandard practice involves using an inappropriate principal part: *I seen it* instead of *I saw it.*   WILLIAM F. IRMSCHER

Related Articles in WORLD BOOK include:

Conjugation	Inflection	Participle	Tense
Gerund	Mood	Person	Voice
Infinitive	Number	Sentence	

VERBAL. See GERUND; PARTICIPLE; INFINITIVE.

VERBENA, *ver BE nuh,* is the name of a group of plants in the vervain family which grow both wild and in the garden. Various kinds of verbena grow from the tropics to the North Temperate Zone. The wild plants, usually called *vervains,* grow in moist meadows. They bloom from June to September.

In tropical countries, some species grow as tall as trees, but those in the temperate climates range from 3 inches (8 centimeters) to over 4 feet (120 centimeters) in height. Almost all of them have four-sided stems, and opposite or alternate leaves. Several wild European species have been introduced into America and are troublesome weeds in many parts of the United States.

Many cultivated verbena have flower clusters of pink, red, white, purple, or any other color except yellow. They are grown as annuals in the northern states. The seeds are planted in pots under glass in the winter. They can also be grown from cuttings. They may be grown in the open in the deep South, and will bloom early in the spring. *Moss verbena* is used for hanging baskets.

J. Horace McFarland
Verbena Flowers

Scientific Classification. Verbenas belong to the vervain family, *Verbenaceae.* The common garden plant is genus *Verbena,* species *V. hybrida.* The moss verbena is *V. tenuisecta.*

VERCHÈRES, *vehr SHAIR,* **MARIE MADELEINE JARRET DE** (1678-1747), was a French-Canadian heroine who led the defense of a fort against an Indian attack. Madeleine de Verchères, as she was called, was only 14 years old at the time. The fort stood on her father's land at Verchères, her birthplace, in what is now the province of Quebec.

On Oct. 22, 1692, about 50 Iroquois Indians attacked Verchères and seized about 20 settlers. Madeleine narrowly escaped capture and ran to the fort, where she organized the defense. Her parents were away, and only one soldier was present. Madeleine held off the Indians with the help of the soldier and some women and children. She fired a cannon shot that frightened the Indians. It also alerted nearby forts, and the alarm signal was passed along, fort by fort, as far as Montreal, about 20 miles (32 kilometers) away. About 100 soldiers came from Montreal, but when they reached Verchères, the Indians had fled.   ANDRÉ VACHON

VERDANDI. See NORNS.

VERDI, GIUSEPPE (1813-1901), was an Italian composer of operas. His works are performed more often today than those of any other opera composer. Between 1851 and 1871, Verdi produced a remarkable series of masterpieces, including *Rigoletto* (1851), *Il Trovatore* (1853), *La Traviata* (1853), *The Sicilian Vespers* (1855), *Simon Boccanegra* (1857, revised 1881), *A Masked Ball* (1859), *La Forza del Destino* (1862), *Don Carlos* (1867), and *Aida* (1871). Verdi wrote 26 operas. He composed all to Italian *librettos* (texts) except the *Sicilian Vespers*

and *Don Carlos*, which he wrote to French librettos.

Verdi gained fame for his mastery of theatrical effect and for the stirring melodic quality of his operas. He took several of his plots from the plays of such great dramatists as Victor Hugo, Friedrich Schiller, and William Shakespeare. Many of the melodies he wrote for soloists, small groups of singers, and choruses remain familiar throughout the world.

Verdi, a fiery Italian patriot, became a symbol of Italy's struggle for independence from Austria in the mid-1800's. He had frequent conflicts with Austrian authorities, who felt that his operas encouraged Italian nationalism. Much of the music of his early operas, particularly of *I Lombardi* (1843), became identified with the Italian nationalist movement.

Verdi was born in Le Roncole, near Parma. He studied music as a boy in Busseto, a nearby town. He tried to enter the Milan Conservatory in 1832 but was refused admission because he was too old and lacked sufficient formal training. He began taking private music lessons in Milan.

Ewing Galloway

Giuseppe Verdi

In 1839, Verdi's first opera, *Oberto*, was a success at its première at La Scala, the leading opera house in Milan. Between 1838 and 1840, his first wife and two small children died. The grief-stricken composer finished a comic opera, *Un Giorno di Regno*, which was a failure when presented in 1840. But his successful third opera, *Nabucco* (1842), made him the foremost Italian composer of his time. After completing *Aida* in 1871, Verdi apparently decided to end his career because of illness and age. During the next 16 years, his only important composition was a *Requiem Mass* (1874), written in memory of the Italian author Alessandro Manzoni.

Verdi returned to opera composing in the mid-1880's through the urging of his friend Arrigo Boito, a noted Italian poet and composer. Boito contributed librettos for Verdi's *Otello* (1887) and *Falstaff* (1893). Many critics have called *Otello* Verdi's greatest tragic opera, and some consider it the greatest of all Italian operas. *Falstaff* was only Verdi's second comic opera, but it ranks as one of the greatest comic operas ever written.

Verdi's only works after *Falstaff* were four beautiful religious compositions for voices called *Quattro Pezzi Sacri* (1898). A period of national mourning was declared in Italy following Verdi's death. *The Complete Operas of Verdi* (1970) by Charles Osborne analyzes the historical, literary, and musical elements of the operas composed by Verdi.   HERBERT WEINSTOCK

See also OPERA (Giuseppe Verdi); BOITO, ARRIGO.

VERDIGRIS, *VUR duh grees* or *VUR duh grihs*, is a poisonous pigment produced by the action of acetic acid on copper. The color of this pigment varies from blue to green. Verdigris is used commercially in dyeing, calico printing, and the manufacture of Paris green and paint. But because the pigment is likely to fade and react

chemically with other substances, it is seldom used. Verdigris is sometimes used in making liniments and salves. It is highly poisonous and so must not be taken internally. In case of poison from verdigris, take milk and egg white.   EDWARD W. STEWART

See also ACETIC ACID.

VERDIN, *VUR duhn*, is a small, yellow-headed bird of the titmouse family. It is about $4\frac{1}{2}$ inches (11 centimeters) long and lives in the arid portions of the southwest-

Cruickshank, National Audubon Society

The Verdin builds its nest of twigs in a thorny tree. The scratchy thorns protect the eggs and young birds from enemies.

ern United States and of Mexico. Its body is ash-colored and the breast is lighter. The verdin's nest is often large, and is shaped like a ball. It is made of twigs and built in a thorny tree. The female lays from three to six eggs, which are greenish-blue with brown specks. The thorny nests give ample protection against most enemies, especially since there is only a small opening on the side as an entrance. Sometimes, the birds build a "porch" around the opening to hide it. They eat spiders and small insects.

Scientific Classification. The verdin is a member of the titmouse family, Paridae. Its scientific name is *Auriparus flaviceps*.   RICHARD F. JOHNSTON

VERDUN, *vair DUHN* or *vur DUHN*, **BATTLES OF.** Verdun, one of the oldest cities of France, has been a battleground ever since Attila the Hun ravaged it in A.D. 450. This city on the Meuse River in northern France is about 50 miles (80 kilometers) from the German border. It has often played an important part in resisting enemy invasion.

The most famous battle took place during World War I. On Feb. 21, 1916, German troops launched a surprise attack, expecting to crush Verdun in a few days. The Germans hoped that, by capturing a key to the French line, they would damage French morale, and could easily defeat other French armies. They also hoped to impress German allies and neutral nations. The French, led by General Henri Pétain, defended the area stubbornly. After 11 months, the Germans withdrew, and the French hailed Pétain as a hero (see PÉTAIN, HENRI P.). During World War II, German forces easily captured Verdun in 1940, and U.S. forces recaptured it in 1944.   STEFAN T. POSSONY

VERDUN, *vair DUHN* or *vur DUHN,* **TREATY OF,** divided Charlemagne's empire into three parts. Charlemagne's grandsons fought over control of the empire after their father died in 840, and finally signed the treaty in 843. Charles the Bald received most of what is now France. Louis the German took almost all the land east of the Rhine, which became modern Germany. Lothair kept the title of emperor, and ruled a strip of land in the middle, from the North Sea to central Italy. As a result of the treaty, the lands that became France and Germany were divided. The section in between remained a battleground for a thousand years. Italy soon fell away from Lothair's kingdom. In later years, part of his kingdom became known as *Lotharingia,* or, later, Lorraine. The partition agreed upon at Verdun marked the end of the political unity of the Christian countries of Western Europe. EDWIN J. WESTERMANN

VÉRENDRYE, SIEUR DE LA. See LA VÉRENDRYE, SIEUR DE.

VERGA, *VAYR gah,* **GIOVANNI,** *joh VAHN nee* (1840-1922), was an Italian novelist, playwright, and short-story writer. His style—dry, matter-of-fact, and impersonal, yet highly effective—influenced many later Italian writers.

Verga was born in Catania, Sicily, and his best work deals with Sicily and its people. In *The House by the Medlar Tree* (1881), Verga described the struggle of a Sicilian fishing family to keep their home and integrity despite tragedy and disaster. Verga planned it as the first of five novels describing people's unsuccessful efforts to improve their lives. The project ended with the second novel, *Mastro Don Gesualdo* (1889).

Verga's literary success began in 1866 with the publication of the first of several romantic novels of middle-class life. He also wrote several short stories set in Sicily. His collection *Life of the Fields* (1880) includes "Cavalleria Rusticana," which Verga adapted into a play. This tale became the basis of an opera by Pietro Mascagni. SERGIO PACIFICI

VERGIL. See VIRGIL.

VERLAINE, *vair LEHN,* **PAUL** (1844-1896), was a French poet born in Metz. He began his career with *Fêtes Galantes* (1869), impressionistic sonnets inspired by the paintings of Antoine Watteau. Verlaine's short poem "Art Poétique" (1871-1873) expressed the spirit of the symbolist movement. In it, he claimed that the suggestive power of music was the essential quality of poetry. See SYMBOLISM.

Verlaine traveled through Great Britain, The Netherlands, and Belgium with the teenage poet Arthur Rimbaud in the early 1870's. Verlaine described the landscapes in dream imagery in *Romances sans Paroles* (*Songs Without Words,* 1874). The friendship ended in 1874 when Verlaine shot and wounded Rimbaud during a quarrel. After Verlaine served a brief prison term for the shooting, he wrote *Sagesse* (*Wisdom,* 1881), poems of self-searching and religious repentance.

Verlaine's many spontaneous and melodious verses—with their images of gray skies, pale moons, and weeping violins—create a melancholy mood. ANNA BALAKIAN

See also RIMBAUD, ARTHUR.

VERMEER, *vuhr MEER,* **JAN,** *yahn* (1632-1675), was a Dutch painter. He was often called Vermeer van Delft to distinguish him from the painter Jan Vermeer van Haarlem. Most of Vermeer's paintings show young,

Officer and Laughing Girl (about 1660), an oil painting on canvas; © The Frick Collection, New York City

A Typical Vermeer Painting shows a quiet scene of middle-class domestic life illuminated by sunlight from an open window.

middle-class people, alone or in small groups, in simply furnished rooms. They sit or stand before light walls, illuminated from a window. Vermeer's painting *Young Woman with a Water Jug* appears in color in the PAINTING article.

There is always an air of quiet and timeless happiness in Vermeer's canvases. The light is clear and soft, and the outlines of all forms seem slightly blurred. His favorite colors, blue and yellow, make a lovely, cool harmony. His two outdoor scenes are among the finest landscapes of the 1600's. Vermeer's works include *The Milk Maid, The Artist in His Studio,* and *View of Delft.* He was born in Delft, and spent his entire life there. Vermeer was a painstaking worker, and he painted only about 40 known pictures. JULIUS S. HELD

VERMICELLI. See PASTA.

VERMICULITE, *vur MIHK yuh lyt,* is a clay mineral which looks like mica. It is found as laminated flakes. In the United States, it is mined chiefly in Montana and South Carolina. When expanded by heat, vermiculite can be used industrially in building materials for insulation and soundproofing. CECIL J. SCHNEER

VERMIFORM APPENDIX. See APPENDIX.

VERMILION, *vuhr MIHL yuhn,* is a pigment or coloring matter used in making paint. Its color varies from crimson to a brilliant yellow-red. Formerly made from the mineral cinnabar, it is now made from mercury and sulfur ground together and treated with caustic-potash solution. This may be heated and stirred to form a black sulfide which yields the pigment, after long steaming. The name *vermilion* comes from a Latin word meaning *little worm,* and refers to the dried bodies of insects from which carmine, another red dye, is obtained. See also CINNABAR. EDWARD W. STEWART

Vermont Village in Winter

VERMONT

THE GREEN MOUNTAIN STATE

VERMONT, a New England state, is famous for its Green Mountains. These tree-covered peaks run the entire length of central Vermont. They divide the state into eastern and western sections. The beauty of the Green Mountains helps make Vermont one of the most scenic states. Every year, the mountains attract thousands of skiers and other tourists. Montpelier is the capital of Vermont, and Burlington is the state's largest city.

Manufacturing is the chief economic activity in Vermont, as it is in all the other New England states. But farming is also important in Vermont. Dairy farming is the state's most valuable source of agricultural income.

Vermont has the lowest percentage of city dwellers of any state in the United States. Only two Vermont cities have more than 15,000 persons. They are Burlington and Rutland. Vermont has the smallest population of any state that lies east of the Mississippi River. It ranks 48th among all the states in population.

Only Alaska and Wyoming have fewer persons than Vermont.

Forests cover about three-fourths of Vermont, and a variety of mineral deposits lie under the ground. These natural resources provide the raw materials for two of the state's main manufacturing industries—wood processing and stone processing. Trees from Vermont's forests supply maple syrup, and wood for making paper, furniture, and many other products. Vermont granite and marble are used in buildings, memorials, and tombs. Slate is used for roofing and for other purposes.

Vermont is the only New England state without a coastline on the Atlantic Ocean. However, water borders more than half the state. The Connecticut River forms Vermont's entire eastern border. Lake Champlain extends along the northern half of the western border of Vermont. In addition to the Green Mountains, Vermont has many other mountains and hills. These include the Granite Hills and the Taconic Mountains.

Maple Sugar Season in Groton

Vermont (blue) ranks 43rd in size among all the states, and 2nd in size among the New England States (gray).

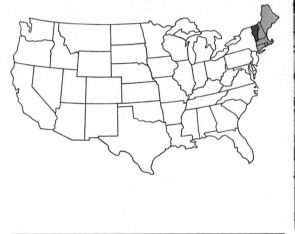

Photos, Dick Smith

Autumn near Peacham

The contributors of this article are J. Rowland Illick, Professor of Geography at Middlebury College; and Gordon Mills, Publisher of the Addison County (Vt.) Independent.

Early in the Revolutionary War, Vermont's Green Mountain Boys, led by Ethan Allen, gained fame for their capture of Fort Ticonderoga from the British. But Vermont was not admitted to the newly formed United States after the war. It remained an independent republic until about 10 years after the last battle. Then, on March 4, 1791, Vermont entered the Union as the 14th state. It was the first state admitted to the Union after the 13 original colonies.

During the 1850's, Vermont began a voting record unequaled by any other state. From then until the 1960's, the voters of Vermont chose only Republicans in elections for President and governor. They also chose Republicans in all elections for the United States Senate and House of Representatives between the mid-1800's and the mid-1900's. No other state has voted so many times in a row for major candidates of the same political party. Two Vermont Republicans, Chester A. Arthur and Calvin Coolidge, became President of the United States.

The word *Vermont* comes from *Vert Mont,* the French words for *Green Mountain.* Vermont's nickname is the *Green Mountain State.*

Facts in Brief

Capital: Montpelier.

Government: *Congress*—U.S. senators, 2; U.S. representatives, 1. *Electoral Votes*—3. *State Legislature*—senators, 30; representatives, 150. *Counties*—14.

Area: 9,614 sq. mi. (24,900 km²), including 341 sq. mi. (883 km²) of inland water; 43rd in size among the states. *Greatest Distances*—north-south, 155 mi. (249 km); east-west, 90 mi. (145 km).

Elevation: *Highest*—Mount Mansfield, 4,393 ft. (1,339 m) above sea level. *Lowest*—Lake Champlain in Franklin County, 95 ft. (29 m) above sea level.

Population: *1980 Census*—511,456; 48th among the states; density, 53 persons per sq. mi. (20 per km²); distribution, 66 per cent rural, 34 per cent urban. *1970 Census*—444,732.

Chief Products: *Agriculture*—milk, beef cattle, eggs, apples, maple products. *Manufacturing*—electric machinery and equipment; nonelectric machinery; printed materials; fabricated metal products; paper products; lumber and wood products. *Mining*—stone, asbestos.

Statehood: March 4, 1791, the 14th state.

State Abbreviations: Vt. (traditional); VT (postal).

State Motto: *Freedom and Unity.*

State Song: "Hail, Vermont!" by Josephine Hovey Perry.

257

Constitution of Vermont was adopted in 1793. Vermont had two earlier constitutions, adopted in 1777 and 1786. The constitution of 1777 was the most liberal of its time. It gave all adult male citizens the right to vote, without regard to their race or religion, or whether or not they owned property. It also forbade slavery.

Amendments (changes) to the Constitution may be proposed every four years by a two-thirds vote of the state Senate. The proposed amendments must be approved by a majority vote in the state House of Representatives. At the next legislative session two years later, the amendments require approval by a majority of both the House and the Senate. Finally, to become law, amendments need the approval of a majority of the people who vote on the proposals in an election.

Executive. The governor of Vermont is elected to a two-year term and receives a $60,000 yearly salary. The governor may be reelected any number of times. Vermont has no official residence for its governor. For a list of all the governors of Vermont, see the *History* section of this article. Vermont voters also elect the lieutenant governor, attorney general, auditor, secretary of state, and treasurer to two-year terms. The governor appoints most other top officials, with senate approval.

Legislature of Vermont is called the *General Assembly*. It consists of a 30-member Senate and a 150-member House of Representatives. The voters in each of Vermont's 13 senatorial districts elect from one to six senators, depending on total population. Voters in each of 106 representative districts and subdistricts elect one or more representatives, depending on voter population. Senators and representatives serve two-year terms. The legislature is scheduled to meet in odd-numbered years but usually meets in even-numbered years as well.

Courts. The Supreme Court, Vermont's highest court, has a chief justice and four associate justices. The legislature elects the Supreme Court justices to six-year terms. It also elects 10 Superior Court judges to six-year terms. It usually reelects these individuals until their death or retirement. Each county has one or two probate courts, whose judges are elected to four-year terms. The governor, with the legislature's approval, appoints the District Court judges to six-year terms.

Local Government in Vermont is centered in towns. Vermont towns are similar to townships in other states. That is, they are geographic areas that may include several communities and large rural districts under one government. In Vermont, there are 237 towns with local governments. Five towns—Averill, Ferdinand, Glastenbury, Lewis, and Somerset—do not have enough inhabitants to have governments. They range in population from no people in Lewis to 15 in Averill. Each of Vermont's nine cities also has a local government.

Vermont towns use the *town meeting* form of government, the purest type of democracy. A town meeting allows citizens to take a direct part in government business. Each March, town voters assemble to elect officials, approve budgets, pass laws, and decide other local business. Vermont cities operate under council-manager or mayor-council governments. The cities must submit changes in their charters to the legislature for approval. The powers of Vermont county governments are limited mainly to judicial affairs.

Peter Miller

Stu Perry

The Vermont House of Representatives occupies a chamber, *above,* in the Vermont State House in Montpelier.

A Town Meeting, *right,* enables Vermont citizens to take a direct part in government. All town voters may attend the annual meetings to elect officials and decide other local matters.

The State Seal

Symbols of Vermont. On the state seal, the 14 branches on the tree represent the 13 original states and Vermont. The wavy lines at the top symbolize the sky, and those on the bottom represent water. The cow and the sheaves of wheat represent dairying and agriculture. The seal was adopted in 1779 but was replaced by a new design in 1821. The original design was re-adopted in 1937. The state flag, adopted in 1923, carries the Vermont coat of arms. It shows a view of the Green Mountains.

Flag, flower, and bird illustrations, courtesy of Eli Lilly and Company

The State Flag

The State Bird
Hermit Thrush

The State Flower
Red Clover

The State Tree
Sugar Maple

Revenue. Taxation provides about half the state government's *general revenue* (income). Almost all the rest comes from federal grants and other U.S. government programs. An individual income tax brings in about a third of the tax revenue. Motor fuel taxes and drivers' license and vehicle registration fees also bring in over a fourth of the tax revenue. Other taxes, in order of importance, include those on sales, corporate income, meals and rooms, tobacco products, and alcoholic beverages.

Politics. Vermont has voted for more Republican presidential nominees than any other state. Since 1856, it has given its electoral votes to the Republican nominee in every presidential election except the 1964 race. That year, Vermont supported Democrat Lyndon B. Johnson. For Vermont's voting record in presidential elections, see ELECTORAL COLLEGE (table).

All of Vermont's U.S. representatives between 1853 and 1959, and all of Vermont's governors between 1854 and 1963 were Republicans. In 1974, Patrick J. Leahy became the first Democrat to be elected to the U.S. Senate from Vermont since the early 1800's.

State House, the seat of state government in Vermont, is in Montpelier. Its dome is covered with gold leaf and topped by a statue of Ceres, the Roman goddess of agriculture. Montpelier has been the state capital since 1805. Many towns served as temporary capitals between 1777 and 1805.

Arthur Griffin

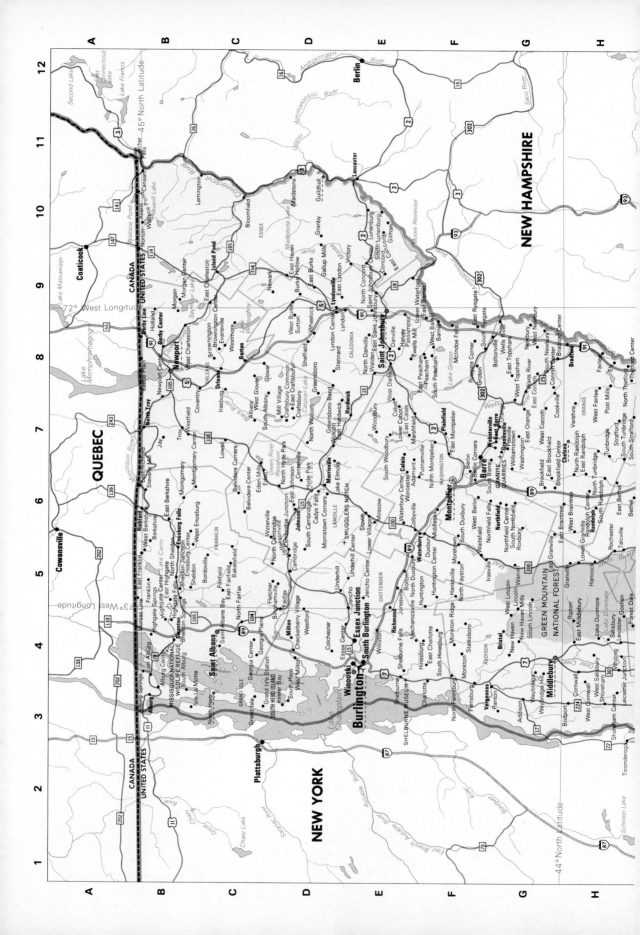

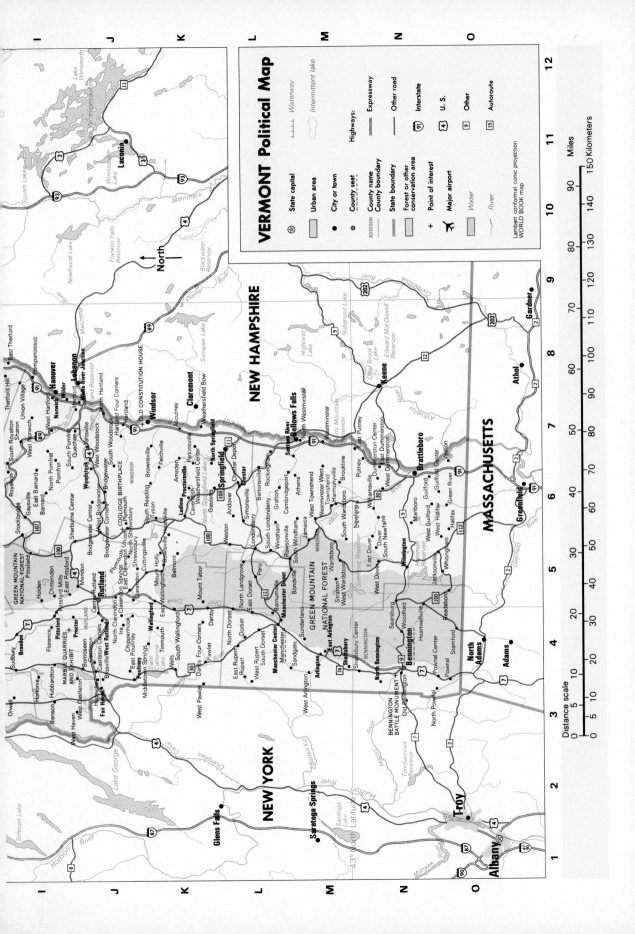

VERMONT Political Map

Legend:

- ⊛ State capital
- ▢ Urban area
- ● City or town
- ○ County seat
- ADDISON — County name
  — County boundary
  — State boundary
- ▤ Forest or other conservation area
- + Point of interest
- ✈ Major airport
- ▨ Water
- River

Highways:
- Expressway
- Other road
- 91 Interstate
- 4 U.S.
- 9 Other
- 15 Autoroute

Waterway
Intermittent lake

Lambert conformal conic projection
WORLD BOOK map

North

Distance scale

Miles
0 10 20 30 40 50 60 70 80 90
Kilometers
0 10 20 30 40 50 60 70 80 90 100 110 120 130 140 150

NEW HAMPSHIRE

NEW YORK

MASSACHUSETTS

GREEN MOUNTAIN NATIONAL FOREST

GREEN MOUNTAIN NATIONAL FOREST

43° North Latitude

Vermont Map Index

Population

511,456 ...Census ... 1980
444,732 ......"...... 1970
389,881 ......"...... 1960
377,747 ......"...... 1950
359,231 ......"...... 1940
359,611 ......"...... 1930
352,428 ......"...... 1920
355,956 ......"...... 1910
343,641 ......"...... 1900
332,422 ......"...... 1890
332,286 ......"...... 1880
330,551 ......"...... 1870
315,098 ......"...... 1860
314,120 ......"...... 1850
291,948 ......"...... 1840
280,652 ......"...... 1830
235,981 ......"...... 1820
217,895 ......"...... 1810
154,465 ......"...... 1800
85,425 ......"...... 1790

Metropolitan Area

Burlington 115,308

Counties

Addison ...... 29,406. .F 4
Bennington ... 33,345. .N 4
Caledonia .... 25,808. .E 8
Chittenden ..115,534. .E 5
Essex .... 6,313. .C 10
Franklin ...... 34,788. .C 5
Grand Isle ..... 4,613. .C 3
Lamoille ...... 16,767. .D 6
Orange ...... 22,739. .H 7
Orleans ...... 23,440. .C 8
Rutland ...... 58,347. .J 4
Washington ... 52,393. .F 6
Windham ...... 36,933. .M 5
Windsor ...... 51,030. .J 6

Cities, Towns, and Villages

Adamant ....E 7
Addison .... 889▲G 3
Albany .... 174 (705▲). .C 7
Alburg .... 496 (1,352▲). .B 3
Alburg Springs ....B 4
Amsden ....K 7
Andover .... 350▲L 6
Arlington ...... 1,309 (2,184▲). .M 4
Ascutney ....K 7
Athens .... 250▲M 6
Averill ....15▲B 10
Averys Gore* ....B 10
Bakersfield ...... 852▲C 5
Baltimore* ...... 181▲K 6
Barnard .... 790▲I 6
Barnet .... 1,338▲F 8
Barnumville ....L 4
Barre* .... 7,090▲F 7
Barre .... 9,824. .F 7
Barton .... 1,062 (2,990▲). .C 8
Bartonsville ....L 6
Beebe Plain ....B 8
Beecher Falls ....B 11
Bellows Falls ... 3,456. .M 7
Belmont ....K 5
Belvidere* ...... 218▲C 6
Bennington .... 9,349 (15,815▲).°N 4
Benson .... 739▲I 3
Berkshire ..... 1,116▲B 5
Berlin .... 2,454▲F 6
Bethel .... 1,016 (1,715▲). .H 6
Blissville ....J 3
Bloomfield ...... 188▲C 10
Bolton .... 715▲E 5
Bomoseen ....J 4
Bondville ....L 5
Bowlsville ....K 5
Bradford .... 831 (2,191▲). .H 8
Braintree* ..... 1,065▲H 6
Brandon ...... 1,925 (4,194▲). .I 4
Brattleboro .... 8,596 (11,886▲). .N 6
Bridgewater ..... 867▲J 6
Bridport .... 997▲H 3
Brighton* ..... 1,557▲C 9
Bristol .... 1,793 (3,293▲). .G 4
Brookfield .... 959▲G 6
Brookline .... 310▲M 6
Brownington ...... 708▲C 8
Brownsville ....K 7
Brunswick* ....82▲C 10
Buel's Gore* ....9. .F 5
Burke* .... 1,385▲D 9
Burke Hollow ....D 9
Burlington .... 37,712.°E 4
Cabot .... 259 (958▲). .E 7
Cadys Falls ....D 6
Calais .... 1,207▲E 7
Cambridge .... 217 (2,019▲). .D 5
Cambridgeport ....L 6
Canaan .... 1,196▲B 11
Castleton ..... 3,637▲J 4
Cavendish ..... 1,355▲K 6
Centerville ....D 6
Charleston* ..... 851▲B 9
Charlotte ...... 2,561▲F 3
Chelsea ...... 1,091▲°H 7
Chester ...... 2,791▲L 6
Chester [-Chester Depot] ...... 1,267. .L 6
Chippenhook ....J 4
Chittenden ...... 927▲I 5
Clarendon ..... 2,372▲J 5
Clarendon Springs .....J 4
Colbyville ....E 6
Colchester ... 12,629▲D 4
Concord ...... 1,125▲E 9
Cookville ....G 7
Corinth* .... 904▲G 8
Corinth Center ....G 8
Cornwall .... 993▲H 4
Coventry .... 674▲C 8
Craftsbury ...... 844▲D 7
Cuttingsville ....J 5
Danby .... 992▲K 4
Danby Four Corners ....K 4
Danville .... 1,705▲E 8
Derby* .... 4,222▲B 8
Derby Center .... 598. .B 8
Derby Line ...... 874. .B 8
Dorset .... 1,648▲L 4
Dover .... 666▲N 5
Dummerston* . 1,574▲N 6
Duxbury .... 877▲F 6
East Barnard ....I 6
East Barre, see Graniteville [-East Barre]
East Burke ....D 9
East Calais ....E 7
East Charleston ....C 9
East Charlotte ....F 4
East Concord ....E 10
East Corinth ....G 8
East Dorset ....L 4
East Dover ....N 5
East Dummerston ......N 6
East Franklin ....B 5
East Granville ....G 5
East Hardwick ....D 7
East Haven ...... 280▲D 9
East Johnson ....D 6
East Lyndon ....D 9
East Middlebury ....H 4
East Montpelier .. 2,205▲F 7
East Orange ....G 7
East Peacham ....F 8
East Poultney ....J 4
East Putney ....M 7
East Randolph ....H 6
East Richford ....B 6
East Rupert ....L 4
East Ryegate ....F 8
East St. Johnsbury ....E 9
East Thetford ....I 8
East Topsham ....G 8
East Wallingford ....K 5
Eden .... 612▲C 6
Eden Mills ....C 7
Elmore* .... 421▲E 7
Ely ....H 8
Enosburg* .... 2,070▲B 5
Enosburg Falls .... 1,207. .B 5
Essex* .... 14,392▲E 4
Essex Junction .... 7,033. .E 4
Evansville ....C 8
Ewells Mill ....E 8
Fair Haven .... 2,363 (2,819▲). .J 3
Fairfax .... 1,805▲D 4
Fairfield .... 1,493▲C 5
Fairlee .... 770▲H 8
Fayston* .... 657▲F 5
Felchville ....K 6
Ferdinand* ....12▲C 10
Ferrisburg ..... 2,117▲F 3
Fletcher .... 626▲D 5
Florence ....I 4
Forest Dale ....H 4
Foxville ....G 7
Franklin .... 1,006▲B 5
Gallup Mills ....D 10
Gassetts ....K 6
Gaysville ....I 6
Georgia* ...... 2,818▲C 4
Georgia Plains ....C 4
Gilman ....E 10
Glastenbury* ....3▲M 4
Glover .... 843▲C 8
Goshen .... 163▲H 4
Grafton .... 604▲L 6
Granby ....70▲D 10
Grand Isle ..... 1,238▲C 3
Graniteville [-East Barre] 2,172. .G 7
Granville .... 288▲H 5
Green River ....O 6
Greensboro ..... 677▲D 8
Greensboro Bend ......D 8
Groton .... 667▲F 8
Guildhall .... 202▲°D 10
Guilford .... 1,532▲N 6
Halifax .... 488▲O 6
Hancock .... 334▲H 5
Hanksville ....F 5
Hardwick ...... 1,476 (2,613▲). .E 7
Harmonyville ....M 6
Hartford ...... 7,963▲I 7
Hartland ...... 2,396▲J 7
Healdville ....K 5
Heartwellville ....N 5
Highgate* ..... 2,493▲B 4
Highgate Falls ....B 4
Highgate Springs ....B 4
Hinesburg ..... 2,690▲F 4
Holden ....I 5
Holland .... 473▲B 9
Hortonia ....I 3
Hubbardton ...... 490▲I 4
Huntington .... 1,161▲F 5
Hyde Park .... 475 (2,021▲).°D 6
Hydeville ....J 3
Ira .... 354▲J 4
Irasburg .... 870▲C 8
Irasville ....F 5
Island Pond .... 1,216. .C 9
Isle La Motte ...... 393▲B 3
Jacksonville ..... 252. .N 5
Jamaica .... 681▲M 5
Jay .... 302▲B 7
Jeffersonville .... 491. .D 5
Jericho .... 1,340 (3,575▲). .E 5
Johnson ...... 1,393 (2,581▲). .D 6
Jonesville ....E 5
Keeler Bay ....D 3
Kirby* .... 282▲E 9
Lake Dunmore ....H 4
Lake Elmore ....D 7
Landgrove* ...... 121▲L 5
Leicester .... 803▲H 4
Lemington ...... 108▲C 11
Lewis* ....B 10
Lincoln .... 870▲G 4
Londonderry .. 1,510▲L 5
Lowell .... 573▲C 7
Lower Granville ....H 5
Lower Village ....E 6
Lower Waterford ....E 9
Ludlow .... 1,352 (2,414▲). .K 6
Lunenburg .... 1,138▲E 10
Lyndon .... 4,924▲D 9
Lyndon Center ....D 9
Lyndonville .... 1,401. .D 9
Maidstone .... 100▲D 10
Manchester .... 563 (3,261▲).°L 4
Manchester Center ...... 1,719. .L 4
Manchester Depot ....L 4
Marlboro .... 695▲N 6
Marshfield ...... 301 (1,267▲). .E 7
McIndoe Falls ....F 8
Mechanicsville ....E 4
Mendon .... 1,056▲J 5
Middlebury .... 5,591 (7,574▲).°G 4
Middlesex ..... 1,235▲F 6
Middletown Springs .... 603▲J 4
Mill Village ....D 7
Milton .... 1,411 (6,829▲). .D 4
Monkton ...... 1,201▲F 4
Monkton Ridge ....F 4
Montgomery ..... 681▲B 6
Montpelier .... 8,241.°F 6
Moretown ..... 1,221▲F 5
Morgan .... 460▲B 9
Morristown* ... 4,448▲D 6
Morrisville ..... 2,074. .D 6
Morses Line ....B 5
Moscow ....E 6
Mount Holly ...... 938▲K 5
Mount Tabor .... 211▲K 5
New Haven ..... 1,217▲G 4
Newark .... 280▲D 9
Newbury .... 425 (1,699▲). .G 9
Newfane .... 119 (1,129▲).°M 6
Newport* ..... 1,319▲B 7
Newport ...... 4,756.°B 8
North Bennington .. 1,685. .N 3
North Concord ....E 9
North Danville ....E 8
North Dorset ....L 4
North Fairfax ....C 4
North Fayston ....F 5
North Ferrisburg ....F 4
North Hero ..... 442▲°C 3
North Landgrove ....L 5
North Montpelier ....F 7
North Pomfret ....I 7
North Pownal ....N 3
North Randolph ....H 6
North Sheldon ....B 5
North Springfield ....K 6
North Troy ...... 717. .B 7
North Tunbridge ....H 7
North Westminster ... 310. .M 7
Northfield ..... 2,033 (5,435▲). .G 6
Norton .... 184▲B 10
Norwich .... 2,398▲I 7
Old Bennington .... 353. .N 4
Orange .... 752▲G 7
Orleans .... 983. .C 8
Orwell .... 901▲I 3
Panton .... 537▲G 3
Passumpsic ....E 9
Pawlet .... 1,244▲K 4
Peacham .... 531▲F 8
Perkinsville ..... 187. .K 6
Peru .... 312▲L 5
Pittsfield .... 396▲I 5
Pittsford .... 666 (2,590▲). .I 4
Pittsford Mills ....I 4
Plainfield .... 599 (1,249▲). .F 7
Plymouth .... 405▲J 6
Pomfret .... 856▲I 6
Pompanoosuc ....I 8
Post Mills ....H 8
Poultney ...... 1,554 (3,196▲). .J 4
Pownal .... 3,269▲O 3
Proctor .... 1,998▲I 4
Proctorsville ..... 481. .K 6
Putnamville ....F 6
Putney .... 1,850▲M 7
Quechee ....I 7
Randolph ..... 2,217 (4,689▲). .H 6
Rawsonville ....L 5
Reading* .... 647▲J 6
Readsboro ...... 402 (638▲). .O 5
Richford ...... 1,471 (2,206▲). .B 6
Richmond .... 865 (3,159▲). .E 4
Ripton .... 327▲H 4
Rochester ..... 1,054▲H 5
Rockingham .... 5,538▲L 7
Roxbury .... 452▲G 6
Royalton ...... 2,100▲I 6
Rupert .... 605▲L 4
Rutland* ...... 3,300▲J 4
Rutland ...... 18,436.°J 5
Ryegate* ...... 1,000▲F 8
St. Albans* .... 3,555▲C 4
St. Albans ..... 7,308.°C 4
St. Albans Bay ....C 4
St. George* ...... 677▲E 4
St. Johnsbury .. 7,150 (7,938▲).°E 9
Salisbury .... 881▲H 4
Sandgate .... 234▲L 4
Saxtons River .... 593. .L 7
Searsburg ....72▲N 5
Shaftsbury .... 3,001▲M 4
Sharon .... 828▲I 7
Sheffield .... 435▲D 8
Shelburne ...... 5,000▲E 4
Shelburne Road Section* ....E 4
Sheldon .... 1,618▲B 5
Sherburne* ...... 891▲I 5
Shoreham .... 972▲H 3
Shrewsbury ..... 866▲J 5
Simonsville ....L 6
Somerset* ....2▲M 5
South Alburg ....B 3
South Barre ... 1,301. .G 7
South Burlington .. 10,679. .E 4
South Cambridge ......D 5
South Duxbury ....F 5
South Hero .... 1,188▲D 3
South Hinesburg ....F 4
South Lincoln ....G 5
South Londonderry ....L 5
South Lunenburg ....E 10
South Newfane ....N 6
South Peacham ....F 8
South Pomfret ....I 6
South Randolph ....H 6
South Royalton ....I 6
South Ryegate ....F 8
South Wallingford ....K 4
South Wardsboro ......M 5
South Windham ....M 6
South Woodbury ....E 7
Springfield .... 5,603 (10,190▲). .L 7
Stamford .... 773▲O 4
Stannard .... 142▲D 8
Starksboro .... 1,336▲F 4
Stevens Mill ....B 6
Stockbridge ..... 508▲I 5
Stowe .... 531 (2,991▲). .E 6
Strafford .... 731▲H 7
Stratton .... 122▲M 5
Sudbury .... 380▲I 4
Sunderland ...... 768▲M 4
Sutton .... 667▲D 9
Swanton ...... 2,520 (5,141▲). .B 4
Taftsville ....J 7
Talcville ....H 5
Thetford* ..... 2,188▲I 8
Tinmouth .... 406▲K 4
Topsham* .... 767▲G 8
Townshend ...... 849▲M 6
Troy .... 1,498▲B 7
Tunbridge .... 925▲H 7
Tyson ....K 6
Underhill ...... 2,172▲D 5
Union Village ....I 8
Vergennes .... 2,273. .F 3
Vernon .... 1,175▲O 7
Vershire .... 442▲H 7
Victory ....56▲E 9
Waits River ....G 8
Waitsfield ..... 1,300▲F 5
Walden .... 575▲E 8
Wallace Pond ....B 10
Wallingford .... 1,141 (1,893▲). .K 5
Waltham* .... 394▲G 4
Wardsboro ...... 505▲M 5
Warners Grant* ....B 9
Warren .... 956▲G 5
Warrens Gore* ....B 9
Washington ..... 855▲G 7
Waterbury ..... 1,892 (4,465▲). .F 6
Waterford* ...... 882▲E 9
Waterville .... 470▲C 6
Weathersfield* .... 2,534▲K 7
Weathersfield Bow .....K 7
Websterville ....G 7
Wells .... 815▲K 4
Wells River ...... 396. .G 8
West Berkshire ....B 5
West Berlin ....F 6
West Braintree ....H 6
West Brattleboro* .... 2,795. .N 6
West Burke ...... 338. .D 9
West Castleton ....J 3
West Charleston ....B 8
West Corinth ....G 7
West Danville ....E 8
West Dover ....N 5
West Fairlee ..... 427▲H 8
West Glover ....C 8
West Hartford ....I 7
West Haven ..... 253▲I 3
West Lincoln ....G 4
West Milton ....D 4
West Newbury ....G 8
West Norwich ....I 7
West Pawlet ....K 3
West Rupert ....L 4
West Rutland ..... 2,169 (2,351▲). .J 4
West Salisbury ....H 4
West Topsham ....G 7
West Townshend ....M 6
West Windsor* ...... 763▲J 7
Westfield .... 418▲B 7
Westford ...... 1,413▲D 4
Westminster ...... 319 (2,493▲). .M 7
Westminster West ......M 6
Westmore .... 257▲C 8
Weston .... 627▲L 5
Weybridge .... 667▲G 4
Wheelock .... 444▲D 8
White River Junction .... 2,582. .J 7
Whiting .... 379▲H 4
Whitingham ... 1,043▲O 5
Wilder .... 1,461. .I 7
Williamstown .. 2,284▲G 6
Williamsville ....N 6
Williston ...... 3,843▲E 4
Williston Road Section* ....E 4
Wilmington ..... 1,808▲N 5
Windham .... 223▲L 6
Windsor .... 4,084▲K 7
Winhall* .... 327▲L 5
Winooski ...... 6,318. .E 4
Wolcott .... 986▲D 7
Woodbury .... 573▲E 7
Woodford .... 314▲N 4
Woodstock ..... 1,178 (3,214▲).°J 6
Worcester .... 727▲E 6

▲Entire town (township), including rural area.
*Does not appear on map; key shows general location.
°County seat.
Source: 1980 census. Places without population figures are unincorporated areas.

VERMONT/People

The 1980 United States census reported that Vermont had 511,456 people. The population had increased 15 per cent over the 1970 census figure, 444,732.

Fewer persons live in Vermont than in any other state east of the Mississippi River. West of the Mississippi, only Alaska and Wyoming have fewer people.

About two-thirds of Vermont's people live in rural areas—a greater percentage than in any other state. Vermont and Maine are the only New England states with a larger rural than urban population.

About a fourth of the people live in the Burlington metropolitan area, Vermont's only metropolitan area (see METROPOLITAN AREA). The city of Burlington is the largest city in the state. It has twice as many people as Rutland, the second largest city. Vermont's seven other cities, in order of size, are South Burlington, Barre, Montpelier, St. Albans, Winooski, Newport, and Vergennes. Vermont has 49 villages and 242 towns. See the separate articles on Vermont's cities, towns, and villages listed in the *Related Articles* at the end of this article.

About 96 of every 100 Vermonters were born in the United States. More than half the people born in other countries came from Canada.

Like other New Englanders, the people of Vermont have long been called *Yankees*. This word is used to mean such traits as thrift, conservative manners, reserved speech, and respect for individual rights.

VERMONT/Education

Schools. The town of Guilford voted funds for a free public school in 1761. Vermont's constitution of 1777 required each town to have a public school. In 1780, Bennington established the state's first secondary school. Vermont's first statewide school fund was approved by the legislature in 1825. Samuel Read Hall, a pioneer educator, established the first teacher-training school in the United States at Concord in 1823.

A state commissioner of education and a seven-member board of education supervise Vermont's public-school system. The governor, with the senate's approval, appoints the board members to six-year terms. The board members, with the governor's approval, appoint the commissioner for an indefinite term.

Vermont's city and town school districts are administered by local boards of directors. The largest districts also have a superintendent of schools. The smaller districts are grouped into *supervisory unions*, each headed by a superintendent. These superintendents work with the boards of directors in managing school affairs.

Vermont law requires children from age 7 through 15 to attend school. For the number of students and teachers in Vermont, see EDUCATION (table).

Libraries. Vermont's first library opened in Brookfield in 1791. It is one of the oldest U.S. libraries still operating. Today, Vermont has over 200 public libraries. The Department of Libraries, in Montpelier, specializes in historical and legal research and reference works, and has the state's best collection of early Vermont newspapers. The Bailey/Howe Library of the University of Vermont is the state's largest.

Population Density

Vermont's population is scattered around its many mountainous areas. About one-fourth of the state's people live in the Burlington metropolitan area. About two-thirds live in rural areas.

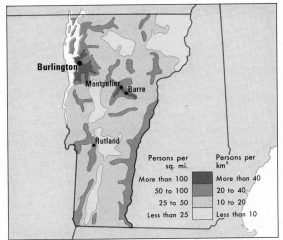

WORLD BOOK map; based on U.S. Bureau of the Census data.

Museums. The Vermont Museum in Montpelier features exhibits on Indian life, life during the Revolutionary War (1775-1783), and rural life in America during the 1800's. It owns one of the oldest globes made in the United States. The globe was made by James Wilson during the early 1800's. The museum also houses one of the first printing presses used in the United States. The Bennington Museum has early American glassware, pottery, Vermont art, and historic flags. The University of Vermont's Robert Hull Fleming Museum in Burlington displays art from many periods. The Saint Johnsbury Athenaeum has fine paintings. The Sheldon Museum in Middlebury houses early Vermont documents, household furnishings, portraits, and tools. The Shelburne Museum is described in the *Places to Visit* section of this article.

Universities and Colleges

Vermont has 17 universities and colleges accredited by the New England Association of Schools and Colleges. For enrollments and further information, see UNIVERSITIES AND COLLEGES (table).

Name	Location	Founded
Bennington College	Bennington	1925
Burlington College	Burlington	1972
Castleton State College	Castleton	1787
Goddard College	Plainfield	1938
Green Mountain College	Poultney	1834
International Training, School for	Brattleboro	1964
Johnson State College	Johnson	1828
Lyndon State College	Lyndonville	1911
Marlboro College	Marlboro	1946
Middlebury College	Middlebury	1800
Norwich University	*	*
St. Joseph the Provider, College of	Rutland	1954
St. Michael's College	Winooski	1903
Southern Vermont College	Bennington	1926
Trinity College	Burlington	1925
Vermont and State Agricultural College, University of	Burlington	1791
Vermont Law School	South Royalton	1972

*For campuses and founding dates, see UNIVERSITIES AND COLLEGES (table).

Side-Wheeler *S.S. Ticonderoga* in Shelburne Museum

Arthur Griffin

Marble Quarry in Proctor

Arthur Griffin

Fishing on the West River

Hanson Carroll

VERMONT/*A Visitor's Guide*

Vermont's mountains, lakes, and streams offer a variety of recreational activities. Visitors to the Green Mountains can hike on the Long Trail. This footpath winds through the mountains from Massachusetts to Canada. Overnight camps lie along the trail every 6 to 8 miles (10 to 13 kilometers). In winter, tourists flock to ski resorts in the Green Mountains and other ranges.

The largest ski resorts are near East Burke, Jay, Manchester, Rutland, Stowe, Waitsfield, and Wilmington. The skiing season usually lasts from mid-December to mid-April. Visitors also enjoy summer boating on the larger lakes and fishing in the state's many streams.

Many vacationers go to Vermont just for the beautiful scenery. In the fall, much of the state is ablaze with the orange, purple, red, and yellow colors of turning leaves. Vermont's quiet towns and villages are other favorite scenes. They are noted for their white churches.

Places to Visit

Following are brief descriptions of some of Vermont's many interesting places to visit:

Bennington Battle Monument, in Bennington, is a granite tower 306 feet (93 meters) high. It honors the colonists who defeated the British in the Battle of Bennington in 1777. The tower is one of the world's highest battle monuments.

Coolidge Birthplace, in Plymouth Notch, is now a combination store and post office. A nearby museum houses possessions of President Calvin Coolidge. A simple gravestone marks his grave in the town cemetery.

Granite Quarries cut deeply into Millstone Hill in Barre. Visitors can watch large granite blocks being quarried, and see granite being sawed, polished, and carved in the world's largest stone-finishing plant.

Marble Quarries and Marble Exhibit are Proctor's chief attractions. The quarries are among the world's largest. The exhibit, in the display rooms of the Vermont Marble Company, features the world's largest collection of various kinds of marble.

Arthur Griffin

George Rockwin, Bruce Coleman Inc.

Bennington Battle Monument   **Winter Carnival at Stowe**

Old Constitution House, in Windsor, is the building in which Vermont's first constitution was written. This two-story frame house, which was originally a tavern, was built in 1772.

Shelburne Museum, in Shelburne, is a reconstruction of an early American village. The museum includes more than 30 historic buildings with such items as carriages, china, dolls, furniture, glass, paintings, pewter, rugs, textiles, and toys. The side-wheeler steamship *Ticonderoga*, which once sailed Lake Champlain, is part of the museum.

Smuggler's Notch, near Stowe, is a wide gap between Mount Mansfield and the Sterling Mountains. The notch got its name during the War of 1812, when smugglers brought goods through the notch from Canada to Boston.

National Forest. Green Mountain National Forest, established in 1911, is located in southern and central Vermont.

State Parks and Forests. There are 45 state parks and 34 state forests in Vermont. For information, write to the Department of Forests and Parks, Montpelier, VT 05602.

Annual Events

Skiing contests rank among Vermont's most popular annual events and take place in many parts of the state throughout the winter. The maple-sugar season begins when the winter snows start melting, usually in March. Many people gather at maple-sugar houses to watch syrup being made from maple sap. Craft fairs, antique shows, and summer theater programs are held statewide during July and August. The best time to see the brilliant colors of Vermont's autumn leaves is from mid-September through mid-October.

Other annual events include the following:

January-June: Stowe Winter Carnival (January); Town Meeting Day, statewide (first Tuesday in March); Vermont Maple Festival in St. Albans (April); Vermont Dairy Festival in Enosburg Falls (June).

July-November: Old-Time Fiddlers Contest in Craftsbury Common (July); Vermont Mozart Festival in Burlington (July-August); Fairs in Barton, Bradford, Essex Junction, Lyndonville, Rutland, and Tunbridge (late July to September); Foliage Festivals, statewide (mid-September to mid-October).

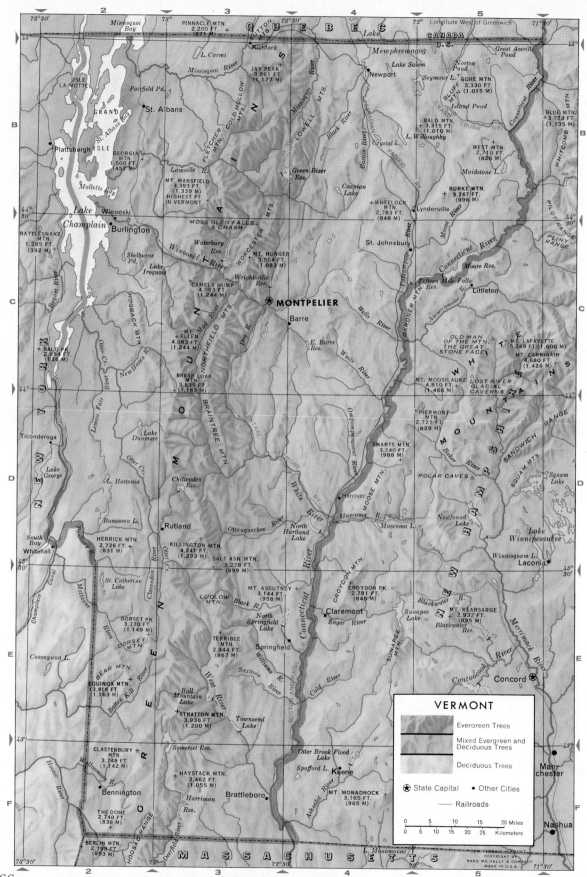

Map Index

VERMONT/*The Land*

Land Regions. Vermont has six main land regions: (1) the White Mountains, (2) the Western New England Upland, (3) the Green Mountains, (4) the Vermont Valley, (5) the Taconic Mountains, and (6) the Champlain Valley.

The White Mountains region covers the northeastern corner of Vermont and parts of New Hampshire and Maine. In Vermont, the region includes a series of *monadnocks*. A monadnock is a mountain of rock that did not wear down when erosion leveled the land around it. The monadnocks have rounded slopes and rise 2,700 to 3,300 feet (823 to 1,010 meters) above sea level. The highest are Gore Mountain (3,330 feet, or 1,015 meters), Burke Mountain (3,267 feet, or 996 meters), and Mount Monadnock (3,140 feet, or 957 meters). Swift streams cut between the monadnocks and flow into the Connecticut and other rivers.

The Western New England Upland covers most of eastern Vermont. It also extends into Massachusetts and Connecticut. This region is sometimes called the *Vermont Piedmont*. In the east, it consists of the broad, fertile lowlands of the Connecticut River Valley. Farmers in the valley raise dairy cattle and grow apples and strawberries. The lowlands rise gradually to hills in the west. The Granite Hills, near Barre, include 1,700-foot (518-meter) Millstone Hill. Many lakes lie among hills in the northern part of the region.

The Green Mountains region covers central Vermont. The famous Green Mountains make up all but the northeastern corner of the region. In the northeast, the Green Mountains taper off into the Northfield, Worcester, and several other low mountain ranges.

Mount Mansfield, one of the Green Mountains, is the highest peak in Vermont. It rises 4,393 feet (1,339 meters) above sea level. Killington Mountain (4,241 feet, or 1,293 meters), Mount Ellen (4,083 feet, or 1,244 meters), and Camels Hump (4,083 feet, or 1,244 meters)—all in the Green Mountains—are Vermont's next tallest peaks. The Green Mountains region is the center of Vermont's tourist industry, and an important source of minerals.

The Vermont Valley is a narrow region that stretches about halfway up western Vermont from the Massachusetts border. The region includes the valleys of several small rivers, including the Batten Kill and the Walloomsac.

The Taconic Mountains region covers a narrow strip in southwestern Vermont. The region also extends into Massachusetts. In Vermont, it includes many mountains. The highest ones are Equinox Mountain (3,816 feet, or 1,163 meters), Dorset Peak (3,770 feet, or 1,149 meters), Little Equinox Mountain (3,320 feet, or 1,012 meters), Mother Myrick Mountain (3,290 feet, or 1,003 meters), and Bear Mountain (3,260 feet, or 994 meters). Swift streams cut through the mountains, and the mountains surround many scenic lakes.

The Champlain Valley, also called the *Vermont Lowland*, borders Lake Champlain. This region includes Burlington, the state's largest city; and some of Vermont's best farmland. The valley has many dairy farms and apple orchards. Farmers in the region also raise corn, hay, oats, and wheat on rolling hills and broad fertile lowlands. Lake Champlain has a series of islands, including Grand Isle and Isle La Motte. These islands are part of Vermont.

Rivers and Lakes. The Connecticut River forms Vermont's entire eastern border. In 1934, a ruling by the Supreme Court of the United States gave control

Land Regions of Vermont

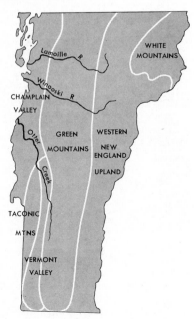

Hanson Carroll

Pleasure Boats ride at anchor on the calm waters of Lake Champlain near South Hero. The lake is the largest in New England.

Dick Smith

A Farm Field adds a golden tint to the countryside surrounding Waterbury Center in Vermont's Green Mountains. The scenic Green Mountains region, which covers central Vermont, attracts many tourists to the state.

of the river to New Hampshire. Its western border is the low water mark on the Vermont side of the river. Otter Creek is the longest river within Vermont. It rises near East Dorset, flows 90 miles (140 kilometers) north, and empties into Lake Champlain. The Batten Kill River also rises near East Dorset. It flows south into New York.

Most other Vermont rivers run down the slopes of the Green Mountains. Some flow down the eastern slopes and empty into the Connecticut River. Others wind down the western slopes and empty into Lake Champlain. Three large rivers—the Missisquoi, the Lamoille, and the Winooski—rise east of the Green Mountains and pass through them. The rivers empty into Lake Champlain.

Vermont has about 430 lakes and ponds. Most of them are in the northeast. Lake Champlain, the largest lake in New England, covers 268 square miles (694 square kilometers) in northwest Vermont. The rest of the 490-square-mile (1,270-square-kilometer) lake lies in New York and Quebec. Vermont's second largest

lake is Lake Memphremagog. About one third of it, or 10 square miles (26 square kilometers), lies in the state, and the rest is in Quebec. Bomoseen Lake, west of Rutland, is the largest lake entirely in Vermont. It covers about 4 square miles (10 square kilometers).

Plant and Animal Life. Forests cover about three-fourths of the state. Common trees include ashes, basswoods, beeches, birches, cedars, hemlocks, maples, pines, poplars, and spruces. Many kinds of ferns grow in the mountain regions of Vermont. Several types of grasses and sedges grow in the forests and lowlands. Anemones, arbutuses, buttercups, daisies, gentians, goldenrods, lilacs, pussy willows, and violets grow throughout the state.

The white-tailed deer is Vermont's most common game animal. Fur-bearing animals found in the state include bears, beavers, bobcats, foxes, minks, muskrats, raccoons, and skunks. Porcupines, rabbits, squirrels, and woodchucks live in the forests.

Grant Heilman

Arthur Griffin

Dairy Cattle Graze along the Connecticut River, *above.* The river forms Vermont's eastern boundary.

Mount Mansfield, *right,* is the highest peak in Vermont. It rises 4,393 feet (1,339 meters) in the Green Mountains.

268

VERMONT / *Climate*

Summers in Vermont are short, with few hot days. Summer nights are cool and crisp, especially in the mountains. Vermont has an average July temperature of 68° F. (20° C). Vernon had the state's highest temperature, 105° F. (41° C), on July 4, 1911.

Vermont winters are long and cold, with an average January temperature of 19° F. (−7° C). Bloomfield had the record low temperature, −50° F. (−46° C), on Dec. 30, 1933. Snowfall in the Connecticut River Valley and the Champlain Valley ranges from 60 to 80 inches (150 to 200 centimeters) yearly. The mountains receive from 80 to 120 inches (200 to 305 centimeters) a year. Snow is important to Vermont's economy. The deep snows on mountains attract thousands of skiers. Yearly *precipitation* (rain, melted snow, and other forms of moisture) averages about 40 inches (100 centimeters).

John H. Harris

The West River winds through the snowy hills in southern Vermont. Snowfall is heavy throughout the state.

SEASONAL TEMPERATURES

January

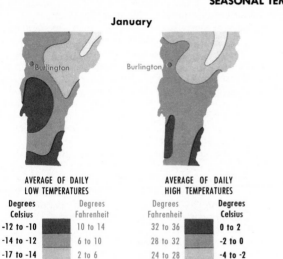

AVERAGE OF DAILY
LOW TEMPERATURES

Degrees Celsius		Degrees Fahrenheit
-12 to -10		10 to 14
-14 to -12		6 to 10
-17 to -14		2 to 6
-19 to -17		-2 to 2

AVERAGE OF DAILY
HIGH TEMPERATURES

Degrees Fahrenheit		Degrees Celsius
32 to 36		0 to 2
28 to 32		-2 to 0
24 to 28		-4 to -2
20 to 24		-7 to -4

July

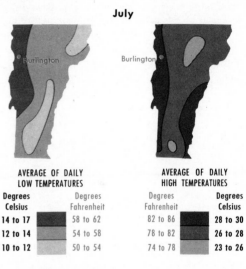

AVERAGE OF DAILY
LOW TEMPERATURES

Degrees Celsius		Degrees Fahrenheit
14 to 17		58 to 62
12 to 14		54 to 58
10 to 12		50 to 54

AVERAGE OF DAILY
HIGH TEMPERATURES

Degrees Fahrenheit		Degrees Celsius
82 to 86		28 to 30
78 to 82		26 to 28
74 to 78		23 to 26

AVERAGE YEARLY PRECIPITATION
(Rain, Melted Snow, and Other Moisture)

Centimeters		Inches
132 to 152		52 to 60
112 to 132		44 to 52
91 to 112		36 to 44
71 to 91		28 to 36

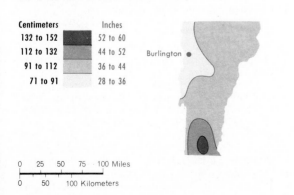

```
0   25   50   75   100 Miles
0      50      100 Kilometers
```

WORLD BOOK maps

AVERAGE MONTHLY WEATHER

BURLINGTON					
	Temperatures				Days of
	F.°		C°		Rain or
	High	Low	High	Low	Snow
JAN.	28	8	-2	-13	13
FEB.	28	8	-2	-13	12
MAR.	39	20	4	-7	13
APR.	53	32	12	0	13
MAY	67	43	19	6	13
JUNE	78	54	26	12	12
JULY	82	58	28	14	12
AUG.	80	56	27	13	11
SEPT.	71	48	22	9	12
OCT.	59	38	15	3	11
NOV.	44	28	7	-2	13
DEC.	31	15	-1	-9	13

Manufacturing is Vermont's single most important economic activity. It accounts for more than one-fourth of the *gross state product*—the total value of all goods and services produced in a state in a year. Tourism and such service industries as wholesale and retail trade are also important to Vermont's economy. Farms and mines are in many parts of the state.

Natural Resources of Vermont include valuable mineral deposits, forests, and some fertile soil.

Soil. Vermont's most fertile areas are its river valleys. Many parts of the state are rocky with little or no soil.

Forests cover about three-fourths of Vermont. The state's hardwood trees include, in order of value, maples, birches, beeches, ashes, poplars, and basswoods. Softwood trees, also in order of value, include spruces, red and white pines, hemlocks and cedars.

Minerals. Large asbestos, granite, marble, and talc deposits make the Green Mountains region Vermont's chief mineral area. Valuable marble deposits are also found in the Vermont Valley and the Taconic Mountains. Most of Vermont's slate comes from the Taconic

Vermont's Gross State Product

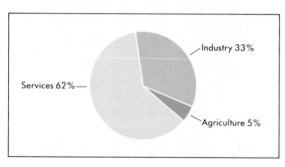

The gross state product (GSP) is the total value of goods and services produced in a state in a year. The GSP measures a state's total economic performance and can also be used to compare the economic output and growth of states. Vermont's GSP was $5,237,000,000 in 1982.

Production and Workers by Economic Activities

Economic Activities	Per Cent of GSP Produced	Employed Workers	
		Number of Persons	Per Cent of Total
Manufacturing	27	47,400	22
Wholesale & Retail Trade	16	43,200	20
Community, Social, & Personal Services	15	49,100	22
Finance, Insurance, & Real Estate	12	8,900	4
Government	11	36,200	17
Transportation, Communication, & Utilities	8	8,700	4
Agriculture	5	12,800	6
Construction	5	10,900	5
Mining	1	600	*
Total	100	217,800	100

*Less than 1 per cent.
Sources: *Employment and Earnings*, May 1984, Bureau of Labor Statistics; Federal Reserve Bank of Boston; 1982 Census of Agriculture, Bureau of the Census.

Mountains. The Granite Hills have granite deposits.

Service Industries account for 62 per cent of the gross state product of Vermont. Most of the service industries are concentrated in Burlington and Rutland, the state's largest cities, and in popular tourist centers. Wholesale and retail trade ranks as the most valuable service industry in Vermont. It accounts for 16 per cent of the gross state product. Trade includes hotel and restaurant services that support the state's thriving tourist industry.

Community, social, and personal services, the state's second most valuable service industry, account for 15 per cent of the gross state product. This industry includes education and health care; advertising; the operation of beauty shops and cleaning establishments; and services in the field of amusement and recreation. Other service industries, in order of importance, are (1) finance, insurance, and real estate, (2) government, and (3) transportation, communication, and utilities.

Manufacturing in Vermont accounts for 27 per cent of the gross state product. Goods manufactured there have a *value added by manufacture* of about $2 billion yearly. Value added by manufacture represents the increase in value of raw materials after they become finished products.

Electrical Machinery and Equipment has an annual value added of about $655 million and is Vermont's most valuable industry. Computer equipment is produced in Essex Junction, and electronic instruments in Bellows Falls and Vergennes.

Nonelectrical Machinery has a value added of about $314 million yearly. Machine tools, such as drills, grinders, and lathes, come chiefly from Springfield and Windsor. Scales are made in Rutland and St. Johnsbury.

Fabricated Metal Products have a value added of about $213 million yearly. Chief products include hand tools, machine parts, ski poles, and weapons for the U.S. armed forces. Burlington is the industry's main production center.

Paper and Related Products. About 350 Vermont factories depend on trees from the state's forests for raw materials. The manufacture of paper and paper products is Vermont's leading wood-processing industry. These products have a yearly value added of about $150 million. They are made throughout the state.

Printed Materials have an annual value added of about $145 million. Brattleboro, Burlington, and Rutland have printing and publishing plants.

Other Industries. Food products are important to the state's economy. Vermont's main food-processing centers include Burlington, Middlebury, Richmond, and St. Albans. The chief processed foods include bakery products; canned fruits; dairy products; and meat products. Vermont's wood-processing industry includes the production of baskets, boxes, building supplies, furniture, lumber, and toys. Factories in many parts of Vermont make building stone, and markers, memorials, and tombs from granite. Barre is the center of the state's granite industry. The manufacture of marble products, including memorials and tile, is also important. Proctor and Rutland are the state's chief marble centers. Other stone products include cement blocks, concrete, and slate.

Agriculture accounts for 5 per cent of Vermont's gross state product. Vermont farmers earn about $425 million yearly. The state's approximately 6,300 farms cover about a fourth of Vermont's land area. Vermont farms average about 250 acres (100 hectares) in size.

Milk earns more than three-fourth's of Vermont's farm income. Cattle in the state produce about 267 million gallons (1,015 million liters) of milk yearly. Other leading livestock products include beef cattle and calves, chickens, eggs, hogs, and turkeys.

Vermont is one of the leading states in producing maple syrup and maple sugar. About 550,000 gallons (2 million liters) of maple syrup come from the state's maple trees each year. Some syrup is made into sugar. Crops are another valuable source of farm income. Potatoes rank as the leading vegetable, and apples as the leading fruit. Hay, oats, and corn grown in Vermont are used as animal feed.

Mining in Vermont accounts for only 1 per cent of the gross state product. The mining industry earns about $42 million yearly. Vermont is a leader in the production of asbestos, granite, marble, slate, and talc. The largest U.S. granite quarries are near Barre. White marble is mined at Danby and West Rutland. Red and green marble occur in a few deposits. Fair Haven is the slate-mining center. One of the country's largest asbestos mines is in Lowell. Sand and gravel are mined in nearly every county. Limestone is mined in Chittenden, Franklin, and Rutland counties. Talc comes from Windham and Windsor counties.

Electric Power. Hydroelectric dams on many Vermont rivers provide power for the state's industries. The four largest power dams are on the Connecticut River between Vermont and New Hampshire. They are the Comerford Dam near Barnet, the Samuel C. Moore Dam near Passumpsic, the Vernon Dam near Vernon, and the Wilder Dam near Wilder. Vermont, Massachusetts, and New Hampshire share the power generated by these dams. Vermont also gets electric power from two sources in New York—the St. Lawrence Power Project and the Niagara Power Project—by overland lines and by underwater cable through Lake Champlain. The Vermont Yankee Nuclear Power Plant in Vernon began operating in 1972.

Transportation. Vermont has about 14,000 miles (22,500 kilometers) of roads and highways, most of which are surfaced. Interstate 89 and Interstate 91 are the chief highways. Interstate 89 extends northwest from White River Junction to the Canadian border at

Farm, Mineral, and Forest Products

This map shows where the state's leading farm, mineral, and forest products are produced. The urban areas (shown on the map in red) are the state's important manufacturing centers.

Highgate. Interstate 91 runs north and south from Guilford to Derby Line. The state has about 25 airports. Five major airlines serve the state. Railroads operate on about 700 miles (1,100 kilometers) of track in Vermont. Twelve rail lines provide freight service. Passenger trains serve seven Vermont cities.

Communication. Vermont has about 30 newspapers, including about 10 dailies. The Vermont Gazette was published in Westminster for a brief period, beginning in 1780. The Rutland Herald is Vermont's oldest continuously published newspaper. It was begun as a weekly in 1794, and is now a daily. The Burlington Free Press and the Rutland Herald are the state's largest dailies. About 30 periodicals are also published in Vermont.

Vermont's first radio station, WSYB, opened in Rutland in 1930. The first television station, WCAX-TV, began broadcasting from Burlington in 1954. Vermont now has about 40 radio and 6 television stations.

Factories in Proctor make memorials, tile, and other products from marble. The manufacture of stone products is one of Vermont's leading industries. Factories throughout Vermont use granite, building stone, and marble from the state's quarries.

Carlos H. Elmer

Confederate Soldiers robbed banks in St. Albans in 1864, and fled into Canada. This was the northernmost action of the Civil War.

St. Albans
● Fairfield

Samuel de Champlain, probably the first white man to reach Vermont, claimed the eastern shores of Lake Champlain for France in 1609.

Gathering Maple Sap became important in Vermont during the late 1700's. The state is famous for sugar and syrup made from maple sap.

★ MONTPELIER

Universal Manhood Suffrage was granted in 1777. Vermont became the first state to include this provision in its constitution.

Vermont Joined the Union in 1791. It was the first territory after the original 13 colonies to become part of the United States.

The Green Mountain Boys, led by Ethan Allen, captured Fort Ticonderoga from the British in 1775.

● Plymouth Notch

HISTORIC VERMONT

Fort Dummer became Vermont's first permanent white settlement in 1724. Colonists built it to warn villages in western Massachusetts of Indian attacks.

Chester A. Arthur
born in Fairfield

Calvin Coolidge
born in Plymouth Notch

Indian Days. Vermont was chiefly an Indian hunting ground before white settlers came. The Abenaki, Mahican, and Penacook tribes of the Algonquian Indian family first claimed the region. Powerful New York Iroquois Indians drove the Algonquian out. The Algonquian returned during the early 1600's. With help from the French, they defeated the Iroquois.

Exploration and Settlement. Samuel de Champlain of France was probably the first white person to explore what is now Vermont. He arrived at Lake Champlain in 1609, and claimed the Vermont region for France. In 1666, the French built a fort dedicated to Saint Anne on Isle La Motte in Lake Champlain. In 1690, Jacobus de Warm led British soldiers from Albany, N.Y., to a point near the site of present-day Middlebury, Vt. De Warm founded a fort at Chimney Point, west of Middlebury. Vermont's first permanent white settlement was made at Fort Dummer, in what is now Brattleboro. Fort Dummer was built by Massachusetts settlers in 1724 to protect that colony's western settlements from raids by the French and Indians.

The Lake Champlain region became a major battleground during the French and Indian War (1754-1763). In this war, England gained from France the control of Vermont and much of the rest of North America. See FRENCH AND INDIAN WARS.

Land Disputes. Benning Wentworth, the royal governor of New Hampshire, made 131 grants of Vermont land between 1749 and 1763. This land was called the *New Hampshire Grants.* But New York claimed the same land and granted it to other settlers. In 1764, England recognized the grants made by New York. England ordered settlers who held New Hampshire Grants to surrender their land or pay New York for it. In 1770, these settlers organized a military force called the *Green Mountain Boys* to defend their land. The Green Mountain Boys attacked many New York settlers and drove them from Vermont. See GREEN MOUNTAIN BOYS.

The Revolutionary War began in Massachusetts in 1775, before the Vermont land disputes were settled. Vermonters united to fight the British. Ethan Allen, Benedict Arnold, and more than 80 Green Mountain Boys captured Fort Ticonderoga from the British in May, 1775. Colonial troops held the fort until 1777, when the British drove them out. The troops retreated south from Fort Ticonderoga, with the British in pursuit. In Hubbardton, a rear guard led by Seth Warner stopped the retreat and fought the British. The rear guard was defeated. But the fighting delayed the British long enough to allow the rest of the colonists to escape.

The Battle of Bennington, on Aug. 16, 1777, was a major Revolutionary War conflict. It is often thought of as a Vermont battle. But it was actually fought just west of Vermont, in New York. The battles of Bennington and Saratoga (also in New York) marked the end of British land operations in the Northern Colonies.

Independent Republic. On Jan. 15, 1777, Vermont settlers declared their territory an independent republic. They named it *New Connecticut.* In July, 1777, Vermont adopted its first constitution and its present name.

New Hampshire and New York still claimed parts of Vermont. But Vermont ignored the claims. In 1783,

Important Dates in Vermont

1609 Samuel de Champlain claimed the Vermont region for France.

1724 Massachusetts established Fort Dummer, the first permanent white settlement in the Vermont region.

1763 England gained control of Vermont.

1775 Ethan Allen and the Green Mountain Boys captured Fort Ticonderoga from the British in the Revolutionary War.

1777 Vermont declared itself an independent republic.

1791 Vermont became the 14th state on March 4.

1823 The opening of the Champlain Canal created a water route from Vermont to New York City.

1864 Confederate soldiers raided St. Albans in the northernmost land action of the Civil War.

1881 Chester A. Arthur, born in Fairfield, became the 21st President of the United States.

1923 Calvin Coolidge, born in Plymouth Notch, became the 30th President of the United States.

1927 Vermont's worst flood killed 60 persons and caused millions of dollars in damage.

1962 Vermonters elected Philip H. Hoff, their first Democratic governor since 1853.

1964 Vermonters voted for Lyndon B. Johnson, the first Democrat they supported in a presidential election since 1824.

1970 The legislature passed the Environmental Control Law, which permitted the state to limit major developments that could harm the environment.

George Washington wrote that he believed it would be necessary to send troops to overthrow the Vermont government. But this never happened, and Vermont remained an independent republic for 14 years. In 1790, Vermont settled its dispute with New York by paying that state $30,000. New Hampshire also gave up its claim to Vermont. Such improved relations with neighboring states helped clear the way for Vermont's admission to the Union. On March 4, 1791, Vermont became the 14th state.

The 1800's. During the War of 1812, Vermont volunteers fought the British in the battles of Chippewa, Lundy's Lane, and Plattsburgh. But the war was unpopular in Vermont, because trade with British-controlled Canada had become important to the state's economy. Hard times came to Vermont after the war. During a prosperous period from 1823 to 1836, many persons moved from Vermont to the growing Midwest. They feared future economic hardships in Vermont.

The Champlain Canal, which opened in 1823, connected Lake Champlain and New York's Hudson River. The canal allowed Vermont farmers to ship their goods by water all the way to New York City, a major market. Farmers in the Champlain Valley prospered, especially those who raised Spanish Merino sheep for wool. By 1840, Vermont had six times as many sheep as persons. Many small, water-powered mills were built in Vermont to process the wool from the sheep. During the mid-1800's, competition from Western states and other countries made wool prices drop. By 1860, Vermont farmers had sold half their sheep to be used as meat. This crisis caused Vermont to change from a sheep-raising state to a dairy-farming state.

During the Civil War (1861-1865), about 34,000 Vermonters served with the Union forces. The northern-

268e

	Party	Term
As an Independent Republic		
Thomas Chittenden	None	1778-1789
Moses Robinson	None	1789-1790
Thomas Chittenden	None	1790-1791
As a State		
Thomas Chittenden	None	1791-1797
Paul Brigham	None	1797
Isaac Tichenor	Federalist	1797-1807
Israel Smith	*Dem.-Rep.	1807-1808
Isaac Tichenor	Federalist	1808-1809
Jonas Galusha	*Dem.-Rep.	1809-1813
Martin Chittenden	Federalist	1813-1815
Jonas Galusha	*Dem.-Rep.	1815-1820
Richard Skinner	*Dem.-Rep.	1820-1823
Cornelius P. Van Ness	*Dem.-Rep.	1823-1826
Ezra Butler	†Nat. Rep.	1826-1828
Samuel C. Crafts	†Nat. Rep.	1828-1831
William A. Palmer	Anti-Masonic	1831-1835
Silas H. Jennison	Whig	1835-1841
Charles Paine	Whig	1841-1843
John Mattocks	Whig	1843-1844
William Slade	Whig	1844-1846
Horace Eaton	Whig	1846-1848
Carlos Coolidge	Whig	1848-1850
Charles K. Williams	Whig	1850-1852
Erastus Fairbanks	Whig	1852-1853
John S. Robinson	Democratic	1853-1854
Stephen Royce	Republican	1854-1856
Ryland Fletcher	Republican	1856-1858
Hiland Hall	Republican	1858-1860
Erastus Fairbanks	Republican	1860-1861
Frederick Holbrook	Republican	1861-1863
J. Gregory Smith	Republican	1863-1865
Paul Dillingham	Republican	1865-1867
John B. Page	Republican	1867-1869
Peter T. Washburn	Republican	1869-1870
George W. Hendee	Republican	1870
John W. Stewart	Republican	1870-1872
Julius Converse	Republican	1872-1874
Asahel Peck	Republican	1874-1876
Horace Fairbanks	Republican	1876-1878
Redfield Proctor	Republican	1878-1880
Roswell Farnham	Republican	1880-1882
John L. Barstow	Republican	1882-1884
Samuel E. Pingree	Republican	1884-1886
Ebenezer J. Ormsbee	Republican	1886-1888
William P. Dillingham	Republican	1888-1890
Carroll S. Page	Republican	1890-1892
Levi K. Fuller	Republican	1892-1894
Urban A. Woodbury	Republican	1894-1896
Josiah Grout	Republican	1896-1898
Edward C. Smith	Republican	1898-1900
William W. Stickney	Republican	1900-1902
John G. McCullough	Republican	1902-1904
Charles J. Bell	Republican	1904-1906
Fletcher D. Proctor	Republican	1906-1908
George H. Prouty	Republican	1908-1910
John A. Mead	Republican	1910-1912
Allen M. Fletcher	Republican	1912-1915
Charles W. Gates	Republican	1915-1917
Horace F. Graham	Republican	1917-1919
Percival W. Clement	Republican	1919-1921
James Hartness	Republican	1921-1923
Redfield Proctor	Republican	1923-1925
Franklin S. Billings	Republican	1925-1927
John E. Weeks	Republican	1927-1931
Stanley C. Wilson	Republican	1931-1935
Charles M. Smith	Republican	1935-1937
George D. Aiken	Republican	1937-1941
William H. Wills	Republican	1941-1945
Mortimer R. Proctor	Republican	1945-1947
Ernest W. Gibson	Republican	1947-1950
Harold J. Arthur	Republican	1950-1951
Lee E. Emerson	Republican	1951-1955
Joseph B. Johnson	Republican	1955-1959
Robert T. Stafford	Republican	1959-1961
F. Ray Keyser, Jr.	Republican	1961-1963
Philip H. Hoff	Democratic	1963-1969
Deane C. Davis	Republican	1969-1973
Thomas P. Salmon	Democratic	1973-1977
Richard A. Snelling	Republican	1977-1985
Madeleine M. Kunin	Democratic	1985-

*Democratic-Republican   †National Republican

most land action of the war took place in Vermont in 1864. A group of 22 Confederate soldiers raided banks in St. Albans, and fled to Canada with over $20,000.

Agriculture declined in Vermont after the war. More and more Vermont farmers left the state for cities, or for better farmland in the Midwest and elsewhere. Most of the French Canadians and Europeans who moved to Vermont settled in cities to work in factories. The late 1800's brought great growth to Vermont's wood-processing and cheese-making industries. Burlington grew rapidly as a port city that processed lumber from Canada and shipped it to U.S. cities. The granite industry boomed in Barre. Vermont's once important textile industry declined during the late 1800's. Many textile mills moved to the South, where labor costs were lower.

The Early 1900's. Manufacturing replaced agriculture as Vermont's most important economic activity during the early 1900's. The value of Vermont's manufactured products more than tripled between 1900 and 1920.

Vermont's tourist industry also grew rapidly during the early 1900's. Many large resort hotels and vacation camps were built. In 1911, Vermont became the first state with an official publicity bureau to attract tourists.

In 1923, Calvin Coolidge, born in Vermont, became the 30th President of the United States. He had been elected Vice-President under President Warren G. Harding, who died in office. Coolidge was a shy man who was quiet in public. To many persons, he seemed to be a "typical Vermont conservative."

The nationwide Great Depression of the 1930's brought severe hardship to Vermont. Many small factories and lumber mills closed. Vermont farmers were hurt by falling prices and reduced sales. Vermont's economy improved during the late 1930's.

The worst flood in Vermont history occurred in November, 1927. Waters from the Winooski River and branches of the Connecticut River swept away entire sections of towns. The flood caused 60 deaths and millions of dollars in damage.

The Mid-1900's. During World War II (1939-1945), Vermont factories again produced war materials. After the war, the state increased its efforts to attract new industries. The Vermont Development Department, established in 1949, promoted industrial development and tourism. The state's Municipal Bond Act of 1955 gave Vermont communities permission to issue revenue bonds. Money from the bonds financed industrial construction programs.

During the 1960's, a few large corporations built factories in Vermont. But most of the industry attracted to Vermont would be considered small in many

other states. Even firms with a dozen or so workers provide economic help to Vermont's small towns. An interstate highway from Massachusetts to the Canadian border, developed during the 1960's, contributed to the growth of industry and tourism in Vermont.

As Vermont manufacturing grew, agriculture became less important to the state's economy. Farms decreased in number and increased in size, and the population began to shift from rural to urban areas. In 1965, the Vermont legislature was *reapportioned* (redivided) to provide more equal representation based on population, and rural residents lost some power. The state Senate was reapportioned again in 1973.

Politically, Vermont remained a Republican center of strength. Republicans held such control in the state that the election of a few Democrats in the 1950's and 1960's made national news. William H. Meyer, elected to the U.S. House of Representatives in 1958, became the state's first Democratic congressman since 1853. Philip H. Hoff, who served as governor of Vermont from 1963 until 1969, was the first Democrat to hold that office since 1854. Since 1856, Vermont has given its electoral votes to the Republican nominee in every presiden-

tial election except the 1964 race. That year, the state's electoral votes went to the Democratic nominee, Lyndon B. Johnson.

Vermont Today. The Democratic Party continued to gain strength in Vermont in the 1970's. In 1974, Patrick J. Leahy became the first Democrat to be elected to the U.S. Senate from Vermont since the early 1880's. Since Governor Philip H. Hoff left office in 1969, two of the four governors have been Democrats.

Manufacturing and tourism continue to contribute greatly to Vermont's economy. The tourist industry, centered in the Green Mountains, brings almost $700 million a year to the state.

One of Vermont's major problems in the 1980's is to attract more industry and tourism and, at the same time, protect the state's natural resources and recreation areas. In 1970, the state legislature passed the Environmental Control Law. This act allows the state to limit major developments that could harm the environment.

J. ROWLAND ILLICK and GORDON MILLS

VERMONT/Study Aids

Related Articles in WORLD BOOK include:

BIOGRAPHIES

Allen, Ethan	Collamer, Jacob	Morrill, Justin S.
Arthur, Chester A.	Coolidge, Calvin	Warner, Seth
Champlain, Samuel de		

CITIES

Burlington	Montpelier	Rutland

PHYSICAL FEATURES

Connecticut River	Green Mountains	Lake Champlain

OTHER RELATED ARTICLES

Green Mountain Boys	Revolutionary War in America

Outline

I. Government
  A. Constitution
  B. Executive
  C. Legislature
  D. Courts
  E. Local Government
  F. Revenue
  G. Politics
II. People
III. Education
  A. Schools
  B. Libraries
  C. Museums
IV. A Visitor's Guide
  A. Places to Visit
  B. Annual Events
V. The Land
  A. Land Regions
  B. Rivers and Lakes
  C. Plant and Animal Life
VI. Climate
VII. Economy
  A. Natural Resources
  B. Service Industries
  C. Manufacturing
  D. Agriculture
  E. Mining
  F. Electric Power
  G. Transportation
  H. Communication
VIII. History

Questions

How long was Vermont an independent republic?
Who were the Green Mountain Boys?
Which U.S. presidents were born in Vermont?
What is Vermont's chief economic activity?

When did Vermont lose its claim to the Connecticut River? What state won this dispute?
How many Vermont towns have no local government? Why do they not have their own government?
What voting record did Vermont set from the 1850's until the 1960's?
Where did the northernmost land action of the Civil War take place?
Where was the first U.S. teacher-training school established? When?
Why was the War of 1812 unpopular with the people of Vermont?

Additional Resources

Level I
CARPENTER, ALLAN. *Vermont.* Rev. ed. Childrens Press, 1979.
CHENEY, CORA. *Vermont: The State with the Storybook Past.* Greene, 1976.
FRADIN, DENNIS B. *Vermont in Words and Pictures.* Childrens Press, 1980.

Level II
HAVILAND, WILLIAM A., and POWER, M. W. *The Original Vermonters: Native Inhabitants, Past and Present.* Univ. Press of New England, 1981.
HILL, RALPH N. *Yankee Kingdom: Vermont and New Hampshire.* Countryman, 1984. Reprint of 1973 edition. *Contrary Country: A Chronicle of Vermont.* Shelburne, 1982. Reprint of 1974 edition.
HOYT, EDWIN P. *The Damndest Yankees: Ethan Allen and His Clan.* Greene, 1976.
JOHNSON, CHARLES W. *The Nature of Vermont: Introduction and Guide to a New England Environment.* Univ. Press of New England, 1980.
JUDD, RICHARD M. *The New Deal in Vermont: Its Impact and Aftermath.* Garland, 1979.
MORRISSEY, CHARLES T. *Vermont: A Bicentennial History.* Norton, 1981.
SWIFT, ESTHER M. *Vermont Place-Names: Footprints of History.* Greene, 1977.
TREE, CHRISTINA, and JENNISON, PETER. *Vermont: An Explorer's Guide.* Countryman, 1983.
VAN DE WATER, FREDERIC F. *The Reluctant Republic: Vermont, 1724-1791.* Countryman, 1974. Reprint of 1941 edition.

VERMONT, UNIVERSITY OF, is a state-supported co-educational school in Burlington, Vt. It has colleges of agriculture; arts and sciences; education and social services; engineering, mathematics, and business administration; and medicine. It also has schools of allied health sciences, home economics, natural resources, and nursing; and a graduate college. The university grants bachelor's, master's, and doctor's degrees. It was the first university in the United States to admit women to the national honor society Phi Beta Kappa.

The University of Vermont was chartered in 1791. The Vermont Agricultural College was chartered in 1864, and joined with the University in 1865 to form the University of Vermont and State Agricultural College. For the enrollment, see UNIVERSITIES AND COLLEGES (table).   Critically reviewed by the UNIVERSITY OF VERMONT

VERNACULAR SCHOOL. See EDUCATION (The Renaissance; The Reformation).

VERNAL EQUINOX. See EQUINOX.

VERNAL FALLS. See YOSEMITE NATIONAL PARK (Waterfalls); WATERFALL (chart).

VERNE, *vurn,* **JULES** (1828-1905), a French novelist, wrote some of the first science-fiction stories. Although his books were written before the invention of the airplane, they have remained popular in the space age. Verne forecast the invention of airplanes, submarines, television, guided missiles, and space satellites. Verne even predicted their uses accurately.

Brown Bros.

Jules Verne

Verne cleverly used realistic detail and believable explanations to support incredible tales of adventure. His fantastic plots took advantage of the widespread interest in science in the 1800's. He carried his readers all over the earth, under it, and above it. Verne's *Twenty Thousand Leagues Under the Sea,* published in 1870, tells about Captain Nemo, a mad sea captain who cruises beneath the oceans in a submarine. In *Around the World in Eighty Days* (1873), Phileas Fogg travels around the earth in the then unheard-of time of 80 days, just to win a bet. Other thrillers include *A Journey to the Center of the Earth* (1864), *From the Earth to the Moon* (1865), and *Around the Moon* (1870).

Verne knew a great deal about geography, and used his knowledge to make his stories realistic. He also wrote several historical novels, including a story about the American Civil War, *North Against South* (1887).

Verne was born in Nantes. He studied law in Paris but decided to become a writer. His first works were plays and the words for operas. Verne's first novel, *Five Weeks in a Balloon* (1863), brought him immediate success. It was based on an essay he wrote describing the exploration of Africa in a balloon. The essay was rejected several times before one publisher suggested that Verne rewrite it as a novel of imagination. The popularity of the book encouraged Verne to continue writing on science-fiction themes.   IRVING PUTTER

VERNIER, *VUR nee uhr,* is an instrument used in measuring lengths and angles. It is named for Pierre Vernier, a French mathematician who invented it in the 1600's.

The most common vernier has a short graduated scale, or "ruler," which slides along a longer scale. The subdivisions on the short rule are nine-tenths as long as the subdivisions on the long scale. Nine small divisions on the large scale are equal to 10 on the small scale.

In using the vernier, the large scale is laid along the material to be measured, a small pipe, for example. The small scale is slid until it reaches the end of the pipe. Now we check to see which of its divisions lines up with one of the divisions on the large scale. Suppose the 5, or fifth division from the zero end of the small scale, lines up with 25 on the large scale. Since each division on the small scale is one-tenth smaller than the large divisions, five divisions are equal to only four and one-half on the large scale. Therefore, the end of the small scale rests at 25 − 4.5, or 20.5 on the large scale.

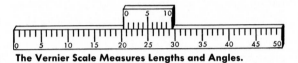

The Vernier Scale Measures Lengths and Angles.

Engineers often use calipers with a vernier attachment (see CALIPER). Some read to $\frac{1}{1000}$ inch (0.0254 millimeter) without a magnifier. The caliper's beam is divided into inches and tenths, and each tenth is divided into fourths. The vernier is divided into 25 parts. The beam may be divided into fiftieths of an inch. The vernier has 20 divisions to each of its 19.   HERMAN J. SHEA

VERNIER, PIERRE. See VERNIER.

VERNON, MOUNT. See MOUNT VERNON (Va.).

VERONA, *vuh ROH nuh* (pop. 261,208), is an Italian city on the Adige River. It lies near the Tyrolese Alps, 71 miles (114 kilometers) west of Venice. For location, see ITALY (political map). Shakespeare used Verona as the scene of his play *Romeo and Juliet.* The house in which Juliet is said to have lived still stands.

Verona presents a fascinating combination of ancient, medieval, and modern civilizations. The city was a prosperous Roman colony before the time of Christ, and still has many Roman ruins, including an amphitheater built by the Emperor Diocletian. In the Middle Ages, Verona was a major art center. It has an active trade in wine, fruits, and marble.   SHEPARD B. CLOUGH

See also ITALY (color picture: Opera).

VERONAL. See BARBITURATE.

VERONESE, *VAY roh NAY say,* **PAOLO,** *PAH oh loh* (1528-1588), painted in and around Venice at the end of the Italian Renaissance. His real name was Paolo Cagliari, but he was called Veronese because he was born in Verona. His art is typically Venetian in its dependence on the poetic effects of color. Veronese became most popular for paintings of historical subjects and myths, and for representations of the life of Venetian aristocrats. He also painted religious subjects and portraits. His figures are robust and handsome, splendidly costumed, and theatrically posed in rich settings. His major works include *Marriage at Cana* in the Louvre in Paris; *Mars and Venus* in the Metropolitan Museum of Art, New York City; and frescoes in the Villa Maser, near Venice.   VERNON HYDE MINOR

VERONICA, *vuh RAHN uh kuh,* **SAINT,** is traditionally supposed to have been one of the women of Jerusalem who followed Christ on His way to Calvary. She is said to have offered Christ her linen veil, to wipe the sweat from His face. Tradition has it that the imprint of His features remained on the cloth, and the miraculous relic is said to have been preserved in Rome since the year 700. It was exhibited in Saint Peter's in 1854. But other cities also claim to possess this relic. Saint Veronica's feast day is July 12.   FULTON J. SHEEN

VERRAZANO, *vehr uh ZAH noh,* **GIOVANNI DA,** *joh VAHN ee dah* (1485?-1528?), an Italian navigator and pirate, is believed to have sailed to America in 1524. About 1521, he is thought to have served France, attacking Spanish ships. In 1523, King Francis I of France supposedly commissioned him to explore the shores of America, and Verrazano may have touched the North Carolina shore. Historians believe he entered New York harbor, reached the Hudson River, and explored the New England coast. Verrazano was born near Florence. It is believed that he was killed by Indians in the West Indies.   FRANKLIN L. FORD

VERRAZANO-NARROWS BRIDGE, *vehr uh ZAH noh,* is one of the world's longest suspension bridges. It spans the Narrows channel between Brooklyn and Staten Island in New York City. The center span of the $325 million bridge is 4,260 feet (1,298 meters) long. See also STATEN ISLAND (picture).   WILLIAM E. YOUNG

VERROCCHIO, *vuh ROH kee OH,* **ANDREA DEL,** *ahn DREH uh dehl* (1435-1488), was an Italian sculptor and painter. One of his early great works is a standing figure of David with the head of Goliath at his feet. The work shows how Verrocchio, by means of his knowledge of anatomy, controlled the muscles of David's body and face to enrich the meaning of his subject. The bronze group, *Christ and St. Thomas,* demonstrates the artist's mastery of psychology in the hesitancy of St. Thomas'

stride and gesture in contrast to the calm and poise of Christ.

Verrocchio's large bronze of Bartolommeo Colleoni is sometimes called the world's finest *equestrian statue* (statue of a man on a horse). It appears in color in the SCULPTURE article. His one unquestioned painting, *The Baptism of Christ,* appears in the JOHN THE BAPTIST article. The angel on the left was probably painted by his pupil Leonardo da Vinci.   G. HAYDN HUNTLEY

VERSAILLES, *vehr SY* or *vehr SAYLZ* (pop. 91,494), is a city in northern France. It lies about 11 miles (18 kilometers) southwest of Paris (see FRANCE [political map]). Versailles is best known as the site of the magnificent Palace of Versailles and the beautiful grounds around it. The palace was built by King Louis XIV during the 1600's and was the royal residence for more than 100 years. It is now a national museum.

The palace stands in the western part of Versailles. It is more than $\frac{1}{4}$ mile (0.4 kilometer) long and has about 1,300 rooms. Many of the rooms have been restored and refurnished to look as they did when royalty lived in them. The palace also has paintings and sculptures by famous European artists.

Many visitors enjoy seeing the bedrooms of the king and queen, the Hall of Mirrors, and the Salon d'Hercule (Room of Hercules). The bedrooms are trimmed with gold-covered wood and furnished with rare antiques. The Hall of Mirrors is a long corridor named for the large mirrors that face each of its windows. The Salon d'Hercule has a high ceiling of about 380 square yards (318 square meters). The ceiling is decorated by a painting of a scene from the life of Hercules, a hero of Greek mythology.

The palace grounds consist of a garden and a park, which cover about 250 acres (101 hectares). In the

© Alain Perceval, Photographic Aerienne

The Palace of Versailles and its grounds make up one of the most beautiful sights in France. The palace was built during the 1600's as the royal residence of France, but today it is a museum. The building has about 1,300 rooms, many of which have been restored and refurnished.

The Treaty of Versailles marked the official end of World War I. Thirty-two Allied countries took part in drawing up the document. The four statesmen shown above took charge of major negotiations. They are, *left to right*, Premier Vittorio Orlando of Italy, Prime Minister David Lloyd George of Great Britain, Premier Georges Clemenceau of France, and President Woodrow Wilson of the United States. The treaty was ratified in 1919 by all the great powers except the United States.

garden, plants are arranged in colorful geometric patterns around fountains and pools. The park includes two small palaces called the Grand Trianon and the Petit Trianon. The Grand Trianon was built by King Louis XIV, who went there to escape the activity of the main palace. Louis XV erected the Petit Trianon. It became the favorite residence of Marie Antoinette, the wife of Louis XVI.

Versailles was originally the site of a hunting lodge built in 1624 by Louis XIII. After he died, his son, Louis XIV, ordered that a palace be constructed on the same site. Work began in 1661 under the direction of Louis Le Vau, a French architect. The palace took more than 40 years to complete. Through the years, later kings added more rooms to the building.

The French Revolution of 1789-1799 led to the overthrow of the French king. Mobs invaded the palace during the revolution and removed or destroyed most of the furniture and art. Little was done to maintain the building until the early 1900's, when restoration work began. This project is still going on.   J. A. LAPONCE

See also FRANCE (picture: Historic French Furniture).

VERSAILLES, TREATY OF, officially ended World War I. Fighting ended when Germany accepted the Armistice of Nov. 11, 1918. But the war did not officially end until the Treaty of Versailles went into effect on Jan. 10, 1920. The treaty was signed on June 28, 1919, in the Hall of Mirrors of the Palace of Versailles, near Paris.

Thirty-two allied countries took part in negotiating the treaty. The United States played an important part in drawing it up. President Woodrow Wilson and Premiers David Lloyd George of Great Britain and Georges Clemenceau of France were known as the "Big Three" because they almost completely controlled the course of negotiations. But the United States never ratified the Versailles Treaty. The Senate refused to give its consent (see WILSON, WOODROW [Opposition to the League; Wilson's Collapse]). Instead, the United States made a separate treaty of peace with Germany in 1921. This treaty reserved for the United States all the advantages it might have had under the Versailles Treaty, but accepted none of the obligations.

Making the Treaty. The people of the defeated countries, and most other people, expected that the treaty of peace would be based upon the famous Fourteen Points set forth by President Wilson in his speech of Jan. 8, 1918 (see WILSON, WOODROW [The Fourteen Points]). They soon learned that this was impossible, for several of the Allies had entered into secret agreements during the war which affected boundaries, the distribution of territory, and many other matters.

From the beginning, it was clear that no one would have much to say about the terms of the treaty except the five "great powers," the United States, Great Britain, France, Italy, and Japan. President Wilson was so eager to see a League of Nations established that he yielded many of the other points in order to protect this one. As a result, most of the provisions of the treaty were compromises that came nearer the desires of France and Great Britain than those of Wilson.

Provisions of the Treaty. The four outstanding provisions of the treaty revised boundaries, set reparations, disarmed Germany, and established the League of Nations (see LEAGUE OF NATIONS). Germany lost the province of Alsace, the German-controlled portion of Lorraine, much of Schleswig, the districts of Eupen and Malmédy, southeastern Silesia, Posen, and a strip of West Prussia, which was granted to Poland as a corridor to the sea. The mouth of the Memel (now Neman)

River and the surrounding territory was ceded to the Allies and later transferred to Lithuania. The city of Danzig (now Gdańsk, Poland) was taken from Germany and became a free city under the jurisdiction of the League of Nations. Germany lost all its overseas colonies, and its rights in Turkey and China. The Saar Valley, with its valuable coal fields, was placed under control of the League of Nations for 15 years. The Rhineland was to be demilitarized. Parts of it were to be occupied for as long as 15 years in order to assure Germany's good behavior.

Reparations. Germany had to turn over to the Allies livestock for the farms the German armies had laid waste, ships, railroad cars, locomotives, and other materials to replace those destroyed during the war, and large quantities of coal to repay France for the losses in its own mines. Germany was also required to pay large yearly sums in cash.

The treaty did not decide on the total amount of these cash payments. Instead, it provided for a reparations commission to determine the actual sum and to arrange the details of payment. In 1921 the figure was set at 132 billion gold marks, or about $33 billion.

Efforts to collect the reparations failed. The Dawes Plan in 1924 and the Young Plan in 1929 also failed to solve this problem. In 1932 the Lausanne Agreement brought reparations payments to an end.

Ratification. The first German representatives sent to sign the peace treaty resigned when they found out what was in it. A few slight changes, such as the provision for a *plebiscite* (popular vote) in Silesia, were made in response to their objections. The Allies also threatened to take over more German territory if the German government refused to sign. A second German delegation signed the treaty, and after hot debate the German Reichstag approved it. All the great Allied powers, except for the United States, ratified the Treaty of Versailles.   DWIGHT E. LEE

See also TRIANON, TREATY OF; WORLD WAR II (Problems Left by World War I).

VERSE, BLANK. See BLANK VERSE.

VERSE, FREE. See FREE VERSE.

VERTEBRA, *VUR tuh bruh,* is any one of the bones that make up the spinal column. A child has 33 vertebrae. But an adult has 26, because several of them unite in later life (see SPINE). Some long-tailed vertebrate animals have many more vertebrae than a child or adult.

A vertebra has a central body with a *pedicle* (bony extension) on each side. The pedicles join bilateral *laminae* to form an *arch* enclosing an opening called the *vertebral foramen.* The spinal cord passes through this opening. A *spinous process* and two *transverse processes* extend from the arch. The transverse processes bear *articular processes* that connect with the articular processes of adjoining vertebra.   GORDON FARRELL

VERTEBRATE, *VUR tuh briht* or *VUR tuh brayt,* is an animal with a backbone and *cranium* (brain case). There are seven living classes of vertebrates: (1) the lamprey and its relatives, *Agnatha;* (2) the shark and other cartilaginous fish, *Chondrichthyes;* (3) the bony fish, *Osteichthyes;* (4) the frog and other amphibians, *Amphibia;* (5) reptiles, *Reptilia;* (6) birds, *Aves;* and (7) mammals, *Mammalia.*

Most vertebrates have a bony backbone called a *spinal column.* The spinal column is made of bones called

vertebrae (see SPINE). But some, such as the shark, do not have bones. Sharks have a spinal column of *cartilage* (waxy tissue). Some scientists prefer to call the group *Craniata* because all vertebrates have a cranium.

All vertebrates are *bilaterally symmetrical.* That is, the left and right sides of the body are alike. The body is usually divided into a head and a trunk. The more advanced land vertebrates have a neck. In *mammals* (animals with milk glands for feeding their young) the trunk is divided into a *thorax* (chest) and abdomen. Vertebrates never have more than two pair of limbs.

Scientific Classification. Vertebrates are classified in the phylum *Chordata,* and make up the subphylum *Vertebrata.*   WILLIAM V. MAYER

Related Articles in WORLD BOOK include:

Amphibian	Invertebrate	Reptile
Amphioxus	Lamprey	Shark
Bird	Mammal	Skate
Chordate	Nervous System	Tail
Fish	(In Vertebrates)	

VERTICAL TAKE-OFF AIRCRAFT. See V/STOL; HELICOPTER.

VERTIGO. See DIZZINESS.

VERVAIN. See VERBENA.

VERWOERD, HENDRIK F. See SOUTH AFRICA (Opposition to Apartheid).

VERY HIGH FREQUENCY WAVE (VHF) refers to the band of electromagnetic waves that range in frequency from 30 megahertz (30 million cycles per second) to 300 megahertz (300 million cycles per second). VHF wave lengths range from 1 to 10 meters. The Federal Communications Commission has assigned portions of the VHF band to TV and FM stations and to "ham" radio operators. The VHF band assigned to TV ranges from 54 to 216 megahertz. The VHF band assigned to FM ranges from 88 to 108 megahertz. VHF waves travel in straight lines, like light waves. For this reason, their transmission is ordinarily limited to line-of-sight paths. Otherwise, obstructions, such as buildings, reflect them.   SAMUEL SEELY

See also FREQUENCY MODULATION; SHORT WAVE; TELEVISION (Broadcasting).

VESALIUS, *vih SAY lee uhs,* **ANDREAS,** *ahn DREH ahs* (1514-1564), was one of the foremost anatomists of all time. His book, *Concerning the Fabric of the Human Body,* or *Fabrica* (1543), contained the first complete description of the human body. For this, Vesalius is called the *father of anatomy.*

Vesalius became a professor at the University of Padua at the age of 23. Because he dared to correct many of Claudius Galen's errors based on animal dissection, followers of Galen bitterly attacked him. Discouraged, he burned most of his writings and resigned from Padua in 1544. He later became physician to Philip II of Spain and Holy Roman Emperor Charles V. Vesalius was born in Brussels, in what is now Belgium. He started his anatomical studies by dissecting the bodies of dead criminals.   CAROLINE A. CHANDLER

See also MEDICINE (The Renaissance; picture: The Scientific Study of Anatomy).

VESEY, *VEE zee,* **DENMARK** (c.1767-1822), a black freedman, planned a slave revolt that involved more blacks than any other uprising in U.S. history. The revolt never took place. But the threat of it caused South

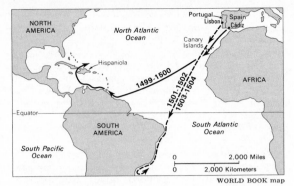

Carolina to pass severe laws restricting the education, movement, and occupation of free blacks and slaves.

In 1822, Vesey organized about 9,000 free blacks and slaves and prepared to attack several South Carolina cities. But some of the slaves told their owners. Several blacks were arrested and gave information that led to the capture of Vesey and several other leaders in the plot. Vesey and about 35 followers were hanged, and about 35 others were sold to West Indian plantation owners.

Historians know little about Vesey's early life. In 1800, he bought his freedom from his owner. He then worked as a carpenter in Charleston, S.C., until he started to plan the revolt.   FRANK OTTO GATELL

VESPASIAN, *vuh SPAY zhee uhn* (A.D. 9-79), was a Roman emperor. Rome prospered under his rule. He set up new taxes and supervised their collection, thereby restoring the empire's financial condition. He built a new forum, the famous Colosseum, and other buildings (see FORUM, ROMAN; COLOSSEUM). He also founded professorships to encourage education.

Vespasian was born near Reate, a city northeast of Rome. His full name was TITUS FLAVIUS VESPASIANUS. He became a general, and in A.D. 67 Emperor Nero sent him to put down a Jewish rebellion in Judea. During the year after Nero's death (A.D. 68), Generals Galba, Otho, and Vitellius followed one another as emperor. Finally, Vespasian's troops proclaimed him emperor in A.D. 69, and he went to Rome. There, the Senate passed the *Lex de imperio Vespasiani,* the first written statement of the powers of a Roman emperor. He was succeeded by his son, Titus. MARY FRANCIS GYLES

VESPER. See EVENING STAR.

VESPERS is the principal evening service of the breviary. Scholars believe that this hour may correspond to the evening sacrifice described in the Old Testament. Some scholars believe that it commemorates the descent from the cross.

VESPUCCI, *veh SPOO chee,* **AMERIGO** (1454-1512), was an Italian-born explorer for whom America was named. He claimed to have explored what is now the American mainland in 1497 and believed he had reached a "New World." Christopher Columbus had sailed to this area in 1492. But Columbus thought he had arrived at islands off the coast of Asia. He did not realize that he had reached a New World until his voyage to the mainland in 1498.

Martin Waldseemüller, a German mapmaker, believed that Vespucci was the first European to reach the New World. In 1507, he suggested that the land

Istituto e Museo di Storia della Scienza, Florence, Italy
Amerigo Vespucci

be named *America.* Soon, this name was used throughout Europe. Today, however, many scholars doubt Vespucci's role in the exploration of America.

Life and Expeditions. Vespucci was born in Florence and studied navigation as a youth. He spent his early

Amerigo Vespucci made three known voyages to America, the first one in 1499. He reported that he also reached America in 1497, but most historians now question this claim.

WORLD BOOK map

career as a merchant in the banking firm of Lorenzo di Pier Francesco de' Medici of Florence. In 1491, Vespucci moved to Seville, Spain, and became connected with a company that equipped ships for long voyages.

Vespucci later claimed that he made four voyages to the New World. After what he called his first voyage, in 1497, he said he had sighted a vast continent (South America). In 1499 and 1500, Vespucci took part in an expedition led by the Spanish explorer Alonso de Ojeda. During this voyage, Vespucci's ship traveled along the coast of Venezuela. In 1501 and 1502, and again in 1503 and 1504, Vespucci sailed with the fleet of Gonçalo Coelho, a Portuguese captain. Both of these expeditions explored the southern coast of Brazil.

Vespucci's reputation came largely from a letter he wrote to Lorenzo di Pier Francesco de' Medici in 1502 or 1503. In it, Vespucci told of his discovery of a new continent and vividly described the land and its people. The letter was published in 1503 or 1504 under the title of *Mundus Novus (New World).* It became extremely popular and later was published in several editions and translations. The letter established Vespucci as a famous explorer.

Vespucci became a Spanish citizen in 1505 and went to work for a government agency that regulated commerce with the New World. He served as chief navigator for the agency from 1508 until his death.

The Controversy. Soon after Vespucci died, scholars began to question his claims of discovery. They found little evidence to support his own reports of making a voyage in 1497. Vespucci also claimed to have led all the expeditions, but he actually had been only a navigator or commander of a single ship. In time, Christopher Columbus became known as the European discoverer of the New World.   CHARLES GIBSON

VESSEL, BLOOD. See BLOOD; ARTERY; VEIN.

VESTA was the goddess of fire on the hearths of home and state in Roman mythology. She resembled the Greek goddess Hestia. She was the oldest daughter of Saturn, the god of the harvest, and Ops, the goddess of the growth of natural things (see SATURN). Vesta was also the sister of Jupiter, the king of the gods (see JUPITER). Vesta never married, but watched over the life of the home, and each house had a shrine to her. She was the symbol of the home, and every meal began and ended with an offering to her.

Every city had a public hearth where a fire burned to

Vesta. People who left the city took some of the old fire with them to start the new fire in their homes. A circular temple to Vesta stood in the center of Rome. A sacred fire, guarded by six young *Vestal Virgins*, burned there constantly. The Romans believed the fire was a safeguard against national disaster.

Living conditions in primitive times partly explain the worship of Vesta. Fires were hard to make, and for that reason, one was always kept burning. People obtained fire from the chief or ruler, whose daughters kept it burning. After fire-making became simple, these customs remained as symbols.

The festivals of Vesta, called *Vestalia*, were held on June 9. The worship of Vesta in homes was closely associated with that of the *Lares*, or the spirits of ancestors, and *Penates*, the gods of the hearth (see LARES AND PENATES). NATHAN DANE II

See also HESTIA.

VESTIBULE. See EAR (The Inner Ear; diagram).

VESUVIUS, *vuh SOO vee uhs*, is the only active volcano on the mainland of Europe. It is probably the most famous volcano in the world. It rises on the Bay of Naples, about 7 miles (11 kilometers) southeast of the city of Naples. Vesuvius has been studied by scientists more than any other volcano because it erupts frequently and is easy to reach.

Vesuvius is a cone within the rim of Mount Somma, a big crater formed when the top of the mountain collapsed in the eruption of A.D. 79. The height of Vesuvius changes with each eruption. In June, 1900, the cone was 4,275 feet (1,303 meters) high. But after the eruption of 1906, it was only 3,842 feet (1,171 meters) high. The top of the active cone is a cup-shaped crater, ranging from 50 to 400 feet (15 to 120 meters) across. Vesuvius spouts columns of steam, cinders, and sometimes small amounts of lava into the air.

Many people live on the lower slopes of the mountain and on the plains at its foot, in spite of Vesuvius' history of disastrous eruptions. The soil is extremely fertile and the area is famous for its vineyards of wine grapes.

Early Eruptions. Prehistoric people probably saw Vesuvius in eruption. Roman legends say that the gods had once used the mountain as a battleground, but at the time of Christ it had been dormant for hundreds of years. A series of earthquakes alarmed the people in the neighborhood of Vesuvius for 16 years following A.D. 63. The first recorded eruption occurred on Aug. 24, A.D. 79, when the cities of Herculaneum, Pompeii, and Stabiae were covered by ashes and lava. An eyewitness account of the disaster was written by a Roman author, Pliny the Younger. His uncle, Pliny the Elder, was killed during the eruption.

In 472, ashes poured from the crater in such great amounts that they were carried by the wind as far as Constantinople (now Istanbul). Streams of lava and boiling water fell on the villages at the foot of the mountain in 1631. About 18,000 people were said to have died. There were other destructive eruptions in 1794, 1822, 1855, 1872, 1880, 1895, 1906, 1929, and 1944.

Recent Eruptions. The greatest destruction in recent years occurred in April 1906, when several towns were destroyed. In the eruption of March 1944, which destroyed the village of San Sebastiano, soldiers of the Allied armies helped the people of nearby towns escape the lava and volcanic dust.

Ewing Galloway

A Plume of White Smoke Drifts from Vesuvius and over the farms and vineyards that nestle on its slopes. Despite the danger of eruptions, farmers make their homes there.

Vesuvius in Eruption is a sight that arouses awe and wonder. Great clouds of volcanic dust are blown from the crater and lava pours over its edges. This is the great eruption of 1944.

U.S. Navy

VETCH

Before the eruption of 1944, thousands of visitors came to Vesuvius every year. They could go down into the crater for some distance and see a crimson stream of lava flow from the cone and turn into a bed of cold stone. A cable railway which took visitors to within 450 feet (137 meters) of the edge of the crater was destroyed in this eruption. Many people still visit the area.

A Royal Observatory was established on the slopes of the mountain in 1844. Since that time scientists have kept a constant watch over the volcano during and between eruptions. One observer lost his life standing by his post.   GORDON A. MACDONALD

See also HERCULANEUM; MOUNTAIN (table; picture chart); NAPLES; POMPEII; VOLCANO (Composite Volcanoes; table).

VETCH is the common name of a group of leguminous plants. Vetches are used for hay, for green manure, as pasture crops, for silage, and as a cover crop for orchards. There are many different kinds of vetch. *Common vetch*, or *tare*, is the most common in the United States, and hairy vetch also grows widely. Purple vetch is becoming important in the Pacific Coast States. Certain flowering vetches are grown for ornamental purposes. Some Europeans eat vetch beans.

N.Y. Botanical Garden

Leaves and Blossoms of Vetch. The plant is highly valuable as a cattle food, and for renewing soil fertility.

Vetches have weak stems which trail across the ground. Farmers often sow oats and rye with vetches because the stiff stems of these plants help to keep the vetch plants off the ground. Vetches require a cool growing season. They grow most successfully in well-drained loam or sandy loam soil. Only hairy vetch can survive a very cold winter. The *vetch bruchid*, a small weevil, destroys the green seed of some vetches.

Scientific Classification. Vetches are of the pea family, Leguminosae. Common vetches are genus *Vicia*, species *V. sativa*. Hairy vetches are *V. villosa*. Purple vetches are *V. atropurpurea*.   ROY G. WIGGANS

VETERANS ADMINISTRATION (VA) administers benefits and services to about 30 million former members of the United States armed forces. The VA also provides these benefits and services for eligible members of the families of deceased veterans. The agency has charge of disability or death pensions and compensation payments, education and training, vocational rehabilitation for disabled veterans, and veterans' hospitals and soldiers' homes. It administers government insurance for former members of the service who served before October 1965, and a mortgage guaranty program for the purchase of homes or farms. The VA also administers national cemeteries for veterans and their spouses and children.

The VA program was created by the Servicemen's Readjustment Act of 1944. It has been amended to give similar benefits to veterans of the Korean War, of the period after the Korean War, and of the Vietnam War. The VA has 58 regional offices, with at least one in each state. There are 172 veterans' hospitals, located in all states except Alaska and Hawaii. These offices and hospitals are staffed by about 220,000 employees.

Benefits and Other Services. The VA pays about $8.8 billion yearly in disability or death compensation or pensions to about 4,900,000 veterans and dependents of deceased veterans. About 185,000 patients receive care every day in VA facilities. More than 7,800,000 members of the service and veterans have VA insurance policies valued at nearly $100 billion.

The agency also guarantees home loans. Loans totaling about $141 billion have been made to about 9,800,000 veterans. The VA provided business loans to World War II and Korean War veterans.

The VA administers an educational training program that has served 7,800,000 World War II and 2,391,000 Korean War veterans at the college and vocational school levels. The Veterans' Readjustment acts of 1966 and 1967 provided similar educational opportunities and loan mortgage privileges for post-Korean War veterans. These laws benefit men and women who have served more than 180 days on active duty, any part of which falls between Jan. 31, 1955, and Jan. 1, 1977. About 7 million such veterans have studied under this program. The VA pays a minimum of $311 a month to veterans attending school full time.

Persons who entered military service after Dec. 31, 1976, may participate in a different VA educational program. To get benefits, they must deposit part of their pay—up to $2,700—in a special savings fund. The government deducts contributions from each person's monthly pay and adds $2 for each $1 the person invests.

History. Veterans of the Revolutionary War received pensions under laws adopted in 1792, 1818, and 1828. Temporary help had already been given to these veterans in the form of cash bonuses and land grants. The office of the Commissioner of Pensions was set up in 1849 to administer all military pension laws under the direction of the secretary of the interior. The first United States Soldiers' Home was established in 1851 in Washington, D.C., to provide a home for invalid or disabled soldiers. Congress established three soldiers' homes in 1866, after the Civil War. Later, 10 more soldiers' homes were set up. A Confederate Soldiers' Home was established in Little Rock, Ark., in 1891, and was taken over by the state in 1893. The Maryland Line Confederate Soldiers' Home, founded in Pikesville, Md., in 1888, was closed in 1932.

Today, the VA operates 16 homes called *domiciliaries* for veterans who do not require hospital care, but who are unable to earn a living and have no adequate means of support. There are also about 90 nursing home units associated with VA hospitals.

During World War I, the Bureau of War Risk Insurance was created under the War Risk Insurance Act. The bureau administered insurance against death or disability of members of the armed forces. The act also set up the Federal Board for Vocational Education to provide vocational rehabilitation for disabled veterans. Five governmental agencies, including the United States Public Health Service, were now serving the needs of veterans. To eliminate the duplication, Congress created the Veterans Bureau in 1920. In 1930, the Veterans Administration was created by combining the Veterans Bureau with the National Home for Disabled Volunteer Soldiers and the Bureau of Pensions.

Critically reviewed by the VETERANS ADMINISTRATION

See also GI BILL OF RIGHTS; PENSION (Military Pensions).

VETERANS DAY honors men and women who have served in the United States armed services. Veterans Day is a legal federal holiday throughout the United States. It is celebrated on November 11. Great Britain celebrates November 11 as Armistice Day. It is not a legal holiday, but special observances celebrate the armistice that ended World War I on Nov. 11, 1918. Canada has a legal holiday called Remembrance Day on November 11.

Veterans Day celebrations in the United States include parades and speeches. Special services are held at the Tomb of the Unknown Soldier in Arlington National Cemetery, Arlington, Va. In 1919, President Woodrow Wilson proclaimed November 11 as Armistice Day to remind Americans of the tragedies of war. A law adopted in 1938 made the day a federal holiday. In 1954, Congress changed the name to Veterans Day to honor all United States veterans. From 1971 through 1977, Veterans Day was celebrated on the fourth Monday in October. RAYMOND HOYT JAHN

VETERANS OF FOREIGN WARS OF THE UNITED STATES (VFW) is one of the largest veterans' organizations in the United States. It seeks to develop comradeship among its members, assist needy veterans and their families, organize memorial services for deceased veterans, and promote patriotism and community activity. The organization has about 1,800,000 members in the United States and in other countries.

Any officer or enlisted man or woman, either on active duty in the armed services or honorably discharged, who fought in any foreign military campaign of the United States, may join the VFW. The membership includes veterans of the Spanish-American War, the Boxer Rebellion, the Philippine Insurrection, campaigns on the Mexican border, Nicaraguan expeditions, World Wars I and II, the Korean War, and the Vietnam War. In 1978, the VFW began to admit women members.

The annual national convention governs the VFW. Convention delegates determine the organization's policies. They also elect a commander in chief to head the VFW. A national council of administration represents the convention between sessions.

The VFW National Home for Veterans' Orphans at Eaton Rapids, Mich., provides care for the children

Bob Dewey, *The Cootie Courier*

The VFW's Military Order of the Cooties is an honor branch. Members devote their time to helping hospitalized veterans.

of deceased veterans. It has family-size houses, a hospital, a swimming pool, a gymnasium, a nursery, and a community social center. VFW posts in the United States sponsor Buddy Poppy sales yearly. Part of the proceeds helps support the home.

The Military Order of the Cooties is the honor branch of the VFW. Only those members who have made outstanding contributions toward furthering the objectives of the VFW may qualify for the order. Members of the Military Order of the Cooties devote their time to helping veterans in hospitals.

The Ladies Auxiliary to the Veterans of Foreign Wars is a woman's organization devoted to community service and patriotism. The auxiliary assists the VFW with many of its programs, including yearly Buddy Poppy sales, and helps support the VFW National Home. Any woman with a close relative who is eligible to join the VFW may join the VFW Auxiliary. Any woman who herself fought in a foreign war may also join. The organization has about 650,000 members in more than 6,800 local units.

National Headquarters, VFW
VFW Emblem

The first attempts to form organizations of veterans of foreign wars began in the late 1890's. Three organizations combined in 1913 to form the VFW. Headquarters are at 34th Street and Broadway, Kansas City, Mo. 64111. Critically reviewed by the VFW

VETERANS' ORGANIZATIONS include former members of a nation's armed services. They may limit membership to veterans who served during a particular war or military campaign. Or they may accept only veterans who fought overseas, or were disabled.

Veterans' organizations have been chiefly patriotic and social in purpose. They try to develop the comradeships formed during war, and to support the laws

and government of the nation. They also provide care for the widows and children of deceased veterans. Veterans' organizations conduct memorial services, and take care of the graves of deceased veterans.

These groups usually have great political influence because of their large membership. The groups use this power to obtain legislation that will benefit veterans, such as pensions, education, and care for disabled veterans.

In the United States, the Society of the Cincinnati was the first veterans' organization. Major General Henry Knox suggested that officers of the continental army should organize a society of veterans who fought in the Revolutionary War. The Society of the Cincinnati began operating in 1783, with George Washington as its first president.

The veterans' organizations formed after the War of 1812 and the Mexican War were not large. After the Civil War, with its large armies, powerful veterans organizations came into existence. The Grand Army of the Republic (GAR), an organization of veterans of the Union Army, began its work in 1866. It had enough influence to control the Republican party for almost 40 years. It reached its highest membership in 1890. The support of the GAR often meant the difference between victory and defeat for candidates in the North. The United Confederate Veterans held a similar position in the South.

Attempts to organize the veterans of foreign military campaigns began in the late 1890's. The United Spanish War Veterans, founded in 1898, included men who fought in the Spanish-American War. Three groups of veterans of foreign wars joined together in 1913 to form the Veterans of Foreign Wars. In 1919, following World War I, men who fought in France formed a veterans' organization called the *American Legion*. The Disabled American Veterans was established in 1920.

After World War II, veterans formed new organizations. The American Veterans of World War II, Korea, and Vietnam (AMVETS) was founded in 1944. It has a membership of about 250,000. The American Veterans Committee (AVC) began in 1944. Its membership is about 25,000.

In Canada, the 500,000-member Royal Canadian Legion is the country's largest veterans' organization. It was founded in 1926, and has about 2,000 branches in Canada. The Army, Navy, and Air Force Veterans in Canada is the country's oldest veterans' group. It was founded in 1837, and ranks second in size. Other Canadian veterans' organizations include the Canadian Corps Association, Canadian Paraplegic Association, Canadian Pensioners Association of the Great War, and the War Amputations of Canada.   H. J. GUINIVAN, JR.

Related Articles in WORLD BOOK include:

VETERANS' READJUSTMENT ACTS. See VETERANS ADMINISTRATION (Benefits and Other Services); GI BILL OF RIGHTS.

© Kirk Kreutzig, Photographics

Caring for Pets is the chief function of veterinarians in cities. The veterinarian shown above is bandaging an injured dog. Vets also provide vaccinations and other preventive care.

VETERINARY MEDICINE, *VEHT uhr uh NEHR ee*, is the branch of medicine that deals with the diseases of animals. Animal doctors are called *veterinarians*. Their work is especially valuable because many animal diseases can be transmitted to human beings. Such diseases are called *zoonoses*. Examples of these are rabies, brucellosis, tuberculosis, *psittacosis* (parrot fever), and *tularemia* (rabbit fever).

In Cities, most veterinarians are associated with pet hospitals. Many animal hospitals contain equipment much like that used in hospitals for human beings. There, animals may be cared for during illnesses, and surgery may be performed if necessary. Veterinarians play an important role in the control of rabies. The proper vaccination of cats and dogs against rabies and the diagnosis of the disease are part of the veterinarian's duties.

Many veterinarians also are associated with the public health services of cities, states, or the federal government. In this service, their special skills and knowledge are helpful in controlling diseases carried by animals. Veterinarians may inspect meat and meat products, or direct some of the operations in slaughtering and packing houses. They may work in laboratories testing milk or other dairy products, or preparing serums and vaccines.

On Farms. Perhaps the most important activity of the veterinarian is the care and treatment of livestock. Veterinarians help keep farm animals in good health to prevent outbreaks of animal diseases. Epidemics of animal diseases, called *epizootics*, may be extremely dangerous, not only to the animals but to human beings as well.

Veterinarians have played an important part in controlling bovine tuberculosis, a form of tuberculosis that can be passed from cows to human beings. In 1917, the federal government began a program to wipe out this disease. A cooperative plan set up by the federal and state governments allows veterinarians to test dairy cattle for tuberculosis. Another project works to control

Rural Veterinarians help keep livestock and other farm animals in good health. The veterinarian shown above is putting a powdered antibiotic into the throat of a cow.

M. P. Kahl, Bruce Coleman Inc.

Zoo Veterinarians specialize in the treatment of wild animals. A vet takes a blood sample from a lion in Africa, *above,* while preparing the beast for shipment to a zoo.

and eradicate bovine brucellosis. This disease also can be transferred to human beings (see BANG'S DISEASE).

Veterinarians give many kinds of inoculations to protect farm animals against disease. For example, they inoculate young pigs against hog cholera. At one time, this dread disease often swept from farm to farm, killing all the hogs in an entire farming community.

Careers in Veterinary Medicine. People who want to become veterinarians must have at least two years of preveterinary college work, followed by four years of study in a college of veterinary medicine. However, many students complete three or four years of preveterinary study. During the four years of veterinary school, they study such subjects as anatomy, surgery, chemistry, physiology, and the breeding of animals.

There are 26 colleges of veterinary medicine in the United States and 3 in Canada that are accredited by the American Veterinary Medical Association. These schools offer courses of study that lead to the degree of Doctor of Veterinary Medicine (D.V.M.) After earning a diploma, the graduate must comply with the license laws of the state in which he or she plans to practice.

After receiving a license, the veterinarian may go into private practice. Veterinarians may also be employed in government service, where they often specialize in the study and treatment of wildlife. A veterinarian interested in research may want to work with the U.S. Public Health Service, the U.S. Department of Agriculture, an agricultural experiment station, or a college. Some veterinarians teach at colleges of veterinary medicine or

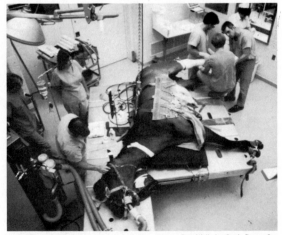

Cary Wolinsky, Stock, Boston, Inc.

A College of Veterinary Medicine has modern operating rooms and equipment. This photograph shows faculty veterinarians teaching students how to fit a cast on the rear leg of a horse.

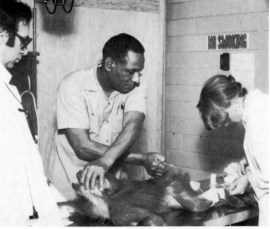

© Kirk Kreutzig, Photographics

Veterinary Research has increased the knowledge of many human diseases. These vets are studying a baboon with *macular degeneration,* an eye disease that also strikes human beings.

279

VETO

work in commercial laboratories that produce serums and vaccines. Other career opportunities for veterinarians include working at animal shelters, race tracks, or zoos, or serving in programs sponsored by such agencies as the Peace Corps and the World Health Organization (WHO).

The American Veterinary Medical Association works to maintain the professional standards of veterinary medicine. Headquarters are at 930 North Meacham Road, Schaumburg, Ill. 60196.

Critically reviewed by the AMERICAN VETERINARY MEDICAL ASSOCIATION

Additional Resources

BERGER, MELVIN. *Animal Hospital*. Day, 1973. For younger readers.

CARAS, ROGER, and others. *Pet Medicine: Health Care and First Aid for All Household Pets*. McGraw, 1977.

GILLUM, HELEN L. *Veterinary Medicine*. Dillon Press, 1976. Suitable for younger readers.

WHITNEY, LEON F. and GEORGE. *Animal Doctor: The History and Practice of Veterinary Medicine*. McKay, 1973.

VETO, is a Latin word which means *I forbid*. In American government, the word *veto* usually refers to the President's power to kill a law that the legislative branch has already passed.

The President of the United States has a *limited* veto power. It is not absolute. A vote of a two-thirds majority of the members present in both houses of Congress can override it. The sovereign of Great Britain still holds the power of *absolute* veto. But no British king or queen has used this power since 1707.

When the two houses of Congress pass a bill or joint resolution, it is presented to the President of the United States. Then one of four things must happen:

The President may approve the bill. If so, the President signs it and it becomes law.

The President may allow the bill to become law without signing it. This can take place under the clause in the Constitution which provides that "if any bill shall not be returned by the President within 10 days (Sundays excepted) after it shall have been presented to him, the same shall be a law in like manner as if he had signed it, unless the Congress by their adjournment prevent its return, in which case it shall not be a law."

The President may retain the bill, in the expectation that Congress will adjourn within 10 days—not including Sundays—and thus the bill will be defeated. This method is called the *pocket veto*. It is used by Presidents who find certain bills unsatisfactory but do not want to veto them openly. Vetoing a congressional bill defeats all parts of it. All provisions and "riders" attached to the bill are vetoed with it.

The President may veto the bill. In that case, the President must send a message to Congress stating the reasons.

Presidents' Use of the Veto. When the Constitution was adopted, Alexander Hamilton declared that Presidents would use the veto power with great caution. Seven Presidents did not veto any bills. Franklin D. Roosevelt, who served as President longer than any other person, vetoed the most bills. Roosevelt used 372 regular vetoes and 263 pocket vetoes. Grover Cleveland ranks second, with 346 regular and 238 pocket vetoes. Congress has overridden only about 5 per cent of all presidential vetoes. For example, 11 of the Presidents who vetoed bills had no vetoes overridden by Congress. Congress reversed only 9 of Roosevelt's 372 regular vetoes and only 2 of the 73 issued by Dwight D. Eisenhower. But it overrode 15 of Andrew Johnson's 21 regular vetoes.

Governors' Veto Power. Most state governors also have a veto power. But in some states, the governor's veto may be overridden by a simple majority of the members present in the houses of the legislature, rather than by a required two-thirds majority. Most governors can veto parts of appropriation bills.   PAYSON S. WILD

See also PRESIDENT OF THE UNITED STATES (Legislative Leader); UNITED NATIONS (Voting); UNITED STATES, GOVERNMENT OF THE (diagram: How a Bill Becomes Law); WASHINGTON, GEORGE (First Veto).

VETTISFOSS, *VEHT uhs FAWS,* is a waterfall in the western part of Norway. It ranks as one of the country's highest waterfalls. Vettisfoss measures 900 feet (274 meters) in height.

VEXILLOLOGY. See FLAG (introduction; table: Flag Terms).

VEZINA TROPHY. See HOCKEY (Professional Leagues).

VFW. See VETERANS OF FOREIGN WARS OF THE UNITED STATES.

VHF WAVE. See VERY HIGH FREQUENCY WAVE.

VIA APPIA or APPIAN WAY. See APPIAN WAY.

VIADUCT, *VY uh duhkt,* is like a bridge, except that it crosses over dry land instead of water. Some viaducts do

International Harvester

Viaducts Help Make the Flow of Traffic Safe and Easy.

cross water, but they also cross dry land instead of merely extending from bank to bank as a bridge does. Most viaducts consist of a series of supports under beam-and-slab or arch construction. Viaducts carry railroad tracks over valleys and gorges. Some viaducts are built higher than the general level of the land to carry railroads over highways or to make a safe crossing for highways over railroads. The ancient Romans built the first viaducts. The aqueducts they built to carry water to cities often also served as roadways.

One of the longest viaducts ever built was a portion of the 110-mile (177-kilometer) Key West extension of the Florida East Coast Railway. Viaducts that extended over the open sea formed 30 miles (48 kilometers) of this extension. Parts were destroyed by a hurricane in 1935, but these were rebuilt as a highway a few years later. The main part of the pier viaduct over the mouth of the River Tay in Scotland has 84 steel spans and is over 2 miles (3.2 kilometers) long. The Tunkhannock viaduct on the Lackawanna Railway is one of the largest steel and concrete viaducts in the world. It is 2,375 feet (724 meters) long and includes 10 spans of 180 feet (55 meters) each. Another famous viaduct is the $3\frac{1}{2}$-mile (5.6-kilometer) Pulaski Skyway between Newark and Jersey City. Other well-known viaducts are the Pecos River viaduct in Texas and the Landwasser viaduct across the Albula Pass, in the canton of Graubünden, Switzerland. ROBERT G. HENNES

VIATICUM, *vy AT uh kuhm,* in the Catholic Church, is the last communion, or Holy Eucharist, administered to the dying or those in danger of death. During a long illness it may be given several times. It is given before Anointing of the Sick. In Latin, the word means *provision for a journey.* In the early Christian Church, it was applied to anything that gave spiritual comfort to the dying. See also ANOINTING OF THE SICK. FULTON J. SHEEN

VIBRATION, in mechanics, indicates to-and-fro motion, or *oscillation,* of a particle. The two types of vibration are *natural* and *artificial.* An earthquake causes a natural vibration. But most vibrations are artificial, because some manufactured device causes them. For example, engineers design special devices called *vibrators* that cause vibration or shaking. Foundries use a special vibrator to loosen a mold that has been placed in sand. Vibrators are also used in medicine to stimulate the circulation and the muscles. If objects did not vibrate, it would be impossible to speak to anyone, because all sound begins with a vibrating object. When speaking, a person's vocal cords begin the vibrations.

Aside from a relatively few valuable uses, vibration is undesirable in industry and in most daily living. It may cause weakening of structures and produce wear and inefficiency. In cities, trucks, subways, elevated trains, and other traffic cause much vibration. These vibrations sometimes enter the steel structure of a large building, and can be felt throughout the building. Engineers deal with this problem by using special materials that absorb vibration. Pneumatic tires are used in an effort to reduce the vibrations on moving automobiles. Automobile engines are mounted on rubber supports to reduce vibration as much as possible. Vibration dampers have also been designed in crankshafts.

Many industries must deal with the problem of vibration and its effect on machinery. Rotating parts of machines give trouble from vibration unless they are accurately balanced, especially at high speeds. The supports of such rotating parts were once bolted to the machine frame or its foundation. To reduce the effect of vibration in machines, the supports for high-speed rotating parts are now sometimes mounted on springs, rubber, or some other kind of flexible connection.

Mechanical vibrations have various frequencies and amplitudes. *Frequency* is the number of complete vibra-

tions during a certain time. *Amplitude* is the maximum distance the particle travels from its normal position of *equilibrium,* or rest. ROBERT L. WEBER

See also SOUND; WAVES.

VIBURNUM, *vy BUR nuhm,* is the name of a group of shrubs and small trees of the honeysuckle family. These plants grow in large numbers throughout North America, Europe, and Asia. They have white or pink flowers, and leaves which sometimes turn various colors in the autumn. Gardeners like viburnum shrubs for borders. See also HONEYSUCKLE.

Scientific Classification. The viburnum belongs to the honeysuckle family, Caprifoliaceae. Some of the common American kinds are *Viburnum acerifolium, V. alnifolium,* and *V. trilobum.* ALFRED C. HOTTES

Carl Mrozek

Viburnum's Beautiful Flowers make it a popular ornamental shrub. The plant also bears bright blue, red, or yellow berries.

VICAR, *VIHK uhr,* is a person who represents and performs duties for a higher official in a church. The term comes from the Latin word *vicarius,* meaning a *substitute.* The pope of the Roman Catholic Church is called the Vicar of Christ on earth. *Vicars apostolic* are bishops who serve as personal representatives of the pope in mission areas. A *vicar general* acts as the deputy of a bishop, and a *vicar capitular* administers a diocese in the absence of a bishop. The Church of England uses the title of vicar for the head of a parish who, for some reason, may not be called the rector. In the Episcopal Church of the United States, the term usually refers to the priest in charge of a parish chapel. R. PIERCE BEAVER and FULTON J. SHEEN

VICAR OF WAKEFIELD. See GOLDSMITH, OLIVER.

VICE ADMIRAL. See RANK IN ARMED SERVICES.

VICE PRESIDENT is the second highest executive officer in the government of some nations. In many countries, the vice president assumes the presidency if the president dies, resigns, is removed from office, or becomes disabled. In some nations, including Argentina and the United States, the vice president also serves as the presiding officer of the national senate.

See also VICE PRESIDENT OF THE UNITED STATES.

VICE PRESIDENT OF THE UNITED STATES

Office of the
Vice President

Seal of the Vice President

VICE PRESIDENT OF THE UNITED STATES is only a heartbeat away from the most powerful elective office in the world. The Vice President must be ready to become President or acting President at a moment's notice if the President dies, resigns, is removed from office, or becomes unable to perform the duties of office.

Thirteen Vice Presidents have become President, eight because of the death of a President. These eight so-called "accidental Presidents" were John Tyler, Millard Fillmore, Andrew Johnson, Chester A. Arthur, Theodore Roosevelt, Calvin Coolidge, Harry S. Truman, and Lyndon B. Johnson. The other Vice Presidents who became President were John Adams, Thomas Jefferson, Martin Van Buren, Richard M. Nixon, and Gerald R. Ford. Ford was the only one to take office because of a President's resignation.

The United States Constitution also provides that the Vice President shall become acting President if the President is disabled. In 1967, the 25th Amendment to the Constitution was ratified. It spelled out procedures

Irving G. Williams, the contributor of this article, is the author of The American Vice-Presidency: New Look *and* Government: Its Structure and Interpretation.

Portrait Gallery of the Vice Presidents

The term of each Vice President, as well as the name of the President under whom the Vice President served, is listed under each picture. The asterisks identify those who later served as President.

*John Adams
1789-1797
Washington

*Thomas Jefferson
1797-1801
J. Adams

Aaron Burr
1801-1805
Jefferson

George Clinton
1805-1812
Jefferson-Madison

Elbridge Gerry
1813-1814
Madison

Daniel D. Tompkins
1817-1825
Monroe

John C. Calhoun
1825-1832
J. Q. Adams-Jackson

*Martin Van Buren
1833-1837
Jackson

Richard M. Johnson
1837-1841
Van Buren

*John Tyler
1841
W. H. Harrison

George M. Dallas
1845-1849
Polk

*Millard Fillmore
1849-1850
Taylor

William R. D. King
1853
Pierce

John C. Breckinridge
1857-1861
Buchanan

Hannibal Hamlin
1861-1865
Lincoln

*Andrew Johnson
1865
Lincoln

Schuyler Colfax
1869-1873
Grant

Henry Wilson
1873-1875
Grant

William A. Wheeler
1877-1881
Hayes

*Chester A. Arthur
1881
Garfield

Thomas A. Hendricks
1885
Cleveland

Levi P. Morton
1889-1893
B. Harrison

282

in case of presidential disability and provided for vice presidential succession (see CONSTITUTION OF THE UNITED STATES [Amendment 25]). Presidents James A. Garfield, Woodrow Wilson, and Dwight D. Eisenhower all had serious illnesses. But their Vice Presidents carefully avoided assuming the duties of the President. In 1985, George Bush became the first Vice President to serve as acting President. He held the office for about eight hours. President Ronald Reagan had designated Bush as acting President when Reagan had surgery.

The Vice President serves as the presiding officer of the United States Senate, and has the title of *president of the Senate*. The Constitution gives the Vice President

no other official duty. For more than a hundred years the absence of political importance of the job caused it to be treated as somewhat of a joke. Some people had humorously suggested that the Vice President be addressed as "Your Superfluous Excellency."

Yet the Founding Fathers had high hopes for the vice presidency. James Iredell of North Carolina, who later served on the Supreme Court of the United States, explained that there would be "two men . . . in office at the same time; the President, who will possess, in the highest degree, the confidence of the country, and the

Facts in Brief About the Vice President

Qualifications: The Constitution provides that a candidate must be a "natural-born" U.S. citizen and must have lived in the United States for at least 14 years. The candidate must be at least 35 years old. No law or court decision has yet defined the exact meaning of the term *natural-born*. Authorities assume that the term applies to all citizens born in the United States and its territories. But they are not certain if the term also includes children born to U.S. citizens in other countries.

How Nominated: By a national political convention. If a vacancy in the vice presidency exists, the President nominates a new Vice President, who takes office upon confirmation by a majority vote of both houses of Congress.

How Elected: By a majority vote of the Electoral College, held in December following the general election held on the first Tuesday after the first Monday in November of every fourth year.

Inauguration: Held at noon, January 20, after election by the Electoral College. If the date falls on Sunday, the ceremony is held on Monday, January 21.

Term: The Vice President is elected for four years, and can serve any number of terms.

Income: $97,900 annual salary, $10,000 expense allowance, and an allowance for staff support.

Removal from Office: Impeachment by a majority vote of the House of Representatives, and trial and conviction by a two-thirds vote of those present in the Senate.

Adlai E. Stevenson
1893-1897
Cleveland

Garret A. Hobart
1897-1899
McKinley

★Theodore Roosevelt
1901
McKinley

Charles W. Fairbanks
1905-1909
T. Roosevelt

James S. Sherman
1909-1912
Taft

Thomas R. Marshall
1913-1921
Wilson

★Calvin Coolidge
1921-1923
Harding

Charles G. Dawes
1925-1929
Coolidge

Charles Curtis
1929-1933
Hoover

John N. Garner
1933-1941
F. Roosevelt

Henry A. Wallace
1941-1945
F. Roosevelt

★Harry S. Truman
1945
F. Roosevelt

Alben W. Barkley
1949-1953
Truman

★Richard M. Nixon
1953-1961
Eisenhower

★Lyndon B. Johnson
1961-1963
Kennedy

Hubert H. Humphrey
1965-1969
Johnson

Spiro T. Agnew
1969-1973
Nixon

★Gerald R. Ford
1973-1974
Nixon

Nelson A. Rockefeller
1974-1977
Ford

Walter F. Mondale
1977-1981
Carter

George H. W. Bush
1981-
Reagan

VICE PRESIDENT OF THE UNITED STATES

Vice President, who is thought to be the next person in the Union most fit to perform this trust."

The prestige of the vice presidency has gradually increased since the early 1920's. Beginning in 1933 with the presidency of Franklin D. Roosevelt, Vice Presidents have regularly attended meetings of the President's Cabinet. Dwight D. Eisenhower and John F. Kennedy did more than any other Presidents to establish the importance of the office of Vice President. Eisenhower's Vice President, Richard M. Nixon, and Kennedy's Vice President, Lyndon B. Johnson, had important duties and responsibilities. When Kennedy was assassinated in 1963, many experts believed that Johnson was the best-prepared "accidental President."

The Vice President has offices in the Capitol, the Richard B. Russell Office Building of the U.S. Senate, and Executive Office Building. All these are in Washington, D.C. In 1974, Congress established a 33-room mansion on the grounds of Washington's Naval Observatory as the Vice President's official residence. Secret Service agents guard the Vice President.

Choosing a Vice President

Nomination of the vice presidential candidate usually comes as an anticlimax to a political convention. The excitement of selecting the presidential nominee is over, but the delegates must still choose a *running mate*. The delegates usually nominate the presidential nominee's preference. A contest develops only if the presidential nominee makes no choice.

Many factors may influence the selection of a vice presidential nominee. After a bitter convention, the winning presidential nominee may support a candidate who can help restore party harmony. The choice for Vice President may be one of the losing candidates for the presidency, or a supporter of one of the losers. In 1844, the Democrats nominated Senator Silas Wright of New York for Vice President. They did this to appease former President Martin Van Buren, who had failed to win the Democratic presidential nomination. But Wright, a close friend of Van Buren, declined the selection. In 1972, the Democratic vice presidential nominee, Senator Thomas F. Eagleton, became the only person ever to withdraw after having accepted a party's nomination at a national convention. He did so following the disclosure that he had received psychiatric treatment. See EAGLETON, THOMAS F.

Often the Vice President comes from one of the states considered to be especially important in the election. This may be a state in which the election outcome is expected to be very close, or it may simply be a state with a large electoral vote. By appealing to local loyalties, the vice presidential candidate may strengthen the party's vote in this "home" state.

Sometimes the vice presidential candidate is chosen because the person is thought to appeal to a large bloc of voters. In 1984, the Democrats nominated Representative Geraldine A. Ferraro of New York for Vice President. She was the first woman and the first person of Italian descent ever chosen as the vice presidential candidate by a major American political party.

The vice presidential choice often is made to *balance the ticket*. If an older candidate is nominated for President, a younger person may be chosen for Vice President. A presidential nominee from the East may be balanced with a vice presidential nominee from the West. If the presidential nominee is known as a conservative, the vice presidential nominee may be a liberal. By balancing the ticket, party leaders hope to win the support of the largest possible number of voters.

The system of selecting a Vice President helps the party win the election. It does not necessarily produce the person best qualified to serve as Vice President. The custom of balancing the ticket with people of conflicting political beliefs has often been criticized. Theodore Roosevelt said early in his political career: "It is an unhealthy thing to have a Vice President and President represented by principles so far apart that the succession of one to the place of the other means a change as radical as any party overturn." This occurred when John Tyler succeeded William Henry Harrison, and when Roosevelt later succeeded William McKinley.

The Campaign. The vice presidential candidate plays an active role in the election campaign. The vice presidential and presidential candidates usually map out separate campaign routes for maximum coverage of the country. They may later change places to cover all strategic areas with repeated campaigning.

Election. Voters select the same electors for the Vice President when they choose presidential electors. They cannot split the ticket. That is, a person cannot vote for electors of the presidential candidate of the Republican Party and for electors of the vice presidential candidate of the Democratic Party. Citizens must vote for a slate of electors pledged to one party's candidates.

The Electoral College elects the President and Vice President on separate ballots (see ELECTORAL COLLEGE). If the Electoral College fails to choose the Vice President by a majority vote, the Senate elects one of the two leading candidates. At least two-thirds of the Senate must be present at the voting, and the winner must receive a majority vote of the entire membership.

The Senate has elected a Vice President only once. In 1837, the Senate elected Richard M. Johnson, a Democrat, by a vote of 33 to 16 over Francis Granger, a Whig. Johnson had fallen one vote short in the Electoral College. He became so controversial that the Democrats refused to renominate him in 1840. In fact, they failed to nominate any vice presidential candidate—the only time any convention has done so.

Inauguration. Until 1933, the Vice President took the oath of office in the Senate. Today, both President and Vice President are inaugurated in the same ceremony in January following their election. The Vice President is sworn into office immediately before the President is inaugurated. The Vice President's oath of office may be administered by the retiring Vice President, by a member of Congress, or by some other government official, such as a justice of the Supreme Court.

In the early days, the Vice President made an inaugural address. This custom has disappeared with the adoption of the combined ceremony in which the President gives the inaugural address.

The 25th Amendment spells out procedures for filling a vacancy in the vice presidency. The office becomes vacant if the Vice President dies, resigns, or is unable to carry out the duties of office. Then the President appoints a new Vice President. The appointment is sub-

The Vice Presidents of the United States

Name	Birthplace	Occupation or Profession	Political Party	Age at Inauguration	Served	President
1. Adams, John (a)	Braintree, Mass.	Lawyer	Federalist	53	1789-1797	Washington
2. Jefferson, Thomas (a)	Albemarle County, Va.	Planter	Democratic-Republican	53	1797-1801	J. Adams
3. Burr, Aaron	Newark, N.J.	Lawyer	Democratic-Republican	45	1801-1805	Jefferson
4. Clinton, George (c)	Little Britain, N.Y.	Soldier	Democratic Republican	65	1805-1809	Jefferson
				69	1809-1812	Madison
5. Gerry, Elbridge (c)	Marblehead, Mass.	Businessman	Democratic-Republican	68	1813-1814	Madison
6. Tompkins, Daniel D.	Fox Meadows, N.Y.	Lawyer	Democratic-Republican	42	1817-1825	Monroe
7. Calhoun, John C. (d)	Abbeville District, S.C.	Lawyer	Democratic-Republican	42	1825-1829	J. Q. Adams
			Democratic	46	1829-1832	Jackson
8. Van Buren, Martin (a)	Kinderhook, N.Y.	Lawyer	Democratic	50	1833-1837	Jackson
9. Johnson, Richard M.	Beargrass, Ky.	Lawyer	Democratic	56	1837-1841	Van Buren
10. Tyler, John (b)	Charles City County, Va.	Lawyer	Whig	50	1841	W. H. Harrison
11. Dallas, George M.	Philadelphia, Pa.	Lawyer	Democratic	52	1845-1849	Polk
12. Fillmore, Millard (b)	Locke, N.Y.	Lawyer	Whig	49	1849-1850	Taylor
13. King, William R. D. (c)	Sampson County, N.C.	Lawyer	Democratic	66	1853	Pierce
14. Breckinridge, John C.	near Lexington, Ky.	Lawyer	Democratic	36	1857-1861	Buchanan
15. Hamlin, Hannibal	Paris, Me.	Lawyer	Republican	51	1861-1865	Lincoln
16. Johnson, Andrew (b)	Raleigh, N.C.	Tailor	National Union (e)	56	1865	Lincoln
17. Colfax, Schuyler	New York, N.Y.	Auditor	Republican	45	1869-1873	Grant
18. Wilson, Henry (c)	Farmington, N.H.	Businessman	Republican	61	1873-1875	Grant
19. Wheeler, William A.	Malone, N.Y.	Lawyer	Republican	57	1877-1881	Hayes
20. Arthur, Chester A. (b)	Fairfield, Vt.	Lawyer	Republican	51	1881	Garfield
21. Hendricks, Thomas A. (c) ..	near Zanesville, O.	Lawyer	Democratic	65	1885	Cleveland
22. Morton, Levi P.	Shoreham, Vt.	Banker	Republican	64	1889-1893	B. Harrison
23. Stevenson, Adlai E.	Christian County, Ky.	Lawyer	Democratic	57	1893-1897	Cleveland
24. Hobart, Garret A. (c)	Long Branch, N.J.	Lawyer	Republican	52	1897-1899	McKinley
25. Roosevelt, Theodore (b) (a)	New York, N.Y.	Author	Republican	42	1901	McKinley
26. Fairbanks, Charles W.	near Unionville Center, O.	Lawyer	Republican	52	1905-1909	T. Roosevelt
27. Sherman, James S. (c)	Utica, N.Y.	Lawyer	Republican	53	1909-1912	Taft
28. Marshall, Thomas R.	North Manchester, Ind.	Lawyer	Democratic	58	1913-1921	Wilson
29. Coolidge, Calvin (b) (a) ...	Plymouth Notch, Vt.	Lawyer	Republican	48	1921-1923	Harding
30. Dawes, Charles G.	Marietta, O.	Lawyer	Republican	59	1925-1929	Coolidge
31. Curtis, Charles	Topeka, Kans.	Lawyer	Republican	69	1929-1933	Hoover
32. Garner, John N.	Red River County, Tex.	Lawyer	Democratic	64	1933-1941	F. Roosevelt
33. Wallace, Henry A.	Adair County, Ia.	Farmer	Democratic	52	1941-1945	F. Roosevelt
34. Truman, Harry S. (b) (a) ...	Lamar, Mo.	Businessman	Democratic	60	1945	F. Roosevelt
35. Barkley, Alben W.	Graves County, Ky.	Lawyer	Democratic	71	1949-1953	Truman
36. Nixon, Richard M. (a)	Yorba Linda, Calif.	Lawyer	Republican	40	1953-1961	Eisenhower
37. Johnson, Lyndon B. (b) (a) .	near Stonewall, Tex.	Teacher	Democratic	52	1961-1963	Kennedy
38. Humphrey, Hubert H.	Wallace, S.Dak.	Pharmacist	Democratic	53	1965-1969	Johnson
39. Agnew, Spiro T. (d)	Towson, Md.	Lawyer	Republican	50	1969-1973	Nixon
40. Ford, Gerald R. (f) (g)	Omaha, Nebr.	Lawyer	Republican	60	1973-1974	Nixon
41. Rockefeller, Nelson A. (f) ..	Bar Harbor, Me.	Businessman	Republican	66	1974-1977	Ford
42. Mondale, Walter F.	Ceylon, Minn.	Lawyer	Democratic	49	1977-1981	Carter
43. Bush, George H. W.	Milton, Mass.	Businessman	Republican	56	1981-	Reagan

(a) Elected to the presidency. (b) Succeeded to the presidency upon the death of the President. (c) Died in office. (d) Resigned. (e) The National Union party consisted of Republicans and War Democrats. Johnson was a Democrat. (f) Became Vice President by filling a vacancy. (g) Succeeded to the presidency upon the resignation of the President. Each Vice President has a separate biography in WORLD BOOK.

ject to the approval of a majority of both houses of Congress. In 1973, House Minority Leader Gerald R. Ford became the first Vice President chosen under terms of the 25th Amendment. He succeeded Vice President Spiro T. Agnew, who resigned. See FORD, GERALD R.

Roles of the Vice President

The Vice President can be only as important as the President chooses. The Vice President has almost no political power, unless the President asks for advice about party policy and political appointments. Even the Vice President's role as a Cabinet member depends on the wishes of the President.

With the active support of the President, the Vice President can exert a tremendous amount of influence. The Vice President's attendance at conferences between the President and congressional leaders strengthens the Vice President's power with the legislative branch. If the President gives the Vice President important diplomatic missions, the Vice President can help shape the foreign policy of the United States.

A Typical Day for the Vice President might begin with a breakfast conference called by the President. A legislative meeting might follow. The two officials confer with their party's congressional leaders about legislation being debated by the Senate and the House

VICE PRESIDENT OF THE UNITED STATES

of Representatives. The Vice President may then work at an office in the White House, the Executive Office Building, or the Senate wing of the Capitol. The Vice President reads and answers mail and sees callers who have appointments. Tourists or unexpected visitors on emergency matters also may arrive. If the Senate is meeting that day, the Vice President enters about noon to preside at the opening of the session. The Vice President may remain at the session, depending on the nature of the day's business and the Vice President's own schedule. If the Vice President leaves, the president *pro tempore* or another senator takes over.

The Vice President spends many evenings away from home. The Vice President must make various kinds of public appearances, many of which require speeches. The Vice President may go to the airport to greet dignitaries from other nations. Ceremonial duties may require the Vice President to dedicate a public-works project, open an athletic tournament, or present an award to a contest-winner.

President of the Senate. When presiding over the Senate, the Vice President performs the duties of chairperson and cannot take part in any Senate debates. Nor can the Vice President vote, except in the rare case of a tie. John Adams cast a deciding vote 29 times, more than did any other Vice President.

The Vice President enforces the rules established by the Senate for its own guidance. Senators can speak only after being recognized by the Vice President or the president *pro tempore*. By using this power of recognition, the Vice President can either aid or hold back legislation by permitting only certain senators to speak. The Vice President also has the power to make rulings in disputes over procedure by interpreting the rules of the Senate. But the Senate can reject such rulings by a majority vote. In 1919, Vice President Thomas R. Marshall ruled three times in one day on a certain point. He was fighting to save the controversial Versailles Treaty and United States membership in the League of Nations. The Senate overruled Marshall three times and finally defeated the treaty.

The president of the Senate also directs the counting of electoral votes for President and Vice President. Early Vice Presidents could decide whether to count or disallow disputed votes. Congress has since assumed this power, leaving the Vice President only formally in charge of counting electoral votes.

Administration and Policymaking. The Vice President attends meetings of the President's Cabinet and is a member of the National Security Council (NSC). The NSC is the highest advisory body to the President on matters of foreign and defense policies. The Vice President also is a member of the Board of Regents of the Smithsonian Institution.

The President may assign the Vice President general counseling and liaison activities. Such duties may involve trips abroad to spread good will, exchange information, and learn about the attitudes of various nations toward the United States. The Vice President may also act as an intermediary between the President and their political party, both in Congress and the party. The Vice President attempts to build party support for the President's program.

Social Duties. One of the oldest functions of the Vice President is to serve as ceremonial assistant to the President. For example, the Vice President attends many receptions and other social events at which the President cannot be present. The Vice President often plays host to dignitaries from other countries.

Some Vice Presidents have enjoyed their ceremonial and social duties, but others have not. Calvin Coolidge took a characteristically philosophic approach. When his hostess at a dinner once remarked to him how annoying it must be to have to dine out so often, Coolidge replied: "Have to eat somewhere." John Nance Garner drew the line on social life. He went to bed early and refused to receive calls from 6 P.M. to 7 A.M., saying these hours "are my own."

History of the Vice Presidency

Early Days. Most historians believe that Alexander Hamilton first proposed the office of Vice President. Not all the delegates to the Constitutional Convention supported the idea. But on Sept. 6, 1787, the convention approved his proposal. The Founding Fathers originally provided that the person who received the

Interesting Facts About the Vice Presidents

Who was the youngest Vice President to be inaugurated? Breckinridge, 36. **The oldest?** Barkley, 71.

Which Vice Presidents were chosen under provisions of the 25th Amendment? Ford, Rockefeller.

Who was the first Vice President to attend meetings of the Cabinet regularly? Coolidge.

Who was the first Vice President to become a regular member of the National Security Council? Barkley.

What Vice President presided over the Senate with a brace of pistols beside him? Van Buren.

Who was the first Vice President to officially serve as acting President? Bush, for 8 hours during President Ronald Reagan's cancer surgery in 1985.

What Vice President-elect died without ever performing the duties of office? King.

Who was the first Vice President to succeed to the presidency, then win the office by election? T. Roosevelt.

Who was the first Vice President to be assigned administrative duties by the President? Wallace.

Who was the only Vice President to succeed to the presidency upon the resignation of the President? Ford.

Which Vice Presidents resigned? Calhoun, Agnew.

What Vice President was selected by the Senate because the Electoral College failed to agree? R. Johnson.

Who was the first Vice President nominated at a national political convention? Van Buren.

What state has produced the most Vice Presidents? New York.

What Vice Presidents died while in office? Clinton, Gerry, King, Wilson, Hendricks, Hobart, Sherman.

Who was the youngest Vice President to succeed to the presidency upon the death of the President? T. Roosevelt, 42. **The oldest?** Truman, 60.

What teams of President and Vice President were re-elected to a second term? Washington and Adams, Monroe and Tompkins, Wilson and Marshall, F. Roosevelt and Garner, Eisenhower and Nixon, Nixon and Agnew, Reagan and Bush.

What Vice Presidents served under two different Presidents? Clinton, Calhoun.

What Vice President took the oath of office in another country? King, in Havana, Cuba.

second highest electoral vote for President should become Vice President. Electors had two votes, which they cast for the two people they considered best qualified for the presidency. Under this system, John Adams became the first Vice President and Thomas Jefferson the second.

Adams and Jefferson developed different views of the vice presidency. Adams wrote his wife: "My country has in its wisdom contrived for me the most insignificant office that ever the invention of man contrived or his imagination conceived." Jefferson declared that "the second office in the government is honorable and easy; the first is but a splendid misery."

The rise of political parties caused the breakdown of this election system. In 1796, the Electoral College gave the greatest number of votes to Adams, a Federalist. Jefferson, a Democratic-Republican, received the next largest number of votes, and became Vice President. The conflicting party loyalties of the two men created discord in the administration.

In 1800, Jefferson and Aaron Burr both ran as Democratic-Republicans. They tied with 73 electoral votes each, and the election was given to the House of Representatives, where each state has one vote in a presidential election. Burr hoped for Federalist support, and tried to be elected President instead of Vice President. But he failed. After 36 ballots, Jefferson won a majority of the votes, and Burr became Vice President. The system's weakness became apparent during this election. In 1804, Congress adopted Amendment 12 to the Constitution, which provided for separate ballots for President and Vice President. This solved the immediate problem, but it also lessened the prestige of the vice presidency. The Vice President was no longer elected as the second choice for the presidency.

In 1832, John C. Calhoun became the first Vice President to resign. He resigned after being elected to fill a U.S. Senate seat from South Carolina.

Tyler Takes Over. The Constitution provides that in case of the death or disability of the President, "the powers and duties" of the office shall devolve on the Vice President. How this would work remained uncertain until 1841, when William Henry Harrison died in office, the first President to do so. His Vice President was John Tyler. Former President John Quincy Adams and other leaders believed Tyler should be called *acting President*, not President. They opposed Tyler's receiving the full presidential salary and even his occupying the White House. Tyler ignored them. He took the oath and title of *President*, occupied the White House, and asserted full presidential powers. His action was not challenged legally, and he thereby established the right of the Vice President to full succession.

Vice Presidents have responded in various ways when a President has become disabled. Vice President Chester A. Arthur did not see James A. Garfield from the day Garfield was shot until he died 80 days later. Arthur received reports of the President's condition from Secretary of State James G. Blaine. He refused to assume the Chief Executive's duties for fear that he would be doing wrong. Vice President Thomas R. Marshall also declined to take up the President's duties during Woodrow Wilson's six-month illness. During Dwight D. Eisenhower's illnesses in 1955 and 1956, Vice President Richard M. Nixon presided at meetings

of the Cabinet and the National Security Council. He kept in close touch with the President. These experiences, and the 1963 assassination of President John F. Kennedy, led to the 25th Amendment to the Constitution. This amendment, ratified in 1967, sets procedures for presidential and vice presidential succession.

Growth of the Vice Presidency. In 1791, Vice President John Adams attended a Cabinet meeting. No other Vice President did so until after World War I. In 1918, President Wilson asked Vice President Marshall to preside over the Cabinet while Wilson was attending the Paris Peace Conference. After Wilson returned home, Marshall was again excluded.

President Warren G. Harding invited Vice President Calvin Coolidge to attend all Cabinet meetings. Coolidge did so until he became President after Harding's death. Vice President Charles G. Dawes declared that he would not attend Cabinet sessions, because if he did so "the precedent might prove injurious to the country." Therefore, Coolidge did not ask him to participate. Nor did President Herbert Hoover invite Vice President Charles Curtis to take part in Cabinet meetings.

Since the first term of President Franklin D. Roosevelt, all Vice Presidents have regularly attended Cabinet meetings. President Eisenhower strengthened the vice presidency further by directing that Vice President Nixon should preside at Cabinet meetings in the President's absence. Previously, the secretary of state had presided at such times. Congress made the Vice President a member of the National Security Council in 1949. Eisenhower directed in 1954 that the Vice President should preside over council meetings when the President was absent.

President John F. Kennedy further extended the duties of the Vice President. His Vice President, Lyndon B. Johnson, served as chairman of the National Aeronautics and Space Council and headed the President's Committee on Equal Employment Opportunity. After he became President, Johnson continued to upgrade the vice presidency. Vice President Hubert H. Humphrey helped unify the Johnson Administration's antipoverty and civil rights programs.

President Richard M. Nixon also gave important duties to his Vice President, Spiro T. Agnew. Agnew promoted the Administration's domestic programs among state and local officials. His outspoken defense of Nixon's policies against criticism by liberals and the news media made Agnew a controversial figure.

In 1973, Agnew became the second Vice President to resign. He left the office when a federal grand jury began to investigate charges that he had participated in widespread graft as an officeholder in Maryland. Nixon nominated House Minority Leader Gerald R. Ford to succeed Agnew. Ford became the first Vice President chosen under terms of the 25th Amendment. In 1974, Nixon resigned. Ford then became the first Vice President to succeed to the presidency because of a President's resignation. Former New York Governor Nelson A. Rockefeller replaced Ford as Vice President. For the first time, three Vice Presidents and two Presidents had held office during one four-year term. Also for the first time, the nation had both an unelected President and Vice President.

VICEROY

President Jimmy Carter continued the trend of using the Vice President for important assignments. His Vice President, Walter F. Mondale, helped develop U.S. policy on southern Africa and helped draft a plan to reorganize U.S. intelligence agencies. He was one of Carter's most influential advisers. Vice President George Bush headed a group of advisers that provided President Ronald Reagan with recommendations on how to respond to specific foreign crises. Bush became the first Vice President to serve as acting President. He held the position for only about eight hours on July 13, 1985, when Reagan had cancer surgery. IRVING G. WILLIAMS

Related Articles. See the biography of each Vice President listed in the *table* in this article. See also:

Address, Forms of	Franking and Penalty
Cabinet	Privileges
Constitution of the U.S.	National Security Council
(Amendment 12; Amendment 20; Amendment 25)	President of the United States
Electoral College	Presidential Succession
Flag (picture: Flags of the U.S. Government)	Senate

Outline

I. Choosing a Vice President
- A. Nomination   C. Election   E. The 25th
- B. The Campaign D. Inauguration   Amendment

II. Roles of the Vice President
- A. A Typical Day
- B. President of the Senate
- C. Administration and Policymaking
- D. Social Duties

III. History of the Vice Presidency

Questions

What is meant by "balancing a ticket"?
What are the legal qualifications for a vice presidential candidate?
What are the official duties of the Vice President?
In what various ways have Vice Presidents responded when a President has become disabled?
What happened in 1800 to bring about a change in the method of electing the Vice President?
How did the vice presidency change after 1804?
How has the vice presidency grown in importance since World War I?
How can a Vice President be removed from office?
How is the Vice President elected if the Electoral College fails to select one by majority vote?

Additional Resources

Level I

FEERICK, JOHN D. and EMALIE P. *The First Book of Vice-Presidents of the United States.* Rev. ed. Watts, 1977.
HOOPES, ROY. *The Changing Vice-Presidency.* Harper, 1981.

Level II

ALOTTA, ROBERT I. *#2: A Look at the Vice Presidency.* Simon & Schuster, 1981.
BARZMAN, SOL. *Madmen and Geniuses: The Vice-Presidents of the United States.* Follett, 1974.
GOLDSTEIN, JOEL K. *The Modern American Vice Presidency: The Transformation of a Political Institution.* Princeton, 1982.
YOUNG, DONALD. *American Roulette: The History and Dilemma of the Vice Presidency.* Rev. ed. Holt, 1972.

VICEROY is an official who rules a province or colony in the name of a king. The term *viceroy* means *in place of the king.* The British governor general of India was a viceroy. Before 1920, the lord lieutenant of Ireland was often called a viceroy.

VICHY, *VIHSH ee* or *vee SHEE* (pop. 30,527), is a resort town on the Allier River in central France (see FRANCE [political map]). During World War II, Vichy was the capital of unoccupied France from July 1940, until November 1942. Marshal Henri Philippe Pétain headed the Vichy government. In November 1942, German troops occupied all France. Vichy remained the seat of the German-controlled French government until 1944, when Allied troops freed the city.

During the months that France was under German occupation, the name *Vichy* came to stand for *collaboration* with the Germans. The name took on this meaning because French government officials in Vichy made compromises and concessions to meet German demands. For many years before World War II, Vichy was famous as a health resort. ROBERT E. DICKINSON

VICKSBURG, Miss. (pop. 25,434), is a major Mississippi River port. It is on the west border of the state (see MISSISSIPPI [political map]). Vicksburg's chief products include chemicals, fabricated metals, and machinery. The Spaniards established an outpost in the area about 1790. In 1825, the settlement was incorporated as Vicksburg. During the Civil War, Vicksburg fell to the Union Army on July 4, 1863, after a 47-day siege (see CIVIL WAR [Vicksburg]). Vicksburg is the seat of Warren County and has a commission form of government. See also MISSISSIPPI (pictures). CHARLOTTE CAPERS

VICKSBURG, BATTLE OF. See CIVIL WAR (Vicksburg; table: Major Battles).

VICTOR EMMANUEL was the name of a king of Sardinia and two kings of Italy.

Victor Emmanuel I (1759-1824) ruled as king of Sardinia from 1814 to 1821. Faced with a revolution in 1821, he abdicated his throne in favor of his brother, Charles Felix, rather than grant his people a constitution and declare war on Austria.

Victor Emmanuel II (1820-1878) was king of Sardinia from 1849 to 1861 and the first king of Italy from 1861 to 1878. He took the leadership of uniting Italy. His first step was to get the Austrians out of Italy. He made an alliance with France, and in 1859 the two countries defeated Austria. Victor Emmanuel gained Lombardy. Revolutions began in central Italy shortly after. In 1860, Giuseppe Garibaldi conquered the Kingdom of the Two Sicilies. As a result, central Italy (except for Rome) and the Kingdom of the Two Sicilies joined Sardinia in 1861 to form a united kingdom of Italy. Victor Emmanuel became king. Venetia joined the kingdom in 1866, and Rome joined in 1870. Victor Emmanuel II was born in Turin, Italy.

Victor Emmanuel III (1869-1947) became king of Italy after the assassination of his father, Humbert I, in 1900. The people honored and respected him during the early years of his reign, but later they came to despise him. Victor Emmanuel refused to proclaim martial law to stop Benito Mussolini's march on Rome in 1922. The king made no protest when Italy became a fascist dictatorship. Victor Emmanuel tried to save the monarchy in 1946 by abdicating in favor of his son, Crown Prince Humbert. But the Italian people voted to abolish the monarchy in a 1946 election. Victor Emmanuel III was born in Naples. R. JOHN RATH

Related Articles in WORLD BOOK include:

Cavour, Count di	Mussolini, Benito	Savoy
Fascism	Papal States	Sicilies,
Garibaldi, Giuseppe	Sardinia,	Kingdom of
Italy (History)	Kingdom of	the Two

VICTORIA (1819-1901) was queen of the United Kingdom of Great Britain and Ireland from 1837 to 1901 and became one of the most famous rulers in English history. Her 63-year reign was the longest in British history. Great Britain reached the height of its power during this period. It built a great colonial empire and enjoyed tremendous industrial expansion at home. As a result, the period of Victoria's reign is often called the Victorian Age.

Early Years. Victoria was born at Kensington Palace in London on May 24, 1819. She was the only child of Edward, Duke of Kent, fourth son of George III, and of Victoria Maria Louisa, daughter of Francis, Duke of Saxe-Coburg-Saalfeld. Victoria's father died before she was a year old, and she was reared by her mother.

Historical Pictures Service
Queen Victoria

Victoria's uncle, King William IV, died on June 20, 1837. He had no heirs, and so she immediately succeeded to the throne. Victoria was crowned queen at Westminster Abbey on June 28, 1838. Lord Melbourne, her first prime minister, educated her in politics and government.

Events of Her Reign. Many important events took place during Victoria's reign. Britain fought in the Opium War (1839-1842) in China and acquired the island of Hong Kong. Britain also fought in the Crimean War (1853-1856) against Russia, and in the Boer War (1899-1902) in order to protect its interests in southern Africa.

In 1858, control of India was transferred from the East India Company, a trading firm, to the British government. Victoria was proclaimed empress of India in 1876. Britain seized control of Egypt and many other areas. British colonies united in Australia and Canada, and these countries became important members of the growing British Empire.

The development of a worldwide colonial empire made Britain the richest country in the world. Britain ended restrictions on foreign trade, and its colonies became both sources of raw materials and markets for its manufactured goods. Britain was called the *workshop of the world*. The British Empire included a fourth of the world's land and a fourth of its people.

The population of Britain itself increased 50 per cent during Victoria's reign, and Britain changed from mainly an agricultural to mainly an industrial nation. More people won the right to vote, and local government became increasingly democratic. The British Parliament passed acts that improved labor conditions, required all children to attend school, and reformed the civil service. In Ireland, the Church of Ireland was separated from the government, and the land system was reformed.

Achievements. The British people had little respect for the throne when Victoria became queen. This situation had developed because of irresponsible conduct by the two kings before her, George IV and William IV. But Victoria showed herself to be a hard-working monarch concerned with the welfare of her people, and she gained their affection and admiration.

Victoria was a wise and capable monarch. But Britain's greatness was due chiefly to her able prime ministers, including Lord Melbourne, Sir Robert Peel, Viscount Palmerston, Benjamin Disraeli, William Gladstone, and the Marquess of Salisbury. Gradually the queen had to accept that the British monarchy would not survive unless its powers were reduced and her ministers in Parliament were allowed to rule the nation. Victoria accepted the switch from political ruler to symbolic ruler. For this reason, Britain's monarchy has survived, while the monarchies of most other countries have not.

Personal Life. In February 1840, Queen Victoria married a cousin, Prince Albert of Saxe-Coburg-Gotha. They had four sons and five daughters. The prince was a scholar, philanthropist, and businessman, and the people came to respect him. He actively assisted his wife in her royal duties. Albert died in 1861, and Victoria never recovered from her grief at his loss. She withdrew from social activities and dressed in black for many years. Victoria died in 1901, and her eldest son became King Edward VII. RICHARD W. DAVIS

Related Articles in WORLD BOOK include:

Albert, Prince
Connaught and Strathearn, Duke of
Edward (VII) of England
English Literature (Victorian Literature)
Great Britain (History)
Windsor

Additional Resources

DRABBLE, MARGARET. *For Queen and Country: Britain in the Victorian Age.* Seabury, 1979. Suitable for younger readers.
LONGFORD, ELIZABETH. *Queen Victoria: Born to Succeed.* Harper, 1964.
WOODHAM-SMITH, CECIL. *Queen Victoria: From Her Birth to the Death of the Prince Consort.* Knopf, 1972.
YOUNG, GEORGE M. *Victorian England: Portrait of an Age.* 2nd ed. Oxford, 1964.

VICTORIA is the smallest state on the Australian mainland. Only the island of Tasmania covers a smaller area among the Australian states. Victoria has a population of 3,832,100. Most of the people are of British descent. About 2 per cent are Aborigines.

Victoria is one of Australia's chief farming regions. It was also the first area in Australia to develop a large-scale manufacturing industry. This activity began in the 1860's. Melbourne, on Port Phillip Bay, is Victoria's capital and also the largest city. About two-thirds of the people live in Melbourne (see MELBOURNE).

Land. Victoria lies at the southeastern tip of Australia. It covers 87,900 square miles (227,600 square kilometers). For detailed maps, see AUSTRALIA. Low hills border Victoria's coastline. Mountains cover much of the eastern, central, and southern parts of the state. The Murray River, Australia's longest waterway, rises in mountains in the east and flows northwestward to form

WORLD BOOK map
Location of Victoria

much of the boundary between Victoria and the state of New South Wales. Plains cover much of western and northern Victoria and part of the south. Port Phillip Bay, one of the largest and deepest bays in the world, covers 875 square miles (2,266 square kilometers). It opens into the Bass Strait, across which lies the island of Tasmania.

Economy. Victoria's chief crops include barley, hay, oats, potatos, wheat, and many kinds of fruit. Livestock raising and dairy farming are also important. Victoria's manufactured products include agricultural implements, chemicals, dyes, iron and steel, leather products, paints, paper, rubber products, textiles, tobacco, and wines. *Lignite* (brown coal), petroleum, and natural gas are the state's chief minerals. A lignite deposit near the coast is believed to be the largest single deposit in the world. Petroleum and natural gas come from offshore deposits.

Government. The British Crown appoints a governor for Victoria, on the advice of the Victorian Parliament. But a premier actually heads the government, assisted by a cabinet of ministers. The legislature consists of a 34-member upper house that serves six years, and a 66-member lower house that serves three years. Victoria sends 10 senators and 33 representatives to the federal Parliament at Canberra.

History. George Bass, a British navigator, sighted the eastern coast of Victoria in 1797. But colonists did not settle permanently until 1835. The territory formed part of New South Wales until 1851, when it became a separate colony. It was named for Queen Victoria.

In 1851, discoveries of gold in Ballarat and Bendigo brought thousands of settlers to Victoria. After the gold rush, many miners became farmers. The settlers won self-government in 1855. Victoria joined the Commonwealth of Australia in 1901.　　　C. M. H. CLARK

VICTORIA (pop. 64,379; met. area pop. 233,481) is the capital of British Columbia and the second largest city of the province. Only Vancouver is larger. A deep harbor at nearby Esquimalt serves as Canada's chief naval base on the west coast. Victoria lies on the southeastern tip of Vancouver Island. For location, see BRITISH COLUMBIA (political map).

About 2 million tourists visit Victoria annually, and many retired people move to the area from other parts of Canada. Victoria's attractions include its scenic surroundings and the "English" appearance of the city itself. Its narrow streets and neat public and private gardens resemble those of England. Victoria also has a milder climate than any other Canadian city. Victoria's temperatures average 40° F. (4° C) in January and 60° F. (16° C) in July.

Description. Victoria covers about 7 square miles (18 square kilometers). Its metropolitan area occupies about 155 square miles (401 square kilometers).

The buildings of the British Columbia Parliament overlook Victoria Harbor. The nearby Empress Hotel is famous for its elegance. The world's finest collection of totem poles may be seen in the British Columbia Provincial Museum and nearby Thunderbird Park. Victoria's modern City Hall borders Centennial Square downtown. The Royal Roads Military College and the University of Victoria lie just outside the city.

About 30 per cent of the workers of the Victoria metropolitan area are employed by the tourist industry or other service fields. About 20 per cent have jobs with the federal, provincial, or local government. Retired people make up about 20 per cent of the population of Victoria.

History. Coast Salish Indians lived in what is now the Victoria area before white settlers arrived there. The Hudson's Bay Company of London, a fur-trading organization, founded Victoria in 1843. The settlement was named for Queen Victoria of Great Britain. It served as the capital of the Colony of Vancouver Island from 1858 to 1866, when the island became part of British Columbia. Victoria has been the capital of British Columbia since 1868.

The city grew steadily through the years. The British Royal Navy established a naval base at the nearby harbor in 1865. Tourism became important to the city after the Canadian Pacific Railway opened the Empress Hotel in 1908. Ferry lines linked the city with railroad terminals on the mainland. The harbor was a key Canadian ship-building center during World War I (1914-1918) and World War II (1939-1945).

During the 1960's and 1970's, Victoria completed several projects that beautified the city and preserved its older areas. These projects included renewal of a historic downtown residential district and construction of new docks and walkways for the harbor. Victoria has a council-manager form of government.　J. B. B. SHAW

See also BRITISH COLUMBIA (pictures); CHRISTMAS (picture: Outdoor Decorations).

VICTORIA (pop. 501,680) is the capital of Hong Kong. Offices and government buildings stand along the waterfront in the central part of Victoria. The crowded Chinese section surrounds the downtown area. See also HONG KONG.

VICTORIA, LAKE. See LAKE VICTORIA.

VICTORIA DAY commemorates the birthday of Queen Victoria on May 24, 1819. The people of the British Commonwealth have always celebrated the birthday of the ruling monarch as a patriotic holiday. During the long lifetime of Queen Victoria, her birthday came to have a special meaning. After Queen Victoria's death, people continued to celebrate her birthday to express their loyalty to the British Empire.

In the early 1900's, the people of Canada celebrated Queen Victoria's birthday as Empire Day. The name was changed to Commonwealth Day in 1947. Canadians now celebrate Victoria Day and the official birthday of the reigning monarch as a legal holiday on the Monday before May 25.　RAYMOND HOYT JAHN

VICTORIA DESERT. See GREAT VICTORIA DESERT.

VICTORIA FALLS is a waterfall that David Livingstone sighted in South Africa in 1855. The explorer named it in honor of Queen Victoria of England. Victoria Falls lies between Zambia and Zimbabwe, about halfway between the mouth and source of the Zambezi River. The Zambezi is about 1 mile (1.6 kilometers) wide at this point and drops suddenly into a deep, narrow chasm. A canyon about 40 miles (64 kilometers) long permits the water to flow out. The height of the falls varies from 256 feet (78 meters) at the right bank to 343 feet (105 meters) in the center.

The mist and spray created by Victoria Falls can be seen for a great distance. This cloud and the constant

roar caused the people of the area to name the falls *Mosi oa Tunya* (smoke that thunders). A hydroelectric plant produces a small amount of power at the falls. A railway bridge crosses the river just below the point where the waters rush out of the chasm.   HARTMUT WALTER

See also ZIMBABWE (picture); WATERFALL (picture chart).

VICTORIA LAND is part of the Antarctic subcontinent. It lies on the shore of the Ross Sea almost due south of New Zealand. Sir James Ross claimed the region for Great Britain during his 1839-1843 expedition. Victoria Land is also called South Victoria Land.

VICTORIAN AGE. See ENGLISH LITERATURE (Victorian Literature); GREAT BRITAIN (History).

VICUÑA, *vih KOON yuh,* is the smallest member of the camel family. It lives in the Andes Mountains of Bolivia, Chile, and Peru, in areas from 12,000 to 18,000 feet (3,600 to 5,490 meters) above sea level. Its home is generally near the snow line. The vicuña and guanaco are the two wild members of the camel family in South America. The other two, the alpaca and llama, are domesticated. None of the four has a hump.

The vicuña is $2\frac{1}{4}$ to 3 feet (69 to 91 centimeters) high at the shoulders and weighs 75 to 140 pounds (34 to 64 kilograms). It has a long, slender neck. Vicuñas eat grass. They usually live in herds which contain one male and 6 to 10 females. They have remarkable sight, speed, and endurance.

Vicuñas have finer fleece than any other wool-bearing animal. The hairs are less than half as thick as the finest sheep's wool. The color of the upper body is reddish yellow to deep tan or reddish brown. The belly and lower legs are white. The fleece grows until it hangs below the flanks and knees. Only the inner fleece is used. It is especially good for high-grade worsted. So many vicuñas were killed for their wool that the species had become rare by the 1960's. Peruvian law now protects the animals. The ancient Inca Indians protected vicuñas and hunted them only once in four years. Only royalty could use the fleece.

Scientific Classification. The vicuña belongs to the camel family, Camelidae. Its scientific name is *Vicugna vicugna.*   DONALD F. HOFFMEISTER

VIDAL, *vee DAHL,* **GORE,** *gawr* (1925-   ), is an American author best known for his novels. Some have historical themes, and others satirize American society. Vidal has also written essays, short stories, and plays.

Vidal's novel *Julian* (1964) deals with the Roman emperor Julian, who lived during the A.D. 300's. It describes Julian's attempt to halt the spread of Christianity and restore the worship of the ancient Greek gods. *Creation* (1981) deals with the adventures of a Persian diplomat in the ancient world during the 400's B.C. The novels *Burr* (1973), *1876* (1976), and *Lincoln* (1984) concern American political history. In *Washington, D.C.* (1967), Vidal satirizes political corruption during the mid-1900's. His novels *Myra Breckinridge* (1968) and *Myron* (1974) explore sexual behavior in Hollywood.

Vidal's *Rocking the Boat* (1962), *Reflections upon a Sinking Ship* (1969), and *The Second American Revolution* (1982) are collections of essays on social and political topics. During the 1950's, Vidal wrote three detective novels under the pen name Edgar Box. His best-known play, *The Best Man* (1960), deals with political intrigue at a presidential nominating convention. He was born in West Point, N.Y.   EUGENE K. GARBER

VIDEO. See TELEVISION; VIDEOTAPE RECORDER.

VIDEO GAME. See ELECTRONIC GAME.

VIDEODISC is a flat, round platter on which material has been prerecorded for reproduction on a tele-

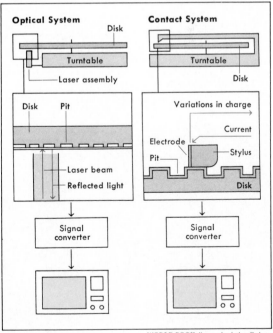

WORLD BOOK diagram by Arthur Grebetz

Videodisc Players convert the material recorded on a disk into television signals. There are two main kinds of disk systems—*optical* and *contact.* An optical player reads a pattern of reflected light. A contact player senses variations in electric charge.

New York Zoological Society

The Vicuña Is a Humpless Member of the Camel Family.

VIDEOTAPE RECORDER

vision set. The word is also spelled *video disk* or *videodisk*. A videodisc is played on a *videodisc player*, which resembles a phonograph and can be hooked up to any TV set. Manufacturers prerecord programs on the disks (or *discs*). Videodisc players cannot record material.

Videodiscs are made of plastic. The disk's surface is covered with microscopic pits that wind in a coil. The pits form a code that represents the recorded pictures and sounds. As the disk spins on the turntable, the player reads the code and converts it into TV signals.

There are two main types of videodisc players—*optical* and *contact*. Each type uses a certain kind of disk and reads it differently. The two kinds of disks are not interchangeable between the players.

The optical player uses a disk that has a reflective metal coating. The player has a device called a *laser*, which aims a concentrated beam of light at the disk. The light reflects off the pits in a pattern that is read by a light-sensitive device in the player. The player converts the pattern, or code, into TV signals. Disks played on optical players do not wear out because only light touches the surface.

The contact player uses a *stylus* (needle) that rests on the spinning disk. An electrode is attached to the stylus. Electric current flows from the electrode to the disk. The pits on the disk vary in their capacity to hold an electric charge. The player senses these variations and converts the charges into TV signals.

Manufacturers began developing videodisc systems in the early 1970's mainly for use as home entertainment. Since the mid-1980's, these systems have been used chiefly in education and industry. Some companies are adapting the optical system to store computer information.   Pamela Hamilton

See also Television (Video Entertainment Systems).

VIDEOTAPE RECORDER is a device that records visual images and sound on magnetic tape. Videotape recorders, also known as *VTR*'s or simply *video recorders*, play back the recorded *video* (picture) and *audio* (sound) information on television sets.

Videotape recorders were first used by the television broadcasting industry during the 1950's. Since then, several other types of VTR's have been developed in addition to the professional models used by TV broadcasters. For example, many schools and businesses use semiprofessional videotape recorders to record educational programs and employee training films. Consumers record TV programs and play back prerecorded cassettes of movies, concerts, and other events on home videotape recorders. Home video recorders, which are also called *video cassette recorders* (VCR's), vary in size. For example, some measure about 18 inches by 13 inches by 3 inches (46 centimeters by 33 centimeters by 8 centimeters). Professional and semiprofessional recorders are much larger. In addition, the various types of video recorders differ in the size of the tape they use and the quality of the pictures they produce.

Videotape consists of a plastic strip coated with particles of iron oxide, a material that is readily magnetized. Videotape recorders record television signals by changing them into magnetic fields that magnetize the particles into patterns. This process is reversed during playback, when the magnetic patterns are changed back into television signals for broadcast on TV sets. For information about where television signals come from and how they are made into a TV picture, see Television (How Television Works).

Videotape has a number of advantages over film. For example, videotape can be played back immediately after being recorded on, but film must be developed before it can be viewed. For this reason, camera operators who use videotape are able to know right away whether a scene needs to be re-recorded. In addition, editing is easier on videotape, because tape can be erased and recorded over, but film cannot.

Uses of Videotape Recorders

In the Home, videotape recorders have become a popular part of home entertainment systems since they first appeared in the 1970's. VCR's are designed to enable consumers to tape television programs while they are away from home. A timer on the recorder is set to turn the recorder on when the program starts and off when it ends. Home recorders can record programs on

© George Hall, Woodfin Camp, Inc.   World Book photo   World Book photo by Dan Miller

Videotape Recorders, also called VTR's, record visual images and sound on magnetic tape. The television industry uses large professional VTR's, *above left,* to record and edit TV programs. Semiprofessional VTR's, *center,* act as a teaching aid in schools and businesses. Families use home recorders, commonly called VCR's, to play back various prerecorded tapes, *above right.*

Transverse Videotape Recording

Most professional videotape recorders record video signals in *transverse* (vertical) tracks. Video tracks consist of lines of magnetized particles on the tape and are created by electromagnets called *video heads.* The video heads rotate on a rapidly spinning *headwheel.* Separate heads record audio and control tracks.

Helical Videotape Recording

Semiprofessional and home videotape recorders record video signals in *helical* (diagonal) tracks on the tape. The video heads on a helical videotape recorder are mounted on a rotating cylinder called a *drum.* Most helical recorders are designed to use tape cassettes.

WORLD BOOK diagrams by Arthur Grebetz

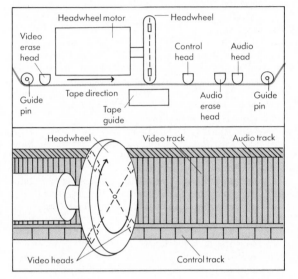

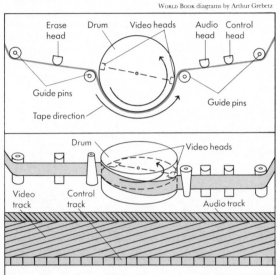

one channel while a person is watching a program on another channel. People also use home recorders to play back prerecorded cassettes of movies, sporting events, concerts, and a variety of other programs. Such cassettes can be either rented or purchased.

Portable videotape recorders, which include a video camera, are used to make home movies. The camera sends audio and video signals through a cable to the recorder. In some portable videotape recorders, the camera and recorder are combined into a single unit.

In Schools, videotape recorders have become a valuable teaching aid. For example, teachers can videotape educational TV programs and then play them back in class at a convenient time. A number of schools also have a *closed-circuit television* system, which allows a videotaped program to be shown in several classrooms at the same time. In some schools, students use portable videotape recorders to produce their own educational programs. Medical school professors use videotape recordings to show students new surgical techniques.

In the Television Industry, videotape recorders have become essential equipment. Commercials, regular TV series, and many other telecasts are recorded on videotape. This practice allows programmers to plan and organize TV schedules ahead of time. It also enables broadcasters to show reruns of programs and to replay commercials. In addition, most television newscasts feature reports recorded on tape, and videotaped *instant replays* have become a routine part of live sports telecasts.

In Other Industries, employers use videotape recorders chiefly to produce training films for employees. Salespeople sometimes study videotapes of their presentation to determine its effectiveness and to see how they appear to their prospects. Video cameras are

used for surveillance in banks, laboratories, and other high-security areas.

How Videotape Recorders Work

Recording. Videotape is a plastic strip covered with particles of iron oxide. As videotape travels through the videotape recorder, the particles are magnetized into patterns that represent television signals. The videotape recorder converts the TV signal into electric current, which travels through wire coils into electromagnets called *heads.* A head is a ring of metal with a gap in it. The current produces a strong magnetic field in the head and over the gap. When videotape is passed over the gap, the magnetic field magnetizes the particles into patterns. The patterns remain until they are removed by an *erase head,* which demagnetizes the tape.

The patterns recorded on videotape consist of three types of *tracks* (lines of magnetized particles). Video tracks contain video signals and take up most of the tape. Audio tracks run along one edge of the tape, and control tracks along the other. Audio tracks contain audio signals, and control tracks ensure that the images from the tape do not tilt or merge into one another when they appear on the TV screen.

Control tracks and audio tracks are recorded by stationary heads. Video tracks are recorded by video heads that are mounted on a rotating metal cylinder called a *drum* or a rotating metal disk called a *headwheel.* The video heads *scan* (pass over) the tape at high speed while recording or playing back video signals. This rapid scanning is necessary for the machine to capture and reproduce such signals, which have a high frequency. If video heads were stationary, a large amount of videotape moving at an extremely fast speed would be needed to record even a small amount of video information.

VIDEOTEX

Most professional videotape recorders are equipped with a headwheel that records video tracks *transversely* (vertically) between edges of the tape. Semiprofessional and home VTR's record such tracks *helically* (diagonally) between edges of tape.

Most professional recorders are designed to use a *supply reel* and a *take-up reel*. The supply reel feeds the tape through the recorder, past the various heads, and onto the take-up reel, where it is wound up. In semiprofessional and home videotape recorders, the supply and take-up reels are contained within a cassette.

Playback. As tape passes over the heads during playback, the tape's magnetic patterns create a magnetic field in the head. When the magnetic field reaches the wire coil, it is converted into patterns of electric current. The current is then changed into audio and video signals and sent to a television set.

History

The development of videotape recorders began during the 1940's. However, the first videotape recorder that was capable of recording a television picture of broadcasting quality on magnetic tape was not invented until 1956. This reel-to-reel machine, produced by the Ampex Corporation of California, recorded transversely with a headwheel that had four video heads.

In 1959, the Toshiba Corporation of Japan introduced the first helical recorder. This VTR, which was smaller and less expensive than previous recorders, helped videotape recording spread outside the television industry. Video cassette recorders were first marketed in the United States in the early 1970's. These machines were designed primarily for use in schools. The first commercially successful home videotape recorder did not appear until 1975. By the mid-1980's, two main types of home VCR systems had been developed. These two systems—called Beta and VHS—operated in basically the same manner, but tapes for one system could not be played on the other. GEORGE W. HRBEK

VIDEOTEX. See TELEVISION (Televised Informational Services).

VIENNA, *vee EHN uh* (pop. 1,515,666), is the capital and largest city of Austria. The city lies in northeastern Austria, on the south bank of the Danube River. For the location of Vienna, see AUSTRIA (political map). Vienna is Austria's leading cultural, economic, and political center. The city's name in German is *Wien*.

Vienna became the capital of the Austrian (later the Austro-Hungarian) Empire under the Hapsburgs (or Habsburgs), a royal family that ruled in central Europe from 1273 to 1918. During the 1700's and 1800's, Vienna won fame as a world center of education, literature, music, and science. The Viennese people became known for their gaiety, wit, and enjoyment of life.

The Austro-Hungarian Empire collapsed after World War I ended in 1918, and Vienna lost much of its importance. After the end of World War II in 1945, Vienna became a center for international conferences and the location of several international agencies.

The City covers about 160 square miles (415 square kilometers) at the eastern end of a narrow plain between the Carpathian Mountains and the Alps. An important mountain gap through the Carpathians is just east of Vienna. The city's location at this transportation crossroads played an important role in its growth and economic development. Trade and communication routes run through Vienna in all directions.

The old "Inner City" forms the center of Vienna. This area includes many of the city's historical buildings and landmarks as well as its most fashionable shopping districts. The famous St. Stephen's Cathedral stands at the heart of the Inner City. Several blocks west is the Hofburg, a palace that consists of both modern buildings and medieval structures. The palace includes the royal apartments, now occupied by the president of Austria; the Imperial Library; several museums; and the Spanish Riding School. Nearby lie two of Vienna's most beautiful parks, the Burggarten and the Volksgarten, which is famed for its rose trees.

A band of streets called the Ringstrassen encircles the Inner City. Some of Vienna's most impressive public buildings line these streets. They include the Museum of Art History, City Hall, the Opera House, the Parliament Building, and the Stock Exchange. These buildings date from the second half of the 1800's.

The older suburban districts of the city lie outside the Ringstrassen. They became part of Vienna during the 1800's. Several important buildings are in the suburbs, including the Karlskirche (Church of St. Charles) and the Belvedere Palace. These structures rank among the finest existing examples of *baroque* architecture, a highly decorative style that developed in the 1600's and 1700's. The noted Austrian architect Johann Bernhard Fischer von Erlach designed several Viennese buildings, including the Karlskirche and the Schönbrunn Palace. The palace stands at the southwestern edge of the city. The Schönbrunn Zoo, which lies on the palace grounds, was established in 1752 and ranks as the world's oldest existing zoo. A long park called the Prater lies north of Vienna along the Danube. The Vienna Woods line the western edge of the city.

The People. Most Viennese are German-speaking Austrians. Many Czechs and Hungarians also live in the city, but nearly all of them speak German in addi-

Joachim Messerschmidt, Bruce Coleman Inc.

Vienna, the capital of Austria, is a leading cultural center of Europe. The city is famous for its art galleries, churches, and theaters. The Burgtheater, *above,* is one of Vienna's many landmarks.

tion to their national language. The Viennese wear clothing much like that worn in the United States, but they dress up somewhat more than Americans do. They wear Austrian folk costumes on holidays and other special occasions. Viennese foods reflect the mixture of nationalities in the city. Many of the people like to drink coffee and eat elegant pastries at pastry shops called *Konditoreien*. They also enjoy visiting the wine houses north of the city to drink freshly made wine, called *Heurigen*.

Most Viennese own or rent apartments in four- or five-story buildings. Some suburban families live in their own homes. The city has built apartment complexes to replace residences that were destroyed during World War II, but housing shortages continue to be a problem.

Education and Cultural Life. Vienna is the home of many fine institutions of higher learning. They include the Academy of Fine Arts, the Academy of Music, the Technical University, and the University of Vienna.

The city has long been known for its excellent museums and art galleries, including the Albertina and the Museum of Art History. The city also has several libraries, among them the National Library. Musical events take place at such opera houses as the Musikverein, the State Opera House, and the Volksoper (see EUROPE [picture: Beautiful Opera Houses]). The famous Vienna Boys' Choir sings every Sunday in the Hofburgkapelle, one of the city's many churches. Major theaters include the Burgtheater, which is financially supported by the Austrian government, and the Theater in der Josefstadt.

A number of famous composers, scientists, and writers have lived in Vienna. Such composers as Ludwig van Beethoven, Johannes Brahms, Joseph Haydn, Wolfgang Amadeus Mozart, Franz Peter Schubert, and Johann Strauss all made their home there.

Economy. Vienna is the chief industrial city of Austria. The city's industries manufacture chemicals, clothing, leatherware, medicine, and radio and television products.

The city has an excellent system of public transportation, with streetcars, elevated and subway trains, and buses. Most of the people use public transportation rather than private automobiles in the city.

History. Prehistoric tribes lived on the site of what is now Vienna. In 15 B.C., the Romans established a frontier post there named Vindobona. After the fall of the Roman Empire in the A.D. 400's, invading Germanic tribes took over the area. During the late 800's, the Magyars, a people from Hungary, gained control of the city, which by then was called Vienna. They lived there until the Germans conquered them in the mid-900's.

In 1273, a member of the Habsburg family became Holy Roman Emperor. The Habsburgs made Vienna their capital, and the city grew rapidly in wealth and importance. The Turks attacked Vienna in 1529 and again in 1683, but they failed to capture the city. Some of Vienna's most beautiful baroque palaces and churches were built during the 1700's.

After World War I, Vienna became the capital of the Austrian republic. German troops occupied Vienna from 1938 to the end of World War II in 1945. The city was badly damaged by Allied bombing during the war. From 1945 to 1955, the people lived under the control of the victorious Allies.

The Viennese rebuilt almost all the destroyed or damaged landmarks, and the city regained much of its former spirit and wealth. During the 1970's, new hotels were built and construction began on an expanded subway system. Also, a United Nations (UN) center consisting of several buildings was constructed in Vienna. The center opened in 1979. The center serves as a UN conference site and provides office space for some UN agencies.   WILLIAM J. McGRATH

See also AUSTRIA (pictures); ARCHITECTURE (Early Modern Architecture in Europe; pictures).

VIENNA, *vee EHN uh,* **CONGRESS OF,** was a meeting of European political leaders in 1814 and 1815. They met after the defeat of Napoleon to restore royal rulers to power and to change the boundaries of European countries. They hoped to return the European political system to the system that existed before 1789. The French Revolution of 1789 had ended royal rule in France. Napoleon had conquered many European countries and had overthrown their rulers in the early 1800's. See FRENCH REVOLUTION; NAPOLEON I.

Prince von Metternich of Austria, William von Humboldt of Prussia, Lord Castlereagh of Great Britain, and Czar Alexander I of Russia plotted to control the congress. But they could not agree on how to divide Poland and Saxony, a Germanic province. French diplomat Talleyrand took advantage of their disagreements to give defeated France a voice at the congress.

The Congress of Vienna changed the borders of countries without considering the wishes of people living in the countries. For example, Belgium and The Netherlands were united in spite of their different languages and customs. Austria took some Italian provinces. Sweden got Norway from Denmark. Austria, Prussia, and Russia took parts of Poland. A Germanic Confederation replaced the Holy Roman Empire. Russia got Finland from Sweden and Bessarabia, in southeastern Europe, from Turkey. The Congress of Vienna also restored to power royal rulers in France, The Netherlands, and several German and Italian states.   ROBERT G. L. WAITE

See also AIX-LA-CHAPELLE, CONGRESS OF.

VIENTIANE, *vyehn TYAHN* (pop. 176,637), is the capital and largest city of Laos. Vientiane lies on the Mekong River near the border between Thailand and Laos (see LAOS [map]).

Vientiane is an important trading center. It has an airport, and ferryboats link the city with a railroad that runs south from nearby Nong Khai, Thailand, to Bangkok, Thailand. River transportation connects Vientiane with towns along the Mekong.

Vientiane formed part of the Kingdom of Lan Xang in the 1300's. During the 1700's, it became an independent kingdom. Siam (now Thailand) annexed the Kingdom of Vientiane in the early 1800's. The French made it part of Laos in 1893 and governed it as part of French Indochina until 1954, when Laos became an independent nation.   DAVID P. CHANDLER

See also LAOS (History); LOUANGPHRABANG.

VIETMINH. See VIETNAM.

The Rice Fields of Vietnam provide the basic food of the Vietnamese people. Most of the people in Vietnam are farmers, and rice is the chief crop.

VIETNAM

VIETNAM, *VEE eht NAHM,* is a tropical country in Southeast Asia. It extends south from China in a long, narrow S-curve. Laos and Kampuchea (Cambodia) lie west of Vietnam, and the South China Sea lies to the east. Vietnam is about as large as California and has about 2½ times as many people as that state. Hanoi is its capital, and Ho Chi Minh City is its largest city.

Most Vietnamese live in villages on the coastal plain and on deltas formed by rivers. They raise rice and a few other crops on the fertile land. Many people who live near the coast catch fish for a living.

In ancient times, the Vietnamese people lived in what is now northern Vietnam. China ruled the area from about 100 B.C. until the A.D. 900's, when the Vietnamese formed an independent state. During the next 900 years, the Vietnamese expanded their territory until they controlled all of what is now Vietnam.

France gained control of Vietnam in the late 1800's. The French governed the country until Japan occupied

Dennis J. Duncanson, the contributor of this article, is Reader in Southeast Asian Studies at the University of Kent in Canterbury, England, and the author of Government and Revolution in Vietnam.

it during World War II. After Japan's defeat in 1945, France tried to regain control of Vietnam. But the *Vietminh,* a group controlled by Communists and headed by Ho Chi Minh, gained power in northern Vietnam. Fighting broke out between French forces and the Vietminh in 1946.

In April 1954, an international conference met in Geneva, Switzerland, to arrange a peace settlement for

Facts in Brief

Capital: Hanoi.

Official Language: Vietnamese.

Official Name: *Cong Hoa Xa Hoi Chu Nghia Viet Nam* (Socialist Republic of Vietnam).

Form of Government: Communist dictatorship.

Area: 127,242 sq. mi. (329,556 km²). *Greatest Distances*—north-south, 1,030 mi. (1,657 km); east-west, 380 mi. (612 km). *Coastline*—1,435 mi. (2,309 km).

Elevation: *Highest*—Fan Si Pan, 10,312 ft. (3,143 m) above sea level. *Lowest*—sea level along the coast.

Population: *Estimated 1986 Population*—60,826,000; distribution, 79 per cent rural, 21 per cent urban; density, 479 persons per sq. mi. (185 per km²). *1979 Census*—52,741,766. *Estimated 1991 Population*—67,487,000.

Chief Products: *Agriculture*—rice. *Manufacturing*—cement, iron and steel, paper, textiles. *Mining*—coal.

Money: *Basic Unit*—dong.

Vietnam. Called the Geneva Conference, it included representatives of the Vietminh and of the French-supported State of Vietnam. France, Great Britain, the United States, China, and Russia also sent representatives. In May, the Vietminh defeated the French. The Geneva Conference then decided to divide Vietnam temporarily into two zones. The Communists received control of the northern zone, called North Vietnam. Non-Communist Vietnamese received control of the southern zone, called South Vietnam. The conference also called for the country to be reunited through elections in 1956. But leaders of the North and the South could not agree on how to conduct the elections.

In 1957, Communists from both South and North Vietnam began attacking villages in South Vietnam. The Communists had as their goal the take-over of South Vietnam. The fighting developed into the Vietnam War. China, Russia, and other Communist countries sent aid to the Vietnamese Communists during the war. Non-Communist countries supported South Vietnam. The United States became the chief ally of the South. It backed the South's war effort with supplies and hundreds of thousands of troops. In 1973, the participants in the Vietnam War agreed to a cease-fire, and the United States withdrew its last combat troops from Vietnam. But North Vietnam soon resumed its war effort. In April 1975, the Communists defeated South Vietnam and took control of it. In 1976, they unified North and South Vietnam into the single nation of Vietnam. See VIETNAM WAR.

Government

Vietnam's leaders call the country a republic and a dictatorship of the working class. In practice, however, the government is tightly controlled by the leaders of the nation's Communist Party.

The Communist Party of Vietnam is officially called the *Dang Lao Dong Viet Nam* (Workers' Party of Vietnam). Its common name is the *Lao Dong Party*. The party's 15-member Politburo is the most powerful governmental unit in Vietnam. It makes all the government's laws and policies.

National Government. Vietnam has a 496-member National Assembly. The Assembly meets twice a year to endorse laws and policies made by the Communist Party. A Council of State—made up of members of the National Assembly—deals with such matters as national defense and the execution of laws. The Council members make up a collective presidency. Members of a Council of Ministers head various departments of the government. The Communist Party chooses—and the National Assembly elects—the members of the Council of State and the Council of Ministers.

Local Government. Vietnam is divided into 35 provinces and three cities independent of provinces. The cities are Haiphong, Hanoi, and Ho Chi Minh City. People's councils conduct government business at the provincial level and on down to the village level in Vietnam. Local government officials must follow Communist Party policies. The Communist Party chooses—and the people elect—the officials of the lower levels of local government. These officials, in turn, elect the members of the higher levels of local government.

Courts. The Communist Party controls the court system of Vietnam. The court system includes the People's

Supreme Court, local people's courts, and military courts.

Armed Forces. Vietnam has an army, navy, and air force. The army has about 685,000 members, the air force about 12,000 members, and the navy about 3,000 members. In addition, about 1½ million Vietnamese serve part-time in the country's militia and other military units.

People

Thousands of years ago, people moved into the Vietnam area from the north and from islands to the south. The Vietnamese people probably developed out of these two groups. Today, they make up almost 90 per cent of Vietnam's population. Chinese, Kampucheans, and Montagnards are the largest minority groups in Vietnam.

Most Vietnamese people have broad faces, high cheekbones, and straight black hair. On the average, the men stand a little over 5 feet (150 centimeters) tall and weigh about 120 pounds (54 kilograms). Most

Vietnam's Flag and Coat of Arms feature a star that stands for Communism. The rice and the cogwheel on the coat of arms represent the importance of agriculture and industry to Vietnam. The flag was adopted by North Vietnam in 1955.

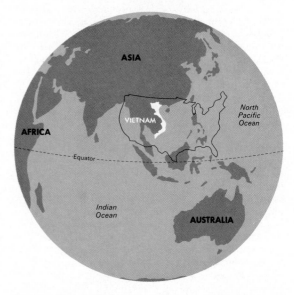

Vietnam lies in Southeast Asia. It has an area about 4 per cent as large as that of the United States, not including Alaska and Hawaii.

James Pickerell, Black Star

Vietnamese Children stand outside a village house on the Mekong Delta of southern Vietnam. Most Vietnamese—like these children—have broad faces, high cheekbones, and straight black hair.

Vietnamese women are slightly smaller than the men.

Most of the Vietnamese people live on the Mekong and Red river deltas and on the coastal plain. The majority of the Chinese live in cities. Most of the Cambodians are farmers in southwestern Vietnam. The Montagnards live in the mountains.

Population. Vietnam has about 61 million people. They include about 3,250,000 Montagnards, 600,000 Chinese, and 600,000 Kampucheans.

Ho Chi Minh City, with a population of about $3\frac{1}{2}$ million, is Vietnam's largest city. Hanoi, the next largest city, has a population of about $2\frac{1}{2}$ million. Haiphong, the third largest, has more than $1\frac{1}{4}$ million people. See DA NANG; HAIPHONG; HANOI; HO CHI MINH CITY; HUE.

Way of Life. The Vietnamese way of life changed little for hundreds of years before the arrival of French colonists in the late 1800's. But since then, the influence of the French and the Communists, and the years of war during the mid-1900's, have brought great changes.

Before the late 1800's, Vietnam was an agricultural society built on strong family ties. Almost all the people lived in villages and farmed the land. People owed loyalty to their families before all else, and held their families' interests above their own. The oldest male was head of the family, and his oldest son was the second most important family member. In many cases, related families lived together. These *extended families* included the parents, their unmarried children, and the oldest married son and his wife and children. Parents chose their children's marriage partners. Families honored their ancestors by performing special ceremonies.

France gained control of Vietnam in the late 1800's. The French brought industry to the country, and many Vietnamese left their farms to work in the new factories in the cities. A new class of wealthy landowners also developed under French rule. They controlled more of the farmland than had any previous group in Vietnam. But the events that most changed the traditional Vietnamese way of life began in the mid-1900's.

The Communists who came to power in Vietnam began transforming the society according to Communist principles. Party leaders extended their control to all walks of life. The Communists forced people to live for the Communist Party instead of their families, and they urged women to perform the same jobs as men. The new rulers discouraged religious worship and the ceremonial honoring of ancestors.

The Vietnam War brought other changes to Vietnamese life. It broke up families as fathers and sons left home to fight. Hundreds of thousands of Vietnamese died in the war. In the north, areas near some cities were heavily bombed, forcing many people to move to the countryside. But almost all the ground fighting took place in rural areas of southern Vietnam. It drove many families from their farm homes to the somewhat safer cities. In the cities of the south, many people learned Western customs from U.S. business people, government workers, and soldiers who came to Vietnam because of the war.

Clothing. The people of Vietnam wear mostly cotton clothing. But the styles differ in northern Vietnam and southern Vietnam.

In cities of the north, most men and women wear plain black trousers with tightly buttoned white or dark-colored jackets. Many people wear sandals made of worn-out automobile tires. In cities of the south, some people wear the same style of clothing. But many people who have lived there since before the Communist takeover wear Western style clothing. In northern rural areas, most women dress in loose-fitting shirts and skirts. Some men wear coatlike garments that hang to the knees. Most rural people go barefoot. Rural men and women in the south usually wear loose-fitting trousers and long-sleeved shirts. Most of the people go barefoot or wear shoes with wooden soles.

Housing in rural areas differs in northern and southern Vietnam because of differences in climate. In the north, which is cooler, many people build simple wood or bamboo houses with tiled roofs. In the warmer south, most families have homes with walls and roofs made of palm leaves or straw. Some of the homes in Vietnamese cities are constructed of brick or stone.

Food. Most Vietnamese eat chiefly fish, rice, and vegetables. Rice has long been the basic food in Vietnam. Rice shortages during the Vietnam War forced many people in Vietnam to substitute foods imported from other countries.

Language. Vietnamese is the official language of Vietnam. The people speak three major *dialects* (local forms) of Vietnamese—northern, central, and southern. But these dialects differ little from one another. Many members of the country's minority groups speak Vietnamese in addition to their own languages. There are about 20 Montagnard languages. Many Vietnamese people, especially those living in the cities, can also speak English, French, Chinese, or Russian.

Education. After the division of Vietnam in 1954, both North and South Vietnam made special efforts to expand their educational systems. But many schools

were destroyed in the Vietnam War, and the war effort required the money and materials needed to build new schools. In addition, Vietnam has a shortage of trained teachers. In spite of such problems, most of the Vietnamese people can read and write.

The Communist Party controls the operation of all schools in Vietnam. The educational system includes general elementary, middle, and high schools and vocational schools, which train skilled workers.

Vietnam has 8 universities and more than 20 colleges and specialized schools. The University of Ho Chi Minh City is the largest school of higher education.

Religion. The Communist leaders of Vietnam discourage all religious practices. Most of the Vietnamese people who practice a religion are Buddhists. Many of these people also worship the spirits of animals and plants and believe in the teachings of Confucianism and Taoism. About 10 per cent of the southern Vietnamese are Roman Catholics. Two small religious groups—the Hoa Hao and the Cao Dai—have developed since 1920 in the south. Hoa Hao is closely related to Buddhism. Cao Dai combines certain beliefs of Taoism and Buddhism with those of several other religions. See BUDDHISM.

The Arts. Poetry has long been the most popular form of literature in Vietnam, and poets have always been highly respected. Most people can recite at least a few verses of "Kim Van Kieu," a poem that tells of an unhappy love affair. This work of more than 3,000 lines was written by the poet Nguyen Du, who lived during the late 1700's and early 1800's. Today, political poems often appear in Vietnamese magazines and newspapers.

Novels began to gain wide popularity in Vietnam during the years of French rule. They remain popular, especially in the south. But the Communist leaders now carefully regulate the books the people may read.

Vietnamese painting shows the influence of both

ancient Chinese and modern French art. Examples of traditional Vietnamese architecture include mostly *pagodas* (temples), tombs, and old royal palaces.

Land and Climate

Vietnam occupies the east coast of the Indochinese Peninsula. The Vietnamese people sometimes describe their country as two rice baskets hanging from opposite ends of a farmer's carrying pole. In the north, the Red River Delta forms one "basket." The Mekong Delta in the south forms the other. A narrow stretch of land in central Vietnam forms the "carrying pole" that connects the deltas.

Vietnam extends about 1,000 miles (1,600 kilometers) from China south to the Gulf of Thailand. At its widest point—in the north—Vietnam extends almost 400 miles (640 kilometers) from Laos to the Gulf of Tonkin. At its narrowest point—in central Vietnam—it is only about 30 miles (48 kilometers) wide.

Vietnam has five main land regions: (1) the Northern Highlands, (2) the Red River Delta, (3) the Annamite Range, (4) the Coastal Lowlands, and (5) the Mekong Delta.

The Northern Highlands are a mountainous region in northwestern Vietnam. The highlands extend into China and Laos. Forests or jungles cover most of the mountains in this thinly populated region. The highest peak in Vietnam, Fan Si Pan, rises 10,312 feet (3,143 meters) above sea level in the highlands.

The Red River Delta extends from the Northern Highlands to the Gulf of Tonkin. It has been formed by the Red River, which flows from southeastern China through northern Vietnam into the gulf. Most of the delta lies 10 feet (3 meters) or less above sea level. The Red River floods much of this densely populated region almost every year. The Red River Delta is northern Vietnam's chief farming area.

The Annamite Range is a chain of mountains. It runs through western Vietnam from the Northern Highlands to about 50 miles (80 kilometers) north of Ho Chi Minh City. Forests cover most of the mountains. Like the highlands, these mountains are thinly populated. Most of the people in this region are Montagnards.

The Coastal Lowlands occupy east-central Vietnam. The lowlands slope from the mountains to the South China Sea and extend from the Red River Delta to the Mekong Delta. Rice is raised throughout most of the region. Many people who live along the coast are fishermen. The lowlands are thickly populated.

The Mekong Delta covers all of Vietnam south of the Annamite Range and the Coastal Lowlands. It has been formed by the Mekong River, which flows from China through Southeast Asia into the South China Sea. The Mekong Delta, like the Red River Delta, lies 10 feet (3 meters) or less above sea level, and much of it is flooded every year. Over half the people of southern Vietnam live on the delta. It is the chief agricultural area of Vietnam. See MEKONG RIVER.

Climate. Vietnam has a tropical climate. *Monsoons* (seasonal winds) affect the weather throughout the year. The summer monsoon brings heavy rains from the southwest. The winter monsoon brings lighter rainfall from the northeast. Most of Vietnam has two seasons—a wet,

Paul J. Quirico
The Market Places of Ho Chi Minh City, Vietnam's largest city, are crowded with peddlers. Many of them display their produce and other goods on the sidewalks in front of stores.

hot summer and a drier, cooler winter. Some areas of northernmost Vietnam have four seasons.

Northern Vietnam has damp weather from November to April. The average January temperature in Hanoi is about 63° F. (17° C). From May to October, the Red River Delta has high temperatures, heavy rains, and some typhoons, which sweep across the Gulf of Tonkin. The average June temperature in Hanoi is about 85° F. (29° C). Hanoi receives about 72 inches (183 centimeters) of rainfall a year.

In southern Vietnam, the humidity remains high throughout the year. Most rain falls in summer. The Ho Chi Minh City area receives about 80 inches (200 centimeters) of rain between April and November. From December through March, the weather is cooler with little rain. The temperature in Ho Chi Minh City ranges from about 79° F. (26° C) in December to 85° F. (29° C) in April.

Most of central Vietnam is drier and cooler than the northern and southern regions. Mountain areas throughout Vietnam generally have lower temperatures and more rainfall than the delta regions and the Coastal Lowlands.

FPG

The Coastal Lowlands extend along much of Vietnam's seacoast. A chain of mountains called the Annamite Range rises in the background beyond the western edge of the lowlands.

Economy

The economy of Vietnam depends on agriculture. About two-thirds of the people are farmers, and farm products—especially rice—are the chief products. All farms, factories, and other businesses in Vietnam are owned and controlled by the Communist government.

Northern Vietnam has most of the country's natural resources. *Anthracite* (hard coal) is the chief mineral resource, and the north has almost all the anthracite fields. Other mineral deposits in the north include gold, iron ore, lead, limestone, phosphates, tin, tungsten, and zinc. Among the mineral deposits in southern Vietnam are gold, limestone, phosphates, and soft coal. Forest products of Vietnam include bamboo, cinnamon, quinine, and timber.

Agriculture. About 15 per cent of the land in northern Vietnam and about 20 per cent of the land in southern Vietnam is used for farming. About another 20 per cent of the land in the south is suitable for growing crops but is not used. Rice is the chief farm product of Vietnam. Other products include coffee, coconuts, corn, cotton, sugar cane, sweet potatoes, tea, tobacco, rubber, and a tropical plant called *cassava*.

Vietnam Map Index

Sources: Census (1976) for provinces and three largest cities; official estimates (1970-1973) and census (1960) for other places.

VIETNAM

Distance scale

0 20 40 60 80 100 Miles

0 40 80 120 Kilometers

✪ National capital

• City or town

— Rail line

CHINA

Wen-shan

Ha Giang
Nan-ning
Yu
Yu-lin

Lao Cai
Bac Quang
Cao Bang

Ou Neua
FAN SI PAN
10,312 FT.
(3,143 M)
Bao Ha
Bac Kan
Na Sam
Ch'in-chou
Mao-ming

Muong
Ou Tay
Bac Quang
Tuyen Quang
Lang
Son
Dinh Lap
Tien Yen
Ho-p'u

Phong Saly
Yen Bai
TONKIN
Thai Nguyen
Bac Giang
Quang
Yen
Cam Pha
Pei-hai

Muong Hun
Xieng Hung
Dien Bien Phu
Phu Tho
Viet Tri
Son Tay
Vinh
Yen
Bac Ninh
Hai Duong
Hon Gay
KAO TAO

BURMA
Muong Sing
Son La
HANOI
Ha Dong
Haiphong
Vung Ha Long
Mandarin
Bay

Houei Sai
Samneua
Hoa Binh
Nam Dinh
XUY NONG
CHAO

Chiang Khong
Muong Sung
Ninh Binh
Thai Binh
DAO BACH
LONG VI
Hainan Strait
Hai-k'ou

Chiang Rai
Louangphrabang
JARRES
PLAIN
Muong
Lan
Thanh
Hoa
Gulf of Tonkin
HAINAN
(CHINA)

Chiang Kham
Muong Soui
HON ME
VIETNAM
+6,165 FT.
(1,879 M)

Nan
Xieng Khouang
PHOU BIA
9,252 FT.
(2,820 M)
PHU XAI LAI LENG
9,059 FT.
(2,761 M)
Ca
Vinh

Phrae
Nan
Borikhane
Nape
Ha Tinh
MUI RON

Paklay
Mekong
Nong Khai
Ba Don
South

Uttaradit
✪Vientiane
Dong Hoi
China

Loei
Udon Thani
HON GIO
CAP LAY
Sea

Phitsanulok
Sakon
Nakhon
Lattan
Muang
Khammouan
Quang Tri

Phichit
Keng Kabao
Sepone
Hue
DEO HAI
VAN

Savannakhet
Muong
Phalane
Da Nang

Nakhon
Sawan
Kalasin
Maha Sarakham
Hoi An
CU LAO CHAM

Chainat
Roi Et
Khemmarat
Khong
Sedone
Saravane
Tam Ky
CU LAO RE

Lop
Buri
Yasothon
THAILAND
PLATEAU
DES
BOLOVENS
LINH
8,524 FT.
(2,598 M)
Quang Ngai

Sara Buri
Mun
Ubon
Ratchathani
Bassac
Muong
May
Attopeu
Hoai Nhon

+KHIEO
4,167 FT.
(1,270 M)
Sisaket
Pakse
Kontum

Phra Nakhon
Si Ayutthaya
Prachin Buri
Khu Khan
Khong
Virachei
Pleiku
An Nhon

Thon
Buri
✪Bangkok
PHANOM DONG RAK MOUNTAINS
Samrong
Khong
San
Qui Nhon

Samut
Sakhon
Chachoengsao
Aranyaprathet
Melouprey
Stung
Treng
Srepok
Hau Bon
Song Cau

Chon Buri
Sisophon
ANGKOR
(RUINS)
Siem Reap
Tuy Hoa

GRAM
Sattahip
Rayong
Chanthaburi
Battambang
Tonle
Sap
Kompong
Kleang
Kompong
Thom
Chinit
Kratie
NUI VONG PHU
6,729 FT.
(2,051 M)
Buon Me Thuot
CAP VARELLA
To Bong
Ben Goi

KO CHANG
Trat
KAMPUCHEA
Pursat
Kompong
Chhnang
Kompong
Cham
Gia Nghia
Nha Trang

KO KUT
Kas Kong
Kompong
Speu
✪Phnom Penh
Prey Veng
Loc Ninh
Phu Giao
Bao Loc
Da Lat
Tung Nghia
Cam Ranh
Cam Ranh
Bay

Gulf
KONG
Takeo
Svay
Rieng
Tay Ninh
Ben Cat
An Loc
Phuoc
Binh
Di Linh
Phan Rang

of
Samit
RONG
Kampot
Kep
Moc Hoa
Phu Cuong
Bien Hoa
Bao Loc
Phan Thiet

Ream
Kompong Som
Chau Phu
PLAIN
OF
REEDS
Tan An
Ho Chi Minh City
Xuan Loc
Ham Tan
South

Thailand
DAO PHU
QUOC
Ha Tien
Long Xuyen
Cao Lanh
My Tho
Truc Giang
Phuoc Le
Vung Tau
MUI VUNG
TAU
GRANDE
CATWICK
CU LAO HON
China

Duong Dong
WAY
Can Tho
Vinh Long
Phu Vinh
POULO SAPATE
Sea

Rach Gia
Vi Thanh
Khanh Hung
Mouths of the Mekong

KO PHANGHAN
Khanh An
Bac Lieu

KO SAMUI
NAM DU
Quan Long
Con Son
CON SON

THO CHAU
LES DEUX FRÈRES

MUI BAI BUNG
HON KHOAI
Longitude East of Greenwich

292c

CM TERRAIN VIETNAM
COPYRIGHT BY
RAND MCNALLY & COMPANY
MADE IN U.S.A.

VIETNAM

Manufacturing. Vietnam lacks the natural resources needed for large-scale industry. The country has a small iron and steel industry. The Vietnamese use the iron and steel to manufacture farm tools, bicycles, and simple machinery. Vietnam also has cement, food-processing, paper, and textile industries.

Foreign Trade. Vietnam imports much more than it exports. Its imports include large amounts of food, machinery, military supplies, petroleum, and vehicles. Rubber is the only major export. Russia is Vietnam's chief trading partner. Russia also gives Vietnam much aid.

Transportation and Communication. Vietnam has an extensive transportation system. The system includes about 20,000 miles (32,000 kilometers) of roads and 2,000 miles (3,200 kilometers) of railroad tracks. During the Vietnam War, the system was heavily damaged. Repairs of the damaged roads and railroad tracks began after the war. The Red River and its branches, and the Mekong and its branches, are important waterways in Vietnam.

The bicycle ranks as the chief means of private transportation in northern Vietnam. The bicycle is also important in the south, but motor scooters are also widely used there.

Many newspapers are published in Vietnam. Before the 1960's, few Vietnamese owned a radio or a TV set. In the 1960's and 1970's, ownership of radios—and to a lesser extent television sets—became fairly widespread in southern Vietnam. In northern Vietnam, relatively few people own either a radio or TV set. Most people listen to radio programs over public loudspeakers. Most of the TV sets in Vietnam are owned by collective farms, workers' organizations, or similar groups.

Vietnam's Communist Party has censored all means of communication since it came to power. It does so in order to promote loyalty to the party.

History

Early Years. In ancient times, the Vietnamese people lived in what is now northern Vietnam. About 200 B.C., a Chinese general named Chao T'o united the area and parts of southeastern China into an independent kingdom called *Nam Viet*. It extended almost as far south as the present city of Hue. In 111 B.C., China conquered Nam Viet and renamed it *Chiao Chih*. In A.D. 679, the Chinese changed the name of Chiao Chih to *Annam*.

By the end of the A.D. 100's, two kingdoms—Funan and Champa—had developed in what is now southern Vietnam. Funan ruled the Mekong Delta and what is now southern Kampuchea. Champa controlled the area between Chiao Chih (Annam) and Funan in central Vietnam. During the 500's and 600's, Khmer people living west of Champa conquered Funan. They built a mighty empire during the next few hundred years.

Independence. In 939, the Chinese left Annam, and the Vietnamese established an independent state. It remained independent for more than 900 years, except for a 20-year period of Chinese control in the early 1400's. During those 900 years, the Vietnamese gradually built a small empire.

In 1009, the Ly family came to power in Annam. The family ruled the country for more than 200 years.

The Ly rulers built a strong army that repeatedly defeated attacking forces from Champa and from the Khmer empire. In 1054, the Vietnamese emperor changed the name of Annam to *Dai Viet*. But for hundreds of years, both names were used for the country.

The Tran family seized power from the Ly rulers in 1225 and governed the country until 1400. During that period, Dai Viet defeated several attacking Mongol armies and fought almost continuously with Champa. China regained control of Dai Viet in 1407. The Vietnamese drove out the Chinese in 1427, and the Le family, which had led the fight against China, came to power. They held the throne until 1787.

In 1471, Le Thanh Ton, the strongest of the Le rulers, conquered Champa. But weak rulers followed Le Thanh Ton, and civil war broke out in Dai Viet during the early 1500's. The war began as two families—the Trinh in the north and the Nguyen in the south—fought for control of the country. Both sides claimed to support the Le rulers. The families finally stopped fighting in 1673, and Dai Viet had peace for about 100 years. During that time, the Nguyen family expanded their territory by seizing parts of the Khmer empire.

In the early 1770's, three brothers in southern Dai Viet led a revolt against the Nguyen family. The brothers called themselves *Tay Son* after the name of their home village. The Tay Son conquered southern Dai Viet and then marched against the Trinh family in the north. In 1787, the brothers conquered the north and removed the Le rulers.

The youngest Tay Son brother became ruler of northern and central Dai Viet. But Nguyen Anh, a member of the defeated Nguyen family, gained control of southern Dai Viet. In 1802, he defeated the Tay Son ruler and declared himself Emperor Gia Long of all Dai Viet, which he renamed *Vietnam*. Members of the Nguyen family remained the emperors of Vietnam until the end of World War II in 1945. But they had little power after the mid-1800's.

French Rule. Roman Catholic missionaries from France began to arrive in Dai Viet in the 1600's. They converted thousands of Vietnamese to Catholicism, but the country's rulers became suspicious of the missionaries. From the 1600's through the early 1800's, Vietnamese rulers continually persecuted the missionaries.

In 1858, French forces began to attack parts of southern Vietnam. France acted partly to stop the persecution of the missionaries and partly because it wanted to become a colonial power in Vietnam. The French seized Saigon (now called Ho Chi Minh City) in 1861 and the rest of southern Vietnam by 1867. They took control of northern Vietnam by 1883. That year, the French forced the Nguyen ruler to sign a treaty that gave France control of all Vietnam. France divided the country into three areas—*Cochin China* (southern Vietnam), *Annam* (central Vietnam), and *Tonkin* (northern Vietnam). France governed the areas as separate parts of French Indochina, which also included Kampuchea and Laos.

Japanese Control. Germany defeated France early in World War II, in June 1940. Japan, one of Germany's allies, soon took control of French Indochina. The Japanese allowed French officials to remain in Vietnam, but they had to govern according to Japan's wishes. Then, in March 1945, the Japanese arrested

all French officials and forced Emperor Bao Dai to announce the independence of Annam and Tonkin from France. Vietnam remained under Japanese control until Japan's defeat in August 1945.

The Indochina War. Ho Chi Minh, a Vietnamese Communist, arrived in Hanoi from China a few days after Japan's defeat. He headed the Revolutionary League for the Independence of Vietnam, commonly called the *Vietminh*. The Vietminh quickly gained control over most of northern Vietnam. They forced Bao Dai to step down as ruler in favor of Ho Chi Minh, who announced formation of the Democratic Republic of Vietnam (DRV) on September 2.

In March 1946, France officially recognized the DRV as the government of Annam and Tonkin. In June, the French approved formation of the Republic of Cochin China by non-Communist Vietnamese leaders. Relations between France and the Vietminh gradually worsened. On Dec. 19, 1946, the Vietminh attacked French forces throughout Vietnam, and the Indochina War began. Starting in 1949, France and other Western powers supported Bao Dai as leader of the State of Vietnam. Its capital was Saigon. Communist nations supported the government of Ho Chi Minh. Each government claimed to represent all Vietnam. In 1953, the Communists began to take control of the farmland in northern Vietnam. They killed or imprisoned landowners they considered enemies of the Communist effort and assigned production quotas to all other farmers.

The Division of Vietnam. In April 1954, representatives of the DRV, the State of Vietnam, Kampuchea, Laos, China, France, Great Britain, Russia, and the United States met in Geneva, Switzerland, to arrange a peace settlement for Vietnam. In May, the Indochina War ended with the defeat of French forces at Dien Bien Phu. The representatives at the Geneva Conference then decided to divide Vietnam temporarily into two parts, North Vietnam and South Vietnam. The confer-

ence also called for elections in 1956 to unite Vietnam under one government. But South Vietnam felt that fair elections could not be held. Its leaders feared the Communists would win a nationwide election because a majority of the Vietnamese lived under Communist control in North Vietnam. See GENEVA ACCORDS.

Ho Chi Minh's government officially took control of North Vietnam. Bao Dai headed South Vietnam. In 1955, the people of South Vietnam elected Ngo Dinh Diem president, and he announced formation of the Republic of Vietnam. Diem and Ho Chi Minh could not agree on how to hold the elections planned for 1956, and Vietnam remained divided.

The Vietnam War Begins. In 1957, Communist guerrillas called *Viet Cong* began to attack villages in South Vietnam. The Viet Cong were supported by North Vietnam and consisted of persons from both the South

Important Dates in Vietnam

111 B.C. The Chinese conquered what is now northern Vietnam.

A.D. 939 China ended its rule over the Vietnamese, who then set up an independent state.

1802 Nguyen Anh united the country and called it *Vietnam.*

1858-1883 France took control of Vietnam.

1940-1945 Japan controlled Vietnam during World War II.

1946 War began between France and the Vietminh.

1954 The Vietminh defeated the French. The Geneva Conference divided Vietnam into two nations.

1957 Communist terrorists began to attack villages in South Vietnam. The fighting developed into the Vietnam War.

1973 U.S. participation in the Vietnam War ended.

1975 The Vietnam War ended on April 30, when South Vietnam surrendered to the Communists.

1976 The Communists unified North and South Vietnam into the nation of Vietnam.

The Indochina Peninsula about A.D. 300

This map shows the early states of Indochina. Chiao Chih was an independent kingdom called *Nam Viet* before it was conquered by China in 111 B.C. Present-day Vietnam is shown in yellow.

WORLD BOOK map

The Indochina Peninsula in 1900

This map shows French Indochina, which included Kampuchea, Laos, and Vietnam. France divided Vietnam into Tonkin, Annam, and Cochin China. Present-day Vietnam is shown in yellow.

WORLD BOOK map

and the North. The fighting gradually developed into a major war that endangered world peace. Communist countries supported North Vietnam, and non-Communist nations supported South Vietnam.

The United States began to send military advisers to South Vietnam in the 1950's. From 1965 to the early 1970's, U.S. combat troops were sent to Vietnam. The U.S. Air Force carried out bombing of the North.

South Vietnam and the War. President Diem signed a new constitution into law in 1956. It declared that South Vietnam was a republic. But Diem and his family actually controlled the government.

Viet Cong attacks in South Vietnam increased during the late 1950's and early 1960's. Diem turned more and more to undemocratic policies to combat the Communists, and South Vietnamese political leaders began to criticize the Diem government. In 1962, Diem declared a national emergency. He established a curfew, the censorship of news, and other restrictions.

On Nov. 1, 1963, a group of army generals led by Duong Van Minh seized the South Vietnamese government. Diem was murdered. A series of military groups held power for brief periods until June 1965. A group led by Nguyen Cao Ky, an air force general, then took control. In 1967, Nguyen Van Thieu, an army general, was elected president. Meanwhile, the Vietnam War grew into a major conflict and battles raged in South Vietnam.

In June 1972, the National Assembly gave Thieu power to rule by *decree* (presidential order) for six months. In August, Thieu ruled that almost all hamlet and village officials would no longer be elected but would be appointed by the national government. This decree ended most local elections in South Vietnam.

North Vietnam and the War. After the division of Vietnam, the Communists completed a take-over of all farms, factories, and other businesses in the North. During the 1960's and early 1970's, North Vietnam concentrated more and more of its agricultural and industrial efforts in support of the war.

Ho Chi Minh served as North Vietnam's president until he died in 1969. Control of the government then passed to the Politburo of the Communist Party.

Communist Victory and Unification. After 1965, South Vietnam depended more and more on American support in its war against the Communists. Beginning in the late 1960's, American involvement in Vietnam became increasingly unpopular in the United States. In January 1973, South Vietnam, the United States, and the Communists signed a cease-fire agreement. Later in the year, the United States removed its last ground troops from Vietnam. But the Communists soon launched another offensive against South Vietnam. On April 30, 1975, Saigon fell to the Communists, and the Communists gained control of South Vietnam. For more details on the conflict, see VIETNAM WAR.

In 1976, the Communists unified North and South Vietnam into the single nation of Vietnam. Communist officials from the North took control of the government of the unified country. They changed the name of Saigon to Ho Chi Minh City.

Recent Developments. In the late 1970's, the Communist government took control of all farms, factories, and other businesses in the South. It also began transferring large numbers of people from cities and towns in the South and North to farm areas in an attempt to increase farm production.

Hundreds of thousands of people have fled Vietnam since the Communist take-over. These refugees include people of both Vietnamese and Chinese ancestry. Many of them, including most of the Chinese refugees, had worked in shops or factories or had owned businesses. They fled after they were ordered to become farmers.

Many refugees left Vietnam in small boats and made dangerous journeys into the open sea. These refugees became known as *boat people*. Many of them drowned at sea, and others sailed to nearby countries. Many of the boat people who reached other countries were admitted on a temporary basis and were housed in crowded refugee camps. Others were not allowed into the countries and were forced to live on their boats. The problems faced by the boat people aroused worldwide concern. Countries in many parts of the world have accepted some of the people as permanent immigrants.

In late 1977, disputes led to fighting between Vietnam and Kampuchea, its neighbor to the west. Kampuchea was ruled by Communists called the Khmer Rouge. Kampuchean Communists who opposed the Khmer Rouge fought on the side of the Vietnamese. In 1979, the Vietnamese and their Kampuchean allies won control of most of Kampuchea. The Kampucheans set up a new government, and many Vietnamese troops remained in Kampuchea. Khmer Rouge forces have continued to fight the Vietnamese and their allies in some parts of Kampuchea.

In 1979, fighting broke out between Vietnam and China, its Communist neighbor to the north. Chinese troops invaded Vietnam in February. The troops left the country in March, and the fighting between the two nations ended. However, in the 1980's, small battles between the two nations flared up from time to time at the border.   DENNIS J. DUNCANSON

Related Articles in WORLD BOOK include:

Outline

I. Government
    A. The Communist Party   D. Courts
    B. National Government   E. Armed Forces
    C. Local Government

II. People
    A. Population   D. Housing   G. Education
    B. Way of Life   E. Food   H. Religion
    C. Clothing   F. Language   I. The Arts

III. Land and Climate
    A. The Northern Highlands   D. The Coastal Lowlands
    B. The Red River Delta   E. The Mekong Delta
    C. The Annamite Cordillera   F. Climate

IV. Economy
    A. Agriculture   D. Transportation
    B. Manufacturing   and Communication
    C. Foreign Trade

V. History

Questions

How did the Vietnam War begin?

What is the chief religion of Vietnam?

What nation controlled Vietnam during World War II?

How has the Vietnamese way of life changed since the late 1800's?

In what ways does the Communist Party control the government of Vietnam?

What is the chief crop of Vietnam?

What are the largest minority groups in Vietnam?

When was Vietnam controlled by China? When was it controlled by France?

How do monsoons affect the weather in Vietnam?

Additional Resources

DUIKER, WILLIAM J. *Vietnam Since the Fall of Saigon.* Ohio Univ. Press, 1981.

LAMB, HELEN B. *Vietnam's Will to Live: Resistance to Foreign Aggression from Early Times Through the Nineteenth Century.* Monthly Review, 1972.

SULLY, FRANÇOIS. *We the Vietnamese: Voices from Vietnam.* Praeger, 1971.

THUY, VUONG. *Getting to Know the Vietnamese and Their Culture.* Ungar, 1976.

VIETNAM WAR was the longest war in which the United States took part. It began in 1957 and ended in 1975. Vietnam, a small country in Southeast Asia, was divided into Communist-ruled North Vietnam and non-Communist South Vietnam. North Vietnam and Communist-trained South Vietnamese rebels fought to take over South Vietnam. The United States and the South Vietnamese army tried to stop the take-over, but failed.

The Vietnam War was actually the second phase of fighting in Vietnam. During the first phase, which began in 1946, the Vietnamese fought France for control of Vietnam. At that time, Vietnam was part of the colony of French Indochina. The United States sent France about $2\frac{1}{2}$ billion in military equipment, but the Vietnamese defeated the French in 1954. Then Vietnam was divided into North and South Vietnam.

U.S. aid to France and later to non-Communist South Vietnam was based on a policy of President Harry S. Truman. He had declared that the United States must help any nation threatened by Communists. Truman's policy was adopted by the next three Presidents —Dwight D. Eisenhower, John F. Kennedy, and Lyndon B. Johnson. They feared that if one Southeast Asian nation fell to the Communists, the others would

Important Dates in the Vietnam War

1957 The Viet Cong began to rebel against the South Vietnamese government headed by President Ngo Dinh Diem.

1963 (Nov. 1) South Vietnamese generals overthrew the Diem government, and Diem was killed the next day.

1964 (Aug. 7) Congress passed the Tonkin Gulf Resolution, which gave the President power to take "all necessary measures" and "to prevent further aggression."

1965 (March 6) President Lyndon B. Johnson sent U.S. Marines to Da Nang, South Vietnam. The Marines were the first U.S. ground troops in the war.

1968 (Jan. 30) North Vietnam and the Viet Cong launched a major campaign against South Vietnamese cities.

1969 (June 8) President Richard M. Nixon announced that U.S. troops would begin to withdraw from Vietnam.

1973 (Jan. 27) The United States, North and South Vietnam, and the Viet Cong signed a cease-fire agreement.

1973 (March 29) The last U.S. ground troops left Vietnam.

1975 (April 30) South Vietnam surrendered.

also fall, one after the other, "like a row of dominoes."

The Communists called the Vietnam War *a war of national liberation.* They saw it as an extension of the struggle with France and as another attempt by a foreign power to rule Vietnam. North Vietnam wanted to end U.S. support of South Vietnam and to unite the north and south into the single nation of Vietnam. China and the Soviet Union, the two largest Communist nations, gave the Vietnamese Communists war materials but not troops.

The Vietnam War had several periods. From 1957 to 1965, it was mainly a struggle between the South Vietnamese army and Communist-trained South Vietnamese rebels known as the Viet Cong. From 1965 to 1969, North Vietnam and the United States did much of the fighting. Australia, New Zealand, the Philippines, South Korea, and Thailand also helped South Vietnam. By 1969, the United States had about 540,000 troops in South Vietnam. But the war seemed endless, and the United States slowly began to withdraw its forces in 1969.

In January 1973, a cease-fire was arranged. The last

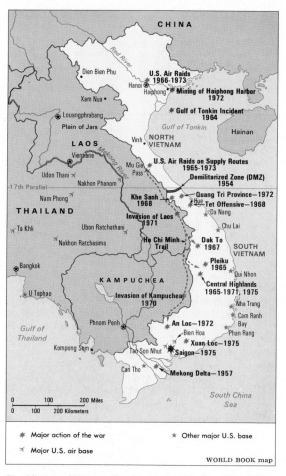

The Vietnam War was fought mainly in North and South Vietnam from 1957 to 1975. Troops also battled in Laos and Kampuchea, and U.S. pilots flew missions from bases in Thailand.

Non-Communist Forces battled in the air and on the ground. American B-52 bombers made thousands of raids on enemy bases in North and South Vietnam, and armed helicopters carried U.S., South Vietnamese, and allied troops into battle. Millions of civilians became refugees.

American ground troops left Vietnam two months later. The fighting began again soon afterward, but U.S. troops did not return to Vietnam. The war ended when South Vietnam surrendered on April 30, 1975.

The Vietnam War was enormously destructive. About 58,000 Americans died in the war. South Vietnamese deaths exceeded a million, and North Vietnam lost between 500,000 and 1 million troops. The war left much of Vietnam in ruin.

Just before the war ended, North Vietnam helped rebels overthrow the government in nearby Kampuchea (widely known in Western nations as Cambodia). After the war, North Vietnam united Vietnam and helped set up a new government in nearby Laos. The U.S. role in the war became one of the most debated issues in the nation's history. Many Americans felt U.S. involvement was necessary and noble. But many others called it cruel, unnecessary, and wrong. Today, many Americans still disagree on the goals, conduct, and lessons of U.S. participation in the Vietnam War.

Background to the War

The Indochina War. Vietnam, Laos, and Kampuchea made up the French colony of Indochina from the late 1800's to the 1940's (see INDOCHINA). Japan occupied Indochina from 1941 to 1945, during World War II. France tried to reestablish control after Japan's defeat in 1945. But Ho Chi Minh, a Vietnamese patriot

and Communist, organized a revolt in northern Vietnam. Ho's *Vietminh* (Revolutionary League for the Independence of Vietnam) declared Vietnam independent. See HO CHI MINH.

A war between France and the Vietminh began in 1946. The Communist take-over of China in 1949 shocked the United States and helped persuade President Harry S. Truman to aid France in Indochina. Truman feared a Vietminh victory would lead to a Communist take-over of Southeast Asia. In 1950, the United States sent troops to South Korea to combat an invasion of that country by Communist North Korea. Later that year, the United States began to give France large amounts of war materials.

In May 1954, the Vietminh captured the great French fortress at Dien Bien Phu in northwestern Vietnam. The war ended in July 1954, when the two sides signed peace agreements at Geneva, Switzerland. The *Geneva Accords* provided that Vietnam be temporarily divided into North and South Vietnam at the 17th parallel and called for national elections in 1956 to reunify the country. See GENEVA ACCORDS.

The Divided Country. Ho Chi Minh established a Communist government in North Vietnam. The territory in the south became the Republic of Vietnam, though it was commonly called South Vietnam. Ngo Dinh Diem, who vigorously opposed Communist control, became president of South Vietnam in 1955. With

the approval of the United States, he refused to go along with the proposed nationwide election. He argued that the Communists would not permit fair elections in North Vietnam. President Dwight D. Eisenhower sent several hundred U.S. civilian and military advisers to assist the Diem government.

Early Stages of the War

The Viet Cong Rebellion. Diem did little to ease the hard life of the peasants in the rural areas of South Vietnam. He became increasingly unpopular in 1956, when he ended local elections and appointed his own village officials. In 1957, members of the Vietminh who had stayed in the south rebelled against Diem's rule. Diem called the rebels the *Viet Cong,* meaning *Vietnamese Communists.* The rebels were under Communist control, but many of them were not Communist Party members.

North Vietnam supported the revolt from its early stages. In 1959, it started to develop a supply route to South Vietnam through Laos and Kampuchea. This system of roads and trails became known as the Ho Chi Minh Trail. Also in 1959, two U.S. military advisers were killed during a battle. They were the first American casualties of the war.

By 1960, discontent with the Diem government was widespread, and the Viet Cong had about 10,000 troops. The rebels soon began to attack South Vietnamese army bases. In 1961, the Viet Cong threatened to overthrow Diem's government. Then President John F. Kennedy greatly expanded economic and military aid to South Vietnam. From 1961 to 1963, he increased the number of U.S. military advisers in Vietnam from about 900 to over 16,000.

The Buddhist Crisis. In May 1963, widespread unrest broke out among Buddhists in South Vietnam's major cities. The Buddhists, who formed a majority of the country's population, complained that the government restricted their religious practices. Buddhist leaders accused Diem, a Roman Catholic, of religious discrimination. A growing number of Buddhist priests staged protests. The government responded with mass arrests, and Diem's brother Ngo Dinh Nhu ordered raids against Buddhist temples.

The Buddhist protests aroused great concern in the United States. Kennedy urged Diem to improve his dealings with the Buddhists, but Diem ignored the advice. Kennedy then supported a group of South Vietnamese generals who opposed Diem's policies. On Nov. 1, 1963, the generals overthrew the Diem government. Against Kennedy's wishes, Diem and Nhu were murdered. See NGO DINH DIEM.

The fall of the Diem government set off a period of political disorder in South Vietnam. New governments rapidly succeeded one another. During this period, North Vietnam stepped up its supply of war materials and began to send units of its own army into the south. By late 1964, the Viet Cong controlled up to 75 per cent of South Vietnam's population.

The Gulf of Tonkin Incident. In 1964, President Lyndon B. Johnson approved secret South Vietnamese naval raids against North Vietnam. On Aug. 4, 1964, he announced that the U.S. destroyers *Maddox* and *C. Turner Joy* had been attacked in the Gulf of Tonkin, off the coast of North Vietnam.

Some Americans doubted that an attack had occurred, and the attack has never been confirmed. Nevertheless, Johnson ordered immediate air strikes against North Vietnam. He also asked Congress for powers to take "all necessary measures to repel any armed attack against the forces of the United States and to prevent further aggression." On August 7, Congress approved these powers in the Tonkin Gulf Resolution. The United States did not declare war on North Vietnam. But Johnson used the resolution as the legal basis for increased U.S. involvement. In March 1965, he sent a group of U.S. Marines to South Vietnam, the first American ground combat forces to enter the war.

The Fighting Intensifies

The Opposing Forces. The war soon became an international conflict. United States forces rose from about 60,000 in mid-1965 to a peak of over 543,000 in 1969. They joined about 800,000 South Vietnamese troops and a total of about 69,000 men from Australia, New Zealand, the Philippines, South Korea, and Thailand. North Vietnam and the Viet Cong had over 300,000 troops, but the exact number is unknown.

The two sides developed strategies to take advantage of their strengths. The United States had the finest of modern weapons and a highly professional military force. Its field commanders were General William C. Westmoreland from 1964 to 1968 and, afterward, Generals Creighton Abrams and Frederick Weyand. The United States did not try to conquer North Vietnam. Instead, American leaders hoped superior U.S. firepower would force the enemy to stop fighting. The United States relied mainly on the bombing of North Vietnam and "search and destroy" ground missions in South Vietnam to achieve its aim.

The United States used giant B-52 bombers as well as smaller planes for the main air strikes against the Communists. American armed helicopters also had a key role in the war. Pilots used them to seek out Viet Cong troops in the jungles and mountains. Helicopters also carried the wounded to hospitals and brought supplies to troops in the field.

In contrast, Viet Cong and North Vietnamese leaders adopted a defensive strategy. Directed by North Vietnam Defense Minister Vo Nguyen Giap, the lightly armed and equipped Communist forces relied on surprise and mobility. They avoided major battles in the open, where heavy U.S. firepower could be decisive. The Viet Cong and North Vietnamese preferred guerrilla tactics, including ambushes and hand-laid bombs (see GUERRILLA WARFARE). Their advantages included a large supply of soldiers, knowledge of the terrain, and large amounts of war materials from Russia and China.

Course of the War. Between 1965 and 1967, the two sides fought to a highly destructive draw. The U.S. bombing of North Vietnam caused tremendous damage, but it did not affect the enemy's willingness or ability to continue fighting. North Vietnam concealed its most vital resources, and the Soviet Union and China helped make up the losses.

American victories in ground battles in South Vietnam also failed to sharply reduce the number of enemy troops there. The U.S. Army and Marines usually won whenever they fought the enemy. But North Vietnam

Wide World

Antiwar Demonstrations took place throughout the United States in the late 1960's and early 1970's. About 50,000 protesters marched in Washington, D.C., in October 1967, *above*.

was able to replace its losses with new troops, and its forces often avoided defeat by retreating into Laos and Kampuchea.

Reactions in the United States. As the war dragged on, it divided many Americans into so-called *hawks* and *doves*. The hawks supported the nation's fight against Communism. But they disliked Johnson's policy of slow, gradual troop increases and urged a decisive defeat of North Vietnam. The doves opposed U.S. involvement and held mass protests. Many doves believed that U.S. security was not at risk. Others charged that the nation was supporting corrupt, undemocratic, and unpopular governments in South Vietnam.

The mounting costs of the war, however, probably did more to arouse public uneasiness than the antiwar movement did. By late 1967, increased casualties and Johnson's request for new taxes helped produce a sharp drop in public support for the war.

The Tet Offensive. North Vietnam and the Viet Cong opened a new phase of the war on Jan. 30, 1968, when they attacked major cities of South Vietnam. The fighting was especially savage in Saigon, South Vietnam's capital, and in Hue. This campaign began at the start of Tet, the Vietnamese New Year celebration.

As a military strategy, the plan failed. The United States and South Vietnam quickly recovered their early losses, and the enemy suffered an enormous number of casualties. But the Tet attacks stunned the American people. The United States had about 500,000 troops in South Vietnam, and U.S. leaders had reported strong gains only a short time before. Tet made the war seem endless. Many Americans wondered whether blocking Communist expansion in South Vietnam was worth the cost in lives and money.

The Tet offensive forced basic changes in Johnson's policies. The President cut back the bombing of North Vietnam and rejected Westmoreland's request for 206,000 additional troops. Johnson also called for peace negotiations and declared that he would not seek reelection in 1968. Peace talks opened in Paris in May.

Vietnamization

The U.S. Withdrawal Begins. The peace talks failed to produce agreement, and more and more Americans became impatient for the war to end. President Richard

M. Nixon felt he had to reduce U.S. involvement in the conflict. On June 8, 1969, he announced a new policy known as Vietnamization. This policy called for stepped-up training programs for South Vietnamese forces and the gradual withdrawal of U.S. troops from South Vietnam. The U.S. troop withdrawal began in July 1969.

The Invasion of Kampuchea. In April 1970, Nixon ordered U.S. and South Vietnamese troops to clear out military supply centers that North Vietnam had set up in Kampuchea. Large stocks of weapons were captured, and the invasion may have delayed a major enemy attack. But many Americans felt the campaign widened the war. The invasion aroused a storm of protest in the United States, especially on college campuses.

The nation was shocked on May 4, 1970, when National Guard units fired into a group of demonstrators at Kent State University in Ohio. The shots killed four students and wounded nine others. Moves began in Congress to force the removal of the troops from Kampuchea by June 30. Nixon ended the campaign in late June.

Renewed Protest. Opposition to the war in the United States grew rapidly during Nixon's presidency. Some of the opposition may have developed as a result of television coverage of the war, which regularly brought scenes of terrified refugees and other war horrors into millions of homes.

In March 1971, the conviction of Lieutenant William L. Calley, Jr., for war crimes raised some of the main moral issues of the conflict. Calley's Army unit had massacred at least 100 and perhaps as many as 200 civilians in 1968 in the hamlet of My Lai in South Vietnam. Calley was found guilty of murder in a trial and was sentenced to a prison term of 10 years. Some war critics used the trial to call attention to the large numbers of civilians killed by U.S. bombing and ground operations in South Vietnam. Others pointed to the vast stretches of South Vietnam's countryside that had been destroyed by the bombing and by the spraying of weedkillers and other chemicals. United States forces used such weedkillers as Agent Orange to reveal Communist hiding places in the jungle and to destroy enemy food crops (see AGENT ORANGE).

Public distrust of the U.S. government deepened in June 1971, when newspapers published a secret government study of the war called *The Pentagon Papers*. This study raised questions about decisions and secret actions of government leaders regarding the war.

Invasion of the South. In March 1972, North Vietnam began a major invasion of South Vietnam. Nixon responded by renewing the bombing of North Vietnam. He also ordered the placing of explosives in the harbor of Haiphong, North Vietnam's major port for importing military supplies. These moves helped stop the invasion, which had nearly reached Saigon by August 1972.

The high cost paid by both sides during the 1972 fighting led to peace negotiations. The talks were conducted by Henry A. Kissinger, Nixon's chief foreign policy adviser, and Le Duc Tho of North Vietnam. On Jan. 27, 1973, a cease-fire agreement was signed in Paris by the United States, South Vietnam, North Vietnam, and the Viet Cong. The pact provided for the withdrawal of all U.S. and allied forces from Vietnam and for the return of all prisoners—both within 60 days. It permitted North Vietnam to leave 150,000 troops in the south and

Yves-Guy Berges, Gamma/Liaison

The War Ended on April 30, 1975, when South Vietnam surrendered in Saigon (now Ho Chi Minh City), *above.* New governments were also established in Kampuchea and Laos in 1975.

called for internationally supervised elections to decide the political future of South Vietnam.

The End of the War. On March 29, 1973, the last U.S. ground forces left Vietnam. But the peace talks soon broke down, and the war resumed. Congress opposed further U.S. involvement, and so no American troops returned to the war. In mid-1973, Congress began to sharply reduce military aid to South Vietnam.

The decreasing U.S. support encouraged North Vietnam. In late 1974, North Vietnamese and Viet Cong troops attacked Phuoc Long, northeast of Saigon, and won an easy victory. In March 1975, they forced South Vietnamese troops to retreat from a region known as the Central Highlands. Thousands of civilians fled with the soldiers and died in the gunfire or from starvation. This retreat became known as the *Convoy of Tears.*

Early in April, President Gerald R. Ford, Nixon's successor, asked Congress for $722 million in military aid for South Vietnam. But Congress provided only $300 million in emergency aid, mainly to evacuate Americans from Saigon. The war ended when South Vietnam surrendered to North Vietnam in Saigon on April 30, 1975. Saigon was then renamed Ho Chi Minh City.

Results of the War

Casualties and Destruction. About 58,000 American men and women died in the war, and approximately 365,000 were wounded. South Vietnamese deaths topped 1 million. North Vietnamese losses ranged between 500,000 and 1 million. Countless numbers of civilians in North and South Vietnam also were killed.

The United States spent over $150 billion on the war. The U.S. bombing in the conflict was about four times greater than the combined U.S.-British bombing of Germany in World War II. The American air strikes destroyed much of North Vietnam's industrial and transportation systems. But South Vietnam, where most of the fighting took place, suffered the most damage. The war made refugees of up to 10 million South Vietnamese, or about half the country's population. The bombing and the use of chemicals to clear forests scarred the landscape and may have permanently damaged much of South Vietnam's cropland and plant and animal life.

Other Effects in Southeast Asia. North Vietnam helped establish Communist governments in Laos and Kampuchea in 1975. In 1976, it officially united North and South Vietnam into the single nation of Vietnam. North Vietnam also ruthlessly forced its culture and political system on the south. To lessen resistance, the North Vietnamese imprisoned hundreds of thousands of South Vietnamese. Nearly a million South Vietnamese have fled the country since 1975.

Vietnam has had little success in rebuilding its shattered economy. Today, the nation still depends heavily on foreign aid from the Soviet Union.

Effects in the United States. The Vietnam War had far-reaching effects in the United States. It was the first foreign war in which U.S. combat forces failed to achieve their goals. This hurt the pride of many Americans and left bitter and painful memories.

The Americans most immediately affected included the approximately 2,700,000 men and women who fought in the war, and their families. Most veterans adjusted smoothly to civilian life. But the war left others with deep psychological problems. These veterans suffered from a high rate of divorce, drug abuse, suicide, involvement in violent crimes, and joblessness.

After World Wars I and II, the country welcomed the returning veterans as heroes. But many of the Americans who opposed the U.S. role in Vietnam criticized or ignored the returning veterans. These reactions shocked the veterans. Many of them felt that the nation neither recognized nor appreciated their sacrifices.

Both Congress and the public became more willing to challenge the President on U.S. military and foreign policy after the Vietnam War. The war also became a new standard of comparison in situations that might involve U.S. troops abroad.

Today, Americans still disagree on the main issues and lessons of the war. Some believe U.S. participation was necessary and just. Many of these people say the war was lost because the United States did not use its full military power and because opposition at home weakened the war effort. But other Americans believe U.S. involvement was immoral and unwise. Some of them feel U.S. leaders stubbornly made the war a test of the nation's power and leadership. Others view the conflict as a civil war that had no importance to U.S. security. Since Vietnam, many Americans have argued that the nation should stay out of wars that do not directly threaten its safety or vital interests.   GEORGE C. HERRING

Related Articles in WORLD BOOK include:

Army, U.S. (pictures)	Laos (History)
Draft, Military	Nguyen Van Thieu
Ford, Gerald R. (The National	Nixon, Richard M. (Foreign
Scene; Foreign Affairs)	Policy; Foreign Affairs)
Johnson, Lyndon B. (The	Vietnam
Widening Vietnam War)	War (table)
Kampuchea (History)	Westmoreland, William C.
Kissinger, Henry A.	

Reading and Study Guide

See *Vietnam War* in the RESEARCH GUIDE/INDEX, Volume 22, for a *Reading and Study Guide.*

Additional Resources

FITZGERALD, FRANCES. *Fire in the Lake: The Vietnamese and the Americans in Vietnam.* Little, Brown, 1972.

VIETNAMIZATION

HARRISON, JAMES P. *The Endless War: Fifty Years of Struggle in Vietnam.* Macmillan, 1982.
HERRING, GEORGE C. *America's Longest War: The United States and Vietnam, 1950-1975.* Wiley, 1979.
KARNOW, STANLEY. *Vietnam: A History.* Viking, 1983.
LAWSON, DON. *The United States in the Vietnam War.* Harper, 1981. For younger readers.
SHEEHAN, NEIL, and others. *The Pentagon Papers as Published by The New York Times.* Quadrangle, 1971. A study of U.S. government documents on the nation's role in Indochina.

VIETNAMIZATION. See VIETNAM WAR (Vietnamization).

VIGÉE-LEBRUN, *vee zhay luh BRUHN,* **ELISABETH,** *ay lee za BEHT* (1755-1842), was a popular French portrait painter. She was the court painter and a personal friend of Queen Marie Antoinette. Vigée-Lebrun painted more than 800 pictures during her long career, many of them portraits of important members of French society. She painted in a graceful and decorative style, using rich colors. Following the custom of her day, Vigée-Lebrun painted portraits that flattered her subjects.

Vigée-Lebrun was born in Paris. She first studied with her father, Louis Vigée, a painter and art teacher. She also knew and received advice from the famous artist Jean Baptiste Greuze. By the time she was in her late teens, she was a professional portrait painter. In 1776, she married Jean Baptiste Lebrun, the most important art dealer of the time.

At the outbreak of the French Revolution in 1789, Vigée-Lebrun was forced to flee from France. For the next 12 years she made a fortune by painting portraits of nobility and royalty in Italy, Austria, Germany, and Russia. Vigée-Lebrun returned to France in the early 1800's.   WILLARD E. MISFELDT

VIGILANTE, *VIHJ uh LAN tee,* is a member of a self-appointed citizen group or vigilance committee. *Vigilante* comes from the Latin verb *vigilare,* which means *to watch.*

During pioneer days of United States history, the authorities often found themselves unable to enforce the laws. Sometimes the only law officer for many miles around was the United States marshal, making it impossible to police all the territory. In these situations, the citizens frequently formed vigilance committees which dealt out swift punishment to persons they considered to be offenders. Sometimes innocent persons were punished. But often the vigilantes were the only force to preserve order.   JOHN R. ALDEN

VIGNY, *vee NYEE,* **ALFRED DE** (1797-1863), a French author, was a leading figure in the romantic movement. He is best known for his lyric and descriptive poetry. From his *Poèmes antiques et modernes* (1826) to *Les Destinées* (1864), Vigny's themes include the solitude of individuals of genius, the alienation of God from humanity, the search for greatness through suffering and resignation, and the nobility of thought as expressed in philosophical poetry. His other works include the play *Chatterton* (1835), the novel *Cinq-Mars* (1826), and a collection of tales, *Military Service and Greatness* (1835).

Vigny was born in Loches. He spent much of his life living in isolation on his estate. An unhappy love affair with an actress and his failure to win political office intensified his sense of loneliness.   JOEL A. HUNT

VIKINGS were fierce pirates and warriors who terrorized Europe from the late 700's to about 1100. During this period, daring Viking sailors also explored the North Atlantic Ocean and even reached America. Such deeds have given this period of European history the name *the Viking Age.*

The Vikings lived in Scandinavia, a region of Europe that includes what are now Denmark, Norway, and Sweden. The Vikings conquered or looted parts of England, France, Germany, Ireland, Italy, Russia, and Spain. At first, they raided these areas to obtain loot. Later, they set up trading centers and trade routes. Viking ships carried settlers to Greenland, which was unknown to Europeans at that time, and to Iceland. Leif Ericson, a Viking explorer, landed in North America about 500 years before Christopher Columbus arrived there in 1492. The Vikings established a settlement in North America, but it lasted only a few years.

The name *Viking* did not come into use until after the Viking Age. It probably came from *Vik,* the name of a pirate center in southern Norway during Viking times. Among the Scandinavians, the expression *to go a-viking* meant *to fight as a pirate or warrior.* Other Europeans called the Scandinavians *Norsemen, Northmen,* or *Danes.* Swedish Vikings settled in eastern Europe, including part of what is now Russia. Some historians believe that the Swedes became known there as the *Rus,* and that Russia was named for them.

Few Scandinavians of the Viking Age spent all their time going a-viking. The majority worked most of the time as farmers or in other peaceful occupations. Today, however, most historians use the term *Vikings* for all Scandinavians of this period.

The Viking Age began after a long period of rapid population growth in Scandinavia. This growth reduced the amount of available farmland. It led many Vikings to leave Scandinavia to find a source of wealth or a new place to live. At the same time, Scandinavians developed new shipbuilding techniques that enabled their ships to travel farther than ever before.

The Vikings had no direct effect on the history of America. But their conquests in Europe influenced relations between England and France for hundreds of years after the Viking Age.

Viking Life

Ancestry and Population. The ancestors of the Vikings were Germanic peoples who once lived in northwestern Europe. Beginning about 2000 B.C., these peoples moved to what are now Denmark, Norway, and Sweden. A separate group of Vikings developed in each of these areas, but the three groups shared the same general culture.

The Vikings spoke a Germanic language that had two major dialects. All the Vikings understood both dialects. The Vikings used an alphabet made up of characters called *runes.* Each rune consisted chiefly of straight lines arranged singly or in combinations of two or more. See RUNE; KENSINGTON RUNE STONE.

Sidney L. Cohen, the contributor of this article, is Associate Professor of History at Louisiana State University in Baton Rouge and the author of Viking Fortresses of the Trelleborg Type.

Fierce Viking Warriors terrorized many seaside and riverside towns in Europe. Their swift, light warships sailed well in either rough seas or shallow rivers and could be easily dragged ashore. These ships made possible the Vikings' surprise attacks and quick retreats.

The Vikings lived in small communities or villages. A king or chief ruled each Viking community. The people were divided into three social classes—nobles, freemen, and slaves. The nobles included the kings, chiefs, and other people who had great wealth or were descendants of highly honored ancestors. The freemen included farmers, merchants, and others who served the ruler or worked for themselves. Many of the slaves were Scandinavians whose ancestors had been enslaved. Others were Europeans who had been captured in Viking raids and battles. The majority of Vikings stayed in one class for life.

Each Viking community had a governing council called a *Thing* or *Folkmoot*. This council, made up of the community's nobles and freemen, made laws, decided whether the community would go to war, and held trials to judge criminals. Its decisions were more important than rulings of the king or chief.

Economic Activities. The great majority of Vikings were farmers. They grew barley, oats, rye, and a variety of fruits and vegetables. They also raised cattle, goats, pigs, and sheep. Other Vikings worked in fishing, metalworking, shipbuilding, and woodcarving. In the largest communities, many people made their living as merchants. Those who were interested mainly in trade traveled widely. They sailed to most parts of the known world and traded farm products, furs, various other goods, and slaves for such products as gold, silk, silver, and weapons.

Family Life. Parents arranged most Viking marriages. The husband ruled the Viking family, but Viking women had more rights than did the women of other European societies of that time. For example, any Viking woman could own land or other property, and a wife had a right to share in the wealth that her husband gained. Viking law permitted a married woman to get a divorce whenever she wished.

Viking men were allowed to have two or more wives at the same time. This custom was most common among wealthy Vikings, who could afford to support more than one wife. Many nobles had three or more wives and large families. Such families helped produce the population boom that became one of the chief causes of the Viking movement out of Scandinavia. The members of a Viking family developed strong ties to one another. Conflicts between individuals of different families often turned into feuds between the families.

The Vikings became known for burial customs that involved great ceremony. Many rich Viking men and women were laid to rest in a ship that was then buried. The Vikings believed that such *ship graves* provided a safe, comfortable journey to the land of the dead. Many of the dead person's possessions, including beds, jewelry, and weapons, were placed in the ship. In some cases, the person's dogs and even slaves were buried alive in a ship grave.

Food. The Vikings ate two meals daily, one in the morning and the other in the evening. They used spoons and knives, but had no forks. Most of the food, including beef, cheese, eggs, and milk, came from their farms.

The Vikings also hunted and fished for food. Hunters supplied meat from deer, elks, polar bears, seals, and whales. The fish catch included cod, herring, salmon, and trout.

Clothing. Most Viking men wore two basic garments—trousers that reached to the knee or ankle, and a long-sleeved pullover shirt that reached below the waist. Viking women wore loose-fitting dresses that were made of linen or wool and hung almost to the ankles. All the Vikings wore leather shoes.

Housing. Most Viking houses were one-story structures with slanted roofs. Some houses had only one room. Others had three or more. Builders made the walls mainly out of wood or stone, and covered the roof with shingles, sod, or straw. Each home included a hearth that provided heat and light as well as a place to cook. Viking houses had no windows. The husband

A Typical Viking Settlement consisted of a small farming community built near a river or *fiord* (inlet to the sea). Most Viking houses had walls made of stone or wood. Many houses were one-room structures as shown above. Others were long buildings with three or more rooms.

used a chair called the *high seat*. The rest of the family sat on benches, which also served as beds.

Religion played an important role in Viking life. The Vikings worshiped a number of gods. The most important ones were Odin, Thor, and Frey.

Odin, also known as Woden, was king of all the Norse gods and goddesses. He was the god of battle and death. Odin lived in a home of the gods that was known as *Asgard*. The Vikings believed that if they died fighting, they would go to a hall in Asgard called *Valhalla*. There, they could fight all day and dine all night.

Wednesday was named in honor of Odin. See ODIN.

Thor, ruler of the sky, was the god of lightning, thunder, rain, storms, and winds. He was the most popular Viking god because his power over the weather had a great effect on the lives of the people. The Vikings prayed to Thor for good harvests and good fortune. *Thursday* was named after Thor. See THOR.

Frey was the god of agriculture and love. Frey and Thor together ensured the success of a harvest and blessed a marriage. See FREY.

Contact between the Vikings and European Chris-

Viking Artifacts

Woodcarving of a Horse's Head, *above,* decorated part of a Viking tent. This carving was done in the 800's.

This Picture Stone was carved on a monument in the 700's. It shows a warrior on horseback and magic symbols.

The Sword was a prized weapon among the Vikings. A sword maker of the 1000's fashioned this handle out of silver.

296

tians led to the end of the Norse religion. English and German missionaries helped make Christianity the chief religion in Scandinavia by the early 1100's.

Cultural Life and Recreation. Poetry was the most popular form of literature among the Vikings. The poets' favorite subjects included the gods and Viking battles. Court poets called *skalds* entertained Viking kings and their guests. Most kings took their skalds into battle so that the poets could recite verses believed to bring good luck and victory.

Many Viking artists used a style in which animals were portrayed with twisted bodies. A favorite subject was the *gripping beast*, which was pictured wildly gripping its throat, sides, or other parts of its body. Swedish artists often carved the gripping beast and other animal figures on limestone rocks called *picture stones*.

The Scandinavians worked skillfully at many crafts, especially metalworking and woodcarving. They produced attractive bracelets, necklaces, pins, and other kinds of jewelry, much of it from silver. Viking woodcarvers decorated homes, ships, and wagons with elegant, detailed carvings of beasts and warriors.

For recreation, the Vikings especially liked rowing, skiing, swimming, and wrestling, and they enjoyed watching horse races. They also played chess and other board games.

Shipbuilding and Navigation

The sea almost surrounded the Vikings' Scandinavian homelands. In addition, hundreds of *fiords* (inlets to the sea) cut into the coastline. As a result, water travel was the main form of transportation in the region, and the Vikings became a seafaring people.

The Vikings as Shipbuilders. The Vikings ranked among the best shipbuilders of their time. They built their ships out of wood that they cut from the vast Scandinavian forests. Viking shipbuilders greatly improved the sailing ability of Scandinavian ships by adding a *keel*, a long, narrow piece of wood attached to the underside of a ship. It extended down into the water along the center of the entire length of the ship. The keel reduced a ship's rolling motion. By doing so, it greatly improved the ship's speed and thus the distance it could travel without stopping for supplies. The keel also made it easier to steer the ship.

The size of a Viking ship varied, depending on whether the ship was used for trade or for battle. Trading ships, called *knorrs*, were about 50 feet (15 meters) long. Warships, also known as *long ships*, ranged in length from about 65 to 95 feet (20 to 29 meters) and were about 17 feet (5 meters) wide.

A Viking warship sailed well in either rough seas or calm waters. It was light enough to enter shallow rivers. At sea, the Vikings depended mainly on the wind and the ship's large woolen sail for power. On a river, rowers powered the ship. A warship had from 15 to over 30 pairs of oars. The *prow* (front end) of a Viking warship curved gracefully upward and ended with a woodcarving of the head of a dragon or snake. See SHIP (Viking Ships; pictures).

The Vikings as Navigators. Early Viking navigators depended primarily on sightings of the sun and the stars to determine direction and approximate location at sea. By the late 900's, however, the Vikings had developed a system that enabled them to determine the latitude in which they were sailing. They made a table of figures that showed the sun's midday height for each week of the year. By using a measuring stick and this table, a navigator could make a sighting and estimate the latitude of the ship's location.

Viking navigators also relied on landmarks. The Vikings sailed from Norway to Greenland using sightings of the Shetland and Faeroe islands and Iceland as landmarks.

Sometimes, Viking sailors found their directions with the help of ravens, which were known for their ability to find land. If the sailors were unsure about the direction of land, they would release a raven from the ship and then sail in the same direction that the bird flew. The raven became a favorite symbol of the Vikings and was shown on their flag. See FLAG (picture: Flags in American History).

Warfare

Viking warriors enjoyed fighting. They were bold and adventurous, but they were also brutal and fearsome. They murdered women and children as well as men. What they did not steal, they burned. The Vikings created such terror in the hearts of other Europeans that a special prayer for protection was offered in the churches: "God, deliver us from the fury of the Northmen."

The cruelest and most feared Viking warrior was called a *berserker* or *berserk*. Some historians believe ber-

© Universitetets Oldsaksamling, Oslo, Norway

This Viking Ship was found buried in a ship grave in Norway. It is about 75 feet (23 meters) long and was built mostly of oak.

VIKINGS

WORLD BOOK illustration by H. Charles McBarron, Jr.

A Viking Warrior fought with a sword that had a broad two-edged blade made of iron or steel. For protection, he carried a round wooden shield and wore a leather helmet.

serkers were raging madmen. Others think they were normal people who became wild and fearless after eating certain mushrooms or other foods that contained drugs. The term *berserk* is still used to describe a person who acts wildly.

Battle Strategy and Tactics. When the Vikings invaded a territory, they launched a fleet of several hundred warships, each probably carrying about 30 warriors. Thousands of fighters landed, overpowered the defenders, and overran the land. In this way, the Vikings conquered land in England and France.

Most Viking warfare, however, was waged by small raiding parties. Such forces consisted of from 2 to 10 ships, also with about 30 raiders on each ship. The chief targets of Viking raids included small, poorly defended towns, isolated farms, and churches and monasteries. The Vikings launched raids mainly to get cattle and horses, food, and valuable objects made of gold or silver. Churches and monasteries were especially prized for such richly ornamented articles as beautiful ivory *croziers* (ornamental staffs) and books covered with gold and precious stones.

The Vikings became known for surprise attacks and quick retreats. They could row their light, swift ships into shallow rivers and then easily drag them ashore. They often struck so fast that their victims had no time to defend themselves.

Weapons and Armor. The Vikings fought mainly with axes, bows and arrows, spears, and swords. The *broad axe* had a long handle and a large flat blade with a curved cutting edge. The Viking warrior used two hands to swing it at an opponent. The Viking sword had a broad two-edged blade made of iron or steel. The fighter swung the sword with a chopping or hack-

ing motion, aiming at an opponent's arms or legs.

Most Viking warriors carried round wooden shields for protection. Many raiders also wore a sort of armor made from thick layers of animal hides, perhaps with bone sewn into them for added protection. Only Viking leaders wore helmets and coats of *mail* (metal armor). Most of the helmets were made of leather and somewhat cone-shaped. Artists have often pictured Viking warriors wearing helmets with cattle horns on the sides, but the Vikings never had such helmets.

Exploration and Conquest

Scholars link the start of the Viking rampage with several conditions in Scandinavia at the time. Perhaps the most important was a rapidly growing population, which led to overcrowding and a shortage of farmland. In addition, family feuds and local wars made life in Scandinavia difficult for many Vikings. Many other Vikings, especially those who were young, poor, or without land of their own, saw in raiding and conquering a means to obtain wealth and honor.

The Norwegian Vikings began the Viking reign of terror. In June 793, Norwegian raiders attacked and looted the monastery of Lindisfarne on an island off the east coast of England. A wave of Norwegian raids against England, Ireland, the Isle of Man, and Scotland followed. Ireland's many fertile farms and rich churches and monasteries made it an especially attractive target. Turgeis, a Norwegian pirate chief, terrorized Ireland from 839 to 845. He founded the town of Dublin and used it as his headquarters.

During the mid-800's, Norwegian raiders struck targets farther from their homeland. They looted and burned towns in France, Italy, and Spain. In the late 800's, many of the Norwegians turned their attention from Europe to the North Atlantic. Norwegian settlers began to migrate to Iceland about 870. About 25,000 Vikings had settled in Iceland by the mid-900's.

About 982, Eric the Red, a Norwegian who had been living in Iceland, sailed with his family to Greenland. About 985, he persuaded several hundred Icelanders to settle in Greenland (see ERIC THE RED). Soon afterward, Bjarni Herjulfsson, a Viking sea captain, became the first known European to see the mainland of North America. He made the sighting after sailing off course during a voyage from Iceland to Greenland. After Herjulfsson reached Greenland, he told the settlers there about the territory he had passed. Having just arrived in Greenland, the settlers were not interested in exploring other lands at that time.

About 10 years later, after all the good cropland in Greenland had been taken, interest began to grow in the land Herjulfsson had sighted. About 1000, Leif Ericson, a son of Eric the Red, led an expedition westward from Greenland to find the new territory. He and his crew landed somewhere on the east coast of North America and spent the winter there. The Vikings made wine from the plentiful supply of grapes they found, and Ericson called the area *Vinland*, or *Wineland*. See ERICSON, LEIF; VINLAND.

The Vikings soon established a colony in Vinland. In time, however, they were driven away by Indians and did not return. Some historians believe that Vinland was located in what is now Maine or Massachusetts. Others think Vinland was in the present-day

Canadian province of Newfoundland. The main evidence of the Vikings' presence on the mainland of North America comes from remains of a Viking settlement found at L'Anse aux Meadows, near St. Lunaire, Nfld., in 1961. According to the *sagas* (stories of heroic deeds) written by Icelanders long after Viking times, a number of settlements were established in Vinland over a period of about 20 years. But no maps or other records of the colony survived.

The Danish Vikings began their raids in the early 800's. They looted and burned towns on the coasts of what are now Belgium, France, and The Netherlands. In 865, the Danes invaded England. They conquered all the English kingdoms except Wessex and settled in the eastern half of the country. In 886, Alfred the Great, king of Wessex, forced the Vikings to withdraw to the eastern third of England (see ALFRED THE GREAT). This area became known as the *Danelaw*.

During the late 800's, Danish Vikings began to attack French towns again. In 886, King Charles II of France paid the Vikings a huge treasure to end their yearlong siege of Paris. In 911, King Charles III of France and a Danish Viking chieftain named Rollo agreed to the treaty of St. Clair-sur-Epte. According to the treaty, Rollo accepted Christianity and pledged to support the French king. In turn, Charles granted the Vikings control of the area in France now known as *Normandy* (Land of the Northmen). See NORMANS.

During the late 900's, the Danish Vikings renewed their interest in England. Ethelred II had become king of England in 978, when he was only about 10 years old. The English nobility refused to support Ethelred, and so England's defense against invasion was much weakened. In 994, Danes led by Sweyn Forkbeard, a son of King Harald Bluetooth of Denmark, went to war against England. In 1016, Sweyn's son Canute finally brought England under Danish control. The Danes ruled England until 1042.

The Swedish Vikings began to raid towns along rivers in eastern Europe during the early 800's. They set up a number of trade centers in this region, which included what is now western Russia. The people of that area were mostly Slavs. The Slavs called the Swedish Vikings the *Rus*.

The Swedes gained control of the key trade routes between the Baltic Sea and the Black Sea. They built forts along these routes to protect traders from wandering raiders. By the late 800's, the Russian towns of Novgorod and Kiev had become Swedish strongholds. In time, Kiev became the first state of Russia.

By the mid-900's, the Rus had adopted many of the customs of the Slavic peoples. About 988, the Rus prince Vladimir I destroyed all the symbols of the Viking religion in Kiev and made Christianity the official religion of the Rus.

Viking Influence

The most important influence of the Viking period was its effect on Scandinavia. The creation of three strong Viking kingdoms in Scandinavia led to the development of three nations—Denmark, Norway, and Sweden. When the Vikings adopted Christianity, they then brought the countries of Scandinavia into the mainstream of European civilization.

The Norsemen also had an enormous influence on developments in England and France. The Viking invasions of England in the 800's and 900's helped unify and strengthen England. The establishment of Normandy in France in 911 was the source of years of conflict between France and England. William the Conqueror, a Norman descendant of the Viking chieftain Rollo, led a Norman army to victory over the English and became king of England in 1066. England and France later fought for control of Normandy during the Hundred Years' War (1337-1453). See WILLIAM (William I, the Conqueror); HUNDRED YEARS' WAR.

The Vikings had a lasting effect on Iceland, where they established a permanent settlement that reflects

The Vikings sailed from Scandinavia in three main directions from the A.D. 700's to the 1000's. The Danes went south and raided Germany, France, England, Spain, and the Mediterranean coast. The Norwegians traveled to North America. The Swedes went to eastern Europe.

WORLD BOOK map

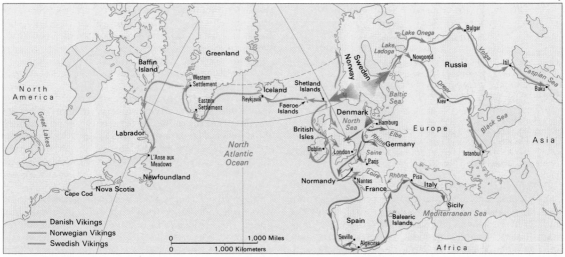

some elements of Viking culture to this day. Although the Vikings established Vinland in North America, they did not influence later European exploration of the New World. Vinland remained unknown to the rest of Europe until long after Columbus had gained credit as the European discoverer of America.   SIDNEY L. COHEN

Related Articles in WORLD BOOK include:

Outline

I. Viking Life
  A. Ancestry and Population
  B. Economic Activities
  C. Family Life
  D. Religion
  E. Cultural Life and
     Recreation

II. Shipbuilding and Navigation
  A. The Vikings as Shipbuilders
  B. The Vikings as Navigators

III. Warfare
  A. Battle Strategy and
     Tactics
  B. Weapons and Armor

IV. Exploration and Conquest
  A. The Norwegian Vikings
  B. The Danish Vikings
  C. The Swedish Vikings

V. Viking Influence

Questions

Why were Viking ships well suited to surprise raids?
What were the three classes of Viking society?
What was a *berserker?*
Why did the Vikings come to North America?
What was a *ship grave?*
What was the occupation of most Vikings?
How did the establishment of Normandy by the Vikings affect the history of France and England?
Why did the Vikings raid churches and monasteries?
Who were the three most important Viking gods?
What were some of the conditions that led to the Viking movement out of Scandinavia?

Reading and Study Guide

See *Vikings* in the RESEARCH GUIDE/INDEX, Volume 22, for a *Reading and Study Guide.*

Additional Resources

Level I
DONOVAN, FRANK R., and the EDITORS OF HORIZON MAGAZINE. *The Vikings.* American Heritage, 1964.
GLUBOK, SHIRLEY. *The Art of the Vikings.* Macmillan, 1978.
GOLDING, MORTON J. *The Mystery of the Vikings in America.* Harper, 1973.

Level II
ATKINSON, IAN. *The Viking Ships.* Cambridge, 1979.
JONES, GWYN. *A History of the Vikings.* Oxford, 1973.
MAGNUSSON, MAGNUS. *Vikings!* Dutton, 1980. Emphasizes their culture, based on archaeological evidence.

VILLA, *VEE yah,* **PANCHO** (1877-1923), was a Mexican bandit chieftain. He sought to control Mexico after the fall of President Porfírio Díaz in 1911. After the murder of President Francisco Madero in 1913, Victoriano Huerta became president. Villa supported him briefly. When Venustiano Carranza moved to gain con-

United Press Int.

Pancho Villa, *right,* and Álvaro Obregón are shown together at a meeting near El Paso, Tex., in 1914. They later became enemies.

trol of Mexico in 1914, Villa attacked him. Álvaro Obregón, who supported Carranza, defeated Villa and helped Carranza become acting chief of Mexico (see MEXICO [The Constitution of 1917]; OBREGÓN, ÁLVARO).

The United States encouraged Villa at first, but President Woodrow Wilson turned to Carranza because of reports of Villa's brutalities. Villa retaliated against Americans in Mexico, stopping trains and shooting those on board. In 1916, he raided Columbus, N. Mex. His cavalry attacked the town, killing 16 people. President Wilson sent United States soldiers under the command of General John J. Pershing into Mexico in pursuit of Villa. Hampered by orders not to use Mexican railroads, Pershing failed to capture Villa. All the people of Mexico, including President Carranza, bitterly resented Pershing's expedition. The expedition was withdrawn from Mexico in 1917 (see WILSON, WOODROW [Crisis in Mexico]).

Obregón drove Carranza from power in 1920 and pacified Villa by a grant of land. Villa was shot from ambush by enemies in 1923. He was born Doroteo Arango in Río Grande, Zacatecas, Mexico. He changed his name to Francisco Villa, and was called Pancho Villa.   DONALD E. WORCESTER

VILLA-LOBOS, *VEE lah LOH boos,* **HEITOR** (1887-1959), was a Brazilian composer, conductor, and educator. His works were among the first serious music to use Brazilian folk and popular melodies, rhythms, and musical instruments. He composed symphonies, ballets, operas, and chamber music. Some of his most popular works are written in forms he invented called the *Bachiana Brasiliera* and *Chôros.*

Villa-Lobos was born in Rio de Janeiro, Brazil. In 1932, he became superintendent of musical education in Rio de Janeiro.   DAVID EWEN

VILLAGE is any small group or community of houses and dwellings. In local government, the term *village* has a more specific meaning. It refers to a community which the state has chartered as a municipality. Such a village is governed by a village president and a board of trustees. The village usually has its own clerk, treasurer, and police official.   H. F. ALDERFER

See also CHARTER; LOCAL GOVERNMENT.

VILLEIN, *VIL in,* was an agricultural worker whose status was midway between that of freeman and slave during the Middle Ages in England. Villeins differed from slaves because villeins were not the property of a master. They differed from freemen because they were

bound to a plot of land that they did not own. In return for the use of this land and protection on it, villeins were required to render certain manual and other services to the lord of the manor. The children of villeins were born into the same bondage as their parents.

Lands held in villeinage often were handed down from father to son until the family acquired a right to them by *prescription* (long use). But the villein still had to serve a master. The villein's sole title to land was a copy of the entries on the court roll. For this reason, villeins came to be called *tenants by copy of court roll*. Tenure of this type was called *copyhold*. This tenure existed until it was practically abolished by the Copyhold Act of 1894. The Property Act of 1925 ended all tenure by copyhold.

Villeinage began to decline in the 1100's when the villein began to exchange labor services for money payments. In the end, the villein became a free tenant who paid a rent for land. By the early 1500's, few villeins were left in England. The contempt in which the villeins were commonly held may be responsible for the fact that we get the word *villain* from the earlier word *villein*. BRYCE LYON

See also FEUDALISM; SERF.

VILLELLA, *vihl EHL uh,* **EDWARD JOSEPH** (1936-), an American dancer, is a leading performer in the New York City Ballet. Villella dances in a style called *bravura,* which means *brilliant and daring.* He performs dramatic leaps and has great strength and speed.

Villella was born in Bayside, N.Y., near Great Neck. He began training at the School of American Ballet when he was 10 years old. In 1957, he joined the New York City Ballet. Villella has been widely praised for his performance of the title role in *Prodigal Son.* He has also danced in such ballets as *Tarantella* (1964), *Harlequinade* (1965), and *Dances at a Gathering* (1969). In addition, Villella composes dances and performs with his own touring company. He has appeared in several dance films made for television. DIANNE L. WOODRUFF

VILLIERS, GEORGE. See BUCKINGHAM, DUKE OF.

VILLON, *vee YAWN,* **FRANÇOIS,** *frahn SWAH* (1431- ?), was a great French poet. His principal works are *Le Petit Testament* and *Grand Testament.* His fast-moving verses bring to life a vivid and colorful description of the sights, sounds, and smells of Paris.

Villon ridiculed the great and the powerful. He poked fun at lawyers, churchmen, and merchants, and laughed at the tricks, shady dealings, and bawdy jokes of sharpsters, thieves, prostitutes, and rowdy students. But Villon also wrote poetry of great tenderness, charm, and melancholy. He was sincerely religious and his deepest themes include brotherhood and love for humanity.

Villon was born in Paris and studied for the clergy at the University of Paris. But he became involved in murder, theft, and street brawls. He was sentenced to be hanged in 1463, but his sentence was reduced to banishment from Paris. Nothing is known of his life after this date. JOEL A. HUNT

VILNIUS, *VIHL nee uhs* (pop. 535,000), is the capital and largest city of Lithuania, one of the 15 republics of the Soviet Union. It lies in southeastern Lithuania, on the Neris (Wilija) River (see LITHUANIA [map]). Vilnius is an important industrial, transportation, and cultural and educational center. Its products include chemicals, furniture, industrial machinery, paper, and textiles.

Railroads pass through the city and an airport is nearby. The V. Kapsukas State University in Vilnius is the oldest university in the Soviet Union. It was founded in 1579.

Vilnius is best known for its many old churches and other buildings that date from between the 1400's and 1800's. The city also has many modern buildings that were erected after World War II ended in 1945.

Vilnius was founded about 1323 by Lithuanian Grand Duke Gediminas. The city was controlled by Russia from 1795 to 1918 and by Poland from 1920 to 1939. In 1939, it was returned to Lithuania, which had claimed it as a capital since 1918. In 1940, Russia seized Lithuania and forced it to become part of the Soviet Union. V. STANLEY VARDYS

See also LITHUANIA (picture).

VIMY RIDGE, *VIHM ee* or *VEE mee,* **BATTLE OF,** was a World War I battle in which Canadian forces scored an important victory over the Germans. In the battle, the Canadians captured Vimy Ridge, a strategically located hill near the town of Arras, in northern France.

The battle began April 9, 1917. The Canadian Corps was part of the British Army, and the battle was part of the British spring offensive. The British attacked Arras while the Canadians attacked the ridge. The chief goal of this offensive was to draw German troops away from Aisne, a town to the south that the French were to attack a week later. The other goal was to win Vimy Ridge and Arras. The Canadians took the ridge on April 14. Of the 100,000 Canadians who took part in the battle, 3,598 were killed and 7,004 wounded. The British offensive succeeded. But the French offensive, and the Allied offensive as a whole, failed. P. B. WAITE

VIÑA DEL MAR, *VEEN yuh dehl MAHR* (pop. 307,308), is the leading seaside resort city of Chile. It lies on the Pacific coast, about 4 miles (6 kilometers) north of Valparaíso. Viña del Mar's mild climate, beaches, hotels, nightclubs, and race tracks make it one of the most popular vacation spots in South America. The city has several food processing plants. Oil refineries are located near the city. Viña del Mar is the second largest city in Chile. Only Santiago has more people. See also CHILE (political map). KALMAN H. SILVERT

VINCENNES, *vihn SEHNZ,* Ind. (pop. 20,857), a manufacturing and trading center in southwestern Indiana, is the oldest city in the state. It lies on the Wabash River, which forms the Indiana-Illinois boundary in the region (see INDIANA [political map]). Vincennes has many historical buildings and memorials. These include the building in which the legislature of the Indiana Territory held its first sessions; the mansion called *Grouseland,* built by William Henry Harrison while he was territorial governor; and the George Rogers Clark Memorial, which stands on the site of old Fort Sackville. The Lincoln Memorial Bridge spans the Wabash River where the Thomas Lincoln family crossed when they went from Indiana to Illinois in 1830.

Industry and Trade. Vincennes is well situated for a manufacturing and trading center. Freight railroads, major highways, and the Wabash River provide good transportation. The city lies in a region which contains coal, and oil and natural-gas fields. The chief industries of Vincennes produce batteries, containers, electronic

instruments, fiberboard, fiberglass products, shoes, structural steel products, and window glass. Vincennes University has its campus in the city.

History. Historians disagree as to the date of the first settlement on the site of Vincennes. Some say settlers came shortly after 1700, which would make Vincennes one of the oldest settlements outside the original 13 colonies. Most historians agree that by about 1731, the French had founded the first permanent settlement in Indiana there.

Around 1733, a fort was built at the village and placed under the command of the Sieur de Vincennes. His name was given to the town soon after Indians captured and put him to death about 1736. The fort became Fort Sackville after France gave up the eastern part of the Mississippi Valley to the British in 1763.

During the Revolutionary War, George Rogers Clark occupied the fort. The British seized Fort Sackville in December, 1778, but, later that winter, Clark recaptured it for the Americans. This victory helped win the old Northwest for the new United States.

Vincennes was the capital of Indiana Territory from 1800 to 1813. The town became the county seat of Knox County early in the territorial period. It was incorporated as a city in 1856. Vincennes has a mayor-council form of government.   PAUL E. MILLION, JR.

VINCENT DE PAUL, SAINT. See SISTERS OF CHARITY.

VINCENT OF BEAUVAIS. See ENCYCLOPEDIA (From the 1200's to the 1600's).

VINCENT'S ANGINA. See TRENCH MOUTH.

VINCI, LEONARDO DA. See DA VINCI, LEONARDO.

VINE usually means a plant that has a weak and flexible stem requiring some kind of support. Some vines can climb walls, trellises, or other plants. Other vines creep along the ground. Some vines have tendrils which wind around their support. Other vines have disks which cling to the object which they are climbing. There are two important kinds of vines—*woody* vines and *herbaceous* vines. Grapes are woody vines. Sometimes the woody vine is fairly short, and can support itself. Then it is somewhat like a shrub. It is often difficult to tell the difference between such a vine and a shrub. Common kinds of herbaceous vines include cucumbers, garden peas, and beans.   WILLIAM C. BEAVER

Related Articles in WORLD BOOK include:

Bean	Cranberry	Morning-Glory
Betel	Gourd	Pea
Bignonia	Grape	Pelican Flower
Bittersweet	Greenbrier	Philodendron
Bramble	Honeysuckle	Smilax
Clematis	Hop	Virginia Creeper
Cowpea	Ivy	Wisteria

VINEGAR is a sour liquid for seasoning foods. It also is used in pickling and processing fruits, vegetables, and meats. The name *vinegar* is from the French word *vinaigre*, which means *sour wine*. But many kinds of vinegar are not made from wine.

Vinegar is a result of the chemical change known as *fermentation*. A *dilute* (weak) alcohol is the raw material from which all vinegar is made. The alcohol may be produced from the fermentation of the juice of any fruits, berries, or even melons. Malt vinegar is made from cereals. Vinegar is also made from sugar solutions, such as molasses, sugar syrup, or honey.

Making Vinegar. Cider vinegar is made from the juice of apples, or *cider*. Fermentation changes the fruit sugar in the juice into alcohol and carbonic gas. The gas evaporates, or passes off, leaving the alcohol and fruit flavors, or *esters*. *Oxidation* changes cider into vinegar. The oxygen in the air comes in contact with the alcohol in the cider, and with the aid of the vinegar bacteria (*mycoderma aceti*) the alcohol changes into vinegar.

The two general methods of making vinegar are the slow, natural process and the quick process. The *slow* process may take from one to two years, depending on temperature and access to air. The fermented liquid may be kept in a special oak barrel, or cask, with holes to permit air circulation. It should be only about four-fifths full, so as to allow ample air space. The alcohol in the cider, being lighter than the other part of the liquid, tends to rise to the top. As the alcohol comes in contact with air, acetic acid is formed. As the top layer changes into acetic acid, it increases in weight and gradually sinks to the bottom of the barrel. This continues until almost all the alcohol becomes vinegar.

In the *quick* method, the fermented cider is circulated continuously through vats called *generators*. The generators are filled with such porous material as corncobs, rattan shavings, or coke. Lukewarm, strong cider vinegar is circulated through the porous material for 24 to 48 hours. Then the fermented cider is fed into the top of the generator through a revolving spray, or *sparger*. The cider is split into drops, and each drop is brought into contact with currents of air that enter through holes near the bottom of the generator. An efficiently run generator converts 1,000 to 2,000 gallons (3,800 to 7,600 liters) of cider into vinegar in 48 to 72 hours.

During the process of converting fermented fruit juices into vinegar, particularly cider vinegar, a slimy scum called *mother of vinegar* (*bacterium xylinum*) forms. Manufacturers try to prevent the formation of vinegar mother. It slows down the circulation of air.

Kinds of Vinegar. The flavors, colors, and odors of various kinds of vinegar come from the substances from which they are made. Cider vinegar has an applelike odor, and is brown or yellow. Distilled vinegar is water-white in color and has no flavor, other than acidity. Most of this vinegar is made from molasses. But some is made from *whey* (liquid part of milk) which contains sugar. Four per cent is the legal minimum acid strength for commercial vinegar.   WALTER H. HILDICK

See also ACETIC ACID; CIDER; FERMENTATION.

VINEGAR EEL is a tiny roundworm that lives in vinegar. Vinegar eels are usually found in barrels or jars of cider vinegar. They feed on fruit pulp and the bacteria which produce the vinegar from the cider. Vinegar eels are harmless when swallowed.

The vinegar eel is slender and threadlike and about $\frac{1}{16}$ inch (1.6 millimeters) long. There are separate males and females. Most females live about ten months and produce as many as 45 tiny larvae which are about $\frac{1}{100}$ inch (0.25 millimeter) long.

Scientific Classification. The vinegar eel is genus *Turbatrix* (*Anguillula*), species *T. aceti*, and belongs to the roundworm class *Nematoda* of the phylum *Aschelminthes*.   JAMES A. MCLEOD

See also ROUNDWORM.

VINEGAR JOE. See STILWELL, JOSEPH WARREN.

VINER, CHARLES. See BLACKSTONE, SIR WILLIAM.

VINEYARD. See Grape.

VINLAND is the name early Scandinavian explorers gave to a region on the east coast of North America. Many historians believe that Norwegian vikings visited this coastal area almost 500 years before Christopher Columbus sailed to America in 1492. Some historians believe Vinland was probably in the region of Cape Cod, Mass. Others believe it was in Newfoundland. In the early 1960's, archaeologists found the remains of a viking settlement near Flower's Cove, Newfoundland.

Early Norse *sagas* (stories of heroic deeds) tell of the explorers' voyages. Many historians do not consider these stories as completely reliable. These tales describe a fertile land with a mild climate. The Norsemen called the region *Vinland* (also spelled *Vineland* or *Wineland*) because of the grapes that grew there. The sagas tell that Leif Ericson, son of Eric the Red, visited Vinland about A.D. 1000. Historians believe the Norsemen had to abandon Vinland because they could not defend their settlements against hostile Indians.　　WILLIAM BARK

VINSON, *VIN s'n,* **FREDERICK MOORE** (1890-1953), became Chief Justice of the United States in 1946. He served as a Democratic member of the United States House of Representatives from Kentucky from 1923 to 1929, and again from 1931 to 1938. He then served until 1943 as associate justice of the United States Court of Appeals for the District of Columbia.

Vinson became director of the Office of Economic Stabilization in 1943, and then director of the Office of War Mobilization and Reconversion. President Harry S. Truman named him Secretary of the Treasury in 1945. Vinson served about a year, and had an important part in arranging financial settlements at the close of World War II. He was born in Louisa, Ky., and studied at Centre College.　　MERLO J. PUSEY

VINYL, *VY nuhl,* is one of the most useful plastics materials ever developed. Vinyl plastics, often called simply *vinyls,* are durable and inexpensive. They can be used in making a wide variety of products, including phonograph records and leatherlike upholstery. Manufacturers make vinyl plastics from such natural substances as natural gas, petroleum, and salt.

Characteristics. Vinyls may have the stiffness of wood or the flexibility of cloth. They may be any color, and they may be transparent. Vinyls do not break or tear easily, and they rarely are harmed by acids, alcohol, oils, or water. Products made of *rigid* (stiff) vinyl may begin to lose their shape at a temperature of about 150° F. (66° C). Most vinyls burn slowly.

Rigid vinyl products include containers, toys, and water pipes. Flexible vinyl items include electrical insulators, floor tiles, garden hoses, shower curtains, and leather-like clothing and luggage. Vinyl coatings keep cardboard milk cartons from becoming soggy and enable wallpaper to resist stains.

All vinyl plastics contain a chemical substance called *vinyl,* which has the formula CH_2CH-. Manufacturers combine vinyl with various other substances to produce several kinds of vinyl plastics. For example, combining vinyl with chlorine produces a gas called *vinyl chloride.* Through the process of *polymerization,* this gas is then used to produce a solid plastic, *polyvinyl chloride* (PVC). See PLASTICS (How Plastics Are Made).

History. In 1927, PVC became the first vinyl plastics material to be manufactured commercially. Through

the years, chemists improved vinyl plastics, and manufacturers found many new uses for these materials. In 1973, U.S. production of vinyl plastics totaled 4.6 billion pounds (2.1 billion kilograms). During the mid-1970's, research indicated that serious illnesses, including a form of liver cancer, may result from breathing air polluted with vinyl chloride, the gas used in making PVC. In 1976, the Environmental Protection Agency required plastics manufacturers to install equipment designed to nearly eliminate vinyl chloride from the air breathed by workers.　　RICHARD F. BLEWITT

See also LINOLEUM (History).

VINYL CHLORIDE. See VINYL.

VIOL is the name of a class of stringed instruments played with a bow. Viols were very popular during the 1500's and 1600's. By about 1750, they had been largely replaced by other stringed instruments, including the viola and the cello. Interest in viol playing revived during the early 1900's as part of a renewed interest in early music.

Viols resemble instruments of the violin family. But unlike violins, viols have a flat back and sloping shoulders. Bows and the way in which a viol player holds the bow also differ. Most viols have six strings that are thinner than violin strings. The instruments are made in several sizes, ranging from soprano—the smallest—to bass—the largest. Players hold the smaller viols upright on their lap and the larger ones between their knees.　　REINHARD G. PAULY

See also BASS; CELLO; VIOLA; VIOLIN.

VIOLA, *vee OH luh,* is a stringed instrument played with a bow. It is similar to a violin in shape and the way it is played. It is larger than the violin and ranges from

WORLD BOOK photo, courtesy Chicago Symphony Orchestra

The Viola looks like a large violin, and the musician holds and plays it like a violin. But the viola has a full, rich tone and a pitch lower than that of a violin.

VIOLENCE

24 to 27 inches (61 to 69 centimeters) in length. The viola is the tenor voice in the string quartet and in the string section of the orchestra. It may be used as a solo instrument. See also VIOLIN.   CHARLES B. RIGHTER

VIOLENCE. See CRIME; REVOLUTION; RIOT; TERRORISM.

VIOLET is the common name of a group of flowering plants. Their blossoms are among the most attractive of all flowers. Violets grow throughout most of the world. They bloom in groups in early spring. Heart-shaped leaves partly conceal the five-petaled flowers. Each flower grows on a slender stalk. There are more than 300 species of violets. About 100 of these grow in the United States. Some varieties of violets bear white and yellow flowers, but the blue and purple violets are world favorites.

Purple violets include the common *meadow*, or *hooded*, *violet*, and the *bird's-foot violet*, whose blue and purple flowers often bloom twice a year, in spring and summer. The bird's-foot violet received its name because its leaves are shaped like birds' feet.

The *dog violet* is so called by the English because it lacks fragrance. The word *dog* is a term of contempt. It is quite different from *dogtooth violet*, a member of the lily family. The pansy is a cultivated kind of violet.

The violet was adopted as state flower by Illinois, New Jersey, Rhode Island, and Wisconsin. The violet is also the flower for the month of March.

The Bird's-Foot Violet Often Blooms Twice a Year.

Scientific Classification. Violets belong to the violet family, *Violaceae*. They are in the genus *Viola*. The blue violet is classified as *V. papilionacea*; the bird's-foot, *V. pedata*; the dog, *V. canina*. The wild form of the cultivated pansy is *V. tricolor*.   THEODOR JUST

See also FLOWER (picture: Garden Perennials); PANSY.

VIOLIN is a stringed instrument that is played with a bow. It is probably the best known and most widely used of all orchestral instruments. Some of the greatest music in the world owes much of its beauty to the violin. Such music may be the sound of a mighty orchestra,

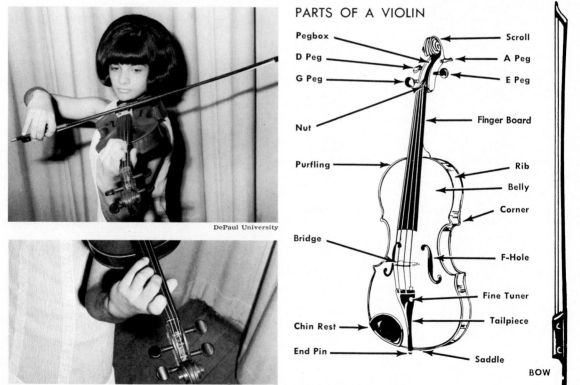

PARTS OF A VIOLIN

Pegbox — Scroll
D Peg — A Peg
G Peg — E Peg
Nut
Purfling — Finger Board
— Rib
— Belly
— Corner
Bridge — F-Hole
— Fine Tuner
Chin Rest — Tailpiece
End Pin — Saddle
BOW

To Play the Violin Properly, tuck the instrument under your chin and rest it on your shoulder. Keep your chin in a straight line with the scroll. Keep your left elbow in close to the body. Cup your fingers over the strings, and place the thumb against the side of the finger board.

with dozens of violins playing together. Or it may be the music produced by one great master playing alone on a violin to a hushed audience.

Several other instruments are similar to the violin in construction and in method of playing. These include the cello and viola. They are considered members of the *violin family.*

Music for the violin covers a wide range. Some composers, such as Johann Sebastian Bach, have written music for the violin alone. Many composers have written pieces for the violin with piano or orchestral accompaniment. The violin also has an important role as part of a group of instruments, as in an orchestra or in a string quartet.

Parts of the Violin. A violin is a special kind of box that *amplifies* (makes louder) the sound of the strings stretched across it. If you stretch a piece of string tightly and then pluck it, you will hear a faint note. If you stretch it across a wooden box, you will hear a much louder note. A violin-maker uses soft pine or spruce for the *belly* (front) of the violin, and maple or sycamore for the *back* and the *ribs* (sides). The *head* (scroll and peg-box) and *neck* are made of maple. The graceful shapes of the back and belly are carved out of solid pieces of wood. The violin-maker cuts two *f-holes* in the belly to allow the sound to escape, and makes the *finger board* and the *tailpiece* (string-holder) of ebony. Ebony is an extremely hard wood that will be long lasting. The violin-maker glues the violin parts together, using no nails or screws.

The violin has four *strings,* which are tuned in fifths. The first (*E*) string is generally made of steel. The second (*A*) string and the third (*D*) string are often made of plain *catgut,* a material made from the intestines of sheep. But most players prefer to use *A* or *D* strings made of a thinner gut over-wound with fine aluminum wire. Synthetic materials such as nylon are also used. The fourth (*G*) string is generally made of gut covered with silver or copper wire. The strings are attached to pegs set in the head. The player tightens the strings with these pegs to tune them to the correct notes.

There are two other important parts of the violin that are not permanently glued to the body. The *bridge* stands on the belly, midway between the two *f*-holes. It supports the strings. A pattern of holes is cut into the bridge to give it greater flexibility. The *sound-post,* a thin rod of pine, is wedged between the back and the belly underneath the bridge, inside the violin. The sound-post conducts the sound from the front to the back of the violin. It also supports the belly against the pressure of the strings. The sound-post is slightly behind one foot of the bridge. The *bass-bar,* a bar of pine that is glued on the underside of the belly, gives further support for the belly. It runs lengthwise underneath the other foot of the bridge.

The Bow is a curved, springy stick about 27 inches (69 centimeters) long that has a flat ribbon of hair attached to it. This ribbon consists of more than 150 horsehairs. The hair is attached to the point of the bow and to a sliding wood block called a *frog* or *nut* at the other end, near the point at which the violinist holds the bow. By turning a screw set into the end of the bow, the player can move the frog back and forth to tighten the hair against the spring of the bow. The bow is made of *Pernambuco wood,* a light, springy wood from a tree that grows in Brazil.

Playing the Violin. The player tucks the end of the violin between the chin and the left shoulder. To obtain a good grip, the player uses a *chin-rest* clamped to the top of the violin, and a *shoulder-rest* or a *pad* between the back of the violin and the shoulder. The violin should be supported entirely without the aid of

HISTORIC VIOLINS

The first reference to stringed instruments appears in Persian and Chinese writings from the 800's. Developments over the next 800 years led to the superb violins of Stradivari.
From *Harvard Dictionary of Music* by Willi Apel, © 1950, Harvard University Press; Lyon & Healy

The Kemantche, an ancient Persian stringed instrument, consisted of a long stick extending through half of a coconut.

The European Rebec, popular in medieval times, resembled a long slender pear. It probably originated in the Orient.

The Vielle ranked as the most important stringed instrument in the 1100's and 1200's. This European fiddle had five strings.

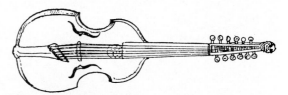

The Viola d'Amore was held and played like the violin of today. It was used in Europe in the 1500's and 1600's.

Violins Made by Antonio Stradivari in the late 1600's and early 1700's have never been surpassed in tone, power, and form.

the player's left hand. The bow is held in the player's right hand.

The player makes the strings of the violin vibrate by drawing the hair of the bow across them. Each of the separate strands of hair on the bow is rough, with minute projections. These projections make the strings vibrate as the bow slides over them. The player can vary the loudness of the tone and get other special effects by the way in which the bow is drawn across the strings. The player can also pluck the strings with the fingers, a form of playing known as *pizzicato*.

The strings of the violin give the player four notes. To obtain other notes, the player shortens the vibrating length of the strings by pressing them down on the finger board with the fingers of the left hand. Flute-like tones called *harmonics* can be produced by touching the strings lightly in certain places.

History. Musicians have used many kinds of stringed instruments, such as harps and lyres, for thousands of years. But no one knows when players began to use bows, instead of just plucking the strings. Chinese players used bowed instruments in the A.D. 900's. A hundred years later, musicians used forms of bowed instruments in many countries of Asia, Europe, and northern Africa. In the 1400's, players started using bows to play instruments of the guitar family. These bowed guitars developed into the instruments called viols.

The first violins date from the 1500's. They were developed from the early bowed instruments, rather than from the viols. For many years, viols and violins developed side by side, each influencing the other. But by the late 1600's, most musicians favored the violin family, and the viols dropped out of use.

The little Italian town of Cremona became an important center of violin making. Members of the Amati family made fine instruments there in the late 1500's and early 1600's. In the 1600's, Antonio Stradivari, a pupil of the Amatis, perfected the design of the violin and produced some of the finest violins ever made. Another great family was that of Guarneri. The violins of Giuseppe Guarneri, who was known as Guarneri del Gesù, rival those of Stradivari for tone. Many great violin-makers worked in Germany. At one time, people considered the violins of the German Jacob Stainer to be finer than those of Stradivari. A Frenchman, François Tourte, perfected the bow in the late 1700's.

In the 1600's, 1700's, and early 1800's, many of the outstanding violinists were also the main composers for violin. Their works led to developments in playing technique. Among the most important of these composers were Arcangelo Corelli, Antonio Vivaldi, Giuseppe Tartini, Giovanni Viotti, Pierre Rode, Rodolphe Kreutzer, and Niccolò Paganini. Viotti has been called the father of modern violin playing. He greatly improved and extended the use of the violin bow. In the 1800's and 1900's, many composers wrote important music for the violin.

Great violin players of the 1900's include Jascha Heifetz, Fritz Kreisler, Yehudi Menuhin, Nathan Milstein, David Oistrakh, Itzhak Perlman, Isaac Stern, and Pinchas Zukerman.   REINHARD G. PAULY

Related Articles in WORLD BOOK include:

VIOLINISTS

Heifetz, Jascha	Perlman, Itzhak
Kreisler, Fritz	Stern, Isaac
Menuhin, Yehudi	Tartini, Giuseppe
Milstein, Nathan	Vivaldi, Antonio
Oistrakh, David	Wieniawski, Henri
Paganini, Niccolò	Zukerman, Pinchas

OTHER RELATED ARTICLES

Amati	Stradivari, Antonio
Bass	Suzuki Method
Cello	Viol
Guarneri	Viola
Music (Stringed Instruments)	

VIOLONCELLO. See CELLO.

VIPER is any one of a group of poisonous snakes. Vipers have a pair of long, hollow fangs in the upper jaw. Many of them have a deep hollow in the side of the head, a little lower than the eye and in front of it. Snakes with this hollow, or pit, are *pit vipers*. Those without it are *true vipers*.

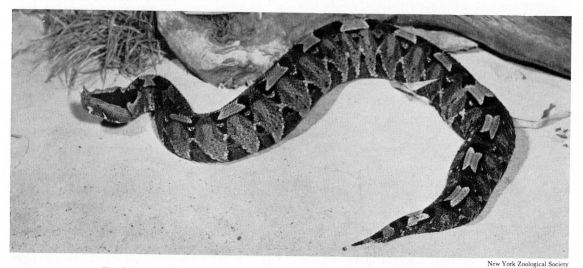

New York Zoological Society

The Rhinoceros Viper Lives in Swamp Areas in the Rain Forests of Central Africa.

True vipers live in Africa, Europe, Asia, and the East Indies. Pit vipers live in the Americas, the East Indies, Asia, and Europe east of the lower Volga River. Of every 100 snakes, about eight are vipers. Over half of the vipers have the pit.

A viper's poison is formed in special glands. The hollow fangs then carry it into the victim's body the way a hypodermic needle injects serum. All vipers can be dangerous to people, but many of the small kinds rarely, if ever, kill anyone with their bite. Certain kinds of large vipers are so harmless that they will not bite unless someone teases or annoys them.

Vipers have a head much broader than the neck, and eyes with catlike pupils, but so do many other snakes. Vipers, therefore, cannot be recognized with any degree of certainty by the shape of the head and pupils. Most vipers have thick bodies and rather short tails.

The facial pit of the pit viper is connected with the brain by a well-developed nerve. The nerve, a sense organ, is highly sensitive to heat. It helps the pit viper to locate and secure its warm-blooded prey.

The most familiar American vipers are the *rattlesnakes, water moccasin, copperhead, bushmaster,* and *fer-de-lance.* The last two live in many parts of tropical America, but not in the United States. Only the bushmaster lays eggs. The others bear their young alive.

The *common viper,* or *adder,* is the only poisonous reptile of Great Britain. Other familiar true vipers include the *Gaboon viper* and *puff adder* of Africa, and *Russell's viper* of Asia and the East Indies. Most true vipers bear their young alive.

Scientific Classification. Vipers make up the viper family, Viperidae. True vipers belong to the subfamily Viperinae. The common European viper, or adder, is genus *Vipera,* species *V. berus.* Other true vipers include the Gaboon viper, *Bitis gabonica;* the puff adder, *B. arietans;* and Russell's viper, *Vipera russeli.* Pit vipers belong to the subfamily Crotalinae. They include the rattlesnakes, which are genera *Crotalus* and *Sistrurus;* the bushmaster, *Lachesis muta;* the copperhead, *Agkistrodon contortrix;* the water moccasin, *A. piscivorus;* and the fer-de-lance, *Bothrops atrox.*   CLIFFORD H. POPE

Related Articles in WORLD BOOK include:

Adder	Copperhead	Rattlesnake Water Moccasin
Bushmaster	Fer-de-Lance	Snake

VIPER'S BUGLOSS, *BYOO glahs,* is a plant that is also known as blue thistle. It has a spotted stem and showy blue flowers. It is a biennial, and seeds planted one year will not produce flowers until the next year. The flowers are reddish when they are budding, but turn blue when they open fully. The viper's bugloss grows widely in the dry pastures of the eastern United States. People once thought viper's bugloss cured viper bites.

Scientific Classification. Viper's bugloss belongs to the borage family, Boraginaceae. It is classified as genus *Echium,* species *E. vulgare.*   WALTER C. MUENSCHER

VIRACOCHA. See INCA (Religion).

VIRCHOW, *FIHR koh,* **RUDOLF** (1821-1902), a German scientist and political leader, is considered the father of *pathology* (the study of diseased body tissue). He did important research in leukemia, tuberculosis, rickets, tumors, and trichinosis. His hygienic reforms in Berlin were important advances in public health.

Virchow entered politics in 1862, and was elected to the Prussian Assembly. After Germany was united, he served in the Reichstag (parliament) until 1893. He became a leader of the Liberal party and a bitter op-

The Yellow-Throated Vireo builds its nest high in the tree-tops. It has a weak but musical song.

ponent of Chancellor Otto von Bismarck. Virchow was born in Pomerania.   ROBERT G. L. WAITE

VIREO, *VIR ee oh,* is the name of a family of small birds. They stay close to the foliage in the forests, and feed on insects. People also call the birds *greenlets* because of their greenish color. Vireos live only in North America, chiefly in the tropics. A few species migrate as far north as the United States and Canada.

The best-known vireo is the red-eyed vireo. People can recognize this bird by its red eyes, which have a white line with a black border above them. The note it sings sounds rather conversational, as if the bird were talking to any listener. Since it repeats this note continually, the vireo is often called the *preacher bird.*

Vireos build cup-shaped nests which hang from forked branches in the trees. The female lays three or four white eggs marked with a few dark specks near the large end. Vireos help man by eating harmful insects.

Scientific Classification. Vireos make up the family *Vireonidae.* The red-eyed vireo is genus *Vireo,* species *V. olivaceus.*   LEONARD W. WING

See also BIRD (picture: Birds of Forests).

VIRGIL, or **VERGIL** (70-19 B.C.), was the greatest poet of ancient Rome and one of the outstanding poets of the world. His masterpiece was the *Aeneid,* the national epic of Rome.

His Life. Virgil was born in Andes, a tiny village near Mantua in northern Italy. His full name in Latin, the language of ancient Rome, was Publius Vergilius Maro. Virgil attended schools in Cremona, Milan, Naples, and Rome. He intended to pursue a law career, but his shyness and awkward manner stood in the way. He turned to poetry instead. His poems attracted the attention of Maecenas, a wealthy patron of the arts and a political adviser to the future emperor, Augustus. Virgil became one of a group of writers who gathered around Maecenas.

Maecenas gave Virgil a house near Naples and encouraged him to write patriotic poems, including the *Aeneid.* Virgil died before he finished the *Aeneid,* and left instructions that the poem be destroyed because he was dissatisfied with it. However, Augustus disregarded Virgil's wish and appointed two of the poet's friends to prepare the *Aeneid* for publication.

His Works. Some scholars attribute a number of minor poems, collected under the title *Virgilian Appendix,* to Virgil's early years. Virgil wrote his first important poems, the *Eclogues,* or *Bucolics,* between 42 and 37 B.C. These 10 poems are *pastorals*—that is, they deal with the lives of shepherds. In writing the *Eclogues,* Virgil imitated the pastoral poems of the Greek poet Theocritus. But Virgil adapted the Greek settings

and themes to the Italian scene. In melodious verse, the *Eclogues* describe the tranquil beauty of country life. The fourth *Eclogue* foretells the birth of a miraculous child who will bring in a new age. Emperor Constantine, Rome's ruler in the early A.D. 300's, and some Christian writers interpreted this prophecy as referring to Jesus Christ.

Virgil spent about seven years writing the *Georgics*, four poems published in 29 B.C. On one level, the *Georgics* are instructive poems about farming. The first poem deals with crops, the second with vines and olives, the third with cattle and horses, and the fourth with bees. But the *Georgics* go beyond practical instruction to celebrate the joy and harmony of farm life. The deep thoughts expressed in the *Georgics* show that Virgil was a philosopher as well as a poet.

For the story of the *Aeneid*, Virgil drew on many sources, the most important being the works of the Greek poet Homer. Virgil based the first six books of the *Aeneid* on Homer's *Odyssey* and the last six on Homer's *Iliad*. Despite Virgil's debt to others, the *Aeneid* is a stately, powerful, and original work.

The *Aeneid* describes the adventures of Aeneas, the legendary Trojan hero who survived the fall of Troy, sailed westward to Italy, and founded the city of Rome. But the *Aeneid* is not just the story of Aeneas. The poem also shows that Rome became great as part of a divine plan. Virgil incorporated in his poem all of Rome's history up to his own time. He represented Augustus as Aeneas' direct descendant and as a leader appointed by the gods. In this way, Virgil glorified Augustus and expressed the emperor's ideals and his hopes for the Roman Empire. Virgil's message was that Rome, led by Augustus and protected by the gods, had a mission—to bring peace and justice to the world.

His Influence. Roman schools used Virgil's works as textbooks by A.D. 100. Copies of the *Aeneid* were kept in Roman temples, and people practiced prophecy by opening the poem at random and interpreting the first words they saw. Later, Christian writers used verses from Virgil's poems to express their own beliefs. During the Middle Ages, people regarded Virgil as a prophet who had foreseen the coming of Christ. They even considered him to have been a magician.

The Italian poet Dante Alighieri based his great epic, the *Divine Comedy* (1321), on the sixth book of the *Aeneid*. Dante regarded Virgil as his literary master, and in the *Divine Comedy* he has Virgil guide him on his journey through hell and purgatory.

During the Renaissance, Virgil's *Eclogues* influenced the pastoral poetry of such writers as Petrarch of Italy, Joachim du Bellay of France, and Sir Philip Sidney of England. From the 1500's through the 1700's, English writers regarded Virgil as the ideal poet. For example, the poet John Milton often imitated Virgil in his own works, especially *Paradise Lost* (1667). The poet John Dryden translated the *Aeneid* into English verse in the late 1600's. Virgil also influenced many writers during the 1800's, including the English poets William Wordsworth and Lord Tennyson.   HERBERT MUSURILLO

See also AENEID.

VIRGIN ISLANDS is the name of two groups of small islands east of Puerto Rico. They lie between the Carib-

bean Sea and the Atlantic Ocean. One of the groups consists of St. Croix, St. John, and St. Thomas islands, together with many nearby islets. This group is called THE VIRGIN ISLANDS OF THE UNITED STATES. It is the easternmost United States possession. The other group includes Anegada, Jost van Dyke, Tortola, and Virgin Gorda islands, with their own surrounding islets. It is called the BRITISH VIRGIN ISLANDS.

Christopher Columbus arrived at the Virgin Islands on his second voyage to America in 1493. The fresh beauty and untouched appearance of their hills rising from the sea charmed him. He named the group the Virgin Islands, in memory of St. Ursula and her 11,000 maidens (see URSULA, SAINT).

Columbus claimed all the islands for Spain, but the Spaniards did not settle there. The British Virgin Islands have been under the British flag since 1672. About that same time, Denmark established a permanent settlement on St. Thomas. The Danes took possession of St. John in 1717, and bought St. Croix from France in 1733. In 1917, Denmark sold its West Indian possessions to the United States for $25 million, or about $295 an acre.

All the Virgin Islands except Anegada and St. Croix are rugged and hilly. A few good harbors in the group make it an important trade center. Watch movements, petroleum products, refined bauxite, rum, and perfume are among the major exports of the American islands. The soil is fertile, but the land has not been intensively cultivated. The islands produce limited amounts of beef cattle and chickens and some fruits and vegetables.

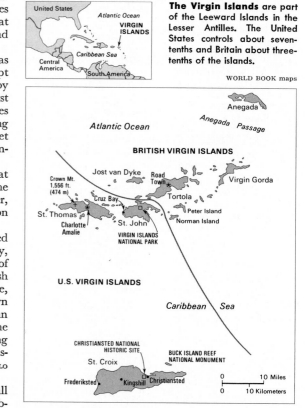

The Virgin Islands are part of the Leeward Islands in the Lesser Antilles. The United States controls about seven-tenths and Britain about three-tenths of the islands.

WORLD BOOK maps

The Territorial Seal

The Virgin Islands of the United States proved to have great military importance during World War II, especially as an outpost to protect the Panama Canal. Today, the island group is a popular tourist and resort area. Congress created the Virgin Islands National Park on Aug. 2, 1956, adding greater interest in the group as a tourist center.

The rest of this article discusses the Virgin Islands of the United States. For information on the British Virgin Islands, see VIRGIN ISLANDS, BRITISH.

The Land and Its Resources

Location and Size. The Virgin Islands of the United States lie about 40 miles (64 kilometers) east of Puerto

The Territorial Flag

Rico, just west of the British Virgin Islands. The group forms the westernmost part of a great chain of West Indian islands called the Lesser Antilles (see WEST INDIES). Miami, Fla., lies about 1,100 miles (1,770 kilometers) to the northwest, and Panama is about 1,200 miles (1,930 kilometers) to the southwest. The Virgin Islands cover 133 square miles (344 square kilometers). Rhode Island, the smallest state in the Union, is over nine times as large. The islands have a general coastline of 117 miles (188 kilometers), and a *tidal shoreline*, including offshore islands, sounds, bays, rivers, and creeks, of 175 miles (282 kilometers).

─────────── FACTS IN BRIEF ───────────

Capital: Charlotte Amalie (since 1917).

Government: *Territorial Legislature*—a one-house legislature of 15 senators.

Area: 133 sq. mi. (344 km²). *Coastline*—117 mi. (188 km).

Elevation: *Highest*—Crown Mt. on St. Thomas, 1,556 ft. (474 m) above sea level; *Lowest*—sea level along the coasts.

Population: *1980 Census*—95,591; density, 719 persons per sq. mi. (278 persons per km²); distribution, 61 per cent urban, 39 per cent rural. *1970 Census*—62,468.

Chief Products: *Agriculture*—beef cattle, chickens, eggs, goats, hogs, milk, vegetables. *Manufacturing*—concrete products, petroleum products, refined bauxite, rum, scientific instruments, textiles, and watches.

Territorial Seal: The coat of arms of the United States, with the American eagle and the shield of the United States, lies in the center of the seal. The words "Government of the Virgin Islands of the United States" encircle the coat of arms. Adopted in 1917.

Territorial Abbreviation: VI (postal).

Territorial Flag: A golden American eagle with the shield of the United States on its breast appears on a white field. The eagle holds a sprig of green laurel in its right talon, and a bundle of blue arrows in its left talon. The blue letters *V* and *I* are to the left and right of the eagle. Adopted in 1917. See FLAG (color picture: Flags of the States and Territories).

Fritz Henle

Virgin Islands Fishing Crews catch bonito, grouper, kingfish, red snapper, and Spanish mackerel to add variety to their menu. Nets are hung on poles when not being used or mended.

307

Scenic Ruins of Princess Plantation, an old sugar-cane farm, are a landmark on St. Croix. Landowners began developing plantations on the islands during the early 1700's.

Islands. All the American islands, except St. Croix, are rugged and hilly. Only three of the islands are inhabited. Hills on the three major islands reach heights of 1,000 to 1,550 feet (300 to 472 meters) or more above sea level. Many bays and inlets cut into the coasts of the islands. Fossils of ancient animals show that the sea once covered the Virgin Islands. The composition of the rocks that form much of the land suggests that volcanoes pushed the islands up from the ocean floor. Some tiny islets are mere rocks jutting from the water. Plant life grows on other islets.

St. Croix—pronounced *saynt kroy*—(pop. 49,013), the largest of the islands, lies about 40 miles (64 kilometers) south of St. Thomas. It covers 82 square miles (212 square kilometers) and makes up about two-thirds of the island group's area. Bauxite processing, petroleum refining, rum production, and tourism are the major economic activities on the island. Christiansted and Frederiksted are the island's only cities. Spanish-speaking people call St. Croix *Santa Cruz*, the name Christopher Columbus gave it.

St. John (pop. 2,360) lies 2 miles (3 kilometers) east of St. Thomas, and less than 1 mile (1.6 kilometers) from British Tortola. It covers 19 square miles (49 square kilometers). The Virgin Islands National Park spreads over about three-fourths of the island (see VIRGIN ISLANDS NATIONAL PARK). Villages are at Cruz Bay and Coral Bay, and a tourist development is at Caneel Bay. Most of the people live on small plots of land and produce their own fruits, vegetables, and poultry. They buy other food products at supermarkets on St. John and on the neighboring island of St. Thomas. Many islanders work for the territorial government and the National Park Service. Others are employed in the tourist industry.

St. Thomas (pop. 44,218) covers 27 square miles (70 square kilometers). Its central range of hills offers lovely views of the ocean. Crown Mountain, the highest point in the entire group, rises 1,556 feet (474 meters) above sea level. The only city on the island is Charlotte Ama-

lie, the capital of the Virgin Islands. The harbor at Charlotte Amalie provides safe anchorage for even the largest ships. Most of the people on the island work for the Virgin Islands government or in tourism-related businesses.

Natural Resources of the Virgin Islands cannot support the people, who must depend on the United States for most of their products. But the excellent climate, attractive beaches, and lovely scenery make the islands a favorite with vacationers. Tropical flowers and trees flourish, including the bougainvillea, canaria, flame tree, and hibiscus. The seas abound with fish. The Virgin Islands mineral production consists mainly of basalt, which is used as roadstone or in making concrete.

An Oil Refinery on the southern coast of St. Croix Island is one of the largest industrial plants in the Virgin Islands.

Climate. The Virgin Islands have a delightful tropical climate the year around. The growing season never ends. Trade winds blow over the islands most of the year, and there are no extremes of heat or cold. The temperature ranges from 70° to 90° F. (21° to 32° C), and averages 78° F. (26° C). The islands receive from 40 to 60 inches (100 to 150 centimeters) of rainfall a year. The amount of rainfall varies widely from island to island, and higher elevations may get from 50 to 60 inches (130 to 150 centimeters) of rainfall a year. The heaviest rains in the Virgin Islands generally occur in spring and fall.

The People

The 1980 U.S. Census reported that the Virgin Islands had a population of 95,591. The population had increased 53 per cent over the 1970 figure of 62,468. Of every 100 islanders, 70 are black and 18 are white. The rest are of mixed race or belong to other races. Of every 100 islanders, 47 were born in the Virgin Islands, 13 in the continental United States, and 6 in Puerto Rico. Most of the rest moved there from other Caribbean islands. Major religious groups include Episcopalians, Lutherans, Methodists, Moravians, and Roman Catholics. The islanders speak and read English.

Charlotte Amalie (pop. 11,756), the capital and largest city in the Virgin Islands, serves as the tourist center of St. Thomas. The city's excellent harbor makes it the chief trade center of the group. Frederiksted (pop. 1,054) is a St. Croix trade center. Christiansted (pop. 2,856) is the local government center on St. Croix. The islands also have several small residential districts.

Work of the People

The Tourist Industry is the Virgin Islands' major industry. About 1 million tourists visit the islands

each year, and they add more than $150 million to the economy of the islands annually. Visitors enjoy excellent bathing beaches, fishing, hotels, restaurants, and shops. Ruins of forts built by Danes and used by pirates during the 1700's are also popular. A popular attraction is the carnival held on St. Thomas at the end of April.

Manufacturing. Two distilleries on the islands make rum. Taxes on exported rum provide over $20 million annually for the government of the Virgin Islands.

Many new industries have been started on the islands. These include an aluminum ore refining plant, an oil refinery, a knitting mill, and factories that make perfume, thermometers, and watches. Watch movements, petroleum products, refined bauxite, rum, and perfume are among the major exports. Most exports are shipped to the United States.

Agriculture. Most of the food Virgin Islanders eat must be imported. But there is some farm income from beef cattle and dairy herds. Eggs are a leading farm product on the islands. There are slaughterhouses on St. Croix and St. Thomas. Farmers grow such vegetables as cucumbers, peppers, and tomatoes. Farmers also grow fruits and raise nuts. Grain sorghum is grown for the feeding of livestock.

Transportation. Two airlines fly from the United States to the Virgin Islands. Several airlines offer service among the islands. About 20 steamship lines serve Charlotte Amalie, Frederiksted, and Christiansted. About 8,000 freighters, liners, and naval vessels dock at island ports each year. All the inhabited islands have paved roads. The Virgin Islands are the only U.S. possession where motorists drive on the left side of the road.

Communication. Newspapers published in the Virgin Islands include the *Daily News* on St. Thomas and the *St. Croix Avis* on St. Croix. The islands have daily

Fritz Henle, U.S. Virgin Islands, Division of Tourism

Christiansted, the largest town on St. Croix Island, lies on a harbor surrounded by hills on the island's northern coast. In the harbor is a smaller island called the Cay, *center.*

Virgin Islands Government Office of Public Relations and Information

Government House at Charlotte Amalie on St. Thomas Island serves as the administrative headquarters of the Virgin Islands. The governor lives and works here.

airmail service and a local telephone system. Telephone cables connect the islands' system with Puerto Rico and the United States mainland. The Virgin Islands also have radio-telegraph service to all parts of the world. St. Croix and St. Thomas have radio and television stations.

Education

The public school system of the Virgin Islands provides education from kindergarten through high school. A nine-member board of education supervises the system, which includes about 35 schools and more than 25,000 students. The board members are elected to two-year terms. Children must attend school between the ages of $5\frac{1}{2}$ and 16. The College of the Virgin Islands is the only accredited institution of higher education in the islands. Its main campus is on St. Thomas and it has a two-year branch campus on St. Croix.

Four public libraries operate in the Virgin Islands, one each on St. John and St. Thomas and two on St. Croix. The islands also have four museums. St. Croix has two and St. John and St. Thomas each have one.

Government

The Virgin Islands are a self-governing territory of the United States. The chief executive officer is a governor elected by the people for a four-year term. The governor may not serve for more than two consecutive terms.

The territorial legislature consists of a *unicameral* (one-house) body of 15 members. The legislature is called the Senate and its members are called senators. The people elect the senators to two-year terms. St. Croix elects seven senators, St. Thomas and St. John together elect seven more, and one is elected at-large. The senator elected at-large must come from St. John. The governor may veto any bills, but the veto may be overridden by a two-thirds majority of the legislature. The legislature meets at Charlotte Amalie on the second Monday in January and continues to meet at various times throughout the year. The governor may also call special sessions of the legislature.

A federal district court known as the District Court of the Virgin Islands heads the judicial system of the islands. This court has jurisdiction over certain local affairs as well as in federal cases. The President appoints the court's two judges with the advice and consent of the U.S. Senate. The judges of the federal district court serve eight-year terms. The governor of the Virgin Islands appoints territorial court judges to six-year terms. These appointments require the advice and consent of the territorial legislature. All residents who are 18 years of age or older and are U.S. citizens may vote in local elections. The islanders send a nonvoting representative to the U.S. Congress. They cannot vote in national elections of any kind.

History

Exploration. Christopher Columbus sighted the Virgin Islands in 1493, during his second voyage to the Americas. Warlike, cannibalistic Carib Indians lived on the islands at that time. They fought with members of Columbus' crew at Sugar Bay on St. Croix. The Caribs continued to attack Europeans during the 1500's. In the mid-1500's, King Charles I of Spain ordered his soldiers to kill the Indians and take their lands. All the Indians had died or left the Virgin Islands by the time the British and Danes began settlement in the 1600's. See CARIB INDIANS.

Early Settlement. A group of English settlers visited the Virgin Islands in 1607 on their way to establish a colony in Jamestown, Va. The Spaniards used the islands as a place to hide their treasure ships from pirates, but never settled there. No Europeans attempted settlement until 1625, when Dutch and English settlers landed on St. Croix. They lived there until the mid-1600's, when Spaniards from Puerto Rico drove them out. Within 20 years, the Spaniards were driven out by the French. The French controlled St. Croix until 1733, when they sold the island to the Danes for $150,000.

The Danes formally claimed St. Thomas in 1666 by establishing a settlement on the island. Eric Smidt was named the first governor of the island, but his colony failed. The Danes made no new settlement on St. Thomas until 1672. In 1717, they settled on St. John.

The Danish West Indies, which included St. Croix, St. John, and St. Thomas, remained under Danish control during most of the years until 1917. They surrendered twice to the British during the Napoleonic Wars. The British quartered thousands of English-speaking soldiers and sailors on the islands during the second

British occupation, from 1807 to 1815. They established English as the common language of the people.

Commercial Development. The Danish West India Company controlled the development of the Virgin Islands for the first hundred years of Danish rule. The Danes made St. Thomas a free port in an effort to develop the islands into an important trade center (see FREE TRADE ZONE). In the early 1700's, landowners used slave labor in developing sugar and cotton plantations.

A bloody slave uprising in 1733 destroyed St. John's economic prospects, because other countries feared using the island's trade facilities. This revolt caused the Danes to increase military authority in the group. An uprising on St. Croix in 1848 caused immediate abolition of slavery on July 3, 1848. Continued efforts by the Danes to develop the islands proved unsuccessful.

On Aug. 4, 1916, Denmark and the United States signed a treaty transferring control of the Virgin Islands to the United States. The treaty was formally ratified on Jan. 17, 1917. Actual control of the islands was transferred on March 31, 1917. The United States paid Denmark $25 million for the islands. James H. Oliver served as the territory's first governor.

Progress Under the United States. In 1927, Congress passed a law making the people of the Virgin Islands citizens of the United States. In 1936, persons who could read and write English were granted the right to vote in local elections. At the close of World War II, the United States set aside $10 million for the further development of the islands. Projects included schools, hospitals, roads, and sewerage and water systems.

In 1954, Congress provided for a regular legislature in the Virgin Islands. In 1956, Congress established the Virgin Islands National Park on St. John. Buck Island Reef National Monument was established near St. Croix in 1961. During the 1960's, the government built health centers, houses, and schools.

In 1958, John D. Merwin became the first native-born governor of the islands. Ralph M. Paiewonsky, also native-born, succeeded him in 1961. Paiewonsky resigned in 1969, and Melvin H. Evans became the first native-born black governor. In 1968, Congress passed a law giving the people the right to elect their own governor. The voters elected Evans in 1970. Cyril E. King won election in 1974 and served until his death in 1978. Juan F. Luis, who had been lieutenant governor, became governor.   RALPH M. PAIEWONSKY

Related Articles in WORLD BOOK include:

Questions

Of what important military value were the Virgin Islands to the United States during World War II?

How does automobile driving in the Virgin Islands differ from that in the United States?

Who was the first white to see the Virgin Islands?

How do the Virgin Islands compare in size with the smallest American state?

How did the Virgin Islands receive their name?

For what is each major island important?

When did Virgin Islanders become U.S. citizens?

What industry provides the largest source of income?

When did Denmark establish its first permanent colony in the Virgin Islands? Where?

Taxes on what product have paid for the original cost of the Virgin Islands?

VIRGIN ISLANDS, BRITISH, are a dependency of Great Britain in the West Indies. They lie near the western end of the Lesser Antilles. A channel called *the Narrows* separates the group from The Virgin Islands of the United States (see VIRGIN ISLANDS [map]).

The islands cover 59 square miles (153 square kilometers) and have a population of 12,000. The group consists of 32 small islands, the largest of which are Anegada, Jost van Dyke, Tortola, and Virgin Gorda islands. Road Town (pop. 3,500) is the capital and only urban area. Major products include beef cattle, fish, fruits and vegetables, and rum. See also BRITISH WEST INDIES; WEST INDIES.   J. ANTONIO JARVIS

VIRGIN ISLANDS NATIONAL PARK lies chiefly on St. John, the smallest of the three chief American-owned Virgin Islands in the Caribbean Sea. The park was authorized on Aug. 2, 1956. Laurance S. Rockefeller donated over 5,000 acres (2,000 hectares) for it.

The park occupies two-thirds of St. John, 15 acres (6 hectares) on St. Thomas Island, and 5,650 acres (2,286 hectares) of waters and smaller islands. For the park's area, see NATIONAL PARK SYSTEM (table: National Parks). Lush tropical vegetation grows throughout the park. The rugged land rises to 1,277 feet (389 meters) at Bordeaux Peak.

Mules and jeeps provide the chief methods of transportation. The park is reached by a 2½-mile (4-kilometer) ferry trip from eastern St. Thomas Island across Pillsbury Sound to Cruz Bay, the main village on St. John. Tourist facilities are limited, but camp grounds, hotels, and cottage colonies are planned.

Virgin Islands National Park has many reminders of the Danish occupation of St. John, which lasted from the 1700's to 1917. Remains of Danish sugar mills and lavish plantations can be found.   OTIS P. STARKEY

VIRGIN MARY. See MARY.

VIRGIN OF GUADALUPE. See MEXICO (Religion).

VIRGINAL is an ancient keyboard instrument in which small pieces of quill or leather pluck a set of strings. It usually has a rectangular case, with the keyboard on the longer side. The virginal has a light, clear, and somewhat tinkling tone. It was particularly popular as a solo instrument in Elizabethan England. Leading composers of the times wrote for it. The *Fitzwilliam Virginal Book*, assembled around 1625 and containing nearly 300 numbers, is the most important collection of music for virginals.   KARL GEIRINGER

George Washington's Home at Mount Vernon

VIRGINIA Old Dominion

VIRGINIA is perhaps the most historic of all the 50 states. Some of the most important events in American history took place there. The first permanent English settlement in America was made at Jamestown in 1607. In 1619, the Jamestown colonists established the first representative legislature in America. Some of the greatest battles of the Revolutionary War and Civil War were fought in Virginia. American independence from Great Britain was assured when George Washington forced Lord Cornwallis to surrender at Yorktown in 1781. The Civil War ended when the Confederate forces surrendered at Appomattox in 1865.

Virginia was named for Queen Elizabeth I of England, the *Virgin Queen*. Historians think the English adventurer Sir Walter Raleigh suggested the name about 1584. That year, Elizabeth gave Raleigh permission to colonize the Virginia region. Virginia is also known as the *Old Dominion*. King Charles II gave it this name because it remained loyal to the crown during the English Civil War of the mid-1600's. Virginia is one of four states officially called *commonwealths*. The others are Kentucky, Massachusetts, and Pennsylvania.

Virginia has the nickname *Mother of Presidents* because eight U.S. Presidents were born there. They include four of the first five Presidents—George Washington, Thomas Jefferson, James Madison, and James Monroe. Other Presidents born in Virginia were William Henry Harrison, John Tyler, Zachary Taylor, and Woodrow Wilson. Virginia also has the nickname *Mother of States*. All or part of eight other states were formed from western territory once claimed by Virginia. These states are Illinois, Indiana, Kentucky, Michigan, Minnesota, Ohio, West Virginia, and Wisconsin.

Tourists from all parts of the United States come to Virginia to see its battlefields, famous old churches, colonial homes, and other historic sites. Famous homes include George Washington's Mount Vernon, Thomas Jefferson's Monticello, and George Mason's Gunston Hall. The Tomb of the Unknown Soldier and the grave of President John F. Kennedy are in Arlington National Cemetery. The cemetery surrounds the mansion of Robert E. Lee and his wife, Mary Custis Lee. Williamsburg, Virginia's second colonial capital, has been restored to look as it did in the 1700's. Antique furnishings, horse-drawn carriages, and guides in colonial costumes add to the historic atmosphere.

Many tourists also come to see Virginia's beautiful scenery. The Skyline Drive along the top of the Blue Ridge offers spectacular views of the Shenandoah Valley. In this fertile valley, General Thomas J. "Stonewall" Jackson won victories over Union armies during the Civil War. Virginia's natural wonders include the Natural Bridge, Natural Chimneys, Natural Tunnel, and many large caves and caverns.

Tobacco has been a leading crop in Virginia since John Rolfe first planted it in early colonial days. Virginia also ranks high among the states in raising apples, broiler chickens, peanuts, and turkeys. Virginia is famous for its Smithfield hams.

Virginia is an example of the industrialization of the South in modern times. Factories produce chemicals, food products, tobacco products, and transportation equipment. Shipyards in the Hampton Roads area build ships for the United States Navy and for commercial use.

Richmond, the capital of the Confederacy from May, 1861, to April, 1865, is Virginia's capital. Norfolk is the largest city.

312

Jack Zehrt, FPG

Springtime in the Blue Ridge Mountains

The contributors of this article are Raymond C. Dingledine, Jr., Head of the History Department at James Madison University, and John E. Leard, former Executive Editor of the Richmond Times-Dispatch *and* Richmond News Leader.

Fox Hunting in Northern Virginia

John Freeman, Publix

Virginia (blue) ranks 36th in size among all the states, and 9th in size among the Southern States (gray).

Facts in Brief

Capital: Richmond.

Government: *Congress*—U.S. senators, 2; U.S. representatives, 10. *Electoral Votes*—12. *State Legislature*—senators, 40; delegates, 100. *Counties*—95.

Area: 40,767 sq. mi. (105,586 km²), including 1,063 sq. mi. (2,753 km²) of inland water but excluding 1,511 sq. mi. (3,913 km²) of Chesapeake Bay; 36th in size among the states. *Greatest Distances*—east-west, 452 mi. (727 km); north-south, 209 mi. (336 km). *Coastline*—112 mi. (180 km).

Elevation: *Highest*—Mount Rogers in Grayson and Smyth counties, 5,729 ft. (1,746 m) above sea level. *Lowest*—sea level.

Population: *1980 Census*—5,346,797; 14th among the states; density, 131 persons per sq. mi. (51 persons per km²);

distribution, 66 per cent urban, 34 per cent rural. *1970 Census*—4,651,448.

Chief Products: *Agriculture*—milk, beef cattle, tobacco, broilers, soybeans. *Fishing Industry*—menhaden, clams, crabs, oysters. *Manufacturing*—tobacco products; chemicals; food products; electrical machinery and equipment; transportation equipment; printed materials; textiles; paper products; rubber and plastic products; nonelectric machinery. *Mining*—coal, stone, lime, sand and gravel.

Statehood: June 25, 1788, the 10th state.

State Abbreviations: Va. (traditional); VA (postal).

State Motto: *Sic Semper Tyrannis* (Thus always to tyrants).

State Song: "Carry Me Back to Old Virginia." Words and music by James A. Bland.

313

Constitution of Virginia became effective in 1971. The state had five earlier constitutions, which went into effect in 1776, 1830, 1851, 1869, and 1902.

Constitutional amendments may be proposed in either house of the state legislature. To become law, the proposed amendments must be approved by a majority of both houses in two successive sessions. Then they must be approved by a majority of persons who vote on the issue. The Constitution may also be amended by a constitutional convention. Such a convention is called by a majority of the legislature with the approval of a majority of Virginia's voters.

Executive. The governor of Virginia is elected to a four-year term. He or she cannot serve two terms in a row. The governor receives a yearly salary of $75,000. For a list of the state's governors, see the *History* section of this article.

The lieutenant governor also is elected to a four-year term. The governor appoints almost all the top state officials, including the secretary of the commonwealth, adjutant general, treasurer, and comptroller. The people of Virginia elect the attorney general to a four-year term. The legislature elects the auditor, who serves a four-year term.

Legislature of Virginia is called the *General Assembly*. It is the oldest representative legislature in America. It traces its history to the House of Burgesses, formed in 1619 (see HOUSE OF BURGESSES).

The General Assembly consists of a 40-member Senate and a 100-member House of Delegates. The Senate and the House of Delegates are apportioned into single-member districts. Voters in each senatorial district elect one senator, and voters in each delegate district elect one delegate. Senators serve four-year terms, and delegates serve two-year terms.

The General Assembly holds regular sessions every year. Sessions begin on the second Wednesday in January. They last up to 60 days in even-numbered years and up to 30 days in odd-numbered years. The governor may call special sessions.

By law, the legislature must *reapportion* (redivide) itself the year after each U.S. census. The redistricting is designed to provide equal representation based on population.

Courts. The state's highest court is the Supreme Court of Virginia. It has seven justices, who are elected by the General Assembly to 12-year terms. The justice who has served longest becomes chief justice for the rest of his or her term.

Circuit courts are the next highest courts in Virginia. The judges of these courts are elected by the General Assembly. Circuit court judges serve eight-year terms. Lower courts in Virginia include juvenile and domestic relations courts and general district courts. The General Assembly elects the judges of these courts to six-year terms.

Local Government. Virginia has 95 counties. Each county except Arlington is governed by a board of supervisors. Arlington has a county board. In most counties, voters elect other officials, including a commissioner of revenue, treasurer, sheriff, commonwealth's attorney, and county clerk. The clerk has an eight-year term. The other officials are elected to four-year terms.

A few counties have a county-manager or county-executive government. In these Virginia counties, a county manager or the board of supervisors appoints executive officials.

Any Virginia town with 5,000 or more persons may become an independent city if the people so wish. Virginia has 41 independent cities. Unlike the cities of most other states, these 41 cities are legally separate from the counties in which they are located. One of the first forms of council-manager government in a U.S. city was established in Staunton in 1908. Today, all Virginia cities have council-manager governments. Some towns in Virginia have council-manager governments, and the others have mayor-council governments.

Revenue. Taxes and license fees bring in about three-fifths of the state government's *general revenue* (income). Virginia collects taxes on motor fuels, and on individual and corporation incomes. It also receives money from the sale of alcoholic beverages in state-owned stores. A general sales tax went into effect in 1966. The federal government provides about 20 per cent of the state's revenue. This money comes in the form of grants and other assistance programs.

Governor's Mansion in Richmond stands northeast of the Capitol. The Federal-style brick home was built in 1813. It replaced an earlier governor's residence built on the same site.

The State Seal

The State Flag

Symbols of Virginia. On the front of the seal, the standing figure represents Virtue dressed as a woman warrior. She is triumphant over Tyranny. The Latin motto means "Thus always to tyrants." On the back of the seal, the figures represent, *left* to *right,* eternity, liberty, and agriculture. The Latin motto means "By persevering." A committee of four men designed the seal. It was first adopted in 1776. The present version was authorized in 1930. The flag probably was first used in the mid-1800's, but it was not adopted until 1930.

Flag and flower illustrations, courtesy of Eli Lilly and Company;
seal, bird, and tree, WORLD BOOK illustrations

Politics. The Democratic Party has controlled Virginia politics throughout most of the state's history. But Republicans began to show strength in 1969, when A. Linwood Holton, Jr., became the first Republican to be elected governor in nearly 100 years. Republicans also won the governorship in 1973 and 1977, but Democrats won in 1981 and 1985.

Virginia Democrats are split into two groups. The larger, more conservative group was headed by Senator Harry F. Byrd, Sr., until he retired in 1965. Its members have been called "Byrd Democrats." Members of the other group, often called "liberal Democrats," have their greatest strength in the north and the east. The conservative Democrats sometimes support Republican candidates in presidential elections. Partly for this reason, Virginia has voted Republican in several national elections. For the state's voting record in presidential elections, see ELECTORAL COLLEGE (table).

The State Bird
Cardinal

State Capitol in Richmond was designed by Thomas Jefferson. The original building was completed in 1792. The Capitol was modeled after a Roman temple in Nîmes, France. The Confederate Congress met in the Capitol during the Civil War. Richmond has been the state capital since 1780. Earlier capitals were Jamestown (1607-1699) and Williamsburg (1699-1780).

Virginia Dept. of Conservation and Economic Development

The State Flower
Flowering Dogwood

The State Tree
Flowering Dogwood

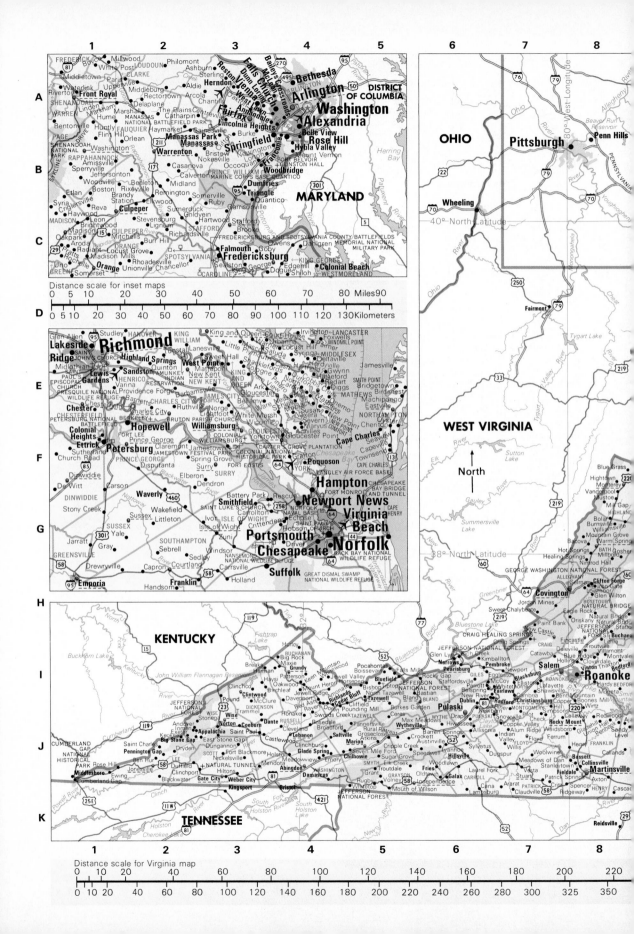

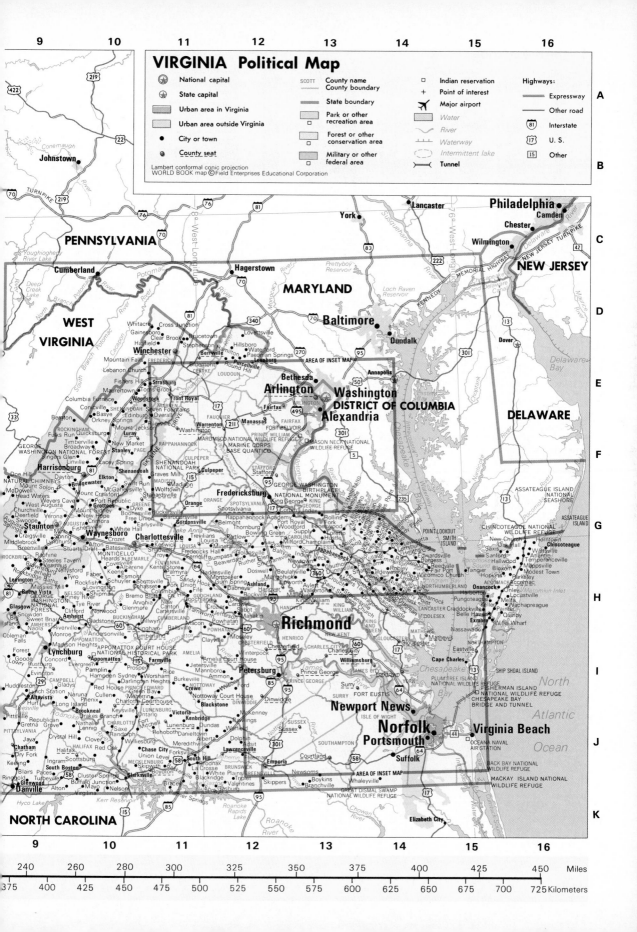

VIRGINIA Political Map

- ⓐ National capital
- ⓑ State capital
- ▓ Urban area in Virginia
- ░ Urban area outside Virginia
- ● City or town
- ● County seat

SCOTT County name
County boundary
State boundary
□ Park or other recreation area
□ Forest or other conservation area
□ Military or other federal area

- □ Indian reservation
- + Point of interest
- ✈ Major airport
- ░ Water
- River
- Waterway
- Intermittent lake
- Tunnel

Highways:
- Expressway
- Other road
- ⑧⑴ Interstate
- ⑰ U.S.
- ⑮ Other

Lambert conformal conic projection
WORLD BOOK map ©Field Enterprises Educational Corporation

PENNSYLVANIA

WEST VIRGINIA

MARYLAND
Baltimore
Dundalk

NEW JERSEY

DELAWARE

Washington
DISTRICT OF COLUMBIA
Arlington
Alexandria

Harrisonburg

Staunton
Waynesboro
Charlottesville

Lynchburg

Richmond

Petersburg

Newport News
Norfolk
Portsmouth
Virginia Beach

Danville

NORTH CAROLINA

North
Atlantic
Ocean

240	260	280	300	325	350	375	400	425	450	Miles

| 375 | 400 | 425 | 450 | 475 | 500 | 525 | 550 | 575 | 600 | 625 | 650 | 675 | 700 | 725 | Kilometers |

Virginia Map Index

Population

5,346,797 . . Census . . 1980
4,651,448 . . . . " 1970
3,966,949 . . . . " 1960
3,318,680 . . . . " 1950
2,677,773 . . . . " 1940
2,421,851 . . . . " 1930
2,309,187 . . . . " 1920
2,061,612 . . . . " 1910
1,854,184 . . . . " 1900
1,655,980 . . . . " 1890
1,512,565 . . . . " 1880
1,225,163 . . . . " 1870
1,219,630 . . . . " 1860
1,119,348 . . . . " 1850
1,025,277 . . . . " 1840
1,044,054 . . . . " 1830
938,261 . . . . " 1820
877,683 . . . . " 1810
807,557 . . . . " 1800
691,737 . . . . " 1790

Metropolitan Areas

Charlottesville 113,568
Danville 111,789
Johnson City-Kingsport (Tenn.)-Bristol . . . 433,638 (343,041 in Tenn.; 90,597 in Va.)
Lynchburg 141,289
Norfolk-Virginia Beach-Newport News . 1,160,311
Richmond-Petersburg 761,311
Roanoke 220,393
Washington, D.C. . . . . 3,250,822 (1,466,305 in Md.; 1,146,184 in Va.; 638,333 in D.C.)

Counties

Accomack . . . . 31,268. .H 15
Albemarle . . . . 55,783. .G 10
Alleghany . . . . 14,333. .H 8
Amelia . . . . 8,405. .I 11
Amherst . . . . . 29,122. .H 9
Appomattox . . 11,971. .I 10
Arlington . . . . 152,599. .E 13
Augusta . . . . . . 53,732. .G 9
Bath . . . . 5,860. .G 8
Bedford . . . . . . 34,927. .I 8
Bland . . . . 6,349. .I 6
Botetourt . . . . 23,270. .H 8
Brunswick . . . . 15,632. .J 12
Buchanan . . . . 37,989. .I 4
Buckingham . . 11,751. .H 10
Campbell . . . . . 45,424. .I 9
Caroline . . . . . 17,904. .G 13
Carroll . . . . 27,270. .J 6
Charles City . . . 6,692. .I 13
Charlotte . . . . . 12,266. .J 10
Chesterfield . 141,372. .I 12
Clarke . . . . 9,965. .E 11
Craig . . . . 3,948. .I 7
Culpeper . . . . . 22,620. .F 11
Cumberland . . . 7,881. .H 11
Dickenson . . . . 19,806. .I 3
Dinwiddie . . . . 22,602. .I 12
Essex . . . . 8,864. .G 13
Fairfax . . . . . . 596,901. .F 12
Fauquier . . . . . 35,889. .E 11
Floyd . . . . 11,563. .J 7
Fluvanna . . . . . 10,244. .H 11
Franklin . . . . . . 35,740. .J 8
Frederick . . . . 34,150. .E 11
Giles . . . . 17,810. .I 6
Gloucester . . . 20,107. .I 14
Goochland . . . 11,761. .H 11
Grayson . . . . . . 16,579. .J 5
Greene . . . . 7,625. .G 10
Greensville . . . 10,903. .J 12
Halifax . . . . 30,599. .J 10
Hanover . . . . . . 50,398. .H 12
Henrico . . . . . 180,735. .I 12
Henry . . . . 57,654. .K 8
Highland . . . . . . 2,937. .G 8
Isle of Wight . . . . . . 21,603. .J 14
James City . . . 22,763. .I 13
King and Queen . . . . . . 5,968. .H 14
King George . . 10,543. .G 13
King William . . . . . . 9,334. .H 13
Lancaster . . . . 10,129. .H 14
Lee . . . . 25,956. .J 2
Loudoun . . . . . 57,427. .E 12
Louisa . . . . 17,825. .G 11
Lunenburg . . . 12,124. .J 11
Madison . . . . . . 10,232. .F 11
Mathews . . . . . . 7,995. .H 14
Mecklenburg . 29,444. .J 10
Middlesex . . . . . 7,719. .H 14
Montgomery . . 63,516. .J 7
Nelson . . . . 12,204. .H 9
New Kent . . . . . 8,781. .H 13
Northampton . 14,625. .I 15
Northumberland . . . . 9,828. .H 14
Nottoway . . . . 14,666. .I 11
Orange . . . . . . 18,063. .G 11
Page . . . . 19,401. .F 10
Patrick . . . . 17,647. .K 7
Pittsylvania . . . 66,147. .J 9
Powhatan . . . . 13,062. .H 11
Prince Edward . . . . 16,456. .I 10
Prince George . . . . 25,733. .I 13
Prince William . . . . 144,703. .F 12
Pulaski . . . . 35,229. .J 6
Rappahannock . 6,093. .F 11
Richmond . . . . . 6,952. .G 13
Roanoke . . . . . 72,945. .I 7
Rockbridge . . . 17,911. .G 9
Rockingham . . 57,038. .F 9
Russell . . . . 31,761. .J 4
Scott . . . . 25,068. .J 3
Shenandoah . . 27,559. .E 10
Smyth . . . . 33,345. .J 5
Southampton . 18,731. .J 13
Spotsylvania . . 34,435. .G 12
Stafford . . . . . 40,470. .F 12
Surry . . . . 6,046. .I 13
Sussex . . . . 10,874. .J 13
Tazewell . . . . . 50,511. .J 5
Warren . . . . . . 21,200. .E 11
Washington . . . 46,487. .J 4
Westmoreland 14,041. .G 13
Wise . . . . 43,863. .J 3
Wythe . . . . 25,522. .J 6
York . . . . 35,463. .I 14

Cities and Towns

Abingdon . . . . . 4,318.°J 4
Accomac . . . . 522.°H 16
Achilles . . . . .F 4
Afton . . . . .G 10
Alberta . . . . 394. .J 11
Aldie . . . . .A 2
Alexandria . .103,217†.E 13
Alfonso . . . . .H 14
Allison Gap* . . . 1,060. .J 4
Altavista . . . . . . 3,849. .I 9
Alton . . . . .K 9
Alum Ridge . . . . .J 7
Amelia Court House . . . .°I 11
Amherst . . . . . . 1,135.°H 9
Amissville . . . . .B 1
Ammon . . . . .I 12
Amonate . . . . .I 5
Andersonville . . . . .I 10
Andover . . . . .J 2
Annandale . . . . 49,524. .A 3
Appalachia . . . . 2,418. .J 2
Appomattox . . . 1,345.°I 10
Aquia Harbor* . . . . . 2,870. .F 12
Ararat . . . . .K 7
Arcola . . . . .A 3
Ark . . . . .E 3
Arlington . . . . 152,599.°E 13
Aroda . . . . .C 1
Arvonia . . . . .H 11
Ashburn . . . . .A 3
Ashland . . . . 4,640. .H 12
Atkins . . . . 1,352. .J 5
Atlantic . . . . .G 16
Augusta Springs . . . . . . .G 9
Austinville . . . . .J 6
Axton . . . . .J 8
Aylett . . . . .H 13
Bacova . . . . .G 8
Baileys Crossroads . 12,564. .A 4
Ballsville . . . . .H 11
Barboursville . . . . .G 11
Barhamsville . . . . .E 3
Barren Springs . . . . .J 6
Baskerville . . . . .J 11
Bassett . . . . 2,034. .J 8
Bastian . . . . .I 5
Basye . . . . .E 10
Batesville . . . . .G 10
Bealeton . . . . .B 2
Beaverdam . . . . .G 12
Bedford . . . . 5,991†°I 8
Bellamy . . . . .E 3
Belle Haven . . . . . 589. .H 15
Belle Haven* . . . . . 6,520. .E 12
Belle View . . . . .B 4
Bellwood* . . . . . 6,439. .I 12
Belmont . . . . . . 1,697. .G 11
Belspring . . . . .I 6
Ben Hur . . . . .J 2
Bensley* . . . . . . 5,299. .I 12
Bent Mountain . . . . .I 7
Bentonville . . . . .A 1
Bergton . . . . .F 9
Berryville . . . . . 1,752.°E 11
Big Island . . . . .H 9
Big Rock . . . . .I 4
Big Stone Gap . . . . 4,748. .J 2
Birchleaf . . . . .I 3
Birdsnest . . . . .E 5
Bishop . . . . .I 5
Blackridge . . . . .J 11
Blacksburg . . . 30,638. .I 7
Blackstone . . . . 3,624. .I 11
Blackwater . . . . .J 2
Blairs . . . . .J 9
Bland . . . .°I 6
Bloxom . . . . 407. .H 16
Blue Grass . . . . .F 8
Blue Ridge . . . . 2,347. .I 8
Bluefield . . . . . . 5,946. .I 5
Bluemont . . . . .E 11
Boissevain . . . . .I 5
Bolar . . . . .G 8
Bon Air* . . . . . 16,224. .H 12
Boones Mill . . . . . . 303. .I 8
Boonesville . . . . .G 10
Boston . . . . .B 1
Bowling Green . . . 665.°G 12
Boyce . . . . 401. .A 1
Boydton . . . . 486.°J 11
Boykins . . . . 791. .K 13
Bracey . . . . .K 11
Branchville . . . . . . 174. .K 13
Brandy Station . . . . .B 2
Breaks . . . . .I 3
Bremo Bluff . . . . .H 11
Bridgewater . . . 3,289. .F 9
Brightwood . . . . .C 1
Bristol . . . . 19,042†.K 4
Bristow . . . . .B 3
Broadford . . . . .J 4
Broadway . . . . . . 1,234. .F 10
Brodnax . . . . 492. .J 11
Brooke . . . . .C 3
Brookneal . . . . . . 1,454. .J 10
Brownsburg . . . . .G 9
Brucetown . . . . .D 11
Buchanan . . . . . . 1,205. .H 8
Buckingham . . . .°H 10
Buena Vista . . . 6,717†.H 9
Buffalo Junction . . . . . . .K 10
Bumpass . . . . .G 12
Burgess . . . . .G 14
Burke . . . . 33,835. .A 3
Burkes Garden . . . . .I 5
Burkeville . . . . 606. .I 11
Burnsville . . . . .G 8
Burr Hill . . . . .C 2
Callands . . . . .J 8
Callao . . . . .G 14
Callaway . . . . .J 8
Calverton . . . . .B 2
Cana . . . . .K 6
Cape Charles . . 1,512. .I 15
Capeville . . . . .F 5
Capron . . . . 238. .H 2
Cardinal . . . . .E 4
Carrollton . . . . .G 3
Carrsville . . . . .H 3
Carson . . . . .F 1
Cartersville . . . . .H 11
Casanova . . . . .B 2
Cascade . . . . .K 8
Cash . . . . .E 4
Castlewood . . . . 2,420. .J 3
Catawba . . . . .I 7
Catharpin . . . . .A 2
Cauthornville . . . . .H 13
Cave Spring* . . . . 21,682. .I 8
Cedar Bluff . . . . 1,550. .I 4
Center Cross . . . . .H 13
Centreville . . . . 7,473. .A 3
Ceres . . . . .J 5
Chamberlayne* . . . . . . 5,136. .H 12
Champlain . . . . .G 13
Chancellor . . . . .C 2
Chantilly . . . . . 12,259. .A 3
Charles City . . . .°I 13
Charlotte Courthouse . . . . 568.°I 10
Charlottesville . . . . . . .39,916†°G 10
Chase City . . . . 2,749. .J 10
Chatham . . . . . . 1,390.°J 9
Check . . . . .J 7
Cheriton . . . . 695. .F 5
Chesapeake . . . .114,486†.G 4
Chester . . . . 11,728. .E 1
Chesterfield . . . .°I 12
Chilesburg . . . . .G 12
Chilhowie . . . . . 1,265. .J 4
Chincoteague . . 1,607. .G 16
Christiansburg . . . . 10,345.°I 7
Church Road . . . . .F 1
Churchville . . . . .G 9
Claremont . . . . 380. .F 2
Clarksville . . . . . 1,468. .J 10
Claudville . . . . .K 7
Claypool Hill* . . 1,295. .I 5
Clayville . . . . .I 12
Clear Brook . . . . .D 11
Cleveland . . . . 360. .J 4
Cliffield . . . . .I 5
Clifford . . . . .H 9
Clifton . . . . 170. .B 3
Clifton Forge . . . . 5,046†.H 8
Clinchburg . . . . .J 4
Clinchco . . . . .I 3
Clinchport . . . . 89. .J 2
Clintwood . . . . . 1,369.°I 3
Clover . . . . 215. .J 10
Cloverdale . . . . .I 8
Cluster Springs . . . . .K 10
Cobbs Creek . . . . .E 4
Coeburn . . . . . . 2,625. .J 3
Cohasset . . . . .H 11
Coleman Falls . . . . .I 9
Coles Point . . . . .G 14
Collinsville . . . . 7,517. .J 8
Cologne . . . . .E 3
Colonial Beach . . . . . . 2,474. .C 4
Colonial Heights . . . . 16,509†.F 1
Columbia . . . . 111. .H 11
Columbia Furnace . . . . . .E 10
Commonwealth* . . . . . 3,505. .G 10
Concord . . . . .I 9
Conicville . . . . .E 10
Copper Hill . . . . .I 7
Copper Valley . . . . .J 7
Corbin . . . . .G 12
Country Club Lake* . . . . 4,098. .F 12
Courtland . . . . 976.°J 13
Covesville . . . . .H 10
Covington . . . . . 9,063†°H 8
Craddockville . . . . .H 15
Craig Springs . . . . .I 7
Craigsville . . . . 845. .G 9
Crewe . . . . 2,325. .I 11
Criglersville . . . . .C 1
Crimora . . . . .G 10
Cripple Creek . . . . .J 6
Crittenden . . . . .G 4
Critz . . . . .K 7
Crockett . . . . .J 5
Cross Junction . . . . .D 11
Crouch . . . . .H 13
Crozet . . . . 2,553. .G 10
Crozier . . . . .H 12
Crystal Hill . . . . .J 10
Cullen . . . . .I 10
Culpeper . . . . . . 6,621.°F 11
Cumberland . . . .°H 11
Dabneys . . . . .H 12
Dahlgren . . . . .C 4
Dale City* . . . . 33,127. .F 12
Daleville . . . . .I 8
Damascus . . . . . 1,330. .J 4
Danieltown . . . . .J 11
Dante . . . . 1,083. .J 3
Danville . . . . . . 45,642†.K 9
Davenport . . . . .I 4
Dayton . . . . 1,017. .F 9
Deerfield . . . . .G 9
Delaplane . . . . .A 2
Deltaville . . . . . . 1,082. .E 4
Dendron . . . . 307. .F 2
De Witt . . . . .F 1
Diggs . . . . .E 4
Dillwyn . . . . 637. .H 10
Dinwiddie . . . .°I 12
Disputanta . . . . .F 2
Doe Hill . . . . .F 9
Dogue . . . . .C 3
Dolphin . . . . .J 12
Dooms* . . . . 1,173. .G 9
Doran . . . . .I 4
Doswell . . . . .H 12
Drakes Branch . . . . 617. .J 10
Draper . . . . .J 6
Drewryville . . . . .H 1
Dry Fork . . . . .J 9
Dryden . . . . .J 2
Dublin . . . . 2,368. .I 6
Duffield . . . . 148. .J 2
Dugspur . . . . .J 6
Dumbarton* . . . 8,149. .H 12
Dumfries . . . . . . 3,214. .B 3
Dundas . . . . .J 11
Dungannon . . . . 339. .J 3
Dunn Loring . . . . 6,077. .A 3
Dunnsville . . . . .H 13
Dutton . . . . .E 4
Dyke . . . . .G 10
Eagle Rock . . . . .H 8
Earlysville . . . . .G 10
East Highland Park* . . . . . 11,797. .H 12
East Stone Gap . . . . .J 3
Eastville . . . . 238.°I 15
Ebony . . . . .K 11
Eclipse . . . . .G 4
Edgehill . . . . .C 4
Edinburg . . . . 752. .E 10
Edwardsville . . . . .G 14
Eggleston . . . . .I 6
Elberon . . . . .F 3
Elk Creek . . . . .J 5
Elk Hill . . . . .H 11
Elkton . . . . 1,520. .F 10
Elkwood . . . . .B 2
Elliston [-Lafayette] . 1,172. .I 7
Emmerton . . . . .G 14
Emory [-Meadowview]2,292. J 4
Emporia . . . . . . 4,840†°J 12
Epworth . . . . .H 13
Esmont . . . . .H 10
Etlan . . . . .B 1
Ettrick . . . . 4,890. .F 1
Evergreen . . . . .I 10
Evington . . . . .I 9
Ewing . . . . .J 1
Exeter . . . . .J 2
Exmore . . . . 1,300. .H 15
Faber . . . . .H 10
Fair Port . . . . .H 14
Fairfax . . . . . . 19,390†°E 12
Fairfield . . . . .H 9
Fairlawn . . . . . . 1,794. .I 7
Falls Church . . . 9,515†.A 4
Falls Mills . . . . .I 5
Falmouth . . . . . . 3,271. .C 3
Farmville . . . . . . 6,067.°I 11
Farnham . . . . .G 14
Ferncliff . . . . .G 11
Ferrum . . . . .J 8
Fieldale . . . . 1,190. .J 8
Fife . . . . .H 11
Fincastle . . . . 282.°I 8
Fishers Hill . . . . .E 10
Fishersville . . . . .G 9
Flint Hill . . . . .B 1
Floyd . . . . 411.°J 7
Foneswood . . . . .G 13
Ford . . . . .I 12
Forest . . . . .I 9
Fork Union . . . . .H 11
Forksville . . . . .J 11
Fort Belvoir . . . . 7,726. .B 4
Fort Blackmore . . . . .J 3
Fort Hunt* . . . 14,294. .F 13
Fort Lee . . . . 9,784. .F 1
Fort Mitchell . . . . .J 10
Foxwells . . . . .D 4
Franconia . . . . . 8,476. .B 4
Franklin . . . . 7,308†.H 2
Fredericks Hall . . . . .G 12
Fredericksburg . . . . . . 15,322†.G 12
Free Union . . . . .G 10
Freeman . . . . .J 12
Fries . . . . 758. .J 6
Front Royal . . . 11,126.°E 11
Fulks Run . . . . .F 10
Gainesboro . . . . .D 11
Gainesville . . . . .A 2
Galax . . . . 6,524†.J 6
Garrisonville . . . . .C 3
Gasburg . . . . .K 11
Gate City . . . . . . 2,494.°J 3
Glade Spring . . 1,722. .J 4
Gladehill . . . . .J 8
Gladstone . . . . .H 10
Gladys . . . . .I 9
Glasgow . . . . . . 1,259. .H 9
Glen Allen . . . . . . 6,202. .D 1
Glen Lyn . . . . 235. .I 6
Glen Wilton . . . . .H 8
Glenmore . . . . .H 10
Glenwood . . . . . 2,276. .K 9
Gloucester . . . . 1,545.°I 14
Gloucester Point 5,841. .F 4
Golansville . . . . .G 12
Goldvein . . . . .C 2
Goochland . . . .°H 11
Goode . . . . .I 9
Gordonsville . . . 1,421. .G 11
Goshen . . . . 134. .G 8
Grafton . . . . .F 4
Graves Mill . . . . .F 11
Gray . . . . .G 1
Great Falls* . . . 2,419. .F 13
Green Bay . . . . .I 11
Greenville . . . . .G 9
Gretna . . . . 1,255. .J 9
Groseclose . . . . .J 5
Grottoes . . . . . . 1,369. .G 10
Groveton* . . . . 18,860. .E 13
Grundy . . . . 1,699.°I 4
Gum Spring . . . . .H 11
Gwynn . . . . .E 4
Hadensville . . . . .H 11
Hague . . . . .G 14
Halifax . . . . 772.°J 10
Hallieford . . . . .E 4
Hallwood . . . . 243. .G 16
Hamilton . . . . 598. .E 12
Hampden Sydney . . . . . 1,011. .I 10
Hampton . . . . 122,617†.F 4
Handsom . . . . .H 2
Hanover . . . .°H 12
Harborton . . . . .H 15
Hardy . . . . .I 8
Hardyville . . . . .E 4
Harrisonburg . . . . . . .19,671†°F 10
Hartfield . . . . .E 4
Hartwood . . . . .C 2
Hayfield . . . . .D 11
Haymarket . . . . . . 230. .A 2
Haynesville . . . . .G 14
Haysi . . . . 371. .I 3
Haywood . . . . .C 1
Head Waters . . . . .G 9
Healing Springs . . . . .G 8
Heards . . . . .H 10
Heathsville . . . .°G 14
Henry . . . . .J 8
Herndon . . . . . 11,449. .A 3
Hessian Hills* . . . . 4,103. .G 10
Highland Springs . . . . 12,146. .E 1
Hightown . . . . .F 8
Hillsboro . . . . 94. .D 12
Hillsville . . . . 2,123.°J 6
Hiltons . . . . .J 3
Hiwassee . . . . .J 6
Hobson . . . . .G 4
Holland . . . . .H 3
Hollins . . . . 12,295. .I 8
Hollymead* . . . . 2,392. .G 10
Holston . . . . .J 4
Honaker . . . . . . 1,475. .J 4
Hopewell . . . . . 23,397†.F 1
Hopkins . . . . .H 15
Horntown . . . . .G 16
Horse Pasture* . . . . 3,650. .J 8
Horsepen . . . . .I 5
Hot Springs . . . . .G 8
Howertons . . . . .H 13
Huddleston . . . . .I 9
Hume . . . . .A 1
Huntington* . . . 5,813. .E 13
Huntly . . . . .A 1

Hurley		I	4
Hurt	1,481	I	9
Hustle		G	13
Hybla Valley	15,533	B	4
Idylwood*	11,982	E	13
Independence	1,112	°K	5
Index		G	13
Indian Neck		H	13
Indian Valley		J	7
Ingram		J	9
Inman		J	2
Iron Gate	620	H	8
Irvington	567	D	4
Isle of Wight		°G	3
Ivanhoe		J	6
Ivor	403	G	3
Jamaica		H	14
Jamestown		F	3
Jamesville		E	5
Jarratt	614	G	1
Java		J	9
Jefferson	24,342	H	11
Jeffersonton		B	1
Jetersville		I	11
Jewell Ridge		I	4
Jewell Valley		I	4
Jonesville	874	°J	2
Jordan Mines		H	7
Keeling		J	9
Keen Mountain		I	4
Keene		H	10
Keller	236	H	15
Kenbridge	1,352	J	11
Kents Store		H	11
Keokee		J	2
Keswick		G	11
Keysville	704	J	10
Kilmarnock	945	H	14
Kimballton		I	6
King and Queen Court House		°D	3
King George		°G	13
King William		°H	13
Kinsale		G	14
Lacey Spring		F	10
La Crosse	734	J	11
Ladysmith		G	12
Lafayette, see Elliston[-Lafayette]			
Lake Barcroft*	8,725	E	13
Lake Ridge*	11,072	F	12
Lakeside	12,289	D	1
Lambsburg		K	6
Lancaster		°H	14
Laneview		H	14
Laurel*	10,569	H	12
Laurel Fork		J	7
Lawrenceville	1,484	°J	12
Lebanon	3,206	°J	4
Lebanon Church		E	10
Leesburg	8,357	°E	12
Lennig		J	10
Leon		C	1
Lewis Gardens		E	1
Lewisetta		G	14
Lexington	7,292†	°H	9
Lightfoot		E	3
Lignum		C	2
Lincolnia*	10,350	E	13
Lincolnia Heights		A	4
Linden		A	1
Linville		F	10
Lithia		I	8
Little Plymouth		D	3
Lively		H	14
Lloyd Place*		J	14
Loch Lomond*	3,608	F	12
Locust Hill		E	4
Locust Grove		C	2
Locustville		H	16
Long Branch*		E	13
Long Island		I	9
Loretto		G	13
Lorton	5,813	B	3
Lottsburg		G	14
Louisa	932	°G	11
Lovettsville	613	D	12
Lovingston		°H	10
Lowmoor		H	8
Lowry		I	9
Lunenburg		°J	11
Luray	3,584	°F	10
Lynch Station		I	9
Lynchburg	66,743†	I	9
Lyndhurst		G	10
Machipongo		E	5
Macon		H	11
Madison	267	°F	11
Madison Heights	14,146	I	9
Madison Mills		C	1
Manakin		H	12
Manassas	15,438†	°E	12
Manassas Park	6,524†	B	3
Mangohick		H	13
Mannboro		I	12
Manquin		H	13
Mantua*	6,523	E	12
Mappsville		H	16
Marion	7,287	°J	5
Markham		A	1
Marshall		A	2
Martinsville	18,149†	°J	8
Maryus		F	4
Mascot		D	3
Massies Mill		H	9
Mathews		°I	14
Matoaca*	1,967	I	12
Mattaponi		E	3
Maurertown		E	10
Max Meadows		J	6
Maxie		I	4
Mayo		K	10
McClure		I	3
McCoy		I	6
McDowell		G	9
McGaheysville		F	10
McKenney	473	J	12
McLean	35,664	A	4
Meadows of Dan		J	7
Meadowview, see Emory [-Meadowview]			
Mechanicsville*	9,269	H	13
Meherrin		I	11
Melfa	391	H	15
Mendota		J	3
Meredithville		J	11
Merrifield*	7,525	E	13
Merry Point		H	14
Middlebrook		G	9
Middleburg	619	A	2
Middletown	841	A	1
Midland		B	2
Midlothian		E	1
Miles		E	4
Milford		G	12
Mill Gap		G	8
Millboro		G	8
Millers Tavern		H	13
Millwood		A	1
Mineral	399	G	11
Mint Spring		G	9
Mitchells		C	1
Mobjack		E	4
Modest Town		H	16
Mollusk		H	14
Moneta		I	8
Monroe		H	9
Monterey	247	°F	8
Montpelier		H	12
Montrose*	5,349	H	12
Montross	456	°G	13
Montvale		I	8
Morattico		H	14
Moseley		I	12
Mount Crawford	315	G	10
Mount Heron		I	4
Mount Jackson	1,419	F	10
Mount Landing		G	13
Mount Sidney		G	9
Mount Solon		F	9
Mount Vernon	24,058	B	4
Mountain Falls		E	10
Mountain Grove		G	8
Mouth of Wilson		K	5
Mundy Point		G	14
Mustoe		G	8
Naola		H	9
Narrows	2,516	I	6
Naruna		I	9
Nassawadox	630	H	15
Nathalie		J	10
Natural Bridge		H	8
Naxera		E	4
Nellysford		H	10
Nelson		K	10
New Canton		H	11
New Castle	213	°H	7
New Church		G	16
New Hope		G	10
New Kent		°E	2
New Market	1,118	F	10
New Point		E	4
New River		I	6
Newbern		J	6
Newington	8,313	B	4
Newport		I	7
Newport News	144,903†	J	14
Newsoms	368	J	13
Newtown		G	13
Nickelsville	464	J	3
Nimrod Hall		G	8
Nokesville		B	2
Nomini Grove		G	14
Norfolk	266,979†	J	15
Norge		E	3
North		E	4
North Pulaski*		J	6
North Springfield*	9,583	E	13
North Tazewell		I	5
Norton	4,757†	J	3
Norwood		H	10
Nottoway Court House		°I	11
Nuttsville		H	14
Oak Hall		G	16
Oakpark		C	1
Oakton	19,150	A	3
Oakwood		I	4
Occoquan	512	B	3
Oilville		H	12
Oldhams		G	14
Oldtown		J	6
Onancock	1,461	H	15
Onemo		E	4
Onley	526	H	15
Ontario		J	10
Orange	2,631	°G	11
Oriskany		H	8
Orkney Springs		E	10
Orlean		B	1
Ottoman		H	14
Overall		E	11
Owens		C	4
Owenton		H	13
Oyster		F	5
Paces		J	9
Paint Bank		H	7
Painter	321	H	15
Palmer		D	4
Palmer Springs		K	11
Palmyra		°H	11
Pamplin	273	I	10
Paris		A	1
Parksley	979	H	16
Parkview*	2,224	F	10
Parrott		I	6
Partlow		G	12
Patrick Springs		K	7
Patterson		I	4
Pearisburg	2,128	°I	6
Pembroke	1,302	I	6
Penhook		J	8
Pennington Gap	1,716	J	2
Petersburg	41,055†	I	12
Phenix	250	I	10
Philomont		A	2
Pilot		J	7
Pimmit Hills*	6,658	E	13
Pinero		E	4
Piney River		H	9
Pittsville		J	9
Plain View		E	3
Plains, The	382	A	2
Pocahontas	708	I	4
Poquoson	8,726†	F	4
Port Republic		G	10
Port Royal	291	G	13
Portsmouth	104,577†	J	14
Pound	1,086	I	3
Pounding Mill		I	4
Powhatan		°H	11
Pratts		C	1
Prince George		°I	13
Prospect		I	10
Providence Forge		E	2
Pulaski	10,106	°J	6
Pulaski North*	1,405	I	6
Pungoteague		H	15
Purcellville	1,567	E	12
Quantico	621	B	3
Quantico Station*	7,121	F	12
Quicksburg		F	10
Quinby		H	15
Quinton		E	2
Radford	13,225†	I	7
Radiant		C	1
Rainswood		G	14
Randolph		J	10
Raphine		G	9
Rappahannock Academy		G	13
Raven	4,000	I	4
Rawlings		J	12
Rectortown		A	2
Red Ash		I	4
Red House		I	10
Red Oak		J	10
Redart		E	4
Redwood		J	8
Reedville		H	14
Rehoboth		J	11
Remington	425	B	2
Republican Grove		J	9
Rescue		G	3
Reston	36,407	A	3
Reva		C	1
Rhoadesville		C	1
Rice		I	11
Rich Creek	746	I	6
Richardsville		C	2
Richlands	5,796	I	4
Richmond	219,214†	°H	12
Ridge		E	1
Ridgeway	858	K	8
Rileyville		F	10
Riner		I	7
Rio*	2,851	G	10
Ringgold		K	9
Riverton		A	1
Riverville		H	10
Rixeyville		B	1
Roanoke	100,220†	I	8
Robley		H	14
Rochelle		C	1
Rockbridge Baths		H	9
Rockfish		H	10
Rockville		H	12
Rocky Gap		I	6
Rocky Mount	4,198	°J	8
Rollins Fork		G	13
Rose Hill	11,926	B	4
Rosedale		J	4
Round Hill	510	E	12
Ruby		B	3
Ruckersville		G	11
Rugby		K	5
Rural Retreat	1,083	J	5
Rushmere*	1,070	I	14
Rustburg		°I	9
Ruther Glen		G	12
Ruthville		E	2
Sabot		H	12
St. Charles	241	J	2
St. Paul	973	J	3
St. Stephens Church		H	13
Salem	23,958†	°I	7
Saltville	2,376	J	4
Saluda		°H	14
Sandston		E	1
Sandy Hook		H	11
Sandy Level		J	8
Sanford		G	15
Saxe		J	10
Saxis	415	G	15
Schley		E	4
Schuyler		H	10
Scottsburg	335	J	10
Scottsville	250	H	10
Sealston		C	3
Seaview		F	5
Sebrell		G	2
Sedley		G	2
Selma		H	8
Seven Corners*	6,058	E	13
Seven Fountains		E	10
Seven Mile Ford		J	5
Severn		F	4
Shacklefords		E	3
Sharps		H	14
Shawsville		I	7
Shenandoah	1,861	F	10
Shiloh		C	4
Shipman		H	10
Shumansville		G	13
Simpsons		J	7
Singers Glen		F	10
Skippers		K	12
Skipwith		J	10
Smithfield	3,718	G	3
Snowden		H	9
Snowville		J	7
Somerset		C	1
Somerville		B	2
South Boston	7,093†	J	10
South Hill	4,347	J	11
Sparta		G	13
Speedwell		J	5
Spencer		K	8
Sperryville		B	1
Spotsylvania		°G	12
Spring Grove		F	2
Springfield	21,435	B	4
Stafford		°F	12
Staffordsville		I	6
Stanardsville	284	°G	10
Stanley	1,204	F	10
Stanleytown	1,761	J	8
Staunton	21,857†	°G	9
Steeles Tavern		G	9
Stephens City*	1,179	E	11
Stephenson		D	11
Sterling		A	3
Sterling Park*	16,080	E	12
Stevens Creek*	1,002	J	6
Stevensburg		C	2
Stevensville		H	13
Stonega		J	2
Stony Creek	329	G	1
Strasburg	2,311	E	11
Stuart	1,131	°J	7
Stuarts Draft	1,776	G	9
Studley	4,674	D	1
Suffolk	47,621†	J	14
Sugar Grove	1,027	J	5
Sugarland Run*	6,258	E	12
Sumerduck		C	2
Supply		G	13
Surry	237	°I	13
Susan		E	4
Sussex		°J	13
Sutherland		F	1
Sweet Briar		H	9
Sweet Chalybeate		H	7
Sweet Hall		E	3
Swift Run		F	10
Swoope		G	9
Swords Creek		J	4
Sylvatus		J	6
Syria		C	1
Syringa		E	4
Tamworth		H	11
Tangier	771	H	15
Tannersville		J	5
Tappahannock	1,821	°G	13
Tazewell	4,468	°I	5
Temperanceville		G	16
Templeman		G	14
Thaxton		I	8
Thornburg		G	12
Tidewater		H	14
Timberlake*	9,697	J	9
Timberville	1,510	F	10
Tiptop		I	5
Toano		E	3
Toms Brook	226	E	10
Townsend		F	5
Trammel		J	3
Trevilians		G	11
Triangle	4,770	B	3
Triplet		J	12
Troutdale	248	J	5
Troutville	496	I	8
Troy		G	11
Tuckahoe*	39,868	H	12
Tunstall		E	2
Turbeville		K	9
Tye River		H	10
Tyro		H	9
Tysons Corner*	10,065	E	13
Union Hall		J	8
Union Level		J	11
Unionville		C	1
University Heights*	6,736	G	10
Uno		C	1
Upperville		A	2
Urbanna	518	D	3
Valentines		K	12
Vanderpool		F	8
Vansant*	2,708	I	4
Varina		E	1
Verona	2,782	G	9
Vesta		J	7
Vesuvius		H	9
Victoria	2,004	J	11
Vienna	15,469	A	3
Vila Heights*	1,264	J	8
Village		G	14
Villamont		I	8
Vint Hill Farms Station*	1,130	F	12
Vinton	8,027	I	8
Virgilina	212	K	10
Virginia Beach	262,199†	J	15
Volney		K	5
Wachapreague	404	H	16
Waidsboro		J	8
Wakefield	1,355	G	2
Walkerton		H	13
Ware Neck		E	4
Warfield		J	12
Warm Springs		°G	8
Warner		D	3
Warrenton	3,907	°F	12
Warsaw	771	°G	14
Washington	247	°F	11
Water View		H	14
Waterford		E	12
Wattsville		G	16
Waverly	2,284	F	2
Waynesboro	15,329†	G	10
Weber City	1,543	J	3
West Augusta		G	9
West Gate*	7,119	F	12
West Lawn		A	3
West Point	2,726	E	3
West Springfield*	25,012	E	13
Westmoreland		G	14
Westover*	3,051	K	9
Weyers Cave		G	10
Whitacre		D	11
White Hall		G	10
White Marsh		F	4
White Plains		J	11
White Post		A	1
White Stone*	409	H	14
Whitetop		K	5
Whitewood		I	4
Wicomico		F	4
Wicomico Church		H	14
Williamsburg	9,870†	°I	14
Williamsville		G	8
Willis		J	7
Willis Wharf		H	15
Wilsons		I	11
Winchester	20,217†	°E	11
Windsor	985	G	3
Winterpock		I	12
Wirtz		I	8
Wise	3,894	°J	3
Wolf Trap*	9,875	E	13
Wolftown		F	11
Woodbridge	24,004	B	3
Woodford		G	12
Woodlawn	1,689	J	6
Woodstock	2,627	°E	10
Woodville		B	1
Woolwine		J	7
Worsham		I	10
Wylliesburg		J	10
Wytheville	7,135	°J	6
Yale		G	1
Yorkshire*	4,940	E	12
Yorktown		°I	14
Zacata		G	13
Zuni		G	3

†Independent city, not part of any county.
*Does not appear on map; key shows general location.
°County seat.
Source: 1980 census. Places without population figures are unincorporated areas.

VIRGINIA/*People*

The 1980 United States census reported that Virginia had 5,346,797 people. The state's population had increased 15 per cent over the 1970 census figure of 4,651,448.

Over two-thirds of Virginia's people live in the state's eight metropolitan areas (see METROPOLITAN AREA). Six of these metropolitan areas lie entirely within Virginia. The areas are: Charlottesville, Danville, Lynchburg, Norfolk-Virginia Beach-Newport News, Richmond-Petersburg, and Roanoke.

Five Virginia counties and five of the state's cities are included in the Washington, D.C. metropolitan area. The Johnson City-Kingsport (Tenn.)-Bristol (Va.) metropolitan area extends into Scott and Washington counties and includes Bristol city in Virginia.

For the population of each of the metropolitan areas, see the *Index* to the political map of Virginia. See also the separate articles on the cities of Virginia listed in the *Related Articles* at the end of this article.

Almost all Virginians were born in the United States. Many of them are of English, German, or Irish ancestry. Blacks make up about 19 per cent of the people of Virginia.

© Mike Williams

Crowds of People Jam the Norfolk Waterfront during Harborfest, a popular event held every spring. Norfolk, a leading Atlantic Coast port, is Virginia's largest city.

Southern Baptists and Methodists make up the largest religious groups in Virginia. Other large religious groups in the state, in order of size from largest to smallest, include Presbyterians, Roman Catholics, and Episcopalians.

Skilled Dancers perform in the Scottish Games and Gathering of the Clans festival in Alexandria. The festival, a favorite annual event among Virginians, is held in July.

Virginia Division of Tourism

Population Density

Most of Virginia's people live in the eastern part of the state—in and around Arlington, Richmond, and Norfolk. Most of the thinly populated areas lie in the central part of the state.

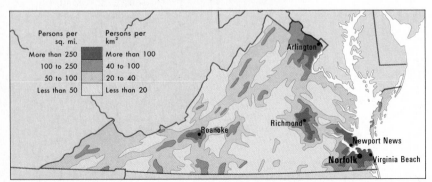

Persons per sq. mi.	Persons per km²
More than 250	More than 100
100 to 250	40 to 100
50 to 100	20 to 40
Less than 50	Less than 20

Arlington

Roanoke

Richmond

Newport News

Norfolk Virginia Beach

WORLD BOOK map;
based on U.S. Bureau of the Census data.

Schools. The Syms Free School was founded in Hampton in 1634, and the Eaton Free School began there about 1640. These were the first free schools in what is now the United States. Some Virginia planters and merchants established private schools called *old-field schools*. They built these schools in open fields. Beginning in the mid-1700's, many *academies* were founded. They were combined elementary and high schools. In 1810, the General Assembly created a Literary Fund to help poor children receive an education.

Virginia's statewide public school system began in 1870. Today, the state board of education supervises Virginia's public school system. The board's nine members are appointed by the governor, subject to the approval of the legislature. The board elects one of its members to serve a two-year term as president.

The state department of education administers the public school system, carrying out state laws and board of education regulations. The department of education is headed by the superintendent of public instruction. This official is appointed by the governor, subject to the approval of the legislature. The superintendent serves during the governor's term of office.

A state law requires children from age 6 through 16 to attend school. For the number of students and teachers in Virginia, see EDUCATION (table).

The College of William and Mary, founded in Williamsburg in 1693, is the second oldest institution of higher learning in the United States. Harvard University is the oldest. Phi Beta Kappa, the honorary scholastic society, was founded at William and Mary in 1776 (see PHI BETA KAPPA).

Libraries and Museums. Virginia's first public library was established in Alexandria in 1794. Today, the state has more than 90 public libraries and about 50 bookmobiles. The State Library in Richmond, founded in 1823, is the largest research library in Virginia that is not connected with a college or university.

The White House of the Confederacy, now known also as The Museum of the Confederacy, was Jefferson Davis' Richmond home. It has more than 16,000 Civil War relics, including the original provisional constitution of the Confederacy. The Virginia Historical Society in Richmond maintains a library of manuscripts and printed books, as well as portraits and mementos of important Virginians.

The Virginia Museum of Fine Arts in Richmond is the nation's oldest state-supported art museum. The Valentine Museum, also in Richmond, has exhibits on Virginia history. The Mariners' Museum in Newport News displays models and paintings of ships, and other items that show the development of shipping. The Edgar Allan Poe Museum in Richmond has exhibits connected with the poet's years in that city. The Science Museum of Virginia in Richmond has many scientific exhibits that emphasize audience participation.

University of Virginia in Charlottesville was founded in 1819 through the efforts of Thomas Jefferson. The school held its first classes in 1825. Jefferson became the institution's first rector, and held this position until his death in 1826. He designed the Rotunda, which was modeled after the Pantheon in Rome.

Universities and Colleges

Virginia has 39 universities and colleges accredited by the Southern Association of Colleges and Schools. For enrollments and further information, see UNIVERSITIES AND COLLEGES (table).

Name	Location	Founded
Averett College	Danville	1859
Bluefield College	Bluefield	1920
Bridgewater College	Bridgewater	1880
Eastern Mennonite College	Harrisonburg	1917
Emory and Henry College	Emory	1836
Ferrum College	Ferrum	1913
George Mason University	Fairfax	1957
Hampden-Sydney College	Hampden-Sydney	1776
Hampton University	Hampton	1868
Hollins College	Roanoke	1842
James Madison University	Harrisonburg	1908
Liberty Baptist College	Lynchburg	1971
Longwood College	Farmville	1839
Lynchburg College	Lynchburg	1903
Mary Baldwin College	Staunton	1842
Mary Washington College	Fredericksburg	1908
Marymount College of Virginia	Arlington	1950
Norfolk State University	Norfolk	1935
Old Dominion University	Norfolk	1930
Presbyterian School of Christian Education	Richmond	1914
Radford University	Radford	1910
Randolph-Macon College	Ashland	1830
Randolph-Macon Woman's College	Lynchburg	1891
Richmond, University of	Richmond	1830
Roanoke College	Salem	1842
St. Paul's College	Lawrenceville	1888
Shenandoah College and Conservatory of Music	Winchester	1875
Sweet Briar College	Sweet Briar	1901
Union Theological Seminary in Virginia	Richmond	1812
Virginia, University of	*	*
Virginia Commonwealth University	Richmond	1837
Virginia Intermont College	Bristol	1884
Virginia Military Institute	Lexington	1839
Virginia Polytechnic Institute and State University	Blacksburg	1872
Virginia State University	Petersburg	1882
Virginia Union University	Richmond	1865
Virginia Wesleyan College	Norfolk	1961
Washington and Lee University	Lexington	1749
William and Mary, College of	*	*

*For campuses and founding dates, see UNIVERSITIES AND COLLEGES (table).

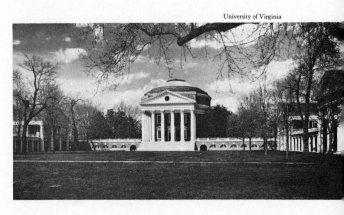

University of Virginia

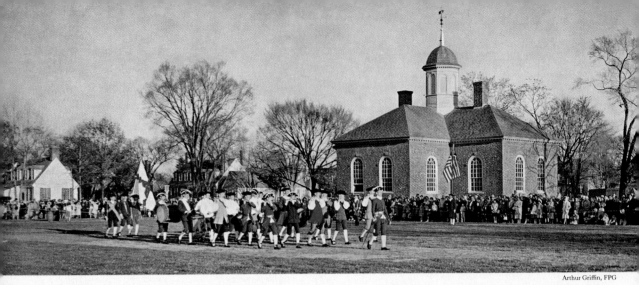

Arthur Griffin, FPG

Boys' Fife and Drum Corps Parade in Williamsburg

VIRGINIA/*A Visitor's Guide*

Virginia is known for its stately old homes and other historic sites. The most popular homes include George Washington's Mount Vernon near Alexandria, and Thomas Jefferson's Monticello near Charlottesville. Williamsburg, Virginia's second colonial capital, has been restored to look as it did in the 1700's. See MONTICELLO; MOUNT VERNON; WILLIAMSBURG.

Many visitors drive along the crest of the Blue Ridge. They travel on the Skyline Drive in the north, and on the Blue Ridge Parkway in the south. In spring, azaleas, dogwoods, and laurels bloom on the mountain slopes. In autumn, the leaves of hardwood trees and shrubs turn bright red, orange, and yellow.

The Atlantic Ocean, Chesapeake Bay, and tidal rivers offer beach sports, fishing, and sailing. Virginia Beach, southeast of Norfolk, is an especially popular ocean resort. Hunters seek game in Dismal Swamp and in the forested highlands.

Places to Visit

Following are brief descriptions of some of Virginia's many interesting places to visit.

Churches. *Bruton Parish Church* (built from 1710 to 1715) in Williamsburg is one of the nation's oldest Episcopal churches. George Washington and Robert E. Lee worshiped at *Christ Church* (1767-1773) in Alexandria. The Second Virginia Convention met in 1775 at *St. John's Church* (1741) in Richmond. There, Patrick Henry gave his famous call for liberty or death. *St. Luke's Church* (1632) near Smithfield is thought to be the oldest brick church in the original 13 states that is still standing. *St. Paul's Church* (1739) in Norfolk was the city's only building to survive a British bombardment during the Revolutionary War (1775-1783). Robert E. Lee and Jefferson Davis worshiped in Richmond's *St. Paul's Episcopal Church* (1844), the "Church of the Confederacy."

Family Entertainment Centers. Kings Dominion, near Richmond, includes an animal preserve where jungle animals roam free. Busch Gardens, near Williamsburg, features sections that reflect the culture of England, France, Germany, and Italy.

Homes. *Berkeley* (1726), near Richmond, was the birthplace of President William Henry Harrison. *Carter's Grove* (1751) is among the most beautiful of the old plantations along the James River. *Gunston Hall* (1755), near Lorton, was the home of George Mason, the author of the Virginia Bill of Rights. The *John Marshall House* (about 1790) in Richmond was long the home of the great Chief Justice of the United States. *Stratford Hall* (about 1730), near Montross, was the birthplace of Robert E. Lee.

Jamestown Festival Park, on the James River, has reproductions of old James Fort and of the three ships that brought the first settlers to Jamestown in 1607.

Natural Bridge is a famous landmark south of Lexington. Water carved away softer rock and left the hard rock that forms the bridge.

Natural Chimneys are seven rock towers. They rise over 100 feet (30 meters) near Mount Solon.

Natural Tunnel, near Gate City, is a giant passageway cut through the Purchase Ridge by the waters of Stock Creek. A railroad runs through the tunnel, which includes a path for visitors.

National Parks, Monuments, and Forests. The National Park Service administers many areas in Virginia. Shenandoah National Park in the Blue Ridge, George Washington Birthplace National Monument in Westmoreland County, and Booker T. Washington National Monument near Roanoke are described under their own names in WORLD BOOK. Virginia has three national historical parks: (1) Appomattox Court House, which includes McLean House, site of the agreement on the terms of surrender in the Civil War; (2) Colonial, which includes Yorktown and most of Jamestown Island; and (3) Cumberland Gap, which extends into Kentucky and Tennessee. See NATIONAL PARK SYSTEM (table).

Manassas National Battlefield Park is the site of the Battles of Manassas, or Bull Run. Other historic sites include Richmond National Battlefield Park; Petersburg National Battlefield; and the Fredericksburg and Spotsylvania County Battlefields Memorial.

Wendell Metzen, Bruce Coleman Inc.

Colorful Sailboats at Virginia Beach

Bruce Coleman Inc.

Thomas Jefferson's Monticello near Charlottesville

Most of George Washington National Forest lies in the northwestern part of the state, along the West Virginia border. Part of this national forest extends into West Virginia. Jefferson National Forest lies in the southwestern part of Virginia.

State Forests and Parks. Virginia has 6 state forests, 25 state parks, an interstate park, and several other historical, natural, and recreational areas. For information on Virginia's state parks, write to Commissioner, Division of Parks, Department of Conservation and Economic Development, 1201 Washington Building, Capital Square, Richmond, VA 23219.

Annual Events

Many of Virginia's most beautiful homes and gardens are open to the public during Historic Garden Week. This event takes place late in April.

Another popular event is Pony Penning on Chincoteague Island, held on the last Wednesday and Thursday in July. The ponies live on nearby Assateague Island. But at Pony Penning time they are driven across the shallow channel to Chincoteague, where some of them are sold.

Other annual events in Virginia include the following:

January-May: Highland County Maple Sugar Festival in Monterey (March); Garden Symposium in Williamsburg (late March); International Azalea Festival in Norfolk (late in April); Dogwood Festival in Charlottesville (late in April); Shenandoah Apple Blossom Festival in Winchester (early May).

June-December: Harborfest in Norfolk (early June); Boardwalk Art Show in Virginia Beach (late June); Jazz Festival in Hampton (late June); Scottish Games and Gathering of the Clans in Alexandria (July); Highlands Arts and Crafts Festival in Abingdon (first two weeks in August); Old Fiddlers' Convention in Galax (August); Neptune Festival in Virginia Beach (late September); Nostalgiafest in Old Towne Petersburg (early October).

Artstreet

Replicas of Sailing Ships in Jamestown Festival Park

Jack Zehrt, FPG

McLean House near Appomattox

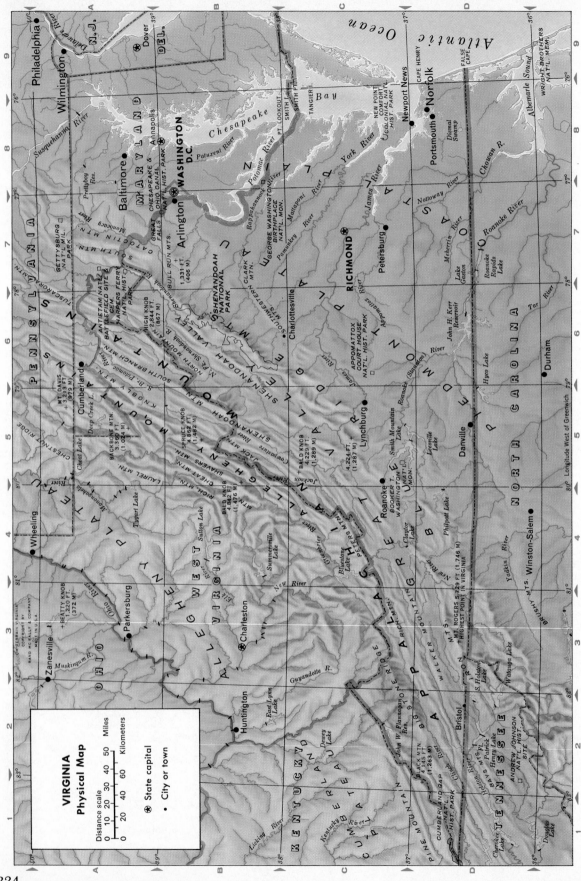

VIRGINIA
Physical Map

Distance scale
Miles
0 10 20 30 40 50
0 20 40 60
Kilometers

⊛ State capital
• City or town

Specially created for **World Book Encyclopedia** by Rand McNally and World Book editors

VIRGINIA/*The Land*

Land Regions. Virginia has five main land regions: (1) the Appalachian Plateau, (2) the Appalachian Ridge and Valley Region, (3) the Blue Ridge, (4) the Piedmont, and (5) the Atlantic Coastal Plain.

The Appalachian Plateau is a rugged region in the southwestern part of the state. It has an average elevation of 2,000 feet (610 meters). Many streams flow westward through the region. In some places, they have cut deep gorges. The plateau is covered with forests and has valuable coal fields.

The Appalachian Ridge and Valley Region consists of a series of parallel mountain ridges that extend northeast and southwest along most of the state's western border. The Great Valley, or Valley of Virginia, lies in the eastern part of this region. The Great Valley is actually a series of separate river valleys. The largest of these is the Shenandoah Valley in the north. A prominent mountain ridge, the Massanutten, divides the Shenandoah Valley into two parts for much of its length. The Appalachian Ridge and Valley Region has many caves and other rock formations created by the action of water on limestone.

The Blue Ridge borders the Appalachian Ridge and Valley Region on the east. It is the main eastern range of the Appalachian Mountain System, and an outstanding feature of Virginia. Northeast of Roanoke, the ridge is narrow and rises sharply from the lower land east and west of it. South of Roanoke, the Blue Ridge broadens into a plateau with mountain peaks, valleys, and deep ravines. The highest peaks in Virginia— Mount Rogers (5,729 feet, or 1,746 meters) and Whitetop Mountain (5,520 feet, or 1,682 meters)—are in the southern part of the Blue Ridge.

The Piedmont, in central Virginia, is the state's largest land region. It is an elevated, gently rolling plain, about 40 miles (64 kilometers) wide in the northeast and widening to about 140 miles (225 kilometers) at the North Carolina border. The Piedmont has an average elevation of 800 to 900 feet (240 to 270 meters) in the west. It slopes gradually to an average elevation of 200 to 300 feet (61 to 91 meters) in the east. Many rivers and streams flow southeastward across the Piedmont. They break

Virginia Dept. of Conservation and Economic Development

Pinnacle Overlook provides a breathtaking view of Cumberland Gap National Historic Park in southwestern Virginia. From this spot, visitors can see parts of Kentucky and Tennessee.

into low waterfalls at the eastern edge of the region, known as the *fall line* (see FALL LINE).

The Atlantic Coastal Plain is a lowland region about 100 miles (160 kilometers) wide that extends north and south along the Atlantic Ocean. It is often called the *Tidewater*, because tidal water flows up its bays, inlets, and rivers. Chesapeake Bay divides the region into a western mainland section and a peninsula called the

Land Regions of Virginia

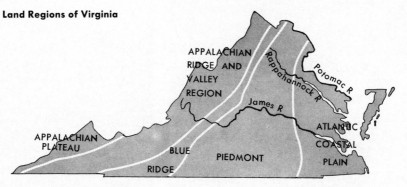

325

Shenandoah Valley is a beautiful rolling area in the Appalachian Ridge and Valley Region of northwest Virginia. Many springs and caverns are scattered through the valley.

Eastern Shore. The region has salt marshes and swamps. The largest is Dismal Swamp, in the southeast.

Coastline. Virginia has a general coastline of 112 miles (180 kilometers). The *tidal shoreline* (including small bays and inlets) is 3,315 miles (5,335 kilometers). Sand bars and islands along the coast have created several lagoons. A long, sandy beach stretches southward from the Norfolk area.

Rivers and Lakes. Several rivers flow from the western mountains and the Piedmont into Chesapeake Bay. These rivers include the Rappahannock, James, and York. They divide the Tidewater area into a series of peninsulas. The Potomac River forms Virginia's northeastern border. It is an important transportation route between Alexandria and Chesapeake Bay. The Shenandoah River flows northward through the Great Valley and empties into the Potomac.

The Roanoke River flows southeastward across the Piedmont into North Carolina. The New River begins in North Carolina and flows north and west through southwestern Virginia into West Virginia. Several rivers in the southwestern corner of the state, including the Clinch, Holston, and Powell, flow southwestward toward the Tennessee Valley.

Virginia's largest natural lake is Lake Drummond (3,200 acres, or 1,290 hectares) in Dismal Swamp.

Many artificial lakes have been formed by damming rivers for hydroelectric power, recreation, or other purposes. The largest of these man-made lakes is Kerr Reservoir on the North Carolina border. About 36,140 acres (14,625 hectares) of this lake are in Virginia.

Plant and Animal Life. Forests cover more than 60 per cent of Virginia. Common trees include ashes, beeches, birches, black tupelos, hemlocks, hickories, locusts, maples, red cedars, spruces, sweet gums, and tulip trees. Flowering dogwood, the state flower, blooms in early spring. Wild azaleas, mountain laurels, redbuds, rhododendrons, and other flowering plants grow in mountain areas. Wild flowers include blue lobelias, lowland laurels, morning-glories, and violets.

Deer and some elk roam the wooded areas of Virginia. Black bears and wildcats live in the western mountains and in Dismal Swamp. Small animals include foxes, muskrats, opossums, rabbits, and raccoons. Virginia has many game birds, including ducks, geese, quails, ruffed grouse, and turkeys.

The state's freshwater fishes include alewife, bass, carp, perch, pickerel, pike, and trout. Drum, flounder, mackerel, menhaden, and shad swim in the Atlantic Ocean, in Chesapeake Bay, and in Virginia's many inlets. Clams, crabs, oysters, and scallops live in Chesapeake Bay and in shallow coastal waters.

Gently Rolling Farmland surrounds the town of Appomattox in the Piedmont, the largest land region in Virginia.

Wild Flowers add brilliant splashes of color to the famous Blue Ridge Mountains of Virginia in Shenandoah National Park.

VIRGINIA / *Climate*

The climate of Virginia is mild. Temperatures vary from east to west as the elevation of the land and the distance from the ocean increase. In January, temperatures average 41° F. (5° C) in the Tidewater area, and about 32° F. (0° C) in parts of the Blue Ridge. July temperatures average 78° F. (26° C) in the Tidewater and about 68° F. (20° C) in the mountains. The state's highest temperature, 110° F. (43° C), occurred at Columbia on July 5, 1900, and at Balcony Falls on July 15, 1954. The record low, −29° F. (−34° C), occurred at Monterey on Feb. 10, 1899.

Virginia's *precipitation* (rain, melted snow, and other forms of moisture) is lightest in the Shenandoah Valley, where it averages about 36 inches (91 centimeters) a year. In the south, it averages about 44 inches (112 centimeters). Snowfall ranges from 5 to 10 inches (13 to 25 centimeters) in the Tidewater to 25 to 30 inches (64 to 76 centimeters) in the western mountains.

FPG

Cool Sea Breezes refresh bathers at Virginia Beach. This popular resort area lies on the Atlantic Coastal Plain.

Seasonal Temperatures

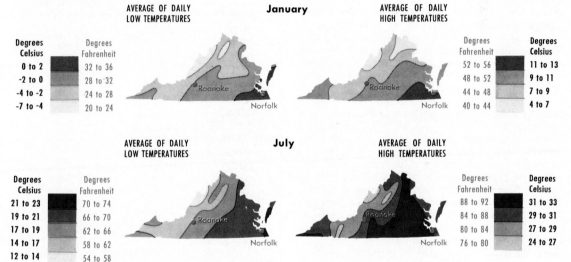

January — AVERAGE OF DAILY LOW TEMPERATURES

Degrees Celsius	Degrees Fahrenheit
0 to 2	32 to 36
-2 to 0	28 to 32
-4 to -2	24 to 28
-7 to -4	20 to 24

January — AVERAGE OF DAILY HIGH TEMPERATURES

Degrees Fahrenheit	Degrees Celsius
52 to 56	11 to 13
48 to 52	9 to 11
44 to 48	7 to 9
40 to 44	4 to 7

July — AVERAGE OF DAILY LOW TEMPERATURES

Degrees Celsius	Degrees Fahrenheit
21 to 23	70 to 74
19 to 21	66 to 70
17 to 19	62 to 66
14 to 17	58 to 62
12 to 14	54 to 58

July — AVERAGE OF DAILY HIGH TEMPERATURES

Degrees Fahrenheit	Degrees Celsius
88 to 92	31 to 33
84 to 88	29 to 31
80 to 84	27 to 29
76 to 80	24 to 27

Average Yearly Precipitation
(Rain, Melted Snow, and Other Moisture)

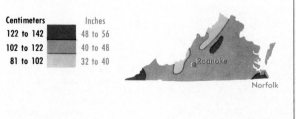

Centimeters	Inches
122 to 142	48 to 56
102 to 122	40 to 48
81 to 102	32 to 40

| 0 | 50 | 100 | 200 Miles |
| 0 | 100 | 200 | 300 Kilometers |

WORLD BOOK maps

Average Monthly Weather

	NORFOLK					ROANOKE				
	Temperatures				Days of Rain or Snow	Temperatures				Days of Rain or Snow
	F° High	F° Low	C° High	C° Low		F° High	F° Low	C° High	C° Low	
JAN.	50	33	10	1	11	47	29	8	-2	11
FEB.	51	33	11	1	11	49	30	9	-1	11
MAR.	59	39	15	4	12	57	36	14	2	12
APR.	66	46	19	8	10	67	44	19	7	10
MAY	75	56	24	13	11	77	53	25	12	11
JUNE	84	65	29	18	11	84	61	29	16	11
JULY	86	69	30	21	12	87	65	31	18	11
AUG.	85	68	29	20	12	85	64	29	18	11
SEPT.	80	64	27	18	8	80	58	27	14	11
OCT.	70	52	21	11	8	70	46	21	8	8
NOV.	60	43	16	6	8	57	37	14	3	10
DEC.	57	34	14	1	10	48	30	9	-1	9

Throughout most of its history, Virginia had an agricultural economy based on tobacco and other plantation crops. Government activities and manufacturing industries grew rapidly after about 1940. Today, government spending is the single most important source of income in Virginia. The government accounts for 23 per cent of the gross state product—the total value of all goods and services produced in a state in a year. Many federal government agencies operate in northern Virginia, near Washington, D.C. Virginia also benefits from the Norfolk Naval Base and other U.S. government installations throughout the state. Government is one of several growing service industries in Virginia.

Virginia's location near highly populated areas of the northeast and the rapidly growing states in the southeast is favorable for manufacturing and trade. Deposits of coal and other natural resources, good transportation by land and water, and a growing population also favor these industries. Millions of tourists visit Virginia each year and spend nearly $4 billion.

Natural Resources of Virginia include varied soils and many mineral deposits.

Soil. Most of the western, mountainous part of Virginia has shallow, rocky soils. The valley soils are stony and not very fertile, except in parts of the Shenandoah Valley and other areas where the soil contains much lime. Soils are stony and shallow in the northern part of the Blue Ridge, but deeper and darker in the southwest. Piedmont soils are generally light in color and have a loamy texture. Most soils in the Atlantic Coastal Plain are sandier than those in other parts of Virginia. The sandy soils are generally deep and easily cultivated.

Minerals. Coal is Virginia's most important mineral resource. Most of the coal is in the southwestern part of the state. *Bituminous* (soft) coal makes up most of these reserves. The famous Pocahontas coal of Buchanan and Tazewell counties is among the bituminous deposits. Virginia has deposits of *semianthracite* (fairly hard coal) in Montgomery and Pulaski counties.

Virginia stones include basalt, granite, limestone, marble, sandstone, shale, slate, and soapstone. Most of the limestone is found in the Appalachian Ridge and Valley Region. The Atlantic Coastal Plain has large deposits of clay, and sand and gravel. Lead and zinc ores occur in Wythe County. Some manganese and iron

Virginia's Gross State Product

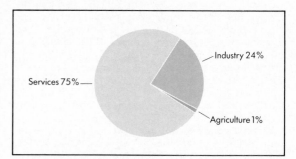

The gross state product (GSP) is the total value of goods and services produced in a state in a year. The GSP measures a state's total economic performance and can also be used to compare the economic output and growth of states. Virginia's GSP was $67,178,600,000 in 1982.

Production and Workers by Economic Activities

Economic Activities	Per Cent of GSP Produced	Employed Workers Number of Persons	Per Cent of Total
Government	22	503,100	22
Manufacturing	17	400,300	18
Community, Social, & Personal Services	16	457,500	20
Wholesale & Retail Trade	15	475,600	21
Finance, Insurance, & Real Estate	13	109,700	5
Transportation, Communication, & Utilities	9	119,200	5
Construction	4	112,700	5
Mining	3	17,500	1
Agriculture	1	73,000	3
Total	100	2,268,600	100

Sources: *Employment and Earnings*, May 1984, Bureau of Labor Statistics; *Farm Labor*, August 1984, USDA; Tayloe Murphy Institute, University of Virginia.

ore occur in the Appalachian Ridge and Valley Region, the Blue Ridge Mountains, and the Piedmont. Other minerals include feldspar, gem stones, gypsum, kyanite, mica, natural gas, petroleum, pyrite, salt, and titanium.

Service Industries account for 75 per cent of Virginia's gross state product. They employ nearly three-

Firestone Synthetic Fibers Company

Polyester Yarns are wound onto huge beams in a Hopewell chemical plant, *left*, before being shipped to textile mills. Synthetic fibers, such as polyesters and acrylics, rank as the chief chemical products manufactured in Virginia. The production of chemicals and related products is the leading industrial activity in the state.

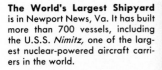

The World's Largest Shipyard is in Newport News, Va. It has built more than 700 vessels, including the U.S.S. *Nimitz*, one of the largest nuclear-powered aircraft carriers in the world.

Newport News Shipbuilding

fourths of the state's workers. Government employs more workers than any other economic activity in the state. About 387,000 Virginians work for the federal government, either in civilian activities or as members of the armed forces. They live chiefly in northern Virginia or in the Hampton Roads area. Many other Virginians work for state or local government agencies.

Community, social, and personal services account for 16 per cent of the gross state product. They form the second most valuable service industry in Virginia. These services include education and health care; advertising and data processing; and the operation of beauty parlors, cleaning establishments, and funeral homes.

Wholesale and retail trade supplies 15 per cent of the gross state product. Richmond ranks as the state's leading center of trade. Petersburg is a market for tobacco and livestock. Charlottesville and Fredericksburg serve as markets for the surrounding farming regions. Roanoke is the trading center for western Virginia.

There are two other important service industries in Virginia. They are (1) finance, insurance, and real estate and (2) transportation, communication, and utilities. Banks, insurance companies, and other financial institutions support the state's industry and international trade. Railroads and trucking companies serve the trading centers. Busy ports at Hampton Roads ship coal, grain, tobacco, and other products worldwide.

Manufacturing accounts for about 17 per cent of Virginia's gross state product. Goods manufactured there have a *value added by manufacture* of about $17\frac{1}{4}$ billion yearly. Value added by manufacture represents the increase in value of raw materials after they become finished products. Virginia's chief manufactured goods, in order of importance, are (1) tobacco products, (2) chemicals, (3) food products, (4) electrical machinery and equipment, and (5) transportation equipment.

Tobacco Products have a value added of about $2\frac{1}{2}$ billion yearly. Cigarettes, the leading tobacco product, are manufactured mainly in Richmond and Petersburg.

Chemicals manufactured and processed in Virginia have a value added of about $2\frac{1}{3}$ billion yearly. The leading chemical products are synthetic fibers, such as nylon. They are made in Front Royal, Hopewell, Martinsville, Narrows, Waynesboro, and Williamsburg, and in Chesterfield County. Elkton, Lynchburg, and Richmond have companies that manufacture drugs.

Food Products account for about $2 billion yearly in value added. Virginia factories produce bakery products, beverages, candy, canned and frozen foods, milk products, and meat products. Factories along Chesapeake Bay process crabs and oysters. Factories there also produce fish meal and oil from menhaden, a kind of fish. Winchester is the center of the apple products industry in the state. Some Virginia factories make livestock and poultry feed.

Electrical Machinery and Equipment has an annual value added of about $1\frac{1}{2}$ billion. The industry's most important products include communication equipment, electronic machinery, and radio and television receiving equipment. Lynchburg, Manassas, Salem, and Waynesboro have large plants that manufacture these items.

Transportation Equipment has a value added of about $1\frac{1}{2}$ billion yearly. The industry's chief products are boats and ships, motor vehicle parts, and trucks. Newport News Shipbuilding is the world's largest shipbuilding and ship-repairing yard. Hampton, Norfolk, and Portsmouth also have shipyards. Motor vehicle parts and trucks are produced in plants throughout the state.

Other Important Industries produce, in order of value, printed materials, textiles, paper products, rubber and plastics products, and nonelectrical machinery.

Mining in Virginia accounts for 3 per cent of the gross state product. The yearly income from mining totals about $1\frac{1}{2}$ billion. Coal is the most important mining product. The state produces about 39 million short tons (35 million metric tons) of coal yearly and ranks among the leading states in coal production. Large amounts of bituminous coal come from Buchanan, Dickenson, Russell, Tazewell, and Wise counties.

Stone production totals about 38 million short tons (35 million metric tons) a year. Limestone from the western valleys is used in making cement and lime. Basalt, granite, marble, sandstone, slate, and talc are also quarried in the state. Sand and gravel production occurs mainly on the Atlantic Coastal Plain. Lead and zinc ores are mined in Wythe County. Virginia also produces brick clay, gemstones, gypsum, iron oxide pigments, kyanite, natural gas, petroleum, and silver.

Agriculture contributes 1 per cent of Virginia's gross state product. The state has a farm income of about $2 billion a year. Virginia has about 50,000 farms, averaging 182 acres (74 hectares) in size.

328a

VIRGINIA

Millions of Apples cover the ground in Winchester in the Shenandoah Valley. Many apples are processed into juice, vinegar, or applesauce. Virginia ranks among the leading states in apple production.

Tom Hollyman, Photo Researchers

FARM, MINERAL, AND FOREST PRODUCTS

This map shows where the state's leading farm, mineral, and forest products are produced. The major urban areas (shown on the map in red) are the state's important manufacturing centers.

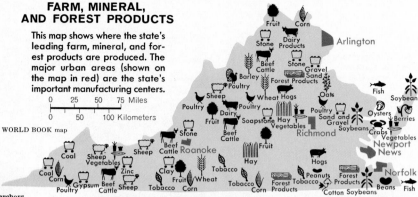

0   25   50   75 Miles

0   50   100 Kilometers

WORLD BOOK map

E. L. Korb, Alpha

A Worker Cuts Tobacco Leaves on a farm in the Piedmont region of southern Virginia. Farmers raise tobacco on only a small part of Virginia's land. But tobacco provides more farm income than any other crop grown in the state.

A Flock of White Turkeys gathers around the feeding trough on a farm in Rockingham County in northwestern Virginia. This county is one of the leading counties in the United States in the production of turkeys. Virginia is also known for its Smithfield hams.

Bradley Smith, Photo Researchers

Livestock, dairying, and poultry raising provide more than half of Virginia's farm income. Farmers raise beef and dairy cattle in all parts of the state. They also raise hogs, horses, and sheep. The state is known for its Smithfield hams. Virginia is a leading producer of turkeys, and also raises large numbers of broiler chickens. Rockingham County is one of the leading counties in the United States in turkey production.

Virginia is a major tobacco-producing state. Farmers grow tobacco on only a small part of Virginia's cropland. But tobacco provides more farm income than any other crop. Most of it is grown in the Piedmont region south of the James River. Other field crops include corn, peanuts, and soybeans. Peanuts are grown in the southeast, especially in Southampton County. Winter wheat is raised mainly east of the Blue Ridge Mountains.

Most commercial production of vegetables takes place near Chesapeake Bay. Virginia's leading vegetable crops include cucumbers, potatoes, snap beans, sweet potatoes, and tomatoes. The state has large apple orchards. Over half the trees are in the Shenandoah Valley. Peaches and strawberries also are grown.

Fishing Industry. Virginia ranks among the leading fishing states. Its yearly fish catch has a value of about $85 million. Virginia is a leading state in crab and oyster production. Other seafoods include clams, croakers, flounders, scallops, sea bass, striped bass, and sea trout. Menhaden are processed into fertilizer and oil.

Electric Power. Most of Virginia's electric power comes from steam plants that burn coal or oil. The main plants are in Virginia and West Virginia. Major hydroelectric plants that supply power to Virginia operate at the Claytor, John H. Kerr, Leesville, and Smith Mountain dams in Virginia, and at the Gaston and Roanoke Rapids dams in North Carolina. Nuclear generating plants in Virginia provide about a third of the state's electric power.

Transportation. The Little River Turnpike was the first U.S. toll road. It was built in the late 1780's from Alexandria to Snicker's Gap in the Blue Ridge. Today, almost all of Virginia's 64,500 miles (103,800 kilo-

meters) of roads and highways are surfaced. Long bridges cross the Tidewater rivers. The Chesapeake Bay Bridge-Tunnel, 23 miles (37 kilometers) long, connects the mainland with the Eastern Shore.

The first Virginia railroad began operating in 1831. It carried coal on flatcars pulled by mules. The wooden track, 12 miles (19 kilometers) long, went from the mines of Chesterfield County to Richmond. Today, railroads operate on over 4,000 miles (6,400 kilometers) of track. More than 15 rail lines provide freight service. Passenger trains serve about 15 Virginia cities.

More than 25 major airlines and about 250 airports serve Virginia. Dulles International Airport, one of the nation's largest, lies near Chantilly. Washington National Airport is near Alexandria.

Large ships can travel on Chesapeake Bay and some distance up the James and Potomac rivers. Hampton Roads, at the junction of the James, Nansemond, and Elizabeth rivers, is an important harbor area. Norfolk, on Hampton Roads, is one of the leading ports in the United States. Other important ports include Newport News on Hampton Roads, Alexandria on the Potomac, and Hopewell and Richmond on the James. The Dismal Swamp Canal and the Albemarle and Chesapeake Canal form part of the Atlantic Intracoastal Waterway (see ATLANTIC INTRACOASTAL WATERWAY).

Communication. In 1736, William Parks, Virginia's public printer, founded the *Virginia Gazette*, the first newspaper in the colony. *The Alexandria Gazette* began in 1784 as a weekly, and became a daily in 1797. It is one of the oldest continuously published dailies in the United States. The *Richmond Times-Dispatch*, *The Richmond News Leader*, and *The Virginian-Pilot* of Norfolk are among the most widely read newspapers in the South.

Virginia's first commercial radio station, WTAR, began in Norfolk in 1923. The state's first television station, WTVR, started in Richmond in 1948. Virginia has about 220 radio stations and over 20 TV stations.

VIRGINIA/History

Indian Days. When the first English colonists arrived in the Virginia region, Indian tribes of three major language groups lived there. The Powhatan, members of the Algonquian language group, lived in the coastal area. The Monacan and Manahoac, who spoke the Siouan language, occupied the Piedmont region. Other Siouan tribes in the Virginia region included the Nahyssan along the James River, and the Occaneechi on the Roanoke River. The Susquehanna near the upper Chesapeake Bay, the Cherokee in the southwest, and the Nottoway in the southeast spoke the Iroquoian language.

Early Settlement. The first Europeans who settled in Virginia were a group of Spanish Jesuits. In 1570, they established a mission, perhaps on the York River. Indians wiped out the settlement a few months later.

In 1584, Queen Elizabeth I of England gave the English adventurer Sir Walter Raleigh permission to establish colonies in America. Raleigh and others soon sent expeditions. These expeditions failed because they did not have enough supplies. Raleigh and the queen

named what is now the eastern United States *Virginia*.

The Jamestown Settlement. In 1606, King James I chartered the Virginia Company of London (often called the London Company) for colonization purposes. In May 1607, colonists sent by the company established the first permanent English settlement in America, at Jamestown. The colony, led by Captain John Smith, survived many hardships. In 1609, Smith was injured and had to return to England. The following winter, so many settlers died from lack of food that the period became known as the *starving time*. In the spring, the discouraged colonists started to leave Jamestown. But they returned after they met the ships of Governor Thomas West, Lord De La Warr, at Hampton Roads. The ships brought supplies and new colonists. After Lord De La Warr returned to England, Thomas Gates and Thomas Dale served as deputy governors.

Progress of the Colony. John Rolfe, one of the colonists, began to raise tobacco in 1612. Rolfe developed a method of curing tobacco. He proved that tobacco

VIRGINIA

could be successfully exported. Tobacco exporting helped save the colony by giving the people a way to support themselves. In 1614, Rolfe married Pocahontas, a daughter of Powhatan, chief of the Indian confederation around Jamestown. Their marriage brought a period of peace between the Indians and the colonists.

By 1619, all free colonists had been granted land of their own. That year, the Virginia Company made plans to send a boatload of young women to the colony to become wives of the lonely settlers. Also in 1619, the first blacks were brought to Jamestown by Dutch traders.

The first representative legislature in America, the House of Burgesses, was formed in 1619. Its first meeting was called by Governor George Yeardley, who acted on instructions from the Virginia Company. The House of Burgesses met with the governor and his council to make laws for the colony. This combined lawmaking body was called the General Assembly of Virginia.

Powhatan, the friendly Indian chief, died in 1618. In 1622, his successor, Chief Opechancanough, led an attack on the colonists and massacred 347 of them.

Royal Governors and Cromwell. In 1624, King James I revoked the Virginia Company's charter and made Virginia a royal colony. The colonists often quarreled with the royal governors sent by England. Sir William Berkeley, governor from 1642 to 1652, had

Important Dates in Virginia

1607 The Virginia Company of London established the colony of Jamestown.

1612 John Rolfe helped save the colony by introducing tobacco growing and exporting.

1619 America's first representative legislature, the House of Burgesses, met in Jamestown. Dutch traders brought the first blacks to Jamestown.

1624 Virginia became a royal colony.

1676 Nathaniel Bacon led a rebellion against the government.

1693 The College of William and Mary was founded.

1775 George Washington became commander in chief of the Continental Army.

1776 Virginia declared its independence and adopted its first constitution. Thomas Jefferson of Virginia wrote the Declaration of Independence.

1781 Lord Cornwallis surrendered at Yorktown in the last major battle of the American Revolutionary War.

1784 Virginia gave up its western land claims to the United States.

1788 Virginia became the 10th state on June 25.

1789 George Washington, a Virginian, became the first President of the United States.

1792 Kentucky was formed from three of Virginia's western counties.

1801-1825 Three Virginians served as President: Thomas Jefferson (1801-1809), James Madison (1809-1817), and James Monroe (1817-1825).

1801-1835 John Marshall of Virginia served as Chief Justice of the United States.

1841 William Henry Harrison, born in Virginia, became President. Harrison died a month later. Vice President John Tyler, also a Virginian, became President.

1849 Zachary Taylor, another Virginian, became President.

1861-1865 Virginia seceded from the Union and became the major battleground of the Civil War.

1863 West Virginia was formed from northwestern Virginia.

1870 Virginia was readmitted to the Union.

1912 Woodrow Wilson became the eighth Virginian to be elected President.

1940-1945 New industries opened during World War II, adding to the state's industrial growth.

1959 The first public school integration in Virginia took place in Arlington County and Norfolk.

1964 The Chesapeake Bay Bridge-Tunnel connecting the mainland and the Eastern Shore was opened.

1969 A. Linwood Holton, Jr., became the first Republican to be elected governor since 1869.

1971 A new state constitution went into effect.

HISTORIC VIRGINIA

Walnut Grove

The Mother of Presidents

Cyrus McCormick invented the reaper near Walnut Grove in 1831.

GEORGE WASHINGTON

THOMAS JEFFERSON

JAMES MADISON

JAMES MONROE

WILLIAM HENRY HARRISON

JOHN TYLER

ZACHARY TAYLOR

WOODROW WILSON

Cumberland Gap was the "Gateway to the West" for many early pioneers. This high pass cuts through the Appalachian Mountains.

Cumberland Gap

good relations with the colonists. But in 1652, Berkeley was forced to surrender Virginia to the rule of Oliver Cromwell, who had overthrown King Charles I.

From 1652 until Charles II became king in 1660, the Virginia colonists were allowed to take almost complete charge of their own government. In spite of the political freedom they enjoyed under Cromwell, most of the colonists remained loyal to the English royalists. Some British supporters of the future King Charles II, called *Cavaliers*, sought refuge in Virginia.

In 1660, after Berkeley had been elected by the royalist Virginia assembly, Charles II reappointed him governor. Berkeley's new term brought widespread discontent. The governor kept the same members of the House of Burgesses in office for 14 years. He also allowed a *Tidewater aristocracy* to rule the colony. This group included the heads of the wealthy eastern families.

Westward Expansion. By the mid-1600's, many small farmers had pushed westward to the eastern edge of the Piedmont. This area is known as the *fall line* (see FALL LINE). The interests of the western farmers differed from those of the Tidewater aristocracy. The westerners

Virginia Military Institute's cadet barracks serve as a backdrop for the parade area. The Lexington college is sometimes called the *West Point of the South*. Its graduates have played an active part in every U.S. war since VMI was founded in 1839.

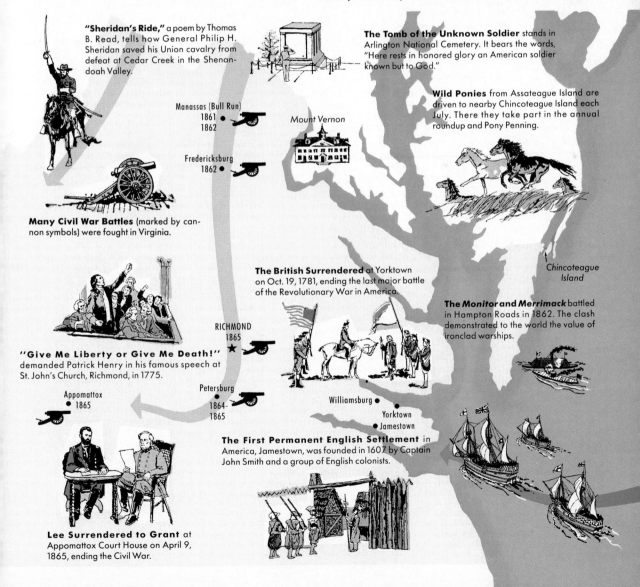

"Sheridan's Ride," a poem by Thomas B. Read, tells how General Philip H. Sheridan saved his Union cavalry from defeat at Cedar Creek in the Shenandoah Valley.

The Tomb of the Unknown Soldier stands in Arlington National Cemetery. It bears the words, "Here rests in honored glory an American soldier known but to God."

Manassas (Bull Run)
1861 •
1862

Mount Vernon

Fredericksburg
1862 •

Wild Ponies from Assateague Island are driven to nearby Chincoteague Island each July. There they take part in the annual roundup and Pony Penning.

Many Civil War Battles (marked by cannon symbols) were fought in Virginia.

Chincoteague Island

The British Surrendered at Yorktown on Oct. 19, 1781, ending the last major battle of the Revolutionary War in America.

The *Monitor* and *Merrimack* battled in Hampton Roads in 1862. The clash demonstrated to the world the value of ironclad warships.

RICHMOND
1865
★

"Give Me Liberty or Give Me Death!" demanded Patrick Henry in his famous speech at St. John's Church, Richmond, in 1775.

Appomattox
• 1865

Petersburg
•
1864-
1865

Williamsburg •

Yorktown
• Jamestown

The First Permanent English Settlement in America, Jamestown, was founded in 1607 by Captain John Smith and a group of English colonists.

Lee Surrendered to Grant at Appomattox Court House on April 9, 1865, ending the Civil War.

wanted protection from the Indians, and fewer political and economic regulations. They resented the British Navigation Acts, which greatly restricted colonial trade (see NAVIGATION ACT). A group of discontented colonists rebelled in 1676. They were led by Nathaniel Bacon, a young planter (see BACON'S REBELLION). In 1699, the capital was moved from Jamestown to Williamsburg.

By 1700, Virginia had a population of about 58,000 and was the largest North American colony. The growing population took up all the land along the tidal rivers and creeks. So, many pioneers moved westward into the Piedmont, the Great Valley, and the mountains. Germans and Scotch-Irish from Pennsylvania also settled in the Great Valley. The westward expansion of the English colonists conflicted with the interests of the French, and led to the French and Indian War of 1754-1763 (see FRENCH AND INDIAN WARS).

During the early 1770's, frequent Indian raids spread terror along the western frontier. In 1774, these attacks led to a campaign against the Indians called Lord Dunmore's War, after Virginia's governor, John Murray, Earl of Dunmore. A group of Virginia soldiers led by Andrew Lewis defeated the Shawnee Indians at Point Pleasant (now in West Virginia) on Oct. 10, 1774. Indian attacks then decreased in western Virginia.

The Course Toward Independence. Like many other colonists, Virginia's leaders were disturbed by the laws passed by the English Parliament without the consent of the colonies (see REVOLUTIONARY WAR IN AMERICA [Causes of the War]). Although most Virginians were loyal to the king, they favored liberty and wanted to govern their own affairs. Virginia's western leaders, including Patrick Henry and Thomas Jefferson, led the way in voicing the complaints of the colonists. Patrick Henry's resolutions, called the Virginia Resolves, helped arouse the colonists against the Stamp Act in 1765 (see STAMP ACT).

In 1774, the English Parliament ordered the port of Boston closed, following the Boston Tea Party in 1773 (see BOSTON TEA PARTY). The House of Burgesses, in sympathy with the Boston colonists, made the day of the port closing a day of fasting and prayer. This action angered Lord Dunmore, and he dissolved the House of Burgesses. Its members then met without official permission on Aug. 1, 1774, in Williamsburg. They called themselves the First Virginia Convention. The members elected delegates to the First Continental Congress (see CONTINENTAL CONGRESS). A Virginia delegate, Peyton Randolph, was chosen president of the congress.

At the Second Virginia Convention, on March 23, 1775, at St. John's Church in Richmond, Patrick Henry made his famous plea for the colonial cause: "Is life so dear or peace so sweet as to be purchased at the price of chains and slavery? Forbid it, Almighty God! I know not what course others may take, but as for me, give me liberty or give me death!"

Independence and Statehood. In 1775, the Second Continental Congress elected George Washington, a Virginian, as commander in chief of the Continental Army. Virginia became an independent commonwealth in June, 1776, when it adopted its first constitution. The constitution included a declaration of rights written by George Mason. This declaration was the first bill of rights in an American constitution. Patrick Henry was elected as the commonwealth's first governor. The capital of the commonwealth was moved from Williamsburg to Richmond in 1780.

Virginia militiamen drove Lord Dunmore from the colony after several skirmishes early in July, 1776. Also in 1776, the colony submitted to the Continental Congress a resolution calling for American independence (see DECLARATION OF INDEPENDENCE).

During the Revolutionary War (1775-1783), a larger proportion of persons in Virginia opposed the English than in any other southern colony. The Declaration of Independence was written by Thomas Jefferson, who later served as the state's second governor. Virginia also contributed the great cavalry leader "Light-Horse Harry" Lee, and Daniel Morgan, the hero of the battles of Saratoga and Cowpens. In 1778, George Rogers Clark won victories in the Northwest Territory. He took from the British Kaskaskia and Cahokia in what is now Illinois, and Vincennes in present-day Indiana. This territory had long been claimed by Virginia. In 1781, American forces won the last major battle of the war on Virginia soil when Lord Cornwallis surrendered to George Washington at Yorktown.

Until 1789, the 13 former colonies were loosely joined under the Articles of Confederation (see ARTICLES OF CONFEDERATION). Virginia had *ratified* (approved) the Articles on July 9, 1778. In order to persuade Maryland to accept the Articles, Virginia promised in 1781 to give up its claim to the Northwest Territory. Virginia did so in 1784 (see NORTHWEST TERRITORY).

The Articles of Confederation soon proved ineffective. James Madison and other Virginians led in creating the Constitution of the United States to replace the Articles. Virginia ratified the Constitution on June 25, 1788, and became the 10th state of the Union. See CONSTITUTION OF THE UNITED STATES.

The Mother of Presidents. Virginia furnished the United States with four of its first five presidents—George Washington, Thomas Jefferson, James Madison, and James Monroe. Washington was elected as the first President in 1789. He appointed Jefferson as the first secretary of state, and Edmund Randolph as the first attorney general. In 1792, the westernmost counties of Virginia became the state of Kentucky.

Thomas Jefferson, James Madison, and James Monroe were often called the *Virginia Dynasty*. During their presidential terms, they strengthened the new nation and added new territory to it. Another Virginian, John Marshall, served as Chief Justice of the United States from 1801 to 1835.

In 1830, Virginia adopted a new constitution, chiefly as a result of growing discontent in the western counties. The new constitution gave the westerners more representation in the general assembly. But eastern leaders kept control of the government.

In 1841, two more Virginians became President. William Henry Harrison and John Tyler had been born in the same Virginia county. Harrison died a month after his inauguration, and Tyler became President. During the Mexican War (1846-1848), Virginia furnished many of the chief military leaders. These men included Thomas J. Jackson, Joseph E. Johnston, Robert E. Lee, and Winfield Scott. General Zachary

Taylor, known as *Old Rough and Ready*, was also born in Virginia. Largely because of his military fame, Taylor was elected President in 1848.

The western counties continued to press for reforms in government. Their demands were incorporated into the constitution of 1851. This constitution gave all white men the right to vote. It also provided for the election of the governor and other officials by popular vote. Until that time, only landowners could vote, and the general assembly had elected the governor.

The Civil War and Reconstruction. South Carolina and six other Southern states withdrew from the Union during the winter of 1860-1861. But Virginia remained in the Union. Most Virginians hoped that compromise could save the Union and prevent war. President Abraham Lincoln called for troops on April 15, 1861. Two days later, a Virginia convention voted to *secede* (withdraw) from the Union. Many westerners in Virginia would not agree to secede. They set up an independent government in northwestern Virginia that stayed loyal to the Union. On June 20, 1863, 48 counties of northwestern Virginia became the state of West Virginia. Two other counties joined them in November 1863.

Richmond was the capital of the Confederacy from May 1861, to April 1865, when it surrendered to Union troops. Danville served briefly as the last headquarters of the Confederacy. Virginia's Robert E. Lee gained lasting fame as the South's outstanding military leader. The state contributed other leading Confederate generals, including Stonewall Jackson, Joseph E. Johnston, George E. Pickett, and Jeb Stuart.

The South won its greatest victories on Virginia battlefields—the first and second battles of Manassas (Bull Run), Jackson's Valley Campaign, and the battles of Fredericksburg and Chancellorsville. More battles were fought in Virginia than in any other state. Union armies repeatedly tried to seize Richmond and the Shenandoah Valley. This fertile valley was called the *Granary of the Confederacy*. The 1862 battle between the *Monitor* and the *Merrimack* (renamed the *Virginia* by the Confederate Navy) at Hampton Roads was the first fight between ironclad warships. This battle marked a turning point in naval warfare. The Civil War, like the Revolutionary War, ended in Virginia. Lee surrendered to General Ulysses S. Grant at Appomattox on April 9, 1865. See CIVIL WAR.

After the war, the federal government passed the Reconstruction Act of 1867, which placed Virginia under army rule as Military District No. 1. This act also provided for a state constitutional convention to draw up a new constitution for Virginia. The constitutional convention, headed by Judge John C. Underwood, met in December 1867. It was controlled by Radical Republicans, and nearly a third of its members were blacks. A constitution was adopted in 1869. It gave blacks

The State Governors of Virginia

	Party	Term		Party	Term
Patrick Henry	None	1776-1779	Henry A. Wise	Democratic	1856-1860
Thomas Jefferson	None	1779-1781	John Letcher	Democratic	1860-1864
William Fleming	None	1781	William Smith	Democratic	1864-1865
Thomas Nelson, Jr.	None	1781	Francis H. Pierpont	Republican	1865-1868
Benjamin Harrison	None	1781-1784	Henry H. Wells	Republican	1868-1869
Patrick Henry	None	1784-1786	Gilbert C. Walker	Republican	1869-1874
Edmund Randolph	None	1786-1788	James L. Kemper	Democratic	1874-1878
Beverley Randolph	None	1788-1791	Frederick W. M. Holliday	Democratic	1878-1882
Henry Lee	Federalist	1791-1794	William E. Cameron	R.-Rep.†	1882-1886
Robert Brooke	Dem.-Rep.*	1794-1796	Fitzhugh Lee	Democratic	1886-1890
James Wood	Dem.-Rep.	1796-1799	Philip W. McKinney	Democratic	1890-1894
James Monroe	Dem.-Rep.	1799-1802	Charles T. O'Ferrall	Democratic	1894-1898
John Page	Dem.-Rep.	1802-1805	James Hoge Tyler	Democratic	1898-1902
William H. Cabell	Dem.-Rep.	1805-1808	Andrew Jackson Montague	Democratic	1902-1906
John Tyler, Sr.	Dem.-Rep.	1808-1811	Claude A. Swanson	Democratic	1906-1910
James Monroe	Dem.-Rep.	1811	William Hodges Mann	Democratic	1910-1914
George William Smith	Dem.-Rep.	1811	Henry Carter Stuart	Democratic	1914-1918
Peyton Randolph	Dem.-Rep.	1811-1812	Westmoreland Davis	Democratic	1918-1922
James Barbour	Dem.-Rep.	1812-1814	Elbert Lee Trinkle	Democratic	1922-1926
Wilson Cary Nicholas	Dem.-Rep.	1814-1816	Harry Flood Byrd	Democratic	1926-1930
James Patton Preston	Dem.-Rep.	1816-1819	John Garland Pollard	Democratic	1930-1934
Thomas Mann Randolph	Dem.-Rep.	1819-1822	George C. Peery	Democratic	1934-1938
James Pleasants	Dem.-Rep.	1822-1825	James H. Price	Democratic	1938-1942
John Tyler, Jr.	Dem.-Rep.	1825-1827	Colgate W. Darden, Jr.	Democratic	1942-1946
William Branch Giles	Democratic	1827-1830	William M. Tuck	Democratic	1946-1950
John Floyd	Democratic	1830-1834	John S. Battle	Democratic	1950-1954
Littleton Waller Tazewell	Whig	1834-1836	Thomas B. Stanley	Democratic	1954-1958
Wyndham Robertson	Whig	1836-1837	J. Lindsay Almond, Jr.	Democratic	1958-1962
David Campbell	Democratic	1837-1840	Albertis S. Harrison, Jr.	Democratic	1962-1966
Thomas Walker Gilmer	Whig	1840-1841	Mills E. Godwin, Jr.	Democratic	1966-1970
John Mercer Patton	Whig	1841	A. Linwood Holton, Jr.	Republican	1970-1974
John Rutherfoord	Whig	1841-1842	Mills E. Godwin, Jr.	Republican	1974-1978
John Munford Gregory	Whig	1842-1843	John N. Dalton	Republican	1978-1982
James McDowell	Democratic	1843-1846	Charles S. Robb	Democratic	1982-1986
William Smith	Democratic	1846-1849	Gerald L. Baliles	Democratic	1986-
John Buchanan Floyd	Democratic	1849-1852			
Joseph Johnson	Democratic	1852-1856			

*Democratic-Republican   †Readjuster-Republican

the right to vote, and provided for a statewide system of public schools. Virginia was readmitted to the Union on Jan. 26, 1870. See RECONSTRUCTION.

A major problem facing Virginia after the war was its debt of about $42 million. The legislature finally provided that this debt should be reduced according to the state's ability to pay. An agreement was reached with the state's creditors in 1892. This agreement reduced the debt to $27 million. It also assigned part of the debt to West Virginia. That state had been a part of Virginia when the debt was acquired (see WEST VIRGINIA [Civil War and Statehood]).

Progress in Government and Industry. Modern industry in Virginia began during the early 1880's, when cigarette factories, cotton textile plants, and shipbuilding plants were built. In 1912, another man born in Virginia, Woodrow Wilson, was elected President. Carter Glass of Lynchburg, then a congressman, became the "father" of the Federal Reserve banking system.

During the early 1900's, many Virginians moved to other states in search of better job opportunities. More than 400,000 persons left the state in the 1920's.

Harry F. Byrd, Sr., served as governor from 1926 to 1930. He used the recommendations of a study commission to reorganize the state government and make it more efficient. In 1933, Byrd was appointed to the U.S. Senate, where he served over 30 years. Throughout this period, Byrd played a leading role in Virginia politics.

The 1930's were an important period of change in Virginia. Federal government activities in the state during the Great Depression created jobs and helped stop the flow of population from the state. Synthetic textile industries were established in many parts of Virginia.

The Mid-1900's. World War II (1939-1945) brought thousands of servicemen and servicewomen to the Virginia suburbs of Washington, D.C., and to the Norfolk area. Many of these people returned to Virginia to live after the war. During the 1940's and 1950's, the state also attracted many other new residents, including federal employees and employees of new industries. By 1955, it had more urban than rural dwellers.

Many Virginia communities built new schools during the 1950's. In the late 1950's, the issue of school integration became critical. In 1954, the Supreme Court of the United States ruled that compulsory segregation in public schools was unconstitutional. In 1956, the Virginia legislature passed so-called "massive resistance" laws to close any public school that the federal courts ordered integrated. In 1959, federal and state courts declared these laws invalid. That same year, public schools in Arlington County and Norfolk became the first in Virginia to integrate. But Prince Edward County closed its public schools in 1959 after a federal court ordered them to integrate. The county reopened the schools in 1964. In the late 1960's, a series of court decisions speeded up integration in the state.

Industry continued to expand in Virginia during the 1960's. The greatest growth occurred in the manufacture of chemicals, clothing, electrical equipment, furniture, and transportation equipment. In 1964, the General Assembly reduced certain taxes to attract new industry. The $200-million Chesapeake Bay Bridge-Tunnel was completed in 1964. This series of bridges, tunnels, and causeways extends 23 miles (37 kilometers), and links the Norfolk area with the Eastern Shore.

The political life of Virginia changed during the 1960's. Conservative Democrats, led by U.S. Senator Harry F. Byrd, Sr., had long controlled Virginia politics. But Byrd retired in 1965, and elections became more competitive. In 1966, Virginia voters elected William B. Spong, Jr., a moderate Democrat, to the U.S. Senate. In 1967, William F. Reid became the first black elected to the state legislature since 1891. The Republican Party also gained strength during the 1960's. In 1969, A. Linwood Holton, Jr., became the first Republican to be elected governor since 1869.

In 1970, Virginia voters approved a new state constitution. The constitution went into effect in 1971.

Virginia Today has a diversified economy. Manufacturing, agriculture, tourism, and activities of the federal government all contribute much to the economy. Virginia's relatively strong economy has kept its unemployment rate below the national average.

In spite of its strong economy, Virginia, like other states, faces a number of problems. It is hard-pressed to build new highways and maintain existing ones because it lacks sufficient transportation revenue. This revenue, which comes mainly from a gasoline tax, has declined since the late 1970's because people have been driving less due to high gasoline costs. Virginia is a leading coal-producing state, and it earns much income from the mineral. However, the use of coal is somewhat restricted because the burning of coal causes air pollution. Scientists are seeking ways to reduce the pollution hazard so more coal can be used.

RAYMOND C. DINGLEDINE, JR., and JOHN E. LEARD

VIRGINIA / Study Aids

Related Articles in WORLD BOOK include:

BIOGRAPHIES

Bacon, Nathaniel	Monroe, James
Berkeley, Sir William	Nelson, Thomas, Jr.
Blair, John	Pickett, George E.
Braxton, Carter	Powhatan
Byrd (family)	Prosser, Gabriel
Byrd, Richard E.	Randolph (family)
Dinwiddie, Robert	Rolfe, John
Glass, Carter	Ruffin, Edmund
Harrison, Benjamin	Seddon, James A.
(1726?-1791)	Smith, John
Harrison, William H.	Spotswood, Alexander
Henry, Patrick	Stuart, James E. B.
Jefferson, Thomas	Taylor, Zachary
Johnston, Joseph E.	Turner, Nat
Lee, Francis L.	Tyler, John
Lee, Henry	Washington, Booker T.
Lee, Richard H.	Washington, George
Lee, Robert E.	Washington, Martha Custis
Madison, James	Wilson, Woodrow
Marshall, John	Wythe, George
Mason, George	

CITIES

Alexandria	Lexington	Richmond
Charlottesville	Newport News	Roanoke
Fredericksburg	Norfolk	Williamsburg
Hampton	Petersburg	Yorktown

HISTORY

MILITARY INSTALLATIONS

PHYSICAL FEATURES

PRODUCTS

For Virginia's rank among the states in production, see the following articles:

OTHER RELATED ARTICLES

Outline

Questions

Why is Virginia called the *Old Dominion*? The *Mother of Presidents*? The *Mother of States*?

What conditions favor Virginia's industrial development?

Why did the population increase in the Virginia suburbs of Washington, D.C., and in the Norfolk area during the 1940's and 1950's?

What are Virginia's chief manufactured products?

What was the *Virginia Dynasty*?

Why is Virginia's General Assembly notable?

What was the *Granary of the Confederacy*?

What are Virginia's chief agricultural products?

What are some of the problems that Virginia faces?

What is Virginia's most important mineral resource?

What points were connected by the first U.S. toll road? When was this road built?

Additional Resources

Level I

BEHRENS, JUNE, and BROWER, PAULINE. *Colonial Farm*. Childrens Press, 1976.

CARPENTER, ALLAN. *Virginia*. Rev. ed. Childrens Press, 1978.

DAVIS, BURKE. *Appomattox: Closing Struggle of the Civil War*. Harper, 1963. *Yorktown: The Winning of American Independence*. 1969. *Getting to Know Jamestown*. Coward, 1971.

FLEMING, THOMAS J. *The Battle of Yorktown*. Harper, 1968.

FRADIN, DENNIS B. *Virginia in Words and Pictures*. Childrens Press, 1976.

GILL, HAROLD B., JR., and FINLAYSON, ANN. *Colonial Virginia*. Nelson, 1973.

LACY, DAN M. *The Colony of Virginia*. Watts, 1973.

TAYLOR, THEODORE. *Rebellion Town: Williamsburg, 1776*. Harper, 1973.

THANE, ELSWYTH. *The Virginia Colony*. Macmillan, 1969.

Level II

BILLINGS, WARREN M., ed. *The Old Dominion in the Seventeenth Century: A Documentary History of Virginia. 1606-1689*. Univ. of North Carolina Press, 1975.

BRIDENBAUGH, CARL. *Jamestown, 1544-1699*. Oxford, 1980.

BUNI, ANDREW. *The Negro in Virginia Politics, 1902-1965*. Univ. Press of Virginia, 1967.

DABNEY, VIRGINIUS. *Virginia: The New Dominion*. Doubleday, 1971.

FLEMING, THOMAS J. *Beat the Last Drum: The Siege of Yorktown, 1781*. St. Martin's, 1963.

FRIDDELL, GUY. *We Began at Jamestown*. Dietz Press, 1968. *The Virginia Way*. Burda, 1973.

GOTTMANN, JEAN. *Virginia in Our Century*. Univ. Press of Virginia, 1969.

ISAAC, RHYS. *The Transformation of Virginia, 1740-1790*. Univ. of North Carolina Press, 1982.

MORGAN, EDMUND S. *American Slavery, American Freedom: The Ordeal of Colonial Virginia*. Norton, 1975.

MORTON, RICHARD L. *Colonial Virginia*. 2 vols. Univ. Press of Virginia, 1960.

NOËL HUME, IVOR. *Here Lies Virginia: An Archaeologist's View of Colonial Life and History*. Knopf, 1963. *Martin's Hundred*. 1982. A record of archaeological discoveries at a colonial Virginia settlement near Williamsburg.

Revolutionary Virginia: The Road to Independence. Ed. by Robert L. Scribner and others. 6 vols. Univ. Press of Virginia, 1973-1981.

ROUSE, PARKE. *Virginia: A Pictorial History*. Scribner, 1975.

RUBIN, LOUIS D., JR. *Virginia: A Bicentennial History*. Norton, 1977.

SHEEHAN, BERNARD W. *Savagism and Civility: Indians and Englishmen in Colonial Virginia*. Cambridge, 1980. How the two groups perceived, and reacted to, each other.

TATE, THADDEUS W., JR. *The Negro in Eighteenth Century Williamsburg*. Rev. Ed. Univ. Press of Virginia, 1965.

VAUGHAN, ALDEN T. *American Genesis: Captain John Smith and the Founding of Virginia*. Little, Brown, 1975.

VIRGINIA, UNIVERSITY OF, is a state-controlled co-educational school in Charlottesville, Va. The university has a college of arts and sciences; schools of architecture, commerce, education, engineering and applied science, law, medicine, and nursing; and graduate schools of arts and sciences and business administration. Courses lead to bachelor's, master's, and doctor's degrees. The university also operates Clinch Valley College in Wise, Va. Clinch Valley grants the bachelor's degree. Thomas Jefferson founded the University of Virginia in 1819. For enrollment, see UNIVERSITIES AND COLLEGES (table).

Critically reviewed by the UNIVERSITY OF VIRGINIA

See also VIRGINIA (picture).

VIRGINIA BEACH (pop. 262,199) is a popular resort and the second largest city in Virginia. Only nearby Norfolk has more people. Virginia Beach lies on the southeastern edge of the state. It is bordered by the Atlantic Ocean and Chesapeake Bay. For location, see VIRGINIA (political map).

About 2 million tourists visit Virginia Beach each year. The city's main attractions are its many beaches and moderate climate. Cape Henry, where the first permanent English settlers in America originally landed in 1607, also is in the city. Many residents of Virginia Beach work at the area's numerous military bases. In the rural southern part of the city, farmers raise grain, hogs, and vegetables and produce dairy products. Virginia Beach was created in 1963, when a small resort town of the same name merged with Princess Anne County. Since the merger, the city's population has more than doubled. Virginia Beach has a council-manager form of government.   DANIEL H. BARKIN

VIRGINIA CITY, Nev., is perhaps the most celebrated and best-preserved ghost town in the West. The American author Mark Twain wrote about the turbulent early days of this former mining center in his book *Roughing It*. The town lies in the Virginia Range, 23 miles (37 kilometers) southeast of Reno. For the location of Virginia City, see NEVADA (political map).

Virginia City was founded in 1859, just two years after the discovery of gold and silver in the surrounding mountains. The town's population swelled to 23,000 in 1876, at the peak of the Comstock Lode's producing power. Today, Virginia City has only about 730 permanent residents. But as many as 40,000 tourists visit the town each week during the summer.   LUCIUS BEEBE

See also COMSTOCK LODE; WESTERN FRONTIER LIFE (Frontier Towns); NEVADA (color picture).

VIRGINIA COMMONWEALTH UNIVERSITY. See UNIVERSITIES AND COLLEGES (table).

VIRGINIA CREEPER is a rambling, creeping plant of the vine family. It grows in most parts of America, and is often called *woodbine*, and *American*, or *five-leaved*, ivy.

The Virginia creeper's strong but slender tendrils have long branches ending in tiny disks. The disks stick to surfaces on which the plant grows. A single tendril with five branches bearing these disks would, even after 10 years' exposure to all sorts of weather, hold up a weight of 10 pounds (5 kilograms).

The Virginia creeper looks somewhat like poison ivy, but the leaves of the poison ivy are made up of three leaflets, and those of the Virginia creeper of five. In the

J. Horace McFarland

Virginia Creeper adds brilliant color to stone fences and bare walls in autumn when its leaves turn a flaming red.

autumn the Virginia creeper has flaming foliage and bunches of dark blue berries.

Scientific Classification. The Virginia creeper belongs to the vine family, *Vitaceae*. It is genus *Parthenocissus*, species *P. quinquefolia*.   J. J. LEVINSON

See also IVY.

VIRGINIA MILITARY INSTITUTE is a state-supported college for men in Lexington, Va. The institute offers majors in biology, chemistry, civil and electrical engineering, economics, English, history, mathematics, modern languages, and physics. Graduates receive the bachelor's degree and either a regular or a reserve commission in one of the branches of the United States armed forces.

Students at the institute are called *cadets*. They lead the lives of soldiers in a highly disciplined atmosphere. They wear uniforms, live in barracks, eat in a mess hall, and take part in drills and field exercises.

Graduates of the institute have played an active part in every U.S. war since the school was founded in 1839. Alumni have also entered almost every civilian field. From 1851 to 1861, Stonewall Jackson was a professor of artillery tactics and natural philosophy at the institute (see JACKSON, STONEWALL). General George C. Marshall graduated from the institute in 1901. The George C. Marshall Research Library on the campus contains the general's papers and souvenirs, as well as military and historical exhibits. General George S. Patton, Jr., and Admiral Richard E. Byrd also attended the institute. For enrollment, see UNIVERSITIES AND COLLEGES (table).

Critically reviewed by the VIRGINIA MILITARY INSTITUTE

VIRGINIA PLAN. See RANDOLPH (Edmund); CONSTITUTION OF THE UNITED STATES (The Compromises).

VIRGINIA POLYTECHNIC INSTITUTE AND STATE UNIVERSITY is a coeducational state-supported institution in Blacksburg, Va. It is commonly called Virginia Tech. The university has undergraduate colleges of agriculture and life sciences, architecture and urban studies, arts and sciences, business, education, engineering, and human resources. It has a professional college of veterinary medicine and a graduate school. Courses lead to bachelor's, master's, and doctor's degrees. Virginia Tech also

offers a full-time military program. The university operates research centers in such fields as agriculture, coal and energy, environmental studies, and water resources. The school was founded in 1872. For enrollment, see UNIVERSITIES AND COLLEGES (table). Critically reviewed by
VIRGINIA POLYTECHNIC INSTITUTE AND STATE UNIVERSITY

VIRGINIA RESOLUTIONS. See KENTUCKY AND VIRGINIA RESOLUTIONS.

VIRGINIUM is a name formerly given to chemical element number 87. The element is now known as francium. See FRANCIUM.

VIRGINIUS MASSACRE was an event in 1873 that almost involved the United States in a war with Spain. During a Cuban revolt against Spain, the Spanish gunboat *Tornado* captured a merchant ship called the *Virginius* on the high seas off Jamaica. A U.S. citizen, Captain John Fry, commanded the *Virginius*, and flew the American flag. The Spanish authorities executed Fry, 36 of the ship's crew members, and 16 passengers. The Spanish claimed that the vessel was aiding the Cuban rebels.

The affair caused great excitement in the United States. But Spain agreed to surrender the ship and survivors, and denied any hostile intent. Later, authorities discovered that the *Virginius* was owned by Cubans, was illegally registered, and had no right to fly the American flag. The vessel was wrecked and left off Cape Fear on its way to the United States. JOHN DONALD HICKS

VIRGO is the sixth sign of the zodiac. Virgo, an earth sign, is symbolized by a virgin. Astrologers believe Virgo

Virgo—The Virgin

Symbol

Birth dates: Aug. 23–Sept. 22.
Group: Earth.
Characteristics: Careful, efficient, modest, orderly, practical, tidy.

Signs of the Zodiac

Aries
Mar. 21–Apr. 19
Taurus
Apr. 20–May 20
Gemini
May 21–June 20
Cancer
June 21–July 22
Leo
July 23–Aug. 22
Virgo
Aug. 23–Sept. 22
Libra
Sept. 23–Oct. 22
Scorpio
Oct. 23–Nov. 21
Sagittarius
Nov. 22–Dec. 21
Capricorn
Dec. 22–Jan. 19
Aquarius
Jan. 20–Feb. 18
Pisces
Feb. 19–Mar. 20

WORLD BOOK illustration by Robert Keys

is ruled by the planet Mercury, which was named for the messenger of the ancient Roman gods.

According to astrologers, people born under the sign of Virgo, from August 23 to September 22, are intelligent, practical, and sensible. They like order and tidiness in all things. Virgoans are good at concentrating on details and tend to find fault with things that other people consider unimportant. They have to be careful that their criticism does not hurt the feelings of others.

Virgoans rely on reason rather than emotion, and they may seem unsympathetic and too proud. They are

not natural leaders but tend to work in the background, where they often become powerful. Virgoans succeed at jobs that require them to be orderly and pay attention to details. They are also successful at skilled crafts. Virgoans have an interest in health, which leads many into the medical professions. CHRISTOPHER MCINTOSH

See also ASTROLOGY; HOROSCOPE; ZODIAC.

VIROLOGY. See BIOLOGY (table); MICROBIOLOGY.

VIRTANEN, ARTTURI. See NOBEL PRIZES (table: Nobel Prizes for Chemistry—1945).

VIRTUAL IMAGE. See LENS.

VIRUS is a microscopic organism that lives in a cell of another living thing. Viruses are the smallest and simplest form of life and are a major cause of disease. Some viruses infect human beings with such diseases as measles, influenza, and the common cold. Others infect animals or plants, and still others attack bacteria. Viruses produce disease in an organism by damaging some of its cells. However, viruses sometimes live in cells without harming them.

Viruses are so primitive that many scientists consider them to be both living and nonliving things. By itself, a virus is a lifeless particle that cannot reproduce. But inside a living cell, a virus becomes an active organism that can multiply hundreds of times.

Viruses are shaped like rods or spheres and range in size from about 0.01 to 0.3 micron. A micron is $\frac{1}{25,400}$ inch or 0.001 millimeter. Most viruses can be seen only with an electron microscope, which magnifies them by thousands of times. The largest virus is about $\frac{1}{10}$ as big as a bacterium of average size.

The study of viruses began in 1898, when a Dutch botanist named Martinus Beijerinck realized that something smaller than bacteria could cause disease. He named this particle a *virus*, a Latin word meaning *poison*. In 1935, Wendell M. Stanley, an American biochemist, showed that viruses contain protein and can be crystallized. This research and many other studies eventually led to the development, during the 1950's, of vaccines for measles, poliomyelitis, and other diseases. *Virologists* (scientists who study viruses) demonstrated in the early 1900's that viruses can cause cancer in animals. During the 1960's and 1970's, experiments with cancer viruses became an important part of biological research.

The Structure of a Virus. Viruses, unlike other organisms, are not made up of cells. Therefore, they lack some of the substances needed to live on their own. To obtain these substances, a virus must enter a cell of another living thing. It then can use the cell's materials to live and reproduce.

A virus has two basic parts, a core of a nucleic acid and an outer coat of protein. The core consists of either *DNA* (deoxyribonucleic acid) or *RNA* (ribonucleic acid). The DNA or RNA enables the virus to reproduce after it has entered a cell (see NUCLEIC ACID). The coat of a virus consists of individual proteins that give the virus its shape. It protects the nucleic acid and helps the DNA or RNA get inside a cell. Some viruses have an outer membrane that provides additional protection.

How a Virus Infects an Organism. Most viruses reproduce in specific cells of certain organisms. For example, viruses that cause colds reproduce in cells of the

human respiratory tract. Viruses cannot live outside their particular cells. They must be carried into the organism by air currents or some other means, and then transported by body fluids to the cells.

When a virus comes into contact with a cell that it can enter, it attaches itself to the cell at areas called *receptors*. Chemicals in the receptors bind the virus to the cell and help bring it or its nucleic acid inside. The nucleic acid then takes control of the cell's protein-making process. Previously, the cell made only the proteins specified by its own *genes*. The genes are the cell's hereditary structures, and they consist of nucleic acid. A cell that has been infected by a virus begins to produce the proteins that are called for by the nucleic acid of the virus. These proteins enable the virus to reproduce itself hundreds or thousands of times.

As new viruses are produced, they are released from the cell and infect other cells. The new viruses become lifeless as soon as they are released. But they return to life after entering another cell. The viruses then start to reproduce and thus spread infection to more cells.

When a virus reproduces, it changes the chemical makeup of a cell. This change usually damages or kills the cell, and disease results if many cells are affected. A few kinds of viruses change a cell only slightly because they do not reproduce.

Virus Diseases in Human Beings include chicken pox; colds; cold sores; hepatitis, a liver disease; influenza; measles; mumps; poliomyelitis; rabies; and yellow fever.

The body protects itself from viruses and other harmful substances by several methods, all of which together are called the *immune system*. For example, white blood cells called *lymphocytes* provide protection in two ways. Some lymphocytes produce substances called *antibodies*, which cover a virus's protein coat and prevent the virus from attaching itself to the receptors of a cell. Other lymphocytes destroy cells that have been infected by viruses and thus kill the viruses before they can reproduce.

Lymphocytes do not start to produce antibodies until several days after a virus has entered the body. However, the body has additional methods of fighting virus infections. For example, the body produces a high fever to combat such virus diseases as chicken pox and measles. The high fever limits the ability of the viruses to reproduce. To fight colds, the body forms large amounts

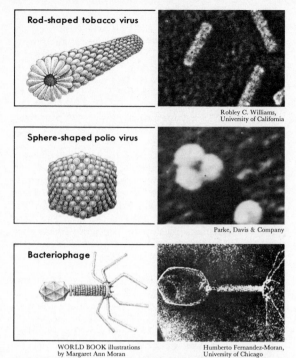

Rod-shaped tobacco virus

Robley C. Williams,
University of California

Sphere-shaped polio virus

Parke, Davis & Company

Bacteriophage

WORLD BOOK illustrations
by Margaret Ann Moran

Humberto Fernandez-Moran,
University of Chicago

Viruses Have Two Basic Shapes. Some, such as tobacco viruses, look like rods. Others, such as polio viruses, resemble spheres. Bacteriophages are sphere-shaped viruses that have a tail.

of mucus in the nose and throat. The mucus traps many cold viruses, which are expelled from the body by sneezing, coughing, and blowing one's nose. The body also makes a protein substance called *interferon* that provides some protection against all types of viruses.

The treatment of a virus disease consists mainly of controlling its symptoms. For example, physicians prescribe aspirin to bring down a high fever. In most cases, doctors cannot attack the cause of the disease itself, because most drugs able to kill or damage a virus also damage healthy cells. The U.S. Food and Drug Administration has approved a few drugs—including iododeoxyuridine (IUDR), adenine arabinoside (ara-A), and acyclovir—for limited use against certain virus diseases. Researchers have found other potential antiviral drugs, but these drugs must undergo further testing before their safety and effectiveness are known.

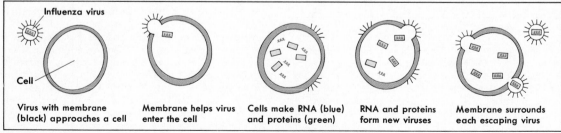

Influenza virus

Cell

Virus with membrane (black) approaches a cell

Membrane helps virus enter the cell

Cells make RNA (blue) and proteins (green)

RNA and proteins form new viruses

Membrane surrounds each escaping virus

WORLD BOOK diagram by David Cunningham

Viruses Reproduce Rapidly Inside Cells. An influenza virus multiplies almost immediately after infecting a cell, *above*. Such rapid reproduction by a virus can lead to disease. Newly formed viruses escape from a cell and infect other cells before the body can stop the process.

Until then, the best way to deal with viruses is immunization before a virus disease strikes. Immunization with vaccines causes the immune system to produce antibodies that resist a virus when it enters the body. Doctors use vaccines to prevent such virus diseases as influenza, measles, and polio. See IMMUNIZATION.

A few viruses are called *slow viruses* because they reproduce more slowly than the others. Many scientists believe such viruses result if an ordinary virus changes slightly. Diseases caused by slow viruses include Creutzfeldt-Jakob disease and Kuru, both of which gradually destroy the cells of the brain. Some researchers believe a slow virus causes multiple sclerosis, a disease of the brain and spinal cord.

Virus Diseases in Animals. Viruses cause hundreds of diseases in animals. These diseases include distemper in dogs, foot-and-mouth disease in cattle, and Newcastle disease in chickens. Most virus diseases in animals occur in certain species. But some of the diseases spread to other species, and a few of them infect human beings. For example, dogs can give people rabies, which destroys nerve cells.

Certain viruses can cause cancer in animals. These viruses do not destroy all the cells they infect. Some of the infected cells have their chemical makeup altered, which causes them to behave abnormally. These altered cells reproduce in an uncontrolled manner, forming masses of tissue called tumors. Cancerous tumors invade and damage surrounding healthy tissue. Researchers have discovered a similarity between some viruses that cause cancer in animals and certain viruses that infect human beings. However, they have not proven that any human cancer is caused by a virus.

Virus Diseases in Plants. Viruses infect all kinds of plants and can cause serious damage to crops. Plant cells have tough walls that a virus cannot penetrate. But insects penetrate the cell walls while feeding on a plant and thus enable viruses to enter. Plant viruses may infect one or two leaves or an entire plant. They produce billions of viruses, which are then carried to other plants by insects or air currents. Common plant virus diseases include tobacco mosaic and turnip yellows mosaic.

Viruses That Attack Bacteria are called *bacteriophages*. The word *bacteriophage* means *bacteria eater*. Bacteria, like plants, have tough cell walls. To penetrate these walls, most bacteriophages have a structure that resembles a hypodermic needle and works in a similar manner. This structure consists of a sphere-shaped head that contains a nucleic acid, and a hollow, rod-shaped tail made of protein. When a bacteriophage enters a bacterium, the tail first penetrates the cell wall. Then the nucleic acid in the head moves through the tail and into the cell.

How Viruses Are Used. Virologists study viruses chiefly to learn how they cause disease and how to control these organisms. Scientists also use viruses for such purposes as (1) insect control, (2) cell research, and (3) development of vaccines.

Insect Control. Certain viruses cause fatal diseases in insects. Virologists are seeking ways to use these viruses to kill insects that damage crops. The use of such viruses may someday replace insecticides, which kill insects but also may harm plants as well as other animals.

Cell Research. Viruses are such simple organisms that scientists can easily study them to gain more knowledge about life itself. Research on bacteriophages has helped biologists understand genes, DNA, and other basic cell structures. Future research may provide further knowledge of how cells function and reproduce.

Development of Vaccines. Scientists produce vaccines from either dead or live viruses. Those used in dead-virus vaccines are killed by chemicals and injected into the body. They cause the body to produce antibodies and other substances that resist viruses. For live-virus vaccines, virologists select very mild forms of living viruses that stimulate the body's immune system but cause no serious harm.   JOHN J. HOLLAND

Related Articles in WORLD BOOK include:

SOME VIRUS DISEASES

Chicken Pox	Measles
Cold, Common	Mosaic Disease
Dengue	Mumps
Distemper	Poliomyelitis
Encephalitis	Rabies
Foot-and-Mouth Disease	Shingles
Hepatitis	Smallpox
Herpes	Yellow Fever
Influenza	

OTHER RELATED ARTICLES

Bacteria	Interferon
Disease (Infectious Diseases)	Rous, Francis
Gnotobiotics	Salk, Jonas E.
Immunization	Stanley, Wendell M.

Additional Resources

ERON, CAROL. *The Virus That Ate Cannibals.* Macmillan, 1981. Gives history of research on various viruses.

KNIGHT, DAVID C. *Viruses: Life's Smallest Enemies.* Morrow, 1981.

LOCKE, DAVID M. *Virus Diseases: A Layman's Handbook.* Crown, 1978.

NOURSE, ALAN E. *Viruses.* Rev. edition, Watts, 1983. For younger readers.

VIRUS PNEUMONIA is an infection of the lungs caused by viruses. These germs are so tiny that only the largest can be seen even under a powerful microscope (see VIRUS). Virus pneumonia has been recognized as a distinct disease only since the early 1900's.

This type of pneumonia is very contagious. Doctors believe it is spread by breathing air containing these germs. Persons with the disease may cough or sneeze, spraying into the air fine droplets with the tiny germs. If another person breathes the air with these germs he or she may contract the disease. X-ray pictures of persons with virus pneumonia show shadows on the lungs. Very sick patients find breathing difficult. They develop *cyanosis*, a blue condition of the skin caused by lack of oxygen. It may take seven days to several months for a person to recover from virus pneumonia.   M. D. ALTSCHULE

See also PNEUMONIA.

VISA, *VEE zuh,* is an endorsement that government officials place on a passport to show that the passport is valid (see PASSPORT). Officials of the country which a traveler is entering grant the visa. It certifies that the passport has been examined and approved. Immigration officers then permit the bearer to enter the country. A government that does not want a person to enter the country can refuse to grant that person a visa.

VISCOSITY, *vihs KAHS uh tee,* is a property of fluids that causes them to resist flowing. It is caused by in-

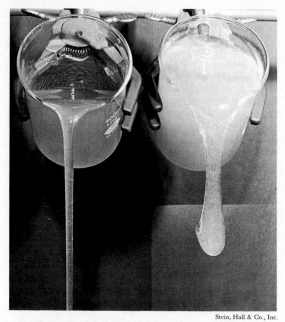

The Viscosity of Liquids causes them to resist flowing. A liquid with low viscosity, *left,* flows much faster than a liquid that has high viscosity, *right.*

Stein, Hall & Co., Inc.

ternal friction from the fluid's molecules moving against each other. Fluids with *high viscosity,* such as molasses, flow more slowly than those with *low viscosity,* such as water. All fluids, including liquids and gases, have some degree of viscosity. Some materials, such as pitch, that appear to be solid are highly viscous and can flow very slowly. The degree of viscosity is important in many applications. For example, the viscosity of motor oil determines how effectively it can lubricate the parts of an automobile engine.

The more strongly a fluid's molecules interact, the more viscous the fluid. Generally, the larger the size or length of a molecule, the greater the interaction. The temperature of a fluid also determines how strongly its molecules interact. Molecules in liquids interact more as the temperature decreases. Thus, hot liquids have lower viscosity than cold liquids. However, gas molecules interact more strongly at high temperatures. Hot gases have higher viscosity than cold gases.

One way to increase a liquid's viscosity is to dissolve *polymers* (long-chain molecules) in it. These molecules become entangled and resist flowing. Putting solid particles in suspension in a liquid also increases viscosity.

E. D. GODDARD

VISCOUNT, *VY kownt,* is a title held by certain British noblemen. A viscount ranks below an earl and above a baron. John Beaumont, an officer and deputy to an earl, was the first to receive the title in 1440. It is usually given to men the ruler wishes to honor.

VISHINSKY, *vih SHIHN skee,* **ANDREI YANU-ARIEVICH,** *ahn DRAY yah nu AHR yuh vihch* (1883-1954), was a Russian prosecutor and diplomat. He became a revolutionary in 1902 and participated in an uprising in 1905.

Vishinsky joined the Communist Party in 1920. From 1933 to 1938, he was a ruthless prosecutor in the Communist Party purge trials. Vishinsky became a deputy commissar of foreign affairs in 1940. He served as foreign minister from 1949 to 1953. As the chief Russian delegate in the United Nations, he became notorious for speeches against the Western world. He was born in Odessa.

ALBERT PARRY

VISHNU, *VIHSH noo,* is one of the two main gods of Hinduism. The other is Shiva. Vishnu has a kindly nature, and Hindus call him *the Preserver.* They believe he tries to ensure the welfare of humanity.

Vishnu sometimes descends from heaven to the earth in one of his *avatars* (physical forms). He does so when a catastrophe faces the universe or if humanity needs comfort and guidance. According to Hindu belief, Vishnu has already appeared in nine principal avatars. The two most important ones were as the Indian prince Rama and the god Krishna. As Rama, Vishnu was the hero of the *Ramayana,* a Hindu epic. As Krishna, Vishnu took part in the *Bhagavad-Gita,* a philosophical dialogue that forms part of the *Mahabharata,* another epic. Hindus believe that Vishnu will return to the earth someday to destroy all evil and begin a new Golden Age of humanity.

CHARLES S. J. WHITE

See also RAMAYANA; BHAGAVAD-GITA; GUPTA DYNASTY (picture); HINDUISM (Divinities); MYTHOLOGY (Hindu Mythology).

Stone statue (A.D. 900's to 1100's) by an unknown Indian sculptor; the Art Institute of Chicago, Gift of Mr. and Mrs. Robert Andrew Brown

Vishnu is an important Hindu god. Hindus believe he someday will descend from heaven to the earth and destroy all evil.

VISIGOTHS. See GOTHS.
VISION. See EYE.
VISTULA RIVER, *VIHS choo luh,* is an important waterway of east central Europe. It carries much of the river traffic in Poland. The Vistula rises in the Carpa-

thian Mountains in southern Poland, and then takes a circular course northward. The river runs through the city of Warsaw. It empties by several branches into the Baltic Sea. Gdańsk lies at the mouth of the Nogat, the westernmost branch. See POLAND (terrain map).

Light boats sail up the river as far as Kraków. The Vistula is frozen two to three months of the year.

Canals connect the Vistula River with the Oder, the Dnepr, and the Neman, all navigable rivers. The Vistula is 678 miles (1,091 kilometers) long and drains an area of about 74,000 square miles (192,000 square kilometers). M. KAMIL DZIEWANOWSKI

VISUAL ACUITY. See EYE (Receiving Regular Eye Examinations).

VISUAL EDUCATION. See AUDIO-VISUAL MATERIALS.

VITAL STATISTICS are a record of the most basic human events—birth, marriage, divorce, sickness, and death. They indicate what is happening or what has happened to the population of a country, state, or other community. Vital statistics can also show what is likely to occur in the future. They come from birth and death certificates, marriage licenses, disease and divorce reports, and other official records. Government officials collect, tabulate, analyze, and publish these records.

Kinds of Vital Statistics. The total number of births, marriages, divorces, sicknesses, and deaths are useful statistics, but the *rate* at which they are happening is often more significant. The rate is the number of human events measured in proportion to part or all of the population. The importance of the rate can be seen in comparing births in the United States and Canada. In 1983, many more births occurred in the United States than in Canada. The United States had about 3,614,000 births, and Canada, about 373,000. But the birth rates in the two countries were almost the same. There were 15.5 births for every 1,000 people in the United States as against 15 in Canada.

The *crude rate* is the number of events in a given year divided by the total population. The crude rate is most often stated as so many occurrences per 1,000 people. It disregards age, sex, and other characteristics of the population. Thus a country that has a large number of young adults has a higher birth rate and a lower death rate than a country that has many older adults.

Sometimes statisticians combine several factors to study vital statistics. For example, they may relate cause of death, place of residence, color, sex, and age. They may determine the specific rate for lung cancer deaths among urban white males 20 to 44 years old per 1,000 such males in the population.

Interpreting Vital Statistics. Government workers, scientists, educators, business people, and others use vital statistics for many purposes. For example, legislators study population trends when they draft housing, employment, and other legislation. Health authorities need various statistics to administer public health. Sociologists study statistics to learn what causes divorces. School administrators use vital statistics in planning facilities for the future. Insurance statisticians use death records to prepare life expectancy tables and life insurance rates. Market researchers study statistics to make marketing plans.

Collecting and Publishing Vital Statistics. In the United States, state laws regulate registration of vital

records. Physicians, funeral directors, members of the clergy, and attorneys most commonly register such records. Doctors or hospital attendants file birth certificates with local registrars. Doctors or coroners return death certificates to funeral directors who file them with local registrars to obtain burial permits. The local registrars send birth and death certificates to their county health department or to the state registrar. Doctors also report cases of disease to local or state health departments.

Town or county clerks issue marriage licenses. After the ceremony, the minister or other marriage officer sends the record certifying the marriage to the license clerk. The licensing office sends the marriage record or a copy to the state registrar. Attorneys file divorce records with the clerk of the court that granted the decree. The court clerk reports the divorce to the state registrar.

State bureaus of vital statistics and state health departments maintain files of vital records and compile statistics. The state governments send reports of births, deaths, *fetal deaths* (stillbirths), diseases, marriages, and divorces to the National Vital Statistics Division of the National Center for Health Statistics. The center is a Public Health Service agency in the United States Department of Health and Human Services. The division tabulates, analyzes, and publishes national data. The Public Health Service publishes the annual *Vital Statistics of the United States*, the *Monthly Vital Statistics Report*, and other statistical data.

The United States and other countries report vital statistics to the Statistical Office of the United Nations. The UN issues the annual *Demographic Yearbook* and other statistical publications.

See also BIRTH AND DEATH RATES; CENSUS; DIVORCE; MARRIAGE; POPULATION.

VITAMIN is a chemical compound that the human body needs in small amounts. Vitamins make up one of the major groups of *nutrients* (food substances necessary for growth and health). Vitamins regulate chemical reactions by which the body converts food into energy and living tissues. There are 13 vitamins. Five of them are produced in the body itself. These vitamins are biotin, niacin, pantothenic acid, vitamin D, and vitamin K. Only biotin, pantothenic acid, and vitamin K, which are made by bacteria in the human intestine, are possibly produced in sufficient quantities to meet the body's needs. Therefore, vitamins must be supplied in a person's daily diet.

Each vitamin has such specific uses that one of the compounds cannot replace, or act for, another. But the lack of one vitamin can interfere with the function of another. The continued lack of one vitamin in an otherwise complete diet results in a *vitamin deficiency disease*. Such diseases include beriberi, pellagra, rickets, or scurvy. Investigators first discovered vitamins while searching for the causes of such diseases. In order to be considered a vitamin, a substance must be required in the diet to prevent a deficiency disease.

The best way for a healthy individual to obtain vitamins is to eat a balanced diet. A daily diet that includes a variety of foods from each of the basic food groups provides an adequate supply of all the vitamins [see NUTRITION (Basic Food Groups)]. A *Recommended Dietary*

VITAMIN

Allowance (RDA) has been established for most vitamins. In order to provide a margin of safety, the RDA is considerably greater than the amount of a vitamin needed daily for good health. The RDA was established by the Food and Nutrition Board of the National Research Council.

Some people take daily vitamin supplements, mostly in the form of vitamin tablets. Most supplements contain doses of one or more vitamins in the range of their RDA's. The vitamins in such preparations are equivalent to those in food. But a person who eats a balanced diet has no need for daily supplements.

A person with a vitamin deficiency disease may be helped by taking one or more preparations that contain large doses of a certain vitamin or of a combination of several vitamins. But individuals should use such preparations only if they are prescribed by a physician. Self-diagnosis and treatment with *megadoses* (doses ten or more times larger than the RDA) can be dangerous.

Kinds of Vitamins

The 13 vitamins are vitamins A; B complex, which is actually a group of 8 vitamins; and vitamins C; D; E; and K. Scientists divide vitamins into two general groups, *fat-soluble vitamins* and *water-soluble vitamins*. The fat-soluble vitamins—vitamins A, D, E, and K—dissolve in fats. The water-soluble vitamins—the B-complex vitamins and vitamin C—dissolve in water.

Vitamin A, also called *retinol*, occurs naturally only in animals. Egg yolk, liver, and milk provide much vitamin A. Some plants contain substances called *carotenes*, or *provitamins A*, which the body converts into vitamin A. These plants include cantaloupes, carrots, sweet potatoes, and green and yellow vegetables.

Vitamin A is essential for the development of babies before birth and the growth of children. It is especially needed for the growth of bones and teeth. Vitamin A keeps the skin healthy and helps produce mucous secretions that build resistance to infection. People who do not get enough vitamin A may develop a condition called *xerophthalmia*, in which the surface of the eye becomes dry and likely to develop infection. Vitamin A also forms part of the two pigments that help the eyes to function normally in light that varies in intensity. Night blindness is an early symptom of a deficiency of vitamin A.

Vitamin B Complex was first believed to be only one vitamin. Researchers later discovered that it consists of eight vitamins—thiamine, riboflavin, niacin, B_6, pantothenic acid, biotin, B_{12}, and folic acid.

Thiamine, or *vitamin B_1*, prevents and cures beriberi, a disease of the nervous system (see BERIBERI). It contains sulfur and nitrogen. Sources of thiamine include green vegetables; meat, especially pork; nuts; soybeans; yeast; and whole-grain and enriched breads and cereals. This vitamin, like vitamin A, is needed for growth. The body also needs it to change carbohydrates into energy.

Riboflavin, or *vitamin B_2*, is most abundant in such foods as eggs, fish, liver, milk, poultry, yeast, and green and leafy vegetables. Direct sunlight destroys riboflavin in milk. This vitamin is needed for growth and for healthy skin and eyes. It promotes the body's use of oxygen in converting food into energy. If a person does not get enough riboflavin, cracks may develop in the skin at the corners of the mouth. The person also may have inflamed lips and a sore tongue, and scaly skin around the nose and ears. The eyes may become extremely sensitive to light.

Niacin, or *nicotinic acid*, helps prevent pellagra (see PELLAGRA). The best sources of niacin are fish, green vegetables, lean meat, poultry, and whole-grain and enriched bread and cereal. Milk and eggs, even though they have little niacin, are good pellagra-preventive foods because they contain *tryptophane*, an amino acid (see AMINO ACID). The body converts some tryptophane into niacin.

Niacin is essential for growth, for healthy tissues, and for the conversion of carbohydrates into energy. It also helps produce fats in the body (see FAT). Without niacin, thiamine and riboflavin cannot function properly. Lack of niacin may cause ailments of the skin and of the digestive and nervous systems.

Vitamin B_6, Pantothenic Acid, and Biotin. A deficiency of these vitamins has never been reported in people who have a healthful diet. Vitamin B_6, or *pyridoxine*, helps the body use amino acids. Lack of this vitamin damages the skin and nervous system. Pantothenic acid is converted by the body into *coenzyme A*, a vital substance that helps the body produce energy from food. Biotin helps the body change fats into fatty acids, which also aid in producing energy.

Vitamin B_{12} and Folic Acid. Vitamin B_{12}, or *cyanocobalamin*, contains cobalt and is essential for the normal functioning of folic acid, also called *folacin*. Vitamin B_{12} and folic acid are needed to produce *deoxyribonucleic acid* (DNA) in the body's cells. DNA carries the "master plans" that govern each cell's activities (see CELL). A deficiency of either of these two vitamins produces anemia (see ANEMIA). Physicians may advise a pregnant woman to supplement her diet with folic acid to prevent anemia. Doctors inject minute amounts of vitamin B_{12} to treat persons with *pernicious anemia*. Lack of vitamin B_{12} also damages the nervous system.

Eggs, liver, milk, and other animal sources of proteins, as well as some microbes, supply vitamin B_{12}. People who eat only vegetables may lack this vitamin. Almost all uncooked foods contain folic acid, but cooking destroys varying amounts of it.

Vitamin C, or *ascorbic acid*. Physicians call vitamin C the *antiscorbutic vitamin* because it prevents and cures scurvy (see SCURVY). The body stores little vitamin C, and so this vitamin must be supplied daily in the diet. Good sources of it include cantaloupe, citrus fruits, raw cabbage, strawberries, and tomatoes. Vitamin C is essential for healthy blood vessels, bones, and teeth. People who lack this vitamin may have sore gums and suffer bleeding under the skin. Vitamin C also helps form *collagen*, a protein that holds tissues together.

Vitamin D helps prevent rickets (see RICKETS). Either a deficiency or an excess of this vitamin can seriously affect the bones. There are several forms of vitamin D. One form, *calciferol*, or *vitamin D_2*, is produced in plants. It is produced from a *sterol*, a type of chemical compound, when a plant is exposed to ultraviolet light. Another form, *cholecalciferol*, or *vitamin D_3*, occurs in the tissues of animals, including human beings. It has been called the "sunshine vitamin" because it forms in the skin when the body is exposed to sunlight. Fish-liver

Vitamin	What It Does	Sources	Recommended Dietary Allowance Adults	Children (ages 1-14)
A (retinol)	Helps maintain skin, eyes, urinary tract, and lining of the nervous, respiratory, and digestive systems. Needed for healthy bones and teeth.	Sweet potatoes, milk, liver, fish liver oils, eggs, butter, green and yellow vegetables.	1000 mcg R.E. (men) 800 mcg R.E. (women)	400-1000 mcg R.E.
Thiamine (B₁)	Needed for carbohydrate metabolism and release of energy from food. Helps heart and nervous system function properly.	Yeast, meat, whole-grain and enriched breads and cereals, nuts, peas, potatoes, most vegetables.	1.2-1.4 mg (men) 1.0-1.1 mg (women)	0.7-1.4 mg
Riboflavin (B₂)	Helps body cells use oxygen. Promotes tissue repair and healthy skin.	Milk, cheese, liver, fish, poultry, green vegetables.	1.4-1.7 mg (men) 1.2-1.3 mg (women)	0.8-1.6 mg
Niacin (nicotinic acid)	Essential for cell metabolism and absorption of carbohydrates. Helps maintain healthy skin.	Liver, yeast, lean meat, whole-grain and enriched breads and cereals.	16-19 mg N.E. (men) 13-14 mg N.E. (women)	9-18 mg N.E.
B₆ (pyridoxine)	Needed for healthy teeth and gums, blood vessels, nervous system, and red blood cells.	Yeast, whole-grain cereals, meat, poultry, fish, most vegetables.	2.0-2.2 mg (men) 2.0 mg (women)	0.9-1.8 mg
Pantothenic Acid	Helps the body convert carbohydrates, fats, and proteins into energy.	Egg yolk, meat, nuts, whole-grain cereals.	4-7 mg*	3-7 mg*
B₁₂	Essential for proper development of red blood cells. Helps proper function of nervous system.	Eggs, meat, milk, milk products.	3 mcg	2-3 mcg
Biotin	Needed for healthy circulatory system and for maintaining healthy skin.	Egg yolk, nuts, liver, kidney, most fresh vegetables; made by intestinal bacteria.	100-200 mcg*	65-200 mcg*
Folic Acid	Needed for production of red blood cells.	Green leafy vegetables, yeast, meat, poultry, fish.	400 mcg	100-400 mcg
C (ascorbic acid)	Essential for sound bones and teeth. Needed for tissue metabolism and wound healing.	Citrus fruits, tomatoes, raw cabbage, potatoes, strawberries, cantaloupe.	60 mg	45-50 mg
D	Essential for calcium and phosphorus metabolism.	Fish liver oils, fortified milk, eggs, tuna, salmon, sunlight.	5-10 mcg	10 mcg
E (tocopherol)	Helps prevent the oxidation of polyunsaturated fatty acids in cell membranes and other body structures.	Whole-grain cereals, lettuce, vegetable oils.	10 mg T.E. (men) 8 mg T.E. (women)	5-8 mg T.E.
K	Needed for normal blood clotting.	Leafy vegetables; made by intestinal bacteria.	70-140 mcg*	15-100 mcg*

mcg = micrograms; mg = milligrams; R.E. = retinol equivalents; N.E. = niacin equivalents; T.E. = tocopherol equivalents
*Estimated Safe and Adequate Dietary Intake. Because there is less information on which to base allowances, these figures are not classified as RDA's. In addition, bacteria in the human intestine produce these vitamins. This bacterial production probably provides a significant portion of the body's requirements.
Source: Food and Nutrition Board, National Academy of Sciences-National Research Council; revised 1979-1980.

oils contain much vitamin D₃, and manufacturers may enrich milk and other animal food products with the oils.

Vitamin E, or *tocopherol*, helps prevent polyunsaturated fatty acids from *oxidizing* (combining with oxygen). Vitamin E thus plays an important role in maintaining cell membranes, which contain substantial amounts of polyunsaturated fatty acids. The best sources of vitamin E are lettuce and wheat-germ oil. Meat, milk, eggs, liver, whole-grain cereals, and most vegetables also contain this vitamin. A deficiency of vitamin E occurs rarely and produces few symptoms.

Vitamin K is essential for blood clotting. Green leafy vegetables, such as cabbage, cauliflower, kale, and spinach, are rich in Vitamin K. Pork liver is also an excellent source. Intestinal bacteria manufacture vitamin K in the body, and so deficiencies of this vitamin rarely result from a poor diet. Doctors sometimes give women vitamin K before childbirth to prevent bleeding in the newborn baby. Babies do not have enough intestinal bacteria to produce adequate amounts of the vitamin until they are about 2 weeks old.

How Vitamins Work

Vitamins function as *catalysts* in the body. A catalyst is a substance that increases the speed of a chemical reaction without being consumed by the reaction. Vitamins help accelerate certain chemical reactions that take place in the body and are essential for health. Without vitamins, these reactions would occur very slowly or not at all.

Most vitamins play the role of either enzymes or

VITAMIN

organic compounds called *coenzymes* (see ENZYME). Enzymes are catalysts that contain protein and regulate certain body processes. An enzyme alters molecules in the body and combines with the molecules to cause a chemical reaction. The enzyme is unchanged by the chemical reaction, and it can repeat the process again and again.

Some vitamins occur in inactive forms that do not influence chemical reactions. The body converts such vitamins into their active forms. Vitamin D is unique because it functions not only as a vitamin, but also as a "chemical messenger," or *hormone* (see HORMONE).

History

Such nutritional diseases as beriberi, pellagra, rickets, and scurvy have been known for centuries. But the idea that they might result from a dietary deficiency is comparatively new. One of the first persons to study the effect of diet on human health was James Lind, a Scottish physician. As early as the 1740's, Lind used lemons and oranges to cure scurvy in sailors, who rarely ate fresh fruits on long voyages. In 1882, a Japanese physician named Kanehiro Takaki cured beriberi among naval crews by adding meat and vegetables to their diet of rice. Christiaan Eijkman, a Dutch scientist, studied beriberi in the Dutch East Indies (now Indonesia). About 1900, he showed that people who ate *polished rice* (rice with the hulls removed) developed the disease. Those who ate whole rice, including the hull, did not. Eijkman concluded that rice hulls contained an *antiberiberi factor* that was essential for health.

In 1912, a Polish biochemist, Casimir Funk, tried but failed to extract the pure antiberiberi factor from rice hulls. Funk thought the substance belonged to a group of chemical compounds called *amines*, and he named it *vitamine*, meaning *amine essential to life*. Meanwhile, research on the effect of diet on the growth of rats was published in 1906 by the British biochemist Frederick G. Hopkins. He demonstrated that certain foods contain substances that are vital for the growth and development of the body. Hopkins called these substances "accessory food factors," to distinguish them from the well-established "basic food factors"—carbohydrates, fats, proteins, minerals, and water. Later, the word *vitamin* (with the *e* dropped) came to be used for all such accessory substances. Together, Hopkins and Funk developed the vitamin theory of deficiency disease.

At first, scientists thought there were only two vitamins, a fat-soluble one and a water-soluble one. By 1922 the American biochemist Elmer V. McCollum had proved that the fat-soluble vitamin actually consisted of a mixture of vitamins. About the same time, Joseph Goldberger, an American physician, showed that the water-soluble vitamin was also a mixture. Since then, vitamins of both types have been identified. Although it is possible that more may be discovered, none of the compounds proposed as vitamins since 1948, when vitamin B_{12} was isolated, has met the required scientific qualifications. VICTOR HERBERT

Related Articles in WORLD BOOK include:

Diet	Goldberger, Joseph	Nutrition
Doisy, Edward A.	McCollum, Elmer V.	Wald, George

Additional Resources

CONSUMER GUIDE. *The Vitamin Book.* Simon & Schuster, 1979.
NOURSE, ALAN E. *Vitamins.* Watts, 1977. For younger readers.
WENTZLER, RICH. *The Vitamin Book.* St. Martin's, 1978.

VITREOUS HUMOR. See EYE (Parts of the Eye; diagram).

VIVALDI, *vih VAHL dee,* **ANTONIO** (1678-1741), was an Italian composer. He was one of the most productive composers of the elaborately rhythmic and melodic music called *baroque music.* Vivaldi wrote nearly 50 operas, much church music, and hundreds of concertos for almost every instrument known at the time.

Vivaldi helped develop the baroque concerto, which influenced Johann Sebastian Bach and other later baroque composers. Bach admired Vivaldi's concertos and arranged 10 of them for the harpsichord and the organ.

Vivaldi was an accomplished violinist and composed his most important works for the violin. Four violin concertos known as *The Four Seasons* (1725) are his best-known compositions. His *L'estro armonico* (1711), a collection of concertos for one, two, and four solo violins, was one of the most influential music publications of the early 1700's. Vivaldi also composed cantatas, oratorios, and solo and trio sonatas. His best-known sacred choral composition is the *Gloria in D Major* (1708).

Vivaldi was born in Venice. He was ordained a priest in 1703 but devoted his life to music. In 1703, he became a violin teacher at the Venetian Ospedale della Pietà, a girls' orphanage with an excellent chorus and orchestra. He composed many of his works for the orphanage musicians. MIRIAM WAGONER BARNDT-WEBB

VIVIPAROUS ANIMAL, *vy VIHP uhr uhs,* is an animal whose young are born alive. This, in general, is true only of the higher animals. Most fish hatch from eggs, but a few, such as the guppy, are born alive. Some snakes bear live young, but others lay eggs.

VIVISECTION. See ANIMAL EXPERIMENTATION.

VIXEN. See Fox (Young).

VIZIER, *vih ZIHR* or *VIHZ yuhr,* is the title some Muslim countries give to certain high officials, such as ministers of state. The word *vizier* comes from the Arabic word *wazir,* which means a *bearer of burdens.* The viziers headed the departments of government in the Ottoman Empire. During the 1800's, the highest officer of the realm was the grand vizier, who was somewhat like a prime minister. SYDNEY N. FISHER

VIZSLA, *VEEZ lah,* is a short-haired hunting dog also known as the *Hungarian pointer.* Vizslas resemble other short-haired pointing breeds except that they have deep, rusty-gold coats. The dog weighs about 50 pounds (23 kilograms) and has a *docked* (shortened) tail.

Dog experts believe the breed is descended from dogs that were brought into central Europe by the Magyars about 1,000 years ago (see MAGYARS). Central Europeans first used the dogs to hunt with falcons, and later to point and retrieve game birds. JOSEPHINE Z. RINE

VLADIMIR I, *VLAD uh mihr* (?-1015), a Russian grand duke, won fame for establishing Christianity as Russia's official religion. In 972, he became ruler of Novgorod in Russia, but had to flee for his life to Scandinavia. Later, he returned, defeated and killed his brother, who was ruling in Kiev, and became grand duke in Kiev.

Vladimir was born a pagan of Viking origin. In about 988, he was converted to Christianity. He married Anna, the sister of the Byzantine emperor Basil II.

Vladimir I founded cities and built churches, schools, and libraries. He promoted trade, established relations with the pope and European rulers, and ably defended Russia against its eastern neighbors. Vladimir I died in 1015, and later was declared a saint. W. KIRCHNER

VLADIVOSTOK, *VLAD uh VAHS tahk* (pop. 590,000), is the most important port of the Soviet Union on the Pacific Ocean. It lies in southeastern Siberia, near the Korean border (see RUSSIA [political map]).

Vladivostok's fine harbor, formed by the Bay of the Golden Horn, has an area of about 2 square miles (5 square kilometers). The harbor is usually frozen between January and March, but icebreakers keep it open. Vladivostok is a base for fishing fleets. Most goods coming to the Soviet Union from Pacific ports pass through Vladivostok. The city has shipyards and fish canneries. It also produces mining equipment. Vladivostok lies near the east end of the railroad line that crosses Siberia (see TRANS-SIBERIAN RAILROAD). Russians founded Vladivostok in 1860. It became a naval base after Russia lost Port Arthur to Japan in 1905. Today, most of its merchant fleet uses the port of Nakhodka. THEODORE SHABAD

VLAMINCK, *vlah MANK,* **MAURICE DE,** *moh REES duh* (1876-1958), was a French artist. With André Derain and Henri Matisse, he was a leader of the fauvist movement in the early 1900's. Vlaminck was influenced by the paintings of the Dutch artist Vincent van Gogh. Like van Gogh, he used slashing brushstrokes and brilliant colors to increase the dramatic impact of his work. However, the exuberant quality of Vlaminck's work contrasted sharply with the feeling of suffering in many of van Gogh's paintings. See FAUVES.

From about 1908 to 1914, Vlaminck painted under the influence of the French artist Paul Cézanne and of cubism. About 1915, he began painting gloomy landscapes that emphasized dark colors and the illusion of deep space. He also created etchings and lithographs in this style. He was born in Paris. WILLARD E. MISFELDT

VOCABULARY is the total number of words in a language. It is also the collection of words a person knows and uses in speaking or writing.

The vocabulary of a language is always changing and

The Vizsla Is a Powerful Hunting Dog.

growing. As life becomes more complex, people devise or borrow new words to describe human activity. No one knows the exact number of English words today, but there are probably about 1 million.

A person has two kinds of vocabularies. The *active* or *use* vocabulary is made up of words used in speaking or writing. The *passive* or *recognition* vocabulary consists of words a person understands when listening or reading. Many people have a recognition vocabulary several times larger than their use vocabulary. This means that they understand words they hear or read but do not habitually use in speaking or writing. For Americans, the average use vocabulary is 10,000 words, but the average recognition vocabulary is 30,000 to 40,000 words.

A person continually builds a vocabulary. Studies have shown that a child entering school may know only from 3,000 to 4,000 words. But by the completion of college, he or she may have a vocabulary of from 10,000 to 30,000 words.

The range of a person's vocabulary is a clue to the person's culture and education. Control over words is often the same as control over the ideas the words represent. The dictionary is an important tool for increasing your vocabulary. If you encounter a word you do not know, look it up and find out what it means and how it is used. GARY TATE

See also BASIC ENGLISH; DICTIONARY; READING; SHAKESPEARE, WILLIAM (Vocabulary).

VOCAL CORD. See LARYNX.

VOCATION. See CAREERS.

VOCATIONAL EDUCATION prepares people for an occupation that does not require a bachelor's degree. It is designed mainly to help meet society's need for workers and to give students more educational options. Courses are taught in such subject areas as agriculture, business, trades and industry, health services, home economics, and technical fields. Courses are classified as either *exploratory* or *occupational*. Exploratory courses provide an introduction to an occupation or to a number of similar jobs. Occupational courses teach entry-level skills necessary for specific semiskilled, skilled, or technical occupations.

Vocational education forms a part of the process of *career education*, which helps students choose and prepare for a career. In kindergarten and elementary school, career education provides information about various jobs and helps children determine their own abilities and interests. In middle school or junior high school, students begin to explore the careers that interest them most. In high school, most students who plan to get a job immediately after graduation take some type of vocational education. About 75 per cent of all high school graduates take at least one course designed to provide preparation for a specific occupation.

Sources of Vocational Education

The chief sources of vocational education are (1) public high schools, (2) proprietary schools, and (3) community and junior colleges. Many business companies, labor unions, the armed forces, and other organizations also provide job training.

Public High Schools are supported by taxes and provide vocational training at little or no charge. They

VOCATIONAL EDUCATION

prepare students for careers in agriculture, carpentry, cosmetology, drafting, home economics, secretarial work, and other fields. Many high schools, called *comprehensive high schools*, offer both vocational training and college preparatory programs. Other institutions, known as *vocational high schools*, specialize in job training. *Technical high schools* are vocational schools that are specially equipped to teach technical subjects, such as automobile repairing and electronics. Many public high schools offer adult-education programs for men and women who want to learn new job skills.

Proprietary Schools include private business colleges, technical institutes, and trade schools. Such schools are owned by individuals or businesses and operate to make a profit. These institutions charge tuition and fees, but they may offer a greater variety of educational opportunities than public schools. Proprietary schools teach clerical skills, data processing, television repairing, and many other subjects. Some schools specialize in training such workers as barbers, dental assistants, truck drivers, or pilots.

Community and Junior Colleges provide advanced training in engineering, health services, and many other semiprofessional and technical fields. Students learn such jobs as those of computer specialist, laboratory technician, pollution control specialist, and medical assistant. Most community and junior colleges receive funds from the local or state government. Therefore, the tuition the students must pay is considerably less than the cost of the instruction.

Other Sources. Labor unions in such skilled trades as bricklaying and printing offer apprenticeship programs for their members. Apprenticeships combine on-the-job experience with individual or classroom instruction. Many businesses and industries also conduct training programs for their employees.

Men and women in the armed forces may be trained in a variety of technical jobs. Many of these people later find a market for their skills in civilian life.

The Job Corps program of the federal government provides work training for disadvantaged youths. Another source of vocational education is a revenue-sharing program established by the Job Training Partnership Act of 1982. Under this law, state and local governments receive federal funds to furnish job training for unskilled, disadvantaged youths and for needy adults.

Vocational Teaching Methods

Vocational education emphasizes a teaching method known as *learning by doing* or *hands-on practice*. Under this method, students learn job skills by practicing them with actual machines or tools. Instruction may take place in a laboratory or in a special classroom called a *shop* that duplicates a real workplace. For example, students in the automotive department of a high school work on automobiles with the same tools used in repair shops. Such equipment makes vocational education one of the most expensive types of education.

Most vocational schools offer individualized instruction, which enables an individual to study the material at his or her own pace. Students work independently with tape recordings, devices called *teaching machines*, computer-assisted instruction, and other materials. The teacher gives individual help.

Another method of vocational education combines classroom studies with work experience. In such *cooperative education*, students attend school part-time and work part-time at a paid or volunteer job. Business firms

City Colleges of Chicago

Vocational Education aims primarily at preparing people for a job. The community college students shown above are training for careers as computer specialists.

338

and other organizations cooperate with schools in employing the students. A faculty member called a *teacher-coordinator* helps students obtain jobs that match their field of study. See COOPERATIVE EDUCATION.

Challenges to Vocational Education

Some people oppose specialized job training at the high school level. They believe that such instruction takes too much time away from academic education. But some educators argue that many students who have difficulty with academic work become more interested in their studies after they begin vocational education. The students realize that mathematics, reading, and other skills are necessary in their working life.

Some members of minority groups charge that vocational education teaches minority students to aim only for what they consider low-level jobs. Leaders of the women's rights movement have also demanded reform of vocational programs, which they claim pressure girls into "women's jobs." Most female students in vocational training take secretarial or consumer and home-making subjects rather than industrial and trade courses.

During the mid-1980's, a national study commission indicated that vocational education experienced challenges that needed to be overcome in 10 areas. It pointed to the need for improvement in the perception of vocational education; access; equity; curriculum; teacher education and recruitment; standards and accountability; articulation; leadership; business, labor, and community involvement; and field-based learning, including cooperative education.

History

Vocational education began in ancient times. Parents and other adults taught children how to provide food, build a shelter, and perform other jobs. Through the centuries, the apprenticeship system of training developed. Under this system, a young person learned a craft or trade by working under a skilled master.

Early Vocational Education in Schools. During the 1800's, schools began to offer vocational education under such names as *manual training* and *mechanical arts*. The Morrill Act of 1862 provided for the establishment of certain colleges and universities to teach agriculture and mechanical arts (see LAND-GRANT COLLEGE OR UNIVERSITY).

In 1868, a Russian educator named Victor Della Vos designed several courses by which schools could teach skilled trades formerly learned through apprenticeships. Della Vos, the director of the Imperial Technical School in Moscow, established blacksmithing, carpentry, and metal-turning shops there.

Della Vos's methods spread to the United States in 1876 at the Philadelphia Centennial Exposition. Two American educators, Calvin M. Woodward and John D. Runkle, saw an exhibition of products made by Russian students. In 1880, Woodward opened the Manual Training School in St. Louis, the first school of its kind in the United States. Runkle, the president of the Massachusetts Institute of Technology, established shop courses there modeled on Della Vos's system.

The 1900's. During the early 1900's, the U.S. government officially recognized the need for vocational education. For example, the Smith-Hughes Act of 1917 financed job training in high schools. During the Great Depression of the 1930's, the federal Civilian Conservation Corps provided on-the-job training for unemployed young men.

During World War II (1939-1945), vocational schools operated around the clock to train the millions of workers needed for war production. After the war, a government program called the GI Bill of Rights provided funds for veterans to attend various types of educational institutions. It created a boom for proprietary schools, where veterans learned a variety of skills.

High unemployment during much of the 1960's and 1970's brought further government support for vocational education. The Manpower Development and Training Act of 1962 furnished federal funds to train unemployed adults. The Vocational Education Act of 1963 provided money for new buildings, programs, and teacher training. The Economic Opportunity Act of 1964 established the Job Corps. The Vocational Education Amendments of 1968 expanded training opportunities for the handicapped and the disadvantaged. The Education Amendments of 1976 required schools receiving federal funds to avoid sex discrimination in vocational education. As a result, many automotive, metalworking, plumbing, and other courses became coeducational for the first time.

Two federal acts passed during the 1980's, the Job Training Partnership Act of 1982 and the Carl D. Perkins Vocational Education Act of 1985, again stressed the importance of overcoming sex bias in vocational education classes. Both acts expanded vocational training opportunities for disadvantaged students.   EDWIN L. HERR

Related Articles in WORLD BOOK include:

Adult Education	Education (Vocational
Agricultural Education	Education)
Apprentice	Handicapped
Business Education	Industrial Arts
Career Education	Job Corps
Careers (Vocational Schools)	Smith-Hughes Act
Cooperative Education	

VOCATIONAL GUIDANCE. See CAREERS.

VOCATIONAL REHABILITATION is a program or service designed to help disabled people become fit for jobs. Vocational rehabilitation programs generally are designed for people age 16 and older who are physically or mentally handicapped. Services are also available for alcoholics and people who have been released from jail or prison. There are three primary activities in vocational rehabilitation. They are (1) rehabilitation counseling, (2) vocational evaluation, and (3) job placement.

Specialists in each of the three main areas of vocational rehabilitation usually work as a team. A rehabilitation counselor advises disabled people about the type of work or training they may need to support themselves financially. A vocational evaluator determines the most suitable specific job or field of training for each person seeking help. This decision is made after the disabled person takes written examinations and is tested on samples. The written examinations measure the person's scholastic achievement and vocational aptitude. The work samples imitate specific job skills and compare the person's performance to standards in that career. A job-placement specialist helps disabled people schedule job

interviews and obtain work suited to their vocational interests and skills.

Vocational rehabilitation programs in the United States developed during the late 1800's, when various government agencies tried to help disabled veterans find jobs. But little else was done until Congress passed the Civilian Vocational Rehabilitation Act of 1920. Since then, numerous federal laws have helped establish vocational rehabilitation as a profession. In Canada, the Vocational Rehabilitation of Disabled Persons Act of 1961 sets guidelines in the field. This law encourages Canada's provinces to develop complete vocational rehabilitation programs. Federal and provincial governments split the cost of the programs.

Today, the demand for qualified vocational rehabilitation specialists exceeds the supply. Careers in vocational rehabilitation generally require at least a bachelor's degree, and most require a master's degree. College students who wish to enter the profession major in rehabilitation, and their courses include counseling, human relations, industrial psychology, statistics, and testing. An internship also is part of the course work.

Vocational rehabilitation specialists may work for public or private agencies. The public agencies consist chiefly of state-operated vocational rehabilitation programs and those serving disabled veterans. Private agencies include nonprofit hospitals and rehabilitation centers and for-profit companies that work with insurance firms representing clients who were injured in industrial accidents.   RAY V. SAKALAS

VOCATIONS. See CAREERS.

VODER, *VOH duhr,* is the name of a device that imitates the sounds of human speech by electrical and electronic means. The name came from the initials of its full name, which is **V**oice **O**peration **D**emonstrator. The voder has a keyboard. When the operator presses certain keys, various sound-producing devices create the effect of human speech. The voder can speak entire sentences, and can even master the pronunciation of such difficult words as *Albuquerque.* The voder can imitate the voice of a man, woman, or child. It can also imitate a sheep's bleat and a pig's grunt. It uses two special vacuum tubes, and can make a total of 23 different and fundamental sounds, with hundreds of combinations of these sounds.   RAYMOND F. YATES

VODKA. See ALCOHOLIC BEVERAGE (Vodka).

VOGELWEIDE, WALTHER VON DER. See WALTHER VON DER VOGELWEIDE.

VOGT, WILLIAM (1902-1968), was an American ecologist and ornithologist. He served as chief of the conservation section of the Pan American Union and became national director of the Planned Parenthood Federation in 1951. Vogt wrote *Road to Survival* (1948), a book dealing with the relationship between world populations and food supplies. Vogt was born in Mineola, N.Y. After he graduated from St. Stephens College (now Bard College), Vogt edited *Bird Lore Magazine.*   ROGERS McVAUGH

VOICE. Almost all animals have voices. A few animals, like the giraffe, rarely use their voices. But most higher animals can bark, cry, howl, groan, growl, chirp, or make some other noise. Many of the animals use their voices to communicate with each other. Birds can make music with their voices. Dogs can express several feelings with their voices. They whimper when begging or when they feel guilty, they growl when angry, and bark eagerly when they are happy. Several of the zoo animals, such as the chimpanzee, also make various sounds to show different feelings. But no animal's voice is as highly developed as a human being's.

The Human Voice can express ideas through a variety of arrangements of consonant and vowel sounds. It can also be used for singing. It can combine speech with music, and sing words. Because the human voice is so highly developed, people have been able to create elaborate languages. These languages allow us to tell one another our most detailed thoughts and actions.

The vocal cords are the main sound producers in human beings. These two small bands of tissue stretch across the *larynx* (voice box). One band stretches on each side of the windpipe opening. Muscles in the larynx stretch and relax the vocal cords.

When we breathe, we relax our vocal cords so they form a V-shaped opening that lets air through. When we speak, we pull the vocal cords by the attached muscles, narrowing the opening. Then, as we drive air from the lungs through the larynx, the air vibrates the tightened vocal cords and sound results.

Varying the Sound. The voice mechanism is so well organized that we use our vocal cords, muscles, and lungs in many combinations without thinking about it. The more tightly the vocal cords are stretched, the

Bell Telephone Laboratories

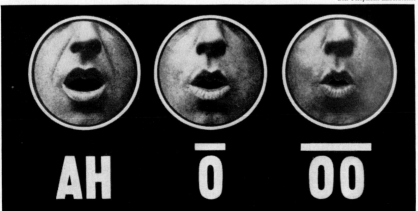

The Lips Help Form Sounds of the voice. They are fairly wide apart, *left,* to shape the sound "ah." They are drawn more closely together to form the long "o," *center,* and puckered with a small opening, *right,* to exclaim "Oo!"

higher are the sounds produced. The more relaxed the cords, the lower the sounds. Even in normal speech we stretch and relax the vocal cords to many degrees. This stretching and relaxing produces variations in the sounds of our voice.

The pitch of the voice is determined by the size of the larynx. Women's voices are usually pitched higher than men's because their vocal cords are shorter. Boys and girls have vocal cords of about the same size until the boys reach puberty. At puberty, the voice boxes of the boys suddenly grow larger. As a result, the boys' voices become lower.

The tongue, lips, and teeth also help shape the sounds of the voice. In addition, the nasal cavity gives resonance and color to the voice. When a person becomes ill with a cold and the nasal passages stop up, the person's voice changes.

Straining the Voice affects the vocal cords. So does a general muscular tension caused by nervousness. In the disease called *laryngitis* the larynx is inflamed, irritated, or infected. Sometimes the sick person cannot speak at all for a day or two. ARTHUR C. GUYTON

Related Articles in WORLD BOOK include:

Laryngitis	Voder
Larynx	Voiceprint
Singing	Windpipe
Stuttering	

VOICE, in grammar, is a feature of verbs. It tells whether the subject of the verb acts or is acted upon. English has two voices, *active* and *passive*.

A verb is in the active voice when its subject is the doer of the action. For example, the verb is in the active voice in the sentence *John sees the picture*, because the subject (*John*) performs the action (*sees*).

A verb is in the passive voice when its subject receives the action. In *The picture was seen by John*, the subject (*picture*) receives the action (*was seen*). The verb is therefore passive. In English, the passive voice consists of some form of the verb *be* (such as *is*, *was*, *were*, or *been*), plus the past participle (such as *seen*). Passive forms of *see* include *is seen*, *was seen*, *were seen*, *will be seen*, *have been seen*, *is being seen*, and *was being seen*. Only *transitive verbs* (verbs that take a direct object) can be changed to passive voice. WILLIAM F. IRMSCHER

See also CONJUGATION; VERB.

VOICE OF AMERICA (VOA) is the worldwide broadcasting division of the United States Information Agency. VOA promotes understanding abroad for the United States. It aims to serve as an objective and reliable source of news, to give a balanced view of all segments of American society, and to describe and discuss U.S. policies.

Each week, VOA broadcasts reach an estimated audience of 110 million people. The programs originate in Washington, D.C., and are broadcast from short-wave transmitters in the United States. Relay stations operate in Europe, the Middle East, South Asia, and East Asia. The broadcasts, in English and about 40 other languages, consist of news and such features as commentaries, discussions, drama, and music. Voice of America was established in 1942.

Critically reviewed by the UNITED STATES INFORMATION AGENCY

See also INFORMATION AGENCY, UNITED STATES.

VOICEPRINT, also called *speech spectrogram*, is a visual record of the sound waves of a human voice. Voice-

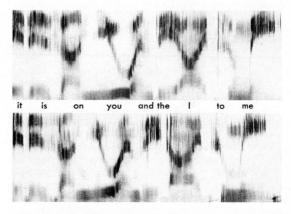

prints and tape recordings of the voices of several people are sometimes compared to identify a certain person's voice. However, some scientists question the reliability of this method as a means of identification. Voiceprints are also used in the study of speech and hearing disorders.

Several police departments in the United States use voiceprint evidence in criminal cases. They believe the voiceprint method is reliable as a method of identification when used in combination with tape recordings. By the early 1970's, voiceprint evidence had been admitted as evidence by the judge in about 70 criminal cases. However, some experts believe voiceprints are difficult to interpret and are not accurate enough for use in a court of law.

Voiceprints are made by running a tape recording of a voice through an instrument called a *sound spectrograph*. A voiceprint shows the duration of spoken words and the loudness, pitch, and quality of the recorded voice.

Three American scientists at the Bell Research Laboratories developed the sound spectrograph in the 1940's. In 1962, the American physicist Lawrence G. Kersta experimented with voiceprints as a means of identification. From 1968 to 1971, the American audiologist Oscar I. Tosi directed an extensive study of voiceprints at Michigan State University. OSCAR I. TOSI

Voiceprints, like fingerprints, can be used as a means of identification. The two voiceprints shown above were made by the same person's saying the same words at different times.

VOILE, *voil*, is a thin, open cloth made of silk, cotton, polyester, rayon, or nylon. It gets its name from the French word *voiler*, which means *to veil*. Voile has a plain weave. Voiles are used in making dresses, curtains, and trimmings. KEITH SLATER

VOJVODINA. See SERBIA.

VOLAPÜK, *VOH luh pook*, was the first widely used universal language. The name of the language comes from two of its words meaning *world* and *speak*. Johann Martin Schleyer, a German priest, created the language in 1879. By 1889, about 200,000 people were using Volapük, but no one uses it today. Volapük combined elements from English, German, Latin, and Romance languages such as French and Italian. ROBERT J. KISPERT

The Eruption of a Volcano can produce spectacular sights. At the left, great clouds of dense gas and dust pour from Surtsey, a volcanic island off the south coast of Iceland. At the right, enormous fountains of glowing lava shoot out of the volcano Kilauea in Hawaii.

VOLCANO

VOLCANO is an opening in the earth's surface through which lava, hot gases, and rock fragments *erupt* (burst forth). Such an opening occurs when melted rock from deep within the earth blasts through the surface. Most volcanoes are atop mountains, particularly cone-shaped mountains. The mountains themselves are also called *volcanoes* and were built up around the opening by lava and other materials thrown out during eruptions.

Eruptions of volcanic mountains are spectacular sights. In some eruptions, huge fiery clouds rise over the mountain, and glowing rivers of lava flow down its sides. In other eruptions, red-hot ash and cinders shoot out the mountaintop, and large chunks of hot rock are blasted high into the air. A few eruptions are so violent they blow the mountain apart.

Some eruptions occur on volcanic islands. Such islands are the tops of volcanic mountains that have been built up from the ocean floor by repeated eruptions. Other eruptions occur along narrow cracks in the ocean floor. In such eruptions, lava flows away from the cracks, building up the sea bottom.

People have always been both fascinated by the spectacle of volcanic eruptions and terrified of their power. Eruptions have caused some of the worst disasters in

---

Frank Press, the contributor of this article, is President of the National Academy of Sciences. He is coauthor of the book Earth.

history, wiping out entire towns and killing thousands of people. In early times, volcanoes played a role in the religious life of some peoples. The word *volcano*, for example, comes from *Vulcan*, the name the ancient Romans gave to their god of fire. The Romans believed the god lived beneath a volcanic island off the Italian coast. They called the island *Vulcano*.

How a Volcano Is Formed

Powerful forces within the earth cause volcanoes. Scientists do not fully understand these forces. But they have developed theories on how the forces create volcanoes. This section describes how most scientists explain the beginning and eruption of a volcano.

The Beginning of a Volcano. A volcano begins as *magma*, melted rock inside the earth. Magma results from the extreme heat of the earth's interior. At certain depths, the heat is so great it partly melts the rock inside the earth. When the rock melts, it produces much gas, which becomes mixed with the magma. Most magma forms 50 to 100 miles (80 to 160 kilometers) beneath the surface. Some develops at depths of 15 to 30 miles (24 to 48 kilometers).

The gas-filled magma gradually rises toward the earth's surface because it is lighter than the solid rock around it. As the magma rises, it melts gaps in the surrounding rock. As more magma rises, it forms a large chamber as close as 2 miles (3 kilometers) to the surface. This *magma chamber* is the reservoir from which volcanic materials erupt.

The Eruption of a Volcano. The gas-filled magma in the reservoir is under great pressure from the weight of the solid rock around it. The pressure causes the magma

to blast or melt a *conduit* (channel) in a fractured or weakened part of the rock. The magma moves up through the conduit to the surface. When the magma nears the surface, the gas in the magma is released. The gas and magma blast out an opening called the *central vent*. Most magma and other volcanic materials then erupt through this vent. The materials gradually pile up around the vent, forming a volcanic mountain, or volcano. After the eruption stops, a bowllike crater generally forms at the top of the volcano. The vent lies at the bottom of the crater.

Once a volcano has formed, not all the magma from later eruptions reaches the surface through the central vent. As the magma rises, some of it may break through the conduit wall and branch out into smaller channels. The magma in these channels may escape through a vent formed in the side of the volcano. Or it may remain below the surface.

Kinds of Volcanic Materials

Three basic kinds of materials may erupt from a volcano. They are (1) lava, (2) rock fragments, and (3) gas. The material that erupts depends chiefly on how sticky or fluid a volcano's magma is.

Lava is the name for magma that has escaped onto the earth's surface. When lava comes to the surface, it is red hot and may have a temperature of more than 2012° F. (1100° C). Highly fluid lava flows rapidly down a volcano's slopes. Sticky lava flows more slowly. As the lava cools, it hardens into many different formations. Highly fluid lava hardens into smooth, folded sheets of rock called *pahoehoe* (pronounced *pah HOH ee HOH ee*). Stickier lava cools into rough, jagged sheets of rock called *aa* (*AH ah*). Pahoehoe and aa cover large areas of Hawaii, where the terms originated.

Other lava formations include *spatter cones* and *lava tubes*. Spatter cones are steep hills up to 100 feet (30 meters) high. They build up from the spatter of fountainlike eruptions of thick lava. Lava tubes are tunnels formed from fluid lava. As the lava flows, its outer surface cools and hardens. But the lava underneath continues to flow. After the flowing lava drains away, it leaves a tunnel.

Rock Fragments, generally called *tephra* (*TEHF ruh*), are formed from sticky magma. Such magma is so sticky that its gas cannot easily escape when the magma approaches the surface or central vent. Finally, the trapped gas builds up so much pressure that it blasts the magma into fragments. Tephra includes, from smallest to largest, *volcanic dust*, *volcanic ash*, and *volcanic bombs*.

Volcanic Dust consists of particles less than $\frac{1}{100}$ inch (0.25 millimeter) in diameter. Volcanic dust can be carried great distances. In 1883, the eruption of the volcano Krakatoa in Indonesia shot such dust as high as 17 miles (27 kilometers) into the air. The dust was carried around the earth several times and produced brilliant red sunsets in many parts of the world. Some scientists believe that large quantities of volcanic dust can affect the climate by reducing the amount of sunlight that reaches the earth.

Volcanic Ash is made up of fragments less than $\frac{1}{5}$ inch (0.5 centimeter) in diameter. Most volcanic ash falls to the surface and becomes welded together as rock called *volcanic tuff*. Sometimes, volcanic ash combines with water in a stream and forms a boiling *mudflow*. Mudflows may reach speeds of 60 miles (97 kilometers) per hour and can be highly destructive.

Volcanic Bombs are large fragments. Most of them range from the size of a baseball to that of a basketball. The largest bombs may measure more than 4 feet (1.2 meters) across and weigh up to 100 short tons (91 metric tons). Small volcanic bombs are generally called *cinders*.

How a Volcanic Mountain Erupts — An eruption begins when *magma* (melted rock inside the earth) rises toward the surface, *left*. The magma collects in a *magma chamber* under the volcano. Pressure on the chamber forces the magma upward through the *conduit, right*. In the volcano shown here, a *composite volcano*, the magma erupts through the central and side vents as gas and mostly lava or mostly *tephra* (dust and other fragments).

WORLD BOOK illustrations by David Cunningham

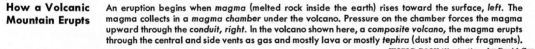

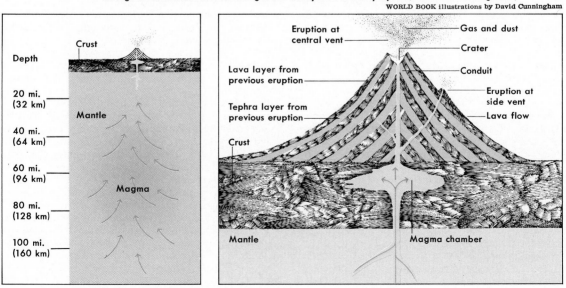

The Three Main Kinds of Volcanoes

Gordon A. Macdonald, Hawaii Institute of Geophysics

Cinder Cones, such as Mexico's Paricutín, *above,* form when mainly tephra erupts from the central vent and piles up around it.

Gordon A. Macdonald, Hawaii Institute of Geophysics

Composite Volcanoes are created by repeated eruptions of lava and tephra. The materials pile up in alternate layers, forming a cone-shaped mountain. Mayon Volcano in the Philippines, *above,* is one of the world's most perfectly shaped volcanoes.

Shield Volcanoes form when lava erupts from several vents, spreads out widely, and builds up a low, broad mountain. Most shield volcanoes, such as Hawaii's Mauna Loa, shown at the left, have many craters on their summit. The larger craters are called *calderas.*

U.S. Air Force

Gas pours out of volcanoes in large quantities during most eruptions. The gas is made up chiefly of steam. But it also includes carbon dioxide, nitrogen, and other gases. Most of the steam comes from a volcano's magma. But some steam may also be produced when rising magma heats water in the ground. Volcanic gas carries a large amount of volcanic dust. This combination of gas and dust looks like black smoke.

Kinds of Volcanoes

Scientists divide volcanoes into three main groups: (1) shield volcanoes, (2) cinder cones, and (3) composite volcanoes. These classifications are based on the shape of the volcanoes and the type of material they are built of.

Shield Volcanoes are formed when a large amount of free-flowing lava spills from a vent and spreads widely. The lava gradually builds up a low, broad, dome-shaped mountain. The famous Mauna Loa in Hawaii is a shield volcano. Thousands of separate, overlapping lava flows, each less than 50 feet (15 meters) thick, formed Mauna Loa.

Cinder Cones build up when mostly tephra erupts from a vent and falls back to earth around the vent.

The accumulated tephra, which is generally cinders, forms a cone-shaped mountain. Paricutín in western Mexico is a well-known cinder cone. It began in 1943, when a crack opened in the ground of a cornfield. When the eruptions ended in 1952, the top of the cone was 1,345 feet (410 meters) above its base.

Composite Volcanoes are formed when both lava and tephra erupt from a central vent. The materials pile up in alternate layers around the vent and form a towering, cone-shaped mountain. Composite volcanoes include Japan's beautiful Mount Fuji; Mayon Volcano in the Philippines; and Italy's Vesuvius, probably the world's most famous volcano. In A.D. 79, Vesuvius erupted, burying the nearby towns of Pompeii, Herculaneum, and Stabiae under an enormous mass of ashes, dust, and cinders.

Occasionally, the magma chamber of a shield volcano, cinder cone, or composite volcano may become nearly empty. This happens when most of a volcano's magma erupts onto the surface. Because the chamber is empty, it can no longer support the volcano above. As a result, a large part of the volcano collapses, forming a huge crater called a *caldera.* Scenic Crater Lake in Oregon is a caldera that has filled with water. It is about

Where Volcanoes Occur

This map shows the location of many volcanoes. It also shows the earth's large, rigid plates. Volcanoes usually occur along the edges of the plates.

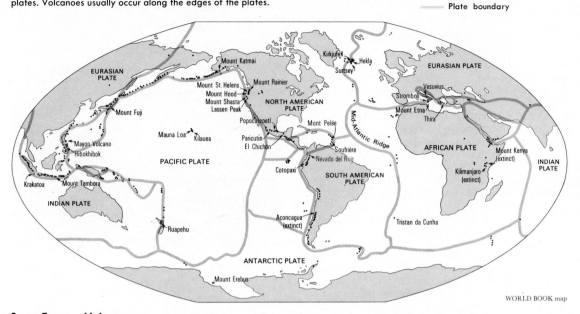

WORLD BOOK map

Some Famous Volcanoes

Name	Location	Height Above Sea Level In feet	In meters	Interesting Facts
*Aconcagua	Argentina	22,831	6,959	Highest mountain in Western Hemisphere; volcano extinct.
*Cotopaxi	Ecuador	19,347	5,897	Eruption in 1877 produced mudflow that traveled about 150 miles (241 kilometers) and killed about 1,000 persons.
El Chichón	Mexico	3,478	1,060	Eruption in 1982 killed 187 persons and released a cloud of dust and sulfur dioxide gas high into the atmosphere.
Hibokhibok	Philippines	4,363	1,330	In 1951, red-hot cloud of gas and dust killed about 500 persons.
*Krakatoa	Indonesia	2,667	813	Great eruption in 1883 heard about 3,000 miles (4,800 kilometers) away; produced sea waves almost 130 feet (40 meters) high that drowned about 36,000 persons on nearby islands.
*Lassen Peak	California	10,457	3,187	One of several volcanoes in the Cascade Range; last erupted in 1921.
*Mauna Loa	Hawaii	13,677	4,169	World's largest volcano; rises almost 30,000 feet (9,100 meters) from ocean floor and is about 60 miles (97 kilometers) wide at its base.
*Mont Pelée	Martinique	4,583	1,397	Glowing cloud from 1902 eruption destroyed town of St. Pierre, killing about 38,000 persons in minutes.
*Mount Etna	Sicily	11,122	3,390	About 20,000 persons killed in 1669 eruption.
Mount Katmai	Alaska	6,715	2,047	Eruption in 1912 produced glowing flood of hot ash that traveled about 15 miles (24 kilometers) and formed Valley of Ten Thousand Smokes.
*Mount St. Helens	Washington	8,364	2,549	In 1980, violent eruptions released large amounts of molten rock and hot ash; killed 60 persons.
Mount Tambora	Indonesia	9,350	2,850	In 1815, eruption released 6 million times more energy than that of an atomic bomb; killed over 12,000 persons.
Nevado del Ruiz	Colombia	17,717	5,400	Eruption in 1985 triggered mud slides and floods; destroyed city of Armero and killed about 25,000 persons.
*Paricutín	Mexico	9,213	2,808	Began in farmer's field in 1943; built cinder cone over 500 feet (150 meters) high in six days.
*Stromboli	Mediterranean Sea	3,031	924	Active since ancient times; erupts constantly for months or even years.
Surtsey	North Atlantic Ocean	568	173	In 1963, underwater eruption began forming island of Surtsey; after last eruption of lava in 1967, island covered more than 1 square mile (2.6 square kilometers).
Thira (formerly Santorin)	Mediterranean Sea	1,850	564	Eruption in about 1500 B.C. may have destroyed Minoan civilization on Crete; legend of lost continent of Atlantis may be based on this eruption.
*Vesuvius	Italy	4,190	1,277	In A.D. 79, produced history's most famous eruption, which destroyed towns of Herculaneum, Pompeii, and Stabiae.

*Has a separate article in WORLD BOOK.

VOLCANO

6 miles (10 kilometers) across at its widest point and 1,932 feet (589 meters) deep.

Why Volcanoes Occur in Certain Places

Most volcanoes are found along a belt, called the *Ring of Fire*, that encircles the Pacific Ocean. Volcanic activity also occurs in such places as Hawaii, Iceland, and southern Europe and at the bottom of the sea.

Scientists have developed a theory, called *plate tectonics*, that explains why most volcanoes—as well as most earthquakes and mountains—occur only in certain places. According to this theory, the earth's outer shell is divided into many rigid sections of rock called *plates*. The plates slide or drift about continuously over a layer of partly melted rock. They move about ½ to 4 inches (1.3 to 10 centimeters) a year. As the plates move, their boundaries collide, spread apart, or slide past one another. Most volcanoes occur at the plate boundaries. The map *Where Volcanoes Occur* shows the plate boundaries and the volcanic activity along them.

Most volcanoes are formed where two plates collide. One of the plates is then forced under the other. As the plate sinks, friction and the earth's heat cause part of it to melt. This melted part then rises as magma. When it reaches the surface, it produces a volcano.

Volcanic activity also occurs when two plates spread apart. Most such movement takes place on the ocean floor. As the two plates move apart, magma from below the crust moves up between the plates. Large amounts of lava pour onto the surface and build up the ocean floor. In some cases, the magma creates an underwater mountain range, such as the enormous Mid-Atlantic Ridge that runs down the length of the Atlantic Ocean. Iceland and the volcanic islands nearby are exposed parts of this ridge.

A number of volcanoes—for example, those in Hawaii—lie far from plate boundaries. Some scientists believe such volcanoes develop when a huge column of magma rises from inside the earth toward the surface. This column, called a *plume*, may measure about 100 miles (160 kilometers) in diameter and rise 5 to 10 inches (13 to 25 centimeters) yearly. In some cases, the plume comes close enough to the surface so that part of the magma breaks through and forms a volcano.

For additional information on the plate tectonics theory, see the article TECTONICS.

The Study of Volcanoes

The scientific study of volcanoes is called *volcanology*. This study includes investigating the nature and causes of eruptions and has saved many lives. To aid them in their work, scientists have set up observatories on the slopes or rim of several volcanoes, including Mount Asama in Japan, Kilauea in Hawaii, and Vesuvius in Italy.

Classifying Volcanic Activity. Scientists classify the activity of a volcano according to how often it erupts. A volcano may thus be classed as (1) active, (2) intermittent, (3) dormant, or (4) extinct.

Active Volcanoes erupt constantly. The eruption is generally quiet but occasionally becomes violent. A famous active volcano is Stromboli, which lies on an island off the coast of Italy.

Intermittent Volcanoes erupt at fairly regular periods.

Sigurgeir Jónasson

The Destructive Force of a volcano can cause many deaths and great property damage. These homes on the Icelandic island of Heimaey were destroyed by lava during an eruption in 1973.

Such volcanoes include Mount Asama in Japan, Mount Etna in Sicily, and Hawaii's Kilauea.

Dormant Volcanoes have become inactive, but not long enough to know whether they will erupt again. Such "sleeping" volcanoes include Lassen Peak in California and Paricutín in Mexico.

Extinct Volcanoes have been inactive since the beginning of recorded history. Aconcagua in Argentina and Kilimanjaro in Tanzania are extinct volcanoes. They probably will not erupt again.

Classifying Volcanic Eruptions. Scientists divide volcanic eruptions into four basic groups: (1) Hawaiian, (2) Strombolian, (3) Vulcanian, and (4) Peléean. These groups are based on the violence of the eruption and the type of material that erupts.

Hawaiian Eruptions are named after the volcanoes in Hawaii and are the least violent type. In such eruptions, highly fluid lava flows quietly from several vents and gradually builds up a shield volcano.

Strombolian Eruptions are named after Stromboli. Such eruptions result from the continuous escape of gas from the magma. As the gas escapes, it produces tephra that piles up into a cinder cone.

Vulcanian Eruptions get their name from Vulcano, a volcanic island off the Italian coast. These eruptions occur when sticky magma plugs up the central vent. The magmatic gas gradually builds up pressure until it blasts the magma into volcanic dust and bombs.

Peléean Eruptions are the most violent. Their name comes from the terrible eruption in 1902 of Mont Pelée on Martinique, an island in the West Indies. The eruption killed about 38,000 persons. A Peléean eruption occurs when the gas in highly sticky magma builds up tremendous pressure. This pressure causes violent explosions that produce glowing clouds of hot ash and dust. Much of the volcano itself blows apart.

Predicting Volcanic Eruptions is one of the chief concerns of volcanology. When a volcano erupts, little

can be done to prevent property damage in the surrounding area. But many lives can be saved if people in the area are evacuated before the eruption begins.

Most volcanic eruptions cannot be predicted. However, some volcanoes, such as those in Hawaii, have a built-in warning system. Before such a volcano erupts, it expands slightly as magma collects in the magma chamber. Then as the magma rises, many small earthquakes occur. The temperature in the surrounding area also begins to increase, and clouds of gas start to pour from the vent.

Scientists use several devices to predict when such a volcano will erupt. They use an instrument called a *tiltmeter* to measure the expansion of a volcano. A device called a *seismograph* helps detect earthquakes. Thermometers check temperature increases in the area, and gas detectors measure the amount of gas.

Benefits of Volcanoes

Volcanoes are among the most destructive natural forces on the earth. Since the 1400's, they have killed almost 200,000 persons. But volcanoes also produce benefits. For example, many volcanic materials have important industrial and chemical uses. Rock formed from lava is commonly used in building roads. *Pumice,* a natural glass that comes from lava, is widely used for grinding and polishing stones, metals, and other materials. Sulfur deposits from volcanoes are used in making chemicals. Weathered volcanic ash greatly improves the fertility of soil.

In many volcanic regions, people use underground steam as a source of energy. This *geothermal* energy is used to produce electricity in such countries as Italy, Mexico, New Zealand, and the United States. In Reykjavík, Iceland, most people heat their homes with water piped from volcanic hot springs.

Finally, volcanoes serve as "windows" to the earth's interior. The materials they erupt help scientists learn about conditions within the earth.   FRANK PRESS

Related Articles in WORLD BOOK include:

VOLCANOES

See the articles on the volcanoes marked by an asterisk in the table *Some Famous Volcanoes* in this article. See also the following articles:

Ararat	Kilimanjaro	Mount Saint
Chimborazo	Mauna Kea	Helens
El Misti	Mount Apo	Mount Shasta
Hekla	Mount Fuji	Orizaba
Ixtacihuatl	Mount Kenya	Pichincha
Kilauea	Mount Rainier	Popocatepetl

OTHER RELATED ARTICLES

Alaska (Land Regions)	El Salvador (picture)	Hot Springs
Cement and Concrete (History)	Fumarole Geology	Igneous Rock Lake (picture: Volcanic
Crater	Geyser	Lakes)
Crater Lake	Hawaii	Lava
Dust	(picture: Molten	Pumice
Earthquake	Lava)	Rock (Igneous Rock)

Outline

I. How a Volcano Is Formed
   A. The Beginning of a Volcano
   B. The Eruption of a Volcano
II. Kinds of Volcanic Materials
   A. Lava   B. Rock Fragments   C. Gas

III. Kinds of Volcanoes
   A. Shield Volcanoes
   B. Cinder Cones
   C. Composite Volcanoes
IV. Why Volcanoes Occur in Certain Places
V. The Study of Volcanoes
   A. Classifying Volcanic Activity
   B. Classifying Volcanic Eruptions
   C. Predicting Volcanic Eruptions
VI. Benefits of Volcanoes

Questions

How is a caldera formed? A spatter cone?
Into what three main groups do scientists divide volcanoes?
What is *magma*? The *magma chamber*?
What three basic kinds of materials may erupt from a volcano?
How do volcanoes help scientists learn about the earth's interior?
What is the *Ring of Fire*?
How does the plate tectonics theory explain the location of most volcanoes?
How are scientists able to predict when some volcanoes are going to erupt?
How was Mauna Loa formed? Paricutín? Mount Fuji?
What is the most violent type of volcanic eruption?

Additional Resources

Level I
BERGER, MELVIN. *Disastrous Volcanoes.* Watts, 1981.
FODOR, RONALD V. *Earth Afire! Volcanoes and Their Activity.* Morrow, 1981.
TIME-LIFE BOOKS EDITORS. *Volcano.* Time Inc., 1982.

Level II
LAMBERT, MAURICE B. *Volcanoes.* Rev. ed. Univ. of Washington Press, 1980. A brief overview, with an extensive bibliography of books and films.
RITTMANN, ALFRED and LOREDANA. *Volcanoes.* Putnam, 1976. Features a listing of the world's volcanoes, with history and statistics on each.
Volcanoes and the Earth's Interior: Readings from "Scientific American." Freeman, 1982.

VOLCANOLOGY. See VOLCANO (The Study of Volcanoes).

VOLCKER, *VOHL kur,* **PAUL ADOLPH** (1927-   ), became chairman of the Board of Governors of the Federal Reserve System (FRS) in 1979. The FRS is an independent federal agency that directs the United States banking system and manages the nation's money supply. Volcker was appointed chairman by President Jimmy Carter, and was reappointed to the position by President Ronald Reagan in 1983.

The United States faced a high rate of inflation when Volcker first became chairman. Under Volcker's leadership, the FRS helped slow down inflation by curbing the growth of the money supply. But many economists believe that Volcker's policy also contributed to the highest unemployment rates since 1941.

Volcker was born in Cape May, N.J. He graduated from Princeton University in 1949 and earned a master's degree from Harvard University in 1951. During his career, Volcker worked for the Chase Manhattan Bank and the United States Department of the Treasury. From 1975 to 1979, he served as president of the Federal Reserve Bank of New York.   LEE THORNTON

VOLE is a mouselike animal. Voles have plump bodies about 5 inches (13 centimeters) long. They have short or medium-length tails, short legs, and tiny ears.

VOLGA RIVER

Rod Planck, Tom Stack & Assoc.

A Vole has a plump, furry body and tiny ears. The meadow vole, *above,* lives in grassy fields of North America. It feeds on seeds, roots, and blades of grass.

Most have gray fur. The many *species* (kinds) are usually named for their *habitats* (places where they live). *Meadow voles* are the most common North American species. They live in grassy fields and eat grass, roots, and seeds. *Water voles* live near water. *Tundra voles* live in cold, swampy plains called *tundra.*

Voles are closely related to lemmings. The vole population changes greatly every three or four years, as does the number of lemmings (see LEMMING). The number of voles may increase by 20 times in this period. Then, presumably because of enemies, diseases, and lack of food, it drops sharply to its original level.

Scientific Classification. Voles are in the New World rat and mouse family, Cricetidae. Meadow voles are genus *Microtus;* a common species is *M. pennsylvanicus.*   DANIEL BRANT

VOLGA RIVER, *VAHL guh* or *VOHL guh,* is the longest river in Europe. It flows 2,193 miles (3,530 kilometers), entirely within the Soviet Union. The Volga begins in the Valdai Hills, about 200 miles (320 kilometers) southeast of Leningrad. It is 748 feet (228 meters) above sea level at its source. It flows southward to the Caspian Sea, where it is 92 feet (28 meters) below sea level (see RUSSIA [physical map]). The Volga delta is about 100 miles (160 kilometers) long, and includes as many as 500 channels and smaller rivers.

The Volga has many tributaries. The most important tributaries are the Kama, the Oka, the Vetluga, and the Sura rivers. The Volga and its tributaries form the Volga river system. The system drains an area of about 525,000 square miles (1,360,000 square kilometers) in the most heavily populated part of the Soviet Union.

The Volga is frozen for most of its length during three months of each year. Canals link it with the Baltic Sea, the White Sea, and the Black Sea via the Sea of Azov.

The fertile river valley is a great wheat-growing region. It is also rich in minerals. The valley is the center of a large petroleum industry. Other minerals include natural gas, salt, and potash. The Volga delta and the nearby Caspian Sea make up one of the world's great fishing grounds. Astrakhan, at the delta, is the center of the caviar industry.

Volgograd (formerly Stalingrad) and Gorki are important manufacturing cities on the banks of the Volga. Saratov, Kazan, and Kuybyshev are other important

cities on the river. Nine major hydroelectric power stations and several large artificial lakes formed by dams lie along the Volga. The largest of the lakes are, from north to south, the Rybinsk, Gorki, Kuybyshev, and Volgograd reservoirs.

The ancient scholar Ptolemy of Alexandria mentioned the Volga in his *Geography.* The river basin was important in the great movements of people from Asia to Europe. A powerful Bulgarian empire once flourished where the Kama River joins the Volga. Volgograd was the scene of the Battle of Stalingrad, the major Soviet victory over Germany in World War II. The deep feeling of the country's people for the Volga has been told many times in their songs and literature. LESZEK A. KOSIŃSKI

VOLGOGRAD, *VAHL guh GRAD* or *VOHL guh GRAD* (pop. 969,000), is an important manufacturing city in Russia. It lies on the west bank of the Volga River, about 250 miles (402 kilometers) above the river's mouth (see RUSSIA [political map]). Volgograd factories make aluminum, and tractors and other machinery.

Volgograd was founded in the 1200's. Its name was originally Tsaritsyn. In 1925, it was renamed Stalingrad in honor of the Soviet leader Joseph Stalin. In 1961, Stalin was downgraded and dishonored throughout Russia, and the city was renamed Volgograd. During World War II, the city was an important point in the German drive into Russia. Soviet armed forces defended the city and finally captured a large German army after a long battle. Following World War II, a large dam and a hydroelectric plant were built on the Volga River just north of the city.   THEODORE SHABAD

See also STALINGRAD, BATTLE OF.

VOLKSWAGEN, *FOHLKS vah guhn,* a West German automobile manufacturer, is one of the world's leading producers of passenger cars. Volkswagen builds more than $2\frac{1}{2}$ million cars yearly and has factories in eight countries throughout the world. Audi-NSU, another West German automobile manufacturer, is a division of Volkswagen. In addition, Volkswagen manufactures trucks, vans, automobile parts, and industrial engines. The company also operates an electronics and office equipment firm and a bank.

The Volkswagen Beetle, also known as the "Bug," became the most popular car ever built. It was designed in the mid-1930's by an Austrian engineer named Ferdinand Porsche, who wanted the Beetle to be a compact, durable car that most people could afford. The German word *Volkswagen* means *the people's car.* The first Beetles were built in 1945, and from then until the mid-1960's, Volkswagen produced chiefly Beetles. The company stopped production of Beetles at its German plants in 1978 but continued to make them in Brazil, Mexico, Nigeria, and South Africa.

The German government established Volkswagen in 1937. Today, the company is owned chiefly by private citizens. Its headquarters are in Wolfsburg, West Germany. The United States branch of Volkswagen, called Volkswagen of America, has its headquarters in Warren, Mich., and operates a car assembly plant in Westmoreland County, Pennsylvania, near New Stanton. The company also owns a sheet-metal stamping plant and an air-conditioner plant. For the assets, sales, and number of employees of Volkswagen, see MANUFACTURING (table: 25 Leading Manufacturers Outside the U.S.).

Critically reviewed by VOLKSWAGEN OF AMERICA, INC.

VOLLEYBALL is a game in which the players hit a ball back and forth across a net with their hands or arms. It is one of the world's most popular team sports.

There are two main forms of volleyball. *Indoor volleyball* is played indoors on a court made of wood or other indoor surface material. It has six players on a team. *Outdoor volleyball*, also called *two-man volleyball* or *two-person volleyball*, is played outdoors on a sand or grass court. It has only two players on a team. The two forms of volleyball have similar rules. This article discusses indoor volleyball.

William G. Morgan, a physical-education instructor at the YMCA in Holyoke, Mass., invented volleyball in 1895. Today, the game is most popular in Asia and Europe. Indoor volleyball became an official sport of the Olympic Games in 1964. More than 150 nations, including the United States and Canada, belong to the International Volleyball Federation. This organization sponsors annual tournaments for men's and women's teams.

The Ball is round and has a cover made of leather. It measures about $8\frac{1}{4}$ inches (21 centimeters) in diameter and weighs about $9\frac{1}{2}$ ounces (270 grams).

The Court. Indoor volleyball is played on a court that measures 60 feet (18 meters) long and 30 feet (9 meters) wide. A net suspended across the center of the court divides it in half. The top of the net is 8 feet (2.4 meters)

high for men's games and 7 feet $4\frac{1}{4}$ inches (2.2 meters) high for women's competition.

There are six positions in indoor volleyball—right back, center back, left back, left forward, center forward, and right forward. Until the ball has been served to start each play, players must assume a position on the court according to the order in which they serve. Two referees and two linespersons serve as officials for the game.

The Game starts with a serve by the right back of the serving team. The ball is served by hitting it with an arm or a hand. The serve must pass over the net into the receiving team's court. The receiving players must return the serve by cleanly hitting it with their hands. They cannot catch, lift, scoop, or throw the ball. A team may hit the ball no more than three times before sending it back over the net.

The players on each team try to hit the ball to the floor of the other team's court. They also try to make it difficult for the other team to return the ball. A player may attempt to *spike* (slam) the ball past the opposing players, who leap and dive to prevent it from touching their floor. No player may touch the ball twice in a row unless the first touch was made in blocking an opponent's spike.

Only the serving team can score. It scores a point each time the ball touches the receiving team's floor or whenever that team hits the ball more than three times. The serving team also scores a point if a member of the receiving team hits the ball out of bounds or commits a foul. The right back continues to serve after each point until a serve hits the net, goes out of bounds, or is faulty in some other way. The serving team also loses the serve if it fails to return the ball. A loss of serve is called a *side out*.

After each side out, the opposing team serves the ball. But first, each of its players rotates clockwise one position. The right forward moves to the right back position, the right back becomes the center back, and so on. The first team to score 15 points wins the game, but it must win by at least 2 points. If the score is 15 to 14, for example, the game continues until one team wins by 2 points. ALBERT M. MONACO, JR.

Additional Resources

LYTTLE, RICHARD B. *Basic Volleyball Strategy: An Introduction for Young Players.* Doubleday, 1979.

ROSENTHAL, GARY. *Volleyball: The Game & How to Play It.* Scribner, 1983.

SULLIVAN, GEORGE. *Better Volleyball for Girls.* Dodd, 1979.

VOLSTEAD ACT, *VAHL stehd,* provided for the enforcing of national prohibition of the use of intoxicating liquors. It was passed by the Congress of the United States in 1919, over the veto of President Woodrow Wilson. The 18th Amendment to the Constitution prohibited the manufacture, sale, or transportation of intoxicating liquors within the United States. It also banned the import or export of such beverages. The Volstead Act provided the means to investigate and punish violators of the amendment. The act took its name from that of Representative Andrew J. Volstead of Minnesota, who introduced it. The act defined intoxicating liquors as beverages which contain "one-half of one per centum or more of alcohol by volume." After the ratification of Amendment 21, which repealed prohibition, the Vol-

United States Volleyball Association

Volleyball Games provide spirited fun and exercise for young people and adults. The players bat a ball back and forth across a high net, and often leap high to *spike* a ball, or drive it downward. Volleyball can be played on both indoor and outdoor courts and by mixed teams of boys and girls. The diagram, *below,* shows the positions for teams of six players.

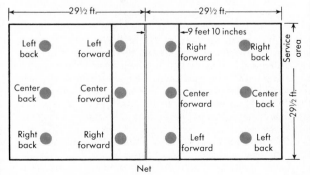

stead Act expired automatically, except in the Territories. See also PROHIBITION.   JOHN A. KROUT

VOLT is a unit of electric measurement in the metric system known as the *International System of Units*. Its symbol is V. One volt is the *potential difference* (difference in the electrical state) between two points if 1 joule of work is done in moving a charge of 1 coulomb between the points (see COULOMB; JOULE).

Differences in potential, often called *voltage*, are related to the energy of the electrical forces that "push" charges through a conductor. One volt of potential difference across a resistance of 1 ohm produces a current of 1 ampere. Most batteries and other sources of electromotive force are labeled according to their voltage. For example, many flashlights use two 1½-volt batteries. The most common instrument used to measure voltage is the *voltmeter*. The volt was named for the Italian scientist Alessandro Volta.   ROBERT B. PRIGO

See also AMPERE; ELECTRIC CURRENT (Conductors and Insulators); OHM; VOLTA, COUNT; VOLTMETER.

VOLTA, *VAHL tah* or *VOHL tuh,* **COUNT** (1745-1827), won fame as the inventor of the electric battery. Volta's discovery of the decomposition of water by an electrical current laid the foundations of electrochemistry. The *volt*, a unit of electrical measurement, is named for him (see VOLT). He also invented the electric condenser (now called a *capacitor*). Volta was born in Como, Italy, into a noble family. His full name was Alessandro Volta. See also BATTERY; ELECTRICITY (Experiments with Electric Charges and Currents).   SIDNEY ROSEN

VOLTAIRE, *vahl TAIR* or *vohl TAIR* (1694-1778), was the pen name of François Marie Arouet, a French author and philosopher. Voltaire's clear style, sparkling wit, keen intelligence, and strong sense of justice made him one of France's most famous writers.

Candide (1759), Voltaire's best-known work, is a brilliant philosophical tale that has been translated into more than 100 languages. On the surface, it describes the adventures of an inexperienced young man as he wanders around the world. Philosophically, *Candide* is a complex inquiry into the nature of good and evil.

Voltaire, the son of a lawyer, was born in Paris. He received an excellent education at a Jesuit school, where many of the students belonged to the nobility. He showed little inclination to study law, and his schooling ended at the age of 16. He soon joined a group of sophisticated aristocrats who had little reverence for anything except wit, pleasure, and literary talent. Paris society sought Voltaire's company because of his cleverness, his remarkable ability to write verses, and his gift for making people laugh. There are several theories about the origin of his pen name, which he adopted in 1718. The most widely accepted one is that *Voltaire* comes from an imperfect arrangement of the letters making up the French equivalent of *Arouet the Younger*.

Imprisonment and Early Success. In 1717, Voltaire was imprisoned in the Bastille for satirical verses that he may or may not have written ridiculing the government. During his 11 months in prison, he finished his tragedy *Oedipe*. The success of the play in 1718 made Voltaire the greatest French playwright of his time. He maintained this reputation—with more than 50 plays—for the rest of his life. While in prison, Voltaire also

worked on *La Henriade*, an epic poem about King Henry IV. This poem, written in the style of the *Aeneid* by the Roman poet Virgil, was published in 1723.

Voltaire became independently wealthy in his early 30's through an inheritance and wise investments. He was also a celebrity who had three plays performed in 1725 to help celebrate the wedding of King Louis XV. Royal pensions and other honors followed. But all this success ended abruptly in 1726 when the Chevalier de Rohan, a powerful young nobleman, scornfully asked: "What is your name anyway? Monsieur de Voltaire or Monsieur Arouet?" His question implied that Voltaire was claiming to be a nobleman while he was in fact of common origin. Voltaire supposedly replied that whatever his name was, he was bringing it honor, which was more than Rohan could say for himself. This answer cost Voltaire a beating by Rohan's men. Challenged to a duel by Voltaire, Rohan had him thrown into the Bastille again. A few days later, Voltaire was allowed to choose between continued imprisonment and exile.

Exile and Return to France. Voltaire chose exile. From 1726 to 1729, he lived in England, for him a land of political and religious freedom. In England he met the great writers Alexander Pope and Jonathan Swift. He also was attracted to the ideas of the philosopher John Locke and the famous scientist Sir Isaac Newton. It has been said that Voltaire went into exile a poet and came back a philosopher.

Voltaire returned to France in 1729, and published several works. The most important ones were *History of Charles XII* (1731) and his best-known play, *Zaïre* (1732). In 1733, his *Letters Concerning the English Nation* appeared in

Detail of a pastel (1736) by Maurice Quentin de La Tour; Palais de Versailles, Versailles, France

Voltaire

England. This book appeared in France the next year in an unauthorized edition called *Philosophical Letters*. Voltaire's praise of English customs, institutions, and style of thought was an indirect criticism of their French counterparts. French authorities condemned the book, and Voltaire fled from Paris.

Voltaire found a home with the Marquise du Châtelet, one of the most cultured and intelligent women of the day. From 1734 to 1749, he lived in her chateau at Cirey in Lorraine. During this period, he wrote several plays, an essay on metaphysics, two works on Sir Isaac Newton, and some poetry. He also wrote two notable philosophical tales. One of them, *Zadig* (1747), explores the problem of human destiny. The other, *Micromégas*, was started at Cirey and was published in 1752. In it, Voltaire used giant visitors from a distant star and from the planet Saturn to discuss the relative insignificance of human pretensions in answering religious questions. In this work, Voltaire also encouraged the use of human reason for the development of science.

Later Years. Following Mme. du Châtelet's death in 1749, Voltaire accepted the invitation of Frederick the Great to settle in Berlin. After three years of living under

the social and intellectual tyranny of the "Philosopher King," as Voltaire called him, Voltaire settled in Switzerland. He lived near Geneva in a chateau that he named Les Délices (The Delights). It is now the Voltaire Institute and Museum. A severe earthquake in Portugal in 1755 inspired Voltaire to write an important philosophical poem, *The Lisbon Disaster*. This work was published with his *Poem on Natural Law* in 1756.

In 1759, Voltaire purchased an estate called Ferney on the French-Swiss border. He lived there until just before his death. In an effort to correct the wrongs he saw in the world, Voltaire produced a constant flow of books, plays, pamphlets, and letters. Ferney soon became the intellectual capital of Europe. There Voltaire wrote *Candide*, added to his *Philosophical Dictionary*, and completed his *Universal History*, also called *Essay on the Manners and Spirit of Nations* (1759-1766). He fought religious intolerance and aided victims of religious persecution. His rallying cry at Ferney was "Écrasez l'infâme" ("Crush the evil thing"), referring to religious superstition.

Voltaire returned to Paris at the age of 83, and was enthusiastically received. There he saw his last play, *Irène* (1778), warmly applauded. But the excitement of the trip was too much for him, and he died in Paris.

The Roman Catholic Church, because of much criticism by Voltaire, refused to allow him to be buried in church ground. However, his body was finally taken to an abbey in Champagne. In 1791, Voltaire's remains were transferred to the Panthéon in Paris, where many of France's greatest are buried.　　　CAROL L. SHERMAN

See also CHÂTELET, MARQUISE DU; PEACE (From the 1400's to the 1700's).

Additional Resources

BESTERMAN, THEODORE. *Voltaire*. 3rd ed. Univ. of Chicago Press, 1977.
MASON, HAYDN. *Voltaire: A Biography*. Johns Hopkins, 1981.
RICHTER, PEYTON E., and RICARDO, ILONA. *Voltaire*. G. K. Hall, 1980. An introduction to Voltaire's writings and philosophy.

VOLTMETER is an instrument that measures the *voltage* (difference in potential) between two points of an electric current. Most commercial voltmeters are galvanometers connected in series with a high resistance. They have scales that read in volts. A typical direct-current voltmeter has a magnet shaped like a horseshoe. To each *pole* (end) of the magnet is attached a semicircular piece of soft iron that also becomes magnetized. These pieces of soft iron direct the magnetic field toward a small iron cylinder placed between the poles of the magnet. Since soft iron becomes highly magnetized, this cylinder concentrates the magnetic field.

Surrounding the cylinder is a coil of thin copper wire wound on a light, rectangular frame. This coil is the movable coil through which the electric current flows. Each end of the wire coil is connected to a small spiral spring. As the coil moves, a needle attached to the coil also moves. This needle moves across a dial and indicates the reading in volts. Another coil of very high resistance, up to several thousand ohms, is connected in series with the movable coil.

When the voltmeter is not in use, the frame does not move and the needle reads "zero." When a current passes through the movable coil, a magnetic field is set up around the coil. As a result, the magnetic field of the horseshoe magnet acts on the current-carrying wires of the coil to produce a force on the coil. This force causes the coil to turn. The springs oppose the motion of the coil and are adjusted so that the position of the needle indicates the correct voltage. In taking voltage readings, a voltmeter is always placed across the part of the circuit to be measured.　　　E. R. WHITEHEAD

See also GALVANOMETER; POTENTIOMETER; VOLT.

VOLUME of a body is the amount of space it occupies. The unit of measurement for volume is the cube, whose edges are of equal length. The volume of a box, for example, may be measured in cubic feet or cubic meters.

There are several ways of measuring the volume of a substance, depending upon the shape of the substance and whether it is a solid or liquid. The volume of a rectangular solid, such as a box, is found by multiplying the length by the width by the depth. This could be stated in the formula, $v = lwd$. A cubic foot equals 1,728 cubic inches, and a cubic meter equals 1,000,000 cubic centimeters.

The volume of a cylinder is determined by multiplying the area of the base by the height, or $v = \pi r^2 h$. The area of the base is obtained by multiplying π (or about 3.1416) by the square of its radius. The volume of a sphere is computed by the formula $v = \frac{\pi D^3}{6}$ (or about .524 D^3), where D is the diameter.

Liquids are usually measured by special glass devices having a graduated scale. In the customary system of measurement, the main units are the gallon, quart, pint, and fluid ounce. A gallon equals four quarts, a quart equals two pints, and a pint equals sixteen fluid ounces. In the metric system, liquids are measured mainly in milliliters and liters. One liter is equal to 1,000 milliliters.　　　E. G. STRAUS

Related Articles in WORLD BOOK include:

Barrel	Gallon	Minim	Quart
Bushel	Hogshead	Peck	Weights and
Density	Liter	Pint	Measures

VOLUNTEERS OF AMERICA is a religious social-welfare organization which provides spiritual and material services to the needy. It has more than 700 program centers throughout the United States. Its spiritual services include missions, Sunday Schools, Bible study groups, and spiritual counseling and guidance.

The organization operates maternity homes and child placement services, summer camps, homes and clubs for the aged, nursing homes and special care facilities, rehabilitation services for the handicapped, residences for working girls, day nurseries, and emergency shelters for the homeless. It sponsors low-cost housing for the poor and the elderly, and has helped establish such housing in many communities. The Volunteers gather clothing and household goods for the needy, and assist prisoners and parolees and their families.

Ballington Booth and his wife, Maud Ballington Booth, founded the Volunteers in New York City in 1896 (see BOOTH, EVANGELINE C.; BOOTH, WILLIAM). The organization's structure is partly military. Officers wear uniforms and hold rank. Headquarters are at 340 W. 85th Street, New York, NY 10024.

Critically reviewed by the VOLUNTEERS OF AMERICA

VOLVOX. See PROTOZOAN (Flagellates).

VOMITING

VOMITING, *VAHM uh tihng,* is the action that expels the contents of the stomach through the mouth. It may indicate something as minor as overeating or as serious as approaching death. Vomiting can result from a wide variety of causes, including anxiety, bacterial infections, chemical irritation of the stomach, pregnancy, radiation, ulcers, unusual motion, or severe pain. Vomiting is usually preceded by *nausea,* an unpleasant sensation in the stomach area (see NAUSEA).

Vomiting can cause death by suffocation in people who accidentally breathe in the *vomitus* (vomited material). This often occurs in intoxicated or unconscious people who vomit while lying on their backs. Repeated vomiting over many hours can cause death by dehydration, especially in infants (see DEHYDRATION). Vomiting after a head injury may indicate damage to the brain stem and should be treated immediately in a hospital.

When a person vomits, the stomach contents are expelled by pressure created by the abdominal muscles and the *diaphragm,* a large muscle at the bottom of the ribs. This muscular activity is called *retching.* Retching involves movement of the diaphragm downward, contraction of the abdominal muscles, and squeezing of the stomach contents upward. A person vomits when retching becomes intense enough to force the stomach contents through the *esophagus*—the tube connecting the stomach and throat. K. E. MONEY

VON BRAUN, *vahn BROWN,* **WERNHER,** *VAIR nuhr* (1912-1977), was one of the world's foremost rocket engineers and a leading authority on space travel. Von Braun directed teams that built the rockets that sent the first American into space and landed the first astronauts on the moon.

Von Braun was born in Wirsitz, Germany (now Wyrzysk, Poland). He experimented with rockets as a child. In 1932, he became an adviser in Germany's rocket program. He played a major role in developing the V-2 rocket, with which Germany bombed Allied cities during World War II (1939-1945). In 1944, Heinrich Himmler, chief of the Nazi secret police, tried to take over the German rocket program. He jailed von Braun, who refused to cooperate. Adolf Hitler, the Nazi dictator, freed von Braun later that year.

NASA

Wernher von Braun

In 1945, von Braun led a group of German scientists who surrendered to the United States Army. Von Braun and 116 of the other scientists were sent to the United States to work on guided missile systems. In 1954, the Army assigned von Braun and his team to the Redstone Arsenal in Huntsville, Ala., to develop the first large U.S. ballistic missile. Von Braun became a United States citizen in 1955.

Von Braun's team developed the four-stage Jupiter rocket that launched *Explorer I,* the first United States earth satellite. Another of the group's rockets, the Redstone, launched America's first astronaut, Alan B. Shep-

ard, Jr., in 1961. Other von Braun projects included the Saturn rockets. In 1969, a Saturn V rocket launched the astronauts who made the first landing on the moon.

In 1960, the Army transferred von Braun and his team to Huntsville's new George C. Marshall Space Flight Center, operated by the National Aeronautics and Space Administration (NASA). In 1970, NASA appointed von Braun deputy associate administrator for planning. In 1972, von Braun resigned from NASA and became an executive of Fairchild Industries, a major aerospace company. From 1975 to 1977, he was president of the National Space Institute, an organization that seeks to promote better public understanding of the U.S. space program. WILLIAM J. CROMIE

See also SPACE TRAVEL (High-Altitude Rockets).

Additional Resources

BERGAUST, ERIK. *Reaching for the Stars.* Doubleday, 1960. A biography. *Wernher Von Braun: The Authoritative and Definitive Biographical Profile of the Father of Modern Space Flight.* Stackpole, 1978.

ORDWAY, FREDERICK I., III, and SHARPE, M. R. *The Rocket Team.* Harper, 1979. The story of the development of modern rocketry by Von Braun and his colleagues.

VONNEGUT, *VAHN uh guht,* **KURT, JR.** (1922-   ), is an American author. Vonnegut uses many devices of science-fiction writing in his works, including space travel and fantastic inventions. Although the tone of his fiction is often playful, he is admittedly a moralizing writer with a gloomy view of humanity.

Vonnegut portrays a universe that is essentially without purpose in such novels as *Player Piano* (1952), *Cat's Cradle* (1963), and *Breakfast of Champions* (1973). In these works, all absolute systems for organizing human activity—whether political, religious, or scientific—are inevitably destructive. Vonnegut's moralizing consists of advice to be kind, to have pity, to seek companionship, and to enjoy the simple human pleasures. Vonnegut also expressed these views in *Palm Sunday* (1981), a collection of nonfiction pieces.

Wide World

Kurt Vonnegut, Jr.

Vonnegut's experiences during World War II (1939-1945) particularly affected his attitudes. While serving in the U.S. Army, he was captured by the Germans and imprisoned in Dresden, Germany. He witnessed that city's destruction by British and American bombing in 1945. His response to that event is reflected throughout his fiction, but dealt with directly only in *Slaughterhouse-Five* (1969), generally considered his most serious work. In that novel, he confronts and accepts what he sees as humanity's tendency to inflict catastrophe on itself. He suggests that our only hope for survival lies in a despairingly comic awareness of human folly.

Vonnegut's other novels include *The Sirens of Titan* (1959), *Mother Night* (1962), *God Bless You, Mr. Rosewater* (1965), *Slapstick* (1976), *Jailbird* (1979), and *Deadeye Dick* (1982). Several of his short stories were collected in *Welcome to the Monkey House* (1968). Vonnegut was born in Indianapolis. MARCUS KLEIN

VON NEUMANN, *vahn NOY mahn,* **JOHN** (1903-1957), was an outstanding mathematician. He wrote *The Mathematical Foundations of Quantum Mechanics* (1944), a treatise which showed that two different theories, Erwin Schrödinger's wave mechanics and Werner Heisenberg's matrix mechanics, were equivalent. Perhaps his best-known book was *The Theory of Games and Economic Behavior* (1944), written with Oskar Morgenstern. In addition, von Neumann helped organize the first research group in numerical weather prediction. See GAME THEORY.

Von Neumann made major contributions to the design of high-speed electronic computers. They were important in the development of the hydrogen bomb. He was appointed to the U.S. Atomic Energy Commission in 1955. Von Neumann was born in Budapest, Hungary. He became an American citizen in 1937.   PHILLIP S. JONES

VON RECKLINGHAUSEN'S DISEASE. See NEUROFIBROMATOSIS.

VON STERNBERG, JOSEF (1894-1969), was an American motion-picture director. He became famous for directing films that starred the German-born actress Marlene Dietrich. These movies feature the vivid, unusual settings and lighting that characterize all Von Sternberg's major films.

Von Sternberg first directed Dietrich in *The Blue Angel,* which was made in Germany in 1930. The success of this movie led to six more Von Sternberg-Dietrich films, all produced in Hollywood. They were *Morocco* (1930), *Dishonored* (1931), *Shanghai Express* (1932), *Blonde Venus* (1932), *The Scarlet Empress* (1934), and *The Devil Is a Woman* (1935).

Von Sternberg, whose real name was Jonas Sternberg, was born in Vienna, Austria. His family moved to the United States when he was 7 years old. He made his debut as a director in *The Salvation Hunters* (1925). Von Sternberg directed three of the earliest gangster films— *Underworld* (1927), *The Drag Net* (1928), and *The Docks of New York* (1928). His other films included *The Last Command* (1928), *An American Tragedy* (1931), *Crime and Punishment* (1935), *The King Steps Out* (1936), and *The Shanghai Gesture* (1941).   JOHN F. MARIANI

VOODOO is a set of beliefs and practices derived from traditional African religions combined with elements of Christianity. Voodoo was developed in Haiti by Africans who were brought there as slaves and by their descendants. People in other West Indian countries, in Brazil, and in the United States also practice forms of voodoo. The word *voodoo* comes from the West African word *vodun,* meaning *god, spirit,* or *sacred object.*

Followers of voodoo, called *voodooists,* believe the world is filled with demons, gods, and spirits of the dead. One of the most dreaded is Baron Samedi, also called *Gèdé Nimbo,* the ruler of graveyard spirits. He wears a black suit and bowler hat.

Voodooists believe they must continually take precautions to protect themselves from magical hazards. For example, voodooists consider noon, when people cast no shadow, a dangerous time. They believe that if a person's shadow disappears, the person's soul has temporarily left its body. A body that loses its soul may become inhabited by unwanted spirits. Voodooists wear magical charms and cast spells to protect themselves. The charms and spells supposedly cure illnesses, expel unwanted spirits, bring success in love, and ward off

magical attacks by enemies. Such attacks may involve a doll made in the victim's likeness. The voodooist sticks pins into the doll or injures it in other ways to bring harm to the person represented.

Odette Mennesson-Rigaud, Photo Researchers

A Voodoo Ceremony in Haiti, *above,* centers around a chalk diagram and includes special prayers. Voodoo was developed in Haiti by Africans brought there as slaves and by their descendants.

Voodoo initiation ceremonies symbolize death and rebirth. The ceremonies involve chanting, drumming, dancing, and animal sacrifices. During the rituals, new converts seem to become temporarily possessed by a god.   CHRISTOPHER MCINTOSH

See also HAITI (People); MAGIC (Contagious Magic).

Additional Resources

DEREN, MAYA. *Divine Horsemen: The Living Gods of Haiti.* McPherson, 1984. Originally published in 1953. An illustrated account of voodoo rites.

KRISTOS, KYLE. *Voodoo.* Harper, 1976. Suitable for younger readers.

VORSTER, *FAWR stuhr,* **BALTHAZAR JOHANNES,** *BAHL ta sahr yoh HAHN uhs* (1915-1983), served as prime minister of South Africa from 1966 to 1978. During his term, South Africa was criticized by many countries for its policy of *apartheid,* a system of strict racial segregation that was officially established in 1948. Vorster's government enforced the policy but relaxed some apartheid laws. For example, it allowed blacks to go to some theaters and nightclubs and to participate with whites in sports. His government also declared two South African areas populated chiefly by blacks to be independent of the government (see SOUTH AFRICA [Black Government]).

Vorster was born in Jamestown, South Africa, near Aliwal North. He graduated from Stellenbosch University and then practiced law. During World War II (1939-1945), he joined a political movement that favored Nazi Germany. Vorster was elected to Parliament in 1953 as a member of the ruling National Party. He became minister of justice in 1961 and helped crush underground activities by blacks against apartheid.

Health problems caused Vorster to resign as prime minister in 1978. He was then named state president, a largely ceremonial office. Vorster resigned from this office in 1979. He had been accused of giving false information to a commission investigating illegal spending by government officials.   L. H. GANN

VORTICELLA. See PROTOZOAN (Ciliates).

VOTING is a method by which people choose their leaders and decide public issues. Most countries give voting rights to their citizens. But nations that do not have a democratic form of government may not allow their voters any real choices. For example, people in many dictatorships may vote—but only for candidates designated by their leaders.

Citizens in democratic countries consider voting one of their most important rights because it allows them to choose who will govern them. In a majority of these countries, most candidates seek office as members of a political party. The voters elect their public officials directly or indirectly. In *direct elections*, the citizens themselves vote for the officials. In *indirect elections*, the voters elect representatives to choose officials. U.S. citizens elect their President indirectly, through the Electoral College (see ELECTORAL COLLEGE).

Citizens in democracies also participate in local and national affairs by voting. The men and women of a community, for example, might vote on whether to levy a tax to build a recreation center.

Some governments give their citizens special voting rights through the *referendum* and *recall*. Legislatures may ask voters to approve or reject proposed laws in special elections called referendums. Voters may remove an official from office through the process of recall. See INITIATIVE AND REFERENDUM; RECALL.

People also vote for purposes other than to elect officials and to settle public matters. In many societies, members of juries and of clubs, labor unions, and other organizations make decisions by voting.

Who May Vote. The 26th Amendment to the United States Constitution grants the vote to U.S. citizens 18 years or older. But the Constitution allows each state to set other qualifications for voting, provided they do not violate other guarantees of the Constitution.

In 1970, Congress passed a law allowing anyone who has lived in a state at least 30 days to vote in presidential elections. The Supreme Court of the United States declared in 1972 that lengthy residency requirements for state and local elections were unconstitutional. In 1973, the court ruled that states can require a person to have lived in the state for 50 days and to have registered before voting in nonpresidential elections.

Before the 26th Amendment was passed in 1971, all but 10 states had limited the vote to citizens who were at least 21. The age had been 18 in Alaska, Georgia, and Kentucky; 19 in Massachusetts, Minnesota, Montana, and Wyoming; and 20 in Hawaii, Maine, and Nebraska.

Congress had passed a law in 1970 lowering the voting age to 18. But the Supreme Court of the United States ruled that the law applied only to national elections. The court said that only individual states or a constitutional amendment could change state and local limits. Congress passed the 26th Amendment in March 1971. By the end of June, the necessary 38 states had ratified the amendment, giving the vote to more than 11 million young men and women.

In Canada, 18-year-olds may vote in national elections. Each province sets voting qualifications for its residents.

Registration is the process by which a person's name is added to the list of eligible voters. On election day, officials check each individual's name against the list before they allow the person to vote.

Voters may register by mail or in person. Many states close registration 30 days before each election. In most states, voters remain registered permanently unless they move or fail to vote for several years. To vote in primary elections, voters in some states must register as members of a political party.

Restrictions on Voting. Even democratic nations deny some people the right to vote. In the United States, most of the states did not allow women to vote until the 19th Amendment to the Constitution was passed in 1920 (see WOMAN SUFFRAGE). American Indians did not gain voting rights in all the states until 1948. Citizens living in Washington, D.C., could not vote in presidential elections until after passage of the 23rd Amendment in 1961.

In the United States and Canada, persons may not vote if they suffer severe mental illness or retardation or have been convicted of certain crimes. Wartime deserters dishonorably discharged from the U.S. armed forces lose the right to vote in national elections.

Several states have tried to deprive blacks of their voting rights. Between 1895 and 1910, seven Southern states added *grandfather clauses* to their constitutions. These clauses violated the 15th Amendment to the Constitution, which prohibits a state from denying a citizen the right to vote because of race. In 1915, the Supreme Court declared such clauses unconstitutional. See GRANDFATHER CLAUSE; FIFTEENTH AMENDMENT.

Some states once required every voter to pay a *poll tax*. Officials in those states often kept blacks and poor whites from voting because they had not paid the tax. The 24th Amendment to the Constitution, adopted in 1964, prohibits poll taxes as voting requirements for national elections. In 1966, the Supreme Court outlawed such taxes for all elections. See POLL TAX.

Many states also once restricted voting rights to citizens who could pass a *literacy test* that indicated a certain level of education. Election officials often tested and disqualified only blacks. In 1970, Congress and the Supreme Court banned these tests.

Voting Districts. In the United States, each county or ward of a state is divided into voting districts called *precincts*. Citizens may vote only at the polling place in the precinct where they live. Election officials at the polling places distribute ballots and count the votes after the polls close.

Methods of Voting. United States citizens consider the secret ballot an important voting right. But in the 1700's, most of the American Colonies conducted oral elections. Later, some states used written ballots but required voters to sign them. Gradually, voting officials realized that oral and signed votes restricted the freedom of voters. Some citizens feared how others would react if they voted as they wished. States began using secret ballots so each voter could choose freely.

During the 1890's, the Australian ballot system—which is used today in the United States and Canada—became popular. Under this system, each voter marks a printed ballot while alone in a screened booth. More than half the voters in the United States use voting machines, which simplify the job of registering and counting votes. See BALLOT; VOTING MACHINE.

Every state and Canadian province allows absentee voting for certain groups of citizens who cannot go to their polling places. These groups include men and women in the armed forces, college students, sick people, and travelers who are abroad on business or vacations. Citizens who wish to vote by absentee ballot get an application from county officials. Most applications must be signed in the presence of a notary public. Qualified absentee voters receive a ballot, envelope, and instructions. They must mark their ballots in the presence of a notary public and return them before election day.

Voting Behavior. Many eligible voters in the United States rarely—or never—vote. During the 1970's and early 1980's, about 55 per cent of the *electorate* (those eligible to vote) voted in presidential elections. In many other democracies, at least 80 per cent of the voters go to the polls in equivalent elections. Some nations prevent low election turnouts by fining or imprisoning those citizens who do not vote.

In general, people vote if they believe they have something to gain or lose from an election. Social scientists have found that some groups of people vote more often than others. Men seem to vote more than women, and persons from 40 to 60 years old vote more frequently than younger or older people. The higher an individual's income or education, the more likely the person is to vote. Family and social background also affects how people vote. For example, many people support the political party that their parents support.

Dramatic national or world events may cause major shifts in voting patterns. During the Great Depression of the 1930's, for example, party loyalties in the United States changed greatly.   GEORGE W. CAREY

Related Articles in WORLD BOOK include:

Civil Rights
Colonial Life in America
 (Voting Requirements)
Congress of the United
 States (Passing a Bill)
Election

Logrolling
Parliamentary Procedure
 (Voting on Motions)
Plebiscite
United Nations (Meetings
 and Voting; Voting)

Additional Resources

ARCHER, JULES. *Winners and Losers: How Elections Work in America.* Harcourt, 1984. Suitable for younger readers.
CLARKE, HAROLD D., and others. *Political Choice in Canada.* McGraw (Scarborough, Ont.), 1979.
DINKIN, ROBERT J. *Voting in Provincial America: A Study of Elections in the Thirteen Colonies, 1689-1776.* Greenwood, 1977. *Voting in Revolutionary America: A Study of Elections in the Original Thirteen States, 1776-1789.* 1982.
WOLFINGER, RAYMOND E., and ROSENSTONE, S. J. *Who Votes?* Yale, 1980.

VOTING MACHINE is a mechanical device for recording and counting votes at an election. It provides an absolutely secret ballot and records it automatically, with accuracy, speed, and economy. Over half of all voters in the United States cast their ballots on voting machines.

Operation. Voting machines may differ in some details, but they all work in much the same way. The

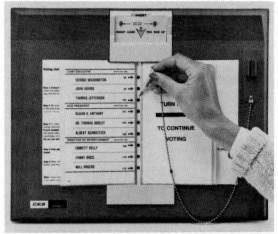

Computer Election Systems

A Computerized Voting System uses a computer card. The voter punches holes in the card, shown above under a mock ballot, and a computer later counts the votes and prints the results.

voter stands in front of the machine and moves a master lever that closes a set of curtains around the voter and unlocks the voting machine. In front of the voter are the names of all the candidates, arranged in rows according to their political party. The candidates are listed next to the titles of the offices they seek. The voter turns a pointer next to the name of each candidate he or she chooses for an office. In some states, a voter may vote a *straight ticket* by pulling a *party lever* at one end of the party's row of candidates. The machine will then register a vote for each candidate in the row. The machine does not register or count any votes until the voter moves the master lever back. This registers and counts the vote, and opens the curtains.

Voting machines also provide for ballots on bond issues or other proposals. The machine registers a *yes* or *no* vote. Modern voting machines have one row of voting pointers for questions, and nine party rows of voting pointers for candidates. They are built in sizes to accommodate 270, 360, 450, or 540 candidates.

Some election districts in the United States use computerized voting machines. Instead of pulling a lever, the voter marks a square or punches a hole on a computer card. The computer totals all valid votes for each candidate or issue and prints out the results.

Advantages. A voting machine is both automatic and impartial. Dishonest officials cannot change it or tamper with its records, although they might "stuff" a ballot box with paper ballots. Fewer election officials are needed, and the cost of printing paper ballots is reduced. The machine also eliminates expensive and possibly inaccurate recounts of hand-counted paper ballots. The savings resulting within a few years often equals the machine's cost. The useful life of a voting machine is often as much as 50 years.

Legislative Voting Machines record the votes for and against proposals in many state legislatures. These electric and mechanical devices reduce the time needed for a roll-call vote of the legislators. Each lawmaker's desk has buttons with which the lawmaker can vote

VOTING RIGHTS ACT OF 1965

either yes or no. When a button is pressed, the vote appears on a counting device at the clerk's or speaker's desk. Many legislatures also have a counting board on one wall of the chamber. As each legislator votes, a colored light is lit opposite the legislator's name on the board. Many legislative voting machines provide a permanent record, showing the total votes cast and the vote of each legislator on each roll-call.

History. Thomas Edison invented the first legislative voting machine in 1868 (see EDISON, THOMAS ALVA [Early Inventions]). Election voting machines developed more slowly. The first practical voting machine used in an actual election was put into service in Lockport, New York, in 1892. Manufacture and distribution of voting machines has continued steadily since that time. Today, voting machines are in use in more than three-fourths of the states. Many states now require the use of voting machines in all elections, including primary elections.

The United States was the first country to conduct elections by machine. Several others began using voting machines in the 1960's. Still other countries are engaged in research on their use. MARIO A. MAZZONETTO

VOTING RIGHTS ACT OF 1965. See BLACK AMERICANS (Political Gains).

VOUCHER SYSTEM. See EDUCATION (Who Should Control Education?).

VOWEL. When a person says "ah" for the doctor, an open sound is made with free passage of breath. This sound is a vowel, as are all the other open and freely breathed sounds in speech. In English, the vowel sounds are represented by the letters, *a, e, i, o, u,* and sometimes *w* and *y* (as in *now, city*). But each letter stands for several sounds. The open quality of vowels distinguishes them from *consonants.* Consonants are formed with the organs of speech more or less closed. A vowel may be a syllable in itself, or it may be joined with one or more consonants to produce a syllable. See also CONSONANT; PRONUNCIATION. GARY TATE

VOYAGEURS NATIONAL PARK, *vwah yah ZHURZ,* lies in northern Minnesota at the United States-Canadian border. The early French-Canadian traders and pioneers known as *voyageurs* traveled the scenic waterways of the area. The park was created in 1971. The park includes an area of many lakes and streams. Waterways are the main means of travel in the park. The major lakes include Kabetogama, Namakan, and Rainy. Bears, deer, timber wolves, wildfowl, and other animals live in the park. For the area of Voyageurs National Park, see NATIONAL PARK SYSTEM (table: National Parks). GEORGE B. HARTZOG, JR.

V/STOL is a type of aircraft that can take off and land (1) vertically or (2) on a very short runway. The term *V/STOL* stands for *Vertical/Short Take-Off and Landing.* A V/STOL plane can take off from or land on a runway that is less than 500 feet (150 meters) long. The largest conventional planes may need more than 5,000 feet (1,500 meters) of runway.

Some V/STOL's, called *VTOL's,* can make only vertical take-offs and landings. Helicopters also take off and land vertically, but they are not considered VTOL's. Unlike a helicopter, which has one or two rotors called *rotary wings,* a VTOL aircraft has *fixed*

wings like those of a conventional airplane. A VTOL also can travel much faster than a helicopter. Other V/STOL's, called *STOL's,* can make only short take-offs and landings.

V/STOL's have great military value because they can land on small airfields near battlefields. Unlike most military planes, V/STOL's can land on ships smaller than aircraft carriers. A V/STOL called the Harrier is used by the armed forces of Great Britain and the United States as a combat plane. It can fly faster than 700 miles (1,100 kilometers) per hour. STOL's also serve as commercial airliners that can operate from small airfields.

V/STOL's can be classified into five main groups, depending on their lift-propulsion system. (1) Tilt-wing aircraft have engines mounted on their wings. The wings of these planes can be tilted to change the direction of the engine thrust. (2) Tilt-engine aircraft have engines that can be moved to direct the engine thrust. (3) Variable-thrust aircraft have special nozzles attached to their engines. The nozzles can be moved to change the direction of the engine thrust. (4) Lift-and-thrust aircraft have two sets of engines. One set provides forward thrust and the other set provides lift. (5) Lift-fan aircraft have *ducted propellers* (see DUCTED PROPELLER). Special controls called *vanes* can be moved to change the direction of the propeller thrust.

The earliest STOL was the Autogiro, which made its first flight in 1923 (see AUTOGIRO). The first modern fixed-wing VTOL was the U.S. Navy Convair XFY-1, or "Pogo Stick." This plane was test-flown in 1954. It landed by backing down onto its tail with its nose in the air (see AIRPLANE [picture]). The first widely used V/STOL was the Harrier, which had its test flights in 1967. During the 1960's and 1970's, aircraft manufacturers developed and tested many experimental V/STOL's, most of them for military use. NORMAN POLMAR

See also AIRPLANE (Special-Purpose Planes; picture: V/STOL's).

VUILLARD, *vwee YAHR,* **EDOUARD,** *ay DWAR* (1868-1940), was a French painter. His pictures portray his private world—a view from a window, or corners of his studio and living room enclosed by walls and furniture. In his interior scenes, he showed figures reading, relaxing, or concentrating on common tasks. He painted his environment both as a place of quiet and rest and as a disturbing situation where even the walls appear menacing. Like his friend and fellow artist Pierre Bonnard, Vuillard was influenced by Japanese art. This influence appears in the brilliantly colored flat patterns of Vuillard's paintings. See BONNARD, PIERRE.

Vuillard was born in Cuiseaux, near Chalon. He lived most of his life withdrawn from society. ALBERT BOIME

VULCAN, *VUHL kuhn,* in Roman mythology, was the god of fire, metalworking, and skilled craftwork in general. He also served as the blacksmith of the gods. Vulcan produced armor, weapons, and many other works. All were perfectly made, and some had magic qualities. Roman metalworkers and other craftworkers worshiped Vulcan as their patron. He closely resembled the Greek god Hephaestus. Many myths about Vulcan are identical with those about Hephaestus.

Vulcan was the son of Jupiter and Juno, the king and queen of the gods. One myth describes Vulcan as being the son of Juno alone, with no father. Vulcan

356

was lame—the only major Roman god who was physically imperfect. Some myths say he was born lame, and others say he became lame from a fall.

Although Vulcan was the least attractive of the gods, he married Venus, the goddess of love and beauty. Venus was unfaithful to Vulcan with both gods and mortal men. Many myths tell of Vulcan's jealousy over his wife's love affairs.

Because of his association with fire, Vulcan's name forms part of the word *vulcanization*, the name of an industrial process of treating rubber with heat. The English word *volcano* comes from the Italian form of Vulcan's name.   PAUL PASCAL

See also HEPHAESTUS; VENUS; PANDORA.

VULCANIZATION. See RUBBER (Discovery of Vulcanization; Vulcanization); TIRE (How Tires Are Made); VULCAN.

VULGATE, *VUHL gayt*, is the name of a Latin translation of the Bible completed in A.D. 405 by Saint Jerome. The Vulgate replaced earlier Latin versions and eventually became the standard Bible of the Roman Catholic Church. The word *vulgate* comes from a Latin word that means *common* or *popular.*

The Council of Trent made the Vulgate the standard Roman Catholic translation in 1546. The official text consisted of a revised edition that was not issued until the 1590's. The traditional English translation of the Vulgate is called the Douay-Rheims, or Douay, Bible. It was named after Douay, France, where the Old Testament was published in 1609 and 1610; and Rheims, France, where the New Testament was published in 1582. Richard Challoner, an English bishop, made major revisions in the Douay Bible from 1749 to 1752. Challoner's edition was the standard Bible of English-speaking Catholics until about 1943. In that year, Pope Pius XII encouraged Catholic Biblical scholars to base modern translations on the original Greek and Hebrew texts. A number of English translations of the Bible are now approved for Catholic use. However, only a few of these are based on the Vulgate.

The Vulgate differs from most English versions of the Bible in the names of some of the books and in the way some chapters and verses have been divided. The Vulgate Old Testament also contains some books that Protestants consider part of the Apocrypha.

From 1969 to 1977, a commission appointed by Pope Paul VI prepared a new Latin translation of the Bible. This translation reflects modern advances in Biblical scholarship but keeps the style and much of the language of the Vulgate.   PATRICK W. SKEHAN

See also BIBLE (The First Translations).

VULTURE is the name of several large birds of prey. They eat *carrion*, or dead animals. Other birds of prey have feathers on their heads, but vultures do not. They have slightly hooked bills and blunt claws which are poor weapons for seizing and carrying off their food. Vultures live in the temperate and tropical regions of America. The vultures of Europe and Asia look like American vultures and have similar habits. But their bodies are different. The Old World vultures belong to a different family, the hawk family.

Vultures are ugly birds, with their naked heads and dark feathers. They not only eat carrion, but they often vomit when they are disturbed. But they are useful, because they eat dead bodies which otherwise might

decay and become dangerous to health. Generally, vultures do not carry disease.

Vultures have a graceful, easy, soaring flight. They sail in broad circles, high in the sky. They have sharp eyes and a keen sense of smell. They can see dead animals from great distances.

Vultures are usually seen in large, mixed flocks, except during breeding season. Then they pair off and nest on the ground under overhanging cliffs, in logs, and in caves. They build no nests. The female vulture lays from 1 to 3 eggs on bare surfaces. The parents bring food in their throats and empty it into the mouth of the young bird.

New World Vultures. There are six species of American vultures. Three live in North America. The turkey vulture, also called *buzzard* or *turkey buzzard*, is found from southern Canada to southern South America. It grows about 30 inches (76 centimeters) long.

The *black vulture* is about 6 inches (15 centimeters) shorter than the turkey vulture. It is found from the central United States to southern South America. This bird is entirely black except for white underwings.

The largest land bird in North America is the vulture called the *California condor*. It is 45 to 55 inches (114 to 140 centimeters) long and has a wingspread of about 9 feet (2.7 meters).

The *king vulture* is the most striking of the three vultures that live in South America. It has a feather ruff around its neck, and its head is yellow, scarlet, white, and blue, with fleshy growths of rich orange. Its bill is orange and black.

The *Andean condor* is about as large as the California condor. It lives high in the Andes of Chile and Peru, and appears on the coats of arms of Bolivia, Chile, Colombia, and Ecuador. The *yellow-headed turkey vulture* of northern South America and Brazil resembles such North American vultures as the turkey buzzard.

Norman Myers

Egyptian Vultures use rocks to break open ostrich eggs. The bird hurls the rock from its beak with a snap of the neck.

Turkey Vulture
Cathartes aura
Found from southern Canada
to southern South America
Body length: 26 to 32 inches
(66 to 81 centimeters)

Black Vulture
Coragyps atratus
Found from central United States to
southern South America
Body length: 23 to 27 inches
(58 to 69 centimeters)

WORLD BOOK illustrations by Guy Tudor

Old World Vultures. There are 14 species of Old World vultures. The *cinereous vulture* grows to about 42 inches (107 centimeters) long. This bird has a bare, pinkish head and black feathers. It is found in southern Europe, northwest Africa, and central Asia.

The *griffon vulture* is about the same size and appearance, and has about the same range. The *Egyptian*, or *white, vulture* is about 25 inches (64 centimeters) long with a naked yellow head and whitish feathers except for the black wings. It lives in the Mediterranean area, as far east as India.

Scientific Classification. New World vultures are in the family *Cathartidae.* The turkey vulture is *Cathartes aura;* the black vulture is *Coragyps atratus;* and the California condor is *Gymnogyps californianus.* The king vulture is *Sarcoramphus papa;* the Andean condor is *Vultur gryphus;* and the yellow-headed turkey vulture is *Cathartes urubitinga.* Old World vultures belong to the family *Accipitridae.* The cinereous vulture is *Aegypius monachus,* the griffon vulture is *Gyps fulvus,* the Egyptian vulture is *Neophron percnopterus,* and the white-rumped vulture is *Gyps africanus.*   OLIN SEWALL PETTINGILL, JR.

See also ANIMAL (color picture: Animals of the Grasslands); BUZZARD; CONDOR; LAMMERGEIER.